10th Anniversary of *Axioms*: Mathematical Analysis

10th Anniversary of *Axioms*: Mathematical Analysis

Editor

Clemente Cesarano

MDPI

Basel • Beijing • Wuhan • Barcelona • Belgrade • Novi Sad • Cluj • Manchester

Editor
Clemente Cesarano
Section of Mathematics
Uninettuno University
Roma
Italy

Editorial Office
MDPI
St. Alban-Anlage 66
4052 Basel, Switzerland

This is a reprint of articles from the Special Issue published online in the open access journal *Axioms* (ISSN 2075-1680) (available at: www.mdpi.com/journal/axioms/special_issues/axioms_10th_anniversary_mathematical_analysis).

For citation purposes, cite each article independently as indicated on the article page online and as indicated below:

Lastname, A.A.; Lastname, B.B. Article Title. *Journal Name* **Year**, *Volume Number*, Page Range.

ISBN 978-3-7258-1254-7 (Hbk)
ISBN 978-3-7258-1253-0 (PDF)
doi.org/10.3390/books978-3-7258-1253-0

Contents

About the Editor

Clemente Cesarano

Clemente Cesarano is a professor of numerical analysis at the Uninettuno University. He coordinates the local Mathematics Section and the doctoral course in technological innovation engineering.

He has carried out teaching and research activities at various Italian and European institutions and universities. He is an associate researcher at the Institute of Complex Systems of the CNR and a member of the National Institute of Higher Mathematics. He has been a visiting professor at European universities, including the University of Linz and the Complutense University of Madrid. He is the author of numerous scientific publications, texts and manuals in the field of approximation theory and mathematical analysis.

He has participated, also as a coordinator, in various national and international funded research projects.

Preface

In this Special Issue, we aim to promote the study of special functions and, particularly the functions of orthogonal polynomials and their applications, not only in the traditional context of mathematical physics equations and integro-differential equations, but also in the contexts of combinatorial theory, analytic number theory and linear analysis. Many articles have recently been published on special sequences of numbers or polynomials in the context of analytic number theory. The analysis of fractional calculus through the concepts and formalism of some classes of orthogonal polynomials (particularly Hermite polynomials) is a further research area for this UIR, as well as the study of extensions in the case of the fractional index of polynomials of Chebyshev, as well as the multidimensional case of pseudo-Chebyshev and pseudo-Lucas, and the generalizations of the numbers of Bernoulli, Euler, Hahn, Bell, etc., also through expressions of polynomials in the form of determinants.

The relationships of multidimensional orthogonal polynomials (particularly Lucas polynomials) with linear algebra and the related applications in the study of linear dynamic systems are now well known and therefore allow for expanding our knowledge in the disciplinary areas considered above.

Clemente Cesarano
Editor

axioms

MDPI

Article

Stability and Hopf Bifurcation Analysis for a Phage Therapy Model with and without Time Delay

Ei Ei Kyaw, Hongchan Zheng * and Jingjing Wang

School of Mathematics and Statistics, Northwestern Polytechnical University, Xi'an 710072, China
* Correspondence: zhenghc@nwpu.edu.cn

Abstract: This study proposes a mathematical model that accounts for the interaction of bacteria, phages, and the innate immune response with a discrete time delay. First, for the non-delayed model we determine the local and global stability of various equilibria and the existence of Hopf bifurcation at the positive equilibrium. Second, for the delayed model we provide sufficient conditions for the local stability of the positive equilibrium by selecting the discrete time delay as a bifurcation parameter; Hopf bifurcation happens when the time delay crosses a critical threshold. Third, based on the normal form method and center manifold theory, we derive precise expressions for determining the direction of Hopf bifurcation and the stability of bifurcating periodic solutions. Finally, numerical simulations are performed to verify our theoretical analysis.

Keywords: phage therapy model; delay; stability; Hopf bifurcation; numerical simulations

MSC: 34K18; 34K20; 34C23

Citation: Kyaw, E.E.; Zheng, H.; Wang, J. Stability and Hopf Bifurcation Analysis for a Phage Therapy Model with and without Time Delay. *Axioms* **2023**, *12*, 772. https://doi.org/10.3390/axioms12080772

Academic Editors: Clemente Cesarano and Feliz Manuel Minhós

Received: 1 June 2023
Revised: 17 July 2023
Accepted: 24 July 2023
Published: 9 August 2023

1. Introduction

Phages are viruses that infect prokaryotic organisms, and are important components of ecological systems [1]. Phages infect bacteria by injecting their genetic material into cells. When the virus enters the cell, it prevents other phages from attacking it and begins to reproduce within the host until the number of new viral particles reaches the bacterial threshold [2,3]. The use of bacteriophages to treat bacterial infections, commonly referred to as phage therapy, dates back to the early 20th century. Phage treatment can be more effective than antibiotics in treating various medical conditions [4]. Moreover, phage therapy has multiple potential applications, and can even be employed in place of antibiotics in certain circumstances [5]. Clinical research on phage therapy has not shown any of the severe side effects such as anaphylaxis that are sometimes associated with antibiotics [6].

Mathematical models are widely used in various fields, including biology, epidemiology, engineering, physics, sciences, business, and computer science. They help us to understand ecosystem dynamics, quantify disease control strategies, and gain new theoretical insights into nature [7]. Nonlinear dynamical systems are commonly used to describe biological systems and relationships between individuals. Researchers have developed nonlinear dynamical systems for various biological phenomena, including stability, persistence, and bifurcation. Mathematical modeling of phage therapy is crucial for understanding bacteria–bacteriophage interactions and their long-term behavior. Various models have been constructed, resulting in numerous beneficial outcomes [2,8–16].

Considering that the evolution of a system is dependent on its present and previous states, time delays must be included in the model. Accordingly, authors have focused on dynamic behaviors such as stability and the existence of Hopf bifurcations in delayed population models [17–20]. The above-mentioned references have investigated the existence and direction of Hopf bifurcations and the stability of positive equilibria. The application of delay differential equations to the modeling of biological phenomena has gained popularity in recent years. In particular, several studies have presented bacteria–bacteriophage models by introducing a time delay to generate more realistic models; see for example [21–26] and references therein. Meanwhile, due to the complexity of the impacts of delay on a system's dynamic behavior, researchers have increasingly focused on the dynamic behavior of delayed phage therapy models, such as their stability and the occurrence of Hopf bifurcations. In a model of a delayed marine bacteriophage infection, Beretta et al. [21] analysed the global and local stability of the equilibrium. Beretta and Solimano [22] expanded upon their previous research [21] to investigate how delay impacts equilibrium stability. In [23], the author addressed models of marine phage infection with delay and stage structure achieving the persistence and extinction of the system under specific conditions. Gakkhar and Sahani [24] proposed a model of bacteria–bacteriophage interaction with a constant delay. They examined a simple Hopf bifurcation for the non-zero equilibrium point and outlined the conditions for a susceptible bacteria-free equilibrium and its stability. Casino et al. [27] identified the optimal lysis time for bacteria–phage interactions in a structured cell population model. Additional delayed bacteria–phage models can be found in [28–31] and the references cited therein. Several significant studies have been published on diffusion-based bacteriophage models [32–34]. Mathematically rigorous studies of stochastic models for bacteriophage infection with and without time delay have been published as well [35–39].

Understanding the interactions between bacteria, phages, and the immune system is essential to developing successful bacteriophage therapeutics. Meanwhile, bacteriophage-based bacterial elimination has therapeutic potential and is currently utilized to treat bacterial infections [40,41]. Mathematical models of bacteria–phage interactions that include immune responses are of growing interest to the authors. Leung and Weitz [42] proposed a nonlinear ODE phage therapy model involving bacterial, phage, and immune system interactions:

$$\begin{cases} \dot{B} = rB\left(1 - \dfrac{B}{K_C}\right) - \phi BP - \dfrac{\epsilon IB}{1 + B/K_D}, \\ \dot{P} = \beta\phi BP - wP, \\ \dot{I} = \alpha I\left(1 - \dfrac{I}{K_I}\right)\dfrac{B}{B + K_N}, \end{cases} \tag{1}$$

where $B(t)$, $P(t)$, and $I(t)$ represent the concentrations of bacteria, phages, and the immune system at time t, respectively, and r and K_C represent the maximum growth rate and carrying capacity of the bacteria, respectively. The phages attach to and infect the bacteria with an adsorption rate of ϕ and release new virus particles with a burst size of β. The phage particles decay with the death rate w. The presence of bacteria with a maximum growth rate α activates the immune system. Meanwhile, the immune carrying capacity is K_I and the killing parameter is ϵ. Finally, K_D is the bacterial density when the host immune response is half-saturated and K_N is the bacterial concentration at which the innate immunity growth rate is at half its maximum.

In [42], Leung and Weitz simplified the above System (1) by employing a quasistatic approximation in which the innate immune response is represented as a constant. This simplification is reasonable considering that the concentrations of bacteria and phages are expected to change more rapidly than the immune response. They applied this approximation when the innate immune response reached its maximum K_I. This resembles a circumstance in which the innate immune response does not control bacterial infection. Phages are then included as an additional treatment. In this case, the model equation in (1) reduces to

$$\begin{cases} \dot{B} = rB\left(1 - \dfrac{B}{K_C}\right) - \phi BP - \dfrac{\epsilon K_I B}{1 + B/K_D}, \\ \dot{P} = \beta\phi BP - wP, \end{cases} \tag{2}$$

with the initial conditions

$$B(0) \geq 0, \;\; P(0) \geq 0.$$

In [42], Leung and Weitz discovered a synergistic regime in which the phage and immune system cooperate to eradicate bacteria. They demonstrated that the interaction between phages and the immune system is essential in order for phage therapy to effectively eliminate bacterial infections. However, they did not discuss the dynamic behaviors of (1) and (2), such as positivity, boundedness, persistence, stability, Hopf bifurcation analysis, etc. In [43], we examined the mathematical dynamics analysis of the model in (1) formulated by Leung and Weitz [42], studied the persistence, non-persistence, and local stability of possible equilibrium solutions, and provided the criteria for the global stability of the planar and positive equilibria. However, the analysis of such dynamics for the model in (2) was not completed in our previous paper [43].

Determining how delays influence the system's stability, dynamics, and bifurcation is a challenging mathematical problem, and nonlinear dynamical bacteria–bacteriophage systems with time delays are extremely challenging because of the application of nonlinear biological phenomena and their dynamic behavior. There are a number of papers in the literature on modeling bacteria–bacteriophage systems using delay differential equations. Inspired by this previous literature, it appears that the model can be made more realistic by incorporating additional terms such as the time delay obtained from the past states of the system. For example, as noted in [21], the introduction of time delay can induce the system to exhibit complex dynamic behaviors, a development that is vital for advancing phage therapy. As far as we know, this model (2) has yet to be studied with the incorporation of a time delay and analysis of its dynamic behavior, making the present study an important one.

Motivated by the above discussion and based on [33], in this paper we assume that the recruitment of phages and the infection of bacteria both require discrete time lags and introduce a discrete time delay into System (2). Such a model is more biologically realistic than existing models. Based on the work of [42], the delay-induced modified model is represented by

$$\begin{cases} \dot{B} = rB\left(1 - \dfrac{B}{K_C}\right) - \phi BP - \dfrac{\epsilon K_I B}{1 + B/K_D}, \\ \dot{P} = \beta\phi B(t-\tau)P(t-\tau) - wP. \end{cases} \tag{3}$$

subject to the initial conditions $B_0(\nu) = \chi_1(\nu) > 0$, $P_0(\nu) = \chi_2(\nu) > 0$ and $\nu \in [-\tau, 0]$, where $\chi_\gamma \in C([-\tau, 0] \longrightarrow \mathbb{R}_+)$ and $(\gamma = 1, 2)$ are given functions and τ is a positive constant.

According to other related studies, for example, [21,26,28,33], etc., the delay can destabilize the coexistence equilibrium and lead to the Hopf bifurcation of the system. Therefore, in this paper there is a real need to pose the important question of whether the delay causes System (3) to display these characteristics. Motivated by this fact, we introduce System (3) by adding a time delay term to System (2), then study the effects of delay on the dynamics of the system.

The remaining sections of this paper are organized as follows: in Section 2, we examine results relating to the non-delayed model, including the local and global stability of the positive equilibrium and the occurrence of Hopf bifurcation; Section 3 discusses similar results along with the stability and the direction of Hopf bifurcation for the delayed model; in Section 4, we conduct numerical simulations to verify our analytical results; finally, Section 5 presents the conclusions of this study.

2. Dynamics of the Non-Delayed Model

2.1. Positivity and Boundedness

In this context, positivity indicates that the population survives and boundedness represents a natural growth restriction due to limited resources. This subsection analyses the positivity and boundedness of the model in (2). In theoretical ecology, the biologically well-behaved nature of a system is established through its positivity and boundedness. Thus, System (2) has the following outcome.

Lemma 1. *System (2) has solutions $(B(t), P(t))$ in the interval $[0, \infty)$ that satisfy $B(t) \geq 0$, $P(t) \geq 0$, and $\forall t \geq 0$.*

Proof. The model in (2) can be written in matrix form:

$$\dot{X} = \mathcal{G}(X),$$
$$X = (x_1, x_2)^T = (B, P)^T \in \mathbb{R}^2$$

where $\mathcal{G}(X)$ is provided by

$$\mathcal{G}(X) = \begin{pmatrix} \mathcal{G}_1(X) \\ \mathcal{G}_2(X) \end{pmatrix} = \begin{pmatrix} rB\left(1 - \frac{B}{K_C}\right) - \phi BP - \frac{\epsilon K_I B}{1+B/K_D} \\ \beta\phi BP - w\,P \end{pmatrix}.$$

Because $\mathcal{G}(X)$ and $\frac{\partial \mathcal{G}}{\partial X}$ are continuous in $\mathbb{R}^2_+$, it is the case that $\mathcal{G} : \mathbb{R}^2_+ \to \mathbb{R}^2$ is locally Lipschitz. By the standard theory of the ODE system, it follows that model (2) has a unique solution for any initial condition $X(0) = X_0 = (B(0), P(0)) \in \mathbb{R}^2_+$.

Further, the model in (2) can be rewritten as

$$\frac{dB}{dt} = B\phi_1(B, P), \quad \frac{dP}{dt} = P\phi_2(B, P),$$

where

$$\phi_1(B, P) = r - \frac{r}{K_C}B - \phi P - \frac{\epsilon K_I}{1 + B/K_D},$$
$$\phi_2(B, P) = \beta\phi B - w.$$
$$\therefore \frac{dB}{dt} = B\phi_1(B, P) \Rightarrow \frac{1}{B}dB = \phi_1(B, P)$$

By integrating, we obtain

$$\ln B = \int \phi_1(B, P)dt + \ln C$$
$$\Rightarrow B = \exp[\int \phi_1(B, P)dt + \ln C] = C\exp[\int \phi_1(B, P)dt].$$

It follows that

$$B(t) = B(0)\exp\left[\int_0^t \phi_1(B(s), P(s))ds\right],$$

where $C = B(0)$. Thus, $B(t)$ is always positive, as $B(0) > 0$. Similarly, from second equation of System (2) we can find the positivity of $P(t)$, as $P(0) > 0$. Hence,

$$B(t) = B(0)\exp\left[\int_0^t \phi_1(B(s), P(s))ds\right] \geq 0,$$
$$P(t) = P(0)\exp\left[\int_0^t \phi_2(B(s), P(s))ds\right] \geq 0.$$

Thus, the solution $X(t) = (B(t), P(t))$ with initial condition $X(0) = X_0 = (B(0), P(0)) \in \mathbb{R}^2_+$ remains positive throughout the region $\mathbb{R}^2_+$. □

We next investigate whether the model in (2) is bounded within a particular region of the dynamical space.

To demonstrate the uniform boundedness of the model in (2), the following comparison lemma [44,45] is needed.

Lemma 2 (Comparison lemma). *If $K(t)$ is an absolutely continuous function which satisfies the differential inequality*

$$\frac{d(K(t))}{dt} + \sigma_1 K(t) \leq \sigma_2, \quad \textit{such that} \quad t \geq 0,$$

where $(\sigma_1, \sigma_2) \in \mathbb{R}^2$ and $\sigma_1 \neq 0$, then for all $t \geq \hat{T} \geq 0$ we have

$$K(t) \leq \frac{\sigma_2}{\sigma_1} - \left(\frac{\sigma_2}{\sigma_1} - K(\hat{T})\right) e^{-\sigma_1(t-\hat{T})}.$$

Remark 1. *All solutions of System (2) initiating in $\mathbb{R}^2_+$ are subject to the region $G = \{(B,P) \in \mathbb{R}^2_+ : \varpi(t) \leq \frac{v}{w}\}$ with $v := \beta\frac{K_C}{4r}(r+w)^2$, as $t \to \infty$ for all positive initial values $(B(0), P(0)) \in \mathbb{R}^2_+$, where $\varpi(t) = \beta B(t) + P(t)$. Using Comparison Lemma 2, we establish the outcome for a delay system. The proof follows in a similar fashion; see Theorem 6 as well.*

2.2. Existence of Equilibrium Points

This subsection demonstrates that the model in (2) has different equilibrium solutions. The following are the probable equilibria of System (2) according to [43] and simple calculation:

1. Trivial equilibrium: $E_0 = (0,0)$
2. Boundary equilibrium (phage-free equilibrium): $E_1 = (\bar{B}, 0)$, where $\bar{B} = \frac{K_C - K_D}{2} + \sqrt{\frac{(K_C+K_D)^2}{4} - \frac{\epsilon K_I K_C K_D}{r}}$ with $K_C > K_D$ and $r > \epsilon K_I$
3. Interior equilibrium: $E_2 = (B^*, P^*)$, where

$$B^* = \frac{w}{\beta\phi}, \quad P^* = \frac{1}{\phi}\left(r(1 - \frac{w}{\beta\phi K_C}) - \frac{\epsilon K_I}{1 + w/\beta\phi K_D}\right) \tag{4}$$

with

$$r > \frac{\epsilon\beta^2\phi^2 K_I K_C K_D}{(\beta\phi K_C - w)(w + \beta\phi K_D)} \quad \text{and} \quad w < \beta\phi K_C \tag{5}$$

2.3. Stability Analysis

Stability refers to a system's ability to resist small perturbations. Stability analysis is an acceptable tool for studying the long-term behavior of dynamic systems. In this subsection, we discuss the local and global stability and bifurcation analysis of System (2).

2.3.1. Stability Analysis of $E_0 = (0,0)$

Theorem 1.
(i) The equilibrium $E_0 = (0,0)$ is locally asymptotically stable if $r < \epsilon K_I$.
(ii) If the parameter r reaches the transcritical threshold $r = r_{tc} = \epsilon K_I$, a transcritical bifurcation arises around E_0 for System (2).

Proof. To acquire the local stability outcomes, we employ the Jacobian matrix related to System (2):

$$J(B,P) = \begin{pmatrix} r - \frac{2r}{K_C}B - \phi P - \frac{\epsilon K_I}{(1+B/K_D)^2} & -\phi B \\ \beta\phi P & \beta\phi B - w \end{pmatrix}.$$

(i) The Jacobian matrix of System (2) at E_0 is

$$J(E_0) = \begin{pmatrix} r - \epsilon K_I & 0 \\ 0 & -w \end{pmatrix}.$$

Thus, the trace and determinant of the matrix $J(E_0)$ are $\mathrm{tr}(J(E_0)) = r - \epsilon K_I - w$ and $\det(J(E_0)) = -w(r - \epsilon K_I)$, respectively. If $r < \epsilon K_I$, then $\mathrm{tr}(J_*(E_0)) < 0$ and $\det(J(E_0)) > 0$, and E_0 is locally asymptotically stable. Hence, E_0 is always unstable (saddle) when $r > \epsilon K_I$.

(ii) To demonstrate Theorem 1 (ii), we can use the transversality criteria based on Sotomayor's theorem [46]. To use Sotomayor's theorem, one of the eigenvalues of the matrix $J(E_0)$ must be zero at the bifurcation point r_{tc}. One eigenvalue of $J(E_0)$ disappears at $r = r_{tc} = \epsilon K_I$, while the other is $-w < 0$. Let $\Delta = (\delta_1, \delta_2)^T$ and $\Upsilon = (\gamma_1, \gamma_2)^T$ represent the eigenvectors of $J(E_0)$ and $J^T(E_0)$ with zero eigenvalue, respectively. Then, $\Delta = \Upsilon = [1,0]^T$.

We define $S(B,P) = \left[V(B,P), W(B,P)\right]^T$.
Therefore,

$$S_r(B,P) = \left[\frac{\partial V(B,P)}{\partial r}, \frac{\partial W(B,P)}{\partial r}\right]^T = \left[B(1-B/K_C), 0\right]^T,$$

which provides

$$Y^T\left[S_r(B,P)\right] = [1,0]\left[B(1-B/K_C), 0\right]^T = B(1-B/K_C).$$

Hence, we have $Y^T\left[S_r(E_0; r_{tc})\right] = 0$.
Now,

$$DS_r := \begin{pmatrix} \frac{\partial V_r}{\partial B} & \frac{\partial V_r}{\partial P} \\ \frac{\partial W_r}{\partial B} & \frac{\partial W_r}{\partial P} \end{pmatrix} = \begin{pmatrix} 1 - \frac{2B}{K_C} & 0 \\ 0 & 0 \end{pmatrix}.$$

Thus, we have $Y^T\left[DS_r(E_0; r_{tc})\Delta\right] = [1,0][1,0]^T = 1 \neq 0$, where

$$DS_r(E_0; r_{tc}) = \begin{pmatrix} 1 & 0 \\ 0 & 0 \end{pmatrix}.$$

Now, we can check the transversality condition.
Here,

$$D^2S(\Delta,\Delta) = \begin{pmatrix} V_{BB}\delta_1\delta_1 + V_{BP}\delta_1\delta_2 + V_{PB}\delta_2\delta_1 + V_{PP}\delta_2\delta_2 \\ W_{BB}\delta_1\delta_1 + W_{BP}\delta_1\delta_2 + W_{PB}\delta_2\delta_1 + W_{PP}\delta_2\delta_2 \end{pmatrix},$$

where $V_{BB}(0,0) = -\frac{2r}{K_C} + \frac{2\epsilon K_I}{K_D}$, $V_{BP}(0,0) = V_{PB}(0,0) = -\phi < 0$, $V_{PP}(0,0) = 0$, $W_{BB}(0,0) = 0$, $W_{BP}(0,0) = W_{PB}(0,0) = \beta\phi > 0$, and $W_{PP}(0,0) = 0$.

Thus, $D^2S((0,0); r_{tc})(\Delta,\Delta) = \left[-\frac{2r}{K_C} + \frac{2\epsilon K_I}{K_D}, 0\right]^T$, meaning that we have

$$Y^T\left[D^2S((0,0); r_{tc})(\Delta,\Delta)\right] = [1,0]\left[-\frac{2r}{K_C} + \frac{2\epsilon K_I}{K_D}, 0\right]^T = \left[-\frac{2r}{K_C} + \frac{2\epsilon K_I}{K_D}\right] \neq 0.$$

Hence, the system undergoes a supercritical transcritical bifurcation at E_0. The proof is now complete. □

Remark 2. *When $r < \epsilon K_I$, it is easy to observe that the trivial equilibrium E_0 is locally asymptotically stable and that the phage-free equilibrium E_1 does not exist. In contrast, the existence of E_1 implies the instability of E_0. Furthermore, the above discussion provides information regarding the experience of transcritical bifurcation around E_0.*

2.3.2. Stability Analysis of $E_1 = (\bar{B}, 0)$

Theorem 2.
(i) The phage-free equilibrium $E_1 = (\bar{B}, 0)$ is locally asymptotically stable if

$$r < \frac{\epsilon K_I K_C K_D^2}{(K_C - 2\bar{B})(\bar{B} + K_D)^2} \text{ and } w > \beta\phi\bar{B}.$$

(ii) The equilibrium $E_1 = (\bar{B}, 0)$ is globally asymptotically stable in the interior of the first quadrant of the plane.

Proof. (i) The variational matrix of the equilibrium $E_1 = (\bar{B}, 0)$ is

$$J(E_1) = \begin{pmatrix} r - \frac{2r}{K_C}\bar{B} - \frac{\epsilon K_I K_D^2}{(\bar{B}+K_D)^2} & -\phi\bar{B} \\ 0 & \beta\phi\bar{B} - w \end{pmatrix}.$$

The roots of $J(E_1)$ are $r - \frac{2r}{K_C}\bar{B} - \frac{\epsilon K_I K_D^2}{(\bar{B}+K_D)^2}$, $\beta\phi\bar{B} - w$. Hence, E_1 is locally asymptotically stable if $r < \frac{\epsilon K_I K_C K_D^2}{(K_C - 2\bar{B})(\bar{B}+K_D)^2}$ and $w > \beta\phi\bar{B}$.

(ii) Let $(B, P) \in \mathbb{R}_+^2 : \{(B, P) \in \mathbb{R}^2 : B > 0, P > 0\}$ and consider the function $L^* : \mathbb{R}_B^2 \longrightarrow \mathbb{R}$,

$$L^*(B, P) = b_1(B - \bar{B} - \bar{B}\ln(B/\bar{B})). \tag{6}$$

The derivative of (6) along the solutions of System (2) is

$$\frac{dL^*}{dt} = b_1\frac{1}{B}(B - \bar{B})\frac{dB}{dt} = b_1(B - \bar{B})\left[r\left(1 - \frac{B}{K_C}\right) - \frac{\epsilon K_I}{1 + B/K_D}\right]. \tag{7}$$

Because $E_2(B^*, P^*)$ satisfies (2), after a simple calculation we obtain

$$r\left(1 - \frac{\bar{B}}{K_C}\right) = \frac{\epsilon K_I}{1 + \bar{B}/K_D}. \tag{8}$$

Replacing (7) with (8), we obtain

$$\begin{aligned} \frac{dL^*}{dt} &= b_1(B - \bar{B})\left[r\left(1 - \frac{B}{K_C}\right) - r\left(1 - \frac{\bar{B}}{K_C}\right)\right] \\ &= b_1(B - \bar{B})\left[-\frac{r}{K_C}(B - \bar{B})\right] \\ &= \frac{-rb_1}{K_C}(B - \bar{B})^2 < 0. \end{aligned}$$

According to the negative coefficients of the square terms, $\frac{dL^*}{dt}$ is less than zero along all trajectories in the plane except $E_2(B^*, P^*)$. Therefore, $E_2(B^*, P^*)$ is globally asymptotically stable. □

2.3.3. Stability and Hopf Bifurcation of $E_2 = (B^*, P^*)$

Theorem 3. *Assume that* $r^* = \frac{\epsilon\beta^2\phi^2 K_I K_C K_D}{(w+\beta\phi K_D)^2}$ *and that (5) holds. The following assertions are obtained:*

(i) The equilibrium E_2 *of System (2) is locally asymptotically stable if* $r > r^*$ *and unstable if* $r < r^*$.

(ii) If $r = r^*$, *System (2) experiences Hopf bifurcation at* E_2, *and* r^* *is the system's critical value.*

Proof. The Jacobian matrix of System (2) at the interior equilibrium $E_2 = (B^*, P^*)$ is

$$J(E_2) = \begin{pmatrix} r - \frac{2r}{K_C}B^* - \phi P^* - \frac{\epsilon K_I}{(1+B^*/K_D)^2} & -\phi B^* \\ \beta\phi P^* & \beta\phi B^* - w \end{pmatrix}.$$

Substituting the values of B^* and P^* described in (4) into $J(E_2)$, we obtain

$$J_*(E_2) = \begin{pmatrix} \frac{\epsilon w\beta\phi K_I K_D}{(w+\beta\phi K_D)^2} - \frac{rw}{\beta\phi K_C} & -\frac{w}{\beta} \\ \frac{r(\beta\phi K_C - w)}{\phi K_C} - \frac{\epsilon\beta^2\phi K_I K_D}{w+\beta\phi K_D} & 0 \end{pmatrix}.$$

The characteristic equation of $J_*(E_2)$ is

$$\lambda^2 - \mathrm{tr}(J_*(E_2))\lambda + \det(J_*(E_2)) = 0, \tag{9}$$

$$\begin{aligned} \mathrm{tr}(J_*(E_2)) &= -\frac{rw}{\beta\phi K_C} + \frac{\epsilon w\beta\phi K_I K_D}{(w+\beta\phi K_D)^2}, \\ \det(J_*(E_2)) &= \frac{w}{\beta}\left[\frac{r(\beta\phi K_C - w)}{\phi K_C} - \frac{\epsilon\beta^2\phi K_I K_D}{w+\beta\phi K_D}\right]. \end{aligned}$$

(i) If $r > r^* = \frac{\epsilon\beta^2\phi^2 K_I K_C K_D}{(w+\beta\phi K_D)^2}$, then $\mathrm{tr}(J_*(E_2)) < 0$, and the existence condition (5) of E_2 implies $\det(J_*(E_2)) > 0$. Thus, the characteristic Equation (9) has negative real parts, as $\mathrm{tr}(J_*(E_2)) < 0$ and $\det(J_*(E_2)) > 0$. Hence, $E_2 = (B^*, P^*)$ is locally asymptotically stable in B-P space for $r > r^*$. Moreover, E_2 is unstable in that space for $r < r^*$.

(ii) It is obvious that if $\mathrm{tr}(J_*(E_2)) = 0$ and $\det(J_*(E_2)) > 0$, then both of the roots must be purely imaginary. Thus, from the implicit function theorem a Hopf bifurcation emerges in which a periodic orbit is generated as the stability of the equilibrium point E_2 varies. The critical value of Hopf bifurcation parameter is defined by $r = r^* = \frac{\epsilon\beta^2\phi^2 K_I K_C K_D}{(w+\beta\phi K_D)^2}$. From the above analysis, it is easy to see that under the given conditions we have the following: (a) $\mathrm{tr}(J_*(E_2)) = 0$, (b) $\det(J_*(E_2)) > 0$, and (c) $\frac{d}{dr}\mathrm{tr}(J_*(E_2)) = -\frac{w}{\beta\phi K_C} \neq 0$ at $r = r^*$. This result guarantees the presence of Hopf bifurcation around the positive equilibrium E_2. The proof is complete. □

2.3.4. Non-Existence of Non-Trivial Periodic Solution of System (2)

It is essential to determine whether an ecological system has a periodic solution, as the existence of such a solution can lead to complex ecological phenomena. On the one hand, the nonexistence of a periodic solution can convert a locally stable equilibrium into a globally stable one. In this subsection, using the Dulac–Bendixon criterion [46], we demonstrate the non-existence of periodic solutions to System (2).

Theorem 4. *If there exists a continuously differentiable function $\Theta(B,P)$ in the interior of $\mathbb{R}^n_+$ such that $\overrightarrow{\nabla} \cdot (\Theta S)$ has constant sign and is not identically zero in any subregion, then system (2) does not possess any limit cycle, and in fact has a closed trajectory which lies entirely within $\mathbb{R}^n_+$.*

Proof. Construct the Dulac function as $\Theta(B,P) = \frac{1}{BP}$ and a C^1 vector field defined in $\mathbb{R}^{20}_+$ as $S(B,P) = (V,W) = \left(rB - \frac{r}{K_C}B^2 - \phi BP - \frac{\epsilon K_I B}{1+B/K_D}, \beta\phi BP - wP\right)$. Clearly, $\Theta \in C^1(\mathbb{R}^{20}_+)$, where $\mathbb{R}^{20}_+$ is the interior of $\mathbb{R}^n_+$. Moreover, it is clear that $\Theta(B,P) > 0$ in $\mathbb{R}^{n0}_+$. We obtain

$$\begin{aligned} \overrightarrow{\nabla} \cdot (\Theta S) &= \frac{\partial}{\partial B}(\Theta V) + \frac{\partial}{\partial P}(\Theta W) \\ &= \frac{1}{P}\frac{\partial}{\partial B}\left(r - \frac{r}{K_C}B - \phi P - \frac{\epsilon K_I}{1+B/K_D}\right) + \frac{1}{B}\frac{\partial}{\partial P}(\beta\phi B - w) \\ &= \frac{1}{P}\left(-\frac{r}{K_C} + \frac{\epsilon K_I K_D}{(B+K_D)^2}\right) \\ &< 0, \text{ provided } r > \frac{\epsilon\beta^2\phi^2 K_I K_C K_D}{(w+\beta\phi K_D)^2}. \end{aligned}$$

Obviously, $\overrightarrow{\nabla} \cdot (\Theta S)$ is neither zero nor changes its sign in the interior $\mathbb{R}^2_+$. Thus, according to the Dulac–Bendixon criterion, System (2) does not have a closed orbit that lies entirely in the interior $\mathbb{R}^2_+$ if $r > \frac{\epsilon\beta^2\phi^2 K_I K_C K_D}{(w+\beta\phi K_D)^2}$. □

2.3.5. Global Stability of $E_2 = (B^*, P^*)$

In this subsection, we provide the global asymptotic stability of the positive equilibrium E_2 by creating a proper Lyapunov function.

Theorem 5. *The positive equilibrium $E_2 = (B^*, P^*)$ is globally asymptotically stable if $\beta < 1$ holds.*

Proof. Define the functional $L(B, P) : \mathbb{R}^2_+ \to \mathbb{R}$ such that

$$L(B, P) = L_1(B) + L_2(P),$$

where $L_1(B) = (B - B^* - B^* \ln(B/B^*)), L_2(P) = (P - P^* - P^* \ln(P/P^*))$. Clearly, $L(B, P)$ is continuous and well-defined on $\mathrm{Int}(\mathbb{R}^2_+)$, while L is positive in the interior of $\mathbb{R}^2_+$ except at $E_2 = (B^*, P^*)$ and $L(B, P)$ disappears at $E_2 = (B^*, P^*)$. As a result of differentiating the function L with respect to the time t along the trajectories of (2), we obtain

$$\frac{dL}{dt} = \frac{dL_1}{dt} + \frac{dL_2}{dt}. \tag{10}$$

Furthermore, the time derivatives of L_1 and L_2 along the solutions of (2) are

$$\frac{dL_1}{dt} = (B - B^*)\left[r\left(1 - \frac{B}{K_C}\right) - \phi P - \frac{\epsilon K_I}{1 + B/K_D}\right], \tag{11}$$

$$\frac{dL_2}{dt} = (P - P^*)(\beta\phi B - w), \tag{12}$$

Because $E_2 = (B^*, P^*)$ satisfies (2), by using a straightforward calculation we can obtain

$$\frac{\epsilon K_I}{1 + B^*/K_D} = r\left(1 - \frac{B^*}{K_C}\right) - \phi P^*, \quad w = \beta\phi B^*. \tag{13}$$

The result of replacing the two values of (13) with (11) and (12) is

$$\frac{dL_1}{dt} = \frac{-r}{K_C}(B - B^*)^2 - \phi(B - B^*)(P - P^*), \tag{14}$$

$$\frac{dL_2}{dt} = \beta\phi(B - B^*)(P - P^*). \tag{15}$$

Using algebraic computation, substituting (14) and (15) into (10) yields

$$\begin{aligned}\frac{dL}{dt} &= \frac{-r}{K_C}(B - B^*)^2 - \phi(B - B^*)(P - P^*) + \beta\phi(B - B^*)(P - P^*)\\ &\leq \frac{1}{2}\left(-\frac{2r}{K_C} - \phi + \beta\phi\right)(B - B^*)^2 + \frac{1}{2}(-\phi + \beta\phi)(P - P^*)^2.\end{aligned}$$

If the requirement in Theorem 5 is satisfied, then $\frac{dL}{dt} < 0$ along all trajectories in $\mathbb{R}^2_+$ except for $E_2 = (B^*, P^*)$. Hence, $E_2 = (B^*, P^*)$ is globally asymptotically stable. □

3. Dynamics of the Delayed Model

3.1. Positivity and Boundedness

Next, we establish the positivity of the system (3). We can express the first equation of (3) as

$$\frac{dB}{B} = \left(r - \frac{rB}{K_C} - \phi P - \frac{\epsilon K_I}{1 + B/K_D}\right)dt.$$

Integrating across the interval $[0, t]$ yields the following result:

$$B(t) = B(0)\exp\left[\int_0^t \left\{r - \frac{r}{K_C}B(s) - \phi P(s) - \frac{\epsilon K_I}{1 + B(s)/K_D}\right\}ds\right],$$

which indicates that $B(t) > 0, \forall\, t$ whenever $B(0) > 0$.

Using the second equation from (3), we can derive

$$P(t) = P(0)\exp\left[\int_0^t \left\{ \frac{\beta\phi B(s-\tau)P(s-\tau)}{P(s)} - \omega \right\} ds\right],$$

which means that $P(t) > 0\ \forall\, t$ whenever $P(0) > 0$. Thus, the interior of the first quadrant is an invariant set for System (3).

Theorem 6. *All solutions of System (3) initiating in $\mathbb{R}_+^2$ are subject to the region $G^* = \{(B,P) \in \mathbb{R}_+^2 : \varrho(t) \le \frac{v}{w}\}$ with $v := \beta\frac{K_C}{4r}(r+w)^2$, as $t \to \infty$ for all positive initial values $(B_0(\theta), P_0(\theta)) \in \mathbb{R}_+^2$, where $\varrho(t) = \beta B(t-\tau) + P(t)$.*

Proof. We define $\varrho(t) = \beta B(t-\tau) + P(t)$; when we differentiate ϱ with respect to t along the trajectories of the model in (3), we obtain

$$\begin{aligned}
\frac{d\varrho}{dt} &= \beta\frac{dB(t-\tau)}{dt} + \frac{dP(t)}{dt} \\
&= r\beta B(t-\tau)\left(1 - \frac{B(t-\tau)}{K_C}\right) - \frac{\beta\epsilon K_I B(t-\tau)}{1 + B(t-\tau)/K_D} - wP(t).
\end{aligned}$$

Hence,

$$\begin{aligned}
\frac{d\varrho}{dt} + w\varrho &= \beta B(t-\tau)\left[(r+w) - \frac{r}{K_C}B(t-\tau)\right] - \frac{\beta\epsilon K_I B(t-\tau)}{1 + B(t-\tau)/K_D} \\
&\le \beta B(t-\tau)\left[(r+w) - \frac{r}{K_C}B(t-\tau)\right] \\
&\le \beta\frac{K_C}{4r}(r+w)^2.
\end{aligned}$$

Now, taking $v = \beta\frac{K_C}{4r}(r+w)^2$, we obtain

$$\frac{d\varrho}{dt} + w\varrho \le v.$$

Using Comparison Lemma 2, we obtain

$$0 \le \varrho(t) \le \frac{v}{w} - \left(\frac{v}{w} - \varrho(t_0)\right)e^{w(t_0 - t)},$$

and for $t \to \infty$ we obtain

$$0 \le \varrho(t) \le \frac{v}{w}.$$

Hence, all solutions of System (3) are bounded. □

3.2. Stability Analysis

To establish the stability of the delayed model, we linearize (3) by replacing $B(t) = B^* + v_1$ and $P(t) = P^* + v_2$ while retaining the first-order terms [20]. The linearized system is provided by

$$\begin{aligned}
\frac{dv_1}{dt} &= \left[-\frac{r}{K_C}B^* + \frac{\epsilon K_I K_D B^*}{(B^* + K_D)^2}\right]v_1 - \phi B^* v_2, \\
\frac{dv_2}{dt} &= \beta\phi P^* v_1(t-\tau) + \beta\phi B^* v_2(t-\tau) - wv_2.
\end{aligned} \tag{16}$$

The variational matrix is

$$J^*(E_2) = \begin{pmatrix} -\frac{r}{K_C}B^* + \frac{\epsilon K_I K_D B^*}{(B^*+K_D)^2} & -\phi B^* \\ \beta\phi P^* e^{-\lambda\tau} & \beta\phi B^* e^{-\lambda\tau} - w \end{pmatrix}.$$

For $\tau = 0$, the characteristic equation of $J^*(E_2)$ is as follows:

$$\lambda^2 - (c_{11} + c_{22})\lambda + c_{11}c_{22} - c_{12}c_{21} = 0, \tag{17}$$

where

$$c_{11} = -\frac{r}{K_C}B^* + \frac{\epsilon K_I K_D B^*}{(B^* + K_D)^2}, \; c_{12} = -\phi B^*, \; c_{21} = \beta\phi P^*, \; c_{22} = \beta\phi B^* - w.$$

Then, Equation (17) is the same as Equation (9) of the non-delayed System (2) examined previously. Hence, when the first condition of Theorem 3(i) is satisfied the interior equilibrium $E_2 = (B^*, P^*)$ is locally asymptotically stable.

Alternatively, according to the Routh–Hurwitz criteria, the roots of Equation (17) have a negative real part, meaning that $E_2 = (B^*, P^*)$ is locally asymptotically stable if

$$\begin{aligned} c_{11} + c_{22} &= -\frac{r}{K_C}B^* + \frac{\epsilon K_I K_D B^*}{(B^* + K_D)^2} + \beta\phi B^* - w < 0, \\ c_{11}c_{22} - c_{12}c_{21} &= \left(-\frac{r}{K_C}B^* + \frac{\epsilon K_I K_D B^*}{(B^* + K_D)^2}\right)(\beta\phi B^* - w) + \beta\phi^2 B^* P^* > 0. \end{aligned} \tag{18}$$

In the case of positive delay, the characteristic equation is

$$D(\lambda) + F(\lambda)\mathrm{e}^{-\lambda\tau} = 0, \tag{19}$$

where

$$D(\lambda) = \lambda^2 + c_1\lambda + c_2; \; F(\lambda) = c_3\lambda + c_4, \tag{20}$$

$$\begin{aligned} c_1 &= w + \frac{r}{K_C}B^* - \frac{\epsilon K_I K_D B^*}{(B^* + K_D)^2}, \\ c_2 &= -w\left(-\frac{r}{K_C}B^* + \frac{\epsilon K_I K_D B^*}{(B^* + K_D)^2}\right), \\ c_3 &= -\beta\phi B^*, \\ c_4 &= \beta\phi B^*\left(-\frac{r}{K_C}B^* + \frac{\epsilon K_I K_D B^*}{(B^* + K_D)^2} + \phi P^*\right). \end{aligned}$$

The characteristic Equation (19) is a transcendental equation with infinite solutions near the positive equilibrium $E_2 = (B^*, P^*)$. As periodic solutions of the system are of interest, the eigenvalues of (19) must be purely imaginary. Substituting $\lambda = i\omega(\omega > 0)$ in (19) yields

$$-\omega^2 + ic_1\omega + c_2 + \mathrm{e}^{-i\omega\tau}(c_3 i\omega) = 0. \tag{21}$$

Separating the real and imaginary parts, we obtain

$$c_4\cos(\omega\tau) + c_3\omega\sin(\omega\tau) = \omega^2 - c_2, \; c_3\omega\cos(\omega\tau) + c_4\sin(\omega\tau) = -c_1\omega, \tag{22}$$

implying that

$$\cos(\omega\tau) = \frac{c_4\omega^2 - c_2c_4 - c_1c_3\omega^2}{c_4^2 + c_3^2\omega^2}, \; \sin(\omega\tau) = \frac{c_3\omega^3 - c_2c_3\omega + c_1c_4\omega}{c_4^2 + c_3^2\omega^2}. \tag{23}$$

Eliminating τ from (22), we obtain

$$\omega^4 + \omega^2(c_1^2 - 2c_2 - c_3^2) + c_2^2 - c_4^2 = 0. \tag{24}$$

Equation (24) is a quadratic equation in ω^2. If we assume that $c_2^2 - c_4^2 < 0$, then (24) can have a positive root. Hence, we obtain a unique non-negative root ω_0 of Equation (24) as follows:

$$\omega_0 = \sqrt{\frac{-(c_1^2 - 2c_2 - c_3^2) + \sqrt{(c_1^2 - 2c_2 - c_3^2)^2 + 4(c_4^2 - c_2^2)}}{2}}. \tag{25}$$

Substituting the value of ω_0 in (23) and solving for τ yields

$$\tan(\omega_0 \tau) = \frac{c_3\omega_0^3 + (c_1c_4 - c_2c_3)\omega_0}{(c_4 - c_1c_3)\omega_0^2 - c_2c_4}. \tag{26}$$

Thus, the critical magnitude τ_s of the delay parameter corresponding to ω_0 is derived as follows:

$$\tau_s = \frac{1}{\omega_0}\arctan\left[\frac{c_3\omega_0^3 + (c_1c_4 - c_2c_3)\omega_0}{(c_4 - c_1c_3)\omega_0^2 - c_2c_4}\right] + \frac{2s\pi}{\omega_0} \tag{27}$$

for $s = 0, 1, 2, 3, \ldots$. For $\tau = 0$, E_2 is stable provided that $c_2^2 - c_4^2 < 0$. Hence, according to Butler's Lemma [47], E_2 remains stable for $\tau < \tau_s$, where $\tau_s = \tau_0$ at $s = 0$.

3.3. *Hopf Bifurcation Analysis*

Biologically, all species that coexist exhibit oscillatory balanced behaviour. Meanwhile, a periodic solution arises in a system when the analyzed equilibrium point changes in stability as a function of its parameters. To capture the oscillating coexistence of populations, we establish the Hopf bifurcation analysis around the coexistence equilibrium point with the discrete delay as a bifurcation parameter. In this subsection, we explore the Hopf bifurcation of the model, which requires the transversality condition $\frac{d(\mathrm{Re}\lambda)}{d\tau}\big|_{\tau=\tau_s} > 0$ to be affirmed [48]. Setting $\lambda = i\omega_0$ into (19), we obtain $|D(i\omega_0)| = |F(i\omega_0)|$, which specifies a probable set of values for ω_0. We focus on the direction of motion of λ as τ varies, which we decide as follows:

$$\Phi = \mathrm{sign}\left[\frac{d(\mathrm{Re}\lambda)}{d\tau}\right]_{\lambda=i\omega_0} = \mathrm{sign}\left[\mathrm{Re}\left(\frac{d\lambda}{d\tau}\right)^{-1}\right]_{\lambda=i\omega_0}.$$

When differentiating (19) with respect to τ, we obtain

$$[(2\lambda + c_1) + c_3 e^{-\lambda\tau} - \tau(c_3\lambda + c_4)e^{-\lambda\tau}]\frac{d\lambda}{d\tau} = (c_3\lambda + c_4)\lambda e^{-\lambda\tau}, \tag{28}$$

$$\begin{aligned}\left(\frac{d\lambda}{d\tau}\right)^{-1} &= \frac{2\lambda + c_1}{\lambda e^{-\lambda\tau}(c_3\lambda + c_4)} + \frac{c_3 e^{-\lambda\tau}}{(c_3\lambda + c_4)\lambda e^{-\lambda\tau}} - \frac{\tau}{\lambda} \\ &= \frac{2\lambda + c_1}{-\lambda(\lambda^2 + c_1\lambda + c_2)} + \frac{c_3}{\lambda(c_3\lambda + c_4)} - \frac{\tau}{\lambda} \\ &= \frac{\lambda^2 - c_2}{-\lambda^2(\lambda^2 + c_1\lambda + c_2)} + \frac{-c_4}{\lambda^2(c_3\lambda + c_4)} - \frac{\tau}{\lambda}.\end{aligned}$$

Thus,

$$\begin{aligned}
\Phi &= \text{sign}\left\{\text{Re}\left[\frac{\lambda^2 - c_2}{-\lambda^2(\lambda^2 + c_1\lambda + c_2)} + \frac{-c_4}{\lambda^2(c_3\lambda + c_4)} - \frac{\tau\lambda}{\lambda^2}\right]\right\}_{\lambda = i\omega_0} \\
&= \frac{1}{\omega_0^2}\text{sign}\left\{\text{Re}\left[\frac{c_2 + \omega_0^2}{\omega_0^2 - ic_1\omega_0 - c_2} + \frac{a_4}{ic_3\omega_0 + c_4}\right]\right\} \\
&= \frac{1}{\omega_0^2}\text{sign}\left\{\left[\frac{(c_2 + \omega_0^2)(\omega_0^2 - c_2)}{(\omega_0^2 - c_2)^2 + c_1^2\omega_0^2} + \frac{c_4^2}{c_4^2 + c_3^2\omega_0^2}\right]\right\} \\
&= \frac{1}{\omega_0^2}\text{sign}\left\{\frac{\omega_0^4 + (c_4^2 - c_2^2)}{c_4^2 + c_3^2\omega_0^2}\right\} > 0 \ (\text{since } c_2^2 - c_4^2 < 0).
\end{aligned}$$

Hence, the transversality criterion is satisfied and the Hopf bifurcation happens at $\omega = \omega_0, \tau = \tau_s$. The biquadratic Equation (24) has a unique non-negative root; therefore, the question of stability switching is irrelevant to our model [49]. The delay-induced phage therapy model provides a periodic solution with a small amplitude that bifurcates from the positive equilibrium point when the bifurcation parameter τ crosses its critical value $\tau = \tau_0$, where τ_0 is the smallest positive value provided by Equation (27). The following theorem summarizes the above results.

Theorem 7. *Suppose that the existence condition (5) of E_2 and the conditions in (18) hold for the model in (3). Then,*
(i) If $\tau < \tau_s$, then the interior equilibrium E_2 is locally asymptotically stable.
(ii) If $\tau > \tau_s$, then the interior equilibrium E_2 is unstable.
(iii) At $\tau = \tau_s$, System (3) undergoes a Hopf bifurcation around $E_2(B^*, P^*)$.

3.4. Direction and Stability of Hopf-Bifurcating Periodic Solution

In the previous section, we determined the conditions for Hopf bifurcation around the positive equilibrium point $E_2(B^*, P^*)$ at the critical value $\tau = \tau_s$. This section aims to determine the direction of Hopf bifurcation and the stability of the bifurcating periodic solutions from the interior equilibrium $E_2(B^*, P^*)$ with the help of the center manifold theorem and the normal form theory created by Hassard et al. [50]. In this section, we assume that System (3) undergoes Hopf bifurcation around the interior equilibrium E_2 at $\tau = \tau_s$, with $\pm i\omega_0$ denoting the corresponding purely imaginary roots of the characteristic equation at E_2.

First, we employ transformation $v_1(t) = B(t) - B^*(t), v_2(t) = P(t) - P^*(t), \tau = \tau_s + \varepsilon$ of System (3) by Taylor series expansion for the positive equilibrium (B^*, P^*); thus, the system becomes

$$\begin{aligned}
\frac{dv_1}{dt} &= d_{10}v_1(t) + d_{01}v_1(t) + \sum_{i+j\geqslant 2} d_{ij}B^iP^j, \\
\frac{dv_2}{dt} &= m_{01}v_2(t) + m_{12}v_1(t-\tau) + m_{21}v_2(t-\tau) + \sum_{i+j+k\geqslant 2} m_{ijk}P^iB^j(t-\tau)P^k(t-\tau),
\end{aligned}$$

where

$$\begin{aligned}
H^{(1)} &= rB\left(1 - \frac{B}{K_C}\right) - \phi BP - \frac{\epsilon K_I B}{1 + B/K_D}, \ H^{(2)} = \beta\phi B(t-\tau)P(t-\tau) - wP, \\
d_{ij} &= \frac{1}{i!j!}\frac{\partial^{i+j}H^{(1)}}{\partial B^i \partial P^j}\bigg|_{(B^*,P^*)}, \ m_{ijk} = \frac{1}{i!j!k!}\frac{\partial^{i+j+k}H^{(2)}}{\partial P^i \partial B^j(t-\tau)\partial P^k(t-\tau)}\bigg|_{(B^*,P^*)}, \\
d_{10} &= -\frac{r}{K_C}B^* + \frac{\epsilon K_I K_D B^*}{(B^* + K_D)^2}, \ d_{01} = -\phi B^*, \ m_{12} = \beta\phi P^*, \ m_{21} = \beta\phi B^*, \ m_{01} = -w,
\end{aligned}$$

substituted by the functional differential (FDE) in $\mathcal{C} = C([-1,0],\mathbf{R}^2)$ as

$$\dot{v}(t) = A_\varepsilon(v_t) + f(\varepsilon, v_t), \tag{29}$$

where $v(t) = (v_1(t), v_2(t))^T \in \mathbf{R}^2$, $v_t(\nu) = v(t+\nu)$ for $\nu \in [-1,0)$, and $A_\varepsilon : C \to \mathbf{R}$, $f : \mathbf{R} \times C \to \mathbf{R}$ are respectively provided by

$$\begin{aligned} A_\varepsilon(\rho) = {} & (\tau_s+\varepsilon)\begin{pmatrix} -\frac{r}{K_C}B^* + \frac{\epsilon K_I K_D B^*}{(B^*+K_D)^2} & -\phi B^* \\ 0 & -w \end{pmatrix} \\ & \begin{pmatrix} \rho_1(0) \\ \rho_2(0) \end{pmatrix} + (\tau_s+\varepsilon)\begin{pmatrix} 0 & 0 \\ \beta\phi P^* & \beta\phi B^* \end{pmatrix}\begin{pmatrix} \rho_1(-1) \\ \rho_2(-1) \end{pmatrix}, \end{aligned} \tag{30}$$

$$f(\varepsilon,\rho) = (\tau_s+\varepsilon)\begin{pmatrix} (-\frac{r}{K_C} + \frac{\epsilon K_I K_D}{(B^*+K_D)^2} - \frac{2\epsilon K_I K_D B^*}{(B^*+K_D)^3})\rho_1^2(0) - \phi\rho_1(0)\rho_2(0) \\ \beta\phi\rho_1(-1)\rho_2(-1) \end{pmatrix}. \tag{31}$$

According to Riesz representation theorem, for $\nu \in [-1,0)$ there exists a bounded variation function $\eta(\nu,\varepsilon)$ such that

$$A_\varepsilon\rho = \int_{-\tau}^{0} d\eta(\nu,0)\rho(0) \ \text{ for } \rho \in C^1[-1,0). \tag{32}$$

In fact, we have a choice:

$$\begin{aligned} \eta(\nu,\varepsilon) = (\tau_s+\varepsilon)\begin{pmatrix} -\frac{r}{K_C}B^* + \frac{\epsilon K_I K_D B^*}{(B^*+K_D)^2} & -\phi B^* \\ 0 & -w \end{pmatrix}\delta(\nu) - (\tau_s+\varepsilon)\begin{pmatrix} 0 & 0 \\ \beta\phi P^* & \beta\phi B^* \end{pmatrix} \\ \delta(\nu+1), \end{aligned} \tag{33}$$

where $\delta(\nu)$ is the Dirac delta function. For $\rho \in C^1([-1,0),\mathbf{R}^2)$, we define

$$M(\varepsilon)\rho(\nu) = \begin{cases} \dfrac{d\rho(\nu)}{d\nu}, & \text{for } \nu \in [-1,0); \\ \displaystyle\int_{-1}^{0} d\eta(\nu,\varepsilon)\rho(\nu), & \text{for } \nu = 0, \end{cases} \tag{34}$$

and

$$Y(\varepsilon)\rho(\nu) = \begin{cases} 0, & \text{for } \nu \in [-1,0); \\ f(\varepsilon,\rho), & \text{for } \nu = 0. \end{cases} \tag{35}$$

Thus, (29) can be recast as

$$\dot{v}_t = M(\varepsilon)v_t + Y(\varepsilon)v_t, \tag{36}$$

where $v_t(\nu) = v(t+\nu)$ for $\nu \in [-1,0)$.

For $\zeta \in C^1([-1,0),(\mathbf{R}^2)^*)$, the adjoint M^* of M can be described as

$$M^*(\varepsilon)\zeta(\kappa) = \begin{cases} -\dfrac{d\zeta}{d\kappa}, & \text{for } \kappa \in (0,1]; \\ \displaystyle\int_{-1}^{0} d\eta^T(t,0)\zeta(-t), & \text{for } \kappa = 0. \end{cases} \tag{37}$$

For $\rho \in [-1,0)$ and $\zeta \in [0,1]$, a bilinear linear form provides

$$\langle\zeta(\kappa),\rho(\nu)\rangle = \bar{\zeta}(0)\rho(0) - \int_{\nu=-1}^{0}\int_{\varphi=0}^{\nu}\bar{\zeta}(\varphi-\nu)d\eta(\nu)\rho(\varphi)d\varphi, \tag{38}$$

where $\eta(\nu) = \eta(\nu,0)$. Thus, $M(0)$ and M^* are adjoint operators. Because $\pm i\omega_0\tau_s$ are the eigenvalues of $M(0)$, $\pm i\omega_0\tau_s$ are the the eigenvalues of M^*.

Proposition 1. *Assume that $q(\nu) = (1,s)^T e^{i\omega_0\tau_s\nu}$ is the eigenvector of $M(0)$ corresponding to $i\omega_0\tau_s$ and that $q^*(\nu) = (1,s^*)^T Q e^{i\omega_0\tau_s\nu}$ is the eigenvector of M^* corresponding to $-i\omega_0\tau_s$. Then, $\langle q^*,\bar{q}\rangle = 0$, $\langle q^*,q\rangle = 1$, with $s = \frac{\beta\phi P^* e^{-i\omega_0\tau_s}}{w+i\omega_0-\beta\phi B^* e^{-i\omega_0\tau_s}}$, $s^* = \frac{\phi B^*}{\beta\phi B^* e^{-i\omega_0\tau_s}-w+i\omega_0}$, $\bar{Q} = [1+\bar{s}^*s+\bar{s}^*\tau_s(\beta\phi P^*+s\beta\phi B^*)e^{-i\omega_0\tau_s}]^{-1}$.*

Proof. Here, we suppose that $q(\nu)$ is the eigenvector of $M(0)$ corresponding to $i\omega_0\tau_s$, $M(0)q(\nu) = i\omega_0\tau_s q(\nu)$. Using the definition of $M(0)$ with (30), (32), and (33), we obtain

$$\begin{pmatrix} -\frac{r}{K_C}B^* + \frac{\epsilon K_I K_D B^*}{(B^*+K_D)^2} - i\omega_0 & -\phi B^* \\ \beta\phi P^* e^{-i\omega_0\tau_s} & \beta\phi B^* e^{-i\omega_0\tau_s} - w - i\omega_0 \end{pmatrix} q(0) = \begin{pmatrix} 0 \\ 0 \end{pmatrix}.$$

It is easy to compute that $q(0) = (1,s)^T$, where

$$q(0) = \begin{pmatrix} 1 \\ s \end{pmatrix} = \begin{pmatrix} 1 \\ \frac{\beta\phi P^* e^{-i\omega_0\tau_s}}{w+i\omega_0-\beta\phi B^* e^{-i\omega_0\tau_s}} \end{pmatrix}.$$

As $q^*(\kappa) = (1,s^*)Qe^{i\omega_0\tau_s\kappa}$ is the eigenvector of M^* associated with $-i\omega_0\tau_s$, we obtain

$$M^*(0)q^*(\kappa) = -i\omega_0\tau_s q^*(\kappa).$$

Through (32), (33), and (37), we have

$$\begin{pmatrix} -\frac{r}{K_C}B^* + \frac{\epsilon K_I K_D B^*}{(B^*+K_D)^2} + i\omega_0 & \beta\phi P^* e^{-i\omega_0\tau_s} \\ -\phi B^* & \beta\phi B^* e^{-i\omega_0\tau_s} - w + i\omega_0 \end{pmatrix} (q^*(0))^T = \begin{pmatrix} 0 \\ 0 \end{pmatrix}.$$

Now,

$$q^*(\kappa) = (1,s^*)Qe^{i\omega_0\tau_s\kappa} = \left(1, \frac{\phi B^*}{\beta\phi B^* e^{-i\omega_0\tau_s} - w + i\omega_0}\right)Qe^{i\omega_0\tau_s\kappa}.$$

To verify $\langle q^*(\kappa), q(\nu)\rangle = 1$, it is necessary to find the expression for Q. From (38), we obtain

$$\begin{aligned}
\langle q^*(\kappa), q(\nu)\rangle &= \bar{Q}(1,\bar{s}^*)(1,s)^T - \int_{\nu=-1}^{0}\int_{\varphi=0}^{\nu} \bar{Q}(1,\bar{s}^*)e^{-i\omega_0\tau_s(\varphi-\nu)}d\eta(\nu)(1,s)^T e^{i\omega_0\tau_s\varphi}d\varphi \\
&= \bar{Q}\left\{(1+\bar{s}^*s) - \int_{\nu=-1}^{0}(1,\bar{s}^*)\nu e^{i\omega_0\tau_s\nu}d\eta(\nu)(1,s)^T\right\} \\
&= \bar{Q}\left\{1+\bar{s}^*s+\bar{s}^*\tau_s(\beta\phi P^*+s\beta\phi B^*)e^{-i\omega_0\tau_s}\right\}.
\end{aligned}$$

Hence, we may decide $\bar{Q}$ as

$$\bar{Q} = [1+\bar{s}^*s+\bar{s}^*\tau_s(\beta\phi P^*+s\beta\phi B^*)e^{-i\omega_0\tau_s}]^{-1}.$$

Moreover, using the adjoint property we have $\langle \xi, M\rho\rangle = \langle M^*\xi,\rho\rangle$.
Thus, $-i\omega_0\tau_s\langle q^*,\bar{q}\rangle = \langle q^*, M\bar{q}\rangle = \langle M^*q^*,\bar{q}\rangle = \langle -i\omega_0\tau_s q^*,\bar{q}\rangle = i\omega_0\tau_s\langle q^*,\bar{q}\rangle$.
Therefore, $\langle q^*,\bar{q}\rangle = 0$ is easy to prove. □

Next, we apply the procedures in [50]; we first calculate the coordinates explaining the center manifold C_0 at $\varepsilon = 0$. Suppose that v_t represents the solution to (36) if $\varepsilon = 0$. We denote

$$g(t) = \langle q^*, v_t\rangle,$$
$$N(t,\nu) = v_t - g(t)q(\nu) - \bar{g}(t)\bar{q}(\nu) = v_t(\nu) - 2\mathrm{Re}\{g(t)q(\nu)\}. \tag{39}$$

On the center manifold C_0, we have $N(t,\nu) = N(g(t), \bar{g}(t), \nu)$, where

$$N(g,\bar{g},\nu) = N_{20}(\nu)\frac{g^2}{2} + N_{11}(\nu)g\bar{g} + N_{02}(\nu)\frac{\bar{g}^2}{2} + N_{30}(\nu)\frac{g^3}{6} + \dots, \tag{40}$$

where $\bar{g}$ and g are local coordinates for the central manifold C_0 in the directions of $\bar{q}^*$ and q^*. Note that if v_t is real, then N is real. We only examine real solutions. Using (39) yields

$$\langle q^*, N\rangle = \langle q^*, v_t - gq - \bar{g}\bar{q}\rangle = \langle q^*, v_t\rangle - g\langle q^*, q\rangle - \bar{g}\langle q^*, \bar{q}\rangle = g - \bar{g} = 0.$$

For $v_t \in C_0$ in (36), as $\varepsilon = 0$, we acquire

$$\begin{aligned}\dot{g}(t) &= \langle q^*, \dot{v}_t\rangle = \langle q^*, M(0)v_t + Y(0)v_t\rangle = \langle M^*(0)q^*, v_t\rangle + \bar{q}^*(0)f(0,v_t) \\ &= \langle -i\omega_0\tau_s q^*, v_t\rangle + \bar{q}^*(0)f_0(g,\bar{g}) = i\omega_0\tau_s g + \bar{q}^*(0)f_0(g,\bar{g}) \\ &= i\omega_0\tau_s g(t) + n(g,\bar{g}),\end{aligned}$$

where

$$n(g,\bar{g}) = \bar{q}^*(0)f_0(g,\bar{g}) = n_{20}\frac{g^2}{2} + n_{11}g\bar{g} + n_{02}\frac{\bar{g}^2}{2} + n_{21}\frac{g^2\bar{g}}{2} + \dots. \tag{41}$$

According to (39) and (40),

$$\begin{aligned}v_t(\nu) &= (v_{1t}(\nu), v_{2t}(\nu)) = N(t,\nu) + 2\mathrm{Re}\{g(t), q(t)\} \\ &= N(g(t), \bar{g}(t), \nu) + gq + \bar{g}\bar{q} \\ &= N_{20}(\nu)\frac{g^2}{2} + N_{11}(\nu)g\bar{g} + N_{02}(\nu)\frac{\bar{g}^2}{2} + g(1,s)^T e^{i\omega_0\tau_s\nu} \\ &\quad + \bar{g}(1,\bar{s})^T e^{-i\omega_0\tau_s\nu} + \dots.\end{aligned} \tag{42}$$

Explicitly, we can state this as

$$\begin{pmatrix} v_{1t}(\nu) \\ v_{2t}(\nu)\end{pmatrix} = \begin{pmatrix} N^{(1)}(\nu) \\ N^{(2)}(\nu)\end{pmatrix} + g\begin{pmatrix} 1 \\ s\end{pmatrix}e^{i\omega_0\tau_s\nu} + \bar{g}\begin{pmatrix} 1 \\ \bar{s}\end{pmatrix}e^{-i\omega_0\tau_s\nu} \equiv \begin{pmatrix}\Gamma_1 \\ \Gamma_2\end{pmatrix},$$

where

$$\Gamma_1 = ge^{i\omega_0\tau_s\nu} + \bar{g}e^{-i\omega_0\tau_s\nu} + N_{20}^{(1)}(\nu)\frac{g^2}{2} + N_{11}^{(1)}(\nu)g\bar{g} + N_{02}^{(1)}(\nu)\frac{\bar{g}^2}{2} + o(|(g,\bar{g})|^3),$$
$$\Gamma_2 = sge^{i\omega_0\tau_s\nu} + \bar{s}\bar{g}e^{-i\omega_0\tau_s\nu} + N_{20}^{(2)}(\nu)\frac{g^2}{2} + N_{11}^{(2)}(\nu)g\bar{g} + N_{02}^{(2)}(\nu)\frac{\bar{g}^2}{2} + o(|(g,\bar{g})|^3).$$

Hence, it follows that

$$v_t(0) = \begin{pmatrix} v_{1t}(\nu) \\ v_{2t}(\nu)\end{pmatrix} \quad \text{and} \quad N(g,\bar{g},\nu) = \begin{pmatrix} N^{(1)}(\nu) \\ N^{(2)}(\nu)\end{pmatrix}.$$

Then,

$$\begin{aligned}
v_{1t}(0) &= g+\bar{g}+N_{20}^{(1)}(0)\frac{g^2}{2}+N_{11}^{(1)}(0)g\bar{g}+N_{02}^{(1)}(0)\frac{\bar{g}^2}{2}+o(|(g,\bar{g})|^3),\\
v_{2t}(0) &= sg+\bar{s}\bar{g}+N_{20}^{(2)}(0)\frac{g^2}{2}+N_{11}^{(2)}(0)g\bar{g}+N_{02}^{(2)}(0)\frac{\bar{g}^2}{2}+o(|(g,\bar{g})|^3),\\
v_{1t}(-1) &= g\mathrm{e}^{-i\omega_0\tau_s}+\bar{g}\mathrm{e}^{i\omega_0\tau_s}+N_{20}^{(1)}(-1)\frac{g^2}{2}+N_{11}^{(1)}(-1)g\bar{g}+N_{02}^{(1)}(-1)\frac{\bar{g}^2}{2}\\
&\quad+o(|(g,\bar{g})|^3),\\
v_{2t}(-1) &= sg\mathrm{e}^{-i\omega_0\tau_s}+\bar{s}\bar{g}\mathrm{e}^{i\omega_0\tau_s}+N_{20}^{(2)}(-1)\frac{g^2}{2}+N_{11}^{(2)}(-1)g\bar{g}+N_{02}^{(2)}(-1)\frac{\bar{g}^2}{2}\\
&\quad+o(|(g,\bar{g})|^3),\\
v_{1t}^2(0) &= g^2+2g\bar{g}+\bar{g}^2+\left(N_{20}^{(1)}(0)+2N_{11}^{(1)}(0)\right)g^2\bar{g}+\text{h.o.t.},\\
v_{1t}(0)v_{2t}(0) &= sg^2+(s+\bar{s})g\bar{g}+\bar{s}\bar{g}^2+\Big(N_{11}^{(2)}(0)+(1/2)N_{20}^{(2)}(0)+sN_{11}^{(1)}(0)\\
&\quad+(\bar{s}/2)N_{20}^{(1)}(0)\Big)g^2\bar{g}+\text{h.o.t.},\\
v_{1t}(-1)v_{2t}(-1) &= sg^2\mathrm{e}^{-2i\omega_0\tau_s}+(s+\bar{s})g\bar{g}+\bar{s}\bar{g}^2\mathrm{e}^{2i\omega_0\tau_s}+\Big(N_{11}^{(2)}(-1)\mathrm{e}^{-i\omega_0\tau_s}\\
&\quad+(1/2)N_{20}^{(2)}(-1)\mathrm{e}^{i\omega_0\tau_s}+sN_{11}^{(1)}(-1)\mathrm{e}^{-i\omega_0\tau_s}\\
&\quad+(\bar{s}/2)N_{20}^{(1)}(-1)\mathrm{e}^{i\omega_0\tau_s}\Big)g^2\bar{g}+\text{h.o.t.}
\end{aligned}$$

From the definition of n and (31), we obtain

$$\begin{aligned}
n(g,\bar{g}) &= \bar{q}^*(0)f_0(g,\bar{g})=\bar{q}^*(0)f(0,v_t)\\
&= \tau_s\bar{Q}(1,\bar{s}^*)\begin{pmatrix}(-\frac{r}{K_C}+\frac{\epsilon K_I K_D}{(B^*+K_D)^2}-\frac{2\epsilon K_I K_D B^*}{(B^*+K_D)^3})v_{1t}^2(0)-\phi v_{1t}(0)v_{2t}(0)\\ \beta\phi v_{1t}(-1)v_{2t}(-1)\end{pmatrix}\\
&= \tau_s\bar{Q}\Bigg\{g^2\Bigg[-\frac{r}{K_C}+\frac{\epsilon K_I K_D}{(B^*+K_D)^2}-\frac{2\epsilon K_I K_D B^*}{(B^*+K_D)^3}-\phi s+s\bar{s}^*\beta\phi\mathrm{e}^{-2i\omega_0\tau_s}\Bigg]\\
&\quad+g\bar{g}\Bigg[-\frac{2r}{K_C}+\frac{2\epsilon K_I K_D}{(B^*+K_D)^2}-\frac{4\epsilon K_I K_D B^*}{(B^*+K_D)^3}-\phi(s+\bar{s})+\bar{s}^*\beta\phi(s+\bar{s})\Bigg]\\
&\quad+\bar{g}^2\Bigg[-\frac{r}{K_C}+\frac{\epsilon K_I K_D}{(B^*+K_D)^2}-\frac{2\epsilon K_I K_D B^*}{(B^*+K_D)^3}-\phi\bar{s}+\bar{s}^*\beta\phi\bar{s}\mathrm{e}^{2i\omega_0\tau_s}\Bigg]\\
&\quad+g^2\bar{g}\Bigg[\Big(-\frac{r}{K_C}+\frac{\epsilon K_I K_D}{(B^*+K_D)^2}-\frac{2\epsilon K_I K_D B^*}{(B^*+K_D)^3}\Big)\Big(N_{20}^{(1)}(0)+2N_{11}^{(1)}(0)\Big)\\
&\quad-\phi\Big(N_{11}^{(2)}(0)+(1/2)N_{20}^{(2)}(0)+sN_{11}^{(1)}(0)+(\bar{s}/2)N_{20}^{(1)}(0)\Big)\\
&\quad+\bar{s}^*\beta\phi\Big(N_{11}^{(2)}(-1)\mathrm{e}^{-i\omega_0\tau_s}+(1/2)N_{20}^{(2)}(-1)\mathrm{e}^{i\omega_0\tau_s}+sN_{11}^{(1)}(-1)\mathrm{e}^{-i\omega_0\tau_s}\\
&\quad+(\bar{s}/2)N_{20}^{(1)}(-1)\mathrm{e}^{i\omega_0\tau_s}\Big)\Bigg]\Bigg\}.
\end{aligned}$$

Comparing the coefficients of g^2, $g\bar{g}$, $\bar{g}^2$, and $g^2\bar{g}$ with (41) yields

$$n_{20} = 2\tau_s \bar{Q}\left[-\frac{r}{K_C} + \frac{\epsilon K_I K_D}{(B^* + K_D)^2} - \frac{2\epsilon K_I K_D B^*}{(B^* + K_D)^3} - \phi s + s\bar{s}^* \beta \phi e^{-2i\omega_0 \tau_s} \right]$$
$$n_{11} = 2\tau_s \bar{Q}\left[-\frac{r}{K_C} + \frac{\epsilon K_I K_D}{(B^* + K_D)^2} - \frac{2\epsilon K_I K_D B^*}{(B^* + K_D)^3} - \phi \mathrm{Re}\{s\} + \bar{s}^* \beta \phi \mathrm{Re}\{s\} \right]$$
$$n_{02} = 2\tau_s \bar{Q}\left[-\frac{r}{K_C} + \frac{\epsilon K_I K_D}{(B^* + K_D)^2} - \frac{2\epsilon K_I K_D B^*}{(B^* + K_D)^3} - \phi \bar{s} + \bar{s}^* \beta \phi \bar{s} e^{2i\omega_0 \tau_s} \right]$$
$$\begin{aligned} n_{21} = 2\tau_s \bar{Q}\Big[&\Big(-\frac{r}{K_C} + \frac{\epsilon K_I K_D}{(B^* + K_D)^2} - \frac{2\epsilon K_I K_D B^*}{(B^* + K_D)^3} \Big) \Big(N_{20}^{(1)}(0) + 2N_{11}^{(1)}(0) \Big) \\ &- \phi \Big(N_{11}^{(2)}(0) + (1/2) N_{20}^{(2)}(0) + s N_{11}^{(1)}(0) + (\bar{s}/2) N_{20}^{(1)}(0) \Big) \\ &+ \bar{s}^* \beta \phi \Big(N_{11}^{(2)}(-1) e^{-i\omega_0 \tau_s} + (1/2) N_{20}^{(2)}(-1) e^{i\omega_0 \tau_s} + s N_{11}^{(1)}(-1) e^{-i\omega_0 \tau_s} \\ &+ (\bar{s}/2) N_{20}^{(1)}(-1) e^{i\omega_0 \tau_s} \Big) \Big]. \end{aligned} \tag{43}$$

Because n_{21} includes N_{11} and N_{20}, we need to calculate their values. From (36) and (39), we obtain

$$\dot{N} = \dot{v}_t - \dot{g}q - \dot{\bar{g}}\bar{q} = \begin{cases} M(0)N - 2\mathrm{Re}\{\bar{q}^*(0) f_0 q(\nu)\}, & \nu \in [-1, 0), \\ M(0)N - 2\mathrm{Re}\{\bar{q}^*(0) f_0 q(\nu)\} + f_0(g, \bar{g}), & \nu = 0, \end{cases}$$

which can be expressed as

$$\dot{N} = M(0)N + H(g, \bar{g}, \nu) \tag{44}$$

with

$$H(g, \bar{g}, \nu) = H_{20}(\nu)\frac{g^2}{2} + H_{11}(\nu) g\bar{g} + H_{02}(\nu)\frac{\bar{g}^2}{2} + \dots . \tag{45}$$

On the other hand, on C_0,

$$\dot{N} = N_g \dot{g} + N_{\bar{g}} \dot{\bar{g}}. \tag{46}$$

Substituting the series of $H(g, \bar{g}, \nu)$ into (44) and comparing the coefficients yields

$$(M(0) - 2i\omega_0 \tau_0) N_{20}(\nu) = -H_{20}(\nu), \quad M(0) N_{11}(\nu) = -H_{11}(\nu), \dots . \tag{47}$$

For $\nu \in [-1, 0)$, the result from (41) and (44) is

$$\begin{aligned} H(g, \bar{g}, \nu) &= -2\mathrm{Re}\{\bar{q}^*(0) f_0(g, \bar{g}) q(\nu)\} = -2\mathrm{Re}\{n(g, \bar{g}) q(\nu)\} \\ &= -n(g, \bar{g}) q(\nu) - \bar{n}(g, \bar{g}) \bar{q}(\nu) \\ &= -\left(n_{20}\frac{g^2}{2} + n_{11} g\bar{g} + n_{02}\frac{\bar{g}^2}{2} + n_{21}\frac{g^2 \bar{g}}{2} + \cdots \right) \times q(\nu) \\ &\quad - \left(\bar{n}_{20}\frac{\bar{g}^2}{2} + \bar{n}_{11} \bar{g} g + \bar{n}_{02}\frac{g^2}{2} + \bar{n}_{21}\frac{\bar{g}^2 g}{2} + \cdots \right) \times \bar{q}(\nu). \end{aligned} \tag{48}$$

Comparing the coefficients of (48) with (45) reveals

$$H_{20}(\nu) = -n_{20} q(\nu) - \bar{n}_{02} \bar{q}(\nu) \tag{49}$$

and

$$H_{11}(\nu) = -n_{11} q(\nu) - \bar{n}_{11} \bar{q}(\nu). \tag{50}$$

From (47) and (49) and the definition of M (i.e., from (34)), we obtain

$$\dot{N}_{20}(\nu) = M(0)N_{20}(\nu) = 2i\omega_0\tau_s N_{20}(\nu) - H_{20}(\nu)$$
$$= 2i\omega_0\tau_s N_{20}(\nu) + n_{20}q(\nu) + \bar{n}_{02}\bar{q}(\nu).$$

Now, taking into account that $q(\nu) = (1, a)^T e^{i\omega_0\tau_s\nu}$, we have

$$\dot{N}_{20}(\nu) = 2i\omega_0\tau_s N_{20}(\nu) + n_{20}q(0)e^{i\omega_0\tau_s\nu} + \bar{n}_{02}\bar{q}(0)e^{-i\omega_0\tau_s\nu}.$$

Solving the above equation, we obtain

$$N_{20}(\nu) = \frac{in_{20}}{\omega_0\tau_s}q(0)e^{i\omega_0\tau_s\nu} + \frac{i\bar{n}_{02}}{3\omega_0\tau_s}\bar{q}(0)e^{-i\omega_0\tau_s\nu} + U_1 e^{2i\omega_0\tau_s\nu}, \tag{51}$$

where $U_1 = \left(U_1^{(1)}, U_1^{(2)}\right) \in \mathbf{R}^2$ is a constant vector. Similarly, based on (47) and (50) together with the definition of M (34), we obtain

$$N_{11}(\nu) = -\frac{in_{11}}{\omega_0\tau_s}q(0)e^{i\omega_0\tau_s\nu} + \frac{i\bar{n}_{11}}{\omega_0\tau_s}\bar{q}(0)e^{-i\omega_0\tau_s\nu} + U_2, \tag{52}$$

where $U_2 = \left(U_2^{(1)}, U_2^{(2)}\right) \in \mathbf{R}^2$ is a two dimensional constant vector.

In the following, we explore relevant U_1 and U_2. Utilizing the definition of M with (34) and (47), we obtain

$$\int_{-1}^{0} d\eta(\nu)N_{20}(\nu) = 2i\omega_0\tau_s N_{20}(\nu) - H_{20}(\nu), \tag{53}$$

and

$$\int_{-1}^{0} d\eta(\nu)N_{11}(\nu) = -H_{11}(\nu) \tag{54}$$

for $\nu = 0$ i.e., $\eta(0,\nu) = \eta(\nu)$.

Now, we can find the formula for $H(g, \bar{g}, \nu)$ by setting $\nu = 0$, which results in

$$\begin{aligned}
H(g, \bar{g}, 0) =& - n(g, \bar{g})q(\nu) - \bar{n}(g, \bar{g})\bar{q}(\nu) + f_0(g, \bar{g}) \\
=& - \left(n_{20}\frac{g^2}{2} + n_{11}g\bar{g} + n_{02}\frac{\bar{g}^2}{2} + n_{21}\frac{g^2\bar{g}}{2} + \cdots\right) \times q(0) \\
& - \left(\bar{n}_{20}\frac{\bar{g}^2}{2} + \bar{n}_{11}\bar{g}g + \bar{n}_{02}\frac{g^2}{2} + \bar{n}_{21}\frac{\bar{g}^2 g}{2} + \cdots\right) \times \bar{q}(0) \\
& + \begin{pmatrix} \Omega_{11}g^2 + \Omega_{12}g\bar{g} + \Omega_{13}\bar{g}^2 + \Omega_{14}g^2\bar{g} + \cdots \\ \Omega_{21}g^2 + \Omega_{22}g\bar{g} + \Omega_{23}\bar{g}^2 + \Omega_{24}g^2\bar{g} + \cdots \end{pmatrix},
\end{aligned}$$

where

$$\begin{aligned}
\Omega_{11} &= -\frac{r}{K_C} + \frac{\epsilon K_I K_D}{(B^* + K_D)^2} - \frac{2\epsilon K_I K_D B^*}{(B^* + K_D)^3} - \phi s, \\
\Omega_{12} &= -\frac{r}{K_C} + \frac{\epsilon K_I K_D}{(B^* + K_D)^2} - \frac{2\epsilon K_I K_D B^*}{(B^* + K_D)^3} - \phi \mathrm{Re}\{s\}, \\
\Omega_{21} &= s\beta\phi e^{-2i\omega_0\tau_s}, \\
\Omega_{22} &= \beta\phi \mathrm{Re}\{s\}.
\end{aligned}$$

For $\nu = 0$, when we compare the coefficients of the above equation with (45) we obtain

$$H_{20}(0) = -n_{20}q(0) - \bar{n}_{20}\bar{q}(0) + 2\tau_s\begin{pmatrix} \Omega_{11} \\ \Omega_{21} \end{pmatrix} \tag{55}$$

and

$$H_{11}(0) = -n_{11}q(0) - \bar{n}_{11}\bar{q}(0) + 2\tau_s\begin{pmatrix} \Omega_{12} \\ \Omega_{22} \end{pmatrix}. \tag{56}$$

According to the definition of M together with (34) and (47), we have

$$\left(i\omega_0\tau_s I - \int_{-1}^{0} e^{i\omega_0\tau_s\nu} d\eta(\nu)\right)q(0) = 0,$$

$$\left(-i\omega_0\tau_s I - \int_{-1}^{0} e^{-i\omega_0\tau_s\nu} d\eta(\nu)\right)\bar{q}(0) = 0.$$

When (51) and (53) are substituted into (55), we obtain

$$\left(2i\omega_0\tau_s I - \int_{-1}^{0} e^{2i\omega_0\tau_s\nu} d\eta(\nu)\right)U_1 = 2\tau_s\begin{pmatrix} \Omega_{11} \\ \Omega_{21} \end{pmatrix},$$

which induces

$$\begin{pmatrix} i\omega_0 + \frac{r}{K_C}B^* - \frac{\epsilon K_I K_D B^*}{(B^*+K_D)^2} & \phi B^* \\ \beta\phi P^* e^{-i\omega_0\tau_s} & i\omega_0 + \beta\phi B^* e^{-i\omega_0\tau_s} + w \end{pmatrix}\begin{pmatrix} U_1^{(1)} \\ U_1^{(2)} \end{pmatrix} = 2\begin{pmatrix} \Omega_{11} \\ \Omega_{21} \end{pmatrix}.$$

Solving for U_1, we find

$$U_1^{(1)} = \frac{2}{\Psi_1}\begin{vmatrix} \Omega_{11} & \phi B^* \\ \Omega_{21} & i\omega_0 + \beta\phi B^* e^{-i\omega_0\tau_s} + w \end{vmatrix},$$

$$U_1^{(2)} = \frac{2}{\Psi_1}\begin{vmatrix} i\omega_0 + \frac{r}{K_C}B^* - \frac{\epsilon K_I K_D B^*}{(B^*+K_D)^2} & \Omega_{11} \\ \beta\phi P^* e^{-i\omega_0\tau_s} & \Omega_{21} \end{vmatrix},$$

with

$$\Psi_1 = \begin{vmatrix} i\omega_0 + \frac{r}{K_C}B^* - \frac{\epsilon K_I K_D B^*}{(B^*+K_D)^2} & \phi B^* \\ \beta\phi P^* e^{-i\omega_0\tau_s} & i\omega_0 + \beta\phi B^* e^{-i\omega_0\tau_s} + w \end{vmatrix}.$$

Similarly, substituting (52) and (54) into (56) yields

$$\begin{pmatrix} -\frac{r}{K_C}B^* + \frac{\epsilon K_I K_D B^*}{(B^*+K_D)^2} & -\phi B^* \\ \beta\phi P^* & \beta\phi B^* - w \end{pmatrix}\begin{pmatrix} U_2^{(1)} \\ U_2^{(2)} \end{pmatrix} = 2\begin{pmatrix} \Omega_{12} \\ \Omega_{22} \end{pmatrix}.$$

Solving for U_2, we obtain

$$U_2^{(1)} = \frac{2}{\Psi_2}\begin{vmatrix} \Omega_{12} & -\phi B^* \\ \Omega_{22} & \beta\phi B^* - w \end{vmatrix},$$

$$U_2^{(2)} = \frac{2}{\Psi_2}\begin{vmatrix} -\frac{r}{K_C}B^* + \frac{\epsilon K_I K_D B^*}{(B^*+K_D)^2} & \Omega_{12} \\ \beta\phi P^* & \Omega_{22} \end{vmatrix},$$

with

$$\Psi_2 = \begin{vmatrix} -\frac{r}{K_C}B^* + \frac{\epsilon K_I K_D B^*}{(B^*+K_D)^2} & -\phi B^* \\ \beta\phi P^* & \beta\phi B^* - w \end{vmatrix}.$$

Then, we can assess $N_{20}(\nu)$ and $N_{11}(\nu)$ from (51) and (52). Further, the parameters and delay can be used to state n_{21} in (43). Accordingly, we can determine the values below:

$$\begin{aligned} \Lambda(0) &= \frac{i}{2\omega_0\tau_s}\left(n_{20}n_{11} - 2|n_{11}|^2 - \frac{|n_{02}|^2}{3}\right) + \frac{n_{21}}{2}, \\ \psi &= -\frac{\mathrm{Re}(\Lambda(0))}{\mathrm{Re}(\lambda'(\tau_s))}, \\ \vartheta &= 2\mathrm{Re}(\Lambda(0)), \\ T &= -\frac{\mathrm{Im}(\Lambda(0)) + \psi\mathrm{Im}(\lambda'(\tau_s))}{\omega_0\tau_s}. \end{aligned} \quad (57)$$

Here, ψ determines the direction of Hopf bifurcation, ϑ determines the stability of the Hopf-bifurcating periodic solutions, and T determines the period of bifurcating periodic solutions at the critical value of $\tau = \tau_s$. Thus, based on the findings of Hassard et al. [50], the properties of the Hopf bifurcation at the crucial value of $\tau = \tau_0$ can be stated as a theorem.

Theorem 8. *In Expression (57), the following outcomes hold:*

(a) The Hopf bifurcation is supercritical (subcritical) if $\psi > 0$ $(\psi < 0)$.

(b) The bifurcating periodic solutions are stable (unstable) if $\vartheta < 0$ $(\vartheta > 0)$.

(c) The period of the bifurcated periodic solution increases (decreases) if $T > 0$ $(T < 0)$.

4. Numerical Simulation

In this section, we validate the theoretical outcomes through numerical simulations. We consider biologically feasible data in order to demonstrate the analytical outcomes, and the parameters are chosen as mentioned in Table 1.

Table 1. Parameter interpretations and their values used in numerical simulations.

Parameter	Description	Data 1	Data 2
ϕ	adsorption rate of phage	0.34	0.34
β	burst size of phage	0.38	0.38
ϵ	killing rate of innate immune response	0.19	0.19
w	decay rate of phage	0.125	0.125
r	intrinsic growth rate of bacteria	0.25	0.5
K_C	carrying capacity of bacteria	7.29	5
K_D	bacterial concentration when innate immune response is half saturated	3.5	3.5
K_I	carrying capacity of innate immune response	0.48	0.48

We take the set of parameter values in Data 1 of Table 1 to correspond to the non-delayed System (2). For this dataset, the positive equilibrium is $E_2 = (0.9675, 0.4276)$. We derive $c_{11} + c_{22} = -0.0177 < 0$ and $c_{11}c_{22} - c_{12}c_{21} = 0.0182 > 0$, which means that the system is locally asymptotically stable (LAS) around E_2. It can be seen that E_2 is stable using the first condition of Theorem 3(i). To analyze the existence of Hopf bifurcation in the case of a non-delayed system, we consider the parameter r as a bifurcation parameter and obtain the value of r as $r^* = 0.1166$ with the same set of parameters stated in Data 1. We can deduce from the second condition of Theorem 3(i) that the positive equilibrium E_2 is destabilized by a Hopf bifurcation when $r = 0.109 < r^*$ (Figure 1a). According to Theorem 3(ii), System (2) undergoes a Hopf bifurcation at E_2 when r passes r^* (Figure 1b), resulting in a stable limit cycle (Figure 1d). In Figure 1c, taking $r = 0.25 > r^*$, we conclude from Theorem 3(i) that E_2 is stable.

To verify the theoretical analysis outcomes in the delayed system (3), we consider the set of parameter values in Data 2 of Table 1. Using these parameter values, we obtain positive equilibrium $E_2(B^*, P^*) = (0.9675, 0.9759)$ and compute $c_1 = 0.2063$, $c_2 = 0.0102$, $c_3 = -0.1250$, and $c_4 = 0.0313$. Furthermore, we compute $\omega_0 = 0.1628$ and $\tau_0 = 3.3270$ using (25) and (27). Thus, we can demonstrate the transversality condition of Hopf bifurcation $\Phi = \text{sign}\left[\text{Re}\left(\frac{d\lambda}{d\tau}\right)^{-1}\right]_{\lambda = i\omega_0} = 42.7388 > 0$ at the critical value of $\tau = \tau_0 = 3.3270$. According to Theorem 7(i), the positive equilibrium $E_2(B^*, P^*)$ is stable when $\tau < \tau_0 = 3.3270$ (Figure 2). Theorem 7(iii) leads us to deduce that System (3) exhibits a Hopf bifurcation at $E_2 = (0.9675, 0.9759)$ when $\tau = \tau_0 = 3.3270$, i.e., there is a periodic solution around $E_2 = (0.9675, 0.9759)$ when τ is close to $\tau_0 = 3.3270$ (Figure 3). When we determine the value of τ as $\tau = 3.5 > \tau_0 = 3.3270$, then $E_2(B^*, P^*)$ is unstable through a Hopf bifurcation and periodic orbits are encountered, as depicted in Figure 4. Figure 5 displays the phase portrait for various τ values, with $\tau = \tau_0 = 3.9$ and $\tau = \tau_0 = 5.5$ producing stable limit cycles.

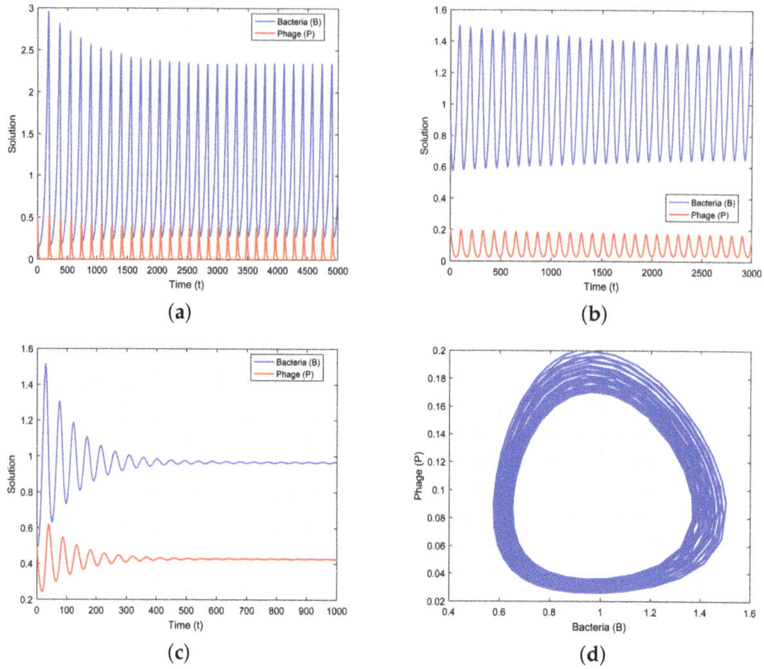

Figure 1. Oscillatory behavior of System (2) with parameter values stated in Data 1 except for r: (**a**) Unstable solution of system when $r = 0.109 < r_*$; (**b**) existence of Hopf bifurcation solution for $r = r_* = 0.1166$; (**c**) stable solution of system when $r = 0.25 > r_*$; (**d**) existence of a stable limit cycle near E_2 when $r = r_*$.

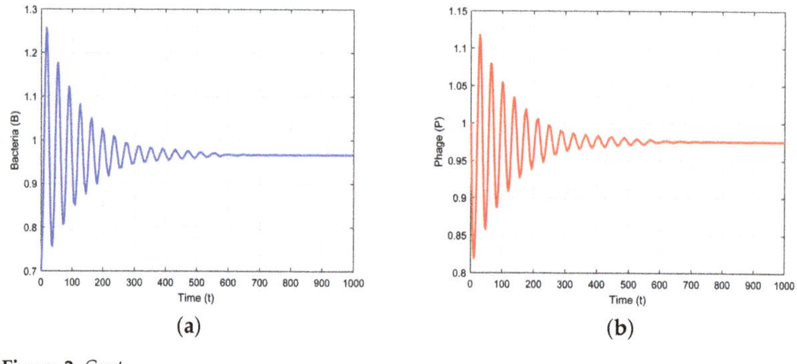

Figure 2. *Cont.*

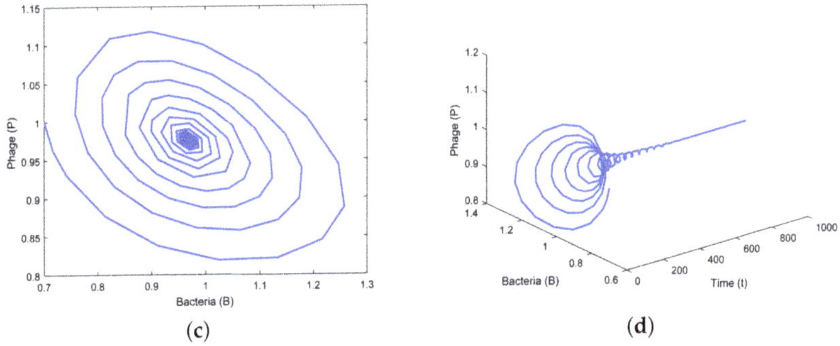

Figure 2. E_2 is asymptotically stable when $\tau = 2.3 < \tau_0$: (**a**,**b**) time series evolution of bacteria and phages; (**c**) phase portrait in B-P plane; (**d**) phase portrait in t-B-P space.

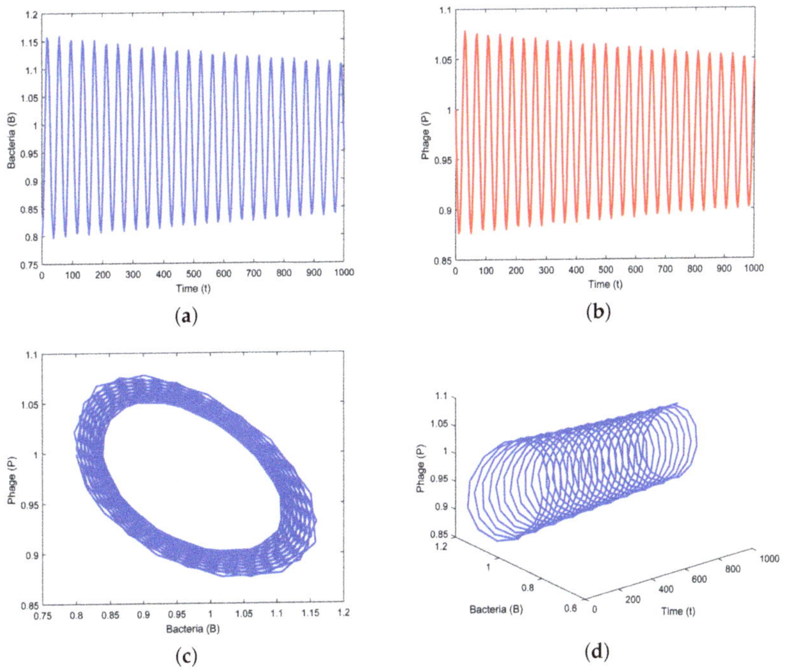

Figure 3. Existence of Hopf bifurcation solution for $\tau = 3.3270 = \tau_0$ around E_2: (**a**,**b**) time series evolution of bacteria and phages; (**c**) presence of a stable limit cycle; (**d**) phase portrait in t-B-P space.

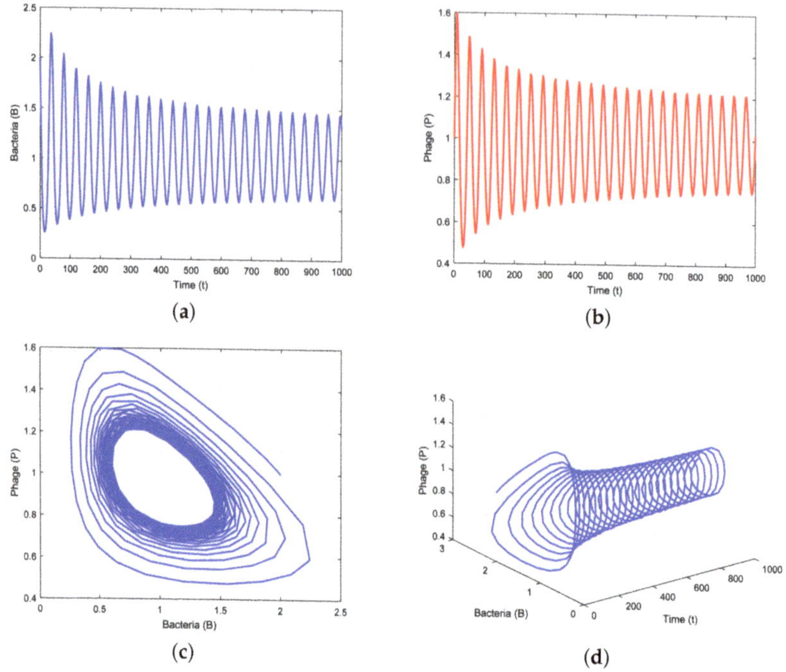

Figure 4. E_2 is unstable when $\tau = 3.5 > \tau_0$: (**a**,**b**) time series evolution of bacteria and phages; (**c**) presence of periodic solution; (**d**) phase portrait in *t*-*B*-*P* space.

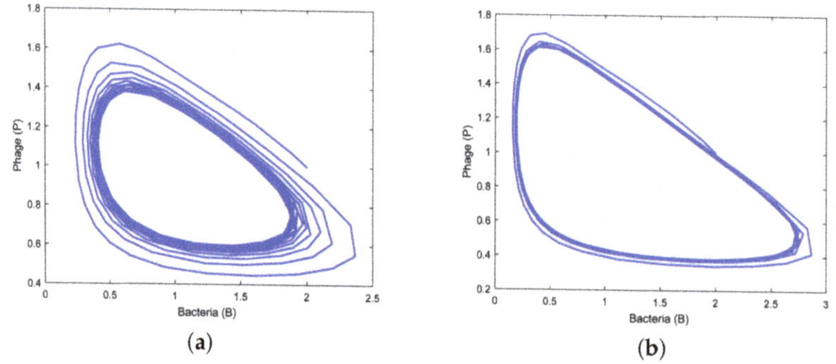

Figure 5. Phase portraits for various values of time delays: (**a**) a stable limit cycle emerges at $\tau = 3.9$ due to Hopf bifurcation; (**b**) a stable limit cycle emerges at $\tau = 5.5$ due to Hopf bifurcation, resulting in stable periodic solutions.

5. Conclusions

In this paper, we modify and analyze the phage therapy model in (2) by including a discrete time delay to obtain its delayed version in (3). This modification is carried out by adding a discrete time delay to the recruitment term of the phages and the infection term of the bacteria. We investigate the dynamic behaviors of the models in (2) and (3), in particular in terms of their stability and Hopf bifurcation. In addition, we examine the Hopf bifurcation properties of System (3), including the bifurcation direction and the stability of a bifurcating periodic solution. Finally, numerical simulations are provided to prove the practical use of the theoretical results.

We consider the positivity and boundedness of both non-delayed and delayed models. The results demonstrate that all of the system's solutions are positive and bounded, indicating that the system is biologically well-behaved.

For the non-delayed model, we explore the necessary conditions for the local stability of all equilibrium solutions and the occurrence of Hopf bifurcation, taking the bacterial intrinsic growth rate r as a bifurcation parameter. In Section 2, the Hopf bifurcation of this model is investigated using Hopf bifurcation theory; it is proved that there exists a critical value of r^* for stability. When the value of r passes through the critical value of r^*, the system loses its stability and Hopf bifurcation occurs. This suggests that the intrinsic growth rate of bacteria has a stabilizing effect on the dynamics of the system.

In Section 4, we demonstrate numerically that the non-delayed System (2) encounters Hopf bifurcation when the parameter r passes a critical value r^* (Figure 1b,d). When the value of r is gradually increased, the positive equilibrium E_2 reaches stability from instability. (Figure 1a,c). The results of our numerical simulations used to depict the analytical results are based on biologically feasible data.

We use the Lyapunov functional method to derive the global stability criteria for the boundary and coexistence equilibrium points in the non-delayed model. The results indicate that the phage burst size β significantly affects the global stability behaviour of the coexistence equilibrium in the phage therapy model. The necessary conditions for the non-existence of periodic solutions to the system are established using the Dulac–Bendixon criterion. This result can be biologically explained as follows: if the bacterial growth rate is greater than the threshold value, then System (2) has no limit cycle.

In the second part of this study, we investigate the system's dynamic behaviour in the presence of a time delay. We use the discrete delay as a bifurcation parameter in the Hopf bifurcation analysis to capture the oscillatory behaviour of the delayed model in (3). In Section 3, using stability theory and Hopf bifurcation theory, the influence of delay on the stability of the equilibrium point is studied along with the existence of Hopf bifurcation. Theorems for the stability and existence of Hopf bifurcation are established. The results show that the time delay destabilizes the system, leading to species coexistence.

It can be inferred from Theorem 7 that Hopf bifurcation arises in System (3) at the critical value $\tau = \tau_0$. When the value of τ is increased to $\tau_0 = 3.3270$, the system loses stability and undergoes Hopf bifurcation (Figure 3). When $\tau > \tau_0$, System (3) enters an unstable equilibrium via Hopf bifurcation at the interior equilibrium E_2, indicating that the densities of bacteria and phages oscillate periodically (Figure 4). However, the system achieves a stable equilibrium state when $\tau < \tau_0$, indicating that the densities of bacteria and phages tend towards a steady state (Figure 2). Our research indicates that oscillatory behavior is feasible in certain circumstances and that a delay can cause a stable equilibrium to evolve into an unstable one.

Furthermore, the direction and stability of the bifurcating periodic solutions are derived by applying normal form theory and the center manifold theorem. Based on Theorem 8, we obtain the formulas for determining the attributes of the Hopf bifurcation of the system. In particular, the Hopf bifurcation is supercritical and the bifurcating periodic solutions are stable under certain conditions.

In summary, this paper has shown that the addition of delay can destabilize the system and induce Hopf bifurcation. These results are in agreement with the destabilization effect that has been observed in previous models when introducing a time delay. From a biomedical perspective, this means that bacteria and phages can coexist under certain conditions if the delay required for phage reproduction and bacterial infection is small or increases to a critical value. This result has a significant effect on determining the most suitable time to introduce phage therapy.

Stochastic differential equations (SDEs) have become popular in modeling ecological and epidemiological models such as the study of population growth and epidemic transmission, as population dynamics vary concern with random perturbation. Population individuals struggle with one another for a restricted amount of nourishment and dwelling space. Environmental noise frequently influences population systems; therefore, it is crucial to determine whether this noise has an impact on the results. As far as we know, the phage therapy population model in (1) has not been studied yet with regard to its stochastic perturbation and asymptotic behavior. Therefore, in the future we intend to consider the behavior of the phage therapy model with stochastic perturbation in order to investigate the impact of random perturbations on model dynamics.

Author Contributions: E.E.K.: conceptualization, methodology, investigation, writing the manuscript. J.W.: reviewing and editing the manuscript. H.Z.: supervision, reviewing and editing the manuscript. All authors have read and agreed to the published version of the manuscript.

Funding: This research received no external funding.

Data Availability Statement: All the data and models employed and/or generated during this study appear in the submitted article.

Acknowledgments: The authors would like to take this chance to thank the editor and the anonymous referees for their very valuable comments, which led to significant improvements over our previous version.

Conflicts of Interest: The authors declare that they have no competing interest.

References

1. Beke, G.; Stano, M.; Klucar, L. Modeling the interaction between bacteriophages and their bacterial hosts. *Math. Biosci.* **2016**, *279*, 27–32. [CrossRef] [PubMed]
2. Beretta, E.; Kuang, Y. Modeling and analysis of a marine bacteriophage infection. *Math. Biosci.* **1998**, *149*, 57–76. [CrossRef]
3. Clokie, M.R.J.; Millard, A.D.; Letarov, A.V.; Heaphy, S. Phages in nature. *Bacteriophage* **2011**, *1*, 31–45. [CrossRef] [PubMed]
4. Sinha, S.; Grewal, R.K.; Roy, S. Modeling bacteria-phage interactions and its implications for phage therapy. *Adv. Appl. Microbiol.* **2018**, *103*, 103–141.
5. Brives, C.; Pourraz, J. Phage therapy as a potential solution in the fight against AMR: Obstacles and possible futures. *Palgrave Commun.* **2020**, *6*, 100. [CrossRef]
6. Styles, K.M.; Brown, A.T.; Sagona, A.P. A review of using mathematical modeling to improve our understanding of bacteriophage, bacteria, and eukaryotic interactions. *Front. Microbiol.* **2021**, *2021*, 2752. [CrossRef]
7. Al-Darabsah, I. Time Delayed Models in Population Biology and Epidemiology. Ph.D. Dissertation, Memorial University of Newfoundland, St. John's, NL, Canada, 2018.
8. Campbell, A. Conditions for the existence of bacteriophage. *Evolution* **1961**, *15*, 153–165. [CrossRef]
9. Levin, B.R.; Stewart, F.M.; Chao, L. Resource-limited growth, competition, and predation: A model and experimental studies with bacteria and bacteriophage. *Am. Nat.* **1977**, *111*, 3–24. [CrossRef]
10. Lenski, R.E.; Levin, B.R. Constraints on the coevolution of bacteria and virulent phage: A model, some experiments, and predictions for natural communities. *Am. Nat.* **1985**, *125*, 585–602. [CrossRef]
11. Smith, H.L.; Trevino, R.T. Bacteriophage infection dynamics: Multiple host binding sites. *Math. Model. Nat. Phenom.* **2009**, *4*, 109–134. [CrossRef]
12. Sahani, S.K.; Gakkhar, S. A mathematical model for phage therapy with impulsive phage dose. *Differ. Equ. Dyn. Syst.* **2020**, *28*, 75–86. [CrossRef]
13. Smith, H.L. Models of virulent phage growth with application to phage therapy. *SIAM J. Appl. Math.* **2008**, *68*, 1717–1737 [CrossRef]
14. Misra, A.K.; Gupta, A.; Venturino, E. Cholera dynamics with bacteriophage infection: A mathematical study. *Chaos Solitons Fract.* **2016**, *91*, 610–621. [CrossRef]
15. Teytsa, H.M.N.; Tsanou, B.; Bowong, S.; Lubuma, J.M. Bifurcation analysis of a phage-bacteria interaction model with prophage induction. *Math. Med. Biol.* **2021**, *38*, 28–58. [CrossRef]
16. Li, X.; Huang, R.; He, M. Dynamics model analysis of bacteriophage infection of bacteria. *Adv. Differ. Equ.* **2021**, *488*, 3–11. [CrossRef]
17. Xu, C.; Tang, X.; Liao, M. Stability and bifurcation analysis of a delayed predator-prey model of prey dispersal in two-patch environments. *Appl. Math. Comput.* **2010**, *216*, 2920–2936. [CrossRef]
18. Liu, Q.; Xu, R. Stability and bifurcation of a Cohen-Grossberg neural network with discrete delays. *Appl. Math. Comput.* **2011**, *218*, 2850–2862. [CrossRef]
19. Li, Y.; Li, C. Stability and Hopf bifurcation analysis on a delayed Leslie–Gower predator-prey system incorporating a prey refuge. *Appl. Math. Comput.* **2013**, *219*, 4576–4589. [CrossRef]
20. Khajanchi, S.; Banerjee, S. Stability and bifurcation analysis of delay induced tumor immune interaction model. *Appl. Math. Comput.* **2014**, *248*, 652–671. [CrossRef]

21. Beretta, E.; Kuang, Y. Modeling and analysis of a marine bacteriophage infection with latency period. *Nonlinear Anal. Real World Appl.* **2001**, *2*, 35–74. [CrossRef]
22. Beretta, E.; Solimano, F. The effect of time delay on stability in a bacteria-bacteriophage model. *Sci. Math. Jpn.* **2003**, *58*, 399–405.
23. Liu, S.; Liu, Z.; Tang, J. A delayed marine bacteriophage infection model. *Appl. Math. Lett.* **2007**, *20*, 702–706. [CrossRef]
24. Gakkhar, S.; Sahani, S.K. A time delay model for bacteria bacteriophage interaction. *J. Biol. Syst.* **2008**, *16*, 445–461. [CrossRef]
25. Smith, H.L.; Thieme, H.R. Persistence of bacteria and phages in a chemostat. *J. Math. Biol.* **2012**, *64*, 951–979. [CrossRef]
26. Aviram, I.; Rabinovitch, A. Bifurcation analysis of bacteria and bacteriophage coexistence in the presence of bacterial debris. *Commun. Nonlinear Sci. Numer. Simul.* **2012**, *17*, 242–254. [CrossRef]
27. Calsina, A.; Palmada, J.M.; Ripoll, J. Optimal latent period in a bacteriophage population model structured by infection-age. *Math. Model. Methods Appl. Sci.* **2011**, *21*, 693–718. [CrossRef]
28. Aviram, I.; Rabinovitch, A. Bacteria and lytic phage coexistence in a chemostat with periodic nutrient supply. *Bull. Math. Biol.* **2014**, *76*, 225–244. [CrossRef]
29. Han, Z.; Smith, H.L. Bacteriophage-resistant and bacteriophage-sensitive bacteria in a chemostat. *Math. Biosci. Eng.* **2012**, *9*, 737–765.
30. Beretta, E.; Solimano, F.; Tang, Y.B. Analysis of a chemostat model for bacteria and virulent bacteriaphage. *Discrete Cont. Dyn. Syst. Ser. B* **2002**, *2*, 495–520.
31. Beretta, E.; Sakakibara, H.; Takeuchi, Y. Stability analysis of time delayed chemostat models for bacteria and virulent phage. *Dyn. Syst. Their Appl. Biol.* **2003**, *36*, 45–58.
32. Czárxaxn, T.; Rattray, F.P.; Möller, C.O.A.; Christensen, B.B. Modelling the influence of metabolite diffusion on non-starter lactic acid bacteria growth in ripening cheddar cheese. *Int. Dairy J.* **2018**, *80*, 35–45.
33. Wang, J.; Zheng, H.; Jia, Y. Dynamical analysis on a bacteria-phages model with delay and diffusion. *Chaos Solitons Fract.* **2021**, *143*, 110597. [CrossRef]
34. Gourley, S.A.; Kuang, Y. A delay reaction-diffusion model of the spread of bacteriophage infection. *SIAM J. Appl. Math.* **2005**, *65*, 550–566. [CrossRef]
35. Carletti, M. On the stability properties of a stochastic model for phage bacteria interaction in open marine environment. *Math. Biosci.* **2002**, *175*, 117–131. [CrossRef]
36. Carletti, M. Mean-square stability of a stochastic model for bacteriophage infection with time delays. *Math. Biosci.* **2007**, *210*, 395–414. [CrossRef]
37. Bardina, X.; Bascompte, D.; Rovira, C.; Tindel, S. An analysis of stochastic model for bacteriophage systems. *Math. Biosci.* **2013**, *241*, 99–108. [CrossRef] [PubMed]
38. Vidurupola, S.W.; Allen, L.J.S. Impact of Variability in Stochastic Models of Bacteria-Phage Dynamics Applicable to Phage Therapy. *Stoch. Anal. Appl.* **2014**, *32*, 427–449. [CrossRef]
39. Vidurupola, S.W. Analysis of deterministic and stochastic mathematical models with resistant bacteria and bacteria debris for bacteriophage dynamics. *Appl. Math. Comput.* **2018**, *316*, 215–228. [CrossRef]
40. Abedon, S.T.; Kuhl, S.J.; Blasdel, B.G.; Kutter, E.M. Phage treatment of human infections. *Bacteriophage* **2011**, *1*, 66–85. [CrossRef]
41. Cisek, A.A.; Dabrowska, I.; Gregorczyk, K.P.; Wyzewski, Z. Phage therapy in bacterial infections treatment: One hundred years after the discovery of bacteriophages. *Curr. Microbiol.* **2017**, *74*, 277–283. [CrossRef]
42. Leung, C.Y.; Weitz, J.S. Modeling the synergistic elimination of bacteria by phage and the innate immune system. *J. Theor. Biol.* **2017**, *429*, 241–252. [CrossRef] [PubMed]
43. Kyaw, E.E.; Zheng, H.; Wang, J.; Hlaing, H.K. Stability analysis and persistence of a phage therapy model. *Math. Biosci. Eng.* **2021**, *18*, 5552–5572. [CrossRef] [PubMed]
44. Birkhoff, G.; Rota, G.C. *Ordinary Differential Equations*; John Wiley and Sons: New York, NY, USA, 1982.
45. Tripathi, J.P.; Tyagi, S.; Abbas, S. Global analysis of a delayed density dependent predator-prey model with Crowley-Martin functional response. *Commun. Nonlinear Sci. Numer. Simul.* **2016**, *30*, 45–69. [CrossRef]
46. Perko, L. *Differential Equations and Dynamical Systems*; Springer Science and Business Media: Berlin/Heidelberg, Germany, 2001.
47. Freedman, H.I.; Rao, V.S.H. The trade-off between mutual interference and time lags in predator-prey ststems. *Bull. Math. Biol.* **1983**, *45*, 991–1004. [CrossRef]
48. Wiggins, S. *Introduction to Applied Nonlinear Dynamical Systems and Chaos*; Springer: New York, NY, USA, 1990.
49. Kuang, Y. *Delay Differential Equation with Applications in Population Dynamics*; Academic Press: New York, NY, USA, 1993.
50. Hassard, B.D.; Kazarinoff, N.D.; Wan, Y.H. *Theory and Applications of Hopf Bifurcation*; University Cambridge: Cambridge, UK, 1981.

axioms

MDPI

Article

Some Hadamard-Type Integral Inequalities Involving Modified Harmonic Exponential Type Convexity

Asif Ali Shaikh [1,2], Evren Hincal [2], Sotiris K. Ntouyas [3], Jessada Tariboon [4,*] and Muhammad Tariq [1]

1 Department of Basic Sciences and Related Studies, Mehran University of Engineering and Technology, Jamshoro 76062, Pakistan; asif.shaikh@faculty.muet.edu.pk (A.A.S.); captaintariq2187@gmail.com (M.T.)
2 Department of Mathematics, Faculty of Arts and Sciences Near East University, Mersin 99138, Turkey; evren.hincal@neu.edu.tr
3 Department of Mathematics, School of Sciences, University of Ioannina, 45110 Ioannina, Greece; sntouyas@uoi.gr
4 Intelligent and Nonlinear Dynamic Innovations Research Center, Department of Mathematics, Faculty of Applied Science, King Mongkut's University of Technology North Bangkok, Bangkok 10800, Thailand
* Correspondence: jessada.t@sci.kmutnb.ac.th

Abstract: The term convexity and theory of inequalities is an enormous and intriguing domain of research in the realm of mathematical comprehension. Due to its applications in multiple areas of science, the theory of convexity and inequalities have recently attracted a lot of attention from historians and modern researchers. This article explores the concept of a new group of modified harmonic exponential s-convex functions. Some of its significant algebraic properties are elegantly elaborated to maintain the newly described idea. A new sort of Hermite–Hadamard-type integral inequality using this new concept of the function is investigated. In addition, several new estimates of Hermite–Hadamard inequality are presented to improve the study. These new results illustrate some generalizations of prior findings in the literature.

Keywords: convex function; m-convexity; Holder's inequality; Hermite–Hadamard inequality

MSC: 26A51; 26A33; 26D07; 26D10; 26D15

Citation: Shaikh, A.A.; Hincal, E.; Ntouyas, S.K.; Tariboon, J.; Tariq, M. Some Hadamard-Type Integral Inequalities Involving Modified Harmonic Exponential Type Convexity. *Axioms* **2023**, *12*, 454. https://doi.org/10.3390/axioms12050454

Academic Editor: Mircea Merca

Received: 22 March 2023
Revised: 26 April 2023
Accepted: 3 May 2023
Published: 5 May 2023

1. Introduction

In recent decades, the theory of convexity and inequalities has become an amazing and deep source of attention and inspiration in different areas of science. The combined study of these terminologies has had not only interesting and deep results in numerous subjects of applied and engineering sciences but also contributed equally towards numerical optimization. The concept of convexity is based and depends on the theory of inequalities and also plays a prominent and meaningful role in this field. The novel literature on inequalities always provides an excellent glimpse of the beauty and fascination of science. Integral inequalities have many applications in probability theory, information technology, statistics, numerical integration, stochastic processes, optimization theory, and integral operator theory. For detailed concepts on inequalities, see [1–19]. In [20], İşcan explores an extended form of convex function, namely the n-polynomial convex function. The harmonic convex set in 2003 was first defined by Shi in [21]. On this harmonic convex set, the harmonic convex function was introduced by Anderson et al. [22]. Noor [23] continued his work on estimations and extensions and investigated the harmonic convex function in a polynomial version and also made some improvements in the frame variational inequality (see [24,25]).

Dragomir [26] was the first to define and research the term "exponential convex function" in the literature. After Dragomir, Awan [27] conducted the study and refined this function.

Kadakal [28] presented a revised definition of exponential convexity. The remarkable significance and applications of exponential convexity are exploited in information sciences, stochastic optimization, data mining, sequential prediction, and statistical learning.

The construction of this manuscript is as follows. In Section 2, we give some basic definitions and concepts which will be required throughout the manuscript's following sections. In Section 3, we introduce the modified harmonic exp s-convex functions and discuss some properties of it. In Section 4, using a newly introduced concept, a new sort of Hadamard-type inequality is achieved. Next, we prove and examine some extensions of the Hadamard-type inequality regarding the new definition with the help of Holder's inequality in Section 5. Finally, in Section 6, future scopes of the present study and a brief conclusion are provided.

2. Preliminaries

For the reader's interest and the quality of the manuscript, it will be best to study and explain some ideas, concepts, definitions, corollaries, theorems, and remarks in this part. The main aim of this part is to mention and discuss some already published definitions and ideas, which we require in our study in the following sections. We start by introducing the convex function and its generalizations in different versions and the Hermite–Hadamard-type inequality. In addition, some theorems regarding harmonic convex functions are added. We sum up this part by stating Holder's and the power mean inequality, which will be needed in our further investigation.

Definition 1 ([1]). *Assume that $\mathbb{X}$ is a convex subset of a real vector space $\mathbb{R}$. A function $Q : \mathbb{X} \to \mathbb{R}$ is convex if*

$$Q(\lambda v_1 + (1-\lambda)v_2) \leq \lambda Q(v_1) + (1-\lambda)Q(v_2), \tag{1}$$

holds $\forall\ v_1, v_2 \in \mathbb{X}$, and $\lambda \in [0,1]$.

The Hermite–Hadamard-type inequality performs a good role in the literature due to its importance and popularity. A lot of scientists have worked on numerous ideas and definitions on the subject of inequalities. In the field of analysis, this inequality has great interest due to its applications. This inequality states that, if function $Q : \mathbb{X} \to \mathbb{R}$ is convex for $v_1, v_2 \in \mathbb{X}$ with the condition $v_1 < v_2$, then

$$Q\left(\frac{v_1+v_2}{2}\right) \leq \frac{1}{v_2 - v_1}\int_{v_1}^{v_2} Q(\chi)d\chi \leq \frac{Q(v_1)+Q(v_2)}{2}. \tag{2}$$

We recommend that readers refer to [29–32].

Definition 2 ([33]). *Let $s \in (0,1]$. A function $Q : [0,+\infty) \to \mathbb{R}$ is s-convex in the second sense if*

$$Q(\lambda v_1 + (1-\lambda)v_2) \leq \lambda^s Q(v_1) + (1-\lambda)^s Q(v_2) \tag{3}$$

holds $\forall\ v_1, v_2 \in [0,+\infty)$, and $\lambda \in [0,1]$.

Definition 3 ([28]). *Let $\mathbb{X}$ be a non-negative real interval. A function $Q : \mathbb{X} \to \mathbb{R}$ is exponentially convex if*

$$Q(\lambda v_1 + (1-\lambda)v_2) \leq \left(e^{\lambda} - 1\right)Q(v_1) + \left(e^{(1-\lambda)} - 1\right)Q(v_2), \tag{4}$$

for all $v_1, v_2 \in \mathbb{X}$, and $\lambda \in [0,1]$.

The notation $EXPC(I)$ represents the family of all exponentially convex functions on the interval $\mathbb{X}$.

Definition 4 ([34]). *Let $\mathbb{X} \subset \mathbb{R} \setminus \{0\}$ be a real interval. A function $\mathrm{Q} : \mathbb{X} \subseteq (0, +\infty) \to \mathbb{R}$ is harmonically convex if*

$$\mathrm{Q}\left(\frac{\mathrm{v}_1\mathrm{v}_2}{\lambda\mathrm{v}_2 + (1-\lambda)\mathrm{v}_1}\right) \leq \lambda\mathrm{Q}(\mathrm{v}_1) + (1-\lambda)\mathrm{Q}(\mathrm{v}_2), \tag{5}$$

holds for all $\mathrm{v}_1, \mathrm{v}_2 \in \mathbb{X}$, and $\lambda \in [0,1]$.

Theorem 1 ([34]). *Assume that a real-valued function Q on $\mathbb{X} \subseteq (0, +\infty) \to \mathbb{R}$ is harmonically convex. If Q is defined on integrable space, i.e., $L[\mathrm{v}_1, \mathrm{v}_2]$, for all $\mathrm{v}_1, \mathrm{v}_2 \in \mathbb{X}$ with $\mathrm{v}_1 < \mathrm{v}_2$, then*

$$\mathrm{Q}\left(\frac{2\mathrm{v}_1\mathrm{v}_2}{\mathrm{v}_1 + \mathrm{v}_2}\right) \leq \frac{\mathrm{v}_1\mathrm{v}_2}{\mathrm{v}_2 - \mathrm{v}_1}\int_{\mathrm{v}_1}^{\mathrm{v}_2} \frac{\mathrm{Q}(x)}{x^2}dx \leq \frac{\mathrm{Q}(\mathrm{v}_1) + \mathrm{Q}(\mathrm{v}_2)}{2}. \tag{6}$$

Definition 5 ([20]). *Let $\mathbb{X}$ be a non-negative real interval. A function $\mathrm{Q} : \mathbb{X} \to [0, \infty)$. Then Q is m-polynomial convex if*

$$\mathrm{Q}(\lambda\mu_1 + (1-\lambda)\mathrm{v}_2) \leq \frac{1}{\mathrm{m}}\sum_{\eta=1}^{\mathrm{m}}[1-(1-\lambda)^\eta]\mathrm{Q}(\mathrm{v}_1) + \frac{1}{\mathrm{m}}\sum_{\eta=1}^{\mathrm{m}}[1-\lambda^\eta]\mathrm{Q}(\mathrm{v}_2), \tag{7}$$

holds for every $\mathrm{v}_1, \mathrm{v}_2 \in \mathbb{X}$, $\mathrm{m} \in \mathbb{N}$, and $\lambda \in [0,1]$.

Definition 6 ([35]). *Assume that $\mathrm{Q} : \mathbb{X} = (0, +\infty) \to [0, \infty)$. Then Q is m-polynomial exponential s-convex if*

$$\mathrm{Q}\Big(\lambda\mathrm{v}_1 + (1-\lambda)\mathrm{v}_2\Big) \leq \frac{1}{\mathrm{m}}\sum_{\eta=1}^{\mathrm{m}}\Big(e^{s\lambda} - 1\Big)^\eta\mathrm{Q}(\mathrm{v}_1) + \frac{1}{\mathrm{m}}\sum_{\eta=1}^{\mathrm{m}}\Big(e^{s(1-\lambda)} - 1\Big)^\eta\mathrm{Q}(\mathrm{v}_2), \tag{8}$$

holds $\forall\, \mathrm{v}_1, \mathrm{v}_2 \in \mathbb{X}$, $\mathrm{m} \in \mathbb{N}$, $s \in [\ln 2.5, 1]$, and $\lambda \in [0,1]$.

Definition 7 ([23]). *Let us assume that $\mathrm{Q} : \mathbb{X} \to [0, \infty)$. Then Q is m-polynomial harmonically convex if*

$$\mathrm{Q}\left(\frac{\mathrm{v}_1\mathrm{v}_2}{\lambda\mathrm{v}_2 + (1-\lambda)\mathrm{v}_1}\right) \leq \frac{1}{\mathrm{m}}\sum_{\eta=1}^{\mathrm{m}}[1-(1-\lambda)^\eta]\mathrm{Q}(\mathrm{v}_1) + \frac{1}{\mathrm{m}}\sum_{\eta=1}^{\mathrm{m}}[1-\lambda^\eta]\mathrm{Q}(\mathrm{v}_2), \tag{9}$$

holds for every $\mathrm{v}_1, \mathrm{v}_2 \in \mathbb{X}$, $\mathrm{m} \in \mathbb{N}$, and $\lambda \in [0,1]$.

Remark 1. *Assume that $\mathrm{m} = 1$; then Definition 7 is referred to Definition 4.*

Remark 2. *If the following inequalities $\lambda \leq \frac{1}{\mathrm{m}}\sum_{\eta=1}^{\mathrm{m}}[1-(1-\lambda)^\eta]$ and $1-\lambda \leq \frac{1}{\mathrm{m}}\sum_{\eta=1}^{\mathrm{m}}[1-\lambda^\eta]$ hold, then every harmonic convex function is an m-polynomial harmonic convex function.*

Definition 8 ([36]). *Let us assume that $\mathrm{Q} : \mathbb{X} \to [0, \infty)$. Then Q is m-polynomial harmonic exponential convex if*

$$\mathrm{Q}\left(\frac{\mathrm{v}_1\mathrm{v}_2}{\lambda\mathrm{v}_2 + (1-\lambda)\mathrm{v}_1}\right) \leq \frac{1}{\mathrm{m}}\sum_{\eta=1}^{\mathrm{m}}\Big(e^{\lambda} - 1\Big)^\eta\mathrm{Q}(\mathrm{v}_1) + \frac{1}{\mathrm{m}}\sum_{\eta=1}^{\mathrm{m}}\Big(e^{1-\lambda} - 1\Big)^\eta\mathrm{Q}(\mathrm{v}_2), \tag{10}$$

holds for every $\mathrm{v}_1, \mathrm{v}_2 \in \mathbb{X}$, $\mathrm{m} \in \mathbb{N}$, and $\lambda \in [0,1]$.

Remark 3 ([36]). *Every nonnegative m-polynomial harmonic convex function is also an m-polynomial harmonic exponential-type convex function. Indeed, for all $\lambda \in [0,1]$ this case is clear from the following inequalities:*

$$\frac{1}{n}\sum_{\eta=1}^{m}[1-(1-\lambda)^{\eta}] \leq \frac{1}{m}\sum_{\eta=1}^{m}(e^{\lambda}-1)^{\eta} \text{ and } \frac{1}{m}\sum_{\eta=1}^{m}[1-\lambda^{\eta}] \leq \frac{1}{m}\sum_{\eta=1}^{m}(e^{1-\lambda}-1)^{\eta}.$$

Theorem 2 ([37]). *Assume that $p > 1$ and $\frac{1}{p}+\frac{1}{q}=1$. If Q_1 and Q_2 are real functions defined on Lebesgue measurable space of a and b, i.e., $L[a,b]$, and if $|Q_1|^p$ and $|Q_2|^q$ are integrable functions on $[a,b]$, then*

$$\int_a^b |Q_1(\nu)Q_2(\nu)|d\nu \leq \left(\int_a^b |Q_1(x)|^p dx\right)^{\frac{1}{p}}\left(\int_a^b |Q_2(x)|^q dx\right)^{\frac{1}{q}}. \tag{11}$$

The equality holds if and only if $A|Q_1|^p = B|Q_2|^q$, almost everywhere, where A and B are constants.

3. Modified Harmonic Exponential *s*-Convex Function and Its Algebraic Properties

The term convexity has gained an amazing image due to many applications in the realms of engineering, optimizations, and applied mathematics. Although many outcomes have been deduced under convexity, the majority of the problems regarding real life are nonconvex in nature. In the 20th century, many researchers gave attention to the term convexity, such as Jensen, Hermite, Holder, and Stolz. Throughout this century, an unprecedented amount of research was carried out, and important results were obtained in the field of convex analysis.

We will provide our basic definition of the modified harmonic exp *s*-convex function and its corresponding features as the main topic of this section.

Definition 9. *Assume that $Q : \mathbb{X} = (0,+\infty) \to [0,\infty)$. Then Q is modified harmonic exponential s-convex if*

$$Q\left(\frac{v_1v_2}{\lambda v_2+(1-\lambda)v_1}\right) \leq \frac{1}{m}\sum_{\eta=1}^{m}\left(e^{s\lambda}-1\right)^{\eta}Q(v_1)+\frac{1}{m}\sum_{\eta=1}^{m}\left(e^{s(1-\lambda)}-1\right)^{\eta}Q(v_2), \tag{12}$$

holds $\forall\, v_1, v_2 \in \mathbb{X}$, $m \in \mathbb{N}$, $s \in [\ln 2.5, 1]$, and $\lambda \in [0,1]$.

Remark 4. *Assume that $m = 1$ in the above inequality (12); then*

$$Q\left(\frac{v_1v_2}{\lambda v_2+(1-\lambda)v_1}\right) \leq \left(e^{s\lambda}-1\right)Q(v_1)+\left(e^{s(1-\lambda)}-1\right)Q(v_2). \tag{13}$$

Remark 5. *Assume that $m = 2$ in the above inequality (12); then*

$$Q\left(\frac{v_1v_2}{\lambda v_2+(1-\lambda)v_1}\right) \leq \left(\frac{e^{2s\lambda}-e^{s\lambda}}{2}\right)Q(v_1)+\left(\frac{e^{2s(1-\lambda)}-e^{s(1-\lambda)}}{2}\right)Q(v_2). \tag{14}$$

Remark 6. *Assume that $s = 1$ in the above inequality (12); we obtain Definition 8.*

Remark 7. *Assume that $m = 1$ and $s = 1$ in the above inequality (12); we obtain Remark 3 in [36].*

Remark 8. *Assume that $m = 2$ and $s = 1$ in the above inequality (12); we obtain Remark 4 in [36].*

That is the best advantage of the novel concept. If we take m and s at their given values, then we obtain the new inequalities and discover their connections with previous results.

Lemma 1. *Let us assume that $\lambda \in [0,1]$ and $s \in [\ln 2.5, 1]$; then $\frac{1}{m}\sum\limits_{\eta=1}^{m}(e^{s\lambda}-1)^{\eta} \geq \lambda$ and $\frac{1}{m}\sum\limits_{\eta=1}^{m}(e^{s(1-\lambda)}-1)^{\eta} \geq (1-\lambda)$ hold.*

Lemma 2. *The following inequalities* $\frac{1}{m}\sum_{\eta=1}^{m}(e^{s\lambda}-1)^{\eta} \geq \frac{1}{n}\sum_{\eta=1}^{m}[1-(1-\lambda)^{\eta}]$ *and* $\frac{1}{m}\sum_{\eta=1}^{m}(e^{s(1-\lambda)}-1)^{\eta} \geq \frac{1}{m}\sum_{\eta=1}^{m}[1-\lambda^{\eta}]$ *hold, for all* $\lambda \in [0,1]$ *and* $s \in [\ln 2.5, 1]$.

Proposition 1. *Every harmonic convex function* $Q : I \subset (0,+\infty) \to [0,\infty)$ *is a modified harmonic exp s-convex function.*

Proof. Since the given function is a harmonic convex, by definition, we have

$$Q\left(\frac{v_1 v_2}{\lambda v_2 + (1-\lambda)v_1}\right) \leq \lambda Q(v_1) + (1-\lambda)Q(v_2).$$

Employing Lemma 1, we have

$$Q\left(\frac{v_1 v_2}{\lambda v_2 + (1-\lambda)v_1}\right) \leq \frac{1}{m}\sum_{\eta=1}^{m}\left(e^{s\lambda}-1\right)^{\eta}Q(v_1) + \frac{1}{m}\sum_{\eta=1}^{m}\left(e^{s(1-\lambda)}-1\right)^{\eta}Q(v_2).$$

□

Proposition 2. *Every* m*-polynomial harmonically convex function is a modified harmonically exp s-convex function.*

Proof. Since the given function is m-polynomial harmonic convex, by definition, we have

$$Q\left(\frac{v_1 v_2}{\lambda v_2 + (1-\lambda)v_1}\right) \leq \frac{1}{m}\sum_{\eta=1}^{m}[1-(1-\lambda)^{\eta}]Q(v_1) + \frac{1}{m}\sum_{\eta=1}^{m}[1-\lambda^{\eta}]Q(v_2).$$

Employing Lemma 2, we have

$$Q\left(\frac{v_1 v_2}{\lambda v_2 + (1-\lambda)v_1}\right) \leq \frac{1}{m}\sum_{\eta=1}^{m}\left(e^{s\lambda}-1\right)^{\eta}Q(v_1) + \frac{1}{m}\sum_{\eta=1}^{m}\left(e^{s(1-\lambda)}-1\right)^{\eta}Q(v_2).$$

□

Next, regarding this new definition, we add some examples.

Example 1. *Let* $Q(x) = x^2 e^{x^2}$ *be a non-decreasing convex function on* $(0,1)$*; then it is harmonic convex (see [38]). Employing Proposition 1, we claim that it is a modified harmonic exp s-convex function.*

Example 2. *Let* $Q(x) = e^x$ *be a non-decreasing convex function; then it is harmonic convex (see [38]). Employing Proposition 1, we claim that it is a modified harmonic exp s-convex function.*

Example 3. *Let* $Q(x) = \sin(-x)$ *be a non-decreasing convex function on* $(0,\frac{\pi}{2})$*; then it is harmonically convex* $\forall x \in (0,\frac{\pi}{2})$ *(see [38]). Employing Proposition 1, it is a modified harmonic exp s-convex function.*

Example 4. *Let* $Q(x) = x$ *be a non-decreasing convex function on* $(0,\infty)$*; then it is harmonically convex for all* $x \in (0,\infty)$ *(see [38]). Employing Remark 2, we claim that it is* m*-polynomial harmonic convex. Employing Proposition 2, we claim that it is a modified harmonic exp s-convex function.*

Example 5. *Let* $Q(x) = \ln x$ *be a harmonic convex on the interval* $(0,\infty)$ *(see [38]). Employing Remark 2 and Proposition 2, we obtain that* $Q(x)$ *is a modified harmonic exp s-convex function.*

In addition, we add some properties regarding the newly introduced idea, namely the modified harmonic exp s-convex function.

Theorem 3. *The sum of two modified harmonic exp s-convex functions is a modified harmonic exp s-convex function.*

Proof. Let us assume that the functions Q and H are modified harmonic exp s-convex and $\lambda \in [0,1]$; then

$$\begin{aligned}
&(\mathsf{Q}+\mathsf{H})\left(\frac{\mathrm{v}_1\mathrm{v}_2}{\lambda\mathrm{v}_2+(1-\lambda)\mathrm{v}_1}\right)\\
&=\mathsf{Q}\left(\frac{\mathrm{v}_1\mathrm{v}_2}{\lambda\mathrm{v}_2+(1-\lambda)\mathrm{v}_1}\right)+\mathsf{H}\left(\frac{\mathrm{v}_1\mathrm{v}_2}{\lambda\mathrm{v}_2+(1-\lambda)\mathrm{v}_1}\right)\\
&\leq\frac{1}{\mathrm{m}}\sum_{\eta=1}^{\mathrm{m}}\left(e^{s\lambda}-1\right)^{\eta}\mathsf{Q}(\mathrm{v}_1)+\frac{1}{\mathrm{m}}\sum_{\eta=1}^{\mathrm{m}}\left(e^{s(1-\lambda)}-1\right)^{\eta}\mathsf{Q}(\mathrm{v}_2)\\
&+\frac{1}{\mathrm{m}}\sum_{\eta=1}^{\mathrm{m}}\left(e^{s\lambda}-1\right)^{\eta}\mathsf{H}(\mathrm{v}_1)+\frac{1}{\mathrm{m}}\sum_{\eta=1}^{\mathrm{m}}\left(e^{s(1-\lambda)}-1\right)^{\eta}\mathsf{H}(\mathrm{v}_2)\\
&=\frac{1}{\mathrm{m}}\sum_{\eta=1}^{\mathrm{m}}\left(e^{s\lambda}-1\right)^{\eta}[\mathsf{Q}(\mathrm{v}_1)+\mathsf{H}(\mathrm{v}_1)]+\frac{1}{\mathrm{m}}\sum_{\eta=1}^{\mathrm{m}}\left(e^{s(1-\lambda)}-1\right)^{\eta}[\mathsf{Q}(\mathrm{v}_2)+\mathsf{H}(\mathrm{v}_2)]\\
&=\frac{1}{\mathrm{m}}\sum_{\eta=1}^{\mathrm{m}}\left(e^{s\lambda}-1\right)^{\eta}(\mathsf{Q}+\mathsf{H})(\mathrm{v}_1)+\frac{1}{\mathrm{m}}\sum_{\eta=1}^{\mathrm{m}}\left(e^{s(1-\lambda)}-1\right)^{\eta}(\mathsf{Q}+\mathsf{H})(\mathrm{v}_2).
\end{aligned}$$

This completes the proof. □

Remark 9. *If we assume that* $\mathrm{m} = 1$*, then we obtain* $\mathsf{Q}+\mathsf{H}$ *as the harmonic exp s-convex function.*

Remark 10. *If we assume that* $s = 1$*, then we obtain* $\mathsf{Q}+\mathsf{H}$ *as a modified harmonic exp convex function.*

Remark 11. *If we assume that* $\mathrm{m} = 1$ *and* $s = 1$*, then we obtain* $\mathsf{Q}+\mathsf{H}$ *as a harmonic exp convex function.*

Theorem 4. *Scalar multiplication of a modified harmonic exp s-convex function is a modified harmonic exp s-convex function.*

Proof. Let assume that the function Q is modified harmonic exp s-convex, $\lambda \in [0,1]$; then

$$\begin{aligned}
&(c\mathsf{Q})\left(\frac{\mathrm{v}_1\mathrm{v}_2}{\lambda\mathrm{v}_2+(1-\lambda)\mathrm{v}_1}\right)\\
&\leq c\left[\frac{1}{\mathrm{m}}\sum_{\eta=1}^{\mathrm{m}}\left(e^{s\lambda}-1\right)^{\eta}\mathsf{Q}(\mathrm{v}_1)+\frac{1}{\mathrm{m}}\sum_{\eta=1}^{\mathrm{m}}\left(e^{s(1-\lambda)}-1\right)^{\eta}\mathsf{Q}(\mathrm{v}_2)\right]\\
&=\frac{1}{\mathrm{m}}\sum_{\eta=1}^{\mathrm{m}}\left(e^{s\lambda}-1\right)^{\eta}c\mathsf{Q}(\mathrm{v}_1)+\frac{1}{\mathrm{m}}\sum_{\eta=1}^{\mathrm{m}}\left(e^{s(1-\lambda)}-1\right)^{\eta}c\mathsf{Q}(\mathrm{v}_2)\\
&=\frac{1}{\mathrm{m}}\sum_{\eta=1}^{\mathrm{m}}\left(e^{s\lambda}-1\right)^{\eta}(c\mathsf{Q})(\mathrm{v}_1)+\frac{1}{\mathrm{m}}\sum_{\eta=1}^{\mathrm{m}}\left(e^{s(1-\lambda)}-1\right)^{\eta}(c\mathsf{Q})(\mathrm{v}_2).
\end{aligned}$$

This completes the proof. □

Remark 12. *If we assume that* $\mathrm{m} = 1$*, then the scalar multiplication of a harmonic exp s-convex function is a harmonic exp s-convex function.*

Remark 13. *If we assume that* $s = 1$, *then the scalar multiplication of the modified harmonic exp convex function is a modified harmonic exp convex function.*

Remark 14. *If we assume that* $m = 1$ *and* $s = 1$, *then scalar multiplication of a harmonically exp convex function is a harmonic exp convex function.*

Theorem 5. *Assume that the function* $Q_1 : \mathbb{X} \to [0, +\infty)$ *is harmonic convex and the function* $Q_2 : [0, +\infty) \to [0, +\infty)$ *is increasing and m-polynomial exp s-convex. Then* $Q_2 \circ Q_1 : \mathbb{X} \to [0, +\infty)$ *is a modified harmonic exp s-convex function.*

Proof. For all $v_1, v_2 \in \mathbb{X}$, and $\lambda \in [0, 1]$, we have

$$\begin{aligned}
&(Q_2 \circ Q_1)\left(\frac{v_1 v_2}{\lambda v_2 + (1-\lambda) v_1}\right) \\
&= Q_2\left(Q_1\left(\frac{v_1 v_2}{\lambda v_2 + (1-\lambda) v_1}\right)\right) \\
&\leq Q_2(\lambda Q_1(v_1) + (1-\lambda) Q_1(v_2)) \\
&\leq \frac{1}{m}\sum_{\eta=1}^{m}\left(e^{s\lambda} - 1\right)^{\eta} Q_2(Q_1(v_1)) + \frac{1}{m}\sum_{\eta=1}^{m}\left(e^{s(1-\lambda)} - 1\right)^{\eta} Q_2(Q_1(v_2)) \\
&= \frac{1}{m}\sum_{\eta=1}^{m}\left(e^{s\lambda} - 1\right)^{\eta} (Q_2 \circ Q_1)(v_1) + \frac{1}{m}\sum_{\eta=1}^{m}\left(e^{s(1-\lambda)} - 1\right)^{\eta} (Q_2 \circ Q_1)(v_2).
\end{aligned}$$

□

Theorem 6. *Let* $0 < v_1 < v_2$ *and assume that non-negative real-valued function* Q_j *is a class of modified harmonic exp s-convex and* $Q(u) = \sup_j Q_j(u)$. *Then the function* Q *is a modified harmonic exp s-convex and* $U = \{u \in [v_1, v_2] : Q(u) < +\infty\}$ *is an interval.*

Proof. Let $v_1, v_2 \in U$ and $\lambda \in [0, 1]$; then

$$\begin{aligned}
&Q\left(\frac{v_1 v_2}{\lambda v_2 + (1-\lambda) v_1}\right) \\
&= \sup_j Q_j\left(\frac{v_1 v_2}{(\lambda v_2 + (1-\lambda) v_1)}\right) \\
&\leq \frac{1}{m}\sum_{\eta=1}^{m}\left(e^{s\lambda} - 1\right)^{\eta} \sup_j Q_j(v_1) + \frac{1}{m}\sum_{\eta=1}^{m}\left(e^{s(1-\lambda)} - 1\right)^{\eta} \sup_j Q_j(v_2) \\
&= \frac{1}{m}\sum_{\eta=1}^{m}\left(e^{s\lambda} - 1\right)^{\eta} Q(v_1) + \frac{1}{m}\sum_{\eta=1}^{m}\left(e^{s(1-\lambda)} - 1\right)^{\eta} Q(v_2) < +\infty.
\end{aligned}$$

This shows simultaneously that U is an interval, since it contains every point between any two of its points, and that Q is a modified harmonic exp s-convex function on U. This is the required proof. □

Theorem 7. *If* $Q : \mathbb{X} \to [0, +\infty)$ *is modified harmonic exp s-convex, then the function* Q *is bounded on* $[v_1, v_2]$.

Proof. Let us assume that $x \in [v_1, v_2]$ and $L = \max\{Q(v_1), Q(v_2)\}$. Then $\exists\, \lambda \in [0,1]$ such that $x = \frac{v_1 v_2}{\lambda v_2 + (1-\lambda) v_1}$. Here, we clearly know about the obvious following inequalities, i.e., $e^{s\lambda} \leq e$ and $e^{s(1-\lambda)} \leq e$; then

$$\begin{aligned} Q(x) &= Q\left(\frac{v_1 v_2}{\lambda v_2 + (1-\lambda) v_1}\right) \\ &\leq \frac{1}{m}\sum_{\eta=1}^{m}\left(e^{s\lambda}-1\right)^{\eta} Q(v_1) + \frac{1}{m}\sum_{\eta=1}^{m}\left(e^{s(1-\lambda)}-1\right)^{\eta} Q(v_2) \\ &\leq \frac{1}{m}\sum_{\eta=1}^{m}\left(e^{s\lambda}-1\right)^{\eta} L + \frac{1}{m}\sum_{\eta=1}^{m}\left(e^{s(1-\lambda)}-1\right)^{\eta} L \\ &\leq \frac{2L}{m}\sum_{\eta=1}^{m}(e-1)^{\eta} = M. \end{aligned}$$

□

4. Generalized Form of Hadamard Inequality via Modified Harmonic Exponential *s*-Convex Function

Convexity is important and crucial in many branches of the pure and applied sciences. Massive generalizations of mathematical inequalities for multiple convex functions have significantly influenced traditional research. Numerous fields, including linear programming, combinatorics, theory of relativity, optimization theory, quantum theory, number theory, dynamics, and orthogonal polynomials are affected by and use integral inequalities. This issue has received much attention from researchers. The Hadamard inequality is the most widely used and popular inequality in the history and literature pertaining to convex theory.

This purpose of this section is to establish a new kind of the Hadamard inequality pertaining to modified harmonic exp s-convexity.

Theorem 8. *Let non-negative real-valued* Q *be modified harmonic exp* s*-convex. If* $Q \in L[v_1, v_2]$, *then*

$$\frac{m}{2\sum_{\eta=1}^{m}\left(\sqrt{e^{s}}-1\right)^{\eta}} Q\left(\frac{2v_1v_2}{v_1+v_2}\right) \leq \frac{v_1v_2}{v_2-v_1}\int_{v_1}^{v_2}\frac{Q(x)}{x^2}dx \leq \left[\mathcal{A}_1 Q(v_1) + \mathcal{A}_2 Q(v_2)\right], \quad (15)$$

where
$\mathcal{A}_1 = \frac{1}{m}\sum_{\eta=1}^{m}\int_0^1 (e^{s\lambda}-1)^{\eta} d\lambda$ *and* $\mathcal{A}_2 = \frac{1}{m}\sum_{\eta=1}^{m}\int_0^1 \left(e^{s(1-\lambda)}-1\right)^{\eta} d\lambda.$

Proof. Since Q is modified harmonic exp s-convex, then we have

$$Q\left(\frac{xy}{\lambda y + (1-\lambda)x}\right) \leq \frac{1}{m}\sum_{\eta=1}^{m}\left(e^{s\lambda}-1\right)^{\eta} Q(x) + \frac{1}{m}\sum_{\eta=1}^{m}\left(e^{s(1-\lambda)}-1\right)^{\eta} Q(y),$$

which leads to

$$Q\left(\frac{2xy}{x+y}\right) \leq \frac{1}{m}\sum_{\eta=1}^{m}\left(\sqrt{e^{s}}-1\right)^{\eta} Q(x) + \frac{1}{m}\sum_{\eta=1}^{m}\left(\sqrt{e^{s}}-1\right)^{\eta} Q(y).$$

Employing the change in variables, we have

$$Q\left(\frac{2v_1v_2}{v_1+v_2}\right) \leq \frac{1}{m}\sum_{\eta=1}^{m}\left[\left(\sqrt{e^{s}}-1\right)^{\eta}\right]\left[Q\left(\frac{v_1v_2}{(\lambda v_2+(1-\lambda)v_1)}\right) + Q\left(\frac{v_1v_2}{(\lambda v_1+(1-\lambda)v_2)}\right)\right]. \quad (16)$$

Integrating inequality (16) w.r.t. λ on $[0,1]$ yields

$$\frac{m}{2\sum_{\eta=1}^{m}\left(\sqrt{e^{s}}-1\right)^{\eta}}Q\left(\frac{2v_1v_2}{v_1+v_2}\right)\leq\frac{v_1v_2}{v_2-v_1}\int_{v_1}^{v_2}\frac{Q(x)}{x^2}dx.$$

This is the required inequality.

For the other inequality, first we suppose $x=\frac{v_1v_2}{\lambda v_2+(1-\lambda)v_1}$ and employ Definition 9 for the function Q; we have

$$\begin{aligned}&\frac{v_1v_2}{v_2-v_1}\int_{v_1}^{v_2}\frac{Q(x)}{x^2}dx\\&=\int_0^1 Q\left(\frac{v_1v_2}{\lambda v_2+(1-\lambda)v_1}\right)d\lambda\\&\leq\int_0^1\left[\frac{1}{m}\sum_{\eta=1}^{m}\left(e^{s\lambda}-1\right)^{\eta}Q(v_1)+\frac{1}{m}\sum_{\eta=1}^{m}\left(e^{s(1-\lambda)}-1\right)^{\eta}Q(v_2)\right]d\lambda\\&=\frac{Q(v_1)}{m}\sum_{\eta=1}^{m}\int_0^1\left(e^{s\lambda}-1\right)^{\eta}d\lambda+\frac{Q(v_2)}{m}\sum_{\eta=1}^{m}\int_0^1\left(e^{s(1-\lambda)}-1\right)^{\eta}d\lambda\\&=\left[\mathcal{A}_1Q(v_1)+\mathcal{A}_2Q(v_2)\right].\end{aligned}$$

This completes the proof. □

Corollary 1. *Assume that $m=1$ in the above inequality (15); then*

$$\frac{1}{2\left(\sqrt{e^{s}}-1\right)}Q\left(\frac{2v_1v_2}{v_1+v_2}\right)\leq\frac{v_1v_2}{v_2-v_1}\int_{v_1}^{v_2}\frac{Q(x)}{x^2}dx\leq\left(\frac{e^{s}-s-1}{s}\right)\left[Q(v_1)+Q(v_2)\right].$$

Remark 15. *Assume that $s=1$ in the above inequality (15); then we obtain Theorem 4.1 in [36].*

5. Refinements of Hadamard Inequality Involving Modified Harmonic Exponential s-Convex Function

In recognition of the importance of convexity, various researchers have created numerous generalizations of convexity and validated a lot of features in these new generalized cases. Convex sequences, their characteristics, and the accompanying inequalities with applications have received increased attention from researchers. The most viewed and discussed inequality in history connected with the field of convex analysis is the Hermite–Hadamard inequality.

Given the following lemma, with the aid of Holder's inequality and involving the newly introduced concept, we obtained some extensions of the Hermite–Hadamard inequality.

Lemma 3 ([23]). *Let us assume that $\rho,\sigma\in[0,1]$ and a non-negative real-valued function Q is a differentiable mapping. If $Q'\in L[v_1,v_2]$, then the following identity holds:*

$$\begin{aligned}&\frac{\rho Q(v_1)+\sigma Q(v_2)}{2}+\frac{2-\rho-\sigma}{2}Q\left(\frac{2v_1v_2}{v_1+v_2}\right)-\frac{v_1v_2}{v_2-v_1}\int_{v_1}^{v_2}\frac{Q(x)}{x^2}dx\\&=\frac{v_1v_2(v_2-v_1)}{4}\int_0^1\left[\frac{4(1-\rho-\lambda)}{((1-\lambda)v_2+(1+\lambda)v_1)^2}Q'\left(\frac{2v_1v_2}{(1-\lambda)v_2+(1+\lambda)v_1}\right)\right.\\&\left.+\frac{4(\sigma-\lambda)}{(\lambda v_1+(2-\lambda)v_2)^2}Q'\left(\frac{2v_1v_2}{\lambda v_1+(2-\lambda)v_2}\right)\right]d\lambda.\end{aligned}\tag{17}$$

For simplicity, we denote

$$A_{v_1,v_2}=(1-\lambda)v_2+(1+\lambda)v_1\quad\text{and}\quad B_{v_1,v_2}=\lambda v_1+(2-\lambda)v_2.\tag{18}$$

The following notations will be used in this way:

$$\Gamma(\mathrm{v}) = \int_0^{+\infty} e^{-\lambda}\lambda^{\mathrm{v}-1}d\lambda, \quad \mathrm{v} > 0;$$

$$\beta(\mathrm{v}_1, \mathrm{v}_2) = \int_0^1 \lambda^{\mathrm{v}_1-1}(1-\lambda)^{\mathrm{v}_2-1}d\lambda, \quad \mathrm{v}_1, \mathrm{v}_2 > 0;$$

This is a hypergeometric function in integral form first introduced by Euler [39]. This function states that

$$\beta(\mathrm{v}_1, \mathrm{v}_2) = \frac{\Gamma(\mathrm{v}_1)\Gamma(\mathrm{v}_2)}{\Gamma(\mathrm{v}_1+\mathrm{v}_2)}, \quad \mathrm{v}_1, \mathrm{v}_2 > 0;$$

$${}_2F_1(\mathrm{v}_1, \mathrm{v}_2; \mathrm{v}_3; \mathrm{v}) = \frac{1}{\beta(\mathrm{v}_2, \mathrm{v}_3 - \mathrm{v}_2)}\int_0^1 \lambda^{\mathrm{v}_2-1}(1-\lambda)^{\mathrm{v}_3-\mathrm{v}_2-1}(1-\mathrm{v}\lambda)^{-\mathrm{v}_1}d\lambda,$$

where $\mathrm{v}_3 > \mathrm{v}_2 > 0$ and $|\mathrm{v}| < 1$.

Theorem 9. *Let us assume that $\rho, \sigma \in [0,1]$ and $\mathrm{Q} : [\mathrm{v}_1, \mathrm{v}_2] \subseteq (0, +\infty) \to \mathbb{R}$ is a differentiable mapping such that $\mathrm{Q}' \in L[\mathrm{v}_1, \mathrm{v}_2]$. Suppose $|\mathrm{Q}'|^q$ is modified harmonic exp s-convex; then for $p, q > 1$ with $\frac{1}{p} + \frac{1}{q} = 1$, we have*

$$\begin{aligned}
&\left|\frac{\rho \mathrm{Q}(\mathrm{v}_1) + \sigma \mathrm{Q}(\mathrm{v}_2)}{2} + \frac{2-\rho-\sigma}{2}\mathrm{Q}\left(\frac{2\mathrm{v}_1\mathrm{v}_2}{\mathrm{v}_1+\mathrm{v}_2}\right) - \frac{\mathrm{v}_1\mathrm{v}_2}{\mathrm{v}_2-\mathrm{v}_1}\int_{\mathrm{v}_1}^{\mathrm{v}_2}\frac{\mathrm{Q}(x)}{x^2}dx\right| \\
&\leq \mathrm{v}_1\mathrm{v}_2(\mathrm{v}_2-\mathrm{v}_1) \qquad (19)\\
&\times \left[\varphi_1^{\frac{1}{p}}\left(\mathfrak{T}_1|\mathrm{Q}'(\mathrm{v}_1)|^q + \mathfrak{T}_2|\mathrm{Q}'(\mathrm{v}_2)|^q\right)^{\frac{1}{q}} + \varphi_2^{\frac{1}{p}}\left(\mathfrak{T}_3|\mathrm{Q}'(\mathrm{v}_1)|^q + \mathfrak{T}_4|\mathrm{Q}'(\mathrm{v}_2)|^q\right)^{\frac{1}{q}}\right],
\end{aligned}$$

where

$$\varphi_1 = \int_0^1 |1-\rho-\lambda|^p d\lambda = \frac{(1-\rho)^{p+1}+\rho^{p+1}}{p+1},$$

$$\varphi_2 = \int_0^1 |\sigma-\lambda|^p d\lambda = \frac{(1-\sigma)^{p+1}+\sigma^{p+1}}{p+1},$$

$$\mathfrak{T}_1 = \frac{1}{2\mathrm{m}}\sum_{\eta=1}^{n}\int_0^1 \frac{1}{A^{2q}_{\mathrm{v}_1,\mathrm{v}_2}}(e^{s(1-\lambda)}-1)^\eta d\lambda, \quad \mathfrak{T}_2 = \frac{1}{2\mathrm{m}}\sum_{\eta=1}^{\mathrm{m}}\int_0^1 \frac{1}{A^{2q}_{\mathrm{v}_1,\mathrm{v}_2}}(e^{s(1+\lambda)}-1)^\eta d\lambda,$$

$$\mathfrak{T}_3 = \frac{1}{2\mathrm{m}}\sum_{\eta=1}^{\mathrm{m}}\int_0^1 \frac{1}{\mathrm{B}^{2q}_{\mathrm{v}_1,\mathrm{v}_2}}(e^{s(2-\lambda)}-1)^\eta d\lambda, \quad \mathfrak{T}_4 = \frac{1}{2\mathrm{m}}\sum_{\eta=1}^{\mathrm{m}}\int_0^1 \frac{1}{\mathrm{B}^{2q}_{\mathrm{v}_1,\mathrm{v}_2}}(e^{s\lambda}-1)^\eta d\lambda,$$

and $A_{\mathrm{v}_1,\mathrm{v}_2}, \mathrm{B}_{\mathrm{v}_1,\mathrm{v}_2}$ are defined from (18).

Proof. From Lemma 3, we have

$$\begin{aligned}
&\left|\frac{\rho \mathrm{Q}(\mathrm{v}_1) + \sigma \mathrm{Q}(\mathrm{v}_2)}{2} + \frac{2-\rho-\sigma}{2}\mathrm{Q}\left(\frac{2\mathrm{v}_1\mathrm{v}_2}{\mathrm{v}_1+\mathrm{v}_2}\right) - \frac{\mathrm{v}_1\mathrm{v}_2}{\mathrm{v}_2-\mathrm{v}_1}\int_{\mathrm{v}_1}^{\mathrm{v}_2}\frac{\mathrm{Q}(x)}{x^2}dx\right| \\
&\leq \frac{\mathrm{v}_1\mathrm{v}_2(\mathrm{v}_2-\mathrm{v}_1)}{4}\left[\int_0^1 \left|\frac{4(1-\rho-\lambda)}{((1-\lambda)\mathrm{v}_2+(1+\lambda)\mathrm{v}_1)^2}\right|\left|\mathrm{Q}'\left(\frac{2\mathrm{v}_1\mathrm{v}_2}{(1-\lambda)\mathrm{v}_2+(1+\lambda)\mathrm{v}_1}\right)\right|d\lambda\right. \\
&\left.+\int_0^1 \left|\frac{4(\sigma-\lambda)}{(\lambda\mu_1+(2-\lambda)\mathrm{v}_2)^2}\right|\left|\mathrm{Q}'\left(\frac{2\mathrm{v}_1\mathrm{v}_2}{\lambda\mathrm{v}_1+(2-\lambda)\mathrm{v}_2}\right)\right|d\lambda\right].
\end{aligned}$$

Employing the property of Hölder's inequality and modified harmonic exp s-convex function, we have

$$\begin{aligned}
&\left|\frac{\rho Q(v_1)+\sigma Q(v_2)}{2}+\frac{2-\rho-\sigma}{2}Q\left(\frac{2v_1v_2}{v_1+v_2}\right)-\frac{v_1v_2}{v_2-v_1}\int_{v_1}^{v_2}\frac{Q(x)}{x^2}dx\right| \\
&\leq v_1v_2(v_2-v_1)\left\{\left(\int_0^1|1-\rho-\lambda|^p d\lambda\right)^{\frac{1}{p}}\right. \\
&\times\left[\int_0^1\frac{1}{A_{v_1,v_2}^{2q}}\left(\frac{1}{2m}\sum_{\eta=1}^{m}\left(e^{s(1-\lambda)}-1\right)^{\eta}|Q'(v_1)|^q+\frac{1}{2m}\sum_{\eta=1}^{m}\left(e^{s(1+\lambda)}-1\right)^{\eta}|Q'(v_2)|^q\right)d\lambda\right]^{\frac{1}{q}} \\
&+\left(\int_0^1|\sigma-\lambda|^p d\lambda\right)^{\frac{1}{p}} \\
&\times\left.\left[\int_0^1\frac{1}{B_{v_1,v_2}^{2q}}\left(\frac{1}{2m}\sum_{\eta=1}^{m}\left(e^{s(2-\lambda)}-1\right)^{\eta}|Q'(v_1)|^q+\frac{1}{2m}\sum_{\eta=1}^{m}\left(e^{s\lambda}-1\right)^{\eta}|Q'(v_2)|^q\right)d\lambda\right]^{\frac{1}{q}}\right\} \\
&=\frac{v_1v_2(v_2-v_1)}{4} \\
&\times\left[\varphi_1^{\frac{1}{p}}\left(\mathfrak{T}_1|Q'(v_1)|^q+\mathfrak{T}_2|Q'(v_2)|^q\right)^{\frac{1}{q}}+\varphi_2^{\frac{1}{p}}\left(\mathfrak{T}_3|Q'(v_1)|^q+\mathfrak{T}_4|Q'(v_2)|^q\right)^{\frac{1}{q}}\right].
\end{aligned}$$

This completes the proof. □

Corollary 2. *Assume that* m = 1 *in inequality (19); then*

$$\begin{aligned}
&\left|\frac{\rho Q(v_1)+\sigma Q(v_2)}{2}+\frac{2-\rho-\sigma}{2}Q\left(\frac{2v_1v_2}{v_1+v_2}\right)-\frac{v_1v_2}{v_2-v_1}\int_{v_1}^{v_2}\frac{Q(x)}{x^2}dx\right| \\
&\leq v_1v_2(v_2-v_1) \\
&\times\left[\varphi_1^{\frac{1}{p}}\left(D_1|Q'(v_1)|^q+D_2|Q'(v_2)|^q\right)^{\frac{1}{q}}+\varphi_2^{\frac{1}{p}}\left(D_3|Q'(v_1)|^q+D_4|Q'(v_2)|^q\right)^{\frac{1}{q}}\right],
\end{aligned}$$

where

$$D_1=\frac{1}{2}\int_0^1\frac{1}{A_{v_1,v_2}^{2q}}(e^{s(1-\lambda)}-1)d\lambda,\quad D_2=\frac{1}{2}\int_0^1\frac{1}{A_{v_1,v_2}^{2q}}(e^{s(1+\lambda)}-1)d\lambda,$$

$$D_3=\frac{1}{2}\int_0^1\frac{1}{B_{v_1,v_2}^{2q}}(e^{s(2-\lambda)}-1)d\lambda,\quad D_4=\frac{1}{2}\int_0^1\frac{1}{B_{v_1,v_2}^{2q}}(e^{s\lambda}-1)d\lambda.$$

Corollary 3. *Assume that* $\rho=\sigma$ *in inequality (19); then*

$$\begin{aligned}
&\left|\rho\frac{Q(v_1)+Q(v_2)}{2}+(1-\rho)Q\left(\frac{2v_1v_2}{v_1+v_2}\right)-\frac{v_1v_2}{v_2-v_1}\int_{v_1}^{v_2}\frac{Q(x)}{x^2}dx\right| \\
&\leq v_1v_2(v_2-v_1)\varphi^{\frac{1}{p}} \\
&\times\left[\left(\mathfrak{T}_1|Q'(v_1)|^q+\mathfrak{T}_2|Q'(v_2)|^q\right)^{\frac{1}{q}}+\left(\mathfrak{T}_3|Q'(v_1)|^q+\mathfrak{T}_4|Q'(v_2)|^q\right)^{\frac{1}{q}}\right],
\end{aligned}$$

where $\varphi_1=\varphi_2=\varphi$.

Corollary 4. *Assume that $\rho = \sigma = 0$ in inequality (19); then*

$$\left|Q\left(\frac{2v_1v_2}{v_1+v_2}\right) - \frac{2v_1v_2}{v_2-v_1}\int_{v_1}^{v_2}\frac{Q(x)}{x^2}dx\right| \leq \frac{v_1v_2(v_2-v_1)}{\sqrt[p]{p+1}}$$
$$\times\left[\left(\mathfrak{T}_1|Q'(v_1)|^q + \mathfrak{T}_2|Q'(v_2)|^q\right)^{\frac{1}{q}} + \left(\mathfrak{T}_3|Q'(v_1)|^q + \mathfrak{T}_4|Q'(v_2)|^q\right)^{\frac{1}{q}}\right].$$

Corollary 5. *Assume that $\rho = \sigma = \frac{1}{2}$ in inequality (19); then*

$$\left|\frac{Q(v_1)+Q(v_2)}{2} + Q\left(\frac{2v_1v_2}{v_1+v_2}\right) - \frac{2v_1v_2}{v_2-v_1}\int_{v_1}^{v_2}\frac{Q(x)}{x^2}dx\right|$$
$$\leq v_1v_2(v_2-v_1)\sqrt[p]{\frac{4}{p+1}}$$
$$\times\left[\left(\mathfrak{T}_1|Q'(v_1)|^q + \mathfrak{T}_2|Q'(v_2)|^q\right)^{\frac{1}{q}} + \left(\mathfrak{T}_3|Q'(v_1)|^q + \mathfrak{T}_4|Q'(v_2)|^q\right)^{\frac{1}{q}}\right].$$

Corollary 6. *Assume that $\rho = \sigma = \frac{1}{3}$ in inequality (19); then*

$$\left|\frac{Q(v_1)+Q(v_2)}{2} + 2\psi\left(\frac{2v_1v_2}{v_1+v_2}\right) - \frac{3v_1v_2}{v_2-v_1}\int_{v_1}^{v_2}\frac{Q(x)}{x^2}dx\right|$$
$$\leq 3v_1v_2(v_2-v_1)\sqrt[p]{4\left(\frac{\left(\frac{2}{3}\right)^{p+1} + \left(\frac{1}{3}\right)^{p+1}}{p+1}\right)}$$
$$\times\left[\left(\mathfrak{T}_1|Q'(v_1)|^q + \mathfrak{T}_2|Q'(v_2)|^q\right)^{\frac{1}{q}} + \left(\mathfrak{T}_3|Q'(v_1)|^q + \mathfrak{T}_4|Q'(v_2)|^q\right)^{\frac{1}{q}}\right].$$

Corollary 7. *Assume that $\rho = \sigma = 1$ in inequality (19); then*

$$\left|\frac{Q(v_1)+Q(v_2)}{2} - \frac{v_1v_2}{v_2-v_1}\int_{v_1}^{v_2}\frac{Q(x)}{x^2}dx\right| \leq \frac{v_1v_2(v_2-v_1)}{\sqrt[p]{p+1}}$$
$$\times\left[\left(\mathfrak{T}_1|Q'(v_1)|^q + \mathfrak{T}_2|Q'(v_2)|^q\right)^{\frac{1}{q}} + \left(\mathfrak{T}_3|Q'(v_1)|^q + \mathfrak{T}_4|Q'(v_2)|^q\right)^{\frac{1}{q}}\right].$$

Theorem 10. *Assume that $\rho, \sigma \in [0,1]$ and $Q : [v_1, v_2] \subseteq (0, +\infty) \to \mathbb{R}$ is a differentiable mapping such that $Q' \in L[v_1, v_2]$. Suppose $|Q'|^q$ is modified harmonic exp s-convex; then for $p, q > 1$ with $\frac{1}{p} + \frac{1}{q} = 1$, we have*

$$\left|\frac{\rho Q(v_1)+\sigma Q(v_2)}{2} + \frac{2-\rho-\sigma}{2}Q\left(\frac{2v_1v_2}{v_1+v_2}\right) - \frac{v_1v_2}{v_2-v_1}\int_{v_1}^{v_2}\frac{Q(x)}{x^2}dx\right|$$
$$\leq \frac{v_1v_2(v_2-v_1)}{4} \tag{20}$$
$$\times\left[\frac{4}{(v_1+v_2)^2}\left({}_2F_1\left(2p,1;2;\frac{v_1-v_2}{v_1+v_2}\right)\right)^{\frac{1}{p}}\left(C_5|Q'(v_1)|^q + C_6|Q'(v_2)|^q\right)^{\frac{1}{q}}\right.$$
$$\left.+\frac{1}{v_1^2}\left({}_2F_1\left(2p,1;2;\frac{v_1-v_2}{2v_1}\right)\right)^{\frac{1}{p}}\left(C_7|Q'(v_1)|^q + C_8|Q'(v_2)|^q\right)^{\frac{1}{q}}\right],$$

where

$$C_5 = \frac{1}{2m}\sum_{\eta=1}^{m}\int_0^1 |1-\rho-\sigma|^q\left(e^{s(1-\lambda)}-1\right)^{\eta}d\lambda,$$

$$C_6 = \frac{1}{2m} \sum_{\eta=1}^{m} \int_0^1 |1-\rho-\sigma|^q (e^{s(1+\lambda)}-1)^\eta d\lambda,$$

$$C_7 = \frac{1}{2m} \sum_{\eta=1}^{m} \int_0^1 |\sigma-\lambda|^q (e^{s(2-\lambda)}-1)^\eta d\lambda,$$

$$C_8 = \frac{1}{2m} \sum_{\eta=1}^{m} \int_0^1 |\sigma-\lambda|^q (e^{s\lambda}-1)^\eta d\lambda.$$

Proof. According to the Lemma 3, we have

$$\begin{aligned}
&\left|\frac{\rho Q(v_1)+\sigma Q(v_2)}{2} + \frac{2-\rho-\sigma}{2} Q\left(\frac{2v_1v_2}{v_1+v_2}\right) - \frac{v_1v_2}{v_2-v_1}\int_{v_1}^{v_2}\frac{Q(x)}{x^2}dx\right| \\
&\leq \frac{v_1v_2(v_2-v_1)}{4}\left[\int_0^1 \left|\frac{4(1-\rho-\lambda)}{((1-\lambda)v_2+(1+\lambda)v_1)^2}\right|\left|Q'\left(\frac{2v_1v_2}{(1-\lambda)v_2+(1+\lambda)v_1}\right)\right| d\lambda \right.\\
&\left. + \int_0^1 \left|\frac{4(\sigma-\lambda)}{(\lambda v_1+(2-\lambda)v_2)^2}\right|\left|Q'\left(\frac{2v_1v_2}{\lambda v_1+(2-\lambda)v_2}\right)\right| d\lambda\right].
\end{aligned}$$

Employing the property of Hölder's inequality and modified harmonic exp s-convex function, we have

$$\begin{aligned}
&\left|\frac{\rho Q(v_1)+\sigma Q(v_2)}{2} + \frac{2-\rho-\sigma}{2} Q\left(\frac{2v_1v_2}{v_1+v_2}\right) - \frac{v_1v_2}{v_2-v_1}\int_{v_1}^{v_2}\frac{Q(x)}{x^2}dx\right| \\
&\leq \frac{v_1v_2(v_2-v_1)}{4}\left\{4\left(\int_0^1 \frac{1}{A^{2p}_{v_1,v_2}} d\lambda\right)^{\frac{1}{p}}\right. \\
&\times\left[\int_0^1 |1-\rho-\sigma|^q\left(\tfrac{1}{2m}\textstyle\sum_{\eta=1}^{m}\left(e^{s(1-\lambda)}-1\right)^\eta |Q'(v_1)|^q + \tfrac{1}{2m}\sum_{\eta=1}^{m}\left(e^{s(1+\lambda)}-1\right)^\eta |Q'(v_2)|^q\right)d\lambda\right]^{\frac{1}{q}} \\
&+4\left(\int_0^1 \frac{1}{B^{2p}_{v_1,v_2}} d\lambda\right)^{\frac{1}{p}} \\
&\times\left.\left[\int_0^1 |\sigma-\lambda|^q\left(\frac{1}{2m}\sum_{\eta=1}^{m}\left(e^{s(2-\lambda)}-1\right)^\eta |Q'(v_1)|^q + \frac{1}{2m}\sum_{\eta=1}^{m}\left(e^{s\lambda}-1\right)^\eta |Q'(v_2)|^q\right)d\lambda\right]^{\frac{1}{q}}\right\} \\
&= \frac{v_1v_2(v_2-v_1)}{4} \\
&\times\left[\frac{4}{(v_1+v_2)^2}\left({}_2F_1\left(2p,1;2;\frac{v_1-v_2}{v_1+v_2}\right)\right)^{\frac{1}{p}}\left(C_5|Q'(v_1)|^q + C_6|Q'(v_2)|^q\right)^{\frac{1}{q}}\right. \\
&\left.+\frac{1}{v_1^2}\left({}_2F_1\left(2p,1;2;\frac{v_1-v_2}{2v_1}\right)\right)^{\frac{1}{p}}\left(C_7|Q'(v_1)|^q + C_8|Q'(v_2)|^q\right)^{\frac{1}{q}}\right].
\end{aligned}$$

This completes the proof. □

Corollary 8. *Assume that* $\mathrm{m} = 1$ *in inequality (20); then*

$$\left|\frac{\rho Q(v_1) + \sigma Q(v_2)}{2} + \frac{2-\rho-\sigma}{2} Q\left(\frac{2v_1v_2}{v_1+v_2}\right) - \frac{v_1v_2}{v_2-v_1}\int_{v_1}^{v_2}\frac{Q(x)}{x^2}dx\right|$$
$$\leq \frac{v_1v_2(v_2-v_1)}{4}$$
$$\times\left[\frac{4}{(v_1+v_2)^2}\left({}_2F_1\left(2p,1;2;\frac{v_1-v_2}{v_1+v_2}\right)\right)^{\frac{1}{p}}\left(D_5|Q'(v_1)|^q + D_6|Q'(v_2)|^q\right)^{\frac{1}{q}}\right.$$
$$\left.+\frac{1}{v_1^2}\left({}_2F_1\left(2p,1;2;\frac{v_1-v_2}{2v_1}\right)\right)^{\frac{1}{p}}\left(D_7|Q'(v_1)|^q + D_8|Q'(v_2)|^q\right)^{\frac{1}{q}}\right],$$

where

$$D_5 = \frac{1}{2}\int_0^1 |1-\rho-\sigma|^q(e^{s(1-\lambda)}-1)d\lambda,$$
$$D_6 = \frac{1}{2}\int_0^1 |1-\rho-\sigma|^q(e^{s(1+\lambda)}-1)d\lambda,$$
$$D_7 = \frac{1}{2}\int_0^1 |\sigma-\lambda|^q(e^{s(2-\lambda)}-1)d\lambda, \quad D_8 = \frac{1}{2}\int_0^1 |\sigma-\lambda|^q(e^{s\lambda}-1)d\lambda.$$

Corollary 9. *Assume that* $\rho = \sigma$ *in inequality (20); then*

$$\left|\rho\frac{Q(v_1) + Q(v_2)}{2} + (1-\rho) Q\left(\frac{2v_1v_2}{v_1+v_2}\right) - \frac{v_1v_2}{v_2-v_1}\int_{v_1}^{v_2}\frac{Q(x)}{x^2}dx\right|$$
$$\leq \frac{v_1v_2(v_2-v_1)}{4}$$
$$\times\left[\frac{4}{(v_1+v_2)^2}\left({}_2F_1\left(2p,1;2;\frac{v_1-v_2}{v_1+v_2}\right)\right)^{\frac{1}{p}}\left(E_1|Q'(v_1)|^q + E_2|Q'(v_2)|^q\right)^{\frac{1}{q}}\right.$$
$$\left.+\frac{1}{v_1^2}\left({}_2F_1\left(2p,1;2;\frac{v_1-v_2}{2v_1}\right)\right)^{\frac{1}{p}}\left(E_3|Q'(v_1)|^q + E_4|Q'(v_2)|^q\right)^{\frac{1}{q}}\right],$$

where

$$E_1 = \frac{1}{2\mathrm{m}}\sum_{\eta=1}^{\mathrm{m}}\int_0^1 |1-2\rho|^q(e^{s(1-\lambda)}-1)^\eta d\lambda,$$
$$E_2 = \frac{1}{2\mathrm{m}}\sum_{\eta=1}^{\mathrm{m}}\int_0^1 |1-2\rho|^q(e^{s(1+\lambda)}-1)^\eta d\lambda,$$
$$E_3 = \frac{1}{2\mathrm{m}}\sum_{\eta=1}^{\mathrm{m}}\int_0^1 |\rho-\lambda|^q(e^{s(2-\lambda)}-1)^\eta d\lambda,$$
$$E_4 = \frac{1}{2\mathrm{m}}\sum_{\eta=1}^{\mathrm{m}}\int_0^1 |\rho-\lambda|^q(e^{s\lambda}-1)^\eta d\lambda.$$

Corollary 10. *Assume that* $\rho = \sigma = 0$ *in inequality (20); then*

$$\left|Q\left(\frac{2v_1v_2}{v_1+v_2}\right) - \frac{v_1v_2}{v_2-v_1}\int_{v_1}^{v_2}\frac{Q(x)}{x^2}dx\right| \leq \frac{v_1v_2(v_2-v_1)}{4}$$
$$\times\left[\frac{4}{(v_1+v_2)^2}\left({}_2F_1\left(2p,1;2;\frac{v_1-v_2}{v_1+v_2}\right)\right)^{\frac{1}{p}}\left(E_5|Q'(v_1)|^q + E_6|Q'(v_2)|^q\right)^{\frac{1}{q}}\right.$$
$$\left.+\frac{1}{v_1^2}\left({}_2F_1\left(2p,1;2;\frac{v_1-v_2}{2v_1}\right)\right)^{\frac{1}{p}}\left(E_7|Q'(v_1)|^q + E_8|Q'(v_2)|^q\right)^{\frac{1}{q}}\right],$$

where

$$E_5 = \frac{1}{2\mathrm{m}} \sum_{\eta=1}^{\mathrm{m}} \int_0^1 (e^{s(1-\lambda)} - 1)^\eta d\lambda,$$

$$E_6 = \frac{1}{2\mathrm{m}} \sum_{\eta=1}^{\mathrm{m}} \int_0^1 (e^{s(1+\lambda)} - 1)^\eta d\lambda,$$

$$E_7 = \frac{1}{2\mathrm{m}} \sum_{\eta=1}^{\mathrm{m}} \int_0^1 \lambda^q (e^{s(2-\lambda)} - 1)^\eta d\lambda,$$

$$E_8 = \frac{1}{2n} \sum_{\eta=1}^{\mathrm{m}} \int_0^1 \lambda^q (e^{s\lambda} - 1)^\eta d\lambda.$$

Corollary 11. *Assume that $\rho = \sigma = \frac{1}{2}$ in inequality (20); then*

$$\left|\frac{\mathrm{Q}(\mathrm{v}_1) + \mathrm{Q}(\mathrm{v}_2)}{2} + \mathrm{Q}\left(\frac{2\mathrm{v}_1\mathrm{v}_2}{\mathrm{v}_1 + \mathrm{v}_2}\right) - \frac{2\mathrm{v}_1\mathrm{v}_2}{\mathrm{v}_2 - \mathrm{v}_1} \int_{\mathrm{v}_1}^{\mathrm{v}_2} \frac{\mathrm{Q}(x)}{x^2} dx\right| \leq \frac{\mathrm{v}_1\mathrm{v}_2(\mathrm{v}_2 - \mathrm{v}_1)}{2}$$
$$\times \left[\frac{1}{\mathrm{v}_1^2}\left({}_2F_1\left(2p, 1; 2; \frac{\mathrm{v}_1 - \mathrm{v}_2}{2\mathrm{v}_1}\right)\right)^{\frac{1}{p}} (E_9|\mathrm{Q}'(\mathrm{v}_1)|^q + E_{10}|\mathrm{Q}'(\mathrm{v}_2)|^q)^{\frac{1}{q}}\right],$$

where

$$E_9 = \frac{1}{2^{q+1}\mathrm{m}} \sum_{\eta=1}^{\mathrm{m}} \int_0^1 |1 - 2\lambda|^q (e^{s(2-\lambda)} - 1)^\eta d\lambda,$$

$$E_{10} = \frac{1}{2^{q+1}\mathrm{m}} \sum_{\eta=1}^{\mathrm{m}} \int_0^1 |1 - 2\lambda|^q (e^{s\lambda} - 1)^\eta d\lambda.$$

Corollary 12. *Assume that $\rho = \sigma = \frac{1}{3}$ in inequality (20); then*

$$\left|\frac{\mathrm{Q}(\mathrm{v}_1) + \mathrm{Q}(\mathrm{v}_2)}{2} + 2\mathrm{Q}\left(\frac{2\mathrm{v}_1\mathrm{v}_2}{\mathrm{v}_1 + \mathrm{v}_2}\right) - \frac{3\mathrm{v}_1\mathrm{v}_2}{\mathrm{v}_2 - \mathrm{v}_1} \int_{\mathrm{v}_1}^{\mathrm{v}_2} \frac{\mathrm{Q}(x)}{x^2} dx\right| \leq \frac{3\mathrm{v}_1\mathrm{v}_2(\mathrm{v}_2 - \mathrm{v}_1)}{4}$$
$$\times \left[\frac{4}{(\mathrm{v}_1 + \mathrm{v}_2)^2}\left({}_2F_1\left(2p, 1; 2; \frac{\mathrm{v}_1 - \mathrm{v}_2}{\mathrm{v}_1 + \mathrm{v}_2}\right)\right)^{\frac{1}{p}} (G_1|\mathrm{Q}'(\mathrm{v}_1)|^q + G_2|\mathrm{Q}'(\mathrm{v}_2)|^q)^{\frac{1}{q}}\right.$$
$$\left. + \frac{1}{\mathrm{v}_1^2}\left({}_2F_1\left(2p, 1; 2; \frac{\mathrm{v}_1 - \mathrm{v}_2}{2\mathrm{v}_1}\right)\right)^{\frac{1}{p}} (G_3|\mathrm{Q}'(\mathrm{v}_1)|^q + G_4|\mathrm{Q}'(\mathrm{v}_2)|^q)^{\frac{1}{q}}\right],$$

where

$$G_1 = \frac{1}{3^q 2\mathrm{m}} \sum_{\eta=1}^{\mathrm{m}} \int_0^1 (e^{s(1-\lambda)} - 1)^\eta d\lambda,$$

$$G_2 = \frac{1}{3^q 2\mathrm{m}} \sum_{\eta=1}^{\mathrm{m}} \int_0^1 (e^{s(1+\lambda)} - 1)^\eta d\lambda,$$

$$G_3 = \frac{1}{3^q 2\mathrm{m}} \sum_{\eta=1}^{\mathrm{m}} \int_0^1 |1 - 3\lambda|^q (e^{s(2-\lambda)} - 1)^\eta d\lambda,$$

$$G_4 = \frac{1}{3^q 2\mathrm{m}} \sum_{\eta=1}^{\mathrm{m}} \int_0^1 |1 - 3\lambda|^q (e^{s\lambda} - 1)^\eta d\lambda.$$

Corollary 13. *Assume that* $\rho = \sigma = 1$ *in inequality (20); then*

$$\left|\frac{Q(v_1)+Q(v_2)}{2} - \frac{v_1 v_2}{v_2 - v_1}\int_{v_1}^{v_2}\frac{Q(x)}{x^2}dx\right| \leq \frac{v_1 v_2 (v_2 - v_1)}{4}$$

$$\times\left[\frac{4}{(v_1+v_2)^2}\left({}_2F_1\left(2p,1;2;\frac{v_1-v_2}{v_1+v_2}\right)\right)^{\frac{1}{p}}\left(G_5|Q'(v_1)|^q + G_6|Q'(v_2)|^q\right)^{\frac{1}{q}}\right.$$

$$\left.+\frac{1}{v_1^2}\left({}_2F_1\left(2p,1;2;\frac{v_1-v_2}{2v_1}\right)\right)^{\frac{1}{p}}\left(G_7|Q'(v_1)|^q + G_8|Q'(v_2)|^q\right)^{\frac{1}{q}}\right],$$

where

$$G_5 = \frac{1}{2m}\sum_{\eta=1}^{m}\int_0^1 (e^{s(1-\lambda)} - 1)^{\eta} d\lambda,$$

$$G_6 = \frac{1}{2m}\sum_{\eta=1}^{m}\int_0^1 (e^{s(1+\lambda)} - 1)^{\eta} d\lambda,$$

$$G_7 = \frac{1}{2m}\sum_{\eta=1}^{m}\int_0^1 |1-\lambda|^q (e^{s(2-\lambda)} - 1)^{\eta} d\lambda,$$

$$G_8 = \frac{1}{2m}\sum_{\eta=1}^{m}\int_0^1 |1-\lambda|^q (e^{s\lambda} - 1)^{\eta} d\lambda.$$

6. Conclusions

The study of integral inequalities in association with convex analysis presents an intriguing and stimulating area of study in the domain of mathematical interpretation. Due to their pivotal role and beneficial importance in many disciplines of science, the subject of inequalities has been described as an attractive field for mathematicians. Many mathematicians try to use and employ new ideas in order to advance the theory of inequalities. A great framework for starting and creating numerical tools for solving and researching challenging mathematical problems is provided by the word inequalities. This work has shown a new variant of Hadamard inequalities involving a new family of convex functions, namely the modified harmonic exp s-convex function. A new class of these functions has been investigated by introducing some algebraic properties. The new family of modified harmonic exp s-convex functions is an extended and generalized class of functions, including convex and harmonically convex functions, which have been proved. Furthermore, the new type of Hadamard-type inequality and its estimations have been achieved. Many researchers add efforts to the term inequality hypotheses to reveal a new dimension of applied analysis because working on this hypothesis has its own importance and wide scope. It is a fascinating and engrossing field of research for researchers. Now is the time to explore the significance of convex analysis and inequalities along with innovative numerical techniques.

Author Contributions: Conceptualization, A.A.S., E.H., S.K.N., J.T. and M.T.; methodology, A.A.S., E.H., S.K.N., J.T. and M.T.; validation, A.A.S., E.H., S.K.N., J.T. and M.T.; formal analysis, A.A.S., E.H., S.K.N., J.T. and M.T.; writing—original draft preparation, A.A.S., E.H., S.K.N., J.T. and M.T. All authors have read and agreed to the published version of the manuscript.

Funding: This research was funded by National Science, Research and Innovation Fund (NSRF) and King Mongkut's University of Technology North Bangkok with Contract no. KMUTNB-FF-66-11.

Institutional Review Board Statement: Not applicable.

Informed Consent Statement: Not applicable.

Data Availability Statement: Not applicable.

Conflicts of Interest: The authors declare no conflicts of interest.

References

1. Niculescu, C.P.; Persson, L.E. *Convex Functions and Their Applications*; Springer: New York, NY, USA, 2006.
2. Özdemir, M.E.; Yildiz, C.; Akdemir, A.O.; Set, E. On some inequalities for s–convex functions and applications. *J. Inequal. Appl.* **2013**, *333*, 2–11. [CrossRef]
3. Butt, S.I.; Rashid, S.; Tariq, M.; Wang, X.H. Novel refinements via n-polynomial harmonically s-type convex functions and Applications in special functions. *J. Funct. Spaces* **2021**, *2021*, 6615948. [CrossRef]
4. Ali, S.; Mubeen, S.; Ali, R.S.; Rahman, G.; Morsy, A.; Nisar, K.S.; Purohit, S.D.; Zakarya, M. Dynamical significance of generalized fractional integral inequalities via convexity. *AIMS Math.* **2021**, *6*, 9705–9730. [CrossRef]
5. Xi, B.Y.; Qi, F. Some integral inequalities of Hermite–Hadamard type for convex functions with applications to means. *J. Funct. Spaces***2012**, *2012*, 980438. [CrossRef]
6. Zhang, X.M.; Chu, Y.M.; Zhang, X.Y. The Hermite–Hadamard type inequality of GA–convex functions and its applications. *J. Inequal. Appl.* **2010**, *2010*, 507560. [CrossRef]
7. Tariq, M. New Hermite–Hadamard type inequalities via p–harmonic exponential type convexity and applications. *Univ. J. Math. Appl.* **2021**, *4*, 59–69.
8. Sahoo, S.K.; Tariq, M.; Ahmad, H.; Nasir, J.; Aydi, H.; Mukheimer, A. New Ostrowski-type fractional integral inequalities via generalized exponential-type convex functions and applications. *Symmetry* **2021**, *13*, 1429. [CrossRef]
9. Butt, S.I.; Pecaric, J.; Rehman, A.U. Exponential convexity of Petrovic and related functional. *J. Inequal. Appl.* **2011**, *89*, 2011. [CrossRef]
10. Zhou, S.S.; Rashid, S.; Noor, M.A.; Noor, K.I.; Safdar, F.; Chu, Y.M. New Hermite-Hadamard type inequalities for exponentially convex functions and applications. *AIMS Math.* **2020**, *5*, 6874–6901. [CrossRef]
11. Omotoyinbo, O.; Mogbodemu, A. Some new Hermite–Hadamard integral inequalities for convex functions. *Int. J. Sci. Innov. Tech.* **2014**, *1*, 1–12.
12. Tariq, M.; Nasir, J.; Sahoo, S.K.; Mallah, A.A. A note on some Ostrowski-type inequalities via generalized exponentially convex function. *J. Math. Anal. Model.* **2021**, *2*, 2021. [CrossRef]
13. Butt, S.I.; Tariq, M.; Aslam, A.; Ahmad, H.; Nofel, T.A. Hermite–Hadamard type inequalities via generalized harmonic exponential convexity. *J. Funct. Spaces* **2021**, *2021*, 5533491. [CrossRef]
14. Rafiq, A.; Mir, N.A.; Ahmad, F. Weighted Chebysev–Ostrowski type inequalities. *Appl. Math. Mech.* **2007**, *28*, 901–906. [CrossRef]
15. Khan, M.A.; Chu, Y.M.; Khan, T.U. Some new inequalities of Hermite–Hadamard type for s–convex functions with applications. *Open Math.* **2017**, *15*, 1414–1430. [CrossRef]
16. Nasir, J.; Qaisar, S.; Butt, S.I.; Aydi, H.; Sen, M.D.L. Hermite-Hadamard like inequalities for fractional integral operator via convexity and quasi-convexity with their applications. *AIMS Math.* **2022**, *7*, 3418–3439. [CrossRef]
17. Aljaaidia, T.A.; Pachpatte, D. New generalization of reverse Minkowski's inequality for fractional integral. *Adv. Theory. Nonlinear Anal. Appl.* **2021**, *1*, 72–81.
18. Aljaaidia, T.A.; Pachpatte, D. Reverse Hermite-Hadamard's inequalities using Q-fractional integral. *Eng. Appl. Sci. Lett.* **2020**, *3*, 75–84. [CrossRef]
19. Aljaaidi, T.A.; Pachpatte, D.B.; Shatanawi, W.; Abdo, M.S.; Abodayeh, K. Generalized proportional fractional integral functional bounds in Minkowski's inequalities. *Adv. Differ. Equ.* **2021**, *2021*, 419.
20. Toplu, T.; Kadakal, M.; İşcan, İ. On n–polynomial convexity and some related inequalities. *AIMS Math.* **2020**, *5*, 1304–1318. [CrossRef]
21. Shi, H.N.; Zhang, J. Some new judgement theorems of Schur geometric and schur harmonic convexities for a class of symmetric function. *J. Inequal. Appl.* **2013**, *2013*, 527. [CrossRef]
22. Anderson, G.D.; Vamanamurthy, M.K.; Vuorinen, M. Generalized convexity and inequalities. *J. Math. Anal. Appl.* **2007**, *335*, 1294–1308. [CrossRef]
23. Awan, M.U.; Akhtar, N.; Iftikhar, S.; Noor, M.A.; Chu, Y.-M. New Hermite–Hadamard type inequalities for n–polynomial harmonically convex functions. *J. Inequal. Appl.* **2020**, *2020*, 125. [CrossRef]
24. Noor, M.A.; Noor, K.I. Harmonic variational inequalities. *Appl. Math. Inf. Sci.* **2016**, *10*, 1811–1814. [CrossRef]
25. Noor, M.A.; Noor, K.I. Some implicit methods for solving harmonic variational inequalities. *Inter. J. Anal. Appl.* **2016**, *12*, 10–14.
26. Dragomir, S.S.; Gomm, I. Some Hermite–Hadamard's inequality functions whose exponentials are convex. *Babes Bolyai Math.* **2015**, *60*, 527–534.
27. Awan, U.; Akhtar, N.; Iftikhar, S.; Noor, M.A.; Chu, Y.M. Hermite–Hadamard type inequalities for exponentially convex functions. *Appl. Math. Inf. Sci.* **2018**, *12*, 405–409. [CrossRef]
28. Kadakal, M.; İşcan, İ. Exponential type convexity and some related inequalities. *J. Inequal. Appl.* **2020**, *2020*, 82. [CrossRef]
29. Alomari, M.; Darus, M.; Kirmaci, U.S. Refinements of Hadamard-type inequalities for quasi-convex functions with applications to trapezoidal formula and to special means. *Comput. Math. Appl.* **2010**, *59*, 225–232. [CrossRef]
30. Chen, F.X.; Wu, S.H. Several complementary inequalities to inequalities of Hermite–Hadamard type for s–convex functions. *J. Nonlinear Sci. Appl.* **2016**, *9*, 705–716. [CrossRef]
31. Samraiz, M.; Saeed, K.; Naheed, S.; Rahman, G.; Nonlaopon, K. On inequalities of Hermite-Hadamard type via n-polynomial exponential type s-convex functions. *AIMS Math.* **2022**, *7*, 14282–14298. [CrossRef]

32. Kashuri, A.; Liko, R. Some new Hermite–Hadamard type inequalities and their applications. *Stud. Sci. Math. Hung.* **2019**, *56*, 103–142. [CrossRef]
33. Set, E.; Ozdemir, M.E.; Sarikaya, M.Z. New inequalities of Ostrowski's type for s-convex functions in the second sense with applications. *Facta Univ. (Nis) Ser. Math.* **2012**, *27*, 67–82.
34. İşcan, İ. Hermite–Hadamard type inequalities for harmonically convex functions. *Hacet. J. Math. Stat.* **2014**, *43*, 935–942. [CrossRef]
35. Tariq, M.; Sahoo, S.K.; Nasir, J.; Aydi, H.; Alsamir, H. Some Ostrowski type inequalities via npolynomial exponentially s-convex functions and their applications. *AIMS Math.* **2021**, *6*, 13272–13290. [CrossRef]
36. Geo, W.; Kashuri, A.; Butt, S.I.; Tariq, M.; Aslam, A.; Nadeem, M. New inequalities via n-polynomial harmonically exponential type functions. *AIMS Math.* **2020**, *5*, 6856–6873. [CrossRef]
37. Mitrinovic, D.S.; Pećaric, J.E.; Fink, A.M. *Classical and New Inequalities in Analysis*; Kluwer Academic: Dordrecht, The Netherlands, 1993.
38. Baloch, I.A.; Sen, M.D.L.; İşcan, İ. Characterizations of classes of harmonic convex functions and applications. *Int. J. Anal. Appl.* **2019**, *17*, 722–733.
39. Abramowitz, M.; Stegun, I.A. *Handbook of Mathematical Functions with Formulas. Graphs, and Mathematical Tables*; Dover: New York, NY, USA, 1965.

axioms MDPI

Article

Gamma-Nabla Hardy–Hilbert-Type Inequalities on Time Scales

Barakah Almarri [1,*] and **Ahmed A. El-Deeb** [2,*]

1 Department of Mathematical Sciences, College of Sciences, Princess Nourah Bint Abdulrahman University, P.O. Box 84428, Riyadh 11671, Saudi Arabia
2 Department of Mathematics, Faculty of Science, Al-Azhar University, Nasr City, Cairo 11884, Egypt
* Correspondence: bjalmarri@pnu.edu.sa (B.A.); ahmedeldeeb@azhar.edu.eg (A.A.E.-D.)

Abstract: We investigated several novel conformable fractional gamma-nabla dynamic Hardy–Hilbert inequalities on time scales in this study. Several continuous inequalities and their corresponding discrete analogues in the literature are combined and expanded by these inequalities. Hölder's inequality on time scales and a few algebraic inequalities are used to demonstrate our findings.

Keywords: Hardy–Hilbert's inequality; dynamic inequality; time scales; conformable fractional nabla calculus

MSC: 26D10; 26D15; 26E70; 34A40

Citation: Almarri, B.; El-Deeb, A.A. Gamma-Nabla Hardy–Hilbert-Type Inequalities on Time Scales. *Axioms* **2023**, *12*, 449. https://doi.org/10.3390/axioms12050449

Academic Editor: Shengda Zeng

Received: 3 April 2023
Revised: 21 April 2023
Accepted: 26 April 2023
Published: 1 May 2023

1. Introduction

This is a statement of the well-known classical extension of Hilbert's double-series theorem [1]:

Theorem 1. *If $\nu, \varpi > 1$ are such that $\frac{1}{\nu} + \frac{1}{\varpi} \leqslant 1$ and $0 < \lambda = 2 - \frac{1}{\nu} - \frac{1}{\varpi} = \frac{1}{\nu'} + \frac{1}{\varpi'} \leqslant 1$, such that ν' and ϖ' present the exponents' conjugate; then,*

$$\sum_{\jmath=1}^{\infty}\sum_{\imath=1}^{\infty}\frac{\vartheta_\jmath \pi_\imath}{(\jmath+\imath)^\lambda} \leqslant K\left(\sum_{\jmath=1}^{\infty}\vartheta_\jmath^\nu\right)^{\frac{1}{\nu}}\left(\sum_{\imath=1}^{\infty}\pi_\imath^\varpi\right)^{\frac{1}{\varpi}}, \tag{1}$$

where $K = K(\nu, \varpi)$ depends on ν and ϖ only.

Readers may find the integral analogue of Theorem 1 in [1].

Theorem 2. *Let $\nu, \varpi, \nu', \varpi'$ and λ be as in Theorem 1. If $\vartheta \in L^\nu(0,\infty)$ and $\theta \in L^\varpi(0,\infty)$, then*

$$\int_0^\infty\int_0^\infty \frac{\vartheta(\imath)\theta(\varsigma)}{(\imath+\varsigma)^\lambda} d\imath d\varsigma \leqslant K\left(\int_0^\infty \vartheta^\nu(\imath)d\imath\right)^{\frac{1}{\nu}}\left(\int_0^\infty \theta^\varpi(\varsigma)d\varsigma\right)^{\frac{1}{\varpi}}, \tag{2}$$

where $K = K(\nu, \varpi)$ depends on ν and ϖ only.

In 2011, Zhao et al. [2] proposed a new inequality similar to Theorem 2.

Theorem 3. *Let $h_i \geqslant 1, \nu_i > 1$ be constants and $\frac{1}{\nu_i} + \frac{1}{\varpi_i} = 1$. Let the differentiable fun. $\vartheta_i(\Im_i)$ on $[0, \iota_i)$, where $\iota_i \in (0, \infty)$, and we use ϑ_i' as a differentiation of ϑ_i. Suppose $\vartheta_i(0) = 0$ for $(i = 1, \ldots, n)$. Then,*

$$\int_0^{\iota_1}\int_0^{\iota_2}\cdots\int_0^{\iota_n} \frac{\prod_{i=1}^n |\vartheta_i^{h_i}(\Im_i)|}{\left(\sum_{i=1}^n \frac{\Im_i}{\varpi_i}\right)^{\sum_{i=1}^n \frac{1}{\varpi_i}}} d\Im_n d\Im_{n-1}\ldots d\Im_1$$
$$\leqslant K\prod_{i=1}^n \left(\int_0^{\iota_i} (\iota_i - \Im_i)|\vartheta_i^{h_i-1}(\Im_i)\vartheta_i'(\Im_i)|^{\nu_i} d\Im_i\right)^{\frac{1}{\nu_i}},$$

where

$$K = \left(n - \sum_{i=1}^n \frac{1}{\nu_i}\right)^{\sum_{i=1}^n \frac{1}{\nu_i} - n} \prod_{i=1}^n h_i \iota_i^{\frac{1}{\varpi_i}}.$$

Moreover, in 2012, Zhoa and Chung [3] proved the following theorem.

Theorem 4. *Let $\nu_i > 1$, be constants and $\frac{1}{\nu_i} + \frac{1}{\varpi_i} = 1$. Let $\vartheta_i(\tau_{1i}, \ldots, \tau_{ni})$ be real-valued nth differentiable functions defined on $[0, \iota_{1i}) \times \cdots \times [0, \iota_{ni})$, where $0 \leqslant \iota_{ji} \leqslant \delta_{ji}$, $\delta_{ji} \in (0, \infty)$ and $i, j = 1, \ldots, n$. Suppose*

$$\vartheta_i(\iota_{1i}, \ldots, \iota_{ni}) = \int_0^{\iota_{1i}}\cdots\int_0^{\iota_{ni}} \frac{\partial^n}{\partial\tau_{1i}\ldots\partial\tau_{ni}} \vartheta_i(\tau_{1i}, \ldots, \tau_{ni}) d\tau_{ni}\ldots d\tau_{1i},$$

then

$$\int_0^{\delta_{11}}\cdots\int_0^{\delta_{n1}}\int_0^{\delta_{12}}\cdots\int_0^{\delta_{n2}}\cdots\int_0^{\delta_{1n}}\cdots\int_0^{\delta_{nn}} \tag{3}$$
$$\frac{\prod_{i=1}^n \left(\int_0^{\iota_{1i}}\cdots\int_0^{\iota_{ni}} \left|\frac{\partial^n}{\partial\tau_{1i}\ldots\partial\tau_{ni}}\vartheta_i(\tau_{1i}, \ldots, \tau_{ni})\right|^{\nu_i} d\tau_{ni}\ldots d\tau_{1i}\right)^{\frac{1}{\nu_i}}}{\left(\sum_{i=1}^n \frac{[\iota_{1i}\ldots\iota_{ni}]}{\varpi_i}\right)^{\sum_{i=1}^n \frac{1}{\varpi_i}}}$$
$$d\iota_{11}\ldots d\iota_{n1} d\iota_{12}\ldots d\iota_{n2}\ldots d\iota_{1n}\ldots d\iota_{nn}$$
$$\leqslant N\prod_{i=1}^n \left(\int_0^{\delta_{1i}}\cdots\int_0^{\delta_{ni}} \prod_{j=1}^n (\delta_{ji} - \iota_{ji})\left|\frac{\partial^n}{\partial\iota_{1i}\ldots\partial\iota_{ni}}\vartheta_i(\iota_{1i}, \ldots, \iota_{ni})\right|^{\nu_i} d\iota_{ni}\ldots d\iota_{1i}\right)^{\frac{1}{\nu_i}},$$

where

$$N = \left(n - \sum_{i=1}^n \frac{1}{\nu_i}\right)^{\sum_{i=1}^n \frac{1}{\nu_i} - n} \prod_{i=1}^n [\delta_{1i}\ldots\delta_{ni}]^{\frac{1}{\varpi_i}}.$$

Pachappte [4] proved the following one:

$$\sum_{m=1}^k \sum_{n=1}^r \frac{\Phi(a_m)\Psi(b_n)}{m+n} \leqslant M(k,r)\left(\sum_{m=1}^k (k-m+1)\left(p_m\Phi\left(\frac{\nabla a_m}{p_m}\right)\right)^2\right)^{\frac{1}{2}} \tag{4}$$
$$\times\left(\sum_{n=1}^r (r-n+1)\left(q_n\Psi\left(\frac{\nabla b_n}{q_n}\right)\right)^2\right)^{\frac{1}{2}},$$

where

$$M(k,r) = \frac{1}{2}\left(\sum_{m=1}^k \left(\frac{\Phi(P_m)}{p_m}\right)^2\right)^{\frac{1}{2}}\left(\sum_{n=1}^r \left(\frac{\Psi(Q_n)}{Q_n}\right)^2\right)^{\frac{1}{2}}$$

$$\int_0^{\vartheta}\int_0^{\varsigma}\frac{\Phi(F(s))\Psi(g(\Im))}{s+\Im}dsdt \leqslant L(\vartheta,\varsigma)\left(\int_0^{\vartheta}(\vartheta-s)\left(p(s)\Phi\left(\frac{F'(s)}{p(s)}\right)^2ds\right)^{\frac{1}{2}}\right)$$
$$\times\left(\int_0^{\varsigma}(\varsigma-\Im)\left(q(\Im)\Psi\left(\frac{g'(\Im)}{q(\Im)}\right)^2dt\right)^{\frac{1}{2}}\right) \quad (5)$$

where

$$L(\vartheta,\varsigma)=\frac{1}{2}\left(\int_0^{\vartheta}\left(\frac{\Phi(P(s))}{P(s)}\right)^2ds\right)^{\frac{1}{2}}\left(\int_0^{\varsigma}\left(\frac{\Psi(Q(\Im))}{Q(\Im)}\right)^2dt\right)^{\frac{1}{2}}.$$

Handley et al. [5] extended (4) and (5) as follows:

$$\sum_{m_1=1}^{k_1}\cdots\sum_{m_n=1}^{k_n}\frac{\prod_{\ell=1}^{n}\Phi_\ell(a_{\ell,m_\ell})}{\left(\sum_{\ell=1}^{n}\gamma'_\ell m_\ell\right)^{\gamma'}} \leqslant M(k_1,\ldots,k_n)\prod_{\ell=1}^{n}\left(\sum_{m_\ell=1}^{k_\ell}(k_\ell-m_\ell+1)\left(p_{\ell,m_\ell}\Phi_\ell\left(\frac{\nabla a_{\ell,m_\ell}}{p_{\ell,m_\ell}}\right)^{\frac{1}{\gamma_\ell}}\right)\right)^{\gamma_\ell} \quad (6)$$

where

$$M(k_1,\ldots,k_n)=\frac{1}{(\gamma')^{\gamma'}}\prod_{\ell=1}^{n}\left(\sum_{m_\ell=1}^{k_\ell}\left(\frac{\Phi_\ell(P_{\ell,m_\ell})}{P_{\ell,m_\ell}}\right)^{\frac{1}{\gamma'_\ell}}\right)^{\gamma'_\ell},$$

and

$$\int_0^{\vartheta_1}\cdots\int_0^{\vartheta_n}\frac{\prod_{\ell=1}^{n}\Phi_\ell(F(s_\ell))}{\left(\sum_{\ell=1}^{n}\gamma'_\ell s_\ell\right)^{\gamma'}}ds_1\ldots ds_n$$
$$\leqslant L(\vartheta_1,\ldots,\vartheta_n)\prod_{\ell=1}^{n}\left(\int_0^{\vartheta_\ell}(\vartheta_\ell-s_\ell)\left(p_\ell(s_\ell)\Phi_\ell\left(\frac{F'(s_\ell)}{p(s_\ell)}\right)^{\frac{1}{\gamma_\ell}}ds_\ell\right)^{\gamma_\ell}\right), \quad (7)$$

where

$$L(\vartheta_1,\ldots,\vartheta_n)=\frac{1}{(\gamma')^{\gamma'}}\prod_{\ell=1}^{n}\left(\int_0^{\vartheta_\ell}\left(\frac{\Phi_\ell(P_\ell(s_\ell))}{P_\ell(s_\ell)}\right)^{\frac{1}{\gamma'_\ell}}ds_\ell\right)^{\gamma'_\ell}.$$

In 2006, Zhao and Cheung [6] proved the following reverse inequality.

$$\int_0^{\vartheta_1}\int_0^{\varsigma_1}\cdots\int_0^{\vartheta_n}\int_0^{\varsigma_n}\prod_{\ell=1}^{n}\frac{\Phi_\ell(F_\ell(s_\ell,\Im_\ell))}{\left(\frac{1}{\gamma'}\sum_{\ell=1}^{n}\gamma'_\ell(s_\ell\Im_\ell)\right)^{\gamma'}}ds_1d\Im_1\ldots ds_nd\Im_n \quad (8)$$
$$\geqslant G(\vartheta_1\varsigma_1,\ldots,\vartheta_n y_n)$$
$$\times\prod_{\ell=1}^{n}\left(\int_0^{\vartheta_\ell}\int_0^{\varsigma_\ell}(\vartheta_\ell-s_\ell)(\varsigma_\ell-\Im_\ell)\left(p_\ell(s_\ell)q_\ell(\Im_\ell)\Phi_\ell\left(\frac{D_2D_1F_\ell(s_\ell,\Im_\ell)}{p_\ell(s_\ell)q_\ell(\Im_\ell)}\right)\right)^{\frac{1}{\gamma_\ell}}ds_\ell d\Im_\ell\right)^{\gamma_\ell}$$

where

$$G(\vartheta_1\varsigma_1,\ldots,\vartheta_n y_n)=\prod_{\ell=1}^{n}\left(\int_0^{\vartheta_\ell}\int_0^{\varsigma_\ell}\left(\frac{\Phi_\ell(P_\ell(s_\ell,\Im_\ell))}{P_\ell(s_\ell,\Im_\ell)}\right)^{\frac{1}{\gamma'_\ell}}ds_\ell d\Im_\ell\right)^{\gamma'_\ell}.$$

and

$$P_\ell(s_\ell,\Im_\ell)=\int_0^{\Im_\ell}\int_0^{s_\ell}p_\ell(\xi_\ell)q_\ell(\tau_\ell)d\xi_\ell d\tau_\ell. \quad (9)$$

In [7], Pachpatte studied the Hilbert version inequalities.

$$\int_0^{\vartheta}\int_0^{\varsigma}\frac{F^h(s)G^l(\Im)}{s+\Im}dsd\Im \leqslant \frac{1}{2}hl(xy)^{\frac{1}{2}}\left(\int_0^{\vartheta}(\vartheta-s)\left(F^{h-1}(s)F(s)\right)^2ds\right)^{\frac{1}{2}} \times\left(\int_0^{\varsigma}(\varsigma-\Im)\left(G^{l-1}g(\Im)\right)^2d\Im\right)^{\frac{1}{2}}, \tag{10}$$

and

$$\int_0^{\vartheta}\int_0^{\varsigma}\frac{\Phi(F(s))\Psi(G(\Im))}{s+\Im}dsd\Im \leqslant L(\vartheta,\varsigma)\left(\int_0^{\vartheta}(\vartheta-s)\left(p(s)\Phi\left(\frac{F(s)}{p(s)}\right)\right)^2ds\right)^{\frac{1}{2}} \times\left(\int_0^{\varsigma}(\varsigma-\Im)\left(q(\Im)\Psi\left(\frac{g(\Im)}{q(\Im)}\right)\right)^2d\Im\right)^{\frac{1}{2}} \tag{11}$$

where

$$L(\vartheta,\varsigma)=\frac{1}{2}\left(\int_0^{\vartheta}\left(\frac{\Phi(P(s))}{P(s)}\right)^2ds\right)^{\frac{1}{2}}\left(\int_0^{\varsigma}\left(\frac{\Psi(Q(\Im))}{Q(\Im)}\right)^2d\Im\right)^{\frac{1}{2}},$$

and

$$\int_0^{\vartheta}\int_0^{\varsigma}\frac{P(s)Q(\Im)\Phi(F(s))\Psi(G(\Im))}{s+\Im}dsd\Im \leqslant \frac{1}{2}(xy)^{\frac{1}{2}}\left(\int_0^{\vartheta}(\vartheta-s)\left(p(s)\Phi\left(F(s)\right)\right)^2ds\right)^{\frac{1}{2}} \times\left(\int_0^{\varsigma}(\varsigma-\Im)\left(q(\Im)\Psi\left(g(\Im)\right)\right)^2d\Im\right)^{\frac{1}{2}}. \tag{12}$$

$$\int_0^{\vartheta_1}\int_0^{\varsigma_1}\cdots\int_0^{\vartheta_n}\int_0^{\varsigma_n}\frac{\prod_{\ell=1}^n\Phi_\ell(F_\ell(s_\ell,\Im_\ell))}{\left(\gamma\sum_{\ell=1}^n\frac{1}{\gamma_\ell}(s_\ell)(\Im_\ell)\right)^{\frac{1}{\gamma}}}ds_1d\Im_1\ldots ds_nd\Im_n \tag{13}$$
$$\geqslant L(\vartheta_1\varsigma_1,\ldots,\vartheta_ny_n) \times\prod_{\ell=1}^n\left(\int_0^{\vartheta_\ell}\int_0^{\varsigma_\ell}(\vartheta_\ell-s_\ell)(\varsigma_\ell-\Im_\ell)\left(p_\ell(s_\ell,\Im_\ell)\Phi_\ell\left(\frac{F_\ell(s_\ell,\Im_\ell)}{p_\ell(s_\ell,\Im_\ell)}\right)\right)^{\beta_\ell}ds_\ell d\Im_\ell\right)^{\frac{1}{\beta_\ell}}.$$

where

$$L(\vartheta_1\varsigma_1,\ldots,\vartheta_ny_n)=\prod_{\ell=1}^n\left(\int_0^{\vartheta_\ell}\int_0^{\varsigma_\ell}\left(\frac{\Phi_\ell(P_\ell(s_\ell,\Im_\ell))}{P_\ell(s_\ell,\Im_\ell)}\right)^{\gamma_\ell}ds_\ell d\Im_\ell\right)^{\frac{1}{\gamma_\ell}}.$$

In [8–10], Yang et al. established some important extensions of a Hardy–Hilbert-type inequality by using the weight coefficient method and techniques of real analysis.

All of the aforementioned findings hold true for both continuous and discrete domains. The purpose of the current research is to provide new, more general conclusions to the time-scale-based disparities previously established. Supreme outcomes, from which many other previous and current results may be taken, would be produced in this way. See the following publications for various dynamic inequalities, integrals of Hilbert's kind, and other categories of inequalities on time scales [11–23].

We hope that the reader has a sufficient background on the nabla conformable fractional on time scales. S. Hilger [24] introduced the time scale theory in 1988 as a way to combine continuous and discrete analysis. A time scale $\mathbb{T}$ is an arbitrary nonempty closed subset of the set of real numbers $\mathbb{R}$. In the manuscript, we use the notation $\nabla^{(\gamma,a)}$ for the nabla conformable fractional derivative on time scales instead of ∇_a^γ for simplification. For more details on nabla conformable fractionals, please see [25].

Definition 1 (Conformable nabla derivative). *Given a function $f : \mathbb{T} \longrightarrow \mathbb{R}$ and $a \in \mathbb{T}$, f is (γ, a)-nabla differentiable at $\xi > a$, if it is nabla differentiable at ξ, and its (γ, a)-nabla derivative is defined by*

$$\nabla_a^{\gamma} f(\xi) = \widehat{G}_{1-\gamma}(\xi, a) f^{\nabla}(\xi) \quad \xi > a, \tag{14}$$

Definition 2 (Conformable nabla integral). *Assume that $0 < \gamma \leqslant 1$, $a, \xi_1, \xi_2 \in \mathbb{T}$, $a \leqslant \xi_1 \leqslant \xi_2$ and $f \in C_{ld}(\mathbb{T})$, and the function f is called (γ, a)-nabla integrable on $[\xi_1, \xi_2]$ if*

$$\begin{aligned} \nabla_a^{-\gamma} f(\xi) &= \int_{\xi_1}^{\xi_2} f(\xi) \nabla_a^{\gamma} \xi \\ &= \int_{\xi_1}^{\xi_2} f(\xi) \widehat{G}_{\gamma-1}(\sigma^{\gamma-1}(\xi), a) \nabla \xi, \end{aligned} \tag{15}$$

exists and is finite.

Lemma 1 (Dynamic Hölder's Inequality [14]). *Let $u, v \in \mathbb{T}$ with $u < v$. If $\vartheta, \theta \in CC_{rd}^1([u, v]_{\mathbb{T}} \times [u, v]_{\mathbb{T}}, \mathbb{R})$ be integrable functions and $\frac{1}{\nu} + \frac{1}{\varpi} = 1$ with $\nu > 1$. Then,*

$$\begin{aligned} \int_u^v \int_u^v |\vartheta(r,\delta)\theta(r,\delta)| \nabla^{(\gamma,a)} r \nabla^{(\gamma,a)} \delta \; &\leq \; \left[\int_u^v \int_u^v |\vartheta(r,\delta)|^{\nu} \nabla^{(\gamma,a)} r \nabla^{(\gamma,a)} \delta \right]^{\frac{1}{\nu}} \\ &\times \left[\int_u^v \int_u^v |\theta(r,\delta)|^{\varpi} \nabla^{(\gamma,a)} r \nabla^{(\gamma,a)} \delta \right]^{\frac{1}{\varpi}}. \end{aligned} \tag{16}$$

This inequality is reversed if $0 < \nu < 1$ and if $\nu < 0$ or $\varpi < 0$.

In this study, we prove a few novel conformable fractional dynamic inequalities of the Hardy–Hilbert type on time scales, which are driven by Theorems 3 and 4 given above. We will also extract the discrete counterparts of the continuous Hilbert inequalities that are present in some special situations of our results. We are now prepared to state and support our key findings.

2. Main Results

Theorem 5. *Let $\mathbb{T}$ be a time scale with $\delta_0, \iota_i, \Im_i, \delta_i \in \mathbb{T}$, $(i = 1, \ldots, n)$. Let $h_i \geqslant 1$, $\nu_i, \varpi_i > 1$ be constants and $\frac{1}{\nu_i} + \frac{1}{\varpi_i} = 1$. Let $\nabla^{(\gamma,a)}$- differentiable functions $\vartheta_i(\Im_i)$ be decreasing on $[\delta_0, \iota_i)_{\mathbb{T}}$, where $\iota_i \in (0, \infty)$. Suppose $\vartheta_i(\delta_0) = 0$. Then,*

$$\begin{aligned} &\int_{\delta_0}^{\iota_1} \int_{\delta_0}^{\iota_2} \cdots \int_{\delta_0}^{\iota_n} \frac{\prod_{i=1}^n |\vartheta_i^{h_i}(\Im_i)|}{\left(\sum_{i=1}^n \frac{(\Im_i - \delta_0)}{\varpi_i} \right)^{\sum_{i=1}^n \frac{1}{\varpi_i}}} \nabla^{(\gamma,a)} \Im_n \nabla^{(\gamma,a)} \Im_{n-1} \ldots \nabla^{(\gamma,a)} \Im_1 \\ &\leqslant K \prod_{i=1}^n \left(\int_{\delta_0}^{\iota_i} (\rho(\iota_i) - \rho(\Im_i)) |\vartheta_i^{h_i - 1}(\Im_i) \vartheta_i^{\nabla^{(\gamma,a)}}(\Im_i)|^{\nu_i} \nabla^{(\gamma,a)} \Im_i \right)^{\frac{1}{\nu_i}}, \end{aligned} \tag{17}$$

where

$$K = K(\iota_1, \ldots, \iota_n) = \left(n - \sum_{i=1}^n \frac{1}{\nu_i} \right)^{\sum_{i=1}^n \frac{1}{\nu_i} - n} \prod_{i=1}^n h_i (\iota_i - \delta_0)^{\frac{1}{\varpi_i}}.$$

Proof. From Hölder inequality (16), one can see that

$$\begin{aligned} \prod_{i=1}^n |\vartheta_i^{h_i}(\Im_i)| \; &\leqslant \; \prod_{i=1}^n h_i \int_{\delta_0}^{\Im_i} |\vartheta_i^{h_i - 1}(\tau_i) \vartheta_i^{\nabla^{(\gamma,a)}}(\tau_i)| \nabla^{(\gamma,a)} \tau_i \\ &\leqslant \prod_{i=1}^n h_i (\Im_i - \delta_0)^{\frac{1}{\varpi_i}} \left(\int_{\delta_0}^{\Im_i} |\vartheta_i^{h_i - 1}(\tau_i) \vartheta_i^{\nabla^{(\gamma,a)}}(\tau_i)|^{\nu_i} \nabla^{(\gamma,a)} \tau_i \right)^{\frac{1}{\nu_i}}. \end{aligned} \tag{18}$$

Using the inequality for the means [26]

$$\left(\prod_{i=1}^{n}\lambda_i^{\frac{1}{\varpi_i}}\right)^{\frac{1}{\sum_{i=1}^{n}\frac{1}{\varpi_i}}} \leqslant \frac{1}{\sum_{i=1}^{n}\frac{1}{\varpi_i}}\sum_{i=1}^{n}\frac{\lambda_i}{\varpi_i}, \quad \lambda_i>0 \quad (i=1,\dots,n), \tag{19}$$

we have

$$\frac{\prod_{i=1}^{n}|\vartheta_i^{h_i}(\Im_i)|}{\left(\sum_{i=1}^{n}\frac{(\Im_i-\delta_0)}{\varpi_i}\right)^{\sum_{i=1}^{n}\frac{1}{\varpi_i}}} \leqslant \left(n-\sum_{i=1}^{n}\frac{1}{\nu_i}\right)^{\sum_{i=1}^{n}\frac{1}{\nu_i}-n}\prod_{i=1}^{n}h_i\left(\int_{\delta_0}^{\Im_i}|\vartheta_i^{h_i-1}(\tau_i)\vartheta_i^{\nabla^{(\gamma,a)}}(\tau_i)|^{\nu_i}\nabla^{(\gamma,a)}\tau_i\right)^{\frac{1}{\nu_i}}. \tag{20}$$

Using the integration of (20) on $\Im_i$ from δ_0 to ι_i $(i=1,\dots,n)$, employing the inequality of Hölder's yields

$$\begin{aligned}
&\int_{\delta_0}^{\iota_1}\int_{\delta_0}^{\iota_2}\cdots\int_{\delta_0}^{\iota_n}\frac{\prod_{i=1}^{n}|\vartheta_i^{h_i}(\Im_i)|}{\left(\sum_{i=1}^{n}\frac{(\Im_i-\delta_0)}{\varpi_i}\right)^{\sum_{i=1}^{n}\frac{1}{\varpi_i}}}\nabla^{(\gamma,a)}\Im_n\nabla^{(\gamma,a)}\Im_{n-1}\dots\nabla^{(\gamma,a)}\Im_1 \\
&\leqslant \left(n-\sum_{i=1}^{n}\frac{1}{\nu_i}\right)^{\sum_{i=1}^{n}\frac{1}{\nu_i}-n}\prod_{i=1}^{n}h_i\int_{\delta_0}^{\iota_i}\left(\int_{\delta_0}^{\Im_i}|\vartheta_i^{h_i-1}(\tau_i)\vartheta_i^{\nabla^{(\gamma,a)}}(\tau_i)|^{\nu_i}\nabla^{(\gamma,a)}\tau_i\right)^{\frac{1}{\nu_i}} \\
&\leqslant K\prod_{i=1}^{n}\left(\int_{\delta_0}^{\iota_i}\int_{\delta_0}^{\Im_i}|\vartheta_i^{h_i-1}(\tau_i)\vartheta_i^{\nabla^{(\gamma,a)}}(\tau_i)|^{\nu_i}\nabla^{(\gamma,a)}\tau_i\nabla^{(\gamma,a)}\Im_i\right)^{\frac{1}{\nu_i}} \\
&= K\prod_{i=1}^{n}\left(\int_{\delta_0}^{\iota_i}(\iota_i-\Im_i)|\vartheta_i^{h_i-1}(\Im_i)\vartheta_i^{\nabla^{(\gamma,a)}}(\Im_i)|^{\nu_i}\nabla^{(\gamma,a)}\Im_i\right)^{\frac{1}{\nu_i}}.
\end{aligned} \tag{21}$$

By exploiting the fact that $\iota_i \leqslant \rho(\iota_i)$, we find that

$$\begin{aligned}
&\int_{\delta_0}^{\iota_1}\int_{\delta_0}^{\iota_2}\cdots\int_{\delta_0}^{\iota_n}\frac{\prod_{i=1}^{n}|\vartheta_i^{h_i}(\Im_i)|}{\left(\sum_{i=1}^{n}\frac{(\Im_i-\delta_0)}{\varpi_i}\right)^{\sum_{i=1}^{n}\frac{1}{\varpi_i}}}\nabla^{(\gamma,a)}\Im_n\nabla^{(\gamma,a)}\Im_{n-1}\dots\nabla^{(\gamma,a)}\Im_1 \\
&\leqslant K\prod_{i=1}^{n}\left(\int_{\delta_0}^{\iota_i}(\rho(\iota_i)-\rho(\Im_i))|\vartheta_i^{h_i-1}(\Im_i)\vartheta_i^{\nabla^{(\gamma,a)}}(\Im_i)|^{\nu_i}\nabla^{(\gamma,a)}\Im_i\right)^{\frac{1}{\nu_i}}.
\end{aligned}$$

This concludes the evidence. □

Remark 1. *In Theorem 5, taking $\mathbb{T}=\mathbb{Z}, \gamma=1, h_i=1$, we obtain the results thanks to the authors of ([2], Theorem 1.1).*

Remark 2. *In Theorem 5, taking $\mathbb{T}=\mathbb{R}, \gamma=1$, we obtain the results thanks to the authors of ([2], Theorem 1.3).*

Corollary 1. *In Theorem 5, taking $n=2$, and $h_1=h_2=1$, if $\nu_1,\nu_2>1$ are such that $\frac{1}{\nu_1}+\frac{1}{\nu_2}\geqslant 1$ and $0<\lambda=2-\frac{1}{\nu_1}-\frac{1}{\nu_2}=\frac{1}{\varpi_1}+\frac{1}{\varpi_2}\leqslant 1$, inequality (17) reduces to*

$$\int_{\delta_0}^{\iota_1}\int_{\delta_0}^{\iota_2}\frac{|\vartheta_1(\Im_1)||\vartheta_2(\Im_2)|}{\Big(\varpi_2(\Im_1-\delta_0)+\varpi_1(\Im_2-\delta_0)\Big)^{\lambda}}\nabla^{(\gamma,a)}\Im_2\nabla^{(\gamma,a)}\Im_1 \leqslant \frac{1}{(\lambda\varpi_1\varpi_2)^{\lambda}}(\iota_1-\delta_0)^{\frac{1}{\varpi_1}}(\iota_2-\delta_0)^{\frac{1}{\varpi_2}} \tag{22}$$

$$\times\left(\int_{\delta_0}^{\iota_1}(\rho(\iota_1)-\rho(\Im_1))|\vartheta_1^{\nabla^{(\gamma,a)}}(\Im_1)|^{\nu_1}\nabla^{(\gamma,a)}\Im_1\right)^{\frac{1}{\nu_1}}\left(\int_{\delta_0}^{\iota_2}(\rho(\iota_2)-\rho(\Im_2))|\vartheta_2^{\nabla^{(\gamma,a)}}(\Im_2)|^{\nu_2}\nabla^{(\gamma,a)}\Im_2\right)^{\frac{1}{\nu_2}}.$$

Remark 3. *In a special case, taking $\mathbb{T}=\mathbb{R},\gamma=1$, in (22), we have that*

$$\int_0^{\iota_1}\int_0^{\iota_2}\frac{|\vartheta_1(\Im_1)||\vartheta_2(\Im_2)|}{(\varpi_2\Im_1+\varpi_1\Im_2)^{\lambda}}d\Im_2 d\Im_1 \leqslant \frac{1}{(\lambda\varpi_1\varpi_2)^{\lambda}}(\iota_1)^{\frac{1}{\varpi_1}}(\iota_2)^{\frac{1}{\varpi_2}}$$
$$\times\left(\int_0^{\iota_1}(\iota_1-\Im_1)|\vartheta_1'(\Im_1)|^{\nu_1}d\Im_1\right)^{\frac{1}{\nu_1}}\left(\int_0^{\iota_2}(\iota_2-\Im_2)|\vartheta_2'(\Im_2)|^{\nu_2}d\Im_2\right)^{\frac{1}{\nu_2}}, \tag{23}$$

which is an interesting variation of the inequality (2).

Remark 4. *In a special case, taking $\mathbb{T}=\mathbb{Z},\gamma=1$, in (22), we have that*

$$\sum_{\Im_1=1}^{m_1}\sum_{\Im_2=1}^{m_2}\frac{|a_1(\Im_1)||a_2(\Im_2)|}{(\varpi_2\Im_1+\varpi_1\Im_2)^{\lambda}} \leqslant \frac{1}{(\lambda\varpi_1\varpi_2)^{\lambda}}(m_1)^{\frac{1}{\varpi_1}}(m_2)^{\frac{1}{\varpi_2}}$$
$$\times\left(\sum_{\Im_1=1}^{m_1}(m_1-\Im_1+1)|\nabla^{(\gamma,a)}a_1(\Im_1)|^{\nu_1}\right)^{\frac{1}{\nu_1}}\left(\sum_{\Im_2=1}^{m_2}(m_2-\Im_2+1)|\nabla^{(\gamma,a)}a_2(\Im_2)|^{\nu_2}\right)^{\frac{1}{\nu_2}}, \tag{24}$$

which is an interesting variation of the inequality (1).

Corollary 2. *In Corollary 1, if $\lambda=1$, then $\frac{1}{\nu_1}+\frac{1}{\nu_2}=\frac{1}{\varpi_1}+\frac{1}{\varpi_2}=1$ and we take $\nu_1=\varpi_2$, $\nu_2=\varpi_1$. In this case, inequality* (22) *reduces to*

$$\int_{\delta_0}^{\iota_1}\int_{\delta_0}^{\iota_2}\frac{|\vartheta_1(\Im_1)||\vartheta_2(\Im_2)|}{\varpi_2(\Im_1-\delta_0)+\varpi_1(\Im_2-\delta_0)}\nabla^{(\gamma,a)}\Im_2\nabla^{(\gamma,a)}\Im_1 \leqslant \frac{1}{\nu_1\varpi_1}(\iota_1-\delta_0)^{\frac{\nu_1-1}{\nu_1}}(\iota_2-\delta_0)^{\frac{\varpi_1-1}{\varpi_1}} \tag{25}$$
$$\times\left(\int_{\delta_0}^{\iota_1}(\rho(\iota_1)-\rho(\Im_1))|\vartheta_1^{\nabla^{(\gamma,a)}}(\Im_1)|^{\nu_1}\nabla^{(\gamma,a)}\Im_1\right)^{\frac{1}{\nu_1}}\left(\int_{\delta_0}^{\iota_2}(\rho(\iota_2)-\rho(\Im_2))|\vartheta_2^{\nabla^{(\gamma,a)}}(\Im_2)|^{\varpi_1}\nabla^{(\gamma,a)}\Im_2\right)^{\frac{1}{\varpi_1}}.$$

Remark 5. *In Corollary 2, if $\mathbb{T}=\mathbb{R},\gamma=1$, we obtain an equivalent formulation of the inequality that Pachpatte presented in ([27], Theorem 2).*

Remark 6. *In Corollary 2, if $\mathbb{T}=\mathbb{Z},\gamma=1$, we obtain an equivalent formulation of the inequality that Pachpatte presented in ([27], Theorem 1).*

Theorem 6. *Let $\mathbb{T}$ be a time scale with $\delta_0,\iota_i,\varsigma_i,\Im_i,\delta_i\in\mathbb{T}$, $(i=1,\ldots,n)$. Let $h_i\geqslant 1,\nu_i,\varpi_i>1$ be constants and $\frac{1}{\nu_i}+\frac{1}{\varpi_i}=1$. Let the $\nabla^{(\gamma,a)}$-differentiable fun. $\vartheta_i(\Im_i,\delta_i)$ be decreasing funs. on $[\delta_0,\iota_i)_{\mathbb{T}}\times[\delta_0,\varsigma_i)_{\mathbb{T}}$ and $\vartheta_i(\delta_0,\delta_i)=\vartheta_i(\Im_i,\delta_0)=0$, for $(i=1,\ldots,n)$. Partial derivatives of ϑ_i are indicated by $\vartheta_i^{\nabla_1^{(\gamma,a)}}$, $\vartheta_i^{\nabla_2^{(\gamma,a)}}$, $\vartheta_i^{\nabla_{12}^{(\gamma,a)}}=\vartheta_i^{\nabla_{21}^{(\gamma,a)}}$. Let*

$$\left(\vartheta_i^{h_i}(\Im_i,\delta_i)\right)^{\nabla_1^{(\gamma,a)}\nabla_2^{(\gamma,a)}}\leqslant\left(h_i\vartheta_i^{h_i-1}(\Im_i,\delta_i).\vartheta_i^{\nabla_1^{(\gamma,a)}}(\Im_i,\delta_i)\right)^{\nabla_2^{(\gamma,a)}}=\vartheta_i^{\nabla_{12}^{(\gamma,a)}}(\Im_i,\delta_i).$$

Then,

$$\int_{\delta_0}^{\iota_1}\int_{\delta_0}^{\varsigma_1}\cdots\int_{\delta_0}^{\iota_n}\int_{\delta_0}^{\varsigma_n}\frac{\prod_{i=1}^{n}|\vartheta_i^{h_i}(\Im_i,\delta_i)|}{\left(\sum_{i=1}^{n}\frac{(\Im_i-\delta_0)(\delta_i-\delta_0)}{\varpi_i}\right)^{\sum_{i=1}^{n}\frac{1}{\varpi_i}}}\nabla^{(\gamma,a)}\delta_n\nabla^{(\gamma,a)}\Im_n\ldots\nabla^{(\gamma,a)}\delta_1\nabla^{(\gamma,a)}\Im_1 \tag{26}$$

$$\leqslant C\prod_{i=1}^{n}\left(\int_{\delta_0}^{\iota_i}\int_{\delta_0}^{\varsigma_i}(\rho(\iota_i)-\rho(\Im_i))(\rho(\varsigma_i)-\rho(\delta_i))|\vartheta_i^{\nabla_{12}^{(\gamma,a)}}(\Im_i,\delta_i)|^{\nu_i}\nabla^{(\gamma,a)}\delta_i\nabla^{(\gamma,a)}\Im_i\right)^{\frac{1}{\nu_i}},$$

where

$$C=C(\iota_1\varsigma_1,\ldots,\iota_n\varsigma_n)=\left(n-\sum_{i=1}^{n}\frac{1}{\nu_i}\right)^{\sum_{i=1}^{n}\frac{1}{\nu_i}-n}\prod_{i=1}^{n}[(\iota_i-\delta_0)(\varsigma_i-\delta_0)]^{\frac{1}{\varpi_i}}.$$

Proof. We can write

$$\begin{aligned}
\vartheta_i^{h_i}(\Im_i,\delta_i) &= \vartheta_i^{h_i}(\Im_i,\delta_i)-\vartheta_i^{h_i}(\delta_0,\delta_i)-\vartheta_i^{h_i}(\Im_i,\delta_0)+\vartheta_i^{h_i}(\delta_0,\delta_0)\\
&= \int_{\delta_0}^{\Im_i}\left(\vartheta_i^{h_i}(\xi_i,\delta_i)\right)^{\nabla_1^{(\gamma,a)}}\nabla_1^{(\gamma,a)}\xi_i-\int_{\delta_0}^{\Im_i}\left(\vartheta_i^{h_i}(\xi_i,\delta_0)\right)^{\nabla_1^{(\gamma,a)}}\nabla^{(\gamma,a)}\xi_i\\
&= \int_{\delta_0}^{\Im_i}\left[\left(\vartheta_i^{h_i}(\xi_i,\delta_i)\right)^{\nabla_1^{(\gamma,a)}}-\left(\vartheta_i^{h_i}(\xi_i,\delta_0)\right)^{\nabla_1^{(\gamma,a)}}\right]\nabla^{(\gamma,a)}\xi_i\\
&\leqslant \int_{\delta_0}^{\Im_i}\int_{\delta_0}^{\delta_i}\left(h_i\vartheta_i^{h_i-1}(\xi_i,\eta_i).\vartheta_i^{\nabla_1^{(\gamma,a)}}(\xi_i,\eta_i)\right)^{\nabla_2^{(\gamma,a)}}\nabla^{(\gamma,a)}\eta_i\nabla^{(\gamma,a)}\xi_i\\
&= \int_{\delta_0}^{\Im_i}\int_{\delta_0}^{\delta_i}\vartheta_i^{\nabla_{12}^{(\gamma,a)}}(\xi_i,\eta_i)\nabla^{(\gamma,a)}\eta_i\nabla^{(\gamma,a)}\xi_i.
\end{aligned} \tag{27}$$

By (27) applying (16) and (28), we obtain

$$\begin{aligned}
\prod_{i=1}^{n}|\vartheta_i^{h_i}(\Im_i,\delta_i)| &\leqslant \prod_{i=1}^{n}\int_{\delta_0}^{\Im_i}\int_{\delta_0}^{\delta_i}|\vartheta_i^{\nabla_{12}^{(\gamma,a)}}(\xi_i,\eta_i)|\nabla_1^{(\gamma,a)}\eta_i\nabla_2^{(\gamma,a)}\xi_i\\
&\leqslant \prod_{i=1}^{n}[(\Im_i-\delta_0)(\delta_i-\delta_0)]^{\frac{1}{\varpi_i}}\left(\int_{\delta_0}^{\Im_i}\int_{\delta_0}^{\delta_i}|\vartheta_i^{\nabla_{12}^{(\gamma,a)}}(\xi_i,\eta_i)|^{\nu_i}\nabla^{(\gamma,a)}\eta_i\nabla^{(\gamma,a)}\xi_i\right)^{\frac{1}{\nu_i}}.
\end{aligned} \tag{28}$$

Using inequality (19), we find that

$$\frac{\prod_{i=1}^{n}|\vartheta_i^{h_i}(\Im_i,\delta_i)|}{\left(\sum_{i=1}^{n}\frac{(\Im_i-\delta_0)(\delta_i-\delta_0)}{\varpi_i}\right)^{\sum_{i=1}^{n}\frac{1}{\varpi_i}}}\leqslant\left(n-\sum_{i=1}^{n}\frac{1}{\nu_i}\right)^{\sum_{i=1}^{n}\frac{1}{\nu_i}-n}\prod_{i=1}^{n}\left(\int_{\delta_0}^{\Im_i}\int_{\delta_0}^{\delta_i}|\vartheta_i^{\nabla_{12}^{(\gamma,a)}}(\xi_i,\eta_i)|^{\nu_i}\nabla^{(\gamma,a)}\eta_i\nabla^{(\gamma,a)}\xi_i\right)^{\frac{1}{\nu_i}}. \tag{29}$$

Integrating (29) with $\Im_i$ and δ_i, and applying (16) and Fubini's theorem, yields

$$\int_{\delta_0}^{\iota_1}\int_{\delta_0}^{\varsigma_1}\cdots\int_{\delta_0}^{\iota_n}\int_{\delta_0}^{\varsigma_n}\frac{\prod_{i=1}^{n}|\vartheta_i^{h_i}(\Im_i,\delta_i)|}{\left(\sum_{i=1}^{n}\frac{(\Im_i-\delta_0)(\delta_i-\delta_0)}{\varpi_i}\right)^{\sum_{i=1}^{n}\frac{1}{\varpi_i}}}\nabla^{(\gamma,a)}\delta_n\nabla^{(\gamma,a)}\Im_n\ldots\nabla^{(\gamma,a)}\delta_1\nabla^{(\gamma,a)}\Im_1$$

$$\leqslant\left(n-\sum_{i=1}^{n}\frac{1}{\nu_i}\right)^{\sum_{i=1}^{n}\frac{1}{\nu_i}-n}$$

$$\times\prod_{i=1}^{n}\left(\int_{\delta_0}^{\iota_i}\int_{\delta_0}^{\varsigma_i}\left(\int_{\delta_0}^{\Im_i}\int_{\delta_0}^{\delta_i}|\vartheta_i^{\nabla_{12}^{(\gamma,a)}}(\xi_i,\eta_i)|^{\nu_i}\nabla^{(\gamma,a)}\eta_i\nabla^{(\gamma,a)}\xi_i\right)^{\frac{1}{\nu_i}}\nabla^{(\gamma,a)}\delta_i\nabla^{(\gamma,a)}\Im_i\right)$$

$$\leqslant\left(n-\sum_{i=1}^{n}\frac{1}{\nu_i}\right)^{\sum_{i=1}^{n}\frac{1}{\nu_i}-n}$$

$$\times\prod_{i=1}^{n}[(\iota_i-\delta_0)(\varsigma_i-\delta_0)]^{\frac{1}{\varpi_i}}\left(\int_{\delta_0}^{\iota_i}\int_{\delta_0}^{\varsigma_i}\left(\int_{\delta_0}^{\Im_i}\int_{\delta_0}^{\delta_i}|\vartheta_i^{\nabla_{12}^{(\gamma,a)}}(\xi_i,\eta_i)|^{\nu_i}\nabla^{(\gamma,a)}\eta_i\nabla^{(\gamma,a)}\xi_i\right)\nabla^{(\gamma,a)}\delta_i\nabla^{(\gamma,a)}\Im_i\right)^{\frac{1}{\nu_i}}$$

$$=C\prod_{i=1}^{n}\left(\int_{\delta_0}^{\iota_i}\int_{\delta_0}^{\varsigma_i}(\iota_i-\Im_i)(\varsigma_i-\delta_i)|\vartheta_i^{\nabla_{12}^{(\gamma,a)}}(\Im_i,\delta_i)|^{\nu_i}\nabla^{(\gamma,a)}\delta_i\nabla^{(\gamma,a)}\Im_i\right)^{\frac{1}{\nu_i}}. \tag{30}$$

By exploiting the fact that $\iota_i \leqslant \rho(\iota_i)$, we obtain

$$\int_{\delta_0}^{\iota_1}\int_{\delta_0}^{\varsigma_1}\cdots\int_{\delta_0}^{\iota_n}\int_{\delta_0}^{\varsigma_n}\frac{\prod_{i=1}^{n}|\vartheta_i^{h_i}(\Im_i,\delta_i)|}{\left(\sum_{i=1}^{n}\frac{(\Im_i-\delta_0)(\delta_i-\delta_0)}{\varpi_i}\right)^{\sum_{i=1}^{n}\frac{1}{\varpi_i}}}\nabla^{(\gamma,a)}\delta_n\nabla^{(\gamma,a)}\Im_n\ldots\nabla^{(\gamma,a)}\delta_1\nabla^{(\gamma,a)}\Im_1$$

$$\leqslant C\prod_{i=1}^{n}\left(\int_{\delta_0}^{\iota_i}\int_{\delta_0}^{\varsigma_i}(\rho(\iota_i)-\rho(\Im_i))(\rho(\varsigma_i)-\rho(\delta_i))|\vartheta_i^{\nabla_{12}^{(\gamma,a)}}(\Im_i,\delta_i)|^{\nu_i}\nabla^{(\gamma,a)}\delta_i\nabla^{(\gamma,a)}\Im_i\right)^{\frac{1}{\nu_i}}.$$

This concludes the evidence. □

Remark 7. *In Theorem 6, if we take $\mathbb{T}=\mathbb{Z},\gamma=1,h_i=1$, we obtain the results thanks to the authors of ([2], Theorem 1.2).*

Remark 8. *In Theorem 6, supposing that $\mathbb{T}=\mathbb{R},\gamma=1$, we obtain the results thanks to the authors of ([2], Theorem 1.4).*

Corollary 3. *Taking $n=2$ and $h_1=h_2=1$ in Theorem 6, we have*

$$\vartheta_1^{\nabla_{12}^{(\gamma,a)}}(\Im_1,\delta_1)=\vartheta^{\nabla_2^{(\gamma,a)}\nabla_1^{(\gamma,a)}}(\Im_1,\delta_1),\qquad \vartheta_2^{\nabla_{12}^{(\gamma,a)}}(\Im_1,\delta_1)=\vartheta^{\nabla_2^{(\gamma,a)}\nabla_1^{(\gamma,a)}}(\Im_2,\delta_2).$$

Moreover, if $\nu_1,\nu_2>1$ satisfy $\frac{1}{\nu_1}+\frac{1}{\nu_2}\geqslant 1$ and $0<\lambda=2-\frac{1}{\nu_1}-\frac{1}{\nu_2}=\frac{1}{\varpi_1}+\frac{1}{\varpi_2}\leqslant 1$, inequality (26) reduces to

$$\int_{\delta_0}^{\iota_1}\int_{\delta_0}^{\varsigma_1}\left(\int_{\delta_0}^{\iota_2}\int_{\delta_0}^{\varsigma_2}\frac{|\vartheta_1(\Im_1,\delta_1)||\vartheta_2(\Im_2,\delta_2)|}{(\nu_1(\Im_1-\delta_0)(\delta_1-\delta_0)+\varpi_1(\Im_2-\delta_0)(\delta_2-\delta_0))^{\lambda}}\nabla^{(\gamma,a)}\Im_2\nabla^{(\gamma,a)}\delta_2\right)\nabla^{(\gamma,a)}\Im_1\nabla^{(\gamma,a)}\delta_1$$

$$\leqslant\frac{1}{(\lambda\varpi_1\varpi_2)^{\lambda}}\left[(\iota_1-\delta_0)(\varsigma_1-\delta_0)\right]^{\frac{1}{\varpi_1}}\left[(\iota_2-\delta_0)(\varsigma_2-\delta_0)\right]^{\frac{\varpi_1-1}{\varpi_1}}$$

$$\times\left(\int_{\delta_0}^{\iota_1}\int_{\delta_0}^{\varsigma_1}(\rho(\iota_1)-\rho(\Im_1))(\rho(\varsigma_1)-\rho(\delta_1))|\vartheta^{\nabla_2^{(\gamma,a)}\nabla_1^{(\gamma,a)}}(\Im_1,\delta_1)|^{\nu_1}\nabla^{(\gamma,a)}\Im_1\nabla^{(\gamma,a)}\delta_1\right)^{\frac{1}{\nu_1}} \tag{31}$$

$$\left(\int_{\delta_0}^{\iota_2}\int_{\delta_0}^{\varsigma_2}(\rho(\iota_2)-\delta_0)(\rho(\varsigma_2)-\delta_0)|\vartheta^{\nabla_2^{(\gamma,a)}\nabla_1^{(\gamma,a)}}(\Im_2,\delta_2)|^{\nu_2}\nabla^{(\gamma,a)}\Im_2\nabla^{(\gamma,a)}\delta_2\right)^{\frac{1}{\nu_2}}.$$

Remark 9. *In a unique scenario, if we take $\mathbb{T} = \mathbb{R}$ in Corollary 3, the inequality* (31) *reduces to*

$$\begin{aligned}
&\int_0^{\iota_1}\int_0^{\varsigma_1}\left(\int_0^{\iota_2}\int_0^{\varsigma_2}\frac{|\vartheta_1(\Im_1,\delta_1)||\vartheta_2(\Im_2,\delta_2)|}{\left(\nu_1\Im_1\delta_1+\varpi_1\Im_2\delta_2\right)^{\lambda}}d\Im_2 d\delta_2\right)d\Im_1 d\delta_1 \\
&\leqslant \frac{1}{(\lambda\varpi_1\varpi_2)^{\lambda}}\left[\iota_1\varsigma_1\right]^{\frac{1}{\varpi_1}}\left[\iota_2\varsigma_2\right]^{\frac{\varpi_1-1}{\varpi_1}} \\
&\times\left(\int_0^{\iota_1}\int_0^{\varsigma_1}(\iota_1-\Im_1)(\varsigma_1-\delta_1)|D_1D_2\vartheta_1(\Im_1,\delta_1)|^{\nu_1}d\Im_1 d\delta_1\right)^{\frac{1}{\nu_1}} \\
&\times\left(\int_0^{\iota_2}\int_0^{\varsigma_2}(\iota_2-\Im_2)(\varsigma_2-\delta_2)|D_1D_2\vartheta_2(\Im_2,\delta_2)|^{\nu_2}d\Im_2 d\delta_2\right)^{\frac{1}{\nu_2}},
\end{aligned} \tag{32}$$

Remark 10. *In a unique scenario, if we take $\mathbb{T} = \mathbb{Z}$ in Corollary 3, the inequality* (31) *reduces to*

$$\begin{aligned}
&\sum_{\Im_1=1}^{m_1}\sum_{\delta_1=1}^{n_1}\left(\sum_{\Im_2=1}^{m_2}\sum_{\delta_2=1}^{n_2}\frac{|a_1(\Im_1,\delta_1)||a_2(\Im_2,\delta_2)|}{\left(\nu_1\Im_1\delta_1+\varpi_1\Im_2\delta_2\right)^{\lambda}}\right) \\
&\leqslant \frac{1}{(\lambda\varpi_1\varpi_2)^{\lambda}}\left[m_1n_1\right]^{\frac{1}{\varpi_1}}\left[m_2n_2\right]^{\frac{\varpi_1-1}{\varpi_1}} \\
&\times\left(\sum_{\Im_1=1}^{m_1}\sum_{\delta_1=1}^{n_1}(n_1-\delta_1)(m_1-\Im_1)|\nabla_1^{(\gamma,a)}\nabla_2^{(\gamma,a)}a_1(\Im_1,\delta_1)|^{\nu_1}\right)^{\frac{1}{\nu_1}} \\
&\times\left(\sum_{\Im_2=1}^{m_2}\sum_{\delta_2=1}^{n_2}(n_2-\delta_2)(m_2-\Im_2))|\nabla_1^{(\gamma,a)}\nabla_2^{(\gamma,a)}a_2(\Im_2,\delta_2)|^{\nu_2}\right)^{\frac{1}{\nu_2}},
\end{aligned} \tag{33}$$

Corollary 4. *In Corollary 3, if $\lambda = 1$, then $\frac{1}{\nu_1}+\frac{1}{\nu_2} = \frac{1}{\varpi_1}+\frac{1}{\varpi_2} = 1$, and we take $\nu_1 = \varpi_2$, $\nu_2 = \varpi_1$. In this case, the inequality* (31) *reduces to*

$$\begin{aligned}
&\int_{\delta_0}^{\iota_1}\int_{\delta_0}^{\varsigma_1}\left(\int_{\delta_0}^{\iota_2}\int_{\delta_0}^{\varsigma_2}\frac{|\vartheta_1(\Im_1,\delta_1)||\vartheta_2(\Im_2,\delta_2)|}{(\nu_1(\Im_1-\delta_0)(\delta_1-\delta_0)+\varpi_1(\Im_2-\delta_0)(\delta_2-\delta_0))}\nabla^{(\gamma,a)}\Im_2\nabla^{(\gamma,a)}\delta_2\right)\nabla^{(\gamma,a)}\Im_1\nabla^{(\gamma,a)}\delta_1 \\
&\leqslant \frac{1}{\nu_1\varpi_1}\left[(\iota_1-\delta_0)(\varsigma_1-\delta_0)\right]^{\frac{\nu_1-1}{\nu_1}}\left[(\iota_2-\delta_0)(\varsigma_2-\delta_0)\right]^{\frac{\varpi_1-1}{\varpi_1}} \\
&\times\left(\int_{\delta_0}^{\iota_1}\int_{\delta_0}^{\varsigma_1}(\rho(\iota_1)-\rho(\Im_1))(\rho(\varsigma_1)-\rho(\delta_1))|\vartheta^{\nabla_2^{(\gamma,a)}\nabla_1^{(\gamma,a)}}(\Im_1,\delta_1)|^{\nu_1}\nabla^{(\gamma,a)}\Im_1\nabla^{(\gamma,a)}\delta_1\right)^{\frac{1}{\nu_1}} \\
&\left(\int_{\delta_0}^{\iota_2}\int_{\delta_0}^{\varsigma_2}(\rho(\iota_2)-\delta_0)(\rho(\varsigma_2)-\delta_0)|\vartheta^{\nabla_2^{(\gamma,a)}\nabla_1^{(\gamma,a)}}(\Im_2,\delta_2)|^{\nu_2}\nabla^{(\gamma,a)}\Im_2\nabla^{(\gamma,a)}\delta_2\right)^{\frac{1}{\nu_2}}.
\end{aligned} \tag{34}$$

Remark 11. *In Corollary 4, if $\mathbb{T} = \mathbb{R}, \gamma = 1$, we obtain an equivalent formulation of the inequality that Pachpatte presented in ([27], Theorem 4).*

Remark 12. *In Corollary 4, if $\mathbb{T} = \mathbb{Z}, \gamma = 1$, we obtain an equivalent formulation of the inequality that Pachpatte presented in ([27], Theorem 3).*

Theorem 7. *Let $\mathbb{T}$ be a time scale with δ_0, ι_{ij}, τ_{ij}, $\delta_{ij} \in \mathbb{T}$, $(i,j = 1,\ldots,n)$. Let $\nu_i, \varpi_i > 1$, be constants and $\frac{1}{\nu_i}+\frac{1}{\varpi_i} = 1$. Let $\vartheta_i(\tau_{1i},\ldots,\tau_{ni})$ be real-valued nth $\nabla^{(\gamma,a)}$-differentiable functions* *also defined on* $[\delta_0, \iota_{1i})_{\mathbb{T}} \times \cdots \times [\delta_0, \iota_{ni})_{\mathbb{T}}$*, where* $\delta_0 \leqslant \iota_{ji} \leqslant \delta_{ji}$*,* $\delta_{ji} \in (0, \infty)$ *and* $i, j = 1, \ldots, n$*. Suppose*

$$\vartheta_i(\iota_{1i}, \ldots, \iota_{ni}) = \int_{\delta_0}^{\iota_{1i}} \cdots \int_{\delta_0}^{\iota_{ni}} \frac{\partial^n}{\nabla^{(\gamma,a)}\tau_{1i} \ldots \nabla^{(\gamma,a)}\tau_{ni}} \vartheta_i(\tau_{1i}, \ldots, \tau_{ni}) \nabla^{(\gamma,a)}\tau_{ni} \ldots \nabla^{(\gamma,a)}\tau_{1i},$$

then

$$\int_{\delta_0}^{\delta_{11}} \cdots \int_{\delta_0}^{\delta_{n1}} \int_{\delta_0}^{\delta_{12}} \cdots \int_{\delta_0}^{\delta_{n2}} \cdots \int_{\delta_0}^{\delta_{1n}} \cdots \int_{\delta_0}^{\delta_{nn}} \tag{35}$$

$$\frac{\prod_{i=1}^n \left(\int_{\delta_0}^{\iota_{1i}} \cdots \int_{\delta_0}^{\iota_{ni}} \left| \frac{\partial^n}{\nabla^{(\gamma,a)}\tau_{1i} \ldots \nabla^{(\gamma,a)}\tau_{ni}} \vartheta_i(\tau_{1i} \ldots \tau_{ni}) \right|^{\nu_i} \nabla^{(\gamma,a)}\tau_{ni} \ldots \nabla^{(\gamma,a)}\tau_{1i} \right)^{\frac{1}{\nu_i}}}{\left(\sum_{i=1}^n \frac{[(\iota_{1i}-\delta_0) \ldots (\iota_{ni}-\delta_0)]}{\varpi_i} \right)^{\sum_{i=1}^n \frac{1}{\varpi_i}}}$$

$$\nabla^{(\gamma,a)}\iota_{11} \ldots \nabla^{(\gamma,a)}\iota_{n1} \ldots \nabla^{(\gamma,a)}\iota_{12} \ldots \nabla^{(\gamma,a)}\iota_{n2} \ldots \nabla^{(\gamma,a)}\iota_{1n} \ldots \nabla^{(\gamma,a)}\iota_{nn}$$

$$\leqslant N \prod_{i=1}^n \left(\int_{\delta_0}^{\delta_{1i}} \cdots \int_{\delta_0}^{\delta_{ni}} \prod_{j=1}^n (\rho(\delta_{ji}) - \iota_{ji}) \left| \frac{\partial^n}{\nabla^{(\gamma,a)}\iota_{1i} \ldots \nabla^{(\gamma,a)}\iota_{ni}} \vartheta_i(\iota_{1i}, \ldots, \iota_{ni}) \right|^{\nu_i} \nabla^{(\gamma,a)}\iota_{1i} \ldots \nabla^{(\gamma,a)}\iota_{ni} \right)^{\frac{1}{\nu_i}},$$

where

$$N = N(\delta_{1i}, \ldots, \delta_{ni}) \left(n - \sum_{i=1}^n \frac{1}{\nu_i} \right)^{\sum_{i=1}^n \frac{1}{\nu_i} - n} \prod_{i=1}^n [(\delta_{1i} - \delta_0) \ldots (\delta_{ni} - \delta_0)]^{\frac{1}{\varpi_i}}.$$

Proof. From the hypothesis of Theorem 7, we have

$$|\vartheta_i(\iota_{1i}, \ldots, \iota_{ni})| \leqslant \int_{\delta_0}^{\iota_{1i}} \cdots \int_{\delta_0}^{\iota_{ni}} \left| \frac{\partial^n}{\nabla^{(\gamma,a)}\tau_{1i} \ldots \nabla^{(\gamma,a)}\tau_{ni}} \vartheta_i(\tau_{1i}, \ldots, \tau_{ni}) \right| \nabla^{(\gamma,a)}\tau_{ni} \ldots \nabla^{(\gamma,a)}\tau_{1i}. \tag{36}$$

On the other hand, by using (19) and Hölder's dynamic inequality, we obtain

$$\begin{aligned}
&\prod_{i=1}^n |\vartheta_i(\iota_{1i}, \ldots, \iota_{ni})| \\
&\leqslant \prod_{i=1}^n \int_{\delta_0}^{\iota_{1i}} \cdots \int_{\delta_0}^{\iota_{ni}} \left| \frac{\partial^n}{\nabla^{(\gamma,a)}\tau_{1i} \ldots \nabla^{(\gamma,a)}\tau_{ni}} \vartheta_i(\tau_{1i}, \ldots, \tau_{ni}) \right| \nabla^{(\gamma,a)}\tau_{ni} \ldots \nabla^{(\gamma,a)}\tau_{1i} \\
&\leqslant \prod_{i=1}^n [(\iota_{1i} - \delta_0) \ldots (\iota_{ni} - \delta_0)]^{\frac{1}{\varpi_i}} \\
&\quad \times \left(\int_{\delta_0}^{\iota_{1i}} \cdots \int_{\delta_0}^{\iota_{ni}} \left| \frac{\partial^n}{\nabla^{(\gamma,a)}\tau_{1i}, \ldots, \nabla^{(\gamma,a)}\tau_{ni}} \vartheta_i(\tau_{1i}, \ldots, \tau_{ni}) \right|^{\nu_i} \nabla^{(\gamma,a)}\tau_{ni} \ldots \nabla^{(\gamma,a)}\tau_{1i} \right)^{\frac{1}{\nu_i}} \\
&\leqslant \frac{\left(\sum_{i=1}^n \frac{[(\iota_{1i}-\delta_0) \ldots (\iota_{ni}-\delta_0)]}{\varpi_i} \right)^{\sum_{i=1}^n \frac{1}{\varpi_i}}}{\left(n - \sum_{i=1}^n \frac{1}{\nu_i} \right)^{n - \sum_{i=1}^n \frac{1}{\nu_i}}} \\
&\quad \times \prod_{i=1}^n \left(\int_{\delta_0}^{\iota_{1i}} \cdots \int_{\delta_0}^{\iota_{ni}} \left| \frac{\partial^n}{\nabla^{(\gamma,a)}\tau_{1i} \ldots \nabla^{(\gamma,a)}\tau_{ni}} \vartheta_i(\tau_{1i}, \ldots, \tau_{ni}) \right|^{\nu_i} \nabla^{(\gamma,a)}\tau_{ni} \ldots \nabla^{(\gamma,a)}\tau_{1i} \right)^{\frac{1}{\nu_i}}.
\end{aligned} \tag{37}$$

Divide (37) by $\left(\sum_{i=1}^n \frac{[(\iota_{1i}-\delta_0) \ldots (\iota_{ni}-\delta_0)]}{\varpi_i} \right)^{\sum_{i=1}^n \frac{1}{\varpi_i}}$, and then integrate it over ι_{ji} from δ_0 to δ_{ji} $(i, j = 1, \ldots, n)$, respectively; using the dynamic Hölder inequality and using the information $\rho(n) \geqslant n$, we obtain

$$\int_{\delta_0}^{\delta_{11}} \cdots \int_{\delta_0}^{\delta_{n1}} \int_{\delta_0}^{\delta_{12}} \cdots \int_{\delta_0}^{\delta_{n2}} \cdots \int_{\delta_0}^{\delta_{1n}} \cdots \int_{\delta_0}^{\delta_{nn}}$$

$$\frac{\prod_{i=1}^{n} \left(\int_{\delta_0}^{\iota_{1i}} \cdots \int_{\delta_0}^{\iota_{ni}} \left| \frac{\partial^n}{\nabla^{(\gamma,a)}\tau_{1i} \ldots \nabla^{(\gamma,a)}\tau_{ni}} \vartheta_i(\tau_{1i}, \ldots, \tau_{ni}) \right|^{\nu_i} \nabla^{(\gamma,a)}\tau_{ni} \ldots \nabla^{(\gamma,a)}\tau_{1i} \right)^{\frac{1}{\nu_i}}}{\left(\sum_{i=1}^{n} \frac{[(\iota_{1i}-\delta_0)\ldots(\iota_{ni}-\delta_0)]}{\omega_i} \right)^{\sum_{i=1}^{n} \frac{1}{\omega_i}}}$$

$$\nabla^{(\gamma,a)}\iota_{11} \ldots \nabla^{(\gamma,a)}\iota_{n1} \nabla^{(\gamma,a)}\iota_{12} \ldots \nabla^{(\gamma,a)}\iota_{n2} \ldots \nabla^{(\gamma,a)}\iota_{1n} \ldots \nabla^{(\gamma,a)}\iota_{nn}$$

$$\leqslant \left(n - \sum_{i=1}^{n} \frac{1}{\nu_i} \right)^{\sum_{i=1}^{n} \frac{1}{\nu_i} - n}$$

$$\times \prod_{i=1}^{n} \int_{\delta_0}^{\delta_{1i}} \cdots \int_{\delta_0}^{\delta_{ni}} \left(\int_{\delta_0}^{\iota_{1i}} \cdots \int_{\delta_0}^{\iota_{ni}} \left| \frac{\partial^n}{\nabla^{(\gamma,a)}\tau_{1i}, \ldots, \nabla^{(\gamma,a)}\tau_{ni}} \vartheta_i(\tau_{1i}, \ldots, \tau_{ni}) \right|^{\nu_i} \nabla^{(\gamma,a)}\tau_{ni} \ldots \nabla^{(\gamma,a)}\tau_{1i} \right)^{\frac{1}{\nu_i}} \nabla^{(\gamma,a)}\iota_{ni} \ldots \nabla^{(\gamma,a)}\iota_{1i}$$

$$\leqslant \left(n - \sum_{i=1}^{n} \frac{1}{\nu_i} \right)^{\sum_{i=1}^{n} \frac{1}{\nu_i} - n} \prod_{i=1}^{n} [(\delta_{1i} - \delta_0) \ldots (\delta_{ni} - \delta_0)]^{\frac{1}{\omega_i}}$$

$$\left(\int_{\delta_0}^{\delta_{1i}} \cdots \int_{\delta_0}^{\delta_{ni}} \left(\int_{\delta_0}^{\iota_{1i}} \cdots \int_{\delta_0}^{\iota_{ni}} \left| \frac{\partial^n}{\nabla^{(\gamma,a)}\tau_{1i} \ldots \nabla^{(\gamma,a)}\tau_{ni}} \vartheta_i(\tau_{1i}, \ldots, \tau_{ni}) \right|^{\nu_i} \nabla^{(\gamma,a)}\tau_{ni} \ldots \nabla^{(\gamma,a)}\tau_{1i} \right) \nabla^{(\gamma,a)}\iota_{ni} \ldots \nabla^{(\gamma,a)}\iota_{1i} \right)^{\frac{1}{\nu_i}}$$

$$= N \prod_{i=1}^{n} \left(\int_{\delta_0}^{\delta_{1i}} \cdots \int_{\delta_0}^{\delta_{ni}} \prod_{j=1}^{n} (\delta_{ji} - \iota_{ji}) \left| \frac{\partial^n}{\nabla^{(\gamma,a)}\iota_{1i} \ldots \nabla^{(\gamma,a)}\iota_{ni}} \vartheta_i(\iota_{1i}, \ldots, \iota_{ni}) \right|^{\nu_i} \nabla^{(\gamma,a)}\iota_{ni} \ldots \nabla^{(\gamma,a)}\iota_{1i} \right)^{\frac{1}{\nu_i}}$$

$$\leqslant N \prod_{i=1}^{n} \left(\int_{\delta_0}^{\delta_{1i}} \cdots \int_{\delta_0}^{\delta_{ni}} \prod_{j=1}^{n} (\rho(\delta_{ji}) - \iota_{ji}) \left| \frac{\partial^n}{\nabla^{(\gamma,a)}\iota_{1i} \ldots \nabla^{(\gamma,a)}\iota_{ni}} \vartheta_i(\iota_{1i}, \ldots, \iota_{ni}) \right|^{\nu_i} \nabla^{(\gamma,a)}\iota_{ni} \ldots \nabla^{(\gamma,a)}\iota_{1i} \right)^{\frac{1}{\nu_i}}.$$

This concludes the evidence. □

Remark 13. *In Theorem 7, supposing $\mathbb{Z} = \mathbb{T}$, andwith$\gamma = 1$, we obtain ([3], Theorem 2.1).*

Remark 14. *In Theorem 7, supposing $\mathbb{R} = \mathbb{T}$, andwith$\gamma = 1$, we obtain ([3], Theorem 2.2).*

Corollary 5. *Let $\vartheta_i(\iota_{1i}, \ldots, \iota_{ni})$ change to $\vartheta_i(\Im_i)$ in Theorem 7 and in view of $\vartheta_i(\delta_0) = 0$, $(i = 1, \ldots, n)$, and then*

$$\int_{\delta_0}^{\iota_1} \int_{\delta_0}^{\iota_2} \cdots \int_{\delta_0}^{\iota_n} \frac{\prod_{i=1}^{n} |\vartheta_i(\Im_i)|}{\left(\sum_{i=1}^{n} \frac{(\Im_i - \delta_0)}{\omega_i} \right)^{\sum_{i=1}^{n} \frac{1}{\omega_i}}} \nabla^{(\gamma,a)}\Im_n \nabla^{(\gamma,a)}\Im_{n-1} \ldots \nabla^{(\gamma,a)}\Im_1$$

$$\leqslant R \prod_{i=1}^{n} \left(\int_{\delta_0}^{\iota_i} (\rho(\iota_i) - \rho(\Im_i)) |\vartheta_i^{\nabla^{(\gamma,a)}}(\Im_i)|^{\nu_i} \nabla^{(\gamma,a)}\tau_i \nabla^{(\gamma,a)}\Im_i \right)^{\frac{1}{\nu_i}}, \tag{38}$$

where

$$R = \left(n - \sum_{i=1}^{n} \frac{1}{\nu_i} \right)^{\sum_{i=1}^{n} \frac{1}{\nu_i} - n} \prod_{i=1}^{n} (\iota_i - \delta_0)^{\frac{1}{\omega_i}}.$$

Remark 15. *Taking $n = 2$, in Corollary 5, if $\nu_1, \nu_2 > 1$ are such that $\frac{1}{\nu_1} + \frac{1}{\nu_2} \geqslant 1$ and $0 < \lambda = 2 - \frac{1}{\nu_1} - \frac{1}{\nu_2} = \frac{1}{\omega_1} + \frac{1}{\omega_2} \leqslant 1$, inequality (38) reduces to inequality (22).*

3. Conclusions

In this work, we used Holder's inequality to prove a number of Hilbert's inequalities on the time scale. Some integer and discrete inequalities were obtained as special cases of the results. This work builds on the multiple inequalities reported by Pachpatte in 1998 and 2000 and by Handley et al. and by Zhao et al. in 2012. Moreover, as a future work, we intend to extend these inequalities by 123 using a-conformable calculus and also by employing alpha-conformable calculus on time scales. Moreover, we will try to obtain the diamond alpha version for these results.

Author Contributions: Resources, methodology and investigations, A.A.E.-D. and B.A.; writing—original draft preparation, A.A.E.-D. and B.A.; conceptualization, writing—review and editing, A.A.E.-D. and B.A. All authors have read and approved the final manuscript.

Funding: Princess Nourah bint Abdulrahman University Researchers Supporting Project number (PNURSP2023R216), Princess Nourah bint Abdulrahman University, Riyadh, Saudi Arabia.

Data Availability Statement: Not applicable.

Conflicts of Interest: The authors declare no conflict of interest.

References

1. Hardy, G.H.; Littlewood, J.E.; Polya, G. *Inequalities Cambridge Univ*; Cambridge University Press: Cambridge, UK, 1952.
2. Zhao, C.-J.; Chen, L.-Y.; Cheung, W. On some new Hilbert-type inequalities. *Math. Slovaca* **2011**, *61*, 15–28. [CrossRef]
3. Zhao, C.; Cheung, W. On Hilbert type inequalities. *J. Inequalities Appl.* **2012**, *2012*, 145. [CrossRef]
4. Pachpatte, B.G. A note on Hilbert type inequality. *Tamkang J. Math.* **1998**, *29*, 293–298. [CrossRef]
5. Handley, G.D.; Koliha, J.J.; Pecaric, J. A Hilbert type inequality. *Tamkang J. Math.* **2000**, *31*, 311–316. [CrossRef]
6. Zhao, C.; Cheung, W. Inverses of new Hilbert-Pachpatte-type inequalities. *J. Inequalities Appl.* **2006**, *2006*, 97860. [CrossRef]
7. Pachpatte, B.G. On some new inequalities similar to Hilbert's inequality. *J. Math. Anal. Appl.* **1998**, *226*, 166–179. [CrossRef]
8. Yang, B.; Rassias, M.T.; Raigorodskii, A. On an extension of a Hardy–Hilbert-type inequality with multi-parameters. *Mathematics* **2021**, *9*, 2432. [CrossRef]
9. Rassias, M.T.; Yang, B. On a Hardy-Hilbert-type inequality with a general homogeneous kernel. *Int. J. Nonlinear Anal. Appl.* **2016**, *7*, 249–269.
10. Rassias, M.T.; Yang, B. A half-discrete Hardy-Hilbert-type inequality with a best possible constant factor related to the hurwitz zeta function. In *Progress in Approximation Theory and Applicable Complex Analysis: In Memory of QI Rahman*; Springer: Cham, Switzerland, 2017; pp. 183–218.
11. Yang, B.; Wu, S.; Chen, Q. A new extension of Hardy-Hilbert's inequality containing kernel of double power functions. *Mathematics* **2020**, *8*, 894. [CrossRef]
12. Yang, B.; Wu, S.; Wang, A. A new Hilbert-type inequality with positive homogeneous kernel and its equivalent forms. *Symmetry* **2020**, *12*, 342. [CrossRef]
13. Liao, J.; Wu, S.; Yang, B. On a new half-discrete Hilbert-type inequality involving the variable upper limit integral and partial sums. *Mathematics* **2020**, *8*, 229. [CrossRef]
14. Agarwal, R.; O'Regan, D.; Saker, S. *Dynamic Inequalities on Time Scales*; Springer: Cham, Switzerland, 2014.
15. Akin-Bohner, E.; Bohner, M.; Akin, F. Pachpatte inequalities on time scales. *JIPAM J. Inequal. Pure Appl. Math.* **2005**, *6*, 6.
16. Bohner, M.; Matthews, T. The Grüss inequality on time scales. *Commun. Math. Anal.* **2007**, *3*, 1–8.
17. Bohner, M.; Matthews, T. Ostrowski inequalities on time scales. *JIPAM J. Inequal. Pure Appl. Math.* **2008**, *9*, 8.
18. Dinu, C. Hermite-Hadamard inequality on time scales. *J. Inequal. Appl.* **2008**, *2008*, 287947. [CrossRef]
19. Hilscher, R. A time scales version of a Wirtinger-type inequality and applications. *J. Comput. Appl. Math.* **2002**, *141*, 219–226. [CrossRef]
20. Li, W.N. Some delay integral inequalities on time scales. *Comput. Math. Appl.* **2010**, *59*, 1929–1936. [CrossRef]
21. Řehák, P. Hardy inequality on time scales and its application to half-linear dynamic equations. *J. Inequal. Appl.* **2005**, *2005*, 942973. [CrossRef]
22. Agarwal, R.P.; Lakshmikantham, V. *Uniqueness and Nonuniqueness Criteria for Ordinary Differential Equations*; Series in Real Analysis; World Scientific Publishing: Singapore, 1993; Volume 6.
23. Li, J.D. Opial-type integral inequalities involving several higher order derivatives. *J. Math. Anal. Appl.* **1992**, *167*, 98–110.
24. Hilger, S. Ein Maßkettenkalkül mit Anwendung auf Zentrumsmannigfaltigkeiten. Ph.D. Thesis, Universität Würzburg, Würzburg, Germany, 1988.
25. Rahmat, M.R.S.; Noorani, M.S.M. A new conformable nabla derivative and its application on arbitrary time scales. *Adv. Differ. Equ.* **2021**, *2021*, 238. [CrossRef]
26. Cloud, M.J.; Drachman, B.C.; Lebedev, L. *Inequalities*; Springer: Berlin/Heidelberg, Germany, 1998.
27. Pachpatte, B.G. Inequalities similar to certain extensions of Hilbert's inequality. *J. Math. Anal. Appl.* **2000**, *243*, 217–227. [CrossRef]

axioms

MDPI

Article

A Study of the Monotonic Properties of Solutions of Neutral Differential Equations and Their Applications

Osama Moaaz [1,2,*] **and Abtehal E. Alhgilan** [1]

[1] Department of Mathematics, College of Science, Qassim University, P.O. Box 6644, Buraydah 51452, Saudi Arabia; 411203459@qu.edu.sa
[2] Department of Mathematics, Faculty of Science, Mansoura University, Mansoura 35516, Egypt
* Correspondence: o.refaei@qu.edu.sa or o_moaaz@mans.edu.eg

Abstract: In this paper, we aim to study the monotonic properties of the solutions of a class of neutral delay differential equations. The importance of this study lies in the fact that the monotonic properties largely control the study of the oscillation and asymptotic behaviour of the solutions to delay differential equations. Then, by using the new properties, we create improved criteria for testing the oscillation of solutions to the studied equation. We also find new criteria that can be applied more than once. Moreover, we discuss the importance and novelty of the results through the application to a special case of the studied equation.

Keywords: delay differential equation; neutral delay; monotonic properties; oscillation

MSC: 34C10; 34K11

Citation: Moaaz, O.; Alhgilan, A.E. A Study of the Monotonic Properties of Solutions of Neutral Differential Equations and Their Applications. *Axioms* **2023**, *12*, 346. https://doi.org/10.3390/axioms12040346

Academic Editors: Delfim F. M. Torres and Wei-Shih Du

Received: 13 February 2023
Revised: 11 March 2023
Accepted: 29 March 2023
Published: 31 March 2023

1. Introduction

Differential equations are the most important link between mathematics and applied sciences, biology, engineering and others. Differential equation models that describe different phenomena enable us to study, analyse and understand these phenomena. However, this requires either solving these models or studying the properties of their solutions. The first aspect is covered by analytical or numerical methods by finding exact or approximate solutions to these models. As for the other side, it is covered by the qualitative theory, which is concerned with investigating the qualitative characteristics of solutions such as oscillation, periodicity, stability, and others.

Oscillation theory is the theory concerned with the investigation of the asymptotic and oscillatory behaviour of solutions to differential equations. This theory is concerned with finding conditions that confirm that all solutions of the equation are oscillatory, guarantee the existence of an oscillatory solution, provide an asymptotic property for non-oscillatory solutions, or study the distance between the zeros of oscillatory solutions.

Neutral differential equations (NDEs) are one type of delay differential equation (DDEs) in which the highest derivative appears on the solution with and without delay. In electrical circuits containing lossless transmission lines and in the study of vibrating masses, models of NDEs appear, see [1]. With the development of new models and the significant technical and scientific advancement that the world is currently experiencing in engineering, biology, and physics, interest in understanding the qualitative properties of DDEs is growing, see [2–5].

In this work, we investigate the asymptotic behaviour of solutions to the even-order NDEs of the form

$$\frac{\mathrm{d}^n}{\mathrm{d}\mathrm{s}^n}\mathcal{U}(\mathrm{s}) + \phi(\mathrm{s})x(\delta(\mathrm{s})) = 0, \qquad (1)$$

where $\mathrm{s} \geq \mathrm{s}_0$, $n \geq 4$ is even, and $\mathcal{U} = x + \varphi \cdot (x \circ \beta)$. We also assume the following conditions:

(C1) φ and ϕ are continuous on $[s_0, \infty)$ and satisfy the conditions: $0 \le \varphi(s) \le \varphi_0$, $\phi(s) > 0$, and ϕ does not vanish identically on any half-line $[s_*, \infty)$, for $s_* \ge s_0$.
(C2) β and δ are continuous delay functions on $[s_0, \infty)$ and fulfil the conditions: $\beta(s) \le s$, $\delta(s) \le s$, $\delta'(s) \ge 0$ and $\lim_{s\to\infty} \beta(s) = \lim_{s\to\infty} \delta(s) = \infty$.

For a solution of (1), we mean a real function $x \in \mathbf{C}([s_*, \infty))$ for $s_* \ge s_0$, which has the property $\mathcal{U} \in \mathbf{C}^n([s_*, \infty))$ and x satisfies (1) on $[s_*, \infty)$. We take into account these solutions x of (1) such that $\sup\{|x(s)| : s \ge s_1\} > 0$ for $s_1 \ge s_*$. A solution x of (1) is said to be non-oscillatoryif it is eventually positive or negative; otherwise, it is said to be oscillatory.

The last decade has witnessed a great development in the study of the oscillatory behaviour of different-order DDEs. Monographs [6–10] have collected the most important results in the oscillation theory of DDEs up to the decade before last.

It is easy to notice the great development in the study of oscillations of second-order DDEs. For example, Bohner et al. [11] and Džurina et al. [12] developed an improved approach to study the oscillation of NDE

$$\left(r(s)(\mathcal{U}'(s))^{\alpha}\right)' + \phi(s)x^{\alpha}(\delta(s)) = 0, \tag{2}$$

in the non-canonical case. Later, Grace et al. [13] extended the approach in [11] to the canonical case of NDE (2). Moaaz et al. [14] presented more efficient criteria for testing the oscillation of NDE (2) in the canonical case based on the definition of two Riccati substitutions. Whereas more recently, Bohner et al. [15] and Jadlovská [16] obtained sharp criteria to ensure the oscillation of NDE (2).

On the other hand, the study of oscillation of higher-order DDEs has also received great attention recently. Agarwal et al. [17] and Li and Rogovchenko [18] introduced criteria for the oscillation of NDE (1). Therefore, from [18], we mention the following result:

Theorem 1. *Assume that $\beta'(s) \ge 0$ and there are functions $\varkappa \in \mathbf{C}([s_0, \infty))$ and $\theta \in \mathbf{C}^1([s_0, \infty))$ such that $\theta'(s) \ge 0$, $\varkappa(s) \to \infty$ and $\theta(s) \to \infty$ as $s \to \infty$,*

$$\max\{\varkappa(s),\ \theta(s)\} \le \delta(s) \text{ and } \max\{\varkappa(s),\ \theta(s)\} < \beta(s).$$

If

$$\liminf_{s\to\infty} \int_{\beta^{-1}(\delta(s))}^{s} \phi(l) K_1(\delta(l)) \left(\beta^{-1}(\varkappa(l))\right)^{n-1} dl > \frac{(n-1)!}{e} \tag{3}$$

and

$$\liminf_{s\to\infty} \int_{\beta^{-1}(\delta(s))}^{s} \left(\int_l^{\infty} \phi(v)(l-v)^{n-3} K_2(\delta(l)) dv\right) \beta^{-1}(\delta(l)) dl > \frac{(n-3)!}{e}, \tag{4}$$

then all solutions of (1) oscillate, where

$$K_1(s) := \frac{1}{\varphi(\beta^{-1}(s))}\left[1 - \frac{\left(\beta^{-1}(\beta^{-1}(s))\right)^{n-1}}{\left(\beta^{-1}(s)\right)^{n-1}\varphi(\beta^{-1}(\beta^{-1}(s)))}\right],$$

and

$$K_2(s) := \frac{1}{\varphi(\beta^{-1}(s))}\left[1 - \frac{\beta^{-1}(\beta^{-1}(s))}{\beta^{-1}(s)\varphi(\beta^{-1}(\beta^{-1}(s)))}\right].$$

The oscillatory behaviour of solutions of the DDE

$$\left(r(s)\left(x^{(n-1)}(s)\right)^{\alpha}\right)' + \phi(s) f(x(\delta(s))) = 0 \tag{5}$$

has been studied by several techniques. In 2012, Baculikova et al. [19] derived criteria for oscillation using comparative principles by comparing DDE (5) with three first-order equations, whereas Zhang et al. [20] and Li and Rogovchenko [21] used the Riccati substitution to obtain criteria for the oscillation of DDE (5) when $f(x) = x^{\beta}$. Moaaz and Muhib [22] used general Riccati substitution to improve the results in [19,20] when $n = 4$. Moaaz et al. [23] improved and simplified the oscillation criteria for (5).

In [24–27], the oscillation of NDE

$$\left(r(s)\left(\mathcal{U}^{(n-1)}(s)\right)^{\alpha}\right)' + \phi(s)f(x(\delta(s))) = 0, \tag{6}$$

or special cases of it, has been studied. Zhang et al. [24] considered DDE (6) when $r(s) = 1$ and $\alpha = 1$, and obtained conditions for oscillation of all solutions. By using the Riccati transformation technique, Baculikova and Dzurina [25] studied the oscillatory behaviour of (6), whereas Baculikova and Dzurina [26] were interested in studying the linear case of (6) by using the comparison technique. Very recently, Salah et al. [27] presented a comparison between the different approaches that relied on the comparison technique to study the oscillation of solutions to (6).

In this article, we find new monotonic properties of a class of positive solutions to DDE (1). Using these properties, we improve the relationship between the solution x and its corresponding function $\mathcal{U}$. To increase positive solutions, the traditional relation $x > (1-\varphi)\mathcal{U}$ is usually used which requires that $\varphi < 1$ be specified. Furthermore, the works that studied the case $\varphi \geq 1$ imposed restrictions on the delay functions in the form $\beta \circ \delta = \delta \circ \beta$. Our results consider the case $\varphi \geq 1$ but do not require the condition $\beta \circ \delta = \delta \circ \beta$. We use the comparison technique to obtain the oscillation theorems that provide criteria ensuring that all solutions of DDE (1) oscillate.

2. Monotonic Properties

Before looking at the oscillation of the DDE, it is known that determining the signs of the derivatives of the solution is necessary. Establishing relationships between derivatives of various orders is also crucial, although doing so may impose further limitations on the study. The most influential factor in the relationships between derivatives is the monotonic properties of the solutions of these equations. Therefore, improving these properties or finding new properties of an iterative nature greatly affects the qualitative study of solutions to these equations.

While presenting the results, we will need the following notations:

$$F_{[1]} := F\ , F_{[i+1]} = F \circ F_{[i]}, \text{ for } i = 1,2,3,....$$

The following lemma can be directly obtained from applying Lemma 2.2.1 in [28].

Lemma 1. *Assume that x is one of the eventually positive solutions of (1). Then $\mathcal{U}(s) > 0$, $\mathcal{U}^{(n-1)}(s) > 0$, $\mathcal{U}^{(n)}(s) \leq 0$, and one of the following possibilities is satisfied, eventually:*

(D_1) $\mathcal{U}^{(i)}(s) > 0$ *for* $i = 1,2,...,n-1$;

(D_2) $(-1)^{i+1}\mathcal{U}^{(i)}(s) > 0$ *for* $i = 1,...,n-2$.

Notation 1. *Solutions x whose corresponding function $\mathcal{U}$ satisfy case (D_1) are indicated by class $\mathcal{F}_*$. Moreover, we will use the following condition to prove the main results:*

(C) *there is a* $\kappa > 0$ *such that* $(1-\varphi(s))s\,\delta^{n-1}(s)\,\phi(s) \geq (n-1)!\,\kappa$.

Lemma 2. *Assume that $x \in \mathcal{F}_*$. Then, eventually,*

$$\mathcal{U}(s) \geq \frac{\epsilon_1 s}{(n-1)} \frac{d}{ds}\mathcal{U}(s), \tag{7}$$

and

$$\mathcal{U}(s) \geq \frac{\epsilon_2 s^{n-1}}{(n-1)!} \frac{d^{n-1}}{ds^{n-1}}\mathcal{U}(s), \tag{8}$$

for all $\epsilon_i \in (0,1)$, $i = 1,2$.

Proof. By using Lemma 1 in [29] and Lemma 2.2.3 in [28], we directly obtain the proof of this lemma. Therefore, it has been left out. □

Lemma 3. *Assume that* $x \in \mathcal{F}_*$ *and* (C) *holds. Then,*

(a) $\lim \frac{\mathcal{U}^{(n-r)}}{s^{r-1}} = 0$,

(b) $\frac{d}{ds}\frac{\mathcal{U}^{(n-r)}}{s^{r-1}} < 0$,

for $r = 1, 2, ..., n$, *eventually.*

Proof. Using the fact that $\mathcal{U}^{(n-1)}$ is a non-increasing positive function, we obtain $\lim_{s\to\infty} \mathcal{U}^{(n-1)} = k \geq 0$. Suppose that $k > 0$. Then, $\mathcal{U}^{(n-1)} \geq k$, for $s \geq s_1$. From Lemma 2, we arrive at

$$x(s) \geq (1 - \varphi(s))\mathcal{U}(s) \geq \frac{k\epsilon_2(1-\varphi(s))}{(n-1)!}s^{n-1},$$

which with (1) and (C) gives

$$\begin{aligned} \frac{d^n}{ds^n}\mathcal{U}(s) &\leq -\frac{k\epsilon_2(1-\varphi(s))}{(n-1)!}\delta^{n-1}(s)\phi(s) \\ &\leq -\frac{k\epsilon_2}{(n-1)!}\frac{1}{s}. \end{aligned} \tag{9}$$

Integrating (9) from s_1 to s gives

$$\begin{aligned} \mathcal{U}^{(n-1)}(s_1) &\geq \mathcal{U}^{(n-1)}(s) + \frac{k\epsilon_2}{(n-1)!}\ln\frac{s}{s_1} \\ &\geq k + \frac{k\epsilon_2}{(n-1)!}\ln\frac{s}{s_1} \to \infty \text{ as } s \to \infty, \end{aligned}$$

which is a contradiction. Thus, $\lim_{s\to\infty} \mathcal{U}^{(n-1)} = 0$. Now, by applying l'Hôpital's rule, we obtain that (a) holds.

Next, we have

$$\begin{aligned} \mathcal{U}^{(n-2)} &= \mathcal{U}^{(n-2)}(s_1) + \int_{s_1}^{s} \mathcal{U}^{(n-1)}(l)dl \\ &\geq \mathcal{U}^{(n-2)}(s_1) + (s - s_1)\mathcal{U}^{(n-1)}(s). \end{aligned} \tag{10}$$

Since $\lim_{s\to\infty} \mathcal{U}^{(n-1)} = 0$, there is an $s_2 \geq s_1$ such that $\mathcal{U}^{(n-2)}(s_1) - s_1\mathcal{U}^{(n-1)}(s) \geq 0$ for $s \geq s_2$. Thus, (10) becomes $\mathcal{U}^{(n-2)} \geq s\mathcal{U}^{(n-1)}$, and so

$$\frac{d}{ds}\frac{\mathcal{U}^{(n-2)}}{s} < 0.$$

Using the fact that $\mathcal{U}^{(n-2)}/s$ is positive and decreasing, we obtain

$$\begin{aligned} \mathcal{U}^{(n-3)}(s) &= \mathcal{U}^{(n-3)}(s_2) + \int_{s_2}^{s} \mathcal{U}^{(n-2)}(l)dl \\ &\geq \mathcal{U}^{(n-3)}(s_2) + \frac{\mathcal{U}^{(n-2)}(s)}{s}\int_{s_2}^{s} l dl \\ &= \mathcal{U}^{(n-3)}(s_2) + \frac{1}{2}\left(s^2 - s_2^2\right)\frac{\mathcal{U}^{(n-2)}(s)}{s}. \end{aligned} \tag{11}$$

Since $\lim_{s\to\infty} \mathcal{U}^{(n-2)}/s = 0$, there is an $s_3 \geq s_2$ such that $\mathcal{U}^{(n-3)}(s_2) - \frac{s_2^2}{2s}\mathcal{U}^{(n-2)}(s) \geq 0$ for $s \geq s_3$. Thus, (11) becomes $\mathcal{U}^{(n-3)} \geq \frac{1}{2}s\mathcal{U}^{(n-2)}$, and hence

$$\frac{d}{ds}\frac{\mathcal{U}^{(n-3)}}{s^2} < 0.$$

By repeating the same approach, we obtain (b). The proof is complete. □

Lemma 4. *Assume that $x \in \mathcal{F}_*$ and (C) holds. Then,*

$$x(s) \geq \sum_{k=1}^{m}\left(\prod_{i=1}^{2k-1}\frac{1}{\varphi\left(\beta_{[i]}^{-1}(s)\right)}\right)\left[1 - \frac{1}{\varphi\left(\beta_{[2k]}^{-1}(s)\right)}\left(\frac{\beta_{[2k]}^{-1}(s)}{\beta_{[2k-1]}^{-1}(s)}\right)^{(n-1)}\right]\mathcal{U}\left(\beta_{[2k-1]}^{-1}(s)\right),$$

for all $\epsilon \in (0,1)$.

Proof. Let $x \in \mathcal{F}_*$. From the definition of $\mathcal{U}$, we arrive at

$$\begin{aligned} x(s) &= \frac{\mathcal{U}(\beta^{-1}(s)) - x(\beta^{-1}(s))}{\varphi(\beta^{-1}(s))} \\ &= \frac{\mathcal{U}(\beta^{-1}(s))}{\varphi(\beta^{-1}(s))} - \frac{\mathcal{U}\left(\beta_{[2]}^{-1}(s)\right) - x\left(\beta_{[2]}^{-1}(s)\right)}{\varphi(\beta^{-1}(s))\varphi\left(\beta_{[2]}^{-1}(s)\right)} \\ &= \frac{\mathcal{U}(\beta^{-1}(s))}{\varphi(\beta^{-1}(s))} - \frac{\mathcal{U}\left(\beta_{[2]}^{-1}(s)\right)}{\varphi\left(\beta_{[1]}^{-1}(s)\right)\varphi\left(\beta_{[2]}^{-1}(s)\right)} + \frac{\mathcal{U}\left(\beta_{[3]}^{-1}(s)\right) - x\left(\beta_{[3]}^{-1}(s)\right)}{\varphi\left(\beta_{[1]}^{-1}(s)\right)\varphi\left(\beta_{[2]}^{-1}(s)\right)\varphi\left(\beta_{[3]}^{-1}(s)\right)}, \end{aligned}$$

and so

$$\begin{aligned} x(s) &= \sum_{k=1}^{2m}\left(\prod_{i=1}^{k}\frac{1}{\varphi\left(\beta_{[i]}^{-1}(s)\right)}\right)(-1)^{k+1}\mathcal{U}\left(\beta_{[k]}^{-1}(s)\right) + x\left(\beta_{[2m]}^{-1}(s)\right)\prod_{i=1}^{2m}\frac{1}{\varphi\left(\beta_{[i]}^{-1}(s)\right)} \\ &\geq \sum_{k=1}^{m}\left(\prod_{i=1}^{2k-1}\frac{1}{\varphi\left(\beta_{[i]}^{-1}(s)\right)}\right)\left[\mathcal{U}\left(\beta_{[2k-1]}^{-1}(s)\right) - \frac{1}{\varphi\left(\beta_{[2k]}^{-1}(s)\right)}\mathcal{U}\left(\beta_{[2k]}^{-1}(s)\right)\right]. \end{aligned} \tag{12}$$

From Lemma 3 and the fact that $\beta(s) \leq s$, we obtain

$$\mathcal{U}\left(\beta_{[2k]}^{-1}(s)\right) \leq \left(\frac{\beta_{[2k]}^{-1}(s)}{\beta_{[2k-1]}^{-1}(s)}\right)^{(n-1)}\mathcal{U}\left(\beta_{[2k-1]}^{-1}(s)\right),$$

which in (12) gives

$$x(s) \geq \sum_{k=1}^{m}\left(\prod_{i=1}^{2k-1}\frac{1}{\varphi\left(\beta_{[i]}^{-1}(s)\right)}\right)\left[1 - \frac{1}{\varphi\left(\beta_{[2k]}^{-1}(s)\right)}\left(\frac{\beta_{[2k]}^{-1}(s)}{\beta_{[2k-1]}^{-1}(s)}\right)^{(n-1)}\right]\mathcal{U}\left(\beta_{[2k-1]}^{-1}(s)\right).$$

The proof is complete. □

3. Oscillation Results

Lemma 5. *Assume that* $\delta(s) \leq \beta(s)$, β^{-1} *is non-decreasing, and* (C) *holds. If*

$$\limsup_{s\to\infty}\left(\beta^{-1}(\delta(s))\right)^{n-1}\sum_{k=1}^{m}\left[\int_{\beta^{-1}(\delta(s))}^{s}\phi(l)\beta_k(\delta(l))\left(\frac{\beta^{-1}_{[2k-1]}(\delta(l))}{\beta^{-1}_{[2k-1]}(\delta(s))}\right)^{(n-1)}\mathrm{d}l+\int_{s}^{\infty}\phi(l)\beta_k(\delta(l))\mathrm{d}l\right] > (n-1)!, \tag{13}$$

for any $m \in \mathbb{N}$, *then* $\mathcal{F}_* = \emptyset$, *where*

$$\beta_k(s) := \left(\prod_{i=1}^{2k-1}\frac{1}{\varphi\left(\beta^{-1}_{[i]}(s)\right)}\right)\left[1-\frac{1}{\varphi\left(\beta^{-1}_{[2k]}(s)\right)}\left(\frac{\beta^{-1}_{[2k]}(s)}{\beta^{-1}_{[2k-1]}(s)}\right)^{(n-1)}\right]. \tag{14}$$

Proof. Let $x \in \mathcal{F}_*$. From Lemma 3, we have (a) and (b) hold. From Lemma 4, Equation (1) becomes

$$\mathcal{U}^{(n)}(s)+\phi(s)\sum_{k=1}^{m}\beta_k(\delta(s))\mathcal{U}\left(\beta^{-1}_{[2k-1]}(\delta(s))\right)\leq 0, \tag{15}$$

An integration of (15) yields

$$\mathcal{U}^{(n-1)}(s)\geq\int_{s}^{\infty}\left(\phi(l)\sum_{k=1}^{m}\beta_k(\delta(l))\mathcal{U}\left(\beta^{-1}_{[2k-1]}(\delta(l))\right)\right)\mathrm{d}l. \tag{16}$$

If $\delta(s) \leq \beta(s)$, then we obtain

$$\begin{aligned}\mathcal{U}^{(n-1)}\left(\beta^{-1}(\delta(s))\right) &\geq \int_{\beta^{-1}(\delta(s))}^{\infty}\left(\phi(l)\sum_{k=1}^{m}\beta_k(\delta(l))\mathcal{U}\left(\beta^{-1}_{[2k-1]}(\delta(l))\right)\right)\mathrm{d}l\\ &= \int_{\beta^{-1}(\delta(s))}^{s}\left(\phi(l)\sum_{k=1}^{m}\beta_k(\delta(l))\mathcal{U}\left(\beta^{-1}_{[2k-1]}(\delta(l))\right)\right)\mathrm{d}l\\ &\quad+\int_{s}^{\infty}\left(\phi(l)\sum_{k=1}^{m}\beta_k(\delta(l))\mathcal{U}\left(\beta^{-1}_{[2k-1]}(\delta(l))\right)\right)\mathrm{d}l.\end{aligned}$$

Using (b) and the fact that $\mathcal{U}'(s) \geq 0$, we find

$$\begin{aligned}&\mathcal{U}^{(n-1)}\left(\beta^{-1}(\delta(s))\right)\\ \geq\;& \sum_{k=1}^{m}\mathcal{U}\left(\beta^{-1}_{[2k-1]}(\delta(s))\right)\left[\int_{\beta^{-1}(\delta(s))}^{s}\phi(l)\beta_k(\delta(l))\left(\frac{\beta^{-1}_{[2k-1]}(\delta(l))}{\beta^{-1}_{[2k-1]}(\delta(s))}\right)^{(n-1)}\mathrm{d}l+\int_{s}^{\infty}\phi(l)\beta_k(\delta(l))\mathrm{d}l\right]\\ \geq\;& \mathcal{U}\left(\beta^{-1}(\delta(s))\right)\sum_{k=1}^{m}\left[\int_{\beta^{-1}(\delta(s))}^{s}\phi(l)\beta_k(\delta(l))\left(\frac{\beta^{-1}_{[2k-1]}(\delta(l))}{\beta^{-1}_{[2k-1]}(\delta(s))}\right)^{(n-1)}\mathrm{d}l+\int_{s}^{\infty}\phi(l)\beta_k(\delta(l))\mathrm{d}l\right].\end{aligned}$$

From (b), we arrive at

$$1\geq\frac{\left(\beta^{-1}(\delta(s))\right)^{n-1}}{(n-1)!}\sum_{k=1}^{m}\left[\int_{\beta^{-1}(\delta(s))}^{s}\phi(l)\beta_k(\delta(l))\left(\frac{\beta^{-1}_{[2k-1]}(\delta(l))}{\beta^{-1}_{[2k-1]}(\delta(s))}\right)^{(n-1)}\mathrm{d}l+\int_{s}^{\infty}\phi(l)\beta_k(\delta(l))\mathrm{d}l\right],$$

which contradicts (13). The proof is complete. □

Lemma 6. *Assume that* (C) *holds and, for any* $m \in \mathbb{N}$, *the DDE*

$$w'(s) + \frac{\epsilon}{(n-1)!}\phi(s)w\left(\beta^{-1}_{[2m-1]}(\delta(s))\right)\sum_{k=1}^{m}\beta_k(\delta(s))\left(\beta^{-1}_{[2k-1]}(\delta(s))\right)^{n-1} = 0, \text{ if } \delta(s) \le \beta_{[2m-1]}(s), \tag{17}$$

or

$$y'(s) + \phi(s)\frac{\epsilon}{(n-1)!}\left(\beta^{-1}(\delta(s))\right)^{n-1} y\left(\beta^{-1}(\delta(s))\right)\sum_{k=1}^{m}\beta_k(\delta(s)) = 0., \text{ if } \delta(s) \le \beta(s), \tag{18}$$

is oscillatory for some $\epsilon \in (0,1)$, *then* $\mathcal{F}_* = \emptyset$, *where* β_k *is defined as in (14).*

Proof. Let $x \in \mathcal{F}_*$. From Lemma 2, we have that (8) holds. Using Lemma 4, Equation (1) reduces to (15). Thus, from (8), we obtain

$$\mathcal{U}^{(n)}(s) + \frac{\epsilon}{(n-1)!}\phi(s)\sum_{k=1}^{m}\beta_k(\delta(s))\left(\beta^{-1}_{[2k-1]}(\delta(s))\right)^{n-1}\mathcal{U}^{(n-1)}\left(\beta^{-1}_{[2k-1]}(\delta(s))\right) \le 0,$$

which, with the facts that $\mathcal{U}^{(n)} \le 0$ and $\beta^{-1}_{[2k-1]}(s) \le \beta^{-1}_{[2m-1]}$ for $k = 1,2,...,m$, gives

$$\mathcal{U}^{(n)}(s) + \frac{\epsilon}{(n-1)!}\phi(s)\mathcal{U}^{(n-1)}\left(\beta^{-1}_{[2m-1]}(\delta(s))\right)\sum_{k=1}^{m}\beta_k(\delta(s))\left(\beta^{-1}_{[2k-1]}(\delta(s))\right)^{n-1} \le 0.$$

Suppose that $w := \mathcal{U}^{(n-1)}$. Then $w > 0$ is a solution of

$$w'(s) + \frac{\epsilon}{(n-1)!}\phi(s)w\left(\beta^{-1}_{[2m-1]}(\delta(s))\right)\sum_{k=1}^{m}\beta_k(\delta(s))\left(\beta^{-1}_{[2k-1]}(\delta(s))\right)^{n-1} \le 0.$$

It follows from Theorem 1 in [30] that Equation (17) also has a positive solution, a contradiction.

On the other hand, using the fact that $\mathcal{U}' > 0$ and $\beta^{-1}(s) \le \beta^{-1}_{[2k-1]}$ for $k = 1,2,...,m$, the inequality in (15) becomes

$$\mathcal{U}^{(n)}(s) + \phi(s)\mathcal{U}\left(\beta^{-1}(\delta(s))\right)\sum_{k=1}^{m}\beta_k(\delta(s)) \le 0.$$

Thus, from (8), we obtain

$$\mathcal{U}^{(n)}(s) + \phi(s)\frac{\epsilon\left(\beta^{-1}(\delta(s))\right)^{n-1}}{(n-1)!}\mathcal{U}^{(n-1)}\left(\beta^{-1}(\delta(s))\right)\sum_{k=1}^{m}\beta_k(\delta(s)) \le 0.$$

Therefore, it follows from Theorem 1 in [30] that Equation (18) has a positive solution, a contradiction. The proof is complete. □

Corollary 1. *Assume that* (C) *holds,*

$$\liminf_{s\to\infty}\int_{\beta^{-1}_{[2m-1]}(\delta(s))}^{s}\left(\phi(l)\sum_{k=1}^{m}\beta_k(\delta(l))\left(\beta^{-1}_{[2k-1]}(\delta(l))\right)^{n-1}\right)dl > \frac{(n-1)!}{e}, \text{ if } \delta(s) \le \beta_{[2m-1]}(s), \tag{19}$$

or

$$\liminf_{s\to\infty}\int_{\beta^{-1}(\delta(s))}^{s}\left(\phi(l)\left(\beta^{-1}(\delta(l))\right)^{n-1}\sum_{k=1}^{m}\beta_k(\delta(l))\right)dl > \frac{(n-1)!}{e},\ if\ \delta(s)\le\beta(s), \tag{20}$$

is oscillatory, then $\mathcal{F}_* = \emptyset$*, where* β_k *is defined as in (14).*

Proof. From Theorem 2 in [31], conditions in (19) and (20) imply the oscillation of Equations (17) and (18), respectively. □

Theorem 2. *Assume that* $\delta(s)\le\beta(s)$, β^{-1} *is non-decreasing, and* (C) *and (13) hold. Then, Equation (1) is oscillatory if (4) holds.*

Proof. Assume that x is an eventually positive solution of (1). From Lemma 1, one of the possibilities (D_1) or (D_2) is satisfied. Using Lemma 5, we have $\mathcal{F}_* = \emptyset$. Then, case (D_2) holds. In exactly the same way as Theorem 2.1 in [18], we obtain a contradiction with (4). The proof is complete. □

Theorem 3. *Assume that* (C) *holds, and one of the conditions in (19) or (20) is satisfied. Then, Equation (1) is oscillatory if (4) holds.*

4. Application and Discussion

Example 1. *Consider the NDE*

$$(x(s)+\varphi_0 x(\mu s))^{(4)} + \frac{\phi_0}{s^4}x(\lambda s) = 0, \tag{21}$$

where $\varphi_0 > 0$, $\lambda < \mu \in (0,1)$, $\phi_0 > 0$, *and* $\mu^3\varphi_0 > 1$. *In the following we will apply the conditions of the theorems in the previous section to check the oscillation of this equation. Conditions in (13), (19) and (20) reduce to*

$$\phi_0\left(\frac{\lambda}{\mu}\right)^3\left[\ln\frac{\mu}{\lambda}+\frac{1}{3}\right]\left[1-\frac{1}{\mu^3\varphi_0}\right]\sum_{k=1}^{m}\frac{1}{\varphi_0^{2k-1}} > 3!, \tag{22}$$

$$\phi_0\lambda^3\left[1-\frac{1}{\mu^3\varphi_0}\right]\ln\left(\frac{\mu^{2m-1}}{\lambda}\right)\sum_{k=1}^{m}\left(\frac{1}{\varphi_0^{2k-1}}\left(\frac{1}{\mu^{2k-1}}\right)^3\right) > \frac{3!}{e},\ if\ \lambda<\mu^{2m-1} \tag{23}$$

and

$$\phi_0\left(\frac{\lambda}{\mu}\right)^3\left[1-\frac{1}{\mu^3\varphi_0}\right]\left(\ln\frac{\mu}{\lambda}\right)\sum_{k=1}^{m}\frac{1}{\varphi_0^{2k-1}} > \frac{3!}{e}, \tag{24}$$

respectively. The condition in (4) becomes

$$\phi_0\frac{1}{3\varphi_0}\frac{\lambda}{\mu}\left[1-\frac{1}{\mu\varphi_0}\right]\ln\frac{\mu}{\lambda} > \frac{1}{e}. \tag{25}$$

By using Theorems 2 and 3, Equation (21) is oscillatory if (25) and one of the conditions in (22), (23) or (24) are satisfied.

Remark 1. *Applying the results in the previous example to the special case of Equation (21), when* $\varphi_0 = 16$, $\mu = 1/2$, *and* $\lambda = 1/6$, *we conclude that Equation (21) is oscillatory if*

$$\phi_0 > \frac{1152}{7e\ln 3},\ [condition\ (25)]$$

and one of conditions (22), (23) or (24) is satisfied, see Table 1.

Table 1. Conditions (22), (23) and (24) when $\varphi_0 = 16$, $\mu = 1/2$, and $\lambda = 1/6$.

Condition	(22)	(23)	(24)
	$\phi_0 > 3606.1$	$\phi_0 > 1736$	$\phi_0 > 1729.1$

Therefore, Equation (21) is oscillatory if $\phi_0 > 1729.1$, while the results of [18] state that (21) is oscillatory if $\phi_0 > 1736$. Thus, our results improve upon those in [18].

Remark 2. *In Example 1, we note that criterion (24) often provides the best results. For comparison between the criteria in (3) and (24), we consider the special case when $\varphi_0 = 1/\mu^4$, and $\lambda = \mu^3$. Conditions in (3) and (24) reduce to*

$$\phi_0 > \frac{3!}{e\mu^{10}\left(\ln \frac{1}{\mu^2}\right)(1-\mu)} \tag{26}$$

and

$$\phi_0 > \frac{3!}{e\mu^{6}\left(\ln \frac{1}{\mu^2}\right)(1-\mu)\sum_{k=1}^{50}\mu^{8k-4}}, \tag{27}$$

respectively. Figure 1 shows a comparison of the lower bounds for the values of ϕ_0 for the conditions in (3) and (24) when $\mu \in (0.7, 0.9)$.

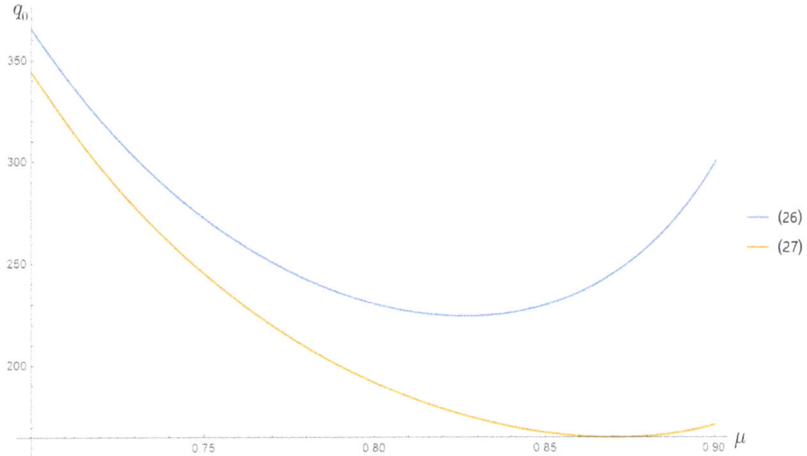

Figure 1. The minimum values of ϕ_0 for which (3) and (24) are satisfied.

5. Conclusions

The study of the oscillatory behaviour of DDEs depends mainly on the monotonic properties of the solutions. These properties control the relationships between the derivatives as well as the relationship between the solution and its corresponding function. Therefore, finding new or improving monotonic properties plays an important role in improving the oscillation parameters.

In this work, we obtained new monotonic properties, through which we were able to obtain a new and improved relationship linking the solution and its corresponding function. Then, we used this relationship to obtain oscillation criteria for the studied equation. Finally, we provided an example and comparisons to illustrate the importance of the results.

Recently, there has been a lot of research activity focused on studying the properties of solutions to fractional differential equations. It would be interesting to extend our results to fractional differential equations.

Author Contributions: Conceptualization, O.M. and A.E.A.; methodology, O.M. and A.E.A.; investigation, O.M. and A.E.A.; writing—original draft, A.E.A.; writing—review and editing, O.M. All authors have read and agreed to the published version of the manuscript.

Funding: The authors gratefully acknowledge Qassim University, represented by the Deanship of Scientific Research, on the financial support for this research under the number (COS-2022-1-1-J-27943) during the academic year 1444 AH/2022 AD.

Acknowledgments: The authors gratefully acknowledge Qassim University, represented by the Deanship of Scientific Research, on the financial support for this research under the number (COS-2022-1-1-J-27943) during the academic year 1444 AH/2022 AD.

Conflicts of Interest: The authors declare no conflict of interest.

References

1. Hale, J.K. Functional differential equations. In *Analytic Theory of Differential Equations*; Springer: Berlin/Heidelberg, Germany, 1971; pp. 9–22.
2. Goldbeter, A. Dissipative structures in biological systems: Bistability, oscillations, spatial patterns and waves. *Philos. Trans. R. Soc. A* **2018**, *376*, 20170376. [CrossRef]
3. Gopalsamy, K. *Stability and Oscillations in Delay Differential Equations of Population Dynamics*; Kluwer: Dordrecht, The Netherlands, 1992.
4. Mackey, M.C.; Glass, L. Oscillations and chaos in physiological control systems. *Science* **1977**, *197*, 287–289. [CrossRef] [PubMed]
5. Rihan, F.A. *Delay Differential Equations and Applications to Biology*; Springer Nature: Singapore, 2021.
6. Gyori, I.; Ladas, G. *Oscillation Theory of Delay Differential Equations with Applications*; Clarendon Press: Oxford, UK, 1991.
7. Erbe, L.H.; Kong, Q.; Zhong, B.G. *Oscillation Theory for Functional Differential Equations*; Marcel Dekker: New York, NY, USA, 1995.
8. Agarwal, R.P.; Grace, S.R.; O'Regan, D. *Oscillation Theory for Second Order Dynamic Equations*; Series in Mathematical Analysis and Applications; Taylor & Francis Ltd.: London, UK, 2003; Volume 5.
9. Agarwal, R.P.; Bohner, M.; Li, W.-T. Nonoscillation and oscillation: Theory for functional differential equations. In *Monographs and Textbooks in Pure and Applied Mathematics*; Marcel Dekker, Inc.: New York, NY, USA, 2004; Volume 267.
10. Saker, S. *Oscillation Theory of Delay Differential and Difference Equations: Second and Third Orders*; LAP Lambert Academic Publishing: Saarbruecken, Germany, 2010.
11. Bohner, M.; Grace, S.R.; Jadlovská, I. Oscillation criteria for second-order neutral delay differential equations. *Electron. J. Qual. Theory Differ. Equ.* **2017**, *60*, 2017. [CrossRef]
12. Džurina, J.; Grace, S.R.; Jadlovska, I.; Li, T. Oscillation criteria for second-order Emden–Fowler delay differential equations with a sublinear neutral term. *Math. Nachr.* **2020** , *293*, 910–922. [CrossRef]
13. Grace, S.R.; Džurina, J.; Jadlovská, I.; Li, T. An improved approach for studying oscillation of second-order neutral delay differential equations. *J. Inequalities Appl.* **2018**, *193*, 2018. [CrossRef] [PubMed]
14. Moaaz, O.; Ramos, H.; Awrejcewicz, J. Second-order Emden–Fowler neutral differential equations: A new precise criterion for oscillation. *Appl. Math. Lett.* **2021**, *118*, 107172. [CrossRef]
15. Bohner, M.; Grace, S.R.; Jadlovská, I. Sharp oscillation criteria for second-order neutral delay differential equations. *Math. Method. Appl. Sci.* **2020**, *43*, 10041–10053. [CrossRef]
16. Jadlovská, I. New criteria for sharp oscillation of second-order neutral delay differential equations. *Mathematics* **2021**, *9*, 2089. [CrossRef]
17. Agarwal, R.P.; Bohner, M.; Li, T.; Zhang, C. A new approach in the study of oscillatory behavior of even-order neutral delay differential equations. *Appl. Math. Comput.* **2013**, *225*, 787–794. [CrossRef]
18. Li, T.; Rogovchenko, Y.V. Oscillation criteria for even-order neutral differential equations. *Appl. Math. Lett.* **2016**, *61*, 35–41. [CrossRef]
19. Baculikova, B.; Dzurina, J.; Graef, J.R. On the oscillation of higher order delay differential equations. *J. Math. Sci.* **2012**, *187*, 13–24. [CrossRef]
20. Zhang, C.; Agarwal, R.P.; Bohner, M.; Li, T. New results for oscillatory behavior of even-order half-linear delay differential equations. *Appl. Math. Lett.* **2013**, *26*, 179–183. [CrossRef]
21. Li, T.; Rogovchenko, Y.V. On asymptotic behavior of solutions to higher-order sublinear Emden–Fowler delay differential equations. *Appl. Math. Lett.* **2017**, *67*, 53–59. [CrossRef]
22. Moaaz, O.; Muhib, A. New oscillation criteria for nonlinear delay differential equations of fourth-order. *Appl. Math. Comput.* **2020**, *377*, 125192. [CrossRef]
23. Moaaz, O.; Muhib, A.; Baleanu, D.; Alharbi, W.; Mahmoud, E.E. Simplified and improved criteria for oscillation of delay differential equations of fourth order. *Adv. Differ. Equ.* **2021**, *2021*, 295. [CrossRef]

24. Zhang, Q.; Yan, J.; Gao, L. Oscillation behavior of even order nonlinear neutral differential equations with variable coefficients. *Comput. Math. Appl.* **2010**, *59*, 426–430. [CrossRef]
25. Baculíková, B.; Dzurina, J.; Li, T. Oscillation results for even-order quasilinear neutral functional differential equations. *Electron. J. Differ. Equ.* **2011**, *2011*, 1–9.
26. Baculíková, B.; Dzurina, J. Oscillation theorems for higher order neutral differential equations. *Appl. Math. Comput .* **2012**, *219*, 3769–3778. [CrossRef]
27. Salah, H.; Moaaz, O.; Cesarano, C.; Elabbasy, E.M. Oscillation of higher-order canonical delay differential equations: Comparison theorems. *Phys. Scr.* **2023**, *98*, 024003. [CrossRef]
28. Agarwal, R.P.; Grace, S.R.; O'Regan, D. *Oscillation Theory for Difference and Functional Differential Equations*; Kluwer Academic: Dordrecht, The Netherlands, 2000.
29. Chatzarakis, G.E.; Grace, S.R.; Jadlovská, I.; Li, T.; Tun ç, E. Oscillation criteria for third-order Emden–Fowler differential equations with unbounded neutral coefficients. *Complexity* **2019**, *2019*, 5691758. [CrossRef]
30. Philos, C.G. On the existence of nonoscillatory solutions tending to zero at ∞ for dif ferential equations with positive delays. *Arch. Math.* **1981**, *36*, 168–178. [CrossRef]
31. Kitamura, Y.; Kusano, T. Oscillation of first-order nonlinear differential equations with deviating arguments. *Proc. Amer. Math. Soc.* **1980**, *78*, 64–68. [CrossRef]

axioms

Article

Mathematical Models of the Processes of Operation, Renewal and Degradation of a Fleet of Complex Technical Systems with Metrological Support

Rustam Khayrullin [1,2], Denis Ershov [2,3,*], Alexander Malahov [2,3] and Tatyana Levina [3]

1 Department of "Fundamental Education", Mytishchy Branch of University, Moscow State University of Civil Engineering, 26, Yaroslavskoye Shosse, 129337 Moscow, Russia
2 Metrology Scientific Head Center, 13 Komarova Street, Moscow Region, 141000 Mytischy, Russia
3 Department of "Standartizaion, Engineering Faculty, Moscow Polytechnic University, Metrology and Sertification", 38, Bolshaya Semenovskaya Street, 107023 Moscow, Russia
* Correspondence: ershov.metrolog@mail.ru

Abstract: (1) Background: The aim of the study is to develop a set of models for managing a fleet of complex technical systems with metrological support, allowing the simulation and management at all the stages of the life cycle of the complex technical systems, as well as to simulate the functioning of large fleets of complex technical systems, including up to several hundred thousand samples; (2) Methods: The authors use methods of mathematical modeling, methods of the theory of Markov and semi-Markov processes, methods of optimization, methods of reliability theory, and methods of probability theory and mathematical statistics; (3) Results: an interconnected set of mathematical models for managing a fleet of complex technical systems with metrological support was developed and the applied software was developed; (4) Conclusions: The set of models presented in the article allows for the adequate simulation of all the stages of the life cycle of large complex technical systems fleets, including up to several hundreds of thousands of samples, to optimize the functioning processes of a fleet of complex technical systems, to form strategies for fleet development, and to assess the risks associated with false and undetected failures, as well as the risks associated with the degradation of complex technical systems.

Keywords: complex technical system; measuring equipment; metrological support; measuring instruments

MSC: 60J20; 60-02

Citation: Khayrullin, R.; Ershov, D.; Malahov, A.; Levina, T. Mathematical Models of the Processes of Operation, Renewal and Degradation of a Fleet of Complex Technical Systems with Metrological Support. *Axioms* **2023**, *12*, 300. https://doi.org/10.3390/axioms12030300

Academic Editor: Clemente Cesarano

Received: 25 January 2023
Revised: 6 March 2023
Accepted: 8 March 2023
Published: 15 March 2023

1. Introduction

A considerable amount of scientific research is devoted to the problem of modeling complex technical systems (CTS) [1–28]. We understand complex technical system as stationary or mobile special-purpose objects with measuring instruments (MI) installed on them, which should be metrologically maintained during long-term operation. In the last half of the century, both CTS themselves and their models have undergone a rather rapid evolution process. Starting from models with 3–5 states and going up to models with up to several hundreds and thousands of states. At the same time, the theoretical base and technical capabilities for modeling CTS with several tens of thousands and even hundreds of thousands of states have been created.

On the qualitative side, simple models allowed modeling only of the basic states of the CTS, which describe the operation processes. The models have been evolving toward a more detailed description of the operation processes (taking into account metrological support technologies, false failure states and undetected failure states), the CTS degradation processes (first degradation level, second degradation level and so on) and the

CTS updating processes (by purchasing the new CTS samples, by upgrading the existing CTS samples, by developing the newest modern CTS samples). Thus, by now there is a need for models that describe all stages of the CTS life cycle. These models should allow the simulation of large CTS fleets, including up to several hundreds of thousands of STS samples. The models should make it possible to manage the process of development of such CTS fleets, taking into account the range of modern tasks to be solved by means of the CTS and the need to solve promising tasks in the future.

Let us first conduct a retrospective comparative analysis of CTS models, with a separate description of the main characteristics of each model, as well as the assumptions underlying their implementation. Let us describe the strengths and weaknesses of the models. Additionally, we will then formulate the goal of our scientific research and we will provide a statement on the problem that will be investigated in this article.

2. Scientific Literature Review

Professor L.I. Volkov [1] proposed the semi-Markov model of aircraft operation control, which has five states: workable status; periodic verifications of the operational status; recovery after the occurrence of the valid state, false failure state; the hidden failure state; the unworkable state (including the hidden failure state); and the state of periodic verifications with hidden failure.

The classical model developed by Professor E.I. Sychev [2], designed to control the process of operation of the CTS with measuring instruments (MI) installed on them to provide metrological support, in contrast to the model by Professor L.I. Volkov, already has six states. Model [2] describes the operation process more correctly. From the fourth unworkable state (including hidden failure), two states were separately highlighted: the state of undetected failure and detected failure. The model takes into account the characteristic features of the CTS with metrological support.

The model [2] assumes the identity of the recovery of the CTS after both a false failure and a valid failure. In practice, for some types of CTS, after a false failure, repeated control is carried out according to the failed technical parameter, and after a detected failure, the system is restored, for example, by adjusting or replacing the faulty element with a serviceable one. In the model [3] developed by Professor V.I. Mishchenko, which already includes seven states, the above-mentioned features and limitations have been eliminated. The model [3] takes into account the intensity of the CTS operation.

Note that the models described above do not take into account the component of maintenance efficiency, determined by the availability of spare parts and their replenishment strategy.

The further direction for the development of the models for the operation of the CTS is to take into account the possibilities of reserving the MI and the possibilities of replenishment with spare parts and tools. In [4], the model of the process for the functioning of the MI with metrological support for doubly redundant MI is proposed, which allows for the taking into account of the features of the maintenance associated with the possibility of providing spare parts, and taking into account the different strategies for replenishing spare parts, tools and accessories. In the model [4], which takes into account eight states, it is assumed: that the detection of failures by the MI occurs only during verification; there are no errors in determining the technical condition of the MI; and the MI in storage do not fail.

In [5], a new approach has been developed to assess the impact of metrological support on achieving the goals of the CTS operation: a graph with an arbitrary number of states is constructed, the edges of the graph that represent possible state transitions are attributed both probabilistic characteristics of the transitions (values of the distribution functions or simply the transition probabilities) and the costs associated with the corresponding transitions. The following states are selected: serviceable, faulty, emergency and catastrophic. The results from the study, on the influence of the volumes of metrological control for various conditions on the effectiveness of the object for its intended purpose, are presented.

As a criterion of efficiency in the various solved tasks, both the readiness coefficient and the technical and economic indicator were used.

It should be noted that all the models analyzed above do not allow modeling and the taking into account of conditions corresponding to the different levels of degradation of the CTS (different levels of deterioration of the metrological reliability characteristics), leading to time and resource costs necessary both for restoring the CTS and bringing it back into working condition. Further development of the CTS operation models takes place in terms of taking into account the aging and degradation processes [6–26] of the CTS (or MI installed on them) and reduction of the metrological reliability.

Thus, in [6] the model with four degradation groups is considered, having one workable state and four states corresponding to the different levels of degradation. This model describes the process of operation of the CTS, for which repair is possible with the restoration of the resource in full. In [7], a model with three degradation groups is considered, which allows for the modeling of the processes of operation, renewal and degradation of the CTS fleet. It is assumed that as a result of the repair, the resource of the CTS cannot be fully restored.

The works analyzed in this section form the basis (starting point) for the research presented in the article. This article summarizes the results of the work [5–8]: a set of models describing the processes of operation, renewal and degradation of the CTS are presented. To describe the operation process, the classical model [2] is used as it is the most adequate for the CTS class considered in the article. To describe the processes of degradation and renewal of the CTS fleet, new additions to the classical model developed by the author are presented (the model of false and undetected failures, the model of degradation and renewal of the fleet, including CTS with full and incomplete restoration of the resource during repair and metrological maintenance).

3. Statement on the Research Problem

It is necessary to develop a set of interrelated mathematical models of CTS fleet management models, allowing for the simulation and management of all stages of the CTS life cycle. The developed set of interrelated models should allow for the simulation of the functioning of large fleets of CTS, including up to several hundreds of thousands of CTS samples. The set of models shall allow for the taking into account of the degradation processes of CTS sample ageing, processes on park development due to the procurement of new samples, the modernization of existing samples and the development of new promising CTS samples. The set of interrelated models should allow for the management of the process of development of such CTS fleets, taking into account a number of modern requirements, and the need to solve promising tasks and problems in the future.

4. Materials and Methods

At first in Section 4.1.1, the results of calculating the readiness coefficient for different failure distribution laws using the classical operation model are presented. The model of false and undetected failures is described in Section 4.1.2. Section 4.1.3 describes and analyzes the models of failure and degradation of the CTS (a fan model, a drift model of the metrological characteristics and two diffusion models). In Section 4.2, the model of operation of the CTS is described, taking into account the degradation processes and the full restoration of the resource, and in Section 4.3, the model of the CTS with incomplete restoration of the resource is described.

4.1. The Classical Model

4.1.1. Construction and Study of the Classical Model for Different Laws on the Distribution of Failures of the Complex Technical System

Let us denote $\{E_i, i = 1, 2, \ldots n\}$ as a finite set of states in which a specific sample of the CTS can be located. The readiness coefficient of the CTS, the operation process of which is described by the semi-Markov model [2], is calculated by the formula:

$$K_A = \sum_{i=1}^{n} \pi_i w_i / \sum_{i=1}^{n} \pi_i \psi_i, \quad (1)$$

where π_i is the relative fraction of the number of steps during which the CTS is in state E_i, w_i is the mathematical expectation of the time of operation of the CTS in state E_i, and ψ_i is the mathematical expectation of the time that the CTS stays in state E_i.

At the same time: $\sum\limits_{i=1}^{n} \pi_i = 1$, $\psi_i = \sum\limits_{i=1}^{n} P_{ij} M(\tau_{ij}) = \sum\limits_{i=1}^{n} P_{ij} \int\limits_{0}^{\infty} \tau_{ij} dF(\tau_{ij})$,

$$w_i = \begin{cases} \psi_i - \text{for workable conditions of CTS} \\ 0 - \text{for unworkable conditions of CTS} \end{cases},$$

where P_{ij} are the elements of the state transition probability matrix $P^* = \left\| P^*_{ij} \right\|$, $F^*(\tau_{ij})$ is the transition probability distribution function, and $M(\tau_{ij})$ is the mathematical expectation of the transition time.

A continuously operating CTS with periodic verification of the technical condition is ready for use at that time τ if it is operational at that moment and is not under verification or repair. The results of the control are used to make a decision on the possibility of further application of the CTS. If the CTS is recognized as workable, according to the results of the verification, then it is included in the work. If the CTS is found to have failed, then its repair is carried out, as a result of which a complete restoration of its operability occurs. The transition graph is shown in Figure 1.

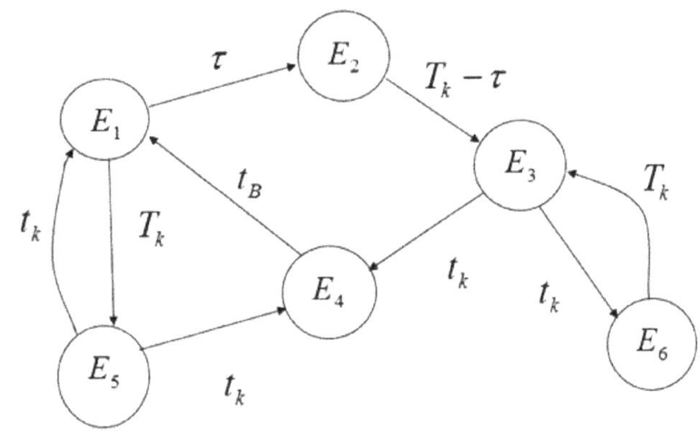

Figure 1. Graph of state transitions.

Possible conditions of the CTS: E_1 is workable, E_2 is unworkable (failure), E_3 is verification of the failed CTS, E_4 is recovery, E_5 is verification of a workable CTS, and E_6 is undetected failure.

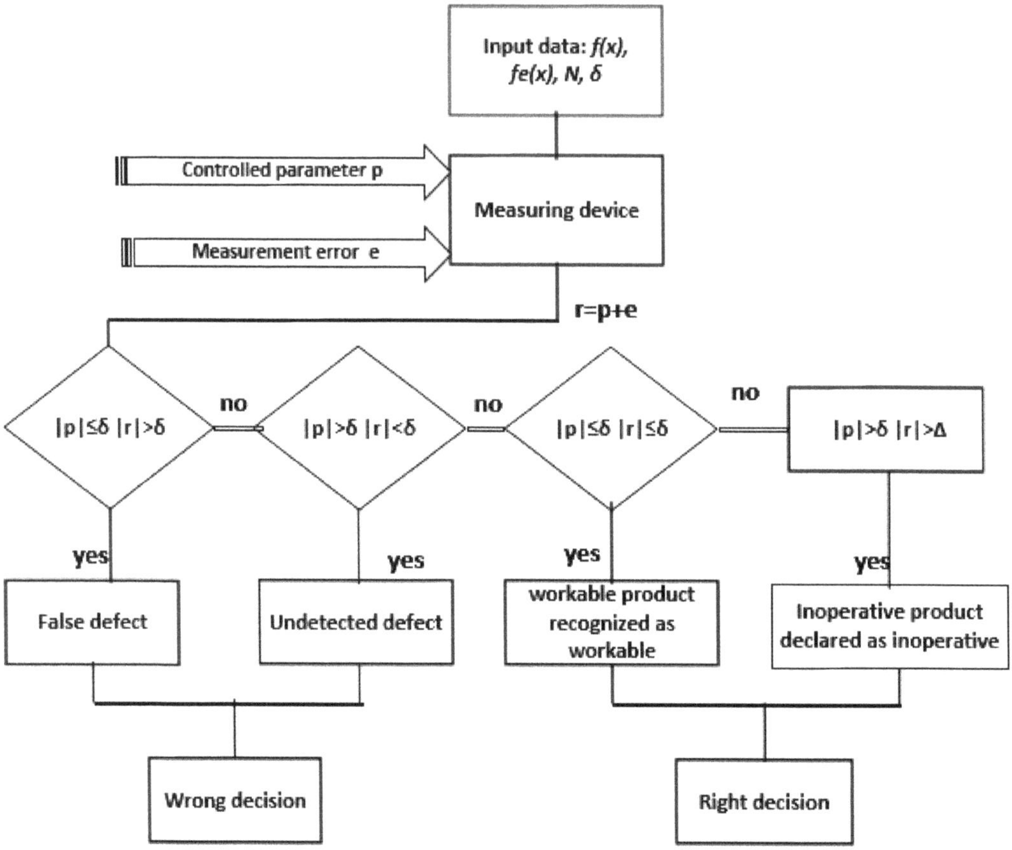

Figure 3. General scheme of diagnostics and decision-making based on the tolerance control method.

Here δ is the tolerance for the controlled parameter, and $f(x)$ and $f_e(x)$ are the distribution density functions of the measured parameter and the measurement error, respectively. It can be seen that the probability of making the right decision can be increased (within certain limits) by reducing the total error of the erroneous decision.

The different physical nature and, consequently, the heterogeneous range of the changes in the measured values leads to the need to introduce dimensionless standardized operational parameters for the MI. As a normalizing element, we take the mean square deviation σ_x of the measured parameter x; $\delta = \Delta/\sigma_x$ is the relative operational tolerance, where Δ is the technical tolerance; $z = \sigma_\varepsilon/\sigma_x$ is the relative parametric measurement error, σ_ε is the mean square deviation of the MI error.

The model is based on formulas for the conditional probabilities of false and undetected failures, respectively [8]:

$$\alpha(\delta,z) = \left\{ \int_{-\delta}^{\delta} f_{cu}(y) \left(\int_{-\infty}^{\frac{-\delta-y}{z}} f_o(\tau)d\tau + \int_{\frac{\delta-y}{z}}^{\infty} f_o(\tau)d\tau \right) dy \right\} / \left\{ \int_{-\delta}^{\delta} f_{cu}(y)dy \right\}, \quad (5)$$

$$\beta(\delta,z)=\left\{\int_{-\infty}^{-\delta} f_{cu}(y)\left(\int_{\frac{-\delta-y}{z}}^{\frac{\delta-y}{z}} f_0(\tau)d\tau\right)dy+\int_{\delta}^{\infty} f_{cu}(y)\left(\int_{\frac{-\delta-y}{z}}^{\frac{\delta-y}{z}} f_0(\tau)d\tau\right)dy\right\}/\left\{\int_{-\infty}^{-\delta} f_{cu}(y)dy+\int_{\delta}^{\infty} f_{cu}(y)dy\right\}, \quad (6)$$

where $f_0(\tau)$ and $f_{cu}(y)$ are the functions of the distribution densities of the measured value and the MI error, respectively.

For normally distributed measured values and MI errors, Formulas (5) and (6) take the form:

$$\alpha(\delta,z)=\frac{1}{2\pi}\left\{\int_{-\delta}^{\delta}\exp\left(-\frac{y^2}{2}\right)\left(\int_{-\infty}^{\frac{-\delta-y}{z}}\exp\left(-\frac{\tau^2}{2}\right)d\tau+\int_{\frac{\delta-y}{z}}^{\infty}\exp\left(-\frac{\tau^2}{2}\right)d\tau\right)dy\right\}/P1, \quad (7)$$

$$\beta(\delta,z)=\frac{1}{2\pi}\left\{\int_{-\infty}^{-\delta}\exp\left(-\frac{y^2}{2}\right)\left(\int_{\frac{-\delta-y}{z}}^{\frac{\delta-y}{z}}\exp\left(-\frac{\tau^2}{2}\right)d\tau\right)dy+\int_{\delta}^{\infty}\exp\left(-\frac{y^2}{2}\right)\left(\int_{\frac{-\delta-y}{z}}^{\frac{\delta-y}{z}}\exp\left(-\frac{\tau^2}{2}\right)d\tau\right)dy\right\}/P2, \quad (8)$$

$$P1=\frac{1}{\sqrt{2\pi}}\int_{-\delta}^{\delta}\exp\left(-\frac{y^2}{2}\right)dy,\ P2=\frac{1}{\sqrt{2\pi}}\left\{\int_{-\infty}^{-\delta}\exp\left(-\frac{y^2}{2}\right)dy+\int_{\delta}^{\infty}\exp\left(-\frac{y^2}{2}\right)dy\right\}$$

For other distribution laws on the measured value and measurement error, the model (5), (6) were investigated in [8].

The dependences of the probabilities $\alpha(\delta,z)$ and $\beta(\delta,z)$, as well as the probability $\alpha(\delta,z)+\beta(\delta,z)$ of an erroneous decision δ on the tolerance value at $z=0.5$ are shown in Figure 4.

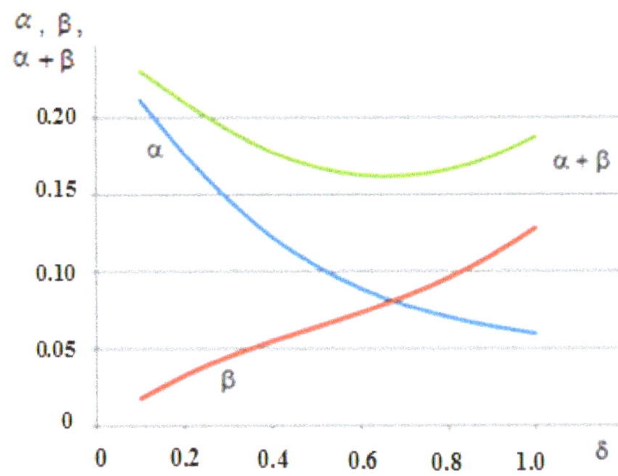

Figure 4. Dependences of the probability of an erroneous decision $(\alpha+\beta)$, as well as the probabilities of false and undetected failures on the value of the reduced tolerance δ on $z=0.5$.

Note also that the error solution function reaches its minimum at some internal point $\delta \in (0;1)$, as is the case with the normal distribution of the measured value and the measurement error.

The two-dimensional dependences of the probabilities of false and undetected failures on the magnitude of the dimensionless measurement error z and the dimensionless tolerance for the controlled parameter δ are shown in Figure 5a,b.

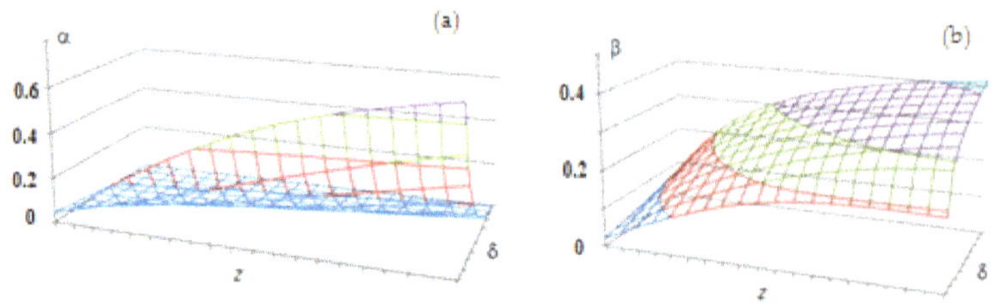

Figure 5. Probability of false failures (**a**); probability of undetected failures (**b**).

4.1.3. Development of the Classical Model: Models of Failures and Degradation of the Complex Technical System

All failure models that allow for the taking into account of the degradation processes occurring in the CTS can be conditionally divided into probabilistic, empirical, and probabilistic physical models, that includes among other things, the Markov models of degradation and failures.

In the fan model [9–11], also called a distribution and belonging to the category of probabilistic models, the defining parameter (DP) is represented as a linear function of time, shown in Figure 6a.

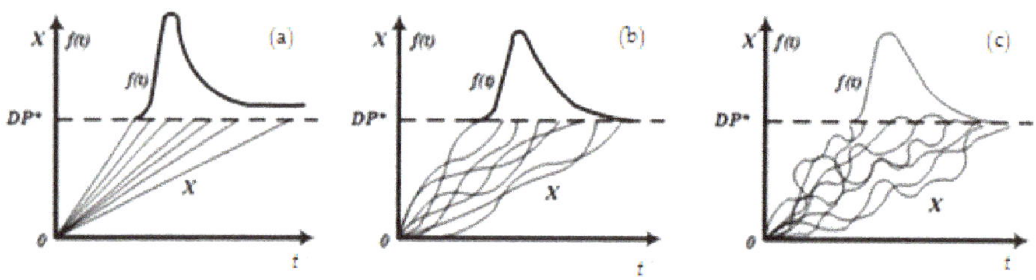

Figure 6. The model of a random degradation process and a scheme for the formation of a time-to-failure distribution: (**a**) α distribution (fan process); (**b**) *DN* distribution law; (**c**) *DM* distribution law.

Here, t is the operating time for the failure; X is random variable of the *DP*; DP^* is the normalized value of the *DP* at which the failure occurs; and f is the function of density of the distribution of the operating time for the failure.

The distribution function of the operating time up to a given level DP^* is given by the distribution function [9–11]:

$$F(t) = \Phi\left(\frac{t-\mu}{vt}\right), \tag{9}$$

where Φ is the normalized normal distribution function; $\mu = 1/a$ is the parameter of the scale of degradation, a is the mathematical expectation of the rate of change of the *DP* (the average rate of the degradation process), normalized to the limit value; and v is the shape parameter (coefficient of the variation of the degradation process).

The empirical model of the "drift of metrological characteristics" [6,7] is based on the assumption on a linear law of change of the MI zero mark and an exponential law of increasing measurement error:

$$m_0(t) = m_{00} + v_m t,\ \sigma(t) = \sigma_0 + \frac{v_z}{a_z}(\exp(a_z t) - 1), \tag{10}$$

where σ_0 is the value of the initial error, v_z is the average initial velocity of the error increase, a_z is the parameter characterizing the acceleration of the error increase, m_{00} is the initial value of the zero drift (usually assumed to be zero), and v_m is the average velocity of the zero drift.

Let us now consider the Markov models of degradation and failures, widely used in applied problems. In these models, it is assumed that the degradation process can be approximated by a continuous Markov process of the diffusion type [9–11] and is described by a stochastic differential equation of the Ito type:

$$dx(t) = A(t)dt + B(t)d\eta(t), \tag{11}$$

where $x(t)$ is the value of the *DP*; $A(t)$ and $B(t)$ are deterministic functions characterizing the change in the mean value and variance of the *DP* (drift coefficient and diffusion coefficient); and $\eta(t)$ is a random variable of the Gaussian type.

The problem of determining the distribution of time before the first failure of the MI, in this case, is reduced to solving the problem of the first achievement of the upper limit of the *DP** (see Figure 6b,c). This problem can be solved if the conditional probability density $\omega(t,x)$ of the process transition from one state to another is known.

For a Markov diffusion-type processes, a partial differential equation (the Fokker–Planck–Kolmogorov equation) follows from (11):

$$\frac{\partial\omega(t,x)}{\partial t} + A(t)\frac{\partial\omega(t,x)}{\partial x} - \frac{(B(t))^2}{2}\frac{\partial^2\omega(t,x)}{\partial x^2} = 0, \tag{12}$$

where $A(t)$ and $B(t)$ are the coefficients of the equation depending on the operating conditions of the MI, and the physical and chemical processes occurring in the materials from which the MI is made. To solve (12), it is necessary to set boundary conditions that depend on the type of implementation of a random process, in particular, on their monotonic nature (Figure 6b) or non-monotonic nature (Figure 6c). You also need to set the initial conditions: $t = t_0$, $x = x_0$.

After finding the function $\omega(t_0, x_0; t, x)$, satisfying the given initial conditions, the density function $f(t)$ of the distribution of the time to reach the boundary *DP** (the density function of the distribution of the time to failure) can be calculated by the formula [11]:

$$f(t) = -\int_{-\infty}^{t} \frac{\partial\omega(t_0, x_0; t, x)}{\partial t} dx$$

In case of one *DP*, Equation (12) can be integrated analytically. The distribution function for the diffusion monotone distribution (*DM* distribution) has the form [11]:

$$F(t) = DM(t;\mu,v) = \Phi\left(\frac{t-\mu}{v\sqrt{\mu t}}\right), \tag{13}$$

Here, $\mu = 1/a$.

The distribution density function $f(t)$ for (13) at $\mu = 0.1$ is shown in Figure 7a.

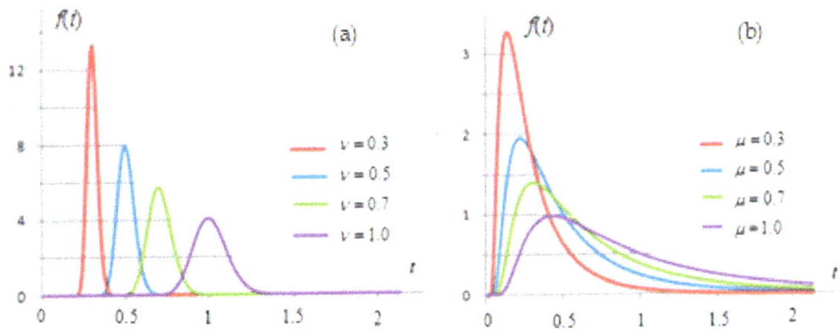

Figure 7. Diffusion distribution functions: (**a**) *DM* distribution; (**b**) *DN* distribution.

The distribution function for the diffusion non-monotonic distribution (*DN* distribution) has the form [11]:

$$F(t) = DN(t;\mu,\nu) = \Phi\left(\frac{t-\mu}{\upsilon\sqrt{\mu t}}\right) + \exp\left(\frac{2}{\nu^2}\right)\Phi\left(-\frac{t-\mu}{\upsilon\sqrt{\mu t}}\right). \quad (14)$$

The corresponding distribution density functions $f(t)$ for (14) at $\nu = 0.8$ are shown in Figure 7b.

The failure rates for *DM* distribution and *DN* distribution have the form:

$$\lambda_{DM}(t) = \frac{(t+\mu)\exp\left(-\frac{(t-\mu)^2}{2\nu^2\mu t}\right)}{2\nu t\sqrt{2\pi\mu t}\cdot\Phi\left(\frac{\mu-t}{\upsilon\sqrt{\mu t}}\right)}, \quad \lambda_{DN}(t) = \frac{\left(\nu t\sqrt{2\pi t}\right)^{-1}\sqrt{\mu}\cdot\exp\left(-\frac{(t-\mu)^2}{2\nu^2\mu t}\right)}{\Phi\left(\frac{\mu-t}{\upsilon\sqrt{\mu t}}\right) - \exp\left(\frac{2}{\nu^2}\right)\cdot\Phi\left(-\frac{\mu-t}{\upsilon\sqrt{\mu t}}\right)}$$

Thus, distribution density functions $f(t)$, distribution functions $F(t)$, and failure rate functions $\lambda(t)$, are calculated using finite analytical formulas using the standard Laplace function $\Phi(t)$.

In case of several *DP* distribution densities $f(t)$, distribution functions $F(t)$, and failure rates $\lambda(t)$, can only be calculated numerically.

The process of degradation of the mechanical components of the CTS, due to the irreversibility of the destruction processes (mechanical wear, fatigue straining, etc.), is considered to be a process with monotonous realizations of a random variable. *DM* distribution is used for CTS nodes containing electromechanical elements (relay and connector contacts, sliding electrical contacts, gears, etc.) [11].

The process of degradation of the CTS, which include integrated circuits and complex electronic devices, also has non-monotonic implementations of a random variable. Therefore, the degradation of such CTS is described by the *DN* distribution [11].

We will analyze the models of failures and degradation of the CTS. Degradation and failures models differ significantly from a physical point of view. In particular, the fan process assumes that its characteristics are completely determined by the initial state (the quality of the manufacturing samples of the components of the CTS), and do not depend on the mechanical, physical and chemical degradation processes occurring in the circuits and mechanisms of the components of the CTS, under the influence of external conditions and time.

The drift model of metrological characteristics [10], clearly demonstrates the departure of the zero mark of the MI and CTS with the increase in measurement error over time. The model assumes preliminary processing of statistical data in order to determine estimates of the drift parameters.

The Markov models (12), (13) are based on the use of probabilistic characteristics, the operating conditions of the CTS, as well as on the use of the physical and chemical properties of the materials. The advantage of Markov models [12,13] is that they have accurate analytical expressions for all statistical characteristics, including statistical moments. In addition, there are no analytical expressions for the statistical moments of the fan α distribution law. These moments are determined by approximate dependencies, which complicates the use of a fan distribution in practice.

The density distribution function of the *DM* distribution occupies an intermediate position between the, widely used in practice, normal distribution (which is symmetrical) and the more elongated distribution.

The density curves of the *DN* distribution have a more significant insensitivity threshold, a more positive kurtosis and are more asymmetric than the *DM* distribution.

The intensities of the diffusion distributions have finite limits:

$$\lim_{t\to\infty}\lambda_{DM}(t) = \lim_{t\to\infty}\lambda_{DN}(t) = \frac{1}{2\mu\nu^2}.$$

Here, are some important properties of diffusion distributions for practical application:

1. Where a random variable T is described by a *DM* distribution of the form $DM(t;\mu,\nu)$, then the random variable $x = cT$ $(c = const)$ is also described by a *DM* distribution of the form $DM(t;c\mu,\nu)$.

2. Where a random variable T is described by a *DM* distribution of the form $DM(t;\mu,\nu)$, then the random variable $\theta = \frac{1}{T}$ is also described by a *DM* distribution of the form $DM\left(t;\frac{1}{\mu},\nu\right)$.

3. Where a random variable T is described by a *DN* distribution of the form $DN(t;\mu,\nu)$, then the random variable $x = cT$ $(c = const)$ is also described by a *DN* distribution of the form $DN(t;c\mu,\nu)$.

4. The sum of n random variables obeying the distribution of the form $DN(t;\mu,\nu_i)$ is described by the *DN* distribution of the form $DN\left(t;n\mu,1/\sqrt{\sum\limits_{i=1}^{n}\nu_i^{-2}}\right)$.

5. The sum of n random variables obeying a distribution of the form $DN(t;\mu_i,\nu)$ is described by a *DN* distribution of the form $DN\left(t;\sum\limits_{i=1}^{n}\mu_i,\nu/\sqrt{n}\right)$.

6. The sum of n random variables obeying the *DN* distribution of the form $DN(t;\mu,\nu)$ is described by the *DN* distribution of the form $DN\left(t;n\mu,\frac{\nu}{\sqrt{n}}\right)$.

The proof of properties 1–6 can be carried out by replacing the variables and definitions of functions (13)–(14).

Some additional properties of diffusion distributions are described in [11].

Analysis of the graphs on the distribution functions shows that distributions (9), (12), (13) have different zones of high reliability. This means that the estimation of small-level quantiles, i.e., the assignment of a gamma-percent resource, significantly depends on the selected type of failure model of the CTS.

Diffusion models can be parameterized quite simply in the presence of statistical information. For example, when parameterizing based on statistical data on the moments of failure $\{t_i,(i = 1,2,\ldots,N)\}$, the estimates of the parameters $\breve{\mu}$ and $\breve{\nu}$ calculated using the maximum likelihood method for the *DM* distribution have the form:

$$\breve{\mu} = \frac{1}{N}\sum_{i=1}^{N} t_i,\ \breve{\nu} = \sqrt{\breve{\mu}}\cdot\sqrt{\frac{1}{N}\sum_{i=1}^{N}\frac{1}{t_i} - N\left(\sum_{i=1}^{N} t_i\right)^{-1}},$$

and for *DN* distributions have the form:

$$\breve{\mu} = N\left(\sum_{i=1}^{N}\frac{1}{t_i}\right)^{-1} + \frac{N}{2}\left(\sum_{i=1}^{N}(\breve{\mu}+t_i)^{-1}\right)^{-1} - \frac{N^2}{4}\left(\sum_{i=1}^{N}(\breve{\mu}+t_i)^{-1}\right)^{-2} - N\left(\sum_{i=1}^{N}\frac{1}{t_i}\right)^{-1}\sqrt{\frac{1}{N}\sum_{i=1}^{N} t_i - N\left(\sum_{i=1}^{N}\frac{1}{t_i}\right)^{-1}},$$

$$\breve{\nu} = \sqrt{\frac{1}{\breve{\mu}N}\sum_{i=1}^{N} t_i + \frac{\breve{\mu}}{N}\sum_{i=1}^{N}\frac{1}{t_i} - 2}$$

Thus, diffusion models are more preferable (adequate), since, unlike the fan distribution and the drift model of metrological characteristics, they can be used to control the degradation and reliability of the CTS, based on the taking into account of the physical patterns implemented through time-dependent variable coefficients $A(t)$ and $B(t)$ in Equation (12). The task of developing models of physical processes for the purpose of constructing coefficients $A(t)$ and $B(t)$ is an independent scientific task and is not considered in this article.

4.2. The Model of Operation of a Complex Technical System Fleet with a Fully Recoverable Resource

The attribution of a set of CTS to one or another degradation group is carried out on the basis of structural and functional analysis of the metrological reliability indicators [2,6,7], which includes the types of failures, the consequences of the failures, as well as determination and analysis of the rational composition of the controlled parameters and an assessment of the required recovery time of the CTS. In this paper, the controlled states of the CTS will be evaluated using the probabilities of a false failure α, an undetected failure β and the time t_B required for recovery after the failure is detected (the recovery time depends on the "severity" of the malfunction detected during monitoring). At low values of these estimated indicators, we will refer the CTS to the first group of degradation. As the degradation increases (as these indicators increase), we will refer the CTS to the second, third and fourth groups of degradation, respectively. Without going into the details of assigning parameters of criteria for attribution to a particular degradation group, we note that the number of degradation levels is determined by a set of types and types of CTS under consideration, their characteristic features, as well as the specific task being solved.

Figure 8a shows a graph with one fully workable state E_1 and four states corresponding to different levels of degradation (malfunction): E_2, E_3, E_4 and E_5 [6]. Let us distinguish the three parts in the classical model [2]: the initial operational state E_1, the failure state E_2 and the subgraph corresponding to the control function (highlighted in Figure 8b by rectangle C2). Then, the classical model can be represented as a "serial connection" E_1, C2 and E_2 [14,15]. The states of the subgraph: K_3 is verification of a failed MI, K_4 is the restoration of the CTS, K_5 is verification of a working MI and K_6 is the state of an undetected failure of the CTS. The probabilistic characteristics of the state transition are the same as in the classical model [2].

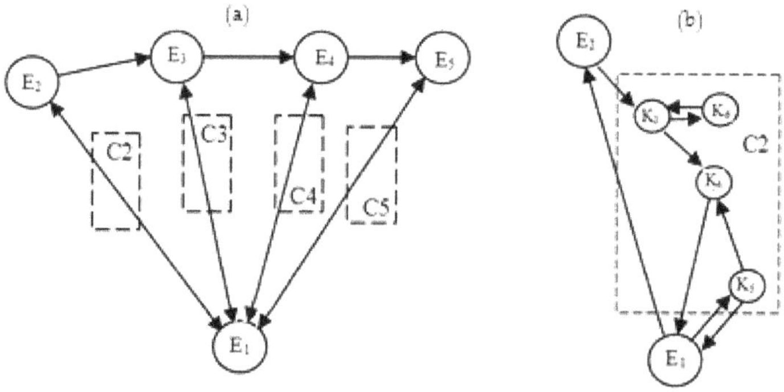

Figure 8. Graphs and subgraphs of the CTS operation model with full resource recovery: (**a**) with the control of four degradation states; (**b**) with the control of one degradation state (classical model).

Note that if the control subgraph is completely removed from the graph in Figure 8b and the probabilistic characteristics are set on the edges of the remaining graph, then a simple model will be obtained that describes the operation of a small gun [6].

Figure 8a uses the notation: E_1 is a fully functional state and four states corresponding to different levels of degradation of the CTS; E_2 is the first group of degradation (functional state with minor deviations of the normalized metrological characteristics); E_3 is the second group of degradation (a state with some deviations of the metrological characteristics, from which it is possible to return to a fully functional state with small resource costs); E_4 is the third group degradation (a state from which it is possible to return to a fully functional state with costs associated with sufficiently resource-intensive maintenance); and E_5 is the fourth "heavier" group of degradation. As the degradation group number increases, returning to the state E_1 becomes more and more resource intensive.

Let us "attach" four metrological control systems, C2, C3, C4 and C5, between the fully functional state E_1 and the other four states, similar to the one shown in Figure 8a ("fan connection"). We will use the corresponding upper indices for the probabilistic and deterministic parameters of the model of each subsystem, describing samples of the CTS with different levels of degradation.

Then, the system of equations describing the semi-Markov stationary model will take the form [6]:

$$\begin{cases} \pi_1^{(1)} = \pi_4^{(1)} + (1-\alpha_1)\pi_5^{(1)} + \pi_4^{(2)} + (1-\alpha_2)\pi_5^{(2)} + \pi_4^{(3)} + (1-\alpha_3)\pi_5^{(3)} + \pi_4^{(4)} + (1-\alpha_4)\pi_5^{(4)} \\ \pi_2^{(1)} = \gamma_1\pi_1 \\ \pi_3^{(1)} = (1-\delta_1)\pi_2^{(1)} + \pi_6^{(1)} \\ \pi_4^{(1)} = (1-\beta_1)\pi_3^{(1)} + \alpha_1\pi_5^{(1)} \\ \pi_5^{(1)} = [1-\gamma_1]\pi_1 \\ \pi_6^{(1)} = \beta_1\pi_3^{(1)} \end{cases},$$

$$\begin{cases} \pi_2^{(2)} = \gamma_2\pi_1 + \delta_1\pi_2^{(1)} \\ \pi_3^{(2)} = (1-\delta_2)\pi_2^{(2)} + \pi_6^{(2)} \\ \pi_4^{(2)} = (1-\beta_2)\pi_3^{(2)} + \alpha_2\pi_5^{(2)} \\ \pi_5^{(2)} = [1-\gamma_2]\pi_1 \\ \pi_6^{(2)} = \beta_2\pi_3^{(2)} \end{cases}, \quad \begin{cases} \pi_2^{(3)} = \gamma_3\pi_1 + \delta_2\pi_2^{(2)} \\ \pi_3^{(3)} = (1-\delta_3)\pi_2^{(3)} + \pi_6^{(3)} \\ \pi_4^{(3)} = (1-\beta_3)\pi_3^{(3)} + \alpha_3\pi_5^{(3)} \\ \pi_5^{(3)} = [1-\gamma_3]\pi_1 \\ \pi_6^{(3)} = \beta_2\pi_3^{(3)} \end{cases}, \quad \begin{cases} \pi_2^{(4)} = \gamma_4\pi_1 + \delta_3\pi_2^{(3)} \\ \pi_3^{(4)} = \pi_2^{(4)} + \pi_6^{(4)} \\ \pi_4^{(4)} = (1-\beta_4)\pi_3^{(4)} + \alpha_4\pi_5^{(4)} \\ \pi_5^{(4)} = [1-\gamma_4]\pi_1 \\ \pi_6^{(4)} = \beta_4\pi_3^{(4)} \end{cases} \quad (15)$$

Here, α_i, $(i = 2,3,4,5)$ is the conditional probability of a false failure, β_i is the conditional probability of an undetected failure and $\gamma_i = F_i(T_K)\delta_j$, $(j = 1,2,3)$ are the probability of a transition from a state of degradation to the next, more severe, state number $j+1$.

Model (15) is a system of 21 equations. The rank of the system is 20. Exclude one of the equations (for example, the last equation of the system (15)) and add a normalization condition, as follows:

$$\pi_1 + \sum_{i=1}^{4}\sum_{j=2}^{6}\pi_j^{(i)} = 1 \quad (16)$$

Then, the resulting system of linear inhomogeneous Equations (15) and (16) will have a unique solution that can be obtained using standard algorithms and methods for solving the corresponding systems [5,6].

Initial data: the total number of states is 21 and the number of degradation levels is four. As the CTS degrades, the duration of the verification and recovery time increase, and reliability decreases.

As generalized parameters characterizing the distribution of the control volumes by the degradation groups, the duration TIBV $T_K^{(i)}$ for each of the four degradation groups was selected. As a result of the calculations, the dependence of the readiness coefficient on the TIBV was constructed:

$$K_A = K_A(T_K^{(1)}, T_K^{(2)}, T_K^{(3)}, T_K^{(4)}), \quad (17)$$

and the analysis of the influence of the TIBV of the different degradation groups (i = 1, 2, 3, 4) on the readiness coefficient was carried out. When constructing the dependence (17), the probabilities of false and undetected failures were set as average values for each of the degradation groups, namely: $\alpha_4 > \alpha_3 > \alpha_2 > \alpha_1$, $\beta_4 > \beta_3 > \beta_2 > \beta_1$.

The calculations have shown that if three arguments out of four are fixed in function (17), for example $T_K^{(2)} = c^{(2)*}$, $T_K^{(3)} = c^{(3)*}$, $T_K^{(4)} = c^{(4)*}$, $c^{(i)*} = const$ then the dependence of function (17) on the remaining variable $T_K^{(1)}$ will have the form shown in Figure 9. If two arguments out of four are fixed in function (17), for example $T_K^{(1)} = c^{(1)*}$ and $T_K^{(2)} = c^{(2)*}$ then the readiness coefficient K_A, as functions of two variables, will be convex upwards (Figure 9). The maximum of the readiness coefficient K_A is reached at a single internal point. Here and further, an asterisk in the upper index means that the corresponding value is set and fixed.

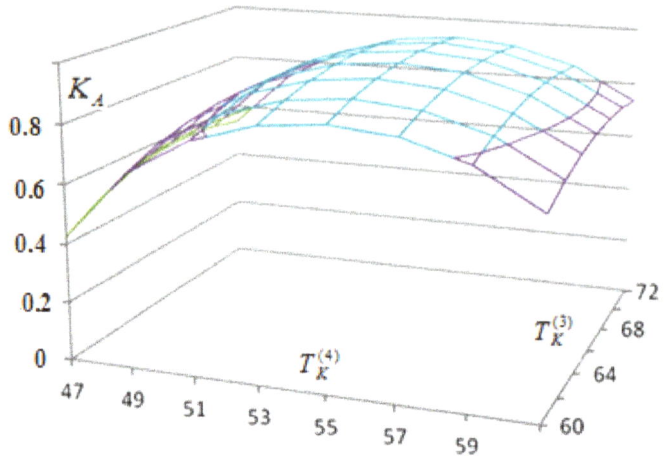

Figure 9. Dependence of the readiness coefficient K_A on the TIBV for technical conditions E_3 and E_4.

The calculations have shown that the maximum value of the readiness coefficient is achieved if the TIBV for the fourth degradation group is about 1.3 times less than for the third group.

The developed model allows us to calculate the optimal duration of the TIBV for the CTS of different degradation groups. If it is impossible to provide optimal TIBV values for some degradation groups in practice, then in (17) "possible" TIBV values should be set for these groups and local optimum TIBV durations for the remaining degradation groups should be calculated.

Note that the model of interaction of the CTS with the MI with a simplified form of technical condition control can be represented as a graph (Figure 8a), if you remove the control subgraphs C2–C5 and set the probabilistic characteristics of the state transitions on the edges of the remaining graph. Such a model, supplemented with a formula for calculating the average total resource costs $SUM = S_{12}p_{12} + S_{23}p_{23} + S_{34}p_{34} + S_{45}p_{45}$ (where $S_{12}, S_{23}, S_{34}, S_{45}$ are unit costs and $p_{12}, p_{23}, p_{34}, p_{45}$ are probabilities of the state transitions), was used in [6] when calculating the technical and economic indicators of the metrological support system, when forming programs for the long-term development of the CTS fleet.

The models described in Section 4.1 and 4.2 do not allow modeling processes of CTS fleet renewal, and do not allow for the taking into account of the procurement of new CTS samples, or the modernization of existing CTS samples and the development of promising CTS samples. The model presented in Section 4.3 of the article allows modeling for all stages of the life cycle, including procurement, modernization and development of advanced CTS samples.

4.3. The Model of Operation of the Complex Technical System Fleet with a Partially Recoverable Resource

Next, we will distribute the CTS into three degradation groups [7]: the first is the start of operation of the CTS, the sample remains operational and the changes are insignificant; the second is where the operation and resource consumption of the CTS sample continue, the changes in characteristics are significant and the rate of change is average; and the third is a long-term operation, where the changes in characteristics are very significant and the rate of change is high. The number of degradation groups is determined by a set of types and the types of CTS under consideration, as well as the specific task being solved.

Figure 10 presents a graph of the operation model of the updated CTS fleet, with three degradation groups and two subgraphs modeling the process of updating the CTS fleet. The upper indices in parentheses indicate the number of the degradation group. Each degradation group will be modeled using the classical model [2], described in Section 4.1.1.

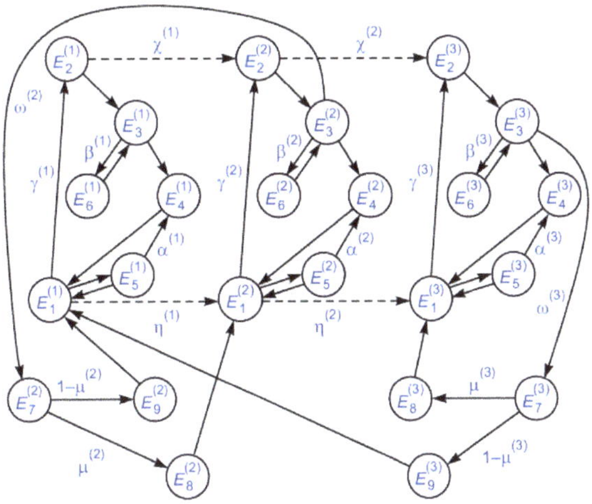

Figure 10. Graph of the model of operation, degradation and renewal of the CTS fleet with incomplete resource recovery.

Each of the two subgraphs describing the upgrade process include three states: $E_7^{(l)}, l = 2, 3$ are the in-depth diagnostics of the technical condition; $E_8^{(l)}, l = 2, 3$ is the repair of the CTS; and $E_9^{(l)}, l = 2, 3$ is the purchase (or development and production) of a new similar model of the CTS. The probabilistic parameters of the main state transitions are shown in Figure 10, in Greek letters. Certain shares of the CTS, from the second $\omega^{(2)}$ and third $\omega^{(3)}$ degradation groups, in case of failure of the CTS are sent for in-depth diagnostics of the technical condition, in order to determine the feasibility of updating (replacing with a new model of the CTS) or continuing operation after repair. To simplify, some probabilistic characteristics are not indicated in Figure 10, but they can be easily restored, taking into account that the sum of the probabilities of the transitions from each vertex of the graph are equal to one. If one edge comes out of the vertex, then the corresponding transition probability is one, and if two edges come out of the vertex, and the probability of one transition is written on the graph, then the probability of the second transition is equal to the difference of one and the known probability of the first transition.

$$\begin{cases} \pi_1^{(1)} = \pi_4^{(1)} + (1-\alpha^{(1)})\pi_5^{(1)} + \pi_9^{(2)} + \pi_9^{(3)} \\ \pi_2^{(1)} = \gamma^{(1)}\pi_1^{(1)} \\ \pi_3^{(1)} = (1-\chi^{(1)})\pi_2^{(1)} + \pi_6^{(1)} \\ \pi_4^{(1)} = (1-\beta^{(1)})\pi_3^{(1)} + \alpha^{(1)}\pi_5^{(1)} \\ \pi_5^{(1)} = \left[1-\gamma^{(1)}-\eta^{(1)}\right]\pi_1^{(1)} \\ \pi_6^{(1)} = \beta^{(1)}\pi_3^{(1)} \end{cases}, \begin{cases} \pi_1^{(2)} = \pi_4^{(2)} + (1-\alpha^{(2)})\pi_5^{(2)} + \eta^{(1)}\pi_1^{(1)} + \pi_8^{(2)} \\ \pi_2^{(2)} = \gamma^{(2)}\pi_1^{(2)} + \chi^{(1)}\pi_2^{(1)} \\ \pi_3^{(2)} = (1-\chi^{(2)})\pi_2^{(2)} + \pi_6^{(2)} \\ \pi_4^{(2)} = (1-\beta^{(2)}-\omega^{(2)})\pi_3^{(2)} + \alpha^{(2)}\pi_5^{(2)} \\ \pi_5^{(2)} = \left[1-\gamma^{(2)}-\eta^{(2)}\right]\pi_1^{(2)} \\ \pi_6^{(2)} = \beta^{(2)}\pi_3^{(2)} \end{cases}$$

$$\begin{cases} \pi_1^{(3)} = \pi_4^{(3)} + (1-\alpha^{(3)})\pi_5^{(3)} + \eta^{(2)}\pi_1^{(2)} + \pi_8^{(3)} \\ \pi_2^{(3)} = \gamma^{(3)}\pi_1^{(3)} + \chi^{(2)}\pi_2^{(2)} \\ \pi_3^{(3)} = \pi_2^{(3)} + \pi_6^{(3)} \\ \pi_4^{(3)} = (1-\beta^{(3)} - \omega^{(3)})\pi_3^{(3)} + \alpha^{(3)}\pi_5^{(3)} \\ \pi_5^{(3)} = \left[1-\gamma^{(3)}\right]\pi_1^{(3)} \\ \pi_6^{(3)} = \beta^{(3)}\pi_3^{(3)} \end{cases}, \quad \begin{cases} \pi_7^{(2)} = \omega^{(2)}\pi_3^{(2)} \\ \pi_8^{(2)} = \mu^{(2)}\pi_3^{(2)} \\ \pi_7^{(3)} = \omega^{(3)}\pi_3^{(3)} \\ \pi_8^{(2)} = \mu^{(3)}\pi_3^{(2)} \\ \pi_9^{(2)} = \left[1-\mu^{(2)}\right]\pi_7^{(2)} \\ \pi_9^{(3)} = \left[1-\mu^{(3)}\right]\pi_7^{(3)} \end{cases} \tag{18}$$

Here $\pi_i^{(j)}$ are the stationary probabilities of finding the CTS in the corresponding states; $\alpha^{(j)}, j = 1, 2, 3$, $\beta^{(j)}, j = 1, 2, 3$ are the conditional probabilities of false and undetected failures, respectively; $\gamma^{(j)} = F_j(T_K)$ is the probability of failure during the time interval T_K between the verifications; $F_j(T)$ is exponential distribution function; and $(\chi^{(j)}, \eta^{(j)}, j = 1, 2)$ are the probabilities of the transitions of the corresponding states from the j degradation group to the next $(j+1)$ group. The first three systems (18) describe the processes of the CTS operation for the three degradation groups, and the fourth system (18) describes the process of updating the CTS fleet.

Model (18) is a homogeneous system of 24 linear algebraic equations. The rank of the system is 23. Exclude one of the equations (for example, the last equation of the system (18)) and add a normalization condition instead, as follows:

$$\sum_{i=1}^{6}\sum_{j=1}^{3}\pi_i^{(j)} + \sum_{i=7}^{9}\sum_{j=2}^{3}\pi_i^{(j)} = 1 \tag{19}$$

Then, the resulting system of linear inhomogeneous algebraic equations (18) will have a unique solution [7].

The readiness coefficient K_A of the fleet of the CTS is calculated by the formula [2]:

$$K_A = \left(\sum_j \pi_1^{(j)}\psi_1^{(j)}\right) / \left(\sum_{i,j} \pi_i^{(j)}\psi_i^{(j)}\right) \tag{20}$$

Here $\psi_i^{(j)}$ is the mathematical expectation of the time (average time) of the CTS being in the corresponding states $E_i^{(j)}$ (assumed to be known). In the numerator (20), summation by index j is performed for all workable states, and in the denominator (20) is the summation by both index i and index j for all states (the index i is responsible for unworkable states).

As parameters characterizing the distribution of the metrological control volumes and the quality of the metrological control by degradation groups, the duration of the TIVB $T_K^{(j)}, j = 1, 2, 3$ for each of the three degradation groups, the relative values of the operational tolerances for the controlled parameters $\delta^{(j)}, j = 1, 2, 3$ and the relative measurement errors $z^{(j)}, j = 1, 2, 3$, were selected.

As a result of the solution for system (18), the dependence of the CTS readiness coefficient for use on the above metrological parameters, organizational, technical and technical parameters is constructed:

$$K_A = K_A(T_K^{(1)}, T_K^{(2)}, T_K^{(3)}, \alpha^{(1)}, \alpha^{(2)}, \alpha^{(3)}, \beta^{(1)}, \beta^{(2)}, \beta^{(3)}, \omega^{(2)}, \omega^{(3)}, \mu^{(2)}, \mu^{(3)}), \tag{21}$$

moreover, the functions of the conditional probabilities of false failures and undetected failures depend on the relative operational tolerance and relative measurement errors:

$$\alpha^{(1)} = \alpha^{(1)}(\delta^{(1)}, z^{(1)}),\ \alpha^{(2)} = \alpha^{(2)}(\delta^{(2)}, z^{(2)}),\ \alpha^{(3)} = \alpha^{(3)}(\delta^{(3)}, z^{(3)}),$$
$$\beta^{(1)} = \beta^{(1)}(\delta^{(1)}, z^{(1)}),\ \beta^{(2)} = \beta^{(2)}(\delta^{(2)}, z^{(2)}),\ \beta^{(3)} = \beta^{(3)}(\delta^{(3)}, z^{(3)})$$

that are calculated using Formulas (5)–(8).

In (21), the following parameters are presented: $\omega^{(2)}$, $\omega^{(3)}$ are the proportion of samples sent for in-depth diagnostics of the CTS samples from the number of samples received for verification; and $\mu^{(2)}$, $\mu^{(3)}$ are the parameters characterizing the process of updating the CTS fleet (so, for example, in special cases $\mu^{(j)} = 0$, where all inoperable CTS samples are changed to new ones, and where $\mu^{(j)} = 1$ they are repaired). The parameters $\omega^{(j)}$, $\mu^{(j)}$ are conditionally attributed to the organizational and technical categories. The readiness coefficient also depends on other technical parameters, for example $\eta^{(1)}$, $\eta^{(2)}$, $\chi^{(1)}$, $\chi^{(2)}$, which characterize the degradation process of the CTS fleet (operational parameters), and the average time $\psi_i^{(j)}$ spent by the CTS sample in various states. These parameters are determined based on the processing of the available statistical information and the relevant criteria for classifying the CTS into different degradation groups.

Note that the parameters $\psi_9^{(j)}$ (time spent in the state $E_9^{(i)}$) allow you to model both the purchase and development of new samples of CTS. To simulate the procurement of new samples of CTS we have to set $\psi_9^{(j)}$ sufficiently small, and to simulate the development of new samples, we have to set the CTS at medium and large.

Note that the constructed dependence (21), like (17), is smooth, so its extreme properties can be effectively investigated using standard gradient methods.

On the basis of solving a series of problems on the extremum of a function of several variables (21), the influence of the TIBV $T_K^{(j)}$ of the CTS from different degradation groups and the relative tolerances on controlled parameters $\delta^{(j)}$ on the readiness coefficient are analyzed K_A.

Consider the effect of the duration of the TIBV on the readiness coefficient K_A. Let us fix all the arguments (21), with the exception of three: $T_K^{(i)}, i = 1, 2, 3$. If we additionally, fix any two arguments $T_K^{(i)}$ out of three, for example $T_K^{(2)} = C_{T_K}^{(2)*}$, $T_K^{(3)} = C_{T_K}^{(3)*}$, then the dependence of function (21) on the remaining argument $T_K^{(1)}$ will have the form given in [2]: convex upwards with a single maximum.

An asterisk in the upper index means that the corresponding value is set and fixed. If one of the three arguments is fixed in function (21) (for example, $T_K^{(3)} = C_{T_K}^{(3)*}$), then the readiness coefficient curve K_A, as well as the functions of the other two arguments, $T_K^{(1)}$ and $T_K^{(2)}$, will be convex upwards (Figure 11). The maximum of the readiness coefficient K_A will be reached at a single internal point in the parameter plane, $T_K^{(1)} \times T_K^{(2)}$. The dependences of the readiness coefficient K_A on the frequency of the control for the first and third groups, and for the second and third groups of degradation, have a similar form.

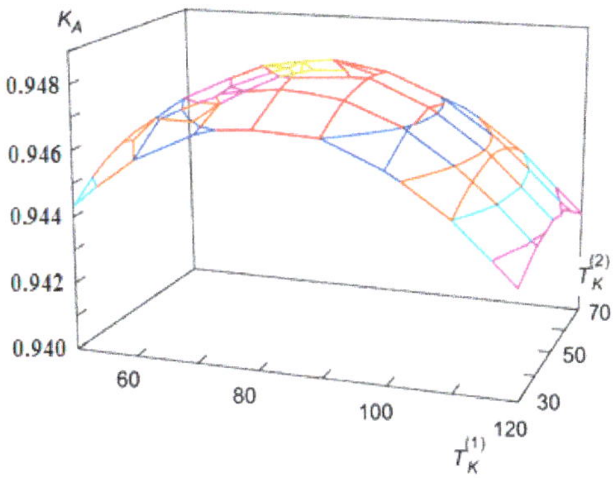

Figure 11. Dependence of the readiness coefficient K_A on the TIBV for the first and second degradation groups.

Optimization (21) for three groups of degradation showed that the characteristic ratio of the TIBV durations is 80:45:30, thus, the higher the degradation group, the more often CTS verifications are required.

Consider the effect of the relative operating tolerances $\delta^{(j)}$, $j = 1, 2, 3$ on K_A. Similarly to the above, we fix all the arguments (21), with the exception of three $\delta^{(j)}$, $j = 1, 2, 3$. Then, the dependence of the readiness coefficient K_A on relative operational tolerances is similar to its dependence on the TIBV, $T_K^{(i)}$, $i = 1, 2, 3$.

The calculations have shown that the general form of dependence K_A on two tolerances, at a fixed value of the third tolerance, has the form of surfaces shown in Figure 12. The surface of the readiness coefficient K_A as a function of two arguments will be convex upwards, where the maximum is reached at a single internal point in the parameter plane, $\delta^{(1)} \times \delta^{(2)}$, $\delta^{(1)} \times \delta^{(3)}$ or $\delta^{(2)} \times \delta^{(3)}$. Optimization of the K_A of three relative tolerances simultaneously showed that their characteristic ratio is 0.07:0.09:0.13, thus, the higher the degradation group, the greater the tolerance.

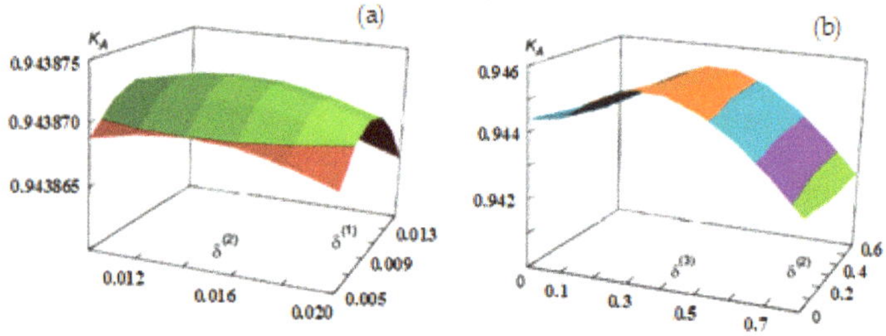

Figure 12. The dependence of the readiness coefficient K_A on the relative operating tolerances for the controlled parameters: (**a**) on $\delta^{(1)}$ and $\delta^{(2)}$; (**b**) on $\delta^{(2)}$ and $\delta^{(3)}$.

The study of the joint dependence K_A on the TIBV and tolerances showed that the maximum of the function of six variables is achieved at a single internal point of a set of parameters, $T_K^{(1)} \times T_K^{(2)} \times T_K^{(3)} \times \delta^{(1)} \times \delta^{(2)} \times \delta^{(3)}$. The optimal values of the arguments were: $T_K^{(1)} = 81.59$, $T_K^{(2)} = 50.46$, $T_K^{(3)} = 32.55$, $\delta^{(1)} = 0.072$, $\delta^{(2)} = 0.0872$ and $\delta^{(3)} = 0.128$. At the same time, the optimal values of the probabilities of false and undetected failures were: $\alpha^{(1)} = 0.227$, $\alpha^{(2)} = 0.267$, $\alpha^{(3)} = 0.347$, $\beta^{(1)} = 0.171$, $\beta^{(2)} = 0.222$ and $\beta^{(3)} = 0.323$. The calculations have shown that with an increase in the number of the degradation group, the TIBV decreases, the tolerances for controlled parameters and the probabilities of false and undetected failures increase. The probabilities of false failures slightly exceed the corresponding probabilities of undetected failures for each degradation group.

We describe the results of a study on the stationary distribution of the CTS samples in different degradation groups, depending on the rate of degradation processes. The rate of degradation is determined using transition probabilities $\chi^{(i)}$, $\eta^{(i)}$. The lower the corresponding probability, the slower the degradation processes proceed. Four variants differing in the rate of degradation were investigated: $\eta^{(1)} = 0.25$, $\chi^{(1)} = 0.2$, $\eta^{(2)} = 0.35$, $\chi^{(2)} = 0.3$ (option 1); $\eta^{(1)} = 0.025$, $\chi^{(1)} = 0.02$, $\eta^{(2)} = 0.35$, $\chi^{(2)} = 0.3$ (option 2); $\eta^{(1)} = 0.025$, $\chi^{(1)} = 0.02$, $\eta^{(2)} = 0.035$, $\chi^{(2)} = 0.03$ (option 3); and $\eta^{(1)} = 0.025$, $\chi^{(1)} = 0.02$; $\eta^{(2)} = 0.035$, $\chi^{(2)} = 0.003$ (option 4). Note that the variants are arranged in order of decreasing degradation rate. The distribution of the proportion of working samples of the CTS by degradation groups at different values of these parameters is shown in Figure 13.

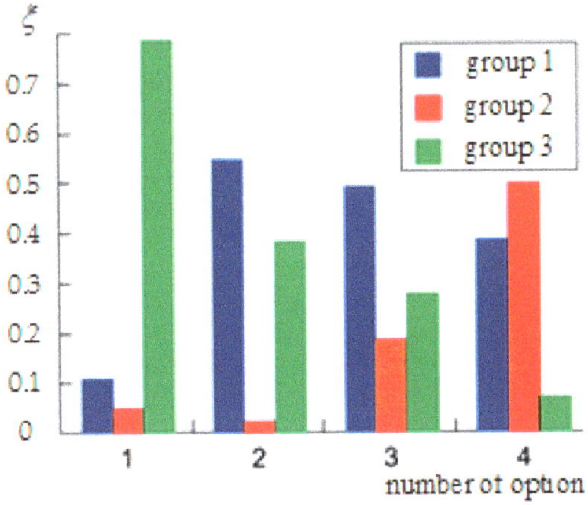

Figure 13. Distribution of workable CTS samples by degradation levels at different values of parameters determining the rate of degradation.

The probability of the CTS staying in the first degradation group for option 2 is about 5.5 times higher compared to option 1. At the same time, the ratio of the probability of being in the third group compared to the probability of being in the first group remains approximately the same.

The probability of the CTS staying in the first degradation group monotonically decreases, and the probability of being in the second group monotonically increases with sequential consideration of options from 2 to 4.

Next, we investigate the dependence K_A on the total production capacity of the metrological units in which the MI and CTS are verified and checked. The production capacity of a metrological unit may be temporarily limited for one reason or another. The specified restriction was set in the form of an inequality, $\sum_j \pi^{(j)}\psi^{(j)} \leq C^{(\pi)*}$, where $C^{(\pi)*}$ is the conditional production capacity of the metrological unit, and the problem of conditional optimization was solved. In Figure 14 the dependences of the TIBV on the total conditional production capacity ζ of the metrological units and the readiness coefficient corresponding to these intervals (in percent) are presented.

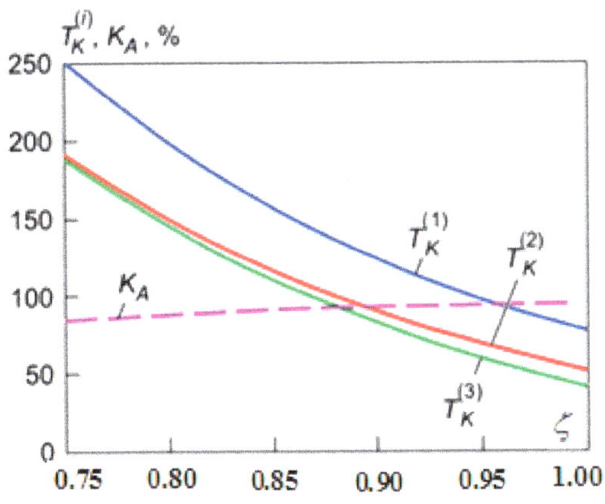

Figure 14. Dependence of the readiness coefficient and the TIBV on the total production capacity of metrological units.

If the production capacities of the metrological division do not allow for the checking of the required number of CTS, then it is possible to operate a fleet of CTS with increased TIBV. With a decrease in the production capacity of the metrological unit from 100% to 75%, the readiness coefficient K_A decreases from 0.9514 to 0.8402.

5. Results

A set of interrelated mathematical models of the processes of operation, renewal and degradation of a fleet of CTS with metrological support was developed. The basis of the developed set of models consists of:

- A basic model of the CTS operation;
- A set of CTS operation models, having different levels of degradation (for different levels of CTS degradation a different number of system states and different variants of system maintenance are used);
- A model of false failures and undetected failures;
- A model of CTS fleet renewal, including such renewal methods as the purchase of new CTS samples, the modernization of existing CTS samples and the development of new promising CTS samples;
- A functional dependence model of the CTS availability factor on a number of technical parameters, organizational and technical parameters, and technological parameters of the CTS belonging to different degradation groups and different methods of CTS stock renewal.

On the basis of the set of interrelated mathematical models presented in the article, the software for modeling the processes of operation, renewal and degradation of the fleet of CTS with metrological support was developed.

6. Discussions

The models developed and implemented as software allow for the parametrical optimization of the processes of CTS fleet functioning for a number of parameters, including metrological parameters, organizational and technical parameters, and technical parameters.

If in practice it is impossible to provide the optimal TIBV values or tolerances for the controlled parameters for some degradation groups, then for these groups the "possible" values of the TIBV and tolerances for the controlled parameters should be established, and the developed models should be used for calculation.

The developed set of models include a model for calculating the probabilities of false failures and undetected failures, for use in cases where the measured parameter and measurement error have a normal distribution law. The set of models developed in the article can also be used for different distribution laws of the measured parameter and measurement error: analytical defined laws, statistical defined laws or analytical and statistical distribution laws.

The constructed functional dependences of the availability factor on metrological, technical, organizational, technical and technological parameters have a smooth character, which makes it possible to effectively investigate the extreme properties of the availability factor using standard gradient methods.

7. Conclusions

Thus, the research goal has been achieved: a set of interrelated models has been developed, which solves the current need for end-to-end modeling of all the main stages of the life cycle of the CTS fleet. The developed set of models makes it possible to adequately simulate large CTS fleets, including those incorporating up to several hundreds of thousands of CTS samples.

The developed set of interrelated models allows:

- Management of the process of development of CTS fleets;
- Optimization of the processes of CTS fleet functioning;
- Identification of problematic issues in the development of CTS fleet and the formation of strategies for CTS fleet development in the presence of various constraints;
- The solving of the problem of conditional optimization in the presence of constraints on the technological parameters of the CTS fleet development (with constraints on part of the arguments of the availability factor function);
- Calculation of the technological and technical–economic parameters of the CTS fleet functioning and development;
- Evaluation of the risks associated with false and undetected failures, as well as the risks associated with CTS degradation;

A set of models is used in the Main Scientific Metrology Center:

- To classify the designed CTS in order to establish the requirements for their metrological support;
- When developing plans for medium-term and long-term development of the CTS fleet.

A set of models and software can be used by design organizations involved in the development of modern and advanced CTS with metrological support.

8. Future Works

At present, a set of models continues to develop in the direction of development and replenishment with models of CTS fleet maintenance; namely, models of workplaces for the verification of MI, taking into account the priorities of the MI samples coming for verification [27,28], as well as models of CTS fleet functioning under such modes of functioning as the mode of high readiness for use, the mode of use in extreme conditions, etc.

Author Contributions: The material is the result of the joint efforts of R.K., D.E., A.M. and T.L. All authors have read and agreed to the published version of the manuscript.

Funding: This research received no external funding.

Institutional Review Board Statement: The study was conducted in accordance with the Declaration of Helsinki, and approved by the Institutional Review Board of Moscow State University of Civil Engineering (protocol № 1, 5 December 2022).

Informed Consent Statement: Not applicable.

Conflicts of Interest: The authors declare no conflict of interest.

References

1. Volkov, L.I. Aircraft Operation Management Moscow: Higher School. 1981. 368p. Available online: https://www.studmed.ru/volkov-l-i-upravlenie-ekspluataciey-letatelnyh-kompleksov_e28fc04269b.html (accessed on 6 March 2023).
2. Sychev, E.I. Metrological Support of Radio-Electronic Equipment (Methods of Analysis). Moscow: RIC "Tatiana's Day". 1994. 277p. Available online: https://rusneb.ru/catalog/000199_000009_001691017/ (accessed on 6 March 2023).
3. Mishchenko, V.I. Evolution of Models of the Process of Operation of Weapons and Military Equipment. *Bull. Acad. Mil. Sci.* **2003**, *4*, 200. Available online: https://militaryarticle.ru/vestnik-akademii-voennykh-nauk/2003-vavn/10460-jevoljucija-modelej-processa-jekspluatacii (accessed on 6 March 2023).
4. Mishchenko, V.I.; Kravtsov, A.N.; Mamleev, T.F. The Semi-Markov Model of Functioning of Redundant Measuring Instruments Taking into Account the Frequency of Verification. *Meas. Equip.* **2021**, *4*, 22–27. Available online: https://link.springer.com/article/10.1007/s11018-021-01931-3 (accessed on 6 March 2023).

5. Khayrullin, R.Z.; Popenkov, A.J. Distribution of Controlling Volumes of Metrological Support for the Objectives of Complex Organizational and Technical Systems with the Use of Semi-Markov Models. In Proceedings of the XI-th International Conference "Management of Large-Scale System Development" (MLSD), Moscow, Russia, 1–3 October 2018; p. 8551917, 5p. Available online: https://www.researchgate.net/publication/329292364_Distribution_of_controlling_volumes_of_metrological_support_for_the_objectives_of_complex_organizational_and_technical_systems_with_the_use_of_semi-Markov_models (accessed on 6 March 2023).
6. Popenkov, A.J.; Fufaeva, O.V.; Khayrullin, R.Z. Analysis of Operation Models of Complex Technical Systems with Degrading Metrological Support. *Proc. Tula State Univ.* **2022**, *7*, 247–254. Available online: https://cyberleninka.ru/article/n/analiz-modeley-ekspluatatsii-slozhnyh-tehnicheskih-sistem-s-degradiruyuschim-metrologicheskim-obespecheniem (accessed on 6 March 2023).
7. Khayrullin, R.Z. Optimization of the Processes of Operation and Renewal of the Park of Measuring Equipment. *Meas. Equip.* **2022**, *8*, 28–34. Available online: https://www.izmt.ru/note.php?type=TAMI_izmt&notes_id=892 (accessed on 6 March 2023).
8. Khayrullin, R.Z.; Kornev, A.S.; Kostoglotov, A.A.; Lazarenko, S.V. Mathematical Simulation of Decision Error Functions in Tolerance Control of the Performance of Measuring Techniques. *Meas. Tech.* **2020**, *63*, 680–685. Available online: https://www.researchgate.net/publication/348442252_Mathematical_Simulation_of_Decision_Error_Functions_in_Tolerance_Control_of_the_Performance_of_Measuring_Techniques (accessed on 6 March 2023). [CrossRef]
9. David, V.; Marie, F.; Zdeněk, V.; Jakub, G. Degradation Process and Failure Estimation of Drilling System Based on Real Data and Diffusion Process Supported by State Space Models. *Measurement* **2020**, *164*, 108076. Available online: https://www.researchgate.net/publication/342137334_Degradation_process_and_failure_estimation_of_drilling_system_based_on_real_data_and_diffusion_process_supported_by_state_space_models (accessed on 6 March 2023).
10. Ma, J.; Fouladirad, M.; Grall, A. Flexible Wind Speed Generation Model: Markov Chain with an Embedded Diffusion Process. *Energy* **2018**, *164*, 316–328. Available online: https://www.researchgate.net/publication/327381227_Flexible_wind_speed_generation_model_Markov_chain_with_an_embedded_diffusion_process (accessed on 6 March 2023). [CrossRef]
11. Azarskov, V.N.; Strelnikov, V.P. Reliability of Control Systems and Automation. Kiev. NAU. 2004. 164p. Available online: https://www.studmed.ru/azarskov-vn-strelnikov-vp-nadezhnost-sistem-upravleniya-i-avtomatiki_881a18fe6fa.html (accessed on 6 March 2023).
12. Khayrullin, R.Z. Methods and Models of Calibration of Vector Network Analyzers. *J. Phys. Conf. Ser.* **2021**, *1921*, 012122. [CrossRef]
13. Abinandhitha, R.; Sakthivel, R.; Kong, F.; Parivalla, A. Robust Non-Fragile Boundary Control for Non-Linear Parabolic PDE Systems with Semi-Markov Switching and Input Quantization. *Eur. J. Control* **2022**, *67*, 100713. Available online: https://www.researchgate.net/publication/362087099_Robust_non-fragile_boundary_control_for_non-linear_parabolic_PDE_systems_with_semi-Markov_switching_and_input_quantization (accessed on 6 March 2023). [CrossRef]
14. Jiang, D.; Chen, T.; Xie, J.; Cui, W.; Song, B. A Mechanical System Reliability Degradation Analysis and Remaining Life Estimation Method with the Example of an Aircraft Hatch Lock Mechanism. *Reliab. Eng. Syst. Saf.* **2023**, *230*, 108922. Available online: https://www.researchgate.net/publication/365098134_A_mechanical_system_reliability_degradation_analysis_and_remaining_life_estimation_method--With_the_example_of_an_aircraft_hatch_lock_mechanism (accessed on 6 March 2023). [CrossRef]
15. Yan, X.; Tang, G.; Wang, X. Bearing Performance Degradation Assessment Based on the Continuous-Scale Mathematical Morphological Particle and Feature Fusion. *Measurement* **2022**, *188*, 110571. Available online: https://www.researchgate.net/publication/356855692_Bearing_Performance_Degradation_Assessment_Based_on_the_Continuous-scale_Mathematical_Morphological_Particle_and_Feature_Fusion (accessed on 6 March 2023). [CrossRef]
16. Yan, T.; Lei, Y.; Li, N.; Wang, B.; Wang, W. Degradation Modeling and Remaining Useful Life Prediction for Dependent Competing Failure Processes. *Reliab. Eng. Syst. Saf.* **2021**, *212*, 107638. Available online: https://www.researchgate.net/publication/350120821_Degradation_Modeling_and_Remaining_Useful_Life_Prediction_for_Dependent_Competing_Failure_Processes (accessed on 6 March 2023). [CrossRef]
17. Fang, G.; Pan, R.; Hong, Y. Copula-Based Reliability Analysis of Degrading Systems with Dependent Failures. *Reliab. Eng. Syst. Saf.* **2020**, *193*, 106618. Available online: https://www.researchgate.net/publication/335646674_Copula-based_Reliability_Analysis_of_Degrading_Systems_with_Dependent_Failures (accessed on 6 March 2023). [CrossRef]
18. Romero, E.E.; Bérenguer, C.; Martinez, J.J. Long-Term Degradation Estimation of Wind Turbine Drive-Train under a Gain-scheduling Control Strategy According to the Weather Conditions. *IFAC-Pap.* **2022**, *55*, 13–18. Available online: https://www.researchgate.net/publication/363895260_Long-term_degradation_estimation_of_wind_turbine_drive-train_under_a_gain-scheduling_control_strategy_according_to_the_weather_conditions (accessed on 6 March 2023). [CrossRef]
19. Jantara, V.L.; Basoalto, H.; Papaelias, M. A damage mechanics approach for lifetime estimation of wind turbine gearbox materials. *Int. J. Fatigue* **2020**, *137*, 105671. [CrossRef]
20. Komusanac, I.; Brindley, G.; Fraile, D.; Ramirez, L. *Wind Energy in Europe*; 2020 Statistics and the Outlook for 2021–2025; Technical Report; WindEurope Business Intelligence: Brussels, Belgium, 2021; Available online: https://www.windenergyhamburg.com/fileadmin/windenergy/2022/pdf/we22_wind-europe-stats2020.pdf (accessed on 6 March 2023).
21. Lee, J.; Zhao, F. GWEC–Global Wind Report 2021. Technical Report. Global Wind Energy Council. 2021. Available online: https://gwec.net/global-wind-report-2021/ (accessed on 6 March 2023).

22. Merainani, B.; Laddada, S.; Bechhoefer, E.; Chikh, M.; Benazzouz, D. An integrated methodology for estimating the remaining useful life of high-speed wind turbine shaft bearings with limited samples. *Renew. Energy* **2022**, *182*, 1141–1151. [CrossRef]
23. Romero, E.E.; Martinez, J.J.; Berenguer, C. Degradation of a Wind-Turbine Drive-Train under Turbulent Conditions: Effect of the Control Law. In Proceedings of the 2021 5th International Conference on Control and Fault-Tolerant Systems (SysTol), Saint-Raphael, France, 29 September–1 October 2021; pp. 335–340. Available online: https://www.researchgate.net/publication/356095568_Degradation_of_a_wind-turbine_drive-train_under_turbulent_conditions_effect_of_the_control_law (accessed on 6 March 2023).
24. Tchakoua, P.; Wamkeue, R.; Ouhrouche, M.; Slaoui, H.; Tameghe, T.; Ekemb, G. Wind Turbine Condition Monitoring: State-of-the-Art Review, New Trends, and Future Challenges. *Energies* **2014**, *7*, 2595–2630. Available online: https://www.researchgate.net/publication/273984269_Wind_Turbine_Condition_Monitoring_State-of-the-Art_Review_New_Trends_and_Future_Challenges (accessed on 6 March 2023). [CrossRef]
25. Kampen, J.K. Reflections on and test of the metrological properties of summated rating, Likert, and other scales based on sums of ordinal variables. *Measurement* **2019**, *137*, 428–434. Available online: https://www.researchgate.net/publication/330828499_Reflections_on_and_test_of_the_metrological_properties_of_summated_rating_Likert_and_other_scales_based_on_sums_of_ordinal_variables (accessed on 6 March 2023). [CrossRef]
26. Chen, H.B.; Zhuang, H.L. A new highly anti-interference regularization method for ill-posed problems. *Vibroeng. Procedia* **2017**, *15*, 128–133. [CrossRef]
27. Ershov, D.S.; Khayrullin, R.Z. Workplace for Verification of Measuring Instruments as a Non-Stationary Service System. *Instrum.-Mak. J.* **2022**, *65*, 701–711. Available online: https://cyberleninka.ru/article/n/matematicheskaya-model-rabochego-mesta-poverki-sredstv-izmereniy-kak-nestatsionarnaya-sistema-obsluzhivaniya (accessed on 6 March 2023).
28. Ershov, D.S.; Malahov, A.V.; Levina, T.A.; Khayrullin, R.Z. To Simulating the Functioning of Workplace for the Verification of Measuring Instruments. *J. Phys. Conf. Ser.* **2022**, *2388*, 012147. Available online: https://www.researchgate.net/publication/366228562_To_simulating_the_functioning_of_workplace_for_the_verification_of_measuring_instruments (accessed on 6 March 2023). [CrossRef]

axioms MDPI

Article

Further Closed Formulae of Exotic ${}_3F_2$-Series

Wenchang Chu [1,2]

[1] School of Mathematics and Statistics, Zhoukou Normal University, Zhoukou 466001, China; wenchang.chu@unisalento.it
[2] Department of Mathematics and Physics, University of Salento, 73100 Lecce, Italy

Abstract: By making use of the linearization method, we examine a class of nonterminating ${}_3F_2$-series with five free integer parameters that yields twenty summation formulae. Under the Kummer and Thomae transformations, six classes of exotic ${}_3F_2$-series are consequently evaluated in closed forms. There are overall 100 identities recorded in the present paper.

Keywords: hypergeometric series; nonterminating exotic ${}_3F_2$-series linearization method; Thomae transformation; Kummer transformation

MSC: Primary 33C20; Secondary 33F10

Citation: Chu, W. Further Closed Formulae of Exotic ${}_3F_2$-Series. *Axioms* **2023**, *12*, 291. https://doi.org/10.3390/axioms12030291

Academic Editors: Gradimir V. Milovanović and Clemente Cesarano

Received: 20 December 2022
Revised: 24 February 2023
Accepted: 9 March 2023
Published: 10 March 2023

1. Introduction and Outline

Denote by $\mathbb{N}$ and $\mathbb{Z}$, respectively, the sets of natural numbers and integers with $\mathbb{N}_0 = \mathbb{N} \cup \{0\}$. The shifted factorials are given by $(x)_0 = \langle x \rangle_0 =\equiv 1$ and

$$\left.\begin{aligned}(x)_n &= x(x+1)\cdots(x+n-1)\\ \langle x\rangle_n &= x(x-1)\cdots(x-n+1)\end{aligned}\right\} \quad \text{for} \quad n \in \mathbb{N}.$$

We can express them, even when $n \in \mathbb{Z}$, as the quotients

$$(x)_n = \frac{\Gamma(x+n)}{\Gamma(x)} \quad \text{and} \quad \langle x\rangle_n = \frac{\Gamma(1+x)}{\Gamma(1+x-n)},$$

where the Γ-function is defined by the Euler integral

$$\Gamma(x) = \int_0^\infty u^{x-1}e^{-u}\mathrm{d}u \quad \text{for} \quad \Re(x) > 0.$$

For brevity, their fractional forms are concisely shortened as

$$\left[\begin{matrix}\alpha, \beta, \cdots, \gamma\\ A, B, \cdots, C\end{matrix}\right]_n = \frac{(\alpha)_n(\beta)_n\cdots(\gamma)_n}{(A)_n(B)_n\cdots(C)_n},$$

$$\Gamma\left[\begin{matrix}\alpha, \beta, \cdots, \gamma\\ A, B, \cdots, C\end{matrix}\right] = \frac{\Gamma(\alpha)\Gamma(\beta)\cdots\Gamma(\gamma)}{\Gamma(A)\Gamma(B)\cdots\Gamma(C)}.$$

According to Bailey [1], the generalized hypergeometric series is defined by

$${}_{1+p}F_p\left[\begin{matrix}a_0, & a_1, & \cdots, & a_p\\ & b_1, & \cdots, & b_p\end{matrix}\middle|\, z\right] = \sum_{n=0}^{\infty} \frac{(a_0)_n(a_1)_n\cdots(a_p)_n}{n!(b_1)_n\cdots(b_p)_n} z^n.$$

When $z = 1$, this series is convergent only if the "parameter excess" (i.e., the difference between the sum of the denominator parameters and that of the numerator ones) has a positive real part.

There exist many strange evaluations of hypergeometric series (cf. [2–8] for example). Recently, Campbell, D'Aurizio and Sondow [9,10] discovered two mysterious-looking formulae (see **D1** and **D12**)

$$
{}_3F_2\left[\begin{matrix}\frac{1}{4}, & \frac{3}{4}, & \frac{1}{2} \\ & 1, & \frac{3}{2}\end{matrix}\,\middle|\,1\right] = \frac{4\ln(1+\sqrt{2})}{\pi},
$$

$$
{}_3F_2\left[\begin{matrix}\frac{1}{4}, & \frac{3}{4}, & -\frac{1}{2} \\ & 1, & \frac{1}{2}\end{matrix}\,\middle|\,1\right] = \frac{\sqrt{2}+\ln(1+\sqrt{2})}{\pi}.
$$

Campbell and Abrarov [11] found, among the others, the following two further ones (see **F10** and **G8**)

$$
{}_3F_2\left[\begin{matrix}\frac{3}{2}, & \frac{3}{4}, & -\frac{1}{4} \\ & 1, & \frac{7}{4}\end{matrix}\,\middle|\,1\right] = \frac{3\sqrt{\pi}\{3\sqrt{2}-\log(1+\sqrt{2})\}}{2\Gamma(\frac{1}{4})^2},
$$

$$
{}_3F_2\left[\begin{matrix}\frac{3}{2}, & \frac{1}{4}, & \frac{5}{4} \\ & 1, & \frac{9}{4}\end{matrix}\,\middle|\,1\right] = \frac{5\sqrt{\pi}\{3\sqrt{2}-\log(1+\sqrt{2})\}}{8\Gamma(\frac{3}{4})^2}.
$$

These series are said "exotic" because one numerator parameter minus a denominator parameter results in a negative integer. By examining carefully these seemingly unrelated series, we find that they are connected, under the Thomae and Kummer transformation (cf. Bailey [1] §3.2 and Page 98), to the following ${}_3F_2$-series

$$
\mathcal{F}(a,c,e;b,d) := {}_3F_2\left[\begin{matrix}1+a, & c, & \frac{1}{2}+e \\ & \frac{3}{4}+b, & \frac{5}{4}+d\end{matrix}\,\middle|\,1\right], \quad \left\{\begin{matrix}\Delta:=\frac{1}{2}+b+d-a-c-e>0 \\ \sigma:=b+d-a-c-e\geq 0\end{matrix}\right\},
$$

where $a,b,c,d,e \in \mathbb{Z}$ satisfying the conditions $a \geq 0$ and $c > 0$ so that the both series involved are nonterminating. When $\sigma = b+d-a-c-e \geq 0$, the series is convergent, because in this case the parameter excess $\Delta = \sigma + \frac{1}{2} > 0$ (i.e., the sum of the denominator parameters minus that of the numerator ones).

Classically, there are three typical summation theorems (for the ${}_3F_2$-series) discovered by Dixon, Watson and Whipple (cf. Bailey [1] §3.1, §3.3 and §3.4). However, neither of them can evaluate the afore-displayed series in closed form. In particular, the formulae for the ${}_3F_2$-series presented in this paper are not present in the recent paper by the author [12], and two useful compendiums: ([13] §8.1.2 and [14] §7.4.4), where numerous closed formulae are collected for the ${}_3F_2(1)$ series with numerical parameters.

By applying the linearization method (cf. [15–18]), we shall transform, in the next section, the evaluation of $\mathcal{F}$-series into the $\Omega_{m,n}$-series treated recently by the author [19]. The main results are summarized in the conclusive theorem as well as twenty closed formulae for the $\mathcal{F}$-series. Finally in Section 3, analytic formulae for six further classes of exotic ${}_3F_2$-series will be provided by employing the Thomae and Kummer transformations (cf. Bailey [1] §3.2 and Page 98) to the $\mathcal{F}$-series.

In order to ensure the accuracy, all the formulae appearing in this paper have been checked numerically by appropriately devised Mathematica commands.

2. Linearization Procedure for the $\mathcal{F}$-Series

In this section, we shall reduce, by means of the linearization method (cf. [15–18]), the $\mathcal{F}$-series to specific instances of a known $\Omega_{m,n}(x,y)$ function, that has recently been examined by the author [19].

2.1. $a = 0$

According to the Chu–Vandermonde convolution identity on binomial coefficients, it is routine to establish the following lemma.

Lemma 1 (Linear relation: $m \in \mathbb{N}_0$).

$$(A+n)_m = \sum_{k=0}^{m}(B+n)_k X_k \quad \textit{where} \quad X_k = \binom{m}{k}(A-B)_{m-k}.$$

Specifying the above relation to the equality

$$(1+n)_a = \sum_{k=0}^{a}(c+n)_k X_k(a) \quad \text{where} \quad X_k(a) = \binom{a}{k}(1-c)_{a-k}$$

and then substituting it into the $\mathcal{F}$-series, we have the double series

$$\begin{aligned}\mathcal{F}(a,c,e;b,d) &= \sum_{n=0}^{\infty}\begin{bmatrix} 1+a, & c, & \frac{1}{2}+e \\ 1, & \frac{3}{4}+b, & \frac{5}{4}+d \end{bmatrix}_n \sum_{k=0}^{a}\frac{(c+n)_k}{(1+n)_a}X_k(a) \\ &= \sum_{k=0}^{a}\frac{(c)_k}{(1)_a}X_k(a)\sum_{n=0}^{\infty}\begin{bmatrix} c+k, & \frac{1}{2}+e \\ \frac{3}{4}+b, & \frac{5}{4}+d \end{bmatrix}_n.\end{aligned}$$

This results in the reduction formula as below.

Proposition 1 (Reduction formula from $a > 0$ to $a = 0$).

$$\mathcal{F}(a,c,e;b,d) = \sum_{k=0}^{a}(-1)^a\binom{-c}{k}\binom{c-1}{a-k}\mathcal{F}(0,c+k,e;b,d).$$

2.2. $b = d$

The $\mathcal{F}$-series can further be reduced to the case $b = d$.
When $b > d$, we can specify Lemma 1 to the equality

$$(\tfrac{5}{4}+d+n)_{b-d} = \sum_{k=0}^{b-d}(c+n)_k Y_k(b,d) \quad \text{where} \quad Y_k(b,d) = \binom{b-d}{k}(\tfrac{5}{4}-c+d)_{b-d-k}.$$

Putting this inside the $\mathcal{F}$-series, we have the double series

$$\begin{aligned}\mathcal{F}(0,c,e;b,d) &= \sum_{n=0}^{\infty}\begin{bmatrix} c, \frac{1}{2}+e \\ \frac{3}{4}+b, \frac{5}{4}+d \end{bmatrix}_n \sum_{k=0}^{b-d}\frac{(c+n)_k}{(\frac{5}{4}+d+n)_{b-d}}Y_k(b,d) \\ &= \sum_{k=0}^{b-d}\frac{(c)_k}{(\frac{5}{4}+d)_{b-d}}Y_k(b,d)\sum_{n=0}^{\infty}\begin{bmatrix} c+k, \frac{1}{2}+e \\ \frac{3}{4}+b, \frac{5}{4}+b \end{bmatrix}_n.\end{aligned}$$

This yields the following reduction formula.

Proposition 2 (Reduction formula from $b > d$ to $b = d$).

$$\mathcal{F}(0,c,e;b,d) = \sum_{k=0}^{b-d}\binom{b-d}{k}\frac{(c)_k(\frac{5}{4}-c+d)_{b-d-k}}{(\frac{5}{4}+d)_{b-d}}\mathcal{F}(0,c+k,e;b,b).$$

Alternatively, for $b < d$, we can specify Lemma 1 to the equality

$$(\tfrac{3}{4}+b+n)_{d-b} = \sum_{k=0}^{d-b}(c+n)_k\mathcal{Y}_k(b,d) \quad \text{where} \quad \mathcal{Y}_k(b,d) = \binom{d-b}{k}(\tfrac{3}{4}+b-c)_{d-b-k}.$$

Substituting this into the $\mathcal{F}$-series, we have the double series

$$\mathcal{F}(0,c,e;b,d) = \sum_{n=0}^{\infty}\left[\begin{matrix} c, \frac{1}{2}+e \\ \frac{3}{4}+b, \frac{5}{4}+d \end{matrix}\right]_n \sum_{k=0}^{d-b} \frac{(c+n)_k}{(\frac{3}{4}+b+n)_{d-b}} \mathcal{Y}_k(b,d)$$
$$= \sum_{k=0}^{d-b} \frac{(c)_k}{(\frac{3}{4}+b)_{d-b}} \mathcal{Y}_k(b,d) \sum_{n=0}^{\infty}\left[\begin{matrix} c+k, \frac{1}{2}+e \\ \frac{3}{4}+d, \frac{5}{4}+d \end{matrix}\right]_n.$$

This gives rise to another reduction formula.

Proposition 3 (Reduction formula from $b < d$ to $b = d$).

$$\mathcal{F}(0,c,e;b,d) = \sum_{k=0}^{d-b} \binom{d-b}{k} \frac{(c)_k(\frac{3}{4}+b-c)_{d-b-k}}{(\frac{3}{4}+b)_{d-b}} \mathcal{F}(0,c+k,e;d,d).$$

2.3. $c = e$

The $\mathcal{F}$-series can further be reduced to the case $c = e$. For this purpose, we have to show the following linearization lemma.

Lemma 2 (Linear relation: $m \in \mathbb{N}_0$).

$$(A+n)_m = \sum_{k=0}^{m} \langle B+2n \rangle_k Z_k \quad \textit{where} \quad Z_k = \sum_{i=0}^{k} \frac{(-1)^{k-i}}{k!} \binom{k}{i} (A - \tfrac{B-i}{2})_m.$$

Proof. By substitution, it suffices to evaluate the double sum

$$\mathcal{S} := \sum_{k=0}^{m} \langle B+2n \rangle_k \sum_{i=0}^{k} \frac{(-1)^{k-i}}{k!} \binom{k}{i} (A - \tfrac{B-i}{2})_m = (A+n)_m.$$

By exchanging the order of summations, we can reformulate it as

$$\mathcal{S} = \sum_{i=0}^{m} \frac{\langle B+2n \rangle_i}{i!} (A - \tfrac{B-i}{2})_m \sum_{k=i}^{m} (-1)^{k-i} \binom{B+2n-i}{k-i}$$
$$= \sum_{i=0}^{m} (-1)^{m-i} \frac{\langle B+2n \rangle_i}{i!} (A - \tfrac{B-i}{2})_m \binom{B+2n-i-1}{m-i}$$
$$= \frac{\langle B+2n \rangle_{m+1}}{m!} \sum_{i=0}^{m} (-1)^{m-i} \binom{m}{i} \frac{(A - \frac{B-i}{2})_m}{B+2n-i}$$
$$= \frac{\langle B+2n \rangle_{m+1}}{m!} \times \frac{m!(A+n)_m}{\langle B+2n \rangle_{m+1}} = (A+n)_m,$$

where the last line is justified by finite difference calculus (cf. [20,21]). □

First for $c < e$, we have from Lemma 2 the equality

$$(\tfrac{1}{2}+c+n)_{e-c} = \sum_{k=0}^{e-c} \left\langle 2b+2n+\tfrac{1}{2} \right\rangle_k \mathcal{Z}_k(b,c,e),$$
$$\text{where} \quad \mathcal{Z}_k(b,c,e) = \sum_{i=0}^{k} \frac{(-1)^{k-i}}{k!} \binom{k}{i} (c-b+\tfrac{1+2i}{4})_{e-c}.$$

By inserting this into the $\mathcal{F}$-series, we obtain the double series below

$$\mathcal{F}(0,c,e;b,b) = \sum_{n=0}^{\infty}\left[\begin{matrix} c, \frac{1}{2}+e \\ \frac{3}{4}+b, \frac{5}{4}+b \end{matrix}\right]_n \sum_{k=0}^{e-c} \frac{\left\langle 2b+2n+\frac{1}{2}\right\rangle_k}{(\frac{1}{2}+c+n)_{e-c}} \mathcal{Z}_k(b,c,e)$$
$$= \sum_{k=0}^{e-c}(-1)^k \frac{(-\frac{1}{2}-2b)_k}{(\frac{1}{2}+c)_{e-c}} \mathcal{Z}_k(b,c,e) \sum_{n=0}^{\infty}\left[\begin{matrix} c, \frac{1}{2}+c \\ \frac{3-2k}{4}+b, \frac{5-2k}{4}+b \end{matrix}\right]_n.$$

Writing the inner sum concerning n in terms of the $\mathcal{F}$-series, we immediately establish the reduction formula as in the following proposition.

Proposition 4 (Reduction formula from $c < e$ to $c = e$).

$$\mathcal{F}(0,c,e;b,b) = \sum_{k=0}^{e-c}(-1)^k \frac{(-\frac{1}{2}-2b)_k}{(\frac{1}{2}+c)_{e-c}} \mathcal{Z}_k(b,c,e)\mathcal{F}(0,c,c;b-\tfrac{k}{2},b-\tfrac{k}{2}).$$

When $c > e$ and $e > 0$, we infer from Lemma 2 that

$$(e+n)_{c-e} = \sum_{k=0}^{c-e}\left\langle 2b+2n+\tfrac{1}{2}\right\rangle_k \mathcal{Z}_k(b,c,e),$$

where $$\mathcal{Z}_k(b,c,e) = \sum_{i=0}^{k} \frac{(-1)^{k-i}}{k!}\binom{k}{i}(e-b+\tfrac{2i-1}{4})_{c-e}. \tag{1}$$

Putting this inside the $\mathcal{F}$-series, we can analogously treat the double series

$$\mathcal{F}(0,c,e;b,b) = \sum_{n=0}^{\infty}\left[\begin{matrix} c, \frac{1}{2}+e \\ \frac{3}{4}+b, \frac{5}{4}+b \end{matrix}\right]_n \sum_{k=0}^{c-e} \frac{\left\langle 2b+2n+\frac{1}{2}\right\rangle_k}{(e+n)_{c-e}} \mathcal{Z}_k(b,c,e)$$
$$= \sum_{k=0}^{c-e}(-1)^k \frac{(-\frac{1}{2}-2b)_k}{(e)_{c-e}} \mathcal{Z}_k(b,c,e) \sum_{n=0}^{\infty}\left[\begin{matrix} e, \frac{1}{2}+e \\ \frac{3-2k}{4}+b, \frac{5-2k}{4}+b \end{matrix}\right]_n.$$

Instead, for $c > e$ and $e \leq 0$, reformulate first the $\mathcal{F}$-series by reindexing

$$\mathcal{F}(0,c,e;b,b) = \mathcal{F}(0,1+c-e,1;1+b-e,1+b-e)$$
$$\times \left[\begin{matrix} c, \frac{1}{2}+e \\ \frac{3}{4}+b, \frac{5}{4}+b \end{matrix}\right]_{1-e} + \sum_{n=0}^{-e}\left[\begin{matrix} c, \frac{1}{2}+e \\ \frac{3}{4}+b, \frac{5}{4}+b \end{matrix}\right]_n.$$

Then according to Lemma 2, we have another equality

$$(1+n)_{c-e} = \sum_{k=0}^{c-e}\langle \tfrac{5}{2}+2b-2e+2n\rangle_k \mathcal{Z}_k(b,c,e),$$

where the connection coefficients $\mathcal{Z}_k(b,c,e)$ coincide with those given by (1). Now, by substitution, we have another double series

$$\mathcal{F}(0,1+c-e,1;1+b-e,1+b-e)$$
$$= \sum_{n=0}^{\infty}\left[\begin{matrix} 1+c-e, \frac{3}{2} \\ \frac{7}{4}+b-e, \frac{9}{4}+b-e \end{matrix}\right]_n \sum_{k=0}^{c-e} \frac{\langle \frac{5}{2}+2b-2e+2n\rangle_k}{(1+n)_{c-e}} \mathcal{Z}_k(b,c,e)$$
$$= \sum_{k=0}^{c-e}(-1)^k \frac{(2e-2b-\frac{5}{2})_k}{(c-e)!} \mathcal{Z}_k(b,c,e) \sum_{n=0}^{\infty}\left[\begin{matrix} 1, \ \frac{3}{2} \\ \frac{7-2k}{4}+b-e, \frac{9-2k}{4}+b-e \end{matrix}\right]_n.$$

Summing up, we have established the reduction formula to the case $c = e$.

Proposition 5 (Reduction formula from $c > e$ to $c = e$).

$$e > 0: \ \mathcal{F}(0,c,e;b,b) = \sum_{k=0}^{c-e}(-1)^k \frac{(-\frac{1}{2}-2b)_k}{(e)_{c-e}} \mathcal{Z}_k(b,c,e)\mathcal{F}(0,e,e;b-\tfrac{k}{2},b-\tfrac{k}{2}),$$

$$e \le 0: \ \mathcal{F}(0,c,e;b,b) = \sum_{n=0}^{-e}\left[\begin{matrix} c, \frac{1}{2}+e \\ \frac{3}{4}+b, \frac{5}{4}+b \end{matrix}\right]_n + \sum_{k=0}^{c-e}(-1)^k \frac{(2e-2b-\frac{5}{2})_k}{(c-e)!} \mathcal{Z}_k(b,c,e)$$
$$\times \left[\begin{matrix} c, \frac{1}{2}+e \\ \frac{3}{4}+b, \frac{5}{4}+b \end{matrix}\right]_{1-e} \mathcal{F}(0,1,1;1+b-e-\tfrac{k}{2},1+b-e-\tfrac{k}{2}).$$

Observe that the parameter excess $\Delta \ge \frac{1}{2}$ for the $\mathcal{F}$-series is not diminished hitherto by the established reduction formulae. Consequently, all the $\mathcal{F}$-series displayed on the right hand sides of Propositions 4 and 5 have the parameter excess $\Delta \ge \frac{1}{2}$, and can be expressed as the following bisection series

$$\mathcal{F}(0,c,c;b,b) = \sum_{n=0}^{\infty} \frac{(2c)_{2n}}{(2b+\frac{3}{2})_{2n}} = \frac{1}{2} \times {}_2F_1\left[\begin{matrix} 1, \ 2c \\ \frac{3}{2}+2b \end{matrix} \,\middle|\, 1\right]$$
$$+\frac{1}{2} \times {}_2F_1\left[\begin{matrix} 1, \ 2c \\ \frac{3}{2}+2b \end{matrix} \,\middle|\, -1\right],$$

where $b, c \in \mathbb{N}$ subject to the condition $b \ge c$. Therefore, to evaluate the $\mathcal{F}$-series explicitly, it suffices to do that for the above bisection series.

2.4. $\Omega_{m,n}$-Series

In a recent paper [19], the author examined a more general series

$$\Omega_{m,n}(x,y) := {}_2F_1\left[\begin{matrix} x, \ \ m-x \\ n+\frac{1}{2} \end{matrix} \,\middle|\, y^2\right] \quad \text{where} \quad m,n \in \mathbb{Z} \tag{2}$$

and proved the following evaluation formula.

Theorem 1 (Chu [19] Theorems 4 and 8: Recurrence formula). *For the two natural numbers m and n satisfying $m < n$, there holds the following formula*

$$\Omega_{m,n}(x,y) = \frac{(\frac{1}{2})_n}{y^{2n}} \sum_{i=0}^{n-m} \binom{n-m}{i} \frac{(x)_i(m-x)_{n-m-i}}{(2x-n+i)_i(m-2x-i)_{n-m-i}}$$
$$\times \sum_{k=0}^{n}(-1)^{n-k}\binom{n}{k} \frac{2x+2i-2k}{(2x+2i-n-k)_{n+1}} \Omega_{0,0}(x+i-k,y),$$

where the series $\Omega_{0,0}$ is evaluated by

$$\Omega_{0,0}(x,y) = {}_2F_1\left[\begin{matrix} x, \ \ -x \\ \frac{1}{2} \end{matrix} \,\middle|\, y^2\right] = \cos(2x \arcsin y).$$

Hence, the $\mathcal{F}$-series can be evaluated in terms of the Ω-series by the theorem below.

Theorem 2 ($b \ge c: \ b, c \in \mathbb{N}$).

$$\mathcal{F}(0,c,c;b,b) = \frac{1}{2} \lim_{x \to 1} \Omega_{2c+1,2b+1}(x,1) + \frac{1}{2} \lim_{x \to 1} \Omega_{2c+1,2b+1}(x,\sqrt{-1})$$

with $\quad \Omega_{0,0}(x,1) = \cos(\pi x) \quad$ *and* $\quad \Omega_{0,0}(x,\sqrt{-1}) = \cosh\left(2x\ln(1+\sqrt{2})\right).$

2.5. Conclusive Theorem and Examples (Class-A)

Based on the preceding reduction formulae, we may evaluate, for any quintuple integers $a, b, c, d, e \in \mathbb{Z}$ subject to $a \geq 0$, $c > 0$ and $\sigma = b + d - a - c - e > 0$, the $\mathcal{F}$-series by carrying out the following procedure:

- **Step-A**: If $a = 0$, go directly to **Step-B**. Otherwise for $a > 0$, according to Proposition 1, express $\mathcal{F}(a, c, e; b, d)$ in terms of $\mathcal{F}(0, c, e; b, d)$, and then go to **Step-B**.
- **Step-B**: By means of Propositions 2 and 3, express $\mathcal{F}(0, c, e; b, d)$ in terms of $\mathcal{F}(0, c, e; b, b)$, and then go to **Step-C**.
- **Step-C**: In virtu of Propositions 4 and 5, express $\mathcal{F}(0, c, e; b, b)$ in terms of $\mathcal{F}(0, c, c; b, b)$, and then go to **Step-D**.
- **Step-D**: Finally by applying Theorems 1 and 2, evaluate $\mathcal{F}(0, c, c; b, b)$ explicitly in terms of the Ω-series.

Therefore, we have validated the conclusive theorem as below.

Theorem 3 (Conclusion). *For any quintuple integers*

$$a, b, c, d, e \in \mathbb{Z} \quad \textit{subject to} \quad a \geq 0,\ c > 0 \quad \textit{and} \quad \sigma = b + d - a - c - e > 0,$$

the nonterminating $\mathcal{F}(a, c, e; b, d)$ *series can always be evaluated by finitely linear sums of trigonometric function* $\cos(\pi x)$ *and hyperbolic function* $\cosh\big(2x\ln(1+\sqrt{2})\big)$, *where* $x \in \mathbb{Z}$ *and the coefficients are rational numbers.*

According to the afore-described procedure, we have written appropriate *Mathematica* commands to determine explicitly closed form expressions for $\mathcal{F}(a, c, e; b, d)$ series. Twenty summation formulae are displayed below, where the argument "1" will be suppressed from the notation of ${}_3F_2$-series for the sake of brevity. We shall call these series "Class-A". Among them, an equivalent form of **A5** has been obtained by Campbell and Abrarov ([11] Equation (18)).

A1. $${}_3F_2\left[1,\ 1,\ \tfrac{1}{2};\ \tfrac{5}{4},\ \tfrac{7}{4}\right] = \tfrac{3}{\sqrt{2}}\log(1+\sqrt{2}).$$

A2. $${}_3F_2\left[1,\ 1,\ \tfrac{1}{2};\ \tfrac{7}{4},\ \tfrac{9}{4}\right] = -5\{1-\sqrt{2}\log(1+\sqrt{2})\}.$$

A3. $${}_3F_2\left[1,\ 1,\ \tfrac{1}{2};\ \tfrac{5}{4},\ \tfrac{11}{4}\right] = \tfrac{-7}{15}\{1-3\sqrt{2}\log(1+\sqrt{2})\}.$$

A4. $${}_3F_2\left[1,\ 1,\ \tfrac{3}{2};\ \tfrac{5}{4},\ \tfrac{11}{4}\right] = \tfrac{7}{12}\{2+3\sqrt{2}\log(1+\sqrt{2})\}.$$

A5. $${}_3F_2\left[1,\ 1,\ \tfrac{3}{2};\ \tfrac{7}{4},\ \tfrac{9}{4}\right] = \tfrac{15}{4}\{2-\sqrt{2}\log(1+\sqrt{2})\}.$$

A6. $${}_3F_2\left[1,\ 1,\ \tfrac{3}{2};\ \tfrac{9}{4},\ \tfrac{11}{4}\right] = \tfrac{35}{6}\{4-3\sqrt{2}\log(1+\sqrt{2})\}.$$

A7. $${}_3F_2\left[1,\ 1,\ -\tfrac{1}{2};\ \tfrac{3}{4},\ \tfrac{5}{4}\right] = \tfrac{1}{3}\{1-\sqrt{2}\log(1+\sqrt{2})\}.$$

A8. $${}_3F_2\left[1,\ 1,\ -\tfrac{1}{2};\ \tfrac{1}{4},\ \tfrac{7}{4}\right] = \tfrac{3}{5}\{1-3\sqrt{2}\log(1+\sqrt{2})\}.$$

A9. $${}_3F_2\left[1,\ 1,\ -\tfrac{1}{2};\ \tfrac{7}{4},\ \tfrac{9}{4}\right] = \tfrac{-3}{7}\{3-4\sqrt{2}\log(1+\sqrt{2})\}.$$

A10. $${}_3F_2\left[1,\ 1,\ -\tfrac{3}{2};\ \tfrac{3}{4},\ \tfrac{5}{4}\right] = \tfrac{1}{35}\{3-4\sqrt{2}\log(1+\sqrt{2})\}.$$

A11. $_3F_2\left[1,\ 2,\ \tfrac{1}{2};\ \tfrac{7}{4},\ \tfrac{9}{4}\right] = \tfrac{5}{8}\{2+\sqrt{2}\log(1+\sqrt{2})\}.$
A12. $_3F_2\left[1,\ 2,\ -\tfrac{1}{2};\ \tfrac{5}{4},\ \tfrac{7}{4}\right] = \tfrac{3}{20}\{2-\sqrt{2}\log(1+\sqrt{2})\}.$
A13. $_3F_2\left[1,\ 2,\ -\tfrac{1}{2};\ \tfrac{3}{4},\ \tfrac{9}{4}\right] = \tfrac{5}{84}\{2-5\sqrt{2}\log(1+\sqrt{2})\}.$
A14. $_3F_2\left[1,\ 2,\ -\tfrac{1}{2};\ \tfrac{7}{4},\ \tfrac{9}{4}\right] = \tfrac{1}{14}\{8+\sqrt{2}\log(1+\sqrt{2})\}.$
A15. $_3F_2\left[1,\ 2,\ -\tfrac{3}{2};\ \tfrac{3}{4},\ \tfrac{9}{4}\right] = \tfrac{-5}{77}\{1+\sqrt{2}\log(1+\sqrt{2})\}.$
A16. $_3F_2\left[2,\ 2,\ \tfrac{1}{2};\ \tfrac{7}{4},\ \tfrac{13}{4}\right] = \tfrac{135}{224}\{6-\sqrt{2}\log(1+\sqrt{2})\}.$
A17. $_3F_2\left[2,\ 2,\ -\tfrac{1}{2};\ \tfrac{5}{4},\ \tfrac{11}{4}\right] = \tfrac{7}{48}\{2-3\sqrt{2}\log(1+\sqrt{2})\}.$
A18. $_3F_2\left[2,\ 2,\ -\tfrac{1}{2};\ \tfrac{9}{4},\ \tfrac{11}{4}\right] = \tfrac{1}{24}\{2+9\sqrt{2}\log(1+\sqrt{2})\}.$
A19. $_3F_2\left[2,\ 2,\ -\tfrac{3}{2};\ \tfrac{7}{4},\ \tfrac{13}{4}\right] = \tfrac{1}{22}\{8-3\sqrt{2}\log(1+\sqrt{2})\}.$
A20. $_3F_2\left[2,\ 2,\ -\tfrac{3}{2};\ \tfrac{11}{4},\ \tfrac{13}{4}\right] = \tfrac{-1}{13}\{13-15\sqrt{2}\log(1+\sqrt{2})\}.$

3. The Thomae and Kummer Transformations

In the classical theory of hypergeometric series, the Thomae and Kummer transformations are fundamental (cf. Bailey [1] §3.2 and Page 98 , where $\sigma = b+d-a-c-e$):

$$ {}_3F_2\left[\begin{matrix} a,c,e \\ b,d \end{matrix}\,\middle|\,1\right] = {}_3F_2\left[\begin{matrix} \sigma, b-a, d-a \\ c+\sigma, e+\sigma \end{matrix}\,\middle|\,1\right]\Gamma\left[\begin{matrix} \sigma,\ \ b,\ \ d \\ a, c+\sigma, e+\sigma \end{matrix}\right] \tag{3}$$

$$ {}_3F_2\left[\begin{matrix} a,c,e \\ b,d \end{matrix}\,\middle|\,1\right] = {}_3F_2\left[\begin{matrix} a, b-c, b-e \\ \sigma+a,\ b \end{matrix}\,\middle|\,1\right]\Gamma\left[\begin{matrix} \sigma,\ \ d \\ \sigma+a, d-a \end{matrix}\right]. \tag{4}$$

They will be applied to the $\mathcal{F}$-series to evaluete six classes of exotic $_3F_2$-series.

3.1. Class B

Applying the Kummer transformation (4), we can express the following "Class-B" series in terms of the $\mathcal{F}$-series (where $\sigma = b+d-a-c-e$):

$$ {}_3F_2\left[\begin{matrix} 1+a, & c+\frac{1}{4}, & e+\frac{3}{4} \\ & b+\frac{3}{2}, & d+\frac{5}{4} \end{matrix}\,\middle|\,1\right] = \Gamma\left[\begin{matrix} b+\frac{3}{2}, \sigma+\frac{3}{4} \\ b-a+\frac{1}{2}, \sigma+a+\frac{7}{4} \end{matrix}\right] \times {}_3F_2\left[\begin{matrix} 1+a, & d-c+1, & d-e+\frac{1}{2} \\ & d+\frac{5}{4}, & \sigma+a+\frac{7}{4} \end{matrix}\,\middle|\,1\right].$$

Then we can derive the following closed formulae for these series (except for divergent series) from those displayed in "Class A".

B1. $_3F_2\left[1,\ \tfrac{1}{4},\ \tfrac{3}{4};\ \tfrac{3}{2},\ \tfrac{5}{4}\right] = \sqrt{2}\log(1+\sqrt{2}).$
B2. $_3F_2\left[1,\ \tfrac{1}{4},\ \tfrac{7}{4};\ \tfrac{5}{2},\ \tfrac{5}{4}\right] = \tfrac{2}{5}\{1+2\sqrt{2}\log(1+\sqrt{2})\}.$
B3. $_3F_2\left[1,\ \tfrac{1}{4},\ \tfrac{7}{4};\ \tfrac{5}{2},\ \tfrac{9}{4}\right] = \tfrac{3}{2}\{2-\sqrt{2}\log(1+\sqrt{2})\}.$
B4. $_3F_2\left[1,\ \tfrac{3}{4},\ \tfrac{5}{4};\ \tfrac{3}{2},\ \tfrac{9}{4}\right] = \tfrac{5}{2}\{2-\sqrt{2}\log(1+\sqrt{2})\}.$
B5. $_3F_2\left[1,\ \tfrac{3}{4},\ \tfrac{5}{4};\ \tfrac{5}{2},\ \tfrac{9}{4}\right] = 5\{4-3\sqrt{2}\log(1+\sqrt{2})\}.$
B6. $_3F_2\left[1,\ \tfrac{7}{4},\ \tfrac{9}{4};\ \tfrac{5}{2},\ \tfrac{13}{4}\right] = \tfrac{9}{5}\{8-5\sqrt{2}\log(1+\sqrt{2})\}.$
B7. $_3F_2\left[2,\ \tfrac{1}{4},\ \tfrac{7}{4};\ \tfrac{7}{2},\ \tfrac{5}{4}\right] = \tfrac{2}{9}\{4+3\sqrt{2}\log(1+\sqrt{2})\}.$
B8. $_3F_2\left[2,\ \tfrac{3}{4},\ \tfrac{5}{4};\ \tfrac{5}{2},\ \tfrac{9}{4}\right] = \tfrac{5}{4}\{-2+3\sqrt{2}\log(1+\sqrt{2})\}.$
B9. $_3F_2\left[2,\ \tfrac{5}{4},\ \tfrac{7}{4};\ \tfrac{7}{2},\ \tfrac{9}{4}\right] = 5\{2-\sqrt{2}\log(1+\sqrt{2})\}.$
B10. $_3F_2\left[2,\ \tfrac{9}{4},\ \tfrac{11}{4};\ \tfrac{9}{2},\ \tfrac{13}{4}\right] = 30\{4-3\sqrt{2}\log(1+\sqrt{2})\}.$

3.2. Class C

By means of the Kummer transformation (4), we can express the "Class-C" series below in terms of the $\mathcal{F}$-series (where $\sigma = b + d - a - c - e$):

$$ {}_3F_2\left[\begin{matrix} 1+a, & c+\frac{1}{4}, & e+\frac{3}{4} \\ & b+\frac{3}{2}, & d+\frac{3}{4} \end{matrix}\middle| 1\right] = \Gamma\left[\begin{matrix} \sigma+\frac{1}{4}, b+\frac{3}{2} \\ \sigma+a+\frac{5}{4}, b-a+\frac{1}{2} \end{matrix}\right] \times {}_3F_2\left[\begin{matrix} 1+a, & d-e, & d-c+\frac{1}{2} \\ & d+\frac{3}{4}, & \sigma+a+\frac{5}{4} \end{matrix}\middle| 1\right]. $$

Then the closed formulae below for these series (except for divergent series) follow directly from those recorded in "Class A".

C1. ${}_3F_2[1, \frac{1}{4}, \frac{3}{4}; \frac{3}{2}, \frac{7}{4}] = \frac{3}{2}\{2 - \sqrt{2}\log(1+\sqrt{2})\}$.

C2. ${}_3F_2[1, \frac{1}{4}, \frac{3}{4}; \frac{5}{2}, \frac{7}{4}] = \frac{3}{5}\{8 - 5\sqrt{2}\log(1+\sqrt{2})\}$.

C3. ${}_3F_2[1, \frac{3}{4}, \frac{5}{4}; \frac{3}{2}, \frac{7}{4}] = 3\sqrt{2}\log(1+\sqrt{2})$.

C4. ${}_3F_2[1, \frac{3}{4}, \frac{9}{4}; \frac{5}{2}, \frac{7}{4}] = \frac{6}{5}\{1 + 2\sqrt{2}\log(1+\sqrt{2})\}$.

C5. ${}_3F_2[1, \frac{5}{4}, -\frac{1}{4}; \frac{3}{2}, \frac{3}{4}] = \frac{2}{3}\{1 - \sqrt{2}\log(1+\sqrt{2})\}$.

C6. ${}_3F_2[1, \frac{5}{4}, -\frac{1}{4}; \frac{3}{2}, \frac{7}{4}] = \frac{1}{4}\{2 + \sqrt{2}\log(1+\sqrt{2})\}$.

C7. ${}_3F_2[1, \frac{5}{4}, -\frac{1}{4}; \frac{5}{2}, \frac{3}{4}] = \frac{2}{7}\{5 - 2\sqrt{2}\log(1+\sqrt{2})\}$.

C8. ${}_3F_2[2, \frac{3}{4}, \frac{5}{4}; \frac{5}{2}, \frac{7}{4}] = \frac{3}{2}\{2 + \sqrt{2}\log(1+\sqrt{2})\}$.

C9. ${}_3F_2[2, \frac{3}{4}, \frac{9}{4}; \frac{7}{2}, \frac{7}{4}] = \frac{6}{7}\{8 + \sqrt{2}\log(1+\sqrt{2})\}$.

C10. ${}_3F_2[2, \frac{3}{4}, \frac{13}{4}; \frac{7}{2}, \frac{11}{4}] = \frac{1}{2}\{2 + 9\sqrt{2}\log(1+\sqrt{2})\}$.

3.3. Class D

By virtue of the Thomae transformation (3), we can express the following "Class-D" series in terms of the $\mathcal{F}$-series (where $\sigma = b + d - a - c - e$):

$$ {}_3F_2\left[\begin{matrix} a+\frac{1}{2}, & c+\frac{1}{4}, & e+\frac{3}{4} \\ & b+1, & d+\frac{1}{2} \end{matrix}\middle| 1\right] = \Gamma\left[\begin{matrix} \sigma, & b+1, & d+\frac{1}{2} \\ a+\frac{1}{2}, & \sigma+c+\frac{1}{4}, & \sigma+e+\frac{3}{4} \end{matrix}\right] \times {}_3F_2\left[\begin{matrix} \sigma, & d-a, & b-a+\frac{1}{2} \\ & \sigma+c+\frac{1}{4}, & \sigma+e+\frac{3}{4} \end{matrix}\middle| 1\right]. \quad (5) $$

Then we find the closed formulae below for these series (except for divergent series) as consequences of those produced in "Class A".

D1. ${}_3F_2[\frac{1}{4}, \frac{3}{4}, \frac{1}{2}; 1, \frac{3}{2}] = \frac{4\log(1+\sqrt{2})}{\pi}$.

D2. ${}_3F_2[\frac{1}{4}, \frac{7}{4}, \frac{1}{2}; 2, \frac{3}{2}] = \frac{8\{\sqrt{2}+3\log(1+\sqrt{2})\}}{9\pi}$.

D3. ${}_3F_2[\frac{1}{4}, \frac{7}{4}, \frac{1}{2}; 1, \frac{5}{2}] = \frac{2\{\sqrt{2}+9\log(1+\sqrt{2})\}}{5\pi}$.

D4. ${}_3F_2[\frac{1}{4}, \frac{7}{4}, \frac{3}{2}; 1, \frac{7}{2}] = \frac{8\{2\sqrt{2}+3\log(1+\sqrt{2})\}}{9\pi}$.

D5. ${}_3F_2[\frac{3}{4}, \frac{5}{4}, \frac{1}{2}; 1, \frac{5}{2}] = \frac{2\{\sqrt{2}+\log(1+\sqrt{2})\}}{\pi}$.

$$\textbf{D6.}\quad {}_3F_2\left[\tfrac{3}{4},\quad \tfrac{5}{4},\quad \tfrac{1}{2};\quad 2,\quad \tfrac{3}{2}\right] = \frac{8\left\{\sqrt{2}-\log(1+\sqrt{2})\right\}}{\pi}.$$

$$\textbf{D7.}\quad {}_3F_2\left[\tfrac{3}{4},\quad \tfrac{5}{4},\quad \tfrac{3}{2};\quad 1,\quad \tfrac{7}{2}\right] = \frac{8\left\{4\sqrt{2}+\log(1+\sqrt{2})\right\}}{7\pi}.$$

$$\textbf{D8.}\quad {}_3F_2\left[\tfrac{5}{4},\quad -\tfrac{1}{4},\quad \tfrac{1}{2};\quad 1,\quad \tfrac{3}{2}\right] = \frac{4\left\{2\sqrt{2}-\log(1+\sqrt{2})\right\}}{3\pi}.$$

$$\textbf{D9.}\quad {}_3F_2\left[\tfrac{5}{4},\quad -\tfrac{1}{4},\quad \tfrac{3}{2};\quad 1,\quad \tfrac{5}{2}\right] = \frac{4\left\{5\sqrt{2}-4\log(1+\sqrt{2})\right\}}{7\pi}.$$

$$\textbf{D10.}\quad {}_3F_2\left[\tfrac{5}{4},\quad \tfrac{7}{4},\quad \tfrac{3}{2};\quad 2,\quad \tfrac{7}{2}\right] = \frac{16\left\{\sqrt{2}-\log(1+\sqrt{2})\right\}}{\pi}.$$

Observing that the parameter excess of the ${}_3F_2$-series displayed on the right hand side of (5) equals $\Delta = \frac{1}{2} + a$, the equality (5) valid only when $a \geq 0$ and $\sigma \geq 0$. It remains a problem to evaluate, for $a < 0$, the ${}_3F_2$-series on the left of (5). This can also be resolved by the linearization method.

According to the Pfaff–Saalschütz summation theorem (cf. Bailey [1] §2.2), it is not hard to confirm the linear relation in the following lemma.

Lemma 3 (Linear relation: $m \in \mathbb{N}_0$).

$$(A+n)_m = \sum_{k=0}^{m} \langle n \rangle_k (B+n)_{m-k} X_k, \quad \textit{where} \quad X_k = (-1)^k \binom{m}{k} \frac{(A)_m (A-B)_k}{(B)_m (A)_k}.$$

By specializing this to the equality

$$(1+b+n)_{-a} = \sum_{k=0}^{-a} \langle n \rangle_k (\tfrac{1}{2}+a+n)_{-a-k} X_a^k,$$

$$\text{where} \quad X_k(a) = \frac{(-a)!}{\left\langle -\frac{1}{2} \right\rangle_{-a}} \binom{a-b-\frac{1}{2}}{k} \binom{b-a}{-a-k}$$

and then substituting it into the ${}_3F_2$-series, we may manipulate the double sum

$$\begin{aligned}
&{}_3F_2\left[\begin{matrix} \frac{1}{2}+a, & \frac{1}{4}+c, & \frac{3}{4}+e \\ & 1+b, & \frac{1}{2}+d \end{matrix} \,\middle|\, 1\right] \\
&= \sum_{n=0}^{\infty} \left[\begin{matrix} \frac{1}{2}+a, \frac{1}{4}+c, \frac{3}{4}+e \\ 1, 1+b, \frac{1}{2}+d \end{matrix}\right]_n \sum_{k=0}^{-a} \frac{\langle n \rangle_k (\frac{1}{2}+a+n)_{-a-k}}{(1+b+n)_{-a}} X_k(a) \\
&= \sum_{k=0}^{-a} \frac{(\frac{1}{2}+a)_{-a-k}}{(1+b)_{-a}} X_k(a) \sum_{n=0}^{\infty} \frac{\langle n \rangle_k}{n!} \left[\begin{matrix} \frac{1}{2}-k, \frac{1}{4}+c, \frac{3}{4}+e \\ 1-a+b, \frac{1}{2}+d \end{matrix}\right]_n.
\end{aligned}$$

Performing the replacement $n \to n+k$, we can express the last sum with respect to n as

$$\left[\begin{matrix} \frac{1}{2}-k, \frac{1}{4}+c, \frac{3}{4}+e \\ 1-a+b, \frac{1}{2}+d \end{matrix}\right]_k {}_3F_2\left[\begin{matrix} \frac{1}{2}, \frac{1}{4}+c+k, \frac{3}{4}+e+k \\ 1-a+b+k, \frac{1}{2}+d+k \end{matrix} \,\middle|\, 1\right].$$

Therefore, we have established, after some simplifications, the following transformation formula.

Theorem 4 (Reduction formula from $a < 0$ to $a = 0$).

$$
{}_3F_2\left[\begin{matrix}\frac{1}{2}+a, & \frac{1}{4}+c, & \frac{3}{4}+e \\ & 1+b, & \frac{1}{2}+d\end{matrix}\Big|1\right] = \sum_{k=0}^{-a}\left[\begin{matrix}a, \frac{1}{2}-a+b, \frac{1}{4}+c, \frac{3}{4}+e \\ 1, 1-a+b, 1+b, \frac{1}{2}+d\end{matrix}\right]_k \times {}_3F_2\left[\begin{matrix}\frac{1}{2}, \frac{1}{4}+c+k, \frac{3}{4}+e+k \\ 1-a+b+k, \frac{1}{2}+d+k\end{matrix}\Big|1\right].
$$

It should be emphasized that under this transformation, the parameter excess $\Delta = \sigma = b+d-a-c-e$ remains invariant for all the ${}_3F_2$-series. However the ${}_3F_2$-series on the right belongs to **Class-D** and can therefore be evaluated by (5). Ten more formulae are recorded below.

D11. ${}_3F_2\left[-\frac{1}{2}, \frac{1}{4}, -\frac{1}{4}; 1, \frac{3}{2}\right] = \frac{13\sqrt{2}+\log(1+\sqrt{2})}{6\pi}$.

D12. ${}_3F_2\left[-\frac{1}{2}, \frac{1}{4}, \frac{3}{4}; 1, \frac{1}{2}\right] = \frac{\sqrt{2}+\log(1+\sqrt{2})}{\pi}$.

D13. ${}_3F_2\left[-\frac{1}{2}, \frac{1}{4}, \frac{3}{4}; 1, \frac{3}{2}\right] = \frac{\sqrt{2}+5\log(1+\sqrt{2})}{2\pi}$.

D14. ${}_3F_2\left[-\frac{1}{2}, \frac{1}{4}, \frac{7}{4}; 1, \frac{3}{2}\right] = \frac{5\sqrt{2}+9\log(1+\sqrt{2})}{6\pi}$.

D15. ${}_3F_2\left[-\frac{1}{2}, \frac{3}{4}, \frac{5}{4}; 1, \frac{3}{2}\right] = \frac{3\sqrt{2}-\log(1+\sqrt{2})}{2\pi}$.

D16. ${}_3F_2\left[-\frac{1}{2}, \frac{3}{4}, -\frac{3}{4}; 1, \frac{1}{2}\right] = \frac{5\sqrt{2}+9\log(1+\sqrt{2})}{3\pi}$.

D17. ${}_3F_2\left[-\frac{1}{2}, \frac{3}{4}, -\frac{3}{4}; 2, \frac{1}{2}\right] = \frac{34\sqrt{2}+42\log(1+\sqrt{2})}{21\pi}$.

D18. ${}_3F_2\left[-\frac{1}{2}, \frac{5}{4}, \frac{7}{4}; 2, \frac{3}{2}\right] = \frac{7\sqrt{2}+3\ln(1+\sqrt{2})}{9\pi}$.

D19. ${}_3F_2\left[-\frac{1}{2}, -\frac{3}{4}, \frac{7}{4}; 1 \ \frac{3}{2}\right] = \frac{43\sqrt{2}+87\log(1+\sqrt{2})}{30\pi}$.

D20. ${}_3F_2\left[-\frac{3}{2}, -\frac{1}{4}, -\frac{3}{4}; 1, \frac{1}{2}\right] = \frac{31\sqrt{2}-37\log(1+\sqrt{2})}{8\pi}$.

Campbell, D'Aurizio and Sondow [9,10,22] discovered some formulae in **Class-D**.

- The formula **D1** has been found by them in ([9] Equation (10)), where they also conjectured **D12**. For this last evaluation, five different proofs have been provided by the same authors [10].
- By making use of beta integrals, Campbell recoded in ([22] Theorems 2,3,7 and Example 12) four formulae. The first one ([22] Theorem 2) is corrected by **D18**. The second one ([22] Theorem 3) is incorrect. The third one ([22] Theorem 7) is simplified by **D2**. The fourth one ([22] Example 12) is too complicated to reproduce here.

3.4. Class E

Again in view of the Thomae transformation (3), we can express the "Class-E" series below in terms of the $\mathcal{F}$-series (where $\sigma = b+d-a-c-e$):

$$
{}_3F_2\left[\begin{matrix}a+\frac{1}{2}, & c+\frac{1}{4}, & e+\frac{3}{4} \\ & b+\frac{1}{2}, & d+\frac{3}{2}\end{matrix}\Big|1\right] = \Gamma\left[\begin{matrix}\sigma+\frac{1}{2}, b+\frac{1}{2}, d+\frac{3}{2} \\ a+\frac{1}{2}, \sigma+c+\frac{3}{4}, \sigma+e+\frac{5}{4}\end{matrix}\right] \times {}_3F_2\left[\begin{matrix}1+d-a, & b-a, & \sigma+\frac{1}{2} \\ & \sigma+c+\frac{3}{4}, & \sigma+e+\frac{5}{4}\end{matrix}\Big|1\right]. \quad (6)
$$

Consequently, the closed formulae below for these series (except for divergent series) can be deduced from those exhibited in "Class A". Among them, **E2** simplifies a formula of Campbell ([22] Example 5).

E1. $\ _3F_2\left[\tfrac{1}{4}, \ \tfrac{3}{4}, \ \tfrac{1}{2}; \ \tfrac{3}{2}, \ \tfrac{3}{2}\right] = 2\sqrt{2} - 2\log(1+\sqrt{2}).$
E2. $\ _3F_2\left[\tfrac{1}{4}, \ \tfrac{7}{4}, \ \tfrac{1}{2}; \ \tfrac{3}{2}, \ \tfrac{3}{2}\right] = \tfrac{1}{3}\{4\sqrt{2} - 2\log(1+\sqrt{2})\}.$
E3. $\ _3F_2\left[\tfrac{1}{4}, \ \tfrac{7}{4}, \ \tfrac{3}{2}; \ \tfrac{5}{2}, \ \tfrac{5}{2}\right] = \tfrac{12}{25}\{8\sqrt{2} - 10\log(1+\sqrt{2})\}.$
E4. $\ _3F_2\left[\tfrac{3}{4}, \ \tfrac{5}{4}, \ \tfrac{1}{2}; \ \tfrac{3}{2}, \ \tfrac{3}{2}\right] = 2\log(1+\sqrt{2}).$
E5. $\ _3F_2\left[\tfrac{3}{4}, \ \tfrac{5}{4}, \ \tfrac{3}{2}; \ \tfrac{5}{2}, \ \tfrac{5}{2}\right] = 4\{4\sqrt{2} - 6\log(1+\sqrt{2})\}.$
E6. $\ _3F_2\left[\tfrac{3}{4}, \ \tfrac{9}{4}, \ \tfrac{1}{2}; \ \tfrac{3}{2}, \ \tfrac{5}{2}\right] = \tfrac{1}{5}\{\sqrt{2} + 9\log(1+\sqrt{2})\}.$
E7. $\ _3F_2\left[\tfrac{5}{4}, \ \tfrac{7}{4}, \ \tfrac{1}{2}; \ \tfrac{3}{2}, \ \tfrac{5}{2}\right] = \sqrt{2} + \log(1+\sqrt{2}).$
E8. $\ _3F_2\left[\tfrac{5}{4}, \ \tfrac{11}{4}, \ \tfrac{1}{2}; \ \tfrac{5}{2}, \ \tfrac{5}{2}\right] = \tfrac{9}{14}\{3\sqrt{2} - \log(1+\sqrt{2})\}.$
E9. $\ _3F_2\left[\tfrac{7}{4}, \ \tfrac{9}{4}, \ \tfrac{3}{2}; \ \tfrac{5}{2}, \ \tfrac{7}{2}\right] = 12\{\sqrt{2} - \log(1+\sqrt{2})\}.$
E10. $\ _3F_2\left[\tfrac{9}{4}, \ \tfrac{11}{4}, \ \tfrac{5}{2}; \ \tfrac{7}{2}, \ \tfrac{9}{2}\right] = 40\{4\sqrt{2} - 6\log(1+\sqrt{2})\}.$

Analogous to the series in **Class-D**, the parameter excess of the $_3F_2$-series displayed on the right hand side of (6) equals $\Delta = \frac{1}{2} + a$, which converges only when $a \geq 0$. We can also evaluate that $_3F_2$-series by reducing the case $a < 0$ to $a = 0$.

By means of Lemma 3, we have the equality

$$\left(\tfrac{1}{2} + b + n\right)_{-a} = \sum_{k=0}^{-a} \langle n\rangle_k \left(\tfrac{1}{2} + a + n\right)_{-a-k} X_a^k,$$
$$\text{where} \quad X_k(a) = \frac{(-a)!}{\left\langle -\frac{1}{2}\right\rangle_{-a}} \binom{a-b}{k}\binom{b-a-\frac{1}{2}}{-a-k}$$

and then insert it in the $_3F_2$-series, we can handle the double sum

$$\begin{aligned}
&{}_3F_2\left[\begin{matrix} \frac{1}{2}+a, & \frac{1}{4}+c, & \frac{3}{4}+e \\ & \frac{1}{2}+b, & \frac{3}{2}+d \end{matrix} \,\middle|\, 1\right] \\
&= \sum_{n=0}^{\infty} \left[\begin{matrix} \frac{1}{2}+a, \frac{1}{4}+c, \frac{3}{4}+e \\ 1, \frac{1}{2}+b, \frac{3}{2}+d \end{matrix}\right]_n \sum_{k=0}^{-a} \frac{\langle n\rangle_k \left(\frac{1}{2}+a+n\right)_{-a-k}}{\left(\frac{1}{2}+b+n\right)_{-a}} X_k(a) \\
&= \sum_{k=0}^{-a} \frac{\left(\frac{1}{2}+a\right)_{-a-k}}{\left(\frac{1}{2}+b\right)_{-a}} X_k(a) \sum_{n=0}^{\infty} \frac{\langle n\rangle_k}{n!} \left[\begin{matrix} \frac{1}{2}-k, \frac{1}{4}+c, \frac{3}{4}+e \\ \frac{1}{2}-a+b, \frac{3}{2}+d \end{matrix}\right]_n.
\end{aligned}$$

Making the replacement $n \to n + k$, we can express the last sum as

$$\left[\begin{matrix} \frac{1}{2}-k, \frac{1}{4}+c, \frac{3}{4}+e \\ \frac{1}{2}-a+b, \frac{3}{2}+d \end{matrix}\right]_k {}_3F_2\left[\begin{matrix} \frac{1}{2}, \frac{1}{4}+c+k, \frac{3}{4}+e+k \\ \frac{1}{2}-a+b+k, \frac{3}{2}+d+k \end{matrix} \,\middle|\, 1\right].$$

After some simplifications, we establish the transformation below.

Theorem 5 (Reduction formula from $a < 0$ to $a = 0$).

$$\begin{aligned}
{}_3F_2\left[\begin{matrix} \frac{1}{2}+a, & \frac{1}{4}+c, & \frac{3}{4}+e \\ & \frac{1}{2}+b, & \frac{3}{2}+d \end{matrix} \,\middle|\, 1\right] &= \sum_{k=0}^{-a} \left[\begin{matrix} a, b-a, \frac{1}{4}+c, \frac{3}{4}+e \\ 1, \frac{1}{2}-a+b, \frac{1}{2}+b, \frac{3}{2}+d \end{matrix}\right]_k \\
&\times {}_3F_2\left[\begin{matrix} \frac{1}{2}, \frac{1}{4}+c+k, \frac{3}{4}+e+k \\ \frac{1}{2}-a+b+k, \frac{3}{2}+d+k \end{matrix} \,\middle|\, 1\right].
\end{aligned}$$

Under this transformation, the parameter excess $\Delta = \sigma = b + d - a - c - e$ remains invariant for all the $_3F_2$-series involved. However the $_3F_2$-series on the right belongs to **Class-E** and can therefore be evaluated by (6). We record ten more examples.

E11. $_3F_2\left[-\tfrac{1}{2}, \tfrac{1}{4}, \tfrac{3}{4}; \tfrac{1}{2}, \tfrac{3}{2}\right] = \frac{6-\sqrt{2}\log(1+\sqrt{2})}{4\sqrt{2}}.$

E12. $_3F_2\left[-\tfrac{1}{2}, \tfrac{1}{4}, \tfrac{7}{4}; \tfrac{1}{2}, \tfrac{3}{2}\right] = \frac{14-5\sqrt{2}\log(1+\sqrt{2})}{12\sqrt{2}}.$

E13. $_3F_2\left[-\tfrac{1}{2}, \tfrac{3}{4}, \tfrac{5}{4}; \tfrac{1}{2}, \tfrac{3}{2}\right] = \frac{2-3\sqrt{2}\log(1+\sqrt{2})}{4\sqrt{2}}.$

E14. $_3F_2\left[-\tfrac{1}{2}, \tfrac{3}{4}, \tfrac{5}{4}; \tfrac{3}{2}, \tfrac{3}{2}\right] = \frac{2+5\sqrt{2}\log(1+\sqrt{2})}{8\sqrt{2}}.$

E15. $_3F_2\left[-\tfrac{1}{2}, \tfrac{5}{4}, \tfrac{7}{4}; \tfrac{1}{2}, \tfrac{5}{2}\right] = \frac{3\left\{2+5\sqrt{2}\log(1+\sqrt{2})\right\}}{-16\sqrt{2}}.$

E16. $_3F_2\left[-\tfrac{1}{2}, \tfrac{5}{4}, \tfrac{7}{4}; \tfrac{3}{2}, \tfrac{3}{2}\right] = \frac{10-7\sqrt{2}\log(1+\sqrt{2})}{24\sqrt{2}}.$

E17. $_3F_2\left[-\tfrac{3}{2}, \tfrac{3}{4}, \tfrac{5}{4}; \tfrac{1}{2}, \tfrac{3}{2}\right] = \frac{10-39\sqrt{2}\log(1+\sqrt{2})}{128\sqrt{2}}.$

E18. $_3F_2\left[-\tfrac{3}{2}, \tfrac{3}{4}, \tfrac{5}{4}; \tfrac{1}{2}, \tfrac{5}{2}\right] = \frac{3\left\{62-37\sqrt{2}\log(1+\sqrt{2})\right\}}{256\sqrt{2}}.$

E19. $_3F_2\left[-\tfrac{3}{2}, \tfrac{5}{4}, \tfrac{7}{4}; \tfrac{3}{2}, \tfrac{3}{2}\right] = \frac{62-37\sqrt{2}\log(1+\sqrt{2})}{512\sqrt{2}}.$

E20. $_3F_2\left[-\tfrac{3}{2}, \tfrac{5}{4}, -\tfrac{1}{4}; \tfrac{1}{2}, \tfrac{3}{2}\right] = \frac{3\left\{42+41\sqrt{2}\log(1+\sqrt{2})\right\}}{128\sqrt{2}}.$

3.5. Class F

By invoking the Kummer transformation (4), we can express the "Class-F" series below in terms of the $\mathcal{F}$-series (where $\sigma = b + d - a - c - e$):

$$
{}_3F_2\left[\begin{matrix} a+\tfrac{1}{2}, & c+\tfrac{3}{4}, & e+\tfrac{3}{4} \\ & b+1, & d+\tfrac{7}{4} \end{matrix}\,\middle|\,1\right] = \Gamma\left[\begin{matrix} b+1, \sigma+\tfrac{3}{4} \\ b-a+\tfrac{1}{2}, \sigma+a+\tfrac{5}{4} \end{matrix}\right]
\times {}_3F_2\left[\begin{matrix} 1+d-c, & 1+d-e, & a+\tfrac{1}{2} \\ & \sigma+a+\tfrac{5}{4}, & d+\tfrac{7}{4} \end{matrix}\,\middle|\,1\right].
$$

Then the closed formulae below for these series (except for divergent series) can be established from those shown in "Class A". Among them, the formula **F10** is due to Campbell and Abrarov ([11] Corollary 5).

F1. $_3F_2\left[-\tfrac{1}{2}, -\tfrac{1}{4}, -\tfrac{1}{4}; 1, \tfrac{3}{4}\right] = \frac{2\sqrt{\pi}\left\{5\sqrt{2}-4\log(1+\sqrt{2})\right\}}{\Gamma(\frac{1}{4})^2}.$

F2. $_3F_2\left[-\tfrac{1}{2}, \tfrac{3}{4}, -\tfrac{1}{4}; 1, \tfrac{7}{4}\right] = \frac{3\sqrt{\pi}\left\{8\sqrt{2}+2\log(1+\sqrt{2})\right\}}{5\Gamma(\frac{1}{4})^2}.$

F3. $_3F_2\left[-\tfrac{1}{2}, \tfrac{3}{4}, \tfrac{3}{4}; 1, \tfrac{7}{4}\right] = \frac{6\sqrt{\pi}\left\{\sqrt{2}+4\log(1+\sqrt{2})\right\}}{5\Gamma(\frac{1}{4})^2}.$

F4. $_3F_2\left[-\tfrac{1}{2}, \tfrac{3}{4}, \tfrac{7}{4}; 1, \tfrac{11}{4}\right] = \frac{7\sqrt{\pi}\left\{4\sqrt{2}+6\log(1+\sqrt{2})\right\}}{15\Gamma(\frac{1}{4})^2}.$

F5. $_3F_2\left[\tfrac{1}{2}, -\tfrac{1}{4}, -\tfrac{1}{4}; 1, \tfrac{3}{4}\right] = \frac{2\sqrt{\pi}\left\{4\sqrt{2}-2\log(1+\sqrt{2})\right\}}{\Gamma(\frac{1}{4})^2}.$

F6. $_3F_2\left[\tfrac{1}{2}, -\tfrac{1}{4}, -\tfrac{1}{4}; 1, \tfrac{7}{4}\right] = \frac{9\sqrt{\pi}\left\{3\sqrt{2}-\log(1+\sqrt{2})\right\}}{4\Gamma(\frac{1}{4})^2}.$

F7. $_3F_2\left[\tfrac{1}{2}, \tfrac{3}{4}, -\tfrac{1}{4}; 1, \tfrac{7}{4}\right] = \frac{3\sqrt{\pi}\left\{\sqrt{2}+\log(1+\sqrt{2})\right\}}{\Gamma(\frac{1}{4})^2}.$

F8. $_3F_2\left[\tfrac{1}{2}, \tfrac{3}{4}, \tfrac{3}{4}; 1, \tfrac{7}{4}\right] = \frac{12\sqrt{\pi}\log(1+\sqrt{2})}{\Gamma(\frac{1}{4})^2}.$

F9. $_3F_2\left[\tfrac{1}{2}, \tfrac{3}{4}, \tfrac{7}{4}; 1, \tfrac{11}{4}\right] = \frac{7\sqrt{\pi}\left\{\sqrt{2}+9\log(1+\sqrt{2})\right\}}{5\Gamma(\frac{1}{4})^2}.$

F10 $_3F_2\left[\tfrac{3}{2}, \tfrac{3}{4}, -\tfrac{1}{4}; 1, \tfrac{7}{4}\right] = \frac{3\sqrt{\pi}\left\{3\sqrt{2}-\log(1+\sqrt{2})\right\}}{2\Gamma(\frac{1}{4})^2}.$

3.6. Class G

Finally, by employing the Kummer transformation (4), we can express the "Class-G" series below in terms of the $\mathcal{F}$-series (where $\sigma = b + d - a - c - e$):

$$ {}_3F_2\left[\begin{matrix} a+\frac{1}{2}, & c+\frac{1}{4}, & e+\frac{1}{4} \\ & b+1, & d+\frac{1}{4} \end{matrix} \middle| 1 \right] = \Gamma\left[\begin{matrix} b+1, \sigma+\frac{1}{4} \\ b-a+\frac{1}{2}, \sigma+a+\frac{3}{4} \end{matrix}\right] $$
$$ \times {}_3F_2\left[\begin{matrix} d-c, & d-e, & a+\frac{1}{2} \\ & d+\frac{1}{4}, & \sigma+a+\frac{3}{4} \end{matrix} \middle| 1 \right]. $$

Then the closed formulae below for these series (except for divergent series) can be shown from those displayed in "Class A". Among them, the formula **G8** is due to Campbell and Abrarov ([11] Corollary 4), who evaluated also another similar series ([11] Corollary 6).

G1. $ {}_3F_2\left[-\frac{3}{2}, \frac{5}{4}, \frac{5}{4}; 1, \frac{13}{4}\right] = \frac{5\sqrt{\pi}\{4\sqrt{2}-3\log(1+\sqrt{2})\}}{44\Gamma(\frac{3}{4})^2}. $

G2. $ {}_3F_2\left[-\frac{1}{2}, \frac{1}{4}, -\frac{3}{4}; 1, \frac{5}{4}\right] = \frac{\sqrt{\pi}\{2\sqrt{2}+3\log(1+\sqrt{2})\}}{6\Gamma(\frac{3}{4})^2}. $

G3. $ {}_3F_2\left[\frac{1}{2}, \frac{1}{4}, -\frac{3}{4}; 1, \frac{5}{4}\right] = \frac{\sqrt{\pi}\{\sqrt{2}+9\log(1+\sqrt{2})\}}{12\Gamma(\frac{3}{4})^2}. $

G4. $ {}_3F_2\left[\frac{1}{2}, \frac{1}{4}, \frac{1}{4}; 1, \frac{5}{4}\right] = \frac{\sqrt{\pi}\log(1+\sqrt{2})}{\Gamma(\frac{3}{4})^2}. $

G5. $ {}_3F_2\left[\frac{1}{2}, \frac{1}{4}, \frac{1}{4}; 2, \frac{5}{4}\right] = \frac{2\sqrt{\pi}\{-\sqrt{2}+6\log(1+\sqrt{2})\}}{9\Gamma(\frac{3}{4})^2}. $

G6. $ {}_3F_2\left[\frac{1}{2}, \frac{1}{4}, \frac{5}{4}; 2, \frac{9}{4}\right] = \frac{5\sqrt{\pi}\{\sqrt{2}-\log(1+\sqrt{2})\}}{3\Gamma(\frac{3}{4})^2}. $

G7. $ {}_3F_2\left[\frac{1}{2}, \frac{5}{4}, \frac{9}{4}; 2, \frac{13}{4}\right] = \frac{3\sqrt{\pi}\{-\sqrt{2}+5\log(1+\sqrt{2})\}}{7\Gamma(\frac{3}{4})^2}. $

G8. $ {}_3F_2\left[\frac{3}{2}, \frac{1}{4}, \frac{5}{4}; 1, \frac{9}{4}\right] = \frac{5\sqrt{\pi}\{3\sqrt{2}-\log(1+\sqrt{2})\}}{8\Gamma(\frac{3}{4})^2} $

G9. $ {}_3F_2\left[\frac{3}{2}, \frac{5}{4}, \frac{5}{4}; 2, \frac{9}{4}\right] = \frac{5\sqrt{\pi}\{2\sqrt{2}-2\log(1+\sqrt{2})\}}{\Gamma(\frac{3}{4})^2}. $

G10. $ {}_3F_2\left[\frac{3}{2}, \frac{5}{4}, \frac{9}{4}; 3, \frac{13}{4}\right] = \frac{6\sqrt{\pi}\{-6\sqrt{2}+10\log(1+\sqrt{2})\}}{\Gamma(\frac{3}{4})^2}. $

Concluding Comments

By combining the linearization method with the Kummer and Thomae transformations, we present 100 explicit formulae for 7 classes of nonterminating ${}_3F_2(1)$-series. They may potentially find applications in mathematics and physics as other mathematical formulae. Further explorations are encouraged to enrich this bank database of hypergeometric series identities.

Funding: This research received no external funding.

Data Availability Statement: Not applicable.

Conflicts of Interest: The author declares no conflict of interest.

References

1. Bailey, W.N. *Generalized Hypergeometric Series*; Cambridge University Press: Cambridge, UK, 1935
2. Asakura, M.; Yabu, T. Explicit logarithmic formulas of special values of hypergeometric functions ${}_3F_2$. *Commun. Contemp. Math.* **2020**, *22*, 1950040. [CrossRef]
3. Chen, K.-W. Explicit formulas for some infinite ${}_3F_2(1)$-Series. *Axioms* **2021**, *10*, 125. [CrossRef]
4. Chu, W. Inversion techniques and combinatorial identities: A unified treatment for the ${}_7F_6$-series identities. *Collect. Math.* **1994**, *45*, 13–43

5. Ekhad, S.B. Forty Strange Computer–Discovered and Computer–Proved (Of Course) Hypergeometric Series Evaluations. Available online: http://www.math.rutgers.edu/~zeilberg/ekhad/ekhad.html (accessed on 10 October 2021).
6. Gessel, I.M. Finding identities with the WZ method. *J. Symbolic Comput.* **1995**, *20*, 537–566 [CrossRef]
7. Gessel, I.M.; Stanton, D. Strange evaluations of hypergeometric series. *SIAM J. Math. Anal.* **1982**, *13*, 295–308 [CrossRef]
8. Zudilin, W. Arithmetic hypergeometric series. *Russ. Math. Surv.* **2011**, *66*, 1–51 [CrossRef]
9. Campbell, J.M.; D'Aurizio, J.; Sondow, J. On the interplay among hypergeometric functions, complete elliptic integrals, and Fourier–Legendre expansions. *J. Math. Anal. Appl.* **2019**, *479*, 90–121. [CrossRef]
10. Campbell, J.M.; D'Aurizio, J.; Sondow, J. Hypergeometry of the parbelos. *Am. Math. Mon.* **2020**, *127*, 23–32 [CrossRef]
11. Campbell, J.M.; Abrarov, S. An Analogue of Ramanujan's Master Theorem. Available online: https://hal.archives-ouvertes.fr/hal-01897255 (accessed on 9 September 2020).
12. Chu, W. Seven hundreds of exotic ${}_3F_2$-series evaluated in π, $\sqrt{2}$ and $\log(1+\sqrt{2})$. *Contemp. Math.* **2021**, *2*, 327–398. [CrossRef]
13. Brychkov, Y.A. *Handbook of Special Functions: Derivatives, Integrals, Series and Other Formulas*; CRC Press: Boca Raton, FL, USA, 2008.
14. Prudnikov, A.P.; Brychkov, Y.A.; Marichev, O.I. *More Special Functions*; Integrals and Series; Gordon & Breach: New York, NY, USA, 1990; Volume 3.
15. Chu, W. Analytical formulae for extended ${}_3F_2$-series of Watson–Whipple–Dixon with two extra integer parameters. *Math. Comp.* **2012**, *81*, 467–479 [CrossRef]
16. Chu, W. Terminating ${}_4F_3$-series extended with two integer parameters. *Integral Transform. Spec. Funct.* **2016**, *27*, 794–805 [CrossRef]
17. Fields, J.L.; Wimp, J. Expansions of hypergeometric functions in hypergeometric functions. *Math. Comp.* **1961**, *15*, 390–395 [CrossRef]
18. Lewanowicz, S. Generalized Watson's summation formula for ${}_3F_2(1)$. *J. Comput. Appl. Math.* **1997**, *86*, 375–386. [CrossRef]
19. Chu, W. Trigonometric expressions for Gaussian ${}_2F_1$-series. *Turk. J. Math.* **2019**, *43*, 1823–1836. [CrossRef]
20. Gessel, I.M. A simple proof of Andrews's ${}_5F_4$ evaluation. *Ramanujan J.* **2015**, *36*, 165–170. [CrossRef]
21. Chu, W. Finite differences and terminating hypergeometric series. *Bull. Irish Math. Soc.* **2016**, *78*, 31–45. [CrossRef]
22. Campbell, J.M. Ramanujan–type series related to Clausen's product. *arXiv* **2011**, arXiv:1010.1941v3.

axioms MDPI

Article

A Note on the Volume Conserving Solution to Simultaneous Aggregation and Collisional Breakage Equation

Farel William Viret Kharchandy [1], Arijit Das [1], Vamsinadh Thota [1], Jitraj Saha [1,*] and Mehakpreet Singh [2,*]

[1] Department of Mathematics, National Institute of Technology Tiruchirappalli, Tamil Nadu 620015, India
[2] Mathematics Applications Consortium for Science and Industry (MACSI), Department of Mathematics and Statistics, University of Limerick, V94 T9PX Limerick, Ireland
* Correspondence: jitraj@nitt.edu (J.S.); mehakpreet.singh@ul.ie (M.S.)

Abstract: A new population balance model is introduced, in which a pair of particles can coagulate into a larger one if their encounter is a completely inelastic collision; otherwise, one of them breaks into multiple fragments (two or more) due to the elastic collision. Mathematically, coagulation and breakage models both manifest nonlinearity behavior. We prove the global existence and uniqueness of the solution to this model for the compactly supported kinetic kernels and an unbounded breakage distribution function. A further investigation dealt with the volume conservation property (necessary condition) of the solution.

Keywords: coagulation; collisional breakage; existence and uniqueness; volume conservation; compact support

MSC: 35Q70; 45K05; 45G05

1. Introduction

Aggregation (coagulation) and fragmentation are fundamental mechanisms that occur in particulate processes such as granulation and crystallization in the pharmaceutical industry [1]. When two particles merge to form a larger one, this process is defined as aggregation. In reverse, fragmentation leads to the formation of smaller particles after the breakup of the mother particle. The aggregation process is inherently nonlinear, while fragmentation is of two types (a) linear, and (b) nonlinear. If fragmentation is spontaneous and driven by an external agent then the process is linear. However, if the process occurs due to the interactions (collisions) between the particles in the system, then it is recognized as a nonlinear fragmentation. The byproducts of the original fragmentation undergo repeated collisions and breakages to drive this process forward. The collisional-induced fragmentation can also be observed in various fields of science and engineering, including the formation of raindrops [2], communication systems [3] and milling processes [4]. Both aggregation and fragmentation mechanisms have been intensively used in the literature for developing mathematical models corresponding to granulation processes [1].

Mathematically, both aggregation and collisional-induced fragmentation mechanisms are represented by a nonlinear integro-partial differential equation. The mathematical expression for tracking the changes in the distribution $\varphi(x,t)$ via these mechanisms can be written as:

$$\begin{aligned}\frac{\partial\varphi(x,t)}{\partial t} =& \frac{1}{2}\int_0^x \mathscr{C}(x-y,y)\varphi(x-y,t)\varphi(y,t)\mathrm{d}y - \varphi(x,t)\int_0^\infty \mathscr{C}(x,y)\varphi(y,t)\mathrm{d}y \\ &+ \int_0^\infty\int_x^\infty \mathscr{K}(y,z)\mathcal{B}(x,y;z)\varphi(y,t)\varphi(z,t)\mathrm{d}y\mathrm{d}z - \varphi(x,t)\int_0^\infty \mathscr{K}(x,y)\varphi(y,t)\mathrm{d}y \end{aligned} \quad (1)$$

with the initial data

$$\varphi(x,0) = \varphi_0(x)(\geq 0), \quad \text{for all} \quad x \in \mathbb{R}_+ = (0,\infty). \quad (2)$$

Citation: Kharchandy, F.W.V.; Das, A.; Thota, V.; Saha, J.; Singh, M. A Note on the Volume Conserving Solution to Simultaneous Aggregation and Collisional Breakage Equation. *Axioms* **2023**, *12*, 181. https://doi.org/10.3390/axioms12020181

Academic Editor: Clemente Cesarano

Received: 15 December 2022
Revised: 19 January 2023
Accepted: 3 February 2023
Published: 9 February 2023

Here, ∂_t stands for the partial derivative with respect to the time t. φ is the number density function for particles of volume x at time t. The kernel $\mathscr{C}(x,y)$ is the aggregation rate at which two particles with particle properties x and y combine to form a larger cluster. $\mathscr{K}(x,y)$ is the collision kernel which describes the rate at which particles of properties x and y are colliding. It is worth noting that both the kernels $\mathscr{C}(x,y)$ and $\mathscr{K}(x,y)$ are symmetric,that is, $\mathscr{C}(x,y) = \mathscr{C}(y,x)$ and $\mathscr{K}(x,y) = \mathscr{K}(y,x)$. $\mathcal{B}(x|y;z)$ is the rate at which particles of property y breaks into fragments of property x due to its impact with a particle of property z. The breakage kernel $\mathcal{B}$ satisfies the following properties.

(i) $\mathcal{B}(x,y;z)$ is non negative and symmetric with respect to y and z, that is

$$\mathcal{B}(x,y;z) = \mathcal{B}(x,z;y).$$

(ii) Volume conservation law

$$\int_0^y x\mathcal{B}(x,y;z)\mathrm{d}x = y \quad and \quad \mathcal{B}(x,y;z) = 0 \quad \text{for all} \quad y \leq x; \tag{3}$$

(iii) Number of particles after fragmentation

$$\int_0^y \mathcal{B}(x,y;z)\mathrm{d}x = \nu(y,z) \leq \bar{N} < \infty \quad \text{for all} \quad y > 0, z > 0. \tag{4}$$

The first integral on the right-hand side of Equation (1) represents the formation of the particle property x due to the merging of particles of properties $(x-y)$ and y. The second term denotes the disappearance of the particle property x from the system. The third integral describes the formation of the particle property x from y due to its collision with another particle z at a specific breakup rate $\mathcal{B}(x,y;z)$. In this term, there is no restriction on the particle property z, which acts as a catalyst, as it collides with the fragmenting particle property y, which leads to the formation of x. The final term explains the disappearance of particle property x due to their collision with the other particles present in the system at a specific collision rate $\mathscr{K}(x,y)$.

To represent the full dynamical systems (specifically granulation and crystallization), it is also required to identify the integral properties such as the total number of particles, total volume in the system and total area of the particles. For this reason, the moments of number density $\varphi(x,t)$ must also be defined. Let $\mathcal{M}_k(t)$ denote the kth order moment of the number density function $\varphi(x,t)$, and it is defined as follows:

$$\mathcal{M}_k(t) = \mathcal{M}_k(\varphi(x,t)) := \int_0^\infty x^k \varphi(x,t)dx. \tag{5}$$

The zeroth order moment gives the total number of particles, whereas the total volume in the system is given by the first order moment. The property of volume conservation is expected to hold during both aggregation and fragmentation events.

Smoluchowski [5] was the first to develop an aggregation kinetics discrete model, now known as the discrete Smoluchowski coagulation equation (SCE). Müller [6] proposed a continuous model for the volume distribution of particles, which included other phenomena such as particle fragmentation. Dubovskiĭ and Stewart [7] established the existence and uniqueness of the solution for this continuous model. In 1988, Cheng and Redner [8,9] were the first to formulate a model on the nonlinear breakage equation. The analytical solutions of the general nonlinear breakage equation were studied by Kostoglou and Karabelas [10]. Ernst and Pagonabarraga [11] studied the collision-induced nonlinear fragmentations caused by binary interactions. Vigil et al. [12] and Ke et al. [13] provided the extensive analysis on coagulation with collision-induced fragmentation. Some other existence and uniqueness studies can also be found in [14,15]. Various numerical approaches in 1D and 2D for solving these models have been discussed in detail by [16–22].

In the SCE, the only possibility for the clusters is to continue growing due to the aggregation mechanism, that is, smaller particles cannot be formed in the system. This restricts the application of only the coagulation process in the granulation process, however, it is still useful for polymerization process. This completely eliminates the possibility of the system to reach a steady state or equilibrium solution. Thus, this presents an opportunity for studying the Smoluchowski equation along with the fragmentation process, allowing the system to reach equilibrium. We have highlighted some of the works conducted in this regard in the above literature review. Our work in this article is another extension of the previously mentioned articles, albeit with the establishment of a new model.

In the present work, we introduce an entirely new model for continuous coagulation with collisional breakage. Earlier works have analysed equations with collsional breakage but this is the first time that such a model has been studied. The model mentioned includes the coagulation terms from the continuous SCE and the fragmentation process is represented by the third and fourth terms in (1). This allows us to study the existence of an equilibrium solution for these mechanisms and discuss the well-posedness of Equation (1). The current research work is majorly focused on establishing this well-posedness for compactly supported kernels. Furthermore, it is hypothesized that the breakage distribution function has the structure of a power law. The volume conservation law and uniqueness of the solution will also be proven to hold true.

Let us now mention the spaces considered in this article. For a fixed $T(>0)$, consider a strip

$$\mathcal{W} := \{(x,t) : 0 < x < \infty, 0 \leq t \leq T\}$$

and define $\Psi_{r,\sigma}(T)$ to be the space of all continuous functions φ with the norm

$$\|\varphi\|_{\Psi} := \sup_{0\leq t\leq T} \int_0^\infty \left(x^r + \frac{1}{x^{2\sigma}}\right)|\varphi(x,t)|\mathrm{d}x, \quad r \geq 1,\ \sigma \geq 0. \tag{6}$$

Furthermore, consider $\Psi^+_{r,\sigma}(T)$ the set of all non-negative functions from $\Psi_{r,\sigma}(T)$. In this article, we prove the existence of strong solutions for the coagulation fragmentation of Equation (1) and (2) under the following assumptions over the kinetic kernels;

(A_1) $\mathscr{K}(x,y)$ is a non-negative and continuous function on $\mathbb{R}_+ \times \mathbb{R}_+$.

(A_2) $\mathcal{B}(x,y;z)$ is a non-negative, continuous function satisfying the condition

$$\int_0^y x^{-\theta\sigma}\mathcal{B}(x,y;z)\mathrm{d}x \leq \Phi(y), \quad \text{where} \quad \Phi(y) = \eta y^{-\theta\sigma},$$

where η and θ are considered to be positive constants.

A breakdown of the various sections of this paper is as follows: In Section 2, we state and provide a detailed proof of the existence of solutions for the IVP (1) and (2). In Section 3, the theoretical results for the volume conservation property of the solution is provided. Meanwhile in Section 4, the uniqueness of the solution is proved. The last section is devoted to some important remarks and conclusions.

2. Existence of Solutions

Theorem 1. *Let the functions $\mathscr{C}(x,y)$, $\mathscr{K}(x,y)$ and $\mathcal{B}(x,y;z)$ be nonnegative and continuous on $\mathbb{R}_+ \times \mathbb{R}_+$, $\mathbb{R}_+ \times \mathbb{R}_+$ and $\mathbb{R}_+ \times \mathbb{R}_+ \times \mathbb{R}_+$ respectively, and satisfy the conditions (A_1), (A_2). Moreover, the kernel $\mathscr{C}$ and $\mathscr{K}$ have compact support for each time $0 \leq t \leq T$. Then, the IVP (1) and (2) has at least one solution $\varphi \in \Psi^+_{r,\sigma}(T)$.*

Proof. We prove the theorem in the following steps;

- Local existence of the solution, that is, there exists a $\tau > 0$ such that the IVP (1) and (2) has at least one solution $\varphi \in \Psi^+_{r,\sigma}(\tau)$;
- Nonnegativity of the local solution;
- Global existence of the unique solution to the space $\Psi^+_{r,\sigma}(T)$.

Existence of local solution: Let us consider that there is a fixed $R(>0)$, the coagulation and fragmentation kernels $\mathscr{C}(x,y)$ and $\mathscr{K}(x,y)$ have compact supports in the intervals $[0,R]\times[0,R]$ for each $t\in[0,T]$. Followed from Equation (1), we have

$$\varphi(x,t)=\varphi_0(x)+\int_0^t\Big[\tfrac{1}{2}\int_0^x\mathscr{C}(x-y,y)\varphi(x-y,\xi)\varphi(y,\xi)\mathrm{d}y-\int_0^\infty\mathscr{C}(x,y)\varphi(x,\xi)\varphi(y,\xi)\mathrm{d}y$$
$$+\int_0^\infty\int_x^\infty\mathscr{K}(y,z)\mathcal{B}(x,y;z)\varphi(y,\xi)\varphi(z,\xi)\mathrm{d}y\mathrm{d}z-\varphi(x,\xi)\int_0^\infty\mathscr{K}(x,y)\varphi(y,\xi)\mathrm{d}y\Big]\mathrm{d}\xi. \tag{7}$$

Hence, the solution to (1) and (2) for $x>2R$ takes the value

$$\varphi(x,t)=\varphi_0(x). \tag{8}$$

The relation (8) provides an approximate solution function beyond the right hand side of the compact domain, where the *tails* of the solution $\varphi(x,t)$, that is, larger size particles, does not alter at all and matches with the *tails* of the initial distribution $\varphi_0(x)$. Let us now focus to show that the local existence of a unique solution for $0<x\le 2R$.

In this regard, let us define the integral operator $\mathcal{H}$ as follows;

$$\mathcal{H}(\varphi)(x,t):=\quad\text{right hand side of Equation (7).}$$

Since $\mathscr{C}$ and $\mathscr{K}$ have compact supports and φ_0 is a nonnegative continuous function,the integral operator $\mathcal{H}$ is well-defined on $\Psi_{r,\sigma}(\tau)$. This result will be proven via the contraction mapping principle. We began this exercise by showing that for small $\tau>0$ there exists a closed ball in $\Psi_{r,\sigma}(\tau)$, which is invariant relatively to the mapping $\mathcal{H}$. Let $L_0(>0)$ be a constant such that

$$\|\varphi\|_\Psi^{(\tau)}:=\sup_{0\le t\le\tau}\int_0^\infty\left(x^r+\frac{1}{x^{2\sigma}}\right)|\varphi(x,t)|\mathrm{d}x\le L_0. \tag{9}$$

Multiplying Equation (7), with $\left(x^r+\frac{1}{x^{2\sigma}}\right)$ on both hand sides and after performing the integration over x, we reached

$$\|\mathcal{H}(\varphi)\|_\Psi^{(\tau)}\le\|\varphi_0\|_\Psi^{(\tau)}+\int_0^t\left[\frac{1}{2}\int_0^\infty\left(x^r+\frac{1}{x^{2\sigma}}\right)\int_0^x\mathscr{C}(x-y,y)\varphi(x-y,\xi)\varphi(y,\xi)\mathrm{d}y\mathrm{d}x\right.$$
$$+\int_0^\infty\left(x^r+\frac{1}{x^{2\sigma}}\right)\int_0^\infty\int_x^\infty\mathscr{K}(y,z)\mathcal{B}(x,y;z)\varphi(y,\xi)\varphi(z,\xi)\mathrm{d}y\mathrm{d}z\mathrm{d}x$$
$$\left.-\int_0^\infty\left(x^r+\frac{1}{x^{2\sigma}}\right)\varphi(x,\xi)\int_0^\infty[\mathscr{C}(x,y)+\mathscr{K}(x,y)]\varphi(y,\xi)\mathrm{d}y\mathrm{d}x\right]\mathrm{d}\xi. \tag{10}$$

Further, we use the application of the Fubini theorem followed by changing the order of integration and considering $\mu:=\max\{\bar{N},\eta\}$, then, one can obtain the following

$$\int_0^\infty\int_0^\infty\int_x^\infty\left(x^r+\frac{1}{x^{2\sigma}}\right)\mathscr{K}(y,z)\mathcal{B}(x,y;z)\varphi(y,\xi)\varphi(z,\xi)\mathrm{d}y\mathrm{d}z\mathrm{d}x$$
$$=\int_0^\infty\int_0^\infty\int_0^y\left(x^r+\frac{1}{x^{2\sigma}}\right)\mathscr{K}(y,z)\mathcal{B}(x,y;z)\varphi(y,\xi)\varphi(z,\xi)\mathrm{d}x\mathrm{d}y\mathrm{d}z$$
$$\le\int_0^\infty\int_0^\infty\int_0^y y^r\mathcal{B}(x,y;z)\mathscr{K}(y,z)\varphi(y,\xi)\varphi(z,\xi)\mathrm{d}x\mathrm{d}y\mathrm{d}z$$
$$+\int_0^\infty\int_0^\infty\int_0^y x^{-2\sigma}\mathcal{B}(x,y;z)\mathscr{K}(y,z)\varphi(y,\xi)\varphi(z,\xi)\mathrm{d}x\mathrm{d}y\mathrm{d}z$$
$$\le\int_0^\infty\int_0^\infty\left[\bar{N}y^r+\eta y^{-2\sigma}\right]y^r\mathscr{K}(y,z)\varphi(y,\xi)\varphi(z,\xi)\mathrm{d}y\mathrm{d}z$$
$$\le\mu\int_0^\infty\int_0^\infty\left(y^r+\frac{1}{y^{2\sigma}}\right)\mathscr{K}(y,z)\varphi(y,\xi)\varphi(z,\xi)\mathrm{d}y\mathrm{d}z$$

Since $\mathscr{C}$ and $\mathscr{K}$ both have compact support, their supremiums exist. Let $\kappa_1 = \sup_{\frac{\zeta}{R}\leq x,y\leq R} \mathscr{C}(x,y)$ and $\kappa_2 = \sup_{\frac{\zeta}{R}\leq x,y\leq R} \mathscr{K}(x,y)$. Applying this inequality in (10), we obtain

$$\begin{aligned}\|\mathcal{H}(\varphi)\|_{\Psi}^{(\tau)} &\leq \|\varphi_0\|_{\Psi}^{(\tau)} + (2^r\kappa_1 + \mu\kappa_2)\int_0^t\int_0^\infty\int_0^\infty \left(y^r + \frac{1}{y^{2\sigma}}\right)\left(z^r + \frac{1}{z^{2\sigma}}\right)\varphi(y,\xi)\varphi(z,\xi)\mathrm{d}y\mathrm{d}z\mathrm{d}\xi \\ &\leq \|\varphi_0\|_{\Psi}^{(\tau)} + (2^r\kappa_1 + \mu\kappa_2)\tau L_0^2 \end{aligned} \tag{11}$$

Further, let $\zeta_1 := \max\{\|\varphi_0\|_{\Psi}^{(\tau)}, (2^r\kappa_1 + \mu\kappa_2)\}$; then, the expression (11) reduces to

$$\|\mathcal{H}(\varphi)\|_{\Psi}^{(\tau)} \leq \zeta_1\left(1 + \tau L_0^2\right).$$

Hence, $\|\mathcal{H}(\varphi)\|_{\Psi}^{(\tau)} \leq L_0$, if $\zeta_1(1 + \tau L_0^2) \leq L_0$. This inequality holds if $\tau < \frac{1}{4\zeta_1^2}$ and

$$\frac{1 - \sqrt{1 - 4\zeta_1^2\tau}}{2\zeta_1\tau} \leq L_0 \leq \frac{1 + \sqrt{1 - 4\zeta_1^2\tau}}{2\zeta_1\tau}. \tag{12}$$

Presently, our focus will be to demonstrate that the mapping of $\mathcal{H}$ is contracting. Using the relation in (7), we have

$$\begin{aligned}\|\mathcal{H}(\varphi) - \mathcal{H}(\psi)\|_{\Psi}^{(\tau)} \leq \int_0^t \Bigg[&\frac{1}{2}\int_0^\infty \left(x^r + \frac{1}{x^{2\sigma}}\right)\int_0^x \mathscr{C}(x-y,y)|\mathcal{A}(x-y,y,\xi)|\mathrm{d}y\mathrm{d}x \\ &+ \int_0^\infty\int_0^\infty\int_x^\infty \left(x^r + \frac{1}{x^{2\sigma}}\right)\mathscr{K}(y,z)\mathcal{B}(x,y;z)|\mathcal{A}(y,z,s)|\mathrm{d}y\mathrm{d}z\mathrm{d}x \\ &+ \int_0^\infty\int_0^\infty \left(x^r + \frac{1}{x^{2\sigma}}\right)(\mathscr{C}(x,y) + \mathscr{K}(x,y))|\mathcal{A}(x,y,s)|\mathrm{d}y\mathrm{d}x\Bigg]\mathrm{d}s \end{aligned} \tag{13}$$

where $\mathcal{A}(x,y,s) = \varphi(x,s)\varphi(y,s) - \psi(x,s)\psi(y,s)$.

The first expression in the above inequality (13) can be estimated, as follows

$$\frac{1}{2}\int_0^\infty \left(x^r + \frac{1}{x^{2\sigma}}\right)\int_0^x \mathscr{C}(x-y,y)|\mathcal{A}(x-y,y,\xi)|\mathrm{d}y\mathrm{d}x \leq 2^r\kappa_1\|\varphi - \psi\|_{\Psi}^{(\tau)}\left[\|\varphi\|_{\Psi}^{(\tau)} + \|\psi\|_{\Psi}^{(\tau)}\right]$$

Furthermore, the second expression in the above inequality (13) is simplified using the Fubini's theorem with respect to z and x followed by interchanging the order of integration with respect to y and x, which gives the following expression

$$\begin{aligned}&\int_0^\infty\int_0^\infty\int_x^\infty \left(x^r + \frac{1}{x^{2\sigma}}\right)\mathscr{K}(y,z)\mathcal{B}(x,y;z)|\mathcal{A}(y,z,s)|\mathrm{d}y\mathrm{d}z\mathrm{d}x \\ &\qquad \leq \int_0^\infty\int_0^\infty\int_0^y x^r\mathscr{K}(y,z)\mathcal{B}(x,y;z)|\mathcal{A}(y,z,s)|\mathrm{d}x\mathrm{d}y\mathrm{d}z \\ &\qquad + \int_0^\infty\int_0^\infty\int_0^y \frac{1}{x^{2\sigma}}\mathscr{K}(y,z)\mathcal{B}(x,y;z)|\mathcal{A}(y,z,s)|\mathrm{d}x\mathrm{d}y\mathrm{d}z \\ &\qquad \leq \mu\int_0^\infty\int_0^\infty \left(y^r + \frac{1}{y^{2\sigma}}\right)\mathscr{K}(y,z)|\mathcal{A}(y,z,s)|\mathrm{d}y\mathrm{d}z \\ &\qquad \leq \mu\kappa_2\int_0^\infty\int_0^\infty \left(y^r + \frac{1}{y^{2\sigma}}\right)|\varphi(z,s)(\varphi(y,s) - \psi(y,s)) \\ &\qquad\qquad + g(y,s)(\varphi(z,s) - \psi(z,s))|\mathrm{d}y\mathrm{d}z \\ &\qquad \leq \kappa_2\mu\|\varphi - \psi\|_{\Psi}^{(\tau)}\left[\|\varphi\|_{\Psi}^{(\tau)} + \|\psi\|_{\Psi}^{(\tau)}\right] \end{aligned}$$

Using this estimation on the relation (13), the following is obtained

$$\|\mathcal{H}(\varphi)-\mathcal{H}(\psi)\|_{\Psi}^{(\tau)} \leq \tau(\kappa_1(2^r+1)+\kappa_2(\mu+1))\|\varphi-\psi\|_{\Psi}^{(\tau)}\left[\|\varphi\|_{\Psi}^{(\tau)}+\|\psi\|_{\Psi}^{(\tau)}\right] \quad (14)$$

Further, let $\zeta_2 := 2[\kappa_1(2^r+1)+\kappa_2(\mu+1)]$, then the inequality (14) reduces to

$$\|\mathcal{H}(\varphi)-\mathcal{H}(\psi)\|_{\Psi}^{(\tau)} \leq \tau\zeta_2 L_0\|\varphi-\psi\|_{\Psi}^{(\tau)}. \quad (15)$$

Thus, the mapping $\mathcal{H}$ is contractive on $\Psi_{r,\sigma}^{+}(\tau)$ for $\tau < [\zeta_2 L_0]^{-1}$. Using this result together with the inequality (12), there exists an invariant ball of radius L_0 for sufficiently small $\tau > 0$ and in this ball, $\mathcal{H}$ is contractive. Consequently, the ball contains a fixed point of $\mathcal{H}$.

Nonnegativity: Case I: Consider $\varphi_0(x) > 0$ for all $x \in (0,R)$. Since φ is continuous, there exists a small strip $\{(x,t) : 0 < x < R, t \in [0,t_0)\}$, where φ is strictly positive. For a particular t_0, we can find an $x_0 \in (0,R)$ such that (x_0,t_0) is the point with the property that

$$\varphi(x_0,t_0) = 0 \text{ and } \varphi(x,t) \neq 0 \text{ for all } 0 < x < \max\{x_0,R\},\ t \in [0,t_0) \quad (16)$$

Since the solution is continuous and satisfies (7) it must be continuously differentiable with respect to t. Therefore,

$$\begin{aligned}\partial_t\varphi(x,t)|_{(x_0,t_0)} =& \frac{1}{2}\int_0^{x_0}\mathscr{C}(x_0-y,y)\varphi(x_0-y,t_0)\varphi(y,t_0)\mathrm{d}y \\ &+\int_0^R\int_{x_0}^R\mathscr{K}(y,z)\mathcal{B}(x_0,y;z)\varphi(y,t)\varphi(z,t)\mathrm{d}y\mathrm{d}z,\end{aligned} \quad (17)$$

- If $x_0 \leq R$, then $\varphi(x,t) > 0$ for all $0 < x \leq R$ and $0 \leq t < t_0$. The positivity of the right hand side of (17) implies $\partial_t\varphi(x,t)|_{(x_0,t_0)} > 0$.
- If $x_0 > R$, we use the property (3) of the breakage function to obtain

$$\begin{aligned}\int_0^R\int_{x_0}^R\mathscr{K}(y,z)\mathcal{B}(x_0,y;z)\varphi(y,t)\varphi(z,t)\mathrm{d}y\mathrm{d}z =& -\int_0^R\int_{x_0}^R\mathscr{K}(y,z)\mathcal{B}(x_0,y;z)\varphi(y,t)\varphi(z,t)\mathrm{d}y\mathrm{d}z \\ =& \ 0\end{aligned}$$

Thus, from the Equation (17), we have $\partial_t\varphi(x,t)|_{(x_0,t_0)} > 0$.

The positive value of the time derivative establishes that there exists a point (x_0,t), with $t < t_0$ such that $\varphi(x_0,t) < 0$. However, this counters the hypothesis that (x_0,t_0) is a point bearing a property provided by relation (16). Hence, the point (x_0,t_0) where the solution vanishes does not exist.

Further, when $x \geq R$ by (7) and the compactly supported kernels $\mathscr{C}$ and $\mathscr{K}$, the solution coincides with the initial data. Hence, again it becomes positive. Consequently, $\varphi(x,t)$ is strictly positive provided that the initial distribution is strictly positive.

Case II: Suppose φ_0 is not strictly positive. Then, we construct the sequence $\{\varphi_0^n\}$ of the positive function to satisfy the conditions listed in Theorem 1, which then converges to φ_0 uniformly in $\Psi_{r,\sigma}(\tau)$ with respect to $t \in [0,\tau]$. We have established earlier that the family of operators $\mathcal{H}_n : \Psi_{r,\sigma}(\tau) \to \Psi_{r,\sigma}(\tau)$, defined as

$$\begin{aligned}\mathcal{H}_n(\varphi)(x,t) =& \varphi_0^n(x)+\int_0^t\left[\frac{1}{2}\int_0^x\mathscr{C}(x-y,y)\varphi(x-y,\xi)\varphi(y,\xi)\mathrm{d}y-\int_0^\infty\mathscr{C}(x,y)\varphi(x,\xi)\varphi(y,\xi)\mathrm{d}y\right. \\ &\left.\int_0^\infty\int_x^\infty\mathscr{K}(y,z)\mathcal{B}(x,y;z)\varphi(y,\xi)\varphi(z,\xi)\mathrm{d}y\mathrm{d}-\varphi(x,\xi)\int_0^\infty\mathscr{K}(x,y)\varphi(y,\xi)\mathrm{d}y\right]\mathrm{d}\xi\end{aligned}$$

is a contraction mapping. Therefore, as $n \to \infty$, we have

$$\sup_{\|\varphi\|_{\Psi}^{(\tau)} \le L} \|\mathcal{H}_n(\varphi) - \mathcal{H}(\varphi)\|_{\Psi}^{(\tau)} \le \int_0^\infty \left(x^r + \frac{1}{x^{2\sigma}}\right)|\varphi_0^n(x) - \varphi_0(x)|\mathrm{d}x \to 0.$$

Since the mapping is contractive in $\Psi_{r,\sigma}(\tau)$, therefore

$$\begin{aligned}\|\varphi^n - \varphi\|_{\Psi}^{(\tau)} = \|\mathcal{H}_n(\varphi^n) - \mathcal{H}(\varphi)\|_{\Psi}^{(\tau)} &\le \|\mathcal{H}_n(\varphi^n) - \mathcal{H}(\varphi^n)\|_{\Psi}^{(\tau)} + \|\mathcal{H}(\varphi^n) - \mathcal{H}(\varphi)\|_{\Psi}^{(\tau)} \\ &\le \|\mathcal{H}_n(\varphi^n) - \mathcal{H}(\varphi^n)\|_{\Psi}^{(\tau)} + \bar{\zeta}\|\varphi^n - \varphi\|_{\Psi}^{(\tau)},\end{aligned}$$

which implies

$$(1-\bar{\zeta})\|\varphi^n - \varphi\|_{\Psi}^{(\tau)} = \|\mathcal{H}_n(\varphi^n) - \mathcal{H}(\varphi^n)\|_{\Psi}^{(\tau)} \to 0 \quad \text{whenever} \quad n \to \infty.$$

This shows that for a positive initial data, the solution φ is also positive.

Global existence of unique solution: Let us first discuss the boundedness of the moments

$$\mathcal{M}_k(t) = \int_0^\infty x^k \varphi(x,t)\mathrm{d}x; \quad \text{where} \quad 0 \le k \le r \quad \text{and} \quad k = -2\sigma,$$

for compactly supported kernels. Simple calculations will lead us to the following results:

$$\mathcal{M}_1(t) \le \bar{m}_1, \quad \mathcal{M}_{-2\sigma}(t) \le \bar{m}_{-2\sigma}, \quad \mathcal{M}_0(t) \le \bar{m}_0, \quad \mathcal{M}_2(t) \le \bar{m}_2, \tag{18}$$

and so on. Here, terms $\bar{m}_k$, $k = -2\sigma, 0, 1, \ldots, r$ are all constants. Furthermore, it is important to note that the boundedness of the kth moment ensures the boundedness of the $(k+1)^{th}$ moment for $k = 2, 3, \ldots, r$. Thus, using the aforementioned results, we can conclude that the

$$\|\varphi\|_{\Psi} \le \bar{m}_r + \bar{m}_{-2\sigma}.$$

implies that the solution of IVP (1) and (2) is bounded in the norm $\|.\|_{\Psi}$. Taking into account the positivity/nonnegativity of the local solution, it is easy to extend it for $0 \le t \le T$. Recalling Theorem 2.2 of [23], the global existence of the unique solution belonging to $\Psi_{r,\sigma}^{+}(T)$ can easily be proved. □

3. Conservation of Volume

In order to show the volume conservation law, let us multiply equation (1) by the x by performing integration over x; the following is obtained

$$\begin{aligned}\frac{\mathrm{d}\mathcal{M}(t)}{\mathrm{d}t} = \frac{\mathrm{d}}{\mathrm{d}t}\int_0^\infty x\varphi(x,t)\mathrm{d}x = &\underbrace{\frac{1}{2}\int_0^\infty\int_0^x x\mathscr{C}(x-y,y)\varphi(x-y,t)\varphi(y,t)\mathrm{d}y}_{M_1} \\ &\underbrace{\int_0^\infty\int_0^\infty\int_x^\infty x\mathscr{K}(y,z)\mathcal{B}(x,y;z)\varphi(y,t)\varphi(z,t)\mathrm{d}y\mathrm{d}z\mathrm{d}x}_{M_2} \\ &\underbrace{-\int_0^\infty\int_0^\infty x(\mathscr{C}(x,y)+\mathscr{K}(x,y))\varphi(x,t)\varphi(y,t)\mathrm{d}y\mathrm{d}x}_{M_3}\end{aligned} \tag{19}$$

Under a suitable transformation, we can estimate the integral M_1, as follows

$$\begin{aligned}M_1 &= \frac{1}{2}\int_0^\infty\int_0^\infty (x+y)\mathscr{C}(x,y)\varphi(x,t)\varphi(y,t)\mathrm{d}y\mathrm{d}x \\ &= \int_0^\infty\int_0^\infty x\mathscr{C}(x,y)\varphi(x,t)\varphi(y,t)\mathrm{d}y\mathrm{d}x\end{aligned} \tag{20}$$

For the integral $\mathcal{N}_1$, using the application of the Fubini's theorem followed by a change in the order of integration with respect to y and x, and using (3), obtains

$$M_2 = \int_0^\infty \int_0^\infty \int_0^y x\mathscr{K}(y,z)\mathcal{B}(x,y;z)\varphi(y,t)\varphi(z,t)\mathrm{d}x\mathrm{d}y\mathrm{d}z$$
$$= \int_0^\infty \int_0^\infty y\mathscr{K}(y,z)\varphi(y,t)\varphi(z,t)\mathrm{d}y\mathrm{d}z$$
$$= \int_0^\infty \int_0^\infty x\mathscr{K}(x,y)\varphi(x,t)\varphi(y,t)\mathrm{d}x\mathrm{d}y \tag{21}$$

Adding the estimations (20) and (21), $M_1 + M_2 = M_3$ are obtained. Hence, by using this relation on (19), we can conclude the volume conservation property of the existing solution.

4. Uniqueness Theory

Theorem 2. *Let the assumptions of Theorem 1 hold true, then the IVP (1) and (2) has a unique solution in* $\Psi^+_{r,\sigma}(T)$.

Proof. Let $t \neq 0$, $\varphi_1(x,t)$ and $\varphi_2(x,t)$ be two distinct solutions of (1), (2) along with $\varphi_1(x,0) = \varphi_2(x,0)$. Further suppose $\mathcal{Q}(x,t) := \varphi_1(x,t) - \varphi_2(x,t)$, and we construct an auxiliary function

$$\mathcal{P}(t) := \int_0^\infty |\mathcal{Q}(x,t)|\mathrm{d}x.$$

Since both the solutions $\varphi_1(x,t)$ and $\varphi_2(x,t)$ satisfy the Equation (7), we have

$$\mathcal{P}(t) \leq \int_0^t \Bigg[\underbrace{\frac{1}{2}\int_0^\infty \int_0^x \mathscr{C}(x-y,y)|\mathcal{A}(x-y,y,\xi)|\mathrm{d}y\mathrm{d}x}_{J_0} + \underbrace{\int_0^\infty \int_0^\infty \int_x^\infty \mathscr{K}(y,z)\mathcal{B}(x,y;z)|\mathcal{A}(y,z,\xi)|\mathrm{d}y\mathrm{d}z\mathrm{d}x}_{J_1} + \underbrace{\int_0^\infty \int_0^\infty (\mathscr{C}(x,y) + \mathscr{K}(x,y))|\mathcal{A}(x,y,\xi)|\mathrm{d}y\mathrm{d}x}_{J_2} \Bigg] \mathrm{d}\xi \tag{22}$$

Further performing the change in the order of integration followed by the application of Fubini's theorem, the integrals J_0 and J_1 can be estimated as

$$J_0 \leq \frac{1}{2}k_1(\|\varphi_1\|_\Psi + \|\varphi_2\|_\Psi)\mathcal{P}(s).$$
$$J_1 \leq k_2\bar{N}(\|\varphi_1\|_\Psi + \|\varphi_2\|_\Psi)\mathcal{P}(s).$$

Similar operations apply for the integral J_2, and when using the relation (22), we obtain

$$\mathcal{N}(t) \leq \Lambda(\|\varphi_1\|_\Psi + \|\varphi_2\|_\Psi)\int_0^t \mathcal{P}(s)\mathrm{d}s., \tag{23}$$

where Λ is a positive constant depending only on k_1, k_2 and $\bar{N}$. Since φ_1 and φ_2 both belong to the space $\Psi^+_{r,\sigma}(T)$, the norms $\|\varphi_1\|_\Psi$ and $\|\varphi_2\|_\Psi$ are uniformly bounded with respect to $0 \leq t \leq T$. Then, by applying Grownwall's inequality on (23), we obtain

$$\mathcal{P}(t) = 0. \quad \text{for all} \quad 0 \leq t \leq T,$$

which concludes the proof. □

5. Concluding Remarks

A new population balance model, including the nonlinear coagulation and fragmentation, was introduced in this paper. The model accounts for a completely inelastic collision between a pair of particles, which leads to the formation of a larger particle. If their encounter is not completely inelastic, then there is a possibility of the formation of smaller particles when they collide. A proof has been given to obtain the existence and the uniqueness of a solution to the purely nonlinear model for a set of kernels with compact support. The results of the existence and uniqueness are further supported by providing the theoretical outcome of the volume conservation law.

Author Contributions: Conceptualization, A.D. and J.S.; methodology, F.W.V.K.; validation, J.S., V.T. and M.S.; formal analysis, F.W.V.K.; investigation, A.D.; resources, J.S.; writing—original draft preparation, F.W.V.K. and A.D.; writing—review and editing, J.S., V.T. and M.S.; visualization, J.S.; supervision, J.S.; project administration, J.S., V.T. and M.S.; funding acquisition, M.S. All authors have read and agreed to the published version of the manuscript.

Funding: FWVK thanks the Council of Scientific & Industrial Research (CSIR), Govt. of India for their funding support during his PhD program. AD thanks Ministry of Education (MoE), Govt. of India for their funding support during his PhD program. JS thanks NITT for their support through the seed grant (file no.: NITT/R & C/SEED GRANT/19-20/P-13/MATHS/JS/E1) during this work. VT thanks NITT for their support through the seed grant (file no.: NITT/R & C/SEED GRANT/19-20/P-15/MATHS/VT/E1-E4) during this work.

Institutional Review Board Statement: Not applicable.

Informed Consent Statement: Not applicable.

Data Availability Statement: This study does not report any data.

Conflicts of Interest: The authors declare no conflict of interest.

References

1. Ismail, H.Y.; Singh, M.; Albadarin, A.B.; Walker, G.M. Complete two dimensional population balance modelling of wet granulation in twin screw. *Int. J. Pharm.* **2020**, *591*, 120018. [CrossRef] [PubMed]
2. Srivastava, R. A simple model of particle coalescence and breakup. *J. Atmos. Sci.* **1982**, *39*, 1317–1322. [CrossRef]
3. Capece, M.; Ecevit, B.; Dave, R. Emergence of falsified kinetics as a consequence of multi-particle interactions in dense-phase comminution processes. *Chem. Eng. Sci.* **2011**, *66*, 5672–5683. [CrossRef]
4. Wibowo, C.; Ng, K. Product-oriented process synthesis and development: Creams and pastes. *AIChE J.* **2001**, *47*, 2746–2767. [CrossRef]
5. von Smoluchowski, M. Drei vortrage uber diffusion, brownsche bewegung und koagulation von kolloidteilchen. *Z. Phys.* **1916**, *17*, 557–585.
6. Müller, H. Zur allgemeinen Theorie ser raschen Koagulation. *Kolloidchem. Beih.* **1928**, *27*, 223–250. [CrossRef]
7. Dubovskiĭ, P.; Stewart, I. Existence, uniqueness and mass conservation for the coagulation–fragmentation equation. *Math. Methods Appl. Sci.* **1996**, *19*, 571–591. [CrossRef]
8. Cheng, Z.; Redner, S. Scaling Theory of Fragmentation. *Phys. Rev. Lett.* **1988**, *60*, 2450–2453. [CrossRef]
9. Cheng, Z.; Redner, S. Kinetics of fragmentation. *J. Phys. A Math. Gen.* **1990**, *23*, 1233–1258. [CrossRef]
10. Kostoglou, M.; Karabelas, A. A study of the nonlinear breakage equation: Analytical and asymptotic solutions. *J. Phys. Math. Gen.* **2000**, *33*, 1221–1232. [CrossRef]
11. Ernst, M.; Pagonabarraga, I. The nonlinear fragmentation equation. *J. Phys. Math. Theor.* **2007**, *40*, F331–F337. [CrossRef]
12. Vigil, R.; Vermeersch, I.; Fox, R. Destructive aggregation: Aggregation with collision-induced breakage. *J. Colloid Interface Sci.* **2006**, *302*, 149–158. [CrossRef]
13. Ke, J.; Lin, Z.; Chen, X. An analytical solution of coagulation processes with collision-induced fragmentation. *J. Phys. A Math. Theor.* **2008**, *41*, 285005. [CrossRef]
14. Das, A.; Saha, J. Existence and uniqueness of mass conserving solutions to the coagulation and collision-induced breakage equation. *J. Anal.* **2022**, *30*, 1323–1340. [CrossRef]
15. Das, A.; Saha, J. On the mass conserving solutions to the singular kernel coagulation with multi-fragmentation. *Jpn. J. Ind. Appl. Math.* **2022**, *40*, 563–588. [CrossRef]
16. Kumar, J.; Peglow, M.; Warnecke, G.; Heinrich, S.; Mörl, L. Improved accuracy and convergence of discretized population balance for aggregation: The cell average technique. *Chem. Eng. Sci.* **2006**, *61*, 3327–3342. [CrossRef]

17. Kumar, J.; Peglow, M.; Warnecke, G.; Heinrich, S. The cell average technique for solving multi-dimensional aggregation population balance equations. *Comput. Chem. Eng.* **2008**, *32*, 1810–1830. [CrossRef]
18. Buffo, A.; Alopaeus, V. Solution of bivariate population balance equations with high-order moment-conserving method of classes. *Comput. Chem. Eng.* **2016**, *87*, 111–124. [CrossRef]
19. Bhoi, S.; Sarkar, D. Hybrid finite volume and Monte Carlo method for solving multi-dimensional population balance equations in crystallization processes. *Chem. Eng. Sci.* **2020**, *217*, 115511. [CrossRef]
20. Singh, D.K.; Brito-Parada, P.R.; Bhutani, G. An open-source computational framework for the solution of the bivariate population balance equation. *Comput. Chem. Eng.* **2022**, *161*, 107780. [CrossRef]
21. Singh, M.; Shirazian, S.; Ranade, V.; Walker, G.M.; Kumar, A. Challenges and opportunities in modelling wet granulation in pharmaceutical industry–A critical review. *Powder Technol.* **2022**, 117380. [CrossRef]
22. Singh, M.; Ranade, V.; Shardt, O.; Matsoukas, T. Challenges and opportunities concerning numerical solutions for population balances: a critical review. *J. Phys. Math. Theor.* **2022**, *55*, 383002. [CrossRef]
23. Dubovskiĭ, P. *Mathematical Theory of Coagulation*; Research Institute of Mathematics, Seoul National University: Seoul, Korea, 1994.

axioms

MDPI

Article

Properties of Differential Subordination and Superordination for Multivalent Functions Associated with the Convolution Operators

Luminiţa-Ioana Cotîrlă [1,*] and Abdul Rahman S. Juma [2]

[1] Department of Mathematics, Technical University of Cluj-Napoca, 400114 Cluj-Napoca, Romania
[2] Department of Mathematics, College of Education for Pure Sciences, University of Anbar, Ramadi 31001, Iraq
* Correspondence: luminita.cotirla@math.utcluj.ro

Abstract: Using convolution (or Hadamard product), we define the El-Ashwah and Drbuk linear operator, which is a multivalent function in the unit disk $U = [w : |w| < 1 \text{ and } w \in ¢]$, and satisfy its specific relationship to derive the subordination, superordination, and sandwich results for this operator by using properties of subordination and superordination concepts.

Keywords: multivalent functions; subordination; Hadamard product; superordination

MSC: 30C45

Citation: Cotîrlă, L.-I.; Juma, A.R.S. Properties of Differential Subordination and Superordination for Multivalent Functions Associated with the Convolution Operators. *Axioms* **2023**, *12*, 169. https://doi.org/10.3390/axioms12020169

Academic Editor: Clemente Cesarano

Received: 8 December 2022
Revised: 1 February 2023
Accepted: 3 February 2023
Published: 7 February 2023

1. Introduction and Definitions

The set $\Omega(U)$ denotes the class of all analytic functions in the open unit disk $U = [w : |w| < 1 \; anq \; w \in ¢]$ and $\Omega[a, k]$ as the subclass of $\Omega(U)$, which consists of the form functions

$$f(w) = a + a_k w^k + a_{k+1} w^{k+1} + \ldots, \; (a \in ¢, \; w \in U, \; k \in N). \tag{1}$$

With $\mathcal{A}_p$ as the class of all multivalent functions in open unit disk U of the form

$$f(w) = w^p + \sum_{k=1+p}^{\infty} a_k w^k, \; w \in U, p \in N. \tag{2}$$

Additionally, we use $\mathcal{A} = \mathcal{A}_1$ to denote the class of analytic functions in the open unit disk U and normalize them with $f(0) = 0$, $f'(0) = 1$.

Additionally, consider $\mathcal{S}$ as the class of the univalent function in U,

Let $\mathcal{S}^*(\varrho)$, $\mathcal{C}(\varrho)$ and $\mathcal{K}$ be the subclasses of $\mathcal{A}$ such that:

$\left\{f \in \mathcal{S}^* : Re\left\{\frac{wf'(w)}{f(w)}\right\} > \varrho\right\}, w \in U, \; (0 < \varrho < 1)$, then f is a starlike function;

$\left\{f \in \mathcal{C} : Re\left\{1 + \frac{wf''(w)}{f'(w)}\right\} > \varrho\right\}, w \in U, \; (0 < \varrho < 1)$, then f is a convex function;

$\left\{f \in \mathcal{K} : Re\left\{\frac{f_1'(w)}{g'(w)}\right\} > 0 : g \in \mathcal{C}\right\}, w \in U$, then f is a close-to-convex function.

If the functions f and g are analytic in U, then we say f is subordinate to g or f is said to be superordinate to f in U, written as $f \prec g$ or $f(w) \prec g(w)$ if there is a Schwarz function $v(w)$ analytic in U, with $|v(w)| < 1$, so that $f(w) = g(v(w))$ and $w \in U$. In particular, if the function g is univalent in U, then the subordination $f \prec g$ is equivalent to $f(0) = g(0)$ and $f(U) \subset g(U)$, (see [1–8]).

If $f, g \in \mathcal{A}_p$, where $f(w)$ is provided by (1) and $g(w)$ is defined by

$$g(w) = w^p + \sum_{k=1+p}^{\infty} a_k w^k, w \in U,$$

the Hadamard product (or convolution) of the function f and g is defined by

$$f(w) \times g(w) = w^p + \sum_{k=1+p}^{\infty} a_k b_k w^k, (w \in U) = (f \times g)(w). \tag{3}$$

Let $\delta > 0,\ a, c \in ¢$ such that $Re(c-a) \geq 0$ and $Rea \geq -\delta p,\ p \in N,\ n \in \mathbb{Z}, \theta \geq 0$ and $\lambda > -p$.

El-Ashwah and Drbuk [5] introduced the linear operator $\mathcal{B}_{p,n}^{\theta,\lambda}(a,c,\delta) : \mathcal{A}_p \to \mathcal{A}_p$ defined by

$$\begin{aligned} &\mathcal{B}_{\theta,\lambda}^{n,\,p}(a,c,\delta)f(w) \\ &= w^p + \tfrac{\Gamma(c+\delta p)}{\Gamma(c+\delta p)} \sum_{k=1+p}^{\infty} \left(\tfrac{p+\lambda+\theta(k-p)}{p+\lambda}\right)^n \tfrac{\Gamma(c+\delta p)}{\Gamma(c+\delta p)} a_k w^k. \end{aligned} \tag{4}$$

It is readily verified from (4) that

$$\begin{aligned} &\mathcal{B}_{\theta,\lambda}^{n+1,\,p}(a,c,\delta)f(w) = \left(1 - \tfrac{p\theta}{p+\lambda}\right)\mathcal{B}_{\theta,\lambda}^{n,\,p}(a,c,\delta)f(w) \\ &+ \tfrac{\theta}{p+\lambda} w \left(\mathcal{B}_{\theta,\lambda}^{n,\,p}(a,c,\delta)f(w)\right)'. \end{aligned} \tag{5}$$

Putting $a = c$ in (4), we obtain the Prajapat operator $J_p^n(\theta,\lambda)$, see [9].

Additionally, when $n = 0$, we obtain the Erdelyi-Kober integral operator $I_{p,\delta}^{a,c}$, see [10].

Definition 1. *Let* $Y\!: ¢^3 \times U \to ¢$ *and* $h\,(w)$ *be univalent in* U*. If* $p\,(w)$ *is analytic in* U*, that fulfils the second-order differential subordination [11]:*

$$Y\Big(p(w), wp'(w),\ w^2 p''(w); w\Big) \prec h(w), \tag{6}$$

then $p(w)$ *is the differential subordination solution of (6).*

Definition 2. *Let* $Y_1\!:\ ¢^3 \times U \to ¢$ *and* $h(w)$ *be univalent in* U*. If* $p(w)$ *and* $Y_1(p(w), wp'(w),\ w^2 p''(w); w)$ *are univalent in* U *and* $p(w)$ *fulfill the second-order differential superordination [11]:*

$$h(w) \prec Y_1\Big(p(w), wp'(w),\ w^2 p''(w); w\Big), \tag{7}$$

then $p(w)$ *is the differential superordination solution of (7).*

Definition 3. *Let* Q *be the collections of functions* f *that are analytic and injective on* $\overline{U}\backslash E(f)$*, when* $E(f) = \left\{\varsigma \in \partial U : \lim_{w \to \varsigma} f(w) = \infty\right\}$ *and* $f'(w) \neq 0$ *for* $\varsigma \in \partial U \backslash E(f)$ *[11].*

Lemma 1. *Let* $p_1(w)$ *be the univalent function in* U *and let* Σ *and* ϑ *be holomorphic in a domain* $p_1(U) \subset D$*, with* $\vartheta(\omega) \neq 0$*, when* $\omega \in p_1\,(U)$*. Set* $\mathcal{O}(w) = w\ p_1{}'(w)\vartheta(p_1(w))$ *and* $\hbar(w) = \Sigma(p_1(w) + \mathcal{O}(w)$*. Suppose that [12]*

(i) $\mathcal{O}$ *is starlike in* U*.*

(ii) $Re\left(\frac{w\hbar'(w)}{\mathcal{O}(w)}\right) > 0,\ w \in\ U$*.*

If $p_2(w)$ *is holomorphic in* U *with* $p_2(0) = p_1(0)$*,* $p_2(U) \subset D$*, and* $\Sigma(p_2(w)) + wp_2{}'(w)\vartheta(p_2(w)) \prec \Sigma(p_1(w)) + wp_1{}'(w)\vartheta(p_1(w))$*, then* $p_2(w) \prec\ p_1(w)$*.*

Lemma 2. *Let* $p_1(w)$ *be convex in* U *and* $\beta_1 \in ¢, \beta_2 \in ¢^*$ *with* $Re\left(1 + \frac{p_1{}''(w)}{p_1{}'(w)}\right) > max\left\{0, -Re\frac{\beta_1}{\beta_2}\right\}$*. If* $p_2(w)$ *is holomorphic in* U *and* $\beta_1 p_2(w) + \beta_2 w p_2{}'(w) \prec \beta_1 p_1(w) + \beta_2 w p_1{}'(w)$*, then* $p_2(w) \prec\ p_1(w)$ *[11].*

Lemma 3. *Let $p_1(w)$ be convex univalent in U and let Σ and ϑ be holomorphic in a domain D, $p_1(U) \subset D$. Suppose that [12]*

(i) $wp_1{}'(w)\vartheta(p_1(w))$ is starlike univalent in U.

(ii) $Re\left(\frac{\Sigma'(p_1(w))}{\vartheta(p_1(w))}\right) > 0$, $w \in U$.

If $p_2(w) \in \mathcal{A}[p_1(0),1] \cap Q$, with $p_2(U) \subset D$, $\Sigma(p_2(w)) + wp_2{}'(w)\vartheta(p_2(w))$ is univalent in U and $\Sigma(p_1(w)) + wp_1{}'(w)\vartheta(p_1(w)) \prec \Sigma(p_2(w)) + wp_2{}'(w)\vartheta(p_2(w))$, then $p_1(w) \prec p_2(w)$.

Lemma 4. *Let $p_1(w)$ be convex in U and $Re(\beta) > 0$.*

If $p_2(w) \in \mathcal{A}[p_1(0),1] \cap Q$, $p_2(w) + \beta wp_2{}'(w)$ is univalent in U and $p_1(w) + \beta wp_1{}'(w) \prec p_2(w) + \beta wp_2{}'(w)$, then $p_1(w) \prec p_2(w)$ [12].

2. Subordination Results

Theorem 1. *Let $b(w)$ be convex univalent in U, with $b(0) = 1$, $a_1 > 0, 0 \neq a_2 \in \mathbb{C}$ and suppose*

$$Re\left(1 + \frac{b''(w)}{b'(w)}\right) > \max\left\{0, -Re\frac{a_1}{a_2}\right\}.$$

If $f \in \mathcal{A}$, it satisfies the subordination:

$$\left(1 - \frac{a_2(p+\lambda)}{\theta}\right)\left(\frac{\mathcal{B}^{n,\,p}_{\theta,\lambda}(a,c,\delta)f(w)}{w^p}\right)^{a_1} + \frac{a_2(p+\lambda)}{\theta}\left(\frac{\mathcal{B}^{n+1,\,p}_{\theta,\lambda}(a,c,\delta)f(w)}{\mathcal{B}^{n,\,p}_{\theta,\lambda}(a,c,\delta)f(w)}\right)^{a_1}\left(\frac{\mathcal{B}^{n,\,p}_{\theta,\lambda}(a,c,\delta)f(w)}{w^p}\right)^{a_1} \prec b(w) + \frac{a_2}{a_1}wb'(w),$$

then

$$\left(\frac{\mathcal{B}^{n,\,p}_{\theta,\lambda}(a,c,\delta)f(w)}{w^p}\right)^{a_1} \prec b(w).$$

Proof. Consider

$$q(w) = \left(\frac{\mathcal{B}^{n,\,p}_{\theta,\lambda}(a,c,\delta)f(w)}{w^p}\right)^{a_1}.$$

Then

$$q'(w) = a_1\left(\frac{\mathcal{B}^{n,\,p}_{\theta,\lambda}(a,c,\delta)f(w)}{w^p}\right)^{a_1}\left(\frac{w^p}{\mathcal{B}^{n,\,p}_{\theta,\lambda}(a,c,\delta)f(w)}\right)$$

$$\left(\frac{w^p\left[\mathcal{B}^{n,\,p}_{\theta,\lambda}(a,c,\delta)f(w)\right]' - pw^{p-1}\left(\mathcal{B}^{n,\,p}_{\theta,\lambda}(a,c,\delta)f(w)\right)}{(w^p)^2}\right)$$

$$= a_1\left(\frac{\mathcal{B}^{n,\,p}_{\theta,\lambda}(a,c,\delta)f(w)}{w^p}\right)^{a_1}\left(\frac{\left[\mathcal{B}^{n,\,p}_{\theta,\lambda}(a,c,\delta)f(w)\right]'}{\mathcal{B}^{n,\,p}_{\theta,\lambda}(a,c,\delta)f(w)} - \frac{p}{w}\right)$$

We have

$$\frac{wq'(w)}{q(w)} = a_1\left(\frac{w\left[\mathcal{B}^{n,\,p}_{\theta,\lambda}(a,c,\delta)f(w)\right]'}{\mathcal{B}^{n,\,p}_{\theta,\lambda}(a,c,\delta)f(w)} - p\right).$$

By using (5) we obtain

$$\frac{wq'(w)}{q(w)}$$
$$= a_1\left(\frac{\frac{(p+\lambda)}{\theta}\left(\mathcal{B}_{\theta,\lambda}^{n+1,\,p}(a,c,\delta)f(w)\right)+p\left(\mathcal{B}_{\theta,\lambda}^{n,\,p}(a,c,\delta)f(w)\right)-\frac{(p+\lambda)}{\theta}\left(\mathcal{B}_{\theta,\lambda}^{n,\,p}(a,c,\delta)f(w)\right)}{\left(\mathcal{B}_{\theta,\lambda}^{n,\,p}(a,c,\delta)f(w)\right)} - p\right)$$
$$= a_1\frac{(p+\lambda)}{\theta}\left(\frac{\left(\mathcal{B}_{\theta,\lambda}^{n+1,\,p}(a,c,\delta)f(w)\right)}{\left(\mathcal{B}_{\theta,\lambda}^{n,\,p}(a,c,\delta)f(w)\right)} - 1\right),$$

and

$$\frac{a_2wq'(w)}{a_1} = \frac{a_2(p+\lambda)}{\theta}\left(\frac{\left(\mathcal{B}_{\theta,\lambda}^{n+1,\,p}(a,c,\delta)f(w)\right)}{\left(\mathcal{B}_{\theta,\lambda}^{n,\,p}(a,c,\delta)f(w)\right)}\right)\left(\frac{\mathcal{B}_{\theta,\lambda}^{n,\,p}(a,c,\delta)f(w)}{w^p}\right)^{a_1}$$
$$-\frac{a_2(p+\lambda)}{\theta}\left(\frac{\mathcal{B}_{\theta,\lambda}^{n,\,p}(a,c,\delta)f(w)}{w^p}\right)^{a_1}.$$

By using the hypothesis, we obtain $q(w) + \frac{a_2}{a_1}wq'(w) \prec b(w) + \frac{a_2}{a_1}wb'(w)$. Additionally, apply Lemma 2, when $\beta_1 = 1$ and $\beta_2 = \frac{a_2}{a_1}$, then

$$\left(\frac{\mathcal{B}_{\theta,\lambda}^{n,\,p}(a,c,\delta)f(w)}{w^p}\right)^{a_1} \prec b(w).$$

□

Corollary 1. *Let $b(w)$ be convex univalent in U, with $b(0) = 1, a_1 > 0, 0 \neq a_2 \in ¢$ and suppose*

$$Re\left(1 + \frac{b''(w)}{b'(w)}\right) > max\left\{0, -Re\frac{a_1}{a_2}\right\}.$$

If $f \in \mathcal{A}$, it satisfies the subordination:

$$\left(1 - \frac{a_2(p+\lambda)}{\theta}\right)\left(\frac{J_p^n(\theta,\lambda)f(w)}{w^p}\right)^{a_1} + \frac{a_2(p+\lambda)}{\theta}\left(\frac{J_p^{n+1}(\theta,\lambda)f(w)}{J_p^n(\theta,\lambda)f(w)}\right)^{a_1}\left(\frac{J_p^n(\theta,\lambda)f(w)}{w^p}\right)^{a_1} \prec b(w) + \frac{a_2}{a_1}wb'(w),$$

then

$$\left(\frac{J_p^n(\theta,\lambda)f(w)}{w^p}\right)^{a_1} \prec b(w).$$

Theorem 2. *Let b be convex univalent in, $b(0) = 1$, and $b(w) \neq 0$ for all $w \in U$, and suppose that b satisfies:*

$$Re\left\{p + \frac{wt\sigma}{w^pa_2} + \frac{w\varepsilon(\sigma+1)}{w^pa_2}(w) + (\sigma-1)\frac{wb'(w)}{b(w)} + \frac{wb''(w)}{b'(w)}\right\} > 0, \quad (8)$$

where $\sigma, \varepsilon, t \in ¢, a_1 > 0, 0 \neq a_2 \in ¢$ and $w \in U$. Suppose that $w^p(b(w))^{\sigma-1}b'(w)$ is a starlike univalent in U.

If $f \in \mathcal{A}$ satisfies the subordination:

$$\mathcal{M}(p,n,\lambda,\theta,\varepsilon,a_1,a_2;w) \prec (t + \varepsilon\, b(w))(b(w))^{\sigma} + a_2(b(w))^{\sigma-1}b'(w)$$

where

$$\mathcal{M}(p,n,\lambda,\theta,\varepsilon,a_1,a_2;w)$$
$$= t\left(\frac{\frac{(p+\lambda)}{\theta}\left(\mathcal{B}_{\theta,\lambda}^{n+1,\,p}(a,c,\delta)f(w)\right)+\left(1-\frac{(p+\lambda)}{\theta}\right)\left(\mathcal{B}_{\theta,\lambda}^{n,\,p}(a,c,\delta)f(w)\right)}{w^p}\right)^{a_1\sigma}$$
$$+\varepsilon\left(\frac{\frac{(p+\lambda)}{\theta}\left(\mathcal{B}_{\theta,\lambda}^{n+1,\,p}(a,c,\delta)f(w)\right)+\left(1-\frac{(p+\lambda)}{\theta}\right)\left(\mathcal{B}_{\theta,\lambda}^{n,\,p}(a,c,\delta)f(w)\right)}{w^p}\right)^{a_1(\sigma+1)}$$
$$+a_2a_1\left(\frac{\frac{(p+\lambda)}{\theta}\left(\mathcal{B}_{\theta,\lambda}^{n+1,\,p}(a,c,\delta)f(w)\right)+\left(1-\frac{(p+\lambda)}{\theta}\right)\left(\mathcal{B}_{\theta,\lambda}^{n,\,p}(a,c,\delta)f(w)\right)}{w^p}\right)^{a_1\sigma}$$
$$\left(\frac{w\frac{(p+\lambda)}{\theta}\left(\mathcal{B}_{\theta,\lambda}^{n+1,\,p}(a,c,\delta)f(w)\right)'+\left(1-\frac{(p+\lambda)}{\theta}\right)\left(\mathcal{B}_{\theta,\lambda}^{n,\,p}(a,c,\delta)f(w)\right)'}{\frac{(p+\lambda)}{\theta}\left(\mathcal{B}_{\theta,\lambda}^{n+1,\,p}(a,c,\delta)f(w)\right)+\left(1-\frac{(p+\lambda)}{\theta}\right)\left(\mathcal{B}_{\theta,\lambda}^{n,\,p}(a,c,\delta)f(w)\right)}-p\right), \tag{9}$$

then

$$\left(\frac{\frac{(p+\lambda)}{\theta}\left(\mathcal{B}_{\theta,\lambda}^{n+1,\,p}(a,c,\delta)f(w)\right)+\left(1-\frac{(p+\lambda)}{\theta}\right)\left(\mathcal{B}_{\theta,\lambda}^{n,\,p}(a,c,\delta)f(w)\right)}{w^p}\right)^{a_1}$$
$$\prec b(w).$$

Proof. Let $H(\beta)=(t+\varepsilon\beta)\beta^{\sigma}$ and $L(\beta)=a_2(\beta)^{\sigma-1}$, $0\neq\beta\in$ ¢, when $H(\beta)$ and $L(\beta)$ are analytic in ¢. □

Then, we obtain $G(w)=wb'(w)L(b(w))=a_2w^p(b(w))^{\sigma-1}b'(w)$ and $y(w)=H(b(w))+G(w)=(t+\varepsilon(b(w)))(b(w))^{\sigma}+a_2w^p(b(w))^{\sigma-1}b'(w)$.

Since $w^p(b(w))^{\sigma-1}b'(w)$ is starlike, then $G(w)$ is starlike in U, and

$$Re\left(\frac{y'(w)}{G(w)}\right)=Re\left\{p+\frac{wt\sigma}{w^pa_2}+\frac{w\varepsilon(\sigma+1)}{w^pa_2}(w)+(\sigma-1)\frac{wb'(w)}{b(w)}+\frac{wb''(w)}{b'(w)}\right\}$$
$$>0$$

Additionally, consider

$$q(w)$$
$$=\left(\frac{\frac{(p+\lambda)}{\theta}\left(\mathcal{B}_{\theta,\lambda}^{n+1,\,p}(a,c,\delta)f(w)\right)+\left(1-\frac{(p+\lambda)}{\theta}\right)\left(\mathcal{B}_{\theta,\lambda}^{n,\,p}(a,c,\delta)f(w)\right)}{w^p}\right)^{a_1}.$$

Then,

$$q'(w)$$
$$=a_1\left(\frac{\frac{(p+\lambda)}{\theta}\left(\mathcal{B}_{\theta,\lambda}^{n+1,\,p}(a,c,\delta)f(w)\right)+\left(1-\frac{(p+\lambda)}{\theta}\right)\left(\mathcal{B}_{\theta,\lambda}^{n,\,p}(a,c,\delta)f(w)\right)}{w^p}\right)^{a_1}$$
$$\left[\frac{\frac{(p+\lambda)}{\theta}\left(\mathcal{B}_{\theta,\lambda}^{n+1,\,p}(a,c,\delta)f(w)\right)'+\left(1-\frac{(p+\lambda)}{\theta}\right)\left(\mathcal{B}_{\theta,\lambda}^{n,\,p}(a,c,\delta)f(w)\right)'}{\frac{(p+\lambda)}{\theta}\left(\mathcal{B}_{\theta,\lambda}^{n+1,\,p}(a,c,\delta)f(w)\right)+\left(1-\frac{(p+\lambda)}{\theta}\right)\left(\mathcal{B}_{\theta,\lambda}^{n,\,p}(a,c,\delta)f(w)\right)}-\frac{1}{w}\right].$$

We obtain

$$t\left(\frac{\frac{(p+\lambda)}{\theta}\left(\mathcal{B}_{\theta,\lambda}^{n+1,\ p}(a,c,\delta)f(w)\right)+\left(1-\frac{(p+\lambda)}{\theta}\right)\left(\mathcal{B}_{\theta,\lambda}^{n,\ p}(a,c,\delta)f(w)\right)}{w^p}\right)^{a_1\sigma}$$

$$+\varepsilon\left(\frac{\frac{(p+\lambda)}{\theta}\left(\mathcal{B}_{\theta,\lambda}^{n+1,\ p}(a,c,\delta)f(w)\right)+\left(1-\frac{(p+\lambda)}{\theta}\right)\left(\mathcal{B}_{\theta,\lambda}^{n,\ p}(a,c,\delta)f(w)\right)}{w^p}\right)^{a_1(\sigma+1)}$$

$$= t(q(w))^{\sigma} + \varepsilon\left[(q(w))^{\sigma}q(w)\right] = (t+\varepsilon q(w))(q(w))^{\sigma}.$$

Since

$$a_1\left(\frac{w\frac{(p+\lambda)}{\theta}\left(\mathcal{B}_{\theta,\lambda}^{n+1,\ p}(a,c,\delta)f(w)\right)' + \left(1-\frac{(p+\lambda)}{\theta}\right)\left(\mathcal{B}_{\theta,\lambda}^{n,\ p}(a,c,\delta)f(w)\right)'}{\frac{(p+\lambda)}{\theta}\left(\mathcal{B}_{\theta,\lambda}^{n+1,\ p}(a,c,\delta)f(w)\right) + \left(1-\frac{(p+\lambda)}{\theta}\right)\left(\mathcal{B}_{\theta,\lambda}^{n,\ p}(a,c,\delta)f(w)\right)} - p\right) = \frac{wq'(w)}{q(w)},$$

That

$$a_2a_1\left(\frac{\frac{(p+\lambda)}{\theta}\left(\mathcal{B}_{\theta,\lambda}^{n+1,\ p}(a,c,\delta)f(w)\right)+\left(1-\frac{(p+\lambda)}{\theta}\right)\left(\mathcal{B}_{\theta,\lambda}^{n,\ p}(a,c,\delta)f(w)\right)}{w^p}\right)^{a_1\sigma}$$

$$\left(\frac{w\frac{(p+\lambda)}{\theta}\left(\mathcal{B}_{\theta,\lambda}^{n+1,\ p}(a,c,\delta)f(w)\right)'+\left(1-\frac{(p+\lambda)}{\theta}\right)\left(\mathcal{B}_{\theta,\lambda}^{n,\ p}(a,c,\delta)f(w)\right)'}{\frac{(p+\lambda)}{\theta}\left(\mathcal{B}_{\theta,\lambda}^{n+1,\ p}(a,c,\delta)f(w)\right)+\left(1-\frac{(p+\lambda)}{\theta}\right)\left(\mathcal{B}_{\theta,\lambda}^{n,\ p}(a,c,\delta)f(w)\right)} - p\right)$$

$$= a_2\, w(q(w))^{\sigma-1}q'(w).$$

From (8) we obtain $(t+\varepsilon q(w))(q(w))^{\sigma} + a_2\ w(q(w))^{\sigma-1}q'(w) \prec (t+\varepsilon b(w))(b(w))^{\sigma} + a_2(b(w))^{\sigma-1}b'(w)$ and using Lemma 1 we obtain $q(w) \prec b(w)$.

Corollary 2. *Let b be convex univalent in, $b(0) = 1$, and $b(w) \neq 0$ for all $w \in U$, and suppose that b satisfies:*

$$Re\left\{p + \frac{wt\sigma}{w^p a_2} + \frac{w\varepsilon(\sigma+1)}{w^p a_2}(w) + (\sigma-1)\frac{wb'(w)}{b(w)} + \frac{wb''(w)}{b'(w)}\right\} > 0,$$

where $\sigma, \varepsilon, t \in ¢, a_1 > 0, 0 \neq a_2 \in ¢$ and $w \in U$.

Suppose that $w^p(b(w))^{\sigma-1}b'(w)$ is a starlike univalent in U.

If $f \in \mathcal{A}$, it satisfies the subordination:

$$\mathcal{M}(\sigma, t, \varepsilon, h_\mu, \mu, a_1, a_2; w) \prec (t+\varepsilon\, b(w))(b(w))^{\sigma} + a_2(b(w))^{\sigma-1}b'(w),$$

then

$$\left(\frac{\frac{(p+\lambda)}{\theta}\left(J_p^{n+1}(\theta,\lambda)f(w)\right) + \left(1-\frac{(p+\lambda)}{\theta}\right)\left(J_p^{n}(\theta,\lambda)f(w)\right)}{w^p}\right)^{a_1} \prec b(w).$$

3. Superordination Results

Theorem 3. *Let $b(w)$ be convex in U, with $b(0) = 1, a_1 > 0$, $Re a_2 > 0$, if $f \in \mathcal{A}$,*

$$\left(\frac{\mathcal{B}_{\theta,\lambda}^{n,\ p}(a,c,\delta)f(w)}{w^p}\right)^{a_1} \in \Omega[q(0),1] \cap Q$$

and

$$\left(1-\frac{a_2(p+\lambda)}{\theta}\right)\left(\frac{\mathcal{B}_{\theta,\lambda}^{n,\,p}(a,c,\delta)f(w)}{w^p}\right)^{a_1}+\frac{a_2(p+\lambda)}{\theta}\left(\frac{\mathcal{B}_{\theta,\lambda}^{n+1,\,p}(a,c,\delta)f(w)}{\mathcal{B}_{\theta,\lambda}^{n,\,p}(a,c,\delta)f(w)}\right)^{a_1}\left(\frac{\mathcal{B}_{\theta,\lambda}^{n,\,p}(a,c,\delta)f(w)}{w^p}\right)^{a_1}$$

is univalent in U and satisfies the superordination.

$$b(w)+\frac{a_2}{a_1}wb'(w)\prec\left(1-\frac{a_2(p+\lambda)}{\theta}\right)\left(\frac{\mathcal{B}_{\theta,\lambda}^{n,\,p}(a,c,\delta)f(w)}{w^p}\right)^{a_1}+\frac{a_2(p+\lambda)}{\theta}\left(\frac{\mathcal{B}_{\theta,\lambda}^{n+1,\,p}(a,c,\delta)f(w)}{\mathcal{B}_{\theta,\lambda}^{n,\,p}(a,c,\delta)f(w)}\right)^{a_1}\left(\frac{\mathcal{B}_{\theta,\lambda}^{n,\,p}(a,c,\delta)f(w)}{w^p}\right)^{a_1}$$

then

$$b(w)\prec\left(\frac{\mathcal{B}_{\theta,\lambda}^{n,\,p}(a,c,\delta)f(w)}{w^p}\right)^{a_1}.$$

Proof. Consider

$$q(w)=\left(\frac{\mathcal{B}_{\theta,\lambda}^{n,\,p}(a,c,\delta)f(w)}{w^p}\right)^{a_1},$$

then

$$q'(w)=a_1\left(\frac{\mathcal{B}_{\theta,\lambda}^{n,\,p}(a,c,\delta)f(w)}{w^p}\right)^{a_1-1}\left(\frac{w^p\left[\mathcal{B}_{\theta,\lambda}^{n,\,p}(a,c,\delta)f(w)\right]'}{(w^p)^2}-\frac{pw^{p-1}\left(\mathcal{B}_{\theta,\lambda}^{n,\,p}(a,c,\delta)f(w)\right)(w)}{(w^p)^2}\right).$$

We have

$$\frac{q'(w)}{q(w)}=a_1\left(\frac{\left[\mathcal{B}_{\theta,\lambda}^{n,\,p}(a,c,\delta)f(w)\right]'}{\left(\mathcal{B}_{\theta,\lambda}^{n,\,p}(a,c,\delta)f(w)\right)}-\frac{1}{w}\right),$$

with the same steps of Theorem 1 and using the hypothesis, we obtain

$$b(w)+\frac{a_2}{a_1}wb'(w)\prec b(w)+\frac{a_2}{a_1}wb'(w).$$

Apply Lemma 4 we obtain

$$b(w)\prec\left(\frac{\mathcal{B}_{\theta,\lambda}^{n,\,p}(a,c,\delta)f(w)}{w^p}\right)^{a_1}.$$

□

Corollary 3. *Let $b(w)$ be convex in U, with $b(0)=1$, $a_1>0$, $Rea_2>0$, if $f\in\mathcal{A}$,*

$$\left(\frac{J_p^n(\theta,\lambda)f(w)}{w^p}\right)^{a_1}\in\Omega[q(0),1]\cap Q$$

and

$$\left(1-\frac{a_2(p+\lambda)}{\theta}\right)\left(\frac{J_p^n(\theta,\lambda)f(w)}{w^p}\right)^{a_1}+\frac{a_2(p+\lambda)}{\theta}\left(\frac{J_p^{n+1}(\theta,\lambda)f(w)}{J_p^n(\theta,\lambda)f(w)}\right)^{a_1}\left(\frac{J_p^n(\theta,\lambda)f(w)}{w^p}\right)^{a_1}$$

is univalent in U and satisfies the superordination

$$b(w)+\frac{a_2}{a_1}wb'(w)\prec\left(1-\frac{a_2(p+\lambda)}{\theta}\right)\left(\frac{J_p^n(\theta,\lambda)f(w)}{w^p}\right)^{a_1}$$
$$+\frac{a_2(p+\lambda)}{\theta}\left(\frac{J_p^{n+1}(\theta,\lambda)f(w)}{J_p^n(\theta,\lambda)f(w)}\right)^{a_1}\left(\frac{J_p^n(\theta,\lambda)f(w)}{w^p}\right)^{a_1},$$

then

$$b(w)\prec\left(\frac{J_p^n(\theta,\lambda)f(w)}{w^p}\right)^{a_1}.$$

Theorem 4. *Let b be convex univalent in $b(0)=1$ and $b(w)\neq 0$ for all $w\in U$ and suppose that b satisfies:*

$$Re\left\{\frac{t\sigma}{a_2}b'(w)+\frac{\varepsilon(\sigma+1)}{a_2}b(w)b'(w)\right\}>0, \tag{10}$$

where, $\varepsilon, t\in ¢, 0\neq a_2\in ¢^*$, $w\in U$, and $w(b(w))^{\sigma-1}b'(w)$ are all starlike univalent in U.

If $f\in\mathcal{A}$, satisfies the condition:

$$\left(\frac{\frac{(p+\lambda)}{\theta}\left(\mathcal{B}_{\theta,\lambda}^{n+1,\,p}(a,c,\delta)f(w)\right)+\left(1-\frac{(p+\lambda)}{\theta}\right)\left(\mathcal{B}_{\theta,\lambda}^{n,\,p}(a,c,\delta)f(w)\right)}{w^p}\right)^{a_1}\in\Omega[b(0),1]\bigcap Q,$$

and $\mathcal{M}(p,n,\lambda,\theta,\varepsilon,a_1,a_2;w)$ is univalent in U.

If $(t+\varepsilon\, b(w))(b(w))^{\sigma}+a_2(b(w))^{\sigma-1}b'(w)\prec\mathcal{M}(\sigma,t,\varepsilon,h_\mu,\mu,a_1,a_2;w)$, then

$$b(w)\prec\left(\frac{\frac{(p+\lambda)}{\theta}\left(\mathcal{B}_{\theta,\lambda}^{n+1,\,p}(a,c,\delta)f(w)\right)+\left(1-\frac{(p+\lambda)}{\theta}\right)\left(\mathcal{B}_{\theta,\lambda}^{n,\,p}(a,c,\delta)f(w)\right)}{w^p}\right)^{a_1}.$$

Proof. Let $H(\beta)=(t+\varepsilon\beta)\beta^{\sigma}$ and $L(\beta)=a_2(\beta)^{\sigma-1}$, $0\neq\beta\in ¢$, when $H(\beta)$ is analytic in ¢ and $L(\beta)\neq 0$ is analytic in $¢/0$. Then, we obtain $G(w)=w^pb'(w)L(b(w))=a_2w^p(b(w))^{\sigma-1}b'(w)$. □

Since $w^p(b(w))^{\sigma-1}b'(w)$ is starlike, then $G(w)$ is starlike in U, and

$$Re\left(\frac{H'(b(w))}{L(b(w))}\right)=Re\left(\frac{\left[(t+\varepsilon(b(w)))(b(w))^{\sigma}\right]'}{a_2(b(w))^{\sigma-1}}\right)=Re\left\{\frac{t\sigma}{a_2}b'(w)+\frac{\varepsilon(\sigma+1)}{a_2}b(w)b'(w)\right\}>0;$$

Now, let

$$q(w)=\left(\frac{\frac{(p+\lambda)}{\theta}\left(\mathcal{B}_{\theta,\lambda}^{n+1,\,p}(a,c,\delta)f(w)\right)+\left(1-\frac{(p+\lambda)}{\theta}\right)\left(\mathcal{B}_{\theta,\lambda}^{n,\,p}(a,c,\delta)f(w)\right)}{w^p}\right)^{a_1}.$$

From (8) we obtain

$$(t+\varepsilon\, b(w))(b(w))^{\sigma}+a_2(b(w))^{\sigma-1}b'(w)$$
$$\prec(t+\varepsilon q(w))(q(w))^{\sigma}+a_2\, w(q(w))^{\sigma-1}q'(w).$$

Using Lemma 3 we obtain $b(w)\prec q(w)$.

Corollary 4. *Let b be convex univalent in U, $b(0) = 1$, and $b(w) \neq 0$ for all $w \in U$, and suppose that b satisfies:*

$$Re\left\{\frac{t\sigma}{a_2}b'(w) + \frac{\varepsilon(\sigma+1)}{a_2}b(w)b'(w)\right\},> 0, \tag{11}$$

where, $\varepsilon, t \in ¢, 0 \neq a_2 \in ¢^*$, $w \in U$, and $w(b(w))^{\sigma-1}b'(w)$ are starlike univalent in U.

Let $f \in \mathcal{A}$, satisfies the condition:

$$\left(\frac{\frac{(p+\lambda)}{\theta}\left(J_p^{n+1}(\theta,\lambda)f(w)\right) + \left(1 - \frac{(p+\lambda)}{\theta}\right)\left(J_p^n(\theta,\lambda)f(w)\right)}{w^p}\right)^{a_1} \in \Omega[b(0),1]\bigcap Q,$$

and $\mathcal{M}(p,n,\lambda,\theta,\varepsilon,a_1,a_2;w)$ is univalent in U.

If $(t+\varepsilon\, b(w))(b(w))^{\sigma} + a_2(b(w))^{\sigma-1}b'(w) \prec \mathcal{M}(\sigma,t,\varepsilon,h_\mu,\mu,a_1,a_2;w)$, then

$$b(w) \prec \left(\frac{\frac{(p+\lambda)}{\theta}\left(J_p^{n+1}(\theta,\lambda)f(w)\right) + \left(1 - \frac{(p+\lambda)}{\theta}\right)\left(J_p^n(\theta,\lambda)f(w)\right)}{w^p}\right)^{a_1}.$$

4. Sandwich Results

By combining the above theories, we obtain the following two sandwich theories.

Theorem 5. *Let b_1, b_2 be convex univalent in U, with $b_1(0) = b_2(0) = 1$ $Rea_2 > 0$ and*

$$Re\left(1 + \frac{q''(w)}{q'(w)}\right) > \max\left\{0, -Re\frac{a_1}{a_2}\right\},$$

where $a_1 > 0, 0 \neq a_2 \in ¢$.

If $f \in \mathcal{A}$ and

$$\left(\frac{\mathcal{B}_{\theta,\lambda}^{n,\,p}(a,c,\delta)f(w)}{w^p}\right)^{a_1} \in \Omega[1,1]\bigcap Q,$$

and

$$\left(1 - \frac{a_2(p+\lambda)}{\theta}\right)\left(\frac{\mathcal{B}_{\theta,\lambda}^{n,\,p}(a,c,\delta)f(w)}{w^p}\right)^{a_1} + \frac{a_2(p+\lambda)}{\theta}\left(\frac{\mathcal{B}_{\theta,\lambda}^{n+1,\,p}(a,c,\delta)f(w)}{\mathcal{B}_{\theta,\lambda}^{n,\,p}(a,c,\delta)f(w)}\right)^{a_1}\left(\frac{\mathcal{B}_{\theta,\lambda}^{n,\,p}(a,c,\delta)f(w)}{w^p}\right)^{a_1}$$

is univalent in U, it satisfies:

$$b_1(w) + \frac{a_2}{a_1}wb'_1(w) \prec \left(1 - \frac{a_2(p+\lambda)}{\theta}\right)\left(\frac{\mathcal{B}_{\theta,\lambda}^{n,\,p}(a,c,\delta)f(w)}{w^p}\right)^{a_1} + \frac{a_2(p+\lambda)}{\theta}\left(\frac{\mathcal{B}_{\theta,\lambda}^{n+1,\,p}(a,c,\delta)f(w)}{\mathcal{B}_{\theta,\lambda}^{n,\,p}(a,c,\delta)f(w)}\right)^{a_1}\left(\frac{\mathcal{B}_{\theta,\lambda}^{n,\,p}(a,c,\delta)f(w)}{w^p}\right)^{a_1} \prec b_2(w) + \frac{a_2}{a_1}wb'_2(w),$$

then $b_1(w) \prec \left(\frac{\mathcal{B}_{\theta,\lambda}^{n,\,p}(a,c,\delta)f(w)}{w^p}\right)^{a_1} \prec b_2(w).$

Theorem 6. *Let b_1, b_2 be convex univalent in U, with $b_1(0) = b_2(0) = 1$, and let $f \in \mathcal{A}$ satisfy the condition:*

$$\left(\frac{\frac{(p+\lambda)}{\theta}\left(\mathcal{B}_{\theta,\lambda}^{n+1,\,p}(a,c,\delta)f(w)\right) + \left(1 - \frac{(p+\lambda)}{\theta}\right)\left(\mathcal{B}_{\theta,\lambda}^{n,\,p}(a,c,\delta)f(w)\right)}{w^p}\right)^{a_1} \in \Omega[1,1]\bigcap Q,$$

and $\mathcal{M}(p,n,\lambda,\theta,\varepsilon,a_1,a_2;w)$ *is univalent in* U.

If

$$(t+\varepsilon\, b_1(w))(b_1(w))^{\sigma}+a_2(b_1(w))^{\sigma-1}{b_1}'(w)\prec\mathcal{M}(p,n,\lambda,\theta,\varepsilon,a_1,a_2;w)$$
$$\prec(t+\varepsilon\, b_2(w))(b_2(w))^{\sigma}+a_2(b_2(w))^{\sigma-1}{b_2}'(w),$$

then

$$b_1(w)\prec\left(\frac{\frac{(p+\lambda)}{\theta}\left(\mathcal{B}^{n+1,\,p}_{\theta,\lambda}(a,c,\delta)f(w)\right)+\left(1-\frac{(p+\lambda)}{\theta}\right)\left(\mathcal{B}^{n,\,p}_{\theta,\lambda}(a,c,\delta)f(w)\right)}{w^p}\right)^{a_1}\prec b_2(w).$$

5. Conclusions

In this paper, using the convolution (or Hadamard product) we defined the El-Ashwah and Drbuk linear operator, which is a multivalent function in the unit disk U and satisfied its specific relationship to derive the subordination, superordination, and some sandwich results for this operator using the properties of subordination and superordination concepts. The interesting results can be obtained for other operators using the same techniques of subordinations and superordinations.

Author Contributions: Conceptualization, L.-I.C. and A.R.S.J. methodology, L.-I.C. and A.R.S.J. software, L.-I.C. and A.R.S.J.; validation, L.-I.C. and A.R.S.J.; formal analysis, L.-I.C. and A.R.S.J.; investigation, L.-I.C. and A.R.S.J.; resources, L.-I.C. and A.R.S.J.; data curation, L.-I.C. and A.R.S.J.; writing—original draft preparation, L.-I.C. and A.R.S.J.; writing—review and editing, L.-I.C. and A.R.S.J.; visualization, L.-I.C. and A.R.S.J.; supervision, L.-I.C. and A.R.S.J.; project administration, L.-I.C. and A.R.S.J.; funding acquisition, L.-I.C. All authors have read and agreed to the published version of the manuscript.

Funding: This research received no external funding.

Data Availability Statement: Not applicable.

Conflicts of Interest: The authors declare no conflict of interest.

References

1. Duren, P.L. Grundlehren der Mathematischen Wissenschaften. In *Univalent Functions*; Springer: New York, NY, USA; Berlin/Heidelberg, Germany; Tokyo, Japan, 1983; Volume 259.
2. El-Ashwah, R.M.; Kota, W.Y. Inclusion and Subordination Properties for Classes of Multivalent Functions Involving Differential-Integral Operator. *Inf. Sci. Lett.* **2022**, *11*, 11.
3. Miller, S.S.; Mocanu, P.T. Briot–Bouquet differential superordinations and sandwich theorems. *J. Math. Anal. Appl.* **2007**, *329*, 327–335. [CrossRef]
4. Cotîrlă, L.I.; Cătaş, A. A Differential Sandwich Theorem for Analytic Functions Defined by an Integral Operator. *Acta Univ. Apulensis* **2020**, *62*, 19–28.
5. Zayed, H.M.; Aouf, M.K.; Mostafa, A.O. Subordination properties for multivalent functions associated with a generalized fractional differential integral operator. *Axioms* **2018**, *7*, 27. [CrossRef]
6. El-Ashwah, R.M.; Drbuk, M.E. Subordination properties of p-valent functions defined by linear operators. *Br. J. Math. Comput. Sci.* **2014**, *21*, 3000–3013. [CrossRef]
7. Atshan, W.G.; Abbas, I.A.; Yalcin, S. New Concept on Fourth-Order Differential Subordination and Superordination with Some Results for Multivalent Analytic Functions. *J. Al-Qadisiyah Comput. Sci. Math.* **2020**, *12*, 96–107.
8. Al-Ameedee, S.A.; Atshan, W.G.; AL-Maamori, F.A.; Yalcin, S. Third-Order Sandwich Results of Multivalent Analytic Functions Involving Catas Operator. *An. Univ. Oradea Fasc. Mat.* **2021**, *28*, 111–129.
9. Prajapat, J. Subordination and superordination preserving properties for generalized multiplier transformation operator. *Math. Comput. Model.* **2012**, *55*, 1456–1465. [CrossRef]
10. Kiryakova, V. *Generalized Fractional Calculus and Applications*; Pitman Research Notes in Mathematics Series; John Wiley & Sons, Inc.: New York, NY, USA, 1994; Volume 301.

11. Shanmugam, T.; Ravichandran, V.; Sivasubramanian, S. Differential sandwich theorems for subclasses of analytic functions. *Aust. J. Math. Anal. Appl.* **2006**, *3*, 1–11.
12. Miller, S.S.; Mocanu, P.T. Subordinates of differential superordinations. *Complex Var. Theory Appl.* **2003**, *48*, 815826.

model SIRD to study the dynamics of Ebola virus disease and developed time-dependent controls in his model. He calculated the basic reproductive number, the equilibrium points, and two boundary equilibria. He implemented the control measures to reduce the Ebola virus disease in specific areas [22]. Ahmed et al. [23] proposed the SEIR model with some new compartments, such as hospitalization, quarantine, and vaccination. In hospitalization and vaccination cases, optimal control strategies are used to control disease transmission and give the powerful impact of vaccination to the infected population. Tulu et al. introduced a mathematical model including quarantine and vaccination to analyze the disease dynamics [24]. They investigated the model using fractional-order derivatives and verified the existence and positive solution of their introduced model. They used Euler and Markov Chain Monte Carlo (MCMC) methods to generate the simulations. Their outcomes illustrated that the quarantine and vaccinations played an important part to control the Ebola outbreak. Area et al. presented a mathematical model with the vaccination of susceptible individuals to control disease transmission [25]. They studied two optimal control problems associated with Ebola disease transmission with vaccination. They considered three vaccination constraints to show the impact of vaccination. A SIR model was constructed with direct and indirect transmissions by Berge et al. [26]. They proved the local and global asymptotic stability of the endemic equilibrium points and developed the nonstandard finite difference scheme, which is dynamically consistent with the model. Kabli et al., in 2018, used the cooperative systems theory to examine the global stability of the epidemic SEIHR model of Ebola disease [27]. Rafiq et al., in 2020, constructed an SEIR model of nonlinear differential equations [28]. They obtained the threshold quantity and equilibrium points and checked the stability of their proposed model. They proved that the equilibrium points are locally asymptotically stable. The Lyapunov function was used to check the global stabilities. They developed a fourth-order Runge–Kutta method and a nonstandard finite difference scheme for the proposed model and demonstrated that the RK-4 method failed at certain step sizes, while the NSFD scheme conserved all the dynamical properties of the model at large step sizes. Okyere et al. examined the optimal control analysis of epidemiological models such as SIR and SEIR using vaccination, treatment, and educational campaigns as time-dependent control functions [29]. They used the forward-backward sweep method with the RK-4 method to explain the optimal system for different control strategies. Ahmed et al. [30], in 2020, established a mathematical model SVEIR by introducing the new sub-population class of vaccinated people into the SEIR model [31]. They also presented the equilibrium points and stability analysis of the model. Both the disease-free and endemic equilibrium points are locally and globally stable. They justified their concluded theoretical outturn by applying RK-4 and NSFD schemes. Their work shows that through voluntary vaccinations, the transmission of the Ebola virus can be controlled. A work regarding a fuzzy epidemic model with an NSFD scheme is presented by Dayan et al. [32].

Some innovative studies for epidemic models in the set of fractional calculus have been conducted. The referred articles are of importance in this connection [33,34]. In the existing theories, advection and diffusion phenomena are considered for the propagation of disease in the defined population. The existing epidemic models deal with the disease dynamics depending on time. However, they do not examine the effect of advection and diffusion factors simultaneously. For that reason, there is no numerical design for this type of model in the running literature, which is, in this context, the generalized epidemic Ebola model, namely the advection–diffusion Ebola model. Moreover, the existing numerical schemes do not preserve the positivity property, which is the essential feature of the solutions to the population systems. Additionally, they lead toward a false steady state. This was a major drawback in some of the present numerical designs. The scheme proposed and developed in this article ensures positive solutions, stability, and convergence toward the true steady state. Hence, the extended model is productive and enriched with disease dynamics.

As far as the limitations of the research work are concerned, the initial and boundary conditions of the underlying model should be continuous functions. If these conditions are discontinuous, piecewise continuous, or nonlocal conditions, then they cannot be considered. The other limitation is related to the existence and uniqueness of the solution. The continuity of the solution lies in a restricted domain. Equivalently, the maximum length of continuity is short.

2. Modified Ebola Virus Model

A compartmental model of the Ebola virus is designed for the numerical study in Section 2. The model under study deals with the spatio-temporal dynamics of the Ebola virus disease. Due to the involvement of space as well as time, the domain for the current model is assumed to be $\Omega = (0, L) \times (0, T) \subseteq \mathbb{R}^2$, where L and T are real numbers, such that $T > 0$. Suppose that the state variables for the system are $S = S(x,t)$, $E = E(x,t)$, $I = I(x,t)$, and $R = R(x,t)$, which are the real functions defined on Ω and are described as the subpopulation sizes of the compartments susceptible, exposed, infected, and recovered, respectively, at any time t. Further, let $S = S(x,t)$, $E = E(x,t)$, $I = I(x,t)$, $R = R(x,t) \in C^{2,1}[\Omega, \mathbb{R}]$. Additionally, suppose that $\zeta_1(x), \zeta_2(x)$ and $\zeta_3(x)$ are three real-valued functions such that $\zeta_1(x), \zeta_2(x)$, and $\zeta_3(x) \in C^1[(0, L), \mathbb{R}]$. The state variables of the model and parameters used in the prescribed system are stated in Table 1.

Table 1. Values of the parameters.

Notations	Description
$S(x,t)$	No. of susceptible individuals at time t and space x
$E(x,t)$	No. of exposed individuals at time t and space x
$I(x,t)$	No. of infected individuals at time t and space x
$R(x,t)$	No. of recovered individuals at time t and space x
p_1	Birth rate as well as death rate
p_2	Contact rate for the individuals from the susceptible with infected class
p_3	Transmission rate of exposed persons to the infected person
p_4	Treatment rate
a_1	Rate of advection for the susceptible class
a_2	Rate of advection for the exposed class
a_3	Rate of advection for the infected class
a_4	Rate of advection for the recovered class
δ_1	Diffusion rate of advection for the susceptible class
δ_2	Diffusion rate of advection for the exposed class
δ_3	Diffusion rate of advection for the infected class
δ_4	Diffusion rate of advection for the recovered class

The spatio-temporal model of Ebola virus disease including advection and diffusion is given as follows [35]:

$$\frac{\partial S(x,t)}{\partial t} + a_1 \frac{\partial S(x,t)}{\partial x} = p_1 - p_2 S(x,t)E(x,t) - p_1 S(x,t) + \delta_1 \frac{d^2 S(x,t)}{dx^2}, \tag{1}$$

$$\frac{\partial E(x,t)}{\partial t} + a_2 \frac{\partial E(x,t)}{\partial x} = p_2 S(x,t)E(x,t) - p_3 E(x,t) - p_1 E(x,t) + \delta_2 \frac{d^2 E(x,t)}{dx^2}, \tag{2}$$

$$\frac{\partial I(x,t)}{\partial t}+a_3\frac{\partial I(x,t)}{\partial x}=p_3E(x,t)-(p_1+p_4)I(x,t)+\delta_3\frac{d^2I(x,t)}{dx^2}, \tag{3}$$

$$\frac{\partial R(x,t)}{\partial t}+a_4\frac{\partial R(x,t)}{\partial x}=p_4I(x,t)-p_1R(x,t)+\delta_4\frac{d^2R(x,t)}{dx^2}. \tag{4}$$

Since all of the above equations are independent of $R(x,t)$, thus, the system (1)–(4) reduces to the system of the first three Equations (1)–(3).

$$\frac{\partial S(x,t)}{\partial t}+a_1\frac{\partial S(x,t)}{\partial x}=p_1-p_2S(x,t)E(x,t)-p_1S(x,t)+\delta_1\frac{d^2S(x,t)}{dx^2}, \tag{5}$$

$$\frac{\partial E(x,t)}{\partial t}+a_2\frac{\partial E(x,t)}{\partial x}=p_2S(x,t)E(x,t)-p_3E(x,t)-p_1E(x,t)+\delta_2\frac{d^2E(x,t)}{dx^2}, \tag{6}$$

$$\frac{\partial I(x,t)}{\partial t}+a_3\frac{\partial I(x,t)}{\partial x}=p_3E(x,t)-(p_1+p_4)I(x,t)+\delta_3\frac{d^2I(x,t)}{dx^2}. \tag{7}$$

Additionally, the initial and boundary conditions

$$S(x,0)=\zeta_1(x),\ \text{for all } x\in[0,L], \tag{8}$$
$$E(x,0)=\zeta_2(x),\ \text{for all } x\in[0,L], \tag{9}$$
$$I(x,0)=\zeta_3(x),\ \text{for all } x\in[0,L], \tag{10}$$

and

$$\frac{\partial\Big(S(x,t)\Big)}{\partial\eta}=\frac{\partial\Big(E(x,t)\Big)}{\partial\eta}=\frac{\partial\Big(I(x,t)\Big)}{\partial\eta}=0, \tag{11}$$

for every ordered pair $(x,t)\in\partial\Omega$, $\frac{\partial}{\partial\eta}$ represent outward normal derivatives on $\partial\Omega$, a boundary of Ω where η is the outward unit normal vector on the boundary. Furthermore, $S(x,t),E(x,t),I(x,t),R(x,t)$ are Lebesgue-integrable functions in the domain mentioned above.

The prescribed system (1)–(4) reflects the dynamical behaviour of the fatal Ebola virus disease, for which $S(x,t),E(x,t),I(x,t)$ and $R(x,t)$ depict the sub-population sizes of respective compartments at point x and time t, respectively. Due to biological reasoning, it is assumed that S,E,I and R are the nonnegative functions of x and t [36–38].

For the equilibrium points, set all instantaneous changes with respect to time and space equal to zero in (5)–(7).

Thus, the Ebola-free equilibrium point of the continuous system is:

$$E_0=(1,0,0,0).$$

Additionally, the endemic equilibrium of the model, obtained by equating all derivatives to zero, is [35]:

$$E_e=(\tilde{S},\tilde{E},\tilde{I},\tilde{R}),$$

where $\tilde{S}=\frac{p_1+p_3}{p_2},\quad \tilde{E}=\frac{p_1(1-\tilde{S})}{p_2\tilde{S}},\quad \tilde{I}=\frac{p_3\tilde{E}}{p_1+p_4},\quad \tilde{R}=\frac{p_4\tilde{I}}{p_1}.$

Additionally, the value of the reproductive number R_0 can be evaluated by using a next-generation matrix.

$$\begin{bmatrix} E' \\ I' \end{bmatrix} = \begin{bmatrix} p_2 S & 0 \\ 0 & 0 \end{bmatrix} \begin{bmatrix} E \\ I \end{bmatrix} - \begin{bmatrix} p_3 + p_1 & 0 \\ -p_3 & p_1 + p_4 \end{bmatrix} \begin{bmatrix} E \\ I \end{bmatrix}.$$

Since $S = 1$

$$F = \begin{bmatrix} p_2 & 0 \\ 0 & 0 \end{bmatrix}, V = \begin{bmatrix} p_3 + p_1 & 0 \\ -p_3 & p_1 + p_4 \end{bmatrix}.$$

Because R_0 is defined as the spectral radius of FV^{-1}, thus,

$$\begin{aligned} R_0 &= \rho(FV^{-1}), \\ &= \frac{p_2}{p_1 + p_3}. \end{aligned}$$

To make the dynamical system more realistic, many researchers examined advection and diffusion phenomena in highly non-linear continuous mathematical models, which reflect the real significance in the dynamics of the systems [39,40]. The current article addresses the advection and diffusive impacts of an epidemic model's compartmental population.

The approach of the nonstandard finite difference scheme for the model (1)–(4) is adopted with the defined initial and boundary conditions in the next section with the supplementary data (8)–(11).

2.1. Optimal Analysis of the Model

The above system (1)–(4) of Ebola disease and its dynamics depend upon the advection and diffusion properties with respect to each of the state variables $S, E, I,$ and R. The first three partial differentials are mutually coupled, while the last partial differential Equation (4) is completely independent of the rest of the coupled system. Since this model primarily describes the population model, where the sum $S + E + I + R = N$ (the total population), therefore, physically, if the total population is known, the three components are computed from the partial differential Equations (1)–(4). Then, obviously, the fourth tuple of the vector of unknown functions is retained without computing the fourth partial differential Equation (4). Thus, potentially, Equation (4) can be set aside for the upcoming existence analysis, the same as it is in the computations. Now, we will consider System (1)–(3) with the conditions (8)–(11). Without any inconvenience, the first time derivative appearing in the system can be inverted, and in concise form, the solutions S, E, I can be written as follows:

$$\begin{aligned} S &= S_0 + \int_0^t F_1\left(S, E, I, \frac{\partial S}{\partial x}, \frac{\partial^2 S}{\partial x^2}\right)(s)ds, \\ E &= E_0 + \int_0^t F_2\left(S, E, I, \frac{\partial E}{\partial x}, \frac{\partial^2 E}{\partial x^2}\right)(s)ds, \\ I &= I_0 + \int_0^t F_3\left(S, E, I, \frac{\partial I}{\partial x}, \frac{\partial^2 I}{\partial x^2}\right)(s)ds. \end{aligned}$$

If we set $\left(S, E, I\right) = \left(u^1, u^2, u^3\right)$, the more compact form of System (1)–(4) and, consequently, Equations (5)–(7) can be written as:

$$\frac{\partial u^i}{\partial t} = F_i\left(u^1, u^2, u^3, \frac{\partial u^i}{\partial x}, \frac{\partial^2 u^i}{\partial x^2}\right), \tag{12}$$

where $u^1, u^2, u^3, i = 1, 2, 3$ represent the unknown functions $S, E,$ and I, respectively.

The classical triple $\left(u^1, u^2, u^3\right)$ needs to be in the function space $C^1[0, \mathcal{T}] \times C^2[a, b]$ for finite numbers a, b and the finite positive number $\mathcal{T}$. The compact embedding of the function spaces leads to the fact that the function space $C^1[0, \mathcal{T}]$ is compactly embedded as $C^0[0, \mathcal{T}]$; consequently, we can have the consideration of the space of continuous functions as our primary Banach space for the solution tuple to be fit in the space $C^0[0, \mathcal{T}]$, equipped with the usual supremum norm. Furthermore, we strictly assume that, with respect to the space variable, this $u^i \in C^2[a, b]$ for $i = 1, 2, 3$, that is, we invert System (12) with the initial conditions (8)–(10) in the form of the Volterra integral equation as follows:

$$u^i = u_0^i + \int_0^t \mathcal{F}_i\left(u^1, u^2, u^3, \frac{\partial u^i}{\partial x}, \frac{\partial^2 u^i}{\partial x^2}\right)(s)ds, \text{ for } i = 1, 2, 3. \tag{13}$$

The integral Equation (13) can be written in the following operator's form:

$$\mathcal{U}^i = u_0^i + \int_0^t \mathcal{F}_i\left(u^1, u^2, u^3, \frac{\partial u^i}{\partial x}, \frac{\partial^2 u^i}{\partial x^2}\right)(s)ds, \text{ for } i = 1, 2, 3. \tag{14}$$

Since System (1)–(4) reduced to (14) is a physical system, prior to the computational technique, we can predict the behaviour of the solution. Besides the many advantages of the existence theory, there is one serious restriction, which is that, in general, the solution does not exist in the large domain. However, we can construct an a priori condition on the bound of the solution in a special environment called the Schauder-type estimates. This fact leads to the nice idea of the optimization of the function space. The following subsection deals with the important dimension of the analysis.

Fixed-Point Optimization in Banach Spaces

Primarily, we will consider the contraction-mapping principle on the space of continuous functions, and we choose the following balls with arbitrary radii $r > 0$ (to be bounded later) defined by

$$B_{r^i}[u_0^i] = \left\{u^i \in C^0[0, \rho], \left\|u^i - u_0^i \leq r^i\right\|\right\}, \quad i = 1, 2, 3. \tag{15}$$

We choose the initial values as the center of the balls, and we set

$$\left\|u^i\right\| \leq r^i + u_0^i.$$

Again, considering the operator Equation (14), we examine the following conditions:

(i) Self-mapping; that is, $\mathcal{U}^i : B_r[u_0^i] \to B_r[u_0^i]$,

(ii) Contractivity; that is, $\left\|\mathcal{U}_1^i - \mathcal{U}_i^2\right\| \leq k_i \left\|u_1^i - u_2^i\right\|$.

To verify the first condition, we take the norm of Equation (14), and we obtain

$$\begin{aligned}\left\|\mathcal{U}^i - u_0^i\right\| &\leq \int_0^t \left\|\mathcal{F}_i\right\| dr, \\ &\leq \mathcal{K}^i(r)\int_0^t ds, \text{ because } \mathcal{F}_i \text{ are bounded and the norm} \\ &\qquad \text{can be estimated by the radius } r. \\ &\leq \mathcal{K}^i(r)\rho, \\ &\leq r.\end{aligned}$$

This implies that

$$\rho \leq \frac{r}{\mathcal{K}^i(r)} \tag{16}$$

The condition (16) is necessary for the existence of a solution and gives explicit bounds for the length of the continuity of intervals of solutions. For contractivity, we take two images $\mathcal{U}_1^i$ and $\mathcal{U}_2^i$ for two pre-images u_1^i and u_2^i, respectively, from (14), and we can rewrite this as follows:

$$\begin{aligned} \mathcal{U}_1^i - \mathcal{U}_2^i &= \int_0^t F_i\left(u_1^i, \frac{\partial u_1^i}{\partial t}, \frac{\partial^2 u_1^i}{\partial t^2}\right)(s)ds - \int_0^t F_i\left(u_2^i, \frac{\partial u_2^i}{\partial x}, \frac{\partial^2 u_2^i}{\partial x^2}\right)(s)ds, \\ \mathcal{U}_1^i - \mathcal{U}_2^i &= \int_0^t \left\{F_i\left(u_1^i, \frac{\partial u_1^i}{\partial x}, \frac{\partial^2 u_1^i}{\partial x^2}\right) - F_i\left(u_2^i, \frac{\partial u_2^i}{\partial x}, \frac{\partial^2 u_2^i}{\partial x^2}\right)\right\}(s)ds. \end{aligned} \tag{17}$$

Now, suppose that $F^i, i = 1,2,3$ all satisfy the Lipschitz condition of spatial type as defined by

$$\left\|F^i(u_1^i) - F_i(u_2^i)\right\| \leq \mathcal{L}^i(r)\left\|u_1^i - u_2^i\right\|_{C^2[a,b]}. \tag{18}$$

Equation (17) implies

$$\left\|\mathcal{U}_i^i - \mathcal{U}_2^i\right\| \leq \rho\mathcal{L}^i(r)\left\|u_1^i - u_2^i\right\|_{C^2[a,b]},$$

and for some positive constant $\mathcal{M}^i$, we can always have

$$\left\|\mathcal{U}_i^i - \mathcal{U}_2^i\right\| \leq \rho\mathcal{M}^i\mathcal{L}^i(r)\left\|u_1^i - u_2^i\right\|_{C^2[a,b]}.$$

For contractivity, we have the following condition:

$$\rho < \frac{1}{\mathcal{M}^i\mathcal{L}^i(r)}, \tag{19}$$

that is, we have more restrictions on the length of the interval of continuity depending on time. For more precise results, the Lipschitz constant must be small enough.

Hence, the following result has been verified.

Theorem 1. *Suppose that the state variables S, E, I and R are in $C^1[0,\mathcal{T}] \times C^2[a,b]$; then, provided that S, E, I and R satisfy the Lipschitz condition of the type of Equation (18), the initial boundary value problem (1)–(4) with (8)–(11) is uniquely solvable.*

Theorem 2. *Suppose that the state variables S, E, I and R are in $C^1[0,\mathcal{T}] \times C^2[a,b]$; then, the continuity and the uniqueness of the solution of System (1)–(4) is given by the inequality,*

$$\rho < \frac{r}{k^i(r)} = \frac{1}{\mathcal{M}^i\mathcal{L}^i(r)}.$$

Since the epidemic models contain a number of parameters, it becomes an uphill task to find the exact solutions of these models. In some cases, it even becomes impossible to evaluate the problem exactly. The numerical solutions then numerical solutions become inevitable for these types of nonlinear epidemic systems.

In the subsequent section, a non-standardized algebraic scheme is designed to attain the numerical solutions of the underlying model.

2.2. Numerical Modeling

Let M and M^* be two natural numbers and $m = \frac{\mathcal{L}}{M}$, $\ell = \frac{\mathfrak{T}}{M^*}$ be the positive real numbers. Additionally, let $[0, \mathcal{L}]$ and $[0, \mathfrak{T}]$ be the spatial and temporal intervals, respectively, for the proposed problem. Thus, the intervals $[0, \mathcal{L}]$ and $[0, \mathfrak{T}]$ are partitioned into m and ℓ subintervals, respectively. Suppose also that the partition norm of the interval $[0, \mathcal{L}]$ is m, while the partition norm for the interval $[0, \mathfrak{T}]$ is ℓ. Define $x_j = jm$ and $t_k = k\ell$, for which $j \in \{0, 1, 2 \ldots, M\}$ and $k \in \{0, 1, 2 \ldots, M^*\}$. Additionally, suppose that S_j^k, E_j^k, I_j^k, and R_j^k are the approximate values of the exact values of the functions $S(x_j, t_k), E(x_j, t_k), I(x_j, t_k)$, and $R(x_j, t_k)$ respectively, at the mesh point $(jm, k\ell)$ for $j \in \mathbb{Z}$ and $0 \le j \le M$ and $k \in \mathbb{Z}$ and $0 \le j \le M^*$. Additionally, if U is the arbitrary function values from the set $\{S, E, I, R\}$, then we define

$$U^k = (U_0^k, U_1^k, \ldots, U_M^k), \quad k \in \mathbb{Z} \text{ and } 0 \le j \le M^*.$$

The continuous model (1)–(3) is converted in to a system of difference equations with the help of some discrete functions. The procedure of conversion is explained as follows:

$$\frac{S_j^{k+1} - S_j^k}{\ell} + a_1\left\{\frac{S_j^{k+1} - S_{j-1}^{k+1}}{m}\right\} = p_1 - p_2 S_j^{k+1} E_j^k - p_1 S_j^{k+1} + \delta_1\left\{\frac{S_{j+1}^{k+1} - 2S_j^{k+1} + S_{j-1}^{k+1}}{m^2}\right\}, \tag{20}$$

$$\frac{E_j^{k+1} - E_j^k}{\ell} + a_2\left\{\frac{E_j^{k+1} - E_{j-1}^{k+1}}{m}\right\} = p_2 S_j^k E_j^k - p_3 E_j^{k+1} - p_1 E_j^{k+1} + \delta_2\left\{\frac{E_{j+1}^{k+1} - 2E_j^{k+1} + E_{j-1}^{k+1}}{m^2}\right\}, \tag{21}$$

$$\frac{I_j^{k+1} - I_j^k}{\ell} + a_3\left\{\frac{I_j^{k+1} - I_{j-1}^{k+1}}{m}\right\} = p_3 E_j^k - (p_1 + p_4) I_j^{k+1} + \delta_3\left\{\frac{I_{j+1}^{k+1} - 2I_j^{k+1} + I_{j-1}^{k+1}}{m^2}\right\}. \tag{22}$$

After simplifications, (20)–(22) gives

$$-(\lambda_1 + \mu_1) S_{j-1}^{k+1} + (1 + \lambda_1 + \ell p_1 + \ell p_2 E_j^k + 2\mu_1) S_j^{k+1} - \mu_1 S_{j+1}^{k+1} = \ell p_1 + S_j^k, \tag{23}$$

$$-(\lambda_2 + \mu_2) E_{j-1}^{k+1} + (1 + \lambda_2 + \ell(p_1 + p_3) + 2\mu_2) E_j^{k+1} - \mu_2 E_{j+1}^{k+1} = E_j^k + p_2 S_j^k E_j^k, \tag{24}$$

$$-(\lambda_3 + \mu_3) I_{j-1}^{k+1} + (1 + \lambda_3 + \ell(p_1 + p_4) + 2\mu_3) I_j^{k+1} - \mu_3 I_{j+1}^{k+1} = I_j^k + p_3 E_j^k, \tag{25}$$

where $\lambda_1 = \frac{a_1\ell}{m}$, $\mu_1 = \frac{\delta_1\ell}{m^2}$, $\lambda_2 = \frac{a_2\ell}{m}$, $\mu_2 = \frac{\delta_2\ell}{m^2}$, $\lambda_3 = \frac{a_3\ell}{m}$ and $\mu_3 = \frac{\delta_3\ell}{m^2}$ for $j \in \{1, 2, \ldots, M\}$ and $k \in \{0, 1, 2, \ldots, M^* - 1\}$.

The auxiliary data are discretized as:

$$\begin{aligned} S_j^0 &= k_1(x_j), \\ E_j^0 &= k_2(x_j), \\ I_j^0 &= k_3(x_j), \quad \text{for} \quad j \in \{1, 2, \ldots, M\}, \end{aligned}$$

and

$$\delta S_1^k = \delta E_1^k = \delta I_1^k = 0,$$
$$\delta S_M^k = \delta E_M^k = \delta I_M^k = 0, \quad \text{for} \quad k \in \{0,1,2,\ldots,M^*\}.$$

A comparison of numerical scheme (20)–(22) with the other existing methods makes it clear that (20)–(22) gives us more reliable results. Thus, to see the strength of our proposed scheme, two well-known schemes are also applied to the proposed system (1)–(3). One is the up-wind implicit scheme, which is constructed as

$$-(\lambda_1+\mu_1)S_{j-1}^{k+1} + (1+\lambda_1+2\mu_1)S_j^{k+1} - \mu_1 S_{j+1}^{k+1} = S_j^k + \ell p_1 - \ell p_2 S_j^k E_j^k - \ell p_1 S_j^k, \tag{26}$$

$$-(\lambda_2+\mu_2)E_{j-1}^{k+1} + (1+\lambda_2+2\mu_2)E_j^{k+1} - \mu_2 E_{j+1}^{k+1} = E_j^k + p_2\ell S_j^k E_j^k - \ell p_3 E_j^k - \ell p_1 E_j^k, \tag{27}$$

$$-(\lambda_3+\mu_3)I_{j-1}^{k+1} + (1+\lambda_3+2\mu_3)I_j^{k+1} - \mu_3 I_{j+1}^{k+1} = I_j^k + p_3\ell E_j^k - p_4 I_j^k - p_1 I_j^k. \tag{28}$$

The second is the Crank–Nicolson method, constructed for System (1)–(3):

$$-\left(\frac{\lambda_1}{4}+\frac{\mu_1}{2}\right)S_{j-1}^{k+1} + (1+\mu_1)S_j^{k+1} + \left(\frac{\lambda_1}{4}-\frac{\mu_1}{2}\right)S_{j+1}^{k+1} = \left(\frac{\lambda_1}{4}+\frac{\mu_1}{2}\right)S_{j-1}^k + \left(1-\ell p_2 E_j^k - \ell p_1 - \mu_1\right)S_j^k + \left(\frac{\mu_1}{2}-\frac{\lambda_1}{4}\right)S_{j+1}^k + \ell p_1, \tag{29}$$

$$-\left(\frac{\lambda_2}{4}+\frac{\mu_2}{2}\right)E_{j-1}^{k+1} + (1+\mu_2)E_j^{k+1} + \left(\frac{\lambda_2}{4}-\frac{\mu_2}{2}\right)E_{j+1}^{k+1} = \left(\frac{\lambda_2}{4}+\frac{\mu_2}{2}\right)E_{j-1}^k + \left(1+\ell p_2 S_j^k - \ell p_3 - \ell p_1 - \mu_2\right)E_j^k + \left(\frac{\mu_2}{2}-\frac{\lambda_2}{4}\right)E_{j+1}^k, \tag{30}$$

$$-\left(\frac{\lambda_3}{4}+\frac{\mu_3}{2}\right)I_{j-1}^{k+1} + (1+\mu_3)I_j^{k+1} + \left(\frac{\lambda_3}{4}-\frac{\mu_3}{2}\right)I_{j+1}^{k+1} = \left(\frac{\lambda_3}{4}+\frac{\mu_3}{2}\right)I_{j-1}^k + \left(1-\ell p_4 - \ell p_1 - \mu_3\right)I_j^k - \left(\frac{\mu_3}{2}-\frac{\lambda_3}{4}\right)I_{j+1}^k + \ell p_3 E_j^k. \tag{31}$$

Remark 1. *The proposed NSFD scheme can be developed by taking unequal step sizes of both time and space.*

3. Physical Features of the Numerical Method

This portion is fixed for the significant characteristics of System (5)–(7). These features play a paramount role to attain the numerical solutions of the nonlinear epidemic models. To discuss these important features, it is important to review some definitions.

Definition 1. *A matrix A with real entries is described as a Z-matrix if every element of it is non-positive except diagonal elements.*

Definition 2. *A square matrix A with real entries is described as an M-matrix if it satisfies the following properties:*

(i) The matrix A is a Z-matrix;
(ii) Every main diagonal entry of the matrix A is positive;
(iii) The matrix A is diagonally dominated, strictly.

The theory of the M-matrix plays an important role in proving the positivity of the state variables involved in the model of various fields of engineering, mathematics, economics, physics, and many more. The subsequent outcome grantees the non-negativity of the numerical solutions to the discrete System (20)–(22). This feature of the numerical scheme can be expressed by applying the M-matrix technique. Moreover, every M-matrix is inverted with real positive entries.

Remark 2. *Every M-matrix has an inversion with positive entries [41].*

The following are the important properties of the proposed scheme for the model under discussion.

3.1. Positivity

For a population dynamical system, the positivity of the state variables plays a vital role. Thus, it must be preserved after employing the numerical scheme on the model. The following theorem reflects the positivity property.

Theorem 3. *Assume that k_1, k_2 and k_3 are the positive real-valued functions depending on x defined in the interval $(0, L)$; then, System (20)–(22), with the supportive data (8)–(11), has a solution $\forall\ m > 0$ and $l > 0$. Moreover, the solutions are positive.*

Proof. Since the left hand sides of (20)–(22) are the implicit relations, we can write it in the vector representation as:

$$US^{k+1} = S_j^k + \ell p_1, \tag{32}$$
$$VE^{k+1} = E_j^k + p_2 S_j^k E_j^k, \tag{33}$$
$$WI^{k+1} = I_j^k + p_3 E_j^k, \tag{34}$$

in which U, V and W are defined as $(M+1)\times(M+1)$ matrices. By using the initial and boundary conditions (8)–(11), we can find the matrices U, V and W. Then,

$$U = \begin{pmatrix} (\gamma_1)_0^k & \gamma_2 & 0 & \cdots & \cdots & \cdots & \cdots & 0 \\ \gamma_3 & (\gamma_1)_1^k & \gamma_4 & \ddots & & & & \vdots \\ 0 & \gamma_3 & (\gamma_1)_2^k & \gamma_4 & \ddots & & & \vdots \\ \vdots & \ddots & \ddots & \ddots & \ddots & \ddots & & \vdots \\ \vdots & & \ddots & \ddots & \ddots & \ddots & \ddots & \vdots \\ \vdots & & & \ddots & \gamma_3 & (\gamma_1)_{M-2}^k & \gamma_4 & 0 \\ \vdots & & & & \ddots & \gamma_3 & (\gamma_1)_{M-1}^k & \gamma_4 \\ 0 & \cdots & \cdots & \cdots & \cdots & 0 & \gamma_3 & (\gamma_1^*)_M^k \end{pmatrix},$$

$$V = \begin{pmatrix} (\xi_1)_0^k & \xi_2 & 0 & \cdots & \cdots & \cdots & \cdots & 0 \\ \xi_3 & (\xi_1)_1^k & \xi_4 & \ddots & & & & \vdots \\ 0 & \xi_3 & (\xi_1)_2^k & \xi_4 & \ddots & & & \vdots \\ \vdots & \ddots & \ddots & \ddots & \ddots & \ddots & & \vdots \\ \vdots & & \ddots & \ddots & \ddots & \ddots & \ddots & \vdots \\ \vdots & & & \ddots & \xi_3 & (\xi_1)_{M-2}^k & \xi_4 & 0 \\ \vdots & & & & \ddots & \xi_3 & (\xi_1)_{M-1}^k & \xi_4 \\ 0 & \cdots & \cdots & \cdots & \cdots & 0 & \xi_3 & (\xi_1^*)_M^k \end{pmatrix},$$

and

$$W = \begin{pmatrix} (\varrho_1)_0^k & \varrho_2 & 0 & \cdots & \cdots & \cdots & \cdots & 0 \\ \varrho_3 & (\varrho_1)_1^k & \varrho_4 & \ddots & & & & \vdots \\ 0 & \varrho_3 & (\varrho_1)_2^k & \varrho_4 & \ddots & & & \vdots \\ \vdots & \ddots & \ddots & \ddots & \ddots & \ddots & & \vdots \\ \vdots & & \ddots & \ddots & \ddots & \ddots & \ddots & \vdots \\ \vdots & & & \ddots & \varrho_3 & (\varrho_1)_{M-2}^k & \varrho_4 & 0 \\ \vdots & & & & \ddots & \varrho_3 & (\varrho_1)_{M-1}^k & \varrho_4 \\ 0 & \cdots & \cdots & \cdots & \cdots & 0 & \varrho_3 & (\varrho_1^*)_M^k \end{pmatrix},$$

where

$$\begin{aligned} (\gamma_1)_j^k &= 1 + \lambda_1 + \ell p_1 + \ell p_2 E_j^k + 2\mu_1, \\ (\xi_1)_j^k &= 1 + \lambda_2 + \ell(p_1 + p_3) + 2\mu_2, \\ (\varrho_1)_j^k &= 1 + \lambda_3 + \ell(p_1 + p_4) + 2\mu_3, \\ (\gamma_1^*)_M^k &= 1 + \lambda_1 + \ell p_1 + \ell p_2 E_M^k + \mu_1, \\ (\xi_1^*)_M^k &= 1 + \lambda_2 + \ell(p_1 + p_3) + \mu_2, \\ (\varrho_1^*)_M^k &= 1 + \lambda_3 + \ell(p_1 + p_4) + \mu_3, \end{aligned}$$

$$\begin{aligned} \gamma_2 &= -(\lambda_1 + 2\mu_1), \ \xi_2 = -(\lambda_2 + 2\mu_2), \ \varrho_2 = -(\lambda_3 + 2\mu_3), \\ \gamma_3 &= -(\lambda_1 + \mu_1), \ \xi_3 = -(\lambda_2 + \mu_2), \ \varrho_3 = -(\lambda_3 + \mu_3), \\ \gamma_4 &= -\mu_1, \qquad \xi_4 = -\mu_2, \qquad \varrho_4 = -\mu_3. \end{aligned}$$

Now, the method of mathematical induction is applied to prove the positivity of the corresponding discrete system of Equations (20)–(22). According to the initial data, S^0, I_A^0 and I_C^0 are positive, so it is assumed that S^k, E^k and I^k, $k \in 0, 1, 2, \ldots, M^* - 1$ are positive component vectors. The above calculation indicates that U, V, and W are the M-matrices, so they are invertible and have positive inverses. Moreover, the expressions that occurred on the right-hand side of each of the equations in System (20)–(22) are positive. Therefore,

$$\begin{aligned} S^{k+1} &= U^{-1}(\ell p_1 + S_j^k), \\ E^{k+1} &= V^{-1}(E_j^k + p_2 S_j^k E_j^k), \\ I^{k+1} &= W^{-1}(I_j^k + p_3 E_j^k), \end{aligned}$$

all the state variables are positive quantities for every $k = 0, 1, 2, \cdots, M^* - 1$.

Hence, the theory of mathematical induction grantees the required solutions. □

Definition 3. *Suppose* $\Omega_m = \Big\{x_j \in R : j \in \mathbb{Z} \mid 0 \leq j \leq M\Big\}$ *is the set of mesh points,* Γ_m *contains the real functions defined on* Ω_m*. Also,* Γ_m *forms a vector space.*
A norm $\|.\|$ *from* Γ_m *to* $\mathbb{R}$ *is defined as:*

$$\|F\| = \sqrt{\sum_{j=1}^{M} |F_j|^2}, \text{ for all } \quad F \in \Gamma_m,$$

and

$$\|F\|_\infty = \max\Big\{|F_j| : j \in \{0, 1, 2, \cdots, M\}\Big\}, \quad \forall \quad F \in \Gamma_m.$$

The consistency of a numerical scheme is an important structural feature since the consistency determines the relationship between the exact solutions of both continuous and corresponding discrete systems. To that end, we define the following differential transformation.

$$\nu_1 = \frac{\partial S(x,t)}{\partial t} + a_1 \frac{\partial S(x,t)}{\partial x} - p_1 + p_2 S(x,t)E(x,t) + p_1 S(x,t) - \delta_1 \nabla^2 S(x,t), \quad (35)$$

$$\nu_2 = \frac{\partial E(x,t)}{\partial t} + a_2 \frac{\partial E(x,t)}{\partial x} - p_2 S(x,t)E(x,t) + p_3 E(x,t) + p_1 E(x,t) - \delta_2 \nabla^2 E(x,t), \quad (36)$$

$$\nu_3 = \frac{\partial I(x,t)}{\partial t} + a_3 \frac{\partial I(x,t)}{\partial x} - p_3 E(x,t) + (p_1 + p_4) I(x,t) - \delta_3 \nabla^2 I(x,t). \quad (37)$$

Moreover, the discrete operator is defined in the following:

$$\nu_1^{*k+1} = \delta_t S_j^{k+1} + \delta_x S_j^{k+1} - p_1 + p_2 S_j^{k+1} E_j^k + p_1 S_j^{k+1} - \delta_1 \delta_{xx} S_j^{k+1}, \quad (38)$$

$$\nu_2^{*k+1} = \delta_t E_j^{k+1} + a_2 \delta_x E_j^{k+1} - p_2 S_j^k E_j^k + p_3 E_j^{k+1} + p_1 E_j^{k+1} - \delta_2 \delta_{xx} E_j^{k+1}, \quad (39)$$

$$\nu_3^{*k+1} = \delta_t I_j^{k+1} + a_3 \delta_x I_j^{k+1} - p_3 E_j^k + (p_1 + p_4) I_j^{k+1} - \delta_3 \delta_{xx} I_j^{k+1}. \quad (40)$$

3.2. Consistency

The accuracy of the proposed numerical scheme is investigated by Taylor's theory. Suppose that

$$\Phi_S = \frac{S(x,t+\ell) - S(x,t)}{\ell} + a_1 \frac{S(x,t+\ell) - S(x-m,t+\ell)}{m} - p_1 + p_2 S(x,t+\ell)E(x,t) + p_1 S(x,t+\ell) - \frac{\delta_1}{m^2}\{S(x+m,t+\ell) - 2S(x,t+\ell) + S(x-m,t+\ell)\}.$$

After applying Taylor's classical theory, we reach the following expression

$$\Phi_S \to \frac{\partial S}{\partial t} + a_1 \frac{\partial S}{\partial x} - p_1 + p_2 SE + p_1 S - \delta_1 \frac{\partial^2 S}{\partial x^2} \quad \text{as} \quad m \to 0, \ell \to 0,$$

and

$$\Phi_E = \frac{E(x,t+\ell)-E(x,t)}{\ell} + a_2\frac{E(x,t+\ell)-E(x-m,t+\ell)}{m} - p_2S(x,t)E(x,t+\ell)+p_1E(x,t+\ell)+p_3E(x,t+\ell) - \frac{\delta_2}{m^2}\{E(x+m,t+\ell)-2E(x,t+\ell)+E(x-m,t+\ell)\},$$

$$\Phi_E \to \frac{\partial E}{\partial t} + a_2\frac{\partial E}{\partial x} - p_2SE + p_1E + p_3E - \delta_2\frac{\partial^2 E}{\partial x^2} \quad \text{as} \quad m \to 0, \ell \to 0.$$

Similarly,

$$\Phi_I \to \frac{\partial I}{\partial t} + a_3\frac{\partial I}{\partial x} - p_3E + p_1I + p_4I - \delta_3\frac{\partial^2 I}{\partial x^2} \quad \text{as} \quad m \to 0, \ell \to 0.$$

Thus, the designed numerical algorithm is consistent with the underlying model of differential Equations (5)–(7).

Using Definition 3 and Equations (35)–(40), the following result may be established.

Theorem 4. *If the state variables $S, E, I, R \in C^{2,2}_{x,t}(\bar{\Omega})$, then there exists $\xi > 0$, which is independent of ℓ and m, with the following inequality:*

$$\max\left\{\|\theta-\theta'\|_\infty, \|\phi-\phi'\|_\infty, \|\psi-\psi'\|_\infty\right\} \le \xi(m+l).$$

3.3. Stability

Since the main purpose of this article is to find the numerical solution of the system of partial differential equations, it is necessary to prove the stability of the numerical scheme. For the stability of the numerical scheme, we consider the propagation of rounding-off errors in the approximate solutions. In other words, we can say that a numerical technique for the system of differential equations is unstable if a minor variation in the initial data produces an abrupt change in the target variables of the model under consideration. Likewise, if the negligible change in the state variable does not lead to a gigantic change in the solution, then the numerical scheme is stable. Von Neumann criteria are applied to investigate the stability of the designed numerical scheme. To that end, we split the numerical error that arose in approximate solutions in the form of Fourier series.

Thus, the linearization of the Equations (20)–(22) and some substitutions leads us to the following expressions:

$$\begin{aligned} S_j^k &= \Psi_1(t)e^{i\omega x}, \\ S_j^{k+1} &= \Psi_1(t+\Delta t)e^{i\omega x}, \\ S_{j+1}^k &= \Psi_1(t)e^{i\omega(x+\Delta x)}, \\ S_{j-1}^k &= \Psi_1(t)e^{i\omega(x-\Delta x)}, \end{aligned}$$

We obtain

$$\left|\frac{\Psi_1(t+\Delta t)}{\Psi_1(t)}\right| \le 1.$$

By substituting

$$\begin{aligned} E_j^k &= \Upsilon + 2(t)e^{i\omega x}, \\ E_j^{k+1} &= \Upsilon_2(t+\Delta t)e^{i\omega x}, \\ E_{j+1}^k &= \Upsilon_2(t)e^{i\omega(x+\Delta x)}, \\ E_{j-1}^k &= \Upsilon_2(t)e^{i\omega(x-\Delta x)}, \end{aligned}$$

we have

$$\left|\frac{\Upsilon_2(t+\Delta t)}{\Upsilon_2(t)}\right| \leq 1.$$

Similarly, from (22), we have

$$\left|\frac{\Upsilon(t+\Delta t)}{\Phi(t)}\right| \leq 1.$$

Hence, the projected scheme is stable in the sense of Von Nuemann.

4. Numerical Illustrations

In the current section, we established two examples: one consists of a model with an unequal birth rate and death rate. The validity of our proposed scheme with the help of empirical data about the outbreak of the Ebola virus that appeared in Liberia in 2014 [42] is performed. In the other example, we consider the equal death rate and birth rate with general numerical simulations for both disease-free equilibrium and endemic equilibrium.

Example 1. *The SEIR advection-reaction-diffusion Ebola model with unequal birth and death rates with vital dynamics is numerically solved.*

$$\begin{aligned} \frac{\partial S(x,t)}{\partial t} + a_1\frac{\partial S(x,t)}{\partial x} &= p_0 - p_2 S(x,t)E(x,t) - p_1 S(x,t) + \\ &\quad \delta_1\frac{d^2 S(x,t)}{dx^2}, \\ \frac{\partial E(x,t)}{\partial t} + a_2\frac{\partial E(x,t)}{\partial x} &= p_2 S(x,t)E(x,t) - p_3 E(x,t) - p_1 E(x,t) + \\ &\quad \delta_2\frac{d^2 E(x,t)}{dx^2}, \\ \frac{\partial I(x,t)}{\partial t} + a_3\frac{\partial I(x,t)}{\partial x} &= p_3 E(x,t) - (p_1 + p_4)I(x,t) + \delta_3\frac{d^2 I(x,t)}{dx^2}, \\ \frac{\partial R(x,t)}{\partial t} + a_4\frac{\partial R(x,t)}{\partial x} &= p_4 I(x,t) - p_1 R(x,t) + \delta_4\frac{d^2 R(x,t)}{dx^2}, \end{aligned}$$

with a birth rate of p_0 and a death rate of p_1.

The threshold quantities for this model are slightly different from Model (1)–(4) and are presented as:

Disease-free equilibrium:

$$\left(\frac{p_0}{p_1}, 0, 0\right),$$

Endemic equilibrium:

$$(S^*, E^*, I^*), \text{ where}$$

$$S^* = \frac{p_1 + p_3}{2}, \quad E^* = \frac{p_0 - p_1 S^*}{p_2 s^*}, \quad I^* = \frac{p_3 E^*}{p_1 + p_4} \tag{41}$$

Note: *Since first, three equations of the above model are independent of R, we can solve only these equations, and also, since the total population is considered bounded, we can estimate the value of R by subtracting the values of S, E, and I from the total population.*

The above model is simulated by using the parameters reported in [43,44]. These parameters are:

$$p_2 = 0.2, \quad p_3 = 0.1887, \quad p_4 = 0.1.$$

These parameters are based on the numerical findings of [43,44] in which susceptible individuals are 88% of the whole population, 7% of the total population is exposed (infected but not infectious), and the infectious are 5%. Additionally, the initial conditions are recorded as:

$$S(0) = 0.88, \quad E(0) = 0.07, \quad I(0) = 0.05.$$

The birth rate p_0 and death rate p_1 are taken from the empirical data about the population of Liberia in 2014 are [45]:

$$p_0 = 0.03507, \quad p_1 = 0.0099.$$

4.1. Simulations

The above figures depict the evolution of the sub-population over time and space. In Figure 1, the graphical resolution of the model gives the value $S^* = 0.99$, which is equal to the theocratical value of S^* calculated from (41). From Figure 2, the evolution of the exposed individuals can be visualized over a time t and space x. When we calculate the value of E^* from the analytical result of (41), it gives the value $E^* = 0.12$. This is exactly the same as the proposed scheme gives in the graph of $E(x,t)$. Similarly, from Figure 3, the value of I^*, in the evolution of infected persons at any point (x,t), can be seen which is equal to 0.217. It coincides with the analytically calculated value from (41). Thus, we can conclude that the numerical solution of the prescribed model using the efficient non-standard finite difference scheme converges to the equilibrium point that is calculated analytically. Finally, Figure 4 reflects the 2-D plot graph of the state variables, and we can observe their convergence to the true steady state.

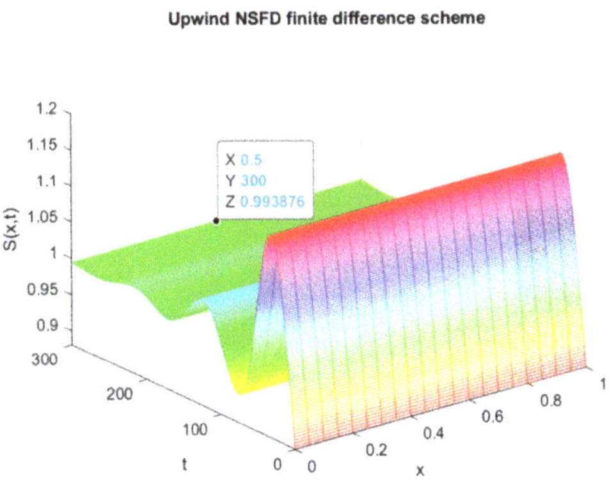

Figure 1. Numerical solution of $S(x,t)$ (susceptible individuals) by employing upwind NSFD technique at endemic equilibrium point with $p_0 = 0.03507, p_1 = 0.0099, p_2 = 0.2, p_3 = 0.1887, p_4 = 0.1$.

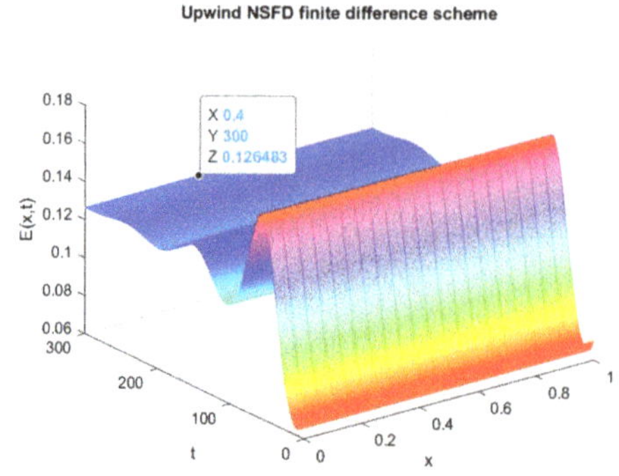

Figure 2. Numerical solution of $E(x,t)$ (exposed individuals) by employing upwind NSFD technique at disease-free point with $p_0 = 0.03507, p_1 = 0.0099, p_2 = 0.2, p_3 = 0.1887, p_4 = 0.1$.

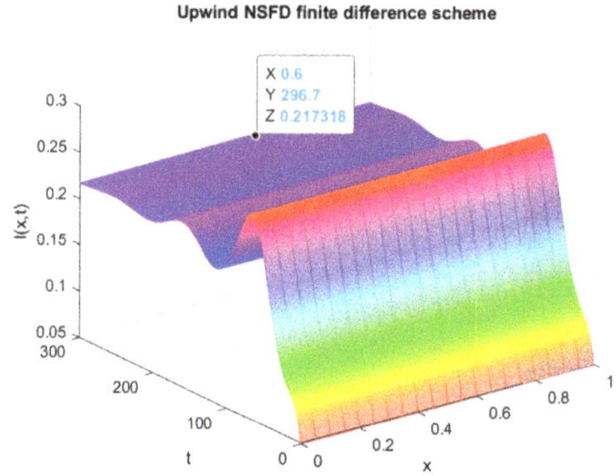

Figure 3. Numerical solution of $I(x,t)$ (infected individuals) by employing upwind NSFD technique at disease-free point with $p_0 = 0.03507, p_1 = 0.0099, p_2 = 0.2, p_3 = 0.1887, p_4 = 0.1$.

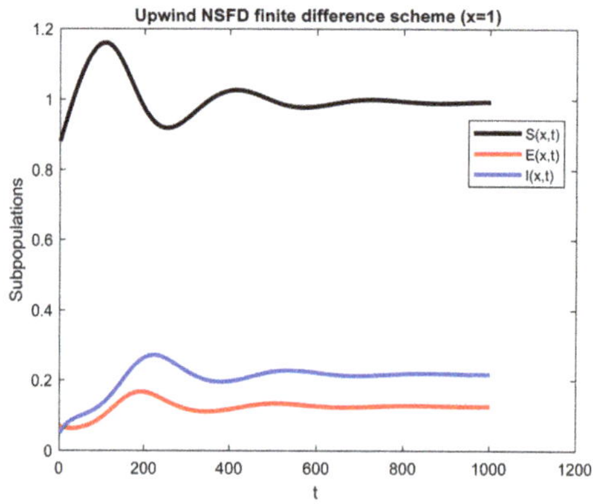

Figure 4. Numerical solution of $S(x,t), E(x,t)$, and $I(x,t)$ by employing upwind NSFD technique at disease-free point with $p_0 = 0.03507, p_1 = 0.0099, p_2 = 0.2, p_3 = 0.1887, p_4 = 0.1$.

Example 2. *The supplementary data are defined as follows:*

$$S(x,0) = \begin{cases} 0.4x & 0 \leq x \leq 1/2, \\ 0.4(1-x) & 1/2 \leq x \leq 1, \end{cases}$$

$$E(x,0) = \begin{cases} 0.3x & 0 \leq x \leq 1/2, \\ 0.3(1-x) & 1/2 \leq x \leq 1, \end{cases}$$

$$I(x,0) = \begin{cases} 0.2x & 0 \leq x \leq 1/2, \\ 0.2(1-x) & 1/2 \leq x \leq 1, \end{cases}$$

The set of parametric values [43,46] chosen in this work are $p_1 = 0.5$, $p_3 = 0.1887$, $p_4 = 0.1$, $\delta_1 = \delta_2 = \delta_3 = 0.02$, *and* $a_1 = a_2 = a_3 = 0.01$.

For the endemic point, we take $p_2 = 0.5$, *and for the infection-free point, we take* $p_2 = 0.9$, *where the physical meanings of these parametric constants may be perceived from the parametric description of the model, stated earlier in Section 2. Now, we present the simulated graphs for ascertaining the pre-results. In the propagation of an infectious disorder, the value of* R_0 *reflects the vital role to determine the stability of the numerical at the steady state of the model. The Ebola virus model with advection and diffusion parameters has two different fixed states, namely the infection-free and disease-persisting steady states, depending upon the value of the basic reproduction number.*

Next, the dynamical behaviour of the state variables at both the steady states is exhibited graphically using the proposed numerical method.

4.2. Disease-Free Point

Figure 5 shows the graphical behavior of the state variables that are involved in the reaction–advection–diffusion ebola model. The values of the parameters associated with the model are selected according to the nature of the disease-free stability point.

The graphical solution illustrated in Figure 5 shows the corresponding values of susceptible individuals for different values of space and time variables; that is, values of $S(x,t)$ are obtained against the variables x and t. There is no abrupt change in the graph, and it converges smoothly toward the true value of the disease-free state. Additionally, in the infection-free state, the values of other state variables become zero, and the whole population becomes susceptible at this stage. This fact is in accordance with the biological procedure of the infection. So, the biological situation strongly supports the numerical situation, obtained by the hybridized upwind nonstandard finite difference scheme.

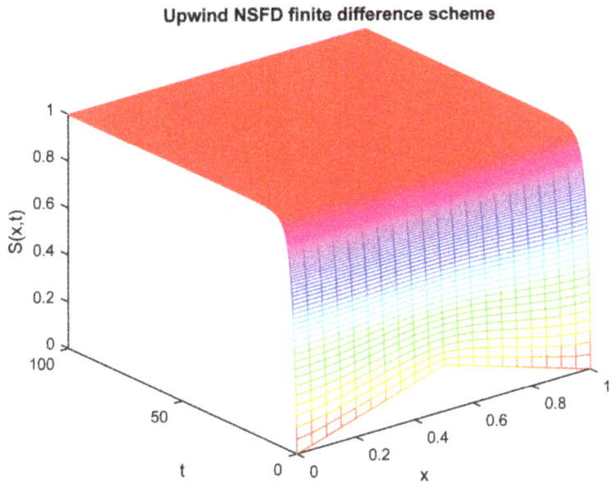

Figure 5. Numerical solution of $S(x,t)$ (susceptible individuals) by employing upwind NSFD technique at disease-free point with $\lambda_1 = \lambda_2 = \lambda_3 = 0.8$ and $\mu_1 = \mu_2 = \mu_3 = 0.02$.

Likewise, Figure 6 shows that the graphical solution obtained by the prescribed scheme ultimately converges towards the acceptable steady state. Additionally, the graph shows that at a certain time $t = 0$, the disease exists in the population in a certain region of the space. However, as time grows, the size of the exposed population gradually becomes zero. This fact is according to the biological scenario because when the disease dies out from a population, the infected individuals become zero. Thus, the numerical solution depicted by Figure 6 is in line with the physical phenomenon of the disease biologically.

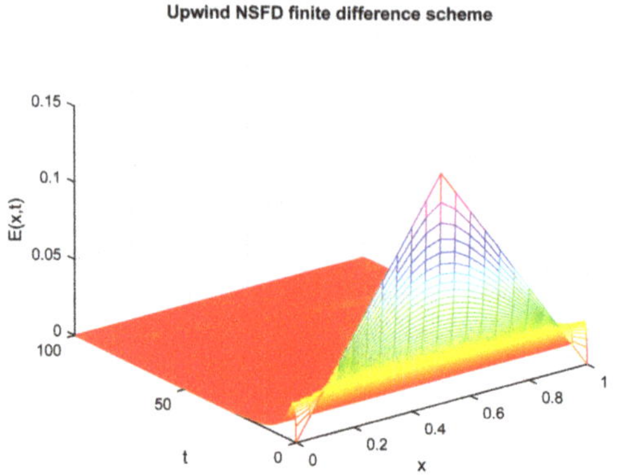

Figure 6. Numerical solution of $E(x,t)$ (exposed individuals) by employing upwind NSFD technique at disease-free point with $\lambda_1 = \lambda_2 = \lambda_3 = 0.8$ and $\mu_1 = \mu_2 = \mu_3 = 0.02$.

The numerical pattern in Figure 7 illustrates the numerical behavior of the infected individuals at a different moment of time and a certain location of space. Certain parametric values are selected to draw this pattern. Initially, the infected individuals take some non-zero values, that is, at $t = 0$ and $x = 0$, $I(x,t) \neq 0$ However, with the passage of time, the state variable $I(x,t)$ approaches zero for the whole space. This is in accordance with biological facts. As the disease dies out, the infected populace becomes zero over the whole space under consideration. Moreover, the proposed design also provides us with the exact solution as computed analytically [47].

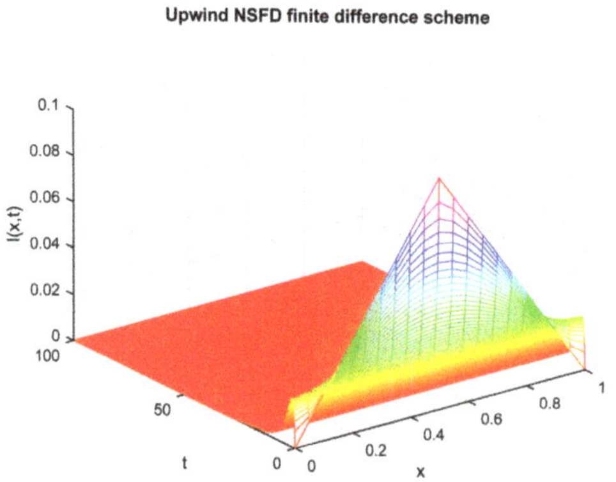

Figure 7. Numerical solution of $I(x,t)$ (infected individuals) by employing upwind NSFD technique at disease-free points with $\lambda_1 = \lambda_2 = \lambda_3 = 0.8$ and $\mu_1 = \mu_2 = \mu_3 = 0.02$.

In Figure 8, 2-D templates of the three populaces, that is, $S(x,t), E(x,t)$ and $I(x,t)$, are presented. Here, space coordinate x is fixed as 1, and the behavior of the different groups of individuals is studied with respect to time. The curved graph behaves according to the mathematical results. Thus, this scheme can be used to predict the behavior of the dynamics of the state variables.

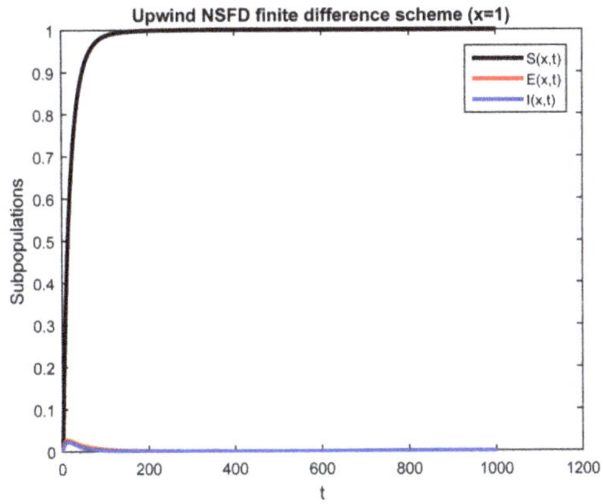

Figure 8. Numerical behavior of all subpopulations by employing upwind NSFD technique at disease-free point with $x = 1$, $\lambda_1 = \lambda_2 = \lambda_3 = 0.8$ and $\mu_1 = \mu_2 = \mu_3 = 0.02$.

4.3. Endemic Point

Figure 9 shows the dynamics of the state variable $S(x,t)$ at the endemic point. The values of the control parameters are selected under specifically defined criteria. One such criterion is that the value of the basic reproductive number is greater than unity. Other conditions are mentioned in the relevant sections. The graph shows that in this case, the whole population is not susceptible, unlike it was in the disease-free case. The mesh graph of $S(x,t)$ also depicts how the susceptible state variable graphically moves toward the endemic state. On the basis of this graph, the prediction of disease dynamics can be made on a certain instant of time and location of space.

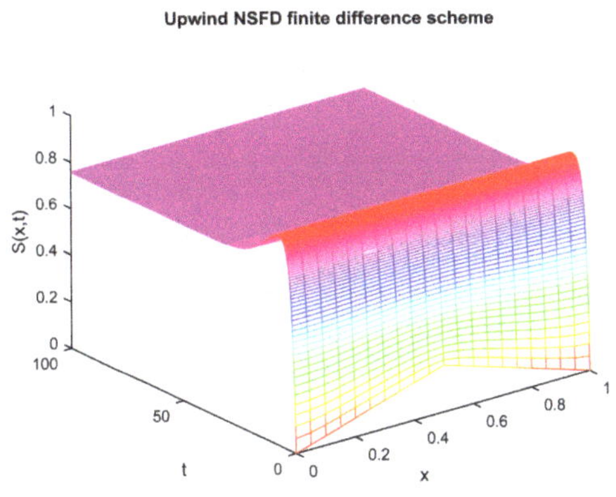

Figure 9. Numerical solution of $S(x,t)$ (susceptible individuals) by employing the proposed scheme at endemic point with $\lambda_1 = \lambda_2 = \lambda_3 = 0.8$ and $\mu_1 = \mu_2 = \mu_3 = 0.02$.

Similarly, Figure 10 is the graphical representation of the exposed persons represented by $E(x,t)$. All the parametric values are kept the same for this state variable $E(x,t)$. The graph shows that the number of exposed individuals has the same positive value because, at the endemic equilibrium point, the value of $E(x,t)$ cannot be zero. Additionally, the graphical value obtained by the numerical scheme coincides with the mathematical value. This graph also reflects the pattern of exposed populace dynamics. Figure 11 shows the numerical solution for the infected individuals in the confined area for a certain time. The graph of the numerical solution is positive and overlaps with the analytical solution. The values of all the parameters are kept fixed for all the state variables at endemic points.

The graph hits the true value of the stable endemic point, which shows that the scheme is quite capable of attaining the exact mathematical value at the infection-free state as well as the endemic state.

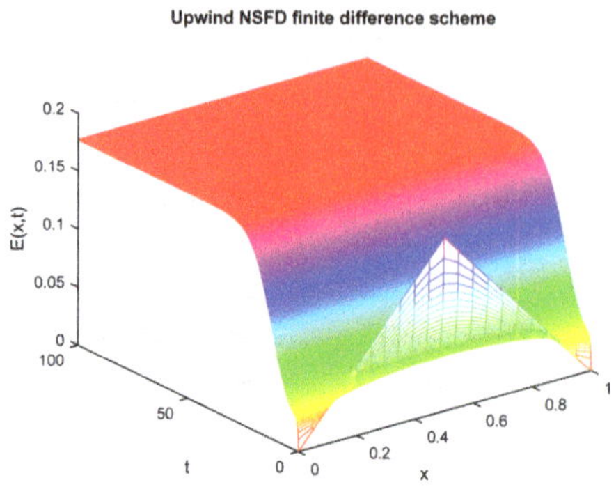

Figure 10. Numerical solution of $E(x,t)$ (exposed individuals) by employing the proposed scheme at an endemic point with $\lambda_1 = \lambda_2 = \lambda_3 = 0.8$ and $\mu_1 = \mu_2 = \mu_3 = 0.02$.

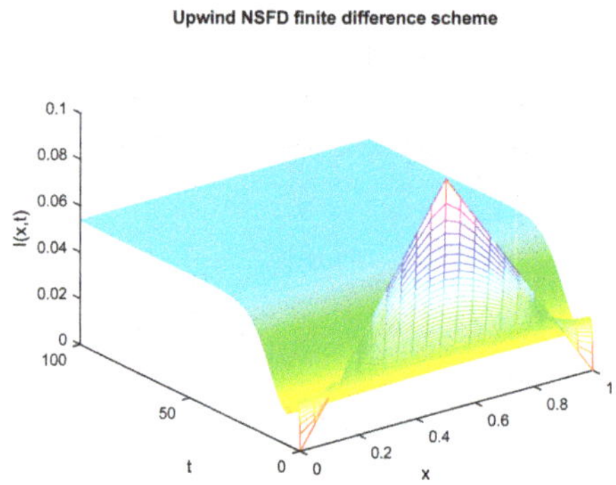

Figure 11. Numerical solution of $I(x,t)$ (infected individuals) by employing the proposed scheme at an endemic point with $\lambda_1 = \lambda_2 = \lambda_3 = 0.8$ and $\mu_1 = \mu_2 = \mu_3 = 0.02$.

Lastly, Figure 12 shows the behavior of the sub-populace for a fixed area over a particular time duration. All other parameters are kept the same to unveil the facts related to the infection propagation. Every population in the graph shows positive and bounded behavior, which are the strong properties of the current numerical scheme. In the end, it is notable that the projected scheme preserves the structure of the system.

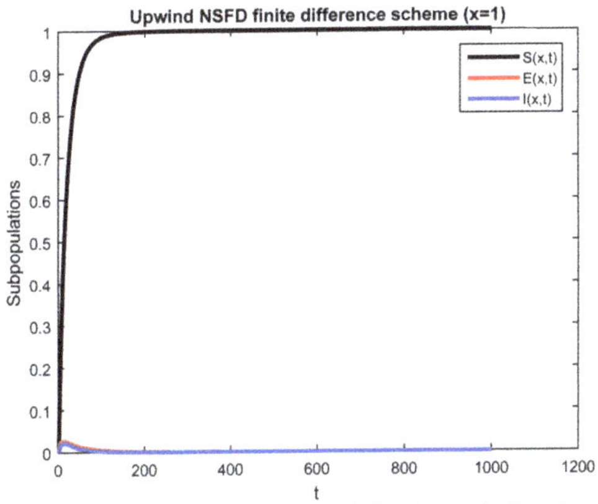

Figure 12. Numerical behavior of all subpopulations by employing upwind NSFD technique at an endemic point with $x = 1$, $\lambda_1 = \lambda_2 = \lambda_3 = 0.8$ and $\mu_1 = \mu_2 = \mu_3 = 0.02$.

4.4. Comparison of Proposed Scheme with Crank Nicolson

This section is devoted to the comparison of our proposed scheme with other existing schemes. Firstly, a comparison of the proposed scheme with the Crank–Nicolson scheme is made. Here, only the graphs of the expected population are compared at both equilibrium points. The plot in Figure 13 shows the negative solution, which is physically meaningless in the current situation. Similarly, Figure 14 reflects the negative behavior at the endemic state by applying the Crank–Nicolson scheme. On the other hand, graphs in Figures 15 and 16 are plotted with the help of the proposed upwind NSFD method. Both the graphs exhibit the positivity property at the disease-free and endemic states, respectively.

The value for each of the parameters mentioned for Figures 13–16 are:
$p_1 = 0.5$, $p_3 = 0.1887$, $p_4 = 0.1$, $\delta_1 = \delta_2 = \delta_3 = 0.02$ and $a_1 = a_2 = a_3 = 0.01$. Now, for the endemic point, we take $p_2 = 0.2$, and for the disease-free point, we take $p_2 = 0.9$.

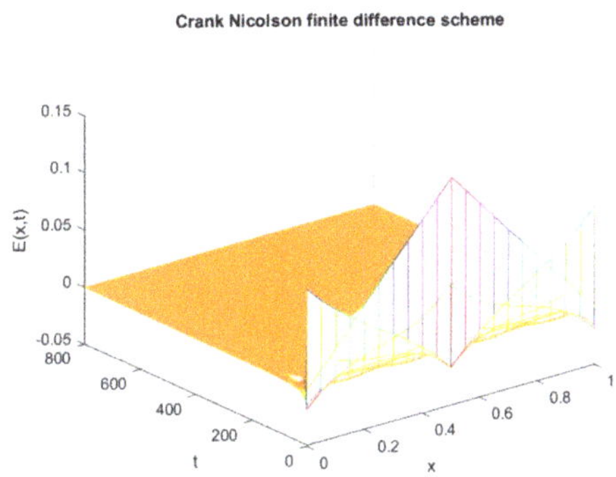

Figure 13. Numerical solution of $E(x,t)$ (exposed individuals) by employing Crank–Nicolson technique at disease-free point with $\lambda_1 = \lambda_2 = \lambda_3 = 0.16$ and $\mu_1 = \mu_2 = \mu_3 = 64$.

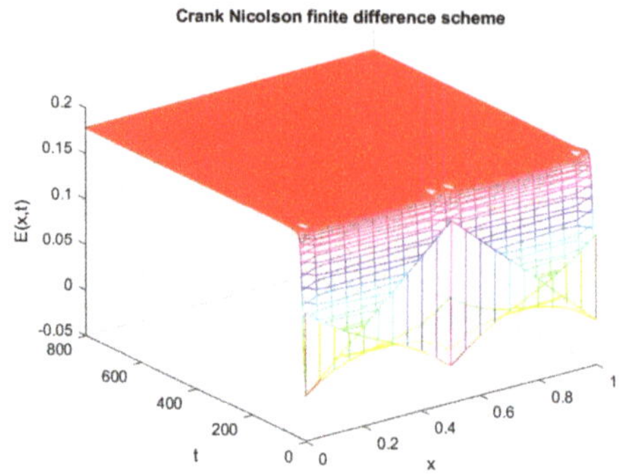

Figure 14. Numerical solution of $E(x,t)$ (exposed individuals) by employing Crank–Nicolson technique at endemic point with $\lambda_1 = \lambda_2 = \lambda_3 = 0.16$ and $\mu_1 = \mu_2 = \mu_3 = 64$.

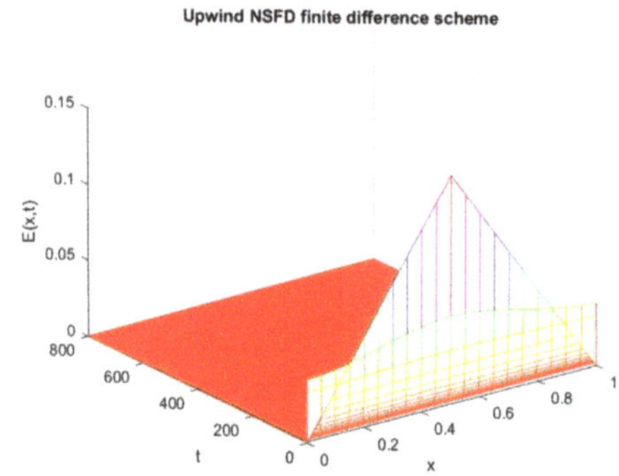

Figure 15. Numerical solution of $E(x,t)$ (exposed individuals) by employing upwind NSFD technique at disease-free point with $\lambda_1 = \lambda_2 = \lambda_3 = 0.16$ and $\mu_1 = \mu_2 = \mu_3 = 64$.

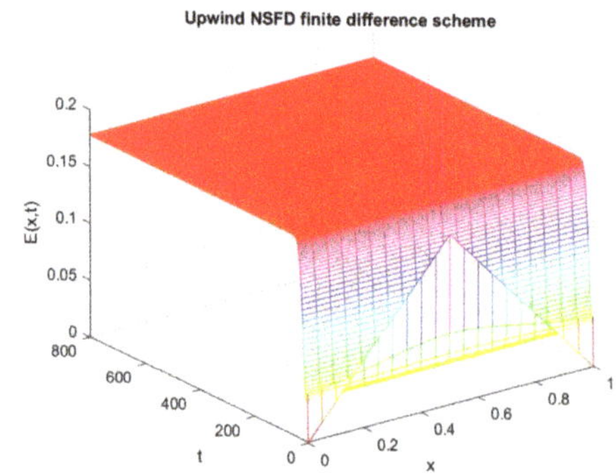

Figure 16. Numerical behavior of $E(x,t)$ (infected individuals) by employing upwind NSFD technique at endemic point with $\lambda_1 = \lambda_2 = \lambda_3 = 0.16$ and $\mu_1 = \mu_2 = \mu_3 = 64$.

4.5. Comparison of Proposed Scheme with Upwind Scheme

The graphs in Figures 17 and 18 show the numerical behavior of the upwind implicit and newly designed NSFD method. It is evident in Figure 17 that the upwind implicit scheme exhibits negative behavior, while the proposed NSFD scheme provides a positive solution for the same parametric values as chosen for the famous upwind technique.

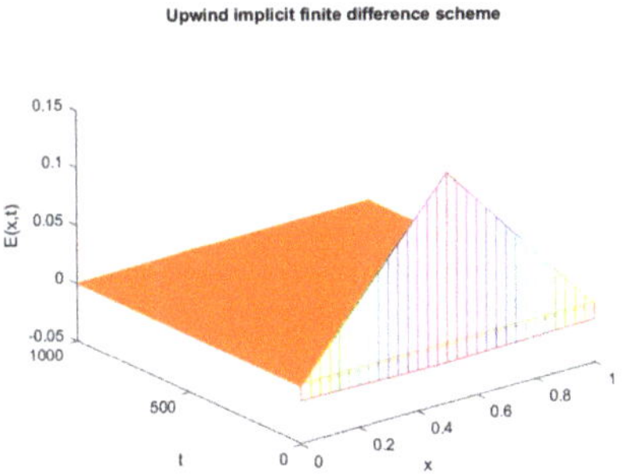

Figure 17. Numerical solution of $E(x,t)$ (exposed individuals) by employing upwind implicit technique at disease-free point with $\lambda_1 = \lambda_2 = \lambda_3 = 0.3$ and $\mu_1 = \mu_2 = \mu_3 = 180$.

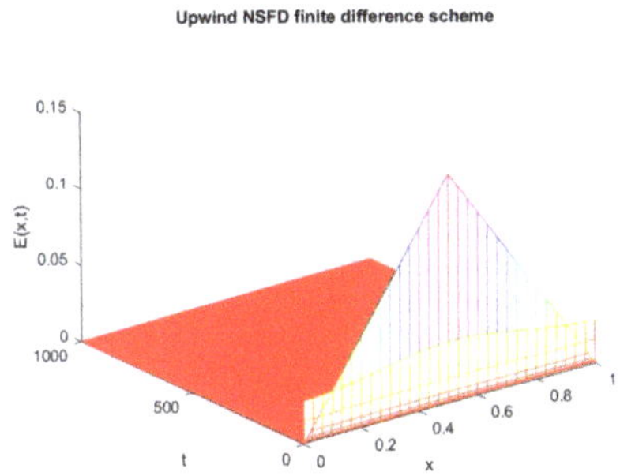

Figure 18. Numerical solution of $E(x,t)$ (exposed individuals) by employing NSFD technique at disease-free point with $\lambda_1 = \lambda_2 = \lambda_3 = 0.3$ and $\mu_1 = \mu_2 = \mu_3 = 180$.

The following values are chosen for the parameters: $p_1 = 0.6$, $p_3 = 0.5887$, $p_4 = 0.5$, $p_2 = 0.01$, $\delta_1 = \delta_2 = \delta_3 = 0.2$, and $a_1 = a_2 = a_3 = 0.01$.

5. Conclusions

The current study deals with the dynamics of the Ebola virus disease by developing an advective–diffusive nonlinear physical system. The present article elucidates the consequential dynamics of a nonlinear epidemic model of a murderous disease known as the Ebola virus disease. The model of this disease is considered in the generic form; that is, in this model, the advective and diffusive transmission of the virus is kept at a constant rate. The existing epidemic models do not consider the random and directed motions simultaneously in their study. Thus, their studies cannot predict the disease dynamics closely. However, this work seems better for investigating the disease dynamics. Additionally, some widely used schemes in the literature provide negative solutions to the state variables, which are physically meaningless. Therefore, it is a novelty of this scheme that it confirms the positivity as well as the other fundamental traits of the numerical solution. Hence, the developed scheme is a reliable tool to solve the nonlinear epidemic model by taking into account the advection and diffusion situation. This article is composed of two main types of analysis: one is optimal existence analysis and the other is numerical analysis. The results regarding the feasible solutions for the proposed Ebola virus epidemic model are formulated. The analysis regarding the solutions to the considered problem is addressed under some special conditions. The supplementary data (auxiliary data) are also examined. As in the dynamical models, the associated solutions of the model's equations belong to the set of continuous functions, but it is expedient to look at the particular subsets of the Banach space. A closed subset is considered for the objective optimal values that are explored. The solutions of the model are guaranteed with the help of Schauder's fixed-point theorem under some feasible constraints. The extension of advection and diffusion terms with constant rates in the equations of the model under study make the study more useful and practical. In the second half of the paper, a numerical analysis is studied. First, the numerical solutions are computed by a well-known nonclassical finite difference template. By adopting the formulas to approximate the derivatives as a function of space and the derivatives as a function of time, a compatible discrete model is designed. It can be observed that the used numerical technique is structure-preserving, which is an important property that should be possessed by the numerical scheme, i.e., the discretized system devised from the numerical template keeps the same features that the associated continuous set of differential equations has retained. We also examined whether a projected formulation is coherent with the planned numerical design. The reliability of the numerical program is validated by applying the Von Neumann condition. Another significant attribute is the non-negativity of the solution variables involved in the model under consideration. Thus, the M-matrix criteria guarantee the positivity of the solutions. Moreover, the assertions are ascertained by some feasible numerical experiments. Numerical simulations of all the considered and proposed schemes are also presented. The simulated graphs depict the various physical features of the relevant scheme. For instance, our scheme provides positive, bounded, and convergent solutions. Thus, all the results reflected by the simulated graphs are in accordance with the pre-assumptions. The results obtained by applying different schemes are also used for comparing the efficacy of the schemes. From the future perspective, this work may be extended to two and three dimensions. The reader should study the physical system by including the advection–diffusion terms in it and construct some structure-preserving numerical schemes for such types of systems.

Author Contributions: Conceptualization, N.S. and N.A.; methodology, T.S.S.; software, N.A. and M.R.; validation, N.A. and A.A.; formal analysis, N.S. and M.A.u.R.; investigation, N.S.; resources, M.D.l.S.; data curation, T.S.S., N.S. and N.A.; writing—original draft preparation, N.S.; writing—review and editing, N.S.; visualization, M.S.I.; supervision, M.A.u.R. and M.S.I.; project administration, N.A. and N.S. All authors have read and agreed to the published version of the manuscript.

Funding: Basque Government, Grants IT1555-22 and KK-2022/00090. MCIN/AEI 269.10.13039/501100011033, Grant PID2021-1235430B-C21/C22.

Data Availability Statement: Not applicable.

Acknowledgments: The authors are grateful to the Basque Government for its support through Grants IT1555-22 and KK-2022/00090 and to MCIN/AEI 269.10.13039/501100011033 for Grant PID2021-1235430B-C21/C22.

Conflicts of Interest: The authors declare no conflict of interest.

References

1. Dhama, K.; Karthik, K.; Khandia, R.; Chakraborty, S.; Munjal, A.; Latheef, S.K.; Kumar, D.; Ramakrishnan, M.A.; Malik, Y.S.; Singh, R.; et al. Advances in designing and developing vaccines, drugs, and therapies to counter Ebola virus. *Front. Immunol.* **2018**, *9*, 1803. [CrossRef]
2. Kourtis, A.P.; Appelgren, K.; Chevalier, M.S.; McElroy, A. Ebola virus disease: Focus on children. *Pediatr. Infect. Dis. J.* **2015**, *34*, 893. [CrossRef] [PubMed]
3. Goeijenbier, M.; Van Kampen, J.J.; Reusken, C.B.; Koopmans, M.P.; Van Gorp, E.C. Ebola virus disease: A review on epidemiology, symptoms, treatment and pathogenesis. *Neth. J. Med.* **2014**, *72*, 442–448. [PubMed]
4. CDC. Outbreaks Chronology: Ebola Virus Disease. Centers for Disease Control and Prevention (CDC), Atlanta, USA. Available online: Phttps://www.cdc.gov/vhf/ebola/history/chronology.html (accessed on 24 November 2022).
5. Center for Disease Control and Prevention. Ebola Outbreak in West Africa—Case Counts. 2014. Available online: https://www.cdc.gov/vhf/\ebola/history/2014-2016-outbreak/index.html#:~:text=The%20impact%20this%20epidemic%20had,outside%20of%20these%20three%20countries (accessed on 24 November 2022).
6. World Health Organization. Ebola Virus Disease, Fact Sheet. June 2017. Available online: https://www.who.int/news-room/fact-sheets/detail/ebola-virus-disease (accessed on 24 November 2022).
7. DRC Ebola Outbreaks: Crisis Update-2019 (Reliefweb). 2 August 2019. Available online: https://reliefweb.int/report/democratic-republic-congo/drc-ebola-outbreaks-crisis-update-2-august-2019 (accessed on 24 November 2022).
8. Leroy, E.M.; Kumulungui, B.; Pourrut, X.; Rouquet, P.; Hassanin, A.; Yaba, P.; Délicat, A.; Paweska, J.T.; Gonzalez, J.P.; Swanepoel, R. Fruit bats as reservoirs of Ebola virus. *Nature* **2015**, *438*, 575–576. [CrossRef]

9. Manguvo, A.; Mafuvadze, B. The impact of traditional and religious practices on the spread of Ebola in West Africa: Time for a strategic shift. *Pan Afr. Med. J.* **2015**, *22* (Suppl. 1), 9. [CrossRef]
10. Feldmann, H.; Sanchez, A.; Geisbert, T. Filoviridae: Marburg and ebola viruses. In *Fields Virology*, 6th ed.; Wolters Kluwer Health Adis (ESP): Alphen aan den Rijn, The Netherlands, 2013.
11. World Health Organization. Ebola Virus Disease. 2020. Available online: https://www.who.int/news-room/fact-sheets/detail/ebola-virus-disease (accessed on 24 November 2022).
12. Legrand, J.; Grais, R.F.; Boelle, P.Y.; Valleron, A.J.; Flahault, A. Understanding the dynamics of Ebola epidemics. *Epidemiol. Infect.* **2007**, *135*, 610–621. [CrossRef] [PubMed]
13. Althaus, C.L. Estimating the reproduction number of Ebola virus (EBOV) during the 2014 outbreak in West Africa. *PLoS Curr.* **2014**, *6*. [CrossRef]
14. Browne, C.; Gulbudak, H.; Webb, G. Modeling contact tracing in outbreaks with application to Ebola. *J. Theor. Biol.* **2015**, *384*, 33–49. [CrossRef] [PubMed]
15. Webb, G.F.; Browne, C.J. A model of the Ebola epidemics in West Africa incorporating age of infection. *J. Biol. Dyn.* **2016**, *10*, 18–30. [CrossRef]
16. Agusto, F.B. Mathematical model of Ebola transmission dynamics with relapse and reinfection. *Math. Biosci.* **2017**, *283*, 48–59. [CrossRef] [PubMed]
17. Bodine, E.N.; Cook, C.; Shorten, M. The potential impact of a prophylactic vaccine for Ebola in Sierra Leone. *Math. Biosci. Eng.* **2018**, *15*, 337. [CrossRef] [PubMed]
18. Weitz, J.S.; Dushoff, J. Modeling post-death transmission of Ebola: Challenges for inference and opportunities for control. *Sci. Rep.* **2015**, *5*, 8751. [CrossRef] [PubMed]
19. Bonyah, E.; Badu, K.; Asiedu-Addo, S.K. Optimal control application to an Ebola model. *Asian Pac. J. Trop. Biomed.* **2016**, *6*, 283–289. [CrossRef] [PubMed]
20. Grigorieva, E.V.; Deignan, P.B.; Khailov, E.N. Optimal control problem for a SEIR type model of ebola epidemics. *Rev. MatemáTica Teor. Apl.* **2017**, *24*, 79–96. [CrossRef]
21. Jiang, S.; Wang, K.; Li, C.; Hong, G.; Zhang, X.; Shan, M.; Li, H.; Wang, J. Mathematical models for devising the optimal Ebola virus disease eradication. *J. Transl. Med.* **2017**, *15*, 124. [CrossRef]
22. Mhlanga, A. Dynamical analysis and control strategies in modelling Ebola virus disease. *Adv. Differ. Equ.* **2019**, *2019*, 458. [CrossRef]
23. Ahmad, M.D.; Usman, M.; Khan, A.; Imran, M. Optimal control analysis of Ebola disease with control strategies of quarantine and vaccination. *Infect. Dis. Poverty* **2016**, *5*, 72. [CrossRef]
24. Tulu, T.W.; Tian, B.; Wu, Z. Modeling the effect of quarantine and vaccination on Ebola disease. *Adv. Differ. Equ.* **2017**, *2017*, 178. [CrossRef]
25. Area, I.; Ndaïrou, F.; Nieto, J.J.; Silva, C.J.; Torres, D.F. Ebola model and optimal control with vaccination constraints. *arXiv* **2017**, arXiv:1703.01368.
26. Berge, T.; Lubuma, J.S.; Moremedi, G.M.; Morris, N.; Kondera-Shava, R. A simple mathematical model for Ebola in Africa. *J. Biol. Dyn.* **2017**, *11*, 42–74. [CrossRef]
27. Kabli, K.; El Moujaddid, S.; Niri, K.; Tridane, A. Cooperative system analysis of the Ebola virus epidemic model. *Infect. Dis. Model.* **2018**, *3*, 145–159. [CrossRef]
28. Rafiq, M.; Ahmad, W.; Abbas, M.; Baleanu, D. A reliable and competitive mathematical analysis of Ebola epidemic model. *Adv. Differ. Equ.* **2020**, *2020*, 540. [CrossRef]
29. Okyere, E.; Ankamah, J.D.; Hunkpe, A.K.; Mensah, D. Deterministic epidemic models for ebola infection with time-dependent controls. *arXiv* **2020**, arXiv:1908.07974.
30. Ahmad, W.; Rafiq, M.; Abbas, M. Mathematical analysis to control the spread of Ebola virus epidemic through voluntary vaccination. *Eur. Phys. J. Plus* **2020**, *135*, 775. [CrossRef]
31. Tahir, M.; Inayat Ali Shah, S.; Zaman, G.; Muhammad, S. Ebola virus epidemic disease its modeling and stability analysis required abstain strategies. *Cogent Biol.* **2018**, *4*, 1488511. [CrossRef]
32. Dayan, F.; Rafiq, M.; Ahmed, N.; Raza, A.; Ahmad, M.O. A dynamical study of a fuzzy epidemic model of Mosquito-Borne Disease. *Comput. Biol. Med.* **2022**, *148*, 105673. [CrossRef]
33. Khan, A.; Zarin, R.; Humphries, U.W.; Akgül, A.; Saeed, A.; Gul, T. Fractional Optimal Control Dynamics of Coronavirus Model with Mittag-Leffler Law. *Ecol. Complex.* **2021**, *45*, 100880.
34. Yadava, S.; Kumar, D.; Singh, J.; Baleanu, D. Analysis and Dynamics of Fractional Order COVID-19 Model with Memory Effect. *Results Phys.* **2021**, *24*, 104017. [CrossRef]
35. Iqbal, Z.; Macías-Díaz, J.E.; Ahmed, N.; Aziz-ur Rehman, M.; Raza, A.; Rafiq, M. A SEIR model with memory effects for the propagation of Ebola-like infections and its dynamically consistent approximation. *Comput. Methods Programs Biomed.* **2021**, *209*, 106322. [CrossRef]
36. Mickens, R.E. Positivity preserving discrete model for the coupled ODE's modeling glycoly-sis. In Proceeding of the fourth International Conference on Dynamical Systems and Differential Equations, Wilmington, NC, USA, 24–27 May 2002; pp. 623–629.
37. Cantrell, R.S.; Cosner, C. *Spatial Ecology via Reaction–Diffusion Equations*; Wiley Ser. Math. Comput. Biol.; John Wiley and Sons: Chichester, UK, 2003.

38. Tang, D.; Ma, L. Existence and uniqueness of a Lotka–Volterra reaction–diffusion model with advection term. *Appl. Math. Lett.* **2018**, *86*, 83–88. [CrossRef]
39. Boztosuna, I.; Charafi, A. An analysis of the linear advection–diffusion equation using mesh-free and mesh-dependent methods. *Eng. Anal. Bound. Elem.* **2002**, *26*, 889–895. [CrossRef]
40. Mojtabi, A.K.; Deville, M. One-Dimensional linear advection–diffusion equation: An-alytical and finite element solutions. *Comput. Fluids* **2015**, *107*, 189–195. [CrossRef]
41. Ervin, V.J.; Macías-Díaz, J.E.; Ruiz-Ramírez, J. A positive and bounded finite element approximation of the generalized Burgers–Huxley equation. *J. Math. Anal. Appl.* **2015**, *424*, 1143–1160. [CrossRef]
42. WHO (World Health Organization). Ebola Data and Statistics. Available online: http://apps.who.int/gho/data/view.ebola-sitrep.ebola-country-LBR (accessed on 24 November 2022). [CrossRef]
43. Rachah, A.; Torres, D.F.M. Dynamics and Optimal Control of Ebola Transmission. *Math. Comput. Sci.* **2016**, *10*, 331–342. https://doi.org/10.1007/s11786-016-0268-y.
44. Rachah, A.; Torres, D.F.M. Mathematical modelling, simulation and optimal control of the 2014 Ebola outbreak in West Africa. *Discret. Dyn. Nat. Soc.* **2015**, *2015*, 842792. [CrossRef]
45. IndexMundi. Available online: http://www.indexmundi.com (accessed on 24 November 2022). [CrossRef]
46. Durojaye M.; Ajie I.J. Mathematical Model of the Spread and Control of Ebola Virus Disease. *Appl. Math.* **2017**, *7*, 23–31. https://doi.org/10.5923/j.am.20170702.02.
47. Fujimoto, T.; Ranade, R. Two characterizations of inverse–positive matrices: The Hawkins–Simon condition and the Le Chatelier—Braun principle. *Electron. J. Linear Algebra* **2004**, *11*, 59–65.

axioms

MDPI

Article

On the Iterative Multivalued ⊥-Preserving Mappings and an Application to Fractional Differential Equation

Muhammad Nazam [1,*], Sumit Chandok [2], Aftab Hussain [3,*] and Hamed H. Al Sulmi [3]

[1] Department of Mathematics, Allama Iqbal Open University, H-8, Islamabad 44000, Pakistan
[2] School of Mathematics, Thapar Institute of Engineering and Technology, Patiala 147004, Punjab, India
[3] Department of Mathematics, King Abdulaziz University, P.O. Box 80203, Jeddah 21589, Saudi Arabia
* Correspondence: muhammad.nazam@aiou.edu.pk (M.N.); aniassuirathka@kau.edu.sa (A.H.)

Abstract: In this paper, we introduce orthogonal multivalued contractions, which are based on the recently introduced notion of orthogonality in the metric spaces. We construct numerous fixed point theorems for these contractions. We show how these fixed point theorems aid in the generalization of a number of recently published findings. Additionally, we offer a theorem that establishes the existence of a fractional differential equation's solution.

Keywords: fixed point; (V, W)-orthogonal contractions; O-complete metric space

MSC: 47H10; 26A18; 26D20

1. Introduction and Preliminaries

The core of the metric fixed-point theory is the exploration of generalized contraction principles to add more applicable fixed-point theorems in the theory. The simplest and most applicable contraction principle is the Banach contraction principle. This contraction principle can be applied to show the existence of solutions to equations representing mathematical models. The contraction principle that appeared in [1] generalizes the Rakotch [2] contraction concept. Furthermore, Matkowski [3], Samet et al. [4], Karapinar et al. [5], and Pasicki [6] have all generalized the Boyd-Wong notion. The concept of F-contraction [7] is another notable generalization of the Banach contraction principle (BCP), and several research articles have been published in the previous decade (see [8–13], and references therein).

The role of fixed point theory in solving real-world problems has been described in many recently published papers. Recently, Turab et al. [14] proposed a generic stochastic functional equation that can be used to describe several psychological and learning theory experiments. The existence, uniqueness, and stability analysis of the suggested stochastic equation are examined by utilizing the notable fixed point theory tools. Khan et al. [15] proposed a fixed-point technique to investigate a system of fractional order differential equations. Rezapour et al. [16] proposed a labeling method for graph vertices, and then presented some existence results for solutions to a family of fractional boundary value problems (FBVPs) on the methyl propane graph by means of Krasnoselskii's and Scheafer's fixed point theorems.

The use of partial order, admissibility of a mapping, graph theory and binary relation are all being effectively utilized in metric fixed point theory. Recently, Gordji et al. [17] presented a special binary relation, termed the orthogonal relation, and presented several examples to clarify the concept of the orthogonal relation and, hence, orthogonal-set (see Ex 2.2 to Ex 2.11). Gordji et al. also presented a generalization of BCP in the *orthogonal metric space*. Later, Baghani et al. [8] generalized the study done in [17] by using the concept of F-contraction, while Nazam et al. [18] broadened the investigation conducted in [8].

Citation: Nazam, M.; Chandok, S.; Hussain, A.; Al Sulmi, H.H. On the Iterative Multivalued ⊥-Preserving Mappings and an Application to Fractional Differential Equation. *Axioms* **2023**, *12*, 53. https://doi.org/10.3390/axioms12010053

Academic Editor: Clemente Cesarano

Received: 6 December 2022
Revised: 21 December 2022
Accepted: 24 December 2022
Published: 3 January 2023

On the other hand, Proinov [19] offered various fixed-point theorems that built on previous work in [1,3–7]. He introduced a generalized class of contractions by operating two functions $V, W : (0, \infty) \to (-\infty, \infty)$ on both sides of the Banach contraction and obtained several fixed point results. The class of contractions given in [19] encapsulate the contractions defined in [4,7,20,21].

In this paper, we extend some results of [19] to multivalued mappings subject to the class of orthogonal contractions. The class of orthogonal contractions generalizes ordered contractions, graphic contractions and α-admissible contractions. We demonstrate that every contraction is orthogonal but not vice versa. Along with several examples to validate the results, we also present an application for solving a fractional differential equation (FDE).

Let $\mathcal{U} \neq \emptyset$ and $\perp \subset \mathcal{U} \times \mathcal{U}$ satisfying the property (P),

$$(\text{P}) : \exists\ \ell_0 \in \mathcal{U} : \text{ either } (\forall \tau \in \mathcal{U}; \ell_0 \perp \tau) \text{ or } (\forall \tau \in \mathcal{U}; \tau \perp \ell_0).$$

We call the pair $(\mathcal{U}, \perp)$ an orthogonal set (abbreviated as, O-set). The concept of orthogonality in an inner-product space is an example of $\perp$.

For the illustration of the orthogonal set, O-sequence, O-Cauchy and its examples, we suggest the reader read the articles [17,22].

Definition 1. *[17] The O-set $(\mathcal{U}, \perp)$ endowed with a metric d is called an O-metric space (in short, OMS) denoted by $(\mathcal{U}, \perp, d)$.*

Definition 2. *[17] Let $(\mathcal{U}, \perp, d)$ be an orthogonal metric space. A mapping $f : \mathcal{U} \to \mathcal{U}$ is said to be an orthogonal contraction if there exists $k \in [0, 1)$ such that*

$$d(fx, fy) \leq kd(x, y)\ \forall x, y \in \mathcal{U} \text{ with } x \perp y.$$

Terms such as continuity and orthogonal continuity, completeness and O-completeness, Banach contraction and orthogonal contraction have been explained in [10,13,17,22]. In the following, we give some comparisons between fundamental notions.

1. The continuity implies orthogonal continuity but the converse is not true. If $f : \mathbb{R} \to \mathbb{R}$ is defined by $f(\ell) = [\ell],\ \forall \ell \in \mathbb{R}$ and the relation $\perp \subseteq \mathbb{R} \times \mathbb{R}$ is defined by
$$\ell \perp g \text{ if } \ell, g \in \left(i + \frac{1}{3}, i + \frac{2}{3}\right), i \in \mathbb{Z} \text{ or } \ell = 0.$$
Then, f is $\perp$-continuous while f is discontinuous on $\mathbb{R}$.
2. The completeness of the metric space implies O-completeness, but the converse is not true. We know that $\mathcal{A} = [0, 1)$ with Euclidean metric d is not a complete metric space. If we define the relation $\perp \subseteq \mathcal{A} \times \mathcal{A}$ by
$$\ell \perp g \iff \ell \leq g \leq \frac{1}{2} \text{ or } \ell = 0,$$
then $(\mathcal{A}, \perp, d)$ is an O-complete.
3. The Banach contraction implies orthogonal contraction but the converse is not true. Let $\mathcal{A} = [0, 10)$ with Euclidean metric d so that $(\mathcal{A}, d)$ is a metric space. If we define the relation $\perp \subseteq \mathcal{A} \times \mathcal{A}$ by
$$\ell \perp g \text{ if } \ell g \leq \ell \vee g,$$
then $(\mathcal{A}, \perp, d)$ is an O-metric space. Define $f : \mathcal{A} \to \mathcal{A}$ by $f(\ell) = \frac{\ell}{2}$ (if $\ell \leq 2$) and $f(\ell) = 0$ (if $\ell > 2$). Since $d(f(3), f(2)) > kd(3, 2)$, f is not a contraction; rather, it is an orthogonal contraction.

Let
$P(\mathcal{U})$— set of non-empty subsets of $\mathcal{U}$.

$P_{cb}(\mathcal{U})$— set of all non-empty bounded and closed subsets of $\mathcal{U}$.
$K(\mathcal{U})$—set of non-empty compact subsets of $\mathcal{U}$.

If we let $E \in P_{cb}(\mathcal{U})$ and $g \in \mathcal{U}$, then $d(g, E) = \inf_{i \in E} d(g, i)$; d is a metric on $\mathcal{U}$. The mapping $H : P_{cb}(\mathcal{U}) \times P_{cb}(\mathcal{U}) \to [0, \infty)$ defined by

$$H(E_1, E_2) = \max\left\{ \sup_{r \in E_1} d(r, E_2), \sup_{w \in E_2} d(w, E_1) \right\} \text{ for all } E_1, E_2 \in P_{cb}(\mathcal{U}),$$

defines a metric on $P_{cb}(\mathcal{U})$. It is also known as the Pompieu-Hausdorff-metric. In the following, we define $\perp$-admissible mapping, $\perp$-preserving mapping and illustrate them with examples. Let $\Lambda = \{(x, y) \in \mathcal{U} \times \mathcal{U} : x \perp y\}$.

Definition 3. *A mapping $f : \mathcal{U} \times \mathcal{U} \to [1, \infty)$ is said to be strictly $\perp$-admissible if $f(a, \theta) > 1$ for all $a, \theta \in \mathcal{U}$ with $a \perp \theta$ and $f(a, \theta) = 1$ otherwise.*

Example 1. *Let $\mathcal{U} = [0, 1)$ and define the relation $\perp \subset \mathcal{U} \times \mathcal{U}$ by*

$$a \perp \theta \text{ if } a\theta \in \{a, \theta\} \subset \mathcal{U}.$$

Then, $\mathcal{U}$ is an O-set. Define $f : \mathcal{U} \times \mathcal{U} \to [1, \infty)$ by

$$f(a, \theta) = \begin{cases} a + \frac{2}{1+\theta} & \text{if } a \perp \theta, \\ 1 & \text{otherwise}. \end{cases}$$

Then, f is $\perp$-admissible.

Definition 4. *Let $\mathcal{U}$ be a non-empty set. A set-valued mapping $L : \mathcal{U} \to P(\mathcal{U})$ satisfying the property (O) is called $\perp$-preserving.*

(O). For each $j \in \mathcal{U}$ and $l \in L(j)$ with $j \perp l$ or $l \perp j$, $\exists\, g \in L(l)$ with $l \perp g$ or $g \perp l$.

Example 2. *Let $\mathcal{U} = [0, 1)$ and define a relation $\perp \subset [0, 1) \times [0, 1)$ by*

$$g \perp h \text{ if } gh \in \{g, h\} \subset [0, 1).$$

Then, $\mathcal{U} := [0, 1)$ is an O-set. Now for a function $t : \mathcal{U} \times \mathcal{U} \to [1, \infty)$ defined by

$$t(g, h) = \begin{cases} g + \frac{2}{1+h} & \text{if } g \perp h, \\ 1 & \text{otherwise}. \end{cases}$$

Then, t is a $\perp$-admissible mapping. The mapping $r : \mathcal{U} \to P(\mathcal{U})$ defined by

$$r(g) = \begin{cases} \left[\frac{g}{15}, \frac{g+1}{7}\right] & \text{if } g \in \mathbb{Q} \cap \mathcal{U}, \\ \{0\} & \text{if } g \in \mathbb{Q}^c \cap \mathcal{U}, \end{cases}$$

is a $\perp$-preserving mapping.

The following facts have been stated in [19] and we carry them for our upcoming results.

Lemma 1. *Let $\{c_\alpha\} \subset (X, d)$ and it obeys the equation $\lim_{\alpha \to \infty} d(c_\alpha, c_{\alpha+1}) = 0$; then, there are subsequences $\{c_{\alpha_l}\}$, $\{c_{\beta_l}\}$ and $q > 0$ (whenever $\{c_\alpha\}$ is not Cauchy) following the equations:*

$$\lim_{l \to \infty} d(c_{\alpha_{l+1}}, c_{\beta_{l+1}}) = q + . \tag{1}$$

$$\lim_{l\to\infty} d(c_{\alpha_l}, c_{\beta_l}) = d(c_{\alpha_{l+1}}, c_{\beta_l}) = d(c_{\alpha_l}, c_{\beta_{l+1}}) = q. \tag{2}$$

The following result appeared in [23] and is very useful for our upcoming results.

Lemma 2. *Let (U, d) and $\ell > 1$, then, for all $w \in Q_1 \subseteq U$, there is a $g \in Q_2 \subseteq U$ following the inequality:*

$$d(w, g) \leq \ell H(Q_1, Q_2).$$

2. Multivalued $(V, W)_\perp$-Contractions

This section deals with the multivalued $(V, W)_\perp$-contractions. To guarantee the presence of fixed points of multivalued $(V, W)_\perp$-contractions, we study a number of constraints on the real valued nonlinear functions (V, W). The multivalued $(V, W)_\perp$-contraction is defined as follows.

Definition 5. *Let $(\mathcal{U}, \perp, d)$ be an OMS. A mapping $\mathcal{S} : \mathcal{U} \to P_{cb}(\mathcal{U})$ is called a multivalued $(V, W)_\perp$-contraction if there exists a strictly $\perp$-admissible function ν such that*

$$V(\nu(q, \ell) H(\mathcal{S}(q), \mathcal{S}(\ell))) \leq W(d(q, \ell)) \tag{3}$$

for all $q, \ell \in \Lambda$ with $H(\mathcal{S}(q), \mathcal{S}(\ell)) > 0$.

Remark 1. *The following observations indicate the generality of multivalued $(V, W)_\perp$ contraction for the specific definitions of the mappings V, W.*

1. *If $V(\ell) = \ell$ and $W(\ell) = \lambda\ell$, where $0 \leq \lambda < 1$, then $\mathcal{S}$ is an orthogonal Nadler contraction [23].*
2. *If $V(\ell) = \ell$, then $\mathcal{S}$ is an orthogonal multivalued Boyd-Wong contraction [1].*
3. *If V is lower semi-continuous and W is upper semi-continuous, then $\mathcal{S}$ is an orthogonal multivalued variant of the contraction defined in [24].*
4. *If $W(\ell) = F(V(\ell))$, then $\mathcal{S}$ is an orthogonal multivalued variant of the contraction defined in [21].*
5. *If $W(\ell) = \alpha(\ell)V(\ell)$ and $V(\ell) = \ell$, then $\mathcal{S}$ is an orthogonal variant of the contraction defined in [25].*
6. *If $W(\ell) = \lambda V(\ell)$, then $\mathcal{S}$ is an orthogonal multivalued variant of the contraction defined in [26].*
7. *If $W(\ell) = F(V(\ell))$ and $F(\ell) = \ell^\alpha$, then $\mathcal{S}$ is an orthogonal multivalued variant of the contraction defined in [20].*
8. *If $W(\ell) = V(\ell) - \tau$, then $\mathcal{S}$ is an orthogonal multivalued variant of the contraction defined in [7].*

Remark 2. It is noted that if $W(c) = V(c) - \tau$ for all $c \in (0, \infty)$, then the contractive condition (3) is a multivalued F-contraction [27]. If $W(c) = V(c) - \tau(c)$ for all $c \in (0, \infty)$, then it is a multivalued (τ, F_T)-contraction [10]. If we set $V(c) = \ln(c)$ for all c, then we have a Nadler contraction [23]. For, if the function $V : (0, \infty) \to (0, \infty)$ is non-decreasing and $p(j) \in (0, 1)$ for all $j \in (0, \infty)$ with $\limsup_{z\to\epsilon^+} p(z) < 1$. Then, defining $W(z) = p(z)V(z)$ and $V(z) = z$ for all $z > 0$, we obtain the contraction defined in [28].

Let $\perp$RCOMS denote a $\perp$-regular complete orthogonal metric space.

The following theorem presents the first formula of this paper for the existence of fixed points.

Theorem 1. *Let $(\mathcal{U}, \perp, d)$ be a $\perp$RCOMS. Suppose that $\mathcal{S} : \mathcal{U} \to P_{cb}(\mathcal{U})$ is a $\perp$-preserving and satisfies (3). If $\perp$ is transitive and functions $V, W : (0, \infty) \to (-\infty, \infty)$ meet the following conditions:*

(i) there exists $c_1 \in \mathcal{S}(c_0)$ such that $c_1 \perp c_0$ or $c_0 \perp c_1$, for any $c_0 \in \mathcal{U}$,

(ii) V *is non-decreasing and* $W(c) < V(c)\ \forall\ c > 0$,
(iii) $\limsup_{c\to\gamma+} W(c) < V(\gamma+)\ (\forall\,\gamma > 0)$.

Then, there exists $c^* \in \mathcal{U}$ *such that* $c^* \in \mathcal{S}(c^*)$.

Proof. By (i), for an arbitrary $c_0 \in \mathcal{U}$, there exists $c_1 \in \mathcal{S}(c_0)$ such that $c_0 \perp c_1$ or $c_1 \perp c_0$. Since the mapping $\mathcal{S}$ is $\perp$-preserving, there exists $c_2 \in \mathcal{S}(c_1)$ such that $c_1 \perp c_2$ or $c_2 \perp c_1$ and, thus, $c_3 \in \mathcal{S}(c_2)$ such that $c_2 \perp c_3$ or $c_3 \perp c_2$. In general, there exists $c_{n+1} \in \mathcal{S}(c_n)$ such that $c_n \perp c_{n+1}$ or $c_{n+1} \perp c_n$ for all $n \geq 0$. Hence, $\nu(c_n, c_{n+1}) > 1$ for all $n \geq 0$. If $c_n \in \mathcal{S}(c_n)$ (for some $n \geq 0$), then c_n is a fixed-point of $\mathcal{S}$. We assume that $c_n \notin \mathcal{S}(c_n)$ $(\forall\, n \geq 0)$. Then, $H(\mathcal{S}c_{n-1}, \mathcal{S}c_n) > 0$. So $\nu(c_n, c_{n+1}) > 1$ and $\mathcal{S}(c_n), \mathcal{S}(c_{n+1}) \in P_{cb}(\mathcal{U})(\forall\, n \geq 0)$. Hence, there exists $c_n \neq c_{n+1} \in \mathcal{S}(c_n)$ such that $d(c_n, c_{n+1}) \leq \nu(c_{n-1}, c_n)H(\mathcal{S}(c_{n-1}), \mathcal{S}(c_n))(\forall\, n \geq 1)$ (see Lemma 2). Since the function V is increasing, by (3), we have

$$V(d(c_n, c_{n+1})) \leq V(\nu(c_{n-1}, c_n)H(\mathcal{S}(c_{n-1}), \mathcal{S}(c_n))) \leq W(d(c_{n-1}, c_n)).$$

Since $W(c) < V(c)$ $(\forall\, c > 0)$, we have

$$V(d(c_n, c_{n+1})) \leq W(d(c_{n-1}, c_n)) < V(d(c_{n-1}, c_n)). \tag{4}$$

The monotonicity of the function V implies $d(c_n, c_{n+1}) < d(c_{n-1}, c_n)$ $(\forall n \geq 1)$ and, thus, the sequence $\{d(c_{n-1}, c_n)\}$ is monotone. Let $\delta \geq 0$ satisfy $\lim_{n\to\infty} d(c_{n-1}, c_n) = \delta+$. If $\delta > 0$, by (4), we have

$$V(\delta+) = \lim_{n\to\infty} V(d(c_n, c_{n+1})) \leq \lim_{n\to\infty} \sup W(d(c_{n-1}, c_n)) \leq \lim_{c\to\delta+} \sup W(c).$$

This is a contradiction to (iii). Thus, $\delta = 0$ and hence the mapping $\mathcal{S}$ is asymptotically-regular.

Now, we show that $\{c_n\}$ is a Cauchy sequence. Contrarily, suppose that the sequence $\{c_n\}$ is not Cauchy. By Lemma 1, there exist two subsequences $\{c_{n_k}\}, \{c_{m_k}\}$ of $\{c_n\}$ and $\epsilon > 0$ such that the equations (1) and (2) hold. By (1), we get that $d(c_{n_k+1}, c_{m_k+1}) > \epsilon$. Since $c_n \perp c_{n+1}$ $(\forall n \geq 0)$, by transitivity of $\perp$, we have $c_{n_k} \perp c_{m_k}$ and, hence, $\nu(c_{n_k}, c_{m_k}) > 1$ $(\forall k \geq 1)$. Setting $q = c_{n_k}$ and $\ell = c_{m_k}$ in (3), we have

$$V(d(c_{n_k+1}, c_{m_k+1})) \leq V(\nu(c_{n_k}, c_{m_k})H(\mathcal{S}c_{n_k}, \mathcal{S}c_{m_k})) \leq W(d(c_{n_k}, c_{m_k})), \text{ for any } k \geq 1.$$

For if $a_k = d(c_{n_k+1}, c_{m_k+1})$ and $b_k = d(c_{n_k}, c_{m_k})$, we have

$$V(a_k) \leq W(b_k), \text{ for any } k \geq 1. \tag{5}$$

By (1) and (2), we have $\lim_{k\to\infty} a_k = \epsilon+$ and $\lim_{k\to\infty} b_k = \epsilon$. By (9), we obtain

$$\lim_{c\to\epsilon+} \inf V(c) \leq \lim_{k\to\infty} \inf V(a_k) \leq \lim_{k\to\infty} \sup W(b_k) \leq \limsup_{c\to\epsilon} W(c). \tag{6}$$

But (6) contradicts (iii), thus, $\{c_n\}$ is a Cauchy sequence in $\mathcal{U}$. Since $(\mathcal{U}, \perp, d)$ is a complete OMS, $\lim_{n\to\infty} c_n = c^*$ for some $c^* \in \mathcal{U}$. Since the space $(\mathcal{U}, \perp, d)$ is $\perp$-regular, we have $c_n \perp c^*$ or $c^* \perp c_n$ such that $\nu(c_n, c^*) > 1$. We need to show that $d(c^*, \mathcal{S}(c^*)) = 0$ and contrarily suppose that $d(c^*, \mathcal{S}(c^*)) > 0$. Then, there exists $n_1 \in \mathbb{N}$ such that $d(c_n, \mathcal{S}(c^*)) > 0$ for all $n \geq n_1$. By (3)

$$V(d(c_{n+1}, \mathcal{S}(c^*))) \leq V(\nu(c_n, c^*)H(\mathcal{S}(c_n), \mathcal{S}(c^*))) \leq W(d(c_n, c^*)) < V(d(c_n, c^*)). \tag{7}$$

By monotonicity of V, we obtain that $d(c_{n+1}, \mathcal{S}(c^*)) < d(c_n, c^*)$. Taking the limit as $n \to \infty$ in (7), we have $d(c^*, \mathcal{S}(c^*)) < 0$, which is a contradiction. Thus, $d(c^*, \mathcal{S}(c^*)) = 0$. Since $\mathcal{S}(c^*)$ is closed, $c^* \in \mathcal{S}(c^*)$. □

The following theorem states another set of terms and conditions ensuring the existence of fixed points of multivalued $(V, W)_\perp$-contractions.

Theorem 2. *Let $(\mathcal{U}, \perp, d)$ be a $\perp$RCOMS with transitive $\perp$. Suppose that $\mathcal{S} : \mathcal{U} \to P_{cb}(\mathcal{U})$ is a $\perp$-preserving and satisfies (3) and the functions $V, W : (0, \infty) \to (-\infty, \infty)$ meet the following conditions:*

(i) *there exists $c_1 \in \mathcal{S}(c_0)$ such that $c_0 \perp c_1$ or $c_1 \perp c_0$, $c_0 \in \mathcal{U}$,*
(ii) *V is non-decreasing and $W(y) < V(y)$ for any $y > 0$,*
(iii) $\inf_{c>\epsilon} V(c) > -\infty$,
(iv) *for the strictly-decreasing sequences $\{V(c_n)\}$ and $\{W(c_n)\}$, if $\lim_{n\to\infty} V(c_n) = \lim_{n\to\infty} W(c_n) = L$, then $\lim_{n\to\infty} c_n = 0$,*
(v) *$\limsup_{c\to\epsilon} W(c) < \liminf_{c\to\epsilon+} V(c)$ for any $\epsilon > 0$,*
(vi) *$\limsup_{c\to\epsilon_1} W(c) < \liminf_{c\to\epsilon} V(c)$ for any $\epsilon, \epsilon_1 > 0$.*
Then, $\mathcal{S}$ admits at least one fixed-point in $\mathcal{U}$.

Proof. By (i), for $c_0 \in \mathcal{U}$, there exists $c_1 \in \mathcal{S}(c_0)$ such that $c_0 \perp c_1$ or $c_1 \perp c_0$. Since T is a $\perp$-preserving mapping, there exists $c_2 \in \mathcal{S}(c_1)$ such that $c_1 \perp c_2$ or $c_2 \perp c_1$ and then $c_3 \in \mathcal{S}(c_2)$ such that $c_2 \perp c_3$ or $c_3 \perp c_2$. In general, there exists $c_{n+1} \in \mathcal{S}(c_n)$ such that $c_n \perp c_{n+1}$ or $c_{n+1} \perp c_n$ $(\forall n \geq 0)$. Hence, $\nu(c_n, c_{n+1}) > 1$ for all $n \geq 0$. If $c_n \in \mathcal{S}(c_n)$ then c_n is a fixed-point of $\mathcal{S}$ $(\forall n \geq 0)$. If $c_n \notin \mathcal{S}(c_n)$ $(\forall n \geq 0)$, then $H(\mathcal{S}c_{n-1}, \mathcal{S}c_n) > 0$. Since $\nu(c_n, c_{n+1}) > 1$ and $\mathcal{S}(c_n), \mathcal{S}(c_{n+1}) \in P_{cb}(\mathcal{U})$, $n \geq 0$, by Lemma 2, there exists $c_{n+1} \in \mathcal{S}(c_n)$ $(c_n \neq c_{n+1})$ such that $d(c_n, c_{n+1}) \leq \nu(c_{n-1}, c_n)H(\mathcal{S}(c_{n-1}), \mathcal{S}(c_n))$ for all $n \geq 1$. By monotonicity of V and (3), we have

$$V(d(c_n, c_{n+1})) \leq V(\nu(c_{n-1}, c_n)H(\mathcal{S}(c_{n-1}), \mathcal{S}(c_n))) \leq W(d(c_{n-1}, c_n)) < V(d(c_{n-1}, c_n)). \quad (8)$$

By (8) we get that $\{V(d(c_{n-1}, c_n))\}$ is a strictly decreasing-sequence.

We have two cases:

Case 1. $\{V(d(c_{n-1}, c_n))\}$ is unbounded below.

By (iii), we have $\inf_{d(c_{n-1},c_n)>\epsilon} V(d(c_{n-1}, c_n)) > -\infty$. This implies that

$$\lim \inf_{d(c_{n-1},c_n)\to\epsilon+} V(d(c_{n-1}, c_n)) > -\infty.$$

Thus, $\lim_{n\to\infty} d(c_{n-1}, c_n) = 0$, otherwise, we have

$$\lim \inf_{d(c_{n-1},c_n)\to\epsilon+} V(d(c_{n-1}, c_n)) = -\infty.$$

This is a contradiction to the assumption (iii).

Case 2. $\{V(d(c_{n-1}, c_n))\}$ is bounded below.

The sequence is convergent and by (8), we have

$$\lim_{n\to\infty} \{W(d(c_{n-1}, c_n))\} = \lim_{n\to\infty} \{V(d(c_{n-1}, c_n))\}.$$

By (iv), we infer $\lim_{n\to\infty} d(c_{n-1}, c_n) = 0$.

Now, contrarily, if we let the sequence $\{c_n\}$ not be Cauchy, then by Lemma 1, there are subsequences $\{c_{n_k}\}$, $\{c_{m_k}\}$ of $\{c_n\}$ and $\epsilon > 0$ such that the Equations (1) and (2) hold. By (1), we get that $d(c_{n_k+1}, c_{m_k+1}) > \epsilon$. Since $c_n \perp c_{n+1}$ $(\forall n \geq 0)$, by transitivity of $\perp$, we have $c_{n_k} \perp c_{m_k}$ and hence $\nu(c_{n_k}, c_{m_k}) > 1$ $(\forall k \geq 1)$. Setting $q = c_{n_k}$ and $\ell = c_{m_k}$ in (3), we have

$$V(d(c_{n_k+1}, c_{m_k+1})) \leq V(\nu(c_{n_k}, c_{m_k})H(\mathcal{S}c_{n_k}, \mathcal{S}c_{m_k})) \leq W(d(c_{n_k}, c_{m_k})), \text{ for any } k \geq 1.$$

For if $a_k = d(c_{n_k+1}, c_{m_k+1})$ and $b_k = d(c_{n_k}, c_{m_k})$, we have

$$V(a_k) \leq W(b_k), \text{ for any } k \geq 1. \quad (9)$$

By (1) and (2), we have $\lim_{k\to\infty} a_k = \epsilon+$ and $\lim_{k\to\infty} b_k = \epsilon$. By (9), we get that

$$\lim \inf_{c\to\epsilon+} V(c) \leq \lim \inf_{k\to\infty} V(a_k) \leq \lim \sup_{k\to\infty} W(b_k) \leq \lim\sup_{c\to\epsilon} W(c). \quad (10)$$

But (10) contradicts (v), thus, $\{c_n\}$ is a Cauchy sequence in $\mathcal{U}$. Since $\mathcal{U}$ is a complete OMS, the sequence $\{c_n\}$ converges to $c^* \in \mathcal{U}$.

We show that c^* is a fixed point of $\mathcal{S}$. There are two possibilities. (P1) If $d(c_{n+1}, \mathcal{S}c^*) = 0$ for a fixed n, then we have

$$d(c^*, \mathcal{S}c^*) \leq d(c^*, c_{n+1}) + d(c_{n+1}, \mathcal{S}c^*) = d(c^*, c_{n+1}).$$

Taking the limit $n \to \infty$, we get $d(c^*, \mathcal{S}c^*) \leq 0$. Thus, $d(c^*, \mathcal{S}(c^*)) = 0$. Since $\mathcal{S}(c^*)$ is closed, $c^* \in \mathcal{S}(c^*)$. (P2) If $d(c_{n+1}, \mathcal{S}c^*) > 0$ for all $n \geq 0$, then the $\perp$-regularity of the space $\mathcal{U}$ implies $c_n \perp c^*$ or $c^* \perp c_n$ and, thus, $\nu(c_n, c^*) > 1$. By the contractive condition (3), for all $n \geq 0$, we have

$$V(d(c_{n+1}, \mathcal{S}c^*)) \leq V(\nu(c_n, c^*)H(\mathcal{S}c_n, \mathcal{S}c^*)) \leq W(d(c_n, c^*)). \tag{11}$$

Set $a_n = d(c_{n+1}, \mathcal{S}c^*)$ and $b_n = d(c_n, c^*)$. Then, by (11), we have

$$V(a_n) \leq W(b_n) \text{ for all } n \geq 0. \tag{12}$$

Suppose that $\epsilon = d(c^*, \mathcal{S}c^*)$ such that $\lim_{n\to\infty} a_n = \epsilon$ and $\lim_{n\to\infty} b_n = 0$. By (12), we have

$$\liminf_{c\to\epsilon} V(c) \leq \liminf_{n\to\infty} V(a_n) \leq \limsup_{n\to\infty} W(b_n) \leq \liminf_{c\to 0} W(c). \tag{13}$$

If $\epsilon > 0$, then (13) contradicts (vi). Thus, we have $d(c^*, \mathcal{S}c^*) = 0$. Hence $c^* \in \mathcal{S}c^*$, that is, c^* is a fixed point of $\mathcal{S}$. □

Remark 3. *If we replace $d(c, \ell)$ with $E(c, \ell)$ in the contractive condition (3), then according to* Ćirić [29], *Theorems 1 and 2 remain true.*

Uniqueness of the fixed point: The following three conditions are essential for the uniqueness of a fixed point of a multivalued mapping.

(U_1). For any multivalued mapping $\mathcal{M} : \mathcal{Q} \to P(\mathcal{Q})$, the set of fixed points of $\mathcal{M}$ ($F(\mathcal{M})$) is totally orthogonal (for any $w, e \in F(\mathcal{M})$ either $w \perp e$ or $e \perp w$).

(U_2). Let

$$\mathcal{Y}_{\mathcal{M}(\ell)}(q) = \{t \in \mathcal{M}(\ell) | d(q, t) = d(\mathcal{M}(\ell), q)\} \text{ for all } q \in \mathcal{Q}.$$

For any $\ell \in \mathcal{Q}$, $\exists\, \theta \in \mathcal{Y}_{\mathcal{M}(\ell)}(q)$ such that $\ell \perp \theta$.

(U_3). For all $i, b, \tau \in \mathcal{Q}$, $d(\tau, i) \geq d(b, i)$, whenever $i \perp b \perp \tau$.

Theorem 3. *Assume that, in addition to conditions stated in Theorem 1 (or Theorem 2), the conditions $(U_1) - (U_3)$ hold. Then, the mapping $\mathcal{M} : \mathcal{Q} \to P_{cb}(\mathcal{Q})$ admits a unique fixed point in $\mathcal{Q}$.*

Proof. Clearly the mapping $\mathcal{M}$ admits at least one fixed point in $\mathcal{Q}$ (by Theorem 1 (or Theorem 2)). Let w and e be two fixed points of $\mathcal{M}$, so that, $w \in \mathcal{M}(w)$ and $e \in \mathcal{M}(e)$. By (U_1), for any $w, e \in (F(\mathcal{M})$, either $w \perp e$ or $e \perp w$. In view of (U_2), $\exists g \in \mathcal{Y}_{\mathcal{M}(\ell)}(q)$ satisfying $\ell \perp g$ and $d(q, g) = d(\mathcal{M}(\ell), q)$. By (U_3), $q \perp \ell \perp g$, implies that $d(g, q) \geq d(\ell, q)$. Since $\ell \in \mathcal{M}(\ell)$ so that $d(g, q) \leq d(\ell, q)$, hence, $d(\mathcal{M}(\ell), q) = d(q, g) = d(\ell, q)$. Now if $\ell \neq q$, then $d(\ell, q) > 0$. Moreover,

$$d(\ell, q) = d(\mathcal{M}(\ell), q) \leq H(\mathcal{M}(\ell), \mathcal{M}(q)) < \nu(\ell, q)H(\mathcal{M}(\ell), \mathcal{M}(q)).$$

By (ii) stated in Theorem 1 and (3), we deduce that

$$V(d(\ell, q)) < V(\nu(\ell, q)H(\mathcal{M}(\ell), \mathcal{M}(q))) \leq W(d(\ell, q)) < V(d(\ell, q)).$$

As V is an increasing mapping, we have $d(\ell, q) < d(\ell, q)$, a contradiction, thus, $\ell = q$. Hence, the multivalued mapping $\mathcal{M}$ has a unique fixed point. □

Examples for the Explanation of Theory

Example 3. *Consider* $X = \{0\} \cup]3, 7]$ *endowed with usual-metric*

$$d(q, \ell) = |q - \ell| \text{ for all } q, \ell \in X.$$

Define the relation $\perp \subset X^2$ *by*

$$a \perp b \text{ if and only if } a \wedge b = 0 \Rightarrow a \vee b \in]5, 7].$$

Then, $\perp$ *is an orthogonal relation and* $(X, d, \perp)$ *is a complete orthogonal metric space. Define* $\mathcal{S} : X \to CB(X)$ *by,*

$$\mathcal{S}(q) = \begin{cases} \{5, 7\}, & q \in]3, 7], \\ \{4, 6\}, & q = 0. \end{cases}$$

Let $A = \{5, 7\}$ *and* $B = \{4, 6\}$*. Since*

$$H(A, B) = \max\{d(A, B), d(B, A)\}, \tag{14}$$

$$\begin{aligned} d(A, B) &= \sup\{d(q, B) : q \in A\} = \inf\{d(q, \ell) : \ell \in B\} \\ d(B, A) &= \sup\{d(\ell, A) : \ell \in B\}. \end{aligned}$$

Consider,

$$\{d(q, B) : q \in A\} = \{d(5, B), d(7, B)\}, \tag{15}$$

where

$$\begin{aligned} d(5, B) &= \inf\{d(5, 4), d(5, 6)\} = \inf\{1, 1\} = 1. \\ d(7, B) &= \inf\{d(7, 4), d(7, 6)\} = \inf\{3, 1\} = 1. \end{aligned}$$

Thus, by (15), we get

$$d(A, B) = \sup\{d(q, B) : q \in A\} = \sup\{1, 1\} = 1. \tag{16}$$

Consider

$$\{d(\ell, A) : \ell \in B\} = \{d(4, A), d(6, A)\}. \tag{17}$$

$$d(4, A) = \inf\{d(4, 5), d(4, 7)\} = \inf\{1, 3\} = 1.$$

$$d(6, A) = \inf\{d(6, 5), d(6, 7)\} = \inf\{1, 1\} = 1.$$

Thus, by (17), we get

$$d(B, A) = \sup\{d(\ell, A) : \ell \in B\} = \sup\{1, 1\} = 1. \tag{18}$$

By virtue of Equations (16) and (18), Equation (14) implies that $H(A, B) = 1 > 0$*. Define* $\nu : X^2 \to [1, \infty)$ *by*

$$\nu(a, b) = \begin{cases} 2 & \text{if } a \perp b, \\ 1 & \text{otherwise}. \end{cases}$$

Then, ν *is* $\perp$*-admissible.*

Case 1: *If* $\ell = 0$ *and* $q \in]5,7]$, *then,* $\ell \perp q$ *and*

$$\frac{1}{294} - \frac{1}{2H(\mathcal{S}q, \mathcal{S}\ell) + 1} \leq \frac{49}{294} - \frac{1}{3} = -\frac{1}{6} < -\frac{1}{d(q,\ell) + 1}. \quad (19)$$

Case 2: *If* $q = 0$ *and* $\ell \in]5,7]$, *then,* $\ell \perp q$ *and*

$$\frac{1}{294} - \frac{1}{2H(\mathcal{S}q, \mathcal{S}\ell) + 1} \leq \frac{49}{294} - \frac{1}{3} = -\frac{1}{6} < -\frac{1}{d(q,\ell) + 1}. \quad (20)$$

By (19) and (20), we deduce that

$$\frac{1}{294} - \frac{1}{2H(\mathcal{S}q, \mathcal{S}\ell) + 1} < -\frac{1}{d(q,\ell) + 1},$$

for all $q, \ell \in X$ *with* $q \perp \ell$. *Thus, by defining* $V(t) = -\frac{1}{t+1}$ *and* $W(t) = V(t) - \tau$ *for all* $t \in (0, \infty)$ *and* $\tau = \frac{1}{294}$, *we see that* V *and* W *satisfy conditions (ii) and (iii) of Theorem 1 and* $\mathcal{S}$ *is a multivalued* $(V, W)_{\perp}$*-contraction:*

$$V(v(q,\ell)H(\mathcal{S}(q), \mathcal{S}(\ell))) \leq W(d(q,\ell)).$$

Here, we note that the fixed point of $\mathcal{S}$ *is 7, because* $7 \in \mathcal{S}(7)$.

Example 4. *Consider* $X =]9, 21]$ *endowed with the usual metric:*

$$d(q,\ell) = |q - \ell| \text{ for all } q, \ell \in X.$$

Define the relation $\perp \subset X^2$ *by*

$$a \perp b \text{ if and only if } a \wedge b = 10 \Rightarrow a \vee b \in]17, 21].$$

Then, $\perp$ *is an orthogonal relation and* $(X, d, \perp)$ *is a complete orthogonal metric space. Define the mapping* $\mathcal{S} : X \to CB(X)$ *by,*

$$\mathcal{S}(q) = \begin{cases} \{20, 21\}, & q \in]9, 21], \\ \{18, 19\}, & q = 10. \end{cases}$$

Let $A = \{20, 21\}$ *and* $B = \{18, 19\}$. *We know that*

$$H(A,B) = \max\{d(A,B), d(B,A)\}; \; d(A,B) = \sup\{d(q,B) : q \in A\} \text{ and } d(B,A) = \sup\{d(\ell, A) : \ell \in B\}. \quad (21)$$

Consider,

$$\{d(q,B) : q \in A\} = \{d(20,B), d(21,B)\}. \quad (22)$$

$$d(q,B) = \inf\{d(q,\ell) : \ell \in B\}$$
$$d(20,B) = \inf\{d(20,18), d(20,19)\} = \inf\{2,1\} = 1.$$
$$d(21,B) = \inf\{d(21,18), d(21,19)\} = \inf\{3,2\} = 2.$$

Thus, by (22), we get

$$d(A,B) = \sup\{d(q,B) : q \in A\} = \sup\{1,2\} = 2. \quad (23)$$

Similarly,

$$\{d(\ell, A) : y \in B\} = \{d(18, A), d(19, A)\}. \quad (24)$$

$d(18, A) = \inf\{d(18, 20), d(18, 21)\} = \inf\{2, 3\} = 2$, *and* $d(19, A) = \inf\{d(19, 20), d(19, 21)\}$ $= \inf\{1, 2\} = 1$. *Thus, by (24), we get*

$$d(B, A) = \sup\{d(\ell, A) : \ell \in B\} = \sup\{2, 1\} = 2. \quad (25)$$

By Equations (23) and (25), the Equation (21) implies that $H(A, B) = 2 > 0$. *Define* $\nu : X^2 \to [1, \infty)$ *by*

$$\nu(a, b) = \begin{cases} 2 & \text{if } a \perp b, \\ 1 & \text{otherwise}. \end{cases}$$

Then, ν *is* $\perp$*-admissible.*

Case 1: *If* $q = 10$ *and* $\ell \in]17, 21]$, *then,* $q \perp \ell$ *and*

$$\begin{aligned} 1 + d(10, \ell) &\geq 8 \geq \frac{3}{2}(1 + 2H(\mathcal{S}10, \mathcal{S}\ell)) \\ \frac{3}{2}(1 + 2H(\mathcal{S}10, \mathcal{S}\ell)) &\leq 1 + d(10, \ell) \\ \ln(\frac{3}{2}(1 + 2H(\mathcal{S}10, \mathcal{S}\ell))) &\leq \ln(1 + d(10, \ell)) \\ \ln(\frac{3}{2}) + \ln(1 + 2H(\mathcal{S}10, \mathcal{S}\ell)) &\leq \ln(1 + d(10, \ell)). \end{aligned}$$

Case 2: *If* $\ell = 10$ *and* $q \in]17, 21]$, *then,* $q \perp \ell$ *and*

$$\begin{aligned} 1 + d(q, 10) &\geq 8 \geq \frac{3}{2}(1 + 2H(\mathcal{S}q, \mathcal{S}10)) \\ \frac{3}{2}(1 + 2H(\mathcal{S}q, \mathcal{S}10)) &\leq 1 + d(q, 10) \\ \ln(\frac{3}{2}(1 + 2H(\mathcal{S}q, \mathcal{S}10))) &\leq \ln(1 + d(q, 10)) \\ \ln(\frac{3}{2}) + \ln(1 + 2H(\mathcal{S}q, \mathcal{S}10)) &\leq \ln(1 + d(q, 10)). \end{aligned}$$

Thus, for all $q, \ell \in X$ *with* $q \perp \ell$, *Thus, by defining* $V(t) = \ln(t + 1)$ *and* $W(t) = V(t) - \tau$ *for all* $t \in (0, \infty)$ *and* $\tau = \ln \frac{3}{2}$, *we see that* V *and* W *satisfy conditions (ii)–(vi) of Theorem 2 and* $\mathcal{S}$ *is a multivalued* $(V, W)_\perp$*-contraction:*

$$V(\nu(q, \ell)H(\mathcal{S}(q), \mathcal{S}(\ell))) \leq W(d(q, \ell)).$$

We note that the fixed point of $\mathcal{S}$ *is 20, because* $20 \in \mathcal{S}(20)$.

3. Consequences

It is noted that the Nadler fixed point theorem [30] is a particular case of Theorems 1 and 2 (let $V(c) = c$ and $W(c) = \lambda c$ for all $c > 0$ and $\lambda \in [0, 1)$). The multivalued version of the Wordowski Theorem can be derived by defining $V(c) = c$ for all $c > 0$ in Theorem 1. If we define $W(c) = V(c) - t$ $(t > 0)$ in Theorems 1 and 2, then we have an improvement of the results presented in [8,12,27,31] as follows:

Corollary 1. *Let* $(\mathcal{U}, \perp, d)$ *be a* $\perp$*RCOMS. Suppose that* $\mathcal{S} : \mathcal{U} \to P_{cb}(\mathcal{U})$ *is* $\perp$*-preserving and there exists a* $\perp$*-admissible function* ν *and* $t > 0$ *such that*

$$H(\mathcal{S}x, \mathcal{S}y) > 0 \text{ implies } t + V(\nu(x, y)H(\mathcal{S}x, \mathcal{S}y)) \leq V(d(x, y))) \text{ for all } x, y \in \mathcal{U}.$$

If there exists $c_1 \in \mathcal{S}(c_0)$ such that $c_0 \perp c_1$ or $c_1 \perp c_0$, $c_0 \in \mathcal{U}$ and $V : (0,\infty) \to \mathbb{R}$ is nondecreasing, then $\mathcal{S}$ admits a fixed point in $\mathcal{U}$.

Defining $W(c) = V(c) - \tau(c)$ for all $c \in (0,\infty)$ in Theorems 1 and 2, we have the following improvement of the result presented in [10].

Corollary 2. *Let $(\mathcal{U},\perp,d)$ be a $\perp$RCOMS. Suppose that $\mathcal{S} : \mathcal{U} \to P_{cb}(\mathcal{U})$ is $\perp$-preserving and there exists a $\perp$-admissible function v such that*

$$H(\mathcal{S}x,\mathcal{S}y) > 0 \text{ implies } \tau(d(x,y)) + V(v(x,y)H(\mathcal{S}x,\mathcal{S}y)) \leq V(d(x,y))) \text{ for all } x,y \in \mathcal{U},$$

$$\lim_{c\to t+}\inf \tau(c) > 0,\ \forall t \geq 0.$$

If there exists $c_1 \in \mathcal{S}(c_0)$ such that $c_0 \perp c_1$ or $c_1 \perp c_0$, $c_0 \in \mathcal{U}$ and $V : (0,\infty) \to \mathbb{R}$ is nondecreasing, then $\mathcal{S}$ admits a fixed point in $\mathcal{U}$.

Defining $W(c) = g(V(c))$ for all $c \in (0,\infty)$ in Theorem 1, we have the following improvement of Moradi's theorem [21].

Corollary 3. *Let $(\mathcal{U},\perp,d)$ be a $\perp$RCOMS. Let $B \subset \mathbb{R}$ and $g : B \to [0,\infty)$ is an upper semi-continuous function satisfying $g(z) < z$ for all $z \in B$. Suppose that $\mathcal{S} : \mathcal{U} \to P_{cb}(\mathcal{U})$ is $\perp$-preserving and there exists a $\perp$-admissible function v such that*

$$H(\mathcal{S}x,\mathcal{S}y) > 0 \text{ implies } V(v(x,y)H(\mathcal{S}x,\mathcal{S}y)) \leq g(V(d(x,y))) \text{ for all } x,y \in \mathcal{U}.$$

If there exists $c_1 \in \mathcal{S}(c_0)$ such that $c_0 \perp c_1$ or $c_1 \perp c_0$, $c_0 \in \mathcal{U}$ and $V : (0,\infty) \to B$ is nondecreasing, then $\mathcal{S}$ admits a fixed point in $\mathcal{U}$.

Defining $g(z) = z^{\omega}$ ($\omega \in (0,1)$) in Corollary 3, we have the following conclusion.

Corollary 4. *Let $(\mathcal{U},\perp,d)$ be a $\perp$RCOMS. Suppose that $\mathcal{S} : \mathcal{U} \to P_{cb}(\mathcal{U})$ is $\perp$-preserving and there exists a $\perp$-admissible function v such that*

$$H(\mathcal{S}x,\mathcal{S}y) > 0 \text{ implies } V(v(x,y)H(\mathcal{S}x,\mathcal{S}y)) \leq (V(d(x,y)))^{\omega} \text{ for all } x,y \in \mathcal{U}$$

and $V : (0,\infty) \to (0,1)$ is nondecreasing. If there exists $c_1 \in \mathcal{S}(c_0)$ such that $c_0 \perp c_1$ or $c_1 \perp c_0$, $c_0 \in \mathcal{U}$, then $\mathcal{S}$ admits a fixed point in $\mathcal{U}$.

Remark 4. *Corollary 4 shows the improvements of fixed point results presented in [20,32].*

If we define $W(y) = \lambda V(y)$ in Theorems 1 and 2, then we have the following improvement of the special case of Skof's fixed point theorem [26].

Corollary 5. *Let $(\mathcal{U},\perp,d)$ be a $\perp$RCOMS. Suppose that $\mathcal{S} : \mathcal{U} \to P_{cb}(\mathcal{U})$ is $\perp$-preserving and there exists a $\perp$-admissible function v such that*

$$H(\mathcal{S}x,\mathcal{S}y) > 0 \text{ implies } V(v(x,y)H(\mathcal{S}x,\mathcal{S}y)) \leq \lambda V(d(x,y)) \text{ for all } x,y \in \mathcal{U},$$

and V is a nondecreasing function that maps positive real numbers to positive real numbers and $\lambda \in (0,1)$. If there exists $c_1 \in \mathcal{S}(c_0)$ such that $c_0 \perp c_1$ or $c_1 \perp c_0$, $c_0 \in \mathcal{U}$, then $\mathcal{S}$ has a unique fixed point in $\mathcal{U}$.

On the other hand, if V is a nondecreasing function that maps positive real numbers to positive real numbers and $\chi : (0,\infty) \to (0,1)$ meets the condition $\limsup_{z\to\epsilon+} \chi(z) < 1$ for any $\epsilon > 0$, and $W(z) = \chi(z)V(z)$ and $V(z) = z$ for all $z > 0$ in Theorem 1, then we have an improvement of a theorem in [25].

Remark 5. *(R1). The $\perp$-admissibility of the mapping $\mathcal{S}$ can be dropped from all of the aforementioned results by replacing $P_{cb}(\mathcal{U})$ with $K(\mathcal{U})$ and the Lemma 2 is no more required.*

(R2). The condition:

$$V(\inf A) = \inf V(A) \text{ for all } A \subseteq (0,\infty) \text{ with } \inf A > 0,$$

can be used as an alternative of the $\perp$-admissibility of $\mathcal{S} : \mathcal{U} \to P_{cb}(\mathcal{U})$ in the above theorems.

The following theorem is a particular case of Theorem 1 and is useful for the upcoming result.

Theorem 4. *Let $\mathcal{S}$ be a $\perp$-preserving self-mapping defined on $\perp$RCOMS such that*

$$t + V(\nu(c,\ell)d(\mathcal{S}(c),\mathcal{S}(\ell))) \leq V(E(c,\ell)) \tag{26}$$

for all $c,\ell \in \Lambda$ with $d(\mathcal{S}(c),\mathcal{S}(\ell)) > 0$ and $V : (0,\infty) \to \mathbb{R}$ is nondecreasing and $t > 0$. If there exists $c_1 = \mathcal{S}(c_0)$ such that $c_0 \perp c_1$ or $c_1 \perp c_0$; $c_0 \in \mathcal{U}$, then $\mathcal{S}$ admits a fixed point.

Proof. Setting $W(y) = V(y) - t$ for all $y > 0$ in Theorem 1, we have the required result. □

Remark 6. *Define $E(c,\ell)$ as any one of the following. Then, Theorem 4 is applicable.*
(1) $\max\{d(c,\ell), d(c,\mathcal{S}(c)), d(\ell,\mathcal{S}(\ell))\}$.
(2) $\max\{d(c,\mathcal{S}(c)), d(\ell,\mathcal{S}(\ell))\}$.
(3) $\max\left\{d(c,\ell), \frac{d(c,\mathcal{S}(c))+d(\ell,\mathcal{S}(\ell))}{2}, \frac{d(\ell,\mathcal{S}(c))+d(c,\mathcal{S}(\ell))}{2}\right\}$.
(4) $a_1 d(c,\ell) + a_2(d(c,\mathcal{S}(c)) + d(\ell,\mathcal{S}(\ell))) + a_3(d(\ell,\mathcal{S}(c)) + d(c,\mathcal{S}(\ell)))$, $\sum_{i=1}^{3} a_i < 1$.
(5) $a_1 d(c,\ell) + a2d(c,\mathcal{S}(c)) + a_3 d(\ell,\mathcal{S}(\ell))$, $\sum_{i=1}^{3} a_i < 1$. *(6)* $d(c,\ell)$.

4. Application of Theorem 4 to FDE

Lacroix (1819) proposed and investigated several fractional differential properties. A number of new Caputo-Fabrizio derivative (CFD) models have recently been discovered and studied by authors in [33–35]. In this section, we will look at one of these models. The following notations are required.

Let $\mathcal{X} =: C[0,1] = \{f|\nu : [0,1] \to (-\infty,\infty)$ and f is continuous$\}$. The function $d : \mathcal{X} \times \mathcal{X} \to [0,\infty)$, defined by

$$d(f,g) = \|f-g\|_\infty = \max_{x\in[0,1]} |f(x) - g(x)|, \text{ for all } f,g \in C[0,1],$$

is a metric on $\mathcal{X}$ and $(\mathcal{X},d)$ is a complete metric space. Define an orthogonal relation $\perp$ on $\mathcal{X}$ by

$$c \perp v \text{ iff } cv \geq 0, \text{ for all } c,v \in \mathcal{X}.$$

Then, $(\mathcal{X},\perp,d)$ is a complete OMS. Let $\nu : \mathcal{X} \times \mathcal{X} \to (1,\infty)$ be defined by

$$\nu(r,t) = e^{\|r+t\|_\infty} \text{ for all } r,t \in \mathcal{X} \text{ with } r \perp t.$$

Then, ν is a strictly $\perp$-admissible mapping. Let $K_1 : [0,1] \times (-\infty,\infty) \to (-\infty,\infty)$ be any mapping. We will apply Theorem 4 to show the existence of the solution to the following FDE:

$$^{CF}D^{\jmath}g(x) = K_1(x,g(x)); g \in \mathcal{X} \tag{27}$$
$$g(0) = 0,\ g'(1) = g'(0).$$

Here, $^{CF}D_0^{\jmath}$ denotes the Caputo-Fabrizio derivative (CFD) of order $\jmath$ defined by

$$^{CF}D_0^{\jmath}g(x) = \frac{1}{\Gamma(\zeta-\jmath)}\int_0^x (x-\theta)^{\zeta-\jmath-1}g(\theta))\,d\theta,$$

where

$$\zeta - 1 < \jmath < \zeta \text{ and } \zeta = [\jmath] + 1.$$

The integral operator is defined by

$$I^{\jmath} g(x) = \frac{1}{\Gamma(\jmath)} \int_0^x (x-\theta)^{\jmath-1} g(\theta)\, d\theta, \text{ with } \jmath > 0.$$

One of the transformations of (27) is as follow:

$$g(x) = \frac{1}{\Gamma(\jmath)} \int_0^x (x-\theta)^{\jmath-1} K_1(\theta, g(\theta))\, d\theta + \frac{2x}{\Gamma(\jmath)} \int_0^1 \int_0^\theta (\theta-u)^{\jmath-1} K_1(u, g(u))\, du d\theta.$$

Let

(I) $\exists\, \alpha > 0$ such that

$$|K_1(\theta, g(\theta)) - K_1(\theta, \ell(\theta))| \le \frac{e^{-\alpha}\Gamma(\jmath+1)}{4M} |g(\theta) - \ell(\theta)| (M = \min\{d(g,\ell)| \quad g, \ell \in \mathcal{X}\}),$$

(II) for an arbitrary $g_0 \in \mathcal{X}$, we have

$$g_0(x) \le \frac{1}{\Gamma(\jmath)} \int_0^x (x-\theta)^{\jmath-1} K_1(\theta, g_0(\theta))\, d\theta + \frac{2x}{\Gamma(\jmath)} \int_0^1 \int_0^\theta (\theta-u)^{\jmath-1} K_1(u, g_0(u))\, du d\theta.$$

Theorem 5. *If the conditions (I)–(II) stated above are satisfied, then the Equation (27) admits a solution in $\mathcal{X}$.*

Proof. Define the operator $\mathcal{S} : \mathcal{X} \to \mathcal{X}$, in line with the above information, by

$$\mathcal{S}(g)(x) = \frac{1}{\Gamma(\jmath)} \int_0^x (x-\theta)^{\jmath-1} K_1(\theta, g(\theta))\, d\theta + \frac{2x}{\Gamma(\jmath)} \int_0^1 \int_0^\theta (\theta-u)^{\jmath-1} K_1(u, g(u))\, du d\theta.$$

We note that whenever $g(x) \perp g(y)$ or $g(y) \perp g(x)$, $\mathcal{S}(g)(x) \perp \mathcal{S}(g)(y)$. By (II), there is an arbitrary function $g_0 \in \mathcal{X}$ such that $g_n = \mathcal{S}^n(g_0))$ with $g_n \perp g_{n+1}$ or $g_{n+1} \perp g_n$ $(\forall n \ge 0)$. We establish (26) of Theorem 4 in the next lines.

$$|\mathcal{S}(g)(x) - \mathcal{S}(\ell)(x)| = \left| \begin{array}{l} \frac{1}{\Gamma(\jmath)} \int_0^x (x-\theta)^{\jmath-1} K_1(\theta, g(\theta))\, d\theta \\ -\frac{1}{\Gamma(\jmath)} \int_0^x (x-\theta)^{\jmath-1} K_1(\theta, \ell(\theta))\, d\theta \\ +\frac{2x}{\Gamma(\jmath)} \int_0^1 \int_0^\theta (\theta-u)^{\jmath-1} K_1(u, g(u))\, du d\theta \\ -\frac{2x}{\Gamma(\jmath)} \int_0^1 \int_0^\theta (\theta-u)^{\jmath-1} K_1(u, \ell(u))\, du d\theta \end{array} \right| \text{ implies}$$

$$
\begin{aligned}
&|\mathcal{S}(g)(x)-\mathcal{S}(\ell)(x)| \\
\leq\ & \left|\int_0^x\left(\frac{1}{\Gamma(\jmath)}(x-\theta)^{\jmath-1}K_1(\theta,g(\theta))-\frac{1}{\Gamma(\jmath)}(x-\theta)^{\jmath-1}K_1(\theta,\ell(\theta))\right)d\theta\right| \\
+\ & \left|\int_0^1\int_0^\theta\left(\frac{2}{\Gamma(\jmath)}(\theta-u)^{\jmath-1}K_1(\theta,g(\theta))-\frac{2}{\Gamma(\jmath)}(\theta-u)^{\jmath-1}K_1(u,\ell(u))\right)dud\theta\right| \\
\leq\ & \frac{1}{\Gamma(\jmath)}\frac{e^{-\alpha}\Gamma(\jmath+1)}{4M}\cdot\int_0^x(x-\theta)^{\jmath-1}(g(\theta)-\ell(\theta))\,d\theta \\
+\ & \frac{2}{\Gamma(\jmath)}\frac{e^{-\alpha}\Gamma(\jmath+1)}{4M}\cdot\int_0^1\int_0^\theta(\theta-u)^{\jmath-1}(\ell(u)-g(u))\,dud\theta \\
\leq\ & \frac{1}{\Gamma(\jmath)}\frac{e^{-\alpha}\Gamma(\jmath+1)}{4M}\cdot d(g,\ell)\cdot\int_0^x(x-\theta)^{\jmath-1}\,d\theta \\
+\ & \frac{2}{\Gamma(\jmath)}\frac{e^{-\alpha}\Gamma(\jmath)\cdot\Gamma(\jmath+1)}{4M\Gamma(s)\cdot\Gamma(\jmath+1)}\cdot d(g,\ell)\cdot\int_0^1\int_0^\theta(\theta-u)^{\jmath-1}\,dud\theta \\
\leq\ & \left(\frac{e^{-\alpha}\Gamma(\jmath)\cdot\Gamma(\jmath+1)}{4M\Gamma(\jmath)\cdot\Gamma(\jmath+1)}\right)\cdot d(g,\ell)+2e^{-\alpha}B(\jmath+1,1)\frac{\Gamma(\jmath)\cdot\Gamma(\jmath+1)}{4M\Gamma(\jmath)\cdot\Gamma(\jmath+1)}\cdot d(g,\ell) \\
\leq\ & \frac{e^{-\alpha}}{4M}d(g,\ell)+\frac{e^{-\alpha}}{2M}d(g,\ell)<\frac{e^{-\alpha}}{M}d(g,\ell),
\end{aligned}
$$

The simplified form is given by

$$
Md(\mathcal{S}(g),\mathcal{S}(\ell))\leq d(g,\ell)d(\mathcal{S}(g),\mathcal{S}(\ell))\leq e^{-\alpha}d(g,\ell). \tag{28}
$$

Define the mapping $V(g(x))=\ln(g(x))$ for all $g,\ell\in\mathcal{X}$. Then, the inequality (28) can be re-written as

$$
\alpha+V(d(g,\ell)d(\mathcal{S}(g),\mathcal{S}(\ell)))\leq V(d(g,\ell)).
$$

By Theorem 4, (27) admits a solution in. □

5. Conclusions

The multivalued contractions introduced in this paper encapsulate so many contractions, including Nadler, F, Boyd-Wong and Geraghty contractions. The results stated in this paper generalize and improve a number of results on the existence of fixed-points of the abovementioned contractions. The orthogonal relation is the useful generalization of binary relation. Fixed point methodology is used to investigate the presence of a solution to a fractional differential equation. Based on the recently developed concept of orthogonality in the metric spaces, we introduce orthogonal multivalued contractions in this study. For these contractions, we derive several fixed point theorems. We demonstrate how these fixed point theorems help to generalize several newly released findings. In addition, we provide a theorem that proves the existence of the solution to a fractional differential equation (FDE).

6. Future Work

The interested readers are suggested to try these results in vector-valued metric spaces or generalized metric spaces.

Author Contributions: Conceptualization, M.N.; methodology, M.N.; software, M.N.; validation, M.N., S.C., H.H.A.S. and A.H.; formal analysis, M.N.; investigation, M.N. and S.C.; resources, H.H.A.S.; writing—original draft preparation, M.N.; writing—review and editing, M.N., S.C. and A.H.; visualization, M.N.; supervision, M.N. and H.H.A.S.; project administration, A.H. and H.H.A.S.; funding acquisition, H.H.A.S. All authors have read and agreed to the published version of the manuscript.

Funding: This research received no external funding.

Institutional Review Board Statement: Not applicable.

Informed Consent Statement: Not applicable.

Data Availability Statement: Not applicable.

Conflicts of Interest: The authors declare that they have no competing interest.

References

1. Boyd, D.W.; Wong, J.S.W. On nonlinear contractions. *Proc. Am. Math. Soc.* **1969**, *20*, 458–464. [CrossRef]
2. Rakotch, E. A note on contractive mappings. *Proc. Am. Math. Soc.* **1962**, *13*, 459–465. [CrossRef]
3. Matkowski, J. Integrable solutions of functional equations. *Diss. Math.* **1975**, *127*, 1–68.
4. Samet, B.; Vetro, C.; Vetro, P. Fixed point theorems for (α, ψ)-contractive type mappings. *Nonlinear Anal.* **2012**, *75*, 2154–2165. [CrossRef]
5. Karapinar, E.; Samet, B. Generalized (α, Ψ)-contractive type mappings and related fixed point theorems with applications. *Abstr. Appl. Anal.* **2012**, *2012*, 793486. [CrossRef]
6. Pasick, L. The Boyd-Wong idea extended. *Fixed Point Theory Appl.* **2016**, *2016*, 63. [CrossRef]
7. Wardowski, D. Fixed point theory of a new type of contractive mappings in complete metric spaces. *Fixed Point Theory Appl.* **2012**, *2012*, 94. [CrossRef]
8. Baghani, H.; Gordji, M.E.; Ramezani, M. Orthogonal sets: The axiom of choice and proof of a fixed point theorem. *J. Fixed Point Theory Appl.* **2016**, *18*, 465–477. [CrossRef]
9. Beg, I.; Mani, G.; Gnanaprakasam, A.J. Fixed point of orthogonal F-Suzuki contraction mapping on O-complete metric spaces with applications. *J. Funct. Spaces* **2021**, *2021*, 6692112. [CrossRef]
10. Chandok, S.; Sharma, R.K.; Radenović, S. Multivalued problems vian orthogonal contraction mappings with application to fractional differential equation. *J. Fixed Point Theory Appl.* **2021**, *23*, 14. [CrossRef]
11. Chandok, S.; Radenović, S. Existence of solution for orthogonal F-contraction mappings via Picard–Jungck sequences. *J. Anal.* **2022**, *30*, 677–690. [CrossRef]
12. Secelean, N.A. Weak F-contractions and some fixed point results. *Bull. Iranian Math. Soc.* **2016**, *42*, 779–798.
13. Sharma, R.K.; Chandok, S. Multivalued problems, orthogonal mappings, and fractional integro-differential equation. *J. Math.* **2020**, *2020*, 6615478. [CrossRef]
14. Turab, A.; Ali, W.; Park, C. A unified fixed point approach to study the existence and uniqueness of solutions to the generalized stochastic functional equation emerging in the psychological theory of learning. *Aims Math.* **2022**, *7*, 5291–5304. [CrossRef]
15. Khan, Z.A.; Ahmad, I.; Shah, K. Applications of Fixed Point Theory to Investigate a System of Fractional Order Differential Equations. *J. Funct. Spaces* **2021**, *2021*, 1399764. [CrossRef]
16. Rezapour, S.; Deressa, C.T.; Hussain, A.; Etemad, S.; George, R.; Ahmad, B. A Theoretical Analysis of a Fractional Multi-Dimensional System of Boundary Value Problems on the Methylpropane Graph via Fixed Point Technique. *Mathematics* **2022**, *10*, 568. [CrossRef]
17. Gordji, M.E.; Rameani, M.; Sen, M.D.L.; Cho, Y. On orthogonal sets and Banach fixed point theorem. *Fixed Point Theory* **2017**, *19*, 569–578. [CrossRef]
18. Nazam, M.; Park, C.; Arshad, M. Fixed point problems for generalized contractions with applications. *Adv. Differ. Equ.* **2021**, *2021*, 247. [CrossRef]
19. Proinov, P.D. Fixed point theorems for generalized contractive mappings in metric spaces. *J. Fixed Point Theory Appl.* **2020**, *22*, 21. [CrossRef]
20. Jleli, M.; Samet, B. A new generalization of the Banach contraction principle. *J. Inequal. Appl.* **2014**, *2014*, 38. [CrossRef]
21. Moradi, S. Fixed point of single-valued cyclic weak φF-contraction mappings. *Filomat* **2014**, *28*, 1747–1752. [CrossRef]
22. Nazam, M.; Aydi, H.; Hussain, A. Existence theorems for (Φ, Ψ)-orthogonal interpolative contractions and an application to fractional differential equations. *Optimization* **2022**, *72*, 1–31. [CrossRef]
23. Nadler, S.B. Multivalued contraction mappings. *Pacific J. Math.* **1969**, *30*, 475–488. [CrossRef]
24. Ran, A.C.M.; Reurings, M.C.B. A fixed point theorem in partially ordered sets and some applications to matrix equations. *Proc. Am. Math. Soc.* **2003**, *132*, 1435–1443. [CrossRef]
25. Geraghty, M.A. On contractive mappings. *Proc. Am. Math. Soc.* **1973**, *40*, 604–608. [CrossRef]
26. Skof, F. Theoremi di punto fisso per applicazioni negli spazi metrici. *Atti. Acad. Sci. Torino Cl. Sci. Fis. Mat. Natur.* **1977**, *111*, 323–329.
27. Acar, O.; Altun, I. Multivalued F-contractive mappings with a graph and some fixed point results. *Publ. Math. Debr.* **2016**, *88*, 305–317. [CrossRef]
28. Afshari, H.; Aydi, H.; Karapinar, E. Some fixed point results for multivalued mappings in b-metric spaces. *East Asian Math. J.* **2016**, *32*, 319–332. [CrossRef]
29. Ćirić, L.B. Generalized contractions and fixed-point theorems. *Publ. Inst. Math.* **1971**, *26*, 19–26.
30. Banach, S. Sur les operations dans les ensembles abstraits et leurs applications aux equations integrales. *Fund. Math.* **1922**, *3*, 133–181. [CrossRef]
31. Durmaz, G.; Altun, I. Fixed point results for α-admissible multivalued F-contractions. *Miskolc Math. Notes* **2016**, *17*, 187–199. [CrossRef]
32. Ahmad, J.; Al-Mazrooei, A.E.; Cho, Y.; Yang, Y. Fixed point results for generalized Θ-contractions. *J. Nonlinear Sci. Appl.* **2017**, *10*, 2350–2358. [CrossRef]

33. Alizadeh, S.; Baleanu, D.; Rezapour, S. Analyzing transient response of the parallel RCL circuit by using the Caputo-Fabrizio fractional derivative. *Adv. Differ. Equ.* **2020**, *2020*, 55. [CrossRef]
34. Baleanu, D.; Jajarmi, A.; Mohammadi, H.; Rezapour, S. A new study on the mathematical modelling of human liver with Caputo-Fabrizio fractional derivative. *Chaos Solitons Fractals* **2020**, *134*, 109705. [CrossRef]
35. Baleanu, D.; Mohammadi, H.; Rezapour, S. Analysis of the model of HIV-1 infection of CD^{4+} T-cell with a new approach of fractional derivative. *Adv. Differ. Equ.* **2020**, *2020*, 71. [CrossRef]

axioms

Article

A Variational Formulation for Fins with Nonzero Contact Thermal Resistance at the Base

Rogério Martins Saldanha da Gama [1,*], Rogério Pazetto Saldanha da Gama [1], Vinicius Vendas Sarmento [2] and Maria Laura Martins-Costa [2]

[1] Mechanical Engineering Department, Universidade do Estado do Rio de Janeiro, Rio de Janeiro 20550-013, Brazil
[2] Mechanical Engineering Department, Universidade Federal Fluminense, Niterói 24210-240, Brazil
* Correspondence: rsgama@terra.com.br

Abstract: This paper considers the steady-state heat transfer process in a fin with a Robin boundary condition at the base (instead of the usual Dirichlet boundary condition at the base). Robin boundary condition models the effect of the thermal resistance between the base of the fin and the surface on which the fin is placed. This work presents an equivalent minimum principle, represented by a convex and coercive functional, ensuring the solution's existence and uniqueness. In order to illustrate the use of the proposed functional for reaching approximations, the heat-transfer process in a trapezoidal fin considering a piecewise linear approximation is simulated. The Appendix presents a case in which the exact solution in a closed form has been achieved.

Keywords: fins; thermal resistance at the base; variational formulation; numerical simulation

MSC: 34B99; 80A21; 80A05

Citation: da Gama, R.M.S.; da Gama, R.P.S.; Sarmento, V.V.; Martins-Costa, M.L. A Variational Formulation for Fins with Nonzero Contact Thermal Resistance at the Base. *Axioms* **2023**, *12*, 54. https://doi.org/10.3390/axioms12010054

Academic Editor: Clemente Cesarano

Received: 27 October 2022
Revised: 21 December 2022
Accepted: 26 December 2022
Published: 3 January 2023

1. Introduction

As more components are placed in a chip, the internal heat generation tends to increase. Since the heat must be rejected to the environment, this increase gives rise to a temperature increase on the surface (as well as a temperature increase in the whole chip). Nevertheless, a maximum allowable temperature exists for each chip (approximately 80 °C on its surface).

Roughly, the heat dissipation is proportional to the difference between the surface temperature and the temperature of the surroundings.

One of the most effective ways to optimize the heat transfer from a device is to increase the effective area of heat transfer. This increase in area is obtained using fins (extended surfaces) and may allow a dissipation increase without a temperature increase [1–4].

Fins are devices found in almost all situations where an improvement of the heat exchange between a given surface and the environment is needed. They act as an artificial enlargement of the original area of a surface, giving rise to a greater actual heat-exchange area. These devices are often the principal tool for avoiding high temperatures that can damage the functionality of a part of a system, such as in circuits involving semiconductors [1–4].

In general, the study of fins, solid or porous, is carried out under the assumption that the temperature of its base is known and coincides with the temperature of the surface in which we fix the fin, giving rise to a Dirichlet boundary condition.

Nevertheless, contact thermal resistance arises when a fin is placed on a given surface, as illustrated in Figure 1. In order to take into account this contact resistance, a Robin boundary condition must replace the previously mentioned Dirichlet boundary condition. This boundary condition takes into account that the temperature of the surface (in which the fin is inserted) is different from the temperature of the base of the fin, giving rise to a relationship between the heat flux and a difference in temperatures caused by the thermal resistance [1–5].

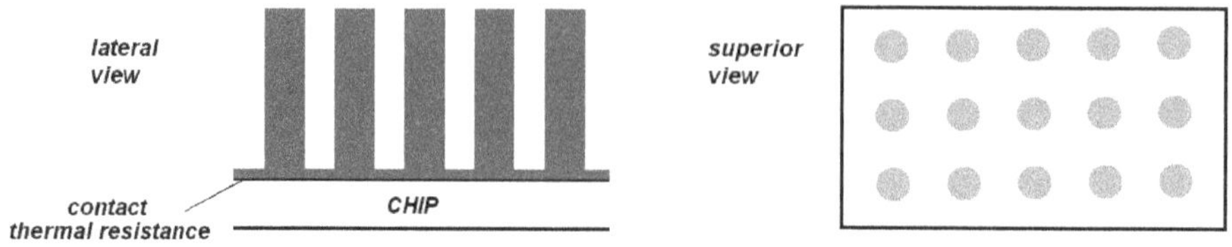

Figure 1. Set of cylindrical fins placed on a chip with the aid of a thermal paste (which gives rise to a thermal contact resistance).

Many studies account for these contact thermal resistances. For instance, Aziz and Arlen [6] analyzed the performance and design of a rectangular fin with the convective base condition and contact resistance, using the numerical package Maple to solve the proposed problem and optimize the geometric parameters to achieve the optimum design. Xie et al. [7] studied T-shaped fins, considering thermal resistance minimization and minimizing geometric parameters according to heat transfer parameters. Their results showed the change of values in the parameters according to the optimization and the degrees of freedom available for change. Taler and Oclón [8] developed a methodology to estimate the thermal resistance of plate-and-tube heat exchangers using experimental data and CFD simulations with ANSYS software. Milman et al. [9] proposed an experimental model to determine the thermal resistance between the tube and the finned wall, accounting for possible errors in this computation, such as surface quality, the possibility of contact corrosion, and welding imperfections.

Fins are designed with the intention of enhancing heat transfer. This heat transfer is, in turn, considerably enlarged by employing porous fins introduced by Kiwan and Al-Nimr [10]. Several authors analyzed significant aspects of porous fins subjected to convection and radiation. For instance, Martins-Costa et al. [11] obtained the temperature distribution in porous fins by minimizing a convex functional. Martins-Costa et al. [12] constructed a solution for the nonlinear problem arising from natural convection and thermal radiation in cylindrical porous fins from a sequence of linear problems, using the parameters suggested by Gorla and Bakier [13].

This work aims to present a mathematical modeling of the heat-transfer process in a fin, accounting for the contact thermal resistance between the base of the fin and the surface in which the fin is placed.

Solid and porous fins are considered to involve convection and radiation heat transfer. All of them possess the prescribed base temperature as a limiting case.

A general mathematical modeling and an equivalent variational principle are presented, enabling the authors to demonstrate the solution's existence and uniqueness.

2. Mathematical Description

The following ordinary differential equation represents the energy balance in a fin:

$$\frac{d}{dx}\left(k\,A\frac{dT}{dx}\right) - p\,f = 0,\; p = \frac{dA_S}{dx},\; x_0 < x < x_L \tag{1}$$

where x represents a spatial position (counted from fin base), A is the sectional area, A_S is the lateral area between the points x_0 and x (for cylindrical fins, p is a constant that represents the perimeter of the section), f represents a heat loss (per unit time and area), and k is the thermal conductivity (assumed here a constant). The function f is a strictly increasing function of the temperature ($f = \hat{f}(T)$), while A and p may depend on the position, but do not depend on the temperature.

The mathematical description represented by the ordinary differential Equation (1) is valid when the temperature distribution can be regarded as a function of only one spatial variable [1].

For instance, for a solid cylindrical fin that exchanges energy with the environment following Newton's law of cooling, the following condition arrives [1–4]:

$$f = h(T - T_\infty),\ A = constant,\ p = constant,\ T_\infty = constant,\ h = constant \quad (2)$$

with $p > 0$, $A > 0$ and $h > 0$.

If it was a solid circular fin (as suggested in Figure 2), with thickness δ, A, A_S, and p would be given by [1–4]:

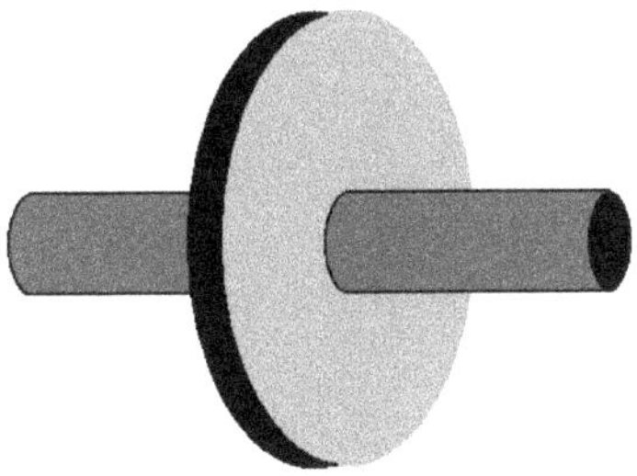

Figure 2. A radial fin with constant thickness δ, installed in a tube with radius $r = x_0$.

$$A = 2\pi x\delta,\ A_S = 2\left(\pi x^2 - \pi x_0^2\right) \Rightarrow p = \frac{d}{dx}A_S = 4\pi x \quad (3)$$

The mathematical structure remains the same as Equation (1) for a porous cylindrical fin subjected to natural convection. However, the meaning of quantities such as A and p changes, as it must be taken into account that the actual area and the actual perimeter are affected by the porosity. In addition, f is not a linear function of T. For a cylindrical porous fin, considering only natural convection, it becomes [12,13]:

$$f = \beta(T - T_\infty)|T - T_\infty|,\ \beta = constant > 0 \quad (4)$$

When thermal radiation is taken into account, additional terms must be considered [11–13].

It is important to note that a differential equation such as Equation (1) describes any one-dimensional heat transfer process in a fin.

In general, the authors consider Equation (1) subjected to the following boundary conditions:

$$\begin{array}{l} T = T_S\ at\ x = x_0 \\ -k\frac{dT}{dx} = \overline{h}(T - T_\infty)\ at\ x = x_L,\ x_L = x_0 + L \end{array} \quad (5)$$

in which L is the fin length and, many times, the non-negative constant $\overline{h}$ is assumed to be zero (insulated tip).

In the current literature, the first condition in Equation (5) (a Dirichlet boundary condition) represents the temperature of the surface on which the fin is installed. Nevertheless, the temperature T_S is not the fin temperature at position $x = x_0$, as there is a contact resistance between the fin and the surface on which the fin is placed. The Dirichlet boundary condition is a limiting case in which the contact resistance is zero (ideal case).

The adequate boundary condition at $x = x_0$ is a Robin boundary condition considering the thermal resistance between the fin and the surface. In other words, instead of Equation (5), the following boundary conditions will be considered:

$$\begin{array}{l} k\frac{dT}{dx} = \gamma(T - T_S)\ at\ x = x_0 \\ -k\frac{dT}{dx} = \overline{h}(T - T_\infty)\ at\ x = x_L,\ x_L = x_0 + L \end{array} \quad (6)$$

The positive constant γ is the inverse of the thermal resistance. When $\gamma \to \infty$ (zero resistance), there is a Dirichlet boundary condition at $x = x_0$.

The resulting problem may be expressed as follows:

$$\begin{array}{l} \frac{d}{dx}\left(k\,A\frac{dT}{dx}\right) - p\,f = 0,\ for\ x_0 < x < x_L,\ A = \widetilde{A}(x),\ p = \widetilde{p}(x),\ f = \hat{f}(T) \\ k\frac{dT}{dx} = \gamma(T - T_S),\ at\ x = x_0 \\ -k\frac{dT}{dx} = \overline{h}(T - T_\infty),\ at\ x = x_L,\ x_L = x_0 + L \end{array} \quad (7)$$

where T_S represents the temperature of the surface (where the fin is placed).

The heat (per unit time) exchanged between the fin and the environment is given by:

$$Q = \left[-kA\frac{dT}{dx}\right]_{x=x_0} = [\gamma A(T_S - T)]_{x=x_0} \quad (8)$$

Furthermore, as shown later, this heat transfer is strongly affected by the contact thermal resistance at the base. The actual temperature at the base of the fin, denoted by T_0, is obtained from Equation (8) after calculating Q, as follows:

$$T_0 = T_S - \frac{Q}{\gamma A} \quad (9)$$

When $\overline{h} \to 0$, an insulated tip is characterized. The most common description for fins considers $\overline{h} \to 0$ and $\gamma \to \infty$. In other words, the most common description assumes a Dirichlet boundary condition at $x = x_0$ and a Neumann boundary condition at $x = x_L$.

It is essential to note that the insulated tip hypothesis ($\overline{h} = 0$) is a conservative approach, as it gives rise to a heat exchange that is smaller than the actual one.

The Appendix presents a linear case's complete (exact) solution, representing a solid cylindrical fin, including the mentioned limiting cases.

3. Variational Formulation

Equation (7) is equivalent to the minimization of the functional $I[w]$, defined as:

$$I[w] = \int_{x_0}^{x_L}\left\{\frac{kA}{2}\left(\frac{dw}{dx}\right)^2 + p\int_0^w \hat{f}(\xi)d\xi\right\}dx + \frac{\gamma}{2}\left[A(w - T_S)^2\right]_{x=x_0} + \frac{\overline{h}}{2}\left[A(w - T_\infty)^2\right]_{x=x_L} \quad (10)$$

In other words, the function T solution of Equation (7) is such that $I[w] \geq I[T]$ for any admissible field w [14].

In order to demonstrate the equivalence between the solution of Equation (7) and the minimization of $I[w]$, the admissible functions w are defined as follows:

$$w = T + \varepsilon\eta \quad (11)$$

in which ε is a parameter and the function η is an admissible but arbitrary variation [14]. Hence, the functional $I[w]$ can be rewritten as follows:

$$\begin{array}{l} I[w] = \int_{x_0}^{x_L}\left\{\frac{kA}{2}\left(\frac{d(T+\varepsilon\eta)}{dx}\right)^2 + p\int_0^{T+\varepsilon\eta}\hat{f}(\xi)d\xi\right\}dx \\ \quad +\frac{1}{2}\gamma\left[A(T + \varepsilon\eta - T_S)^2\right]_{x=x_0} + \frac{1}{2}\overline{h}\left[A(T + \varepsilon\eta - T_\infty)^2\right]_{x=x_L} \end{array} \quad (12)$$

In order to show that $w = T$ corresponds to an extremum of $I[w]$, let us calculate the derivative with respect to ε, for $\varepsilon = 0$, equaling the result to zero for any η. The derivative of $I[w]$ is given by:

$$\begin{aligned}\frac{d}{d\varepsilon}\{I[w]\} &= \frac{d}{d\varepsilon}\int_{x_0}^{x_L}\left\{\frac{kA}{2}\left(\frac{d(T+\varepsilon\eta)}{dx}\right)^2 + p\int_0^{T+\varepsilon\eta}\hat{f}(\xi)d\xi\right\}dx \\ &\quad +\frac{1}{2}\gamma\left[A\frac{d}{d\varepsilon}(T+\varepsilon\eta-T_S)^2\right]_{x=x_0} + \frac{1}{2}\overline{h}\left[A\frac{d}{d\varepsilon}(T+\varepsilon\eta-T_\infty)^2\right]_{x=x_L} \\ &= \int_{x_0}^{x_L}\left\{kA\left(\frac{d(T+\varepsilon\eta)}{dx}\right)\frac{d\eta}{dx} + \eta p\hat{f}(T+\varepsilon\eta)\right\}dx \\ &\quad +\gamma[A\eta(T+\varepsilon\eta-T_S)]_{x=x_0} + \overline{h}[A\eta(T+\varepsilon\eta-T_\infty)]_{x=x_L}\end{aligned} \tag{13}$$

So, when $\varepsilon = 0$, this yields:

$$\left[\frac{d}{d\varepsilon}I[w]\right]_{\varepsilon=0} = \int_{x_0}^{x_L}\left\{kA\left(\frac{dT}{dx}\right)\frac{d\eta}{dx} + \eta p\hat{f}(T)\right\}dx + \gamma[A\eta(T-T_S)]_{x=x_0} + \overline{h}[A\eta(T-T_\infty)]_{x=x_L} \tag{14}$$

Because [15]:

$$A\left(\frac{dT}{dx}\right)\frac{d\eta}{dx} = \frac{d}{dx}\left(\eta A\frac{dT}{dx}\right) - \eta\frac{d}{dx}\left(A\frac{dT}{dx}\right) \tag{15}$$

It becomes:

$$\begin{aligned}&\left[\frac{d}{d\varepsilon}\{I[w]\}\right]_{\varepsilon=0} = \int_{x_0}^{x_L}\left\{\frac{d}{dx}\left(\eta kA\frac{dT}{dx}\right) - \eta\frac{d}{dx}\left(kA\frac{dT}{dx}\right) + \eta p\hat{f}(T)\right\}dx \\ &+\gamma[\eta(T-T_S)]_{x=x_0} + \overline{h}[\eta(T-T_\infty)]_{x=x_L} = -\int_{x_0}^{x_L}\left\{\frac{d}{dx}\left(kA\frac{dT}{dx}\right) - p\hat{f}(T)\right\}\eta dx \\ &+\left[\eta kA\frac{dT}{dx}\right]_{x=x_L} - \left[\eta kA\frac{dT}{dx}\right]_{x=x_0} + \gamma[A\eta(T-T_S)]_{x=x_0} + \overline{h}[A\eta(T-T_\infty)]_{x=x_L}\end{aligned} \tag{16}$$

Therefore, to ensure that the derivative of $I[w]$ is zero at $\varepsilon = 0$ (corresponding to the first variation of $I[w]$), taking into account that the function η is arbitrary, Equation (17) must take place [14]:

$$\begin{aligned}&\frac{d}{dx}\left(kA\frac{dT}{dx}\right) - p\hat{f}(T) = 0 \rightarrow \textit{Euler} - \textit{Lagrange equation} \\ &-\left[kA\frac{dT}{dx}\right]_{x=x_0} + \gamma[A(T-T_S)]_{x=x_0} = 0 \rightarrow \textit{natural boundary condition at } x = x_0 \\ &\left[kA\frac{dT}{dx}\right]_{x=x_L} + \overline{h}[A(T-T_\infty)]_{x=x_L} = 0 \rightarrow \textit{natural boundary condition at } x = x_L\end{aligned} \tag{17}$$

It is important to remark that Equation (17) corresponds exactly to Equation (7).

The existence of the functional defined in (10) is a powerful tool for reaching numerical approximations.

4. Existence and Uniqueness

Calculating the second derivative of $I[w]$ with respect to ε, the following equation is obtained:

$$\begin{aligned}\frac{d^2}{d\varepsilon^2}\{I[w]\} &= \frac{d}{d\varepsilon}\int_{x_0}^{x_L}\left\{kA\left(\frac{d(T+\varepsilon\eta)}{dx}\right)\frac{d\eta}{dx} + \eta p\hat{f}(T+\varepsilon\eta)\right\}dx \\ &= \int_{x_0}^{x_L}\left\{kA\left(\frac{d\eta}{dx}\right)^2 + \eta^2 p\frac{df}{dw}\right\}dx\end{aligned} \tag{18}$$

Because f is an increasing function of T, the second derivative of $I[w]$ is positive-valued for any η different from zero. Consequently, $I[w]$ is a strictly convex functional, and its extremum (if it exists) is a minimum and unique.

Now, to show the existence of the minimum, it is sufficient to demonstrate the coerciveness of $I[w]$. The coerciveness can be ensured provided that [16]:

$$\lim_{\lambda\to\infty}\frac{I[\lambda w]}{\lambda}=+\infty,\ \|w\|=1 \tag{19}$$

in which the norm $\|w\|$ is defined as (Sobolev space $H^1(x_1,x_2)$ [17]):

$$\|w\|=\int_{x_0}^{x_L}\left\{\left(\frac{dw}{dx}\right)^2+w^2\right\}^{1/2}dx \tag{20}$$

Evaluating the limit, the following equation is achieved:

$$\begin{aligned}\lim_{\lambda\to\infty}\tfrac{I[\lambda w]}{\lambda}=&\lim_{\lambda\to\infty}\int_{x_0}^{x_L}\left\{\lambda\tfrac{kA}{2}\left(\tfrac{dw}{dx}\right)^2+\tfrac{1}{\lambda}p\int_0^{\lambda w}\hat{f}(\xi)d\xi\right\}dx\\&+\lim_{\lambda\to\infty}\left\{\tfrac{1}{2\lambda}\gamma\left[A(\lambda w-T_S)^2\right]_{x=x_0}+\tfrac{1}{2\lambda}\overline{h}\left[A(\lambda w-T_\infty)^2\right]_{x=x_L}\right\}\end{aligned} \tag{21}$$

Because $\hat{f}(\xi)$ is a strictly increasing function of ξ, there exist two constants a and b such that:

$$\int_0^T\hat{f}(\xi)d\xi>aT+b \tag{22}$$

Therefore, it may be concluded that there exists a constant C such that:

$$\lim_{\lambda\to\infty}\frac{1}{\lambda}p\int_0^{\lambda w}\hat{f}(\xi)d\xi>C \tag{23}$$

Hence,

$$\begin{aligned}&\lim_{\lambda\to\infty}\int_{x_0}^{x_L}\left\{\lambda\tfrac{kA}{2}\left(\tfrac{dw}{dx}\right)^2+\tfrac{1}{\lambda}p\int_0^{\lambda w}\hat{f}(\xi)d\xi\right\}dx\\&+\lim_{\lambda\to\infty}\left\{\tfrac{1}{2\lambda}\gamma\left[A(\lambda w-T_S)^2\right]_{x=x_0}+\tfrac{1}{2\lambda}\overline{h}\left[A(\lambda w-T_\infty)^2\right]_{x=x_L}\right\}=+\infty\end{aligned} \tag{24}$$

Therefore, the functional is coercive [16]. This coerciveness ensures the existence of the minimum. Because the minimum for the solution to the original problem (Equation (7)) was obtained, the solution's existence was ensured [16].

5. An Example: Longitudinal Trapezoidal Fin

In addition to the classical solid cylindrical fin (with the constant area and perimeter—see Appendix A) that exchanges energy following Newton's law of cooling (the case in which $f=h(T-T_\infty)$), other interesting situations could be considered, such as, for instance, the longitudinal trapezoidal fin with width W, illustrated in Figure 3.

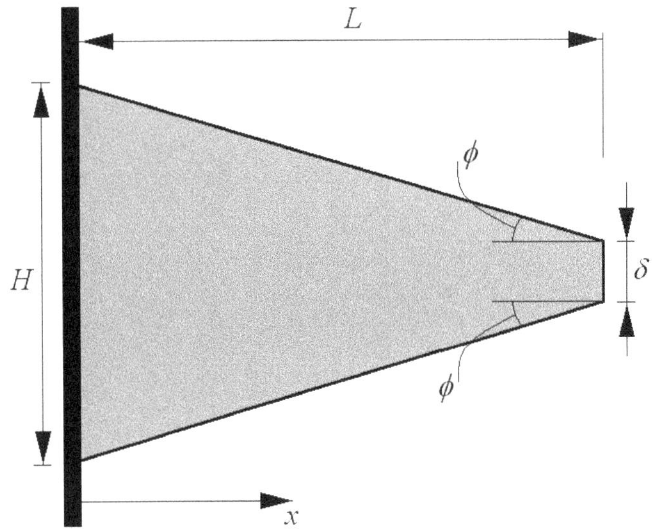

Figure 3. Lateral view of a longitudinal trapezoidal fin with width W.

In this case, p and A are defined as:

$$\begin{aligned} p &= \tfrac{d}{dx}A_S = 2W\sqrt{1+\left(\tfrac{H-\delta}{2L}\right)^2} + 2\left(H - \tfrac{x}{L}(H-\delta)\right) \\ A &= W\left(H - \tfrac{H-\delta}{L}x\right) \end{aligned} \tag{25}$$

and, therefore, the differential equation becomes:

$$\frac{d}{dx}\left(kW\left(H-\frac{H-\delta}{L}x\right)\frac{dT}{dx}\right) - \left(2W\sqrt{1+\left(\frac{H-\delta}{2L}\right)^2} + 2\left(H-\frac{H-\delta}{L}x\right)\right)f = 0,\ 0<x<L \tag{26}$$

Clearly, when $H=\delta$, a cylindrical fin is characterized (in which p and A are constants).

Now, the fin will be considered black, with a constant thermal conductivity, surrounded by an atmosphere-free space, and with an insulated tip. Following these hypotheses, only thermal conduction and thermal radiation are present. Under these assumptions, the process will be described as follows:

$$\begin{aligned} & k\tfrac{d}{dx}\left(W\left(H-\tfrac{H-\delta}{L}x\right)\tfrac{dT}{dx}\right) \\ & \quad -\left(2W\sqrt{1+\left(\tfrac{H-\delta}{2L}\right)^2} + 2\left(H-\tfrac{H-\delta}{L}x\right)\right)\sigma|T|^3T = 0,\ 0<x<L \\ & k\tfrac{dT}{dx} = \gamma(T-T_S)\ at\ x=0 \\ & \tfrac{dT}{dx} = 0\ at\ x=L \end{aligned} \tag{27}$$

In which σ is the classical Stefan–Boltzmann constant [18–20].

In this case, the functional $I[w]$ becomes:

$$\begin{aligned} I[w] &= \int_0^L \left\{\tfrac{kW}{2}\left(H-\tfrac{H-\delta}{L}x\right)\left(\tfrac{dw}{dx}\right)^2\right\}dx \\ &+ \int_0^L \left\{\left(2W\sqrt{1+\left(\tfrac{H-\delta}{2L}\right)^2} + 2\left(H-\tfrac{H-\delta}{L}x\right)\right)\sigma\tfrac{|w|^5}{5}\right\}dx + \tfrac{\gamma}{2}\left[HW(w-T_S)^2\right]_{x=0} \end{aligned} \tag{28}$$

Equation (27) may be conveniently rewritten in a dimensionless form as:

$$\begin{aligned}&\tfrac{d}{dX}\left(\tfrac{WH}{L^2}\left(1-\tfrac{H-\delta}{H}X\right)\tfrac{d\theta}{dX}\right)\\&\quad-\left(2\sqrt{1+\left(\tfrac{H-\delta}{2L}\right)^2}+2\tfrac{H}{W}\left(1-\tfrac{H-\delta}{H}X\right)\right)\tfrac{W\sigma T_S^3}{k}|\theta|^3\theta=0,\ 0<X<1\\&\tfrac{d\theta}{dX}=\tfrac{\gamma L}{k}(\theta-1)\ at\ X=0\\&\tfrac{d\theta}{dX}=0\ at\ X=1\end{aligned}\tag{29}$$

in which the following dimensionless position and temperature are defined:

$$\begin{aligned}X&=\tfrac{x}{L}\\\theta&=\tfrac{T}{T_S}\end{aligned}\tag{30}$$

Hence the functional $I[w]$ presented in Equation (28) can be written as:

$$\begin{aligned}I[w]&=\int_0^1\left\{\tfrac{WH}{2L^2}\left(1-\tfrac{H-\delta}{H}X\right)\left(\tfrac{dw}{dX}\right)^2\right\}dX\\&+\int_0^1\left\{\left(2\sqrt{1+\left(\tfrac{H-\delta}{2L}\right)^2}+2\tfrac{H}{W}\left(1-\tfrac{H-\delta}{H}X\right)\right)\tfrac{W\sigma T_S^3}{5k}|w|^5\right\}dX+\tfrac{\gamma HW}{2kL}\left[(w-1)^2\right]_{X=0}\end{aligned}\tag{31}$$

At this point, the following approximation for the solution θ is considered:

$$\theta=(\theta_{i+1}-\theta_i)\frac{X-X_i}{X_{i+1}-X_i}+\theta_i,\ i=1,2,\ldots,N,\ X_i\le X\le X_{i+1}\tag{32}$$

in which the constants θ_i are those obtained from the minimization of the functional defined in Equation (31). In other words, the constants θ_i are obtained from the following system:

$$\begin{aligned}&\tfrac{5kH}{4\sigma L^2T_S^3}\tfrac{\partial}{\partial\theta_j}\left(\sum_{i=1}^N\int_{X_i}^{X_{i+1}}\left\{\left(1-\tfrac{H-\delta}{H}X\right)\left(\tfrac{\theta_{i+1}-\theta_i}{X_{i+1}-X_i}\right)^2\right\}dX\right)+\tfrac{5\gamma H}{4L\sigma T_S^3}\left(\tfrac{\partial}{\partial\theta_j}(\theta_1-1)^2\right)\\&+\tfrac{\partial}{\partial\theta_j}\sum_{i=1}^N\int_{X_i}^{X_{i+1}}\left\{\left(\sqrt{1+\left(\tfrac{H-\delta}{2L}\right)^2}+\tfrac{H}{W}\left(1-\tfrac{H-\delta}{H}X\right)\right)\left|(\theta_{i+1}-\theta_i)\tfrac{X-X_i}{X_{i+1}-X_i}+\theta_i\right|^5\right\}dX=0\\&j=1,2,3,\ldots,N,N+1.\end{aligned}\tag{33}$$

in which:

$$\frac{5kH}{4\sigma L^2T_S^3}=\frac{5}{4}\frac{\left(\frac{W}{L}\right)\left(\frac{H}{L}\right)}{\left(\frac{\sigma T_S^3W}{k}\right)}\ \text{and}\ \frac{5\gamma H}{4L\sigma T_S^3}=\frac{5}{4}\frac{\left(\frac{\gamma L}{k}\right)\left(\frac{W}{L}\right)\left(\frac{H}{L}\right)}{\left(\frac{\sigma T_S^3W}{k}\right)}\tag{34}$$

Figures 4 and 5 present some results obtained with $N=100$, considering $X_{i+1}-X_i=\Delta x=\text{constant}=1/N$, illustrating the effect of the contact resistance and the effect of the thermal conductivity.

In both figures, distinct values of the geometric parameters L/H, δ/H, and W/H and of the parameter associated with radiation and conduction, $\sigma T_S^3W/k$, are considered. Figures 4 and 5 show the effect of varying the dimensionless thermal resistance inverse $\gamma L/k$ from 0.1 to 1000.0, along with the distinct geometric parameters and the parameter associated with radiation and conduction. Regardless of the chosen values for the geometric parameters and the parameter associated with radiation and conduction, in both figures the higher the thermal resistance, the smaller the fin's base temperature and the temperature along the fin.

The case of the red continuous line (corresponding to $\gamma L/k=1000.0$) denotes practically a Dirichlet boundary condition ($\theta=1$ at $X=0$).

The main factor leading to smaller temperatures as shown in Figure 5, compared with those shown in Figure 4, is the parameter associated with radiation and conduction, given by $\sigma T_S^3 W/k = 50.0$ in the former and $\sigma T_S^3 W/k = 1.0$ in the latter.

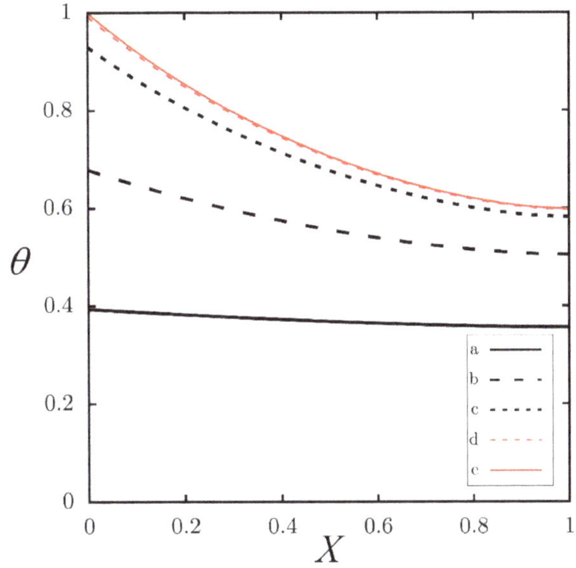

Figure 4. θ *vs* X with $L/H = 3.0$, $\delta/H = 0.2$, $W/H = 1.0$, $\sigma T_S^3 W/k = 1.0$ and five values of $\gamma L/k$ ($a \rightarrow \gamma L/k = 0.1$, $b \rightarrow \gamma L/k = 1.0$, $c \rightarrow \gamma L/k = 10.0$, $d \rightarrow \gamma L/k = 100.0$ and $e \rightarrow \gamma L/k = 1000.0$).

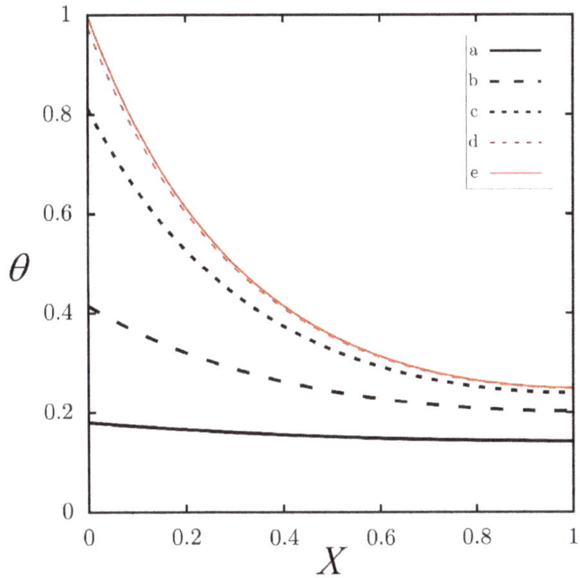

Figure 5. θ *vs* X with $L/H = 200.0$, $\delta/H = 0.4$, $W/H = 1.0$, $\sigma T_S^3 W/k = 50.0$ and five values of $\gamma L/k$ ($a \rightarrow \gamma L/k = 0.1$, $b \rightarrow \gamma L/k = 1.0$, $c \rightarrow \gamma L/k = 10.0$, $d \rightarrow \gamma L/k = 100.0$ and $e \rightarrow \gamma L/k = 1000.0$).

When comparing this methodology to others, the main advantage of this method is the equivalence between a minimum principle and the original problem. This equivalence provides a convenient tool for carrying out numerical simulations by means of a minimization process.

6. Conclusions

The thermal resistance present in real engineering problems involving fins accounts for the different temperatures of the surface (in which the fin is installed) and the temperature of the fin's base. This work studied this problem—namely, a heat-transfer problem with the Robin boundary condition at the fin's base. This article presented a general mathematical model that may involve convection and radiation and proposed an equivalent minimum principle.

A convex and coercive functional represents this minimum principle, ensuring the solution's existence and uniqueness.

It is essential to notice that the formulation developed in this work allows a simplified treatment of realistic heat-transfer problems, because real problems involve thermal resistance between the surface and the fin's base. In addition, this proposed minimum principle involves solely natural boundary conditions. In a broad sense, the Dirichlet boundary condition could be considered a limit of the Robin boundary condition when $\gamma \to \infty$ (zero thermal resistance). When only natural boundary conditions are considered, the space of functions needs no restriction on the boundaries.

As an example, the proposed functional was employed to study the heat transfer in a longitudinal trapezoidal fin, accounting for thermal resistance at the fin's base. This problem accounted for thermal radiation (non-participant environment and black body assumption). It was simulated using piecewise linear approximations.

The Appendix presents an exact closed solution for a solid cylindrical fin.

Author Contributions: Conceptualization, R.M.S.d.G. and M.L.M.-C.; methodology, R.M.S.d.G.; software, R.P.S.d.G.; validation, R.M.S.d.G. and V.V.S.; formal analysis, R.M.S.d.G. and M.L.M.-C.; writing—original draft preparation, R.M.S.d.G. and M.L.M.-C.; writing—review and editing, R.M.S.d.G. and M.L.M.-C.; supervision, R.M.S.d.G. and M.L.M.-C.; funding acquisition, R.M.S.d.G. All authors have read and agreed to the published version of the manuscript.

Funding: This research was funded by CNPq grant number [306364/2018-1] and by Brazilian Agency CAPES (finance code 001).

Data Availability Statement: Not applicable.

Conflicts of Interest: The authors declare no conflict of interest.

Appendix A. An Exact Solution

When Equation (2) holds, the problem represented by Equation (7) becomes:

$$
\begin{aligned}
&\frac{d}{dx}\left(k\,A\frac{dT}{dx}\right) - p\,h(T - T_\infty) = 0,\ for\ x_0 < x < x_L \\
&k\frac{dT}{dx} = \gamma(T - T_S),\ at\ x = x_0 \\
&-k\frac{dT}{dx} = \overline{h}(T - T_\infty),\ at\ x = x_L,\ x_L = x_0 + L
\end{aligned}
\tag{A1}
$$

and admits the exact solution:

$$
\begin{aligned}
T = T_\infty + (T_S - T_\infty)&\left\{\frac{\frac{\overline{h}}{k}\tanh(mL) + m}{m\left\{\frac{mk}{\gamma}\tanh(mL)\right\} + \frac{\overline{h}}{k}\left(\frac{mk}{\gamma}\right) + \frac{\overline{h}}{k}\tanh(mL) + m}\right\}\cosh(m(x - x_0)) \\
+(T_S - T_\infty)&\left\{\frac{-\left(\frac{\overline{h}}{k\tanh(mL)} + m\right)\tanh(mL)}{m\left\{\frac{mk}{\gamma}\tanh(mL)\right\} + \frac{\overline{h}}{k}\left(\frac{mk}{\gamma}\right) + \frac{\overline{h}}{k}\tanh(mL) + m}\right\}\sinh(m(x - x_0))
\end{aligned}
\tag{A2}
$$

in which $m = \sqrt{hp/(kA)}$.

The heat (per unit time) exchanged between the fin and the environment, in this case, is given by:

$$Q = \left[-kA\frac{dT}{dx} \right]_{x=x_0} \tag{A3}$$

The contact thermal resistance at the base strongly affects this heat exchange.
Taking into account (A2), Equation (A3) gives rise to:

$$Q = \left[-kA\frac{dT}{dx} \right]_{x=x_0} = kA(T_S - T_\infty)\left\{ \frac{m\left(\frac{\bar{h}}{k\tanh(mL)} + m\right)\tanh(mL)}{m\left\{\frac{mk}{\gamma}\tanh(mL)\right\} + \frac{\bar{h}}{k}\left(\frac{mk}{\gamma}\right) + \frac{\bar{h}}{k}\tanh(mL) + m} \right\} \tag{A4}$$

The temperature at the base of the fin, denoted by T_0, is obtained from:

$$Q = \left[-kA\frac{dT}{dx} \right]_{x=x_0} = \gamma A(T_S - T_0) \tag{A5}$$

and is given by:

$$T_0 = T_S - \frac{Q}{\gamma A} = T_S - \frac{k}{\gamma}(T_S - T_\infty)\left\{ \frac{m\left(\frac{\bar{h}}{k\tanh(mL)} + m\right)\tanh(mL)}{m\left\{\frac{mk}{\gamma}\tanh(mL)\right\} + \frac{\bar{h}}{k}\left(\frac{mk}{\gamma}\right) + \frac{\bar{h}}{k}\tanh(mL) + m} \right\} \tag{A6}$$

In order to illustrate this influence, the case with the fin insulated at the tip is considered. In such case $\bar{h} \to 0$, and (A2) reduces to:

$$T = T_\infty + \frac{\gamma(T_S - T_\infty)}{mk\tanh(mL) + \gamma}\{\cosh(m(x - x_0)) - \tanh(mL)\sinh(m(x - x_0))\} \tag{A7}$$

In the classical literature, Equation (A1) is solved assuming $\gamma \to \infty$ (no thermal resistance at the base). When $\gamma \to \infty$, the solution reduces to:

$$\begin{aligned} T = {} & T_\infty + (T_S - T_\infty)\cosh(m(x - x_0)) \\ & + (T_S - T_\infty)\left\{ \frac{-\left(\frac{1}{\tanh(mL)} + \frac{mk}{\bar{h}}\right)\tanh(mL)}{\tanh(mL) + \frac{mk}{\bar{h}}} \right\}\sinh(m(x - x_0)) \end{aligned} \tag{A8}$$

and, consequently, $T_0 = T_S$.

When, in addition to $\gamma \to \infty$, it is supposed that $\bar{h} \to 0$ (insulated tip), the solution reduces to one of the most known results in heat transfer, given by:

$$T = T_\infty + (T_S - T_\infty)\{\cosh(m(x - x_0)) - \tanh(mL)\sinh(m(x - x_0))\} \tag{A9}$$

In this case, the heat flux is given by:

$$Q = \left[-kA\frac{dT}{dx} \right]_{x=x_0} = (T_S - T_\infty)\sqrt{hpkA}\tanh\left(\sqrt{\frac{hp}{kA}}L\right) \tag{A10}$$

When, in addition to $\gamma \to \infty$, it is assumed that $\bar{h} \to \infty$ (prescribed temperature at $x = x_L$),the following temperature is obtained:

$$T = T_\infty + (T_S - T_\infty)\left\{ \cosh(m(x - x_0)) - \frac{1}{\tanh(mL)}\sinh(m(x - x_0)) \right\} \tag{A11}$$

and the heat flux is given by:

$$Q = \left[-kA\frac{dT}{dx} \right]_{x=x_0} = (T_S - T_\infty)\sqrt{hpkA}\left(\tanh\left(\sqrt{\frac{hp}{kA}}L\right)\right)^{-1} \tag{A12}$$

Equations (A9)–(A12) represent classical results (found in most heat-transfer books [1–4]). For very long fins (i.e., $\tanh(mL) \cong 1$), it becomes:

$$T = T_\infty + (T_S - T_\infty)\left\{\frac{\gamma}{mk+\gamma}\right\}\exp(-m(x-x_0)) \tag{A13}$$

and:

$$Q = \left[-kA\frac{dT}{dx}\right]_{x=x_0} = (T_S - T_\infty)\left\{\frac{\gamma}{mk+\gamma}\right\}\sqrt{hpkA} \tag{A14}$$

References

1. Holman, J.P. *Heat Transfer*, 10th ed.; McGraw-Hill: New York, NY, USA, 2009.
2. Kreith, F.; Manglik, R.M. *Principles of Heat Transfer*, 8th ed.; CENGAGE Learning: Boston, MA, USA, 2016.
3. Incropera, F.P.; Dewitt, D.P.; Bergmann, T.L.; Lavine, A.S. *Fundamentals of Heat and Mass Transfer*, 6th ed.; Thermal Contact Resistance; John Wiley: Hoboken, NJ, USA, 2007; pp. 101–103.
4. John, H.; Lienhard, I.V. *A Heat Transfer Textbook*, 5th ed.; Phlogiston Press: Cambridge, MA, USA, 2020.
5. Yovanovich, M.M. Conduction and Thermal Contact Resistances (Conductances). In *Handbook of Heat Transfer*; Rohsenow, W.M., Hartnett, J.P., Cho, Y.I., Eds.; McGraw-Hill: New York, NY, USA, 1998; pp. 3.1–3.73.
6. Aziz, A.; Beers-Green, A.B. Performance and optimum design of convective–radiative rectangular fin with convective base heating, wall conduction resistance, and contact resistance between the wall and the fin base. *Energy Convers. Manag.* **2009**, *50*, 2622–2631. [CrossRef]
7. Xie, Z.; Chen, L.; Sun, F. Comparative study on constructal optimizations of T-shaped fin based on entransy dissipation rate minimization and maximum thermal resistance minimization. *Sci. China Technol. Sci.* **2011**, *54*, 1249–1258. [CrossRef]
8. Taler, D.; Oclón, P. Thermal contact resistance in plate fin-and-tube heat exchangers, determined by experimental data and CFD simulations. *Int. J. Therm. Sci.* **2014**, *84*, 309–322. [CrossRef]
9. Milman, O.O.; Yankov, G.G.; Kondratev, A.V.; Ptakhin, A.V.; Krylov, V.S.; Korlyakova, E.J.; Zhilin, A.E. Approximate estimation of the thermal resistance of the terms in the process of heat transfer through the finned wall. *J. Physics: Conf. Ser.* **2017**, *891*, 012137. [CrossRef]
10. Kiwan, S.; Al-Nimr, M.A. Using porous fins for heat transferenhancement. *J. Heat Transf.* **2001**, *123*, 790–795. [CrossRef]
11. Martins-Costa, M.L.; Vendas Sarmento, V.; Morares de Lira, A.; Gama, R.M.S. Temperature distribution in porous fins, subjected to convection and radiation, obtained from the minimization of a convex functional. *Mathem. Problems. Engng.* **2020**, *2020*, 8613717. [CrossRef]
12. Martins-Costa, M.L.; Vendas Sarmento, V.; Saldanha da Gama, R.P.; Saldanha da Gama, R.M. Solution construction for the nonlinear heat transfer problem in a cylindrical porous fin. *J. Porous Media* **2022**, *25*, 1–19. [CrossRef]
13. Gorla, R.S.R.; Bakier, A. Thermal analysis of natural convection and radiation in porous fins. *Int. Commun. Heat Mass Transf.* **2011**, *38*, 638–645. [CrossRef]
14. Sagan, H. *Introduction to the Calculus of Variations*; Dover: New York, NY, USA, 1992.
15. Wylie, C.R. *Advanced Engineering Mathematics*; McGraw-Hill Kogakusha: Tokyo, Japan, 1975.
16. Berger, M.S. *Nonlinearity & Functional Analysis: Lectures on Nonlinear Problems in Mathematical Analysis*; Academic Press: London, UK, 1977.
17. Adams, R.A. *Sobolev Spaces*; Academic Press: New York, NY, USA, 1975.
18. Sparrow, E.M.; Cess, R.D. *Radiation Heat Transfer*; McGraw-Hill: New York, NY, USA, 1978.
19. Gama, R.M.S. An Alternative Mathematical Modelling for Coupled Conduction/Radiation Energy Transfer Phenomenon in a System of Gray Bodies Surrounded by a Vacuum. *Int. J. Non-Linear Mech.* **1995**, *30*, 433–447. [CrossRef]
20. Gama, R.M.S. Simulation of the steady-state energy transfer in rigid bodies, with convective/radiative boundary conditions, employing a minimum principle. *J. Comput. Phys. New York* **1992**, *99*, 310–320. [CrossRef]

axioms

Article

Hyers Stability in Generalized Intuitionistic P-Pseudo Fuzzy 2-Normed Spaces

Ehsan Movahednia [1,*] and Manuel De la Sen [2,*]

[1] Department of Mathematics, Behbahan Khatam Alanbia University of Technology, Behbahan 6361663973, Iran
[2] Department of Electricity and Electronics, Institute of Research and Development of Processes, University of Basque Country, Campus of Leioa (Bizkaia), 48080 Bilbao, Spain
* Correspondence: movahednia@bkatu.ac.ir (E.M.); manuel.delasen@ehu.eus (M.D.l.S.)

Abstract: In this article, we defined the generalized intuitionistic P-pseudo fuzzy 2-normed spaces and investigated the Hyers stability of m-mappings in this space. The m-mappings are interesting functional equations; these functional equations are additive for $m = 1$, quadratic for $m = 2$, cubic for $m = 3$, and quartic for $m = 4$. We have investigated the stability of four types of functional equations in generalized intuitionistic P-pseudo fuzzy 2-normed spaces by the fixed point method.

Keywords: intuitionistic fuzzy 2-normed space; Hyers–Ulam–Rassias stability; fuzzy mathematics

MSC: 39B82; 39B52; 46S40; 47H10

Citation: Movahednia, E.; De la Sen, M. Hyers Stability in Generalized Intuitionistic P-Pseudo Fuzzy 2-Normed Spaces. *Axioms* **2023**, *12*, 28. https://doi.org/10.3390/axioms12010028

Academic Editor: Clemente Cesarano

Received: 27 November 2022
Revised: 16 December 2022
Accepted: 19 December 2022
Published: 26 December 2022

1. Introduction

Functional equations generalize the subject of a modern branch of mathematics. The first articles in the field of functional equations were published by J. D'Alembert during 1747–1750. The apparent simplicity and harmonic nature have caused the subject of functional equations to be studied by many mathematicians. In the fall of 1940, Ulam [1] presented several unsolved problems in his famous speech at the University of Wisconsin. This lecture became the starting point for the theory of stability of functional equations. The question raised by Ulam was as follows: When is it true that a function which approximately satisfies a functional equation D must be close to an exact solution of D? If the problem admits a solution, we say that equation D is stable.

Ulam's problem was solved by Hyers [2] for additive mappings in 1941, and Hyers's results were generalized by Rassias [3] for linear mappings by various control functions. The results of Rassias had a great impact on the issue of the stability of functional equations. Today this type of stability is called the Hyers–Ulam–Rassias stability.

Mathematicians have proposed and proved many other theorems in the field of stability by changing the type of functional equation, control function, and space in the above theorem. In some of the articles in this field, the control function ϵ has been replaced by another function, and the stability theorem has been re-examined with new conditions. Similarly, by changing the type of functional equation in the above theorem from additive to quadratic, cubic, Jensen, etc., or replacing the functional equation with a differential or integral equation, the conditions of the stability theorem have been investigated and proven. We refer readers to [4–13] references for consideration of the stability of various functional equations in different spaces.

L. Zadeh [14] proposed the concept of fuzzy sets in 1965. The fuzzy metric space was introduced by Kromosil and Michalek [15]. This space is a generalization of the probabilistic metric space. In 1986, Atanasos [16] founded the concept of intuitionistic fuzzy sets by developing fuzzy sets. The idea of intuitionistic fuzzy normed space by Saadati and Park [17] was introduced in 2006.

In 2012, Gordji et al. [4] introduced the following functional equation

$$f(ru+v)+f(ru-v) = r^{m-2}[f(u+v)+f(u-v)] \\ +2\left(r^2-1\right)\left[r^{m-2}f(u)+\frac{(m-2)(1-(m-2)^2)}{6}f(v)\right] \quad (1)$$

for every fixed integer r with $r \neq 0, \pm 1$. It is easily proven that $f(u) = cu^m (u \in \mathbb{R}, m = 1, 2, 3, 4)$ satisfies the functional Equation (1). More precisely, if $m = 1$, the functional Equation (1) is additive, if $m = 2$, then it is quadratic, if $m = 3, 4$, then it is the cubic and quartic functional equation, respectively. We call a solution of the functional Equation (1) m-mapping.

Theorem 1 ([18]). *If (Δ, d) is a complete generalized metric space and $\mathcal{Z} : \Delta \to \Delta$ is a strictly contractive mapping with Lipschitz constant $\kappa < 1$, then for each element $u \in \Delta$, either*

$$d(\mathcal{Z}^n u, \mathcal{Z}^{n+1} u) = +\infty,$$

for every non-negative integer n, or there exists a $n_0 \in \mathbb{Z}^+$ such that
(1) $d(\mathcal{Z}^n u, \mathcal{Z}^{n+1} u) < +\infty$ for every $n \geq n_0$;
(2) The sequence $\{\mathcal{Z}^n u\} \to v^*$, where v^* is a fixed point of $\mathcal{Z}$;
(3) v^* is the unique fixed point of $\mathcal{Z}$ in the set $V = \{v \in \Delta \mid d(\mathcal{Z}^{n_0} u, v) < +\infty\}$.
(4) $d(v, v^*) \leq \frac{1}{1-\kappa} d(v, \mathcal{Z}v)$ for every $v \in V$.

Let Δ be a linear space over the field $\mathcal{F}$ and $\bigstar$ be a continuous t-norm and $\blacklozenge$ be a continuous t-conorm, in the following; we define the concepts of fuzzy and anti-fuzzy 2-norm.

Definition 1 ([19]). *A fuzzy subset μ of $\Delta \times \Delta \times \mathbb{R}$ is said to be a fuzzy 2-norm on Δ if and only if for $u, v, w \in \Delta$, $p, q \in \mathbb{R}$, and $\alpha \in \mathcal{F}$ the following items hold.*
(FT1) $\mu(u, v, p) = 0$ if $p \leq 0$.
(FT2) $\mu(u, v, p) = 1$ if and only if u, v are linearly dependent for all $p > 0$.
(FT3) $\mu(u, v, p)$ is invariant under any permutation of u, v.
(FT4) $\mu(u, \alpha v, p) = \mu\left(u, v, \frac{p}{|\alpha|}\right)$, for all $p > 0$ and $\alpha \neq 0$.
(FT5) $\mu(u + w, v, p + q) \geq \mu(u, v, p) \bigstar \mu(w, v, q)$ for all $p, q > 0$.
(FT6) $\mu(u, v, .)$ is a non-decreasing function on $\mathbb{R}$ and

$$\lim_{p \to \infty} \mu(u, v, p) = 1.$$

In this case, the (Δ, μ) is said to be a fuzzy 2-normed space.

Example 1 ([19]). *Let $(\Delta, \|., .\|)$ be a 2-normed linear space. Define*

$$\mu(u, v, p) = \begin{cases} \frac{p}{p+\|u,v\|} & p > 0 \\ 0 & p \leq 0 \end{cases}$$

where $u, v \in \Delta$ and $p \in \mathbb{R}$. Then (Δ, μ) is a fuzzy 2-normed linear space.

Definition 2 ([20]). *A fuzzy subset ν of $\Delta \times \Delta \times \mathbb{R}$ is said to be an anti fuzzy 2-norm on Δ if and only if for all $u, v, w \in \Delta$, $p, q \in \mathbb{R}$ and $\alpha \in \mathcal{F}$, the following items hold.*
(FN1) $\nu(u, v, p) = 1$, for every $p \leq 0$.
(FN2) $\nu(u, v, p) = 0$ if and only if u, v are linearly dependent for all $p > 0$.
(FN3) $\nu(u, v, p)$ is invariant under any permutation of u, v.
(FN4) $\nu(u, \alpha v, p) = \nu\left(u, v, \frac{p}{|\alpha|}\right)$ for every $p > 0, \alpha \neq 0$.

(FN5) $\nu(u, v+w, p+q) \leq \nu(u, v, p) \blacklozenge \nu(u, w, q)$ for all $p, q > 0$.
(FN6) $\nu(u, v, .)$ is a non-increasing function and

$$\lim_{p \to \infty} \nu(u, v, p) = 0.$$

In this case, the (Δ, ν) is said to be an anti-fuzzy 2-normed linear space.

Example 2 ([20]). *Let $(\Delta, \|., .\|)$ be a 2-normed linear space. Define*

$$\nu(u, v, p) = \begin{cases} \frac{\|u,v\|}{p+\|u,v\|} & p > 0 \\ 1 & p \leq 0 \end{cases}$$

where $u, v \in \Delta$ and $p \in \mathbb{R}$. Then (Δ, ν) is an anti-fuzzy 2-normed linear space.

Lemma 1 ([20]). *We define the set Y^* and operation $\leq_{Y^*}$ by*

$$Y^* = \left\{(\sigma_1, \sigma_2) : (\sigma_1, \sigma_2) \in [0,1]^2 \text{ and } \sigma_1 + \sigma_2 \leq 1\right\}$$
$$(\sigma_1, \sigma_2) \leq_{Y^*} (\pi_1, \pi_2) \Longleftrightarrow \sigma_1 \leq \pi_1, \sigma_2 \geq \pi_2$$

for all $(\sigma_1, \sigma_2), (\pi_1, \pi_2) \in Y^*$. Then $(Y^*, \leq_{Y^*})$ is a complete lattice.

Definition 3 ([20]). *A continuous t-norm τ on $Y = [0,1]^2$ is said to be continuous t-representable if there is a continuous t-norm $\bigstar$ and a continuous t-conorm $\blacklozenge$ on $[0,1]$ such that, for every $\sigma = (\sigma_1, \sigma_2), \pi = (\pi_1, \pi_2) \in Y$*

$$\tau(\sigma, \pi) = (\sigma_1 \bigstar \pi_1, \sigma_2 \blacklozenge \pi_2)$$

2. Main Results

2.1. Generalized Intuitionistic P-Pseudo Fuzzy 2-Normed Space

In this section, we introduce generalized intuitionistic P-pseudo fuzzy 2-normed space, and then we investigate the stability of functional equations in this space.

Definition 4 ([8]). *Let Δ be a linear space over the field $\mathcal{F}$, μ and ν be a fuzzy 2-norm and anti fuzzy 2-norm, respectively, such that $\nu(u, v, p) + \mu(u, v, p) \leq 1$, τ is a continuous $t-$representable, and*

$$\rho_{\mu,\nu} : \Delta \times \Delta \times \mathbb{R} \to Y^*$$
$$\rho_{\mu,\nu}(u, v, p) = (\mu(u, v, p), \nu(u, v, p))$$

is a function satisfying the following condition for all $u, v, w \in \Delta$, $p, q \in \mathbb{R}$ and $\alpha \in \mathcal{F}$

(P1) $\rho_{\mu,\nu}(u, v, p) = (0, 1) = 0_{Y^*}$ for all $p \leq 0$.
(P2) $\rho_{\mu,\nu}(u, v, p) = (1, 0) = 1_{Y^*}$ if and only if u, v are linearly dependent for all $p > 0$.
(P3) $\rho_{\mu,\nu}(\alpha u, v, p) = \rho_{\mu,\nu}\left(u, v, \frac{p}{|\alpha|}\right)$ for all $p > 0$ and $\alpha \neq 0$.
(P4) $\rho_{\mu,\nu}(u, v, p)$ is invariant under any permutation of u, v.
(P5) $\rho_{\mu,\nu}(u+w, v, p+q) \geq_{Y^*} \tau(\rho_{\mu,\nu}(u, v, p), \rho_{\mu,\nu}(w, v, q))$ for all $p, q > 0$.
(P6) $\rho_{\mu,\nu}(u, v, .)$ is continuous and

$$\lim_{p \to 0} \rho_{\mu,v}(u, v, p) = 0_{Y^*} \quad \text{and} \quad \lim_{p \to \infty} \rho_{\mu,v}(u, v, p) = 1_{Y^*}$$

Then $\rho_{\mu,\nu}$ is said to be an intuitionistic fuzzy 2-norm on a linear space Δ, and the 3-tuple $(\Delta, \rho_{\mu,\nu}, \tau)$ is called to be an intuitionistic fuzzy 2-normed space (for short IF2NS).

Example 3. *Let* $(\Delta, \|.,.\|)$ *be a 2-normed space,*

$$\tau(r,s) = (r_1 s_1, \min(r_2 + s_2, 1))$$

be a continuous t-representable for all $r = (r_1, r_2), s = (s_1, s_2) \in \Upsilon^*$ *and* μ *be a fuzzy 2-norm and* ν *be an anti fuzzy 2-norm. We put*

$$\rho_{\mu,\nu}(u,v,p) = \left(\frac{p}{p + m\|u,v\|}, \frac{\|u,v\|}{p + m\|u,v\|}\right)$$

for all $p \in \mathbb{R}^+$ *in which* $m > 1$*. Then* $(\Delta, \rho_{\mu,\nu}, \tau)$ *is an IF2NS.*

Definition 5 ([8]). *A sequence* $\{u_n\}$ *in* $(\Delta, \rho_{\mu,\nu}, \tau)$ *is said to be convergent to a point* $u \in \Delta$*, if*

$$\lim_{n\to\infty} \rho_{\mu,\nu}(u_n - u, v, p) = 1_{\Upsilon^*} \quad (v \in \Delta)$$

for all $p > 0$*.*

Definition 6. *In Definition (4), we replace condition* $(P5)$ *with the following condition; in this case,* $(\Delta, \rho_{\mu,\nu}, \tau)$ *is called to be an intuitionistic pseudo fuzzy 2-normed space.*

$$(P5') \ \rho_{\mu,\nu}(u + w, v, K(p+q)) \geq_{\Upsilon^*} \tau(\rho_{\mu,\nu}(u,v,p), \rho_{\mu,\nu}(w,v,q))$$

for constant $K \geq 1$*.*

Definition 7. *The intuitionistic pseudo fuzzy 2-normed space* $(\Delta, \rho_{\mu,\nu}, \tau)$ *is called generalized intuitionistic P-pseudo fuzzy 2-normed space, if for all* $u, v \in \Delta$*,* $p, q > 0$ *and* $0 < P \leq 1$*, the following inequality holds.*

$$\rho_{\mu,\nu}(u + w, v, \sqrt[P]{p+q}) \geq_{\Upsilon^*} \tau\left(\rho_{\mu,\nu}(u, v, \sqrt[P]{t}), \rho_{\mu,\nu}(w, v, \sqrt[P]{s})\right)$$

Example 4. *Let* $(\Delta, \|.,.\|)$ *be a 2-normed space with conditions of Example (3); we define*

$$\rho_{\mu,\nu}(u,v,p) = \left(\frac{p}{p + m\|u,v\|}, \frac{\|u,v\|}{p + m\|u,v\|}\right),$$

then $(\Delta, \rho_{\mu,\nu}, \tau)$ *is a generalized intuitionistic P-pseudo fuzzy 2-normed space.*

It follows from $(P2)$ and $(P5')$ that in a generalized intuitionistic P-pseudo fuzzy 2-normed space $(\Delta, \rho_{\mu,\nu}, \tau)$ for all $q > p > 0$ and $u, v \in \Delta$, we have

$$\begin{aligned} \rho_{\mu,\nu}(u,v,q) = \rho_{\mu,\nu}(u + 0, v, \sqrt[P]{p^P + (q^P - p^P)}) \geq_{\Upsilon^*} \\ \tau\{\rho_{\mu,\nu}(u,v,p), \rho_{\mu,\nu}(0, v, \sqrt[P]{q^P - p^P})\} = \rho_{\mu,\nu}(u,v,p). \end{aligned} \tag{2}$$

Therefore, $\rho_{\mu,\nu}(u,v,.)$ is a non-decreasing function on $\mathbb{R}^+$ for all $u, v \in \Delta$. Next, we present the following concepts of convergence and Cauchy sequences in a generalized intuitionistic P-pseudo fuzzy 2-normed space $(\Delta, \rho_{\mu,\nu}, \tau)$.

Definition 8. *A sequence* $\{u_n\}$ *in* Δ *is said to be convergent if there exists* $u \in \Delta$ *such that*

$$\lim_{n\to\infty} \rho_{\mu,\nu}(u_n - u, v, p) = 1_{\Upsilon^*} \quad (v \in \Delta)$$

for all $p > 0$*. In this case, we write*

$$u_n \xrightarrow{\rho_{\mu,\nu}} u \ \text{ or } \ u := \rho_{\mu,\nu} - \lim_{n\to\infty} u_n.$$

Definition 9. *A sequence $\{u_n\}$ in Δ is called to be Cauchy sequence, if for each $0 < \epsilon < 1$ and $p > 0$ there exists $n_0 \in \mathbb{N}$, such that*

$$\rho_{\mu,\nu}(u_n - u_m, v, p) \geq_{\Upsilon^*} (1-\epsilon, \epsilon) \ (n, m \geq n_0) \ (v \in \Delta)$$

If any Cauchy sequence is convergent, then generalized intuitionistic P-pseudo fuzzy 2-normed space $(\Delta, \rho_{\mu,\nu}, \tau)$ is said to be complete and the complete generalized intuitionistic P-pseudo fuzzy 2-normed space is said to be a Banach generalized intuitionistic P-pseudo fuzzy 2-normed space.

2.2. Stability of m-Mapping in Generalized Intuitionistic P-Pseudo Fuzzy 2-Normed Space

In this section, using the fixed point theorem, we investigate the stability of m-mapping in a generalized intuitionistic P-pseudo fuzzy 2-normed space. We suppose that $0 < P \leq 1$ and $Q = \frac{1}{P}$, Δ is a real vector space, $(\Theta, \rho_{\mu,\nu}, \tau)$ and is a Banach generalized intuitionistic P-pseudo fuzzy 2-normed space and $(\chi, \rho'_{\mu,\nu}, \tau')$ is generalized intuitionistic P-pseudo fuzzy 2-normed space. Furthermore, let $f : \Delta \to \Theta$ be a mapping. We define

$$\begin{aligned} D_m f(u,v) := {} & f(ru+v) + f(ru-v) - r^{m-2}[f(u+v) + f(u-v)] \\ & -2\left(r^2-1\right)\left[r^{m-2}f(u) + \frac{(m-2)(1-(m-2)^2)}{6}f(v)\right] \end{aligned} \tag{3}$$

for all $u, v \in \Delta$, fixed integer number $r \neq 0, \pm 1$ and $0 < m < 5$.

Theorem 2. *Let $\varphi_m, \psi_m : \Delta \times \Delta \to \chi$ be two functions such that for all $u, v \in \Delta$ and $p > 0$, the following relations are satisfied,*

$$\rho'_{\mu,\nu}(\varphi_m(ru, rv), \psi_m(ru, rv), p) \geq_{\Upsilon^*} \rho'_{\mu,\nu}(\varphi_m(u,v), \psi_m(u,v), \tfrac{p}{\alpha}) \tag{4}$$

moreover,

$$\lim_{n\to\infty}\left(\varphi_m(r^n u, r^n u), \psi_m(r^n u, r^n u), \tfrac{r^{mn}p}{2\alpha^n}\right) = 1, \tag{5}$$

where $\alpha > 0$ and $\alpha^2 < r^m$. Let $\xi : \Delta \to \Theta$ be a function so that

$$\xi(ru) = \tfrac{1}{\alpha}\xi(u), \tag{6}$$

for all $u \in \Delta$ and, $f : \Delta \to \Theta$ be a mapping such that,

$$\begin{aligned} \rho_{\mu,\nu}(D_m f(u,v), \xi(u), p+q) \geq_{\Upsilon^*} \tau'\{ & \rho'_{\mu,\nu}(\varphi_m(u,u), \psi_m(u,u), p), \\ & \rho'_{\mu,\nu}(\varphi_m(v,v), \psi_m(v,v), q)\}. \end{aligned} \tag{7}$$

Then there exists a unique m-mapping $F : \Delta \to \Theta$ such as that satisfied in (1), and

$$\rho_{\mu,\nu}(f(u) - F(u), \xi(u), p) \geq \rho'_{\mu,\nu}\left(\varphi_m(u,u), \psi_m(u,u), (r^{mP} - \alpha^{2P})^Q\right) \tag{8}$$

Proof. Putting $v = 0$ and $p = q$ in (7), we have

$$\begin{aligned} \rho_{\mu,\nu}(2f(ru) - 2r^m f(u), \xi(u), 2p) & \geq_{\Upsilon^*} \tau'\left[\rho'_{\mu,\nu}(\varphi_m(u,u), \psi_m(u,u), p), 1\right] \\ & = \rho'_{\mu,\nu}(\varphi_m(u,u), \psi_m(u,u), p), \end{aligned} \tag{9}$$

therefore,

$$\rho_{\mu,\nu}(f(ru) - r^m f(u), \xi(u), p) \geq_{\Upsilon^*} \rho'_{\mu,\nu}(\varphi_m(u,u), \psi_m(u,u), p). \tag{10}$$

Now, we define the set $\mathcal{S}$ and the function d on it as follows

$$\mathcal{S} := \{g : \ g : \Delta \to \Theta, \ \ g(0) = 0\}$$

$$d(g,h) := \inf\Big\{\delta \in \mathbb{R}^+ \mid \rho_{\mu,\nu}(g(u) - h(u), \xi(u), \delta^Q t) \geq_{Y^*} \rho'_{\mu,\nu}(\varphi_m(u,u), \psi_m(u,u), p), \ \forall u \in \Delta\,, \ \forall p > 0\Big\}, \tag{11}$$

where $\inf \emptyset = +\infty$. The following shows that $(\mathcal{S}, d)$ is a complete generalized metric space.

(1) It is obvious that d has a symmetry property, i.e., $d(g,h) = d(h,g)$.

(2) Using Definition (11), we have

$$d(g,g) := \inf\Big\{\delta \in \mathbb{R}^+ \mid \underbrace{\rho_{\mu,\nu}(g(u) - g(u), \xi(u), \delta^Q p)}_{=1_{Y^*}} \geq_{Y^*} \rho'_{\mu,\nu}(\varphi_m(u,u), \psi_m(u,u), p), \ \forall u \in \Delta\,, \ \forall p > 0\Big\} \tag{12}$$

The right side of the above definition is satisfied for every $\delta \in \mathbb{R}^+$, then $d(g,g) = 0$.

(3) Let $d(g,h) = 0$, using the definition of d, the following inequality holds, for every constant u and $p > 0$.

$$\rho_{\mu,\nu}(g(u) - h(u), \xi(u), p) \geq_{Y^*} \rho'_{\mu,\nu}\Big(\varphi_m(u,u), \psi_m(u,u), \frac{p}{\delta^Q}\Big).$$

As $\delta \to 0$, by $(P6)$, we have

$$\rho_{\mu,\nu}(g(u) - h(u), \xi(u), p) \geq_{Y^*} 1 \Rightarrow g(u) = h(u),$$

for all $u \in \Delta$ and $p > 0$.

(4) Triangular inequality: Let $g, h, j \in \mathcal{S}$ such that $d(g,h) \leq \eta_1$ and $d(j,h) \leq \eta_2$. Using (7), we have

$$\begin{aligned}\rho_{\mu,\nu}(g(u) - h(u), \xi(u), \eta_1^Q p) &\geq_{Y^*} \rho_{\mu,\nu}(g(u) - h(u), \xi(u), \delta^Q p) \\ &\geq_{Y^*} \rho'_{\mu,\nu}(\varphi_m(u,u), \psi_m(u,u), p)\end{aligned} \tag{13}$$

and

$$\begin{aligned}\rho_{\mu,\nu}(h(u) - j(u), \xi(u), \eta_1^Q p) &\geq_{Y^*} \rho_{\mu,\nu}(h(u) - j(u), \xi(u), \delta^Q p) \\ &\geq_{Y^*} \rho'_{\mu,\nu}(\varphi_m(u,u), \psi_m(u,u), p).\end{aligned} \tag{14}$$

Therefore, for all $u \in \Delta$ and $p > 0$, we obtain

$$\begin{aligned}\rho_{\mu,\nu}(g(u) - j(u), \xi(u), (\eta_1 + \eta_2)^Q p) &= \rho_{\mu,\nu}(g(u) - j(u), \xi(u), \sqrt[P]{(\eta_1 + \eta_2) p^P}) \\ &\geq_{L^*} \tau\Big(\rho_{\mu,\nu}(g(u) - j(u), \xi(u), \sqrt[P]{\eta_1 p^P}), \rho_{\mu,\nu}(g(u) - j(u), \xi(u), \sqrt[P]{\eta_2 p^P})\Big) \\ &= \tau\Big(\rho_{\mu,\nu}(g(u) - j(u), \xi(u), \sqrt[P]{\eta_1} p), \rho_{\mu,\nu}(g(u) - j(u), \xi(u), \sqrt[P]{\eta_2} p)\Big) \\ &\geq \rho'_{\mu,\nu}\Big(\varphi_m(u,u), \psi_m(u,u), p\Big),\end{aligned}$$

by (11), we have

$$d(g,j) \leq \eta_1 + \eta_2 \Rightarrow d(g,j) \leq d(g,h) + d(h,j), \tag{15}$$

that is, the property of triangular inequality holds, then d is a generalized metric on $\mathcal{S}$. Next, we show that $(\mathcal{S},d)$ is a complete generalized metric space. For this, we prove that every Cauchy sequence $\{g_n\}$ in $\mathcal{S}$ is convergent to $g \in \mathcal{S}$. Let $u \in \Delta$ be fixed and $\varepsilon > 0$, $\epsilon \in (0,1)$ and $p > 0$ be given, such that

$$\rho'_{\mu,\nu}\Big(\varphi_m(u,u), \psi_m(u,u), p\Big) > 1 - \epsilon.$$

Since $\{g_n\}$ is a Cauchy sequence in $\mathcal{S}$ for $\delta^Q < \frac{\varepsilon}{p}$ there exists $n_0 \in \mathbb{N}$ such that

$$d(g_n, g_m) < \tfrac{\varepsilon}{p} \ \forall n,m \geq n_0,$$

therefore, we have

$$\begin{aligned}\rho_{\mu,\nu}\Big(g_n(u) - g_m(u), \xi(u), \varepsilon\Big) &\geq_{\Upsilon^*} \rho_{\mu,\nu}\Big(g_n(u) - g_m(u), \xi(u), \delta^Q p\Big)\\ &\geq_{\Upsilon^*} \rho'_{\mu,\nu}\Big(\varphi_m(u,u), \psi_m(u,u), p\Big) > 1 - \epsilon.\end{aligned} \tag{16}$$

Hence, the sequence $\{g_n(u)\}$ is a Cauchy sequence in Θ since Θ is a Banach space, so $\{g_n(u)\}$ is a convergent sequence. It means that there exists $g : \Delta \to \Theta$ such that

$$\lim_{n\to\infty} g_n(u) = g(u).$$

It is enough to show that $g \in \mathcal{S}$. Assume that $\alpha, \beta > 0$ be given. There is $n_0 \in \mathbb{N}$ such that the following inequality holds for all $n \geq n_0$ and $m > 0$.

$$\rho_{\mu,\nu}\Big(g_n(u) - g_{n+m}(u), \xi(u), \alpha^Q p\Big) \geq_{\Upsilon^*} \rho'_{\mu,\nu}\Big(\varphi_m(u,u), \psi_m(u,u), p\Big).$$

Fix $n \geq n_0$ and $p > 0$, we have

$$\begin{aligned}&\rho_{\mu,\nu}(g_n(u) - g_{n+m}(u), \xi(u), (\alpha+\beta)^Q p)\\ &\quad= \rho_{\mu,\nu}(g_n(u) - g_{n+m}(u), \xi(u), \sqrt[P]{(\alpha+\beta)p^P})\\ &\quad\geq_{\Upsilon^*} \tau\Big[\rho_{\mu,\nu}(g_n(u) - g_{n+m}(u), \xi(u), \alpha^Q p), \rho_{\mu,\nu}(g_{n+m}(u) - g(u), \xi(u), \beta^Q p)\Big]\\ &\quad\geq_{\Upsilon^*} \tau\Big[\rho'_{\mu,\nu}(\varphi_m(u,u), \psi_m(u,u), p), \rho_{\mu,\nu}(g_{n+m}(u) - g(u), \xi(u), \beta^Q p)\Big].\end{aligned}$$

By passing $m \to \infty$, so

$$\begin{aligned}\rho_{\mu,\nu}(g_n(u) - g_{n+m}(u), \xi(u), (\alpha+\beta)^Q p) &\geq_{\Upsilon^*} \tau\Big[\rho'_{\mu,\nu}(\varphi_m(u,u), \psi_m(u,u), p), 1\Big]\\ &= \rho'_{\mu,\nu}(\varphi_m(u,u), \psi_m(u,u), p).\end{aligned} \tag{17}$$

By (11), we can deduce that $g \in \mathcal{S}$. Hence, $(\mathcal{S},d)$ is a complete generalized metric space. Next, we define the mapping $\mathcal{Z} : \mathcal{S} \to \mathcal{S}$ by

$$\mathcal{Z}g(u) := \frac{1}{r^m} g(ru), \quad \forall g \in \mathcal{S}, u \in \Delta.$$

Assume that $g, h \in \mathcal{S}$, such that $d(g,h) < \delta$, where $\delta \in (0,\infty)$ is an arbitrary constant. Then, by (11) we obtain

$$\rho_{\mu,\nu}(g(u) - h(u), \xi(u), \delta^{Q} p) \succeq_{\Upsilon^*} \rho'_{\mu,\nu}(\varphi_m(u,u), \psi_m(u,u), p), \ \forall u \in \Delta, \ p > 0. \tag{18}$$

Replacing ru by u in (18), we have

$$\rho_{\mu,\nu}(g(ru) - h(ru), \xi(ru), \delta^{Q} p) \succeq_{\Upsilon^*} \rho'_{\mu,\nu}(\varphi_m(ru,ru), \psi_m(ru,ru), p). \tag{19}$$

Therefore, using $(P3)$ and Definition (6), we have

$$\rho_{\mu,\nu}\left(\frac{1}{r^m} g(ru) - \frac{1}{r^m} h(ru), \frac{1}{\alpha}\xi(u), \frac{\delta^{Q} p}{r^m}\right) \succeq_{\Upsilon^*} \rho'_{\mu,\nu}(\varphi_m(ru,ru), \psi_m(ru,ru), p). \tag{20}$$

It means that

$$\begin{aligned}\rho_{\mu,\nu}\left(\mathcal{Z}g(u) - \mathcal{Z}h(u), \xi(u), \frac{\alpha}{r^m}\delta^{Q} p\right) &\succeq_{\Upsilon^*} \rho'_{\mu,\nu}(\varphi_m(ru,ru), \psi_m(ru,ru), p) \\ &\succeq_{\Upsilon^*} \rho'_{\mu,\nu}\left(\varphi_m(u,u), \psi_m(u,u), \frac{p}{\alpha}\right).\end{aligned} \tag{21}$$

Hence,

$$\rho_{\mu,\nu}\left(\mathcal{Z}g(u) - \mathcal{Z}h(u), \xi(u), \frac{\alpha^2}{r^m}\delta^{Q} p\right) \succeq_{\Upsilon^*} \rho'_{\mu,\nu}(\varphi_m(u,u), \psi_m(u,u), p). \tag{22}$$

Therefore, by (11), we have

$$d(\mathcal{Z}g, \mathcal{Z}h) \leq \left(\frac{\alpha^2}{r^m}\right)^P \delta.$$

It means that $\mathcal{Z}$ is a strictly contractive self-mapping on $\mathcal{S}$ with the Lipschitz constant $L = \left(\frac{\alpha^2}{r^m}\right)^P < 1$.

Moreover, by (10), we obtain

$$d(f, \mathcal{Z}f) \leq \left(\frac{1}{r^m}\right)^P.$$

It follows from (1) that the $\{\mathcal{Z}^n f\}$ converges to a fixed point F of $\mathcal{Z}$. Therefore,

$$\begin{aligned} &F : \Delta \to \Theta \\ &F(u) := \rho_{\mu,\nu} - \lim_{n\to\infty} \mathcal{Z}^n f(u) = \lim_{n\to\infty} \frac{1}{r^{mn}} f(r^n u),\end{aligned} \tag{23}$$

for all $u \in \Delta$ and $p > 0$. Furthermore,

$$F(ru) = r^m F(u). \tag{24}$$

Also, F is the unique fixed point of $\mathcal{Z}$ in the set $S^* = \{g \in S \ : \ d(f,g) < \infty\}$. Hence, there exists a $\delta \in \mathbb{R}^+$ such that

$$\rho_{\mu,\nu}\left(g(u) - f(u), \xi(u), \delta^{Q} p\right) \succeq_{\Upsilon^*} \rho'_{\mu,\nu}\left(\varphi_m(u,u), \psi_m(u,u), \frac{p}{\alpha}\right) \tag{25}$$

for all $u \in \Delta$ and $p > 0$. Furthermore,

$$d(f, F) \leq \frac{1}{1-L} d(f, \mathcal{Z}f) \leq \frac{1}{r^{mP} - \alpha^{2P}}.$$

It means that (8) holds. It is enough to show that F satisfies (1). Putting $p = q$, $v := r^n v$ and $u := r^n u$ in (7), we obtain

$$\rho_{\mu,\nu}(D_m f(r^n u, r^n v), \xi(r^n u), 2p) \geq_{Y^*} \tau'\Big\{\rho'_{\mu,\nu}(\varphi_m(r^n u, r^n u), \psi_m(r^n u, r^n u), p), \rho'_{\mu,\nu}(\varphi_m(r^n v, r^n v), \psi_m(r^n v, r^n v), p)\Big\}. \quad (26)$$

According to $(P3)$, we have

$$\rho_{\mu,\nu}\left(\frac{1}{r^{mn}} D_m f(r^n u, r^n v), \xi(u), p\right) \geq_{L^*} \tau'\left\{\rho'_{\mu,\nu}\left(\varphi_m(r^n u, r^n u), \psi_m(r^n u, r^n u), \frac{r^{mn} p}{2\alpha^n}\right), \rho'_{\mu,\nu}\left(\varphi_m(r^n v, r^n v), \psi_m(r^n v, r^n v), \frac{r^{mn} p}{2\alpha^n}\right)\right\}. \quad (27)$$

By letting $n \to \infty$ and using (5) and (23), we have

$$\rho_{\mu,\nu}(D_m F(u,v), \xi(u), p) \geq_{Y^*} 1 \xrightarrow{(P2)} D_m F(u,v) = 0, \ \forall u, v \in \Delta, p > 0.$$

Thus, F satisfies (3) and as a result, F is an $m-$mapping. □

Corollary 1. *Let α be a real positive number with $\alpha > r^m$, such that the mappings φ_m, ψ_m: $\Delta \times \Delta \to \chi$ satisfy in the following inequality, for all $u, v \in \Delta$ and $p > 0$.*

$$\rho'_{\mu,\nu}\left(\varphi_m\left(\frac{u}{r}, \frac{v}{r}\right), \psi_m\left(\frac{u}{r}, \frac{v}{r}\right), p\right) \geq_{Y^*} \rho'_{\mu,\nu}(\varphi_m(u,v), \psi_m(u,v), \alpha p). \quad (28)$$

Furthermore, suppose that $\xi : \Delta \to \Theta$ is a function that satisfies

$$\xi(ru) = \frac{1}{\alpha}\xi(u), \quad (29)$$

for all $u \in \Delta$. If $f : \Delta \to \Theta$ is a mapping satisfying $f(0) = 0$ and the inequality (7), then there exists a unique $m-$mapping $F : \Delta \to \Theta$ satisfying (3) such that

$$\rho_{\mu,\nu}(f(u) - F(u), \xi(u), p) \geq \rho'_{\mu,\nu}\left(\varphi_m(u,u), \psi_m(u,u), (\alpha^P - r^{mP})Q\right) \quad (30)$$

for all $u \in \Delta$ and $p > 0$.

Proof. It is similar to the proof of the above theorem. □

Corollary 2. *Let φ, ψ be functions from $\Delta \times \Delta$ to χ such that for all $u, v \in \Delta$ and $p > 0$, the following inequality is held.*

$$\rho'_{\mu,\nu}(\varphi(u,v), \psi(u,v), p) \geq_{Y^*} \rho'_{\mu,\nu}(\varphi(2u, 2v), \psi_m(2u, 2v), 5p). \quad (31)$$

Furthermore, assume that $\xi : \Delta \to \Theta$ is a function satisfying

$$\xi(u) = 5\xi(2u), \quad (32)$$

for all $u \in \Delta$. *If* $f : \Delta \to \Theta$ *is a mapping satisfying* $f(0) = 0$ *and the inequality*

$$\rho_{\mu,\nu}\big(f(2x+y)+f(2x-y) - f(x+y) - f(x-y) - 6f(x),\ \xi(u),\ p+q\big) \\ \geq_{Y^*} \tau'\{\rho'_{\mu,\nu}(\varphi(u,u),\psi(u,u),p),\rho'_{\mu,\nu}(\varphi(v,v),\psi(v,v),q)\}. \quad (33)$$

Then there exists a unique quadratic mapping $F : \Delta \to \Theta$ *such that*

$$\rho_{\mu,\nu}(f(u) - F(u),\xi(u),p) \geq \rho'_{\mu,\nu}\Big(\varphi_m(u,u),\psi_m(u,u),(5^P - 4^P)^Q\Big) \quad (34)$$

for all $u \in \Delta$ *and* $p > 0$.

Proof. Putting $m = r = 2$ and $\alpha = 5$ in the above theorem, we can easily show the stability of quadratic functional equations in generalized intuitionistic P-pseudo fuzzy 2-normed space. □

3. Conclusions

In this paper, we defined the generalized intuitionistic P-pseudo fuzzy 2-normed space and investigated its features. Furthermore, we defined the convergent and Cauchy sequences in this space; then, we investigated the stability of m-mapping in this space by the fixed point method. By changing m and choosing the appropriate r, α from Theorem 2.1, we can prove the stability of the additive, cubic and quartic functional equation.

Author Contributions: Methodology, E.M. and M.D.l.S.; validation, M.D.l.S.; investigation, E.M. and M.D.l.S.; writing—original draft, E.M.; project administration, M.D.l.S.; funding acquisition, M.D.l.S. All authors have read and agreed to the published version of the manuscript.

Funding: This work is supported by the Basque Government under Grants IT1555-22 and KK-2022/00090 and MCIN/AEI 269.10.13039/501100011033 under Grant PID2021-1235430B-C21/C22.

Informed Consent Statement: Not applicable.

Data Availability Statement: Not applicable.

Acknowledgments: The authors are grateful to the Basque Government for its support through Grants IT1555-22 and KK-2022/00090 and to MCIN/AEI 269.10.13039/501100011033 for Grant PID2021-1235430B-C21/C22.

Conflicts of Interest: The authors declare no conflict of interest.

References

1. Ulam, S.M. *Problems in Modern Mathematics*; Courier Corporation: North Chelmsford, MA, USA, 2004.
2. Hyers, H.D. On the stability of the linear functional equation. *Proc. Natl. Acad. Sci. USA* **1941**, *27*, 222–224. [CrossRef] [PubMed]
3. Rassias, T.M. On the stability of the linear mapping in Banach spaces. *Proc. Am. Math. Soc.* **1978**, *72*, 297–300. [CrossRef]
4. Gordji, M.E.; Alizadeh, Z.; Khodaei, H.; Park, C. On approximate homomorphisms: A fixed point approach. *Math. Sci.* **2012**, *6*, 1–8. [CrossRef]
5. Mirmostafaee, A.K.; Mirzavaziri, M.; Moslehian, M.S. Fuzzy stability of the Jensen functional equation. *Fuzzy Sets Syst.* **2008**, *159*, 730–738. [CrossRef]
6. Mirmostafaee, A.K.; Moslehian, M.S. Fuzzy versions of Hyers-Ulam-Rassias theorem. *Fuzzy Sets Syst.* **2008** *159*, 720–729. [CrossRef]
7. Mosadegh, S.M.S.; Movahednia, E. Stability of preserving lattice cubic functional equation in Menger probabilistic normed Riesz spaces. *J. Fixed Point Theory Appl.* **2018**, *20*, 34. [CrossRef]
8. Movahednia, E.; Mursaleen, M. Stability of a generalized quadratic functional equation in intuitionistic fuzzy 2-normed space. *Filomat* **2016**, *30*, 449–457. [CrossRef]
9. Movahednia, E.; Cho, Y.; Park, C.; Paokanta, S. On approximate solution of lattice functional equations in Banach f-algebras. *AIMS Math.* **2020**, *5*, 5458–5469. [CrossRef]
10. Jung, S.M. Hyers-Ulam-Rassias stability of Jensen's equation and its application. *Proc. Am. Math. Soc.* **1998**, *126*, 3137–3143. [CrossRef]
11. Park, C.; Gorgji, M.E.; Saadati, R. Random homomorphisms and random derivations in random normed algebras via fixed point method. *J. Inequal. Appl.* **2012**, *194*, 1–13. [CrossRef]

12. Sahoo, P.K.; Palaniappan, K. *Introduction to Functional Equations*; CRC Press: Boca Raton, FL, USA, 2011.
13. Salehi, N.; Modarres, S.M.S. A fixed point method for stability of involutions on multi-Banach algebra. *J. Fixed Point Theory Appl.* **2020**, *22*, 20. [CrossRef]
14. Zadeh, L.A. Fuzzy sets. *Inf. Control* **1965**, *8*, 338–353. [CrossRef]
15. Kramosil, I.; Michalek, J. Fuzzy metric and statistical metric spaces. *Kybernetika* **1975**, *11*, 326–334.
16. Atanassov, K.T. Intuitionistic fuzzy sets. *Fuzzy Sets Syst.* **1986**, *20*, 87–96. [CrossRef]
17. Saadati, R.; Park, J.H. On the intuitionistic fuzzy topological spaces. *Chaos Solitons Fractals* **2006**, *27*, 331–344. [CrossRef]
18. Diaz, J.; Margolis, B. A fixed point theorem of the alternative for contractions on a generalized complete metric space. *Bull. Amer. Math. Soc.* **1968**, *74*, 305–309. [CrossRef]
19. Samanta, T.K.; Jebril, I.H. Finite Dimensional Intuitionistic Fuzzy Normed Linear Space. *Int. J. Open Probl. Compt. Math.* **2009**, *4*, 574–591.
20. Mursaleen, M.; Lohani, Q.M.D. Intuitionistic fuzzy 2-normed space and some related concepts. *Chaos Solitons Fractals* **2009**, *42*, 224–234. [CrossRef]

axioms

MDPI

Article

Nonhomogeneous Dirichlet Problems with Unbounded Coefficient in the Principal Part

Dumitru Motreanu

Département de Mathématiques, Université de Perpignan, 66860 Perpignan, France; motreanu@univ-perp.fr

Abstract: The main result of the paper establishes the existence of a bounded weak solution for a nonlinear Dirichlet problem exhibiting full dependence on the solution u and its gradient ∇u in the reaction term, which is driven by a p-Laplacian-type operator with a coefficient $G(u)$ that can be unbounded. Through a special Moser iteration procedure, it is shown that the solution set is uniformly bounded. A truncated problem is formulated that drops that $G(u)$ be unbounded. The existence of a bounded weak solution to the truncated problem is proven via the theory of pseudomonotone operators. It is noted that the bound of the solution for the truncated problem coincides with the uniform bound of the original problem. This estimate allows us to deduce that for an appropriate choice of truncation, one actually resolves the original problem.

Keywords: p-Laplacian with unbounded coefficient; convection term; truncated problem; uniform bound; weak solution; pseudomonotone operator

MSC: 35J70; 35J92; 47H30

Citation: Motreanu, D. Nonhomogeneous Dirichlet Problems with Unbounded Coefficient in the Principal Part. *Axioms* **2022**, *11*, 739. https://doi.org/10.3390/axioms11120739

Academic Editor: Clemente Cesarano

Received: 20 November 2022
Accepted: 15 December 2022
Published: 17 December 2022

1. Introduction

In this paper, we study the following Dirichlet problem:

$$\begin{cases} -\mathrm{div}(G(u)|\nabla u|^{p-2}\nabla u) = F(x,u,\nabla u) & \text{in } \Omega \\ u = 0 & \text{on } \partial\Omega \end{cases} \tag{1}$$

on a bounded domain Ω in $\mathbb{R}^N$ with a Lipschitz boundary $\partial\Omega$. In (1) we have a continuous function $G : \mathbb{R} \to [a_0, +\infty)$, with $a_0 > 0$, a number $p \in (1, +\infty)$ with $N > p$, and a Carathéodory function $F : \Omega \times \mathbb{R} \times \mathbb{R}^N \to \mathbb{R}$ (i.e., $F(\cdot, t, \xi)$ is measurable on Ω for each $(t, \xi) \in \mathbb{R} \times \mathbb{R}^N$ and $F(x, \cdot, \cdot)$ is continuous on $\mathbb{R} \times \mathbb{R}^N$ for almost all $x \in \Omega$). The notation ∇u stands for the gradient of u in the distributional sense. It is seen that the driving operator in Equation (1) is the p-Laplacian with a coefficient $G(u)$ depending on the solution u. The notation $G(u)$ in Equation (1) means the composition of the functions $G : \mathbb{R} \to \mathbb{R}$ and $u : \Omega \to \mathbb{R}$, that is, $G(u)(x) = G(u(x))$ for $x \in \Omega$. The main point is that $G(u)$ can be unbounded from above, which does not permit to apply any standard method. It is also worth mentioning that problem (1) is not in variational form.

The space underlying the Dirichlet problem (1) is the Banach space $W_0^{1,p}(\Omega)$ endowed with the norm

$$\|u\| := \left(\int_\Omega |\nabla u(x)|^p dx\right)^{\frac{1}{p}}, \quad \forall u \in W_0^{1,p}(\Omega).$$

The dual space of $W_0^{1,p}(\Omega)$ is denoted $W^{-1,p'}(\Omega)$. Since it was supposed that $N > p$, the critical Sobolev exponent is $p^* = Np/(N-p)$. Refer to [1] for the background related to the space $W_0^{1,p}(\Omega)$.

The (negative) p-Laplacian is the nonlinear operator $-\Delta_p : W_0^{1,p}(\Omega) \to W^{-1,p'}(\Omega)$ (linear for $p = 2$) defined by

$$\langle -\Delta_p(u), v\rangle := \int_\Omega |\nabla u|^{p-2}\nabla u \nabla v dx, \quad \forall u, v \in W_0^{1,p}(\Omega). \tag{2}$$

Due to the unbounded function $G(u)$, one cannot build a definition as in (2) corresponding to the term $-\mathrm{div}(G(u)|\nabla u|^{p-2}\nabla u)$ in (1). A major tool in our arguments is the first eigenvalue λ_1 of $-\Delta_p$, which is positive and isolated in the spectrum of $-\Delta_p$, and is given by

$$\lambda_1 := \inf_{u \in W_0^{1,p}(\Omega),\, u \neq 0} \frac{\int_\Omega |\nabla u|^p dx}{\int_\Omega |u|^p dx}. \tag{3}$$

For the the rest of the paper, in order to simplify the notation we make the notational convention that for any real number $r > 1$ we denote $r' := r/(r-1)$ (the Hölder conjugate of r).

The Carathéodory function $F : \Omega \times \mathbb{R} \times \mathbb{R}^N \to \mathbb{R}$ determining the reaction term $F(x, u, \nabla u)$ is subject to the following hypotheses.

Hypothesis 1 (H1). *There exist constants $c_1 \geq 0$, $c_2 \geq 0$, $c_3 \geq 0$, and $r \in (p, p^*)$ such that*

$$|F(x,t,\xi)| \leq c_1|\xi|^{\frac{p}{r'}} + c_2|t|^{r-1} + c_3 \textit{ for a.e. } x \in \Omega,\ \forall t \in \mathbb{R},\ \forall \xi \in \mathbb{R}^N.$$

Hypothesis 2 (H2). *There exist constants $d_1 \geq 0$ and $d_2 \geq 0$ with $d_1 + \lambda_1^{-1}d_2 < a_0$, and a function $\sigma \in L^1(\Omega)$ such that*

$$F(x,t,\xi)t \leq d_1|\xi|^p + d_2|t|^p + \sigma(x) \textit{ for a.e. } x \in \Omega,\ \forall t \in \mathbb{R},\ \forall \xi \in \mathbb{R}^N,$$

where λ_1 denotes the first eigenvalue of $-\Delta_p$.

The main result of this paper is stated as follows.

Theorem 1. *Assume that $G : \mathbb{R} \to [a_0, +\infty)$, with $a_0 > 0$, is a continuous function and $F : \Omega \times \mathbb{R} \times \mathbb{R}^N \to \mathbb{R}$ is a Carathéodory function satisfying the conditions (H1) and (H2). Then problem* (1) *has at least a bounded weak solution $u \in W_0^{1,p}(\Omega)$ in the following sense:*

$$\int_\Omega G(u)|\nabla u|^{p-2}\nabla u \nabla v dx = \int_\Omega F(x,u,\nabla u) v dx, \quad \forall v \in W_0^{1,p}(\Omega). \tag{4}$$

Under hypothesis (H1), the integrals in (4) exist. The proof of Theorem 1 is presented in Section 3. In order to see the effective applicability of Theorem 1, we provide an example.

Example 1. *On a bounded domain Ω in $\mathbb{R}^N$ with a Lipschitz boundary $\partial\Omega$, we state the Dirichlet problem*

$$\begin{cases} -\mathrm{div}(e^{u^2}|\nabla u|^{p-2}\nabla u) = b_1|u|^{p-2}u + b_2\frac{u}{u^2+1}|\nabla u|^{\frac{p(r-1)}{r}} & \textit{in } \Omega \\ u = 0 & \textit{on } \partial\Omega, \end{cases} \tag{5}$$

with constants $p \in (1, +\infty)$, $r \in (p, p^*)$, $b_1 \geq 0$, $b_2 \geq 0$, provided that $N > p$ and $1 > b_2 + \lambda_1^{-1}b_1$, where λ_1 is given by (3)*. We readily check that* (5) *fits into the framework of problem* (1) *taking $G(t) = e^{t^2}$ for all $t \in \mathbb{R}$ and*

$$F(x,t,\xi) = b_1|t|^{p-2}t + b_2\frac{t}{t^2+1}|\xi|^{\frac{p(r-1)}{r}}, \quad \forall (x,t,\xi) \in \Omega \times \mathbb{R} \times \in \mathbb{R}^N.$$

Indeed, one has $G(t) \geq a_0 := 1$ *for all* $t \in \mathbb{R}$,

$$|F(x,t,\xi)| \leq b_1(|t|^{r-1}+1) + b_2|\xi|^{\frac{p}{r'}}, \quad \forall (x,t,\xi) \in \Omega \times \mathbb{R} \times \mathbb{R}^N,$$

$$F(x,t,\xi)t \leq b_1|t|^p + b_2(|\xi|^p+1), \quad \forall (x,t,\xi) \in \Omega \times \mathbb{R} \times \in \mathbb{R}^N.$$

Assumption (H1) is verified with $c_1 = b_2$, $c_2 = c_3 = b_1$, *while assumption (H2) holds with* $d_1 = b_2$, $d_2 = b_1$, $\sigma(x) \equiv b_2$. *Theorem 1 applies because* $a_0 > d_1 + \lambda_1^{-1} d_2$.

The inspiration for the present work comes from the recent paper [2] that deals with the Dirichlet problem

$$\begin{cases} -\mathrm{div}(a(x)g(|u|)|\nabla u|^{p-2}\nabla u) = f(x,u,\nabla u) & \text{in } \Omega \\ u = 0 & \text{on } \partial\Omega \end{cases} \tag{6}$$

for a positive $a \in L^1_{loc}(\Omega)$, a continuous function $g : [0,+\infty) \to [a_0,+\infty)$, with $a_0 > 0$, and a Carathéodory function $f : \Omega \times \mathbb{R} \times \mathbb{R}^N \to \mathbb{R}$. The standing point in that work was to use the theory of weighted Sobolev spaces in [3] (see also [4]) with the weight $a \in L^1_{loc}(\Omega)$ requiring the condition

$$a^{-s} \in L^1(\Omega) \ \text{ for some } s \in \left(\frac{N}{p}, +\infty\right) \cap \left[\frac{1}{p-1}, +\infty\right).$$

If we consider our problem (1) as a particular case of (6) taking $a(x) \equiv 1$ on Ω and apply the result in [2], the issue is that one obtains a solution of (1) belonging to the space $W_0^{1,p_s}(\Omega)$ with

$$p_s = \frac{ps}{s+1}. \tag{7}$$

and not to the space $W_0^{1,p}(\Omega)$ as it would be natural according to the statement of (1). In this respect, by (7) we note that $p_s < p$, so $W_0^{1,p}(\Omega)$ is strictly contained in $W_0^{1,p_s}(\Omega)$. Moreover, the assumptions admitted therein for the reaction $f(x,u,\nabla u)$ in (6) are more restrictive than here because they are formulated in terms of p_s corresponding to some s and not with p as in conditions (H1)–(H2) for $F(x,u,\nabla u)$. All of this shows that the treatment in [2] does not provide the right approach to obtain Theorem 1. For this reason, we develop a direct study for problem (1) relying just on the classical Sobolev space $W_0^{1,p}(\Omega)$. The present paper is the first work studying problem (1) with unbounded coefficient $G(u)$ in the Soboleev space $W_0^{1,p}(\Omega)$. Certainly, we use some previous ideas but with substantial modifications and in a different functional setting. The technique relies on truncation, which is needed because the coefficient $G(u)$ in the principal part of Equation (1) is unbounded. Other important tools in our study are a special version of Moser iteration and the surjectivity theorem for pseudomonotone operators.

We mention a few relevant works in the area of our paper. A large amount of results in the field is based on variational smooth or nonsmooth methods for which we refer to the recent publications [5–7]. They cannot be applied to problem (1) taking into account the lack of variational structure. Nonvariational problems with convection terms have been investigated in recent years through theoretic operator techniques, sub-supersolution and approximation (see, e.g., [8–12]). The main point in these works lies in the dependence of the reaction term with respect to the gradient of the solution without weakening the ellipticity condition of the driving operator. In this connection, we also cite papers dealing with the equations and inclusions driven by the (p,q)-Laplacian operators, such as, for instance [13,14]. As an extension of this setting, the paper [15] deals with degenerate (p,q)-Laplacian problems, but without dependence on the solution u in the principal part of the equation. An advance in this direction is ref. [2], where there is dependence on solution u in the principal part of the equation of type (6) subject to a weight $a(x)$. Here, we drop the dependence on weight $a(x)$ and allow to have a unbounded coefficient $G(u)$ in problem (1).

Regarding the rest of the paper, Section 2 focuses on the bounded solutions to problem (1), and Section 3 contains the proof of Theorem 1.

2. Bounded Solutions to Problem (1)

Our first goal is to estimate the solutions in $W_0^{1,p}(\Omega)$.

Lemma 1. *Assume that condition (H2) holds. Then the set of solutions to problem* (1) *is bounded in* $W_0^{1,p}(\Omega)$ *with a bound that depends on function G only through the lower bound* a_0 *of G.*

Proof. Let $u \in W_0^{1,p}(\Omega)$ be a solution of (1). Inserting $v = u$ in (4) yields

$$\int_\Omega G(u)|\nabla u|^p dx = \int_\Omega F(x,u,\nabla u)u dx.$$

Invoking hypothesis (H2) and (3), we arrive at

$$a_0\|u\|^p \leq (d_1 + d_2\lambda_1^{-1})\|u\|^p + \|\sigma\|_{L^1(\Omega)}.$$

Since by hypothesis $d_1 + d_2\lambda_1^{-1} < a_0$, the stated result is true. □

We are now able to find a uniform bound for the solutions of (1).

Theorem 2. *Assume that conditions (H1) and (H2) are satisfied. Then the solution set of problem* (1) *is uniformly bounded, that is, there exists a constant* $C > 0$ *such that* $\|u\|_{L^\infty(\Omega)} \leq C$ *for every weak solution* $u \in W_0^{1,p}(\Omega)$ *to problem* (1). *The dependence of the uniform bound C on the data in problem* (1) *and hypotheses (H1) and (H2) is indicated as* $C = C(N, p, \Omega, a_0, c_1, c_2, c_3, d_1, d_2, \|\sigma\|_{L^1(\Omega)})$. *In particular, the uniform bound C depends on G only through its lower bound* a_0.

Proof. Given a weak solution $u \in W_0^{1,p}(\Omega)$ to problem (1), we have the representation $u = u^+ - u^-$ with $u^+ = \max\{u, 0\}$ (the positive part of u) and $u^- = \max\{-u, 0\}$ (the negative part of u). We prove the uniform boundedness separately for u^+ and u^-. We only give the proof for u^+, noting that we can argue similarly in the case of u^-.

We proceed by using in (4) the test function $v = u^+u_h^{kp} \in W_0^{1,p}(\Omega)$, where $u_h := \min\{u^+, h\}$ with arbitrary constants $h > 0$ and $k > 0$. The fact that $v \in W_0^{1,p}(\Omega)$ follows from $u \in L^p(\Omega)$ and u_h is bounded, while the distributional partial derivatives

$$\frac{\partial v}{\partial x_i} = u_h^{kp}\frac{\partial u^+}{\partial x_i} + kpu_h^{kp-1}u^+\frac{\partial u_h}{\partial x_i}, \quad \forall i = 1, \cdots, N,$$

belong to $L^p(\Omega)$ because $u, \partial u_h/\partial x_i \in L^p(\Omega)$ and u_h is bounded. This gives

$$\int_\Omega G(u)|\nabla u|^{p-2}\nabla u\nabla(u^+u_h^{kp})dx = \int_\Omega F(x,u,\nabla u)u^+u_h^{kp}dx. \tag{8}$$

The left-hand side of (8) can be estimated as follows:

$$\begin{aligned}&\int_\Omega G(u)|\nabla u|^{p-2}\nabla u\nabla(u^+u_h^{kp})dx\\&=\int_\Omega G(u)|\nabla u|^{p-2}\nabla u(u_h^{kp}\nabla(u^+)+kpu^+u_h^{kp-1}\nabla(u_h))dx\\&\geq a_0\left[\int_\Omega u_h^{kp}|\nabla(u^+)|^p dx+kp\int_{\{0<u<h\}}u_h^{kp}|\nabla(u^+)|^p dx\right].\end{aligned}\tag{9}$$

For the right-hand side of (8), by hypothesis (H1), we obtain

$$\begin{aligned}&\int_\Omega F(x,u,\nabla u)u^+u_h^{kp}dx\\&\leq c_1\int_\Omega|\nabla u|^{\frac{p}{r'}}u_h^{kp}u^+dx+c_2\int_\Omega|u|^{r-1}u_h^{kp}u^+dx+c_3\int_\Omega u_h^{kp}u^+dx.\end{aligned}\tag{10}$$

By Young's inequality, for each $\varepsilon>0$ there is a constant $c(\varepsilon)>0$ such that

$$\begin{aligned}c_1\int_\Omega|\nabla u|^{\frac{p}{r'}}u_h^{kp}u^+dx&=c_1\int_\Omega(|\nabla(u^+)|^{\frac{p}{r'}}u_h^{\frac{kp}{r'}})(u_h^{\frac{kp}{r}}u^+)dx\\&\leq\varepsilon\int_\Omega u_h^{kp}|\nabla(u^+)|^p dx+c(\varepsilon)\int_\Omega u_h^{kp}(u^+)^r dx.\end{aligned}\tag{11}$$

It is clear that

$$\int_\Omega|u|^{r-1}u_h^{kp}u^+dx=\int_\Omega u_h^{kp}(u^+)^r dx\tag{12}$$

and, since $r>1$ and $u_h\leq u^+$,

$$\begin{aligned}\int_\Omega u_h^{kp}u^+dx&=\int_{\{u^+\geq1\}}u_h^{kp}u^+dx+\int_{\{u^+<1\}}u_h^{kp}u^+dx\\&\leq\int_\Omega u_h^{kp}(u^+)^r dx+|\Omega|,\end{aligned}\tag{13}$$

where $|\Omega|$ denotes the Lebesgue measure of Ω.

If $\varepsilon>0$ is sufficiently small, we deduce from (8), in conjunction with (9), (10), (11), (12), and (13) that

$$\begin{aligned}&\int_\Omega u_h^{kp}|\nabla(u^+)|^p dx+kp\int_{\{0<u<h\}}u_h^{kp}|\nabla(u^+)|^p dx\\&\leq b\left(\int_\Omega u_h^{kp}(u^+)^r dx+1\right),\end{aligned}\tag{14}$$

with a constant $b>0$. The last integral exists because $r<p^*$.

On the other hand, by Bernoulli's inequality and since $u_h=u^+$ on $\{0<u<h\}$, we derive

$$\begin{aligned}&\int_\Omega u_h^{kp}|\nabla(u^+)|^p dx+kp\int_{\{0<u<h\}}u_h^{kp}|\nabla(u^+)|^p dx\\&=\int_{\{u\geq h\}}|\nabla(u_h^k u^+)|^p dx+\int_{\{u<h\}}|\nabla(u_h^k u^+)|^p dx+\frac{kp}{(k+1)^p}\int_{\{0<u<h\}}|\nabla(u_h^k u^+)|^p dx\\&=\int_{\{u\geq h\}}|\nabla(u_h^k u^+)|^p dx+\frac{kp+1}{(k+1)^p}\int_{\{0<u<h\}}|\nabla(u_h^k u^+)|^p dx\\&\geq\frac{kp+1}{(k+1)^p}\int_\Omega|\nabla(u_h^k u^+)|^p dx.\end{aligned}\tag{15}$$

Combining (14) and (15) leads to

$$\frac{kp+1}{(k+1)^p}\int_\Omega |\nabla(u_h^k u^+)|^p dx \le b\Big(\int_\Omega u_h^{kp}(u^+)^r dx + 1\Big). \tag{16}$$

At this point, we choose $q \in (p, r)$ with

$$\frac{(r-p)q}{q-p} < p^*. \tag{17}$$

The validity of such a choice holds in view of $p < r < p^*$ as postulated in condition (H1). Then (17), the Sobolev embedding theorem, Hölder's inequality with $(q-p)/q + p/q = 1$, and Lemma 1 imply

$$\int_\Omega u_h^{kp}(u^+)^r dx = \int_\Omega (u^+)^{r-p}(u_h^k u^+)^p dx$$

$$\le \Big(\int_\Omega (u^+)^{\frac{(r-p)q}{q-p}} dx\Big)^{\frac{q-p}{q}} \Big(\int_\Omega (u_h^k u^+)^q dx\Big)^{\frac{p}{q}} \le K\|u_h^k u^+\|^p_{L^q(\Omega)},$$

with a constant $K > 0$.

On the basis of the previous inequality and the Sobolev embedding theorem, we obtain from (16) that

$$c_0 \frac{kp+1}{(k+1)^p}\|u_h^k u^+\|^p_{L^{p^*}(\Omega)} \le b\Big(\|(u^+)^{k+1}\|^p_{L^q(\Omega)} + 1\Big),$$

with a constant $c_0 > 0$. Then Fatou's lemma letting $h \to +\infty$ entails

$$c_0 \frac{kp+1}{(k+1)^p}\|u^+\|^{p(k+1)}_{L^{p^*(k+1)}(\Omega)} \le b\Big(\|(u^+)^{k+1}\|^p_{L^q(\Omega)} + 1\Big).$$

By some arrangements, we obtain for a constant $C_1 > 0$ the estimate

$$\|u^+\|_{L^{(k+1)p^*}(\Omega)} \le C_1^{\frac{1}{k+1}}(k+1)^{\frac{1}{k+1}}\Big(\|(u^+)^{k+1}\|^p_{L^q(\Omega)} + 1\Big)^{\frac{1}{(k+1)p}}.$$

Noticing that the sequence $(k+1)^{\frac{1}{\sqrt{k+1}}}$ is bounded, we find a constant $C_0 > 0$ for which it holds

$$\|u^+\|_{L^{(k+1)p^*}(\Omega)} \le C_0^{\frac{1}{\sqrt{k+1}}}\Big(\|u^+\|^{(k+1)p}_{L^{(k+1)q}(\Omega)} + 1\Big)^{\frac{1}{(k+1)p}}. \tag{18}$$

We claim that there exists a constant $C > 0$ independent of the solution u to (1) such that

$$\|u^+\|_{L^d(\Omega)} \le C, \quad \forall d \ge 1. \tag{19}$$

In the case where $\|u^+\|_{L^{(k+1)q}(\Omega)} \le 1$ for infinitely many k, it is straightforward to show the validity of the claim. Therefore, we may suppose that $\|u^+\|_{L^{(k+1)q}(\Omega)} > 1$ for all $k \ge k_0$,

If $\|u^+\|_{L^{(k+1)q}(\Omega)} > 1$ for all k, we see that (18) takes the form

$$\|u^+\|_{L^{(k+1)p^*}(\Omega)} \le C_1^{\frac{1}{\sqrt{k+1}}}\|u^+\|_{L^{(k+1)q}(\Omega)}, \tag{20}$$

with a constant $C_1 > 0$. Through (20), we are able to carry on a Moser iteration, setting inductively $(k_n+1)q = (k_{n-1}+1)p^*$ with the initial step $(k_1+1)q = p^*$. Applying repeatedly (20), it turns out that

$$\|u^+\|_{L^{(k_n+1)p^*}(\Omega)} \leq C_1^{\sum_{1\leq i\leq n} \frac{1}{\sqrt{k_i+1}}} \|u^+\|_{L^{(k_1+1)q}(\Omega)}, \quad \forall n \geq 1. \tag{21}$$

The series $\sum_{n\geq 1} \frac{1}{\sqrt{k_n+1}}$ converges because $q < p^*$ and $k_n \to +\infty$ as $n \to \infty$. Consequently, we can obtain (19) letting $n \to \infty$ in (21).

It remains to handle the case when the number k_0 is such that $\|u^+\|_{L^{(k_0+1)q}(\Omega)} \leq 1$ and $\|u^+\|_{L^{(k+1)q}(\Omega)} > 1$ for all $k > k_0$. In this case, the Moser iteration reads as $(k_n+1)q = (k_{n-1}+1)p^*$ with the initial step $(k_1+1)q = k_0$ if $k_0 < p^*$ and $(k_1+1)q = p^*$ if $k_0 \geq p^*$. In any case, we are led to (21) from which (19) can be established as before.

We can pass to the limit as $d \to \infty$ in (19) obtaining $\|u^+\|_{L^\infty(\Omega)} \leq C$ for each weak solution $u \in W_0^{1,p}(\Omega)$ to problem (1). Analogously, we can prove that $\|u^-\|_{L^\infty(\Omega)} \leq C$ for all weak solutions $u \in W_0^{1,p}(\Omega)$ to problem (1). Altogether, we have the uniform bound $\|u\|_{L^\infty(\Omega)} \leq C$ for the solution set of problem (1).

A careful reading of the above proof reveals the dependence of the uniform bound C on the data in problem (1) and on the coefficients, entering assumptions (H1) and (H2). Precisely, we have to check how the constants b, q, K, c_0, C_1, and C_0 arising in the proof depend on the data given in (1), (H1), and (H2). Collecting all these renders the dependence $C = C(N, p, \Omega, a_0, c_1, c_2, c_3, d_1, d_2, \|\sigma\|_{L^1(\Omega)})$. This completes the proof. □

3. Truncation Problem and Proof of Theorem 1

The method of proof relies on the truncation of the coefficient $G(u)$ of the p-Laplacian in problem (1) to drop its unboundedness. This idea was used in [2] in the context of the degenerate p-Laplacian. Specifically, for any number $R > 0$, we introduce the truncation

$$G_R(t) = \begin{cases} G(t) & \text{if } |t| \leq R \\ G(R) & \text{if } t > R \\ G(-R) & \text{if } t < -R. \end{cases} \tag{22}$$

By (22), we obtain a continuous function $G_R : \mathbb{R} \to [a_0, +\infty)$. We also consider the associated operator $\mathcal{A}_R : W_0^{1,p}(\Omega) \to W_0^{-1,p'}(\Omega)$ given by

$$\langle \mathcal{A}_R(u), v\rangle = \int_\Omega G_R(u)|\nabla u|^{p-2}\nabla u \nabla v dx, \quad \forall u, v \in W_0^{1,p}(\Omega). \tag{23}$$

The notation $G_R(u)|$ in Equation (23) means the composition of the functions $G_R : \mathbb{R} \to \mathbb{R}$ and $u : \Omega \to \mathbb{R}$, that is $G_R(u)(x) = G_R(u(x))$ for $x \in \Omega$. The next proposition discusses the properties of $\mathcal{A}_R$.

Proposition 1. *The nonlinear operator $\mathcal{A}_R$ in* (23) *is well defined, bounded (i.e., it maps bounded sets into bounded sets), continuous, and satisfies the S_+ property, that is, any sequence $\{u_n\} \subset W_0^{1,p}(\Omega)$ with $u_n \rightharpoonup u$ in $W_0^{1,p}(\Omega)$ and*

$$\limsup_{n\to\infty} \langle \mathcal{A}_R(u_n), u_n - u\rangle \leq 0 \tag{24}$$

fulfills $u_n \to u$ in $W_0^{1,p}(\Omega)$.

Proof. The continuity of the function G combined with (22), (23), and Hölder's inequality ensures

$$|\langle \mathcal{A}_R(u), v\rangle| \leq \max_{t\in[-R,R]} G(t)\|u\|^{p-1}\|v\|.$$

for all $u, v \in W_0^{1,p}(\Omega)$. It follows that the operator $\mathcal{A}_R$ is well-defined and bounded.

In order to show the continuity of $\mathcal{A}_R$ let $u_n \to u$ in $W_0^{1,p}(\Omega)$. By the continuity of G, (22), (23), Hölder's inequality, and (2), we find

$$\begin{aligned}
&|\langle \mathcal{A}_R(u_n) - \mathcal{A}_R(u), v\rangle| \\
&\leq \left|\int_\Omega G_R(u_n)(|\nabla u_n|^{p-2}\nabla u_n - |\nabla u|^{p-2}\nabla u)\nabla v dx\right| \\
&+\left|\int_\Omega (G_R(u_n) - G_R(u))|\nabla u|^{p-2}\nabla u \nabla v dx\right| \\
&\leq \max_{t\in[-R,R]} G(t)|\langle -\Delta_p(u_n) - (-\Delta_p(u)), v\rangle| \\
&+\left(\int_\Omega |G_R(u_n) - G_R(u)|^{\frac{p}{p-1}}|\nabla u|^p dx\right)^{\frac{p-1}{p}}\|v\|
\end{aligned}$$

for all $v \in W_0^{1,p}(\Omega)$. We infer that

$$\begin{aligned}
&\|\mathcal{A}_R(u_n) - \mathcal{A}_R(u)\|_{W^{-1,p'}(\Omega)} \\
&\leq \max_{t\in[-R,R]} G(t)\| - \Delta_p(u_n) - (-\Delta_p(u))\|_{W^{-1,p'}(\Omega)} \\
&+\left(\int_\Omega |G_R(u_n) - G_R(u)|^{\frac{p}{p-1}}|\nabla u|^p dx\right)^{\frac{p-1}{p}}.
\end{aligned}$$

The continuity of the p-Laplacian Δ_p implies that $-\Delta_p(u_n) \to -\Delta_p(u)$ in $W^{-1,p'}(\Omega)$. By Lebesgue's dominated convergence theorem, we derive

$$\lim_{n\to\infty}\int_\Omega |G_R(u_n) - G_R(u)|^{\frac{p}{p-1}}|\nabla u|^p dx = 0,$$

whence $\mathcal{A}_R(u_n) \to \mathcal{A}_R(u)$ in $W^{-1,p'}(\Omega)$, so the continuity of $\mathcal{A}_R$ is proven.

Now we show the S_+ property for the operator $\mathcal{A}_R$. Let a sequence $\{u_n\}$ satisfy $u_n \rightharpoonup u$ in $W^{1,p}(a, \Omega)$ and (24). It is seen that

$$\limsup_{n\to\infty}\langle \mathcal{A}_R(u_n) - \mathcal{A}_R(u), u_n - u\rangle \leq 0. \tag{25}$$

Taking into account (23) and the monotonicity of $-\Delta_p$, we have

$$\begin{aligned}
&\langle \mathcal{A}_R(u_n) - \mathcal{A}_R(u), u_n - u\rangle \\
=\ & \int_\Omega G_R(u_n)(|\nabla u_n|^{p-2}\nabla u_n - |\nabla u|^{p-2}\nabla u)\nabla(u_n - u)dx \\
+\ & \int_\Omega (G_R(u_n) - G_R(u))|\nabla u|^{p-2}\nabla u\nabla(u_n - u)dx \\
\geq\ & a_0\langle -\Delta_p(u_n) - (-\Delta_p(u)), u_n - u\rangle \\
+\ & \int_\Omega (G_R(u_n) - G_R(u))|\nabla u|^{p-2}\nabla u\nabla(u_n - u)dx.
\end{aligned} \tag{26}$$

We claim that

$$\lim_{n\to\infty}\int_\Omega (G_R(u_n)-G_R(u))|\nabla u|^{p-2}\nabla u\nabla(u_n-u)dx=0. \tag{27}$$

To this end, by Hölder's inequality and since the sequence $\{u_n\}$ is bounded in $W_0^{1,p}(\Omega)$, we find a constant $C>0$ such that

$$\begin{aligned} &\left|\int_\Omega (G_R(u_n)-G_R(u))|\nabla u|^{p-2}\nabla u\nabla(u_n-u)dx\right| \qquad (28)\\ \leq\ & C\Big(\int_\Omega |G_R(u_n)-G_R(u)|^{\frac{p}{p-1}}|\nabla u|^p dx\Big)^{\frac{p-1}{p}}. \end{aligned}$$

By Lebesgue's dominated convergence theorem, it holds

$$\lim_{n\to\infty}\int_\Omega |G_R(u_n)-G_R(u)|^{\frac{p}{p-1}}|\nabla u|^p dx=0. \tag{29}$$

This is true because G_R is continuous, $u_n\to u$ in $L^p(\Omega)$ and there is the domination

$$|G_R(u_n)-G_R(u)|^{\frac{p}{p-1}}|\nabla u|^p\leq 2^{\frac{1}{p-1}}(\max_{t\in[-R,R]}G(t))^{\frac{p}{p-1}}|\nabla u|^p\in L^1(\Omega).$$

Then (25), (26), (27), (28), (29), and $u_n\rightharpoonup u$ in $W^{1,p}(\Omega)$ yield

$$\lim_{n\to\infty}\langle -\Delta_p(u_n),u_n-u\rangle=0. \tag{30}$$

Since it holds,

$$\begin{aligned} \|u_n\|^p &= \langle -\Delta_p(u_n),u\rangle+\langle -\Delta_p(u_n),u_n-u\rangle\\ &\leq \|u_n\|^{p-1}\|u\|+\langle -\Delta_p(u_n),u_n-u\rangle, \end{aligned}$$

Equation (30) results in $\limsup_{n\to\infty}\|u_n\|\leq\|u\|$. Recalling that space $W_0^{1,p}(\Omega)$ is uniformly convex, we conclude that $u_n\to u$ in $W_0^{1,p}(\Omega)$, which proves the S_+ property of the operator $\mathcal{A}_R$. The proof is thus complete. □

For any $R>0$ and the truncation G_R in (22), let us consider the auxiliary problem

$$\begin{cases} -\mathrm{div}(G_R(u)|\nabla u|^{p-2}\nabla u)=F(x,u,\nabla u) & \text{in } \Omega,\\ u=0 & \text{on } \partial\Omega. \end{cases} \tag{31}$$

The solvability and a priori estimates for problem (31) are now studied.

Theorem 3. *Assume that $G:[0,+\infty)\to[a_0,+\infty)$ is a continuous function with $a_0>0$, and that $F:\Omega\times\mathbb{R}\times\mathbb{R}^N\to\mathbb{R}$ is a Carathéodory function satisfying the conditions (H1) and (H2). Then, for every $R>0$, the auxiliary problem* (31) *has a weak solution $u_R\in W_0^{1,p}(\Omega)$ in the sense that*

$$\int_\Omega G_R(u_R)|\nabla u_R|^{p-2}\nabla u_R\nabla v dx=\int_\Omega F(x,u_R,\nabla u_R)v dx,\quad \forall v\in W_0^{1,p}(\Omega). \tag{32}$$

Moreover, the solution u_R is uniformly bounded and fulfills the a priori estimate $\|u_R\|_{L^\infty(\Omega)}\leq C$ with the constant $C=C(N,p,\Omega,a_0,c_1,c_2,c_3,d_1,d_2,\|\sigma\|_{L^1(\Omega)})$ provided by Theorem 2.

Proof. Fix an $R > 0$. In view of (23), equality (32) reads as

$$\langle \mathcal{A}_R(u_R), v\rangle = \int_\Omega F(x, u_R, \nabla u_R) v dx, \quad \forall v \in W_0^{1,p}(\Omega). \tag{33}$$

Through hypothesis (H1) and Hólder's inequality, we find

$$\left|\int_\Omega F(x, u, \nabla u) v dx\right| \leq \int_\Omega |F(x, u, \nabla u)||v| dx$$

$$\leq \int_\Omega (c_1 |\nabla u|^{\frac{p}{r'}} |v| + c_2 |u|^{r-1} |v| + c_3 |v|) dx$$

$$\leq c_1 \|u\|^{\frac{p}{r'}} \|v\|_{L^r(\Omega)} + c_2 \|u\|^{r-1}_{L^r(\Omega)} \|v\|_{L^r(\Omega)} + c_3 |\Omega|^{\frac{1}{r'}} \|v\|_{L^r(\Omega)}$$

for all $u \in W_0^{1,p}(\Omega)$ and $v \in L^r(\Omega)$. We deduce that the mapping

$$u \in W_0^{1,p}(\Omega) \mapsto F(\cdot, u(\cdot), \nabla u(\cdot)) \in L^{r'}(\Omega) \tag{34}$$

is well-defined and bounded. Furthermore, by Krasnoselskii's theorem for Nemytskii operators, the mapping in (34) is continuous from $W_0^{1,p}(\Omega)$ to $L^{r'}(\Omega)$, so continuous from $W_0^{1,p}(\Omega)$ to $W^{-1,p'}(\Omega)$ due to the continuous embedding $W_0^{1,p}(\Omega) \subset L^r(\Omega)$.

Let us define the mapping $\mathcal{B}_R : W_0^{1,p}(\Omega) \to W^{-1,p'}(\Omega)$ by

$$\mathcal{B}_R(u) = \mathcal{A}_R(u) - F(\cdot, u(\cdot), \nabla u(\cdot)), \quad \forall u \in W_0^{1,p}(\Omega). \tag{35}$$

On account of Proposition 1 and on what was said regarding the mapping in (34), we are entitled to assert that $\mathcal{B}_R : W_0^{1,p}(\Omega) \to W_0^{-1,p'}(\Omega)$ introduced in (35) is well-defined, bounded and continuous.

The next step in the proof is to show that the mapping $\mathcal{B}_R : W_0^{1,p}(\Omega) \to W^{-1,p'}(\Omega)$ is a pseudomonotone operator, which means that if $u_n \rightharpoonup u$ in $W_0^{1,p}(\Omega)$ and

$$\limsup_{n\to\infty} \langle \mathcal{B}_R(u_n), u_n - u\rangle \leq 0, \tag{36}$$

then

$$\langle \mathcal{B}_R(v), u - v\rangle \leq \liminf_{n\to\infty} \langle \mathcal{B}_R(u_n), u_n - v\rangle \text{ for all } v \in W_0^{1,p}(\Omega). \tag{37}$$

To this end, let $\{u_n\}$ be a sequence as above. By the Rellich–Kondrachov theorem, we derive from $u_n \rightharpoonup u$ in $W_0^{1,p}(\Omega)$ that $u_n \to u$ in $L^r(\Omega)$. As noted before, the sequence $\{F(\cdot, u_n(\cdot), \nabla u_n(\cdot))\}$ is bounded in $L^{r'}(\Omega)$. Therefore, we have

$$\lim_{n\to\infty} \int_\Omega F(x, u_n(x), \nabla u_n(x))(u_n(x) - u(x)) dx = 0.$$

Then (36) entails that (24) holds true. As Proposition 1 guarantees that $\mathcal{A}_R$ has the S_+ property, we can conclude that $u_n \to u$ in $W_0^{1,p}(\Omega)$. From here, it can be readily shown (37) thanks to the continuity and boundedness properties stated in Proposition 1 and those related to (34). This amounts to saying that $\mathcal{B}_R$ is a pseudomonotone operator.

In the following, we prove that the operator $\mathcal{B}_R : W_0^{1,p}(\Omega) \to W_0^{-1,p'}(\Omega)$ is coercive, that is

$$\lim_{\|u\|\to\infty} \frac{\langle \mathcal{B}_R(u), u\rangle}{\|u\|} = +\infty. \tag{38}$$

Toward this we infer from (35), (33), (22), (3), Hölder's inequality and hypothesis (H2) that

$$\begin{aligned}\langle \mathcal{B}_R(u), u\rangle &= \int_\Omega G_R(u)|\nabla u|^p dx - \int_\Omega F(x,u,\nabla u)u dx \\ &\geq (a_0 - d_1 - d_2\lambda_1^{-1})\|u\|^p - \|\sigma\|_{L^1(\Omega)}\end{aligned}$$

for all $u \in W_0^{1,p}(\Omega)$. Since $p > 1$ and $a_0 - d_1 - d_2\lambda_1^{-1} > 0$ as known from hypothesis (H2), we confirm the validity of (38).

We showed on the reflexive Banach space $W_0^{1,p}(\Omega)$ that the operator $\mathcal{B}_R : W_0^{1,p}(\Omega) \to W_0^{-1,p'}(\Omega)$ defined in (35) is bounded, pseudomonotone and coercive. According to the main theorem for pseudomonotone operators (see, for example, [16], Th. 2.99), we can conclude that the mapping $\mathcal{B}_R$ is surjective. So, in particular, there exists $u_R \in W_0^{1,p}(\Omega)$ such that $\mathcal{B}_R(u_R) = 0$, which is exactly (32). Therefore u_R is a weak solution of auxiliary problem (31).

Let us point out that the function G and its truncation G_R take values in the same set $[a_0, +\infty)$, and function F is the same in both problems (1) and the (31). Consequently, Theorem 2 can be applied to the auxiliary problem (31) and provides the same uniform bound $C = C(N, p, \Omega, a_0, c_1, c_2, c_3, d_1, d_2, \|\sigma\|_{L^1(\Omega)})$ of the solution set as for the original problem (1). This ensures that $\|u_R\|_{L^\infty(\Omega)} \leq C$, which completes the proof. □

Relying on Theorem 3, we are now able to prove Theorem 1.

Proof of Theorem 1. It was established in Theorem 2 that the solution set of problem (1) is uniformly bounded by a constant $C = C(N, p, \Omega, a_0, c_1, c_2, c_3, d_1, d_2, \|\sigma\|_{L^1(\Omega)})$, where a_0 is a lower bound of the function G. Since the truncated function G_R has the lower bound a_0 too for all $R > 0$ (see (22)) and the reaction term $F(x,t,\xi)$ is unchanged in problems (1) and (31) and is subject to the same hypotheses (H1)-(H2), Theorem 2 applies to the truncated problem (31) and provides the same bound C for its solution set whenever $R > 0$. In particular, the solution $u_R \in W_0^{1,p}(\Omega)$ of problem (31) provided by Theorem 3 satisfies the estimate $\|u_R\|_{L^\infty(\Omega)} \leq C$.

Owing to the crucial information that C is independent of $R > 0$, we can choose $R \geq C$. Hence, the estimate $\|u_R\|_{L^\infty(\Omega)} \leq C$ and (22) render that the functions G_R and G coincide along the values $u_R(x)$ for all $x \in \Omega$. According to Theorem 3, $u_R \in W_0^{1,p}(\Omega)$ solves problem (31), and thus it becomes a bounded weak solution of the original problem (1). The conclusion of Theorem 1 is achieved. □

Funding: This research received no external funding.

Institutional Review Board Statement: Not applicable.

Informed Consent Statement: Not applicable.

Data Availability Statement: Not applicable.

Conflicts of Interest: The author declares no conflict of interest.

References

1. Brezis, H. *Functional Analysis, Sobolev Spaces and Partial Differential Equations;* Universitext; Springer: New York, NY, USA, 2011.
2. Motreanu, D.; Tornatore, E. Nonhomogeneous degenerate quasilinear problems with convection. *Nonlinear Anal. Real World Appl.* **2023**, *71*, 103800. [CrossRef]
3. Drabek, P.; Kufner, A.; Nicolosi, F. *Quasilinear Eliptic Equations with Degenerations and Singularities;* De Gruyter Series in Nonlinear Analysis and Applications; Walter de Gruyter & Co.: Berlin, Germany, 1997; Volume 5.
4. Kufner, A. *Weighted Sobolev Spaces;* John Wiley & Sons, Inc.: New York, NY, USA, 1985.
5. Alves, C.D.; Moameni, A. Super-critical Neumann problems on unbounded domains. *Nonlinearity* **2020**, *33*, 4568–4589. [CrossRef]

6. Costea, N.; Kristaly, A.; Varga, C. Variational and monotonicity methods in nonsmooth analysis. In *Frontiers in Mathematics*; Birkhäuser/ Springer: Cham, Switzerland, 2021.
7. Moameni, A. Critical point theory on convex subsets with applications in differential equations and analysis. *J. Math. Pures Appl.* **2020**, *141*, 266–315. [CrossRef]
8. de Araujo, A.L.A.; Faria, L.F.O. Positive solutions of quasilinear elliptic equations with exponential nonlinearity combined with convection term. *J. Differ. Equ.* **2019**, *267*, 4589–4608. [CrossRef]
9. Faraci, F.; Puglisi, D. Nodal solutions of semi-linear elliptic equations with dependence on the gradient. *Bull. Sci. Math.* **2022**, *175*, 103101. [CrossRef]
10. Gasinski, L.; Winkert, P. Existence and uniqueness results for double phase problems with convection term. *J. Differ. Equ.* **2021**, *268*, 4183–4193. [CrossRef]
11. Guarnotta, U.; Marano, S.A. Infinitely many solutions to singular convective Neumann systems with arbitrarily growing reactions. *J. Differ. Equ.* **2021**, *271*, 849–863. [CrossRef]
12. Zeng, S.; Bai, Y.; Gasinski, L. Nonlinear nonhomogeneous obstacle problems with multivalued convection term. *J. Geom. Anal.* **2022**, *32*, 75. [CrossRef]
13. Bobkov, V.; Tanaka, M. Multiplicity of positive solutions for (p,q)-Laplace equations with two parameters. *Commun. Contemp. Math.* **2022**, *24*, 2150008. [CrossRef]
14. Zeng, S.; Radulescu, V.D.; Winkert, P. Double phase implicit obstacle problems with convection and multivalued mixed boundary value conditions. *SIAM J. Math. Anal.* **2022**, *54*, 1898–1926. [CrossRef]
15. Motreanu, D. Degenerated and competing Dirichlet problems with weights and convection. *Axioms* **2021**, *10*, 271. [CrossRef]
16. Carl, S.; Le, V.K.; Motreanu, D. Nonsmooth variational problems and their inequalities. In *Comparison Principles and Applications*; Springer: New York, NY, USA, 2007.

axioms

MDPI

Article

Amended Criteria for Testing the Asymptotic and Oscillatory Behavior of Solutions of Higher-Order Functional Differential Equations

Barakah Almarri [1], Fahd Masood [2], Osama Moaaz [3,4,*] and Ali Muhib [4]

[1] Department of Mathematical Sciences, College of Sciences, Princess Nourah bint Abdulrahman University, P.O. Box 84428, Riyadh 11671, Saudi Arabia
[2] Faculty of Science, Mansoura University, Mansoura 35516, Egypt
[3] Department of Mathematics, College of Science, Qassim University, P.O. Box 6644, Buraydah 51452, Saudi Arabia
[4] Department of Mathematics, Faculty of Science, Mansoura University, Mansoura 35516, Egypt
* Correspondence: o_moaaz@mans.edu.eg

Abstract: Our interest in this article is to develop oscillation conditions for solutions of higher order differential equations and to extend recent results in the literature to differential equations of several delays. We obtain new asymptotic properties of a class from the positive solutions of an even higher order neutral delay differential equation. Then we use these properties to create more effective criteria for studying oscillation. Finally, we present some special cases of the studied equation and apply the new results to them.

Keywords: oscillatory; nonoscillatory; even-order; neutral; delay; differential equation

Citation: Almarri, B.; Masood, F.; Moaaz, O.; Muhib, A. Amended Criteria for Testing the Asymptotic and Oscillatory Behavior of Solutions of Higher-Order Functional Differential Equations. *Axioms* **2022**, *11*, 718. https://doi.org/10.3390/axioms11120718

Academic Editor: Delfim F. M. Torres

Received: 23 October 2022
Accepted: 26 November 2022
Published: 12 December 2022

1. Introduction

When modeling the length of time required to accomplish some hidden activities, the concept of delay in systems is considered as playing a crucial role. When the predator birth rate is influenced by historical levels of predators or prey rather than only present levels, the predator-prey model exhibits a delay. Sending measured signals to the remote control center has been much easier because to the quick development of communication technologies. The primary challenge for engineers, nevertheless, is the inescapable lag between the measurement and the signal received by the controller. To minimize the possibility of experimental instability and potential harm, this lag must be taken into account at the design stage. Delay differential equations (DDE) appear when modeling such phenomena, and others, see [1,2].

Many biological, chemical, and physical phenomena have mathematical models that use differential equations of the fourth-order delay. Examples of these applications include soil settlement and elastic issues. The oscillatory traction of a muscle, which takes place when the muscle is subjected to an inertial force, is one model that can be modeled by a fourth-order oscillatory equation with delay, see [3]. Heterogeneity in the Fisher-KPP reaction term is a research topic of interest. Palencia et al. [4] studied the existence of solutions, uniqueness, and travelling wave oscillatory properties.

Over the past few years, research has consistently focused on identifying necessary conditions for the oscillatory and non-oscillatory features of fourth and higher-order differential equations; see for example [5–9].

Below, we review in more detail some of the works that contributed to the development of the oscillation theory of higher order DDEs.

In 1998, Zafer [10] presented an oscillation criterion for the neutral differential equation (NDE)

$$(x(\ell)+p(\ell)x(\vartheta(\ell)))^{(n)}+G(\ell,x(\ell),x(h(\ell)))=0, \tag{1}$$

where $G(\ell,u,v)\in([0,\infty)\times\mathbb{R}\times\mathbb{R})$ and $vG(\ell,u,v)>0$ for $uv>0$.

Li et al. [11] and Zhang et al. [12] created and developed criteria for oscillation of the NDE

$$(x(\ell)+p(\ell)x(\vartheta(\ell)))^{(n)}+q(\ell)H(x(h(\ell)))=0, \tag{2}$$

The results obtained are an improvement and generalization of the results [10].

It is known that studies of the oscillatory behavior of solutions of differential equations are classified into two types, depending on the convergence or divergence of the integration $\int_{\ell_1}^{\ell} r^{-1/\alpha}(\mathfrak{a})\mathrm{d}\mathfrak{a}$ as $\ell\to\infty$. This is a result of the effect of this influence on the behavior of the positive solutions of the equation. In the case of equations with even orders, we find that the divergence of this integration means that there are no positive decreasing solutions.

Baculikova and Dzurina [13] studied the asymptotic and oscillation behavior of the solutions of the higher order delay differential equations

$$\left(r(\ell)\left(x'(\ell)\right)^{\alpha}\right)^{(n-1)}+q(\ell)x^{\alpha}(\vartheta(\ell))=0, \tag{3}$$

They set some oscillation conditions for (3) under the canonical condition

$$\int_{\ell_1}^{\ell} r^{-1/\alpha}(\mathfrak{a})\mathrm{d}\mathfrak{a}\to\infty \text{ as } \ell\to\infty. \tag{4}$$

where α is the ratio of two positive odd integers.

Sun et al. [14] studied the oscillation of NDE

$$(r(\ell)(x(\ell)+p(\ell)x(\vartheta(\ell))))^{(n)}+q(\ell)f(x(h(\ell)))=0, \tag{5}$$

under both the canonical condition (4) and non-canonical condition

$$\int_{\ell_0}^{\infty}\frac{1}{r^{1/\alpha}(\mathfrak{a})}\mathrm{d}\mathfrak{a}<\infty, \tag{6}$$

where $f(u)/u\geq k>0$.

Moaaz et al. [15] investigated the oscillatory properties of NDE

$$\left(r(\ell)\left((x(\ell)+p(\ell)x(\vartheta(\ell)))^{(n-1)}\right)^{\alpha}\right)'+q(\ell)x^{\alpha}(h(\ell))=0, \tag{7}$$

in the noncanonical case. They derived criteria for improving conditions that exclude the decreasing positive solutions of the considered equation.

In this study, we consider the more general neutral differential equation (NDE) of higher order and with several delays,

$$\frac{\mathrm{d}}{\mathrm{d}\ell}\left(r(\ell)\left(\frac{\mathrm{d}^{n-1}}{\mathrm{d}\ell^{n-1}}[x(\ell)+p(\ell)x(\vartheta(\ell))]\right)^{\alpha}\right)+\sum_{i=1}^{J}q_i(\ell)x^{\alpha}(h_i(\ell))=0,\ \ell\geq\ell_0, \tag{8}$$

which includes many of the previous equations as special cases. We deal with the oscillatory behavior of the solutions of Equation (8), so that we introduce new criteria that guarantee the oscillation of all solutions of this equation in the non-canonical condition. For this, we assume the following for n and α:

(H_1) $n\in\mathbb{N}$, $n\geq 4$, and $\alpha\in Q^{+}_{odd}:=\{a/b: a,b\in\mathbb{Z}^{+}$ and a,b are odd$\}$.

Moreover, r, p and q_i are continuous real functions on $[\ell_0,\infty)$, and r is differentiable, which satisfy the conditions:

(H_2) $r(\ell)>0$, $r'(\ell)\geq 0$, $0\leq p(\ell)<1$ and $q_i(\ell)\geq 0$ for $i=1,2,\ldots,J$.

Furthermore, ϑ and h_i are continuous delay functions on $[\ell_0,\infty)$ and h_i is differentiable, which satisfy the conditions:

(H3) $\vartheta(\ell) \leq \ell$, $h_i(\ell) \leq \ell$, $h_i'(\ell) > 0$. and $\lim_{\ell\to\infty}\vartheta(\ell) = \lim_{\ell\to\infty} h_i(\ell) = \infty$ for $i = 1,2,\ldots,J$.

For convenience, we define the corresponding function $\mathcal{B} := x + p\cdot(x\circ\vartheta)$. A solution to Equation (8) is defined as a real differentiable function on $[\ell_x,\infty)$, $\ell_x \geq \ell_0$, which satisfies the properties $\mathcal{B} \in C^{(n-1)}([\ell_x,\infty))$, $r(\mathcal{B}^{(n-1)})^\alpha \in C^1([\ell_x,\infty))$ and x satisfies (8) on $[\ell_x,\infty)$. We will consider the eventually non-zero solutions, that is, $\sup\{|x(\ell)| : \ell \geqslant \ell_*\} > 0$, for $\ell_* \geq \ell_x$. A solution of (8) is said to be oscillatory if it is neither eventually positive nor eventually negative. Otherwise, it is said to be nonoscillatory.

This article aims to extend recent previous results from the literature (see for example [16–19]) to differential equations with even-order and several delays, and to develop oscillation criteria for solutions of even order differential equations. For a class of positive solutions of NDE (8), we derive new asymptotic properties. Then, we construct better criteria for evaluating oscillation using these properties. We then apply the new results to a some particular cases of the equation under study.

2. Previous Results

In this part, we review some results from the literature.

Below, we review the most important results of paper [10], which studies the oscillatory behavior of solutions to Equation (1).

Theorem 1 ([10]). *Assume that $\psi(\ell) \in C([\ell_0,\infty),[0,\infty))$ and that $F \in C^1([\ell_0,\infty),[0,\infty))$ such that $F' \geq 0$,*

$$|G(\ell,u,v)| \geq \psi(\ell)F\left(\frac{|v|}{(1-p(h(\ell)))h^{n-1}(\ell)}\right),$$

and

$$\int_{\ell_0}^{\zeta} \frac{1}{F(\mathfrak{a})}\mathrm{d}\mathfrak{a} < \infty \text{ for all } \zeta > 0.$$

Then, all solutions of Equation (1) are oscillatory if

$$\int_{\ell_0}^{\infty} \psi(\mathfrak{a})\mathrm{d}\mathfrak{a} = \infty,$$

In the following theorem we give the oscillation condition of Equation (2).

Theorem 2 ([12]). *Suppose that $|H(u)| \geq |u|$, for all $|u| \geq u_0 > 0$. Then, all solutions of Equation (2) are oscillatory if there is a $\lambda \in (0,1)$ such that the first-order DDE*

$$Y'(\ell) + \frac{\lambda}{(n-1)!}q(\ell)h^{n-1}(\ell)(1-p(h(\ell)))Y(h(\ell)) = 0,$$

is oscillatory.

Now, we present one of the results of the oscillation of the Equation (3).

Theorem 3 ([13]). *All solutions of Equation (3) are oscillatory if the first-order DDE*

$$Y'(\ell) + \frac{\alpha^\alpha\lambda^\alpha}{(n-2)!(n-2+\alpha)^\alpha}\frac{q(\ell)\vartheta^{n-2+\alpha}(\ell)}{r(\vartheta(\ell))}Y(\vartheta(\ell)) = 0,$$

is oscillatory, for some $\lambda \in (0,1)$.

In the following two theorems, Sun et al. [14] provide two different criteria for the volatility of the Equation (5).

Theorem 4 ([14]). *Suppose that (4) holds and*

$$h(\ell) \le \vartheta(\ell),\ p(\ell) \le p_0,\ \vartheta'(\ell) \ge \vartheta_0 > 0 \text{ and } \vartheta \circ h = h \circ \vartheta. \tag{9}$$

Then, all solutions of Equation (5) are oscillatory if

$$\liminf_{\ell\to\infty} \int_{\vartheta^{-1}(h(\ell))}^{\ell} \frac{h^{n-1}(\mathfrak{a})}{r(h(\mathfrak{a}))} Q(\mathfrak{a}) d\mathfrak{a} > (n-1)! \frac{(p_0+\vartheta_0)}{k\vartheta_0 e}, \tag{10}$$

where $Q(\ell) = \min\{q(\ell), q(\vartheta(\ell))\}$.

Theorem 5 ([14]). *Suppose that (6) and (9) hold. Then, all solutions of Equation (5) are oscillatory if (10) and*

$$\limsup_{\ell\to\infty} \int_{\ell_0}^{\ell} \left(\frac{\lambda}{(n-2)!} \xi(\mathfrak{a}) Q(\mathfrak{a}) h^{n-2}(\mathfrak{a}) - \frac{1+p_0/\vartheta_0}{4} \frac{1}{r(\mathfrak{a})\xi(\mathfrak{a})} \right) d\mathfrak{a} = \infty,$$

for $\lambda \in (0,1)$, *where* $\xi(\ell) := \int_{\ell}^{\infty} r^{-1/\alpha}(\mathfrak{a}) d\mathfrak{a}$.

Finally, we present one of the results that guarantees the oscillation of Equation (7) in the non-canonical case.

Theorem 6 ([15]). *Suppose that*

$$\limsup_{\ell\to\infty} \int_{\ell_0}^{\ell} \left[q(\mathfrak{a}) \left(1 - p(h(\mathfrak{a})) R_0(\mathfrak{a}) \frac{\lambda h^{n-2}(\mathfrak{a})}{(n-2)!} \right)^{\alpha} - \frac{\frac{\alpha^{\alpha+1}}{(\alpha+1)^{\alpha+1}}}{r^{1/\alpha}(\mathfrak{a}) R_0(\mathfrak{a})} \right] d\mathfrak{a} = \infty,$$

holds for some constant $\lambda \in (0,1)$ *and*

$$\limsup_{\ell\to\infty} \left(R_{n-2}^{\alpha}(\ell) \int_{\ell_1}^{\ell} q(\mathfrak{a}) \widetilde{p}^{\alpha}(h(\mathfrak{a})) d\mathfrak{a} \right) > 1.$$

Then all solutions of (7) are oscillatory, where

$$R_0(\ell) := \int_{\ell}^{\infty} \frac{1}{r^{1/\alpha}(\mathfrak{a})} d\mathfrak{a},\ R_{n-2}(\ell) := \int_{\ell}^{\infty} R_{n-3}(\mathfrak{a}) d\mathfrak{a},$$

and

$$\widetilde{p}(\ell) = 1 - p(\ell) \frac{R_{n-2}(\vartheta(\ell))}{R_{n-2}(\ell)} > 0.$$

In the next part, we review some lemmas from the literature that we will need in the proof of our results.

Lemma 1 ([20]). *Suppose that* $Y(\ell) \in C^m([\ell_0,\infty), \mathbb{R}^+)$, $Y^{(m)}(\ell)$ *is of constant sign and not identically zero on* $[\ell_0,\infty)$. *Assume also that* $Y^{(m-1)}(\ell) Y^{(m)}(\ell) \le 0$, *eventually, and* $\lim_{u\to\infty} Y(\ell) \ne 0$. *Then, eventually,*

$$Y(\ell) \ge \frac{\lambda}{(m-1)!} u^{m-1} \left| Y^{(m-1)}(\ell) \right|, \text{ for } \lambda \in (0,1).$$

Lemma 2 ([21]). *Assume that* ϱ_1 *and* ϱ_2 *are real numbers,* $\varrho_1 > 0$, *then,*

$$\varrho_1 H^{(\alpha+1)/\alpha} - \varrho_2 H \ge -\frac{\alpha^{\alpha}}{(\alpha+1)^{\alpha+1}} \frac{\varrho_2^{\alpha+1}}{\varrho_1^{\alpha}}. \tag{11}$$

The following lemma classifies the positive solutions depending on the sign of their derivatives, which is a modification of Lemma 1.1 in [22] for the studied equation.

Lemma 3. *Suppose that $x \in C([\ell_0,\infty),\mathbb{R}^+)$ is a solution to (8). Then, $\mathcal{B}$ is positive, $r \cdot \left(\mathcal{B}^{(n-1)}\right)^{\alpha}$ is decreasing, and $\mathcal{B}$ satisfies one of the following cases:*

$$(\mathbf{N}_1)\ \mathcal{B}^{(r)}(\ell) > 0 \text{ for } r = 1,2,\ldots,n-1 \text{ and } \mathcal{B}^{(n)}(\ell) < 0;$$
$$(\mathbf{N}_2)\ \mathcal{B}^{(r)}(\ell) > 0 \text{ for } r = 1,2,\ldots,n-2 \text{ and } \mathcal{B}^{(n-1)}(\ell) < 0;$$
$$(\mathbf{N}_3)\ (-1)^r\mathcal{B}^{(r)}(\ell) > 0 \text{ for } r = 0,1,2,\ldots,n-1,$$

eventually.

3. Auxiliary Results

Next, we provide the following notations to help us display the results easily:

$$h(\ell) := \min\{h_i(\ell),\ i = 1,\ldots,J\},$$

$$R_0(\ell) := \int_\ell^\infty \frac{1}{r^{1/\alpha}(\mathfrak{a})}\mathrm{d}\mathfrak{a},$$

$$R_m(\ell) := \int_\ell^\infty R_{m-1}(\mathfrak{a})\mathrm{d}\mathfrak{a},\ m = 1,2,\ldots,n-2,$$

$$Q(\ell) := \sum_{i=1}^{J} q_i(\ell)(1 - p(h_i(\ell)))^\alpha$$

and

$$Q^*(\ell) := \sum_{i=1}^{J} q_i(\ell)\left(1 - p(h_i(\ell))\frac{R_{n-2}(\vartheta(h_i(\ell)))}{R_{n-2}(h_i(\ell))}\right)^\alpha.$$

Further, we denote the set of all eventually positive solutions of (8) which $\mathcal{B}(\ell)$ satisfies $\mathbf{N}_2$ by Ω.

Lemma 4. *Assume that $x \in \Omega$, then,*

$$\left(r(\ell)\left(\mathcal{B}^{(n-1)}(\ell)\right)^\alpha\right)' \leq -Q(\ell)\mathcal{B}^\alpha(h(\ell)).$$

Proof. Assume that $x \in \Omega$, we find $\mathcal{B}'(\ell) > 0$. Since $\vartheta(\ell) \leq \ell$,then we have $x(\vartheta(\ell)) \leq \mathcal{B}(\vartheta(\ell)) \leq \mathcal{B}(\ell)$, therefore, we get

$$\begin{aligned} x(\ell) &= \mathcal{B}(\ell) - p(\ell)x(\vartheta(\ell)) \geq \mathcal{B}(\ell) - p(\ell)\mathcal{B}(\vartheta(\ell)) \\ &\geq (1 - p(\ell))\mathcal{B}(\ell). \end{aligned} \tag{12}$$

From (8) and (12), we have

$$\begin{aligned} \left(r(\ell)\left(\mathcal{B}^{(n-1)}(\ell)\right)^\alpha\right)' &= -\sum_{i=1}^{J} q_i(\ell)x^\alpha(h_i(\ell)) \leq -\sum_{i=1}^{J} q_i(\ell)(1 - p(h_i(\ell)))^\alpha\mathcal{B}^\alpha(h_i(\ell)) \\ &\leq -\mathcal{B}^\alpha(h(\ell))\sum_{i=1}^{J} q_i(\ell)(1 - p(h_i(\ell)))^\alpha \leq -\mathcal{B}^\alpha(h(\ell))Q(\ell). \end{aligned} \tag{13}$$

The proof of the lemma is complete. □

Lemma 5. *Assume that $x \in \Omega$, then, $\mathcal{B}^{(n-2)}(\ell)/R_0(\ell)$ is increasing.*

Proof. Assume that $x \in \Omega$. From (8) we find that $r(\ell)\left(\mathcal{B}^{(n-1)}(\ell)\right)^\alpha$ is decreasing.

Now, since

$$\mathcal{B}^{(n-2)}(\ell) \geq -\int_{\ell}^{\infty} \frac{r^{1/\alpha}(\mathfrak{a})}{r^{1/\alpha}(\mathfrak{a})} \mathcal{B}^{(n-1)}(\mathfrak{a}) d\mathfrak{a} \geq -R_0(\ell) r^{1/\alpha}(\ell) \mathcal{B}^{(n-1)}(\ell), \tag{14}$$

and so

$$\left(\frac{\mathcal{B}^{(n-2)}(\ell)}{R_0(\ell)}\right)' = \frac{1}{r^{1/\alpha}(\ell) R_0^2(\ell)} \left(R_0(\ell) r^{1/\alpha}(\ell) \mathcal{B}^{(n-1)}(\ell) + \mathcal{B}^{(n-2)}(\ell)\right) \geq 0. \tag{15}$$

The proof of the lemma is complete. □

Lemma 6. *Assume that $x \in \Omega$, and there are $\gamma > 0$ and $\ell_1 \geq \ell_0$ such that*

$$\frac{1}{\alpha} r^{1/\alpha}(\ell) R_0^{1+\alpha}(\ell) \left(h^{n-2}(\ell)\right)^{\alpha} Q(\ell) \geq ((n-2)!)^{\alpha} \gamma, \tag{16}$$

then

$$\lim_{\ell \to \infty} \mathcal{B}^{(n-2)}(\ell) = 0,$$

where $\beta_0 = \mu_0 \gamma^{1/\alpha}$.

Proof. Assume that $x \in \Omega$, using Lemma 1 with $f = \mathcal{B}$ and $m = n-1$, we have

$$\mathcal{B}(\ell) \geq \frac{\mu_0}{(n-2)!} \ell^{n-2} \mathcal{B}^{(n-2)}(\ell), \tag{17}$$

for all $\mu_0 \in (0,1)$. Now, since $\mathcal{B}^{(n-2)}(\ell)$ is a positive decreasing function, we conclude that $\lim_{\ell \to \infty} \mathcal{B}^{(n-2)}(\ell) = c_1 \geq 0$. We claim that $c_1 = 0$. If not, then $\mathcal{B}^{(n-2)}(\ell) \geq c_1 > 0$ eventually, which with (17) gives

$$\mathcal{B}(\ell) \geq \frac{\mu_0}{(n-2)!} \ell^{n-2} \mathcal{B}^{(n-2)}(\ell) \geq \frac{\mu_0 c_1}{(n-2)!} \ell^{n-2},$$

for all $\mu_0 \in (0,1)$. Therefore, from (13), we have

$$\begin{aligned} \left(r(\ell)\left(\mathcal{B}^{(n-1)}(\ell)\right)^{\alpha}\right)' &\leq -Q(\ell) \mathcal{B}^{\alpha}(h(\ell)) \leq -\left(\frac{\mu_0 c_1}{(n-2)!} h^{n-2}(\ell)\right)^{\alpha} Q(\ell) \\ &\leq -\mu_0^{\alpha} c_1^{\alpha} \frac{\left(h^{n-2}(\ell)\right)^{\alpha}}{((n-2)!)^{\alpha}} Q(\ell), \end{aligned}$$

which with (16) becomes

$$\left(r(\ell)\left(\mathcal{B}^{(n-1)}(\ell)\right)^{\alpha}\right)' \leq -\alpha c_1^{\alpha} \mu_0^{\alpha} \gamma \frac{1}{r^{1/\alpha}(\ell) R_0^{1+\alpha}(\ell)} \leq -\alpha c_1^{\alpha} \beta_0^{\alpha} \frac{1}{r^{1/\alpha}(\ell) R_0^{1+\alpha}(\ell)}. \tag{18}$$

Integrating (18) from ℓ_2 to ℓ, we have

$$\begin{aligned} r(\ell)\left(\mathcal{B}^{(n-1)}(\ell)\right)^{\alpha} &\leq r(\ell_2)\left(\mathcal{B}^{(n-1)}(\ell_2)\right)^{\alpha} - \alpha c_1^{\alpha} \beta_0^{\alpha} \int_{\ell_2}^{\ell} \frac{1}{r^{1/\alpha}(\mathfrak{a}) R_0^{1+\alpha}(\mathfrak{a})} d\mathfrak{a} \\ &\leq \beta_0^{\alpha} c_1^{\alpha} \left(\frac{1}{R_0^{\alpha}(\ell_2)} - \frac{1}{R_0^{\alpha}(\ell)}\right). \end{aligned} \tag{19}$$

Since $R_0^{-\alpha}(\ell) \to \infty$ as $\ell \to \infty$, there is a $\ell_3 \geq \ell_2$ such that $R_0^{-\alpha}(\ell) - R_0^{-\alpha}(\ell_2) \geq \epsilon R_0^{-\alpha}(\ell)$ for all $\epsilon \in (0,1)$. Therefore, (19) becomes

$$\mathcal{B}^{(n-1)}(\ell) \leq -c_1 \epsilon^{1/\alpha} \beta_0 \frac{1}{r^{1/\alpha}(\ell) R_0(\ell)}, \tag{20}$$

for all $\ell \geq \ell_3$. Integrating (20) from ℓ_3 to ℓ, we have

$$\begin{aligned} \mathcal{B}^{(n-2)}(\ell) &\leq \mathcal{B}^{(n-2)}(\ell_3) - c_1 \epsilon^{1/\alpha} \beta_0 \int_{\ell_3}^{\ell} \frac{1}{r^{1/\alpha}(\mathfrak{a}) R_0(\mathfrak{a})} d\mathfrak{a} \\ &\leq \mathcal{B}^{(n-2)}(\ell_3) - c_1 \epsilon^{1/\alpha} \beta_0 \ln \frac{R_0(\ell_3)}{R_0(\ell)} \to -\infty \text{ as } \ell \to \infty, \end{aligned}$$

which is a contradiction. Then, $c_1 = 0$. The proof of the lemma is complete. □

Lemma 7. *Assume that $x \in \Omega$, and (16) holds, then*

$$\mathcal{B}^{(n-2)}(\ell)/R_0^{\beta_0}(\ell) \text{ is decreasing} \tag{21}$$

and

$$\mathcal{B}^{(n-2)}(\ell)/R_0^{1-\beta_0}(\ell) \text{ is increasing} \tag{22}$$

for $\ell \geq \ell_0$, where $\beta_0 = \mu_0 \gamma^{1/\alpha}$, $\mu_0 \in (0,1)$ and $\alpha \leq 1$.

Proof. Assume that $x \in \Omega$, from (13), (16) and (17), we obtain

$$\left(r(\ell) \left(\mathcal{B}^{(n-1)}(\ell) \right)^{\alpha} \right)' \leq -\frac{\alpha \beta_0^{\alpha}}{r^{1/\alpha}(\ell) R_0^{1+\alpha}(\ell)} \left(\mathcal{B}^{(n-2)}(h(\ell)) \right)^{\alpha}. \tag{23}$$

By integrating (23) from ℓ_1 to ℓ and using the fact $\mathcal{B}^{(n-1)}(\ell) < 0$, we have

$$\begin{aligned} r(\ell)\left(\mathcal{B}^{(n-1)}(\ell)\right)^{\alpha} &\leq r(\ell_1)\left(\mathcal{B}^{(n-1)}(\ell_1)\right)^{\alpha} - \alpha \beta_0^{\alpha} \int_{\ell_1}^{\ell} \frac{1}{r^{1/\alpha}(\mathfrak{a}) R_0^{1+\alpha}(\mathfrak{a})} \left(\mathcal{B}^{(n-2)}(h(\mathfrak{a}))\right)^{\alpha} d\mathfrak{a} \\ &\leq r(\ell_1)\left(\mathcal{B}^{(n-1)}(\ell_1)\right)^{\alpha} - \alpha \beta_0^{\alpha} \left(\mathcal{B}^{(n-2)}(\ell)\right)^{\alpha} \int_{\ell_1}^{\ell} \frac{1}{r^{1/\alpha}(\mathfrak{a}) R_0^{1+\alpha}(\mathfrak{a})} d\mathfrak{a} \\ &\leq r(\ell_1)\left(\mathcal{B}^{(n-1)}(\ell_1)\right)^{\alpha} + \frac{\beta_0^{\alpha}}{R_0^{\alpha}(\ell_1)} \left(\mathcal{B}^{(n-2)}(\ell)\right)^{\alpha} - \frac{\beta_0^{\alpha}}{R_0^{\alpha}(\ell)} \left(\mathcal{B}^{(n-2)}(\ell)\right)^{\alpha}. \end{aligned}$$

Since $\mathcal{B}^{(n-2)}(\ell) \to 0$ as $\ell \to \infty$ there is a $\ell_2 \geq \ell_1$ such that

$$r(\ell_1)\left(\mathcal{B}^{(n-1)}(\ell_1)\right)^{\alpha} + \frac{\beta_0^{\alpha}}{R_0^{\alpha}(\ell_1)} \left(\mathcal{B}^{(n-2)}(\ell)\right)^{\alpha} \leq 0,$$

for $\ell \geq \ell_2$. Therefore, we get

$$r(\ell)\left(\mathcal{B}^{(n-1)}(\ell)\right)^{\alpha} \leq -\frac{\beta_0^{\alpha}}{R_0^{\alpha}(\ell)} \left(\mathcal{B}^{(n-2)}(\ell)\right)^{\alpha},$$

and so

$$r^{1/\alpha}(\ell) \mathcal{B}^{(n-1)}(\ell) R_0(\ell) + \beta_0 \mathcal{B}^{(n-2)}(\ell) \leq 0, \tag{24}$$

then

$$\left(\frac{\mathcal{B}^{(n-2)}(\ell)}{R_0^{\beta_0}(\ell)} \right)' = \frac{R_0(\ell) r^{1/\alpha}(\ell) \mathcal{B}^{(n-1)}(\ell) + \beta_0 \mathcal{B}^{(n-2)}(\ell)}{r^{1/\alpha}(\ell) R_0^{1+\beta_0}(\ell)} \leq 0.$$

Now, from (13), (16), (17) and (24), we obtain

$$\begin{aligned}\left(r(\ell)\left(\mathcal{B}^{(n-1)}(\ell)\right)^{\alpha}\right)' &\le -\left(\frac{\mu_0}{(n-2)!}h^{n-2}(\ell)\right)^{\alpha} Q(\ell)\left(\mathcal{B}^{(n-2)}(h(\ell))\right)^{\alpha} \\ &\le -\alpha\beta_0^{\alpha}\frac{1}{r^{1/\alpha}(\ell)R_0^{1+\alpha}(\ell)}\left(\mathcal{B}^{(n-2)}(h(\ell))\right)^{\alpha} \end{aligned} \tag{25}$$

and

$$r^{1/\alpha}(\ell)\mathcal{B}^{(n-1)}(\ell) \le -\beta_0\frac{\mathcal{B}^{(n-2)}(\ell)}{R_0(\ell)},$$

and so

$$\left(r^{1/\alpha}(\ell)\mathcal{B}^{(n-1)}(\ell)\right)^{1-\alpha} \ge \left(\beta_0\frac{\mathcal{B}^{(n-2)}(\ell)}{R_0(\ell)}\right)^{1-\alpha}, \tag{26}$$

Now, we find

$$\begin{aligned}&\left(r^{1/\alpha}(\ell)\mathcal{B}^{(n-1)}(\ell)R_0(\ell)+\mathcal{B}^{(n-2)}(\ell)\right)' \\ &= \left(r^{1/\alpha}(\ell)\mathcal{B}^{(n-1)}(\ell)\right)'R_0(\ell)-\mathcal{B}^{(n-1)}(\ell)+\mathcal{B}^{(n-1)}(\ell) \\ &= \left(r^{1/\alpha}(\ell)\mathcal{B}^{(n-1)}(\ell)\right)'R_0(\ell) \\ &= \frac{1}{\alpha}\left(r(\ell)\left(\mathcal{B}^{(n-1)}(\ell)\right)^{\alpha}\right)'\left(r^{1/\alpha}(\ell)\mathcal{B}^{(n-1)}(\ell)\right)^{1-\alpha}R_0(\ell),\end{aligned}$$

from (25) and (26), we get

$$\begin{aligned}\left(r^{1/\alpha}(\ell)\mathcal{B}^{(n-1)}(\ell)R_0(\ell)+\mathcal{B}^{(n-2)}(\ell)\right)' &\le -\beta_0^{\alpha}\frac{\left(\mathcal{B}^{(n-2)}(h(\ell))\right)^{\alpha}}{r^{1/\alpha}(\ell)R_0^{1+\alpha}(\ell)}\left(\beta_0\frac{\mathcal{B}^{(n-2)}(\ell)}{R_0(\ell)}\right)^{1-\alpha}R_0(\ell) \\ &\le -\beta_0^{\alpha}\frac{\left(\mathcal{B}^{(n-2)}(\ell)\right)^{\alpha}}{r^{1/\alpha}(\ell)R_0^{\alpha}(\ell)}\left(\beta_0\frac{\mathcal{B}^{(n-2)}(\ell)}{R_0(\ell)}\right)^{1-\alpha} \\ &\le \frac{-\beta_0}{r^{1/\alpha}(\ell)R_0(\ell)}\mathcal{B}^{(n-2)}(\ell).\end{aligned}$$

Integrating the last inequality from ℓ to ∞ and using (14), we obtain

$$-r^{1/\alpha}(\ell)\mathcal{B}^{(n-1)}(\ell)R_0(\ell)-\mathcal{B}^{(n-2)}(\ell) \le -\beta_0\int_{\ell}^{\infty}\frac{1}{r^{1/\alpha}(\mathfrak{a})R_0(\mathfrak{a})}\mathcal{B}^{(n-2)}(\mathfrak{a})\mathrm{d}\mathfrak{a},$$

and so

$$\begin{aligned}r^{1/\alpha}(\ell)\mathcal{B}^{(n-1)}(\ell)R_0(\ell)+\mathcal{B}^{(n-2)}(\ell) &\ge \beta_0\int_{\ell}^{\infty}\frac{1}{r^{1/\alpha}(\mathfrak{a})R_0(\mathfrak{a})}\mathcal{B}^{(n-2)}(\mathfrak{a})\mathrm{d}\mathfrak{a} \\ &\ge \beta_0\frac{\mathcal{B}^{(n-2)}(\ell)}{R_0(\ell)}\int_{\ell}^{\infty}\frac{1}{r^{1/\alpha}(\mathfrak{a})}\mathrm{d}\mathfrak{a} \\ &\ge \beta_0\mathcal{B}^{(n-2)}(\ell),\end{aligned}$$

which means that

$$r^{1/\alpha}(\ell)\mathcal{B}^{(n-1)}(\ell)R_0(\ell)+(1-\beta_0)\mathcal{B}^{(n-2)}(\ell) \ge 0.$$

Then

$$\left(\frac{\mathcal{B}^{(n-2)}(\ell)}{R_0^{1-\beta_0}(\ell)}\right)' = \frac{R_0(\ell)r^{1/\alpha}(\ell)\mathcal{B}^{(n-1)}(\ell)+(1-\beta_0)\mathcal{B}^{(n-2)}(\ell)}{r^{1/\alpha}(\ell)R_0^{2-\beta_0}(\ell)} \ge 0. \tag{27}$$

The proof of the lemma is complete. □

Lemma 8. *Assume that $x \in \Omega$, and (16) holds, then*

$$\lim_{\ell\to\infty} \mathcal{B}^{(n-2)}(\ell)/R_0^{\beta_0}(\ell) = 0.$$

Proof. Since $\mathcal{B}^{(n-2)}(\ell)/R_0^{\beta_0}(\ell)$ is a positive decreasing function, $\lim_{\ell\to\infty} \mathcal{B}^{(n-2)}(\ell)/R_0^{\beta_0}(\ell) = c_2 \geq 0$. We claim that $c_2 = 0$. If not, then $\mathcal{B}^{(n-2)}(\ell)/R_0^{\beta_0}(\ell) \geq c_2 > 0$ eventually. Now, we introduce the function

$$w(\ell) = \frac{\mathcal{B}^{(n-2)}(\ell) + R_0(\ell) r^{1/\alpha}(\ell)\mathcal{B}^{(n-1)}(\ell)}{R_0^{\beta_0}(\ell)}.$$

From (16), we note that $w(\ell) > 0$ and

$$\begin{aligned} w'(\ell) &= \frac{\mathcal{B}^{(n-1)}(\ell) + R_0(\ell)\left(r^{1/\alpha}(\ell)\mathcal{B}^{(n-1)}(\ell)\right)' - \mathcal{B}^{(n-1)}(\ell)}{R_0^{\beta_0}(\ell)} \\ &\quad + \beta_0 \frac{\mathcal{B}^{(n-2)}(\ell) + R_0(\ell) r^{1/\alpha}(\ell)\mathcal{B}^{(n-1)}(\ell)}{r^{1/\alpha}(\ell) R_0^{1+\beta_0}(\ell)} \\ &= \frac{\left(r^{1/\alpha}(\ell)\mathcal{B}^{(n-1)}(\ell)\right)'}{R_0^{\beta_0-1}(\ell)} + \beta_0 \frac{\mathcal{B}^{(n-2)}(\ell)}{r^{1/\alpha}(\ell) R_0^{1+\beta_0}(\ell)} + \beta_0 \frac{\mathcal{B}^{(n-1)}(\ell)}{R_0^{\beta_0}(\ell)} \\ &= \frac{1}{\alpha} \frac{\left(r(\ell)\left(\mathcal{B}^{(n-1)}(\ell)\right)^{\alpha}\right)' \left(r^{1/\alpha}(\ell)\mathcal{B}^{(n-1)}(\ell)\right)^{1-\alpha}}{R_0^{\beta_0-1}(\ell)} \\ &\quad + \beta_0 \frac{\mathcal{B}^{(n-2)}(\ell)}{r^{1/\alpha}(\ell) R_0^{1+\beta_0}(\ell)} + \beta_0 \frac{\mathcal{B}^{(n-1)}(\ell)}{R_0^{\beta_0}(\ell)}. \end{aligned}$$

using (25) and (26), we have

$$\begin{aligned} w'(\ell) &\leq -\frac{\beta_0^{\alpha}}{R_0^{\beta_0-1}(\ell)} \frac{1}{r^{1/\alpha}(\ell) R_0^{1+\alpha}(\ell)} \left(\mathcal{B}^{(n-2)}(h(\ell))\right)^{\alpha} \left(\beta_0 \frac{\mathcal{B}^{(n-2)}(\ell)}{R_0(\ell)}\right)^{1-\alpha} \\ &\quad + \beta_0 \frac{\mathcal{B}^{(n-2)}(\ell)}{r^{1/\alpha}(\ell) R_0^{1+\beta_0}(\ell)} + \beta_0 \frac{\mathcal{B}^{(n-1)}(\ell)}{R_0^{\beta_0}(\ell)}. \end{aligned}$$

Since $\mathcal{B}^{(n-1)}(\ell) < 0$, $h(\ell) \leq \ell$, we find $\mathcal{B}^{(n-2)}(h(\ell)) \geq \mathcal{B}^{(n-2)}(\ell)$, and then

$$\begin{aligned} w'(\ell) &\leq -\frac{\beta_0^{\alpha}}{R_0^{\beta_0-1}(\ell)} \frac{1}{r^{1/\alpha}(\ell) R_0^{1+\alpha}(\ell)} \left(\mathcal{B}^{(n-2)}(\ell)\right)^{\alpha} \left(\beta_0 \frac{\mathcal{B}^{(n-2)}(\ell)}{R_0(\ell)}\right)^{1-\alpha} \\ &\quad + \beta_0 \frac{\mathcal{B}^{(n-2)}(\ell)}{r^{1/\alpha}(\ell) R_0^{1+\beta_0}(\ell)} + \beta_0 \frac{\mathcal{B}^{(n-1)}(\ell)}{R_0^{\beta_0}(\ell)} \\ &\leq -\beta_0 \frac{\mathcal{B}^{(n-2)}(\ell)}{r^{1/\alpha}(\ell) R_0^{1+\beta_0}(\ell)} + \beta_0 \frac{\mathcal{B}^{(n-2)}(\ell)}{r^{1/\alpha}(\ell) R_0^{1+\beta_0}(\ell)} + \beta_0 \frac{\mathcal{B}^{(n-1)}(\ell)}{R_0^{\beta_0}(\ell)} \\ &\leq \beta_0 \frac{\mathcal{B}^{(n-1)}(\ell)}{R_0^{\beta_0}(\ell)}. \end{aligned}$$

Since $\mathcal{B}^{(n-2)}(\ell)/R_0^{\beta_0}(\ell) \geq c_2$, and (24) holds, we obtain

$$\begin{aligned} w'(\ell) &\leq \beta_0 \frac{\mathcal{B}^{(n-1)}(\ell)}{R_0^{\beta_0}(\ell)} \leq -\frac{\mathcal{B}^{(n-2)}(\ell)}{R_0^{\beta_0}(\ell)} \frac{\beta_0^2}{r^{1/\alpha}(\ell)R_0(\ell)} \\ &\leq \frac{-c_2\beta_0^2}{r^{1/\alpha}(\ell)R_0(\ell)} < 0. \end{aligned} \tag{28}$$

The function $w(\ell)$ converges to a non-negative constant because it is a positive decreasing function. Integrating (28) from ℓ_3 to ∞, we have

$$-w(\ell_3) \leq -\beta_0^2 c_2 \lim_{\ell\to\infty} \ln \frac{R_0(\ell_3)}{R_0(\ell)},$$

and so

$$w(\ell_3) \geq \beta_0^2 c_2 \lim_{\ell\to\infty} \ln \frac{R_0(\ell_3)}{R_0(\ell)} \to \infty,$$

which is a contradiction and we get that $c_2 = 0$. The proof of the lemma is complete. □

If $\beta_0 \leq 1/2$, we can improve the properties in Lemma 7, as in the following lemma.

Lemma 9. *Assume that $x \in \Omega$, and (16) holds. If*

$$\lim_{\ell\to\infty} \frac{R_0(h(\ell))}{R_0(\ell)} = \delta < \infty, \tag{29}$$

and there exists an increasing sequence $\{\beta_r\}_{r=1}^{m}$ defined as

$$\beta_r := \beta_0 \frac{\delta^{\beta_{r-1}}}{(1-\beta_{r-1})^{1/\alpha}},$$

with $\alpha \leq 1$, $\beta_0 = \mu_0\gamma^{1/\alpha}$, $\beta_{m-1} \leq 1/2$ and β_m, $\mu_0 \in (0,1)$, then,

$$\mathcal{B}^{(n-2)}(\ell)/R_0^{\beta_m}(\ell) \text{ is decreasing.} \tag{30}$$

Proof. Since $x \in \Omega$, from Lemma 7, we have that (21) and (22) hold.

Now, assume that $\beta_0 \leq 1/2$ and

$$\beta_1 := \beta_0 \frac{\delta^{\beta_0}}{(1-\beta_0)^{1/\alpha}}.$$

Next, we will prove (30) at $m = 1$. As in the proof of Lemma 7 we find

$$\left(r(\ell)\left(\mathcal{B}^{(n-1)}(\ell)\right)^{\alpha}\right)' \leq -\alpha\beta_0^{\alpha} \frac{1}{r^{1/\alpha}(\ell)R_0^{1+\alpha}(\ell)} \left(\mathcal{B}^{(n-2)}(h(\ell))\right)^{\alpha}. \tag{31}$$

Integrating (31) from ℓ_1 to ℓ, and using (21) and (29), we have

$$
\begin{aligned}
& r(\ell)\left(\mathcal{B}^{(n-1)}(\ell)\right)^{\alpha} \\
& \leq r(\ell_1)\left(\mathcal{B}^{(n-1)}(\ell_1)\right)^{\alpha} - \alpha\beta_0^{\alpha}\int_{\ell_1}^{\ell}\frac{\left(\mathcal{B}^{(n-2)}(h(\mathfrak{a}))\right)^{\alpha}}{r^{1/\alpha}(\mathfrak{a})R_0^{1+\alpha}(\mathfrak{a})}d\mathfrak{a} \\
& \leq r(\ell_1)\left(\mathcal{B}^{(n-1)}(\ell_1)\right)^{\alpha} - \alpha\beta_0^{\alpha}\int_{\ell_1}^{\ell}\frac{R_0^{\alpha\beta_0}(h(\mathfrak{a}))}{r^{1/\alpha}(\mathfrak{a})R_0^{1+\alpha}(\mathfrak{a})}\left(\frac{\mathcal{B}^{(n-2)}(\mathfrak{a})}{R_0^{\beta_0}(\mathfrak{a})}\right)^{\alpha}d\mathfrak{a} \\
& \leq r(\ell_1)\left(\mathcal{B}^{(n-1)}(\ell_1)\right)^{\alpha} - \alpha\beta_0^{\alpha}\left(\frac{\mathcal{B}^{(n-2)}(\ell)}{R_0^{\beta_0}(\ell)}\right)^{\alpha}\int_{\ell_1}^{\ell}\frac{R_0^{-1-\alpha+\alpha\beta_0}(\mathfrak{a})}{r^{1/\alpha}(\mathfrak{a})}\frac{R_0^{\alpha\beta_0}(h(\mathfrak{a}))}{R_0^{\alpha\beta_0}(\mathfrak{a})}d\mathfrak{a} \\
& \leq r(\ell_1)\left(\mathcal{B}^{(n-1)}(\ell_1)\right)^{\alpha} - \alpha\beta_0^{\alpha}\delta^{\alpha\beta_0}\left(\frac{\mathcal{B}^{(n-2)}(\ell)}{R_0^{\beta_0}(\ell)}\right)^{\alpha}\int_{\ell_1}^{\ell}\frac{R_0^{-1-\alpha+\alpha\beta_0}(\mathfrak{a})}{r^{1/\alpha}(\mathfrak{a})}d\mathfrak{a} \\
& \leq r(\ell_1)\left(\mathcal{B}^{(n-1)}(\ell_1)\right)^{\alpha} - \frac{\beta_0^{\alpha}\delta^{\alpha\beta_0}}{1-\beta_0}\left(\frac{\mathcal{B}^{(n-2)}(\ell)}{R_0^{\beta_0}(\ell)}\right)^{\alpha}\left(\frac{1}{R_0^{\alpha(1-\beta_0)}(\ell)} - \frac{1}{R_0^{\alpha(1-\beta_0)}(\ell_1)}\right) \\
& \leq r(\ell_1)\left(\mathcal{B}^{(n-1)}(\ell_1)\right)^{\alpha} + \beta_1^{\alpha}\frac{1}{R_0^{\alpha(1-\beta_0)}(\ell_1)}\left(\frac{\mathcal{B}^{(n-2)}(\ell)}{R_0^{\beta_0}(\ell)}\right)^{\alpha} - \beta_1^{\alpha}\left(\frac{\mathcal{B}^{(n-2)}(\ell)}{R_0(\ell)}\right)^{\alpha}.
\end{aligned}
$$

Since $\mathcal{B}^{(n-2)}(\ell)/R_0^{\beta_0}(\ell) \to 0$ as $\ell \to \infty$, we get

$$
r(\ell_1)\left(\mathcal{B}^{(n-1)}(\ell_1)\right)^{\alpha} + \beta_1^{\alpha}\frac{1}{R_0^{\alpha(1-\beta_0)}(\ell_1)}\left(\frac{\mathcal{B}^{(n-2)}(\ell)}{R_0^{\beta_0}(\ell)}\right)^{\alpha} \leq 0.
$$

Hence, we have

$$
r(\ell)\left(\mathcal{B}^{(n-1)}(\ell)\right)^{\alpha} \leq -\beta_1^{\alpha}\left(\frac{\mathcal{B}^{(n-2)}(\ell)}{R_0(\ell)}\right)^{\alpha},
$$

and so

$$
r^{1/\alpha}(\ell)\mathcal{B}^{(n-1)}(\ell)R_0(\ell) + \beta_1\mathcal{B}^{(n-2)}(\ell) \leq 0,
$$

then

$$
\left(\frac{\mathcal{B}^{(n-2)}(\ell)}{R_0^{\beta_1}(\ell)}\right)' = \frac{R_0(\ell)r^{1/\alpha}(\ell)\mathcal{B}^{(n-1)}(\ell) + \beta_1\mathcal{B}^{(n-2)}(\ell)}{r^{1/\alpha}(\ell)R_0^{1+\beta_1}(\ell)} \leq 0.
$$

By repeating the same approach used previously, we can prove that

$$
\left(\frac{\mathcal{B}^{(n-2)}(\ell)}{R_0^{1-\beta_1}(\ell)}\right)' \geq 0.
$$

Similarly, if $\beta_{k-1} < \beta_k \leq 1/2$, then we can prove

$$
r^{1/\alpha}(\ell)\mathcal{B}^{(n-1)}(\ell)R_0(\ell) + \beta_k\mathcal{B}^{(n-2)}(\ell) \leq 0, \tag{32}
$$

for $k = 2, 3, \ldots, m$. The proof of the lemma is complete. □

Lemma 10. *Assume that x is a positive solution of (8) and $\mathcal{B}$ satisfies $\mathbf{N}_3$. Then*

$$
\left(\frac{\mathcal{B}(\ell)}{R_{n-2}(\ell)}\right)' \geq 0. \tag{33}
$$

Proof. Assume that x is a positive solution of (8) and $\mathcal{B}$ satisfies $\mathbf{N}_3$. From (8), we find $r(\ell)\left(\mathcal{B}^{(n-1)}(\ell)\right)^{\alpha}$ is decreasing, and so

$$r^{1/\alpha}(\ell)\mathcal{B}^{(n-1)}(\ell)\int_{\ell}^{\infty}\frac{1}{r^{1/\alpha}(\mathfrak{a})}d\mathfrak{a} \geq \int_{\ell}^{\infty}\frac{1}{r^{1/\alpha}(\mathfrak{a})}r^{1/\alpha}(\mathfrak{a})\mathcal{B}^{(n-1)}(\mathfrak{a})d\mathfrak{a} = \lim_{\ell\to\infty}\mathcal{B}^{(n-2)}(\ell) - \mathcal{B}^{(n-2)}(\ell). \quad (34)$$

Since $\mathcal{B}^{(n-2)}(\ell)$ is a positive decreasing function, we have that $\mathcal{B}^{(n-2)}(\ell)$ converges to a nonnegative constant when $\ell \to \infty$. Thus, (34) becomes

$$-\mathcal{B}^{(n-2)}(\ell) \leq r^{1/\alpha}(\ell)\mathcal{B}^{(n-1)}(\ell)R_0(\ell), \quad (35)$$

from (35), we get

$$\left(\frac{\mathcal{B}^{(n-2)}(\ell)}{R_0(\ell)}\right)' = \frac{\left(r^{1/\alpha}(\ell)R_0(\ell)\mathcal{B}^{(n-1)}(\ell) + \mathcal{B}^{(n-2)}(\ell)\right)}{r^{1/\alpha}(\ell)R_0^2(\ell)} \geq 0,$$

which leads to

$$-\mathcal{B}^{(n-3)}(\ell) \geq \int_{\ell}^{\infty}\frac{\mathcal{B}^{(n-2)}(\mathfrak{a})}{R_0(\mathfrak{a})}R_0(\mathfrak{a})d\mathfrak{a} \geq \frac{\mathcal{B}^{(n-2)}(\ell)}{R_0(\ell)}\int_{\ell}^{\infty}R_0(\mathfrak{a})d\mathfrak{a} = \frac{\mathcal{B}^{(n-2)}(\ell)}{R_0(\ell)}R_1(\mathfrak{a}).$$

This implies

$$\left(\frac{\mathcal{B}^{(n-3)}(\ell)}{R_1(\ell)}\right)' = \frac{R_1(\ell)\mathcal{B}^{(n-2)}(\ell) + \mathcal{B}^{(n-3)}(\ell)R_0(\ell)}{R_1^2(\ell)} \leq 0.$$

Similarly, we repeat the same previous process $(n-4)$ times, we have

$$\left(\frac{\mathcal{B}'(\ell)}{R_{n-3}(\ell)}\right)' \leq 0.$$

Now,

$$-\mathcal{B}(\ell) \leq \int_{\ell}^{\infty}\frac{\mathcal{B}'(\mathfrak{a})}{R_{n-3}(\mathfrak{a})}R_{n-3}(\mathfrak{a})d\mathfrak{a} \leq \frac{\mathcal{B}'(\ell)}{R_{n-3}(\ell)}\int_{\ell}^{\infty}R_{n-3}(\mathfrak{a})d\mathfrak{a} = \frac{\mathcal{B}'(\ell)}{R_{n-3}(\ell)}R_{n-2}(\ell).$$

This implies

$$\left(\frac{\mathcal{B}(\ell)}{R_{n-2}(\ell)}\right)' = \frac{R_{n-2}(\ell)\mathcal{B}'(\ell) + \mathcal{B}(\ell)R_{n-3}(\ell)}{R_{n-2}^2(\ell)} \geq 0.$$

The proof of the lemma is complete. □

4. Main Results

In the following theorems, we prove that there are no positive solutions that satisfy case $\mathbf{N}_2$.

Theorem 7. *Assume that (16) holds. If*

$$\beta_0 > 1/2, \quad (36)$$

for some $\mu_0 \in (0,1)$, then the class Ω is empty, where β_0 is defined as in Lemma 7.

Proof. Assume the contrary that $x \in \Omega$. From Lemma 7, we have that the functions $\mathcal{B}^{(n-2)}(\ell)/R_0^{\beta_0}(\ell)$ and $\mathcal{B}^{(n-2)}(\ell)/R_0^{1-\beta_0}(\ell)$ are decreasing and increasing for $\ell \geq \ell_1$, respectively. In another meaning, we have

$$r^{1/\alpha}(\ell)\mathcal{B}^{(n-1)}(\ell)R_0(\ell) + \beta_0\mathcal{B}^{(n-2)}(\ell) \leq 0 \tag{37}$$

and

$$r^{1/\alpha}(\ell)\mathcal{B}^{(n-1)}(\ell)R_0(\ell) + (1-\beta_0)\mathcal{B}^{(n-2)}(\ell) \geq 0. \tag{38}$$

from (37) and (38), we get

$$\begin{aligned} 0 &\leq r^{1/\alpha}(\ell)\mathcal{B}^{(n-1)}(\ell)R_0(\ell) + (1-\beta_0)\mathcal{B}^{(n-2)}(\ell) \\ &= r^{1/\alpha}(\ell)\mathcal{B}^{(n-1)}(\ell)R_0(\ell) + \beta_0\mathcal{B}^{(n-2)}(\ell) + \mathcal{B}^{(n-2)}(\ell) - 2\beta_0\mathcal{B}^{(n-2)}(\ell) \\ &\leq (1-2\beta_0)\mathcal{B}^{(n-2)}(\ell). \end{aligned}$$

Since $\mathcal{B}^{(n-2)}(\ell) > 0$, must be $1 - 2\beta_0 \geq 0$, which measn that

$$\beta_0 \leq 1/2,$$

a contradiction. The proof of the theorem is complete. □

Theorem 8. *Assume that (16) and (29) hold. If there exists a positive integer number m such that*

$$w'(\ell) + \frac{1}{\alpha}\frac{\mu_0^\alpha \beta_m^{1-\alpha}}{((n-2)!)^\alpha (1-\beta_m)}\frac{R_0(\ell)}{R_0^{1-\alpha}(h(\ell))}\left(h^{n-2}(\ell)\right)^\alpha Q(\ell)w(h(\ell)) = 0, \tag{39}$$

then the class Ω is empty, where $\alpha \leq 1$ and β_m is defined as in Lemma 9.

Proof. Assume the contrary, that $x \in \Omega$. From Lemma 9, we have that (30) holds.
Now, we define the function

$$w(\ell) = r^{1/\alpha}(\ell)\mathcal{B}^{(n-1)}(\ell)R_0(\ell) + \mathcal{B}^{(n-2)}(\ell).$$

It follows from (14) that $w(\ell) > 0$ for $\ell \geq \ell_1$. From (30), we obtain

$$r^{1/\alpha}(\ell)\mathcal{B}^{(n-1)}(\ell)R_0(\ell) \leq -\beta_m\mathcal{B}^{(n-2)}(\ell).$$

Then, from the definition of $w(\ell)$, we find

$$\begin{aligned} w(\ell) &= r^{1/\alpha}(\ell)\mathcal{B}^{(n-1)}(\ell)R_0(\ell) + \beta_m\mathcal{B}^{(n-2)}(\ell) - \beta_m\mathcal{B}^{(n-2)}(\ell) + \mathcal{B}^{(n-2)}(\ell) \\ &\leq (1-\beta_m)\mathcal{B}^{(n-2)}(\ell). \end{aligned} \tag{40}$$

From (17) and (13), we get

$$\begin{aligned} w'(\ell) &= \left(r^{1/\alpha}(\ell)\mathcal{B}^{(n-1)}(\ell)\right)' R_0(\ell) \leq \frac{1}{\alpha}\left(r(\ell)\left(\mathcal{B}^{(n-1)}(\ell)\right)^\alpha\right)'\left(r^{1/\alpha}(\ell)\mathcal{B}^{(n-1)}(\ell)\right)^{1-\alpha} R_0(\ell) \\ &\leq -\frac{1}{\alpha}Q(\ell)\mathcal{B}^\alpha(h(\ell))\left(r^{1/\alpha}(\ell)\mathcal{B}^{(n-1)}(\ell)\right)^{1-\alpha} R_0(\ell) \\ &\leq -\frac{1}{\alpha}Q(\ell)\mathcal{B}^\alpha(h(\ell))\left(\beta_m\frac{\mathcal{B}^{(n-2)}(\ell)}{R_0(\ell)}\right)^{1-\alpha} R_0(\ell) \\ &\leq -\frac{1}{\alpha}\beta_m^{1-\alpha}Q(\ell)R_0(\ell)\mathcal{B}^\alpha(h(\ell))\left(\frac{\mathcal{B}^{(n-2)}(\ell)}{R_0(\ell)}\right)^{1-\alpha} \\ &\leq -\frac{1}{\alpha}\beta_m^{1-\alpha}Q(\ell)R_0(\ell)\left(\frac{\mu_0}{(n-2)!}h^{n-2}(\ell)\right)^\alpha\left(\mathcal{B}^{(n-2)}(h(\ell))\right)^\alpha\left(\frac{\mathcal{B}^{(n-2)}(\ell)}{R_0(\ell)}\right)^{1-\alpha}, \end{aligned}$$

from (15), we note that $\mathcal{B}^{(n-2)}(\ell)/R_0(\ell)$ is increasing, then

$$\frac{\mathcal{B}^{(n-2)}(h(\ell))}{R_0(h(\ell))} \leq \frac{\mathcal{B}^{(n-2)}(\ell)}{R_0(\ell)}$$

and

$$\left(\frac{\mathcal{B}^{(n-2)}(h(\ell))}{R_0(h(\ell))}\right)^{1-\alpha} \leq \left(\frac{\mathcal{B}^{(n-2)}(\ell)}{R_0(\ell)}\right)^{1-\alpha},$$

then, we have

$$\begin{aligned} w'(\ell) &\leq -\frac{1}{\alpha}\beta_m^{1-\alpha}Q(\ell)R_0(\ell)\left(\frac{\mu_0}{(n-2)!}h^{n-2}(\ell)\right)^{\alpha}\left(\mathcal{B}^{(n-2)}(h(\ell))\right)^{\alpha}\left(\frac{\mathcal{B}^{(n-2)}(h(\ell))}{R_0(h(\ell))}\right)^{1-\alpha} \\ &\leq -\frac{1}{\alpha}\frac{\beta_m^{1-\alpha}\mu_0^{\alpha}}{((n-2)!)^{\alpha}}Q(\ell)\frac{R_0(\ell)}{R_0^{1-\alpha}(h(\ell))}\left(h^{n-2}(\ell)\right)^{\alpha}\mathcal{B}^{(n-2)}(h(\ell)), \end{aligned}$$

which, from (40), gives

$$w'(\ell) + \frac{1}{\alpha}\frac{\mu_0^{\alpha}\beta_m^{1-\alpha}}{((n-2)!)^{\alpha}(1-\beta_m)}\frac{R_0(\ell)}{R_0^{1-\alpha}(h(\ell))}\left(h^{n-2}(\ell)\right)^{\alpha}Q(\ell)w(h(\ell)) \leq 0. \tag{41}$$

Hence, $w(\ell)$ is a positive solution of (41). Using [[23], Corollary 1], we see that (39) also has a positive solution, a contradiction. This contradiction completes the proof of the theorem. □

Corollary 1. *Assume that (16) and (29) hold. If*

$$\liminf_{\ell\to\infty}\int_{h(\ell)}^{\ell}\frac{1}{\alpha}\frac{R_0(\mathfrak{a})\left(h^{n-2}(\mathfrak{a})\right)^{\alpha}Q(\mathfrak{a})}{R_0^{1-\alpha}(h(\mathfrak{a}))}\mathrm{d}\mathfrak{a} > \frac{\beta_m^{\alpha-1}(1-\beta_m)((n-2)!)^{\alpha}}{\mathrm{e}}, \tag{42}$$

holds, then the class Ω is empty.

Theorem 9. *Assume that (16) and (29) hold. If*

$$\limsup_{\ell\to\infty}\int_{\ell_0}^{\ell}\left[\left(\frac{\lambda h^{n-2}(\mathfrak{a})}{(n-2)!}\right)^{\alpha}\frac{R_0^{\alpha\beta_m}(h(\mathfrak{a}))}{R_0^{-\alpha(1-\beta_m)}(\mathfrak{a})}Q(\mathfrak{a}) - \frac{\alpha^{\alpha+1}}{(1+\alpha)^{1+\alpha}}\frac{1}{R_0(\mathfrak{a})r^{1/\alpha}(\mathfrak{a})}\right]\mathrm{d}\mathfrak{a} = \infty, \tag{43}$$

holds for some constant $\lambda \in (0,1)$, then the class Ω is empty.

Proof. Assume the contrary that $x \in \Omega$. Define the function w by

$$w(\ell) = \frac{r(\ell)\left(\mathcal{B}^{(n-1)}(\ell)\right)^{\alpha}}{\left(\mathcal{B}^{(n-2)}(\ell)\right)^{\alpha}},\ \ell \geq \ell_1. \tag{44}$$

Then $w(\ell) < 0$ for $\ell \geq \ell_1$. Since $r(\ell)\left(\mathcal{B}^{(n-1)}(\ell)\right)^{\alpha}$ is decreasing, we have

$$r^{1/\alpha}(\mathfrak{a})\mathcal{B}^{(n-1)}(\mathfrak{a}) \leq r^{1/\alpha}(\ell)\mathcal{B}^{(n-1)}(\ell),$$

for $\mathfrak{a} \geq \ell \geq \ell_1$. By dividing the last inequality by $r^{1/\alpha}(\mathfrak{a})$ and integrating it from ℓ to ∞, we obtain

$$0 \leq \mathcal{B}^{(n-2)}(\ell) + r^{1/\alpha}(\ell)\mathcal{B}^{(n-1)}(\ell)\int_{\ell}^{l}\frac{1}{r^{1/\alpha}(\mathfrak{a})}\mathrm{d}\mathfrak{a},$$

and so

$$0 \leq \mathcal{B}^{(n-2)}(\ell) + r^{1/\alpha}(\ell)\mathcal{B}^{(n-1)}(\ell)R_0(\ell),$$

which produces

$$-\frac{r^{1/\alpha}(\ell)\mathcal{B}^{(n-1)}(\ell)}{\mathcal{B}^{(n-2)}(\ell)}R_0(\ell) \leq 1.$$

Hence, from (44), we find

$$-w(\ell)R_0^{\alpha}(\ell) \leq 1. \tag{45}$$

From (44), we have

$$\begin{aligned} w'(\ell) &= \frac{\left(r(\ell)\left(\mathcal{B}^{(n-1)}(\ell)\right)^{\alpha}\right)'}{\left(\mathcal{B}^{(n-2)}(\ell)\right)^{\alpha}} - \alpha\frac{r(\ell)\left(\mathcal{B}^{(n-1)}(\ell)\right)^{\alpha+1}}{\left(\mathcal{B}^{(n-2)}(\ell)\right)^{\alpha+1}} \\ &\leq -\frac{Q(\ell)\mathcal{B}^{\alpha}(h(\ell))}{\left(\mathcal{B}^{(n-2)}(\ell)\right)^{\alpha}} - \alpha\frac{w^{(\alpha+1)/\alpha}}{r^{1/\alpha}(\ell)}. \end{aligned}$$

Using Lemma 1, we get

$$\mathcal{B}(h(\ell)) \geq \frac{\lambda}{(n-2)!}h^{n-2}(\ell)\mathcal{B}^{(n-2)}(h(\ell)),$$

for every $\lambda \in (0,1)$ and for all sufficiently large ℓ. Then,

$$w'(\ell) \leq -Q(\ell)\left(\frac{\lambda}{(n-2)!}h^{n-2}(\ell)\right)^{\alpha}\frac{\left(\mathcal{B}^{(n-2)}(h(\ell))\right)^{\alpha}}{\left(\mathcal{B}^{(n-2)}(\ell)\right)^{\alpha}} - \alpha\frac{w^{(\alpha+1)/\alpha}(\ell)}{r^{1/\alpha}(\ell)}.$$

Since $\mathcal{B}^{(n-2)}(\ell)/R_0^{\beta_m}(\ell)$ is decreasing, then

$$\mathcal{B}^{(n-2)}(\ell) \leq \frac{\mathcal{B}^{(n-2)}(h(\ell))}{R_0^{\beta_m}(h(\ell))}R_0^{\beta_m}(\ell), \tag{46}$$

for $h(\ell) \leq \ell$, thus

$$w'(\ell) \leq -Q(\ell)\frac{R_0^{\alpha\beta_m}(h(\ell))}{R_0^{\alpha\beta_m}(\ell)}\left(\frac{\lambda}{(n-2)!}h^{n-2}(\ell)\right)^{\alpha} - \alpha\frac{w^{(\alpha+1)/\alpha}(\ell)}{r^{1/\alpha}(\ell)}. \tag{47}$$

Multiplying (47) by $R_0^{\alpha}(\ell)$ and integrating it from ℓ_1 to ℓ, we obtain

$$\begin{aligned} &R_0^{\alpha}(\ell)w(\ell) - R_0^{\alpha}(\ell_1)w(\ell_1) + \alpha\int_{\ell_1}^{\ell}\frac{R_0^{\alpha-1}(\mathfrak{a})}{r^{1/\alpha}(\mathfrak{a})}w(\mathfrak{a})d\mathfrak{a} \\ &+\int_{\ell_1}^{\ell}Q(\mathfrak{a})\frac{R_0^{\alpha\beta_m}(h(\mathfrak{a}))}{R_0^{-\alpha(1-\beta_m)}(\mathfrak{a})}\left(\frac{\lambda h^{n-2}(\mathfrak{a})}{(n-2)!}\right)^{\alpha}d\mathfrak{a} + \alpha\int_{\ell_1}^{\ell}\frac{w^{(\alpha+1)/\alpha}(\mathfrak{a})}{r^{1/\alpha}(\mathfrak{a})}R_0^{\alpha}(\mathfrak{a})d\mathfrak{a} \leq 0. \end{aligned}$$

Using (11) with

$$\varrho_1 := \frac{R_0^{\alpha}(\mathfrak{a})}{r^{1/\alpha}(\mathfrak{a})},\ \varrho_2 := \frac{R_0^{\alpha-1}(\mathfrak{a})}{r^{1/\alpha}(\mathfrak{a})} \text{ and } u := -w(\mathfrak{a}),$$

we have

$$\begin{aligned} \int_{\ell_1}^{\ell}\left[\left(\frac{\lambda h^{n-2}(\mathfrak{a})}{(n-2)!}\right)^{\alpha}\frac{R_0^{\alpha\beta_m}(h(\mathfrak{a}))}{R_0^{-\alpha(1-\beta_m)}(\mathfrak{a})}Q(\mathfrak{a}) - \frac{\alpha^{\alpha+1}}{(1+\alpha)^{1+\alpha}}\frac{1}{R_0(\mathfrak{a})r^{1/\alpha}(\mathfrak{a})}\right]d\mathfrak{a} \\ \leq R_0^{\alpha}(\ell_1)w(\ell_1) + 1, \end{aligned}$$

due to (45), which contradicts (43). This completes the proof of the theorem. □

In the following theorems, we establish new oscillation criteria for (8).

Theorem 10. *Let (16) and (29) hold. Assume that*

$$\liminf_{\ell\to\infty}\int_{h(\ell)}^{\ell} Q(\mathfrak{a})\frac{\left(h^{n-1}(\mathfrak{a})\right)^{\alpha}}{r(h(\mathfrak{a}))}\mathrm{d}\mathfrak{a} > \frac{((n-1)!)^{\alpha}}{\mathrm{e}}, \tag{48}$$

(43) and

$$\limsup_{\ell\to\infty}\int_{\ell_1}^{\ell}\left[Q^{*}(\mathfrak{a})R_{n-2}^{\alpha}(\mathfrak{a}) - \frac{\alpha^{\alpha+1}}{(\alpha+1)^{\alpha+1}}\frac{R_{n-3}(\mathfrak{a})}{R_{n-2}(\mathfrak{a})}\right]\mathrm{d}\mathfrak{a} = \infty, \tag{49}$$

hold for some constant $\lambda \in (0,1)$, then, every solution of (8) is oscillatory.

Proof. Assume that Equation (8) has a non-oscillatory solution x. Without loss of generality, we may assume that x is eventually positive. It follows from Equation (8) that there exist three possible cases as in Lemma 3.

Assume that $\mathbf{N}_1$ holds. Using Lemma 1, we have

$$\mathcal{B}(\ell) \geq \frac{\lambda\ell^{n-1}}{(n-1)!r^{1/\alpha}(\ell)}\left(r^{1/\alpha}(\ell)\mathcal{B}^{(n-1)}(\ell)\right), \tag{50}$$

for every $\lambda \in (0,1)$ and for all sufficiently large ℓ. Using (8) and (50), we obtain

$$\begin{aligned}\left(r(\ell)\left(\mathcal{B}^{(n-1)}(\ell)\right)^{\alpha}\right)' &= -\sum_{i=1}^{J} q_i(\ell)x^{\alpha}(h_i(\ell))\\ &\leq -Q(\ell)\mathcal{B}^{\alpha}(h(\ell))\\ &\leq -Q(\ell)\frac{\lambda^{\alpha}\left(h^{n-1}(\ell)\right)^{\alpha}}{((n-1)!)^{\alpha}r(h(\ell))}r(h(\ell))\left(\mathcal{B}^{(n-1)}(h(\ell))\right)^{\alpha}.\end{aligned}$$

Letting $w(\ell) := r(\ell)\left(\mathcal{B}^{(n-1)}(\ell)\right)^{\alpha}$, we find

$$w'(\ell) + Q(\ell)\frac{\lambda^{\alpha}\left(h^{n-1}(\ell)\right)^{\alpha}}{((n-1)!)^{\alpha}r(h(\ell))}w(h(\ell)) \leq 0. \tag{51}$$

This is a contradiction because condition (48) guarantees that (51) has no positive solution according to Theorem 2.1.1 in [24].

Assume that case $\mathbf{N}_2$ holds. The proof of the $\mathbf{N}_2$ is the same as that of Theorem 9.

Assume that $\mathbf{N}_3$ holds. Since $r(\ell)\left(\mathcal{B}^{(n-1)}(\ell)\right)^{\alpha}$ is decreasing, we have

$$r^{1/\alpha}(\mathfrak{a})\mathcal{B}^{(n-1)}(\mathfrak{a}) \leq r^{1/\alpha}(\ell)\mathcal{B}^{(n-1)}(\ell),$$

for $\mathfrak{a} \geq \ell \geq \ell_1$. By dividing the last inequality by $r^{1/\alpha}(\mathfrak{a})$ and integrating it from ℓ to ∞, we have

$$0 \leq \mathcal{B}^{(n-2)}(\ell) + r^{1/\alpha}(\ell)\mathcal{B}^{(n-1)}(\ell)\int_{\ell}^{\infty}\frac{1}{r^{1/\alpha}(\mathfrak{a})}\mathrm{d}\mathfrak{a},$$

and so

$$0 \leq \mathcal{B}^{(n-2)}(\ell) + r^{1/\alpha}(\ell)\mathcal{B}^{(n-1)}(\ell)R_0(\ell),$$

which leads to

$$\mathcal{B}^{(n-2)}(\ell) \geq -r^{1/\alpha}(\ell)\mathcal{B}^{(n-1)}(\ell)R_0(\ell). \tag{52}$$

Integrating (52) from ℓ to ∞ yields

$$\begin{aligned} -\mathcal{B}^{(n-3)}(\ell) &\geq -\int_\ell^\infty r^{1/\alpha}(\mathfrak{a})\mathcal{B}^{(n-1)}(\mathfrak{a})R_0(\mathfrak{a})d\mathfrak{a} \geq -r^{1/\alpha}(\ell)\mathcal{B}^{(n-1)}(\ell)\int_\ell^\infty R_0(\mathfrak{a})d\mathfrak{a} \\ &\geq -r^{1/\alpha}(\ell)\mathcal{B}^{(n-1)}(\ell)R_1(\ell). \end{aligned} \tag{53}$$

Similarly, Integrating (53) from ℓ to ∞ a total of $(n-4)$ times, we have

$$-\mathcal{B}'(\ell) \geq -r^{1/\alpha}(\ell)\mathcal{B}^{(n-1)}(\ell)R_{n-3}(\ell). \tag{54}$$

Integrating (54) from ℓ to ∞ provides

$$\mathcal{B}(\ell) \geq -r^{1/\alpha}(\ell)\mathcal{B}^{(n-1)}(\ell)R_{n-2}(\ell). \tag{55}$$

Now, define the function w by

$$w(\ell) = \frac{r(\ell)\left(\mathcal{B}^{(n-1)}(\ell)\right)^\alpha}{\mathcal{B}^\alpha(\ell)},\ \ell \geq \ell_1. \tag{56}$$

Then $w(\ell) < 0$ for $\ell \leq \ell_1$. Differentiating (56), we obtain

$$w'(\ell) = \frac{\left(r(\ell)\left(\mathcal{B}^{(n-1)}(\ell)\right)^\alpha\right)'}{\mathcal{B}^\alpha(\ell)} - \alpha\frac{r(\ell)\left(\mathcal{B}^{(n-1)}(\ell)\right)^\alpha\mathcal{B}'(\ell)}{\mathcal{B}^{\alpha+1}(\ell)}.$$

It follows from (8) and (56) that

$$w'(\ell) \leq -\frac{\sum_{i=1}^J q_i(\ell)x^\alpha(h_i(\ell))}{\mathcal{B}^\alpha(\ell)} - \alpha\frac{r(\ell)\left(\mathcal{B}^{(n-1)}(\ell)\right)^\alpha}{\mathcal{B}^\alpha(\ell)}\frac{r^{1/\alpha}(\ell)\mathcal{B}^{(n-1)}(\ell)}{\mathcal{B}(\ell)}R_{n-3}(\ell). \tag{57}$$

Since

$$x(\ell) = \mathcal{B}(\ell) - p(\ell)x(\vartheta(\ell)) \geq \mathcal{B}(\ell) - p(\ell)\mathcal{B}(\vartheta(\ell)), \tag{58}$$

from (33), we see that $\mathcal{B}(\ell)/R_{n-2}(\ell)$ is increasing, consequently

$$\frac{\mathcal{B}(\ell)}{R_{n-2}(\ell)} \geq \frac{\mathcal{B}(\vartheta(\ell))}{R_{n-2}(\vartheta(\ell))},$$

for $\vartheta(\ell) \leq \ell$. From (58), we have

$$x(\ell) \geq \left(1 - p(\ell)\frac{R_{n-2}(\vartheta(\ell))}{R_{n-2}(\ell)}\right)\mathcal{B}(\ell),$$

and

$$x(h_i(\ell)) \geq \left(1 - p(h_i(\ell))\frac{R_{n-2}(\vartheta(h_i(\ell)))}{R_{n-2}(h_i(\ell))}\right)\mathcal{B}(h_i(\ell))$$

also

$$\begin{aligned} \sum_{i=1}^J q_i(\ell)x^\alpha(h_i(\ell)) &\geq \sum_{i=1}^J q_i(\ell)\left(1 - p(h_i(\ell))\frac{R_{n-2}(\vartheta(h_i(\ell)))}{R_{n-2}(h_i(\ell))}\right)^\alpha\mathcal{B}^\alpha(h_i(\ell)) \\ &\geq \mathcal{B}^\alpha(h(\ell))\sum_{i=1}^J q_i(\ell)\left(1 - p(h_i(\ell))\frac{R_{n-2}(\vartheta(h_i(\ell)))}{R_{n-2}(h_i(\ell))}\right)^\alpha \\ &= Q^*(\ell)\mathcal{B}^\alpha(h(\ell)). \end{aligned}$$

Now, we see that (57) becomes

$$w'(\ell) \leq -Q^*(\ell)\frac{\mathcal{B}^\alpha(h(\ell))}{\mathcal{B}^\alpha(\ell)} - \alpha\frac{r(\ell)\left(\mathcal{B}^{(n-1)}(\ell)\right)^\alpha}{\mathcal{B}^\alpha(\ell)}\frac{r^{1/\alpha}(\ell)\mathcal{B}^{(n-1)}(\ell)}{\mathcal{B}(\ell)}R_{n-3}(\ell). \tag{59}$$

Multiplying (59) by $R^\alpha_{n-2}(\ell)$ and integrating it from ℓ_1 to ℓ, we have

$$R^\alpha_{n-2}(\ell)w(\ell) - R^\alpha_{n-2}(\ell_1)w(\ell_1) + \alpha\int_{\ell_1}^{\ell} R^{\alpha-1}_{n-2}(\mathfrak{a})R_{n-3}(\mathfrak{a})w(\mathfrak{a})d\mathfrak{a}$$
$$+\int_{\ell_1}^{\ell} Q^*(\mathfrak{a})R^\alpha_{n-2}(\mathfrak{a})d\mathfrak{a} + \alpha\int_{\ell_1}^{\ell} R_{n-3}(\mathfrak{a})R^\alpha_{n-2}(\mathfrak{a})w^{(\alpha+1)/\alpha}(\mathfrak{a})d\mathfrak{a} \leq 0.$$

Using (11) with

$$\varrho_1 := R_{n-3}(\mathfrak{a})R^\alpha_{n-2}(\mathfrak{a}),\ \varrho_2 := R^{\alpha-1}_{n-2}(\mathfrak{a})R_{n-3}(\mathfrak{a}) \text{ and } u := -w(\mathfrak{a}),$$

we get

$$\int_{\ell_1}^{\ell}\left[Q^*(\mathfrak{a})R^\alpha_{n-2}(\mathfrak{a}) - \frac{\alpha^{\alpha+1}}{(\alpha+1)^{\alpha+1}}\frac{R_{n-3}(\mathfrak{a})}{R_{n-2}(\mathfrak{a})}\right]d\mathfrak{a} \leq R^\alpha_{n-2}(\ell_1)w(\ell_1) + 1,$$

due to (55), which contradicts (49). Therefore, every solution of (8) is oscillatory. □

Theorem 11. *Let (16) and (29) hold. Assume that (42), (48) and (49) hold for some constant $\lambda \in (0,1)$, then, every solution of (8) is oscillatory.*

Example 1. *Consider the NDE*

$$\left(\ell^{4\alpha}\left(\left(x(\ell) + p_0x(\vartheta_0\ell)\right)'''\right)^\alpha\right)' + \sum_{i=1}^{J} q_0\ell^{\alpha-1}x^\alpha(h_i\ell) = 0,\ \ell \geq 1, \tag{60}$$

where $0 \leq p_0 < 1$, ϑ_0, $h_0 \in (0,1)$ and $q_0 > 0$. By comparing (8) and (60) we see that $n = 4$, $r(\ell) = \ell^{4\alpha}$, $q_i(\ell) = q_0\ell^{\alpha-1}$, $p(\ell) = p_0$, $\vartheta(\ell) = \vartheta_0\ell$, $h_i(\ell) = h_i\ell$. It is easy to find that

$$R_0(\ell) = \frac{1}{3\ell^3},\ R_1(\ell) = \frac{1}{6\ell^2},\ R_2(\ell) = \frac{1}{6\ell}$$

and

$$Q(\ell) = Jq_0\ell^{\alpha-1}(1-p_0)^\alpha.$$

For (16), we set

$$\gamma = \frac{J}{\alpha}\frac{h_0^{2\alpha}q_0}{2^\alpha 3^{\alpha+1}}(1-p_0)^\alpha,$$

where $h_0\ell = \min\{h_i\ell, i = 1,\ldots,J\}$. From (29), we get

$$\delta = \frac{1}{h_0^3}.$$

Now, we define the sequence $\{\beta_r\}_{r=1}^m$ as

$$\beta_r = \beta_0\frac{1}{(1-\beta_{r-1})^{1/\alpha}}\left(\frac{1}{h_0}\right)^{3\beta_{r-1}},$$

with

$$\beta_0 = \frac{J^{1/\alpha}\mu_0 q_0^{1/\alpha}}{6\alpha^{1/\alpha}3^{1/\alpha}}h_0^2(1-p_0).$$

Then, condition (36) reduces to

$$q_0 > \frac{3^{\alpha+1}\alpha}{\left(J\mu_0 h_0^2(1-p_0)\right)^{\alpha}}, \tag{61}$$

and condition (42) becomes

$$\begin{aligned}
&\liminf_{\ell\to\infty}\int_{h(\ell)}^{\ell}\frac{1}{\alpha}\frac{R_0(\ell)\left(h^{n-2}(\mathfrak{a})\right)^{\alpha}Q(\mathfrak{a})}{R_0^{1-\alpha}(h(\ell))}\mathrm{d}\mathfrak{a}\\
=&\liminf_{\ell\to\infty}\int_{h_0\ell}^{\ell}\frac{1}{\alpha}\frac{1}{3\mathfrak{a}^3}h_0^{2\alpha}\mathfrak{a}^{2\alpha}3^{1-\alpha}\mathfrak{a}^{3-3\alpha}h_0^{3-3\alpha}Jq_0\mathfrak{a}^{\alpha-1}(1-p_0)^{\alpha}\mathrm{d}\mathfrak{a}\\
=&\frac{1}{\alpha}\frac{J}{3^{\alpha}}h_0^{3-\alpha}q_0(1-p_0)^{\alpha}\ln\frac{1}{h_0},
\end{aligned}$$

which leads to

$$\frac{1}{\alpha}\frac{J}{6^{\alpha}}h_0^{3-\alpha}q_0(1-p_0)^{\alpha}\ln\frac{1}{h_0} > \frac{\beta_m^{\alpha-1}(1-\beta_m)}{\mathrm{e}}, \tag{62}$$

while condition (43) becomes

$$\begin{aligned}
&\limsup_{\ell\to\infty}\int_{\ell_0}^{\ell}\left[\left(\frac{\lambda h^{n-2}(\mathfrak{a})}{(n-2)!}\right)^{\alpha}\frac{R_0^{\alpha\beta_m}(h(\mathfrak{a}))}{R_0^{-\alpha(1-\beta_m)}(\mathfrak{a})}Q(\mathfrak{a})-\frac{\alpha^{\alpha+1}}{(1+\alpha)^{1+\alpha}}\frac{1}{R_0(\mathfrak{a})r^{1/\alpha}(\mathfrak{a})}\right]\mathrm{d}\mathfrak{a}\\
=&\limsup_{\ell\to\infty}\int_{\ell_0}^{\ell}\left[\frac{\lambda^{\alpha}}{2^{\alpha}}h_0^{2\alpha}\mathfrak{a}^{2\alpha}\frac{1}{3^{\alpha}\mathfrak{a}^{3\alpha}}\frac{1}{h_0^{3\alpha\beta_m}}Jq_0\mathfrak{a}^{\alpha-1}(1-p_0)^{\alpha}-\frac{\alpha^{\alpha+1}}{(1+\alpha)^{1+\alpha}}3\mathfrak{a}^3\frac{1}{\mathfrak{a}^4}\right]\mathrm{d}\mathfrak{a}\\
=&\left[\frac{\lambda^{\alpha}}{6^{\alpha}}\frac{J}{h_0^{3\alpha\beta_m-2\alpha}}q_0(1-p_0)^{\alpha}-\frac{3\alpha^{\alpha+1}}{(1+\alpha)^{1+\alpha}}\right]\limsup_{\ell\to\infty}\ln\frac{\ell}{\ell_0}=\infty,
\end{aligned}$$

which is achieved if

$$\frac{\lambda^{\alpha}}{6^{\alpha}}\frac{J}{h_0^{3\alpha\beta_m-2\alpha}}q_0(1-p_0)^{\alpha} > \frac{3\alpha^{\alpha+1}}{(1+\alpha)^{1+\alpha}}. \tag{63}$$

Using Theorem 7, Corollary 1 and Theorem 9, we note that the class Ω is empty if either (61), (62) or (63) holds, respectively.

Example 2. *Consider the NDE (60) where $\alpha = 1$, $p_0 = 1/2$, $2\vartheta_0 > 1$ and $J = 3$, then (60) becomes*

$$\left(\ell^4\left(\left(x(\ell)+\frac{1}{2}x(\vartheta_0\ell)\right)'''\right)\right)' + q_0(x(h_1u)+x(h_2u)+x(h_3u)) = 0,\ \ell \geq 1. \tag{64}$$

Clearly

$$h(\ell) = \min\{h_i(\ell),\ i = 1,2,3\} = h_0\ell$$

and

$$Q(\ell) = \frac{3}{2}q_0.$$

For (16), we set

$$\gamma = \frac{1}{12}h_0^2 q_0.$$

Form (29), we have $\delta = 1/h_0^3$. Now, we define the sequence $\{\beta_r\}_{r=1}^{m}$ as

$$\beta_r = \beta_0\frac{1}{(1-\beta_{r-1})^{1/\alpha}}\left(\frac{1}{h_0}\right)^{3\beta_{r-1}},$$

with

$$\beta_0 = \frac{1}{12}\mu_0 h_0^2 q_0.$$

Then, condition (36) reduces to

$$q_0 > \frac{6}{\mu_0 h_0^2}, \tag{65}$$

and condition (48) becomes

$$\begin{aligned} \liminf_{\ell\to\infty} \frac{1}{(n-1)!} \int_{h(\ell)}^{\ell} Q(\mathfrak{a}) \frac{h^{n-1}(\mathfrak{a})}{r(h(\mathfrak{a}))} d\mathfrak{a} &= \liminf_{\ell\to\infty} \frac{1}{6} \int_{h_0\ell}^{\ell} \frac{3}{2} q_0 \frac{h_0^3 \mathfrak{a}^3}{h_0^4 \mathfrak{a}^4} d\mathfrak{a} \\ &= \frac{1}{4} \frac{q_0}{h_0} \ln \frac{1}{h_0}, \end{aligned}$$

which leads to

$$\frac{1}{4} \frac{q_0}{h_0} \ln \frac{1}{h_0} > \frac{1}{e}, \tag{66}$$

while condition (49) is abbreviated to

$$\begin{aligned} &\limsup_{\ell\to\infty} \int_{\ell_1}^{\ell} \left[Q^*(\mathfrak{a}) R_{n-2}^{\alpha}(\mathfrak{a}) - \frac{\alpha^{\alpha+1}}{(\alpha+1)^{\alpha+1}} \frac{R_{n-3}(\mathfrak{a})}{R_{n-2}(\mathfrak{a})} \right] d\mathfrak{a} \\ &= \limsup_{\ell\to\infty} \int_{\ell_1}^{\ell} \left[3q_0 \left(1 - \frac{1}{2}\frac{1}{\vartheta_0}\right) \frac{1}{6} - \frac{1}{4} \right] \frac{1}{\mathfrak{a}} d\mathfrak{a} \\ &= \left[\frac{1}{2} q_0 \left(1 - \frac{1}{2}\frac{1}{\vartheta_0}\right) - \frac{1}{4} \right] \limsup_{\ell\to\infty} \ln \frac{\ell}{\ell_1} = \infty, \end{aligned}$$

which is achieved when

$$q_0 \left(1 - \frac{1}{2}\frac{1}{\vartheta_0}\right) > \frac{1}{2}. \tag{67}$$

From Theorem 10 we see that every solution of (64) is oscillatory if (65), (66) and (67) holds.

5. Conclusions

In this paper, we have investigated the asymptotic properties of positive solutions of even-order neutral differential equations in the non-canonical case. We introduced several auxiliaries and important results on which our results depend. We used different techniques, including the Recati technique, and the comparison method to create the oscillation criteria for the studied equation. Finally, we provided some examples as special cases of the studied equation to illustrate the possibility of applying the results we obtained. Our obtained theorems not only generalize the existing results in the literature but also can be used to plan future research papers in a variety of directions. For example:

(1) One can consider Equation (8) with

$$\mathcal{B} := x + p_1 \cdot (x \circ \vartheta) + p_2 \cdot (x \circ \tau)$$

where $\tau(\ell) \leq \ell$.

(2) It would be of interest to extend the results of this paper for higher order equations of type (8), where $n \geq 3$ is an odd natural number.

Author Contributions: Conceptualization, B.A. and O.M.; methodology, F.M.; validation, B.A., F.M. and A.M.; formal analysis, O.M.; investigation, F.M.; writing—original draft preparation, B.A.; writing—review and editing, A.M. All authors have read and agreed to the published version of the manuscript.

Funding: Princess Nourah bint Abdulrahman University Researchers Supporting Project number (PNURSP2022R216), Princess Nourah bint Abdulrahman University, Riyadh, Saudi Arabia.

Acknowledgments: This research was supported by Princess Nourah bint Abdulrahman University Researchers Supporting Project number (PNURSP2022R216), Princess Nourah bint Abdulrahman University, Riyadh, Saudi Arabia.

Conflicts of Interest: The authors declare no conflict of interest.

References

1. Hale, J.K. Functional differential equations. In *Analytic Theory of Differential Equations*; Springer: Berlin/Heidelberg, Germany, 1971; pp. 9–22.
2. Gopalsamy, K. *Stability and Oscillations in Delay Differential Equation in Delay Differential Equations of Population Dynamics*; Springer: Dordrecht, The Netherlands, 1992.
3. Oguztoreli, M.N.; Stein, R.B. An analysis of oscillations in neuro-muscular systems. *J. Math. Biol.* **1975**, *2*, 87–105. [CrossRef]
4. Palencia, J.L.D.; González, J.R.; Sánchez, A.S. Study of Solutions for a Degenerate Reaction Equation with a High Order Operator and Advection. *Mathematics* **2022**, *10*, 1729. [CrossRef]
5. Almarri, B.; Ramos, H.; Moaaz, O. New monotonic properties of the class of positive solutions of even-order neutral differential equations. *Mathematics* **2022**, *10*, 1470. [CrossRef]
6. Elabbasy, E.M.; Moaaz, O.; Ramos, H.; Muhib, A. Improved criteria for oscillation of noncanonical neutral differential equations of even order. *Adv. Differ. Equ.* **2021**, *2021*, 412. [CrossRef]
7. Moaaz, O.; Muhib, A.; Zakarya, M.; Abdel-Aty, A.-H. Delay differential equation of fourth-order: Asymptotic analysis and oscillatory behavior. *Alex. Eng. J.* **2022**, *61*, 2919–2924. [CrossRef]
8. Muhib, A.; Moaaz, O.; Cesarano, C.; Askar, S.S. New conditions for testing the oscillation of fourth-order differential equations with several delays. *Symmetry* **2022**, *14*, 1068. [CrossRef]
9. Ramos, H.; Moaaz, O.; Muhib, A.; Awrejcewicz, J. More effective results for testing oscillation of non-canonical neutral delay differential equations. *Mathematics* **2021**, *9*, 1114. [CrossRef]
10. Zafer, A. Oscillation criteria for even order neutral differential equations. *Appl. Math. Lett.* **1998**, *11*, 21–25. [CrossRef]
11. Li, T.; Han, Z.; Zhao, P.; Sun, S. Oscillation of even-order neutral delay differential equations. *Adv. Differ. Equ.* **2010**, *2010*, 184180. [CrossRef]
12. Zhang, Q.; Yan, J.; Gao, L. Oscillation behavior of even-order nonlinear neutral differential equations with variable coefficients. *Comput. Math. Appl.* **2010**, *59*, 426–430. [CrossRef]
13. Baculikova, B.; Dzurina, J. Asymptotic and oscillatory behavior of higher order quasilinear delay differential equations. *Electron. J. Qual. Theory Differ. Equ.* **2012**, *89*, 1–10. [CrossRef]
14. Sun, Y.; Han, Z.; Sun, S.; Zhang, C. Oscillation criteria for even order nonlinear neutral differential equations. *Electron. J. Qual. Theory Differ. Equ.* **2012**, *30*, 1–12. [CrossRef]
15. Moaaz, O.; Almarri, B.; Masood, F.; Atta, D. Even-order neutral delay differential equations with noncanonical operator: New oscillation criteria. *Fractal Fract.* **2022**, *6*, 313. [CrossRef]
16. Hassan, T.S.; Moaaz, O.; Nabih, A.; Mesmouli, M.B.; El-Sayed, A.M.A. New sufficient conditions for oscillation of second-order neutral delay differential equations. *Axioms* **2021**, *10*, 281. [CrossRef]
17. Jadlovská, I. New Criteria for Sharp Oscillation of Second-Order Neutral Delay Differential Equations. *Mathematics* **2021**, *9*, 2089. [CrossRef]
18. Jadlovská, I.; Džurina, J. Kneser-type oscillation criteria for second-order half-linear delay differential equations. *Appl. Math. Comput.* **2020**, *380*, 125289. [CrossRef]
19. Moaaz, O.; Elabbasy, E.M.E.; Awrejcewicz, J.; Abdelnaser, A. Criteria for the oscillation of solutions to linear second-order delay differential equation with a damping term. *Axioms* **2021**, *10*, 246. [CrossRef]
20. Agarwal, R.P.; Grace, S.R.; O'Regan, D. *Oscillation Theory for Difference and Functional Differential Equations*; Kluwer Academic: Dordrecht, The Netherlands, 2000.
21. Zhang, C.; Agarwal, R.; Bohner, M.; Li, T. New results for oscillatory behavior of even-order half-linear delay differential equations. *Appl. Math. Lett.* **2013**, *26*, 179–183. [CrossRef]
22. Kiguradze, I.; Chanturia, T. Asymptotic properties of solutions of nonautonomous ordinary differential equations. In *Mathematics and Its Applications (Soviet Series)*; Translated from the 1985 Russian Original; Kluwer Academic Publishers Group: Dordrecht, The Netherlands, 1993; Volume 89.
23. Philos, C.G. On the existence of nonoscillatory solutions tending to zero at ∞ for differential equations with positive delays. *Arch. Math.* **1981**, *36*, 168–178. [CrossRef]
24. Ladde, G.; Lakshmikantham, S.V.; Zhang, B.G. *Oscillation Theory of Differential Equations with Deviating Arguments*; Marcel Dekker: New York, NY, USA, 1987.

axioms

MDPI

Article

Inexact Restoration Methods for Semivectorial Bilevel Programming Problem on Riemannian Manifolds

Jiagen Liao *,† and Zhongping Wan †

School of Mathematics and Statistics, Wuhan University, Wuhan 430072, China
* Correspondence: jiagenliao@163.com
† These authors contributed equally to this work.

Abstract: For a better understanding of the bilevel programming on Riemannian manifolds, a semivectorial bilevel programming scheme is proposed in this paper. The semivectorial bilevel programming is firstly transformed into a single-level programming problem by using the Karush–Kuhn–Tucker (KKT) conditions of the lower-level problem, which is convex and satisfies the Slater constraint qualification. Then, the single-level programming is divided into two stages: restoration and minimization, based on which an Inexact Restoration algorithm is developed. Under certain conditions, the stability and convergence of the algorithm are analyzed.

Keywords: Riemannian manifolds; semivectorial bilevel programming; Inexact Restoration algorithm

MSC: 58C05; 90C25; 90C29

Citation: Liao, J.; Wan, Z. Inexact Restoration Methods for Semivectorial Bilevel Programming Problem on Riemannian Manifolds. *Axioms* **2022**, *11*, 696. https://doi.org/10.3390/axioms11120696

Academic Editor: Clemente Cesarano

Received: 30 September 2022
Accepted: 2 December 2022
Published: 5 December 2022

1. Introduction

The bilevel optimization problem on Euclidean spaces has been shown to be NP-hard, and even the verification of the local optimality for a feasible solution is in general NP-hard. Bilevel optimization problems are often nonconvex optimization problems, and this makes the computation of an optimal solution a challenging task. Thus, it is natural to consider the bilevel optimization problems on Riemannian manifolds. Actually, studying optimization problems on Riemannian manifolds has many advantages. Some constrained optimization problems on Euclidean spaces can be seen as unconstrained ones from the Riemannian geometry viewpoint. Moreover, some nonconvex optimization problems in the setting of Euclidean spaces may become convex optimization problems by introducing an appropriate Riemannian metric. See for instance [1,2]. The aim of this paper is to study the bilevel optimization problem on Riemannian manifolds.

In order to study the bilevel optimization problem on Riemannian manifolds, it is reasonable to have some idea of solving the bilevel optimization problem in Euclidean spaces. An approach to investigate bilevel optimization problems on Euclidean spaces is to replace the lower-level problem by its (under certain necessary and sufficient assumptions) KKT optimality conditions. In a recent article [3], the authors presented the KKT reformulation of the bilevel optimization problems on Riemannian manifolds. Moreover, it has been shown that global optimal solutions of the KKT reformulation correspond to global optimal solutions of the bilevel problem on the Riemannian manifolds provided the lower level convex problem satisfies Slater's constraint qualification. On this basis, we consider a semivectorial bilevel optimization problem on Riemannian manifolds with a multiobjective problem in the lower-level problem. Since the Inexact Restoration (IR) algorithm [4,5] was introduced to solve constrained optimization problems and if we transform the semivectorial bilevel optimization problem into a single-level problem, it also can be solved by using the IR algorithm as a constrained optimization problem.

For the convenience of the readers, let us review the IR algorithm on Euclidean spaces firstly. Each iteration of the IR algorithm consists of two phases: restoration and minimization. Consider the following nonlinear programming:

$$\begin{aligned} \min \quad & f(x) \\ \text{s.t.} \quad & C(x) \leq 0, \quad x \in \Omega, \end{aligned} \tag{1}$$

where $f : \mathbb{R}^n \to \mathbb{R}$ and $C : \mathbb{R}^n \to \mathbb{R}^m$ are continuous differentiable functions and the set $\Omega \subset \mathbb{R}^m$ is closed convex. The algorithm generates feasible iterates with respect to Ω, $x^k \in \Omega$ (for all $k = 0, 1, 2 \ldots$).

In the restoration step, which is executed once per iteration, an intermediate point $y^k \in \Omega$ is found such that the infeasibility at y^k is a fraction of the infeasibility at x^k. Immediately after restoration, we construct an approximation π_k of the feasible region using available information at y^k. In the minimization step, we compute a trial point $z^{ki} \in \pi_k$ such that $f(z^{ki}) \ll f(y^k)$. Here, the symbol $\ll$ means sufficiently smaller than, and $\|z^{ki} - y^k\| \leq \delta_{ki}$, where δ_{ki} is a trust-region radius. The trial point z^{ki} is accepted as a new iteration one if the value of a nonsmooth (exact penalty) merit function at z^{ki} is sufficiently smaller than its value at x^k. If z^{ki} is not acceptable, the trust-region radius is reduced.

The IR algorithm is related to classical feasible methods for nonlinear programming, such as the generalized reduced gradient (GRG) and the family of sequential gradient restoration algorithms. There are several studies on the numerical characteristics of the IR algorithm. For example, this method was applied to the general constraint problem in [6], and good results were obtained. In addition, the IR algorithm using the regularization strategy was proposed in [7], in which the problem of derivative-free optimization was effectively solved. The IR algorithms are especially useful when there is some natural way to restore feasibility. One of the most successful applications of the IR algorithm is electronic structure calculation, as shown in [8]. Moreover, the IR algorithm has also been successful applied to optimization problems with the box constraint in [9] and problems with multiobjective constraints under weighted-sum scalarization in [10]. For more applications, please see [11,12].

Since the IR algorithm is so important in applications, many researches have been trying to improve it from different angles. The restoration phase improves feasibility, and in the minimization step, optimality is improved as a linear tangent approximation of the constraints. When a sufficient descent criterion does not hold, the trial point is modified in such a way that, eventually, acceptance occurs at a point that may be close to the solution of the restoration (first) phase. The acceptance criterion may use merit functions [4,5] or filters [13]. The minimization step consists of an inexact (approximate) minimization of f with linear constraints. In this case, the restoration step represents also an inexact minimization of infeasibility with linear constraints. Therefore, the available algorithms for (large-scale) linearly constrained minimization can be fully exploited; see the published articles [14–16]. Furthermore, IR techniques for constrained optimization were improved, extended, and analyzed in [7,17–19], among others.

Inspired and motivated by the research works [4,10,20–25], we introduce a kind of bilevel programming with a multiobjective problem in the lower level on Riemannian manifolds, the so-called semivectorial bilevel programming. Then, we transform the semivectorial bilevel programming into a single-level programming by using the KKT optimality conditions of the lower-level problem, which is convex and satisfies the Slater constraint qualification. Finally, we divide the single-level programming into two stages: restoration and minimization, and give an IR algorithm for semivectorial bilevel programming. Under certain conditions, we analyze the well-definiteness and convergence of the presented algorithm.

The remainder of this paper is organized as follows: In Section 2, some basic concepts, notations, and important results of Riemannian geometry are presented. In Section 3, we propose the semivectorial bilevel programming on the Riemannian manifold and give the KKT reformulation, and then, we present an algorithm by using the IR technique for solving the semivectorial bilevel programming on Riemannian manifolds. In Section 4, its convergence properties are studied. The conclusions are given in Section 5.

2. Preliminaries

An m-dimensional Riemannian manifold is a pair (M, g), where M stands for an m-dimensional smooth manifold and g stands for a smooth, symmetric positive definite $(0,2)$-tensor field on M, called a Riemannian metric on M. If (M, g) is a Riemannian manifold, then for any point $x \in M$, the restriction $g_x : T_xM \times T_xM \to \mathbb{R}$ is an inner product on the tangent space T_xM. The tangent bundle TM over M is $TM := \bigcup_{x \in M} T_xM$, and a vector field on M is a section of the tangent bundle, which is a mapping $X : M \to TM$ such that, for any $x \in M$, $X(x) \equiv X_x \in T_xM$.

We denote $\langle \cdot, \cdot \rangle_x$ by the scalar product on T_xM with the associated norm $\|.\|_x$. The length of a tangent vector $v \in T_xM$ is defined by $\|v\|_x = \langle v, v \rangle^{\frac{1}{2}}$. Given a piecewise smooth curve $\gamma : [a,b] \subset \mathbb{R} \to M$ joining x to y, i.e., $\gamma(a) = x$ and $\gamma(b) = y$, then its length is defined by $L(\gamma) = \int_a^b \|\dot{\gamma}(t)\|_{\gamma(t)} dt$, where $\dot{\gamma}$ means the first derivative of γ with respect to t. Let x and y be two points in Riemannian manifold (M, g) and $\Gamma_{x,y}$ the set of all piecewise smooth curves joining x and y. The function:

$$\mathrm{d} : M \times M \to \mathbb{R}, \mathrm{d}(x,y) := \inf\{L(\gamma) : \gamma \in \Gamma_{x,y}\}$$

is a distance on M, and the induced metric topology on M coincides with the topology of M as the manifold.

Let ∇ be the Levi-Civita connection associated with the Riemannian metric and γ be a smooth curve in M. A vector field X is said to be parallel along $\gamma : [0,1] \to M$ if $\nabla_{\dot{\gamma}} X = 0$. If $\dot{\gamma}$ itself is parallel along γ joining x to y,

$$\gamma(0) = x, \gamma(1) = y \text{ and } \nabla_{\dot{\gamma}}\dot{\gamma} = 0 \text{ on } [0,1],$$

then we say that γ is a geodesic, and in this case, $\|\dot{\gamma}\|$ is constant. When $\|\dot{\gamma}\| = 1$, γ is said to be normalized. A geodesic joining x to y in M is said to be minimal if its length equals $\mathrm{d}(x,y)$.

By the Hopf–Rinow theorem, we know that, if M is complete, then any pair of points in M can be joined by a minimal geodesic. Moreover, (M, d) is a complete metric space, and the bounded closed subsets are compact. Furthermore, for the exponential mapping at x, $\exp_x : T_xM \to M$ is well defined on T_xM. Clearly, a curve $\gamma : [0,1] \to M$ is a minimal geodesic joining x to y if and only if there exists a vector $v \in T_xM$ such that $\|v\| = \mathrm{d}(x,y)$ and $\gamma(t) = \exp_x(tv)$ for each $t \in [0,1]$.

Set $p \in M$ and $V_p := \{v \in T_pM : \gamma_v \text{ defined in } [0,1]\}$. The exponential mapping $\exp_p : V_p \to M$ is defined by $\exp_p(v) = \gamma_v(1), \forall v \in V_p$. The exponential mapping $\exp_p : T_pM \to M$ at $p \in M$ is well posed on the tangent space T_pM. Obviously, a curve $\gamma : [0,1] \to M$ joining p and q is a minimum geodesic, if and only if there is a vector $v \in T_pM$ such that $\|v\| = \mathrm{d}(p,q)$ and $\gamma(t) = \exp_p(tv)$ hold for every $t \in [0,1]$.

The gradient of a differentiable function $f : M \to \mathbb{R}$ with respect to the Riemannian metric g is the vector field $\mathrm{grad}f$ defined by $g(\mathrm{grad}f, X) = df(X), \forall X \in TM$, where df denotes the differential of the function f.

In this normal coordinate system, the geodesics through p are represented by lines passing through the origin. Moreover, the matrix (g_{ij}) associated with the bilinear form g at the point p in this orthonormal basis reduces to the identity matrix, and the Christoffel symbols vanish. Thus, for any smooth function $f : M \to \mathbb{R}$, in normal coordinates around p, we obtain

$$\mathrm{grad}f(p) = \sum_i \frac{\partial f}{\partial x^i}(p) \frac{\partial}{\partial x^i} \,.$$

Now, consider a smooth function $f : M \to R$ and the real-valued function $T_pM \ni v \mapsto f_p(v) := f(\exp_p v)$ defined around 0 in T_pM.

It is easy to see that

$$\frac{\partial f_p}{\partial x^i}(0) = \frac{\partial f}{\partial x^i}(p).$$

The Taylor–Young formula (for Euclidean spaces) applied to f_p around the origin can be written using matrices as

$$f_p(v) = f_p(0) + J_{f_p}(0)v + \frac{1}{2}v^T \mathrm{Hess}_{f_p}(0)v + o(\|v\|^2),$$

where

$$\begin{aligned} v &= [v^1 \dots v^n]^T, \\ J_{f_p}(0) &= \left[\frac{\partial f}{\partial x^1}(p) \dots \frac{\partial f}{\partial x^n}(p)\right], \\ \mathrm{Hess}_{f_p}(0) &= \left(\frac{\partial^2 f}{\partial x^i \partial x^j}(p)\right) = \mathrm{Hess}_p f(v, v). \end{aligned}$$

In other words, we have the following Taylor–Young expansion for f around p:

$$f(\exp_p v) = f(p) + g_p(\mathrm{grad} f, v) + \frac{1}{2}\mathrm{Hess}_p f(v, v) + o(\|v\|_p^2)$$

which holds in any coordinate system.

The set $A \subset M$ is said to be convex if it contains a geodesic segment γ whenever it contains the end points of γ, that is $\gamma((1-t)a + tb)$ is in A whenever $x = \gamma(a)$ and $y = \gamma(b)$ are in A, and $t \in [0,1]$. A function $f : M \to \mathbb{R}$ is said to be convex if its restriction to any geodesic curve $\gamma : [a,b] \to M$ is convex in the classical sense, such that the one real variable function $f \circ \gamma : [a,b] \to \mathbb{R}$ is convex. Let P_A denote the projection on $A \subset M$, that is, for each $x \in M$,

$$P_A x = \left\{ \bar{x} \in A : \mathrm{d}(x, \bar{x}) = \inf_{z \in A} \mathrm{d}(x, z) \right\}. \tag{2}$$

For more details and complete information on the fundamentals in Riemannian geometry, see [1,26–28].

3. Inexact Restoration Algorithm

We study an optimistic bilevel programming on an m-dimensional Riemannian manifold (M, g), where the lower-level problem is a multi-objective problem, the so-called semivectorial bilevel programming. The problem is formulated below:

$$\begin{aligned} \min \quad & F(x) \\ \text{s.t.} \quad & x \in \mathrm{Sol(MOP)}, \end{aligned} \tag{3}$$

where $F : M \to \mathbb{R}$ and $\mathrm{Sol(MOP)}$ is the effective solution set of the following multi-objective problem (MOP):

$$\begin{aligned} \min \quad & \{f_1(x), \dots, f_p(x)\} \\ \text{s.t.} \quad & h(x) = 0, \\ & x \in M, \end{aligned} \tag{4}$$

where $f = \{f_1(x), \dots, f_p(x)\} : M \to \mathbb{R}^p$, $I := \{1, \dots, p\}$, $h : M \to \mathbb{R}^n$, and $D = \{x \in M : h(x) = 0\}$ denote the feasible solution of the MOP.

Definition 1. *Let $f : M \to \mathbb{R}^p$ be a vectorial function on Riemannian manifold M. Then, f is said to be convex on M if, for every $x, y \in M$ and every geodesic segment $\gamma : [0, 1] \to M$ joining x to y, i.e., $\gamma(0) = x$ and $\gamma(1) = y$, it holds that*

$$f(\gamma(t)) \preceq (1-t)f(x) + tf(y), \quad t \in [0, 1].$$

The above definition is a natural extension of the definition of convexity in Euclidean space to the Riemannian context; see [29].

Definition 2. *A point $x \in M$ is said to be Pareto critical of f on Riemannian manifold M if, for any $v \in T_xM$, there are an index $i \in I$ and $u \in \mathrm{grad} f_i(x)$, such that*

$$\langle u, v \rangle \geq 0.$$

Definition 3. *(a) A point $x^* \in M$ is a Pareto-optimal point of f on Riemannian manifold M if there is no $x \in M$ with $f(x) \preceq f(x^*)$. (b) A point $x^* \in M$ is a weak Pareto-optimal point of f on Riemannian manifold M if there is no $x \in M$ with $f(x) \prec f(x^*)$.*

We know that criticality is a necessary, but not a sufficient condition for optimality. Under the convexity of the vectorial function f, the following proposition shows that criticality is equivalent to weak optimality.

Proposition 1 ([29]). *Let $f : M \to \mathbb{R}^p$ be a convex function given by $f = \{f_1(x), \dots, f_p(x)\}$. A point $x \in M$ is a critical Pareto-optimal point of the function f if and only if it is a weak Pareto-optimal point of the function f.*

We assume that the functions $f = \{f_1(x), \dots, f_p(x)\} : M \to \mathbb{R}^p$ and $h : M \to \mathbb{R}^n$ are twice continuously differentiable and consider the weighted sun scaling problem related to the MOP, as follows.

Let $\omega_i \geq 0,\ i = 1, \dots, p$ such that $\sum\limits_{i=1}^{p} \omega_i = 1$:

$$\begin{aligned} \min_x \quad & \sum_{i=1}^{p} \omega_i f_i(x) \\ \text{s.t.} \quad & h(x) = 0, \\ & x \in M. \end{aligned} \tag{5}$$

Note that, if $\omega_i \geq 0, i = 1, \dots, p$ such that $\sum_{i=1}^{p} \omega_i = 1$, then the weak Pareto-optimal solution sets of Problem (4) are equivalent to the union of the optimal solution sets of Problem (5). Meanwhile, if $f_i : M \to \mathbb{R}, i = 1, \dots, p$ is the convex function on the Riemannian manifold, then the function $\sum\limits_{i=1}^{p} \omega_i f_i(x)$ is also convex. Thus, the bilevel programming (3)–(4) can be transformed into the following problem:

$$\begin{aligned} \min_{x,\omega} \quad & F(x) \\ \text{s.t.} \quad & \sum_{i=1}^{p} \omega_i = 1, \\ & \omega_i \geq 0,\ i \in I, \\ & x \in \arg\min \left\{ \begin{aligned} \min \quad & \sum_{i=1}^{p} \omega_i f_i(x) \\ \text{s.t.} \quad & h(x) = 0, \\ & x \in M. \end{aligned} \right\}. \end{aligned} \tag{6}$$

A strategy to solve the bilevel problem (6) on the Riemannian manifolds is to replace the lower-level problem with the KKT conditions. When the lower-level problem is convex and satisfies the Slater constraint qualification, the global optimal solutions of the KKT reformulation correspond to the global optimal solutions of the bilevel problem on the Riemannian manifolds. See Theorems 4.1 and 4.2 in [3].

In the following, we give the KKT reformulation of the semivectorial bilevel programming on Riemannian manifolds.

$$\begin{aligned} \min_{x,\omega} \quad & F(x) \\ \text{s.t.} \quad & \omega \in W, \\ & \sum_{i=1}^{p} \omega_i \text{grad}_x f_i(x) + \text{grad}_x h(x)\mu = 0, \\ & h(x) = 0, \\ & x \in M, \end{aligned} \tag{7}$$

where

$$W = \left\{ \omega \in \mathbb{R}^p : \sum_{i=1}^{p} \omega_i = 1, \omega_i \geq 0, i = 1, \ldots, p \right\}$$

is a convex and compact set, $\mu \in \mathbb{R}^n$, and M is a complete m-dimensional Riemannian manifold.

We will adopt an IR method to solve the optimization problem in two stages, first pursuing feasibility and optimality, keeping a certain control over the feasibility that has been realized. Consequently, the approach exploits the inherent minimization structure of the problem, especially in the feasibility phase, so that it can obtain better solutions. Moreover, in the feasibility phase of the IR strategy, the user is free to choose the method of his/her choice, as long as the recovered iteration satisfies some mild assumptions [4,5].

For simplicity, we introduce the following notations:

$$C(x, \omega, \mu) = \begin{pmatrix} \sum_{i=1}^{p} \omega_i \text{grad}_x f_i(x) + \text{grad}_x h(x)\mu \\ h(x) \end{pmatrix} \in \mathbb{R}^{m+n} \tag{8}$$

and

$$L(x, \omega, \mu, \lambda) = F(x) + C(x, \omega, \mu)^T \lambda, \ \ \lambda \in \mathbb{R}^{m+n}. \tag{9}$$

We write shortly $s = (x,\ \omega,\ \mu) \in M \times W \times \mathbb{R}^n$ and give the Jacobian of C as follows:

$$C'(s) = \begin{pmatrix} \sum_{i=1}^{p} \omega_i \text{Hess}_x f_i + \sum_{j=1}^{n} \mu_j \text{Hess}_x h_j & \text{grad}_x f_1 & \cdots & \text{grad}_x f_p & \text{grad}_x h \\ \text{grad}_x h^T & 0 & \cdots & 0 & 0 \end{pmatrix}. \tag{10}$$

Thus, the semivectorial bilevel programming can be reduced:

$$\begin{aligned} \min \quad & F(s) \\ \text{s.t.} \quad & C(s) = 0, \\ & s \in M \times W \times \mathbb{R}^n. \end{aligned} \tag{11}$$

Before giving a rigorous description of the algorithm, let us start with an overview of each step.

Restoration step: We apply any globally convergent optimization algorithm to solve the lower-level minimization problem parameterized by $z^k = (\bar{x}, \omega^k, \bar{\mu})$. Once an approximate minimizer $\bar{x}$ and a pair of corresponding estimated Lagrange multiplier vectors are obtained, then we compute the current set π_k and the direction d^k_{tan}.

Approximate linearized feasible region: The set π_k is a linear approximation of the region described by KKT$(\bar{x})$ containing $z^k = (\bar{x}, \omega^k, \bar{\mu})$. This auxiliary region is given by

$$\pi_k = \{s \in M \times W \times \mathbb{R}^n : \langle C'(z^k), \dot{\gamma}_{s,z^k}(0) \rangle = 0\}.$$

Descent direction: Using the projection on Riemannian manifolds, the projection defined on π_k is represented as follows:

$$P_{\pi_k}(z^k) = P_k\Big(\exp_{z^k}\Big(-\eta \mathrm{grad}_s L(z^k, \lambda^k)\Big)\Big),$$

where $\eta > 0$ is an arbitrary scaling parameter independent of k. It turns out that

$$d^k_{\tan} = P_k\Big(\exp_{z^k}\Big(-\eta \mathrm{grad}_s L(z^k, \lambda^k)\Big)\Big) - z^k$$

which is a feasible descent direction on π_k.

Minimization step: The objective of the minimization step is to obtain $v^{k,i} \in \pi_k$ such that $L(v^{k,i}, \lambda^k) < L(z^k, \lambda^k)$ and $v^{k,i} \in B_{k,i} = \{v : \mathrm{d}(v, z^k) \leq \delta_{k,i}\}$, where $\delta_{k,i}$ is a trust-region radius. The first trial point at each iteration is obtained using a trust-region radius $\delta_{k,0}$. A successive trust-region radius is tried until a point $v^{k,i}$ is found such that the merit function at this point is sufficiently smaller than the merit function at s^k.

Merit function and penalty parameter: We decided to use a variant of the sharp Lagrangian merit function, given by

$$\Psi(s, \lambda, \theta) = \theta L(s, \lambda) + (1 - \theta)|C(s)|,$$

where $\theta \in (0, 1]$ is a penalty parameter used to give different weights to the objective function and the feasibility objective. The choice of the parameter θ at each iteration depends on practical and theoretical considerations. Roughly speaking, we wish the merit function at the new point to be less than the merit function at the current point s^k.

That is, we want $\mathrm{Ared}_{k,i} > 0$, where $\mathrm{Ared}_{k,i}$ is the actual reduction of the merit function, defined by

$$\mathrm{Ared}_{k,i} = \Psi(s^k, \lambda^k, \theta_{k,i}) - \Psi(v^{k,i}, \lambda^k, \theta_{k,i}).$$

So,

$$\mathrm{Ared}_{k,i} = \theta_{k,i}\Big[L(s^k, \lambda^k) - L(v^{k,i}, \lambda^{k,i})\Big] + (1 - \theta_{k,i})\Big[|C(s^k)| - |C(v^{k,i})|\Big].$$

However, merely a reduction of the merit function is not sufficient to guarantee convergence. In fact, we need a sufficient reduction of the merit function, which will be defined by the satisfaction of the following test:

$$\mathrm{Ared}_{k,i} \geq 0.1 \mathrm{Pred}_{k,i},$$

where $\mathrm{Pred}_{k,i}$ is a positive predicted reduction of the merit function $\Psi(s, \lambda, \theta)$ between s^k and $v^{k,i}$. It is defined by

$$\begin{aligned} \mathrm{Pred}_{k,i} =& \theta_{k,i}\Big[L(s^k, \lambda^k) - L(v^{k,i}, \lambda^k) - C(z^k)^T(\lambda^{k,i} - \lambda^k)\Big] + \\ & (1 - \theta_{k,i})\Big[|C(s^k)| - |C(z^k)|\Big]. \end{aligned}$$

The quantity $\mathrm{Pred}_{k,i}$ defined above can be nonpositive depending on the value of the penalty parameter. Fortunately, if $\theta_{k,i}$ is small enough, $\mathrm{Pred}_{k,i}$ is arbitrarily close to

$\left[|C(s^k)| - |C(z^k)|\right]$, which is necessarily nonnegative. Therefore, we will always be able to choose $\theta_{k,i} \in (0,1]$ such that

$$\text{Pred}_{k,i} \geq \frac{1}{2}\left[|C(s^k)| - |C(z^k)|\right].$$

When the criterion $\text{Ared}_{k,i} \geq 0.1\text{Pred}_{k,i}$ is satisfied, we accept $v^{k,i} = z^k$. Otherwise, we reduce the trust-region radius.

To establish IR methods for semivectorial bilevel programming on Riemannian manifolds, we adapt the IR method presented in [4]. In the presented algorithm, the parameters $\eta > 0$, $N > 0$, $\theta_{-1} \in (0,1)$, $\delta_{\min} > 0$, $\tau_1 > 0$, and $\tau_2 > 0$ are given. The initial approximations $s^0 \in W \times M \times \mathbb{R}^n$, $\lambda^0 \in \mathbb{R}^{m+n}$, as well as a sequence $\{\omega^k\}$ such that $\sum_{k=0}^{+} \infty\omega^k < +\infty$ are also given.

4. Convergence Results

Using the method for studying the convergence of the IR algorithm in Euclidean spaces [20,22], the convergence results of IR algorithms for semivectorial bilevel programming on Riemannian manifolds are given under the following assumptions. From now on, we assume that the semivectorial bilevel optimization problems on Riemannian manifolds satisfy assumptions H_1–H_3 stated below:

H_1 There exists L_1 such that, for all (x,ω), $(\bar{x},\bar{\omega}) \in M \times W$, $\mu, \bar{\mu} \in \mathbb{R}^n$, and $\xi \in [0, \xi_{\max}]$,

$$|C'(x,\omega,\mu) - C'(\bar{x},\bar{\omega},\bar{\mu})| \leq L_1 \text{d}((x,\omega,\mu),(\bar{x},\bar{\omega},\bar{\mu})).$$

H_2 There exists L_2 such that, for all $x, \bar{x} \in M$,

$$|\text{gard}_x F(x) - \text{gard}_x F(\bar{x})| \leq L_2 \text{d}((x,\bar{x})).$$

H_3 There exists $r \in [0,1)$, independently of k, such that the point $z^k = (\bar{x},\bar{\omega},\bar{\mu})$ obtained at the restoration phase satisfies

$$|C(z^k)| \leq r|C(s^k)|,$$

where $s^k = (x^k, \omega^k, \mu^k)$. Moreover, if $C(s^k) = 0$, then $z^k = s^k$.

Theorem 1 (Well-definiteness). *Under assumptions H_1–H_3, IR Algorithm 1 for bilevel programming is well defined.*

Algorithm 1: Inexact Restoration algorithm

1 *Define* $\theta_k^{\min} = \min\{1, \theta_{k-1}, \ldots, \theta_{-1}\}$, $\theta_k^{\text{large}} = \min\{1, \theta_k^{\min} + \omega^k\}$, *and* $\theta_{k,-1} = \theta_k^{\text{large}}$.

2 **(Restoration phase)** *Find an approximate minimizer $\bar{x}$ and multipliers $\bar{\mu} \in \mathbb{R}^n$ for the problem:*

$$\begin{aligned} \min_x \ & \sum_{i=1}^{p} \omega_i^k f_i(x) \\ \text{s.t.} \ & h(x) = 0, \\ & x \in M, \end{aligned}$$

and define $z^k = (\bar{x}, \omega^k, \bar{\mu})$.

Algorithm 1: *Cont.*

3 (**Direction**) *Compute*

$$d_{\tan}^{k} = P_k\Big(\exp_{z^k}\Big(-\eta \operatorname{grad}_s L(z^k, \lambda^k)\Big)\Big) - z^k,$$

where P_k *is the projection on*

$$\pi_k = \{s \in M \times W \times \mathbb{R}^n : \langle C'(z^k), \dot{\gamma}_{s,z^k}(0)\rangle = 0\},$$

and $P_k\Big(\exp_{z^k}\Big(-\eta \operatorname{grad}_s L(z^k, \lambda^k)\Big)\Big)$ *is a solution of the following problem:*

$$\begin{aligned} \min_{y \in M \times W \times \mathbb{R}^n} \quad & \frac{1}{2}\Big\|y - \exp_{z^k}\Big(-\eta \operatorname{grad}_s L(z^k, \lambda^k)\Big)\Big\|^2 \\ \text{s.t.} \quad & \langle C'(z^k), \dot{\gamma}_{y,z^k}(0)\rangle = 0. \end{aligned}$$

If $z^k = s^k$, $d_{\tan}^k = 0$, *then stop and return* x^k *as a solution of Problem (7). Otherwise, we set* $i \leftarrow 0$ *and choose* $\delta_{k,0} \geq \delta_{\min}$.

4 (**Minimization phase**) *If* $d_{\tan}^k = 0$, *then we take* $v^{k,i} = z^k$. *Otherwise, we take* $t_{\text{break}}^{k,i} = \min\Big\{1, \frac{\delta_{k,i}}{d_{\tan}^k}\Big\}$ *and find* $v^{k,i} \in \pi_k$ *such that, for some* $0 < t < t_{\text{break}}^{k,i}$, *we have*

$$L(v^{k,i}, \lambda^k) \leq \max\Big\{L(z^k + t d_{\tan}^k, \lambda^k), L(z^k, \lambda^k) - \tau_1 \delta_{k,i}, L(z^k, \lambda^k) - \tau_2\Big\}$$

and $\mathrm{d}(v^{k,i}, z^k) \leq \delta_{k,i}$.

5 *If* $d_{\tan}^k = 0$, *define* $\lambda^{k,i} = \lambda^k$. *Otherwise, we take* $\lambda^{k,i} \in \mathbb{R}^{n+m}$ *such that* $|\lambda^{k,i}| \leq N$.

6 *For all* $\theta \in [0, 1]$, *we define*

$$\begin{aligned} \operatorname{Pred}_{k,i}(\theta) = & \theta\Big[L(s^k, \lambda^k) - L(v^{k,i}, \lambda^k) - C(z^k)^T(\lambda^{k,i} - \lambda^k)\Big] + \\ & (1-\theta)\Big[|C(s^k)| - |C(z^k)|\Big]. \end{aligned}$$

We take $\theta_{k,i}$ *as the maximum* $\theta \in [0, \theta_{k,i-1}]$ *that it satisfies:*

$$\operatorname{Pred}_{k,i}(\theta) \geq \frac{1}{2}\Big[|C(s^k)| - |C(z^k)|\Big], \tag{12}$$

and define $\operatorname{Pred}_{k,i} = \operatorname{Pred}_{k,i}(\theta_{k,i})$.

Algorithm 1: *Cont.*

7 *Compute*

$$\text{Ared}_{k,i} = \theta_{k,i}\Big[L(s^k,\lambda^k) - L(v^{k,i},\lambda^{k,i})\Big] + (1-\theta_{k,i})\Big[|C(s^k)| - |C(v^{k,i})|\Big].$$

If

$$\text{Ared}_{k,i} \geq 0.1\text{Pred}_{k,i},$$

then we take

$$s^{k+1} = v^{k,i},\quad \lambda^{k+1} = \lambda^{k,i},\quad \theta_k = \theta_{k,i},\quad \delta_k = \delta_{k,i},$$
$$\text{Ared}_k = \text{Ared}_{k,i},\quad \text{Pred}_k = \text{Pred}_{k,i}.$$

and finish the current kth *iteration. Otherwise, we choose* $\delta_{k,i+1} \in [0.1\delta_{k,i}, 0.9\delta_{k,i}]$, *set* $i \leftarrow i+1$, *and go to Step 4.*

Proof. According to Step 6 and Step 7 of Algorithm 1, it can be calculated that

$$\begin{aligned}
\text{Ared}_{k,i} - 0.1\text{Pred}_{k,i} &= 0.9\text{Pred}_{k,i} + (1-\theta_{k,i})[|C(z^k)| - |C(v^{k,i})|] \\
&+ \theta_{k,i}\Big[L(v^{k,i},\lambda^k) - L(v^{k,i},\lambda^{k,i}) + C(z^k)^T(\lambda^{k,i} - \lambda^k)\Big] \\
&= 0.9\text{Pred}_{k,i} + (1-\theta_{k,i})[|C(z^k)| - |C(v^{k,i})|] \\
&+ \theta_{k,i}\Big[C(v^{k,i})^T\lambda^k - C(v^{k,i})^T\lambda^{k,i} + C(z^k)^T(\lambda^{k,i} - \lambda^k)\Big] \\
&= 0.9\text{Pred}_{k,i} + (1-\theta_{k,i})[|C(z^k)| - |C(v^{k,i})|] \\
&+ \theta_{k,i}\Big(C(z^k) - C(v^{k,i})\Big)^T(\lambda^{k,i} - \lambda^k).
\end{aligned}$$

Through the condition (12), we have

$$\begin{aligned}
\text{Ared}_{k,i} - 0.1\text{Pred}_{k,i} &\geq 0.45\Big[|C(s^k)| - |C(z^k)|\Big] + (1-\theta_{k,i})[|C(z^k)| - |C(v^{k,i})|] \\
&+ \theta_{k,i}\Big(C(z^k) - C(v^{k,i})\Big)^T(\lambda^{k,i} - \lambda^k).
\end{aligned} \tag{13}$$

Then, from the assumption H_3,

$$\begin{aligned}
\text{Ared}_{k,i} - 0.1\text{Pred}_{k,i} &= 0.45(1-r)|C(s^k)| + (1-\theta_{k,i})[|C(z^k)| - |C(v^{k,i})|] \\
&+ \theta_{k,i}\Big(C(z^k) - C(v^{k,i})\Big)^T(\lambda^{k,i} - \lambda^k).
\end{aligned}$$

If $C(s^k) \neq 0$, due to the continuity of C and $\delta_{k,i} \to 0$, we have $|C(z^k)| - |C(v^{k,i})| \to 0$. Thus, there exists a positive constant $\delta_{k,i}$ such that

$$\text{Ared}_{k,i} - 0.1\text{Pred}_{k,i} \geq 0.$$

This means that the algorithm is well defined when $C(s^k) \neq 0$.

If $C(s^k) = 0$, then s^k is feasible. Since the algorithm does not terminate at the kth iteration, we know that $d^k_{\tan} \neq 0$. Therefore, we have

$$z^k = s^k \text{ and } C(z^k) = C(s^k) = 0.$$

Combining the condition (12), it follows that

$$\text{Pred}_{\text{k,i}}(\theta) = \theta\Big[L(s^k, \lambda^k) - L(v^{k,i}, \lambda^k)\Big] \geq 0,$$

and independent of θ, for all i, $\theta_{k,i} = \theta_{k,-1}$. In terms of the inequality (13), when $\delta_{k,i}$ is sufficiently small, we obtain

$$\text{Ared}_{k,i} - 0.1\text{Pred}_{k,i} \geq 0.$$

Therefore, Algorithm 1 is well defined. □

The next theorem is an important tool for proving the convergence of Algorithm 1. We prove that the actual reduction Ared_{k,i^*}, with i^* the accepted value of i, achieved at each iteration necessarily tends to 0.

Theorem 2. *Under the assumptions H_1–H_3, if Algorithm 1 generates an infinite sequence, then*

$$\lim_{k\to+\infty} \text{Ared}_k = 0, \lim_{k\to+\infty} |C(s^k)| = 0.$$

The same results above occur when $\lambda^k = 0$, for all k.

Proof. Let us prove that $\lim_{k\to+\infty} \text{Ared}_k = 0$, i.e., we need to prove

$$\lim_{k\to+\infty}\Big[\theta_k\Big[L(s^k,\lambda^k) - L(s^{k+1},\lambda^{k+1})\Big] + (1-\theta_k)\Big[|C(s^k)| - |C(s^{k+1})|\Big]\Big] = 0,$$

that is

$$\lim_{k\to+\infty}\Big[\theta_k L(s^k,\lambda^k) + (1-\theta_k)|C(s^k)| - \Big[\theta_k L(s^{k+1},\lambda^{k+1}) + (1-\theta_k)|C(s^{k+1})|\Big]\Big] = 0,$$

namely

$$\lim_{k\to+\infty}\left[\Psi(s^k,\theta_k) - \Psi(s^{k+1},\theta_k)\right] = 0,$$

where $\Psi(s^k,\theta_k) = \theta_k L(s^k,\lambda^k) + (1-\theta_k)|C(s^k)|$.

By contradiction, suppose that there is an infinite indicator set $T_1 \subset \{0,1,2\dots\}$ and a positive constant $\zeta > 0$ such that, for any $k \in T_1$, we have

$$\Psi(s^{k+1},\theta_k) \leq \Psi(s^k,\theta_k) - \zeta.$$

Let $\Psi_k = \Psi(s^k,\theta_k)$, then

$$\begin{aligned}
\Psi_{k+1} &= \theta_{k+1}L(s^{k+1},\lambda^{k+1}) + (1-\theta_{k+1})|C(s^{k+1})| \\
&= \theta_{k+1}L(s^{k+1},\lambda^{k+1}) + (1-\theta_{k+1})|C(s^{k+1})| \\
&- \theta_k L(s^{k+1},\lambda^{k+1}) + (1-\theta_k)|C(s^{k+1})| \\
&+ \theta_k L(s^{k+1},\lambda^{k+1}) + (1-\theta_k)|C(s^{k+1})| \\
&= (\theta_{k+1}-\theta_k)L(s^{k+1},\lambda^{k+1}) + (\theta_k-\theta_{k+1})|C(s^{k+1})| \\
&+ \theta_k L(s^{k+1},\lambda^{k+1}) + (1-\theta_k)|C(s^{k+1})| \\
&\leq (\theta_k-\theta_{k+1})\Big[\|C(s^{k+1})\| - L(s^{k+1},\lambda^{k+1})\Big] \\
&+ \theta_k L(s^k,\lambda^k) + (1-\theta_k)|C(s^k)| - \zeta_k.
\end{aligned}$$

Equivalently,

$$\Psi_{k+1} \leq (\theta_k-\theta_{k+1})\Big[|C(s^{k+1})| - L(s^{k+1},\lambda^{k+1})\Big] + \Psi_k - \zeta_k, \tag{14}$$

where $\zeta_k > 0$ and $\zeta_k > \zeta > 0, k \in T_1$.

According to the definition of $\theta_{k,-1}$,

$$\theta_k - \theta_{k+1} + \omega_k \geq 0, \quad k \in T_1.$$

There is an upper bound $c > 0$, such that

$$|C(s^k)| - \|L(s^{k+1}, \lambda^{k+1})\| \leq c. \tag{15}$$

Combining the inequalities (14) and (15), it follows that

$$\begin{aligned}\Psi_{j+1} &\leq (\theta_j - \theta_{j+1} + \omega_j)\Big[|C(s^{j+1})| - L(s^{j+1}, \lambda^{j+1})\Big] \\ &\quad + \Psi_j - \zeta_j - \omega_j\Big[|C(s^{j+1})| - L(s^{j+1}, \lambda^{j+1})\Big] \\ &\leq (\theta_j - \theta_{j+1} + \omega_j)c + \Psi_j - \zeta_j + \omega_j c \\ &\leq (\theta_j - \theta_{j+1})c + \Psi_j - \zeta_j + 2\omega_j c.\end{aligned}$$

Then, for all $k \geq 1$, we have

$$\begin{aligned}\Psi_k &\leq \Psi_0 + (\theta_0 - \theta_{k+1})c + -\sum_{j=0}^{k-1}\zeta_j + \sum_{j=0}^{k-1}2\omega_j c \\ &\leq \Psi_0 + 2c + -\sum_{j=0}^{k-1}\zeta_j + \sum_{j=0}^{k-1}2\omega_j c.\end{aligned}$$

Since $\sum_{j=0}^{k-1} 2\omega_j$ is the convergence and ζ_j is bounded away from zero, this implies that Ψ_k is unbounded. This is a contradiction. Thus, we have that $\lim_{k\to+\infty} \text{Ared}_k = 0$. In addition, in a similar way, we can prove $\lim_{k\to+\infty} |C(s^k)| = 0$. □

According to Theorem 2, it means that the point generated by the IR algorithm for the KKT transformation (7) will converge to a feasible point eventually. Then, we prove that d^k_{tan} cannot be bounded away from zero under the following assumption H_4. This means that the point generated by the IR algorithm will converge to a weak Pareto solution of Problem (7):

H_4 There exists $\beta > 0$, independently of k, such that

$$\text{d}(s^k, z^k) \leq \beta|C(s^k)|.$$

Theorem 3. *Suppose that the assumptions H_1, H_2, H_3, and H_4 hold. If $\{s^k\}$ is an infinite sequence generated by Algorithm 1, $\{z^k\}$ is the sequence defined at the restoration phase in Algorithm 1, then:*

1 $\left|C(s^k)\right| \to 0$.
2 *There exists a limit point s^* of $\{s^k\}$.*
3 *Every limit point of $\{s^k\}$ is a feasible point of the KKT reformulation (7).*
4 *If, for all ω, a global solution of the lower-level problem is found, then any limit point (x^*, ω^*) is feasible for the weighted semivectorial bilevel programming (6).*
5 *If s^* is a limit point of $\{s^k\}$, there exists an infinite set $K \subset \mathbb{N}$ such that*

$$\lim_{k\in K} s^k = \lim_{k\in K} z^k = s^*, \quad C(s^*) = 0, \quad \lim_{k\in K} d^k_{tan} = 0.$$

Proof. We can prove the first two items from Theorem 2 and the assumption H_1–H_3. Based on the conclusions of the first two terms, the third and forth items are valid. The fifth item follows from the assumption H_4 and the first item. □

The above conclusions give the well-definiteness and convergence of the algorithm proposed for semivectorial bilevel programming on Riemannian manifolds. From the point of view of the assumption put forward in this paper, the assumptions H_3 and H_4 are related to the sequences generated by the IR algorithm. Therefore, it is worth studying establishing sufficient conditions to ensure their effectiveness. Two assumptions about the lower-level problem are given below to verify the hypotheses H_3 and H_4:

H_5 For every solution $s = (x, \omega, \mu)$ of $C(x, \omega, \mu) = 0$, such that the gradients $\text{grad}h_i(x)$, $i = 1, \ldots, n$ of the active lower level constraints are linearly independent.

H_6 For every solution $s = (x, \omega, \mu)$ of $C(x, \omega, \mu) = 0$ such that the matrix:

$$H(x, \omega, \mu) = \sum_{i=1}^{p} \omega_i \text{Hess}_x f_i(x) + \sum_{i=1}^{n} \mu_i \text{Hess}_x h_i(x),$$

is positive definite in the following set:

$$Z(x) = \{d \in \mathbb{R}^n | \text{grad}h(x)^T d = 0,\ d_j = 0 \text{ for all } j\}.$$

For convenience, to verify H_3 and H_4, we define the following matrix:

$$D'(s) = \begin{pmatrix} \sum_{i=1}^{p} \omega_i \text{Hess}_x f_i + \sum_{i=1}^{n} \mu_i \text{Hess}_x h_i & \text{grad}_x h \\ \text{grad}_x h^T & 0 \end{pmatrix}.$$

Lemma 1. *The matrix $D'(s)$ is non-singular for any solution $s = (x, \omega, \mu)$ of $C(x, \omega, \mu) = 0$.*

Proof. Assuming that there exist $u \in \mathbb{R}^m$ and $v \in \mathbb{R}^p$ such that

$$D'(s) \begin{pmatrix} u \\ v \end{pmatrix} = 0,$$

then we have

$$\Big(\sum_{i=1}^{p} \omega_i \text{Hess}_x f_i + \sum_{i=1}^{n} \mu_i \text{Hess}_x h_i\Big) u + \text{grad}_x h v = 0, \tag{16}$$

$$\text{grad}_x h u = 0. \tag{17}$$

According to the assumptions H_5–H_6 and Equalities (16) and (17), it follows that $u = 0$ and $v = 0$. This means that the matrix $D'(s)$ is non-singular for any solution $s = (x, \omega, \mu)$ of $C(x, \omega, \mu) = 0$. □

Let $D(s)$ be defined on $M \times W \times \mathbb{R}^n$, for each $\omega \in W$, a solution $u(\omega) = (x(\omega), \mu(\omega))$ of $C(x, \omega, \mu) = 0$ such that the function $v(\omega) = u(\omega)$ is continuous on W. Now, we fix the function $v(\omega)$, by Lemma 1, and we can define a function $\Upsilon(\omega) = D'(\omega, v(\omega))^{-1}$ over the set W. Let $V(v(\omega), \alpha) = \{v \in M \times \mathbb{R}^n : \text{d}(v, v(\omega)) \leq \alpha\}$. Furthermore, the following lemma can be obtained.

Lemma 2. *There exist $\alpha > 0$ and $\beta > 0$, such that, for all $\omega \in W$, it holds $|\Upsilon(\omega)| < \beta$, and for all $v \in V(v(\omega), \alpha)$, $\Upsilon(\omega)$ coincides with the local inverse operator of $D'(\omega, \cdot)$.*

Proof. Since $D'(\omega, v)$ is continuous on (ω, v), $v(\omega)$ is continuous on W, and $\Upsilon(\omega)$ is continuous with respect to $\omega \in W$, there exists $\beta > 0$, such that, for all $\omega \in W$, $|\Upsilon(\omega)| < \beta$.

For each fixed value of $\omega \in W$, associated with each v, the continuously differentiable operator of the vector $C(\omega, v)$ verifies the assumption of the inverse function theorem at $v(\omega)$. Hence, there exists $\alpha > 0$ such that $C(\omega, \cdot)$ has a continuously differentiable local inverse operator $G(\omega) : C(\omega, V(v(\omega), \alpha)) \mapsto V(v(\omega), \alpha)$, and the Jacobian matrix $[G(\omega)]'$ is consistent with $Y(\omega)$. This ends the proof. □

Finally, we state that H_3 and H_4 hold under the assumptions H_5 to H_6. The next theorem summarizes this fact, and it can be proven as follows.

Theorem 4. *Let $r \in [0,1)$, $(\omega, u) \in W \times M \times \mathbb{R}^n$ be such that $C(\omega, u) \neq 0$. If the assumptions H_5-H_6 hold, then there exist $\beta > 0$, $\omega \in W$, and $\bar{u} = (\bar{x}, \bar{\mu}) \in M \times \mathbb{R}^n$ such that*

$$|C(\omega, \bar{u})| \leq r|C(\omega, u)|,$$

and

$$d((\omega, u), (\omega, \bar{u})) \leq \beta|C(\omega, u)|.$$

Proof. According to Lemmas 1 and 2, combining the assumptions H_5 and H_6, by using Taylor expansions of the functions on Riemannian manifolds, the statement follows from the results of [20]. This ends the proof. □

Example 1. *We consider the particular case $M = \mathbb{R}^2_+ := \{(x_1, x_2) \in \mathbb{R}^2 | x_1 > 0, x_2 > 0\}$ with the metric g given in Cartesian coordinates (x_1, x_2) around the point $x \in M$ by the matrix:*

$$M \ni y \mapsto (g_{ij})_y = \left(g\left(\frac{\partial}{\partial y_i}, \frac{\partial}{\partial y_j}\right)\right) := \operatorname{diag}\left(x_1^{-1}, x_2^{-1}\right).$$

In other words, for any vectors $u = (u_1, u_2)$ and $v = (v_1, v_2)$ in the tangent plane at $x \in M$, denoted by $T_y M$, which coincides with $\mathbb{R}^2$, we have

$$g(u, v) = \frac{u_1 v_1}{x_1} + \frac{u_2 v_2}{x_2}.$$

Let $a = (a_1, a_2) \in M$ and $v = (v_1, v_2) \in T_a M$. It is easy to see that the (minimizing) geodesic curve $t \mapsto \gamma(t)$ verifying $\gamma(0) = a$, $\gamma(0) = v$ is given by

$$\mathbb{R} \ni t \mapsto (a_1 e^{\frac{v_1}{a_1} t}, a_2 e^{\frac{v_2}{a_2} t}).$$

Hence, M is a complete Riemannian manifold. Furthermore, the (minimizing) geodesic segment $\gamma : [0,1] \to M_2$ joining the points $a = (a_1, a_2)$ and $b = (b_1, b_2)$, i.e., $\gamma(0) = a$, $\gamma(1) = b$ is given by $\gamma_i(t) = a_1^{1-t} b_i^t$, $i = 1, 2$. Thus, the distance d on the metric space (M_2, g_2) is given by

$$\begin{aligned} d(a,b) &= \int_0^1 \|\dot{\gamma}(t)\|_{\gamma(t)} dt = \int_0^1 \sqrt{(\frac{\dot{\gamma}_1(t)}{\gamma_1(t)})^2 + (\frac{\dot{\gamma}_2(t)}{\gamma_2(t)})^2} dt \\ &= \sqrt{(\ln \frac{a_1}{b_1})^2 + (\ln \frac{a_2}{b_2})^2}. \end{aligned}$$

It follows easily that the closed ball $\mathbb{B}(a; R)$ centered in $a \in M$ of radius $R \geq 0$ verifies

$$\left[a_1 e^{-\frac{R}{\sqrt{2}}}, a_1 e^{-\frac{R}{\sqrt{2}}}\right] \times \left[a_2 e^{-\frac{R}{\sqrt{2}}}, a_2 e^{-\frac{R}{\sqrt{2}}}\right] \subset \mathbb{B}(a; R);$$

thus, every closed rectangle $[\rho_1, \eta_1] \times [\rho_2, \eta_2]$ $(\rho_1 > 0, \rho_2 > 0)$ is bounded in the metric space (M, g) with the distance d.

Next, we consider the functions $F: M \to \mathbb{R}$, $f: M \to \mathbb{R}^2$ and $h: M \to \mathbb{R}$ given for any $x \in M$ by

$$\begin{aligned} F(x) &= -x_1, \\ f_1(x) &= \frac{1}{2}(x_1-1)^2 - \frac{3}{4}\ln x_1 + \frac{3}{8}(x_2-1)^2, \\ f_2(x) &= \frac{1}{4}(x_1-1)^2 - \frac{3}{8}\ln x_1 + \frac{3}{16}(x_2-1)^2, \\ h(x) &= \frac{1}{3}(x_1-1)^2 + \frac{1}{3}(x_2-1)^2 - \frac{1}{3}. \end{aligned}$$

It is easy to see that, for $x \in M$ and any geodesic segment $\gamma: [0,1] \to M$ with $\gamma(0) = a$, $\gamma(1) = b$, the functions $f_i(x), i = 1,2$, and $h(x)$ are all convex on M with the Riemannian metric g. Moreover, the function $h(x)$ satisfies the Slater constraint qualification.

We then consider the corresponding KKT reformulation of the semivectorial bilevel programming on Riemannian manifolds:

$$\begin{aligned} \min_{x,\omega} \quad & F(x) = -x_2 \\ \text{s.t.} \quad & \omega \in W, \\ & \sum_{i=1}^{2} \omega_i \mathrm{grad}_x f_i(x) + \mathrm{grad}_x h(x)\mu = 0, \\ & h(x) = 0, \\ & x \in M. \end{aligned}$$

By the definition of the gradient of a differentiable function with respect to the Riemannian metric g, let $\omega_1 = \frac{1}{3}$, $\omega_2 = \frac{2}{3}$, $\omega_1 + \omega_2 = 1$, and $\mu = (\frac{1}{2}, \frac{3}{4})^T \in \mathbb{R}^2$; we have

$$\begin{aligned} \min_{x,\omega} \quad & F(x) = -x_1 \\ \text{s.t.} \quad & (x_1 - \frac{1}{2})^2 + (x_2 - \frac{1}{2})^2 - 1 = 0, \\ & \frac{1}{3}(x_1-1)^2 + \frac{1}{3}(x_2-1)^2 - \frac{1}{3} = 0, \\ & x \in M. \end{aligned}$$

It is easy to see that the unique optimal solution of the KKT reformulation is $x = (\frac{3-\sqrt{7}}{4}, \frac{3+\sqrt{7}}{4})$.

According to Algorithm 1, we first give the initial approximations $s^0 \in W \times M \times \mathbb{R}^2$, $\lambda^0 \in \mathbb{R}^2$, and a sequence $\{\omega^k\}$. In the restoration phase, find an approximate minimizer $\bar{x} = (\bar{x_1}, \bar{x_2}) \in M$ and multiplier $\bar{\mu} = (\bar{\mu_1}, \bar{\mu_2}) \in \mathbb{R}^2$ for the problem:

$$\begin{aligned} \min_{x} \quad & \omega_1^k f_1(x) + \omega_2^k f_2(x) \\ \text{s.t.} \quad & h(x) = 0, \\ & x \in M, \end{aligned}$$

and define $z^k = (\bar{x}, \omega^k, \bar{\mu})$.

We then compute the direction by using the exponential mapping and the projection defined on Riemannian manifold M.

$$\begin{aligned} d_{\tan}^k &= P_k\left(\exp_{z^k}\left(-\eta \mathrm{grad}_s L(z^k, \lambda^k)\right)\right) - z^k, \\ &= P_k\left(z_1^k e^{-\eta \frac{\mathrm{grad}_s L(z^k,\lambda^k)}{z_1^k}}, z_2^k e^{-\eta \frac{\mathrm{grad}_s L(z^k,\lambda^k)}{z_2^k}}\right) - z^k, \end{aligned}$$

axioms

MDPI

Article

A Novel Approach for the Approximate Solution of Wave Problems in Multi-Dimensional Orders with Computational Applications

Muhammad Nadeem [1,*], Ali Akgül [2,3,4], Liliana Guran [5] and Monica-Felicia Bota [6,*]

[1] School of Mathematics and Statistics, Qujing Normal University, Qujing 655011, China
[2] Department of Computer Science and Mathematics, Lebanese American University, Beirut 1102 2801, Lebanon
[3] Art and Science Faculty, Department of Mathematics, Siirt University, 56100 Siirt, Turkey
[4] Department of Mathematics, Mathematics Research Center, Near East University, Near East Boulevard, Mersin 10, 99138 Nicosia, Turkey
[5] Department of Pharmaceutical Sciences, "Vasile Goldis" Western University of Arad, L. Rebreanu Street, No. 86, 310048 Arad, Romania
[6] Department of Mathematics, Babes-Bolyai University, M. Kogălniceanu Street, No. 1, 400084 Cluj-Napoca, Romania
* Correspondence: nadeem@mail.qjnu.edu.cn (M.N.); monica.bota@ubbcluj.ro (M.-F.B.)

Abstract: The main goal of this paper is to introduce a new scheme, known as the Aboodh homotopy integral transform method (𝔸HITM), for the approximate solution of wave problems in multi-dimensional orders. The Aboodh integral transform (𝔸IT) removes the restriction of variables in the recurrence relation, whereas the homotopy perturbation method (HPM) derives the successive iterations using the initial conditions. The convergence analysis is provided to study a wave equation with multiple dimensions. Some computational applications are considered to show the efficiency of this scheme. Graphical representation between the approximate and the exact solution predicts the high rate of convergence of this approach.

Keywords: Aboodh integral transform; homotopy perturbation method; wave problems; series results

MSC: 35L05; 35A22

Citation: Nadeem, M.; Akgül, A.; Guran, L.; Bota, M.-F. A Novel Approach for the Approximate Solution of Wave Problems in Multi-Dimensional Orders with Computational Applications. *Axioms* **2022**, *11*, 665. https://doi.org/10.3390/axioms11120665

Academic Editor: Clemente Cesarano

Received: 8 November 2022
Accepted: 21 November 2022
Published: 24 November 2022

1. Introduction

In the real world, partial differential equations (PDEs) are used to analyze a wide range of physical phenomena that occur in different branches of applied sciences, including fluid dynamics, mathematical biology, quantum physics, chemical kinetics, and linear optics [1–3]. Various approaches have been introduced to obtain the analytical solutions of these PDEs. Although the calculations for these strategies are pretty straightforward, their limitations are predicated on the assumption of small parameters. As a result, many researchers developed some novel methods to get around these restrictions. Numerous scientists have studied multiple innovative and unique methods to obtain analytical solutions that are reasonably close to the precise solutions, such as the homotopy analysis method [4], modified extended tanh method [5], new Kudryashov method [6], Chun-Hui He's iteration method [7], the sub-equation method [8], Exp-function method [9], modified exponential rational method [10], homotopy asymptotic method [11], modified extended tanh expansion [12], fractal variational iteration transform method [13], residual power series (RPS) method [14] and Adomian decomposition method [15]. In the past, many experts and researchers established the application of the homotopy perturbation method (HPM) [16–18] in various physical problems and showed the performance of this approach in consistently transforming the challenging issues into a straightforward resolution.

The wave equation is a partial differential equation for a scalar function that describes the propagation phenomenon in different areas of engineering, physics, and scientific applications [19,20]. Wazwaz [21] studied linear and nonlinear problems in bounded and unbounded domains using the variational iteration method. Ghasemi et al. [22] employed the homotopy perturbation method to derive the numerical solution of two-dimensional nonlinear differential equations. Keskin and Oturanc [23] applied the reduced differential transform method to various wave equations. Ullah et al. [24] proposed the optimal homotopy asymptotic method to obtain the analytic series solution of wave equations. Adwan et al. [25] presented the numerical solutions of multi-dimensional wave equations and showed the accuracy of the proposed techniques. Jleli et al. [26] studied the framework of the homotopy perturbation transform method for analytic treatment of wave equations. Mullen and Belytschko [27] provided the finite element scheme for the examination of two-dimensional wave equations and considered some semi-discretizations. These schemes have many limitations and assumptions in finding the approximate solutions of the problems. To overcome these limitations and restrictions of variables, we introduce a new iterative strategy for the approximate solutions of multi-dimensional wave problems.

The variational iteration method (VIM), Laplace transform and homotopy analysis method (HAM) have some limitations, such as the VIM involving integration and producing the constant of integration, the Laplace transform involving the convolution theorem and the HAM also considering some assumptions. The Aboodh integral transform is very easy to implement for differential problems. The purpose of this paper is to apply the $\mathbb{A}$HITM with a combination of the Abdooh integral transform and the HPM for wave problems of different dimensions. Less computations, fast convergence and significant results make this scheme unique and different from other approaches in the literature. This strategy derives a series of solutions with fast convergence and yields an approximate solution very close to the precise solution. This paper is structured as follows. In Section 2, we give brief details about the Abdooh integral transform. In Section 3, we present the formulation of the $\mathbb{A}$HITM for solving multi-dimension problems. We provide the convergence analysis in Section 4. Some computational applications are demonstrated to show the effectiveness in Section 5, and finally, we discuss the conclusions in Section 6.

2. Preliminary Definitions of $\mathbb{A}$IT

In this section, we describe a few fundamental characteristics and concepts of $\mathbb{A}$IT that are very helpful in the formulation of this scheme:

Definition 1. *If we let $\vartheta(\phi)$ be a function precise for $\sigma \geq 0$, then*

$$\mathcal{L}\{\vartheta(\phi)\} = F(s) = \theta \int_0^{\infty} \vartheta(\phi) e^{-\sigma\phi} d\phi, \tag{1}$$

is called a Laplace transform.

Definition 2. *The $\mathbb{A}$IT of a function $\vartheta(\phi)$ is defined as* [28]

$$\mathbb{A}[\vartheta(\phi)] = R(\sigma) = \frac{1}{\sigma} \int_0^{\infty} \vartheta(\phi) e^{-\sigma\phi} d\phi. \ \ \phi \geq 0, \ \ k_1 \leq \sigma \leq k_2 \tag{2}$$

where $\mathbb{A}$ represents the symbol of $\mathbb{A}$IT, k_1 and k_2 are constants and σ is the independent variable of the transformed function ϕ. Conversely, since $R(\sigma)$ is the $\mathbb{A}$IT of function $\vartheta(\phi)$, then

$$\mathbb{A}^{-1}[R(\sigma)] = \vartheta(\phi), \quad \mathbb{A}^{-1}$$

is called the inverse $\mathbb{A}$IT.

Proposition 1. *If we let* $\mathbb{A}\{\vartheta_1(\phi)\} = R_1(\sigma)$ *and* $\mathbb{A}\{\vartheta_2(\phi)\} = R_2(\sigma)$, *then* [29]

$$\begin{aligned} &\mathbb{A}\{au_1(\phi) + bu_2(\phi)\} = aS\{\vartheta_1(\phi)\} + bS\{\vartheta_2(\phi)\}, \\ \Rightarrow \quad &\mathbb{A}\{au_1(\phi) + bu_2(\phi)\} = aR_1(\sigma) + bR_2(\sigma). \end{aligned} \tag{3}$$

Proposition 2. *If* $\mathbb{A}\{\vartheta(\phi)\} = R(\sigma)$, *then the differential properties are defined as follows* [29,30]:

$$\begin{aligned} &(1) \quad \mathbb{A}\{\vartheta'(\phi)\} = \sigma R(\sigma) - \frac{\vartheta(0)}{\sigma}; \\ &(2) \quad \mathbb{A}\{\vartheta''(\phi)\} = \sigma^2 R(\sigma) - \vartheta(0) - \frac{\vartheta'(0)}{\sigma}; \\ &(3) \quad \mathbb{A}\{\vartheta^m(\phi)\} = \sigma^m R(\sigma) - \frac{\vartheta(0)}{\sigma^{2-m}} - \frac{\vartheta'(0)}{\sigma^{3-m}} - \cdots - \frac{\vartheta^{m-1}(0)}{\sigma}. \end{aligned} \tag{4}$$

3. Formulation of $\mathbb{A}$HITM

In this segment, we formulate the strategy of the $\mathbb{A}$HITM for finding the approximate solutions of 1D, 2D and 3D wave equation flows. We observe that this strategy is independent of integration and any hypotheses during the formulation of this scheme. We consider a differential problem such that

$$\vartheta''(\varsigma,\phi) = \vartheta(\varsigma,\phi) + g(\vartheta) + g(\varsigma,\phi), \tag{5}$$

with the initial condition

$$\vartheta(\varsigma,0) = a_1, \qquad \vartheta_\phi(\varsigma,0) = a_2, \tag{6}$$

where ϑ denotes the function in a region of time ϕ and $g(\vartheta)$ is considered a nonlinear term with the source term $g(\varsigma,\phi)$ of arbitrary constat a. Employing the $\mathbb{A}$IT in Equation (5) yields

$$\mathbb{A}[\vartheta''(\varsigma,\phi)] = \mathbb{A}[\vartheta(\varsigma,\phi) + g(\vartheta) + g(\varsigma,\phi)].$$

Using the proposition in Equation (4) for the $\mathbb{A}$IT, we obtain

$$\sigma^2 R(\sigma) - \vartheta(\varsigma,0) - \frac{\vartheta'(\varsigma,0)}{\sigma} = \mathbb{A}[\vartheta(\varsigma,\phi) + g(\vartheta) + g(\varsigma,\phi)].$$

Hence, $R(\sigma)$ is evaluated such that

$$R[\sigma] = \frac{\vartheta(\varsigma,0)}{\sigma^2} + \frac{\vartheta'(\varsigma,0)}{\sigma^3} + \frac{1}{\sigma^2}\mathbb{A}[\vartheta(\varsigma,\phi) + g(\vartheta) + g(\varsigma,\phi)]. \tag{7}$$

By using the inverse $\mathbb{A}$IT on Equation (7), we obtain

$$\vartheta(\varsigma,\phi) = \vartheta(\varsigma,0) + \phi\vartheta'(\varsigma,0) + \mathbb{A}^{-1}\left[\frac{1}{\sigma^2}\mathbb{A}\Big\{\vartheta(\varsigma,\phi) + g(\vartheta) + g(\varsigma,\phi)\Big\}\right],$$

Using the initial conditions, we obtain

$$\vartheta(\varsigma,\phi) = a_1 + \phi a_2 + \mathbb{A}^{-1}\left[\frac{1}{\sigma^2}\mathbb{A}\Big\{\vartheta(\varsigma,\phi) + g(\vartheta) + g(\varsigma,\phi)\Big\}\right].$$

Using the proposition in Equation (3), we obtain

$$\vartheta(\varsigma,\phi) = a_1 + \phi a_2 + \mathbb{A}^{-1}\left[\frac{1}{\sigma^2}\mathbb{A}\Big\{g(\varsigma,\phi)\Big\}\right] + \mathbb{A}^{-1}\left[\frac{1}{\sigma^2}\mathbb{A}\Big[\vartheta(\varsigma,\phi) + g(\vartheta)\Big]\right].$$

This implies that

$$\vartheta(\varsigma,\phi) = G(\varsigma,\phi) + \mathbb{A}^{-1}\left[\frac{1}{\sigma^2}\mathbb{A}\Big[\vartheta(\varsigma,\phi) + g(\vartheta)\Big]\right] \tag{8}$$

where

$$G(\varsigma,\phi) = a_1 + \phi a_2 + \mathbb{A}^{-1}\Big[\frac{1}{\sigma^2}\mathbb{A}\Big\{g(\varsigma,\phi)\Big\}\Big].$$

Equation (8) is called the recurrence relation, which is now suitable for the implementation of the HPM such that

$$\vartheta(\varsigma,\phi) = \sum_{i=0}^{\infty} p^i \vartheta_i(\varsigma,\phi) = \vartheta_0 + p^1\vartheta_1 + p^2\vartheta_2 + \cdots, \tag{9}$$

The nonlinear terms $g(\vartheta)$ are evaluated by considering the algorithm

$$g(\vartheta) = \sum_{i=0}^{\infty} p^i H_i(\vartheta) = H_0 + p^1 H_1 + p^2 H_2 + \cdots, \tag{10}$$

where the H_n polynomials are derived as follows:

$$H_n(\vartheta_0 + \vartheta_1 + \cdots + \vartheta_n) = \frac{1}{n!}\frac{\partial^n}{\partial p^n}\left(g\Big(\sum_{i=0}^{\infty} p^i \vartheta_i\Big)\right)_{p=0}, \quad n = 0,1,2,\cdots \tag{11}$$

We use Equations (9)–(11) in Equation (8) to compare the identical power of p such that

$$\begin{aligned}
p^0 &: \vartheta_0(\varsigma,\phi) = G(\varsigma,\phi), \\
p^1 &: \vartheta_1(\varsigma,\phi) = \mathbb{A}^{-1}\left[\frac{1}{\sigma^2}\mathbb{A}\Big\{\vartheta_0(\varsigma,\phi) + H_0(\vartheta)\Big\}\right], \\
p^2 &: \vartheta_2(\varsigma,\phi) = \mathbb{A}^{-1}\left[\frac{1}{\sigma^2}\mathbb{A}\Big\{\vartheta_1(\varsigma,\phi) + H_1(\vartheta)\Big\}\right], \\
p^3 &: \vartheta_3(\varsigma,\phi) = \mathbb{A}^{-1}\left[\frac{1}{\sigma^2}\mathbb{A}\Big\{\vartheta_2(\varsigma,\phi) + H_2(\vartheta)\Big\}\right], \\
&\vdots
\end{aligned}$$

Proceeding with this process yields

$$\vartheta(\varsigma,\phi) = \vartheta_0 + \vartheta_1 + \vartheta_2 + \cdots = \sum_{i=0}^{\infty} \vartheta_i. \tag{12}$$

Thus, Equation (12) is the approximate result of the differential problem in Equation (5).

4. Convergence Analysis

Statement: *Let P and Q be Banach spaces where $X : P \to Q$ is a nonlinear mapping. If the series produced by HPM is*

$$\vartheta_n(P,\varsigma) = X(\vartheta_{n-1}(P,\varsigma)) = \sum_{i=0}^{n-1} \vartheta_i(P,\varsigma), \quad n = 1,2,3\ldots$$

then the following conditions must be true:

(1) $\|\vartheta_n(P,\varsigma) - \vartheta(P,\varsigma)\| \leq \varphi^n \|\vartheta(P,\varsigma) - \vartheta(P,\varsigma)\|$;
(2) $\vartheta_n(P,\varsigma)$ *is forever in the neighborhood of* $\vartheta(P,x)$ *meaning* $\vartheta_n(P,\varsigma) \in B(\vartheta(P,\varsigma),r) = \{\vartheta^*(P,\varsigma)/\|\vartheta^*(P,\varsigma) - \vartheta(P,\varsigma)\|\}$;
(3) $\lim_{n\to\infty} \vartheta_n(P,x) = \vartheta(P,\varsigma)$.

Proof.

(1) **Consider** condition **(1)** by recognition of n such that $\|\vartheta_1 - \vartheta\| = \|T(\vartheta_0) - \vartheta\|$, and the Banach fixed point theorem states that X has a fixed point ϑ (i.e., $X(\vartheta) = \vartheta$). Therefore, we have

$$\|\vartheta_1 - \vartheta\| = \|G(\vartheta_0) - \vartheta\| = \|G(\vartheta_0) - G(\vartheta)\| \leq \varphi\|\vartheta_0 - \vartheta\| = \varphi\|\vartheta(P,\varsigma) - \vartheta\|.$$

where X is a nonlinear mapping. By considering that $\|\vartheta_{n-1} - \vartheta\| \leq \varphi^{n-1}\|\vartheta(P,0) - \vartheta(P,x)\|$ is an induction hypothesis, then

$$\|\vartheta_n - \vartheta\| = \|G(\vartheta_{n-1}) - G(\vartheta)\| \leq \varphi\|\vartheta_{n-1} - \vartheta\| \leq \varphi\varphi^{n-1}\|\vartheta(P,\varsigma) - \vartheta\|.$$

(2) Our initial challenge is to demonstrate $\vartheta(P,\varsigma) \in B(\vartheta(P,\varsigma),r)$, which is attained by replacing m. Thus, for $m = 1, \|\vartheta(P,\varsigma) - \vartheta(P,\varsigma)\| = \|\vartheta(P,0) - \vartheta(P,\varsigma)\| \leq r$ with $\vartheta(P,0)$ as an initial condition. Consider that $\|\vartheta(P,x) - \vartheta(P,\varsigma)\| \leq r$ for $m - 2$ is an induction theory. Thus, we have

$$\begin{aligned}
\|\vartheta(P,\varsigma) - \vartheta(P,\varsigma)\| &= \vartheta_{m-2}(P,\varsigma) - \frac{f_m(P)}{\Gamma(\delta - m + 1)}x^{\delta - m}\| \\
&\leq \|\vartheta_{m-1}(P,\varsigma) - \vartheta(P,\varsigma)\| + \left\|\frac{f_m(P)}{\Gamma(\delta - m + 1)}x^{\delta - m}\right\| \\
&= r.
\end{aligned}$$

Now, $\forall\, n \geq 1$, using **(1)**, we obtain

$$\|\vartheta_n - \vartheta\| \leq \varphi^n\|\vartheta(P,\varsigma) - \vartheta\| \leq \varphi^n r \leq r.$$

(3) Using condition **(2)** and $\lim_{n\to\infty} \varphi^n = 0$, it follows that $\lim_{n\to\infty}\|\vartheta_n - \vartheta\| = 0$, and hence

$$\lim_{n\to\infty} \vartheta_n = \vartheta,$$

Thus, ϑ converges.

□

5. Computational Applications

We illustrate some computational applications to check the validity and authenticity of the $\mathbb{A}$HITM. We observe that this strategy is extremely convenient to utilize and generates the series of convergence much easier than other schemes. We also study the physical behaviors of the these surface solutions. The error distribution is obtained graphically to show that the results obtained by the $\mathbb{A}$HITM are very close to the precise results.

5.1. Example 1

Suppose a one-dimensional wave equation

$$\frac{\partial^2\vartheta}{\partial\phi^2} = \frac{\partial^2\vartheta}{\partial\varsigma^2} - 3\vartheta, \tag{13}$$

with the initial condition

$$\vartheta(\varsigma, 0) = 0, \qquad \vartheta_\phi(\varsigma, 0) = 2\cos(\varsigma), \tag{14}$$

and boundary condition

$$\vartheta(0, \phi) = \sin(2\phi), \qquad \vartheta_\varsigma(\pi, \phi) = -\sin(2\phi). \tag{15}$$

Using the $\mathbb{A}$IT on Equation (13), we obtain $R(\sigma)$ such that

$$R[\sigma] = \frac{\vartheta(\varsigma, 0)}{\sigma^2} + \frac{\vartheta'(\varsigma, 0)}{\sigma^3} + \frac{1}{\sigma^2}\mathbb{A}\Big[\frac{\partial^2 \vartheta}{\partial \varsigma^2} - 3\vartheta\Big].$$

Using the inverse $\mathbb{A}$IT yields

$$\vartheta(\varsigma, \phi) = \vartheta(\varsigma, 0) + \phi\vartheta_\phi(\varsigma, 0) + \mathbb{A}^{-1}\Big[\frac{1}{\sigma^2}\mathbb{A}\Big\{\frac{\partial^2 \vartheta}{\partial \varsigma^2} - 3\vartheta\Big\}\Big].$$

Now, we apply the HPM to obtain a relation such that

$$\sum_{i=0}^{\infty} p^i \vartheta_i(\varsigma, \phi) = 2\phi\cos(\varsigma) + \mathbb{A}^{-1}\Big[\frac{1}{\sigma^2}\mathbb{A}\Big\{\sum_{i=0}^{\infty} p^i \frac{\partial^2 \vartheta_i}{\partial \varsigma^2} - 3\sum_{i=0}^{\infty} p^i \vartheta\Big\}\Big]. \tag{16}$$

When evaluating similar components of p, we obtain

$$\begin{aligned}
p^0 &: \vartheta_0(\varsigma, \phi) = \vartheta(\varsigma, 0) = 2\phi\cos(\varsigma),\\
p^1 &: \vartheta_1(\varsigma, \phi) = \mathbb{A}^{-1}\left[\frac{1}{\sigma^2}\mathbb{A}\left\{\frac{\partial^2 \vartheta_0}{\partial \varsigma^2} - 3\vartheta_0\right\}\right] = -\frac{(2\phi)^3}{3!}\cos(\varsigma),\\
p^2 &: \vartheta_2(\varsigma, \phi) = \mathbb{A}^{-1}\left[\frac{1}{\sigma^2}\mathbb{A}\left\{\frac{\partial^2 \vartheta_1}{\partial \varsigma^2} - 3\vartheta_1\right\}\right] = \frac{(2\phi)^5}{5!}\cos(\varsigma),\\
p^3 &: \vartheta_3(\varsigma, \phi) = \mathbb{A}^{-1}\left[\frac{1}{\sigma^2}\mathbb{A}\left\{\frac{\partial^2 \vartheta_2}{\partial \varsigma^2} - 3\vartheta_2\right\}\right] = -\frac{(2\phi)^7}{7!}\cos(\varsigma),\\
p^4 &: \vartheta_4(\varsigma, \phi) = \mathbb{A}^{-1}\left[\frac{1}{\sigma^2}\mathbb{A}\left\{\frac{\partial^2 \vartheta_3}{\partial \varsigma^2} - 3\vartheta_3\right\}\right] = \frac{(2\phi)^9}{9!}\cos(\varsigma),\\
&\vdots
\end{aligned}$$

In a similar way, we can consider the approximate series such that

$$\begin{aligned}
\vartheta(\varsigma, \phi) &= \vartheta_0(\varsigma, \phi) + \vartheta_1(\varsigma, \phi) + \vartheta_2(\varsigma, \phi) + \vartheta_3(\varsigma, \phi) + \vartheta_4(\varsigma, \phi) + \cdots,\\
&= \cos(\varsigma)\left(2\phi - \frac{(2\phi)^3}{3!} + \frac{(2\phi)^5}{5!} - \frac{(2\phi)^7}{7!} + \frac{(2\phi)^9}{9!}\right) + \cdots.
\end{aligned} \tag{17}$$

which can approach

$$\vartheta(\varsigma, \phi) = \cos(\varsigma)\sin(2\phi). \tag{18}$$

Figure 1 contains two diagrams: (a) the $\mathbb{A}$HITM results of $\vartheta(\varsigma, \phi)$ and (b) the exact results of $\vartheta(\varsigma, \phi)$ at $-2 \leq \varsigma \leq 2$ and $0 \leq \phi \leq 0.5$ for a 1D wave problem. Figure 2 represents the graphical error of the 1D wave equation between the approximate and precise solutions at $0 \leq \varsigma \leq 20$ with $\phi = 0.5$. Table 1 presents the absolute error between the approximate solution obtained by the $\mathbb{A}$HITM and the exact solution at $\varsigma = 0.5, 1$ and $0.25, 0.50, 0.75, 1$. We observe that the current approach demonstrated strong agreement with a precise answer to the problem (Section 5.1) only after a few iterations. The rate of convergence shows that the $\mathbb{A}$HITM is a relatable approach for $\vartheta(\varsigma, \phi)$. This means that we can effectively model any surface in accordance with the desired physical processes appearing in science and engineering.

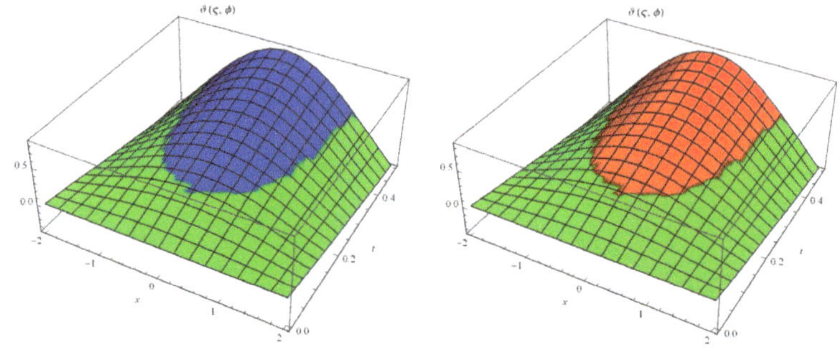

(a) (b)

Figure 1. Surface solutions of 1D wave equation. (**a**) Surface plot for approximate results. (**b**) Surface plot for precise results.

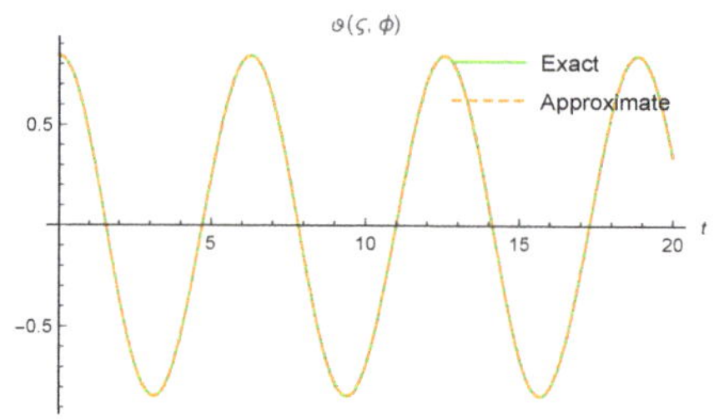

Figure 2. Graphical error between the approximate and precise results of $\vartheta(\varsigma, \phi)$.

Table 1. Absolute error between the approximate and exact solutions for Example 1.

ς	ϕ	Approximate	Exact	Absolute Error
0.5	0.25	0.420735	0.420735	1×10^{-8}
	0.50	0.73846	0.73846	1.7×10^{-7}
	0.75	0.875386	0.875384	2×10^{-6}
	1.0	0.798027	0.797984	4.3×10^{-5}
1.0	0.25	0.259035	0.259035	1×10^{-9}
	0.5	0.454649	0.454649	1.5×10^{-8}
	0.75	0.53895	0.538949	2.3×10^{-7}
	1.0	0.491323	0.491295	2.8×10^{-6}

5.2. Example 2

Suppose a two-dimensional wave equation

$$\frac{\partial^2 \vartheta}{\partial \phi^2} = 2\left(\frac{\partial^2 \vartheta}{\partial \varsigma^2} + \frac{\partial^2 \vartheta}{\partial \xi^2}\right) + 6\phi + 2\varsigma + 4\xi, \tag{19}$$

with the initial condition

$$\vartheta(\varsigma, \xi, 0) = 0, \qquad \vartheta_\phi(\varsigma, \xi, 0) = 2\sin(\varsigma)\sin(\xi), \tag{20}$$

and boundary condition

$$\begin{aligned} \vartheta(0,\xi,\phi) &= \phi^3 + 2\phi^2\xi, & \vartheta_{\varsigma}(\pi,\xi,\phi) &= \phi^3 + \pi\phi^2 + 2\phi^2\xi, \\ \vartheta(\varsigma,0,\phi) &= \phi^3 + \phi^2\varsigma, & \vartheta_{\varsigma}(\varsigma,\pi,\phi) &= \phi^3 + 2\pi\phi^2 + \phi^2\varsigma. \end{aligned} \tag{21}$$

By using the $\mathbb{A}$IT on Equation (19), we obtain $R(\sigma)$ such that

$$R[\sigma] = \frac{6}{\sigma^5} + \frac{2\varsigma}{\sigma^4} + \frac{4\xi}{\sigma^4} + \frac{\vartheta(0)}{\sigma^2} + \frac{\vartheta'(0)}{\sigma^3} + \frac{1}{\sigma^2}\mathbb{A}\Big[2\Big(\frac{\partial^2\vartheta}{\partial\varsigma^2} + \frac{\partial^2\vartheta}{\partial\xi^2}\Big].$$

Using the inverse $\mathbb{A}$IT yields

$$\vartheta(\varsigma,\xi,\phi) = \phi^3 + \varsigma\phi^2 + 2\xi\phi^2 + \vartheta(\varsigma,0) + \phi\vartheta_{\phi}(\varsigma,0) + \mathbb{A}^{-1}\Big[\frac{1}{\sigma^2}\mathbb{A}\Big\{2\Big(\frac{\partial^2\vartheta}{\partial\varsigma^2} + \frac{\partial^2\vartheta}{\partial\xi^2}\Big\}\Big].$$

Now, we apply the HPM to obtain a relation such that

$$\sum_{i=0}^{\infty} p^i\vartheta_i(\varsigma,\xi,\phi) = \phi^3 + \varsigma\phi^2 + 2\xi\phi^2 + 2\phi\sin(\varsigma)\sin(\xi) + \mathbb{A}^{-1}\Big[\frac{1}{\sigma^2}\mathbb{A}\Big\{2\Big(\sum_{i=0}^{\infty} p^i\frac{\partial^2\vartheta_i}{\partial\varsigma^2} + \sum_{i=0}^{\infty} p^i\frac{\partial^2\vartheta_i}{\partial\xi^2}\Big)\Big\}\Big]. \tag{22}$$

By evaluating similar components of p, we obtain

$$\begin{aligned}
p^0 &: \vartheta_0(\varsigma,\xi,\phi) = \vartheta(\varsigma,0) = \phi^3 + \varsigma\phi^2 + 2\xi\phi^2 + 2\phi\sin(\varsigma)\sin(\xi), \\
p^1 &: \vartheta_1(\varsigma,\xi,\phi) = \mathbb{A}^{-1}\left[\frac{1}{\sigma^2}\mathbb{A}\left\{\frac{\partial^2\vartheta_0}{\partial\varsigma^2} + \frac{\partial^2\vartheta_0}{\partial\xi^2}\right\}\right] = -\frac{(2\phi)^3}{3!}\sin(\varsigma)\sin(\xi), \\
p^2 &: \vartheta_2(\varsigma,\xi,\phi) = \mathbb{A}^{-1}\left[\frac{1}{\sigma^2}\mathbb{A}\left\{\frac{\partial^2\vartheta_1}{\partial\varsigma^2} + \frac{\partial^2\vartheta_1}{\partial\xi^2}\right\}\right] = \frac{(2\phi)^5}{5!}\sin(\varsigma)\sin(\xi), \\
p^3 &: \vartheta_3(\varsigma,\xi,\phi) = \mathbb{A}^{-1}\left[\frac{1}{\sigma^2}\mathbb{A}\left\{\frac{\partial^2\vartheta_2}{\partial\varsigma^2} + \frac{\partial^2\vartheta_2}{\partial\xi^2}\right\}\right] = -\frac{(2\phi)^7}{7!}\sin(\varsigma)\sin(\xi), \\
p^4 &: \vartheta_4(\varsigma,\xi,\phi) = \mathbb{A}^{-1}\left[\frac{1}{\sigma^2}\mathbb{A}\left\{\frac{\partial^2\vartheta_3}{\partial\varsigma^2} + \frac{\partial^2\vartheta_3}{\partial\xi^2}\right\}\right] = \frac{(2\phi)^9}{9!}\sin(\varsigma)\sin(\xi), \\
&\vdots
\end{aligned}$$

In a similar way, we can consider the approximate series such that

$$\begin{aligned} \vartheta(\varsigma,\xi,\phi) &= \vartheta_0(\varsigma,\xi,\phi) + \vartheta_1(\varsigma,\xi,\phi) + \vartheta_2(\varsigma,\xi,\phi) + \vartheta_3(\varsigma,\xi,\phi) + \vartheta_4(\varsigma,\xi,\phi) + \cdots, \\ &= \phi^3 + \varsigma\phi^2 + 2\xi\phi^2 + \sin(\varsigma)\sin(\xi)\left(2\phi - \frac{(2\phi)^3}{3!} + \frac{(2\phi)^5}{5!} - \frac{(2\phi)^7}{7!} + \frac{(2\phi)^9}{9!}\right) + \cdots. \end{aligned} \tag{23}$$

which can approach

$$\vartheta(\varsigma,\xi,\phi) = \phi^3 + \varsigma\phi^2 + 2\xi\phi^2 + \sin(\varsigma)\sin(\xi)\sin(2\phi). \tag{24}$$

Figure 3 contains two diagrams: (a) the $\mathbb{A}$HITM results of $\vartheta(\varsigma,\xi,\phi)$ and (b) the exact results of $\vartheta(\varsigma,\xi,\phi)$ at $-1 \le \varsigma \le 1$ and $0 \le \phi \le 0.1$ with $\xi = 0.5$ for the 2D wave problem. Figure 4 represents the graphical error of the 2D wave equation between the approximate and precise solutions at $0 \le \varsigma \le 20$ with $\xi = 0.01$ and $\phi = 0.01$. Table 2 presents the absolute error between the approximate solution obtained by the $\mathbb{A}$HITM and the exact solution at $\varsigma = 0.5, 1$ and $0.25, 0.50, 0.75, 1$, where $\xi = 0.5$. We observe that the current approach demonstrated strong agreement with the precise answer to the problem (Section 5.2) only after a few iterations. The rate of convergence shows that the $\mathbb{A}$HITM is a reliable approach for $\vartheta(\varsigma, \xi, \phi)$. This means that we can effectively model any surface in accordance with the desired physical processes appearing in nature.

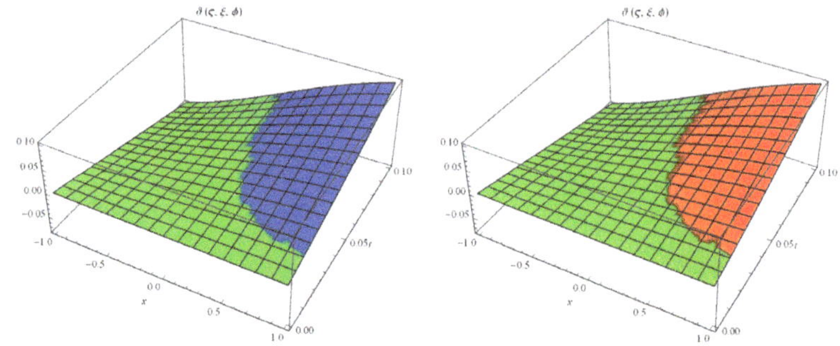

(a) (b)

Figure 3. Surface solutions of 2D wave equation. (**a**) Surface plot for approximate results. (**b**) Surface plot for precise results.

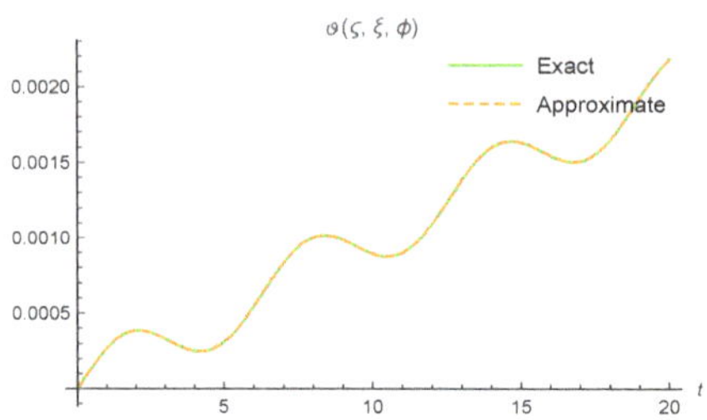

Figure 4. Graphical error between the approximate and precise results of $\vartheta(\varsigma, \xi, \phi)$.

Table 2. Absolute error between the approximate and exact solutions for Example 2.

ς	ϕ	Approximate	Exact	Absolute Error
0.5	0.25	0.365286	0.365286	1×10^{-7}
	0.50	1.08947	1.08947	1×10^{-7}
	0.75	2.23054	2.23054	1.5×10^{-6}
	1.0	3.86685	3.86683	2×10^{-5}
1.0	0.25	0.542593	0.542593	1×10^{-8}
	0.5	1.47082	1.47082	1.2×10^{-7}
	0.75	2.81568	2.81567	2.3×10^{-6}
	1.0	4.64388	4.64385	3×10^{-5}

5.3. Example 3

Consider the three-dimensional wave problem

$$\frac{\partial^2 \vartheta}{\partial \phi^2} = \frac{\varsigma^2}{18} \frac{\partial^2 \vartheta}{\partial \varsigma^2} + \frac{\xi^2}{18} \frac{\partial^2 \vartheta}{\partial \xi^2} + \frac{\eta^2}{18} \frac{\partial^2 \vartheta}{\partial \eta^2} - \vartheta, \tag{25}$$

with the initial condition

$$\vartheta(\varsigma, \xi, \eta, 0) = 0, \qquad \vartheta_\phi(\varsigma, \xi, \eta, 0) = \varsigma^4 \xi^4 \eta^4, \tag{26}$$

and boundary condition

$$\begin{aligned} \vartheta(0,\xi,\eta,\phi) &= 0, & \vartheta(1,\xi,\eta,\phi) &= \xi^4\eta^4\sinh(\phi), \\ \vartheta(\varsigma,0,\eta,\phi) &= 0, & \vartheta(\varsigma,1,\eta,\phi) &= \varsigma^4\eta^4\sinh(\phi), \\ \vartheta(\varsigma,\xi,0,\phi) &= 0, & \vartheta(\varsigma,\xi,1,\phi) &= \varsigma^4\xi^4\sinh(\phi). \end{aligned} \tag{27}$$

By using the $\mathbb{A}$IT in Equation (25), we obtain $R(\sigma)$ such that

$$R[\sigma] = \frac{\vartheta(\varsigma,0)}{\sigma^2} + \frac{\vartheta'(\varsigma,0)}{\sigma^3} + \frac{1}{\sigma^2}\mathbb{A}\Big[\frac{\varsigma^2}{18}\frac{\partial^2\vartheta}{\partial\varsigma^2} + \frac{\xi^2}{18}\frac{\partial^2\vartheta}{\partial\xi^2} + \frac{\eta^2}{18}\frac{\partial^2\vartheta}{\partial\eta^2} - \vartheta\Big].$$

Using the inverse $\mathbb{A}$IT yields

$$\vartheta(\varsigma,\xi,\eta,\phi) = \vartheta(\varsigma,0) + \phi\vartheta_\phi(\varsigma,0) + \mathbb{A}^{-1}\left[\frac{1}{\sigma^2}\mathbb{A}\left\{\frac{\varsigma^2}{18}\frac{\partial^2\vartheta}{\partial\varsigma^2} + \frac{\xi^2}{18}\frac{\partial^2\vartheta}{\partial\xi^2} + \frac{\eta^2}{18}\frac{\partial^2\vartheta}{\partial\eta^2} - \vartheta\right\}\right].$$

Now, we apply the HPM to obtain a relation such that

$$\sum_{i=0}^{\infty} p^i\vartheta(\varsigma,\xi,\eta,\phi) = \phi\varsigma^4\xi^4\eta^4 + \mathbb{A}^{-1}\left[\frac{1}{\sigma^2}\mathbb{A}\left\{\sum_{i=0}^{\infty} p^i\frac{\varsigma^2}{18}\frac{\partial^2\vartheta_i}{\partial\varsigma^2} + \sum_{i=0}^{\infty} p^i\frac{\xi^2}{18}\frac{\partial^2\vartheta_i}{\partial\xi^2} + \sum_{i=0}^{\infty} p^i\frac{\eta^2}{18}\frac{\partial^2\vartheta_i}{\partial\eta^2} - \sum_{i=0}^{\infty} p^i\vartheta\right\}\right]. \tag{28}$$

By evaluating similar components of p, we obtain

$$\begin{aligned}
p^0 &: \vartheta_0(\varsigma,\xi,\eta,\phi) = \vartheta(\varsigma,\xi,\eta,0) = \phi\varsigma^4\xi^4\eta^4, \\
p^1 &: \vartheta_1(\varsigma,\xi,\phi) = \mathbb{A}^{-1}\left[\frac{1}{\sigma^2}\mathbb{A}\left\{\frac{\varsigma^2}{18}\frac{\partial^2\vartheta_0}{\partial\varsigma^2} + \frac{\xi^2}{18}\frac{\partial^2\vartheta_0}{\partial\xi^2} + \frac{\eta^2}{18}\frac{\partial^2\vartheta_0}{\partial\eta^2} - \vartheta_0\right\}\right] = \frac{\phi^3}{3!}\varsigma^4\xi^4\eta^4, \\
p^2 &: \vartheta_2(\varsigma,\xi,\phi) = \mathbb{A}^{-1}\left[\frac{1}{\sigma^2}\mathbb{A}\left\{\frac{\varsigma^2}{18}\frac{\partial^2\vartheta_1}{\partial\varsigma^2} + \frac{\xi^2}{18}\frac{\partial^2\vartheta_1}{\partial\xi^2} + \frac{\eta^2}{18}\frac{\partial^2\vartheta_1}{\partial\eta^2} - \vartheta_1\right\}\right] = \frac{\phi^5}{5!}\varsigma^4\xi^4\eta^4, \\
p^3 &: \vartheta_3(\varsigma,\xi,\phi) = \mathbb{A}^{-1}\left[\frac{1}{\sigma^2}\mathbb{A}\left\{\frac{\varsigma^2}{18}\frac{\partial^2\vartheta_2}{\partial\varsigma^2} + \frac{\xi^2}{18}\frac{\partial^2\vartheta_2}{\partial\xi^2} + \frac{\eta^2}{18}\frac{\partial^2\vartheta_2}{\partial\eta^2} - \vartheta_2\right\}\right] = \frac{\phi^7}{7!}\varsigma^4\xi^4\eta^4, \\
p^4 &: \vartheta_4(\varsigma,\xi,\phi) = \mathbb{A}^{-1}\left[\frac{1}{\sigma^2}\mathbb{A}\left\{\frac{\varsigma^2}{18}\frac{\partial^2\vartheta_3}{\partial\varsigma^2} + \frac{\xi^2}{18}\frac{\partial^2\vartheta_3}{\partial\xi^2} + \frac{\eta^2}{18}\frac{\partial^2\vartheta_3}{\partial\eta^2} - \vartheta_3\right\}\right] = \frac{\phi^9}{9!}\varsigma^4\xi^4\eta^4, \\
&\vdots
\end{aligned}$$

In a similar way, we can consider the approximate series such that

$$\begin{aligned} \vartheta(\varsigma,\xi,\eta,\phi) &= \vartheta_0(\varsigma,\xi,\eta,\phi) + \vartheta_1(\varsigma,\xi,\eta,\phi) + \vartheta_2(\varsigma,\xi,\eta,\phi) + \vartheta_3(\varsigma,\xi,\eta,\phi) + \vartheta_4(\varsigma,\xi,\eta,\phi) + \cdots, \\ &= \varsigma^4\xi^4\eta^4\Big(\phi + \frac{\phi^3}{3!} + \frac{\phi^5}{5!} + \frac{\phi^7}{7!} + \frac{\phi^9}{9!}\Big) + \cdots. \end{aligned} \tag{29}$$

which can approach

$$\vartheta(\varsigma,\xi,\eta,\phi) = \varsigma^4\xi^4\eta^4\sinh(\phi). \tag{30}$$

Figure 5 contains two diagrams: (a) the $\mathbb{A}$HITM results of $\vartheta(\varsigma,\xi,\eta,\phi)$ and (b) the exact results of $\vartheta(\varsigma,\xi,\eta,\phi)$ at $-5 \leq \varsigma \leq 5$ and $0 \leq \phi \leq 0.05$ with $\xi = 0.5$ and $\eta = 0.5$ for the 3D wave problem. Figure 6 represents the graphical error of the 3D wave equation between the approximate and precise solutions at $0 \leq \varsigma \leq 10$ with $\varsigma = 0.5$, $\xi = 0.5$ and $\phi = 0.1$. Table 3 presents the absolute error between the approximate solution obtained by the $\mathbb{A}$HITM and the exact solution at $\varsigma = 0.5, 1$ and $0.25, 0.50, 0.75, 1$, where $\xi = 0.5$ and $\eta = 0.5$. We observe that the current approach demonstrated the strong agreement, with a precise answer to the problem (Section 5.3) only after a few iterations. The rate of convergence shows that the $\mathbb{A}$HITM is a reliable approach for $\vartheta(\varsigma, \xi, \eta, \phi)$. This means that we can effectively model any surface in accordance with the desired physical processes appearing in nature.

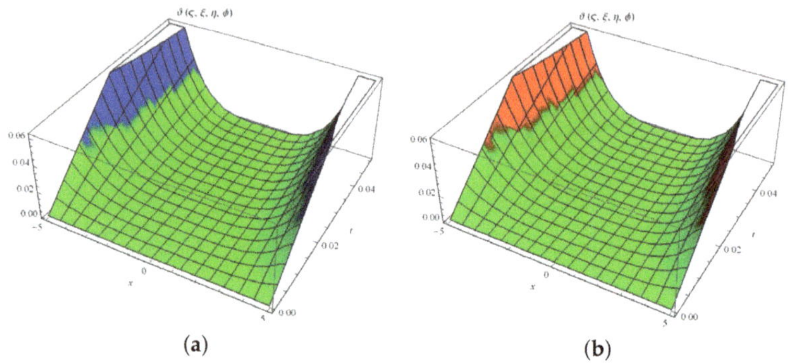

Figure 5. Surface solutions of 3D wave equation. (**a**) Surface plot for approximate results. (**b**) Surface plot for precise results.

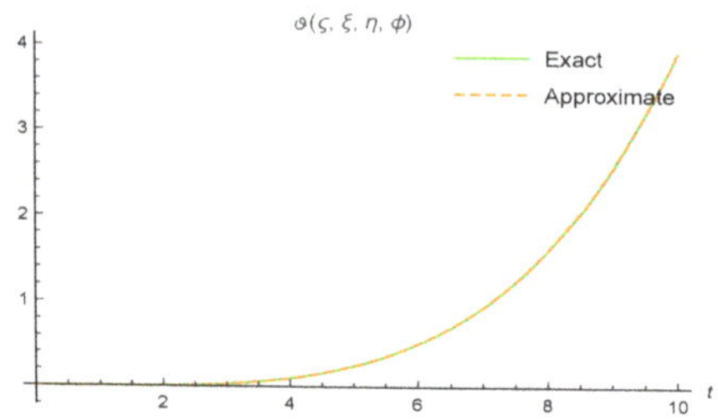

Figure 6. Graphical error between the approximate and precise results of $\vartheta(\varsigma, \xi, \eta, \phi)$.

Table 3. Absolute error between the approximate and exact solutions for Example 3.

ς	ϕ	Approximate	Exact	Absolute Error
0.5	0.25	0.0157883	0.0157883	1×10^{-9}
	0.50	0.0325685	0.0325685	1.2×10^{-9}
	0.75	0.0513948	0.0513948	1.4×10^{-8}
	1.0	0.0734501	0.0734501	2×10^{-7}
1.0	0.25	0.252612	0.252612	1×10^{-9}
	0.5	0.521095	0.521095	1.8×10^{-8}
	0.75	0.822317	0.822317	2.5×10^{-7}
	1.0	1.1752	1.1752	2.9×10^{-6}

6. Conclusions

In this paper, we employed the $\mathbb{A}$HITM for obtaining the approximate solutions to 1D, 2D and 3D wave equations. The main advantage of the $\mathbb{A}$IT is that the recurrence relation produces the iteration without any assumption of a small parameter. The HPM helps to produce successive iterations in the recurrence relation. The obtained results show that this approach is very simple to utilize and derives the series solution in convergence form. The graphical error of plot distortion shows that the $\mathbb{A}$HITM had the best agreement between the approximate solution and the exact solution. We encourage readers to extend this scheme for the numerical solution of a nonlinear coupled system of a fractional order in science and engineering for their future works.

Author Contributions: Investigation, methodology, software and writing—original draft, M.N.; writing—review and editing and supervision, A.A.; validation and visualization, L.G.; conceptualization, formal analysis and funding acquisition, M.-F.B. All authors have read and agreed to the published version of the manuscript.

Funding: This research received no external funding.

Institutional Review Board Statement: Not applicable.

Informed Consent Statement: Not applicable.

Data Availability Statement: Not applicable.

Acknowledgments: The publication of this paper was partially supported by AGC grants of Babes-Bolyai University, Cluj-Napoca, Romania.

Conflicts of Interest: The authors declare no conflict of interest.

References

1. Liu, M.Z.; Cao, X.Q.; Zhu, X.Q.; Liu, B.N.; Peng, K.C. Variational Principles and Solitary Wave Solutions of Generalized Nonlinear Schrödinger Equation in the Ocean. *J. Appl. Comput. Mech.* **2021**, *7*, 1639–1648.
2. Cakmak, M.; Alkan, S. A numerical method for solving a class of systems of nonlinear Pantograph differential equations. *Alex. Eng. J.* **2022**, *61*, 2651–2661. [CrossRef]
3. Momani, S.; Odibat, Z. Analytical approach to linear fractional partial differential equations arising in fluid mechanics. *Phys. Lett. A* **2006**, *355*, 271–279. [CrossRef]
4. Dehghan, M.; Manafian, J.; Saadatmandi, A. The solution of the linear fractional partial differential equations using the homotopy analysis method. *Z. Naturforschung-A* **2010**, *65*, 935.
5. Raslan, K.; Ali, K.K.; Shallal, M.A. The modified extended tanh method with the Riccati equation for solving the space-time fractional EW and MEW equations. *Chaos Solitons Fractals* **2017**, *103*, 404–409. [CrossRef]
6. Rezazadeh, H.; Ullah, N.; Akinyemi, L.; Shah, A.; Mirhosseini-Alizamin, S.M.; Chu, Y.M.; Ahmad, H. Optical soliton solutions of the generalized non-autonomous nonlinear Schrödinger equations by the new Kudryashov's method. *Results Phys.* **2021**, *24*, 104179. [CrossRef]
7. Khan, W.A. Numerical simulation of Chun-Hui He's iteration method with applications in engineering. *Int. J. Numer. Methods Heat Fluid Flow* **2021**, *32*, 944–955. [CrossRef]
8. Gepreel, K.A.; Al-Thobaiti, A. Exact solutions of nonlinear partial fractional differential equations using fractional sub-equation method. *Indian J. Phys.* **2014**, *88*, 293–300. [CrossRef]
9. Zhang, S.; Zhang, Y.; Xu, B. Exp-function Method and Reduction Transformations for Rogue Wave Solutions of the Davey-Stewartson Equations. *J. Appl. Comput. Mech.* **2021**, *7*, 102–108.
10. Althobaiti, A.; Althobaiti, S.; El-Rashidy, K.; Seadawy, A.R. Exact solutions for the nonlinear extended KdV equation in a stratified shear flow using modified exponential rational method. *Results Phys.* **2021**, *29*, 104723. [CrossRef]
11. Fiza, M.; Ullah, H.; Islam, S.; Shah, Q.; Chohan, F.I.; Mamat, M.B. Modifications of the multistep optimal homotopy asymptotic method to some nonlinear KdV-equations. *Eur. J. Pure Appl. Math.* **2018**, *11*, 537–552. [CrossRef]
12. Nuruddeen, R.I.; Aboodh, K.S.; Ali, K.K. Analytical investigation of soliton solutions to three quantum Zakharov-Kuznetsov equations. *Commun. Theor. Phys.* **2018**, *70*, 405. [CrossRef]
13. Wang, K. New variational theory for coupled nonlinear fractal Schrödinger system. *Int. J. Numer. Methods Heat Fluid Flow* **2021**, *32*, 589–597. [CrossRef]
14. Alaroud, M.; Al-Smadi, M.; Rozita Ahmad, R.; Salma Din, U.K. An analytical numerical method for solving fuzzy fractional Volterra integro-differential equations. *Symmetry* **2019**, *11*, 205. [CrossRef]
15. Duan, J.S.; Rach, R.; Wazwaz, A.M. Higher order numeric solutions of the Lane–Emden-type equations derived from the multi-stage modified Adomian decomposition method. *Int. J. Comput. Math.* **2017**, *94*, 197–215. [CrossRef]
16. Biazar, J.; Ghazvini, H. Convergence of the homotopy perturbation method for partial differential equations. *Nonlinear Anal. Real World Appl.* **2009**, *10*, 2633–2640. [CrossRef]
17. Mohyud-Din, S.T.; Noor, M.A. Homotopy perturbation method for solving partial differential equations. *Z. Naturforschung* **2009**, *64*, 157–170. [CrossRef]
18. He, J.H.; El-Dib, Y.O.; Mady, A.A. Homotopy perturbation method for the fractal toda oscillator. *Fractal Fract.* **2021**, *5*, 93. [CrossRef]
19. Jornet, M. Exact solution to a multidimensional wave equation with delay. *Appl. Math. Comput.* **2021**, *409*, 126421. [CrossRef]
20. Akinyemi, L.; Şenol, M.; Iyiola, O.S. Exact solutions of the generalized multidimensional mathematical physics models via sub-equation method. *Math. Comput. Simul.* **2021**, *182*, 211–233. [CrossRef]
21. Wazwaz, A.M. The variational iteration method: A reliable analytic tool for solving linear and nonlinear wave equations. *Comput. Math. Appl.* **2007**, *54*, 926–932. [CrossRef]

22. Ghasemi, M.; Kajani, M.T.; Davari, A. Numerical solution of two-dimensional nonlinear differential equation by homotopy perturbation method. *Appl. Math. Comput.* **2007**, *189*, 341–345. [CrossRef]
23. Keskin, Y.; Oturanc, G. Reduced differential transform method for solving linear and nonlinear wave equations. *Iran. J. Sci. Technol. Trans.-Sci.* **2010**, *34*, 113–122.
24. Ullah, H.; Islam, S.; Dennis, L.; Abdelhameed, T.; Khan, I.; Fiza, M. Approximate solution of two-dimensional nonlinear wave equation by optimal homotopy asymptotic method. *Math. Probl. Eng.* **2015**, *2015*, 380104. doi: 10.1155/2015/380104. [CrossRef]
25. Adwan, M.; Al-Jawary, M.; Tibaut, J.; Ravnik, J. Analytic and numerical solutions for linear and nonlinear multidimensional wave equations. *Arab. J. Basic Appl. Sci.* **2020**, *27*, 166–182. [CrossRef]
26. Jleli, M.; Kumar, S.; Kumar, R.; Samet, B. Analytical approach for time fractional wave equations in the sense of Yang-Abdel-Aty-Cattani via the homotopy perturbation transform method. *Alex. Eng. J.* **2020**, *59*, 2859–2863. [CrossRef]
27. Mullen, R.; Belytschko, T. Dispersion analysis of finite element semidiscretizations of the two-dimensional wave equation. *Int. J. Numer. Methods Eng.* **1982**, *18*, 11–29. [CrossRef]
28. Ojo, G.O.; Mahmudov, N.I. Aboodh transform iterative method for spatial diffusion of a biological population with fractional-order. *Mathematics* **2021**, *9*, 155. [CrossRef]
29. Aggarwal, S.; Chauhan, R. A comparative study of Mohand and Aboodh transforms. *Int. J. Res. Advent Technol.* **2019**, *7*, 520–529. [CrossRef]
30. Aggarwal, S.; Sharma, S.D. Solution of Abel's integral equation by Aboodh transform method. *J. Emerg. Technol. Innov. Res.* **2019**, *6*, 317–325.

axioms

MDPI

Article

Some New Generalized Inequalities of Hardy Type Involving Several Functions on Time Scale Nabla Calculus

A. I. Saied [1], Ghada AlNemer [2,*], Mohammed Zakarya [3,4], Clemente Cesarano [5] and Haytham M. Rezk [6]

1 Department of Mathematics, Faculty of Science, Benha University, Benha 13511, Egypt
2 Department of Mathematical Science, College of Science, Princess Nourah bint Abdulrahman University, P.O. Box 84428, Riyadh 11671, Saudi Arabia
3 Department of Mathematics, College of Science, King Khalid University, P.O. Box 9004, Abha 61413, Saudi Arabia
4 Department of Mathematics, Faculty of Science, Al-Azhar University, Assiut 71524, Egypt
5 Section of Mathematics, Università Telematica Internazionale Uninettuno, 00186 Rome, Italy
6 Department of Mathematics, Faculty of Science, Al-Azhar University, Nasr City 11884, Egypt
* Correspondence: gnnemer@pnu.edu.sa

Abstract: In this article, we establish several new generalized Hardy-type inequalities involving several functions on time-scale nabla calculus. Furthermore, we derive some new multidimensional Hardy-type inequalities on time scales nabla calculus. The main results are proved by applying Minkowski's inequality, Jensen's inequality and Arithmetic Mean–Geometric Mean inequality. As a special case of our results, when $\mathbb{T} = \mathbb{R}$, we obtain refinements of some well-known continuous inequalities and when $\mathbb{T} = \mathbb{N}$, the results which are essentially new.

Keywords: Hardy-type inequality; time scales nabla calculus; weighted functions; inequalities; arithmetic mean–geometric mean inequality.

MSC: 26D10; 26D15; 34N05; 42B25; 42C10; 47B38

Citation: Saied, A.I.; AlNemer, G.; Zakarya, M.; Cesarano, C.; Rezk, H.M. Some New Generalized Inequalities of Hardy Type Involving Several Functions on Time Scale Nabla Calculus. *Axioms* **2022**, *11*, 662. https://doi.org/10.3390/axioms11120662

Academic Editor: Chris Goodrich

Received: 17 September 2022
Accepted: 15 November 2022
Published: 22 November 2022

1. Introduction

In [1], Hardy proved that

$$\sum_{l=1}^{\infty}\left(\frac{1}{l}\sum_{i=1}^{l}a(i)\right)^{q} \leq \left(\frac{q}{q-1}\right)^{q}\sum_{l=1}^{\infty}a^{q}(l), \quad q>1, \tag{1}$$

where $a(l) \geq 0$ for $l \geq 1$ and $\sum_{l=1}^{\infty} a^{q}(l) < \infty$.

In [2], Hardy proved the continuous case of (1) in the following form

$$\int_{0}^{\infty}\left(\frac{1}{\theta}\int_{0}^{\theta}f(\tau)d\tau\right)^{q}d\theta \leq \left(\frac{q}{q-1}\right)^{q}\int_{0}^{\infty}f^{q}(\theta)d\theta, \quad q>1, \tag{2}$$

where $f \geq 0$ and integrable over any finite interval $(0,\theta)$, $\theta \in (0,\infty)$, $f \in L^{q}(0,\infty)$ and the constant $(q/(q-1))^{q}$ in (1) and (2) is sharp.

In [3], Kaijser et al. established that if Φ is a convex function on $\mathbb{R}^{+}$, then

$$\int_{0}^{\infty}\Phi\left(\frac{1}{\lambda}\int_{0}^{\lambda}\varpi(\eta)d\eta\right)\frac{d\lambda}{\lambda} \leq \int_{0}^{\infty}\Phi(\varpi(\lambda))\frac{d\lambda}{\lambda}, \tag{3}$$

where $\varpi : \mathbb{R}^{+} \to \mathbb{R}^{+}$ is a locally integrable positive function. In [4], Čižmešija et al. generalized (3) in the following form

$$\int_{0}^{r}\varkappa(\lambda)\Phi\left(\frac{1}{\lambda}\int_{0}^{\lambda}\varpi(\eta)d\eta\right)\frac{d\lambda}{\lambda} \leq \int_{0}^{r}\omega(\lambda)\Phi(\varpi(\lambda))\frac{d\lambda}{\lambda},$$

where $\varkappa : (0,r) \to \mathbb{R}$, $0 < r \leq \infty$, is a non-negative function, such that $\lambda \to \varkappa(\lambda)/\lambda^2$ is locally integrable, Φ is a convex function, $\varpi : (0,r) \to \mathbb{R}\ \forall\lambda \in (0,r)$ and

$$\omega(\eta) = \eta \int_\eta^r \frac{\varkappa(\lambda)}{\lambda^2} d\lambda, \quad \text{for} \quad \eta \in (0,r).$$

In [5], Kaijser et al. explicated that if $\varkappa : (0,r) \to \mathbb{R}$, $\varrho : (0,r) \times (0,r) \to \mathbb{R}$, $0 < r \leq \infty$ are positive functions, such that $0 < \Lambda(\eta) = \int_0^\eta \varrho(\eta,\vartheta)d\vartheta < \infty$, $\eta \in (0,r)$, Φ is a convex function on $I \subseteq \mathbb{R}$, and

$$\omega(\lambda) = \lambda \int_\lambda^r \varkappa(\eta) \frac{\varrho(\eta,\lambda)}{\Lambda(\eta)} \frac{d\eta}{\eta} < \infty, \quad \lambda \in (0,r),$$

then

$$\int_0^r \varkappa(\lambda)\Phi(A_\varrho\varpi(\lambda))\frac{d\lambda}{\lambda} \leq \int_0^r \omega(\lambda)\Phi(\varpi(\lambda))\frac{d\lambda}{\lambda}, \tag{4}$$

where $\varpi : (0,r) \to \mathbb{R}$ is a function with values in I, and

$$A_\varrho\varpi(\lambda) = \frac{1}{\Lambda(\lambda)} \int_0^\lambda \varrho(\lambda,\vartheta)\varpi(\vartheta)d\vartheta,\ \lambda \in (0,r).$$

Additionally, in [5] it is established that if $1 < p \leq q < \infty$, $s \in (1,p)$ and $0 < r < \infty$, $\varrho : \mathbb{R}^+ \times \mathbb{R}^+ \to \mathbb{R}^+$ is a non-negative kernel, $\varkappa(\lambda) \geq 0$ and $\omega(\lambda) \geq 0$ are weighted functions, and

$$\left(\int_0^r [\Phi(A_\varrho\varpi(\lambda))]^q \varkappa(\lambda)\frac{d\lambda}{\lambda}\right)^{\frac{1}{q}} \leq C\left[\int_0^r \Phi^p(\varpi(\lambda))\omega(\lambda)\frac{d\lambda}{\lambda}\right]^{\frac{1}{p}}, \tag{5}$$

holds for all $\varpi(\lambda) \geq 0$, $\lambda \in [0,r]$ and $C > 0$, if

$$A(s) = \sup_{0<\vartheta<r} [\Omega(\vartheta)]^{\frac{s-1}{p}} \left(\int_\vartheta^r \left(\frac{\varrho(\lambda,\vartheta)}{\Lambda(\lambda)}\right)^q [\Omega(\lambda)]^{\frac{q(p-s)}{p}} \varkappa(\lambda)\frac{d\lambda}{\lambda}\right)^{\frac{1}{q}} < \infty,$$

where

$$\Omega(\vartheta) = \int_0^\vartheta [\omega(\eta)]^{\frac{-1}{p-1}} \eta^{\frac{1}{p-1}} d\eta.$$

In the last few decades, researchers discovered the time-scale calculus which unifies the continuous and discrete calculus. A time scale $\mathbb{T}$ is an arbitrary, non-empty closed subset of the real numbers $\mathbb{R}$. Many authors established some new dynamic inequalities on $\mathbb{T}$; see the books [6,7] and the papers [8–12].

In [13], Özkan et al. demonstrated that if $0 \leq r < y \leq \infty$, $u \in C_{rd}([r,y),\mathbb{R})$ is a non-negative function, such that $\int_t^y \frac{u(\lambda)}{(\lambda-r)(\sigma(\lambda)-r)}\Delta\lambda$ exists as a finite number, Φ is continuous and convex, $f \in C_{rd}([r,y),\mathbb{R})$ and

$$v(t) = (t-r)\int_t^y \frac{u(\lambda)}{(\lambda-r)(\sigma(\lambda)-r)}\Delta\lambda, \quad t \in [r,y),$$

then

$$\int_r^y u(\lambda)\Phi\left(\frac{1}{\sigma(\lambda)-r}\int_r^{\sigma(\lambda)} f(t)\Delta t\right)\frac{\Delta\lambda}{\lambda-r} \leq \int_r^y v(\lambda)\Phi(f(\lambda))\frac{\Delta\lambda}{\lambda-r}. \tag{6}$$

They also proved that if $u \in C_{rd}([y,\infty),\mathbb{R})$ is a non-negative function, and

$$v(t) = \frac{1}{t}\int_b^t u(\lambda)\Delta\lambda, \quad t \in [y,\infty),$$

then
$$\int_r^y u(\lambda)\Phi\left(\frac{1}{\sigma(\lambda)-r}\int_r^{\sigma(\lambda)} f(t)\Delta t\right)\frac{\Delta\lambda}{\lambda-r} \leq \int_r^y v(\lambda)\Phi(f(\lambda))\frac{\Delta\lambda}{\lambda-r},$$
holds for all $f \in C_{rd}([y,\infty),\mathbb{R})$.

In [14], the authors proved the time-scale version of (4) as follows. Let $k(\lambda,\theta) \in C_{rd}([r,y)\times[r,y),\mathbb{R})$, $u \in C_{rd}([r,y),\mathbb{R})$ be non-negative functions, $f \in C_{rd}([r,y),\mathbb{R})$, Φ is a continuous and convex function, and
$$v(t) = (t-r)\int_t^y \frac{k(\lambda,t)}{K(\sigma(\lambda),\lambda)}u(\lambda)\frac{\Delta\lambda}{\lambda-r}, \quad t \in [r,y).$$

Then,
$$\int_r^y u(\lambda)\Phi(A_k f(\sigma(\lambda),\lambda))\frac{\Delta\lambda}{\lambda-r} \leq \int_r^y v(\lambda)\Phi(f(\lambda))\frac{\Delta\lambda}{\lambda-r}, \tag{7}$$
where
$$A_k f(t,\beta) = \frac{1}{K(t,\beta)}\int_r^t k(\beta,\theta)f(\theta)\Delta\theta, \quad K(t,\beta) := \int_r^t k(\beta,\theta)\Delta\theta.$$

Our aim in this study is to generalize (4) on time-scale nabla calculus of power $\eta \geq 1$ in the form
$$\int_r^y \chi^\eta(A_\varrho\varpi(\zeta))\frac{\varkappa(\zeta)}{\rho(\zeta)-r}\nabla\zeta \leq \left(\frac{B}{A}\right)^\eta\left(\int_r^y \chi(\varpi(\vartheta))\frac{\omega(\vartheta)}{\rho(\vartheta)-r}\nabla\vartheta\right)^\eta,$$
where A, B are positive constants. We will also establish the last inequality for several functions. Furthermore, we will prove the last inequality in multidimensions on time-scales nabla calculus.

The paper proceeds as follows. In Section 2, we state some properties concerning the time-scales nabla calculus needed in Section 3, where we prove the main results. Our main results when $\mathbb{T} \to \mathbb{R}$, we obtain (4) proved by Kaijser et al. [5] and when $\mathbb{T} \to \mathbb{N}$, we obtain a new discrete inequality.

2. Preliminaries and Basic Lemmas

For a time scale $\mathbb{T}$, we define the backward jump operator as $\rho(\gamma) = \sup\{s \in \mathbb{T} : s < \gamma\}$. Additionally, we define a mapping $\nu : \mathbb{T} \to \mathbb{R}^+$ by $\nu(\gamma) = \gamma - \rho(\gamma)$, such that if ϖ is nabla differentiable at γ, then $\nu(\gamma)\varpi^\nabla(\gamma) = \varpi(\gamma) - \varpi^\rho(\gamma)$. For more details about $\mathbb{T}$ calculus, see ([6,7]).

The nabla derivative of $\varkappa\omega$ and $\varkappa/\omega$ (where $\omega(\gamma)\omega^\rho(\gamma) \neq 0$) are given by
$$\begin{aligned}(\varkappa\omega)^\nabla(\gamma) &= \varkappa^\nabla(\gamma)\omega(\gamma) + \varkappa^\rho(\gamma)\omega^\nabla(\gamma)\\ &= \varkappa(\gamma)\omega^\nabla(\gamma) + \varkappa^\nabla(\gamma)\omega^\rho(\gamma),\end{aligned}$$
and
$$\left(\frac{\varkappa}{\omega}\right)^\nabla(\gamma) = \frac{\varkappa^\nabla(\gamma)\omega(\gamma) - \varkappa(\gamma)\omega^\nabla(\gamma)}{\omega(\gamma)\omega^\rho(\gamma)}.$$

Definition 1 ([6]). *A function $F : \mathbb{T} \to \mathbb{R}$ is a nabla antiderivative of $\varpi : \mathbb{T} \to \mathbb{R}$ if $F^\nabla(t) = \varpi(t)$ holds $\forall t \in \mathbb{T}$. Hence, we have*
$$\int_r^t \varpi(\gamma)\nabla\gamma = F(t) - F(r) \quad \forall t \in \mathbb{T}.$$

Theorem 1 ([6]). *0If $r, y \in \mathbb{T}$, $\alpha \in \mathbb{R}$ and ϖ, λ are ld-continuous functions, then*
(1) $\int_r^y [\varpi(\gamma) + \lambda(\gamma)]\nabla\gamma = \int_r^y \varpi(\gamma)\nabla\gamma + \int_r^y \lambda(\gamma)\nabla\gamma$;
(2) $\int_r^y \alpha\varpi(\gamma)\nabla\gamma = \alpha\int_r^y \varpi(\gamma)\nabla\gamma$;
(3) $\int_r^r \varpi(\gamma)\nabla\gamma = 0$.

The integration by parts formula on time scales nabla calculus [6] is

$$\int_r^y \varkappa(\gamma)\omega^{\nabla}(\gamma)\nabla\gamma = [\varkappa(\gamma)\omega(\gamma)]_r^y - \int_r^y \varkappa^{\nabla}(\gamma)\omega^{\rho}(\gamma)\nabla\gamma. \tag{8}$$

The Arithmetic Mean–Geometric Mean inequality is given by

$$[\lambda_1(\zeta)\lambda_2(\zeta)...\lambda_n(\zeta)]^{\frac{1}{n}} \leq \frac{\sum_{k=1}^{n}\lambda_k(\zeta)}{n}. \tag{9}$$

where $\lambda_1(\zeta), ..., \lambda_n(\zeta)$, $n \geq 1$ are non-negative functions.

In 2008, Ferreira et al. [15] proved Minkowski's inequality on diamond alpha time scales. As a special case of this inequality (when $\alpha = 0$), we get Minkowski's inequality on time-scale nabla calculus as follows.

Lemma 1 ([15]). *Let $r, y \in \mathbb{T}$ and f, g be non-negative functions. Then,*

$$\left(\int_r^y (f(\gamma)+g(\gamma))^p \nabla\gamma\right)^{\frac{1}{p}} \leq \left(\int_r^y f^p(\gamma)\nabla\gamma\right)^{\frac{1}{p}} + \left(\int_r^y g^p(\gamma)\nabla\gamma\right)^{\frac{1}{p}}, \tag{10}$$

for $p \geq 1$.

Lemma 2 ([16]). *Let $\varkappa, \omega$ and ϖ be non-negative functions on Ω, Υ and $\Omega \times \Upsilon$, respectively. If $\alpha \geq 1$, then*

$$\begin{aligned}
&\left(\int_\Omega \varkappa(\lambda)\left(\int_\Upsilon \varpi(\lambda,\vartheta)\omega(\vartheta)\nabla\vartheta\right)^{\alpha}\nabla\lambda\right)^{\frac{1}{\alpha}} \\
&\leq \int_\Upsilon \omega(\vartheta)\left(\int_\Omega \varpi^{\alpha}(\lambda,\vartheta)\varkappa(\lambda)\nabla\lambda\right)^{\frac{1}{\alpha}}\nabla\vartheta.
\end{aligned} \tag{11}$$

Theorem 2 ([16]). *Let $\varepsilon_i, \varsigma_i \in \mathbb{T}$, $i = 1, 2, .., m$, $\gamma \geq 1$, $\varkappa : \mathbb{T}^m \times \mathbb{T}^m \to \mathbb{R}$ and $w, h : \mathbb{T}^m \to \mathbb{R}$ be non-negative rd-continuous functions. Then,*

$$\begin{aligned}
&\left[\int_{\varepsilon_1}^{\varsigma_1} ... \int_{\varepsilon_m}^{\varsigma_m} w(\mathbf{y})\left(\int_{\varepsilon_1}^{\varsigma_1} ... \int_{\varepsilon_m}^{\varsigma_m} h(\mathbf{z})\varkappa(\mathbf{y},\mathbf{z})\nabla\mathbf{z}\right)^{\gamma}\nabla\mathbf{y}\right]^{\frac{1}{\gamma}} \\
&\leq \int_{\varepsilon_1}^{\varsigma_1} ... \int_{\varepsilon_m}^{\varsigma_m} h(\mathbf{z})\left(\int_{\varepsilon_1}^{\varsigma_1} ... \int_{\varepsilon_m}^{\varsigma_m} w(\mathbf{y})\varkappa^{\gamma}(\mathbf{y},\mathbf{z})\nabla\mathbf{y}\right)^{\frac{1}{\gamma}}\nabla\mathbf{z},
\end{aligned} \tag{12}$$

where $\nabla\mathbf{y} = \nabla y_1...\nabla y_m$, $\varkappa(\mathbf{y},\mathbf{z}) = \varkappa(y_1, ..., y_m, z_1, ..., z_m)$, $w(\mathbf{z}) = w(z_1, ..., z_m)$ and $h(\mathbf{z}) = h(z_1, ..., z_m)$.

In [17], Jensen's inequality is proved for the diamond$-\alpha$ time scale. In the case, $\alpha = 0$, this inequality can be written in nabla time-scale calculus as follows.

Lemma 3 ([17]). *Let $r, y \in \mathbb{T}$, $h \in C_{ld}([r,y]_{\mathbb{T}}, \mathbb{R})$, $u : [r,y]_{\mathbb{T}} \to (c,d)$, $c, d \in \mathbb{R}$ be ld-continuous and Φ be continuous and convex. Then,*

$$\Phi\left(\frac{1}{\int_r^y h(\vartheta)\nabla\vartheta}\int_r^y h(\gamma)u(\gamma)\nabla\gamma\right) \leq \frac{1}{\int_r^y h(\vartheta)\nabla\vartheta}\int_r^y h(\gamma)\Phi(u(\gamma))\nabla\gamma. \tag{13}$$

If Φ is a concave function, then (13) will be reversed.

Theorem 3 ([17]). *Let $\varepsilon_i, \varsigma_i \in \mathbb{T}, i = 1, 2, ..., m, g : \mathbb{T}^m \to (c, d), c, d \in \mathbb{R}$ be ld-continuous and Φ be continuous and convex. Then,*

$$\Phi\left(\frac{1}{\int_{\varepsilon_1}^{\varsigma_1} ... \int_{\varepsilon_m}^{\varsigma_m} \varrho(\mathbf{y}, \mathbf{z}) \nabla \mathbf{z}} \int_{\varepsilon_1}^{\varsigma_1} ... \int_{\varepsilon_m}^{\varsigma_m} \varrho(\mathbf{y}, \mathbf{z}) g(\mathbf{z}) \nabla \mathbf{z}\right) \leq \frac{1}{\int_{\varepsilon_1}^{\varsigma_1} ... \int_{\varepsilon_m}^{\varsigma_m} \varrho(\mathbf{y}, \mathbf{z}) \nabla \mathbf{z}} \int_{\varepsilon_1}^{\varsigma_1} ... \int_{\varepsilon_m}^{\varsigma_m} \varrho(\mathbf{y}, \mathbf{z}) \Phi(g(\mathbf{z})) \nabla \mathbf{z}, \tag{14}$$

where $\nabla \mathbf{z} = \nabla z_1 ... \nabla z_m$, $\varrho(\mathbf{y}, \mathbf{z}) = \varrho(y_1, ..., y_m, z_1, ..., z_m)$ and $g(\mathbf{z}) = g(z_1, ..., z_m)$.

3. Main Results

Throughout this section, we will assume that the functions (without mention) are non-negative ld-continuous functions and the integrals in the statements of the theorems are convergent. We define the general Hardy operator A_ϱ as follows

$$A_\varrho \varpi(\lambda) = \frac{1}{\Lambda(\lambda)} \int_r^y \varrho(\lambda, \vartheta) \varpi(\vartheta) \nabla \vartheta, \quad \Lambda(\lambda) = \int_r^y \varrho(\lambda, \vartheta) \nabla \vartheta,$$

where $\lambda > r$ and $\varpi \in C_{ld}([r, y]_{\mathbb{T}}, \mathbb{R}^+)$ and $\varrho(\lambda, \vartheta) \in C_{ld}([r, y]_{\mathbb{T}} \times [r, y]_{\mathbb{T}}, \mathbb{R}^+)$.

Now, we state and prove our main results.

Theorem 4. *Let $r, y \in \mathbb{T}$, $\eta \geq 1$ and $\varkappa, \omega$ be weighted functions, such that*

$$\omega(\vartheta) = (\rho(\vartheta) - r)\left(\int_r^y \left(\frac{\varrho(\lambda, \vartheta)}{\Lambda(\lambda)}\right)^\eta \frac{\varkappa(\lambda)}{\rho(\lambda) - r} \nabla \lambda\right)^{\frac{1}{\eta}}. \tag{15}$$

Furthermore, assume that χ, ξ defined on (c, d), $-\infty < c < d < \infty$ and ξ is a convex function, such that

$$A\xi(\lambda) \leq \chi(\lambda) \leq B\xi(\lambda), \quad c < \lambda < d, \tag{16}$$

where A, B are positive constants; then

$$\int_r^y \chi^\eta(A_\varrho \varpi(\lambda)) \frac{\varkappa(\lambda)}{\rho(\lambda) - r} \nabla \lambda \leq \left(\frac{B}{A}\right)^\eta \left(\int_r^y \chi(\varpi(\vartheta)) \frac{\omega(\vartheta)}{\rho(\vartheta) - r} \nabla \vartheta\right)^\eta, \tag{17}$$

holds for the non-negative function ϖ.

Proof. Using (16) and applying (13) (where ξ is convex), we have

$$\begin{aligned}
&\int_r^y \chi^\eta(A_\varrho \varpi(\lambda)) \varkappa(\lambda) \frac{\nabla \lambda}{\rho(\lambda) - r} \\
&= \int_r^y \chi^\eta\left(\frac{1}{\Lambda(\lambda)} \int_r^y \varrho(\lambda, \vartheta) \varpi(\vartheta) \nabla \vartheta\right) \frac{\varkappa(\lambda)}{\rho(\lambda) - r} \nabla \lambda \\
&\leq B^\eta \int_r^y \xi^\eta\left(\frac{1}{\Lambda(\lambda)} \int_r^y \varrho(\lambda, \vartheta) \varpi(\vartheta) \nabla \vartheta\right) \frac{\varkappa(\lambda)}{\rho(\lambda) - r} \nabla \lambda \\
&\leq B^\eta \int_r^y \frac{1}{\Lambda^\eta(\lambda)} \left(\int_r^y \varrho(\lambda, \vartheta) \xi(\varpi(\vartheta)) \nabla \vartheta\right)^\eta \frac{\varkappa(\lambda)}{\rho(\lambda) - r} \nabla \lambda.
\end{aligned} \tag{18}$$

Applying (11) on the term

$$\int_r^y \frac{1}{\Lambda^\eta(\lambda)} \left(\int_r^y \varrho(\lambda, \vartheta) \xi(\varpi(\vartheta)) \nabla \vartheta\right)^\eta \frac{\varkappa(\lambda)}{\rho(\lambda) - r} \nabla \lambda,$$

with $\eta \geq 1$, we see that

$$\left(\int_r^y \frac{1}{\Lambda^\eta(\lambda)}\left(\int_r^y \varrho(\lambda,\vartheta)\xi(\varpi(\vartheta))\nabla\vartheta\right)^\eta \frac{\varkappa(\lambda)}{\rho(\lambda)-r}\nabla\lambda\right)^{\frac{1}{\eta}}$$
$$\leq \int_r^y \xi(\varpi(\vartheta))\left(\int_r^y \left(\frac{\varrho(\lambda,\vartheta)}{\Lambda(\lambda)}\right)^\eta \frac{\varkappa(\lambda)}{\rho(\lambda)-r}\nabla\lambda\right)^{\frac{1}{\eta}}\nabla\vartheta,$$

then

$$\int_r^y \frac{1}{\Lambda^\eta(\lambda)}\left(\int_r^y \varrho(\lambda,\vartheta)\xi(\varpi(\vartheta))\nabla\vartheta\right)^\eta \frac{\varkappa(\lambda)}{\rho(\lambda)-r}\nabla\lambda$$
$$\leq \left[\int_r^y \xi(\varpi(\vartheta))\left(\int_r^y \left(\frac{\varrho(\lambda,\vartheta)}{\Lambda(\lambda)}\right)^\eta \frac{\varkappa(\lambda)}{\rho(\lambda)-r}\nabla\lambda\right)^{\frac{1}{\eta}}\nabla\vartheta\right]^\eta$$
$$= \left[\int_r^y \xi(\varpi(\vartheta))\frac{1}{\rho(\vartheta)-r}(\rho(\vartheta)-r)\left(\int_r^y \left(\frac{\varrho(\lambda,\vartheta)}{\Lambda(\lambda)}\right)^\eta \frac{\varkappa(\lambda)}{\rho(\lambda)-r}\nabla\lambda\right)^{\frac{1}{\eta}}\nabla\vartheta\right]^\eta. \quad (19)$$

Substituting (19) into (18), we have from (15) that

$$\int_r^y \chi^\eta(A_\varrho\varpi(\lambda))\varkappa(\lambda)\frac{\nabla\lambda}{\rho(\lambda)-r}$$
$$\leq B^\eta\left[\int_r^y \xi(\varpi(\vartheta))\frac{1}{\rho(\vartheta)-r}(\rho(\vartheta)-r)\left(\int_r^y \left(\frac{\varrho(\lambda,\vartheta)}{\Lambda(\lambda)}\right)^\eta \frac{\varkappa(\lambda)}{\rho(\lambda)-r}\nabla\lambda\right)^{\frac{1}{\eta}}\nabla\vartheta\right]^\eta$$
$$= B^\eta\left[\int_r^y \xi(\varpi(\vartheta))\frac{1}{\rho(\vartheta)-r}\omega(\vartheta)\nabla\vartheta\right]^\eta,$$

and then, we get from (16) that

$$\int_r^y \chi^\eta(A_\varrho\varpi(\lambda))\varkappa(\lambda)\frac{\nabla\lambda}{\rho(\lambda)-r} \leq \left(\frac{B}{A}\right)^\eta\left[\int_r^y \chi(\varpi(\vartheta))\frac{1}{\rho(\vartheta)-r}\omega(\vartheta)\nabla\vartheta\right]^\eta,$$

which is (17). □

Corollary 1. *If $A = B$ and $\eta = 1$, then*

$$\int_r^y \chi(A_\varrho\varpi(\lambda))\frac{\varkappa(\lambda)}{\rho(\lambda)-r}\nabla\lambda \leq \left(\int_r^y \chi(\varpi(\vartheta))\frac{\omega(\vartheta)}{\rho(\vartheta)-r}\nabla\vartheta\right),$$

where

$$\omega(\vartheta) = (\rho(\vartheta)-r)\left(\int_r^y \left(\frac{\varrho(\lambda,\vartheta)}{\Lambda(\lambda)}\right)\frac{\varkappa(\lambda)}{\rho(\lambda)-r}\nabla\lambda\right).$$

Remark 1. *If $\mathbb{T} = \mathbb{N}$, $r = 0$, then $\rho(n) = n-1$ and (17) reduces to*

$$\sum_{n=1}^N \chi\left(\frac{1}{\sum_{m=1}^n \varrho(n,m)}\sum_{m=1}^n \varrho(n,m)\varpi(m)\right)\frac{\varkappa(n)}{n-1}$$
$$\leq \left[\sum_{n=1}^N \chi(\varpi(n))\frac{\omega(n)}{n-1}\right], \quad \text{for } N \in \mathbb{N}.$$

Remark 2. *If $\mathbb{T} = \mathbb{R}$, $r = 0$, then $\rho(\zeta) = \zeta$, and we have*

$$\int_r^y \chi(A_\varrho\varpi(\lambda))\frac{\varkappa(\lambda)}{\lambda}d\lambda \leq \left(\int_r^y \chi(\varpi(\vartheta))\frac{\omega(\vartheta)}{\vartheta}d\vartheta\right),$$

where

$$\omega(\vartheta) = \vartheta\left(\int_r^y \left(\frac{\varrho(\lambda,\vartheta)}{\Lambda(\lambda)}\right)\frac{\varkappa(\lambda)}{\lambda}d\lambda\right).$$

Remark 3. *If* $\varrho(\lambda,\vartheta) = \begin{cases} 0 & ,\ \lambda \in [r,\vartheta), \\ f(\lambda,\vartheta), & \lambda \in [\vartheta, y]. \end{cases}$ *, we get the inequality (4) proved by Kaijser et al. [5].*

The following theorem is proved for several functions.

Theorem 5. *Let* $r, y \in \mathbb{T}$, $\eta \geq 1$ *and* $\varkappa, \omega$ *be as in Theorem 4, such that*

$$\omega(\vartheta) = (\rho(\vartheta) - r)\left(\int_r^y \left(\frac{\varrho(\lambda,\vartheta)}{\Lambda(\lambda)}\right)^{\eta}\frac{\varkappa(\lambda)}{\rho(\lambda)-r}\nabla\lambda\right)^{\frac{1}{\eta}}. \tag{20}$$

Furthermore, assume that $\varpi_k, k = 1, 2, ..., n$ *and* χ, ξ *are as in Theorem 4, such that*

$$A\xi(\lambda) \leq \chi(\lambda) \leq B\xi(\lambda), \tag{21}$$

where A, B *are positive constants, then*

$$\begin{aligned} &\int_r^y [\Pi_{k=1}^n \chi(A_\varrho\varpi_k(\lambda))]^{\frac{\eta}{n}} \varkappa(\lambda)\frac{\nabla\lambda}{\rho(\lambda)-r} \\ &\leq \left(\frac{B}{nA}\right)^{\eta}\left(\sum_{k=1}^{n}\left[\int_r^y \chi(\varpi_k(\vartheta))\frac{1}{\rho(\vartheta)-r}\omega(\vartheta)\nabla\vartheta\right]\right)^{\eta}, \end{aligned} \tag{22}$$

holds for $n \geq 1$.

Proof. Applying (Arithmetic Mean–Geometric Mean) inequality (9), we see that

$$\begin{aligned} &[\Pi_{k=1}^n \chi(A_\varrho\varpi_k(\lambda))]^{\frac{1}{n}} \\ &= [\chi(A_\varrho\varpi_1(\lambda))\chi(A_\varrho\varpi_2(\lambda))...\chi(A_\varrho\varpi_n(\lambda))]^{\frac{1}{n}} \\ &\leq \frac{\sum_{k=1}^n \chi(A_\varrho\varpi_k(\lambda))}{n}. \end{aligned}$$

Then, we obtain

$$\begin{aligned} &\int_r^y [\Pi_{k=1}^n \chi(A_\varrho\varpi_k(\lambda))]^{\frac{\eta}{n}} \varkappa(\lambda)\frac{\nabla\lambda}{\rho(\lambda)-r} \\ &\leq \int_r^y \left(\frac{\sum_{k=1}^n \chi(A_\varrho\varpi_k(\lambda))}{n}\right)^{\eta}\varkappa(\lambda)\frac{\nabla\lambda}{\rho(\lambda)-r} \\ &= \left(\frac{1}{n}\right)^{\eta}\int_r^y \left(\sum_{k=1}^n \chi(A_\varrho\varpi_k(\lambda))\right)^{\eta}\varkappa(\lambda)\frac{\nabla\lambda}{\rho(\lambda)-r}. \end{aligned} \tag{23}$$

By applying (10) (where $\eta \geq 1$), we observe that

$$\begin{aligned}
&\left(\int_r^y \left(\sum_{k=1}^n \chi(A_\varrho \varpi_k(\lambda))\right)^\eta \varkappa(\lambda) \frac{\nabla\lambda}{\rho(\lambda)-r}\right)^{\frac{1}{\eta}} \\
&= \left(\int_r^y \frac{\varkappa(\lambda)}{\rho(\lambda)-r}[\chi(A_\varrho \varpi_1(\lambda)) + \ldots + \chi(A_\varrho \varpi_n(\lambda))]^\eta \nabla\lambda\right)^{\frac{1}{\eta}} \\
&\leq \left(\int_r^y \frac{\varkappa(\lambda)}{\rho(\lambda)-r}\chi^\eta(A_\varrho \varpi_1(\lambda))\nabla\lambda\right)^{\frac{1}{\eta}} + \ldots + \left(\int_r^y \frac{\varkappa(\lambda)}{\rho(\lambda)-r}\chi^\eta(A_\varrho \varpi_n(\lambda))\nabla\lambda\right)^{\frac{1}{\eta}} \\
&= \sum_{k=1}^n \left(\int_r^y \frac{\varkappa(\lambda)}{\rho(\lambda)-r}\chi^\eta(A_\varrho \varpi_k(\lambda))\nabla\lambda\right)^{\frac{1}{\eta}},
\end{aligned}$$

and then

$$\begin{aligned}
&\int_r^y \left(\sum_{k=1}^n \chi(A_\varrho \varpi_k(\lambda))\right)^\eta \varkappa(\lambda) \frac{\nabla\lambda}{\rho(\lambda)-r} \\
&\leq \left[\sum_{k=1}^n \left(\int_r^y \frac{\varkappa(\lambda)}{\rho(\lambda)-r}\chi^\eta(A_\varrho \varpi_k(\lambda))\nabla\lambda\right)^{\frac{1}{\eta}}\right]^\eta.
\end{aligned} \tag{24}$$

Substituting (24) into (23), we have that

$$\begin{aligned}
&\int_r^y \left[\Pi_{k=1}^n \chi(A_\varrho \varpi_k(\lambda))\right]^{\frac{\eta}{n}} \varkappa(\lambda) \frac{\nabla\lambda}{\rho(\lambda)-r} \\
&\leq \left(\frac{1}{n}\right)^\eta \left[\sum_{k=1}^n \left(\int_r^y \frac{\varkappa(\lambda)}{\rho(\lambda)-r}\chi^\eta(A_\varrho \varpi_k(\lambda))\nabla\lambda\right)^{\frac{1}{\eta}}\right]^\eta.
\end{aligned} \tag{25}$$

Using (21) and applying (13), we get

$$\begin{aligned}
&\int_r^y \chi^\eta(A_\varrho \varpi_k(\lambda))\varkappa(\lambda) \frac{\nabla\lambda}{\rho(\lambda)-r} \\
&= \int_r^y \chi^\eta\left(\frac{1}{\Lambda(\lambda)}\int_r^y \varrho(\lambda,\vartheta)\varpi_k(\vartheta)\nabla\vartheta\right)\frac{\varkappa(\lambda)}{\rho(\lambda)-r}\nabla\lambda \\
&\leq B^\eta \int_r^y \xi^\eta\left(\frac{1}{\Lambda(\lambda)}\int_r^y \varrho(\lambda,\vartheta)\varpi_k(\vartheta)\nabla\vartheta\right)\frac{\varkappa(\lambda)}{\rho(\lambda)-r}\nabla\lambda \\
&\leq B^\eta \int_r^y \frac{1}{\Lambda^\eta(\lambda)}\left(\int_r^y \varrho(\lambda,\vartheta)\xi(\varpi_k(\vartheta))\nabla\vartheta\right)^\eta \frac{\varkappa(\lambda)}{\rho(\lambda)-r}\nabla\lambda.
\end{aligned} \tag{26}$$

Applying (11) on the term

$$\int_r^y \frac{1}{\Lambda^\eta(\lambda)}\left(\int_r^y \varrho(\lambda,\vartheta)\xi(\varpi_k(\vartheta))\nabla\vartheta\right)^\eta \frac{\varkappa(\lambda)}{\rho(\lambda)-r}\nabla\lambda,$$

with $\eta \geq 1$, we see that

$$\begin{aligned}
&\left(\int_r^y \frac{1}{\Lambda^\eta(\lambda)}\left(\int_r^y \varrho(\lambda,\vartheta)\xi(\varpi_k(\vartheta))\nabla\vartheta\right)^\eta \frac{\varkappa(\lambda)}{\rho(\lambda)-r}\nabla\lambda\right)^{\frac{1}{\eta}} \\
&\leq \int_r^y \xi(\varpi_k(\vartheta))\left(\int_r^y \left(\frac{\varrho(\lambda,\vartheta)}{\Lambda(\lambda)}\right)^\eta \frac{\varkappa(\lambda)}{\rho(\lambda)-r}\nabla\lambda\right)^{\frac{1}{\eta}}\nabla\vartheta,
\end{aligned}$$

then

$$\begin{aligned}
&\int_r^y \frac{1}{\Lambda^\eta(\lambda)}\left(\int_r^y \varrho(\lambda,\vartheta)\xi(\varpi_k(\vartheta))\nabla\vartheta\right)^\eta \frac{\varkappa(\lambda)}{\rho(\lambda)-r}\nabla\lambda \\
&\le \left[\int_r^y \xi(\varpi_k(\vartheta))\left(\int_r^y \left(\frac{\varrho(\lambda,\vartheta)}{\Lambda(\lambda)}\right)^\eta \frac{\varkappa(\lambda)}{\rho(\lambda)-r}\nabla\lambda\right)^{\frac{1}{\eta}}\nabla\vartheta\right]^\eta \\
&= \left[\int_r^y \xi(\varpi_k(\vartheta))\frac{1}{\rho(\vartheta)-r}(\rho(\vartheta)-r)\right. \\
&\times\left.\left(\int_r^y \left(\frac{\varrho(\lambda,\vartheta)}{\Lambda(\lambda)}\right)^\eta \frac{\varkappa(\lambda)}{\rho(\lambda)-r}\nabla\lambda\right)^{\frac{1}{\eta}}\nabla\vartheta\right]^\eta. \qquad (27)
\end{aligned}$$

Substituting (27) into (26) and using (20), we get

$$\begin{aligned}
&\int_r^y \chi^\eta(A_\varrho\varpi_k(\lambda))\varkappa(\lambda)\frac{\nabla\lambda}{\rho(\lambda)-r} \\
&\le B^\eta\left[\int_r^y \xi(\varpi_k(\vartheta))\frac{1}{\rho(\vartheta)-r}(\rho(\vartheta)-r)\right. \\
&\times\left.\left(\int_r^y \left(\frac{\varrho(\lambda,\vartheta)}{\Lambda(\lambda)}\right)^\eta \frac{\varkappa(\lambda)}{\rho(\lambda)-r}\nabla\lambda\right)^{\frac{1}{\eta}}\nabla\vartheta\right]^\eta \\
&= B^\eta\left[\int_r^y \xi(\varpi_k(\vartheta))\frac{1}{\rho(\vartheta)-r}\omega(\vartheta)\nabla\vartheta\right]^\eta.
\end{aligned}$$

From (21), we obtain

$$\begin{aligned}
&\int_r^y \chi^\eta(A_\varrho\varpi_k(\lambda))\varkappa(\lambda)\frac{\nabla\lambda}{\rho(\lambda)-r} \\
&\le \left(\frac{B}{A}\right)^\eta\left[\int_r^y \chi(\varpi_k(\vartheta))\frac{1}{\rho(\vartheta)-r}\omega(\vartheta)\nabla\vartheta\right]^\eta.
\end{aligned}$$

Substituting the last inequality into (25), we get

$$\begin{aligned}
&\int_r^y \left[\Pi_{k=1}^n \chi(A_\varrho\varpi_k(\lambda))\right]^{\frac{\eta}{n}}\varkappa(\lambda)\frac{\nabla\lambda}{\rho(\lambda)-r} \\
&\le \left(\frac{B}{nA}\right)^\eta\left(\sum_{k=1}^n\left[\int_r^y \chi(\varpi_k(\vartheta))\frac{1}{\rho(\vartheta)-r}\omega(\vartheta)\nabla\vartheta\right]\right)^\eta,
\end{aligned}$$

which is (22). □

Remark 4. *If $n = 1$, we get Theorem 4.*

Multidimensional Inequalities on Time Scales

In the following section, we define

$$A_\varrho\varpi(\mathbf{y}) = \frac{1}{\Lambda(\mathbf{y})}\int_{\varepsilon_1}^{\epsilon_1}\ldots\int_{\varepsilon_m}^{\epsilon_m}\varrho(\mathbf{y},\mathbf{z})\varpi(\mathbf{z})\nabla\mathbf{z}, \quad \Lambda(\mathbf{y}) = \int_{\varepsilon_1}^{\epsilon_1}\ldots\int_{\varepsilon_m}^{\epsilon_m}\varrho(\mathbf{y},\mathbf{z})\nabla\mathbf{z},$$

where $\varrho(\mathbf{y},\mathbf{z}) = \varrho(y_1,\ldots,y_m,z_1,\ldots,z_m)$, $\nabla\mathbf{y} = \nabla y_1\ldots\nabla y_m$ and $\varpi(\mathbf{z}) = \varpi(z_1,\ldots,z_m)$.

Theorem 6. *Let $\varepsilon_i, \epsilon_i \in \mathbb{T}$, $i = 1, 2, ..., m$, $\eta \geq 1$ and $\varkappa, \omega$ be as in Theorem 4, such that*

$$\omega(\mathbf{z}) = (\rho(z_1) - \varepsilon_1)...(\rho(z_m) - \varepsilon_m) \times \left(\int_{\varepsilon_1}^{\epsilon_1} ... \int_{\varepsilon_m}^{\epsilon_m} \left(\frac{\varrho(\mathbf{y}, \mathbf{z})}{\Lambda(\mathbf{y})} \right)^{\eta} \frac{\varkappa(\mathbf{y})}{(\rho(y_1) - \varepsilon_1)...(\rho(y_m) - \varepsilon_m)} \nabla \mathbf{y} \right)^{\frac{1}{\eta}}. \tag{28}$$

In addition, assume that χ, ξ are as in Theorem 4, such that

$$A\xi(\mathbf{y}) \leq \chi(\mathbf{y}) \leq B\xi(\mathbf{y}), \tag{29}$$

where A, B are positive constants, then

$$\begin{aligned} &\int_{\varepsilon_1}^{\epsilon_1} ... \int_{\varepsilon_m}^{\epsilon_m} \chi^{\eta} (A_{\varrho}\varpi(\mathbf{y})) \varkappa(\mathbf{y}) \frac{\nabla \mathbf{y}}{(\rho(y_1) - \varepsilon_1)...(\rho(y_m) - \varepsilon_m)} \\ &\leq \left(\frac{B}{A} \right)^{\eta} \left[\int_{\varepsilon_1}^{\epsilon_1} ... \int_{\varepsilon_m}^{\epsilon_m} \chi(\varpi(\mathbf{z})) \frac{1}{(\rho(z_1) - \varepsilon_1)...(\rho(z_m) - \varepsilon_m)} \omega(\mathbf{z}) \nabla \mathbf{z} \right]^{\eta}, \end{aligned} \tag{30}$$

holds for the non-negative function ϖ.

Proof. Using (29) and applying (14), we get

$$\begin{aligned} &\int_{\varepsilon_1}^{\epsilon_1} ... \int_{\varepsilon_m}^{\epsilon_m} \chi^{\eta} (A_{\varrho}\varpi(\mathbf{y})) \varkappa(\mathbf{y}) \frac{\nabla \mathbf{y}}{(\rho(y_1) - \varepsilon_1)...(\rho(y_m) - \varepsilon_m)} \\ &= \int_{\varepsilon_1}^{\epsilon_1} ... \int_{\varepsilon_m}^{\epsilon_m} \chi^{\eta} \left(\frac{1}{\Lambda(\mathbf{y})} \int_{\varepsilon_1}^{\epsilon_1} ... \int_{\varepsilon_m}^{\epsilon_m} \varrho(\mathbf{y}, \mathbf{z}) \varpi(\mathbf{z}) \nabla \mathbf{z} \right) \\ &\times \frac{\varkappa(\mathbf{y})}{(\rho(y_1) - \varepsilon_1)...(\rho(y_m) - \varepsilon_m)} \nabla \mathbf{y} \\ &\leq B^{\eta} \int_{\varepsilon_1}^{\epsilon_1} ... \int_{\varepsilon_m}^{\epsilon_m} \xi^{\eta} \left(\frac{1}{\Lambda(\mathbf{y})} \int_{\varepsilon_1}^{\epsilon_1} ... \int_{\varepsilon_m}^{\epsilon_m} \varrho(\mathbf{y}, \mathbf{z}) \varpi(\mathbf{z}) \nabla \mathbf{z} \right) \\ &\times \frac{\varkappa(\mathbf{y})}{(\rho(y_1) - \varepsilon_1)...(\rho(y_m) - \varepsilon_m)} \nabla \mathbf{y} \\ &\leq B^{\eta} \int_{\varepsilon_1}^{\epsilon_1} ... \int_{\varepsilon_m}^{\epsilon_m} \frac{1}{\Lambda^{\eta}(\mathbf{y})} \left(\int_{\varepsilon_1}^{\epsilon_1} ... \int_{\varepsilon_m}^{\epsilon_m} \varrho(\mathbf{y}, \mathbf{z}) \xi(\varpi(\mathbf{z})) \nabla \mathbf{z} \right)^{\eta} \\ &\times \frac{\varkappa(\mathbf{y})}{(\rho(y_1) - \varepsilon_1)...(\rho(y_m) - \varepsilon_m)} \nabla \mathbf{y}. \end{aligned} \tag{31}$$

Applying (12) on the term

$$\begin{aligned} &\int_{\varepsilon_1}^{\epsilon_1} ... \int_{\varepsilon_m}^{\epsilon_m} \frac{1}{\Lambda^{\eta}(\mathbf{y})} \left(\int_{\varepsilon_1}^{\epsilon_1} ... \int_{\varepsilon_m}^{\epsilon_m} \varrho(\mathbf{y}, \mathbf{z}) \xi(\varpi(\mathbf{z})) \nabla \mathbf{z} \right)^{\eta} \\ &\times \frac{\varkappa(\mathbf{y})}{(\rho(y_1) - \varepsilon_1)...(\rho(y_m) - \varepsilon_m)} \nabla \mathbf{y}, \end{aligned}$$

with $\eta \geq 1$, we see that

$$\begin{aligned} &\left[\int_{\varepsilon_1}^{\epsilon_1} ... \int_{\varepsilon_m}^{\epsilon_m} \frac{1}{\Lambda^{\eta}(\mathbf{y})} \left(\int_{\varepsilon_1}^{\epsilon_1} ... \int_{\varepsilon_m}^{\epsilon_m} \varrho(\mathbf{y}, \mathbf{z}) \xi(\varpi(\mathbf{z})) \nabla \mathbf{z} \right)^{\eta} \right. \\ &\left. \times \frac{\varkappa(\mathbf{y})}{(\rho(y_1) - \varepsilon_1)...(\rho(y_m) - \varepsilon_m)} \nabla \mathbf{y} \right]^{\frac{1}{\eta}} \\ &\leq \int_{\varepsilon_1}^{\epsilon_1} ... \int_{\varepsilon_m}^{\epsilon_m} \xi(\varpi(\mathbf{z})) \left(\int_{\varepsilon_1}^{\epsilon_1} ... \int_{\varepsilon_m}^{\epsilon_m} \left(\frac{\varrho(\mathbf{y}, \mathbf{z})}{\Lambda(\mathbf{y})} \right)^{\eta} \frac{\varkappa(\mathbf{y})}{(\rho(y_1) - \varepsilon_1)...(\rho(y_m) - \varepsilon_m)} \nabla \mathbf{y} \right)^{\frac{1}{\eta}} \nabla \mathbf{z}, \end{aligned}$$

then

$$\int_{\varepsilon_1}^{\epsilon_1} \dots \int_{\varepsilon_m}^{\epsilon_m} \frac{1}{\Lambda^{\eta}(\mathbf{y})} \left(\int_{\varepsilon_1}^{\epsilon_1} \dots \int_{\varepsilon_m}^{\epsilon_m} \varrho(\mathbf{y},\mathbf{z}) \xi(\varpi(\mathbf{z})) \nabla \mathbf{z} \right)^{\eta}$$
$$\times \frac{\varkappa(\mathbf{y})}{(\rho(y_1)-\varepsilon_1)\dots(\rho(y_m)-\varepsilon_m)} \nabla \mathbf{y}$$
$$\leq \left[\int_{\varepsilon_1}^{\epsilon_1} \dots \int_{\varepsilon_m}^{\epsilon_m} \xi(\varpi(\mathbf{z})) \right.$$
$$\left. \times \left(\int_{\varepsilon_1}^{\epsilon_1} \dots \int_{\varepsilon_m}^{\epsilon_m} \left(\frac{\varrho(\mathbf{y},\mathbf{z})}{\Lambda(\mathbf{y})} \right)^{\eta} \frac{\varkappa(\mathbf{y})}{(\rho(y_1)-\varepsilon_1)\dots(\rho(y_m)-\varepsilon_m)} \nabla \mathbf{y} \right)^{\frac{1}{\eta}} \nabla \mathbf{z} \right]^{\eta}. \tag{32}$$

Substituting (32) into (31), we have from (28) that

$$\int_{\varepsilon_1}^{\epsilon_1} \dots \int_{\varepsilon_m}^{\epsilon_m} \chi^{\eta}(A_{\varrho}\varpi(\mathbf{y})) \varkappa(\mathbf{y}) \frac{\nabla \mathbf{y}}{(\rho(y_1)-\varepsilon_1)\dots(\rho(y_m)-\varepsilon_m)}$$
$$\leq B^{\eta} \left[\int_{\varepsilon_1}^{\epsilon_1} \dots \int_{\varepsilon_m}^{\epsilon_m} \xi(\varpi(\mathbf{z})) \right.$$
$$\left. \times \left(\int_{\varepsilon_1}^{\epsilon_1} \dots \int_{\varepsilon_m}^{\epsilon_m} \left(\frac{\varrho(\mathbf{y},\mathbf{z})}{\Lambda(\mathbf{y})} \right)^{\eta} \frac{\varkappa(\mathbf{y})}{(\rho(y_1)-\varepsilon_1)\dots(\rho(y_m)-\varepsilon_m)} \nabla \mathbf{y} \right)^{\frac{1}{\eta}} \nabla \mathbf{z} \right]^{\eta}$$
$$= B^{\eta} \left[\int_{\varepsilon_1}^{\epsilon_1} \dots \int_{\varepsilon_m}^{\epsilon_m} \xi(\varpi(\mathbf{z})) \frac{1}{(\rho(z_1)-\varepsilon_1)\dots(\rho(z_m)-\varepsilon_m)} \omega(\mathbf{z}) \nabla \mathbf{z} \right]^{\eta},$$

and then we have from (29) that

$$\int_{\varepsilon_1}^{\epsilon_1} \dots \int_{\varepsilon_m}^{\epsilon_m} \chi^{\eta}(A_{\varrho}\varpi(\mathbf{y})) \varkappa(\mathbf{y}) \frac{\nabla \mathbf{y}}{(\rho(y_1)-\varepsilon_1)\dots(\rho(y_m)-\varepsilon_m)}$$
$$\leq \left(\frac{B}{A} \right)^{\eta} \left[\int_{\varepsilon_1}^{\epsilon_1} \dots \int_{\varepsilon_m}^{\epsilon_m} \chi(\varpi(\mathbf{z})) \frac{1}{(\rho(z_1)-\varepsilon_1)\dots(\rho(z_m)-\varepsilon_m)} \omega(\mathbf{z}) \nabla \mathbf{z} \right]^{\eta},$$

which is (30). □

Remark 5. *If $\mathbb{T} = \mathbb{R}$, $\rho(\vartheta) = \vartheta$ and $A = B = 1$, then*

$$\int_{\varepsilon_1}^{\epsilon_1} \dots \int_{\varepsilon_m}^{\epsilon_m} \chi^{\eta}(A_{\varrho}\varpi(\mathbf{y})) \frac{\varkappa(\mathbf{y})}{(y_1-\varepsilon_1)\dots(y_m-\varepsilon_m)} d\mathbf{y}$$
$$\leq \left(\int_{\varepsilon_1}^{\epsilon_1} \dots \int_{\varepsilon_m}^{\epsilon_m} \chi(\varpi(\mathbf{z})) \frac{\omega(\mathbf{z})}{(z_1-\varepsilon_1)\dots(z_m-\varepsilon_m)} d\mathbf{z} \right)^{\eta},$$

where $\varpi(\mathbf{z}) = \varpi(z_1, z_2, \dots, z_m)$, $\varrho(\mathbf{y},\mathbf{z}) = \varrho(y_1, \dots, y_m, z_1, \dots, z_m)$ and

$$A_{\varrho}\varpi(\mathbf{y}) = \frac{1}{\Lambda(\mathbf{y})} \int_{\varepsilon_1}^{\epsilon_1} \dots \int_{\varepsilon_m}^{\epsilon_m} \varrho(\mathbf{y},\mathbf{z}) \varpi(\mathbf{z}) d\mathbf{z}, \quad \Lambda(\mathbf{y}) = \int_{\varepsilon_1}^{\epsilon_1} \dots \int_{\varepsilon_m}^{\epsilon_m} \varrho(\mathbf{y},\mathbf{z}) d\mathbf{z},$$

with

$$\omega(\mathbf{z}) = (z_1-\varepsilon_1)\dots(z_m-\varepsilon_m)$$
$$\times \left(\int_{\varepsilon_1}^{\epsilon_1} \dots \int_{\varepsilon_m}^{\epsilon_m} \left(\frac{\varrho(\mathbf{y},\mathbf{z})}{\Lambda(\mathbf{y})} \right)^{\eta} \frac{\varkappa(\mathbf{y})}{(y_1-\varepsilon_1)\dots(y_m-\varepsilon_m)} d\mathbf{y} \right)^{\frac{1}{\eta}}.$$

Remark 6. *If* $\mathbb{T} = \mathbb{N}$, $\rho(\vartheta) = \vartheta - 1$ *and* $A = B = 1$, *then*

$$\sum_{\varepsilon_1}^{\varepsilon_1} \dots \sum_{\varepsilon_m}^{\varepsilon_m} \chi^{\eta}(A_{\varrho}\varpi(\mathbf{y})) \frac{\varkappa(\mathbf{y})}{(y_1 - \varepsilon_1 - 1)\dots(y_m - \varepsilon_m - 1)}$$
$$\leq \left[\sum_{\varepsilon_1}^{\varepsilon_1} \dots \sum_{\varepsilon_m}^{\varepsilon_m} \chi(\varpi(\mathbf{z})) \frac{1}{(z_1 - \varepsilon_1 - 1)\dots(z_m - \varepsilon_m - 1)} \omega(\mathbf{z}) \right]^{\eta},$$

where $\varpi(\mathbf{z}) = \varpi(z_1, z_2, \dots, z_m)$, $\varrho(\mathbf{y}, \mathbf{z}) = \varrho(y_1, \dots, y_m, z_1, \dots, z_m)$ *and*

$$A_{\varrho}\varpi(\mathbf{y}) = \frac{1}{\Lambda(\mathbf{y})} \sum_{\varepsilon_1}^{\varepsilon_1} \dots \sum_{\varepsilon_m}^{\varepsilon_m} \varrho(\mathbf{y}, \mathbf{z})\varpi(\mathbf{z}), \quad \Lambda(\mathbf{y}) = \sum_{\varepsilon_1}^{\varepsilon_1} \dots \sum_{\varepsilon_m}^{\varepsilon_m} \varrho(\mathbf{y}, \mathbf{z}),$$

with

$$\omega(\mathbf{z}) = (z_1 - \varepsilon_1 - 1)\dots(z_m - \varepsilon_m - 1)$$
$$\times \left(\sum_{\varepsilon_1}^{\varepsilon_1} \dots \sum_{\varepsilon_m}^{\varepsilon_m} \left(\frac{\varrho(\mathbf{y}, \mathbf{z})}{\Lambda(\mathbf{y})} \right)^{\eta} \frac{\varkappa(\mathbf{y})}{(y_1 - \varepsilon_1 - 1)\dots(y_m - \varepsilon_m - 1)} \right)^{\frac{1}{\eta}}.$$

4. Conclusions

In this research, we generalize some new inequalities on time-scale nabla calculus. We will also establish some dynamic inequalities for several functions. Furthermore, we will establish these inequalities in multiple dimensions on time-scales nabla calculus. All of these inequalities can be proved by applying Minkowski's inequality, Jensen's inequality and Arithmetic Mean–Geometric Mean inequality. In the future, we hope to study these dynamic inequalities via conformable nabla fractional calculus on time scales.

Author Contributions: Software and Writing—original draft, A.I.S., G.A. and C.C.; Writing—review and editing M.Z. and H.M.R. All authors have read and agreed to the published version of the manuscript.

Funding: Princess Nourah bint Abdulrahman University, Riyadh, Saudi Arabia.

Data Availability Statement: Not applicable.

Acknowledgments: Princess Nourah bint Abdulrahman University Researchers Supporting Project number (PNURSP2022R45), Princess Nourah bint Abdulrahman University, Riyadh, Saudi Arabia.

Conflicts of Interest: The authors declare no conflict of interest.

References

1. Hardy, G.H. Notes on a theorem of Hilbert. *Math. Z.* **1920**, *6*, 314–317. [CrossRef]
2. Hardy, G.H. Notes on some points in the integral calculus, LX. An inequality between integrals. *Mess. Math.* **1925**, *54*, 150–156.
3. Kaijser, S.; Persson, L.E.; öberg, A. On Carleman and Knopp's inequalities. *J. Approx. Theory* **2002**, *117*, 140–151. [CrossRef]
4. Cižmešija, A.; Pečarić, J.; Persson, L.E. On strengthened Hardy and Pólya-Knopp's inequalities. *J. Approx. Theory* **2003**, *125*, 74–84. [CrossRef]
5. Kaijser, S.; Nikolova, L.; Persson, L.E.; Wedestig, A. Hardy type inequalities via convexity. *Math. Inequal. Appl.* **2005**, *8*, 403–417. [CrossRef]
6. Bohner, M.; Peterson, A. *Dynamic Equations on Time Scales: An Introduction with Applications*; Birkhäuser: Boston, MA, USA, 2001.
7. Bohner, M.; Peterson, A. *Advances in Dynamic Equations on Time Scales*; Birkhäuser: Boston, MA, USA, 2003.
8. Rezk, H.M.; Saied, A.I.; AlNemer, Ġ.; Zakarya, M. On Hardy–Knopp type inequalities with kernels via time scale calculus. *J. Math.* **2022**, *2022*, 1–13. [CrossRef]
9. Saker, S.H.; Rezk, H.M. Islam Abohela and Dumitru Baleanu, Refinement Multidimensional Dynamic Inequalities with General Kernels and Measures. *J. Inequalities Appl.* **2019**,306, 1–16.
10. Zakarya, M.; Nemer, G.A.L.; Saied, A.I.; Butush, R.; Rezk, O.B.H.M. Generalized Inequalities of Hilbert-Type on Time Scales Nabla Calculus. *Symmetry* **2022**, *14*, 1512. [CrossRef]
11. Zakarya, M.; Saied, A.I.; Nemer, G.A.L.; Rezk, H.M. A study on some new reverse Hilbert-type inequalities and its generalizations on time scales. *J. Math.* **2022**, *2022*, 1–12. [CrossRef]

12. Rashid, S.; Noor, Ṁ.A.; Noor, K̇.I.; Safdar, Ḟ.; Chu, Y.M. Hermite-Hadamard type inequalities for the class of convex functions on time scale. *Mathematics 2019*, *7*, 956. [CrossRef]
13. Özkan, U.M.; Yildirim, H. Hardy-Knopp type inequalities on time scales. *Dyn. Syst. Appl.* **2008**, *17*, 477–486.
14. Özkan, U.M.; Yildirim, H. Time scale Hardy-Knopp type integral inequalities. *Commun. Math.* **2009**, *6*, 36–41.
15. Ferreira, R.A.; Ammi, M.R.S.; Torres, D.F. Diamond-alpha integral inequalities on time scales. *arXiv* **2008**, arXiv:0805.0242.
16. Bibi, R.; Bohner, M.; Pećarixcx, J.; Varošanec, S. Minkowski and Beckenbach-Dresher inequalities and functionals on time scales. *J. Math. Inequal.* **2013**, *7*, 299–312. [CrossRef]
17. Ammi, M.R.S.; Ferreira, R.A.; Torres, D. Diamond$-\alpha$ Jensen's inequality on time scales. *J. Inequal. Appl.* **2008**, *2008*, 1–13.

axioms

MDPI

Article

On Some New Dynamic Inequalities Involving C-Monotonic Functions on Time Scales

Ghada AlNemer [1], A. I. Saied [2], A. M. Hassan [2], Clemente Cesarano [3], Haytham M. Rezk [4,*] and Mohammed Zakarya [5,6,*]

1 Department of Mathematical Sciences, College of Science, Princess Nourah bint Abdulrahman University, P.O. Box 84428, Riyadh 11671, Saudi Arabia
2 Department of Mathematics, Faculty of Science, Benha University, Benha 13511, Egypt
3 Section of Mathematics, Università Telematica Internazionale Uninettuno, 00186 Rome, Italy
4 Department of Mathematics, Faculty of Science, Al-Azhar University, Nasr City 11884, Egypt
5 Department of Mathematics, College of Science, King Khalid University, P.O. Box 9004, Abha 61413, Saudi Arabia
6 Department of Mathematics, Faculty of Science, Al-Azhar University, Assiut 71524, Egypt
* Correspondence: haythamrezk@azhar.edu.eg (H.M.R.); mzibrahim@kku.edu.sa (M.Z.)

Abstract: In this paper, we establish some new dynamic inequalities involving C-monotonic functions with $C \geq 1$, on time scales. As a special case of our results when $C = 1$, we obtain the inequalities involving increasing or decreasing functions (where for $C = 1$, the 1-decreasing function is decreasing and the 1-increasing function is increasing). The main results are proved by applying the properties of C-monotonic functions and the chain rule formula on time scales. As a special case of our results, when $\mathbb{T} = \mathbb{R}$, we obtain refinements of some well-known continuous inequalities and when $\mathbb{T} = \mathbb{N}$, to the best of the authors' knowledge, the results are essentially new.

Keywords: C-monotonic functions; time scales; chain rule on time scales; inequalities

MSC: 26D10; 26D15; 34N05

Citation: AlNemer, G.; Saied, A.I.; Hassan, A.M.; Cesarano, C.; Rezk, H.M.; Zakarya, M. On Some New Dynamic Inequalities Involving C-Monotonic Functions on Time Scales. *Axioms* **2022**, *11*, 644. https://doi.org/10.3390/axioms11110644

Academic Editor: Wei-Shih Du

Received: 9 October 2022
Accepted: 4 November 2022
Published: 15 November 2022

1. Introduction

In 1995, Heinig and Maligranda [1] proved that if $-\infty \leq \varepsilon < \epsilon \leq \infty$, $\omega, \varpi \geq 0$, ω is decreasing on $[\varepsilon, \epsilon]$ and ϖ is increasing on $[\varepsilon, \epsilon]$ with $\varpi(\varepsilon) = 0$, then for any $\delta \in (0, 1]$,

$$\int_{\varepsilon}^{\epsilon} \omega(\vartheta) d\varpi(\vartheta) \leq \left(\int_{\varepsilon}^{\epsilon} \omega^{\delta}(\vartheta) d\left[\varpi^{\delta}(\vartheta)\right] \right)^{\frac{1}{\delta}}. \tag{1}$$

The inequality (1) is reversed when $1 \leq \delta < \infty$. In addition, the authors of [1] proved that if ω is increasing on $[\varepsilon, \epsilon]$ and ϖ is decreasing on $[\varepsilon, \epsilon]$ with $\varpi(\epsilon) = 0$, then for any $\delta \in (0, 1]$,

$$\int_{\varepsilon}^{\epsilon} \omega(\vartheta) d[-\varpi(\vartheta)] \leq \left(\int_{\varepsilon}^{\epsilon} \omega^{\delta}(\vartheta) d\left[-\varpi^{\delta}(\vartheta)\right] \right)^{\frac{1}{\delta}}. \tag{2}$$

We define that if $s \leq \theta$ implies $\omega(\theta) \leq C\omega(s)$ with $C \geq 1$, then ω is C-decreasing and if $s \leq \theta$ implies $\omega(s) \leq C\omega(\theta)$, $C \geq 1$, then ω is C-increasing. We observe that for $C = 1$, the 1-decreasing function is the normal decreasing function and the 1-increasing function is the normal increasing function.

By using the definition of C-monotonic functions, Pečarić et al. [2] generalized (1) and (2) for C-monotone functions with $C \geq 1$. they proved that if $0 < p < q < \infty$, ω is C-decreasing on $[\varepsilon, \epsilon]$ for $C \geq 1$ and ϖ is increasing and differentiable on $[\varepsilon, \epsilon]$, such that $\varpi(\varepsilon) = 0$, then

$$\left(\int_{\varepsilon}^{\epsilon} \omega^{q}(\vartheta) d[\varpi^{q}(\vartheta)] \right)^{\frac{1}{q}} \leq C^{1-p/q} \left(\int_{\varepsilon}^{\epsilon} \omega^{p}(\vartheta) d[\varpi^{p}(\vartheta)] \right)^{\frac{1}{p}}. \tag{3}$$

In addition, they proved that if $0 < p < q < \infty$, ω is C-increasing on $[\varepsilon, \epsilon]$ for $C \geq 1$ and ϖ is increasing and differentiable on $[\varepsilon, \epsilon]$, such that $\varpi(\varepsilon) = 0$, then

$$\left(\int_{\varepsilon}^{\epsilon} \omega^{q}(\vartheta) d[\varpi^{q}(\vartheta)]\right)^{\frac{1}{q}} \geq C^{p/q-1}\left(\int_{\varepsilon}^{\epsilon} \omega^{p}(\vartheta) d[\varpi^{p}(\vartheta)]\right)^{\frac{1}{p}}. \tag{4}$$

The authors of [2] proved that if $0 < p < q < \infty$, ω is C-increasing on $[\varepsilon, \epsilon]$ with $C \geq 1$ and ϖ is decreasing and differentiable on $[\varepsilon, \epsilon]$, such that $\varpi(\epsilon) = 0$, then

$$\left(\int_{\varepsilon}^{\epsilon} \omega^{q}(\vartheta) d[-\varpi^{q}(\vartheta)]\right)^{\frac{1}{q}} \leq C^{1-p/q}\left(\int_{\varepsilon}^{\epsilon} \omega^{p}(\vartheta) d[-\varpi^{p}(\vartheta)]\right)^{\frac{1}{p}}, \tag{5}$$

and they also proved that if $0 < p < q < \infty$, ω is C-decreasing on $[\varepsilon, \epsilon]$ for $C \geq 1$ and ϖ is decreasing and differentiable on $[\varepsilon, \epsilon]$, such that $\varpi(\epsilon) = 0$, then

$$\left(\int_{\varepsilon}^{\epsilon} \omega^{q}(\vartheta) d[-\varpi^{q}(\vartheta)]\right)^{\frac{1}{q}} \geq C^{p/q-1}\left(\int_{\varepsilon}^{\epsilon} \omega^{p}(\vartheta) d[-\varpi^{p}(\vartheta)]\right)^{\frac{1}{p}}. \tag{6}$$

In the last decades, some authors have been interested in finding some discrete results on $l^{p}(\mathbb{N})$ analogues to $L^{p}(\mathbb{R})$-bounds in different fields in analysis and, as a result, this subject becomes a topic of ongoing research. One reason for this upsurge of interest in the discrete case is also due to the fact that discrete operators may even behave differently from their continuous counterparts. In this paper, we obtain the discrete inequalities as special cases of the results with a general domain called the time scale $\mathbb{T}$. The time scale $\mathbb{T}$ is an arbitrary nonempty closed subset of the real numbers $\mathbb{R}$. These results contain the classical continuous and discrete inequalities as special cases when $\mathbb{T} = \mathbb{R}$ and $\mathbb{T} = \mathbb{N}$ and can be extended to different inequalities on different time scales such as $\mathbb{T} = h\mathbb{N}$, $h > 0$, $\mathbb{T} = q^{\mathbb{N}}$ for $q > 1$, etc. In recent years, the study of dynamic inequalities on time scales has received a lot of attention and become a major field in pure and applied mathematics. For more details about the dynamic inequalities on time scales, we refer the reader to the papers [3–16]. For example, Saker et al. [17] proved some dynamic inequalities for C-monotonic functions and proved that if ω is C-decreasing on $[\varepsilon, \epsilon] \cap \mathbb{T}$ with $C \geq 1$ and ϖ is increasing on $[\varepsilon, \epsilon] \cap \mathbb{T}$, such that $\varpi(\varepsilon) = 0$, then

$$\varphi\left(C\int_{\varepsilon}^{\epsilon} \omega(\vartheta)\varpi^{\Delta}(\vartheta)\Delta\vartheta\right) \leq C\int_{\varepsilon}^{\epsilon} \omega(\vartheta)\varpi^{\Delta}(\vartheta)\varphi'[\omega(\vartheta)\varpi(\vartheta)]\Delta\vartheta,$$

and if ω is C-increasing on $[\varepsilon, \epsilon] \cap \mathbb{T}$ for $C \geq 1$ and ϖ is increasing on $[\varepsilon, \epsilon] \cap \mathbb{T}$, such that $\varpi(\varepsilon) = 0$, then

$$\varphi\left(\frac{1}{C}\int_{\varepsilon}^{\epsilon} \omega(\vartheta)\varpi^{\Delta}(\vartheta)\Delta\vartheta\right) \geq \frac{1}{C}\int_{\varepsilon}^{\epsilon} \omega(\vartheta)\varpi^{\Delta}(\vartheta)\varphi'[\omega^{\sigma}(\vartheta)\varpi^{\sigma}(\vartheta)]\Delta\vartheta.$$

In addition, they proved that if ω is C-increasing on $[\varepsilon, \epsilon] \cap \mathbb{T}$ with $C \geq 1$ and ϖ is decreasing on $[\varepsilon, \epsilon] \cap \mathbb{T}$, such that $\varpi(\epsilon) = 0$, then

$$\varphi\left(C\int_{\varepsilon}^{\epsilon} \omega(\vartheta)[-\varpi(\vartheta)]^{\Delta}\Delta\vartheta\right) \leq C\int_{\varepsilon}^{\epsilon} \omega(\vartheta)[-\varpi(\vartheta)]^{\Delta}\varphi'[\omega^{\sigma}(\vartheta)\varpi^{\sigma}(\vartheta)]\Delta\vartheta,$$

and if ω is C-decreasing on $[\varepsilon, \epsilon] \cap \mathbb{T}$ with $C \geq 1$ and ϖ is decreasing on $[\varepsilon, \epsilon] \cap \mathbb{T}$, such that $\varpi(\epsilon) = 0$, then

$$\varphi\left(\frac{1}{C}\int_{\varepsilon}^{\epsilon} \omega(\vartheta)[-\varpi(\vartheta)]^{\Delta}\Delta\vartheta\right) \geq \frac{1}{C}\int_{\varepsilon}^{\epsilon} \omega(\vartheta)[-\varpi(\vartheta)]^{\Delta}\varphi'[\omega(\vartheta)\varpi(\vartheta)]\Delta\vartheta.$$

Our aim in this paper is to generalize the inequalities (1)–(6) on time scales by establishing some new dynamic inequalities involving C-monotonic functions.

The paper is organized as follows. In Section 2, we present some preliminaries concerning the theory of time scales and the definitions of C-monotonic functions. In Section 3, we prove the main results using the chain rule on time scales and the properties of C-monotonic functions. Our results when $\mathbb{T} = \mathbb{R}$ give the inequalities (1)–(6) proved by Heinig, Maligranda, Pečarić, Perić and Persson, respectively. Our results for $\mathbb{T} = \mathbb{N}$ are essentially new.

2. Preliminaries and Basic Lemmas

In this section, we recall the following concepts related to the notion of time scales. A time scale $\mathbb{T}$ is an arbitrary nonempty closed subset of the real numbers $\mathbb{R}$. For more details of time scale analysis, we refer the reader to the two books by Bohner and Peterson [18,19] which summarize and organize much of the time scale calculus. We define the time scale interval $[\varepsilon, \epsilon]_{\mathbb{T}}$ by $[\varepsilon, \epsilon]_{\mathbb{T}} := [\varepsilon, \epsilon] \cap \mathbb{T}$. A function $\omega : \mathbb{T} \to \mathbb{R}$ is said to be right-dense continuous (rd-continuous) provided that ω is continuous at right-dense points and at left-dense points in $\mathbb{T}$, left-hand limits exist and are finite. The set of all such rd-continuous functions is denoted by $C_{rd}(\mathbb{T}) = C_{rd}(\mathbb{T}, \mathbb{R})$. The product and quotient rules for the derivative of the product $\omega\varpi$ and the quotient ω/ϖ (where $\varpi\varpi^\sigma \neq 0$, here $\varpi^\sigma = \varpi \circ \sigma$) of two differentiable functions ω and ϖ are given by

$$(\omega\varpi)^\Delta = \omega\varpi^\Delta + \omega^\Delta\varpi^\sigma = \omega^\Delta\varpi + \omega^\sigma\varpi^\Delta, \text{ and } \left(\frac{\omega}{\varpi}\right)^\Delta = \frac{\omega^\Delta\varpi - \omega\varpi^\Delta}{\varpi\,\varpi^\sigma}.$$

Let $\omega : \mathbb{R} \to \mathbb{R}$ be continuously differentiable and suppose that $\varpi : \mathbb{T} \to \mathbb{R}$ is delta-differentiable. Then, $\omega \circ \varpi : \mathbb{T} \to \mathbb{R}$ is delta-differentiable and there exists ξ in the real interval $[\theta, \sigma(\theta)]$ with

$$(\omega \circ \varpi)^\Delta(\theta) = \omega'(\varpi(\xi))\varpi^\Delta(\theta).$$

In addition, the formula

$$(\omega \circ \varpi)^\Delta(\theta) = \left\{\int_0^1 \omega'\Big(\varpi(\theta) + h\mu(\theta)\varpi^\Delta(\theta)\Big)dh\right\}\varpi^\Delta(\theta), \tag{7}$$

holds. A special case of (7) is

$$\left[u^\lambda(\theta)\right]^\Delta = \lambda\int_0^1 [hu^\sigma + (1-h)u]^{\lambda-1}u^\Delta(\theta)dh.$$

In this paper, we will refer to the (delta) integral which we can define as follows. If $G^\Delta(\theta) = \varpi(\theta)$, then the Cauchy (delta) integral of ϖ is defined by $\int_\varepsilon^\theta \varpi(\vartheta)\Delta\vartheta := G(\theta) - G(\varepsilon)$. It can be shown (see [18]) that if $\varpi \in C_{rd}(\mathbb{T})$, then the Cauchy integral $G(\theta) := \int_{\theta_0}^\theta \varpi(\vartheta)\Delta\vartheta$ exists, $\theta_0 \in \mathbb{T}$ and satisfies $G^\Delta(\theta) = \varpi(\theta)$, $\theta \in \mathbb{T}$. The integration on discrete time scales is defined by $\int_\varepsilon^\epsilon \varpi(\theta)\Delta\theta = \sum_{\theta\in[\varepsilon,\epsilon)} \mu(\theta)\varpi(\theta)$. In case $\mathbb{T} = \mathbb{R}$, we have

$$\sigma(\theta) = \rho(\theta) = \theta,\ \mu(\theta) = 0,\ \omega^\Delta = \omega', \text{ and } \int_\varepsilon^\epsilon \omega(\theta)\Delta\theta = \int_\varepsilon^\epsilon \omega(\theta)d\theta,$$

and in case $\mathbb{T} = \mathbb{Z}$, we have

$$\sigma(\theta) = \theta + 1,\ \rho(\theta) = \theta - 1,\ \mu(\theta) = 1,\ \omega^\Delta = \Delta\omega, \text{ and } \int_\varepsilon^\epsilon \omega(\theta)\Delta\theta = \sum_{\theta=\varepsilon}^{\epsilon-1} \omega(\theta).$$

The integration by parts formula on time scale is given by

$$\int_\varepsilon^\epsilon u^\Delta(\theta)v^\sigma(\theta)\,\Delta\theta = u(\theta)v(\theta)|_\varepsilon^\epsilon - \int_\varepsilon^\epsilon u(\theta)v^\Delta(\theta)\Delta\theta.$$

In addition, we have for $\omega \in C_{rd}$ and $\theta \in \mathbb{T}$ that

$$\int_{\theta}^{\sigma(\theta)} \omega(\tau)\Delta\tau = \mu(\theta)\omega(\theta).$$

Definition 1. *Assume that $\mathbb{T}$ is a time scale and $\omega : \mathbb{T} \to \mathbb{R}$. If $s \leq \theta$ implies $\omega(\theta) \leq \omega(s)$, then ω is decreasing and if $s \leq \theta$ implies $\omega(s) \leq \omega(\theta)$, then ω is increasing.*

We can generalize the definition of the increasing and decreasing function to be C-increasing and C-decreasing, respectively, which is given in the following.

Definition 2 ([17]). *Assume that $\mathbb{T}$ is a time scale, $\omega : \mathbb{T} \to \mathbb{R}$ and $C \geq 1$. If $s \leq \theta$ implies $\omega(\theta) \leq C\omega(s)$, then ω is C-decreasing. If $s \leq \theta$ implies $\omega(s) \leq C\omega(\theta)$, then ω is C-increasing.*

As a special case, when $C = 1$, we observe that the 1-decreasing function is decreasing and the 1-increasing function is increasing.

Lemma 1. *Let $0 < q < \infty$. If ω is C-decreasing for $C \geq 1$, then ω^q is C^q-decreasing and if ϖ is C-increasing, then ϖ^q is C^q-increasing.*

Proof. Since ω is C-decreasing, we have for $s \leq \theta$ that $\omega(\theta) \leq C\omega(s)$, and then, we obtain (where $q > 0$) that

$$\omega^q(\theta) \leq C^q\omega^q(s).$$

Thus, ω^q is C^q-decreasing.

Since ϖ is C-increasing, we have for $s \leq \theta$ that $\varpi(s) \leq C\varpi(\theta)$, and then, we see (where $q > 0$) that

$$\varpi^q(s) \leq C^q\varpi^q(\theta),$$

which indicates that ϖ^q is C^q-increasing. The proof is completed. □

3. Main Results

Throughout the paper, we assume that the functions (without mentioning) are rd-continuous nonnegative and Δ-differentiable functions, locally Δ-integrable on $[\varepsilon, \infty)_{\mathbb{T}}$, and the considered integrals are assumed to exist.

In this section, we state and prove our main results.

Theorem 1. *Assume that $\mathbb{T}$ is a time scale with $\varepsilon, \epsilon \in \mathbb{T}$, $q > 0$ and $0 < \delta < 1$. Furthermore, assume that if χ is C^q-decreasing on $[\varepsilon, \epsilon]_{\mathbb{T}}$, $C \geq 1$ and λ is increasing on $[\varepsilon, \epsilon]_{\mathbb{T}}$, such that $\lambda(\varepsilon) = 0$. If*

$$\lambda^{\delta-1}(\sigma(\theta))\lambda^{1-\delta}(\theta) \geq 1, \tag{8}$$

then

$$\left(\int_{\varepsilon}^{\epsilon} \chi(\vartheta)[\lambda(\vartheta)]^{\Delta}\Delta\vartheta\right) \leq C^{q(1-\delta)}\left(\int_{\varepsilon}^{\epsilon} \chi^{\delta}(\vartheta)\left[\lambda^{\delta}(\vartheta)\right]^{\Delta}\Delta\vartheta\right)^{\frac{1}{\delta}}. \tag{9}$$

Proof. Since λ is an increasing function with $\lambda(\varepsilon) = 0$ and χ is C^q-decreasing function, we have for $\vartheta \leq \theta$ that $\chi(\theta) \leq C^q\chi(\vartheta)$, and then,

$$\begin{aligned}
\textstyle\int_{\varepsilon}^{\theta} \chi^{\delta}(\vartheta)\left[\lambda^{\delta}(\vartheta)\right]^{\Delta}\Delta\vartheta \geq{} & \left(\tfrac{1}{C}\right)^{q\delta} \textstyle\int_{\varepsilon}^{\theta} \chi^{\delta}(\theta)\left[\lambda^{\delta}(\vartheta)\right]^{\Delta}\Delta\vartheta \\
={} & \left(\tfrac{1}{C}\right)^{q\delta} \chi^{\delta}(\theta) \textstyle\int_{\varepsilon}^{\theta}\left[\lambda^{\delta}(\vartheta)\right]^{\Delta}\Delta\vartheta \\
={} & \left(\tfrac{1}{C}\right)^{q\delta} \chi^{\delta}(\theta)\left[\lambda^{\delta}(\theta) - \lambda^{\delta}(\varepsilon)\right] \\
={} & \left(\tfrac{1}{C}\right)^{q\delta} \chi^{\delta}(\theta)\lambda^{\delta}(\theta),
\end{aligned} \tag{10}$$

and then,

$$\chi^{\delta}(\theta)\lambda^{\delta}(\theta) \leq C^{q\delta} \int_{\varepsilon}^{\theta} \chi^{\delta}(\vartheta)\left[\lambda^{\delta}(\vartheta)\right]^{\Delta} \Delta\vartheta. \tag{11}$$

Consider the function

$$\Lambda(\theta) = C^{q(1-\delta)}\left(\int_{\varepsilon}^{\theta} \chi^{\delta}(\vartheta)\left[\lambda^{\delta}(\vartheta)\right]^{\Delta} \Delta\vartheta\right)^{\frac{1}{\delta}} - \int_{\varepsilon}^{\theta} \chi(\vartheta)[\lambda(\vartheta)]^{\Delta} \Delta\vartheta. \tag{12}$$

By applying chain rule formula on the term

$$\left(\int_{\varepsilon}^{\theta} \chi^{\delta}(\vartheta)\left[\lambda^{\delta}(\vartheta)\right]^{\Delta} \Delta\vartheta\right)^{\frac{1}{\delta}},$$

we have for $\xi \in [\theta, \sigma(\theta)]$ that

$$\begin{aligned} &\left[\left(\int_{\varepsilon}^{\theta} \chi^{\delta}(\vartheta)\left[\lambda^{\delta}(\vartheta)\right]^{\Delta} \Delta\vartheta\right)^{\frac{1}{\delta}}\right]^{\Delta} \\ &= \frac{1}{\delta}\left(\int_{\varepsilon}^{\xi} \chi^{\delta}(\vartheta)\left[\lambda^{\delta}(\vartheta)\right]^{\Delta} \Delta\vartheta\right)^{\frac{1}{\delta}-1} \chi^{\delta}(\theta)\left[\lambda^{\delta}(\theta)\right]^{\Delta}. \end{aligned} \tag{13}$$

Again, by applying the chain rule formula on the term $\lambda^{\delta}(\theta)$, we obtain

$$\left[\lambda^{\delta}(\theta)\right]^{\Delta} = \delta\lambda^{\delta-1}(\xi)\lambda^{\Delta}(\theta), \tag{14}$$

where $\xi \in [\theta, \sigma(\theta)]$. From (12), we observe that

$$\Lambda^{\Delta}(\theta) = C^{q(1-\delta)}\left[\left(\int_{\varepsilon}^{\theta} \chi^{\delta}(\vartheta)\left[\lambda^{\delta}(\vartheta)\right]^{\Delta} \Delta\vartheta\right)^{\frac{1}{\delta}}\right]^{\Delta} - \chi(\theta)\lambda^{\Delta}(\theta). \tag{15}$$

Substituting (13) and (14) into (15), we get

$$\begin{aligned} \Lambda^{\Delta}(\theta) &= \frac{1}{\delta}C^{q(1-\delta)}\left(\int_{\varepsilon}^{\xi} \chi^{\delta}(\vartheta)\left[\lambda^{\delta}(\vartheta)\right]^{\Delta} \Delta\vartheta\right)^{\frac{1}{\delta}-1} \chi^{\delta}(\theta)\left[\lambda^{\delta}(\theta)\right]^{\Delta} - \chi(\theta)\lambda^{\Delta}(\theta) \\ &= C^{q(1-\delta)}\lambda^{\delta-1}(\xi)\left(\int_{\varepsilon}^{\xi} \chi^{\delta}(\vartheta)\left[\lambda^{\delta}(\vartheta)\right]^{\Delta} \Delta\vartheta\right)^{\frac{1}{\delta}-1} \chi^{\delta}(\theta)\lambda^{\Delta}(\theta) - \chi(\theta)\lambda^{\Delta}(\theta) \\ &= \lambda^{\Delta}(\theta)\left[C^{q(1-\delta)}\lambda^{\delta-1}(\xi)\left(\int_{\varepsilon}^{\xi} \chi^{\delta}(\vartheta)\left[\lambda^{\delta}(\vartheta)\right]^{\Delta} \Delta\vartheta\right)^{\frac{1}{\delta}-1} \chi^{\delta}(\theta) - \chi(\theta)\right]. \end{aligned} \tag{16}$$

Since $\xi \in [\theta, \sigma(\theta)]$, $0 < \delta < 1$ and λ is an increasing function, then

$$\begin{aligned} &\lambda^{\delta-1}(\xi)\left(\int_{\varepsilon}^{\xi} \chi^{\delta}(\vartheta)\left[\lambda^{\delta}(\vartheta)\right]^{\Delta} \Delta\vartheta\right)^{\frac{1}{\delta}-1} \\ &\geq \lambda^{\delta-1}(\sigma(\theta))\left(\int_{\varepsilon}^{\theta} \chi^{\delta}(\vartheta)\left[\lambda^{\delta}(\vartheta)\right]^{\Delta} \Delta\vartheta\right)^{\frac{1}{\delta}-1}. \end{aligned} \tag{17}$$

Substituting (17) into (16), we observe that

$$\Lambda^{\Delta}(\theta) \geq \lambda^{\Delta}(\theta)\left[C^{q(1-\delta)}\lambda^{\delta-1}(\sigma(\theta))\left(\int_{\varepsilon}^{\theta} \chi^{\delta}(\vartheta)\left[\lambda^{\delta}(\vartheta)\right]^{\Delta} \Delta\vartheta\right)^{\frac{1}{\delta}-1} \chi^{\delta}(\theta) - \chi(\theta)\right]. \tag{18}$$

Substituting (11) into (18), we get

$$\begin{aligned} \Lambda^{\Delta}(\theta) \geq\ & \lambda^{\Delta}(\theta)\left[\lambda^{\delta-1}(\sigma(\theta))\left[\chi^{\delta}(\theta)\lambda^{\delta}(\theta)\right]^{\frac{1}{\delta}-1}\chi^{\delta}(\theta)-\chi(\theta)\right] \\ =\ & \lambda^{\Delta}(\theta)\left[\lambda^{\delta-1}(\sigma(\theta))\lambda^{1-\delta}(\theta)\chi(\theta)-\chi(\theta)\right]. \end{aligned} \tag{19}$$

By using (8) and λ is an increasing function, we have from (19) that

$$\Lambda^{\Delta}(\theta) \geq 0,$$

and then, the function Λ is increasing on $[\varepsilon, \epsilon]_{\lesssim}$.

Since Λ is an increasing function, we have for $\epsilon > \varepsilon$ that $\Lambda(\epsilon) \geq \Lambda(\varepsilon)$ and then (note that $\Lambda(\varepsilon) = 0$),

$$\int_{\varepsilon}^{\epsilon} \chi(\vartheta)[\lambda(\vartheta)]^{\Delta}\Delta\vartheta \leq C^{q(1-\delta)}\left(\int_{\varepsilon}^{\epsilon} \chi^{\delta}(\vartheta)\left[\lambda^{\delta}(\vartheta)\right]^{\Delta}\Delta\vartheta\right)^{\frac{1}{\delta}},$$

which is the desired inequality (9). The proof is completed. □

Corollary 1. *When $\mathbb{T} = \mathbb{R}$, $\sigma(\theta) = \theta$, $C = 1$, we observe that (8) holds already with equality and we get the inequality (1) proved by Heinig and Maligranda* [1].

As a special case of Theorem 1, when $0 < p < q < \infty$ such that $0 < \delta = p/q < 1$, $\chi(\vartheta) = \omega^{q}(\vartheta)$ and $\lambda(\vartheta) = \varpi^{q}(\vartheta)$, we have the following corollary.

Corollary 2. *Assume that $0 < p < q < \infty$, ω is C-decreasing on $[\varepsilon, \epsilon]_{\mathbb{T}}$, $C \geq 1$ and ϖ is increasing on $[\varepsilon, \epsilon]_{\mathbb{T}}$, such that $\varpi(\varepsilon) = 0$. If*

$$[\varpi^{\sigma}(\theta)]^{p-q}\varpi^{q-p}(\theta) \geq 1, \tag{20}$$

then

$$\left(\int_{\varepsilon}^{\epsilon} \omega^{q}(\vartheta)[\varpi^{q}(\vartheta)]^{\Delta}\Delta\vartheta\right)^{\frac{1}{q}} \leq C^{1-\frac{p}{q}}\left(\int_{\varepsilon}^{\epsilon} \omega^{p}(\vartheta)[\varpi^{p}(\vartheta)]^{\Delta}\Delta\vartheta\right)^{\frac{1}{p}}. \tag{21}$$

Corollary 3. *In Corollary 2, when $\mathbb{T} = \mathbb{R}$, $\sigma(\theta) = \theta$, we observe that (20) holds with equality and then we obtain the inequality (3) proved by Pečarić et al.* [2].

Corollary 4. *In Corollary 2, when $\mathbb{T} = \mathbb{N}$, $\sigma(n) = n+1$, we have that if $\varepsilon, \epsilon \in \mathbb{N}$, $0 < p < q < \infty$, ω is C-decreasing sequence for $C \geq 1$ and ϖ is increasing with $\varpi(\varepsilon) = 0$ such that*

$$[\varpi(n+1)]^{p-q}\varpi^{q-p}(n) \geq 1,$$

then

$$\left(\sum_{n=\varepsilon}^{\epsilon} \omega^{q}(n)\Delta[\varpi^{q}(n)]\right)^{\frac{1}{q}} \leq C^{1-\frac{p}{q}}\left(\sum_{n=\varepsilon}^{\epsilon} \omega^{p}(n)\Delta[\varpi^{p}(n)]\right)^{\frac{1}{p}}.$$

Theorem 2. *Assume that $\mathbb{T}$ is a time scale with $\varepsilon, \epsilon \in \mathbb{T}$, $q > 0$ and $0 < \delta < 1$. Furthermore assume that χ is C^{q}-increasing on $[\varepsilon, \epsilon]_{\mathbb{T}}$ with $C \geq 1$ and λ is increasing on $[\varepsilon, \epsilon]_{\mathbb{T}}$, such that $\lambda(\varepsilon) = 0$. If*

$$\lambda^{\delta-1}(\theta)[\lambda^{\sigma}(\theta)]^{1-\delta}[\chi^{\sigma}(\theta)]^{1-\delta}\chi^{\delta}(\theta) \leq \chi(\theta), \tag{22}$$

then

$$\left(\int_{\varepsilon}^{\epsilon} \chi(\vartheta)[\lambda(\vartheta)]^{\Delta}\Delta\vartheta\right) \geq C^{q(\delta-1)}\left(\int_{\varepsilon}^{\epsilon} \chi^{\delta}(\vartheta)\left[\lambda^{\delta}(\vartheta)\right]^{\Delta}\Delta\vartheta\right)^{\frac{1}{\delta}}. \tag{23}$$

Proof. Since λ is an increasing function with $\lambda(\varepsilon) = 0$ and χ is a C^q-increasing function, we have for $\vartheta \leq \theta$ that $\chi(\vartheta) \leq C^q \chi(\theta)$, and thus,

$$\begin{aligned} \int_\varepsilon^\theta \chi^\delta(\vartheta)\left[\lambda^\delta(\vartheta)\right]^\Delta \Delta\vartheta \leq & \; C^{q\delta} \int_\varepsilon^\theta \chi^\delta(\theta)\left[\lambda^\delta(\vartheta)\right]^\Delta \Delta\vartheta \\ = & \; C^{q\delta}\chi^\delta(\theta) \int_\varepsilon^\theta \left[\lambda^\delta(\vartheta)\right]^\Delta \Delta\vartheta \\ = & \; C^{q\delta}\chi^\delta(\theta)\left[\lambda^\delta(\theta) - \lambda^\delta(\varepsilon)\right] \\ = & \; C^{q\delta}\chi^\delta(\theta)\lambda^\delta(\theta), \end{aligned} \tag{24}$$

and then,

$$\chi^\delta(\theta)\lambda^\delta(\theta) \geq \frac{1}{C^{q\delta}} \int_\varepsilon^\theta \chi^\delta(\vartheta)\left[\lambda^\delta(\vartheta)\right]^\Delta \Delta\vartheta. \tag{25}$$

Consider the function

$$\Lambda(\theta) = C^{q(\delta-1)}\left(\int_\varepsilon^\theta \chi^\delta(\vartheta)\left[\lambda^\delta(\vartheta)\right]^\Delta \Delta\vartheta\right)^{\frac{1}{\delta}} - \int_\varepsilon^\theta \chi(\vartheta)[\lambda(\vartheta)]^\Delta \Delta\vartheta. \tag{26}$$

By applying the chain rule formula on the term

$$\left(\int_\varepsilon^\theta \chi^\delta(\vartheta)\left[\lambda^\delta(\vartheta)\right]^\Delta \Delta\vartheta\right)^{\frac{1}{\delta}},$$

we have for $\xi \in [\theta, \sigma(\theta)]$ that

$$\begin{aligned} & \left[\left(\int_\varepsilon^\theta \chi^\delta(\vartheta)\left[\lambda^\delta(\vartheta)\right]^\Delta \Delta\vartheta\right)^{\frac{1}{\delta}}\right]^\Delta \\ & = \tfrac{1}{\delta}\left(\int_\varepsilon^\xi \chi^\delta(\vartheta)\left[\lambda^\delta(\vartheta)\right]^\Delta \Delta\vartheta\right)^{\frac{1}{\delta}-1} \chi^\delta(\theta)\left[\lambda^\delta(\theta)\right]^\Delta. \end{aligned} \tag{27}$$

Again, by applying the chain rule formula on the terms $\lambda^\delta(\theta)$, we obtain

$$\left[\lambda^\delta(\theta)\right]^\Delta = \delta\lambda^{\delta-1}(\xi)\lambda^\Delta(\theta), \tag{28}$$

where $\xi \in [\theta, \sigma(\theta)]$. From (26), we observe that

$$\Lambda^\Delta(\theta) = C^{q(\delta-1)}\left[\left(\int_\varepsilon^\theta \chi^\delta(\vartheta)\left[\lambda^\delta(\vartheta)\right]^\Delta \Delta\vartheta\right)^{\frac{1}{\delta}}\right]^\Delta - \chi(\theta)\lambda^\Delta(\theta). \tag{29}$$

Substituting (27) and (28) into (29), we get

$$\begin{aligned} \Lambda^\Delta(\theta) = & \; \tfrac{1}{\delta}C^{q(\delta-1)}\left(\int_\varepsilon^\xi \chi^\delta(\vartheta)\left[\lambda^\delta(\vartheta)\right]^\Delta \Delta\vartheta\right)^{\frac{1}{\delta}-1} \chi^\delta(\theta)\left[\lambda^\delta(\theta)\right]^\Delta - \chi(\theta)\lambda^\Delta(\theta) \\ = & \; C^{q(\delta-1)}\lambda^{\delta-1}(\xi)\left(\int_\varepsilon^\xi \chi^\delta(\vartheta)\left[\lambda^\delta(\vartheta)\right]^\Delta \Delta\vartheta\right)^{\frac{1}{\delta}-1} \chi^\delta(\theta)\lambda^\Delta(\theta) - \chi(\theta)\lambda^\Delta(\theta) \\ = & \; \lambda^\Delta(\theta)\left[C^{q(\delta-1)}\lambda^{\delta-1}(\xi)\left(\int_\varepsilon^\xi \chi^\delta(\vartheta)\left[\lambda^\delta(\vartheta)\right]^\Delta \Delta\vartheta\right)^{\frac{1}{\delta}-1} \chi^\delta(\theta) - \chi(\theta)\right]. \end{aligned} \tag{30}$$

Since $\xi \in [\theta, \sigma(\theta)]$, $0 < \delta < 1$ and λ is an increasing function, then

$$\begin{aligned}&\lambda^{\delta-1}(\xi)\left(\int_{\varepsilon}^{\xi} \chi^{\delta}(\vartheta)\left[\lambda^{\delta}(\vartheta)\right]^{\Delta}\Delta\vartheta\right)^{\frac{1}{\delta}-1} \\ &\leq \lambda^{\delta-1}(\theta)\left(\int_{\varepsilon}^{\sigma(\theta)} \chi^{\delta}(\vartheta)\left[\lambda^{\delta}(\vartheta)\right]^{\Delta}\Delta\vartheta\right)^{\frac{1}{\delta}-1}.\end{aligned} \tag{31}$$

Substituting (31) into (30), we see that

$$\Lambda^{\Delta}(\theta) \leq \lambda^{\Delta}(\theta)\left[C^{q(\delta-1)}\lambda^{\delta-1}(\theta)\left(\int_{\varepsilon}^{\sigma(\theta)} \chi^{\delta}(\vartheta)\left[\lambda^{\delta}(\vartheta)\right]^{\Delta}\Delta\vartheta\right)^{\frac{1}{\delta}-1}\chi^{\delta}(\theta) - \chi(\theta)\right]. \tag{32}$$

Substituting (25) into (32), we get

$$\begin{aligned}\Lambda^{\Delta}(\theta) \leq\ & \lambda^{\Delta}(\theta)\left[\lambda^{\delta-1}(\theta)\left[\chi^{\delta}(\sigma(\theta))\lambda^{\delta}(\sigma(\theta))\right]^{\frac{1}{\delta}-1}\chi^{\delta}(\theta) - \chi(\theta)\right] \\ =\ & \lambda^{\Delta}(\theta)\left[\lambda^{\delta-1}(\theta)\left[\lambda^{\sigma}(\theta)\right]^{1-\delta}\left[\chi^{\sigma}(\theta)\right]^{1-\delta}\chi^{\delta}(\theta) - \chi(\theta)\right].\end{aligned} \tag{33}$$

By using (22) and λ is an increasing function, the inequality (33) becomes

$$\Lambda^{\Delta}(\theta) \leq 0,$$

and then, the function Λ is decreasing on $[\varepsilon, \epsilon]_{\mathbb{T}}$.

Since Λ is a decreasing function, then we have for $\epsilon > \varepsilon$ that $\Lambda(\epsilon) \leq \Lambda(\varepsilon)$ and then (note that $\Lambda(\varepsilon) = 0$),

$$C^{q(\delta-1)}\left(\int_{\varepsilon}^{\epsilon} \chi^{\delta}(\vartheta)\left[\lambda^{\delta}(\vartheta)\right]^{\Delta}\Delta\vartheta\right)^{\frac{1}{\delta}} \leq \int_{\varepsilon}^{\epsilon} \chi(\vartheta)[\lambda(\vartheta)]^{\Delta}\Delta\vartheta,$$

which is the desired inequality (23). The proof is completed. □

As a special case of Theorem 2, when $0 < p < q < \infty$ such that $0 < \delta = p/q < 1$, $\chi(\vartheta) = \omega^{q}(\vartheta)$ and $\lambda(\vartheta) = \varpi^{q}(\vartheta)$, we get the following corollary.

Corollary 5. *Assume that $\mathbb{T}$ is a time scale with $\varepsilon, \epsilon \in \mathbb{T}$ and $0 < p < q < \infty$. Furthermore, if ω is C-increasing on $[\varepsilon, \epsilon]_{\mathbb{T}}$ for $C \geq 1$ and ϖ is increasing on $[\varepsilon, \epsilon]_{\mathbb{T}}$, with $\varpi(\varepsilon) = 0$, such that*

$$\varpi^{p-q}(\theta)[\varpi^{\sigma}(\theta)]^{q-p}[\omega^{\sigma}(\theta)]^{q-p}\omega^{p}(\theta) \leq \omega^{q}(\theta), \tag{34}$$

then

$$\left(\int_{\varepsilon}^{\epsilon} \omega^{q}(\vartheta)[\varpi^{q}(\vartheta)]^{\Delta}\Delta\vartheta\right)^{\frac{1}{q}} \geq C^{p/q-1}\left(\int_{\varepsilon}^{\epsilon} \omega^{p}(\vartheta)[\varpi^{p}(\vartheta)]^{\Delta}\Delta\vartheta\right)^{\frac{1}{p}}.$$

Corollary 6. *As a special case of Corollary 5, when $\mathbb{T} = \mathbb{R}$, $\sigma(\theta) = \theta$, we have that (34) holds already with equality and we get the inequality (4) proved by Pečarić et al.* [2].

Corollary 7. *In Corollary 5, when $\mathbb{T} = \mathbb{N}$, $\sigma(n) = n+1$, we have that if $\varepsilon, \epsilon \in \mathbb{N}$, $0 < p < q < \infty$, ω is a C-increasing sequence for $C \geq 1$ and ϖ is increasing with $\varpi(\varepsilon) = 0$, such that*

$$\varpi^{p-q}(n)\varpi^{q-p}(n+1)\omega^{q-p}(n+1)\omega^{p}(n) \leq \omega^{q}(n),$$

then

$$\left(\sum_{n=\varepsilon}^{\epsilon} \omega^{q}(n)\Delta\varpi^{q}(n)\right)^{\frac{1}{q}} \geq C^{p/q-1}\left(\sum_{n=\varepsilon}^{\epsilon}\int_{\varepsilon}^{\epsilon} \omega^{p}(n)\Delta\varpi^{p}(n)\right)^{\frac{1}{p}}.$$

Theorem 3. *Assume that $\mathbb{T}$ is a time scale with $\varepsilon, \epsilon \in \mathbb{T}$, $q > 0$ and $0 < \delta < 1$. Furthermore, if χ is C^q-increasing on $[\varepsilon, \epsilon]_{\mathbb{T}}$, $C \geq 1$ and λ is decreasing on $[\varepsilon, \epsilon]_{\mathbb{T}}$, with $\lambda(\epsilon) = 0$ such that*

$$\chi(\theta) \leq \lambda^{\delta-1}(\theta)[\lambda^{\sigma}(\theta)]^{1-\delta}\chi^{\delta}(\theta)[\chi^{\sigma}(\theta)]^{1-\delta}, \tag{35}$$

then

$$\int_{\varepsilon}^{\epsilon} \chi(\vartheta)[-\lambda(\vartheta)]^{\Delta}\Delta\vartheta \leq C^{q(1-\delta)}\left(\int_{\varepsilon}^{\epsilon} \chi^{\delta}(\vartheta)\left[-\lambda^{\delta}(\vartheta)\right]^{\Delta}\Delta\vartheta\right)^{\frac{1}{\delta}}. \tag{36}$$

Proof. Since λ is a decreasing function with $\lambda(\epsilon) = 0$ and χ is a C^q-increasing function, we have for $\vartheta \geq \theta$ that $\chi(\theta) \leq C^q\chi(\vartheta)$, and thus,

$$\begin{aligned} \int_{\theta}^{\epsilon} \chi^{\delta}(\vartheta)\left[-\lambda^{\delta}(\vartheta)\right]^{\Delta}\Delta\vartheta \geq& \frac{1}{C^{q\delta}}\int_{\theta}^{\epsilon} \chi^{\delta}(\theta)\left[-\lambda^{\delta}(\vartheta)\right]^{\Delta}\Delta\vartheta \\ =& \frac{1}{C^{q\delta}}\chi^{\delta}(\theta)\int_{\theta}^{\epsilon}\left[-\lambda^{\delta}(\vartheta)\right]^{\Delta}\Delta\vartheta \\ =& \frac{1}{C^{q\delta}}\chi^{\delta}(\theta)\left[\lambda^{\delta}(\theta) - \lambda^{\delta}(\epsilon)\right] \\ =& \frac{1}{C^{q\delta}}\chi^{\delta}(\theta)\lambda^{\delta}(\theta). \end{aligned} \tag{37}$$

Consider the function

$$\Lambda(\theta) = C^{q(1-\delta)}\left(\int_{\theta}^{\epsilon} \chi^{\delta}(\vartheta)\left[-\lambda^{\delta}(\vartheta)\right]^{\Delta}\Delta\vartheta\right)^{\frac{1}{\delta}} - \int_{\theta}^{\epsilon} \chi(\vartheta)[-\lambda(\vartheta)]^{\Delta}\Delta\vartheta. \tag{38}$$

By applying the chain rule formula on the term

$$\left(\int_{\theta}^{\epsilon} \chi^{\delta}(\vartheta)\left[-\lambda^{\delta}(\vartheta)\right]^{\Delta}\Delta\vartheta\right)^{\frac{1}{\delta}},$$

we have for $\xi \in [\theta, \sigma(\theta)]$ that

$$\begin{aligned} &\left[\left(\int_{\theta}^{\epsilon} \chi^{\delta}(\vartheta)\left[-\lambda^{\delta}(\vartheta)\right]^{\Delta}\Delta\vartheta\right)^{\frac{1}{\delta}}\right]^{\Delta} \\ &= \frac{1}{\delta}\left(\int_{\xi}^{\epsilon} \chi^{\delta}(\vartheta)\left[-\lambda^{\delta}(\vartheta)\right]^{\Delta}\Delta\vartheta\right)^{\frac{1}{\delta}-1}\chi^{\delta}(\theta)\left[\lambda^{\delta}(\theta)\right]^{\Delta}. \end{aligned} \tag{39}$$

Again by applying the chain rule formula on the terms $\lambda^{\delta}(\theta)$, we obtain

$$\left[\lambda^{\delta}(\theta)\right]^{\Delta} = \delta\lambda^{\delta-1}(\xi)\lambda^{\Delta}(\theta), \tag{40}$$

where $\xi \in [\theta, \sigma(\theta)]$. From (38), we observe that

$$\Lambda^{\Delta}(\theta) = C^{q(1-\delta)}\left[\left(\int_{\theta}^{\epsilon} \chi^{\delta}(\vartheta)\left[-\lambda^{\delta}(\vartheta)\right]^{\Delta}\Delta\vartheta\right)^{\frac{1}{\delta}}\right]^{\Delta} - \chi(\theta)\lambda^{\Delta}(\theta). \tag{41}$$

Substituting (39) and (40) into (41), we get

$$\begin{aligned} \Lambda^{\Delta}(\theta) =& \frac{1}{\delta}C^{q(1-\delta)}\left(\int_{\xi}^{\epsilon} \chi^{\delta}(\vartheta)\left[-\lambda^{\delta}(\vartheta)\right]^{\Delta}\Delta\vartheta\right)^{\frac{1}{\delta}-1}\chi^{\delta}(\theta)\left[\lambda^{\delta}(\theta)\right]^{\Delta} - \chi(\theta)\lambda^{\Delta}(\theta) \\ =& C^{q(1-\delta)}\lambda^{\delta-1}(\xi)\left(\int_{\xi}^{\epsilon} \chi^{\delta}(\vartheta)\left[-\lambda^{\delta}(\vartheta)\right]^{\Delta}\Delta\vartheta\right)^{\frac{1}{\delta}-1}\chi^{\delta}(\theta)\lambda^{\Delta}(\theta) - \chi(\theta)\lambda^{\Delta}(\theta) \\ =& \left[-\lambda^{\Delta}(\theta)\right]\left[-C^{q(1-\delta)}\lambda^{\delta-1}(\xi)\left(\int_{\xi}^{\epsilon} \chi^{\delta}(\vartheta)\left[-\lambda^{\delta}(\vartheta)\right]^{\Delta}\Delta\vartheta\right)^{\frac{1}{\delta}-1}\chi^{\delta}(\theta) + \chi(\theta)\right]. \end{aligned} \tag{42}$$

Since $\xi \in [\theta, \sigma(\theta)]$, $0 < \delta < 1$ and λ is a decreasing function, then

$$\begin{aligned} &\lambda^{\delta-1}(\xi)\left(\int_\xi^\epsilon \chi^\delta(\vartheta)\left[-\lambda^\delta(\vartheta)\right]^\Delta \Delta\vartheta\right)^{\frac{1}{\delta}-1} \\ &\geq \lambda^{\delta-1}(\theta)\left(\int_{\sigma(\theta)}^\epsilon \chi^\delta(\vartheta)\left[-\lambda^\delta(\vartheta)\right]^\Delta \Delta\vartheta\right)^{\frac{1}{\delta}-1}. \end{aligned} \tag{43}$$

Substituting (43) into (42), we see that

$$\Lambda^\Delta(\theta) \leq \left[-\lambda^\Delta(\theta)\right]\left[-C^{q(1-\delta)}\lambda^{\delta-1}(\theta)\left(\int_{\sigma(\theta)}^\epsilon \chi^\delta(\vartheta)\left[-\lambda^\delta(\vartheta)\right]^\Delta \Delta\vartheta\right)^{\frac{1}{\delta}-1}\chi^\delta(\theta) + \chi(\theta)\right]. \tag{44}$$

Substituting (37) into (44), we get

$$\Lambda^\Delta(\theta) \leq \left[-\lambda^\Delta(\theta)\right]\left[-\lambda^{\delta-1}(\theta)[\lambda^\sigma(\theta)]^{1-\delta}\chi^\delta(\theta)[\chi^\sigma(\theta)]^{1-\delta} + \chi(\theta)\right]. \tag{45}$$

By using (35) and λ is a decreasing function, we have from (45) that

$$\Lambda^\Delta(\theta) \leq 0,$$

and then, the function Λ is decreasing on $[\varepsilon, \epsilon]_{\mathbb{T}}$.

Since Λ is a decreasing function, we have for $\epsilon > \varepsilon$ that $\Lambda(\epsilon) \leq \Lambda(\varepsilon)$ and then (note that $\Lambda(\epsilon) = 0$),

$$\int_\varepsilon^\epsilon \chi(\vartheta)[-\lambda(\vartheta)]^\Delta \Delta\vartheta \leq C^{q(1-\delta)}\left(\int_\varepsilon^\epsilon \chi^\delta(\vartheta)\left[-\lambda^\delta(\vartheta)\right]^\Delta \Delta\vartheta\right)^{\frac{1}{\delta}},$$

which is the desired inequality (36). The proof is completed. □

Corollary 8. *As a special case of Theorem 3, when $\mathbb{T} = \mathbb{R}$, $\sigma(\theta) = \theta$ and $C = 1$, we observe that (35) holds with equality, and then, we get the inequality (2) proved by Heinig and Maligranda* [1].

As a special case of Theorem 3, when $0 < p < q < \infty$ such that $0 < \delta = p/q < 1$, $\chi(\vartheta) = \omega^q(\vartheta)$ and $\lambda(\vartheta) = \varpi^q(\vartheta)$, we get the following corollary.

Corollary 9. *If $0 < p < q < \infty$, ω is C-increasing on $[\varepsilon, \epsilon]_{\mathbb{T}}$, $C \geq 1$ and ϖ is decreasing on $[\varepsilon, \epsilon]_{\mathbb{T}}$ with $\varpi(\epsilon) = 0$ such that*

$$\omega^q(\theta) \leq \varpi^{p-q}(\theta)[\varpi^\sigma(\theta)]^{q-p}\omega^p(\theta)[\omega^\sigma(\theta)]^{q-p}, \tag{46}$$

then

$$\left(\int_\varepsilon^\epsilon \omega^q(\vartheta)[-\varpi^q(\vartheta)]^\Delta \Delta\vartheta\right)^{\frac{1}{q}} \leq C^{1-p/q}\left(\int_\varepsilon^\epsilon \omega^p(\vartheta)[-\varpi^p(\vartheta)]^\Delta \Delta\vartheta\right)^{\frac{1}{p}}.$$

Corollary 10. *As a special case of Corollary 9, when $\mathbb{T} = \mathbb{R}$, $\sigma(\theta) = \theta$, we observe that (46) holds already with equality and we get the inequality (5) proved by Pečarić et al.* [2].

Corollary 11. *In Corollary 9, when $\mathbb{T} = \mathbb{N}$, $\sigma(n) = n + 1$, we have that if $\varepsilon, \epsilon \in \mathbb{N}$, $0 < p < q < \infty$, ω is C-increasing sequence for $C \geq 1$ and ϖ is decreasing with $\varpi(\epsilon) = 0$, such that*

$$\omega^q(n) \leq \varpi^{p-q}(n)\varpi^{q-p}(n+1)\omega^p(n)\omega^{q-p}(n+1),$$

then

$$\left(\sum_{n=\varepsilon}^{\epsilon} \omega^q(n)\Delta[-\varpi^q(n)]\right)^{\frac{1}{q}} \leq C^{1-p/q}\left(\sum_{n=\varepsilon}^{\epsilon} \omega^p(n)\Delta[-\varpi^p(n)]\right)^{\frac{1}{p}}.$$

Theorem 4. *Assume that* $\mathbb{T}$ *is a time scale with* $\varepsilon, \epsilon \in \mathbb{T}$, $q > 0$ *and* $0 < \delta < 1$. *Furthermore, if* χ *is* C^q*-decreasing on* $[\varepsilon, \epsilon]_{\mathbb{T}}$, $C \geq 1$ *and* λ *is decreasing on* $[\varepsilon, \epsilon]_{\mathbb{T}}$ *with* $\lambda(\epsilon) = 0$ *such that*

$$\lambda^{1-\delta}(\theta)[\lambda^{\sigma}(\theta)]^{\delta-1} \leq 1, \tag{47}$$

then

$$\int_{\varepsilon}^{\epsilon} \chi(\vartheta)[-\lambda(\vartheta)]^{\Delta}\Delta\vartheta \geq C^{q(\delta-1)}\left(\int_{\varepsilon}^{\epsilon} \chi^{\delta}(\vartheta)\left[-\lambda^{\delta}(\vartheta)\right]^{\Delta}\Delta\vartheta\right)^{\frac{1}{\delta}}. \tag{48}$$

Proof. Since λ is a decreasing function with $\lambda(\epsilon) = 0$ and χ is a C^q-decreasing function, we have for $\vartheta \geq \theta$ that $\chi(\vartheta) \leq C^q\chi(\theta)$, and then,

$$\begin{aligned} \int_{\theta}^{\epsilon} \chi^{\delta}(\vartheta)\left[-\lambda^{\delta}(\vartheta)\right]^{\Delta}\Delta\vartheta \leq & \ C^{q\delta} \int_{\theta}^{\epsilon} \chi^{\delta}(\theta)\left[-\lambda^{\delta}(\vartheta)\right]^{\Delta}\Delta\vartheta \\ = & \ C^{q\delta}\chi^{\delta}(\theta) \int_{\theta}^{\epsilon}\left[-\lambda^{\delta}(\vartheta)\right]^{\Delta}\Delta\vartheta \\ = & \ C^{q\delta}\chi^{\delta}(\theta)\left[\lambda^{\delta}(\theta) - \lambda^{\delta}(\epsilon)\right] \\ = & \ C^{q\delta}\chi^{\delta}(\theta)\lambda^{\delta}(\theta). \end{aligned} \tag{49}$$

Consider the function

$$\Lambda(\theta) = C^{q(\delta-1)}\left(\int_{\theta}^{\epsilon} \chi^{\delta}(\vartheta)\left[-\lambda^{\delta}(\vartheta)\right]^{\Delta}\Delta\vartheta\right)^{\frac{1}{\delta}} - \int_{\theta}^{\epsilon} \chi(\vartheta)[-\lambda(\vartheta)]^{\Delta}\Delta\vartheta. \tag{50}$$

By applying the chain rule formula on the term

$$\left(\int_{\theta}^{\epsilon} \chi^{\delta}(\vartheta)\left[-\lambda^{\delta}(\vartheta)\right]^{\Delta}\Delta\vartheta\right)^{\frac{1}{\delta}},$$

we have for $\xi \in [\theta, \sigma(\theta)]$ that

$$\begin{aligned} & \left[\left(\int_{\theta}^{\epsilon} \chi^{\delta}(\vartheta)\left[-\lambda^{\delta}(\vartheta)\right]^{\Delta}\Delta\vartheta\right)^{\frac{1}{\delta}}\right]^{\Delta} \\ & = \frac{1}{\delta}\left(\int_{\xi}^{\epsilon} \chi^{\delta}(\vartheta)\left[-\lambda^{\delta}(\vartheta)\right]^{\Delta}\Delta\vartheta\right)^{\frac{1}{\delta}-1} \chi^{\delta}(\theta)\left[\lambda^{\delta}(\theta)\right]^{\Delta}. \end{aligned} \tag{51}$$

Again, by applying the chain rule formula on the terms $\lambda^{\delta}(\theta)$, we obtain

$$\left[\lambda^{\delta}(\theta)\right]^{\Delta} = \delta\lambda^{\delta-1}(\xi)\lambda^{\Delta}(\theta), \tag{52}$$

where $\xi \in [\theta, \sigma(\theta)]$. From (50), we observe that

$$\Lambda^{\Delta}(\theta) = C^{q(\delta-1)}\left[\left(\int_{\theta}^{\epsilon} \chi^{\delta}(\vartheta)\left[-\lambda^{\delta}(\vartheta)\right]^{\Delta}\Delta\vartheta\right)^{\frac{1}{\delta}}\right]^{\Delta} - \chi(\theta)\lambda^{\Delta}(\theta). \tag{53}$$

Substituting (51) and (52) into (53), we get

$$\begin{aligned} \Lambda^{\Delta}(\theta) = & \ \frac{1}{\delta}C^{q(\delta-1)}\left(\int_{\xi}^{\epsilon} \chi^{\delta}(\vartheta)\left[-\lambda^{\delta}(\vartheta)\right]^{\Delta}\Delta\vartheta\right)^{\frac{1}{\delta}-1}\chi^{\delta}(\theta)\left[\lambda^{\delta}(\theta)\right]^{\Delta} - \chi(\theta)\lambda^{\Delta}(\theta) \\ = & \ C^{q(\delta-1)}\lambda^{\delta-1}(\xi)\left(\int_{\xi}^{\epsilon} \chi^{\delta}(\vartheta)\left[-\lambda^{\delta}(\vartheta)\right]^{\Delta}\Delta\vartheta\right)^{\frac{1}{\delta}-1}\chi^{\delta}(\theta)\lambda^{\Delta}(\theta) - \chi(\theta)\lambda^{\Delta}(\theta) \\ = & \ \left[-\lambda^{\Delta}(\theta)\right]\left[-C^{q(\delta-1)}\lambda^{\delta-1}(\xi)\left(\int_{\xi}^{\epsilon} \chi^{\delta}(\vartheta)\left[-\lambda^{\delta}(\vartheta)\right]^{\Delta}\Delta\vartheta\right)^{\frac{1}{\delta}-1}\chi^{\delta}(\theta) + \chi(\theta)\right]. \end{aligned} \tag{54}$$

Since $\xi \in [\theta, \sigma(\theta)]$, $0 < \delta < 1$ and λ is a decreasing function, we obtain

$$\begin{aligned} &\lambda^{\delta-1}(\xi)\left(\int_{\xi}^{\epsilon} \chi^{\delta}(\vartheta)\left[-\lambda^{\delta}(\vartheta)\right]^{\Delta}\Delta\vartheta\right)^{\frac{1}{\delta}-1} \\ &\leq \lambda^{\delta-1}(\sigma(\theta))\left(\int_{\theta}^{\epsilon} \chi^{\delta}(\vartheta)\left[-\lambda^{\delta}(\vartheta)\right]^{\Delta}\Delta\vartheta\right)^{\frac{1}{\delta}-1}. \end{aligned} \tag{55}$$

Substituting (55) into (54), we observe that

$$\Lambda^{\Delta}(\theta) \geq \left[-\lambda^{\Delta}(\theta)\right]\left[-C^{q(\delta-1)}\lambda^{\delta-1}(\sigma(\theta))\left(\int_{\theta}^{\epsilon} \chi^{\delta}(\vartheta)\left[-\lambda^{\delta}(\vartheta)\right]^{\Delta}\Delta\vartheta\right)^{\frac{1}{\delta}-1}\chi^{\delta}(\theta) + \chi(\theta)\right]. \tag{56}$$

Substituting (49) into (56), we get

$$\Lambda^{\Delta}(\theta) \geq \left[-\lambda^{\Delta}(\theta)\right]\left[-\lambda^{\delta-1}(\sigma(\theta))\lambda^{1-\delta}(\theta)\chi(\theta) + \chi(\theta)\right]. \tag{57}$$

By using (47) and λ is a decreasing function, we have from (57) that

$$\Lambda^{\Delta}(\theta) \geq 0,$$

and then, the function Λ is increasing on $[\varepsilon, \epsilon]_{\mathbb{T}}$.

Since Λ is an increasing function, we have for $\epsilon > \varepsilon$ that $\Lambda(\epsilon) \geq \Lambda(\varepsilon)$ and then (note that $\Lambda(\epsilon) = 0$),

$$\int_{\varepsilon}^{\epsilon} \chi(\vartheta)[-\lambda(\vartheta)]^{\Delta}\Delta\vartheta \geq C^{q(\delta-1)}\left(\int_{\varepsilon}^{\epsilon} \chi^{\delta}(\vartheta)\left[-\lambda^{\delta}(\vartheta)\right]^{\Delta}\Delta\vartheta\right)^{\frac{1}{\delta}},$$

which is the desired inequality (48). The proof is completed. □

As a special case of Theorem 4, when $0 < p < q < \infty$ such that $0 < \delta = p/q < 1$, $\chi(\vartheta) = \omega^{q}(\vartheta)$ and $\lambda(\vartheta) = \varpi^{q}(\vartheta)$, we get the following corollary.

Corollary 12. *Assume that $\mathbb{T}$ is a time scale with $\varepsilon, \epsilon \in \mathbb{T}$ and $0 < p < q < \infty$. Furthermore, if ω is C-decreasing on $[\varepsilon, \epsilon]_{\mathbb{T}}$, $C \geq 1$ and ϖ is decreasing on $[\varepsilon, \epsilon]_{\mathbb{T}}$ with $\varpi(\epsilon) = 0$ such that*

$$\varpi^{q-p}(\theta)[\varpi^{\sigma}(\theta)]^{p-q} \leq 1, \tag{58}$$

then

$$\left(\int_{\varepsilon}^{\epsilon} \omega^{q}(\vartheta)[-\varpi^{q}(\vartheta)]^{\Delta}\Delta\vartheta\right)^{\frac{1}{q}} \geq C^{p/q-1}\left(\int_{\varepsilon}^{\epsilon} \omega^{p}(\vartheta)[-\varpi^{p}(\vartheta)]^{\Delta}\Delta\vartheta\right)^{\frac{1}{p}}.$$

Corollary 13. *As a special case of Corollary 12, when $\mathbb{T} = \mathbb{R}$, $\sigma(\theta) = \theta$, we have that (58) holds already with equality and we also get the inequality (6) proved by Pečarić et al.* [2].

Corollary 14. *In Corollary 12, when $\mathbb{T} = \mathbb{N}$, $\sigma(n) = n + 1$, we have that if $\varepsilon, \epsilon \in \mathbb{N}$, $0 < p < q < \infty$, ω is a C-decreasing sequence for $C \geq 1$ and ϖ is decreasing with $\varpi(\epsilon) = 0$, such that*

$$\varpi^{q-p}(n)\varpi^{p-q}(n+1) \leq 1,$$

then

$$\left(\sum_{n=\varepsilon}^{\epsilon} \omega^{q}(n)\Delta[-\varpi^{q}(n)]\right)^{\frac{1}{q}} \geq C^{p/q-1}\left(\sum_{n=\varepsilon}^{\epsilon} \omega^{p}(n)\Delta[-\varpi^{p}(n)]\right)^{\frac{1}{p}}.$$

4. Conclusions and Future Work

In this paper, we establish some new dynamic inequalities involving C-monotonic functions with $C \geq 1$, on time scales. It is known that if $C = 1$, then the 1-decreasing function is decreasing and the 1-increasing function increasing. Thus, our results are special cases when $C = 1$ and give the inequalities involving increasing or decreasing functions. These results can be proved by applying the properties of C-monotonic functions and the chain rule formula on time scales. In the future, we hope to study the dynamic inequalities involving C-monotonic functions via conformable delta fractional calculus on time scales.

Author Contributions: Software and writing—original draft, M.Z., G.A., A.I.S. and A.M.H.; writing—review and editing C.C., H.M.R. and M.Z. All authors have read and agreed to the published version of the manuscript.

Funding: Princess Nourah bint Abdulrahman University, Riyadh, Saudi Arabia.

Data Availability Statement: Not applicable.

Acknowledgments: Princess Nourah bint Abdulrahman University Researchers Supporting Project number (PNURSP2022R45), Princess Nourah bint Abdulrahman University, Riyadh, Saudi Arabia.

Conflicts of Interest: The authors declare no conflict of interest.

References

1. Heinig, H.; Maligranda, L. Weighted inequalities for monotone and concave functions. *Stud. Math.* **1995**, *116*, 133–165.
2. Pečarić, J.; Perixcx, I.; Persson, L.E. Integral inequalities for monotone functions. *J. Math. Anal. Appl.* **1997**, *215*, 235–251. [CrossRef]
3. AlNemer, G.; Saied, A.I.; Zakarya, M.; El-Hamid, H.A.A.; Bazighifan, O.; Rezk, H.M. Some New Reverse Hilbert's Inequalities on Time Scales. *Symmetry* **2021**, *13*, 2431. [CrossRef]
4. Bibi, R.; Bohner, M.; Pečarić, J.; Varošanec, S. Minkowski and Beckenbach-Dresher inequalities and functionals on time scales. *J. Math. Inequal* **2013**, *7*, 299–312. [CrossRef]
5. Bohner, M.; Nosheen, A.; Pečarić, J.; Younis, A. Some dynamic Hardy-type inequalities with general kernels. *Math. Ineq. Appl.* **2014**, *8*, 185–199. [CrossRef]
6. Bohner, M.; Georgiev, S.G. Multiple integration on time scales. In *Multivariable Dynamic Calculus on Time Scales*; Springer: Cham, Switzerland, 2016; pp. 449–515.
7. Donchev, T.; Nosheen, A.; Pečarić, J.E. Hardy-type inequalities on time scales via convexity in several variables. *ISRN Math. Anal.* **2013**, *2013*, 1–9. [CrossRef]
8. Fabelurin, O.O.; Oguntuase, J.A. Multivariat Hardy—Type inequalities on time scales via superquadraticity. *Proc. A. Razm. Math. Inst.* **2015**, *167*, 29–42.
9. El-Deeb, A.A.; Elsennary, H.A.; Cheung, W. Some reverse Hölder inequalities with Specht's ratio on time scales. *J. Nonlinear Sci. Appl.* **2018**, *11*, 444–455. [CrossRef]
10. Oguntuase, J.A.; Persson, L.E. Time scales Hardy-type inequalities via superquadracity. *Ann. Funct. Anal.* **2014**, *5*, 61–73. [CrossRef]
11. Řehak, P. Hardy inequality on time scales and its application to half-linear dynamic equations. *J. Inequalities Appl.* **2005**, *2005*, 495–507. [CrossRef]
12. Rezk, H.M.; AlNemer, G.; Saied, A.I.; Bazighifan, O.; Zakarya, M. Some New Generalizations of Reverse Hilbert-Type Inequalities on Time Scales. *Symmetry* **2022**, *14*, 750. [CrossRef]
13. Rezk, H.M.; Saied, A.I.; AlNemer, G.; Zakarya, M. On Hardy–Knopp Type Inequalities with Kernels via Time Scale Calculus. *J. Math.* **2022**, *2022*, 1–13. [CrossRef]
14. Saker, S.H.; Saied, A.I.; Krnić, M. Some new dynamic Hardy-type inequalities with kernels involving monotone functions. *Rev. Real Acad. Cienc. Exactas Fis. Nat. Ser. A. Mat.* **2020**, *114*, 1–16. [CrossRef]
15. Saker, S.H.; Saied, A.I.; Krnić, M. Some New Weighted Dynamic Inequalities for Monotone Functions Involving Kernels. *Mediterr. Math.* **2020**, *17*, 1–18. [CrossRef]
16. Wong, F.H.; Yeh, C.C.; Yu, S.L.; Hong, C.H. Young's inequality and related results on time scales. *Appl. Math. Lett.* **2005**, *18*, 983–988. [CrossRef]
17. Saker, S.H.; Awwad, E.; Saied, A.I. Some new dynamic inequalities involving monotonic functions on time scales. *J. Funct. Spaces* **2019**, *2019*, 1–11. [CrossRef]
18. Bohner, M.; Peterson, A. *Dynamic Equations on Time Scales: An Introduction with Applications*; Birkhäuser: Boston, MA, USA, 2001.
19. Bohner, M.; Peterson, A. *Advances in Dynamic Equations on Time Scales*; Springer Science & Business Media: New York, USA, 2002.

axioms

MDPI

Article

New Fractional Integral Inequalities Pertaining to Caputo–Fabrizio and Generalized Riemann–Liouville Fractional Integral Operators

Muhammad Tariq [1], Omar Mutab Alsalami [2], Asif Ali Shaikh [1], Kamsing Nonlaopon [3,*] and Sotiris K. Ntouyas [4,5]

1 Department of Basic Sciences and Related Studies, Mehran University of Engineering and Technology, Jamshoro 76062, Pakistan
2 Department of Electrical Engineering, College of Engineering, Taif University, Taif 21944, Saudi Arabia
3 Department of Mathematics, Faculty of Science, Khon Kaen University, Khon Kaen 40002, Thailand
4 Department of Mathematics, University of Ioannina, 451 10 Ioannina, Greece
5 Nonlinear Analysis and Applied Mathematics (NAAM) Research Group, Department of Mathematics, Faculty of Science, King Abdulaziz University, Jeddah 21589, Saudi Arabia
* Correspondence: nkamsi@kku.ac.th; Tel.: +66-8-6642-1582

Abstract: Integral inequalities have accumulated a comprehensive and prolific field of research within mathematical interpretations. In recent times, strategies of fractional calculus have become the subject of intensive research in historical and contemporary generations because of their applications in various branches of science. In this paper, we concentrate on establishing Hermite–Hadamard and Pachpatte-type integral inequalities with the aid of two different fractional operators. In particular, we acknowledge the critical Hermite–Hadamard and related inequalities for n-polynomial s-type convex functions and n-polynomial s-type harmonically convex functions. We practice these inequalities to consider the Caputo–Fabrizio and the k-Riemann–Liouville fractional integrals. Several special cases of our main results are also presented in the form of corollaries and remarks. Our study offers a better perception of integral inequalities involving fractional operators.

Keywords: Hermite–Hadamard inequality; convex function; harmonically convex function; Caputo–Fabrizio fractional operator; fractional integral inequality

Citation: Tariq, M.; Alsalami, O.M.; Shaikh, A.A.; Nonlaopon, K.; Ntouyas, S.K. New Fractional Integral Inequalities Pertaining to Caputo–Fabrizio and Generalized Riemann–Liouville Fractional Integral Operators. *Axioms* **2022**, *11*, 618. https://doi.org/10.3390/axioms11110618

Academic Editor: Simeon Reich

Received: 28 September 2022
Accepted: 31 October 2022
Published: 7 November 2022

Publisher's Note: MDPI stays neutral with regard to jurisdictional claims in published maps and institutional affiliations.

1. Introduction

The convex function is a class of significant functions popularly accepted in mathematical analysis. This class represents prominent parts of the theory of inequality. Moreover, convex functions have been widely used in many research fields such as optimization, engineering, physics, financial activities, etc. In optimization, the concept of generalized convexity along with inequality theory is often used. Hermite–Hadamard integral inequalities containing convex functions are an intense research topic for many mathematicians because of their relevance and efficiency in use.

Convex functions have a very strong association with integral inequalities. Recently, several mathematicians have explored the close relationship and correlated work on symmetry and convexity. It is also explained that while working on any one of the concepts, work tends to be applied to the other one too. Many familiar and relevant inequalities are modifications of convex functions. In the literature, there are some well-known inequalities such as the Hermite–Hadamard inequality and the Jensen inequality that interpret the geometrical meaning of convex functions. In this paper, we concentrate on presenting new versions of fractional integral inequalities through n-polynomial s-type convex functions and n-polynomial s-type harmonically convex functions. To begin the discussion, let us recall the definition of a convex function.

In 1905, Jensen presented the meaning of convex function as follows:

Definition 1 ([1,2]). *A function $\Phi\colon [\mathfrak{a}_1, \mathfrak{a}_2] \to \mathbb{R}$ is called convex if*

$$\Phi(\ell x + (1-\ell)y) \leq \ell\Phi(x) + (1-\ell)\Phi(y),$$

holds for every $x, y \in [\mathfrak{a}_1, \mathfrak{a}_2]$ and $\ell \in [0,1]$.

The well-known Hermite–Hadamard inequality is given as follows:

Theorem 1 (see [3]). *Consider $\Phi : \mathbb{T} \subseteq \mathbb{R} \to \mathbb{R}$ to be a convex function with $\mathfrak{a}_1 < \mathfrak{a}_2$ and $\mathfrak{a}_1, \mathfrak{a}_2 \in \mathbb{T}$. Then, the following inequality holds:*

$$\Phi\left(\frac{\mathfrak{a}_1 + \mathfrak{a}_2}{2}\right) \leq \frac{1}{\mathfrak{a}_2 - \mathfrak{a}_1}\int_{\mathfrak{a}_1}^{\mathfrak{a}_2} \Phi(x)\mathrm{d}x \leq \frac{\Phi(\mathfrak{a}_1) + \Phi(\mathfrak{a}_2)}{2}. \tag{1}$$

Definition 2 (see [4]). *A function $\Phi\colon \mathbb{T} \to \mathbb{R}$ is said to be a harmonically convex function if*

$$\Phi\left(\frac{\mathfrak{a}_1\mathfrak{a}_2}{\ell\mathfrak{a}_1 + (1-\ell)\mathfrak{a}_2}\right) \leq \ell\Phi(\mathfrak{a}_2) + (1-\ell)\Phi(\mathfrak{a}_2), \tag{2}$$

holds for all $\mathfrak{a}_1, \mathfrak{a}_2 \in \mathbb{T}$ and $\ell \in [0,1]$.

2. Preliminaries

The set $\mathbb{T} \subseteq \mathbb{R} \setminus \{0\}$ is called convex if $\ell x + (1-\ell)y \in \mathbb{T}$ for $x, y \in \mathbb{T}$ and $\ell \in [0,1]$ and the set $\mathbb{S} \subseteq \mathbb{R} \setminus \{0\}$ as harmonically convex if $\frac{xy}{\ell x + (1-\ell)y} \in \mathbb{S}$ for all $x, y \in \mathbb{S}$ and $\ell \in [o,1]$. From now on, we always assume $\mathbb{T}$ to be a convex set and $\mathbb{S}$ as a harmonically convex set.

Many researchers have generalized and extended the Hermite–Hadamard inequality using different convexities. For example, Dragomir et al. [5], Qi et al. [6] and Kirmaci et al. [7] proved some refinements of Hermite–Hadamard inequality for differentiable functions and presented some applications of the main results for special means and trapezoidal rules. Furthermore, the related inequalities for s-convex functions were investigated in articles [8,9]. Özcan et al. [10] improved the refinements of Hermite–Hadamard type inequalities using improved Holder's inequality. Moreover, this inequality was also improved for interval-valued preinvex functions in [11]. Recently, a group of mathematicians, namely Toplu, Kadakal and İşcan [12], presented a very important class of convex function, i.e., the n-polynomial convex function, which is given as:

Let $n \in \mathbb{N}$. A function $\Phi : \mathbb{T} \to \mathbb{R}$ is said to be an n-polynomial convex function on $\mathbb{T}$, if

$$\Phi(\ell x + (1-\ell)y) \leq \frac{1}{n}\sum_{\wp=1}^{n}\left[1 - (1-\ell)^{\wp}\right]\Phi(x) + \frac{1}{n}\sum_{\wp=1}^{n}\left[1 - \ell^{\wp}\right]\Phi(y),$$

for all $x, y \in \mathbb{T}$ and $\ell \in [0,1]$.

In the same paper, they also proved the following Hermite–Hadamard inequality employing this new generalized notion of convexity.

Theorem 2 (see [12]). *Suppose $\Phi\colon \mathbb{T} \to \mathbb{R}$ is an n-polynomial convex function, $\mathfrak{a}_1, \mathfrak{a}_2 \in \mathbb{T}$ with $\mathfrak{a}_1 < \mathfrak{a}_2$ and Φ is a Lebesgue integrable function on $[\mathfrak{a}_1, \mathfrak{a}_2]$. Then the following integral inequality holds:*

$$\frac{2^{-1}n}{n + 2^{-n} - 1}\Phi\left(\frac{\mathfrak{a}_1 + \mathfrak{a}_2}{2}\right) \leq \frac{1}{\mathfrak{a}_2 - \mathfrak{a}_1}\int_{\mathfrak{a}_1}^{\mathfrak{a}_2} \Phi(x)\mathrm{d}x \leq \frac{\Phi(\mathfrak{a}_1) + \Phi(\mathfrak{a}_2)}{n}\sum_{\wp=1}^{n}\frac{\wp}{\wp + 1}. \tag{3}$$

If we set $n = 1$ in the inequality (3), *then the classical Hermite–Hadamard inequality* (1) *for a convex function is recovered.*

Inspired by the above-mentioned article, Awan et al. [13], extended the concept of n-polynomial convexity and presented a generalized version of a harmonically convex function, i.e., an n-polynomial harmonically convex function, given as:

A function $\Phi : \mathbb{S} \to \mathbb{R}^+$ is said to be an n-polynomial harmonically convex if for all $x, y \in \mathbb{S}$, $n \in N$ and $\ell \in [0,1]$, the following inequality holds.

$$\Phi\left(\frac{\mathfrak{a}_1\mathfrak{a}_2}{\ell\mathfrak{a}_1 + (1-\ell)\mathfrak{a}_2}\right) \le \frac{1}{n}\sum_{\wp=1}^{n}(1-(1-\ell)^{\wp})\Phi(\mathfrak{a}_2) + \frac{1}{n}\sum_{\wp=1}^{n}\left[1-\ell^{\wp}\right]\Phi(\mathfrak{a}_1).$$

In the same paper, the following new version of Hermite–Hadamard inequality was established.

Theorem 3 (see [13]). *Suppose $\Phi\colon \mathbb{S} \to \mathbb{R}^+$ is an n-polynomial harmonically convex function. If $\mathfrak{a}_1, \mathfrak{a}_2 \in \mathbb{S}$ with $0 < \mathfrak{a}_1 < \mathfrak{a}_2$ and $\Phi \in \mathcal{L}[\mathfrak{a}_1, \mathfrak{a}_2]$, then the following integral inequality holds.*

$$\frac{2^{-1}n}{n+2^{-n}-1}\Phi\left(\frac{2\mathfrak{a}_1\mathfrak{a}_2}{\mathfrak{a}_1+\mathfrak{a}_2}\right) \le \frac{\mathfrak{a}_1\mathfrak{a}_2}{\mathfrak{a}_2-\mathfrak{a}_1}\int_{\mathfrak{a}_1}^{\mathfrak{a}_2}\frac{\Phi(x)}{x^2}dx \le \frac{\Phi(\mathfrak{a}_1)+\Phi(\mathfrak{a}_2)}{n}\sum_{\wp=1}^{n}\frac{\wp}{\wp+1}.$$

Definition 3 ([14]). *A function $\Phi\colon \mathbb{T} \to \mathbb{R}$ is said to be an n-polynomial s-type convex function for $n \in \mathbb{N}$. If for $\mathfrak{a}_1, \mathfrak{a}_2 \in \mathbb{T}$ with $\ell, s \in [0,1]$, the following inequality satisfies.*

$$\Phi(\ell x + (1-\ell)y) \le \frac{1}{n}\sum_{\wp=1}^{n}\left[1-(s(1-\ell))^{\wp}\right]\Phi(x) + \frac{1}{n}\sum_{\wp=1}^{n}\left[1-(s\ell)^{\wp}\right]\Phi(y). \tag{4}$$

Theorem 4 (see [14]). *Let $\Phi\colon \mathbb{S} \to \mathbb{R}$ be an n-polynomial s-type convex function. If $\mathfrak{a}_1, \mathfrak{a}_2 \in \mathbb{T}$ with $\mathfrak{a}_1, \mathfrak{a}_2 \in \mathbb{T}$ with $\mathfrak{a}_1 < \mathfrak{a}_2$. If $\Phi \in \mathcal{L}[\mathfrak{a}_1, \mathfrak{a}_2]$, then the following integral inequality holds.*

$$\frac{2^{-1}}{\sum_{\wp=1}^{n}\left[1-\left(\frac{s}{2}\right)^{\wp}\right]}\Phi\left(\frac{\mathfrak{a}_1+\mathfrak{a}_2}{2}\right) \le \frac{1}{\mathfrak{a}_2-\mathfrak{a}_1}\int_{\mathfrak{a}_1}^{\mathfrak{a}_2}\Phi(x)dx \le \frac{\Phi(\mathfrak{a}_1)+\Phi(\mathfrak{a}_2)}{n}\sum_{\wp=1}^{n}\left[\frac{\wp+1-s^{\wp}}{\wp+1}\right]. \tag{5}$$

Integral inequalities have been indispensable in establishing the uniqueness of solutions for certain fractional differential equations. Sarikaya et al. [15] introduced the fractional version of Hermite–Hadamard inequality employing a Riemann–Liouville fractional operator. Motivated by this article many mathematicians used different notions of fractional operators to generalize inequalities such as Hermite–Hadamard, Ostrowski, Simpson, Opial, Jensen-Mercer, etc. To carry forward our investigation about fractional calculus, we start with the notion of the Caputo–Fabrizio fractional operator.

Note: From now on, we will use $\mathcal{M}(\lambda) > 0$ as a normalization function satisfying $\mathcal{M}(0) = \mathcal{M}(1) = 1$.

Let $\mathcal{L}^2(\mathfrak{a}_1, \mathfrak{a}_2)$ be the space of square integrable function on the interval $(\mathfrak{a}_1, \mathfrak{a}_2)$ and

$$H'(\mathfrak{a}_1, \mathfrak{a}_2) = \left\{g/g \in \mathcal{L}^2(\mathfrak{a}_1, \mathfrak{a}_2) \quad and \quad g' \in \mathcal{L}^2(\mathfrak{a}_1, \mathfrak{a}_2)\right\}.$$

If $\Phi \in H'(\mathfrak{a}_1, \mathfrak{a}_2)$, $\mathfrak{a}_1 < \mathfrak{a}_2$ and $\lambda) \in [0,1]$, then the left- and right-sided Caputo–Fabrizio fractional integral operator ${}^{CF}\mathrm{I}^{\lambda}_{\mathfrak{a}_1}$ and ${}^{CF}\mathrm{I}^{\lambda}_{\mathfrak{a}_2}$ are defined as:

Definition 4 (see [16,17]). *Let $\Phi \in H'(\mathfrak{a}_1, \mathfrak{a}_2)$, $\mathfrak{a}_1 < \mathfrak{a}_2$, $\lambda \in [0,1]$, then the definition of the left fractional integral in the sense of Caputo and Fabrizio becomes*

$$\left({}^{\mathcal{CF}}_{\mathfrak{a}_1}\mathrm{I}^{\lambda}\Phi\right)(\varphi) = \frac{(1-\lambda)}{\mathcal{M}(\lambda)}\Phi(\varphi) + \frac{\lambda}{\mathcal{M}(\lambda)}\int_{\mathfrak{a}_1}^{\varphi}\Phi(x)\mathrm{d}x, \tag{6}$$

$$\left({}^{\mathcal{CF}}\mathrm{I}^{\lambda}_{\mathfrak{a}_2}\Phi\right)(\varphi) = \frac{(1-\lambda)}{\mathcal{M}(\lambda)}\Phi(\varphi) + \frac{\lambda}{\mathcal{M}(\lambda)}\int_{\varphi}^{\mathfrak{a}_2}\Phi(x)\mathrm{d}x, \tag{7}$$

where $\mathcal{M} : [0,1] \to (0,\infty)$ is a normalization function satisfying $\mathcal{M}(0) = \mathcal{M}(1) = 1$.

Gürbüz et al. [16] used Caputo–Fabrizio fractional integrals to establish the following Hermite–Hadamard inequality.

Theorem 5 (see [16]). *Let $\Phi : \mathbb{T} \to \mathbb{R}$ be a convex function on $\mathbb{T}$. If $\mathfrak{a}_1, \mathfrak{a}_2 \in \mathbb{T}$ with $\mathfrak{a}_1 < \mathfrak{a}_2$ and Φ is a Lebesgue integral function on $[\mathfrak{a}_1, \mathfrak{a}_2]$, then the following double inequality holds:*

$$\Phi\left(\frac{\mathfrak{a}_1 + \mathfrak{a}_2}{2}\right) \leq \frac{\mathcal{M}(\lambda)}{\lambda(\mathfrak{a}_2 - \mathfrak{a}_1)}\left[\left({}^{C\mathcal{F}}\mathrm{I}^{\lambda}_{\mathfrak{a}_1}\Phi\right)(k) + \left({}^{C\mathcal{F}}\mathrm{I}^{\lambda}_{\mathfrak{a}_2}\Phi\right)(k) - \frac{2(1-\lambda)}{\mathcal{M}(\lambda)}\Phi(k)\right] \leq \frac{\Phi(\mathfrak{a}_1) + \Phi(\mathfrak{a}_2)}{2},$$

where $\lambda \in [0,1], k \in [\mathfrak{a}_1, \mathfrak{a}_2]$.

Theorem 6. *Let $\Phi : \mathbb{T} \to \mathbb{R}$ be a Lebesgue integrable function on $[\mathfrak{a}_1, \mathfrak{a}_2]$ with $\mathfrak{a}_1 < \mathfrak{a}_2$ and $\mathfrak{a}_1, \mathfrak{a}_2 \in \mathbb{T}$. If Φ is an n-polynomial convex function then,*

$$\frac{2^{-1}n}{n + 2^{-n} - 1}\Phi\left(\frac{\mathfrak{a}_1 + \mathfrak{a}_2}{2}\right) \leq \frac{\mathcal{M}(\lambda)}{\lambda(\mathfrak{a}_2 - \mathfrak{a}_1)}\left[{}^{CF}\mathrm{I}^{\lambda}_{\mathfrak{a}_1}\Phi(r) + {}^{CF}\mathrm{I}^{\lambda}_{\mathfrak{a}_2}\Phi(r) - \frac{2(1-\lambda)}{\mathcal{M}(\lambda)}\Phi(r)\right] \leq \frac{\Phi(\mathfrak{a}_1) + \Phi(\mathfrak{a}_2)}{n}\sum_{\wp=1}^{n}\frac{\wp}{\wp+1},$$

where $\lambda \in [0,1], r \in [\mathfrak{a}_1, \mathfrak{a}_2]$ and $\mathcal{M}(\lambda) > 0$, is a normalization function.

Fractional derivatives and integral operators have recently been used to generalize existing kernels. Nwaeze et al. [18] proved fractional versions of Hermite–Hadamard inequality for n-polynomial convex and n-polynomial harmonically convex functions. Sahoo et al. [19] established some new Hermite–Hadamard type fractional inequalities for (h-m) convex functions. Abdeljawad et al. [20] used local fractional integrals to present inequalities for generalized (s,m)-convex functions. Ostrowski-type inequalities are also investigated using fractional operators in [21,22]. Further refinements of Hermite–Hadamard inequalities are done for Wright-generalized Bessel functions [23], polynomial convex functions [24] and for strongly convexity via Atangana–Baleanu operators [25].

The Caputo–Fabrizio fractional derivative was introduced by Caputo and Fabrizio [26] in 2015. The advantage of this proposition was due to the necessity of accepting a model that describes structures with various scales. Recently, it has been seen that many mathematicians are showing their interest in using the Caputo fractional derivative and Caputo–Fabrizio fractional integral to establish fractional integral inequalities such as Hermite–Hadamard, Ostrowski, etc. The persistence of this article is to employ the Caputo–Fabrizio fractional integral operator and k-Riemann–Liouville fractional operator to investigate some new types of integral inequalities involving n-polynomial convex and n-polynomial harmonically convex functions, which have been presented earlier using various fractional operators such as Riemann–Liouville, Atangana–Baleanu, Katugampola, generalized fractional operators, etc. The results presented could be remedial to prove the existence and uniqueness of some fractional differential equations.

Now we recall that the left- and right-side k-Riemann–Liouville fractional operator ${}_k\mathrm{I}^{\lambda}_{\mathfrak{a}_1^+}$ and ${}_k\mathrm{I}^{\lambda}_{\mathfrak{a}_2^-}$ of order $\lambda > 0$ for a real valued continuous function $\Phi(x)$ are defined by (see [27,28]).

$${}_k\mathrm{I}^{\lambda}_{\mathfrak{a}_1^+}\Phi(x) = \frac{1}{k\Gamma(\lambda)}\int_{\mathfrak{a}_1}^{x}(x-t)^{\frac{\lambda}{k}-1}\Phi(\ell)dt \quad x > \mathfrak{a}_1,$$

and

$${}_k\mathrm{I}^{\lambda}_{\mathfrak{a}_2^-}\Phi(x) = \frac{1}{k\Gamma(\lambda)}\int_{x}^{\mathfrak{a}_2}(t-x)^{\frac{\lambda}{k}-1}\Phi(\ell)dt \quad x < \mathfrak{a}_2.$$

When $k > 0$ and Γ_k is the k-gamma function given by

$$\Gamma_k(x) = \int_0^{x}\ell^{x-1}\exp^{\frac{-\ell^k}{k}}d\ell \quad Re(x) > 0,$$

with the properties $\Gamma_k(x+k) = x\Gamma_k(x)$ and $\Gamma_k(k) = 1$ if $k = 1$ we simply write ${}_1\mathrm{I}^{\lambda}_{\mathfrak{a}_1^+}\Phi = \mathrm{I}^{\lambda}_{\mathfrak{a}_1^+}\Phi$ and ${}_1\mathrm{I}^{\lambda}_{\mathfrak{a}_1^+}\Phi = \mathrm{I}^{\lambda}_{\mathfrak{a}_1^+}\Phi$. The beta function is defined by

$$\beta(u,v) = \int_0^1 \ell^{u-1}(1-\ell)^{v-1}d\ell \quad for \quad R_e(u) > 0, R_e(v) > 0. \tag{8}$$

The novelty of this article is that it deals with inequalities of Hermite–Hadamard and Pachpatte type for higher-order convexity, i.e., n-polynomial s-type convex and n-polynomial s-type harmonically convex functions employing two different types of fractional integral operators. The rest of the article has the following structure: after studying some necessary concepts about fractional calculus and Hermite–Hadamard type inequalities, in Section 3, we present new variants of Hermite–Hadamard-type inequality via Caputo–Fabrizio fractional operators for n-polynomial s-type convex functions. Next, Section 4 is dedicated to establishing Hermite–Hadamard inequalities for n-polynomial s-type harmonically convex functions via k-Riemann–Liouville fractional operators. A brief conclusion and future scopes of the present work is given in the last Section 5.

3. Main Results

Theorem 7. *Let $\Phi : \mathbb{T} \to \mathbb{R}$ be an n-polynomial s-type convex function on $\mathbb{T}$ with $\mathfrak{a}_1 < \mathfrak{a}_2$ and $\mathfrak{a}_1, \mathfrak{a}_2 \in \mathbb{T}$. If Φ is a Lebesgue integrable function on $[\mathfrak{a}_1, \mathfrak{a}_2]$, then*

$$\frac{2^{-1}n}{\sum\limits_{\wp=1}^{n}\left[1-\left(\frac{s}{2}\right)^{\wp}\right]}\Phi\left(\frac{\mathfrak{a}_1+\mathfrak{a}_2}{2}\right) \le \frac{\mathcal{M}(\lambda)}{\lambda(\mathfrak{a}_2-\mathfrak{a}_1)}\left[{}^{CF}\mathrm{I}^{\lambda}_{\mathfrak{a}_1}\Phi(r) + {}^{CF}\mathrm{I}^{\lambda}_{\mathfrak{a}_2}\Phi(r) - \frac{2(1-\lambda)}{\mathcal{M}(\lambda)}\Phi(r)\right]$$
$$\le \frac{\Phi(\mathfrak{a}_1)+\Phi(\mathfrak{a}_2)}{n}\sum_{\wp=1}^{n}\frac{\wp+1-s^{\wp}}{\wp+1},$$

where $\lambda \in [0,1], s \in [0,1], r \in [0,1]$ and $\mathcal{M}(\lambda) > 0$ is a normalization function.

Proof. Given that Φ is n-polynomial s-type convex function. It follows from Equation (5) that

$$\frac{n}{\sum\limits_{\wp=1}^{n}\left[1-\left(\frac{s}{2}\right)^{\wp}\right]}\Phi\left(\frac{\mathfrak{a}_1+\mathfrak{a}_2}{2}\right) \le \frac{2}{\mathfrak{a}_2-\mathfrak{a}_1}\int_{\mathfrak{a}_1}^{\mathfrak{a}_2}\Phi(x)dx$$
$$= \frac{2}{\mathfrak{a}_2-\mathfrak{a}_1}\left[\int_{\mathfrak{a}_1}^{r}\Phi(x)dx + \int_{r}^{\mathfrak{a}_2}\Phi(x)dx\right]. \tag{9}$$

Multiplying both sides of Equation (9) by $\frac{\lambda(\mathfrak{a}_2-\mathfrak{a}_1)}{2\mathcal{M}(\lambda)}$ gives

$$\frac{\lambda(\mathfrak{a}_2-\mathfrak{a}_1)}{2\mathcal{M}(\lambda)}\frac{n}{\sum\limits_{\wp=1}^{n}\left[1-\left(\frac{s}{2}\right)^{\wp}\right]}\Phi\left(\frac{\mathfrak{a}_1+\mathfrak{a}_2}{2}\right) \le \frac{\lambda}{\mathcal{M}(\lambda)}\left[\int_{\mathfrak{a}_1}^{r}\Phi(x)dx + \int_{r}^{\mathfrak{a}_2}\Phi(x)dx\right]. \tag{10}$$

By adding $\frac{2(1-\lambda)}{\mathcal{M}(\lambda)}\Phi(r)$ to both sides of Equation (10), we obtain

$$\frac{2(1-\lambda)}{\mathcal{M}(\lambda)}\Phi(r) + \frac{\lambda(\mathfrak{a}_2-\mathfrak{a}_1)}{2\mathcal{M}(\lambda)}\frac{n}{\sum_{\wp=1}^{n}\left[1-\left(\frac{s}{2}\right)^{\wp}\right]}\Phi\left(\frac{\mathfrak{a}_1+\mathfrak{a}_2}{2}\right) \le \frac{2(1-\lambda)}{\mathcal{M}(\lambda)}\Phi(r)$$
$$+\frac{\lambda}{\mathcal{M}(\lambda)}\left[\int_{\mathfrak{a}_1}^{r}\Phi(x)dx + \int_{r}^{\mathfrak{a}_2}\Phi(x)dx\right]$$
$$= \left[\frac{(1-\lambda)}{\mathcal{M}(\lambda)}\Phi(r) + \frac{\lambda}{\mathcal{M}(\lambda)}\int_{\mathfrak{a}_1}^{r}\Phi(x)dx\right] + \left[\frac{(1-\lambda)}{\mathcal{M}(\lambda)}\Phi(r) + \frac{\lambda}{\mathcal{M}(\lambda)}\int_{r}^{\mathfrak{a}_2}\Phi(x)dx\right]$$
$$= {}^{CF}\mathrm{I}^{\lambda}_{\mathfrak{a}_1}\Phi(r) + {}^{CF}\mathrm{I}^{\lambda}_{\mathfrak{a}_2}\Phi(r).$$

This implies that

$$\frac{2(1-\lambda)}{\mathcal{M}(\lambda)}\Phi(r)+\frac{\lambda(\mathfrak{a}_2-\mathfrak{a}_1)}{2\mathcal{M}(\lambda)}\frac{n}{\sum_{\wp=1}^{n}\left[1-\left(\frac{s}{2}\right)^{\wp}\right]}\Phi\left(\frac{\mathfrak{a}_1+\mathfrak{a}_2}{2}\right)\leq {}^{CF}\mathrm{I}^{\lambda}_{\mathfrak{a}_1}\Phi(r)+{}^{CF}\mathrm{I}^{\lambda}_{\mathfrak{a}_2}\Phi(r). \tag{11}$$

On the other hand from Equation (5), we also obtain

$$\frac{2}{\mathfrak{a}_2-\mathfrak{a}_1}\int_{\mathfrak{a}_1}^{\mathfrak{a}_2}\Phi(x)dx\leq\frac{\Phi(\mathfrak{a}_1)+\Phi(\mathfrak{a}_2)}{n}\sum_{\wp=1}^{n}\left[\frac{\wp+1-s^{\wp}}{\wp+1}\right]. \tag{12}$$

If we multiply Equation (12) by $\frac{\lambda(\mathfrak{a}_2-\mathfrak{a}_1)}{2\mathcal{M}(\lambda)}$ and then add $\frac{2(1-\lambda)}{\mathcal{M}(\lambda)}\Phi(r)$ to the resulting inequality, we obtain

$${}^{CF}\mathrm{I}^{\lambda}_{\mathfrak{a}_1}\Phi(r)+{}^{CF}\mathrm{I}^{\lambda}_{\mathfrak{a}_2}\Phi(r)\leq\frac{\lambda(\mathfrak{a}_2-\mathfrak{a}_1)}{\mathcal{M}(\lambda)}\frac{\Phi(\mathfrak{a}_1)+\Phi(\mathfrak{a}_2)}{n}\sum_{\wp=1}^{n}\left[\frac{\wp+1-s^{\wp}}{\wp+1}\right]+\frac{2(1-\lambda)}{\mathcal{M}(\lambda)}\Phi(r). \tag{13}$$

Hence, the desired result is obtained by combining Equations (11) and (13). □

Remark 1. *By taking $s=1$, Theorem 7 becomes Theorem 6.*

Corollary 1. *By taking $n=1$, Theorem 7 becomes the following inequality,*

$$\Phi\left(\frac{\mathfrak{a}_1+\mathfrak{a}_2}{2}\right)$$
$$\leq\frac{2-s}{\lambda}\frac{\mathcal{M}(\lambda)}{\mathfrak{a}_2-\mathfrak{a}_1}\left[{}^{CF}_{\mathfrak{a}_1}I^{\lambda}\Phi(r)+{}^{CF}\mathrm{I}^{\lambda}_{\mathfrak{a}_2}\Phi(r)-\frac{2(1-\lambda)}{\mathcal{M}(\lambda)}\Phi(r)\right]\leq\frac{(2-s)^2}{2}[\Phi(\mathfrak{a}_1)+\Phi(\mathfrak{a}_2)].$$

Remark 2. *By taking $n=s=1$, then Theorem 7 becomes Theorem 5.*

Theorem 8. *Suppose $\Phi,\Upsilon:\mathbb{T}\to\mathbb{R}$ is functions such that $\Phi\,\Upsilon$ is integrable on $[\mathfrak{a}_1,\mathfrak{a}_2]$ with $\mathfrak{a}_1<\mathfrak{a}_2$ and $\mathfrak{a}_1,\mathfrak{a}_2\in\mathbb{T}$. If Φ is n_1-polynomial s-type convex function and Φ is an n_2-polynomial s-type convex function, then the following inequality holds:*

$$\frac{\mathcal{M}(\lambda)}{\lambda(\mathfrak{a}_2-\mathfrak{a}_1)}\left[{}^{CF}_{\mathfrak{a}_1}I^{\lambda}\Phi(r)\Upsilon(r)+{}^{CF}\mathrm{I}^{\lambda}_{\mathfrak{a}_2}\Phi(r)\Upsilon(r)-\frac{2(1-\lambda)}{\mathcal{M}(\lambda)}\Phi(r)\Upsilon(r)\right]$$
$$\leq\int_0^1[\Delta_1(\ell)\Phi(\mathfrak{a}_1)\Upsilon(\mathfrak{a}_1)+\Delta_2(\ell)\Phi(\mathfrak{a}_2)\Upsilon(\mathfrak{a}_2)+\Delta_3(\ell)\Phi(\mathfrak{a}_2)\Upsilon(\mathfrak{a}_1)+\Delta_4(\ell)\Phi(\mathfrak{a}_1)\Upsilon(\mathfrak{a}_2)]d\ell,$$

where $\lambda\in[0,1]$ and $r\in[\mathfrak{a}_1,\mathfrak{a}_2]$ and $\mathcal{M}(\lambda)>0$ is a normalization function and

$$\Delta_1(\ell)=\frac{1}{n_1}\frac{1}{n_2}\sum_{\wp=1}^{n_1}[1-(s(1-\ell))^{\wp}]\sum_{\wp=1}^{n_2}[1-(s(1-\ell))^{\wp}],$$
$$\Delta_2(\ell)=\frac{1}{n_1}\frac{1}{n_2}\sum_{\wp=1}^{n_1}[1-(s\ell)^{\wp}]\sum_{\wp=1}^{n_2}[1-(s\ell)^{\wp}],$$
$$\Delta_3(\ell)=\frac{1}{n_1}\frac{1}{n_2}\sum_{\wp=1}^{n_1}[1-(s\ell)^{\wp}]\sum_{\wp=1}^{n_2}[1-(s(1-\ell))^{\wp}],$$
$$\Delta_4(\ell)=\frac{1}{n_1}\frac{1}{n_2}\sum_{\wp=1}^{n_1}[1-(s(1-\ell))^{\wp}]\sum_{\wp=1}^{n_2}[1-(s\ell)^{\wp}].$$

Proof. Let Φ be n_1-polynomial s-type convex function and Υ is n_2-polynomial s-type convex function

$$\Phi\left(\ell\mathfrak{a}_1+(1-\ell)\mathfrak{a}_2\right)\leq\frac{1}{n_1}\sum_{\wp=1}^{n_1}\left[1-(s(1-\ell))^{\wp}\right]\Phi(\mathfrak{a}_1)+\frac{1}{n_1}\sum_{\wp=1}^{n_1}\left[1-(s\ell)^{\wp}\right]\Phi(\mathfrak{a}_2). \tag{14}$$

$$\Upsilon\Big(\ell\mathfrak{a}_1+(1-\ell)\mathfrak{a}_2\Big)\le\frac{1}{n_2}\sum_{\wp=1}^{n_2}\Big[1-(s(1-\ell))^{\wp}\Big]\Upsilon(\mathfrak{a}_1)+\frac{1}{n_2}\sum_{\wp=1}^{n_2}\Big[1-(s\ell)^{\wp}\Big]\Upsilon(\mathfrak{a}_2). \quad (15)$$

Multiplying (14) and (15).

$$\begin{aligned}
&\Phi\Big(\ell\mathfrak{a}_1+(1-\ell)\mathfrak{a}_2\Big)\Upsilon\Big(\ell\mathfrak{a}_1+(1-\ell)\mathfrak{a}_2\Big)\\
&\le\frac{1}{n_1}\frac{1}{n_2}\sum_{\wp=1}^{n_2}\Big[1-(s(1-\ell))^{\wp}\Big]\sum_{\wp=1}^{n_1}\Big[1-(s(1-\ell))^{\wp}\Big]\Phi(\mathfrak{a}_1)\Upsilon(\mathfrak{a}_1)\\
&+\frac{1}{n_1}\frac{1}{n_2}\sum_{\wp=1}^{n_2}\Big[1-(s\ell)^{\wp}\Big]\sum_{\wp=1}^{n_1}\Big[1-(s\ell)^{\wp}\Big]\Phi(\mathfrak{a}_1)\Upsilon(\mathfrak{a}_2)\\
&+\frac{1}{n_1}\frac{1}{n_2}\sum_{\wp=1}^{n_1}\Big[1-(s\ell)^{\wp}\Big]\sum_{\wp=1}^{n_2}\Big[1-(s(1-\ell))^{\wp}\Big]\Phi(\mathfrak{a}_2)\Upsilon(\mathfrak{a}_1)\\
&+\frac{1}{n_1}\frac{1}{n_2}\sum_{\wp=1}^{n_1}\Big[1-(s\ell)^{\wp}\Big]\sum_{\wp=1}^{n_2}\Big[1-(s(1-\ell))^{\wp}\Big]\Phi(\mathfrak{a}_2)\Upsilon(\mathfrak{a}_1). \quad (16)\\
&=\Delta_1(\ell)\Phi(\mathfrak{a}_1)\Upsilon(\mathfrak{a}_1)+\Delta_2(\ell)\Phi(\mathfrak{a}_2)\Upsilon(\mathfrak{a}_2)+\Delta_3(\ell)\Phi(\mathfrak{a}_2)\Upsilon(\mathfrak{a}_1)+\Delta_4(\ell)\Phi(\mathfrak{a}_1)\Upsilon(\mathfrak{a}_2).
\end{aligned}$$

This implies that

$$\begin{aligned}
&\Phi\Big(\ell\mathfrak{a}_1+(1-\ell)\mathfrak{a}_2\Big)\Upsilon\Big(\ell\mathfrak{a}_1+(1-\ell)\mathfrak{a}_2\Big)\\
&\quad\le\Delta_1(\ell)\Phi(\mathfrak{a}_1)\Upsilon(\mathfrak{a}_1)+\Delta_2(\ell)\Phi(\mathfrak{a}_2)\Upsilon(\mathfrak{a}_2)+\Delta_3(\ell)\Phi(\mathfrak{a}_2)\Upsilon(\mathfrak{a}_1)+\Delta_4(\ell)\Phi(\mathfrak{a}_1)\Upsilon(\mathfrak{a}_2).
\end{aligned}$$

Integrating both sides of (16) with respect to over $[0,1]$ results to

$$\begin{aligned}
\frac{2}{\mathfrak{a}_2-\mathfrak{a}_1}\int_{\mathfrak{a}_1}^{\mathfrak{a}_2}\Phi(x)\Upsilon(x)dx&\le2\int_0^1\Big[\Delta_1(\ell)\Phi(\mathfrak{a}_1)\Upsilon(\mathfrak{a}_1)+\Delta_2(\ell)\Phi(\mathfrak{a}_2)\Upsilon(\mathfrak{a}_2)\\
&\quad+\Delta_3(\ell)\Phi(\mathfrak{a}_2)\Upsilon(\mathfrak{a}_1)+\Delta_4(\ell)\Phi(\mathfrak{a}_1)\Upsilon(\mathfrak{a}_2)\Big]d\ell\\
&=N(\mathfrak{a}_1,\mathfrak{a}_2).
\end{aligned}$$

Consequently,

$$\frac{2}{\mathfrak{a}_2-\mathfrak{a}_1}\left[\int_{\mathfrak{a}_1}^{r}\Phi(x)\Upsilon(x)dx+\int_{r}^{\mathfrak{a}_2}\Phi(x)\Upsilon(x)dx\right]\le N(\mathfrak{a}_1,\mathfrak{a}_2). \quad (17)$$

Now, multiplying (17) by $\frac{\lambda(\mathfrak{a}_2-\mathfrak{a}_1)}{2\mathcal{M}(\lambda)}$ and then adding $\frac{2(1-\lambda)}{\mathcal{M}(\lambda)}\Phi(r)$ to the result, we obtain

$$\begin{aligned}
&\frac{\lambda}{\mathcal{M}(\lambda)}\left[\int_{\mathfrak{a}_1}^{r}\Phi(x)\Upsilon(x)dx+\int_{r}^{\mathfrak{a}_2}\Phi(x)\Upsilon(x)dx\right]+\frac{2(1-\lambda)}{\mathcal{M}(\lambda)}\Phi(r)\Upsilon(r)\\
&\le\frac{\lambda(\mathfrak{a}_2-\mathfrak{a}_1)}{2\mathcal{M}(\lambda)}N(\mathfrak{a}_1,\mathfrak{a}_2)+\frac{2(1-\lambda)}{\mathcal{M}(\lambda)}\Phi(r)\Upsilon(r).
\end{aligned}$$

Hence,

$${}^{CF}_{\mathfrak{a}_1}\mathrm{I}^{\lambda}\Phi(r)\Upsilon(r)+{}^{CF}\mathrm{I}^{\lambda}_{\mathfrak{a}_2}\Phi(r)\Upsilon(r)\le\frac{\lambda(\mathfrak{a}_2-\mathfrak{a}_1)}{2\mathcal{M}(\lambda)}N(\mathfrak{a}_1,\mathfrak{a}_2)+\frac{2(1-\lambda)}{\mathcal{M}(\lambda)}\Phi(r)\Upsilon(r).$$

From which we obtain the intended inequality. □

Remark 3. *If we put $s=1$ in Theorem 8, we get Theorem 6.*

Remark 4. *If we put $n_1=n_2=1, s=1$ in Theorem 8, we obtain Theorem 4.*

Corollary 2. *If we put $n_1 = n_2 = 1$, in Theorem 8, then*

$$\frac{2\mathcal{M}(\lambda)}{\lambda(\mathfrak{a}_2-\mathfrak{a}_1)}\left[{}^{CF}_{\mathfrak{a}_1}\mathrm{I}^{\lambda}\Phi(r)\Upsilon(r)+{}^{CF}\,\mathrm{I}^{\lambda}_{\mathfrak{a}_2}\Phi(r)\Upsilon(r)-\frac{2(1-\lambda)}{\mathcal{M}(\lambda)}\Phi(r)\Upsilon(r)\right]$$
$$\leq\frac{2}{3}(3(1-s)+s^3)[\Phi(\mathfrak{a}_1)\Upsilon(\mathfrak{a}_1)+\Phi(\mathfrak{a}_2)\Upsilon(\mathfrak{a}_2)]$$
$$+\frac{1}{3}(6(1-s)+s^2)[\Phi(\mathfrak{a}_1)\Upsilon(\mathfrak{a}_2)+\Phi(\mathfrak{a}_2)\Upsilon(\mathfrak{a}_1)].$$

4. Further Estimations via n-Polynomial Harmonically s-Type Convex Function

Theorem 9. *Suppose $\Phi:\mathbb{S}\to\mathbb{R}^+$ be an n-polynomial harmonically s-type convex function on $\mathbb{S}$ with $\mathfrak{a}_1<\mathfrak{a}_2$ and $\Phi\in\mathcal{L}[\mathfrak{a}_1,\mathfrak{a}_2]$ and $\mathfrak{a}_1,\mathfrak{a}_2>0$, $s\in[0,1]$. Then, the following fractional inequality holds:*

$$\frac{1}{\sum\limits_{\wp=1}^{n}\left[1-\left(\frac{s}{2}\right)^{\wp}\right]}$$
$$\leq\Phi\left(\frac{2\mathfrak{a}_1\mathfrak{a}_2}{\mathfrak{a}_1+\mathfrak{a}_2}\right)\frac{\Gamma_k(\lambda)+k)}{n}\left(\frac{\mathfrak{a}_1\mathfrak{a}_2}{\mathfrak{a}_2-\mathfrak{a}_1}\right)^{\frac{\lambda}{k}}\left[\mathrm{I}^{\lambda}_{k\ \frac{1}{\mathfrak{a}_2}+}\Phi\circ\Psi\left(\frac{1}{\mathfrak{a}_1}\right)+_k\mathrm{I}^{\lambda}_{\frac{1}{\mathfrak{a}_1}-}\Phi\circ\Psi\left(\frac{1}{\mathfrak{a}_2}\right)\right]$$
$$\leq\frac{\Phi(\mathfrak{a}_1)+\Phi(\mathfrak{a}_2)}{n^2}\sum_{\wp=1}^{n}\left[2-\frac{s^{\wp}\lambda}{\lambda+ik}-\frac{s^{\wp\lambda}}{k}\beta\left(\frac{\lambda}{k},\wp+1\right)\right],$$

where $\Psi(r)=\frac{1}{r}$ and β is the beta function.

Proof. Given that Φ is n-polynomial s-type convex function,

$$\Phi\left(\frac{2xy}{x+y}\right)\leq\frac{1}{n}\sum_{\wp=1}^{n}\left[1-\left(\frac{s}{2}\right)^{\wp}\right][\Phi(x)+\Phi(y)]. \tag{18}$$

Now, let $x=\frac{\mathfrak{a}_1\mathfrak{a}_2}{\ell\mathfrak{a}_1+(1-\ell)\mathfrak{a}_2}$ and $y=\frac{\mathfrak{a}_1\mathfrak{a}_2}{\ell\mathfrak{a}_2+(1-\ell)\mathfrak{a}_1}$ then (18) becomes,

$$\Phi\left(\frac{2\mathfrak{a}_1\mathfrak{a}_2}{\mathfrak{a}_1+\mathfrak{a}_2}\right)\leq\frac{1}{n}\sum_{\wp=1}^{n}\left[1-\left(\frac{s}{2}\right)^{\wp}\right]\left\{\Phi\left(\frac{\mathfrak{a}_1\mathfrak{a}_2}{\ell\mathfrak{a}_1+(1-\ell)\mathfrak{a}_2}\right)+\Phi\left(\frac{\mathfrak{a}_1\mathfrak{a}_2}{\ell\mathfrak{a}_2+(1-\ell)\mathfrak{a}_1}\right)\right\}. \tag{19}$$

Multiplying both sides of Equation (19) by $\ell^{\frac{\lambda}{k}-1}$ and integrating with respect to ℓ over $[0,1]$, we obtain

$$\int_0^1\ell^{\frac{\lambda}{k}-1}\Phi\left(\frac{2\mathfrak{a}_1\mathfrak{a}_2}{\mathfrak{a}_1+\mathfrak{a}_2}\right)d\ell$$
$$\leq\frac{1}{n}\sum_{\wp=1}^{n}\left[1-\left(\frac{s}{2}\right)^{\wp}\right]\int_0^1\ell^{\frac{\lambda}{k}-1}\left\{\Phi\left(\frac{\mathfrak{a}_1\mathfrak{a}_2}{\ell\mathfrak{a}_1+(1-\ell)\mathfrak{a}_2}\right)+\Phi\left(\frac{\mathfrak{a}_1\mathfrak{a}_2}{\ell\mathfrak{a}_2+(1-\ell)\mathfrak{a}_1}\right)\right\}d\ell$$
$$=\frac{1}{n}\sum_{\wp=1}^{n}\left[1-\left(\frac{s}{2}\right)^{\wp}\right]\left\{\int_0^1\ell^{\frac{\lambda}{k}-1}\Phi\left(\frac{\mathfrak{a}_1\mathfrak{a}_2}{\ell\mathfrak{a}_1+(1-\ell)\mathfrak{a}_2}\right)+\int_0^1\ell^{\frac{\lambda}{k}-1}\Phi\left(\frac{\mathfrak{a}_1\mathfrak{a}_2}{\ell\mathfrak{a}_2+(1-\ell)\mathfrak{a}_1}\right)d\ell\right\}$$
$$=\frac{1}{n}\sum_{\wp=1}^{n}\left[1-\left(\frac{s}{2}\right)^{\wp}\right]$$
$$\times\left[\left(\frac{\mathfrak{a}_1\mathfrak{a}_2}{\mathfrak{a}_2-\mathfrak{a}_1}\right)^{\frac{\lambda}{k}}\int_{\frac{1}{\mathfrak{a}_2}}^{\frac{1}{\mathfrak{a}_1}}\left(\frac{1}{\mathfrak{a}_1}-r\right)^{\frac{\lambda}{k}-1}\Phi\left(\frac{1}{r}\right)dr+\left(\frac{\mathfrak{a}_1\mathfrak{a}_2}{\mathfrak{a}_2-\mathfrak{a}_1}\right)^{\frac{\lambda}{k}}\int_{\frac{1}{\mathfrak{a}_2}}^{\frac{1}{\mathfrak{a}_1}}\left(r-\frac{1}{\mathfrak{a}_2}\right)^{\frac{\lambda}{k}-1}\Phi\left(\frac{1}{r}\right)dr\right]$$

$$= \frac{k\Gamma_k(\lambda)}{n}\sum_{\wp=1}^{n}\left[1-\left(\frac{s}{2}\right)^{\wp}\right]\left(\frac{\mathfrak{a}_1\mathfrak{a}_2}{\mathfrak{a}_2-\mathfrak{a}_1}\right)^{\frac{\lambda}{k}}$$
$$\times\left[\frac{1}{k\Gamma_k(\lambda)}\int_{\frac{1}{\mathfrak{a}_2}}^{\frac{1}{\mathfrak{a}_1}}\left(\frac{1}{\mathfrak{a}_1}-r\right)^{\frac{\lambda}{k}-1}\Phi\left(\frac{1}{r}\right)dr+\frac{1}{k\Gamma_k}(\lambda)\int_{\frac{1}{\mathfrak{a}_2}}^{\frac{1}{\mathfrak{a}_1}}\left(r-\frac{1}{\mathfrak{a}_2}\right)^{\frac{\lambda}{k}-1}\Phi\left(\frac{1}{r}\right)dr\right]$$

$$= \frac{k\Gamma_k(\lambda)}{n}\sum_{\wp=1}^{n}\left[1-\left(\frac{s}{2}\right)^{\wp}\right]\left(\frac{\mathfrak{a}_1\mathfrak{a}_2}{\mathfrak{a}_2-\mathfrak{a}_1}\right)^{\frac{\lambda}{k}}\left[{}_kI^{\lambda}_{(\frac{1}{\mathfrak{a}_2})^+}(\Phi\circ\Psi)(\frac{1}{\mathfrak{a}_1})+{}_kI^{\lambda}_{(\frac{1}{\mathfrak{a}_1})^-}(\Phi\circ\Psi)(\frac{1}{\mathfrak{a}_2})\right],$$

where $\Psi(r)=\frac{1}{r}$, this implies that

$$\frac{1}{\sum_{\wp=1}^{n}[1-(\frac{s}{2})^{\wp}]}\Phi\left(\frac{2\mathfrak{a}_1\mathfrak{a}_2}{\mathfrak{a}_1+\mathfrak{a}_2}\right)$$
$$\leq\frac{\Gamma_k(\lambda+k)}{n}\left(\frac{\mathfrak{a}_1\mathfrak{a}_2}{\mathfrak{a}_2-\mathfrak{a}_1}\right)^{\frac{\lambda}{k}}\left[{}_kI^{\lambda}_{(\frac{1}{\mathfrak{a}_2})^+}(\Phi\circ\Psi)(\frac{1}{\mathfrak{a}_1})+{}_kI^{\lambda}_{(\frac{1}{\mathfrak{a}_1})^-}(\Phi\circ\Psi)(\frac{1}{\mathfrak{a}_2})\right]. \tag{20}$$

Next, substituting $x=\mathfrak{a}_1, y=\mathfrak{a}_2$ in (4) gives

$$\Phi\left(\frac{\mathfrak{a}_1\mathfrak{a}_2}{\ell\mathfrak{a}_1+(1-\ell)\mathfrak{a}_2}\right)\leq\frac{1}{n}\sum_{\wp=1}^{n}[1-s(1-\ell)^{\wp}]\Phi(\mathfrak{a}_2)+\frac{1}{n}\sum_{\wp=1}^{n}[1-(s\ell)^{\wp}]\Phi(\mathfrak{a}_1). \tag{21}$$

Reversing the role of $\mathfrak{a}_1$ and $\mathfrak{a}_2$ in (21)

$$\Phi\left(\frac{\mathfrak{a}_1\mathfrak{a}_2}{\ell\mathfrak{a}_2+(1-\ell)\mathfrak{a}_1}\right)\leq\frac{1}{n}\sum_{\wp=1}^{n}[1-(s(1-\ell)^{\wp})]\Phi(\mathfrak{a}_1)+\frac{1}{n}\sum_{\wp=1}^{n}[1-(s\ell)^{\wp}]\Phi(\mathfrak{a}_2). \tag{22}$$

Adding (20) and (21) and multiplying the resulting inequality by $\ell^{\frac{\lambda}{k}-1}$, then integrating with respect to $\ell\in[0,1]$, we obtain

$$\int_0^1\ell^{\frac{\lambda}{k}-1}\left\{\Phi\left(\frac{\mathfrak{a}_1\mathfrak{a}_2}{\ell\mathfrak{a}_1+(1-\ell)\mathfrak{a}_2}\right)+\Phi\left(\frac{\mathfrak{a}_1\mathfrak{a}_2}{\ell\mathfrak{a}_2+(1-\ell)\mathfrak{a}_1}\right)\right\}d\ell$$
$$\leq\frac{\Phi(\mathfrak{a}_1)+\Phi(\mathfrak{a}_2)}{n}\sum_{\wp=1}^{n}\int_0^1\left[2\ell^{\frac{\lambda}{k}-1}-\ell^{\frac{\lambda}{k}-1}(s(1-\ell))^{\wp}-(s\ell)^{\wp}\ell^{\frac{\lambda}{k}-1}\right]d\ell$$
$$\leq\frac{\Phi(\mathfrak{a}_1)+\Phi(\mathfrak{a}_2)}{n}\sum_{\wp=1}^{n}\left[2\frac{k}{\lambda}-\frac{s^{\wp}k}{\lambda+ik}-s^{\wp}\beta\left(\frac{\lambda}{k},\wp+1\right)\right]. \tag{23}$$

Again from (23), one has

$$\frac{\Gamma_k(\lambda+k)}{n}\left(\frac{\mathfrak{a}_1\mathfrak{a}_2}{\mathfrak{a}_2-\mathfrak{a}_1}\right)^{\frac{\lambda}{k}}\left[{}_kI^{\lambda}_{(\frac{1}{\mathfrak{a}_2})^+}(\Phi\circ\Psi)(\frac{1}{\mathfrak{a}_1})+{}_kI^{\lambda}_{(\frac{1}{\mathfrak{a}_1})^-}(\Phi\circ\Psi)(\frac{1}{\mathfrak{a}_2})\right]$$
$$\leq\frac{\Phi(\mathfrak{a}_1)+\Phi(\mathfrak{a}_2)}{n^2}\sum_{\wp=1}^{n}\left[2-\frac{s^{\wp}\lambda}{\lambda+ik}-\frac{s^{\wp}\lambda}{k}\beta\left(\frac{\lambda}{k},\wp+1\right)\right].$$

Combining (20) and (22) leads us to the desired result. □

Remark 5. *If we take $s=1$ and $\lambda=k=1$, then Theorem 9 reduces to Theorem 3.*

Remark 6. *If we take $\lambda=k=1$, then Theorem 9 reduces to Theorem 4.*

Remark 7. *If we take $n=1$, $s=1$ $\lambda=k=1$ in Theorem 9, then the classical Hermite–Hadamard type inequality for harmonic convex function is recovered.*

Remark 8. *If we take $n = \lambda = k = 1$ in Theorem 9, then the classical Hermite–Hadamard inequality for harmonic s-type convex function is recovered.*

Corollary 3. *If we set $n = 1$ in Theorem 9, then we have the following inequality.*

$$\begin{aligned}
&\frac{1}{[1-(\frac{s}{2})]}\Phi\left(\frac{\mathfrak{a}_1\mathfrak{a}_2}{\mathfrak{a}_1+\mathfrak{a}_2}\right)\\
&\leq \frac{\Gamma_k(\lambda+k)}{n}\left(\frac{\mathfrak{a}_1\mathfrak{a}_2}{\mathfrak{a}_2-\mathfrak{a}_1}\right)^{\frac{\lambda}{k}}\left[{}_k\mathrm{I}^{\lambda}_{(\frac{1}{\mathfrak{a}_2})^+}(\Phi\circ\Psi)(\frac{1}{\mathfrak{a}_1})+{}_k\mathrm{I}^{\lambda}_{(\frac{1}{\mathfrak{a}_1})^-}(\Phi\circ\Psi)(\frac{1}{\mathfrak{a}_2})\right]\\
&\leq [\Phi(\mathfrak{a}_1)+\Phi(\mathfrak{a}_2)]\left[2-\frac{s\lambda}{\lambda+k}-\frac{s\lambda}{k}\beta\left(\frac{\lambda}{k},2\right)\right].
\end{aligned}$$

Theorem 10. *Suppose $\Phi,\Psi : S \to \mathbb{R}^+$ be two functions such that $\Phi\Psi \in \mathcal{L}[\mathfrak{a}_1,\mathfrak{a}_2]$ and $\mathfrak{a}_1,\mathfrak{a}_2 > 0$, $\mathfrak{a}_1,\mathfrak{a}_2 \in S$. If Φ is an n_1-polynomial harmonically s-type convex function and Ψ is an n_2-polynomial harmonically s-type convex function with $\lambda, k > 0$, then the following inequality holds:*

$$\begin{aligned}
&\left(\frac{\mathfrak{a}_1\mathfrak{a}_2}{\mathfrak{a}_2-\mathfrak{a}_1}\right)^{\frac{\lambda}{k}}\left[{}_k\mathrm{I}^{\lambda}_{(\frac{1}{\mathfrak{a}_2})^+}(\Phi\Psi\circ h)(\frac{1}{\mathfrak{a}_1})+{}_k\mathrm{I}^{\lambda}_{(\frac{1}{\mathfrak{a}_1})^-}(\Phi\Psi\circ h)(\frac{1}{\mathfrak{a}_2})\right]\\
&\leq \frac{D(\mathfrak{a}_1,\mathfrak{a}_2)}{k\Gamma_k(\lambda)}\int_0^1 \ell^{\frac{\lambda}{k}-1}[\Delta_1(\ell)+\Delta_4(\ell)]d\ell+\frac{F(\mathfrak{a}_1,\mathfrak{a}_2)}{k\Gamma_k(\lambda)}\int_0^1 \ell^{\frac{\lambda}{k}-1}[\Delta_2(\ell)+\Delta_4(\ell)]d\ell,
\end{aligned}$$

where $D(\mathfrak{a}_1,\mathfrak{a}_2) = \Phi(\mathfrak{a}_1)\Psi(\mathfrak{a}_1)+\Phi(\mathfrak{a}_2)\Psi(\mathfrak{a}_2)$, $F(\mathfrak{a}_1,\mathfrak{a}_2) = \Phi(\mathfrak{a}_1)\Psi(\mathfrak{a}_2)+\Phi(\mathfrak{a}_2)\Psi(\mathfrak{a}_1)$, $h(r) = \frac{1}{r}$ and $\Delta_1(\ell),\Delta_2(\ell),\Delta_3(\ell)$ and $\Delta_4(\ell)$ are defined in Theorem 8.

Proof. Since Φ is an n_1-polynomial harmonically s-type convex function and Ψ is an n_2-polynomial harmonically s-type convex function, we have

$$\begin{aligned}
&\Phi\left(\frac{\mathfrak{a}_1\mathfrak{a}_2}{\ell\mathfrak{a}_1+(1-\ell)\mathfrak{a}_2}\right)\Psi\left(\frac{\mathfrak{a}_1\mathfrak{a}_2}{\ell\mathfrak{a}_1+(1-\ell)\mathfrak{a}_2}\right)\\
&\leq \frac{1}{n_1}\frac{1}{n_2}\sum_{\wp=1}^{n_1}\left[1-(s(1-\ell))^{\wp}\right]\sum_{\wp=1}^{n_2}\left[1-(s(1-\ell))^{\wp}\right]\Phi(\mathfrak{a}_2)\Psi(\mathfrak{a}_2)\\
&+\frac{1}{n_1}\frac{1}{n_2}\sum_{\wp=1}^{n_1}\left[1-(s(1-\ell))^{\wp}\right]\sum_{\wp=1}^{n_2}\left[1-(s\ell)^{\wp}\right]\Phi(\mathfrak{a}_2)\Psi(\mathfrak{a}_1)\\
&+\frac{1}{n_1}\frac{1}{n_2}\sum_{\wp=1}^{n_2}\left[1-(s\ell)^{\wp}\right]\sum_{\wp=1}^{n_1}\left[1-(s(1-\ell))^{\wp}\right]\Phi(\mathfrak{a}_1)\Psi(\mathfrak{a}_2)\\
&+\frac{1}{n_1}\frac{1}{n_2}\sum_{\wp=1}^{n_1}\left[1-(s\ell)^{\wp}\right]\sum_{\wp=1}^{n_2}\left[1-(s\ell)^{\wp}\right]\Phi(\mathfrak{a}_1)\Psi(\mathfrak{a}_1)\\
&=\Delta_1(\ell)\Phi(\mathfrak{a}_2)\Psi(\mathfrak{a}_2)+\Delta_2(\ell)\Phi(\mathfrak{a}_2)\Psi(\mathfrak{a}_1)+\Delta_3(\ell)\Phi(\mathfrak{a}_1)\Psi(\mathfrak{a}_2)+\Delta_4(\ell)\Phi(\mathfrak{a}_1)\Psi(\mathfrak{a}_1).
\end{aligned}$$

This gives

$$\begin{aligned}
&\Phi\left(\frac{\mathfrak{a}_1\mathfrak{a}_2}{\ell\mathfrak{a}_1+(1-\ell)\mathfrak{a}_2}\right)\Psi\left(\frac{\mathfrak{a}_1\mathfrak{a}_2}{\ell\mathfrak{a}_1+(1-\ell)\mathfrak{a}_2}\right)\\
&\leq \Delta_1(\ell)\Phi(\mathfrak{a}_2)\Psi(\mathfrak{a}_2)+\Delta_2(\ell)\Phi(\mathfrak{a}_2)\Psi(\mathfrak{a}_1)+\Delta_3(\ell)\Phi(\mathfrak{a}_1)\Psi(\mathfrak{a}_2)+\Delta_4(\ell)\Phi(\mathfrak{a}_1)\Psi(\mathfrak{a}_1). \quad (24)
\end{aligned}$$

Similarly, we also have

$$\begin{aligned}
&\Phi\left(\frac{\mathfrak{a}_1\mathfrak{a}_2}{\ell\mathfrak{a}_2+(1-\ell)\mathfrak{a}_1}\right)\Psi\left(\frac{\mathfrak{a}_1\mathfrak{a}_2}{\ell\mathfrak{a}_2+(1-\ell)\mathfrak{a}_1}\right)\\
&\leq \Delta_1(\ell)\Phi(\mathfrak{a}_1)\Psi(\mathfrak{a}_1)+\Delta_2(\ell)\Phi(\mathfrak{a}_1)\Psi(\mathfrak{a}_2)+\Delta_3(\ell)\Phi(\mathfrak{a}_2)\Psi(\mathfrak{a}_1)+\Delta_4(\ell)\Phi(\mathfrak{a}_2)\Psi(\mathfrak{a}_2). \quad (25)
\end{aligned}$$

Adding (24) and (25)

$$\Phi\left(\frac{\mathfrak{a}_1\mathfrak{a}_2}{\ell\mathfrak{a}_1+(1-\ell)\mathfrak{a}_2}\right)\Psi\left(\frac{\mathfrak{a}_1\mathfrak{a}_2}{\ell\mathfrak{a}_1+(1-\ell)\mathfrak{a}_2}\right)+\Phi\left(\frac{\mathfrak{a}_1\mathfrak{a}_2}{\ell\mathfrak{a}_2+(1-\ell)\mathfrak{a}_1}\right)\Psi\left(\frac{\mathfrak{a}_1\mathfrak{a}_2}{\ell\mathfrak{a}_2+(1-\ell)\mathfrak{a}_1}\right)$$
$$\leq(\Phi(\mathfrak{a}_1)\Psi(\mathfrak{a}_1)+\Phi(\mathfrak{a}_2)\Psi(\mathfrak{a}_2))[\Delta_1(\ell)+\Delta_4(\ell)]$$
$$+(\Phi(\mathfrak{a}_1)\Psi(\mathfrak{a}_2)+\Phi(\mathfrak{a}_2)\Psi(\mathfrak{a}_1))[\Delta_2(\ell)+\Delta_3(\ell)].$$

Multiplying both sides of (17) by $\ell^{\frac{\lambda}{k}-1}$ and then integrating with respect to ℓ over [0,1], one obtains

$$k\Gamma_k(\lambda)\left(\frac{\mathfrak{a}_1\mathfrak{a}_2}{\mathfrak{a}_2-\mathfrak{a}_1}\right)^{\frac{\lambda}{k}}\left[{}_kI^{\lambda}_{(\frac{1}{\mathfrak{a}_2})^+}(\Phi\Psi\circ h)(\frac{1}{\mathfrak{a}_1})+{}_kI^{\lambda}_{(\frac{1}{\mathfrak{a}_1})^-}(\Phi\Psi\circ h)(\frac{1}{\mathfrak{a}_2})\right]$$
$$\int_0^1\ell^{\frac{\lambda}{k}-1}\Phi\left(\frac{\mathfrak{a}_1\mathfrak{a}_2}{\ell\mathfrak{a}_1+(1-\ell)\mathfrak{a}_2}\right)\Psi\left(\frac{\mathfrak{a}_1\mathfrak{a}_2}{\ell\mathfrak{a}_1+(1-\ell)\mathfrak{a}_2}\right)d\ell$$
$$+\int_0^1\ell^{\frac{\lambda}{k}-1}\Phi\left(\frac{\mathfrak{a}_1\mathfrak{a}_2}{\ell\mathfrak{a}_2+(1-\ell)\mathfrak{a}_1}\right)\Psi\left(\frac{\mathfrak{a}_1\mathfrak{a}_2}{\ell\mathfrak{a}_2+(1-\ell)\mathfrak{a}_1}\right)d\ell$$
$$\leq(\Phi(\mathfrak{a}_1)\Psi(\mathfrak{a}_1)+\Phi(\mathfrak{a}_2)\Psi(\mathfrak{a}_2))\int_0^1\ell^{\frac{\lambda}{k}-1}[\Delta_1(\ell)+\Delta_4(\ell)]d\ell$$
$$+(\Phi(\mathfrak{a}_1)\Psi(\mathfrak{a}_2)+\Phi(\mathfrak{a}_2)\Psi(\mathfrak{a}_1))\int_0^1\ell^{\frac{\lambda}{k}-1}[\Delta_2(\ell)+\Delta_3(\ell)]d\ell$$
$$=D(\mathfrak{a}_1,\mathfrak{a}_2)\int_0^1\ell^{\frac{\lambda}{k}-1}[\Delta_1(\ell)+\Delta_4(\ell)]d\ell+F(\mathfrak{a}_1,\mathfrak{a}_2)\int_0^1\ell^{\frac{\lambda}{k}-1}[\Delta_2(\ell)+\Delta_3(\ell)]d\ell.$$

Hence, the proof is completed. □

Corollary 4. *Suppose $\Phi,\Psi\colon S\to\mathbb{R}^+$ are functions such that $\Phi\Psi\in\mathcal{L}[\mathfrak{a}_1,\mathfrak{a}_2]$ and $\mathfrak{a}_1,\mathfrak{a}_2>0$, $\mathfrak{a}_1,\mathfrak{a}_2\in S$. If Φ and Ψ are n_1-polynomial harmonically s-type convex functions, then the following fractional inequality holds:*

$$\left(\frac{\mathfrak{a}_1\mathfrak{a}_2}{\mathfrak{a}_2-\mathfrak{a}_1}\right)^{\frac{\lambda}{k}}\left[{}_kI^{\lambda}_{(\frac{1}{\mathfrak{a}_2})^+}(\Phi\Psi\circ h)(\frac{1}{\mathfrak{a}_1})+{}_kI^{\lambda}_{(\frac{1}{\mathfrak{a}_1})^-}(\Phi\Psi\circ h)(\frac{1}{\mathfrak{a}_2})\right]$$
$$\leq\frac{D(\mathfrak{a}_1,\mathfrak{a}_2)}{\Gamma_k(\lambda)}\left[\frac{1+(1-s)^2}{\lambda}+\frac{2s^2}{\lambda+2k}-\frac{2s^2}{\lambda+k}\right]+\frac{F(\mathfrak{a}_1,\mathfrak{a}_2)}{\Gamma_k(\lambda)}\left[\frac{2(1-s)}{\lambda}+\frac{2s^2}{\lambda+k}-\frac{2s^2}{\lambda+2k}\right].$$

Proof. Let $n_1=n_2=1$ $\quad\Delta_1(\ell)=[1-s(1-\ell)]^2$, $\Delta_4(\ell)=[1-s\ell]^2$ and $\Delta_3(\ell)=\Delta_4(\ell)=[(1-s)+s^2(\ell-\ell^2)]$.

The result follows using Theorem 10. □

Remark 9. *If we put $s=1$ in Corollary 4, then Corollary 2 [18] is recovered.*

Theorem 11. *Suppose $\Phi,\Psi\colon \mathrm{S}\to\mathbb{R}^+$ be functions such that $\Phi\Psi\in\mathcal{L}[\mathfrak{a}_1,\mathfrak{a}_2]$ with $\mathfrak{a}_1,\mathfrak{a}_2>0$ and $\mathfrak{a}_1,\mathfrak{a}_2\in\mathrm{S}$. If Φ is n_1-polynomial harmonically s-type convex function, Ψ is n_2-polynomial harmonically s-type convex function and $\lambda,k>0$. Then the following fractional inequality holds:*

$$\frac{n_1n_2}{\sum_{\wp=1}^{n_1}[1-(\frac{2}{s})]\sum_{\wp=1}^{n_2}[1-(\frac{2}{s})]}\Phi\left(\frac{2\mathfrak{a}_1\mathfrak{a}_2}{\mathfrak{a}_1+\mathfrak{a}_2}\right)\Psi\left(\frac{2\mathfrak{a}_1\mathfrak{a}_2}{\mathfrak{a}_1+\mathfrak{a}_2}\right)$$
$$\leq\Gamma_k(\lambda+k)\left(\frac{\mathfrak{a}_1\mathfrak{a}_2}{\mathfrak{a}_2-\mathfrak{a}_1}\right)^{\frac{\lambda}{k}}\left[{}_kI^{\lambda}_{(\frac{1}{\mathfrak{a}_2})^+}(\Phi\Psi\circ h)(\frac{1}{\mathfrak{a}_1})+{}_kI^{\lambda}_{(\frac{1}{\mathfrak{a}_1})^-}(\Phi\Psi\circ h)(\frac{1}{\mathfrak{a}_2})\right]$$
$$+\frac{\lambda}{k}\int_{0^1}\ell^{\frac{\lambda}{k}-1}\Big\{[\Lambda_{n_1}(\ell)\bar{\Lambda}_{n_2}(\ell)+\bar{\Lambda}_{n_1}(\ell)\Lambda_{n_2}(\ell)]D(\mathfrak{a}_1,\mathfrak{a}_2)$$
$$+[\Lambda_{n_1}(\ell)\Lambda_{n_2}(\ell)+\bar{\Lambda}_{n_1}(\ell)\bar{\Lambda}_{n_2}(\ell)]F(\mathfrak{a}_1,\mathfrak{a}_2)\Big\}d\ell,$$

where h is defined as in Theorem 9, $\Lambda_n = \frac{1}{n}\sum_{\wp=1}^{n}[1-(s(1-\ell))^{\wp}]$ *and* $\bar{\Lambda}_n = \frac{1}{n}\sum_{\wp=1}^{n}[1-(s\ell)^{\wp}]$.

Proof. Please note that $\bar{\Lambda}_n\left(\frac{1}{2}\right) = \Lambda_n\left(\frac{1}{2}\right) = E_n = \frac{\sum_{\wp=1}^{n}\left[1-\left(\frac{s}{2}\right)^{\wp}\right]}{n}$.

Now, let $\ell \in [0,1]$, hence from (10), one obtains

$$\Phi\left(\frac{2\mathfrak{a}_1\mathfrak{a}_2}{\mathfrak{a}_1+\mathfrak{a}_2}\right) \le E_{n_1}\left\{\Phi\left(\frac{\mathfrak{a}_1\mathfrak{a}_2}{\ell\mathfrak{a}_1+(1-\ell)\mathfrak{a}_2}\right)+\Phi\left(\frac{\mathfrak{a}_1\mathfrak{a}_2}{\ell\mathfrak{a}_2+(1-\ell)\mathfrak{a}_1}\right)\right\},$$

and

$$\Psi\left(\frac{2\mathfrak{a}_1\mathfrak{a}_2}{\mathfrak{a}_1+\mathfrak{a}_2}\right) \le E_{n_2}\left\{\Psi\left(\frac{\mathfrak{a}_1\mathfrak{a}_2}{\ell\mathfrak{a}_1+(1-\ell)\mathfrak{a}_2}\right)+\Psi\left(\frac{\mathfrak{a}_1\mathfrak{a}_2}{\ell\mathfrak{a}_2+(1-\ell)\mathfrak{a}_1}\right)\right\}.$$

Now,

$$\begin{aligned}
&\Phi\left(\frac{2\mathfrak{a}_1\mathfrak{a}_2}{\mathfrak{a}_1+\mathfrak{a}_2}\right)\Psi\left(\frac{2\mathfrak{a}_1\mathfrak{a}_2}{\mathfrak{a}_1+\mathfrak{a}_2}\right)\\
&\le E_{n_1}E_{n_2}\left\{\Phi\left(\frac{\mathfrak{a}_1\mathfrak{a}_2}{\ell\mathfrak{a}_1+(1-\ell)\mathfrak{a}_2}\right)\Psi\left(\frac{\mathfrak{a}_1\mathfrak{a}_2}{\ell\mathfrak{a}_1+(1-\ell)\mathfrak{a}_2}\right)\right.\\
&\left.+\Phi\left(\frac{\mathfrak{a}_1\mathfrak{a}_2}{\ell\mathfrak{a}_2+(1-\ell)\mathfrak{a}_1}\right)\Psi\left(\frac{\mathfrak{a}_1\mathfrak{a}_2}{\ell\mathfrak{a}_2+(1-\ell)\mathfrak{a}_1}\right)\right\}\\
&+E_{n_1}E_{n_2}\left\{\Phi\left(\frac{\mathfrak{a}_1\mathfrak{a}_2}{\ell\mathfrak{a}_1+(1-\ell)\mathfrak{a}_2}\right)\Psi\left(\frac{\mathfrak{a}_1\mathfrak{a}_2}{\ell\mathfrak{a}_2+(1-\ell)\mathfrak{a}_1}\right)\right.\\
&\left.+\Phi\left(\frac{\mathfrak{a}_1\mathfrak{a}_2}{\ell\mathfrak{a}_2+(1-\ell)\mathfrak{a}_1}\right)\Psi\left(\frac{\mathfrak{a}_1\mathfrak{a}_2}{\ell\mathfrak{a}_1+(1-\ell)\mathfrak{a}_2}\right)\right\}\\
&\le E_{n_1}E_{n_2}\left\{\Phi\left(\frac{\mathfrak{a}_1\mathfrak{a}_2}{\ell\mathfrak{a}_1+(1-\ell)\mathfrak{a}_2}\right)\Psi\left(\frac{\mathfrak{a}_1\mathfrak{a}_2}{\ell\mathfrak{a}_1+(1-\ell)\mathfrak{a}_2}\right)\right.\\
&\left.+\Phi\left(\frac{\mathfrak{a}_1\mathfrak{a}_2}{\ell\mathfrak{a}_2+(1-\ell)\mathfrak{a}_1}\right)\Psi\left(\frac{\mathfrak{a}_1\mathfrak{a}_2}{\ell\mathfrak{a}_2+(1-\ell)\mathfrak{a}_1}\right)\right\}\\
&+E_{n_1}E_{n_2}\left\{[\Lambda_{n_1}(\ell)\Phi(\mathfrak{a}_2)+\bar{\Lambda}_{n_1}(\ell)\Phi(\mathfrak{a}_2)][\Lambda_{n_2}(\ell)\Psi(\mathfrak{a}_1)+\bar{\Lambda}_{n_2}(\ell)\Psi(\mathfrak{a}_2)]\right.\\
&\left.+[\Lambda_{n_1}(\ell)\Phi(\mathfrak{a}_1)+\bar{\Lambda}_{n_1}(\ell)\Phi(\mathfrak{a}_2)][\Lambda_{n_2}(\ell)\Psi(\mathfrak{a}_2)+\bar{\Lambda}_{n_2}(\ell)\Psi(\mathfrak{a}_1)]\right\}\\
&=E_{n_1}E_{n_2}\left\{\Phi\left(\frac{\mathfrak{a}_1\mathfrak{a}_2}{\ell\mathfrak{a}_1+(1-\ell)\mathfrak{a}_2}\right)\Psi\left(\frac{\mathfrak{a}_1\mathfrak{a}_2}{\ell\mathfrak{a}_1+(1-\ell)\mathfrak{a}_2}\right)\right.\\
&\left.+\Phi\left(\frac{\mathfrak{a}_1\mathfrak{a}_2}{\ell\mathfrak{a}_2+(1-\ell)\mathfrak{a}_1}\right)\Psi\left(\frac{\mathfrak{a}_1\mathfrak{a}_2}{\ell\mathfrak{a}_2+(1-\ell)\mathfrak{a}}\right)\right\}\\
&+E_{n_1}E_{n_2}\left\{[\Lambda_{n_1}(\ell)\bar{\Lambda}_{n_2}(\ell)+\bar{\Lambda}_{n_1}(\ell)\Lambda_{n_2}(\ell)]D(\mathfrak{a}_1,\mathfrak{a}_2)\right.\\
&\left.+[\Lambda_{n_1}(\ell)\Lambda_{n_2}(\ell)+\bar{\Lambda}_{n_1}(\ell)\bar{\Lambda}_{n_2}(\ell)]F(\mathfrak{a}_1,\mathfrak{a}_2)\right\}.
\end{aligned}$$

Consequently, we have

$$\begin{aligned}
\Phi\left(\frac{2\mathfrak{a}_1\mathfrak{a}_2}{\mathfrak{a}_1+\mathfrak{a}_2}\right)\Psi\left(\frac{2\mathfrak{a}_1\mathfrak{a}_2}{\mathfrak{a}_1+\mathfrak{a}_2}\right) &\le E_{n_1}E_{n_2}\left\{\Phi\left(\frac{\mathfrak{a}_1\mathfrak{a}_2}{\ell\mathfrak{a}_1+(1-\ell)\mathfrak{a}_2}\right)\Psi\left(\frac{\mathfrak{a}_1\mathfrak{a}_2}{\ell\mathfrak{a}_1+(1-\ell)\mathfrak{a}_2}\right)\right.\\
&\left.+\Phi\left(\frac{\mathfrak{a}_1\mathfrak{a}_2}{\ell\mathfrak{a}_2+(1-\ell)\mathfrak{a}_1}\right)\Psi\left(\frac{\mathfrak{a}_1\mathfrak{a}_2}{\ell\mathfrak{a}_2+(1-\ell)\mathfrak{a}_1}\right)\right\}\\
&+E_{n_1}E_{n_2}\left\{[\Lambda_{n_1}(\ell)\bar{\Lambda}_{n_2}(\ell)+\bar{\Lambda}_{n_1}(\ell)\Lambda_{n_2}(\ell)]D(\mathfrak{a}_1,\mathfrak{a}_2)\right.\\
&\left.+[\Lambda_{n_1}(\ell)\Lambda_{n_2}(\ell)+\bar{\Lambda}_{n_1}(\ell)\bar{\Lambda}_{n_2}(\ell)]F(\mathfrak{a}_1,\mathfrak{a}_2)\right\}. \quad (26)
\end{aligned}$$

Multiplying both sides of (26) by $\ell^{\frac{\lambda}{k}-1}$ and integrating the resulting inequality with respect to ℓ over $[0,1]$ one has

$$\begin{aligned}
&\frac{k}{\lambda}\Phi\left(\frac{2\mathfrak{a}_1\mathfrak{a}_2}{\mathfrak{a}_1+\mathfrak{a}_2}\right)\Psi\left(\frac{2\mathfrak{a}_1\mathfrak{a}_2}{\mathfrak{a}_1+\mathfrak{a}_2}\right)\\
&=\int_0^1 \ell^{\frac{\lambda}{k}-1}\Phi\left(\frac{2\mathfrak{a}_1\mathfrak{a}_2}{\mathfrak{a}_1+\mathfrak{a}_2}\right)\Psi\left(\frac{2\mathfrak{a}_1\mathfrak{a}_2}{\mathfrak{a}_1+\mathfrak{a}_2}\right)\\
&\leq E_{n_1}E_{n_2}\int_0^1 \ell^{\frac{\lambda}{k}-1}\left\{\Phi\left(\frac{\mathfrak{a}_1\mathfrak{a}_2}{\ell\mathfrak{a}_1+(1-\ell)\mathfrak{a}_2}\right)\Psi\left(\frac{\mathfrak{a}_1\mathfrak{a}_2}{\ell\mathfrak{a}_1+(1-\ell)\mathfrak{a}_2}\right)\right.\\
&\left.+\Phi\left(\frac{\mathfrak{a}_1\mathfrak{a}_2}{\ell\mathfrak{a}_2+(1-\ell)\mathfrak{a}_1}\right)\Psi\left(\frac{\mathfrak{a}_1\mathfrak{a}_2}{\ell\mathfrak{a}_2+(1-\ell)\mathfrak{a}_1}\right)\right\}\\
&+E_{n_1}E_{n_2}\int_0^1 \ell^{\frac{\lambda}{k}-1}\Big\{[\Lambda_{n_1}(\ell)\bar{\Lambda}_{n_2}(\ell)+\bar{\Lambda}_{n_1}(\ell)\Lambda_{n_2}(\ell)]D(\mathfrak{a}_1,\mathfrak{a}_2)\\
&+[\Lambda_{n_1}(\ell)\Lambda_{n_2}(\ell)+\bar{\Lambda}_{n_1}(\ell)\bar{\Lambda}_{n_2}(\ell)]F(\mathfrak{a}_1,\mathfrak{a}_2)\Big\}.\\
&=E_{n_1}E_{n_2}\left\{k\Gamma_k(\lambda)\left(\frac{\mathfrak{a}_1\mathfrak{a}_2}{\mathfrak{a}_2-\mathfrak{a}_1}\right)^{\frac{\lambda}{k}}\left[{}_kI^{\lambda}_{(\frac{1}{\mathfrak{a}_2})^+}(\Phi\Psi\circ h)(\frac{1}{\mathfrak{a}_1})+{}_kI^{\lambda}_{(\frac{1}{\mathfrak{a}_1})^-}(\Phi\Psi\circ h)(\frac{1}{\mathfrak{a}_2})\right]\right\}\\
&+E_{n_1}E_{n_2}\int_{0^1} \ell^{\frac{\lambda}{k}-1}\Big\{[\Lambda_{n_1}(\ell)\bar{\Lambda}_{n_2}(\ell)+\bar{\Lambda}_{n_1}(\ell)\Lambda_{n_2}(\ell)]D(\mathfrak{a}_1,\mathfrak{a}_2)\\
&+[\Lambda_{n_1}(\ell)\Lambda_{n_2}(\ell)+\bar{\Lambda}_{n_1}(\ell)\bar{\Lambda}_{n_2}(\ell)]F(\mathfrak{a}_1,\mathfrak{a}_2)\Big\}d\ell.
\end{aligned}$$

The required result follows. □

Corollary 5. *Let $\Phi,\Psi : S \to \mathbb{R}^+$ be two functions such that $\Phi\Psi \in \mathcal{L}[\mathfrak{a}_1,\mathfrak{a}_2]$ and $\mathfrak{a}_1,\mathfrak{a}_2 > 0$, $\mathfrak{a}_1,\mathfrak{a}_2 \in S$. If Φ and Ψ are n_1-polynomial harmonically s-type convex functions with $\lambda, k > 0$, then*

$$\begin{aligned}
&\Phi\left(\frac{2\mathfrak{a}_1\mathfrak{a}_2}{\mathfrak{a}_1+\mathfrak{a}_2}\right)\Psi\left(\frac{2\mathfrak{a}_1\mathfrak{a}_2}{\mathfrak{a}_1+\mathfrak{a}_2}\right)\\
&\leq\left(1-\frac{s}{2}\right)\Gamma_k(\lambda+k)\left(\frac{\mathfrak{a}_1\mathfrak{a}_2}{\mathfrak{a}_2-\mathfrak{a}_1}\right)^{\frac{\lambda}{k}}\left[{}_kI^{\lambda}_{(\frac{1}{\mathfrak{a}_2})^+}(\Phi\Psi\circ h)(\frac{1}{\mathfrak{a}_1})+{}_kI^{\lambda}_{(\frac{1}{\mathfrak{a}_1})^-}(\Phi\Psi\circ h)(\frac{1}{\mathfrak{a}_2})\right]\\
&+\left(1-\frac{s}{2}\right)^2\left\{\left[2(1-s)+\frac{2s^2\lambda}{\lambda+k}-\frac{2s^2\lambda}{\lambda+2k}\right]D(\mathfrak{a}_1,\mathfrak{a}_2)\right.\\
&\left.+\left[(1+(1-s))^2-\frac{2s^2\lambda}{\lambda+k}+\frac{2s^2\lambda}{\lambda+2k}\right]F(\mathfrak{a}_1,\mathfrak{a}_2)\right\}.
\end{aligned}$$

Proof. Let $n_1 = n_2 = 1$, then $\Lambda_{n_1}(\ell) = \Lambda_{n_2}(\ell) = 1 - s(1-\ell)$ and $\bar{\Lambda}_{n_1}(\ell) = \bar{\Lambda}_{n_2}(\ell) = 1 - s\ell$. The intended result follows using Theorem 11. □

Remark 10. *If we put $s = 1$ in Corollary 5, then we obtain Corollary 3 [18].*

5. Conclusions and Future Scope

As per recent trends, incorporating different fractional operators into the theory of inequalities is a new area of interest among several researchers. Several mathematicians have worked on the generalizations of some well-known inequalities to offer new bounds and new applications using new methods. In this manuscript:

(1) We presented and concentrated several fractional inequalities of the Caputo–Fabrizio operator for an n-polynomial s-type convex function and k-Riemann–Liouville fractional integral operator for an n-polynomial harmonically s-type convex function.

(2) New version of Hermite–Hadamard inequality and Pachpatte-type inequality are obtained via Caputo–Fabrizio fractional integral operators.

(3) Some special cases of the presented results have been in the form of corollaries and remarks.

In the future, we intend to generalize the theory of inequality for concepts such as interval-valued analysis, quantum calculus, fuzzy interval-valued calculus and time-scale calculus.

Author Contributions: Conceptualization, M.T. and A.A.S.; Data curation, O.M.A. and S.K.N.; Formal analysis, M.T.; Funding acquisition, K.N.; Investigation, S.K.N.; Methodology, K.N. and S.K.N.; Resources, M.T. and O.M.A.; Software, M.T. and K.N.; Supervision, K.N.; Validation, A.A.S. and S.K.N.; Visualization, M.T.; Writing—original draft, M.T.; Writing—review and editing, M.T. and O.M.A. All authors have read and agreed to the published version of the manuscript.

Funding: This research was supported by the Fundamental Fund of Khon Kaen University, Thailand.

Data Availability Statement: Not applicable.

Acknowledgments: The authors would like to thank the Khon Kaen University, Thailand.

Conflicts of Interest: The authors declare no conflict of interest.

References

1. Jensen, J.L.W.V. Sur les fonctions convexes et les inegalites entre les valeurs moyennes. *Acta Math.* **1905**, *30*, 175–193. [CrossRef]
2. Niculescu, C.P.; Persson, L.E. *Convex Functions and Their Applications*; Springer: New York, NY, USA, 2006.
3. Hadamard, J. Étude sur les propriétés des fonctions entiéres en particulier d'une fonction considérée par Riemann. *J. Math. Pures Appl.* **1893**, *58*, 171–215.
4. İşcan, İ. Hermite-Hadamard type inequalities for harmonically convex functions. *Hacet. J. Math. Stat.* **2014**, *43*, 935–942. [CrossRef]
5. Dragomir, S.S.; Agarwal, R.P. Two inequalities for differentiable mappings and applications to special means fo real numbers and to trapezoidal formula. *Appl. Math. Lett.* **1998**, *11*, 91–95 [CrossRef]
6. Xi, B.Y.; Qi, F. Some integral inequalities of Hermite–Hadamard type for convex functions with applications to means. *J. Funct. Spaces. Appl.* **2012**, *2012*, 980438. [CrossRef]
7. Kirmaci, U.S.; Özdemir, M.E. On some inequalities for differentiable mappings and applications to special means of real numbers and to midpoint formula. *Appl. Math. Comput.* **2004**, *153*, 361–368. [CrossRef]
8. Hudzik, H.; Maligranda, L. Some remarks on *s*–convex functions. *Aequationes Math.* **1994**, *1994*, 48100–48111.
9. Dragomir, S.S.; Fitzpatrik, S. The Hadamard inequality for *s*–convex functions in the second sense. *Demonstr. Math.* **1999**, *32*, 687–696. [CrossRef]
10. Özcan, S.; İşcan, İ. Some new Hermite-Hadamard type integral inequalities for the *s*–convex functions and theirs applications. *J. Inequal. Appl.* **2019**, *201*, 201. [CrossRef]
11. Srivastava, H.M.; Sahoo, S.K.; Mohammed, P.O.; Baleanu, D.; Kodamasingh, B. Hermite–Hadamard Type Inequalities for Interval-Valued Preinvex Functions via Fractional Integral Operators. *Int. J. Comput. Intell. Syst.* **2022**, *15*, 8. [CrossRef]
12. Toplu, T.; Kadakal, M.; İşcan, İ. On n-polynomial convexity and some relatd inequalities. *AIMS Math.* **2020**, *5*, 1304–1318. [CrossRef]
13. Awan, M.U.; Akhtar, N.; Iftikhar, S.; Noor, M.A.; Chu, Y.M. New Hermite?Hadamard type inequalities for n-polynomial harmonically convex functions. *J. Inequl. Appl.* **2020**, *2020*, 125. [CrossRef]
14. Rashid, S.; İşcan, İ.; Baleanu, D.; Chu, Y.M. Generation of new fractional inequalities via n–polynomials s–type convexity with applications. *Adv. Differ. Equ.* **2020**, *2020*, 264. [CrossRef]
15. Sarikaya, M.Z.; Set, E.; Yaldiz, H.; Başak, N. Hermite–Hadamard inequalities for fractional integrals and related fractional inequalities. *Math. Comput. Model.* **2013**, *57*, 2403–2407. [CrossRef]
16. Gürbüz, M.; Akdemir, A.O.; Rashid, S.; Set, E. Hermite-Hadamard inequality for fractional integrals of Caputo-Fabrizio type and related inequalities. *J. Inequl. Appl.* **2020**, *2020*, 172. [CrossRef]
17. Abdeljawad, T.; Baleanu, D. On fractional derivatives with exponential kernel and their discrete versions. *Rep. Math. Phys.* **2017**, *80*, 11–27. [CrossRef]
18. Nwaeze, E.R.; Khan, M.A.; Ahmadian, A.; Ahmad, M.N.; Mahmood, A.K. Fractional inequalities of the Hermite-Hadamard type for m-polynomial convex and harmonically convex functions. *AIMS Math.* **2021**, *6*, 1889–1904. [CrossRef]
19. Sahoo, S.K.; Ahmad, H.; Tariq, M.; Kodamasingh, B.; Aydi, H.; De la Sen, M. Hermite-Hadamard type inequalities involving k-fractional operator for $(\bar{h}, m)$-convex functions. *Symmetry* **2021**, *13*, 1686. [CrossRef]
20. Abdeljawad, T.; Rashid, S.; Hammouch, Z.; Chu, Y.M. Some new local fractional inequalities associated with generalized (s, m)-convex functions and applications. *Adv. Differ. Equ.* **2020**, *2020*, 406. [CrossRef]
21. Sahoo, S.K.; Tariq, M.; Ahmad, H.; Nasir, J.; Aydi, H.; Mukheimer, A. New Ostrowski-type fractional integral inequalities via generalized exponential-type convex functions and applications. *Symmetry* **2021**, *13*, 1429. [CrossRef]
22. Tariq, M.; Sahoo, S.K.; Nasir, J.; Aydi, H.; Alsamir, H. Some Ostrowski type inequalities via n-polynomial exponentially s-convex functions and their applications. *AIMS Math.* **2021**, *6*, 13272–13290. [CrossRef]

23. Ali, S.; Mubeen, S.; Ali, R.S.; Rahman, G.; Morsy, A.; Nisar, K.S.; Purohit, S.D.; Zakarya, M. Dynamical significance of generalized fractional integral inequalities via convexity. *AIMS Math.* **2021**, *6*, 9705–9730. [CrossRef]
24. Akdemir, A.O.; Butt, S.I.; Nadeem, M.; Alessandra, M. Some new integral inequalities for a general variant of polynomial convex functions. *AIMS Math.* **2022**, *7*, 20461–20489. [CrossRef]
25. Kizil, S.; Ardic, M.A. Inequalities for strongly convex functions via Atangana-Baleanu Integral Operators. *Turk. J. Sci.* **2021**, *6*, 96–109.
26. Caputo, M.; Fabrizio, M. A new definition of fractional derivative without singular kernel. *Prog. Fract. Differ. Appl.* **2015**, *1*, 73–85.
27. Wu, S.; Iqbal, S.; Aamir, M.; Samraiz, M.; Younus, A. On some Hermite-Hadamard inequalities involving k-fractional operators. *J. Ineq. Appl.* **2021**, *2021*, 32. [CrossRef]
28. Mubeen, S.; Habibullah, G.M. k-Fractional integrals and application. *Int. J. Contemp. Math. Sci.* **2012**, *7*, 89–94.

axioms

MDPI

Article

Variational Iteration Method for Solving Fractional Integro-Differential Equations with Conformable Differointegration

Mondher Damak [1] and Zaid Amer Mohammed [2,*]

[1] Faculty of Sciences of Sfax, University of Sfax, P.O. Box 1171, Sfax 3000, Tunisia; mondher_damak@yahoo.com
[2] Economic and Administration College, Al-Iraqia University, Baghdad 10071, Iraq
* Correspondence: zaid.amer84@yahoo.com

Abstract: Multidimensional integro-differential equations are obtained when the unknown function of several independent variable and/or its derivatives appear under an integral sign. When the differentiation or integration operators or both are of fractional order, the integral equation in this case is called a multidimensional fractional integro-differential equation. Such equations are difficult to solve analytically; therefore, as the main objective of this paper, an approximate method—which is the variational iteration method—will be used to solve this type of equation with conformable fractional-order derivatives and integrals. First, we drive the iterative sequence of approximate solutions using the proposed method, and then, under certain conditions over the kernel of the integro-differential equation, prove its convergence to the exact solution. Two illustrative examples, linear and nonlinear, are given, and their approximated solutions are simulated using computer programs in order to verify from the reliability and applicability of the proposed method.

Keywords: multidimensional integro-differential equations; conformable fractional diffrointegrations; variational iteration method; convergence of the iterative method; general Lagrange multiplier

Citation: Damak, M.; Mohammed, Z.A. Variational Iteration Method for Solving Fractional Integro-Differential Equations with Conformable Differointegration. *Axioms* **2022**, *11*, 586. https://doi.org/10.3390/axioms11110586

Academic Editor: Clemente Cesarano

Received: 8 September 2022
Accepted: 15 October 2022
Published: 24 October 2022

1. Introduction

Recently, fractional differential equations, fractional calculus and fractional differential integral equations became highly important in several branches of science and engineering because many mathematical models are used to formulate different phenomena, such as mechanics, physics, chemical kinetics, astronomy, biology, economics, potential theory and electrostatistics, which are modeled using integro-differential equations [1–6]. In 2016, Shi [7] introduced a formula of mild solutions for impulsive fractional evolution equations.

Many academic researchers continue to be interested in the use of fractional differential equations and/or integral equations, which are based on the development and applications of fractional calculus [8,9]. Nonlinear fractional integral equations and integro-differential equations are notoriously difficult to solve analytically. Moreover, accurate solutions for these equations are extremely rare. As a result, various authors have taken an interest in numerically solving these problems, particularly after the big revolution in computer application. Among the techniques used to solve integro-differential equations are the multi-step methods [10], Adomian decomposition method (ADM) [11], homotopy perturbation method (HPM) [12–14], homotopy analysis method (HAM) [15], variational iteration method (VIM) [16] and so on.

The VIM has been successfully applied to solve many problems in different fields of mathematics and its applications. For example, He was the first researcher to propose the use of VIM to solve linear and nonlinear differential and integral equations [17]. In 1998, He used VIM to solve the classical Blasius equation, ref. [18] and in 1999, he provided the approximate solutions for some well-known nonlinear problems [19]. In 2000, He used the VIM to solve autonomous ordinary differential equations. Moreover, in 2006, Soliman applied the VIM to solve the kdv-Burger's and Lax's seventh-order kdv equations. In the same year, VIM was applied by Abulwafa and Momani [20] to solve a nonlinear coagulation problem with mass loss and Odibat et al. employed the VIM to solve nonlinear differential equations of fractional order in 2006. In 2006, the VIM was also utilised by Bildiki et al. to solve a variety of problems, including nonlinear partial differential equations, Dehghan and Tateri's Fokker–Plank equation and quadratic Riccati differential equations with constant coefficients. Wang [21] used the VIM to solve integro-differential equations in 2009, while Sweilam used the VIM to solve both linear and nonlinear boundary value problems of the fourth-order integro-differential equations.

In 2009, Wen-Hua Wang used the VIM to solve certain types of fractional integro-differential equations [21]. In 2011, Muhammet and Adin used the VIM to solve the problem of nonlinear fractional integro-differential equations [20].

If an exact solution exists, the VIM provides rapidly convergent consecutive approximations to the precise solution; otherwise, a few approximations might be employed for numerical results.

In this paper, we shall present the VIM used to solve integro–differential equations with conformable fractional order differointegration of the form:

$$T_x^{\alpha} u(x,y) = g(x,y) + I_x^{\beta} I_y^{\gamma} K(x,y,s,t,u(x,y)) \tag{1}$$

where K is given continuous function, $0 < \alpha \leq 1$, $\beta, \gamma > 0$, $x, y \in [a,b] \times [c,d]$ here, T^{α} is understood as a conformable fractional derivative of order α, while I^{β} and I^{γ} stands for conformable fractional-order integrals of order β and γ, respectively.

2. Main Concepts of Factional Calculus

Among the most important definitions of fractional-order derivatives or integrals which will be used next in this paper is the conformable type, which is more simple than other definitions and more stable in comparison with the nonfractional (or integer order) derivatives and integrals.

Definition 1 (Conformable Fractional-Order Derivative [22]**).** *Given a function $f : [a,\infty) \to \mathbb{R}$, then the left conformable fractional derivative of order α can be defined as:*

$$(T_{\alpha}^{a}(f))(x) = \lim_{\varepsilon \to 0} \frac{f(x + \varepsilon(x-a)^{1-\alpha}) - f(x)}{\varepsilon}$$

for all $x > 0, \alpha \in (0,1]$. When $a = 0$, we write T_{α}. If $(T_{\alpha}^{a}(f))(x)$ exist on the interval (a,b), then define:

$$(T_{\alpha}^{a}(f))(a) = \lim_{x \to a^{+}} f^{(\alpha)}(x)$$

The right conformable fractional derivative of order $\alpha \in (0,1]$ terminating at b of f, is defined by:

$${}_{\alpha}^{b}T(f)(x) = \lim \frac{f(x + \varepsilon(b-x)^{1-\alpha}) - f(x)}{\varepsilon}$$

If ${}_{\alpha}^{b}(T(f)(x))$ exist on the interval (a,b), then define:

$${}_{\alpha}^{b}(T(f))(b) = \lim_{x \to b^{-}} {}^{b}T_{\alpha}(f)(x)$$

Definition 2 (Conformable Fractional-Order Integral [23]**).** *Given a continuous function $f : [a,\infty) \to R$, then the left conformable fractional integral of order α of f is:*

$$(I_{\alpha}^{a}(f))(x) = \int_a^x f(s) d\alpha(s,a) = \int_a^x \frac{f(s)}{(s-a)^{1-\alpha}} ds \tag{2}$$

where the integral is considered as the usual Riemann improper integral and $a \geq 0$. *On the other hand, in the right case, we have:*

$$ {}^{b}_{\alpha}I_x(f)(x) = \int_x^b f(s)d\alpha(b,s) = \int_x^b \frac{f(s)}{(b-s)^{1-\alpha}}ds \tag{3}$$

Among some different properties concerning fractional integrals and derivative which are very useful in applications are the following, where T^α and I^α refer to fractional-order conformable and integral, respectively:

1. $T^\alpha(c_1f + bc_2) = c_1T^\alpha(f) + c_2T^\alpha(g)$, for all $c_1, c_2 \in \mathbb{R}$.
2. $T^\alpha(c_1f + c_2g) = c_1T^\alpha f + c_2T^\alpha g$.
3. $T^\alpha(c_1f + bc_2) = c_1T^\alpha(f) + c_2T^\alpha(g)$, for all $c_1, c_2 \in \mathbb{R}$.
4. $T^\alpha(x^p) = px^{p-\alpha}$, for all $p \in \mathbb{R}$.
5. $T^\alpha(\lambda) = 0$, for all constant functions $f(x) = \lambda$.
6. $T^\alpha(fg) = fT^\alpha(g) + gT^\alpha(f)$
7. $T^\alpha\left(\frac{f}{g}\right) = \frac{gT^\alpha(f) - fT^\alpha(g)}{g^2}, g \neq 0$.
8. If, in addition, f is differentiable, then $T^\alpha(f)(x) = x^{1-\alpha}\frac{df}{dt}(x)$.
9. $T^a_{\alpha x}I^a_\alpha(f)(x) = f(x)$, for $x > a$, where f is any continuous function in the domain of I^a_α and ${}^{b}_{\alpha}T^b_\alpha I_x(f)(x) = f(x)$, for $x < b$, where f is any continuous function in the domain of ${}^{b}_{\alpha}I$.

3. Variational Iteration Method

The essential aspect of the VIM, as previously stated in the literature, is that the solution of a mathematical problem under the linearization assumption is utilized as a starting approximation or trial function for the next successive approximate solution to the problem under certain conditions [2].

Consider the following general nonlinear equation in operator form to demonstrate the VIM's essential concept [3]:

$$Au(x) = g(x) \tag{4}$$

and suppose that Equation (1) may be decomposed as:

$$L(u(x)) + N(u(x)) = g(x), x \in [a,b] \tag{5}$$

where A is any operator that may be decomposed into linear and nonlinear operators L and N, respectively, and $g(x)$ is any function that is referred to as the nonhomogeneous term. Equation (5) may be solved iteratively using the VIM by using the correction functional defined by:

$$u_{n+1}(x) = u_n(x) + \int_{x_a}^{a} \lambda(x,s)\{L(u_n(s) + N(\tilde{u}_n(s)) - g(s)\}ds, n = 0,1,\ldots \tag{6}$$

where λ is the general Lagrange multiplier that may ideally be discovered using variational theory the nth approximation of the subscript n denotes the solution u, and $\tilde{u}_n$ is considered a restricted variation, i.e., $\delta\tilde{u}_n = 0$ where the δ is the first variation [3].

4. Applications of the Vim for Multidimensional Integro-Differential Equations of Fractional Order

Consider the fractional integro-differential Equation (1), which may be written as:

$$T^\alpha_x u(x,y) - I^\beta_x I^\gamma_y K(x,y,s,t,u(s,t)) - g(x,y) = 0 \tag{7}$$

Multiplying Equation (7) by a general Lagrange multiplier λ, yields to:

$$\lambda(s,t)\{T^\alpha_x u(x,y) - I^\beta_x I^\gamma_y K(x,y,s,t,u(s,t)) - g(x,y)\} = 0 \tag{8}$$

Now, take I_x^α to both sides of Equation (8), which give:

$$I_x^\alpha[\lambda(s,t)\{T_x^\alpha u(x,y) + I_x^\beta I_y^\alpha K(x,y,s,t,u(s,t))\} - g(x,y)] = 0 \tag{9}$$

Then, the correction functional with respect to x will be read as follows:

$$u_{n+1}(x,y) = u_n(x,y) + I_x^\alpha[\lambda(w,y)\{T_w^\alpha u(w,y) - I_w^\beta I_y^\gamma K(w,y,s,t,u(s,t)) - g(w,y)\}] = 0 \tag{10}$$

and the problem now is to evaluate λ. The problem of evaluating λ is difficult, since Equation (10) consists of functional derivatives and integrals, so to avoid this difficulty, approximate I_x^α and T_w^a for $0 < \alpha \leqslant 1$ by the first integral and derivative. Hence:

$$u_{n+1}(x,y) = u_n(x,y) + \int_a^x \left[\lambda\left(x,y)(\frac{\partial u_n}{\partial w}(w,y) - g(w,y) - I_w^\beta I_y^\gamma k(w,y,s,t,\widetilde{u_n}(s,t))\right)\right]dw \tag{11}$$

Now, taking the first variation of Equation (11) with respect to u_n, give:

$$\delta u_{n+1}(x,y) = \delta u_n(x,y) + \delta \int_{x_0}^x \left[\lambda\left(\frac{\partial u_n}{\partial s} - g - I_x^\beta I_y^y k(s,t,u_n(s,t))\right)\right]dw \tag{12}$$

$$= \delta u_n(x,y) + \delta \int_{x_a}^x \lambda(w,y)\left(\frac{\partial u_n(w,y)}{\partial w}\right)dw \tag{13}$$

$$= \delta u_n(x,y) + \int_a^x \lambda(w,y)\delta\left(\frac{\partial u_n(w,y)}{\partial w}\right)dw \tag{14}$$

Using integration by parts,

$$\delta u_{n+1}(x,y) = \delta u_n(x,y) + \delta u_n(w,y)|_{w=x} - \int \frac{\partial \lambda(w,y)}{\partial w}\delta u_n dw \tag{15}$$

$$= (1+\lambda)\delta u_n(w,y)|_{w=x} - \int \frac{\partial \lambda}{\partial w}\delta u_n(w,y)ds \tag{16}$$

$$\frac{\partial \lambda}{\partial w}(w,y)|_{w=x} = 0 \tag{17}$$

$$1 + \lambda(w,y)|_{w=x} = 0 \tag{18}$$

Solving this equation will give $\lambda(w,y) = -1$, and substituting in Equation (10), we get:

$$u_{n+1}(x,y) = u_n(x,y) - I_x^\alpha\left[T_w^\alpha u_n(w,y) - g(w,y) - I_w^\beta I_y^\gamma K\left(w,y,s,t,u_n(s,t)\right)\right] \tag{19}$$

Theorem 1. *Let $u, u_n \in C_x^m([a,b] \times [c,d])$, which is a Banach space with a m-th-order continuous partial derivative with respect to x, be the exact and approximate solutions of the integro-differential equation of fractional order (1). If $E_n(x,y) = u_n(x,y) - u(x,y)$ and the kernel K satisfy Lipschitz with respect to u, with constant L satisfying*

$$L < \left[\frac{\theta(2\theta+1)(3\theta+1)\dots(n\theta+1)\gamma(2\gamma+1)(3\gamma+1)\dots(n\gamma+1)}{(b-a)^{n\theta+1}(d-c)^{n\gamma+1}}\right]^{1/n}$$

then, the sequences solutions of approximation $\{u_n\}$ converge to the exact solution u.

Proof. Consider the integro-differential equation of fractional order:

$$T_x^\alpha u(x,y) = g(x,y) + I_x^\beta I_y^\gamma K(x,y,s,t,u(s,t)), \text{ where } u(0,y) = u_0$$

The approximate solution using the VIM is given by:

$$u_{n+1}(x,y) = u_n(x,y) - I_x^{\alpha}\{T_w^{\alpha}u_n(w,y) - g(w,y) - I_w^{\beta}I_y^{\gamma}k(x,y,s,t,u(s,t)\} \quad (20)$$

Since u is the exact solution of the integro-differential of the fractional order,

$$u(x,y) = u(x,y) - I_x^{\alpha}\{T_w^{\alpha}u(w,y) - g(x,y) - I_w^{\beta}I_y^{\gamma}k(x,y,s,t,u(s,t)\} \quad (21)$$

Then, subtracting Equation (21) from Equation (20), we get:

$$E_{n+1}(x,y) = E_n(x,y) - I_x^{\alpha}T_w^{\alpha}u_n(w,y) - g(x,y) + g(x,y) \quad (22)$$
$$-I_w^{\beta}I_y^{\gamma}ku_n(x,y,s,t,u_n(s,t) - T_w^{\beta}u(w,y) + I_w^{\beta}I_y^{\gamma}K(x,y,s,t,u(s,t) + g(x,y))$$

$$= E_n(x,y) - I_x^{\alpha}\{T_w^{\beta}E_n(w,y) - I_w^{\beta}I_y^{\gamma}\{K(w,y,s,t,u_n(s,t) - K(x,y,s,t,u_n(s,t)\}$$

From property (3), $I_x^{\alpha}I_w^{\alpha}E_n(x,y) = E_n(x,y) - E_n(0,y)$ and since $E_n(0,y) = 0$, then

$$E_{n+1}(x,y) = E_n(x,y) - E_n(x,y) + I_x^{\alpha}I_x^{\beta}I_y^{\gamma}\ [K(x,y,s,t,u_n(s,t)) - K(x,y,s,t,u_n(s,t))]$$

If $\theta = \alpha + \beta$, then:

$$E_{n+1}(x,y) = I_x^{\theta}I_y^{\gamma}[K(x,y,s,t,u_n(s,t)) - K(x,y,s,t,u(s,t))] \quad (23)$$

Now, taking the supermum norm for both sides of Equation (23)

$$\| E_{n+1}(x,y)\| \leq I_x^{\theta}I_y^{\gamma}\| K(x,y,s,t,u_n(s,t) - K(x,y,s,t,u(s,t)\|$$

where the K (kernel function) satisfies the Lipschitz condition with constant L, then:

$$\| E_{n+1}(x,y)\| \leq LI_x^{\theta}I_y^{\gamma}\| u_n - u\|$$
$$= LI_x^{\theta}I_y^{\gamma}\|E_n(x,y)\| \quad (24)$$

Using the conformable definition of integrals in Equation (24) implies:

$$\| E_{n+1}(x,y)\| \leq L\int_a^x (s-a)^{\theta-1}\int_c^y (t-c)^{\gamma-1}\| E_n(s,t)\|dsdt$$
$$= L\int_c^x\int_a^y (s-a)^{\theta-1}(t-c)^{\gamma-1}\|E_n(x,y)\|dsdt \quad (25)$$

Now, applying mathematical induction over the last inequality:
If $n = 0$

$$\| E_1(x,y)\| \leq L\int_a^x\int_c^y (s-a)^{\theta-1}(t-c)^{\gamma-1}\| E_0(x,y)\|dsdt$$
$$= L\frac{(s-a)^{\theta}}{\theta}\bigg|_a^x\frac{(t-c)^{\gamma}}{\gamma}\bigg|_c^y\| E_0(x,y)\|$$
$$\leq L\frac{(x-a)^{\theta}}{\theta}\frac{(y-c)^{\gamma}}{\gamma}\| E_0(x,y)\|$$

If $n = 1$, then:

$$\| E_2(x,y)\| \leq L\int_a^x\int_c^y (s-a)^{\theta-1}(t-c)^{\gamma-1}\| E_1(x,y)\|dsdt$$

$$\leq L\int_a^x\int_c^y (s-a)^{\theta-1}(t-c)^{\gamma-1}L\frac{(s-a)^{\theta}}{\theta}\ \frac{(t-c)^{\gamma}}{\gamma}\| E_0(x,y)\|\ dsdt$$

$$=\frac{L^2}{\theta\gamma}\int_a^x\int_c^y (s-a)^{2\theta}(t-c)^{2\gamma-1}\| E_0(x,y)\|dsdt$$

$$=\frac{L^2}{\theta\gamma}\frac{(s-a)^{2\theta+1}}{2\theta+1}\Bigg|_a^x\frac{(t-c)^{2\gamma+1}}{2\gamma+1}\Bigg|_c^y\| E_0(x,y)\|$$

$$=\frac{L^2}{\theta(2\theta+1)\gamma(2\gamma+1)}(x-a)^{2\theta+1}(y-c)^{2\gamma+1}\| E_0(x,y)\|$$

If $n=2$

$$\| E_3(x,y)\|\leq L\int_a^x\int_c^y (s-a)^{\theta-1}(t-c)^{\gamma-1}\| E_2(x,y)\|dsdt$$

$$\leq L\int_a^x\int_c^y (s-a)^{\theta-1}(t-c)^{\gamma-1}\frac{L^2}{w(2\theta+1)\gamma(2\gamma+1)}(s-a)^{2\theta+1}(t-c)^{2\gamma+1}\| E_0(x,y)\|dsdt$$

$$=\frac{L^3}{\theta(2\theta+1)\gamma(2\gamma+1)}\int_a^x\int_c^y (s-a)^{3\theta}(t-c)^{3\gamma}\ \| E_0(x,y)\|dsdt$$

$$=\frac{L^3}{\theta(2\theta+1)\gamma(2\gamma+1)}\frac{(s-a)^{3\theta+1}}{3\theta+1}\Bigg|_a^x\frac{(t-c)^{3\gamma+1}}{3\gamma+1}\Bigg|_c^y\| E_0(x,y)\|$$

$$=\frac{L^3}{\theta(2\theta+1)(3\theta+1)\gamma(2\gamma+1)(3\gamma+1)}(x-a)^{3\theta+1}(y-c)^{3\gamma+1}\| E_0(x,y)\|$$

Hence, by induction, we have:

$$\| E_{n+1}(x,y)\|\leq \frac{L^n}{\theta(2\theta+1)(3\theta+1)\dots(n\theta+1)\gamma(2\gamma+1)(3\gamma+1)\dots(n\gamma+1)}(x-a)^{n\theta+1}(y-c)^{n\gamma+1}\| E_0(x,y)\|$$

and upon taking the supremum values of x and y, over $[a,b]\times[c.d]$, getting:

$$\| E_{n+1}(x,y)\|\leq \frac{L^n}{\theta(2\theta+1)(3\theta+1)\dots(n\theta+1)\gamma(2\gamma+1)(3\gamma+1)\dots(n\gamma+1)}(b-a)^{n\theta+1}(d-c)^{n\gamma+1}\| E_0(x,y)\|$$

Since

$$\frac{L^n(b-a)^{n\theta+1}(d-c)^{n\gamma+1}}{\theta(2\theta+1)(3\theta+1)\dots(n\theta+1)\gamma(2\gamma+1)(3\gamma+1)\dots(n\gamma+1)}<1$$

Because

$$L<\left[\frac{\theta(2\theta+1)(3\theta+1)\dots(n\theta+1)\gamma(2\gamma+1)(3\gamma+1)\dots(n\gamma+1)}{(b-a)^{n\theta+1}(d-c)^{n\gamma+1}}\right]^{1/n}$$

Hence as *as* $n\to\infty$, we have $\| E_n(x,y)\|\to 0$, i.e., $u_n(x,y)\to u(x,y)$ *as* $n\to\infty$. □

5. Illustrative Examples

Two examples of using the VIM to solve linear and nonlinear integro-differential equations with conformable fractional order differo-integration are presented in this section.

Example 1. *Consider the linear integral equation of fractional order:*

$$T_x^{\alpha} u(x,y) = g(x,y) + I_x^{\beta} I_y^{\gamma} [(x-y)u(x,y)]$$

where $g(x,y) = T_x^{\alpha} u(x,y) - I_x^{\beta} I_y^{\gamma} [(x-y)u(x,y)]$.

The exact solution is given for comparison purpose by $u_e(x,y) = x^3 y$

Hence, starting with the initial guess solution:

$$u_0(x,y) = g(x,y) \; = 3yx^{3-\alpha} - \frac{x^{\beta+4}}{\beta+4} \cdot \frac{y^{\gamma+1}}{\gamma+1} + \frac{x^{\beta+3}}{\beta+3} \cdot \frac{y^{\gamma+2}}{\gamma+2}$$

then, to find $u_1(x,y)$, *if* $n = 1$, *getting:*

$$\begin{aligned} u_1(x,y) &= u_0(x,y) - I_x^{\alpha} [T_x^{\alpha} u_0(x,y) - g(x,y) - I_x^{\beta} I_y^{\gamma} [(x-y)u(x,y)] \\ &= 3yx^{2-\alpha} - \tfrac{x^{\beta+4}}{\beta+4} \cdot \tfrac{y^{\gamma+1}}{\gamma+1} + \tfrac{x^{\beta+3}}{\beta+3} \\ &\cdot \tfrac{y^{\gamma+2}}{\gamma+2} - I_x^{\alpha} [(9-3\alpha) y^{3-2\alpha} - x^{\beta+4-\alpha} . \tfrac{y^{\gamma+1}}{\gamma+1} + x^{\beta+3-\alpha} . \\ &\tfrac{y^{\gamma+2}}{\gamma+2} - 3yx^{2-\alpha} - \tfrac{x^{\beta+4}}{\beta+4} \cdot \tfrac{y^{\gamma+1}}{\gamma+1} + \tfrac{x^{\beta+3}}{\beta+3} \cdot \tfrac{y^{\gamma+2}}{\gamma+2} - I_x^{\beta} I_y^{\gamma} \\ &\left[3yx^{2-\alpha} + \tfrac{x^{\beta+5}}{\beta+4} \cdot \tfrac{y^{\gamma+1}}{\gamma+1} + \tfrac{x^{\beta+4}}{\beta+3} \cdot \tfrac{y^{\gamma+2}}{\gamma+2} + 3y^2 x^{3-\alpha} + \tfrac{x^{\beta+4}}{\beta+4} \cdot \tfrac{y^{\gamma+2}}{\gamma+1} - \tfrac{x^{\beta+3}}{\beta+3} \cdot \tfrac{y^{\gamma+3}}{\gamma+2} \right] \end{aligned} \tag{26}$$

and carrying out recursively fractional-order integrals of the order γ *represent to* y, *of order* β *with respect to* x *and of order of* α *represent to* y, *we get the final form of* $u_1(x,y)$, *which is as follows: when* $\alpha = 0.8$, $\beta = 0.5$ *and* $\gamma = 0.75$ *substitution in Equation (26).*

We get the following result of $u_1(x,y)$ *approximate up to six decimals*

$$\begin{aligned} u_1(x,y) \cong\; & 0.024161885 x^{4.3} y^{2.75} + \\ & 1.0 x^{3.0} y + 0.1029601 x^{4.5} y^{1.75} - 0.0012449424 x^{6.8} y^{2.5} - 0.023959269 x^{5.3} y^{1.75} \\ & -0.11544012 x^{3.5} y^{2.75} + 0.0022746821 x^{5.8} y^{3.5} + 2.1684043 e^{-19} x^{2.2} y - 0.0012025012 x^{4.8} y^{4.5} \end{aligned}$$

Similarly to the calculations $u_1(x,y)$, *we may find new approximation solution up to three iterations, which are found to be*

$$\begin{aligned} u_2(x,y) = \; & 9.09495e - 10x^{4.3} y^{2.75} - 0.000199751 x^{5.6} y^{4.5} + 1.0 x^{3.0} y \\ & -0.00000507162 x^{9.1} y^{3.25} + 2.96859e - 9x^{4.5} y^{1.75} + 0.00100941 x^{6.8} y^{2.5} + \\ & 5.67525e - 10x^{5.3} y^{1.75} + 0.00000595113 x^{6.1} y^{6.25} - 0.0000148071 x^{7.1} y^{5.25} + 4.5693e- \\ & 9x^{3.5} y^{2.75} - 0.000185443 x^{7.6} y^{2.5} - 0.00215173 x^{5.8} y^{3.5} + 0.000359167 x^{6.6} y^{3.5} + \\ & 0.0000140055 x^{8.1} y^{4.25} + 9.31323e - 10x^{2.2} y + \\ & 0.00133611 x^{4.8} y^{4.5} \end{aligned}$$

$$\begin{aligned} u_3(x,y) = \; & 0.0241619 x^{4.3} y^{2.75} + 1.0 x^{3.0} y + 2.00089e - 11x^{6.8} y^{2.5} - 0.0239593 \\ & x^{5.3} y^{1.75} + 9.41681e - 12x^{3.5} y^{2.75} + 6.36646e - 12x^{5.8} y^{3.5} - \left(-0.386473 x^{2.3} y^{0.75} + 0.879121 x^{1.3} y^{1.75} \right). \end{aligned}$$

$$(0.00000525264x^{8.1}y^{3.25}+4.0829e-11x^{5.8}y^{2.5}-7.91503e-7x^{8.9}y^{3.25}$$
$$+0.0379687x^{4.3}y^{1.75}+0.00000787187x^{6.1}y^{5.25}-0.0000113188x^{7.1}y^{4.25}+$$
$$5.946e-12x^{6.6}y^{2.5}+6.78554e-11x^{4.8}y^{3.5}-9.03963e-7x^{6.9}y^{5.25}+$$
$$0.00000150668x^{7.9}y^{4.25}-3.86567e-8x^{8.4}y^{6}+9.63085e-$$
$$12x^{5.6}y^{3.5}+3.465e-8x^{9.4}y^{5}-1.26994e-8x^{10.4}y^{4}+$$
$$1.3112e-20x^{3.5}y^{1.75}+1.74071e-8x^{7.4}y^{7})+9.31323e-10x^{2.2}y+4.77485e-$$
$$11x^{4.8}y^{4.5}$$

Figure 1 shows the comparison between the exact and the approximated solution for different values of y.

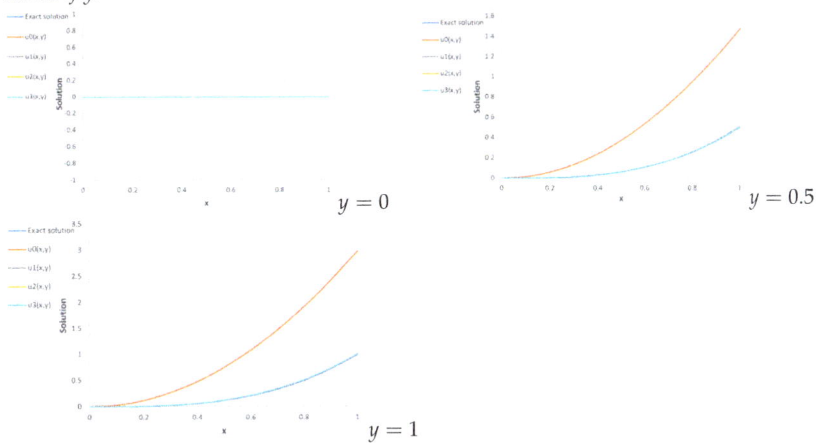

Figure 1. Exact and approximate solutions of Example 1.

Example 2. *Let the non-linear equation is:*

$$T_x^{\alpha}u(x,y)=g(x,y)+I_x^{\beta}I_y^{\gamma}\left[(xy)e^{u(x,y}\right]$$

When the exact solution $u_e(x,y)=x^2y^2$.

For the simplicity of calculations and in order to use the properties of conformable and integrations e^u *by the Tayler series*

$$e^u=1+u+\frac{u^2}{2!}+\ldots$$

After tow terms, we have $e^u\cong 1+u$.

By calculus of variation, the initial condition to

$$u_0(x,y)=g(x,y)\ =2y^2x^{2-\alpha}-\frac{x^{\beta+1}}{\beta+1}\cdot\frac{y^{\gamma+1}}{\gamma+1}+\frac{x^{\beta+3}}{\beta+3}\cdot\frac{y^{\gamma+3}}{\gamma+3}$$

Now, using the variation iteration method to find the next approximation solution as follows:

$$u_1(x,y)=u_0(x,y)-I_x^{\alpha}[T_x^{\alpha}u_0(x,y)-g(x,y)-I_x^{\beta}I_y^{\gamma}[xy(1+u_0(x,y))]$$

$$= 2y^2x^{2-\alpha} - \frac{x^{\beta+1}}{\beta+1}.\frac{y^{\gamma+1}}{\gamma+1} + \frac{x^{\beta+3}}{\beta+3}$$
$$.\frac{y^{\gamma+3}}{\gamma+3} - I_y^{\alpha}[T_x^{\alpha}2y^2x^{2-\alpha} - \frac{x^{\beta+1}}{\beta+1}.\frac{y^{\gamma+1}}{\gamma+1} + \frac{x^{\beta+3}}{\beta+3}.$$
$$\frac{y^{\gamma+3}}{\gamma+3} - [2y^2x^{2-\alpha} - \frac{x^{\beta+1}}{\beta+1}.\frac{y^{\gamma+1}}{\gamma+1} + \frac{x^{\beta+3}}{\beta+3}.$$
$$\frac{y^{\gamma+3}}{\gamma+3}] - I_x^{\beta}I_y^{\gamma}\left[xy + 2y^3x^{1-\alpha} - \frac{x^{\beta+2}}{\beta+1}.\frac{y^{\gamma+2}}{\gamma+1} + \frac{x^{\beta+4}}{\beta+3}.\frac{y^{\gamma+4}}{\gamma+3}\right] \quad (27)$$

Carrying out recursively order integrals of order γ to represent y, of order β to represent x and of order α to represent y, we get the final from of $u_1(x,y)$, which is as follows.

When $\alpha = 0.8$, $\beta = 0.5$ and $\gamma = 0.75$ substitution in Equation (27)

We get the following result of $u_1(x,y)$, which is approximate up to six decimals

$$u_1(x,y) = 1.81826e - 8x^{5.5}y^{5.75} - 0.000477683x^{5.8}y^{5.5}$$
$$-0.0177187x^{4.3}y^{3.75} + 1.0x^{2.0}y^2 - 0.00250957x^{6.3}y^{5.75} +$$
$$9.31323e^{-10}x^{1.2}y^2 + 0.0564374x^{3.5}y^{3.75} - 0.00954771x^{3.8}y^{3.5}$$
$$-0.0000386088x^{7.8}\,y^{7.5}$$

If n = 1, we get

$$u_2(x,y) = 7.27596e - 12x^{5.5}y^{5.75} + 0.000353838x^{5.8}y^{5.5}$$
$$-0.00000111428x^{8.1}y^{7.25} - 0.0000562515x^{6.1}y^{5.25} - 4.65079e - 8x^{4.3}y^{3.75}$$
$$-0.00000498821x^{8.6}y^{7.5} + 1.0x^{2.0}y^2 - 0.00250957$$
$$x^{6.3}y^{5.75} - 0.0000841583x^{6.6}y^{5.5} - 2.42514e^{-15}x^{1.2}y^2$$
$$+5.82077e^{-11}x^{3.5}y^{3.75} - 4.94072e^{-8}x^{9.6}y^{9.25}$$

If n = 2, we get

$$u_3(x,y) = -4.89841e^{-9}x^{10.9}y^{9.25} - 7.20333e^{-12}x^{5.5}y^{5.75} + 2.27374e^{-13}$$
$$x^{5.8}y^{5.5} + 8.25388e^{-7}x^{8.1}y^{7.25} - 1.61021e^{-7}x^{8.9}y^{7.25} - 7.27596e^{-12}x^{4.3}$$
$$y^{3.75} - 0.00000498821x^{8.6}y^{7.5} + 1.0x^{2.0}y^2 - 0.00250957x^{6.3}y^{5.75}$$
$$-3.03032e^{-10}x^{6.6}y^{5.5} - 1.25876e^{-7}x^{8.4}y^7 - 1.7528e^{-21}x^{1.2}y^2 -$$
$$1.24008e^{-9}x^{10.4}y^9 - 3.40038e^{-11}x^{11.9}y^{11} + 1.77679e^{-14}x^{7.8}y^{7.5}$$

Figure 2 compares the exact and the approximated solutions for different values of y.

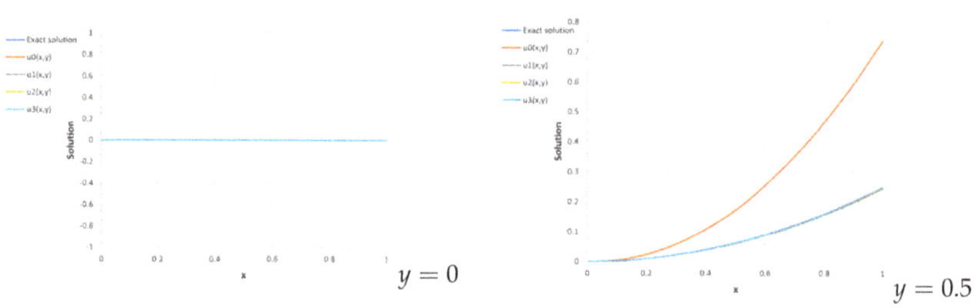

Figure 2. *Cont.*

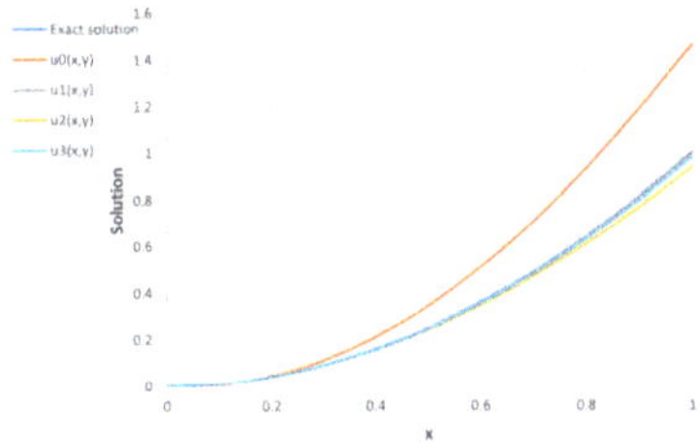

$y = 1$

Figure 2. Exact and approximate solutions of Example 2.

6. Conclusions

The present study shows that VIM is a very accurate method that gives the exact solution in a few steps. In some cases, however, it requires more calculations, which will add some difficulties to the problem under consideration. This work may be improved in future by including integro-differential equations with kernels including fractional-order derivatives of the unknown function, in addition to considering fractional-order derivatives greater than 1.

Author Contributions: Conceptualization, M.D. and Z.A.M.; methodology, M.D.; software, Z.A.M.; validation, M.D. and Z.A.M.; formal analysis, M.D.; investigation, Z.A.M.; resources, Z.A.M.; data curation, Z.A.M.; writing—original draft preparation, M.D.; writing—review and editing, Z.A.M.; visualization, Z.A.M.; supervision, M.D.; project administration, M.D. All authors have read and agreed to the published version of the manuscript.

Funding: This research received no external funding.

Institutional Review Board Statement: Not applicable.

Informed Consent Statement: Not applicable.

Data Availability Statement: Not applicable.

Conflicts of Interest: The authors declare no conflict of interest.

References

1. Bagley, R.L.; Torvik, P.J. A theoretical basis for the application of fractional calculus to viscoelasticity. *J. Rheol.* **1983**, *27*, 201–210. [CrossRef]
2. Karthikeyan, K.; Karthikeyan, P.; Baskonus, H.M.; Venkatachalam, K.; Chu, Y.M. Almost sectorial operators on psi-Hilfer derivative fractional impulsive integro-differential equations. *Math. Methods Appl. Sci.* **2022**, *45*, 8045–8059. [CrossRef]
3. Kurulay, M.; Secer, A. Variational Iteration Method for Solving Nonlinear Fractional Integro-Differential Equations. *Int. J. Comput. Sci. Emerg. Technol.* **2011**, *2*, 18–20.
4. Khaleel, O. I. Variational Iteration Method for Solving Multi-Fractional Integro Differential Equations. *J. Sci.* **2014**, *55*, 1086–1094.
5. Fang, J.; Nadeem, M.; Habib, M.; Akgül, A. Numerical Investigation of Nonlinear Shock Wave Equations with Fractional Order in Propagating Disturbance. *Symmetry* **2022**, *14*, 1179. [CrossRef]
6. Partohaghighi, M.; Akgül, A.; Guran, L.; Bota, M.F. Novel Mathematical Modelling of Platelet-Poor Plasma Arising in a Blood Coagulation System with the Fractional Caputo–Fabrizio Derivative. *Symmetry* **2022**, *14*, 1128. [CrossRef]
7. Shi, Y. A study on the mild solution of impulsive fractional evolution equations. *Appl. Math. Comput.* **2016**, *273*, 465–476. [CrossRef]
8. Mainardi, F. *Fractional Calculus: Some Basic Problems in Continuum and Statistical Mechanics, in Fractals and Fractional Calculus in Continuum Mechanics*; Springer: Vienna, Austria, 1997; Volume 378, pp. 291–348.
9. Khan, Y.; Khan, A.; Shaeel, M.; Akgül, A. Two Dimensional Laplace Transform Coupled with the Marichev-Saigo-Maeda Integral Operator and the Generalized Incomplete Hypergeometric Function. *Symmetry* **2021**, *13*, 2420. [CrossRef]
10. Hajiseyedazizi, S.N.; Samei, M.E.; Alzabut, J.; Chu, Y.M. On multi-step methods for singular fractional q-integro-differential equations. *Open Math.* **2021**, *19*, 1378–1405. [CrossRef]
11. Rossikhin, Y.A.; Shitikova, M.V. Applications of fractional calculus to dynamic problems of linear and nonlinear hereditary mechanics of solids. *Appl. Mech. Rev.* **1997**, *50*, 15–67. [CrossRef]
12. Larsson, S.; Racheva, M.; Saedpanah, F. Discontinuous Galerkin method for an integro-differential equation modeling dynamic fractional order viscoelasticity. *Comput. Methods Appl. Mech. Eng.* **2015**, *283*, 196–209. [CrossRef]

13. Liu, J.; Nadeem, M.; Habib, M.; Akgül, A. Approximate Solution of Nonlinear Time-Fractional Klein-Gordon Equations Using Yang Transform. *Symmetry* **2022**, *14*, 907. [CrossRef]
14. Zhu, S.D.; Chu, Y.M.; Qiu, S.L. The homotopy perturbation method for discontinued problems arising in nanotechnology. *Comput. Math. Appl.* **2009**, *58*, 2398–2401. [CrossRef]
15. Batiha, B.; Noorani, M.S.; Hashim, I. Numerical solutions of the nonlinear integro- differential equations. *J. Open Probl. Compt. Math.* **2008**, *1*, 34–41.
16. He, J.H. Variational Iteration Method; Some Recent Results and New Interpretations. *J. Comput. Appl. Math.* **2007**, *207*, 3–17. [CrossRef]
17. He, J.H. A new approach to nonlinear partial differential equations. *Commun. Nonlinear Sci. Numer. Simul.* **1997**, *2*, 230–235. [CrossRef]
18. He, J.H. A variational iteration approach to nonlinear problems and its applications. *Mech. Appl.* **1998**, *20*, 30–31.
19. He, J.H. Variational iteration method—A kind of non-linear analytical technique: Some examples. *Int. J.-Non-Linear Mech.* **1999**, *34*, 699–708. [CrossRef]
20. Abbasbandy, S.; Shivanian, E. Application of the Variational Iteration Method for System of Nonlinear Volterra's Integro-Differential Equations. *J. Math. Comput. Appl.* **2009**, *14*, 147–158. [CrossRef]
21. Wang, W.-H. An Effective Method for Solving Fractional Integro-Differential Equations. *Acta Univ. Apulensis* **2009**, *20*, 229–235.
22. Hammad, M.A.; Khalil, R. Conformable fractional heat differential equations. *Int. J. Pure Appl. Math.* **2014**, *94*, 215–221. [CrossRef]
23. Khader , A.H. The Conformable Laplace Transform of the Fractional Chebyshev and Legendre Polynnomials. Ph.D. Thesis, Zarqa University, Zarqa, Jordan, 2017.

axioms

MDPI

Article

Some New Refinements of Trapezium-Type Integral Inequalities in Connection with Generalized Fractional Integrals

Muhammad Tariq [1], Soubhagya Kumar Sahoo [2,3], Sotiris K. Ntouyas [4,5], Omar Mutab Alsalami [6], Asif Ali Shaikh [1] and Kamsing Nonlaopon [7,*]

1 Department of Basic Sciences and Related Studies, Mehran University of Engineering and Technology, Jamshoro 76062, Pakistan
2 Department of Mathematics, Institute of Technical Education and Research, Siksha O Anusandhan University, Bhubaneswar 751030, India
3 Department of Mathematics, Aryan Institute of Engineering and Technology, Bhubaneswar 752050, India
4 Department of Mathematics, University of Ioannina, 451 10 Ioannina, Greece
5 Nonlinear Analysis and Applied Mathematics (NAAM)-Research Group, Department of Mathematics, Faculty of Science, King Abdulaziz University, Jeddah 21589, Saudi Arabia
6 Department of Electrical Engineering, College of Engineering, Taif University, Taif 21944, Saudi Arabia
7 Department of Mathematics, Faculty of Science, Khon Kaen University, Khon Kaen 40002, Thailand
* Correspondence: nkamsi@kku.ac.th; Tel.: +66-8-6642-1582

Abstract: The main objective of this article is to introduce a new notion of convexity, i.e., modified exponential type convex function, and establish related fractional inequalities. To strengthen the argument of the paper, we introduce two new lemmas as auxiliary results and discuss some algebraic properties of the proposed notion. Considering a generalized fractional integral operator and differentiable mappings, whose initial absolute derivative at a given power is a modified exponential type convex, various improvements of the Hermite–Hadamard inequality are presented. Thanks to the main results, some generalizations about the earlier findings in the literature are recovered.

Keywords: convex function; Hölder's inequality; power-mean integral inequality; m–type convexity; exponential convex function

MSC: 26A51; 26A33; 26D07; 26D10; 26D15

Citation: Tariq, M.; Sahoo, S.K.; Ntouyas, S.K.; Alsalami, O.M.; Shaikh, A.A.; Nonlaopon, K. Some New Refinements of Trapezium-Type Integral Inequalities in Connection with Generalized Fractional Integrals. *Axioms* **2022**, *11*, 508. https://doi.org/10.3390/axioms11100508

Academic Editor: Patricia J. Y. Wong

Received: 24 August 2022
Accepted: 21 September 2022
Published: 27 September 2022

1. Introduction

Convexity theory has had a substantial and crucial influence on the development of numerous disciplines such as economics [1], financial mathematics [2], engineering [3], and optimization [4] in modern mathematics. This theory gives a fantastic framework for initiating and developing numerical tools for tackling and studying complex mathematical problems.

In the current decade, many mathematicians have been merging new ideas with fractional analysis to bring new dimensions with different features to the field of mathematical analysis. Fractional analysis has many applications in modeling [5,6], epidemiology [7], fluid flow [8], nanotechnology [9], mathematical biology [10], and control systems [11]. It is particularly crucial while studying optimization problems because it has a variety of useful inequalities. This explains why convex functions and convex sets have such a robust theoretical foundation. There are numerous practical uses for convex functions in optimization, circuit design, controller design, modeling, etc. Because it has gained so much attention, the concept of "convexity" has developed into a fertile area of research and inspiration.

The theory of inequalities has been expanded and generalized during the past few decades, and this has been made possible by the concept of convex analysis. Inequalities theory and the theory of convexity are strongly related to one another. Many mathematicians and research scientists have made considerable efforts and contributions to the study of this inequality over the last few decades. Some authors have also studied dynamic inequalities [12–17] to further strengthen the theory of convexity and inequality. As a result, there is a rich and insightful literature on convexity and inequalities; for further information, see the references at [18–21].

Many mathematicians and scientists in a wide range of applied and scientific areas have been fascinated and inspired by fractional calculus. Because of its ability to interpolate between operators of integer order, fractional integrals and derivatives have a rich history and are used frequently in practical situations. Given its wide range of applications in the mathematical modeling of numerous complicated and nonlocal nonlinear systems, fractional calculus has become a crucial topic of research. The nonlocal nature of fractional-order operators, which explains the hereditary characteristics of the underlying phenomena, is an important property of these operators. A macroscopic stress–strain relation expressed in terms of fractional differential operators results from the interactions between macromolecules in damping phenomena. Its appeal in modeling different transport characteristics in complicated heterogeneous and disordered media is largely due to the fact that it offers a suitable context for describing processes with memory and is fractal or multi-fractal in origin.

We organized the study in the following manner in light of the aforementioned findings and literature on inequality theory: We review some well-known concepts and definitions in Section 2. We describe the idea and algebraic characteristics of modified exponential type convex functions in Section 3. The H–H inequality, whose first derivatives in absolute value at a given power is of the modified exponential type convex, and additional extensions of it are developed in Section 4. Finally, we provide a brief conclusion in Section 5.

2. Preliminaries

Because there are so many theorems and definitions in the preliminary section, it will be advisable to examine and investigate it for the sake of thoroughness. We will review a few well-known terms, definitions, and findings in this section that we will be required for our inquiry in subsequent sections. Convex functions, Hermite–Hadamard type inequality, m-convex functions, and exponential type convex functions are introduced first. We recall here the Riemann–Liouville fractional integral operator, its k-generalization, and certain crucial functions, such as the incomplete gamma function and gamma function, which will be needed in our investigations.

Definition 1 ([22])**.** *If* $\mathrm{G} : \mathbb{X} \subset \mathbb{R} \to \mathbb{R}$, *then an inequality of the form*

$$\mathrm{G}(\mathrm{g}_1\varrho + (1-\varrho)\mathrm{g}_2) \leq \varrho\mathrm{G}(\mathrm{g}_1) + (1-\varrho)\mathrm{G}(\mathrm{g}_2), \tag{1}$$

is said to be convex if for all $\mathrm{g}_1, \mathrm{g}_2 \in \mathbb{X}$ *and* $\varrho \in [0,1]$.

The well-known Hermite–Hadamard inequality must be mentioned in any paper on Hermite inequalities. This inequality claims that, if $\mathrm{G} : \mathbb{X} \subset \mathbb{R} \to \mathbb{R}$ is convex in $\mathbb{X}$ for $\mathrm{g}_1, \mathrm{g}_2 \in \mathbb{X}$ and $\mathrm{g}_1 < \mathrm{g}_2$, then

$$\mathrm{G}\left(\frac{\mathrm{g}_1+\mathrm{g}_2}{2}\right) \leq \frac{1}{\mathrm{g}_2-\mathrm{g}_1}\int_{\mathrm{g}_1}^{\mathrm{g}_2} \mathrm{G}(\chi)d\chi \leq \frac{\mathrm{G}(\mathrm{g}_1)+\mathrm{G}(\mathrm{g}_2)}{2}. \tag{2}$$

Interested readers can refer to [23–26].

In 1985, the famous mathematician G. Toader [27] first considered and examined the new version of convexity, namely the m-convex function.

Definition 2 ([27]). *Let* $\mathsf{G} : [0, b] \to \mathbb{R}$, $b > 0$ *and* $m \in (0, 1]$. *An inequality of the form*

$$\mathsf{G}(\varrho \mathrm{g}_1 + m(1-\varrho)\mathrm{g}_2) \leq \varrho \mathsf{G}(\mathrm{g}_1) + m(1-\varrho)\mathsf{G}(\mathrm{g}_2), \tag{3}$$

is then said to be m–convex if $\forall\, \mathrm{g}_1, \mathrm{g}_2 \in [0, b]$ *and* $\varrho \in [0, 1]$. *Otherwise,* G *is m–concave if* $(-\mathsf{G})$ *is m–convex.*

Definition 3 ([28]). *Let* G *be a nonnegative function.* $\mathsf{G} : \mathbb{X} \to \mathbb{R}$, *is then said to be a exponential type convex if*

$$\mathsf{G}(\varrho \mathrm{g}_1 + (1-\varrho)\mathrm{g}_2) \leq (e^{\varrho} - 1)\mathsf{G}(\mathrm{g}_1) + \left(e^{(1-\varrho)} - 1\right)\mathsf{G}(\mathrm{g}_2) \tag{4}$$

holds $\forall\, \mathrm{g}_1, \mathrm{g}_2 \in \mathbb{X}$, *and* $\varrho \in [0, 1]$.

Definition 4 (Hölder Integral Inequality [29]). *If* G *and* H *be two integrable functions, then the Hölder inequality is given by*

$$\int_0^1 |\mathsf{G}(\nu)\mathsf{H}(\nu)| d\nu \leq \left(\int_0^1 |\mathsf{G}(x)|^p dx\right)^{\frac{1}{p}} \left(\int_0^1 |\mathsf{H}(x)|^q dx\right)^{\frac{1}{q}}. \tag{5}$$

Definition 5 (Power-mean integral inequality [30]). *If* G *and* H *be two integrable functions, then power mean inequality is given by*

$$\int_0^1 |\mathsf{G}(\nu)\mathsf{H}(\nu)| d\nu \leq \left(\int_0^1 |\mathsf{G}(x)| dx\right)^{1-\frac{1}{q}} \left(\int_0^1 |\mathsf{G}(x)| dx \int_0^1 |\mathsf{H}(x)|^q dx\right)^{\frac{1}{q}}. \tag{6}$$

The concept of fractional integral inequalities have many applications in applied sciences. Such types of inequalities have always been established and have managed the uniqueness of solutions to some fractional partial differential equations. Additionally, they offer upper and lower bounds for the solutions to the fractional boundary value problems. In order to study specific extensions and generalizations, scholars in the subject of integral inequalities have used fractional calculus operators; for further information, see [31–34].

Let $\mathsf{G} \in L[\mathrm{g}_1, \mathrm{g}_2]$. Riemann–Liouville fractional integrals of order $\alpha > 0$ with $\mathrm{g}_1 \geq 0$ are then defined as follows:

$$J^{\alpha}_{\mathrm{g}_1^+}\mathsf{G}(x) = \frac{1}{\Gamma(\alpha)} \int_{\mathrm{g}_1}^{x} (x-\chi)^{\alpha-1}\, \mathsf{G}(\chi)\, d\chi, \quad x > \mathrm{g}_1$$

and

$$J^{\alpha}_{\mathrm{g}_2^-}\mathsf{G}(x) = \frac{1}{\Gamma(\alpha)} \int_{x}^{\mathrm{g}_2} (\chi - x)^{\alpha-1}\, \mathsf{G}(\chi)\, d\chi, \quad x < \mathrm{g}_2.$$

For further details, one may see [35–40].

In [41,42], there is a given definition of k—fractional Riemann–Liouville integrals. Let $\mathsf{G} \in L[\mathrm{g}_1, \mathrm{g}_2]$. $k-$fractional integrals of order $\alpha, k > 0$ with $\mathrm{g}_1 \geq 0$ are then defined as follows:

$${}^{k}J^{\alpha}_{\mathrm{g}_1^+}\mathsf{G}(x) = \frac{1}{k\Gamma_k(\alpha)} \int_{\mathrm{g}_1}^{x} (x-\chi)^{\frac{\alpha}{k}-1}\, \mathsf{G}(\chi)\, d\chi \quad x > \mathrm{g}_1,$$

and

$${}^{k}J^{\alpha}_{\mathrm{g}_2^-}\mathsf{G}(x) = \frac{1}{k\Gamma_k(\alpha)} \int_{x}^{\mathrm{g}_2} (\chi - x)^{\frac{\alpha}{k}-1}\, \mathsf{G}(\chi)\, d\chi, \quad x < \mathrm{g}_2,$$

where $\Gamma_k(\alpha)$ is the k—Gamma function defined as

$$\Gamma_k(\alpha) = \int_0^{+\infty} \chi^{\alpha-1} e^{-\frac{\chi^k}{k}} d\chi.$$

We can notice that

$$\Gamma_k(\alpha + k) = \alpha\Gamma_k(\alpha)$$

and

$${}^1J^0_{\mathrm{g}_1^+}\psi(x) = {}^1J^0_{\mathrm{g}_2^-}\psi(x) = \psi(x).$$

By choosing $k = 1$, the above k—fractional integrals yield Riemann–Liouville integrals. The incomplete gamma function $\gamma(\vartheta, \varrho)$ is defined for $\vartheta > 0$ and $\varrho \geq 0$ by integral

$$\gamma(\vartheta, \varrho) = \int_0^{\varrho} e^{-\mu}\, \mu^{\vartheta-1}\, d\mu.$$

The gamma function $\Gamma(\vartheta)$ is defined for $\vartheta > 0$ by integral

$$\Gamma(\vartheta) = \int_0^{+\infty} e^{-\mu}\, \mu^{\vartheta-1}\, d\mu.$$

3. The Modified Exponential Type Convex Function and Its Associated Algebraic Properties

There has recently been a rise in interest in information theory involving exponentially convex functions because of the substantial and valuable research on big data analysis and extended learning. As a result, other mathematicians, including Antczak (2001), Pecaric (2013), Dragomir (2015), Pal (2017), Alirezaei (2018), Awan (2018), Saima (2019), Noor (2019), and Kadakal (2020), worked on the idea of exponential type convexity in various ways and made contributions to the field of analysis.

The main attention of this section is to present a new definition of modified exponential type convex function and its associated properties.

Definition 6. *Let* G *be a nonnegative function.* $\mathsf{G} : \mathbb{X} \to \mathbb{R}$, *is then said to be a modified exponential type convex if*

$$\mathsf{G}(\varrho \mathrm{g}_1 + m(1-\varrho)\mathrm{g}_2) \leq (e^{\varrho} - 1)\mathsf{G}(\mathrm{g}_1) + m\left(e^{1-\varrho} - 1\right)\mathsf{G}(\mathrm{g}_2), \tag{7}$$

holds $\forall\ \mathrm{g}_1, \mathrm{g}_2 \in \mathbb{X}$, $m \in [0,1]$, *and* $\varrho \in [0,1]$.

We will denote by MEXPC($\mathbb{X}$) the class of modified exponential type convex functions on interval $\mathbb{X}$.

Remark 1. *For* $m = 1$, *we attain exponential type convexity, which is explored by İşcan in* [28].

Remark 2. *The range of the MEXP convex functions for* $m \in [0,1]$ *is* $[0, +\infty)$.

Proof. The proof is obvious. □

We explore some relations between the class of MEXPC functions and other classes of generalized convex functions.

Lemma 1. *The following inequalities* $(e^{\varrho} - 1) \geq \varrho$ *and* $(e^{1-\varrho} - 1) \geq (1 - \varrho)$ *hold* $\forall \varrho \in [0,1]$.

Proof. The proof is obvious, so omitted. □

Proposition 1. *If $m \in [0,1]$, then every nonnegative m–convex function is an MEXPC function.*

Proof. Since $m \in [0,1]$, by using Lemma 1, we have

$$\begin{aligned} & \mathsf{G}(\varrho \mathrm{g}_1 + m(1-\varrho)\mathrm{g}_2) \leq \varrho \mathsf{G}(\mathrm{g}_1) + m(1-\varrho)\mathsf{G}(\mathrm{g}_2) \\ \leq \; & (e^{\varrho} - 1)\mathsf{G}(\mathrm{g}_1) + m\left(e^{1-\varrho} - 1\right)\mathsf{G}(\mathrm{g}_2). \end{aligned}$$

□

Theorem 1. *The sum of two MEXPC functions is an MEXPC function.*

Proof. Let G and P be MEXPC functions. It follows that

$$\begin{aligned} & (\mathsf{G}+\mathsf{P})\left[(\varrho \mathrm{g}_1 + m(1-\varrho)\mathrm{g}_2)\right] \\ = \; & \mathsf{G}(\varrho \mathrm{g}_1 + m(1-\varrho)\mathrm{g}_2) + \mathsf{P}(\varrho \mathrm{g}_1 + m(1-\varrho)\mathrm{g}_2) \\ \leq \; & (e^{\varrho} - 1)\mathsf{G}(\mathrm{g}_1) + m\left(e^{1-\varrho} - 1\right)\mathsf{G}(\mathrm{g}_2) \\ & +(e^{\varrho} - 1)\mathsf{P}(\mathrm{g}_1) + m\left(e^{1-\varrho} - 1\right)\mathsf{P}(\mathrm{g}_2) \\ = \; & (\mathrm{e}^{\varrho} - 1)[\mathsf{G}(\mathrm{g}_1) + \mathsf{P}(\mathrm{g}_1)] + m\left(e^{1-\varrho} - 1\right)[\mathsf{G}(\mathrm{g}_2) + \mathsf{P}(\mathrm{g}_2)] \\ = \; & (e^{\varrho} - 1)(\mathsf{G}+\mathsf{P})(\mathrm{g}_1) + m\left(e^{1-\varrho} - 1\right)(\mathsf{G}+\mathsf{P})(\mathrm{g}_2), \end{aligned}$$

which implies that $\mathsf{G} + \mathsf{P}$ is an MEXP convex function. □

Theorem 2. *Scalar multiplication of the MEXPC function is also an MEXPC function.*

Proof. Let G be an MEXPC function. It follows that

$$\begin{aligned} & (c\mathsf{G})\left[(\varrho \mathrm{g}_1 + m(1-\varrho)\mathrm{g}_2)\right] \\ & = c\left[\mathsf{G}(\varrho \mathrm{g}_1 + m(1-\varrho)\mathrm{g}_2)\right] \\ & \leq c\left[(e^{\varrho} - 1)\mathsf{G}(\mathrm{g}_1) + m\left(e^{1-\varrho} - 1\right)\mathsf{G}(\mathrm{g}_2)\right] \\ & = (e^{\varrho} - 1)c\mathsf{G}(\mathrm{g}_1) + m\left(e^{1-\varrho} - 1\right)c\mathsf{G}(\mathrm{g}_2) \\ & = (e^{\varrho} - 1)(c\mathsf{G})(\mathrm{g}_1) + m\left(e^{1-\varrho} - 1\right)(c\mathsf{G})(\mathrm{g}_2), \end{aligned}$$

which implies that $c\mathsf{G}$ is an MEXPC function. □

Theorem 3. *Let $\mathsf{P} : [0,b] \to J$ be an m–convex function for $b > 0$ and $m \in [0,1]$, and $\mathsf{G} : \mathbb{X} \to \mathbb{R}$ is non-decreasing and an MEXPC function. It follows that the function $\mathsf{G} \circ \mathsf{P} : [0,b] \to \mathbb{R}$ is an MEXPC function.*

Proof. $\forall g_1, g_2 \in [0, b]$, $m \in [0,1]$, and $\varrho \in [0,1]$, we have

$$\begin{aligned}
&(\mathsf{G} \circ \mathsf{P})(\varrho g_1 + m(1-\varrho)g_2) \\
&= \mathsf{G}(\mathsf{P}(\varrho g_1 + m(1-\varrho)g_2)) \\
&\leq \mathsf{G}(\varrho \mathsf{P}(g_1) + m(1-\varrho)\mathsf{P}(g_2)) \\
&\leq (e^{\varrho} - 1)\mathsf{G}(\mathsf{P})(g_1) + m\left(e^{1-\varrho} - 1\right)\mathsf{G}(\mathsf{P})(g_2) \\
&= (e^{\varrho} - 1)(\mathsf{G} \circ \mathsf{P})(g_1) + m\left(e^{1-\varrho} - 1\right)(\mathsf{G} \circ \mathsf{P})(g_2),
\end{aligned}$$

which implies that $\mathsf{G} \circ \mathsf{P}$ is an MEXPC function. □

Theorem 4. *Let $\mathsf{G}_i : [g_1, g_2] \to \mathbb{R}$ be a class of MEXP convex functions for $m \in [0,1]$ and let $\mathsf{G}(g) = \sup_i \mathsf{G}_i(g)$. If $E = \{g \in [g_1, g_2] : \mathsf{G}(g) < +\infty\} \neq \emptyset$, then E is an interval, and G is an MEXP convex function on E.*

Proof. For all $g_1, g_2 \in E$, $m \in [0,1]$, and $\varrho \in [0,1]$, we have

$$\begin{aligned}
\mathsf{G}(\varrho g_1 + m(1-\mathsf{G})g_2) &= \sup_i \mathsf{G}_i(\varrho g_1 + m(1-\varrho)g_2) \\
\leq\ & \sup_i \left[(e^{\varrho} - 1)\mathsf{G}_i(g_1) + m\left(e^{1-\varrho} - 1\right)\mathsf{G}_i(g_2)\right] \\
\leq\ & (e^{\varrho} - 1)\sup_i \mathsf{G}_i(g_1) + m\left(e^{1-\varrho} - 1\right)\sup_i \mathsf{G}_i(g_2) \\
=\ & (e^{\varrho} - 1)\mathsf{G}(g_1) + m\left(e^{1-\varrho} - 1\right)\mathsf{G}(g_2) < +\infty.
\end{aligned}$$

□

Theorem 5. *If the function $\mathsf{G} : [g_1, g_2] \to \mathbb{R}$ is an MEXPC function for $m \in [0,1]$, then G is bounded on $[g_1, mg_2]$.*

Proof. Suppose $x \in [g_1, g_2]$ is a point, $m \in [0,1]$, and $L = \max\{\mathsf{G}(g_1), m\mathsf{G}(g_2)\}$. It follows that $\exists\ \varrho \in [0,1]$ such that $x = \varrho g_1 + m(1-\varrho)g_2$. Thus, since $e^{\varrho} \leq e$ and $e^{1-\varrho} \leq e$, we have

$$\begin{aligned}
\mathsf{G}(x) &= \mathsf{G}(\varrho g_1 + m(1-\varrho)g_2) \\
&\leq (e^{\varrho} - 1)\mathsf{G}(g_1) + m\left(e^{1-\varrho} - 1\right)\mathsf{G}(g_2) \\
&\leq (e-1)L + m(e-1)L = L(m+1)(e-1) = M.
\end{aligned}$$

□

4. Refinements of (H–H) Type Inequality for the *k*-Fractional Integral

Numerous academics across a wide range of fields have been studying fractional calculus and its applications in depth for a very long time, and interest in this topic has increased significantly. The notion of fractional derivatives and integrals has been used to propose numerous extensions of them, and authors have obtained new perspectives in a variety of fields, including engineering, physics, economics, biology, and statistics. Here, the term "Riemann–Liouville fractional integral" and its k-generalization are used, as well as some of the theorems that will be mentioned in this section.

Here, we first introduce and demonstrate two new lemmas. We achieve certain improvements of the trapezium type inequality for functions whose first derivative in absolute value at a specific power is an MEXPC function based on these new lemmas.

Lemma 2. *Let $0 < w \leq 1$, and $\mathsf{G} : [mw\mathsf{g}_1, \mathsf{g}_2] \to \mathbb{R}$ is a differentiable mapping on $(mw\mathsf{g}_1, \mathsf{g}_2)$ with $0 < m\mathsf{g}_1 < \mathsf{g}_2$ and $m \in (0,1]$. If $\mathsf{G}' \in L_1[mw\mathsf{g}_1, \mathsf{g}_2]$, then the following equality for k—fractional integral holds true:*

$$\begin{aligned} &\frac{\mathsf{G}(mw\mathsf{g}_1) + \frac{\alpha}{k}\mathsf{G}(\mathsf{g}_2)}{\frac{\alpha}{k}+1} - \frac{\Gamma_k(\alpha+k)}{(\mathsf{g}_2 - mw\mathsf{g}_1)^{\frac{\alpha}{k}}}\, {}^kJ^{\alpha}_{\mathsf{g}_2^-}\mathsf{G}(mw\mathsf{g}_1) \\ =& \left(\frac{\mathsf{g}_2 - mw\mathsf{g}_1}{\frac{\alpha}{k}+1}\right)\int_0^1 \left[\left(\frac{\alpha}{k}+1\right)\varrho^{\frac{\alpha}{k}} - 1\right] \mathsf{G}'(mw(1-\varrho)\mathsf{g}_1 + \varrho\mathsf{g}_2)\, d\varrho, \end{aligned} \tag{8}$$

where $\alpha, k > 0$ and $\Gamma(\cdot)$ is the Euler Gamma function.

Proof. Applying integrating by parts, we have

$$\begin{aligned} &\left(\frac{\mathsf{g}_2 - mw\mathsf{g}_1}{\frac{\alpha}{k}+1}\right)\int_0^1 \left[\left(\frac{\alpha}{k}+1\right)\varrho^{\frac{\alpha}{k}} - 1\right] \mathsf{G}'(mw(1-\varrho)\mathsf{g}_1 + \varrho\mathsf{g}_2)\, d\varrho \\ =& \left(\frac{\mathsf{g}_2 - mw\mathsf{g}_1}{\frac{\alpha}{k}+1}\right)\left\{\int_0^1 \left(\frac{\alpha}{k}+1\right)\varrho^{\frac{\alpha}{k}}\mathsf{G}'(mw(1-\varrho)\mathsf{g}_1 + \varrho\mathsf{g}_2)\, d\varrho \right. \\ &\left. - \int_0^1 \mathsf{G}'(mw(1-\varrho)\mathsf{g}_1 + \varrho\mathsf{g}_2)\, d\varrho\right\} \\ =& \left(\frac{\mathsf{g}_2 - mw\mathsf{g}_1}{\frac{\alpha}{k}+1}\right)\left[\left(\frac{\alpha}{k}+1\right)\left\{\frac{\varrho^{\frac{\alpha}{k}}\mathsf{G}(mw(1-\varrho)\mathsf{g}_1 + \varrho\mathsf{g}_2)}{\mathsf{g}_2 - mw\mathsf{g}_1}\bigg|_0^1 \right.\right. \\ &\left.\left. - \int_0^1 \frac{\mathsf{G}(mw(1-\varrho)\mathsf{g}_1 + \varrho\mathsf{g}_2)}{\mathsf{g}_2 - mw\mathsf{g}_1}\frac{\alpha}{k}\varrho^{\frac{\alpha}{k}-1}\, d\varrho\right\} - \frac{\mathsf{G}(mw(1-\varrho)\mathsf{g}_1 + \varrho\mathsf{g}_2)}{\mathsf{g}_2 - mw\mathsf{g}_1}\bigg|_0^1\right] \\ =& \left(\frac{\mathsf{g}_2 - mw\mathsf{g}_1}{\frac{\alpha}{k}+1}\right)\left[\left(\frac{\alpha}{k}+1\right)\right. \\ &\times\left\{\frac{\mathsf{G}(\mathsf{g}_2)}{\mathsf{g}_2 - mwa_1} - \frac{\alpha}{k(\mathsf{g}_2 - mw\mathsf{g}_1)}\int_0^1 \varrho^{\frac{\alpha}{k}-1}\mathsf{G}(mw(1-\varrho)\mathsf{g}_1 + \varrho\mathsf{g}_2)\, d\varrho\right\} \\ &\left. - \frac{\mathsf{G}(\mathsf{g}_2) - \mathsf{G}(mw\mathsf{g}_1)}{\mathsf{g}_2 - mw\mathsf{g}_1}\right] \\ =& \frac{\mathsf{G}(mw\mathsf{g}_1) + \frac{\alpha}{k}\mathsf{G}(\mathsf{g}_2)}{\frac{\alpha}{k}+1} - \frac{\Gamma_k(\alpha+k)}{(\mathsf{g}_2 - mw\mathsf{g}_1)^{\frac{\alpha}{k}}}\, {}^kJ^{\alpha}_{\mathsf{g}_2^-}\mathsf{G}(mw\mathsf{g}_1), \end{aligned}$$

which completes the proof. □

Lemma 3. *Let $0 < w \leq 1$, and $\mathsf{G} : [mw\mathsf{g}_1, \mathsf{g}_2] \to \mathbb{R}$ is a differentiable mapping on $(mw\mathsf{g}_1, \mathsf{g}_2)$ with $0 < m\mathsf{g}_1 < \mathsf{g}_2$ and $m \in (0,1]$. If $\mathsf{G}' \in L_1[mw\mathsf{g}_1, \mathsf{g}_2]$, then the following equality for k—fractional integral holds true:*

$$\begin{aligned} &\frac{\mathsf{G}(mw\mathsf{g}_1) + \mathsf{G}(\mathsf{g}_2)}{w+1} - \frac{\Gamma_k(\alpha+k)}{(w+1)(\mathsf{g}_2 - mw\mathsf{g}_1)^{\frac{\alpha}{k}}}\left\{{}^kJ^{\alpha}_{\mathsf{g}_1^+}\mathsf{G}(\mathsf{g}_2) + {}^kJ^{\alpha}_{\mathsf{g}_2^-}\mathsf{G}(mw\mathsf{g}_1)\right\} \\ =& \left(\frac{\mathsf{g}_2 - mw\mathsf{g}_1}{w+1}\right)\int_0^1 \left[\varrho^{\frac{\alpha}{k}} - (1-\varrho)^{\frac{\alpha}{k}}\right]\mathsf{G}'(mw(1-\varrho)\mathsf{g}_1 + \varrho\mathsf{g}_2)d\varrho. \end{aligned} \tag{9}$$

Proof. Applying integrating by parts, we have

$$\begin{aligned}
&\left(\frac{g_2 - mwg_1}{w+1}\right)\int_0^1\left[\varrho^{\frac{\alpha}{k}} - (1-\varrho)^{\frac{\alpha}{k}}\right]G'(mw(1-\varrho)g_1 + \varrho g_2)d\varrho \\
=\ &\left(\frac{g_2 - mwg_1}{w+1}\right)\left[\int_0^1 \varrho^{\frac{\alpha}{k}}G'(mw(1-\varrho)g_1 + \varrho g_2)d\varrho\right. \\
&\left.-\int_0^1 (1-\varrho)^{\frac{\alpha}{k}}G'(mw(1-\varrho)g_1 + \varrho g_2)d\varrho\right] \\
=\ &\left(\frac{g_2 - mwg_1}{w+1}\right)[I_1 - I_2], \qquad (10)
\end{aligned}$$

where

$$\begin{aligned}
I_1 &= \int_0^1 \varrho^{\frac{\alpha}{k}}G'(mw(1-\varrho)g_1 + \varrho g_2)d\varrho \\
&= \frac{\varrho^{\frac{\alpha}{k}}G(mw(1-\varrho)g_1 + \varrho g_2)}{g_2 - mwg_1}\Bigg|_0^1 - \int_0^1 \frac{G(mw(1-\varrho)g_1 + \varrho g_2)}{g_2 - mwg_1}\frac{\alpha}{k}\varrho^{\frac{\alpha}{k}-1}\,d\varrho \\
&= \frac{G(g_2)}{g_2 - mwg_1} - \frac{\alpha}{k(g_2 - mwg_1)}\int_0^1 \varrho^{\frac{\alpha}{k}-1}G(mw(1-\varrho)g_1 + \varrho g_2)\,d\varrho \\
&= \frac{G(g_2)}{g_2 - mwg_1} - \frac{\Gamma_k(\alpha+k)}{(g_2 - mwg_1)^{\frac{\alpha}{k}+1}}\,{}^kJ^{\alpha}_{g_2^-}G(mwg_1) \qquad (11)
\end{aligned}$$

and

$$\begin{aligned}
I_2 &= \int_0^1 (1-\varrho)^{\frac{\alpha}{k}}\,G'(mw(1-\varrho)g_1 + \varrho g_2)d\varrho \\
&= \frac{(1-\varrho)^{\frac{\alpha}{k}}G(mw(1-\varrho)g_1 + \varrho g_2)}{g_2 - mwg_1}\Bigg|_0^1 \\
&\quad - \int_0^1 \frac{G(mw(1-\varrho)g_1 + \varrho g_2)}{g_2 - mwg_1}\frac{\alpha}{k}(1-\varrho)^{\frac{\alpha}{k}-1}\,(-1)\,d\varrho \\
&= -\frac{G(mwg_1)}{g_2 - mwg_1} + \frac{\alpha}{k(g_2 - mwg_1)}\int_0^1 (1-\varrho)^{\frac{\alpha}{k}-1}\,G(mw(1-\varrho)g_1 + \varrho g_2)\,d\varrho \\
&= -\frac{G(mwg_1)}{g_2 - mwg_1} + \frac{\Gamma_k(\alpha+k)}{(g_2 - mwg_1)^{\frac{\alpha}{k}+1}}\,{}^kJ^{\alpha}_{g_1^+}G(g_2). \qquad (12)
\end{aligned}$$

Combining Equations (11) and (12) in (10) and multiplying it by $\frac{g_2 - wg_1}{w+1}$, we obtain (9), which completes the proof. □

Theorem 6. *Let $0 < w \leq 1$, and $G : \left(0, \frac{g_2}{mw}\right] \to \mathbb{R}$ is a differentiable mapping on $\left(0, \frac{g_2}{mw}\right)$ with $0 < g_1 < g_2$. If $|G'|^q$ is an MEXPC function on $\left(0, \frac{g_2}{mw}\right]$ for $q > 1$ and $q^{-1} + p^{-1} = 1$, then for some fixed $m \in (0,1]$ the following inequality for k—fractional integral holds true:*

$$\begin{aligned}
&\left|\frac{G(mwg_1) + \frac{\alpha}{k}G(g_2)}{\frac{\alpha}{k}+1} - \frac{\Gamma_k(\alpha+k)}{(g_2 - mwg_1)^{\frac{\alpha}{k}}}\,{}^kJ^{\alpha}_{g_2^-}G(mwg_1)\right| \\
\leq\ &\left(\frac{g_2 - mwg_1}{\frac{\alpha}{k}+1}\right)[U_1(\alpha,k,p) + U_2(\alpha,k,p)]^{\frac{1}{p}}\left[(e-2)\left(m|G'(wg_1)|^q + |G'(g_2)|^q\right)\right]^{\frac{1}{q}}, \qquad (13)
\end{aligned}$$

where

$$U_1(\alpha,k,p) = \int_0^{\frac{1}{\sqrt[\alpha]{(\frac{\alpha}{k}+1)^k}}} \left(1-\left(\frac{\alpha}{k}+1\right)\varrho^{\frac{\alpha}{k}}\right)^p d\varrho,$$
$$U_2(\alpha,k,p) = \int_{\frac{1}{\sqrt[\alpha]{(\frac{\alpha}{k}+1)^k}}}^1 \left(\left(\frac{\alpha}{k}+1\right)\varrho^{\frac{\alpha}{k}}-1\right)^p d\varrho.$$

Proof. Using Lemma 2, with the help of Hölder's inequality and the MEXPC function of $|G'|^q$, we obtain

$$\begin{aligned}
&\left|\frac{G(mwg_1)+\frac{\alpha}{k}G(g_2)}{\frac{\alpha}{k}+1} - \frac{\Gamma_k(\alpha+k)}{(g_2-mwg_1)^{\frac{\alpha}{k}}}\, {}^kJ^{\alpha}_{g_2^-}G(mwg_1)\right| \\
\le\ & \left(\frac{g_2-mwg_1}{\frac{\alpha}{k}+1}\right)\int_0^1\left|\left(\frac{\alpha}{k}+1\right)\varrho^{\frac{\alpha}{k}}-1\right|\,|G'(mw(1-\varrho)g_1+\varrho g_2)|\,d\varrho \\
\le\ & \left(\frac{g_2-mwg_1}{\frac{\alpha}{k}+1}\right)\left(\int_0^1\left|\left(\frac{\alpha}{k}+1\right)\varrho^{\frac{\alpha}{k}}-1\right|^p d\varrho\right)^{\frac{1}{p}}\left(\int_0^1|G'(mw(1-\varrho)g_1+\varrho g_2)|^q d\varrho\right)^{\frac{1}{q}} \\
\le\ & \left(\frac{g_2-mwg_1}{\frac{\alpha}{k}+1}\right)\left(\int_0^1\left|\left(\frac{\alpha}{k}+1\right)\varrho^{\frac{\alpha}{k}}-1\right|^p d\varrho\right)^{\frac{1}{p}} \\
&\times\left(\int_0^1\left[m\left(e^{1-\varrho}-1\right)|G'(wg_1)|^q+(e^{\varrho}-1)|G'(g_2)|^q\right]d\varrho\right)^{\frac{1}{q}} \\
=\ & \left(\frac{g_2-mwg_1}{\frac{\alpha}{k}+1}\right)[U_1(\alpha,k,p)+U_2(\alpha,k,p)]^{\frac{1}{p}}\left[(e-2)\left(m|G'(wg_1)|^q+|G'(g_2)|^q\right)\right]^{\frac{1}{q}},
\end{aligned}$$

which completes the proof. □

Theorem 7. *Let $0 < w \le 1$, and $G : (0, \frac{g_2}{mw}] \to \mathbb{R}$ is a differentiable mapping on $(0, \frac{g_2}{mw})$ with $0 < g_1 < g_2$. If $|G'|^q$ is an MEXPC function on $(0, \frac{g_2}{mw}]$ for $q \ge 1$, then for some fixed $m \in (0,1]$ the following inequality for k—fractional integral holds true:*

$$\begin{aligned}
&\left|\frac{G(mwg_1)+\frac{\alpha}{k}G(g_2)}{\frac{\alpha}{k}+1} - \frac{\Gamma_k(\alpha+k)}{(g_2-mwg_1)^{\frac{\alpha}{k}}}\, {}^kJ^{\alpha}_{g_2^-}G(mwg_1)\right| \\
\le\ & \left(\frac{g_2-mwg_1}{\frac{\alpha}{k}+1}\right)\left(\frac{2\alpha}{k(\frac{\alpha}{k}+1)^{\frac{k}{\alpha}+1}}\right)^{1-\frac{1}{q}} \\
&\times\Bigg[m|G'(wg_1)|^q\Bigg\{-\frac{2\alpha}{k(\frac{\alpha}{k}+1)^{\frac{k}{\alpha}+1}}-2e^{\left(1-\frac{1}{\sqrt[\alpha]{(\frac{\alpha}{k}+1)^k}}\right)} \\
&-\left(\frac{\alpha}{k}+1\right)e\,\gamma\left(\frac{\alpha}{k}+1,\frac{1}{\sqrt[\alpha]{(\frac{\alpha}{k}+1)^k}}\right) \\
&+\left(\frac{\alpha}{k}+1\right)e\,\gamma_{1-\frac{1}{\sqrt[\alpha]{(\frac{\alpha}{k}+1)^k}}}\left(\frac{\alpha}{k}+1,\frac{1}{\sqrt[\alpha]{(\frac{\alpha}{k}+1)^k}}\right)+1\Bigg\} \\
&+|G'(g_2)|\Bigg\{2e^{\frac{1}{\sqrt[\alpha]{(\frac{\alpha}{k}+1)^k}}}-\frac{2\alpha}{k(\frac{\alpha}{k}+1)^{\frac{k}{\alpha}+1}}+\left(\frac{\alpha}{k}+1\right)\gamma\left(\frac{\alpha}{k}+1,\frac{1}{\sqrt[\alpha]{(\frac{\alpha}{k}+1)^k}}\right) \\
&-\left(\frac{\alpha}{k}+1\right)\gamma_{1-\frac{1}{\sqrt[\alpha]{(\frac{\alpha}{k}+1)^k}}}\left(\frac{\alpha}{k}+1,\frac{1}{\sqrt[\alpha]{(\frac{\alpha}{k}+1)^k}}\right)-e\Bigg\}\Bigg]^{\frac{1}{q}}.
\end{aligned} \tag{14}$$

Proof. Using Lemma 2, with the help of power mean inequality and the MEXPC function of $|\mathsf{G}'|^q$, we obtain

$$
\begin{aligned}
&\left|\frac{\mathsf{G}(mwg_1)+\frac{\alpha}{k}\mathsf{G}(g_2)}{\frac{\alpha}{k}+1}-\frac{\Gamma_k(\alpha+k)}{(g_2-mwg_1)^{\frac{\alpha}{k}}}\,{}^kJ^{\alpha}_{g_2^-}\mathsf{G}(mwg_1)\right| \\
\leq\; & \left(\frac{g_2-mwg_1}{\frac{\alpha}{k}+1}\right)\int_0^1\left|\left(\frac{\alpha}{k}+1\right)\varrho^{\frac{\alpha}{k}}-1\right|\left|\mathsf{G}'(mw(1-\varrho)g_1+\varrho g_2)\right|d\varrho \\
\leq\; & \left(\frac{g_2-mwg_1}{\frac{\alpha}{k}+1}\right)\left(\int_0^1\left|\left(\frac{\alpha}{k}+1\right)\varrho^{\frac{\alpha}{k}}-1\right|d\varrho\right)^{1-\frac{1}{q}} \\
&\times\left(\int_0^1\left|\left(\frac{\alpha}{k}+1\right)\varrho^{\frac{\alpha}{k}}-1\right|\left|\mathsf{G}'(mw(1-\varrho)g_1+\varrho g_2)\right|^q d\varrho\right)^{\frac{1}{q}} \\
\leq\; & \left(\frac{g_2-mwg_1}{\frac{\alpha}{k}+1}\right)\left(\int_0^1\left|\left(\frac{\alpha}{k}+1\right)\varrho^{\frac{\alpha}{k}}-1\right|d\varrho\right)^{1-\frac{1}{q}} \\
&\times\left(\int_0^1\left|\left(\frac{\alpha}{k}+1\right)\varrho^{\frac{\alpha}{k}}-1\right|\left[m\left(e^{1-\varrho}-1\right)\left|\mathsf{G}'(wg_1)\right|^q+(e^{\varrho}-1)\left|\mathsf{G}'(g_2)\right|^q\right]d\varrho\right)^{\frac{1}{q}} \\
=\; & \left(\frac{g_2-mwg_1}{\frac{\alpha}{k}+1}\right)\left(\frac{2\alpha}{k(\frac{\alpha}{k}+1)^{\frac{k}{\alpha}+1}}\right)^{1-\frac{1}{q}}\left[m\left|\mathsf{G}'(wa_1)\right|^q\left\{-\frac{2\alpha}{k(\frac{\alpha}{k}+1)^{\frac{k}{\alpha}+1}}-2e^{\left(1-\frac{1}{\sqrt[\alpha]{(\frac{\alpha}{k}+1)^k}}\right)}\right.\right. \\
&-\left(\frac{\alpha}{k}+1\right)e\gamma\left(\frac{\alpha}{k}+1,\frac{1}{\sqrt[\alpha]{(\frac{\alpha}{k}+1)^k}}\right)+\left(\frac{\alpha}{k}+1\right)e\gamma_{1-\frac{1}{\sqrt[\alpha]{(\frac{\alpha}{k}+1)^k}}}\left(\frac{\alpha}{k}+1,\frac{1}{\sqrt[\alpha]{(\frac{\alpha}{k}+1)^k}}\right)+1\Bigg\} \\
&+\left|\mathsf{G}'(g_2)\right|\left\{2e^{\frac{1}{\sqrt[\alpha]{(\frac{\alpha}{k}+1)^k}}}-\frac{2\alpha}{k(\frac{\alpha}{k}+1)^{\frac{k}{\alpha}+1}}+\left(\frac{\alpha}{k}+1\right)\gamma\left(\frac{\alpha}{k}+1,\frac{1}{\sqrt[\alpha]{(\frac{\alpha}{k}+1)^k}}\right)\right. \\
&\left.\left.-\left(\frac{\alpha}{k}+1\right)\gamma_{1-\frac{1}{\sqrt[\alpha]{(\frac{\alpha}{k}+1)^k}}}\left(\frac{\alpha}{k}+1,\frac{1}{\sqrt[\alpha]{(\frac{\alpha}{k}+1)^k}}\right)-e\right\}\right]^{\frac{1}{q}},
\end{aligned}
$$

which completes the proof. □

Theorem 8. *Let $0 < w \leq 1$, and $\mathsf{G} : (0, \frac{g_2}{m}] \to \mathbb{R}$ is a differentiable mapping on $(0, \frac{g_2}{m})$ with $0 < g_1 < g_2$. If $|\mathsf{G}'|^q$ is an MEXPC function on $(0, \frac{g_2}{m}]$ for $q > 1$ and $q^{-1} + p^{-1} = 1$, then for some fixed $m \in (0, 1]$ the following inequality for k—fractional integral holds true:*

$$
\begin{aligned}
&\left|\frac{\mathsf{G}(mwg_1)+\mathsf{G}(g_2)}{w+1}-\frac{\Gamma_k(\alpha+k)}{(w+1)(g_2-mwg_1)^{\frac{\alpha}{k}}}\left\{{}^kJ^{\alpha}_{g_1^+}\mathsf{G}(g_2)+{}^kJ^{\alpha}_{g_2^-}\mathsf{G}(mwg_1)\right\}\right| \\
\leq\; & \frac{2(g_2-mwg_1)}{w+1}\left(\frac{k}{\alpha p+k}\right)^{\frac{1}{p}}\left[(e-2)\left(m\left|\mathsf{G}'(wg_1)\right|^q+\left|\mathsf{G}'(g_2)\right|^q\right)\right]^{\frac{1}{q}}. \qquad (15)
\end{aligned}
$$

Proof. Using Lemma 3, with the help of Hölder's inequality and the MEXPC function of $|G'|^q$, we obtain

$$
\begin{aligned}
&\left|\frac{G(mwg_1)+G(g_2)}{w+1}-\frac{\Gamma_k(\alpha+k)}{(w+1)(g_2-mwg_1)^{\frac{\alpha}{k}}}\left\{{}^kJ^{\alpha}_{g_1^+}G(g_2)+{}^kJ^{\alpha}_{g_2^-}G(mwg_1)\right\}\right| \\
\le\;&\left(\frac{g_2-mwg_1}{w+1}\right)\int_0^1\left|\varrho^{\frac{\alpha}{k}}-(1-\varrho)^{\frac{\alpha}{k}}\right|\left|G'(mw(1-\varrho)g_1+\varrho g_2)\right|d\varrho \\
\le\;&\left(\frac{g_2-mwg_1}{w+1}\right)\left[\int_0^1\varrho^{\frac{\alpha}{k}}\left|G'(mw(1-\varrho)g_1+\varrho g_2)\right|d\varrho\right. \\
&\left.+\int_0^1(1-\varrho)^{\frac{\alpha}{k}}\left|G'(mw(1-\varrho)g_1+\varrho g_2)\right|d\varrho\right] \\
\le\;&\left(\frac{g_2-mwg_1}{w+1}\right)\left[\left(\int_0^1\varrho^{\frac{\alpha}{k}p}d\varrho\right)^{\frac{1}{p}}\left(\int_0^1\left|G'(mw(1-\varrho)g_1+\varrho g_2)\right|^q d\varrho\right)^{\frac{1}{q}}\right. \\
&\left.+\left(\int_0^1(1-\varrho)^{\frac{\alpha}{k}p}d\varrho\right)^{\frac{1}{p}}\left(\int_0^1\left|G'(mw(1-\varrho)a_1+\varrho g_2)\right|^q d\varrho\right)^{\frac{1}{q}}\right] \\
\le\;&\left(\frac{g_2-mwg_1}{w+1}\right)\left[\left(\int_0^1\varrho^{\frac{\alpha}{k}p}d\varrho\right)^{\frac{1}{p}}\right. \\
&\times\left(\int_0^1\left[m\left(e^{1-\varrho}-1\right)\left|G'(wg_1)\right|^q+(e^{\varrho}-1)\left|G'(g_2)\right|^q\right]d\varrho\right)^{\frac{1}{q}}+\left(\int_0^1(1-\varrho)^{\frac{\alpha}{k}p}d\varrho\right)^{\frac{1}{p}} \\
&\left.\times\left(\int_0^1\left[m\left(e^{1-\varrho}-1\right)\left|G'(wg_1)\right|^q+(e^{\varrho}-1)\left|G'(g_2)\right|^q\right]d\varrho\right)^{\frac{1}{q}}\right] \\
=\;&\frac{2(g_2-mwg_1)}{w+1}\left(\frac{k}{\alpha p+k}\right)^{\frac{1}{p}}\left[(e-2)\left(m\left|G'(wg_1)\right|^q+\left|G'(g_2)\right|^q\right)\right]^{\frac{1}{q}},
\end{aligned}
$$

which completes the proof. □

Theorem 9. *Let $0<w\le 1$, and $G:(0,\frac{a_2}{m}]\to\mathbb{R}$ is a differentiable mapping on $(0,\frac{g_2}{m})$ with $0<g_1<g_2$. If $|G'|^q$ is an MEXPC function on $(0,\frac{g_2}{m}]$ for $q\ge 1$, then for some fixed $m\in(0,1]$ the following inequality for k—fractional integral holds true:*

$$
\begin{aligned}
&\left|\frac{G(mwg_1)+G(g_2)}{w+1}-\frac{\Gamma_k(\alpha+k)}{(w+1)(g_2-mwg_1)^{\frac{\alpha}{k}}}\left\{{}^kJ^{\alpha}_{g_1^+}G(g_2)+{}^kJ^{\alpha}_{g_2^-}G(mwg_1)\right\}\right| \\
\le\;&\left(\frac{a_2-mwg_1}{w+1}\right)\left(\frac{k}{\alpha+k}\right)^{1-\frac{1}{q}}\left[\left\{m\left|G'(wg_1)\right|^q\left(\Gamma\left(\frac{\alpha}{k}+1\right)-\Gamma\left(\frac{\alpha}{k}+1,1\right)e-\frac{1}{\frac{\alpha}{k}+1}\right)\right.\right. \\
&\left.+\left|G'(g_2)\right|^q\left(\Gamma\left(\frac{\alpha}{k}+1,-1\right)-\Gamma\left(\frac{\alpha}{k}+1\right)-\frac{1}{\frac{\alpha}{k}+1}\right)\right\}^{\frac{1}{q}} \\
&+\left\{m\left|G'(wg_1)\right|^q\left((-1)^{\frac{\alpha}{k}-1}\left(\Gamma\left(\frac{\alpha}{k}+1\right)-\Gamma\left(\frac{\alpha}{k}+1,-1\right)\right)-\frac{1}{\frac{\alpha}{k}+1}\right)\right. \\
&\left.\left.+\left|G'(g_2)\right|^q\left(\frac{(\frac{\alpha}{k}+1)ek(\Gamma(\frac{\alpha}{k}+1,1)-\Gamma(\frac{\alpha}{k}+1))}{k+\alpha}-\frac{1}{\frac{\alpha}{k}+1}\right)\right\}^{\frac{1}{q}}\right].
\end{aligned}
\tag{16}
$$

Proof. Using Lemma 3 with the help of power mean inequality and the MEXPC function of $|G'|^q$, we obtain

$$\begin{aligned}
&\left|\frac{G(mwg_1)+G(g_2)}{w+1} - \frac{\Gamma_k(\alpha+k)}{(w+1)(g_2-mwg_1)^{\frac{\alpha}{k}}}\left\{{}^kJ^{\alpha}_{g_1^+}G(g_2) + {}^kJ^{\alpha}_{g_2^-}G(mwg_1)\right\}\right| \\
\leq\;& \left(\frac{g_2-mwg_1}{w+1}\right)\int_0^1\left|\varrho^{\frac{\alpha}{k}}-(1-\varrho)^{\frac{\alpha}{k}}\right|\left|G'(mw(1-\varrho)g_1+\varrho g_2)\right|d\varrho \\
\leq\;& \left(\frac{g_2-mwg_1}{w+1}\right) \\
&\times\left[\int_0^1\varrho^{\frac{\alpha}{k}}\left|G'(mw(1-\varrho)g_1+\varrho g_2)\right|d\varrho+\int_0^1(1-\varrho)^{\frac{\alpha}{k}}\left|G'(mw(1-\varrho)g_1+\varrho g_2)\right|d\varrho\right] \\
\leq\;& \left(\frac{g_2-mwg_1}{w+1}\right)\left[\left(\int_0^1\varrho^{\frac{\alpha}{k}}d\varrho\right)^{1-\frac{1}{q}}\left(\int_0^1\varrho^{\frac{\alpha}{k}}\left|G'(mw(1-\varrho)g_1+\varrho g_2)\right|^q d\varrho\right)^{\frac{1}{q}}\right. \\
&\left.+\left(\int_0^1(1-\varrho)^{\frac{\alpha}{k}}d\varrho\right)^{1-\frac{1}{q}}\left(\int_0^1(1-\varrho)^{\frac{\alpha}{k}}\left|G'(mw(1-\varrho)g_1+\varrho g_2)\right|^q d\varrho\right)^{\frac{1}{q}}\right] \\
\leq\;& \left(\frac{g_2-mwg_1}{w+1}\right)\left(\int_0^1\varrho^{\frac{\alpha}{k}}d\varrho\right)^{1-\frac{1}{q}} \\
&\times\left[\left(\int_0^1\varrho^{\frac{\alpha}{k}}\left[m\left(e^{1-\varrho}-1\right)\left|G'(wg_1)\right|^q+(e^{\varrho}-1)\left|G'(g_2)\right|^q\right]d\varrho\right)^{\frac{1}{q}}\right. \\
&\left.+\left(\int_0^1(1-\varrho)^{\frac{\alpha}{k}}\left[m\left(e^{1-\varrho}-1\right)\left|G'(wg_1)\right|^q+(e^{\varrho}-1)\left|G'(g_2)\right|^q\right]d\varrho\right)^{\frac{1}{q}}\right] \\
=\;& \left(\frac{a_2-mwg_1}{w+1}\right)\left(\frac{k}{\alpha+k}\right)^{1-\frac{1}{q}} \\
&\times\left[\left\{m\left|G'(wg_1)\right|^q\left(\Gamma\left(\frac{\alpha}{k}+1\right)-\Gamma\left(\frac{\alpha}{k}+1,1\right)e-\frac{1}{\frac{\alpha}{k}+1}\right)\right.\right. \\
&\left.+\left|G'(g_2)\right|^q\left(\Gamma\left(\frac{\alpha}{k}+1,-1\right)-\Gamma\left(\frac{\alpha}{k}+1\right)-\frac{1}{\frac{\alpha}{k}+1}\right)\right\}^{\frac{1}{q}} \\
&+\left\{m\left|G'(wg_1)\right|^q\left((-1)^{\frac{\alpha}{k}-1}\left(\Gamma\left(\frac{\alpha}{k}+1\right)-\Gamma\left(\frac{\alpha}{k}+1,-1\right)\right)-\frac{1}{\frac{\alpha}{k}+1}\right)\right. \\
&\left.\left.+\left|G'(g_2)\right|^q\left(\left(\frac{\alpha}{k}+1\right)ek\left(\Gamma\left(\frac{\alpha}{k}+1,1\right)-\Gamma\left(\frac{\alpha}{k}+1\right)\right)k+\alpha-\frac{1}{\frac{\alpha}{k}+1}\right)\right\}^{\frac{1}{q}}\right],
\end{aligned}$$

which completes the proof. □

5. Conclusions

In this study, some fresh evaluations of the (H − H) type inequality for a new generalized convex function are presented. Recently, many mathematicians have worked on the inequality hypothesis to provide a new dimension to mathematical analysis. To proceed in this direction, we have generalized a new definition and have established related inequalities. Since it is simple and convenient to move forward by application of the expectation, we contend that the novel mathematical thoughts, concepts, and strategies we have introduced here are more natural than those currently presented in the literature. In future, we intend to work on concepts such as interval valued analysis, time scale calculus, and quantum calculus for this new convexity and improve inequalities, including the Opial, Simpson, Bullen, Newton, Fejé, Mercer, and Ostrowski types.

Author Contributions: Conceptualization, M.T. and S.K.S.; methodology, M.T., S.K.S. and S.K.N.; software, M.T. and S.K.S.; validation, M.T., S.K.S., S.K.N., and A.A.S.; formal analysis, S.K.S., S.K.N., O.M.A. and K.N.; investigation, M.T., S.K.S. and K.N.; resources, S.K.S. and O.M.A.; data curation, O.M.A., A.A.S. and K.N.; writing—original draft preparation, M.T. and S.K.S.; writing—review and editing, M.T., S.K.S. and A.A.S.; supervision, S.K.S., S.K.N. and A.A.S.; project administration, S.K.S.; funding acquisition, K.N. All authors have read and agreed to the published version of the manuscript.

Funding: This research was supported by the Fundamental Fund of Khon Kaen University, Thailand.

Data Availability Statement: Not applicable.

Conflicts of Interest: The authors declare that they have no conflict of interest.

References

1. Green, J.; Walter P.H. Mathematical analysis and convexity with applications to economics. In *Handbook of Mathematical Economics*; North-Holland Publishing Co.: Amsterdam, The Netherlands, 1981; Volume 1, pp. 15–52.
2. Föllmer, A.; Schied, A. Convex measures of risk and trading constraints. *Financ. Stoch.* **2002**, *6*, 429–447.
3. Pełczyński, J. Application of the theory of convex sets for engineering structures with uncertain parameters. *Appl. Sci.* **2020**, *10*, 6864. [CrossRef]
4. Pennanen, T. Convex duality in stochastic optimization and mathematical finance. *Math. Oper. Res.* **2011**, *36*, 340–362. [CrossRef]
5. El Shaed, M.A. Fractional calculus model of semilunar heart valve vibrations. In Proceedings of the International Mathematica Symposium, London, UK, 7–11 July 2003.
6. Hoan, L.V.C.; Akinlar, M.A.; Inc, M.; Gomez-Aguilar, J.F.; Chu, Y.M.; Almohsen, B. A new fractional-order compartmental disease model. *Alex. Eng. J.* **2020**, *59*, 3187–3196.
7. Atangana, A. Application of fractional calculus to epidemiology. *Fract. Dyn.* **2016**, 174–190.
8. Kulish, V.V.; Lage, J.L. Application of fractional calculus to fluid mechanics. *J. Fluids Eng.* **2002**, *124*, 803–806. [CrossRef]
9. Baleanu, D.; Güvenç, Z.B.; Machado, J.T. *New Trends in Nanotechnology and Fractional Calculus Applications*; Springer: New York, NY, USA, 2010.
10. Magin, R.L. *Fractional Calculus in Bio-Engineering*; Begell House Inc. Publishers: Danbury, CT, USA, 2006.
11. Axtell, M.; Bise, M.E. Fractional calculus application in control systems. In Proceedings of the IEEE Conference on Aerospace and Electronics, Dayton, OH, USA, 21–25 May 1990; pp. 563–566.
12. AlNemer, G.; Zakarya, M.; Abd El-Hamid, H.A.; Kenawy, M.R.; Rezk, H.M. Dynamic Hardy-type inequalities with non-conjugate parameters. *Alex. Eng. J.* **2020**, *59*, 4523–4532. [CrossRef]
13. Abd El-Hamid, H.A.; Rezk, H.M.; Ahmed, A.M.; AlNemer, G.; Zakarya, M.; El Saify, H.A. Dynamic inequalities in quotients with general kernels and measures. *J. Funct. Spaces.* **2020**, *2020*, 5417084.
14. Zakarya, M.; Altanji, M.; AlNemer, G.; Abd El-Hamid, H.A.; Cesarano, C.; Rezk, M. Fractional reverse coposn's inequalities via conformable calculus on Time Scales. *Symmetry*, **2021**, *13*, 542. [CrossRef]
15. Rezk, H.M.; Albalawi, W.; Abd El-Hamid, H.A.; Ahmed, I.S.; Bazighifan, O.; Mohamed, M.S.; Zakarya, M. Hardy-Leindler type inequalities via conformable delta fractional calculus. *J. Funct. Spaces.* **2022**, *2022*, 2399182. [CrossRef]
16. Srivastava, H.M.; Murugusundaramoorthy, G.; El-Deeb, S.M. Faber polynomial coefficient estimates of bi-close-to-convex functions connected with the Borel distribution of the Mittag-Leffler type. *J. Nonlinear Var. Anal.* **2021**, *5*, 103–118.
17. Wang, H. Certain integral inequalities related to $(\varphi, \varrho^{\alpha})$-Lipschitzian mappings and generalized h-convexity on fractal sets. *J. Nonlinear Funct. Anal.* **2021**, *2021*, 12.
18. Omotoyinbo, O.; Mogbodemu, A. Some new Hermite–Hadamard integral inequalities for convex functions. *Int. J. Sci. Innovation Tech.* **2014**, *1*, 1–12.
19. Butt, S.I.; Tariq, M.; Aslam, A.; Ahmad, H.; Nofel, T.A. Hermite–Hadamard type inequalities via generalized harmonic exponential convexity. *J. Funct. Spaces.* **2021**, *2021*, 5533491. [CrossRef]
20. Rafiq, A.; Mir, N.A.; Ahmad, F. Weighted Chebysev–Ostrowski type inequalities. *Appl. Math. Mech.* **2007**, *28*, 901–906. [CrossRef]
21. Khan, M.A.; Chu, Y.M.; Khan, T.U. Some new inequalities of Hermite–Hadamard type for s–convex functions with applications. *Open Math.* **2017**, *15*, 1414–1430. [CrossRef]
22. Niculescu, C.P.; Persson, L.E. *Convex Functions and Their Applications*; Springer: New York, NY, USA, 2006.
23. Alomari, M.; Darus, M.; Kirmaci, U.S. Refinements of Hadamard-type inequalities for quasi-convex functions with applications to trapezoidal formula and to special means. *Comput. Math. Appl.* **2010**, *59*, 225–232. [CrossRef]
24. Chen, F.X.; Wu, S.H. Several complementary inequalities to inequalities of Hermite–Hadamard type for s–convex functions. *J. Nonlinear Sci. Appl.* **2016**, *9*, 705–716. [CrossRef]
25. Tariq, M. New Hermite–Hadamard type and some related inequalities via s-type p-convex function. *IJSER* **2020**, *11*, 498–508.
26. Kashuri, A.; Liko, R. Some new Hermite–Hadamard type inequalities and their applications. *Stud. Sci. Math. Hung.* **2019**, *56*, 103–142.

27. Toader, G. Some generalizations of the convexity. In Proceedings of the Colloquium on Approximation and Optimization, Cluj-Napoca, Romania, 25–27 October 1985; pp. 329–338.
28. Kadakal, M.; İşcan, İ. Exponential type convexity and some related inequalities. *J. Inequal. Appl.* **2020**, *2020*, 82. [CrossRef]
29. Mitrinovic, D.S.; Pećaric, J.E.; Fink, A.M. *Classical and New Inequalities in Analysis*; Kluwer Academic: Dordrecht, The Netherlands, 1993.
30. Kadakal, M.; İscan, İ.; Kadakal, H. On improvements of some integral inequalities. *Honam Math. J.* **2021**, *43*, 441–452.
31. Anastassiou, G.A. *Advanced Inequalities*; World Scientifc: Singapore, 2011.
32. Kilbas, A.A.; Srivastava, H.M.; Trujillo, J.J. *Theory and Applications of Fractional Differential Equations*; Elsevier: Amsterdam, The Netherlands, 2006.
33. Sahoo, S.K.; Ahmad, H.; Tariq, M.; Kodamasingh, B.; Aydi, H.; De la Sen, M. Hermite–Hadamard type inequalities involving k-fractional operator for $(\bar{h}, m)$-convex Functions. *Symmetry* **2021**, *13*, 1686. [CrossRef]
34. Ahmad, H; Tariq, M.; Sahoo, S.K.; Baili, J.; Cesarano, C. New estimations of Hermite–Hadamard type integral inequalities for special functions. *Fractal Fract.* **2021**, *5*, 144.
35. Gorenflo, R.; Mainardi, F. *Fractional Calculus: Integral and Differential Equations of Fractional Order*; Springer: Vienna, Austria, 1997.
36. Miller, K.; Ross, B. *An Introduction to the Fractional Calculus and Fractional Differential Equations*; John Wiley and Sons, Inc.: New York, NY, USA, 1993.
37. Podlubni, I. *Fractional Differential Equations*; Academic Press: San Diego, CA, USA, 1999.
38. Özdemir, M.E.; Yildiz, C.; Akdemir, A.O.; Set, E. On some inequalities for *s*–convex functions and applications. *J. Inequal. Appl.* **2013**, *333*, 2–11. [CrossRef]
39. Xi, B.Y.; Qi. F. Some integral inequalities of Hermite–Hadamard type for convex functions with applications to means. *J. Funct. Spaces Appl.* **2012**, *2012*, 980438. [CrossRef]
40. Sahoo, S.K.; Tariq, M.; Ahmad, H.; Nasir, J.; Aydi, H.; Mukheimer, A. New Ostrowski-type fractional integral inequalities via generalized exponential-type convex functions and applications. *Symmetry* **2021**, *13*, 1429. [CrossRef]
41. Mubeen, S.; Habibullah, G.M. *k*-Fractional integrals and applications. *Int. Contemp. Math Sci.* **2012**, *7*, 89–94.
42. Farid, G.; Rehman, A.U.; Zahra, M. On Hadamard inequalities for k-fractional integrals. *Nonlinear Funct. Anal. Appl.* **2016**, *21*, 463–478.

axioms

Article

Analytical Solutions of Temperature Distribution in a Rectangular Parallelepiped

Dinesh Kumar [1,†], Frédéric Yves Ayant [2,3,†] and Clemente Cesarano [4,*,†]

1 Department of Applied Sciences, College of Agriculture-Jodhpur, Agriculture University Jodhpur, Jodhpur 342304, India
2 Collége Jean L'herminier, Allée des Nymphéas, 83500 La Seyne-sur-Mer, France
3 Department VAR, Avenue Joseph Raynaud le Parc Fleuri, 83140 Six-Fours-les-Plages, France
4 Section of Mathematics, Luciano Modica, International Telematic University Uninettuno, Corso Vittorio Emanuele II, 00186 Roma, Italy
* Correspondence: clemente.cesarano@uninettunouniversity.net; Tel.: +39-0669207675
† These authors contributed equally to this work.

Abstract: In the present article, we give analytical solutions for temperature distribution in a rectangular parallelepiped with the help of a multivariable I-function. The results established in this paper are of a general character from which several known and new results can be deduced. We also give the special and particular cases of our main findings.

Keywords: multivariable I-function; multivariable H-function; temperature distribution

Citation: Kumar, D.; Ayant, F.Y.; Cesarano, C. Analytical Solutions of Temperature Distribution in a Rectangular Parallelepiped. *Axioms* **2022**, *11*, 488. https://doi.org/10.3390/axioms11090488

Academic Editor: Mircea Merca

Received: 23 August 2022
Accepted: 15 September 2022
Published: 19 September 2022

1. Introduction and Preliminaries

Fractional calculus is three centuries old—as old as conventional calculus. Its importance has been highlighted by many researchers in recent years.

Fractional calculus is based on integrals and the derivatives of non-integer arbitrary order, fractional differential equations and methods of their solution, approximations and implementation techniques. The concept of differentiation and integration to non-integer order is by no means new. Interest in this subject was evident almost as soon as the ideas of classical calculus were known. For the past three centuries, this subject was considered by mathematicians, and only in the last few years has it been applied to the fields of engineering, science and economics. As is well known, several physical phenomena are often better described by fractional derivatives. However, recent attempts have been made to define the fractional derivative as a local operator in fractal science theory.

In recent years, several authors have studied the functions of two or more variables, for example, see [1–5]. Recent expansion in the theory of I-functions has become important due to the introduction of the multivariable I-function which has been studied by many authors (for recent work, see [6,7]). Recently, Kumar & Ayant [8] provided an application of the Jacobi polynomial and multivariable Aleph-function in heat conduction in a non-homogeneous moving rectangular parallelepiped. Prasad & Pati [9] used the modified multivariable H-function and provided the temperature distribution in a rectangular parallelepiped. In the present paper, we provide an application of the multivariable I-function for temperature distribution in a rectangular parallelepiped.

The multivariable I-function is defined in terms of the multiple Mellin–Barnes-type integral, and is given in the following manner [10]:

$$I(z_1,\cdots,z_r)=I^{0,n_2;0,n_3;\cdots;0,n_r:m',n';\cdots;m^{(r)},n^{(r)}}_{p_2,q_2,p_3,q_3;\cdots;p_r,q_r:p',q';\cdots;p^{(r)},q^{(r)}}\left(\begin{array}{c} z_1 \\ \cdot \\ \cdot \\ z_r \end{array}\middle|\begin{array}{l}\left(a_{2j};\alpha^{(1)}_{2j},\alpha^{(2)}_{2j}\right)_{1,p_2};\cdots; \\ \left(b_{2j};\beta^{(1)}_{2j},\beta^{(2)}_{2j}\right)_{1,q_2};\cdots;\end{array}\right.$$

$$\left.\begin{array}{l}\left(a_{rj};\alpha^{(1)}_{rj},\cdots,\alpha^{(r)}_{rj}\right)_{1,p_r}:\left(a^{(1)}_j,\alpha^{(1)}_j\right)_{1,p^{(1)}};\cdots;\left(a^{(r)}_j,\alpha^{(r)}_j\right)_{1,p^{(r)}} \\ \left(b_{rj};\beta^{(1)}_{rj},\cdots,\beta^{(r)}_{rj}\right)_{1,q_r}:\left(b^{(1)}_j,\beta^{(1)}_j\right)_{1,q^{(1)}};\cdots;\left(b^{(r)}_j,\beta^{(r)}_j\right)_{1,q^{(r)}}\end{array}\right),$$

$$=\frac{1}{(2\pi\omega)^r}\int_{\mathcal{L}_1}\cdots\int_{\mathcal{L}_r}\xi(s_1,\cdots,s_r)\left\{\prod_{i=1}^{r}\phi_i(s_i)\,z_i^{s_i}\right\}\mathrm{d}s_1\cdots\mathrm{d}s_r, \tag{1}$$

where $z_i\neq 0$, $\omega=\sqrt{-1}$, and

$$\phi_i(s_i)=\frac{\left\{\prod_{j=1}^{m^{(i)}}\Gamma\left(b^{(i)}_j-\beta^{(i)}_j s_i\right)\right\}\left\{\prod_{j=1}^{n^{(i)}}\Gamma\left(1-a^{(i)}_j+\alpha^{(i)}_j s_i\right)\right\}}{\left\{\prod_{j=m^{(i)}+1}^{q^{(i)}}\Gamma\left(1-b^{(i)}_j+\beta^{(i)}_j s_i\right)\right\}\left\{\prod_{j=n^{(i)}+1}^{p^{(i)}}\Gamma\left(a^{(i)}_j-\alpha^{(i)}_j s_i\right)\right\}}\ \text{(for all } i\in\{1,\cdots,r\}), \tag{2}$$

$$\xi(s_1,\cdots,s_r)=\frac{\prod_{k=2}^{r}\left\{\prod_{j=1}^{n_k}\Gamma\left(1-a_{kj}+\sum_{i=1}^{k}\alpha^{(i)}_{kj}s_i\right)\right\}}{\prod_{k=2}^{r}\left\{\prod_{j=n_k+1}^{p_k}\Gamma\left(a_{kj}-\sum_{i=1}^{k}\alpha^{(i)}_{kj}s_i\right)\right\}}$$
$$\times\frac{1}{\prod_{k=2}^{r}\left\{\prod_{j=1}^{q_k}\Gamma\left(1-b_{kj}+\sum_{i=1}^{k}\beta^{(i)}_{kj}s_i\right)\right\}}. \tag{3}$$

For the existence and convergence conditions of (1) (the reader may wish to refer to work by Prasad [10]).

The absolute convergence condition of the multiple Mellin–Barnes-type contour (1) can be obtained by extension of the corresponding conditions for the multivariable H-function, given by

$$|\arg z_i|<\frac{1}{2}\Omega_i\,\pi,$$

where

$$\Omega_i=\sum_{k=1}^{n^{(i)}}\alpha^{(i)}_k-\sum_{k=n^{(i)}+1}^{p^{(i)}}\alpha^{(i)}_k+\sum_{k=1}^{m^{(i)}}\beta^{(i)}_k-\sum_{k=m^{(i)}+1}^{q^{(i)}}\beta^{(i)}_k+\left(\sum_{k=1}^{n_2}\alpha^{(i)}_{2k}-\sum_{k=n_2+1}^{p_2}\alpha^{(i)}_{2k}\right)$$
$$+\left(\sum_{k=1}^{n_r}\alpha^{(i)}_{rk}-\sum_{k=n_r+1}^{p_r}\alpha^{(i)}_{rk}\right)-\left(\sum_{k=1}^{q_2}\beta^{(i)}_{2k}+\sum_{k=1}^{q_3}\beta^{(i)}_{3k}+\cdots+\sum_{k=1}^{q_r}\beta^{(i)}_{rk}\right), \tag{4}$$

where $i=1,\cdots,r$.

Throughout the present paper, we assume the existence and absolute convergence conditions of the multivariable I-function.

We may establish the asymptotic expansion in the following convenient form:

$$I(z_1,\cdots,z_r)=O\left(|z_1|^{\alpha'_1},\cdots,|z_r|^{\alpha'_r}\right),\ \max(|z_1|,\cdots,|z_r|)\to 0$$

$$I(z_1,\cdots,z_r)=O\left(|z_1|^{\beta'_1},\cdots,|z_r|^{\beta'_s}\right),\ \min(|z_1|,\cdots,|z_r|)\to +\infty$$

where $k=1,\cdots,z;\ \alpha'_k=\min\left[\Re\left(b^{(k)}_j/\beta^{(k)}_j\right)\right]$, $j=1,\cdots,m^{(k)}$ and

$$\beta'_k=\max\left[\Re\left(\left(a^{(k)}_j-1\right)/\alpha^{(k)}_j\right)\right],\ j=1,\cdots,n^{(k)}.$$

We use the following notations in this paper:

$$U = p_2, q_2; p_3, q_3; \cdots ; p_{r-1}, q_{r-1}; \;\; V = 0, n_2; 0, n_3; \cdots ; 0, n_{r-1}, \tag{5}$$

$$W = \left(p^{(1)}, q^{(1)}\right); \cdots ; \left(p^{(r)}, q^{(r)}\right); \;\; X = \left(m^{(1)}, n^{(1)}\right); \cdots ; \left(m^{(r)}, n^{(r)}\right), \tag{6}$$

$$A = \left(a_{2k}, \alpha_{2k}^{(1)}, \alpha_{2k}^{(2)}\right)_{1,p_2}; \cdots ; \left(a_{(r-1)k}, \alpha_{(r-1)k}^{(1)}, \alpha_{(r-1)k}^{(2)}, \cdots, \alpha_{(r-1)k}^{(r-1)}\right)_{1,p_{r-1}}, \tag{7}$$

$$B = \left(b_{2k}, \beta_{2k}^{(1)}, \beta_{2k}^{(2)}\right)_{1;q_2}; \cdots ; \left(b_{(r-1)k}, \beta_{(r-1)k}^{(1)}, \beta_{(r-1)k}^{(2)}, \cdots, \beta_{(r-1)k}^{(r-1)}\right)_{1,q_{r-1}}, \tag{8}$$

$$\mathbb{A} = \left(a_{rk}; \alpha_{rk}^{(1)}, \alpha_{rk}^{(2)}, \cdots, \alpha_{rk}^{(r)}\right)_{1,p_r} : \left(a_k^{(1)}, \alpha_k^{(1)}\right)_{1,p'}; \cdots ; \left(a_k^{(r)}, \alpha_k^{(r)}\right)_{1,p^{(r)}}, \tag{9}$$

$$\mathbb{B} = \left(b_{rk}; \beta_{rk}^{(1)}, \beta_{rk}^{(2)}, \cdots, \beta_{rk}^{(r)}\right)_{1,q_r} : \left(b_k^{(1)}, \beta_k^{(1)}\right)_{1,q'}; \cdots ; \left(b_k^{(r)}, \beta_k^{(r)}\right)_{1,q^{(r)}}. \tag{10}$$

2. Formulation of the Problem

The temperature $\theta(x, y, z, t)$ at any point of a rectangular parallelepiped of edges a, b, c, can be represented by the following partial differential equation:

$$\frac{\partial \theta}{\partial t} = K_1\left(\frac{\partial^2 \theta}{\partial x^2} + \frac{\partial^2 \theta}{\partial y^2} + \frac{\partial^2 \theta}{\partial z^2}\right) + \psi(x, y, z, t) + c_0\, \theta(x, y, z, t), \tag{11}$$

where t is the time, $K_1 = \frac{K}{\rho c}$, in which K is the thermal conductivity of the rectangular parallelepiped, ρ is the density, c is the specific heat and ψ is the heat source within it; K, ρ, c and c_0 are constants.

The initial and boundary conditions are taken as

$$\theta(x, y, z, 0) = f(x, y, z), \tag{12}$$

$$\theta(a, y, z, t) = g_1(y, z), \tag{13}$$

$$\theta(x, b, z, t) = h_1(x, z), \tag{14}$$

$$\theta(x, y, c, t) = r_1(x, y), \tag{15}$$

$$\theta(0, y, z, t) = g_2(y, z), \tag{16}$$

$$\theta(x, 0, z, t) = h_2(x, z), \tag{17}$$

$$\theta(x, y, 0, t) = r_2(x, y), \tag{18}$$

3. Solution of the Problem

Required Integral

We will need the following result:

Lemma 1.

$$\int_0^b \sin\left(\frac{n\pi y}{b}\right) e^{-\mu y} \mathrm{d}y = \frac{\pi n b}{(\mu^2 b^2 + n^2 \pi^2)}\left[(-)^{n+1} e^{-\mu b} + 1\right]. \tag{19}$$

For the solution of (11) under the conditions (12)–(18), we take the triple finite Fourier transform which is represented as follows:

$$\bar{\theta}(m, n, q, t) = \int_0^a \int_0^b \int_0^c \theta(x, y, z, t) \sin\left(\frac{m\pi x}{a}\right) \sin\left(\frac{n\pi y}{b}\right) \sin\left(\frac{q\pi z}{c}\right) \mathrm{d}x\, \mathrm{d}y\, \mathrm{d}z. \tag{20}$$

Now, multiplying both sides of (11) by $\sin\left(\frac{m\pi x}{a}\right)\sin\left(\frac{n\pi y}{b}\right)\sin\left(\frac{q\pi z}{c}\right)$, and integrating over the whole rectangular parallelepiped, we get

$$
\begin{aligned}
&\int_0^a\int_0^b\int_0^c \frac{\partial\theta}{\partial t}\sin\left(\frac{m\pi x}{a}\right)\sin\left(\frac{n\pi y}{b}\right)\sin\left(\frac{q\pi z}{c}\right)\mathrm{d}x\,\mathrm{d}y\,\mathrm{d}z\\
&= K_1\int_0^a\int_0^b\int_0^c\left[\frac{\partial\theta^2}{\partial x^2}+\frac{\partial\theta^2}{\partial y^2}+\frac{\partial\theta^2}{\partial z^2}\right]\sin\left(\frac{m\pi x}{a}\right)\sin\left(\frac{n\pi y}{b}\right)\sin\left(\frac{q\pi z}{c}\right)\mathrm{d}x\,\mathrm{d}y\,\mathrm{d}z\\
&+\int_0^a\int_0^b\int_0^c \psi(x,y,z,t)\sin\left(\frac{m\pi x}{a}\right)\sin\left(\frac{n\pi y}{b}\right)\sin\left(\frac{q\pi z}{c}\right)\mathrm{d}x\,\mathrm{d}y\,\mathrm{d}z\\
&+c_0\int_0^a\int_0^b\int_0^c \theta(x,y,z,t)\sin\left(\frac{m\pi x}{a}\right)\sin\left(\frac{n\pi y}{b}\right)\sin\left(\frac{q\pi z}{c}\right)\mathrm{d}x\,\mathrm{d}y\,\mathrm{d}z. \qquad (21)
\end{aligned}
$$

By the application of results of (20), (13)–(18) and Sneddon [11], the equation (21) is transformed to

$$
\begin{aligned}
&\frac{\mathrm{d}\bar{\theta}}{\mathrm{d}t}+K_1\pi^2\left[\frac{m^2}{a^2}+\frac{n^2}{b^2}+\frac{q^2}{c^2}-\frac{c_0}{K_1}\right]\bar{\theta} = K_1[K_2\bar{F}_1(n,q)+K_3\bar{F}_2(m,q)+K_4\bar{F}_3(m,n)]\\
&+K_1[K_5\bar{F}_4(n,q)+K_6\bar{F}_5(m,q)+K_7\bar{F}_6(m,n)]+\bar{\psi}(m,n,q,t), \qquad (22)
\end{aligned}
$$

where,

$$\bar{F}_1(n,q) = \int_0^b\int_0^c g_1(y,z)\sin\left(\frac{n\pi y}{b}\right)\sin\left(\frac{q\pi z}{c}\right)\mathrm{d}y\,\mathrm{d}z, \qquad (23)$$

$$\bar{F}_2(m,q) = \int_0^a\int_0^c h_1(x,z)\sin\left(\frac{m\pi x}{a}\right)\sin\left(\frac{q\pi z}{c}\right)\mathrm{d}x\,\mathrm{d}z, \qquad (24)$$

$$\bar{F}_3(m,n) = \int_0^a\int_0^b r_1(x,y)\sin\left(\frac{m\pi x}{a}\right)\sin\left(\frac{n\pi y}{b}\right)\mathrm{d}x\,\mathrm{d}y, \qquad (25)$$

$$\bar{F}_4(n,q) = \int_0^b\int_0^c g_2(y,z)\sin\left(\frac{n\pi y}{b}\right)\sin\left(\frac{q\pi z}{c}\right)\mathrm{d}y\,\mathrm{d}z, \qquad (26)$$

$$\bar{F}_5(m,q) = \int_0^a\int_0^c h_2(x,z)\sin\left(\frac{m\pi x}{a}\right)\sin\left(\frac{q\pi z}{c}\right)\mathrm{d}x\,\mathrm{d}z, \qquad (27)$$

$$\bar{F}_6(m,n) = \int_0^a\int_0^b r_2(x,y)\sin\left(\frac{m\pi x}{b}\right)\sin\left(\frac{n\pi y}{b}\right)\mathrm{d}x\,\mathrm{d}y, \qquad (28)$$

$$K_2 = (-)^{m+1}\frac{m\pi}{a}, \qquad (29)$$

$$K_3 = (-)^{n+1}\frac{n\pi}{b}, \qquad (30)$$

$$K_4 = (-)^{q+1}\frac{q\pi}{c}, \qquad (31)$$

$$K_5 = \frac{m\pi}{a}, \qquad (32)$$

$$K_6 = \frac{n\pi}{b}, \qquad (33)$$

$$K_7 = \frac{n\pi}{c}. \qquad (34)$$

The Equation (22) can be written as

$$
\begin{aligned}
&\frac{d\bar{\theta}}{dt}+K_1B\bar{\theta} = K_1[K_2\bar{F}_1(n,q)+K_3\bar{F}_2(m,q)+K_4\bar{F}_3(m,n)]\\
&+K_1[K_5\bar{F}_4(n,q)+K_6\bar{F}_5(m,q)+K_7\bar{F}_6(m,n)]+\bar{\psi}(m,n,q,t), \qquad (35)
\end{aligned}
$$

where,

$$B = \pi^2\left[\frac{m^2}{a^2}+\frac{n^2}{b^2}+\frac{q^2}{c^2}-\frac{c_0}{K_1}\right], \qquad (36)$$

here c_0 is chosen that $B > 0$.

Applying the boundary condition (12) on the linear differential equation (35), we get the following result:

$$\bar{\theta}(m,n,q,t) = \bar{f}(m,n,q)\, e^{-K_1 B t} + \frac{1}{B}[K_2\bar{F}_1(n,q) + K_3\bar{F}_2(m,q) + K_4\bar{F}_3(m,n)]$$
$$+ K_1[K_5\bar{F}_4(n,q) + K_6\bar{F}_5(m,q) + K_7\bar{F}_6(m,n)]\left(1 - e^{-K_1 B t}\right)$$
$$+ \int_0^t e^{-K_1 B(t-\tau)}\bar{\psi}(m,n,q,\tau)\,d\tau, \qquad (37)$$

where,

$$\bar{f}(m,n,q) = \int_0^a \int_0^b \int_0^c f(x,y,z)\, \sin\left(\frac{m\pi x}{a}\right) \sin\left(\frac{n\pi y}{b}\right) \sin\left(\frac{q\pi z}{c}\right) dx\, dy\, dz. \qquad (38)$$

Using the theorem for the finite sine transform and the result of Sneddon [11], we get the following solution:

$$\theta(x,y,z,t) = \frac{8}{abc}\sum_{m,n,q=1}^{+\infty} \bar{f}(m,n,q)\, e^{-K_1 B t} \sin\left(\frac{m\pi x}{a}\right) \sin\left(\frac{n\pi y}{b}\right) \sin\left(\frac{q\pi z}{c}\right)$$
$$+ \frac{8}{abc}\sum_{m,n,q=1}^{+\infty} \frac{K_2}{B}\bar{F}_1(n,q)\left(1 - e^{-K_1 B t}\right) \sin\left(\frac{m\pi x}{a}\right) \sin\left(\frac{n\pi y}{b}\right) \sin\left(\frac{q\pi z}{c}\right)$$
$$+ \frac{8}{abc}\sum_{m,n,q=1}^{+\infty} \frac{K_3}{B}\bar{F}_2(m,q)\left(1 - e^{-K_1 B t}\right) \sin\left(\frac{m\pi x}{a}\right) \sin\left(\frac{n\pi y}{b}\right) \sin\left(\frac{q\pi z}{c}\right)$$
$$+ \frac{8}{abc}\sum_{m,n,q=1}^{+\infty} \frac{K_4}{B}\bar{F}_3(m,n)\left(1 - e^{-K_1 B t}\right) \sin\left(\frac{m\pi x}{a}\right) \sin\left(\frac{n\pi y}{b}\right) \sin\left(\frac{q\pi z}{c}\right)$$
$$+ \frac{8}{abc}\sum_{m,n,q=1}^{+\infty} \frac{K_5}{B}\bar{F}_4(n,q)\left(1 - e^{-K_1 B t}\right) \sin\left(\frac{m\pi x}{a}\right) \sin\left(\frac{n\pi y}{b}\right) \sin\left(\frac{q\pi z}{c}\right)$$
$$+ \frac{8}{abc}\sum_{m,n,q=1}^{+\infty} \frac{K_6}{B}\bar{F}_5(m,q)\left(1 - e^{-K_1 B t}\right) \sin\left(\frac{m\pi x}{a}\right) \sin\left(\frac{n\pi y}{b}\right) \sin\left(\frac{q\pi z}{c}\right)$$
$$+ \frac{8}{abc}\sum_{m,n,q=1}^{+\infty} \frac{K_7}{B}\bar{F}_6(m,n)\left(1 - e^{-K_1 B t}\right) \sin\left(\frac{m\pi x}{a}\right) \sin\left(\frac{n\pi y}{b}\right) \sin\left(\frac{q\pi z}{c}\right)$$
$$+ \frac{8}{abc}\sum_{m,n,q=1}^{+\infty} \sin\left(\frac{m\pi x}{a}\right) \sin\left(\frac{n\pi y}{b}\right) \sin\left(\frac{q\pi z}{c}\right) \int_0^t e^{-K_1 B(t-\tau)}\, \bar{\psi}(m,n,q,\tau)\,d\tau. \qquad (39)$$

4. Particular Case

On taking $g_1(y,z) = g_2(y,z) = h_1(x,z) = h_2(x,z) = r_1(x,y) = r_2(x,y) = 0$, the six faces of the rectangular parallelepiped are kept at zero temperature, the solution (39) reduces to

$$\theta(x,y,z,t) = \frac{8}{abc}\sum_{m,n,q=1}^{+\infty} \bar{f}(m,n,q)e^{-K_1 B t} \sin\left(\frac{m\pi x}{a}\right) \sin\left(\frac{n\pi y}{b}\right) \sin\left(\frac{q\pi z}{c}\right)$$
$$+ \frac{8}{abc}\sum_{m,n,q=1}^{+\infty} \sin\left(\frac{m\pi x}{a}\right) \sin\left(\frac{n\pi y}{b}\right) \sin\left(\frac{q\pi z}{c}\right) \int_0^t e^{-K_1 B(t-\tau)}\, \bar{\psi}(m,n,q,\tau)\,d\tau. \qquad (40)$$

Example

Since the multivariable I-function defined by Prasad [10] is the generalized function in the field of special functions, we are interested in obtaining a particular solution of the

Equation (40) by assuming both the initial temperature distribution at any point (x, y, z) and the heat source of general character in terms of the multivariable I-function.

For the first attempt, let us take (variables separation method)

$$f(x, y, z) = f_1(x) f_2(y) f_3(z), \tag{41}$$

where, $f_2(y) = e^{-\mu y}, f_3(z) = e^{-\delta z}$ and

$$f_1(x) = I^{V;0,n_r:X}_{U;p_r,q_r:W} \left(\begin{array}{c|c} c_1 x^{m_1} & A; \mathbb{A} \\ \vdots & \\ c_r x^{m_r} & B; \mathbb{B} \end{array} \right). \tag{42}$$

We obtain

$$\begin{aligned} &\bar{f}(m, n, p) \\ &= \sum_{r_1=0}^{+\infty} \frac{(-)^{r_1} (m\pi)^{2r_1+1}}{(2r_1+1)!} \frac{\pi^2 nqbc}{(\mu^2 b^2 + n^2\pi^2)(\delta^2 c^2 + q^2\pi^2)} \left[(-)^{n+1} e^{-\mu b} + 1 \right] \left[(-)^{q+1} e^{-\delta c} + 1 \right] \\ &\times I^{V;0,n_r+1:X}_{U;p_r+1,q_r+1:W} \left(\begin{array}{c|c} c_1 a^{m_1} & A; (-2r_1 - 2; m_1, \cdots, m_r), \mathbb{A} \\ \vdots & \\ c_r a^{m_r} & B; (-2r_1 - 1; m_1, \cdots, m_r), \mathbb{B} \end{array} \right), \end{aligned} \tag{43}$$

provided that $\min\{\mu, \delta, m_i\} > 0$ $(i = 1, \cdots, r)$, $2 + \sum_{i=1}^r m_i \min_{1 \leqslant j \leqslant m^{(i)}} \Re\left(\frac{b_j^{(i)}}{\beta_j^{(i)}} \right) > 0$, and $|\arg c_i| < \frac{1}{2}\Omega_i \pi$, where Ω_i is defined by (4).

Proof of (43). Considering the relation (41) and applying Lemma 19, according to (39), we have

$$\begin{aligned} \bar{f}(m, n, q) &= \int_0^a \int_0^b \int_0^c f(x, y, z) \sin\left(\frac{m\pi x}{a}\right) \sin\left(\frac{n\pi y}{b}\right) \sin\left(\frac{q\pi z}{c}\right) \mathrm{d}x\mathrm{d}y\mathrm{d}z \\ &= \frac{\pi^2 nqbc}{(\mu^2 b^2 + n^2\pi^2)(\delta^2 c^2 + q^2\pi^2)} \left[(-)^{n+1} e^{-\mu b} + 1 \right] \left[(-)^{q+1} e^{-\delta c} + 1 \right] \\ &\times \int_0^a \sin\left(\frac{m\pi x}{a}\right) f_1(x)\, \mathrm{d}x. \end{aligned} \tag{44}$$

Now, replacing $f_1(x)$ by the multivariable I-function with the help of (42), we have

$$\begin{aligned} \bar{f}(m, n, q) &= \frac{\pi^2 nqbc}{(\mu^2 b^2 + n^2\pi^2)(\delta^2 c^2 + q^2\pi^2)} \left[(-)^{n+1} e^{-\mu b} + 1 \right] \left[(-)^{q+1} e^{-\delta c} + 1 \right] \\ &\times \int_0^a \sin\left(\frac{m\pi x}{a}\right) I^{V;0,n_r:X}_{U;p_r,q_r:W} \left(\begin{array}{c|c} c_1 x^{m_1} & A; \mathbb{A} \\ \vdots & \vdots \\ c_r x^{m_r} & B; \mathbb{B} \end{array} \right) \mathrm{d}z, \end{aligned} \tag{45}$$

using the integrals representation of the multivariable I-function with the help of (1), and interchanging the order of integrations, which is justified under the conditions mentioned above, then we arrive at

$$\begin{aligned} \bar{f}(m, n, q) &= \frac{\pi^2 nqbc}{(\mu^2 b^2 + n^2\pi^2)(\delta^2 c^2 + q^2\pi^2)} \left[(-)^{n+1} e^{-\mu b} + 1 \right] \left[(-)^{q+1} e^{-\delta c} + 1 \right] \\ &\times \frac{1}{(2\pi\omega)^r} \int_{L_1} \cdots \int_{L_r} \xi(s_1, \cdots, s_r) \prod_{i=1}^r \phi_i(s_i) z_i^{s_i} c_i^{s_i} \int_0^a \sin\left(\frac{m\pi x}{a}\right) x^{\sum_{i=1}^r c_i s_i}\, \mathrm{d}x\, \mathrm{d}s_1 \cdots \mathrm{d}s_r. \end{aligned} \tag{46}$$

On the other hand, we have the following relation:

$$\sin\left(\frac{m\pi x}{a}\right) = \sum_{r_1=0}^{+\infty} \frac{(-1)^{2r_1+1}}{(2r_1+1)!}\left(\frac{m\pi x}{a}\right)^{2r_1+1}, \tag{47}$$

By using the above relation and interchanging the order of integration and summation, which is permissible under the stated validity conditions, then we get

$$\begin{aligned} \bar{f}(m,n,q) &= \frac{\pi^2 nqbc}{(\mu^2b^2+n^2\pi^2)(\delta^2c^2+q^2\pi^2)}\left[(-)^{n+1}e^{-\mu b}+1\right]\left[(-)^{q+1}e^{-\delta c}+1\right] \\ &\times \sum_{r_1=0}^{+\infty} \frac{(m\pi)^{2r_1+1}(-1)^{2r_1+1}}{a^{2r_1+1}(2r_1+1)!}\frac{1}{(2\pi\omega)^r}\int_{L_1}\cdots\int_{L_r}\xi(s_1,\cdots,s_r)\prod_{i=1}^{r}\phi_i(s_i)z_i^{s_i}c_i^{s_i} \\ &\times \int_0^a x^{\sum_{i=1}^r c_is_i+2r_1+1}\,\mathrm{d}x\,\mathrm{d}s_1\cdots\mathrm{d}s_r. \end{aligned} \tag{48}$$

Evaluating the inner integral and using the relation $\frac{1}{a} = \frac{\Gamma(a)}{\Gamma(a+1)}$, then

$$\begin{aligned} \bar{f}(m,n,q) &= \frac{\pi^2 nqbc}{(\mu^2b^2+n^2\pi^2)(\delta^2c^2+q^2\pi^2)}\left[(-)^{n+1}e^{-\mu b}+1\right]\left[(-)^{q+1}e^{-\delta c}+1\right] \\ &\times \sum_{r_1=0}^{+\infty} \frac{(-1)^{2r_1+1}}{(2r_1+1)!}(m\pi)^{2r_1+1}\frac{1}{(2\pi\omega)^r}\int_{L_1}\cdots\int_{L_r}\xi(s_1,\cdots,s_r) \\ &\times \prod_{i=1}^{r}\phi_i(s_i)z_i^{s_i}c_i^{s_i}\frac{\Gamma(\sum_{i=1}^r c_is_i+2r_1+2)}{\Gamma(\sum_{i=1}^r c_is_i+2r_1+3)}\,a^{\sum_{i=1}^r c_is_i}\,\mathrm{d}s_1\cdots\mathrm{d}s_r. \end{aligned} \tag{49}$$

Now, interpreting the multiple integrals (49) in terms of the I-function of r-variables, we obtain the required result (43). □

Again, for the heat source, let

$$\psi(x,y,z,t) = e^{-\alpha t}\psi'(x,y,z). \tag{50}$$

For the first attempt, let us take (variables separation method)

$$\psi'(x,y,z) = \psi_1(x)\psi_2(y)\psi_3(z), \tag{51}$$

where, $\psi_2(y) = e^{-\mu' y}$, $\psi_3(z) = e^{-\delta' z}$ and

$$\psi_1(x) = I^{V';0,n'_r:X'}_{U';p'_r,q'_r:W'}\left(\begin{array}{c|c} c'_1x^{m'_1} & A';\mathbb{A}' \\ \vdots & \\ c'_rx^{m'_r} & B';\mathbb{B}' \end{array}\right), \tag{52}$$

where,

$$U' = p'_2,q'_2;p'_3,q'_3;\cdots;p'_{r-1},q'_{r-1};\;\; V' = 0,n'_2;0,n'_3;\cdots;0,n'_{r-1}. \tag{53}$$

$$W' = \left(p'^{(1)},q'^{(1)}\right);\cdots;\left(p'^{(r)},q'^{(r)}\right);\;\; X = \left(m'^{(1)},n'^{(1)}\right);\cdots;\left(m'^{(r)},n'^{(r)}\right). \tag{54}$$

$$A' = \left(a'_{2k};\alpha'^{(1)}_{2k},\alpha'^{(2)}_{2k}\right)_{1,p'_2};\cdots;\left(a'^{(1)}_{(r-1)};\alpha'^{(1)}_{(r-1)k},\alpha'^{(2)}_{(r-1)k},\cdots,\alpha'^{(r-1)}_{(r-1)k}\right)_{1,p'_{r-1}}. \tag{55}$$

$$B' = \left(b'_{2k};\beta'^{(1)}_{2k},\beta'^{(2)}_{2k}\right)_{1,q'_2};\cdots;\left(b'^{(1)}_{(r-1)};\beta'^{(1)}_{(r-1)k},\beta''^{(2)}_{(r-1)k},\cdots,\beta'^{(r-1)}_{(r-1)k}\right)_{1,q'_{r-1}}. \tag{56}$$

$$\mathbb{A}' = \left(a'_{rk};\alpha'^{(1)}_{rk},\alpha'^{(2)}_{rk},\cdots,\alpha'^{(r)}_{rk}\right)_{1,p'_r}:\left(a'^{(1)}_k;\alpha'^{(1)}_k\right)_{1,p'^{(1)}},\cdots;\left(a'^{(r)}_k;\alpha'^{(r)}_k\right)_{1,p'^{(r)}}. \tag{57}$$

$$\mathbb{B}' = \left(b'_{rk}; \beta'^{(1)}_{rk}, \beta'^{(2)}_{rk}, \cdots, \beta'^{(r)}_{rk}\right)_{1,q'_r} : \left(b'^{(1)}_k; \beta'^{(1)}_k\right)_{1,q'^{(1)}}, \cdots ; \left(\beta'^{(r)}_k; \beta'^{(r)}_k\right)_{1,q'^{(r)}}. \tag{58}$$

Using the value of $\psi(x,y,z,t)$ in the Equation (20) and integrating ψ with respect to τ between the limits 0 and t, then we obtain

$$\int_0^t e^{-K_1B(t-\tau)}\,\bar{\psi}(m,n,q,\tau)\,\mathrm{d}\tau = \sum_{r_1=0}^{+\infty} \frac{(-)^{r_1}(m\pi)^{2r_1+1}}{(2r_1+1)!} \frac{\pi^2 nqbc}{(\mu'^2b^2+n^2\pi^2)(\delta'^2c^2+q^2\pi^2)}$$
$$\times \left[(-)^{n+1}e^{-\mu'b}+1\right]\left[(-)^{q+1}e^{-\delta'c}+1\right]\frac{e^{-K_1Bt}}{K_1B-\alpha}\left(e^{(K_1B-\alpha)t}-1\right)$$
$$\times I^{V';0,n'_r+1:X'}_{U';p'_r+1,q'_r+1:W'}\left(\begin{array}{c|c} c'_1a^{m_1} & A';(-2r_1-2;m'_1,\cdots,m'_r),\mathbb{A}' \\ \vdots & \vdots \\ c'_ra^{m_r} & B';(-2r_1-1;m'_1,\cdots,m'_r),\mathbb{B}' \end{array}\right), \tag{59}$$

provided that $\min\{\alpha,\mu',\delta',m'_i\} > 0\ (i=1,\cdots,r), 2+\sum_{i=1}^r m'_i \min_{1\leqslant j\leqslant m'^{(i)}} \Re\left(\frac{b'^{(i)}_j}{\beta'^{(i)}_j}\right) > 0$, and $|\arg c'_i| < \frac{1}{2}\Omega'_i\pi$, where

$$\Omega'_i = \sum_{k=1}^{n^{(i)}} \alpha'^{(i)}_k - \sum_{k=n^{(i)}+1}^{p^{(i)}} \alpha'^{(i)}_k + \sum_{k=1}^{m^{(i)}} \beta'^{(i)}_k - \sum_{k=m^{(i)}+1}^{q^{(i)}} \beta'^{(i)}_k + \left(\sum_{k=1}^{n_2} \alpha'^{(i)}_{2k} - \sum_{k=n_2+1}^{p_2} \alpha'^{(i)}_{2k}\right)$$
$$+ \left(\sum_{k=1}^{n_r} \alpha'^{(i)}_{rk} - \sum_{k=n_r+1}^{p_r} \alpha'^{(i)}_{rk}\right) - \left(\sum_{k=1}^{q_2} \beta'^{(i)}_{2k} + \sum_{k=1}^{q_3} \beta'^{(i)}_{3k} + \cdots + \sum_{k=1}^{q_r} \beta'^{(i)}_{rk}\right). \tag{60}$$

The proof of (59) is similar to (43).

Now, putting the known values of $\bar{f}(m,n,p)$ and $\int_0^t e^{-K_1B(t-\tau)}\,\bar{\psi}(m,n,q,\tau)\,\mathrm{d}\tau$ in Equation (40), we obtain the solution of our problem, defined as

$$\theta(x,y,z,t) = \frac{8}{abc}\sum_{m,n,q=1}^{+\infty}\sum_{r_1=0}^{+\infty} \frac{(-)^{r_1}(m\pi)^{2r_1+1}}{(2r_1+1)!} \frac{\pi^2 nqbc}{(\mu^2b^2+n^2\pi^2)(\delta^2c^2+q^2\pi^2)}$$
$$\times \left[(-)^{n+1}e^{-\mu b}+1\right]\left[(-)^{q+1}e^{-\delta c}+1\right]e^{-K_1Bt}\sin\left(\frac{m\pi x}{a}\right)\sin\left(\frac{n\pi y}{b}\right)\sin\left(\frac{q\pi z}{c}\right)$$
$$\times I^{V;0,n_r+1:X}_{U;p_r+1,q_r+1:W}\left(\begin{array}{c|c} c_1a^{m_1} & A;(-2r_1-2;m_1,\cdots,m_r),\mathbb{A} \\ \vdots & \\ c_ra^{m_r} & B;(-2r_1-1;m_1,\cdots,m_r),\mathbb{B} \end{array}\right)$$
$$+ \frac{8}{abc}\sum_{m,n,q=1}^{+\infty}\sum_{r_1=0}^{+\infty} \frac{(-)^{r_1}(m\pi)^{2r_1+1}}{(2r_1+1)!} \frac{\pi^2 nqbc}{(\mu'^2b^2+n^2\pi^2)(\delta'^2c^2+q^2\pi^2)}$$
$$\times \left[(-)^{n+1}e^{-\mu'b}+1\right]\left[(-)^{q+1}e^{-\delta'c}+1\right]$$
$$\times \frac{e^{-K_1Bt}}{K_1B-\alpha}\left(e^{(K_1B-\alpha)t}-1\right)\sin\left(\frac{m\pi x}{a}\right)\sin\left(\frac{n\pi y}{b}\right)\sin\left(\frac{q\pi z}{c}\right)$$
$$\times I^{V';0,n'_r+1:X'}_{U';p'_r+1,q'_r+1:W'}\left(\begin{array}{c|c} c'_1a^{m_1} & A';(-2r_1-2;m'_1,\cdots,m'_r),\mathbb{A}' \\ \vdots & \\ c'_ra^{m_r} & B';(-2r_1-1;m'_1,\cdots,m'_r),\mathbb{B}' \end{array}\right), \tag{61}$$

provided that $\min\{\mu,\delta,m_i\} > 0,\ \min\{\alpha,\mu',\delta',m'_i\} > 0$ for $i=1,\cdots,r, 2+\sum_{i=1}^r m_i \min_{1\leqslant j\leqslant m'^{(i)}} \Re\left(\frac{b^{(i)}_j}{\beta^{(i)}_j}\right) > 0,\ 2+\sum_{i=1}^r m'_i \min_{1\leqslant j\leqslant m'^{(i)}} \Re\left(\frac{b'^{(i)}_j}{\beta'^{(i)}_j}\right) > 0$, $|\arg c_i| < \frac{1}{2}\Omega_i\pi$, and $|\arg c'_i| < \frac{1}{2}\Omega'_i\pi$.

5. Special Cases

If $U_r = V_r = A = B = U_r' = V_r' = A' = B' = 0$, then the multivariable I-functions reduce to multivariable H-functions as defined by Srivastava et al. [12–15]. We have the following result:

Corollary 1.

$$\theta(x,y,z,t) = \frac{8}{abc}\sum_{m,n,q=1}^{+\infty}\sum_{r_1=0}^{+\infty}\frac{(-)^{r_1}(m\pi)^{2r_1+1}}{(2r_1+1)!}\frac{\pi^2 nqbc}{(\mu^2b^2+n^2\pi^2)(\delta^2c^2+q^2\pi^2)}$$
$$\times\left[(-)^{n+1}e^{-\mu b}+1\right]\left[(-)^{q+1}e^{-\delta c}+1\right]e^{-K_1Bt}\sin\left(\frac{m\pi x}{a}\right)\sin\left(\frac{n\pi y}{b}\right)\sin\left(\frac{q\pi z}{c}\right)$$
$$\times H^{0,n_r+1:X}_{p_r+1,q_r+1:W}\left(\begin{array}{c|c} c_1a^{m_1} & (-2r_1-2;m_1,\cdots,m_r),\mathbb{A} \\ \vdots\, c_ra^{m_r} & (-2r_1-1;m_1,\cdots,m_r),\mathbb{B}\end{array}\right)$$

$$+\frac{8}{abc}\sum_{m,n,q=1}^{+\infty}\sum_{r_1=0}^{+\infty}\frac{(-)^{r_1}(m\pi)^{2r_1+1}}{(2r_1+1)!}\frac{\pi^2 nqbc}{(\mu'^2b^2+n^2\pi^2)(\delta'^2c^2+q^2\pi^2)}$$
$$\times\left[(-)^{n+1}e^{-\mu' b}+1\right]\left[(-)^{q+1}e^{-\delta' c}+1\right]$$
$$\times\frac{e^{-K_1Bt}}{K_1B-\alpha}\left(e^{(K_1B-\alpha)t}-1\right)\sin\left(\frac{m\pi x}{a}\right)\sin\left(\frac{n\pi y}{b}\right)\sin\left(\frac{q\pi z}{c}\right)$$
$$\times H^{0,n_r'+1:X'}_{p_r'+1,q_r'+1:W'}\left(\begin{array}{c|c} c_1'a^{m_1} & (-2r_1-2;m_1',\cdots,m_r'),\mathbb{A}' \\ \vdots & \\ c_r'a^{m_r} & (-2r_1-1;m_1',\cdots,m_r'),\mathbb{B}'\end{array}\right), \tag{62}$$

under the same conditions that (61) *with* $U_r = V_r = A = B = U_r' = V_r' = A' = B' = 0$.

Corollary 2. *The heat source* $\psi(x,y,z,t)$ *vanishes, and the formal solution is given by*

$$\theta(x,y,z,t) = \frac{8}{abc}\sum_{m,n,q=1}^{+\infty}\sum_{r_1=0}^{+\infty}\frac{(-)^{r_1}(m\pi)^{2r_1+1}}{(2r_1+1)!}\frac{\pi^2 nqbc}{(\mu^2b^2+n^2\pi^2)(\delta^2c^2+q^2\pi^2)}$$
$$\times\left[(-)^{n+1}e^{-\mu b}+1\right]\left[(-)^{q+1}e^{-\delta c}+1\right]e^{-K_1Bt}\sin\left(\frac{m\pi x}{a}\right)\sin\left(\frac{n\pi y}{b}\right)\sin\left(\frac{q\pi z}{c}\right)$$
$$\times I^{V;0,n_r+1:X}_{U;p_r+1,q_r+1:W}\left(\begin{array}{c|c} c_1a^{m_1} & A;(-2r_1-1;m_1,\cdots,m_r),\mathbb{A} \\ \vdots & \vdots \\ c_ra^{m_r} & B;(-2r_1-2;m_1,\cdots,m_r),\mathbb{B}\end{array}\right), \tag{63}$$

under the conditions (43).

Corollary 3. *Consider the above formula, if* $U_r = V_r = A = B = 0$*, then we have*

$$\theta(x,y,z,t) = \frac{8}{abc}\sum_{m,n,q=1}^{+\infty}\sum_{r_1=0}^{+\infty}\frac{(-)^{r_1}(m\pi)^{2r_1+1}}{(2r_1+1)!}\frac{\pi^2 nqbc}{(\mu^2b^2+n^2\pi^2)(\delta^2c^2+q^2\pi^2)}$$
$$\times\left[(-)^{n+1}e^{-\mu b}+1\right]\left[(-)^{q+1}e^{-\delta c}+1\right]e^{-K_1Bt}\sin\left(\frac{m\pi x}{a}\right)\sin\left(\frac{n\pi y}{b}\right)\sin\left(\frac{q\pi z}{c}\right)$$
$$\times H^{0,n+1:X}_{p+1,q+1:W}\left(\begin{array}{c|c} c_1a^{m_1} & (-2r_1-1;m_1,\cdots,m_r),\mathbb{A} \\ \vdots & \vdots \\ c_ra^{m_r} & (-2r_1-2;m_1,\cdots,m_r),\mathbb{B}\end{array}\right), \tag{64}$$

under the conditions (43) *and* $U_r = V_r = A = B = 0$.

6. Conclusions

The significance of our findings lies in its generality. By specializing the various parameters and variables of the multivariable I-function in our results, we can obtain new results in the form of various special functions of one and several variables. Thus, the result obtained in this paper can yield a large number of results, involving a large variety of special functions and polynomials, concerning the problem of temperature distribution in a rectangular parallelepiped.

Author Contributions: All authors contributed substantially to the research. Conceptualization: D.K. and F.Y.A.; original draft preparation, D.K. and F.Y.A.; formal analysis, D.K., F.Y.A. and C.C.; review and editing, C.C.; validation, D.K., F.Y.A. and C.C.; funding acquisition, C.C. All authors have read and agreed to the published version of the manuscript.

Funding: This research received no external funding.

Institutional Review Board Statement: Not applicable.

Informed Consent Statement: Not applicable.

Data Availability Statement: Not applicable.

Acknowledgments: The author (DK) would like to thank the Agriculture University, Jodhpur, for supporting and encouraging this work.

Conflicts of Interest: The authors declare no conflict of interest.

References

1. Choi, J.; Daiya, J.; Kumar, D.; Saxena, R.K. Fractional differentiation of the product of Appell function F_3 and multivariable H-function. *Commun. Korean Math. Soc.* **2016**, *31*, 115–129. [CrossRef]
2. Daiya, J.; Ram, J.; Kumar, D. The multivariable H-function and the general class of Srivastava polynomials involving the generalized Mellin-Barnes contour integrals. *Filomat* **2016**, *30*, 1457–1464. [CrossRef]
3. Kumar, D. *Generalized Fractional Calculus Operators with Special Functions*, 1st ed.; LAP LAMBERT Academic Publishing: Saarbrücken, Germany, 2017.
4. Kumar, D.; Purohit, S.D.; Choi, J. Generalized fractional integrals involving product of multivariable H-function and a general class of polynomials. *J. Nonlinear Sci. Appl.* **2016**, *9*, 8–21. [CrossRef]
5. Ram, J.; Kumar, D. Generalized fractional integration involving Appell hypergeometric of the product of two H-functions. *Vijanana Parishad Anusandhan Patrika* **2011**, *54*, 33–43.
6. Kumar, D.; Ayant, F.Y. Fractional calculus pertaining to multivariable I-function defined by Prathima. *J. Appl. Math. Stat. Inform.* **2019**, *15*, 61–73. [CrossRef]
7. Kumar, D.; Ayant, F.Y. Some double integrals involving multivariable I-function. *Acta Univ. Apulensis Math. Inform.* **2019**, *58*, 35–43.
8. Kumar, D.; Ayant, F.Y. Application of Jacobi polynomial and multivariable Aleph-function in heat conduction in non-homogeneous moving rectangular parallelepiped. *Kragujevac J. Math.* **2021**, *45*, 439–447. [CrossRef]
9. Prasad, Y.N.; Pati, R. Application of modified multivariable H-function in temperature distribution in a rectangular parallelepiped. *Proc. Nat. Acad. Sci. Indian* **1982**, *52*, 52–62.
10. Prasad, Y.N. Multivariable I-function. *Vijnana Parishad Anusandhan Patrika* **1986**, *29*, 231–237.
11. Sneddon, I.N. *Fourier Transforms*; McGraw-Hill: New York, NY, USA, 1951.
12. Srivastava, H.M.; Panda, R. Some expansion theorems and generating relations for the H-function of several complex variables. *Comment. Math. Univ. St. Paul.* **1975**, *24*, 119–137.
13. Srivastava, H.M.; Panda, R. Some expansion theorems and generating relations for the H-function of several complex variables II. *Comment. Math. Univ. St. Paul.* **1976**, *25*, 167–197.
14. Mátyás, L.; Barna, I.F. General Self-Similar Solutions of Diffusion Equation and Related Constructions. *Rom. J. Phys.* **2022**, *67*, 1–16.
15. Wang, K.J.; Wang, G.D. Gamma function method for the nonlinear cubic-quintic Duffing oscillators. *J. Low Freq. Noise Vib. Act. Control* **2022**, *41*, 216–222.

axioms

MDPI

Article

Existence and Uniqueness of Solution to a Terminal Value Problem of First-Order Differential Equation

Yuqiang Feng [1,*], Qian Pan [2] and Jun Jiang [2]

[1] School of Science, Wuhan University of Science and Technology, Wuhan 430081, China
[2] Hubei Province Key Laboratory of Systems Science in Metallurgical Process, Wuhan 430081, China
* Correspondence: yqfeng6@126.com

Abstract: The terminal value problem of differential equations has an important application background. In this paper, we are concerned with the terminal value problem of a first-order differential equation. Some sufficient conditions are given to obtain the existence and uniqueness results of solutions to the problem. Firstly, some comparison lemmas are established; secondly, an iterative technique and fixed point method are used to set up the main results; Finally, an example is provided to illustrate the application of the main results.

Keywords: terminal value problem; existence; uniqueness; comparison lemma; solution

MSC: 34C99; 34A40; 34A45

Citation: Feng, Y.; Pan, Q.; Jiang, J. Existence and Uniqueness of Solution to a Terminal Value Problem of First-Order Differential Equation. *Axioms* **2022**, *11*, 435. https://doi.org/10.3390/axioms11090435

Academic Editor: Delfim F. M. Torres

Received: 29 July 2022
Accepted: 25 August 2022
Published: 26 August 2022

1. Introduction

The terminal value problem (also called the final value problem, initial inverse problem, backward in time problem, abbrev. **TVP**) is an exciting topic within differential equations. It has important applications in many fields, such as aerospace science, mathematical economics, optimal control, and differential games, etc. For example, in aerospace science, the question of how to design the flight path of a spacecraft given its landing site on a planet can be reduced to the terminal value problem of a differential equation.

With the development of nonlinear functional analysis, scholars have made significant progress with the use of the fixed point theory method in the study of the terminal value problem of differential equations. For example, Wang [1] transformed the terminal value problem of fractional differential equations into initial value problems based on the shooting method, and then used the theoretical results of the initial value problem of fractional differential equations in solving the terminal value problem. Finally, the effectiveness of this method to solve the final value problem of fractional differential equations was verified by numerical simulation. Zhang [2] used Monch's fixed point theorem to study the terminal value problem of first-order differential equations in Banach space, obtained a new existence theorem under looser conditions, and improved and generalized some known results. Wang [3] studied the existence and uniqueness of the solution to the terminal value problem of first-order differential equations with discontinuous terms in Banach space by using semi-order theory and the mixed monotone iteration technique, without involving compact conditions, and presented an error estimate of the iterative sequence of approximations to the solution. Zhou [4] used the new comparison results and semi-order theory to study the existence of the minimum and maximum solutions of the terminal value problem of first-order nonlinear differential equations in Banach space, and improved and generalized some known results. In [5], combining the generalized quasi-linearization technique with the upper and lower solutions method, Yakar and Arslan obtained a unique solution to the fractional causal terminal value problem. In [6], Shah and Rehman established a sufficient condition for the existence and uniqueness of the solution of a class of fractional differential equations over infinite intervals. In [7], the authors discussed the terminal value differential inequality, the existence of extreme value solutions of differential equations, and the corresponding comparison principle. In [8], Benchohra et al. presented the existence results and uniqueness of solutions for a class of boundary value problems of the terminal type for fractional differential equations with the Hilfer–Katugampola fractional derivative. The reasoning was mainly based upon different types of classical fixed point theorems, such as the Banach contraction principle and Krasnoselskii's fixed point theorem. In [9], Li et al. were concerned with the well-posedness and efficient numerical algorithm for a terminal value problem with a generalized Caputo fractional derivative. They investigated the existence and uniqueness of the solution of the terminal value problem and considered the continuous dependence of the solutions on the given data. In [10], Babak and Wu tempered fractional differential equations with terminal value problems. Discretized collocation methods on piecewise polynomial spaces were proposed for solving these equations. Regularity results were constructed on weighted spaces, and convergence order was studied.

The above results are mainly based on the properties of compact operators or increasing operators.

In this paper, we are concerned with the following **TVP**,

$$u'(t) = f(t, u(t)) \quad t \in [0, T], \quad u(T) = u_T,$$

where $T > 0, u_T \in R$ are two constants and $f : [0, T] \times R \to R$ is continuous.

By the properties of decreasing operators, we obtain the existence and uniqueness of the solution to this problem. Our contributions are the following:

(1) we present some comparison lemmas for (**TVP**);

(2) we establish the existence and uniqueness results of solutions for (**TVP**);

(3) we set up an iterative scheme of approximation solutions for (**TVP**).

The paper is organized as follows. In Section 2, some comparison lemmas are established; the existence and uniqueness results of (**TVP**) are presented in Section 3 via the iterative technique and fixed point method; an example shown in Section 4 illustrates the application of the results obtained.

2. Comparison Lemmas

The following comparison lemmas are of importance throughout this paper.

Lemma 1. *If $v \in C^1[0, T]$ satisfies*

$$v'(t) + \lambda v(t) \geqslant 0 \quad v(T) \leqslant 0 \quad t \in [0, T]$$

where $\lambda \in R$ is a constant, then $v(t) \leqslant 0$ for $t \in [0, T]$.

Proof. Since $v'(t) + \lambda v(t) \geqslant 0$, we have

$$e^{\lambda t}(v'(t) + \lambda v(t)) \geqslant 0$$

that is,

$$\left(v(t)e^{\lambda t}\right)' \geqslant 0$$

which implies that $v(t)e^{\lambda t}$ is increasing on $[0, T]$. Hence, for $\forall t \in [0, T]$,

$$v(t)e^{\lambda t} \leqslant v(T)e^{\lambda T} \leqslant 0$$

i.e., $v(t) \leqslant 0, t \in [0, T]$. □

Lemma 2. *Let $v, w \in C^1[0, T]$, and $\lambda \in R$ be a constant. If*

$$w'(t) + \lambda w(t) \leqslant v'(t) + \lambda v(t) \quad v(T) \leq u_T \leq w(T) \quad t \in [0, T],$$

then $v(t) \leqslant w(t)$ *for* $t \in [0, T]$.

Proof. Let $h(t) = v(t) - w(t)$, then we have

$$h'(t) + \lambda h(t) \geqslant 0 \quad h(T) \leqslant 0 \quad t \in [0, T].$$

By Lemma 1, we know $h(t) \leqslant 0, t \in [0, T]$, i.e., $v(t) \leqslant w(t)$ for $t \in [0, T]$. □

Lemma 3. *Let* $w \in C^1[0, T], h \in C[0, 1]$, *and* $\lambda \in R$ *be a constant. If*

$$w'(t) + \lambda w(t) \leqslant h(t) \quad w(T) \geq u_T \quad t \in [0, T],$$

then

$$w(t) \geq u_T e^{\lambda(T-t)} - \int_t^T e^{\lambda(s-t)} h(s)\, ds$$

for $t \in [0, T]$.

Proof. If $v \in C^1[0, 1]$ is a solution to the following terminal value problem

$$v'(t) + \lambda v(t) = h(t) \quad v(T) = u_T \quad t \in [0, T],$$

then we have

1.
$$v(t) = u_T e^{\lambda(T-t)} - \int_t^T e^{\lambda(T-t)} h(s)\, ds$$

2.
$$w'(t) + \lambda w(t) \leq v'(t) + \lambda v(t), \quad v(T) = u_T \leq w(T) \quad t \in [0, T].$$

By Lemma 2, we obtain

$$w(t) \geq v(t) = u_T e^{\lambda(T-t)} - \int_t^T e^{\lambda(T-t)} h(s)\, ds.$$

□

3. Main Results

In this section, we give some sufficient conditions to ensure the existence and uniqueness of the (**TVP**).

Firstly, we transform the (**TVP**) to a fixed point problem; secondly, we construct an iterative sequence by the integral operator; finally, by using comparison lemmas, we verify that the sequence is uniformly convergent to the unique solution of the (**TVP**).

Let $u, v \in C[0, T]$; if $u(t) \leq v(t)$ for $\forall t \in [0, T]$, we denote $u \leq v$. The order interval $[u, v] = \{x \in C[0, T] | u(t) \leq x(t) \leq v(t), \forall t \in [0, T]\}$.

The main result of this paper is the following.

Theorem 1. *Let us say that there exist* $v, w \in C^1[0, T]$, $v \leqslant w$ *and a constant* λ *such that*

1. *for* $\forall t \in [0, T]$, $x, y \in [v, w]$, $x \leqslant y$,

$$f(t, y(t)) - f(t, x(t)) \geqslant -\lambda(y(t) - x(t))$$

2. *for* $\forall t \in [0, T]$, $0 \leqslant \ell \leqslant 1$ *and* $x, y \in [v, w]$,

$$f(t, lx(t) + (1-l)y(t)) \geqslant l f(t, x(t)) + (1-l) f(t, y(t))$$

3. *for* $\forall t \in [0, T]$,

$$\begin{aligned} (v+w)'(t) + \lambda(v-w)(t) &\geqslant 2f(t, w(t)) \\ f(t, v(t)) &\geqslant w'(t) + \lambda(w-v)(t) \end{aligned} \tag{1}$$

4. $v(T) = u_T = w(T)$.

Then, (TVP) has a unique solution $\tilde{x}$ *satisfying* $v(t) \leq \tilde{x}(t) \leq w(t), t \in [0, T]$ *(abbr.* $\tilde{x} \in [v, w]$*).*

Proof. Let $x \in C[0, 1]$. If $h \in C^1[0, T]$ be a solution to the following terminal value problem:

$$h'(t) + \lambda h(t) = f(t, x(t)) + \lambda x(t),\ h(t) = u_T$$

Then,

$$h(t) = u_T e^{\lambda(T-t)} - \int_t^T e^{\lambda(T-t)}[f(s, x(s)) + \lambda x(s)]\, ds$$

Define a mapping T on $C[0, T]$ as follows:

$$(Tx)(t) = u_T e^{\lambda(T-t)} - \int_t^T e^{\lambda(s-t)}[f(s, x(s)) + \lambda x(s)]\, ds, \quad x \in C[0, 1].$$

It is easy to verify that T maps $C[0, T]$ into $C[0, T]$, and (TVP) has a solution if and only if T has a fixed point in $C[0, T]$.

By Assumptions (1) and (2), we know that T is decreasing and convex on $[v, w]$.

By the first inequality in (1), we have

$$\begin{cases} \left(\dfrac{v+w}{2}\right)'(t) + \lambda\left(\dfrac{v+w}{2}\right) \geqslant f(t \cdot w(t)) + \lambda w(t), \\ \left(\dfrac{v+w}{2}\right)(T) = u_T. \end{cases}$$

Due to the second inequality in (1), we obtain

$$\begin{cases} w'(t) + \lambda w(t) \leqslant f(t, v(t)) + \lambda v(t), \\ w(T) = u_T. \end{cases}$$

Let $x_0(t)$ be a solution to the following terminal value problem:

$$\begin{cases} u'(t) + \lambda u(t) = f(t, w(t)) + \lambda w(t), \\ u(T) = u_T, \end{cases}$$

Then,

$$x_0(t) = u_T e^{\lambda(T-t)} - \int_t^T e^{\lambda(s-t)}[f(s, w(s)) + \lambda w(s)]\, ds.$$

Construct an iterative sequence $\{x_n(t)\}$ as follows:

$$\begin{cases} x'_{n+1}(t) + \lambda x_{n+1}(t) = f(t, x_n(t)) + \lambda x_n(t) \\ x_{n+1}(T) = u_T \end{cases} \qquad n = 0, 1, 2, \cdots$$

i.e.,

$$x_{n+1}(t) = u_T e^{\lambda(T-t)} - \int_t^T e^{\lambda(s-t)}[f(s, x_n(s)) + \lambda x_n(s)]\, ds.$$

In what follows, we prove that $\{x_n\}$ is a Cauchy sequence in $C[0, T]$, and converges to the solution of the (**TVP**) in $C[0, T]$.

Step 1. We assert

$$w(t) \geqslant x_0(t) \geqslant \left(\frac{w+v}{2}\right)(t) \geqslant v(t) \quad t \in [0,T].$$

In virtue of

$$\left(\frac{w+v}{2}\right)'(t) + \lambda\left(\frac{v+w}{2}\right)(t) \geqslant x_0'(t) + \lambda x_0(t)$$

and

$$\left(\frac{u+v}{2}\right)(T) = u_T = x_0(T)$$

and Lemma 2, we obtain

$$x_0(t) \geqslant \left(\frac{w+v}{2}\right)(t).$$

Moreover,

$$\begin{aligned} w'(t) + \lambda w(t) \leqslant & f(t, v(t)) + \lambda v(t) \\ \leqslant & f(t, w(t)) + \lambda w(t) \\ = & x_0'(t) + \lambda x_0(t), \\ w(T) = & u_T = x_0(T). \end{aligned}$$

Hence, by Lemma 2, we have $x_0(t) \leqslant w(t)$, and

$$w \geqslant x_0 \geqslant \frac{w+v}{2} \geqslant v.$$

Step 2. For $n = 0, 1, 2, \cdots$,

$$w(t) \geqslant x_{2n+1}(t) \geqslant x_{2n}(t) \geqslant \left(\frac{w+v}{2}\right)(t) \geqslant v(t).$$

On the one hand, since

$$\begin{aligned} x_1(t) = & u_T e^{\lambda(T-t)} - \int_t^T e^{\lambda(s-t)}[f(s, x_0(s)) + \lambda x_0(s)]\, ds \\ = & (Tx_0)(t) \end{aligned}$$

and T is decreasing, we obtain

$$Tw \leqslant Tx_0 = x_1 \leqslant T\left(\frac{\omega+v}{2}\right) \leqslant Tv.$$

Noting that $x_0 = Tw$, we have

$$x_0 \leqslant x_1.$$

On the other hand, by the second inequality in (1), we have

$$w'(t) + \lambda w(t) \leqslant f(t, v(t)) + \lambda v(t) \leqslant x_1'(t) + \lambda x_1 t = f(t_1, x_0(t)) + \lambda x_0(t)$$

which means

$$x_1'(t) + \lambda x_1(t) \geqslant w'(t) + \lambda w'(t)$$

By the comparison Lemma 2, there holds $x_1(t) \leqslant w(t)$. Hence,

$$x_0 \leqslant x_1 \leqslant w.$$

Noting that $x_0 \geqslant \frac{w+v}{2}$, we have $w \geqslant x_1 \geqslant x_0 \geqslant \frac{w+v}{2} \geqslant v$, which implies that the assertion holds for $n = 0$.

Suppose that when $n = k$,

$$w(t) \geqslant x_{2k+1}(t) \geqslant x_{2k}(t) \geqslant \left(\frac{v+w}{2}\right)(t) \geqslant v(t)$$

then

$$\begin{aligned} f(t, w(t)) + \lambda w(t) &\geqslant f(t, x_{2k+1}(t)) + \lambda x_{2k+1}(t) \\ &\geqslant f(t, x_{2k}(t)) + \lambda x_{2k}(t) \\ &\geqslant f(t \cdot v(t)) + \lambda v(t). \end{aligned}$$

Hence, we have

$$\begin{aligned} \left(\frac{v+w}{2}\right)'(t) + \lambda\left(\frac{v+w}{2}\right)(t) &\geqslant x'_{2k+2}(t) + \lambda x_{2k+2}(t) \\ &\geqslant x'_{2k+1}(t) + \lambda x_{2k+1}(t) \\ &\geqslant w'(t) + \lambda w(t). \end{aligned}$$

By the comparison Lemma 2,

$$\frac{v+w}{2} \leqslant x_{2k+2}(t) \leqslant x_{2k+1}(t) \leqslant w(t).$$

Repeating this process, we can verify

$$\frac{v+w}{2} \leqslant x_{2k+2}(t) \leqslant x_{2_{k+3}}(t) \leqslant w(t),$$

which means the assertion holds for $n = k + 1$.

Hence, for all n, there holds

$$w(t) \geqslant x_{2n+1}(t) \geqslant x_{2n}(t) \geqslant \left(\frac{v+w}{2}\right)(t) \geqslant v(t)$$

Step 3. $\{x_{2n}(t)\}$ is increasing, while $\{x_{2n+1}(t)\}$ is decreasing.

Since

$$u(t) \leqslant \left(\frac{v+w}{2}\right)(t) \leqslant x_1(t) \leqslant w(t),$$

then

$$\begin{aligned} f(t, v(t)) + \lambda v(t) &\leqslant f(t, x_1(t)) + \lambda x_1(t) \\ &\leqslant f(t, \lambda w(t)) + \lambda w(t)) \end{aligned}$$

and

$$w'(t) + \lambda w(t) \leqslant x'_2(t) + \lambda x_2(t) \leqslant x'_0(t) + \lambda x_0(t)$$

By the comparison Lemma 2,

$$x_0(t) \leqslant x_2(t) \leqslant w(t)$$

In a similar way to Step 2, we can prove

$$\{x_{2n}(t)\} \text{ is increasing}, \{x_{2n+1}(t)\} \text{ is decreasing.}$$

Step 4. $\{x_n(t)\}$ is uniformly convergent on $[0, 1]$.

By Steps 1–3, we know that $\{x_n(t)\}$ satisfies

$$v(t) \leqslant \left(\frac{v+w}{2}\right)(t) \leqslant x_0(t) \leqslant x_2(t) \leqslant \cdots \leqslant x_{2n}(t) \leqslant \cdots \leqslant x_{2n+1}(t) \leqslant \cdots \leqslant x_1(t) \leqslant w(t)$$

Let $Z_n(t) = x_n(t) - v(t)$. We have

$$0 \leqslant \left(\frac{w-v}{2}\right)(t) \leqslant Z_0(t) \leqslant Z_2 t \leqslant \cdots \leqslant Z_{2n}(t) \leqslant \cdots \leqslant Z_{2n+1}(t) \leqslant \cdots \leqslant Z_1(t)$$
$$\leqslant (w-v)(t).$$

Define

$$r_n = \sup\{r \in R \mid Z_{2n}(t) \geqslant r Z_{2n+1}(t)\}$$

Then, the sequence $\{r_n\}$ is well defined, $\frac{1}{2} \leqslant r_n \leqslant 1$, and $\{r_n\}$ is increasing.

Since

1. $$Z_{2n}(t) \geqslant \frac{1}{2}(w-v)(t) \geqslant \frac{1}{2} Z_{2n+1}(t)$$
   we have $r_n \geqslant \frac{1}{2}$
2. $$Z_{2n}(t) \geqslant Z_{2n+1}(t)$$
   and we obtain $r_n \leqslant 1$.
3. If r satisfies $Z_{2n}(t) \geqslant r Z_{2n+1}(t)$, then the monotonicity of $\{Z_{2n}\}$ and $\{Z_{2n+1}\}$ implies
   $$Z_{2n+2}(t) \geqslant Z_{2n}(t) \geqslant r Z_{2n+1}(t) \geqslant r Z_{2n+3}(t)$$

i.e., $\{r \in R \mid Z_{2n}(t) \geqslant r Z_{2n+1}(t)\} \subset \{r \in R \mid Z_{2n+2}(t) \geqslant r Z_{2n+3}(t)\}$.

By (1–3), we know that $\{r_n\}$ is convergent. Denote $r_0 = \lim_{n\to\infty} r_n$.

By the comparison Lemma 3,

$$\begin{aligned}
Z_{2n+3}(t) &\leqslant Z_{2n+1}(t) = x_{2n+1}(t) - v(t) \\
&= u_T e^{\lambda(T-t)} - \int_t^T e^{\lambda(s-t)}[f(s, x_{2n}(s)) + \lambda x_{2n}(s)]\, ds - v(t) \\
&= u_T e^{\lambda(T-t)} - \int_t^T e^{\lambda(s-t)}[f(s, Z_{2n}(s) + v(s))) + \lambda(Z_{2n} + v(s))\, ds - v(t) \\
&\leqslant u_T e^{\lambda(T-t)} - \int_t^T e^{\lambda(s-t)}[f(s, (r_n Z_{2n+1} + v)(s)) + \lambda(r_n Z_{2n+1} + v)(s)]\, ds - v(t) \\
&= u_T e^{\lambda(T-t)} - \int_t^T e^{\lambda(s-t)} \begin{bmatrix} f(s, (r_n x_{2n+1} + (1-r_n)v(s)))+ \\ \lambda(r_n x_{2n+1} + (1-r_n)v(s)) \end{bmatrix} ds - v(t) \\
&\leqslant u_T e^{\lambda(T-t)} - \int_t^T e^{\lambda(s-t)} \begin{bmatrix} r_n(f(s, x_{2n+1}(s)) + \lambda x_{2n+1}(s))+ \\ (1-r_n)(f(s, v(s)) + \lambda v(s)) \end{bmatrix} ds - v(t) \\
&= r_n\left[u_T e^{\lambda(T-t)} - \int_t^T e^{\lambda(s-t)}[f(s, x_{2n+1}(s)) + \lambda x_{2n+1}(s)\, ds - v(t)]\right] \\
&\quad + (1-r_n)\left[u_T e^{\lambda(T-t)} - \int_t^T e^{\lambda(s-t)}[f(s, v(s)) + \lambda v(s)]\, ds - v(t)\right] \\
&\leqslant r_n[x_{2n+2}(t) - v(t)] + (1-r_n)[w(t) - v(t)] \\
&= r_n Z_{2n+2} + 2(1-r_n)(\frac{w-v}{2})(t) \\
&\leqslant r_n Z_{2n+2} + 2(1-r_n) Z_{2n+2} \\
&= (2-r_n) Z_{2n+2},
\end{aligned}$$

then

$$r_{n+1} = \sup\{r \in R \mid Z_{2n+3}(t) \geqslant r Z_{2n+2}(t)\} \geqslant \frac{1}{2-r_n}.$$

Taking the limit on both sides, we obtain

$$r_0 \geqslant \frac{1}{2-r_0}.$$

Noting that $\frac{1}{2} \leqslant r_0 \leqslant 1$, we know $r_0 = 1$.
Then, for an even number p,

$$0 \leqslant Z_{2n+p} - Z_{2n} \leqslant Z_{2n+1} - Z_{2n} \leqslant (1-r_n)Z_{2n+1} \leqslant (1-r_n)(v-u).$$

Since $r_n \to 1$, $\{Z_{2n}\}$ is convergent. In a similar way, we obtain that $\{Z_{2n+1}\}$ is convergent, and

$$\lim_{n\to\infty} Z_{2n} = \lim_{n\to\infty} Z_{2n+1}.$$

Hence, $\{Z_n\}$ is convergent.
Let $Z = \lim_{n\to\infty} Z_n$ and $\bar{x} = Z + v$, and then

$$\begin{aligned}\lim_{n\to\infty} x_n(t) =&\bar{x}(t)\\ =&\lim_{n\to\infty} x_{n+1}(t)\\ =&\lim_{n\to\infty}\left[u_T e^{\lambda(T-t)} - \int_t^T [f(s,x_n(s)) + \lambda x_n(s)]\,ds\right]\\ =&u_T e^{\lambda(T-t)} - \int_t^T [f(s,\bar{x}(s)) + \lambda \bar{x}(s)]\,ds\\ =&(T\bar{x})(t),\end{aligned}$$

which means that $\bar{x}(t)$ is a fixed point of T.
Step 5. $\bar{x}$ is the unique fixed point of T in $[v,w]$.
In fact, if $\tilde{x}$ is a fixed point of T in $[v,w]$, then

$$\begin{aligned}v \leqslant \tilde{x} \leqslant w \Rightarrow& Tv \geqslant T\tilde{x} \geqslant Tw\\ \Rightarrow& w \geqslant Tv \geqslant \tilde{x} \geqslant x_0.\end{aligned}$$

Continuing this process, we have

$$x_{2n}(t) \leqslant \tilde{x}(t) \leqslant x_{2n+1}(t).$$

Taking the limit on both sides, we obtain

$$\tilde{x}(t) = \bar{x}(t).$$

Hence, $\bar{x}$ is the unique fixed point of T in $[v,w]$, i.e., $\bar{x}$ is the unique solution of (TVP) in $[v,w]$. □

Remark 1. *Let*

$$y_0(t) = u_T e^{\lambda(T-t)} - \int_t^T e^{\lambda(s-t)}[f(s,v(s)) + \lambda v(s)]\,ds$$

Define

$$y_{n+1}(t) = u_T e^{\lambda(T-t)} - \int_t^T e^{\lambda(s-t)}[f(s,y_n(s)) + \lambda y_n(s)]ds, n = 0,1,2,\cdots$$

In the same way as in Theorem 1, we can prove that $\{y_n\}$ is uniformly convergent to $\bar{x}$ on $[0,1]$.

Corollary 1. *Assume that there exist two constants $c > 0$ and $\lambda \in R$ satisfying the following:*

1. $f(t,0) - \lambda c(T-t) \geqslant -c \geqslant 2f(t, c(T-t)) + \lambda c(T-t)$;
2. *for* $\forall t \in [0,T]$, $f(t,\cdot)$ *is concave;*
3. *for* $\forall t \in [0,T]$, $x, y \in [0, c(T-t)]$, $x \leqslant y$,

$$f(t,y) - f(t,x) \geqslant -\lambda(y-x),$$

and then (TVP)

$$\begin{cases} x'(t) = f(t, x(t)) \\ x(T) = 0 \end{cases}$$

has a unique solution $\bar{x}(t)$ satisfying

$$0 \leqslant \bar{x}(t) \leqslant c(T-t),\ t \in [0,T].$$

Proof. Choose $v(t) = 0, w(t) = c(T-t)$, and we can verify that all conditions of Theorem 1 are fulfilled. □

Consider the following terminal value problem.

$$\begin{cases} x'(t) = t + g(x(t))\ t \in [0,1] \\ x(1) = 0 \end{cases}$$

Corollary 2. *Let $g \in C^2[0,1]$. If the following conditions are satisfied*

1. $g(0) \geq -2$;
2. *for* $\forall x \in [0,1]$, $g(x) \leq \frac{3}{2}x - \frac{3}{2}$;
3. *for* $\forall x \in [0,1]$, $g'(x) \geq 1$;
4. *for* $\forall x \in [0,1]$, $g''(x) \leq 0$.

Then the above (TVP) has a unique solution $\bar{x}(t)$ satisfying

$$0 \leqslant \bar{x}(t) \leqslant 1-t, t \in [0,1].$$

Proof. Let

$$f(t,x) = t + g(x).$$

and $c = T = 1, \lambda = -1$; we can verify that

$$\begin{aligned} f(t,0) - \lambda c(T-t) \geq& t + (-2) + 1 - t \\ =& -1 = -c \\ 2f(t, c(T-t)) + \lambda c(T-t) =& 2[t + g(1-t)] - (1-t) \\ \leq& 2[t + \frac{3}{2}(1-t) - \frac{3}{2}] - (1-t) \leqslant -1 = -c, \end{aligned}$$

which implies that assumption (1) of Corollary 1 is satisfied.

Moreover,

$$f''_{xx}(t,x) = g''(x) \leq 0$$

means that $f(t,.)$ is concave, i.e., Assumption (2) of Corollary 1 is fulfilled. Noting that

$$f'_x(t,x) = g'(x) \geqslant 1, \quad x \in [0,1],$$

hence, f meets condition (3) of Corollary 1.

By Corollary 1, we know that this terminal problem has a unique solution $\bar{x}(t)$ satisfying

$$0 \leqslant \bar{x}(t) \leqslant 1 - t.$$

□

4. Application

Example 1. *Let $g(x) = x + sinx - 2$. We can verify that all assumptions of Corollary 2 hold. Hence, the terminal value problem*

$$\begin{cases} x'(t) = t + x(t) + sinx(t) - 2 \\ x(1) = 0 \end{cases}$$

has a unique solution $\bar{x}(t)$ satisfying

$$0 \leqslant \bar{x}(t) \leqslant 1 - t.$$

Let $T = 1, \lambda = -1, v_0(t) = 0$. Define

$$v_{n+1}(t) = u_T e^{\lambda(T-t)} - \int_t^T e^{\lambda(s-t)}[f(s, v_n(s)) + \lambda v_n(s)]ds, n = 0, 1, 2, \cdots.$$

Then, the approximate solutions of the above TVP are

$$\begin{aligned} v_1(t) &= (t-2)\left[e^{(t-1)} - 1\right] \\ v_2(t) &= \left\{t + \sin\left\{(t-2)\left[e^{(t-1)} - 1\right]\right\} - 2\right\} \cdot \left[e^{(t-1)} - 1\right] \\ &\cdots \end{aligned}$$

The image of the approximate solutions of v_1, v_2 is the Figure 1.

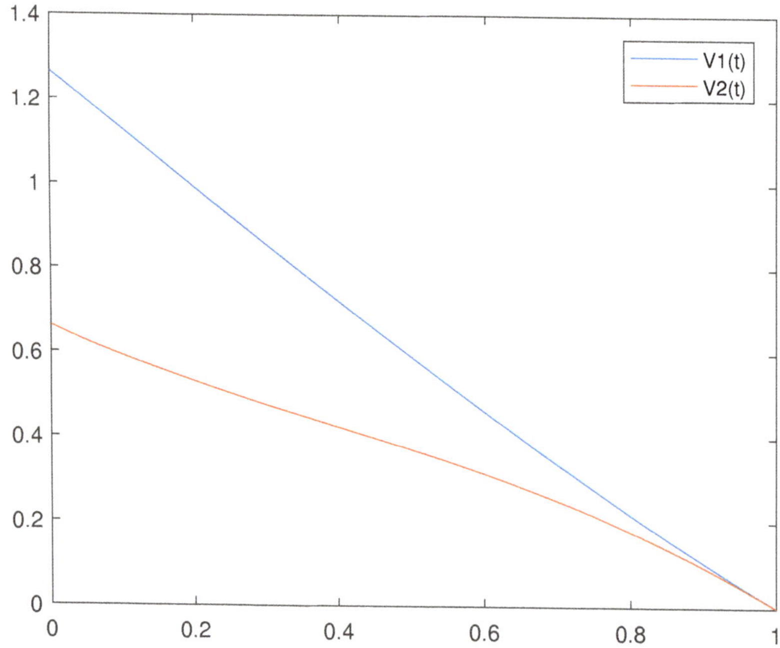

Figure 1. Image of the approximate solutions of v_1, v_2.

5. Discussion

In this paper, we have constructed an iterative monotone sequence and verified that this sequence is convergent to a solution of problem (**TVP**). Other assumptions ensure the uniqueness of this solution. Our uniqueness result is a **local result**, which means that the problem may have multiple solutions in the space $C[0, T]$.

6. Conclusions

In this paper, we have used comparison lemmas, an iterative technique and a fixed point method to obtain the existence and uniqueness results of solutions for a terminal value problem of the first-order differential equation. Our discussion lies in a bounded interval. It is an interesting problem to extend the study to an unbounded interval, i.e.,

$$\begin{cases} x'(t) & = f(t, x(t)) \\ x(\infty) & = \lim_{t\to\infty} x(t) = u_\infty \end{cases}$$

We will try to find appropriate conditions to ensure the existence and uniqueness of the solution to the above problem.

Author Contributions: Methodology, Y.F. and Q.P.; writing—original draft preparation, Q.P.; writing—review and editing, Y.F. and J.J.; funding acquisition, Y.F. All authors have read and agreed to the published version of the manuscript.

Funding: This research is partially supported by the National Natural Science Foundation of China (72031009).

Institutional Review Board Statement: Not applicable.

Informed Consent Statement: Not applicable.

Data Availability Statement: Not applicable.

Acknowledgments: The authors thank the anonymous referees for their valuable constructive comments and suggestions, which improved the quality of this paper in the present form.

Conflicts of Interest: The authors declare no conflict of interest.

References

1. Wang, L.; Wu, Y.; Liu, M.; Meng, Y.; Cao, M. Hybrid collocation method for solving terminal value problemsof a class of fractional differential eqautions. *J. Jilin Univ. (Sci. Ed.)* **2018**, *56*, 897–900.
2. Zhang, H. Existence of solutions of terminal value problem for nonlinear first order differential equations systems in Banach spaces. *J. Chuzhou Univ.* **2010**, *12*, 4–6.
3. Wang, F.; Cui, Y.; Zhang, F. The method of quasi-upper and lower solutions for terminal value problems of differential equations with discontinuous terms. *J. Math. Study* **2009**, *42*, 68–74.
4. Zhou, Y. Maximal and minmal solutions of terminal value problems for differential eqautions in Banach spaces. *J. Syst. Sci. Math. Sci.* **1999**, *19*, 264–267.
5. Yakar, C.; Arslan, M. Terminal value problem for causal differential equations with a caputofractional derivative. *Turk. J. Math.* **2017**, *41*, 1042–1052. [CrossRef]
6. Shah, S.; Rehman, M.U. A note on terminal value problems for fractional differential equations on infinite interval. *Appl. Math. Lett.* **2016**, *52*, 118–125. [CrossRef]
7. Aftabizadeh, A.; Lakshmikantham, V. On the theory of terminal value problems for ordinary differential equations. *Nonlinear Anal. Theory Methods Appl.* **1981**, *5*, 1173–1180. [CrossRef]
8. Benchohra, M.; Bouriah, S.; Nieto, J.J. Terminal value problem for differential equations with Hilfer–Katugampola fractional derivative. *Symmetry* **2019**, *11*, 672. [CrossRef]
9. Li, C.; Li, M.M.; Zhou, H. Terminal value problem for a generalized fractional ordinary differential equation. *Math. Methods Appl. Sci.* **2021**, *44*, 12963–12979. [CrossRef]
10. Babak, S.; Wu, G.C.; Dumitru, B. Collocation methods for terminal value problems of tempered fractional differential equations. *Appl. Numer. Math.* **2020**, *156*, 385–395.

axioms

MDPI

Article

Dirichlet Problem with $L^1(S)$ Boundary Values

Alexander G. Ramm

Department of Mathematics, Kansas State University, Manhattan, KS 66506, USA; ramm@ksu.edu

Abstract: Let D be a connected bounded domain in $\mathbb{R}^2$, S be its boundary, which is closed and C^2-smooth. Consider the Dirichlet problem $\Delta u = 0$ in $D, u|_S = h$, where $h \in L^1(S)$. The aim of this paper is to prove that the above problem has a solution for an arbitrary $h \in L^1(S)$, and this solution is unique. The result is new. The method of its proof is new. The definition of the $L^1(S)$-boundary value of a harmonic in the D function is given. No embedding theorems are used. The history of the Dirichlet problem goes back to 1828. The result in this paper is, to the author's knowledge, the first result in the 194 years of research (since 1828) that yields the existence and uniqueness of the solution to the Dirichlet problem with the boundary values in $L^1(S)$.

Keywords: Dirichlet problem; $L^1(S)$ boundary values

MSC: 31A05; 35J25

Citation: Ramm, A.G. Dirichlet Problem with $L^1(S)$ Boundary Values. *Axioms* **2022**, *11*, 371. https://doi.org/10.3390/axioms11080371

Academic Editor: Clemente Cesarano

Received: 20 June 2022
Accepted: 22 July 2022
Published: 28 July 2022

1. Introduction

Let D be a connected bounded domain on the complex plane, S be its boundary, which is closed and C^2-smooth.

The aim of this paper is to prove that an arbitrary $h \in L^1(S)$ can be the boundary value of a harmonic in the D function. The boundary value $h \in L^1(S)$ uniquely determines the harmonic function in D.

There is a large body of literature on the Dirichlet problem for elliptic equations going back to 1828; see references. There are three basic directions of research: non-smooth domains, non-smooth coefficients and non-smooth boundary values. This paper deals with smooth domains, the simplest elliptic operator, the Laplacean and non-smooth boundary values. In the published papers and books, the boundary values of harmonic functions were always assumed to be smoother than $L^1(S)$. For example, the maximal non-smoothness, allowed in [1], is bounded continuous function h on S with finitely many points of discontinuity of the first kind. In [2], the boundary conditions in $L^1(S)$ are not considered at all.

We deal with the smooth two-dimensional domains ($n = 2$) for definiteness. In the two-dimensional case, the kernel of the integral equation of the potential theory is continuous, and the corresponding integral operator A is compact in $L^1(S)$. The compactness of A in $L^1(S)$ holds for any finite dimension $n \geq 2$, but the kernel $A(t,s)$ of A, defined below formula (2), is not continuous for $n > 2$. This does not prevent A from being compact in $L^1(S)$. Our arguments are based on the new definition of the boundary values of a harmonic function in $L^1(S)$; see Definition 1 below. To our knowledge, in this paper, the $L^1(S)$-boundary values of harmonic functions are considered for the first time.

The problem we study is:

$$\Delta u = 0 \text{ in } D, \quad u|_S = h. \tag{1}$$

This problem has been studied in many papers and books for a long time. We mention only a few names: G. Green (1828), Gauss, Thomson, Dirichlet (1850), Hilbert (1900). One of the methods to solve this problem is based on the potential theory. Let us look for the solution in the form of the double-layer potential

$$u(x) = \int_S \frac{\partial g(x,s)}{\partial N}\mu(s)ds, \quad N := N_s. \tag{2}$$

Here $g = -\frac{1}{2\pi}\ln r$, $r := r_{xy} = |x-y|$, $x, y \in \mathbb{R}^2$, $A(t,s) := \frac{\partial g(t,s)}{\partial N} = -\frac{1}{2\pi}\frac{N_s \cdot r^0}{r_{ts}}$, $r^0 = \frac{s-t}{|s-t|}$, $N = N_s$ is the unit normal to S at the point s, N is directed out of D, $\mu = \mu(s)$ is the unknown function. The kernel $A(t,s)$ is a continuous function of t and s on $S \times S$ when $D \subset \mathbb{R}^2$ and S is C^2-smooth. We could assume S to be $C^{1,a}-$ smooth, $a \in (0,1]$, but this is not important in this paper.

In our case, operator

$$A\mu = \int_S A(t,s)\mu(s)ds \tag{3}$$

is well defined as an operator in $L^1(S)$ and is compact in this space, see [3–5] for the compactness test of $L^1(S)$.

Let us check that the kernel $A(t,s)$ is continuous on $S \times S$ if $n = 2$ and $S \in C^2$. For $|t-s| > \epsilon$ this kernel is C^1-smooth. Therefore, only its behavior as $t \to s$ should be considered. This behavior is determined by the function $\frac{N_s \cdot r^0}{-2\pi r_{ts}}$. Choose the coordinate system in which the $y-$axis is directed along N_t, so $N_t = j$, where i and j are the orthogonal unit vectors of the coordinate system. The equation of S in a neighborhood of t in this system is $y = f(x)$, $f(0) = f'(0) = 0$, the vector $t = (0,0)$, the vector $s = xi + jf(x)$, the vector $s - t = xi + jf(x)$, $r^0 = \frac{xi + f(x)j}{(x^2 + f^2(x))^{1/2}}$, $N_s = \frac{f'(x)i - j}{(1+(f')^2)^{1/2}}$, $N_s \cdot r^0 = \frac{xf'(x) - f(x)}{(x^2+f^2(x))^{1/2}(1+(f')^2)^{1/2}}$. Denote $\frac{N_s \cdot r^0}{r_{ts}} := J$. In our coordinate system $f(0) = f'(0) = 0$, so $f(x) \sim \frac{f''(0)x^2}{2}$ as $x \to 0$. Therefore, one gets $J(0) = -\lim_{x\to 0}\frac{f''(0)x^2}{2x^2} = -\frac{f''(0)}{2}$. Thus, the kernel $A(t,s)$ is continuous as $t \to s$. Therefore, it is continuous on $S \times S$.

If $D \subset \mathbb{R}^n$, $n > 2$, and S is smooth, then the kernel $A(t,s)$ is $O(\frac{1}{r_{ts}^{n-2}})$. Therefore, if $n > 2$, operator A is compact in $L^1(S)$, but the kernel is not continuous on $S \times S$.

If one looks for the solution to Equation (1) of the form (2) and $\mu \in C^1(S)$, then the integral equation for μ is:

$$h(t) = -\frac{\mu(t)}{2} + \int_S A(t,s)\mu(s)ds. \tag{4}$$

Equation (4) holds everywhere with respect to the Lebesgue measure on S if $A(t,s)$ is continuous. See, for example, [6], where the derivation of Equation (4) under the assumption $\mu \in C^1(S)$ is given. It is well known that the set $C^1(S)$ is dense in $L^1(S)$ in the norm of $L^1(S)$. Equation (4) holds almost everywhere with respect to Lebesgue's measure on S if $h \in L^1(S)$.

Let us recall M. Riesz's compactness criterion for sets in $L^1(S)$:

Proposition 1. *For a bounded set $M \subset L^1(S)$ to be compact in $L^1(S)$, it is necessary and sufficient that for an arbitrary small $\epsilon > 0$ there exists a $\delta > 0$ such that if $|\sigma| \le \delta$, then for any $h \in M$ one has $||h(s+\sigma) - h(s)|| < \epsilon$, where $s + \sigma \in S$.*

Here and below, the norm is the $L^1(S)$ norm, $||h|| = \int_S |h(s)|ds$. Proofs of Proposition 1 can be found in [3,5].

Lemma 1. *If $A(t,s)$ is continuous on $S \times S$ and a set $M \in L^1(S)$ is bounded, then the set AM is compact in $L^1(S)$.*

Proof. By Proposition 1, it is sufficient to check that $\|(Ah)(t+\sigma)-(Ah)(t)\| \leq \epsilon$ for $|\sigma| \leq \delta$, where $h \in M$ is arbitrary. Let $|S|$ denote the length of S. One has

$$\|(Ah)(t+\sigma)-(Ah)(t)\| \leq |S| \sup_{s,t\in S} |A(t+\sigma,s)-A(t,s)|\|h\| \leq c\epsilon, \tag{5}$$

provided that $|\sigma| \leq \delta$. Here $c > 0$ does not depend on δ, it comes from the bound $\|h\| \leq c_1$ for all $h \in M$, $c = |S|c_1$. We have used the continuity of $A(t,s)$ on $S \times S$ to conclude that

$$\sup_{s,t} |A(t+\sigma,s)-A(t,s)| \leq \epsilon, \tag{6}$$

if $|\sigma|$ is sufficiently small. Lemma 1 is proven. □

We want to make sense of the method of integral equation for solving the Dirichlet problem (1), assuming that $h \in L^1(S)$.

Lemma 2. *Operator A is compact in $L^1(S)$. Operator $-\frac{I}{2}+A$ is Fredholm-type, where I is the identity operator. The null-space of operator $-\frac{I}{2}+A$ is trivial.*

Proof. Operator $A: L^1(S) \to L^1(S)$ is compact by Lemma 1. This is also true if $n > 2$ and $A(t,s) = O(|t-s|^{-(n-2)})$. Operator $-\frac{I}{2}+A$, where I is the identity operator, is bounded and continuous as an operator from $L^1(S)$ into itself. It is known (see, e.g., ref. [1]) that the homogeneous problem (1) has only the trivial solution in the space $C(S)$. We claim that the same is true in the space $L^1(S)$. Indeed, if μ solves the homogeneous Equation (4) and $n = 2$, then $\mu \in C(S)$ because $(A\mu) \in C(S)$ if $\mu \in L^1(S)$ since the kernel $A(t,s) \in C(S \times S)$. Therefore, the null-space of operator $-\frac{I}{2}+A$ is trivial in $L^1(S)$ as well.

Since A is compact and the null-space of operator $-\frac{I}{2}+A$ is trivial, the Fredholm alternative holds: the inverse operator $(-\frac{I}{2}+A)^{-1}$ exists, is bounded, and it maps $L^1(S)$ onto itself. This means not only that Equation (4) makes sense for $\mu \in L^1(S)$ and $h \in L^1(S)$, but also that μ depends continuously on h in the norm of $L^1(S)$.

Lemma 2 is proved. □

Remark 1. *It follows from Lemma 2 that the only solution in $L^1(S)$ of the homogeneous problem* (1) *is $u = 0$. This result is new because $L^1(S)$ boundary values of harmonic functions were not considered earlier.*

Remark 2. *One can find a harmonic function u in the circle $D = \{x,y : (x-1)^2+y^2 < 1\}$, which is zero on $S = \{x,y : (x-1)^2+y^2 = 1\}$, except at one point $x = 0$, $y = 0$, and which is not zero in D. For example, $u = 1 - 2Re\, z^{-1}$, $z = x+iy$. Of course, $u|_S$ in this example does not belong to $L^1(S)$.*

To check this, write $u = \frac{(x-y)^2}{x^2+y^2}$ and use the polar coordinates $x-1 = r\cos\phi$, $y = r\sin\phi$. Then S has representation $x = 1+\cos\phi$, $y = \sin\phi$ and the point $(0,0)$ has coordinates $r = 1$, $\phi = \pi$. One has

$$\int_0^{2\pi} \frac{(x-y)^2}{x^2+y^2} d\phi = \int_0^{2\pi} \frac{1-\sin(2\phi)}{2+2\cos\phi} d\phi.$$

The integrand in the above integral is not absolutely integrable in a neighborhood of the point $\phi = \pi$. The function $(x-y)^2 = 0$ on S because the equation $(x-1)^2+y^2 = 1$ of S is equivalent to the equation $(x-y)^2 = 0$.

This example shows that the assumption $h \in L^1(S)$ is necessary for the uniqueness of the solution to the Dirichlet problem (1).

Our next step is to define the $\lim_{x\to t} A_x\mu$ *for* $\mu \in L^1(S)$, *where*

$$A_x\mu := \int_S A(x,s)\mu(s)ds, \tag{7}$$

and the kernel of operator A_x *is* $A(x,s) := \frac{\partial g(x,s)}{\partial N_s}$.

By $x \to t$ we mean *a non-tangential limit* $x \to t$, where $x \in D$ and $t \in S$.

Let $h \in L^1(S)$ be arbitrary. Choose any sequence $h_\delta \in C^1(S)$ such that

$$\lim_{\delta\to 0} \|h - h_\delta\| = 0. \tag{8}$$

By Lemma 2, Equation (8) implies

$$\lim_{\delta\to 0} \|\mu - \mu_\delta\| = 0, \tag{9}$$

where μ_δ is the unique solution to the equation:

$$-\frac{\mu_\delta(t)}{2} + \int_S \frac{\partial g(t,s)}{\partial N_s}\mu_\delta(s)ds := h_\delta. \tag{10}$$

Definition 1. *We define*

$$A_x\mu := \lim_{\delta\to 0} A_x\mu_\delta, \quad x \in D, \tag{11}$$

and

$$A_t\mu := \lim_{\delta\to 0}\lim_{x\to t} \int_S \frac{\partial g(x,s)}{\partial N_s}\mu_\delta(s)ds, \quad t \in S. \tag{12}$$

This definition gives meaning to the boundary condition in Equation (1) if $h \in L^1(S)$. The existence of the limit

$$\lim_{\delta\to 0} \int_S \frac{\partial g(x,s)}{\partial N}\mu_\delta(s)ds = \int_S \frac{\partial g(x,s)}{\partial N}\mu(s)ds$$

is obvious for $x \in D$ because of relation (9) and because kernel $\frac{\partial g(x,s)}{\partial N}$ is smooth when $x \in D$.

The existence of the limit

$$\lim_{x\to t} \int_S \frac{\partial g(x,s)}{\partial N}\mu_\delta(s)ds = -\frac{\mu_\delta(t)}{2} + A\mu_\delta \tag{13}$$

is known from the potential theory if $\mu_\delta \in C^1(S)$, see, for example, ref. [6], pp. 148–152. The existence of the limit

$$\lim_{\delta\to 0}\Big(-\frac{\mu_\delta(t)}{2} + A\mu_\delta\Big) = -\frac{\mu(t)}{2} + A\mu \tag{14}$$

is clear from relation (9) and Lemma 2.

For the convenience, of the reader we sketch a proof of Equation (13) following [6]. The proof is shorter than in [6] because the kernel $\frac{\partial g(t,s)}{\partial N}$ is continuous if $n = 2$.

Note that $J(x) := \lim_{x\to t} \int_S \frac{\partial g(x,s)}{\partial N} ds = -1$ if $x \in D$; $J(x) = 0$ if $x \in D'$, where D' is defined by the formula: $D' := \mathbb{R}^3 \setminus \bar{D}$; $J(x) = -\frac{1}{2}$ if $x = t \in S$. This result is well known and is proven by applying Green's formula and the equation $\Delta g(x,y) = -\delta(x-y)$, where $\delta(x)$ is the delta function.

Let $\mu_\delta \in C^1(S)$. Then,

$$M := \int_S \frac{\partial g(x,s)}{\partial N}\mu_\delta(s)ds = J(x)\mu_\delta(t) + \int_S \frac{\partial g(x,s)}{\partial N}[\mu_\delta(s) - \mu_\delta(t)]ds := J(x)\mu_\delta(t) + K.$$

One has (the $+$ sign denotes the non-tangential to S limit when $x \in D$, $x \to t \in S$ and the $-$ sign denotes the similar limit when $x \in D'$, $x \to t \in S$):

$$M_+ = -\mu_\delta(t) + \lim_{x\to t, x\in D} K := J_+, \quad M_- = 0 + \lim_{x\to t, x\in D'} K := J_-. \quad M_0 = -\frac{1}{2}\mu_\delta(t) + K.$$

If one proves that K is continuous when x passes t along the normal N_t, then $M_0 = -\frac{1}{2}\mu_\delta + K(t)$ and the desired statement is proven. Here $K(t) = \int_S \frac{\partial g(t,s)}{\partial N}[\mu_\delta(s) - \mu_\delta(t)]ds$.

If $\mu_\delta \in C^1(S)$, then $|\mu_\delta(s) - \mu_\delta(t)| \le c|s-t|$. Therefore,

$$|K(x) - K(t)| \le c\int_S \Big|\frac{N\cdot r^0_{xs}}{|x-s|} - \frac{N\cdot r^0_{ts}}{|t-s|}\Big||t-s|ds := L.$$

The function r^0_{xs} is continuous with respect to x. The function $|t-s|/|x-s|$ is continuous with respect to x when $x \to t$ along the normal N_t. This implies continuity of L when x crosses t along N_t. Therefore, M is a continuous function of x when x crosses t along N_t, as we claimed.

Since operator A is compact in $L^1(S)$, the Fredholm alternative yields the unique solution to Equation (4) with an arbitrary $h \in L^1(S)$, because Equation (4) with $h = 0$ has only the trivial solution in $L^1(S)$. Given an arbitrary $h \in L^1(S)$, one finds $h_\delta \in C^1(S)$ such that

$$\lim_{\delta\to 0} ||h_\delta - h|| = 0.$$

If $\lim_{\delta\to 0} ||h_\delta - h|| = 0$, then $\lim_{\delta\to 0} ||\mu_\delta - \mu|| = 0$ since the inverse operator $\Big(-\frac{I}{2} + A\Big)^{-1}$ is continuous and defined on all of $L^1(S)$. The function $u(x) = A_x\mu$, where μ is the unique solution to Equation (4), solves the Dirichlet problem (1). We have proven the following result:

Theorem 1. *Assume that $h \in L^1(S)$ is arbitrary. Then there exists a unique harmonic in the D function $u = A_x\mu$, $x \in D$, such that $u = h$ on S. The boundary value of u on S is defined by formula* (12).

2. Conclusions

The history of the Dirichlet problem goes back to 1828. The result in this paper is, to the author's knowledge, the first result in the 194 years of research since 1828 that yields the existence and uniqueness of the solution to the Dirichlet problem with the boundary values in $L^1(S)$.

It is proven that the Dirichlet problem (1) with the boundary function $h \in L^1(S)$ has a solution, and this solution is unique.

Open problem. Let us keep our assumption about D. Given a harmonic function $u(x,y)$ in D; one can use the Schwarz operator to construct the conjugate harmonic function $v(x,y)$ (up to an additive constant) and to get the corresponding analytic function $f(z) = u + iv$, $z = x + iy$, in D. The open problem is:

What is the set of boundary values of $f(z)$ on S when the values h of u on S run through all of $L^1(S)$?

The Schwarz operator is known explicitly if, for example, D is the unit disc; see, for example, ref. [7]. In [8,9], one can find information about the action of singular integral operators in Lebesgue's spaces $L^p(S)$, $1 < p < \infty$.

Funding: This research received no external funding.

Conflicts of Interest: The author declares no conflict of interest.

References

1. Lavrent'ev M.A.; Shabat B.V. *Methods of the Theory of Functions of Complex Variable*; GIFML: Moscow, Russia, 1958. (In Russian)
2. Gilbarg, D.; Trudinger, N. *Elliptic Partial Differential Equations of Second Order*; Springer: New York, NY, USA, 1983.
3. Hanche-Olsen, H.; Holden, H. The Kolmogorov-Riesz compactness theorem. *Expo. Math.* **2010**, *28*, 385–394. [CrossRef]
4. Kolmogorov, A.N. Über Kompaktheit der Funktionenmengen bei der Konvergenz im Mittel. *Nachr. Ges. Wiss. Göttingen* **1931**, *9*, 60–63.
5. Riesz, M. Sur les ensembles compacts de fonctions sommables. *Acta Szeged Sect. Math.* **1933**, *6*, 136–142. (In French)
6. Ramm, A.G. *Scattering of Acoustic and Electromagnetic Waves by Small Bodies of Arbitrary Shapes: Applications to Creating New Engineered Materials*; Momentum Press: New York, NY, USA, 2013.
7. Gahov, F. *Boundary Value Problems*; Nauka: Moscow, Russia, 1977. (In Russian)
8. Khvedelidze, B. Linear discontinuous boundary value problems of function theory, singular integral equations and some applications. *Tr. Tbil. Math. Instituta Akad. Nauk Grusinskoi SSR* **1956**, *23*, 3–158.
9. Mikhlin, S.; Prössdorf, S. *Singular Integral Operators*; Springer: New York, NY, USA, 1986.

axioms MDPI

Article

New Type of Degenerate Changhee–Genocchi Polynomials

Maryam Salem Alatawi [1] and Waseem Ahmad Khan [2,*]

[1] Department of Mathematics, Faculty of Science, University of Tabuk, Tabuk 71491, Saudi Arabia; msoalatawi@ut.edu.sa
[2] Department of Mathematics and Natural Sciences, Prince Mohammad Bin Fahd University, P.O. Box 1664, Al Khobar 31952, Saudi Arabia
* Correspondence: wkhan1@pmu.edu.sa

Abstract: A remarkably large number of polynomials and their extensions have been presented and studied. In this paper, we consider a new type of degenerate Changhee–Genocchi numbers and polynomials which are different from those previously introduced by Kim. We investigate some properties of these numbers and polynomials. We also introduce a higher-order new type of degenerate Changhee–Genocchi numbers and polynomials which can be represented in terms of the degenerate logarithm function. Finally, we derive their summation formulae.

Keywords: degenerate Genocchi polynomials and numbers; degenerate Changhee–Genocchi polynomials; higher-order degenerate Changhee–Genocchi polynomials and numbers; Stirling numbers

MSC: 11B83; 11B73; 05A19

Citation: Alatawi, M.S.; Khan, W.A. New Type of Degenerate Changhee–Genocchi Polynomials. *Axioms* **2022**, *11*, 355. https://doi.org/10.3390/axioms11080355

Academic Editor: Clemente Cesarano

Received: 28 June 2022
Accepted: 21 July 2022
Published: 23 July 2022

1. Introduction

Carlitz first proposed the idea of degenerate numbers and polynomials which are associated with Bernoulli and Euler numbers and polynomials (see [1,2]). After Carlitz introduced the degenerate polynomials, many researchers studied the degenerate polynomials related to unique polynomials in diverse regions (see [3]). Recently, Kim et al. [4–6], Sharma et al. [7,8], Muhiuddin et al. [9,10] gave same new and thrilling identities of degenerate special numbers and polynomials which are derived from the non-differential equation. These identities and technical approach are very useful for reading some issues which can be associated with mathematical physics. This paper aims to introduce a new type of degenerate version of the Changhee–Genocchi polynomials and numbers, the so-called new type of degenerate Changhee–Genocchi polynomials and numbers, constructed from the degenerate logarithm function. We derive some explicit expressions and identities for those numbers and polynomials. Additionally, we introduce a new type of higher-order degenerate Changhee–Genocchi polynomials and establish some properties of these polynomials.

The ordinary Euler and Genocchi polynomials are defined by (see [3,11–15])

$$\frac{2}{e^{\tau}+1}e^{\xi\tau} = \sum_{\omega=0}^{\infty} \mathbb{E}_{\omega}(\xi)\frac{\tau^{\omega}}{\omega!} \quad |\,\tau\,|< \pi, \tag{1}$$

and

$$\frac{2\tau}{e^{\tau}+1}e^{\xi\tau} = \sum_{\omega=0}^{\infty} \mathbb{G}_{\omega}(\xi)\frac{\tau^{\omega}}{\omega!} \quad |\,\tau\,|< \pi, \tag{2}$$

respectively.

In the case when $\xi = 0$, $\mathbb{E}_{\omega} = \mathbb{E}_{\omega}(0)$ and $\mathbb{G}_{\omega} = \mathbb{G}_{\omega}(0)$ are called the Euler and Genocchi numbers, respectively.

We note that
$$\mathbb{G}_0(\xi) = 0, \quad \mathbb{E}_\omega(\xi) = \frac{\mathbb{G}_{\omega+1}(\xi)}{\omega+1} \quad (\omega \geq 0).$$

For any non-zero $\lambda \in \mathbb{R}$ (or $\mathbb{C}$), the degenerate exponential function is defined by (see [14,15])
$$e_\lambda^\xi(\tau) = (1+\lambda\tau)^{\frac{\xi}{\lambda}}, \; e_\lambda^1(\tau) = (1+\lambda\tau)^{\frac{1}{\lambda}}. \tag{3}$$

By binomial expansion, we obtain
$$e_\lambda^\xi(\tau) = \sum_{\omega=0}^{\infty} (\xi)_{\omega,\lambda} \frac{\tau^\omega}{\omega!}, \tag{4}$$
where $(\xi)_{0,\lambda} = 1$, $(\xi)_{\omega,\lambda} = (\xi-\lambda)(\xi-2\lambda)\cdots(\xi-(\omega-1)\lambda)$ $(\omega \geq 1)$.

Note that
$$\lim_{\lambda\to 0} e_\lambda^\xi(\tau) = \sum_{\omega=0}^{\infty} \xi^\omega \frac{\tau^\omega}{\omega!} = e^{\xi\tau}.$$

In [1], Carlitz considered the degenerate Euler polynomials given by
$$\frac{2}{(1+\lambda\tau)^{\frac{1}{\lambda}}+1}(1+\lambda\tau)^{\frac{\xi}{\lambda}} = \sum_{\omega=0}^{\infty} \mathbb{E}_{\omega,\lambda}(\xi)\frac{\tau^\omega}{\omega!} \quad (\lambda \in \mathbb{R}). \tag{5}$$

When $\xi = 0, \mathbb{E}_{\omega,\lambda} = \mathbb{E}_{\omega,\lambda}(0)$ are called degenerate Euler numbers. The falling factorial sequence is given by
$$(\xi)_0 = 1, (\xi)_\omega = \xi(\xi-1)...(\xi-\omega+1) \quad (\omega \geq 1). \tag{6}$$

As is well known, the higher-order degenerate Euler polynomials are considered by L. Carlitz as follows (see [2]):
$$\left(\frac{2}{(1+\lambda\tau)^{\frac{1}{\lambda}}+1}\right)^r (1+\lambda\tau)^{\frac{\xi}{\lambda}} = \sum_{\omega=0}^{\infty} \mathbb{E}_{\omega,\lambda}^{(r)}(\xi)\frac{\tau^\omega}{\omega!}. \tag{7}$$

At the point $\xi = 0$, $\mathbb{E}_{\omega,\lambda}^{(r)} = \mathbb{E}_{\omega,\lambda}^{(r)}(0)$ are called the higher-order degenerate Euler numbers. Note that $\lim_{\lambda\to 0}\mathbb{E}_{\omega,\lambda}^{(r)}(\xi) = \mathbb{E}_\omega^{(r)}(\xi)$ $(\omega \geq 0)$.

The degenerate Genocchi polynomials $\mathbb{G}_\omega(\xi;\lambda)$ are defined by (see [16,17])
$$\frac{2\tau}{e_\lambda(\tau)+1}e_\lambda^\xi(\tau) = \sum_{\omega=0}^{\infty} \mathbb{G}_\omega(\xi,\lambda)\frac{\tau^\omega}{\omega!}. \tag{8}$$

In the case when $\xi = 0$, $\mathbb{G}_\omega(\lambda) = \mathbb{G}_\omega(0,\lambda)$ are called degenerate Genocchi numbers.

For $\lambda \in \mathbb{R}$, the degenerate logarithm function $\log_\lambda(1+\tau)$, which is the inverse of the degenerate exponential function $e_\lambda(\tau)$, is defined by (see [6])
$$\log_\lambda(1+\tau) = \sum_{\omega=1}^{\infty} \lambda^{\omega-1}(1)_{\omega,1/\lambda}\frac{\tau^\omega}{\omega!}. \tag{9}$$

It is easy to show that
$$\lim_{\lambda\to 0}\log_\lambda(1+\tau) = \sum_{\omega=1}^{\infty}(-1)^{\omega-1}\frac{\tau^\omega}{\omega!} = \log(1+\tau).$$

Note that $e_\lambda(\log_\lambda(1+\tau)) = \log_\lambda(e_\lambda(1+\tau)) = 1+\tau$.

The degenerate Stirling numbers of the first kind are defined by (see [5,6,18])
$$\frac{1}{\nu!}(\log_\lambda(1+\tau))^\nu = \sum_{\omega=\nu}^{\infty} S_{1,\lambda}(\omega,\nu)\frac{\tau^\omega}{\omega!} \quad (\nu \geq 0). \tag{10}$$

Note here that $\lim_{\lambda\to 0} S_{1,\lambda}(\omega,\nu) = S_1(\omega,\nu)$, where $S_1(\omega,\nu)$ are called the Stirling numbers of the first kind given by

$$\frac{1}{\nu!}(\log(1+\tau))^{\nu} = \sum_{\omega=\nu}^{\infty} S_1(\omega,\nu)\frac{\tau^{\omega}}{\omega!} \ (\nu \geq 0).$$

The degenerate Stirling numbers of the second kind (see [19]) are given by

$$\frac{1}{\nu!}(e_{\lambda}(\tau)-1)^{\nu} = \sum_{\omega=\nu}^{\infty} S_{2,\lambda}(\omega,\nu)\frac{\tau^{\omega}}{\omega!} \ (\nu \geq 0). \tag{11}$$

It is clear that $\lim_{\lambda\to 0} S_{2,\lambda}(\omega,\nu) = S_2(\omega,\nu)$, where $S_2(\omega,\nu)$ are called the Stirling numbers of the second kind given by

$$\frac{1}{\nu!}(e^{\tau}-1)^{\nu} = \sum_{\omega=\nu}^{\infty} S_2(\omega,\nu)\frac{\tau^{\omega}}{\omega!} \ (\nu \geq 0).$$

The Daehee polynomials are defined by (see [13])

$$\frac{\log(1+\tau)}{\tau}(1+\tau)^{\xi} = \sum_{\omega=0}^{\infty} D_{\omega}(\xi)\frac{\tau^{\omega}}{\omega!}. \tag{12}$$

When $\xi = 0$, $D_{\omega} = D_{\omega}(0)$ are called the Daehee numbers.

Recently, Kim et al. [5] introduced the new type degenerate Daehee polynomials defined by

$$\frac{\log_{\lambda}(1+\tau)}{\tau}(1+\tau)^{\xi} = \sum_{\omega=0}^{\infty} D_{\omega,\lambda}(\xi)\frac{\tau^{\omega}}{\omega!}. \tag{13}$$

When $\xi = 0$, $D_{\omega,\lambda} = D_{\omega,\lambda}(0)$ are called the degenerate Daehee numbers.

The Changhee polynomials are defined by (see [4])

$$\frac{2}{2+\tau}(1+\tau)^{\xi} = \sum_{\omega=0}^{\infty} Ch_{\omega}(\xi)\frac{\tau^{\omega}}{\omega!}. \tag{14}$$

When $\xi = 0$, $Ch_{\omega} = Ch_{\omega}(0)$ are called the Changhee numbers.

The higher-order Changhee polynomials are defined by (see [4])

$$\left(\frac{2}{2+\tau}\right)^{k}(1+\tau)^{\xi} = \sum_{\omega=0}^{\infty} Ch_{\omega}^{(k)}(\xi)\frac{\tau^{\omega}}{\omega!}. \tag{15}$$

When $\xi = 0$, $Ch_{\omega}^{(k)} = Ch_{\omega}^{(k)}(0)$ are called the higher-order Changhee numbers.

The Changhee–Genocchi polynomials are defined by the generating function (see [20])

$$\frac{2\log(1+\tau)}{2+\tau}(1+\tau)^{\xi} = \sum_{\omega=0}^{\infty} CG_{\omega}(\xi)\frac{\tau^{\omega}}{\omega!}. \tag{16}$$

When $\xi = 0$, $CG_{\omega} = CG_{\omega}(0)$ are called Changhee–Genocchi numbers.

Recently, Kim et al. [20] introduced the modified Changhee–Genocchi polynomials defined by

$$\frac{2\tau}{2+\tau}(1+\tau)^{\xi} = \sum_{\omega=0}^{\infty} CG_{\omega}^{*}(\xi)\frac{\tau^{\omega}}{\omega!}. \tag{17}$$

When $\xi = 0$, $CG_{\omega}^{*} = CG_{\omega}^{*}(0)$ are called the modified Changhee–Genocchi numbers.

From (1) and (17), we see that

$$\frac{2\tau}{2+\tau}(1+\tau)^{\xi} = \frac{2\tau}{e^{\log(1+\tau)}+1}e^{\xi\log(1+\tau)}$$

$$= \tau \sum_{\nu=0}^{\infty} \mathbb{E}_\nu(\xi) \frac{1}{\nu!} (\log(1+\tau))^\nu$$

$$= \tau \sum_{\omega=0}^{\infty} \left(\sum_{\nu=0}^{\omega} \mathbb{E}_\nu(\xi) S_1(\omega,\nu) \right) \frac{\tau^\omega}{\omega!}. \tag{18}$$

Thus, from (17) and (18), we obtain

$$\frac{CG^*_{\omega+1}(\xi)}{\omega+1} = \sum_{\nu=0}^{\omega} \mathbb{E}_\nu(\xi) S_1(\omega,\nu) \quad (\omega \geq 0).$$

The λ-Changhee–Genocchi polynomials are defined by (see [21])

$$\frac{2\log(1+\tau)}{(1+\tau)^\lambda + 1} (1+\tau)^{\lambda\xi} = \sum_{\omega=0}^{\infty} CG_{\omega,\lambda}(\xi) \frac{\tau^\omega}{\omega!}. \tag{19}$$

In the case $\xi = 0$, $CG_{\omega,\lambda} = CG_{\omega,\lambda}(0)$ are called the λ-Changhee–Genocchi numbers.

Motivated by the works of Kim et al. [6,20], we first define a new type of degenerate Changhee–Genocchi numbers and polynomials. We investigate some new properties of these numbers and polynomials and derive some new identities and relations between the new type of degenerate Changhee–Genocchi numbers and polynomials and Stirling numbers of the first and second kind. We also define a new type of higher-order Changhee–Genocchi polynomials and investigate some properties of these polynomials.

2. New Type of Degenerate Changhee–Genocchi Polynomials

In this section, we introduce a new type of degenerate Changhee–Genocchi polynomials and investigate some explicit expressions for degenerate Changhee–Genocchi polynomials and numbers. We begin with the following definition as.

For $\lambda \in \mathbb{R}$, we consider the new type of degenerate Changhee–Genocchi polynomials as defined by means of the following generating function

$$\frac{2\log_\lambda(1+\tau)}{2+\tau} (1+\tau)^{\xi} = \sum_{\omega=0}^{\infty} CG_{\omega,\lambda}(\xi) \frac{\tau^\omega}{\omega!}. \tag{20}$$

At the point $\xi = 0$, $CG_{\omega,\lambda} = CG_{\omega,\lambda}(0)$ are called the new type of degenerate Changhee–Genocchi numbers.

It is clear that

$$\sum_{\omega=0}^{\infty} \lim_{\lambda \to 0} CG_{\omega,\lambda}(\xi) \frac{\tau^\omega}{\omega!} = \lim_{\lambda \to 0} \frac{2\log_\lambda(1+\tau)}{2+\tau} (1+\tau)^{\xi}$$

$$= \frac{2\log(1+\tau)}{2+\tau} (1+\tau)^{\xi} = \sum_{\omega=0}^{\infty} CG_{\omega}(\xi) \frac{\tau^\omega}{\omega!}, \tag{21}$$

where $CG_\omega(\xi)$ are called the Changhee–Genocchi polynomials (see Equation (1)).

Theorem 1. *For $\omega \geq 0$, we have*

$$CG_{\omega,\lambda}(\xi) = \sum_{\nu=0}^{\omega} \mathbb{G}_\nu(\xi,\lambda) S_{1,\lambda}(\omega,\nu).$$

Proof. Using (8), (10) and (20), we note that

$$\sum_{\omega=0}^{\infty} CG_{\omega,\lambda}(\xi) \frac{\tau^\omega}{\omega!} = \frac{2\log_\lambda(1+\tau)}{e_\lambda(\log_\lambda(1+\tau)) + 1} e_\lambda^{\xi \log_\lambda(1+\tau)}$$

$$= \sum_{\nu=0}^{\infty} \mathbb{G}_{\nu}(\xi,\lambda)\frac{1}{\nu!}(\log_{\lambda}(1+\tau))^{\nu}$$
$$= \sum_{\nu=0}^{\infty} \mathbb{G}_{\nu}(\xi,\lambda)\sum_{\omega=\nu}^{\infty} S_{1,\lambda}(\omega,\nu)\frac{\tau^{\omega}}{\omega!}$$
$$= \sum_{\omega=0}^{\infty}\left(\sum_{\nu=0}^{\omega} \mathbb{G}_{\nu}(\xi,\lambda)S_{1,\lambda}(\omega,\nu)\right)\frac{\tau^{\omega}}{\omega!}. \quad (22)$$

Therefore, by (20) and (22), we obtain the result. □

Theorem 2. *For $\omega \geq 0$, we have*

$$CG_{\omega,\lambda}(\xi) = \sum_{\sigma=0}^{\omega}\sum_{\nu=0}^{\sigma}\binom{\omega}{\sigma}CG_{\omega-\sigma,\lambda}(\xi)_{\nu,\lambda}S_{1,\lambda}(\sigma,\nu).$$

Proof. By using (4), (10) and (20), we see that

$$\sum_{\omega=0}^{\infty} CG_{\omega,\lambda}(\xi)\frac{\tau^{\omega}}{\omega!} = \frac{2\log_{\lambda}(1+\tau)}{2+t}e_{\lambda}^{\xi\log_{\lambda}(1+\tau)} \quad (23)$$
$$= \sum_{\omega=0}^{\infty} CG_{\omega,\lambda}\frac{\tau^{\omega}}{\omega!}\sum_{\nu=0}^{\infty}(\xi)_{\nu,\lambda}\frac{(\log_{\lambda}(1+\tau))^{\nu}}{\nu!}$$
$$= \sum_{\omega=0}^{\infty} GG_{\omega,\lambda}\frac{\tau^{\omega}}{\omega!}\sum_{\sigma=0}^{\infty}\sum_{\omega=0}^{\sigma}(\xi)_{\sigma,\lambda}S_{1,\lambda}(\sigma,\nu)\frac{\tau^{\sigma}}{\sigma!}$$
$$= \sum_{\omega=0}^{\infty}\left(\sum_{\sigma=0}^{\omega}\sum_{\nu=0}^{\sigma}\binom{\omega}{\sigma}CG_{\omega-\sigma,\lambda}(\xi)_{\nu,\lambda}S_{1,\lambda}(\sigma,\nu)\right)\frac{\tau^{\omega}}{\omega!}. \quad (24)$$

Therefore, by (20) and (24), we obtain the result. □

Theorem 3. *For $\omega \geq 0$, we have*

$$\mathbb{G}_{\omega}(\xi,\lambda) = \sum_{\nu=0}^{\omega} CG_{\nu,\lambda}(\xi)S_{2,\lambda}(\omega,\nu).$$

Proof. By replacing τ by $e_{\lambda}(\tau)-1$ in (20) and using (8) and (11), we obtain

$$\sum_{\nu=0}^{\infty} CG_{\nu,\lambda}(\xi)\frac{1}{\nu!}(e_{\lambda}(\tau)-1)^{\nu} = \frac{2\tau}{e_{\lambda}(\tau)+1}e_{\lambda}^{\xi}(\tau)$$
$$= \sum_{\omega=0}^{\infty} \mathbb{G}_{\omega}(\xi,\lambda)\frac{\tau^{\omega}}{\omega!}. \quad (25)$$

On the other hand,

$$\sum_{\nu=0}^{\infty} CG_{\nu,\lambda}(\xi)\frac{1}{\nu!}(e_{\lambda}(\tau)-1)^{\tau} = \sum_{\nu=0}^{\infty} CG_{\nu,\lambda}(\xi)\sum_{\nu=\omega}^{\infty} S_{2,\lambda}(\omega,\nu)\frac{\tau^{\omega}}{\omega!}$$
$$= \sum_{\omega=0}^{\infty}\left(\sum_{\nu=0}^{\omega} CG_{\nu,\lambda}(\xi)S_{2,\lambda}(\omega,\nu)\right)\frac{\tau^{\omega}}{\omega!}. \quad (26)$$

Therefore, by (25) and (26), we obtain the required result. □

Theorem 4. *For $\omega \geq 0$, we have*

$$CG_{\omega,\lambda}(\xi) = \sum_{\nu=0}^{\omega} \mathbb{G}_{\nu}(\xi,\lambda) S_{1,\lambda}(\omega,\nu).$$

Proof. Replacing τ by $\log_{\lambda}(1+\tau)$ in (8) and applying (10), we obtain

$$\begin{aligned}
\frac{2\log_{\lambda}(1+\tau)}{2+\tau}(1+\tau)^{\xi} &= \sum_{\nu=0}^{\infty} \mathbb{G}_{\nu}(\xi,\lambda)\frac{1}{\nu!}(\log_{\lambda}(1+\tau))^{\nu} \\
&= \sum_{\nu=0}^{\infty} \mathbb{G}_{\nu}(\xi,\lambda) \sum_{\omega=\nu}^{\infty} S_{1,\lambda}(\omega,\nu)\frac{\tau^{\omega}}{\omega!} \\
&= \sum_{\omega=0}^{\infty}\left(\sum_{\nu=0}^{\omega} \mathbb{G}_{\nu}(\xi,\lambda) S_{1,\lambda}(\omega,\nu)\right)\frac{\tau^{\omega}}{\omega!}. \quad (27)
\end{aligned}$$

By using (20) and (27), we acquire the desired result. □

Theorem 5. *For $\omega \geq 0$, we have*

$$CG_{\omega,\lambda}(\xi) = \sum_{\nu=0}^{\omega} \binom{\omega}{\nu} CG^{*}_{\omega-\nu}(\xi) D_{\nu,\lambda}.$$

Proof. From (13), (17) and (20), we note that

$$\begin{aligned}
\sum_{\omega=0}^{\infty} CG_{\omega,\lambda}(\xi)\frac{\tau^{\omega}}{\omega!} &= \frac{2\log_{\lambda}(1+\tau)}{2+\tau}(1+\tau)^{\xi} \\
&= \frac{2\tau}{2+\tau}(1+\tau)^{\xi}\frac{\log_{\lambda}(1+\tau)}{\tau} \\
&= \sum_{\omega=0}^{\infty} CG^{*}_{\omega}(\xi)\frac{\tau^{\omega}}{\omega!}\sum_{\nu=0}^{\infty} D_{\nu,\lambda}\frac{\tau^{\nu}}{\nu!} \\
&= \sum_{\omega=0}^{\infty}\left(\sum_{\nu=0}^{\omega}\binom{\omega}{\nu} CG^{*}_{\omega-\nu}(\xi) D_{\nu,\lambda}\right)\frac{\tau^{\omega}}{\omega!}. \quad (28)
\end{aligned}$$

Therefore, by (20) and (28), we obtain the result. □

Theorem 6. *For $\omega \geq 0$, we have*

$$\frac{CG_{\omega+1,\lambda}(\xi)}{\omega+1} = \sum_{\sigma=0}^{\omega}\sum_{\nu=0}^{\sigma}\binom{\omega}{\sigma}\mathbb{E}_{\nu}(\xi) S_{1}(\sigma,\nu) D_{\omega-\sigma,\lambda}.$$

Proof. From (1), (13) and (20), we note that

$$\begin{aligned}
\sum_{\omega=1}^{\infty} CG_{\omega,\lambda}(\xi)\frac{\tau^{\omega}}{\omega!} &= \frac{2\log_{\lambda}(1+\tau)}{2+\tau}(1+\tau)^{\xi} \\
&= \frac{2\tau}{e^{\log(1+\tau)}+1} e^{\xi\log(1+\tau)}\frac{\log_{\lambda}(1+\tau)}{\tau} \\
&= \tau\sum_{\nu=0}^{\infty}\mathbb{E}_{\nu}(\xi)\frac{(\log(1+\tau))^{\nu}}{\nu!}\sum_{\omega=0}^{\infty} D_{\omega,\lambda}\frac{\tau^{\omega}}{\omega!} \\
&= \tau\sum_{\sigma=0}^{\infty}\sum_{\nu=0}^{\sigma}\mathbb{E}_{\nu}(\xi) S_{1}(\sigma,\nu)\frac{\tau^{\sigma}}{\sigma!}\sum_{\omega=0}^{\infty} D_{\omega,\lambda}\frac{\tau^{\omega}}{\omega!}
\end{aligned}$$

$$= \sum_{\omega=1}^{\infty}\left(\sum_{\sigma=0}^{\omega}\sum_{\nu=0}^{\sigma}\binom{\omega}{\sigma}\mathbb{E}_{\nu}(\xi)S_1(\sigma,\nu)D_{\omega-\sigma,\lambda}\right)\frac{\tau^{\omega}}{\omega!}. \tag{29}$$

By (20) and (29), we obtain the result. □

Theorem 7. *For $\omega \geq 0$, we have*

$$CG_{\omega,\lambda}(\xi) = \sum_{\sigma=0}^{\omega}\sum_{\nu=0}^{\sigma}\binom{\omega}{\sigma}(\nu+1)(\xi)_{\nu,\lambda}\frac{S_{1,\lambda}(\sigma+1,\nu+1)}{\sigma+1}CG^{*}_{\omega-\sigma}.$$

Proof. By using (10), (17) and (20), we see that

$$\begin{aligned}
&\frac{2\log_{\lambda}(1+\tau)}{2+\tau}e_{\lambda}^{\xi\log_{\lambda}(1+\tau)} \\
&= \frac{2\log_{\lambda}(1+\tau)}{2+\tau}\sum_{\nu=0}^{\infty}(\xi)_{\nu,\lambda}\frac{(\log_{\lambda}(1+\tau))^{\nu}}{\nu!} \\
&= \frac{2\tau}{2+\tau}\frac{1}{\tau}\sum_{\nu=0}^{\infty}(\nu+1)(\xi)_{\nu,\lambda}\frac{(\log_{\lambda}(1+\tau))^{\nu+1}}{(\nu+1)!} \\
&= \sum_{\omega=0}^{\infty}CG^{*}_{\omega}\frac{\tau^{\omega}}{\omega!}\frac{1}{\tau}\sum_{\nu=0}^{\infty}(\nu+1)(\xi)_{\nu,\lambda}\sum_{\sigma=\nu+1}^{\infty}S_{1,\lambda}(\sigma,\nu+1)\frac{\tau^{\sigma}}{\sigma!} \\
&= \sum_{\omega=0}^{\infty}CG^{*}_{\omega}\frac{\tau^{\omega}}{\omega!}\sum_{\sigma=0}^{\infty}\sum_{\nu=0}^{\sigma}(\nu+1)(\xi)_{\nu,\lambda}\frac{S_{1,\lambda}(\sigma+1,\nu+1)}{\sigma+1}\frac{\tau^{\sigma}}{\sigma!} \\
&= \sum_{\omega=0}^{\infty}\left(\sum_{\sigma=0}^{\omega}\sum_{\nu=0}^{\sigma}\binom{\omega}{\sigma}(\nu+1)(\xi)_{\nu,\lambda}\frac{S_{1,\lambda}(\sigma+1,\nu+1)}{\sigma+1}CG^{*}_{\omega-\nu}\right)\frac{\tau^{\omega}}{\omega!}.
\end{aligned} \tag{30}$$

Therefore, by (20) and (30), we obtain the result. □

For $d \in \mathbb{N}$ with $d \equiv 1$ (mod 2), the following identity is (see [21])

$$\sum_{a=0}^{d-1}(-1)^{a}(1+\tau)^{a} = \frac{1+(1+\tau)^{d}}{2+\tau}. \tag{31}$$

Theorem 8. *For $d \in \mathbb{N}$ with $d \equiv 1$ (mod 2), we have the following identity*

$$CG_{\omega,\lambda}(\xi) = \sum_{a=0}^{d-1}(-1)^{a}CG_{\omega,\lambda}\left(\frac{a+\xi}{d}\right).$$

Proof. Thus, for such $d \equiv 1$ (mod 2), from (19), (20) and (31), we see that

$$\begin{aligned}
\sum_{\omega=0}^{\infty}CG_{\omega,\lambda}(\xi)\frac{\tau^{\omega}}{\omega!} &= \frac{2\log_{\lambda}(1+\tau)}{2+\tau}(1+\tau)^{\xi} \\
&= \sum_{a=0}^{d-1}(-1)^{a}\frac{2\log_{\lambda}(1+\tau)}{(1+\tau)^{d}+1}(1+\tau)^{d(\frac{a+\xi}{d})} \\
&= \sum_{a=0}^{d-1}(-1)^{a}\sum_{\omega=0}^{\infty}CG_{\omega,\lambda}\left(\frac{a+\xi}{d}\right)\frac{\tau^{\omega}}{\omega!} \\
&= \sum_{\omega=0}^{\infty}\left(\sum_{a=0}^{d-1}(-1)^{a}CG_{\omega,\lambda}\left(\frac{a+\xi}{d}\right)\right)\frac{\tau^{\omega}}{\omega!}.
\end{aligned} \tag{32}$$

By (20) and (32), we obtain the result. □

Theorem 9. *For $d \in \mathbb{N}$ with $d \equiv 1 \pmod 2$, we have the following identity*

$$2\sum_{a=0}^{d-1}(-1)^a D_{\omega,\lambda}(a) = \frac{CG_{\omega+1,\lambda}}{\omega+1} + \frac{CG_{\omega+1,\lambda}(d)}{\omega+1}.$$

Proof. By using (13), (20) and (31), we see that

$$2\log_\lambda(1+\tau)\sum_{a=0}^{d-1}(-1)^a(1+\tau)^a = \frac{2\log_\lambda(1+\tau)}{2+\tau} + \frac{2\log_\lambda(1+\tau)}{2+\tau}(1+\tau)^d$$

$$= \frac{2\log_\lambda(1+\tau)}{\tau}\left(\sum_{a=0}^{d-1}(-1)^a(1+\tau)^a\right)$$

$$= \sum_{\omega=0}^{\infty} CG_{\omega,\lambda}\frac{\tau^{\omega-1}}{\omega!} + \sum_{\omega=0}^{\infty} CG_{\omega,\lambda}(d)\frac{\tau^{\omega-1}}{\omega!}$$

$$= \left(2\sum_{a=0}^{d-1}(-1)^a D_{\omega,\lambda}(a)\right)\frac{\tau^\omega}{\omega!}$$

$$= \sum_{\omega=0}^{\infty}\left(\frac{CG_{\omega+1,\lambda}}{\omega+1} + \frac{CG_{\omega+1,\lambda}(d)}{\omega+1}\right)\frac{\tau^\omega}{\omega!}. \tag{33}$$

By comparing the coefficients of τ^ω on both sides, we obtain the result. □

Theorem 10. *For $\omega \geq 1$, we have*

$$\omega CG_{\omega-1,\lambda} + 2CG_{\omega,\lambda} = 2(\lambda)^{\omega-1}(1)_{\omega,1/\lambda},$$

with $CG_{0,\lambda} = 0$.

Proof. From (20), we note that

$$2\log_\lambda(1+\tau) = \sum_{\omega=0}^{\infty} CG_{\omega,\lambda}\frac{\tau^\omega}{\omega!}(\tau+2)$$

$$= \sum_{\omega=1}^{\infty} CG_{\omega,\lambda}\frac{\tau^{\omega+1}}{\omega!} + 2\sum_{\omega=0}^{\infty} CG_{\omega,\lambda}\frac{\tau^\omega}{\omega!}$$

$$= \sum_{\omega=2}^{\infty} \omega CG_{\omega-1,\lambda}\frac{\tau^\omega}{\omega!} + 2\sum_{\omega=0}^{\infty} CG_{\omega,\lambda}\frac{\tau^\omega}{\omega!}$$

$$= 2CG_{1,\lambda}(\tau) + \sum_{\omega=2}^{\infty}(\omega CG_{\omega-1,\lambda} + 2CG_{\omega,\lambda})\frac{\tau^\omega}{\omega!}. \tag{34}$$

On the other hand,

$$2\log_\lambda(1+\tau) = 2\sum_{\omega=1}^{\infty}(\lambda)^{\omega-1}(1)_{\omega,1/\lambda}\frac{\tau^\omega}{\omega!}. \tag{35}$$

Therefore, by (34) and (35), we obtain the result. □

We now consider a new type of higher-order degenerate Changhee–Genocchi polynomials by the following definition.

Let $r \in \mathbb{N}$, and we consider that a new type of higher-order degenerate Changhee–Genocchi polynomials is given by the following generating function

$$\left(\frac{2\log_\lambda(1+\tau)}{2+\tau}\right)^r (1+\tau)^\xi = \sum_{\omega=0}^{\infty} CG_{\omega,\lambda}^{(r)}(\xi)\frac{\tau^\omega}{\omega!}. \tag{36}$$

When $\xi = 0, CG^{(r)}_{\omega,\lambda} = CG^{(r)}_{\omega,\lambda}(0)$ are called the new type of higher-order degenerate Changhee–Genocchi numbers.

It is worth noting that

$$\lim_{\lambda\to 0} CG^{(r)}_{\omega,\lambda}(\xi) = CG^{(r)}_{\omega}(\xi),$$

are called higher-order Changhee–Genocchi polynomials.

Theorem 11. *For $\omega \geq 0$, we have*

$$CG^{(r+1)}_{\omega,\lambda}(\xi) = \sum_{\nu=0}^{\omega} \binom{\omega}{\nu} CG_{\nu,\lambda} CG^{(r)}_{\omega-\nu,\lambda}(\xi).$$

Proof. From (20) and (36), we note that

$$\frac{2\log_\lambda(1+\tau)}{2+\tau} \sum_{\omega=0}^{\infty} CG^{(r)}_{\omega,\lambda}(\xi)\frac{\tau^\omega}{\omega!} = \frac{2\log_\lambda(1+\tau)}{2+\tau}\left(\frac{2\log_\lambda(1+\tau)}{2+\tau}\right)^r (1+\tau)^\xi$$

$$\left(\sum_{\nu=0}^{\infty} CG_{\nu,\lambda}\frac{\tau^\omega}{\omega!}\right)\left(\sum_{\omega=0}^{\infty} CG^{(r)}_{\omega,\lambda}(\xi)\frac{\tau^\omega}{\omega!}\right) = \sum_{\omega=0}^{\infty} CG^{(r+1)}_{\omega,\lambda}(\xi)\frac{\tau^\omega}{\omega!}$$

$$\sum_{\omega=0}^{\infty}\left(\sum_{\nu=0}^{\omega}\binom{\omega}{\nu} CG_{\nu,\lambda} CG^{(r)}_{\omega-\nu,\lambda}(\xi)\right)\frac{\tau^\omega}{\omega!} = \sum_{\omega=0}^{\infty} CG^{(r+1)}_{\omega,\lambda}(\xi)\frac{\tau^\omega}{\omega!}. \tag{37}$$

Comparing the coefficients of τ in above equation, we obtain the result. □

Theorem 12. *For $r, k \in \mathbb{N}$, with $r > k$, we have*

$$CG^{(r)}_{\omega,\lambda}(\xi) = \sum_{\sigma=0}^{\omega}\binom{\omega}{\sigma} CG^{(r-k)}_{\sigma,\lambda} CG^{(k)}_{\omega-\sigma,\lambda}(\xi) \quad (\omega \geq 0).$$

Proof. By (36), we see that

$$\begin{aligned}
&\left(\frac{2\log_\lambda(1+\tau)}{2+\tau}\right)^r (1+\tau)^\xi \\
&= \left(\frac{2\log_\lambda(1+\tau)}{2+\tau}\right)^{r-k}\left(\frac{2\log_\lambda(1+\tau)}{2+\tau}\right)^k (1+\tau)^\xi \\
&= \left(\sum_{\sigma=0}^{\infty} CG^{(r-k)}_{\sigma,\lambda}\frac{\tau^\sigma}{\sigma!}\right)\left(\sum_{\omega=0}^{\infty} CG^{(k)}_{\omega,\lambda}(\xi)\frac{\tau^\omega}{\omega!}\right) \\
&= \sum_{\omega=0}^{\infty}\left(\sum_{\sigma=0}^{\omega}\binom{\omega}{\sigma} CG^{(r-k)}_{\sigma,\lambda} CG^{(k)}_{\omega-\sigma,\lambda}(\xi)\right)\frac{\tau^\omega}{\omega!}.
\end{aligned} \tag{38}$$

Therefore, by (36) and (38), we obtain the result. □

Theorem 13. *For $\omega \geq 0$, we have*

$$CG^{(r)}_{\omega,\lambda}(\xi+\eta) = \sum_{\nu=0}^{\omega}\binom{\omega}{\nu} CG^{(r)}_{\omega-\nu,\lambda}(\xi)(\eta)_\nu.$$

Proof. Now, we observe that

$$\sum_{\omega=0}^{\infty} CG^{(r)}_{\omega,\lambda}(\xi+\eta)\frac{\tau^\omega}{\omega!} = \left(\frac{2\log_\lambda(1+\tau)}{2+\tau}\right)^r (1+\tau)^{\xi+\eta}$$

$$= \left(\sum_{\sigma=0}^{\infty} CG_{\sigma,\lambda}^{(r)}(\xi)\frac{\tau^{\sigma}}{\sigma!}\right)\left(\sum_{\nu=0}^{\infty}(\eta)_{\nu}\frac{\tau^{\nu}}{\nu!}\right)$$

$$= \sum_{\omega=0}^{\infty}\left(\sum_{\nu=0}^{\omega}\binom{\omega}{\nu}CG_{\omega-\nu,\lambda}^{(r)}(\xi)(\eta)_{\nu}\right)\frac{\tau^{\omega}}{\omega!}. \tag{39}$$

Equating the coefficients of τ^{ω} on both sides, we obtain the result. □

Theorem 14. *For $\omega \geq 0$, we have*

$$CG_{\omega,\lambda}^{(r)} = \sum_{\nu=0}^{\omega}\binom{\omega}{\nu}CG_{\nu}^{(*,r)}D_{\omega-\nu,\lambda}^{(r)}.$$

Proof. By making use of (36), we have

$$\left(\frac{2\log_{\lambda}(1+\tau)}{2+\tau}\right)^{r} = \left(\frac{2t}{2+\tau}\right)^{r}\left(\frac{\log_{\lambda}(1+\tau)}{\tau}\right)^{r}$$

$$= \left(\sum_{\nu=0}^{\infty}CG_{\nu}^{(*,r)}\frac{\tau^{\nu}}{\nu!}\right)\left(\sum_{\omega=0}^{\infty}D_{\omega,\lambda}^{(r)}\frac{\tau^{\omega}}{\omega!}\right)$$

$$= \sum_{\omega=0}^{\infty}\left(\sum_{\nu=0}^{\omega}\binom{\omega}{\nu}CG_{\nu}^{(*,r)}D_{\omega-\nu,\lambda}^{(r)}\right)\frac{\tau^{\omega}}{\omega!}. \tag{40}$$

Therefore, by (36) and (40), we obtain the result. □

3. Conclusions

Motivated by the research work of [6,20,21], we defined a new type of degenerating Changhee–Genocchi polynomials which turned out to be classical ones in the special cases. We also derived their explicit expressions and some identities involving them. Later, we introduced the higher-order degenerate Changhee–Genocchi polynomials and deduced their explicit expressions and some identities by making use of the generating functions method, analytical means and power series expansion.

Author Contributions: Conceptualization, M.S.A. and W.A.K.; methodology, W.A.K.; software, M.S.A.; validation, M.S.A.; formal analysis, W.A.K.; investigation, M.S.A.; resources, W.A.K.; data curation, M.S.A.; writing—original draft preparation, W.A.K; writing—review and editing, W.A.K.; visualization, M.S.A.; supervision, W.A.K. All authors have read and agreed to the published version of the manuscript.

Funding: There is no external funding.

Institutional Review Board Statement: Not applicable.

Informed Consent Statement: Not applicable.

Data Availability Statement: Not applicable.

Acknowledgments: The authors wish to express their appreciation to the reviewers for their helpful suggestions which greatly improved the presentation of this paper.

Conflicts of Interest: The authors declare no conflict of interest.

References

1. Carlitz, L. Degenerate Stirling Bernoulli and Eulerian numbers. *Util.Math.* **1979**, 15, 51–88.
2. Carlitz, L. A degenerate Staud-Clausen theorem. *Arch. Math.* **1956**, 7, 28–33. [CrossRef]
3. Khan, W.A.; Muhiuddin, G.; Muhyi, A.; Al-Kadi, D. Analytical properties of type 2 degenerate poly-Bernoulli polynomials associated with their applications. *Adv. Diff. Equ.* **2021**, *2021*, 420. [CrossRef]
4. Kim, D.S.; Kim, T. Higher-order Changhee numbers and polynomials. *Adv. Studies Theor. Phys.* **2014**, *8*, 365–373. [CrossRef]

5. Kim, T.; Kim, D.S.; Kim, H.-Y.; Kwon, J. Some results on degenerate Daehee and Bernoulli numbers and polynomials. *Adv. Diff. Eq.* **2020**, *2020*, 311. [CrossRef]
6. Kim, D.S.; Kim, T. A note on a new type of degenerate Bernoulli numbers. *Russ. J. Math. Phys.* **2020**, *27*, 227–235. [CrossRef]
7. Sharma, S.K.; Khan, W.A.; Araci, S.; Ahmed, S.S. New type of degenerate Daehee polynomials of the second kind. *Adv. Differ. Equ.* **2020**, *2020*, 428. [CrossRef]
8. Sharma, S.K.; Khan, W.A.; Araci, S.; Ahmed, S.S. New construction of type 2 of degenerate central Fubini polynomials with their certain properties. *Adv. Differ. Equ.* **2020**, *2020*, 587. [CrossRef]
9. Muhiuddin, G.; Khan, W.A.; Muhyi, A.; Al-Kadi, D. Some results on type 2 degenerate poly-Fubini polynomials and numbers. *Comput. Model. Eng. Sci.* **2021**, *29*, 1051–1073. [CrossRef]
10. Muhiuddin, G.; Khan, W.A.; Al-Kadi, D. Construction on the degenerate poly-Frobenius-Euler polynomials of complex variable. *J. Function Spaces* **2021**, *2021*, 3115424. [CrossRef]
11. Khan, W.A.; Acikgoz, M.; Duran, U. Note on the type 2 degenerate multi-poly-Euler polynomials. *Symmetry* **2020**, *12*, 1691. [CrossRef]
12. Khan, W.A.; Haroon, H. Some symmetric identities for the generalized Bernoulli, Euler and Genocchi polynomials associated with Hermite polynomials. *Springer Plus* **2016**, *5*, 1920. [CrossRef] [PubMed]
13. Khan, W.A.; Nisar, K.S.; Duran, U.; Acikgoz, M.; Araci, S. Multifarious implicit summation formulae of Hermite-based poly-Daehee polynomials. *Appl. Math. Inf. Sci.* **2018**, *12*, 305–310. [CrossRef]
14. Khan, W.A.; Muhyi, A.; Ali, R.; Alzobydi, K.A.H.; Singh, M.; Agarwal, P. A new family of degenerate poly-Bernoulli polynomials of the second kind with its certain related properties. *AIMS Math.* **2021**, *6*, 12680–12697. [CrossRef]
15. Khan, W.A.; Ali, R.; Alzobydi, K.A.H.; Ahmed, N. A new family of degenerate poly-Genocchi polynomials with its certain properties. *J. Funct. Spaces* **2021**, *2021*, 6660517. [CrossRef]
16. Lim, D. Some identities of degenerate Genocchi polynomials. *Bull. Korean Math. Soc.* **2016**, *53*, 569–579. [CrossRef]
17. Sharma, S.K. A note on degenerate poly-Genocchi polynomials. *Int. J. Adv. Appl. Sci.* **2020**, *7*, 1–5. [CrossRef]
18. Kwon, H.-I.; Kim, T.; Park, J.W. A note on degenerate Changhee-Genocchi polynomials and numbers. *Glob. J. Pure Appl. Math.* **2016**, *12*, 4057–4064.
19. Kim, T. A note on degenerate Stirling numbers of the second kind. *Proc. Jangjeon Math. Soc.* **2018**, *21*, 589–598.
20. Kim, B.M.; Jang, L-.C.; Kim, W.; Kwon, H.I. Degenerate Changhee-Genocchi numbers and polynomials. *J. Ineq. Appl.* **2017**, *2017*, 294. [CrossRef]
21. Kim, B.M.; Jeong, J.; Rim, S.H. Some explicit identities on Changhee-Genocchi polynomials and numbers. *Adv. Diff. Equ.* **2016**, *2016*, 202. [CrossRef]

axioms

MDPI

Article

The Influence of Multiplicative Noise and Fractional Derivative on the Solutions of the Stochastic Fractional Hirota–Maccari System

Farah M. Al-Askar [1], Wael W. Mohammed [2,3,*], Clemente Cesarano [4] and M. El-Morshedy [5,6]

1 Department of Mathematical Science, Collage of Science, Princess, Nourah Bint Abdulrahman University, P.O. Box 84428, Riyadh 11671, Saudi Arabia; famalaskar@pnu.edu.sa
2 Department of Mathematics, Faculty of Science, University of Ha'il, Ha'il 2440, Saudi Arabia
3 Department of Mathematics, Faculty of Science, Mansoura University, Mansoura 35516, Egypt
4 Section of Mathematics, International Telematic University Uninettuno, Corso Vittorio Emanuele II, 39, 00186 Roma, Italy; c.cesarano@uninettunouniversity.net
5 Department of Mathematics, College of Science and Humanities in Al-Kharj, Prince Sattam Bin Abdulaziz University, Al-Kharj 11942, Saudi Arabia; m.elmorshedy@psau.edu.sa
6 Department of Statistics and Computer Science, Faculty of Science, Mansoura University, Mansoura 35516, Egypt
* Correspondence: wael.mohammed@mans.edu.eg

Abstract: We address here the space-fractional stochastic Hirota–Maccari system (SFSHMs) derived by the multiplicative Brownian motion in the Stratonovich sense. To acquire innovative elliptic, trigonometric and rational stochastic fractional solutions, we employ the Jacobi elliptic functions method. The attained solutions are useful in describing certain fascinating physical phenomena due to the significance of the Hirota–Maccari system in optical fibers. We use MATLAB programm to draw our figures and exhibit several 3D graphs in order to demonstrate how the multiplicative Brownian motion and fractional derivative affect the exact solutions of the SFSHMs. We prove that the solutions of SFSHMs are stabilized by the multiplicative Brownian motion around zero.

Keywords: fractional Hirota–Maccari system; stochastic Hirota–Maccari system; Jacobi elliptic functions method

Citation: Al-Askar, F.M.; Mohammed, W.W.; Cesarano, C.; El-Morshedy, M. The Influence of Multiplicative Noise and Fractional Derivative on the Solutions of the Stochastic Fractional Hirota–Maccari System. *Axioms* **2022**, *11*, 357. https://doi.org/10.3390/axioms11080357

Academic Editor: Hans J. Haubold

Received: 29 June 2022
Accepted: 22 July 2022
Published: 23 July 2022

1. Introduction

Recently, numerous significant phenomena have been represented by fractional derivatives, including electro-magnetic, image processing, acoustics, electrochemistry and anomalous diffusion phenomena [1–6]. One benefit of fractional models is that they may be stated more specifically than integer models, which encourages us to construct a number of significant and practical fractional models. On the other hand, the advantages of taking random influences into account in the analysis, simulation, prediction and modeling of complex processes have been highlighted in several fields including chemistry, geophysics, fluid mechanics, biology, atmosphere, physics, climate dynamics, engineering and other fields [7–10]. Since noise may produce statistical features and significant phenomena, it cannot be ignored. In general, it is more difficult to obtain exact solutions to fractional PDEs forced by a stochastic term than to classical ones.

Recently, finding approximate and exact solutions to PDEs using a variety of approaches has become the main objective for many scientists. Many effective methods, including the sine-Gordon expansion method [11], the trial equation method [12], (G'/G)-expansion [13,14], semi-inverse variational principle [15], the ansatz approach [16], perturbation methods [17,18], Darboux transformation [19], tanh-sech [20,21], $exp(-\phi(\varsigma))$-expansion [22] and the Jacobi elliptic function [23,24], have been devised to obtain exact solutions to PDEs.

As a result, we study here the following stochastic fractional-space Hirota–Maccari system (SFSHMs) with multiplicative noise in the Stratonovich sense:

$$i\Phi_t + \mathcal{D}^{\alpha}_{xy}\Phi + i\mathcal{D}^{\alpha}_{xxx}\Phi + \Phi\Psi - i\Phi\mathcal{D}^{\alpha}_{x}(|\Phi|^2) + i\sigma\Phi \circ W_t = 0, \quad (1)$$

$$3\mathcal{D}^{\alpha}_{x}\Psi + \mathcal{D}^{\alpha}_{y}(|\Phi|^2) = 0, \quad (2)$$

where $\Psi(x,y,t)$ denotes the real field of scalars and $\Phi(x,y,t)$ is the complex scalar field, x, y are independent spatial variables and t is the temporal variable. $\mathcal{D}^{\alpha}_{x}$ is the conformable derivative (CD) for $\alpha \in (0,1]$ [25]. $W_t = \frac{dW}{dt}$ is the time derivative of Brownian motion $W(t)$ and σ is a noise strength.

The stochastic integral $\int_0^t \Phi(s)dW(s)$ is called the Stratonovich stochastic integral (denoted by $\int_0^t \Phi(s) \circ dW(s)$), if we calculate the stochastic integral at the middle, while the stochastic integral $\int_0^t \Phi(s)dW(s)$ is called Itô (denoted by $\int_0^t \Phi(s)dW(s)$) when we calculate it at the left end [26]. The relation between the Stratonovich integral and Itô integral is:

$$\int_0^t \Phi(s, Z_s)dW(s) = \int_0^t \Phi(s, Z_s) \circ dW(s) - \frac{1}{2}\int_0^t \Phi(s, Z_s)\frac{\partial \Phi(s, Z_s)}{\partial z}ds. \quad (3)$$

The conformable derivative for the function $\phi : (0, \infty) \to \mathbb{R}$ is defined for $\alpha \in (0,1]$ as

$$\mathcal{D}^{\alpha}_{x}\phi(x) = \lim_{\kappa \to 0} \frac{\phi(x + \kappa x^{1-\alpha}) - \phi(x)}{\kappa}. \quad (4)$$

The important property of CD is the following chain rule:

$$\mathcal{D}^{\alpha}_{x}(\phi_1 \circ \phi_2)(x) = x^{1-\alpha}\phi_2'(x)\phi_1'(\phi_2(x)).$$

The Hirota–Maccari system (1-2), with $\sigma = 0$ and $\alpha = 1$, was derived by Maccari [27]. There are several physical applications of the integrable Hirota–Maccari system including the transmission of optical pulses across nematic liquid crystal waveguides and for a certain parameter regime, the transmission of femtosecond pulses through optical fibers. Due to the importance of the Hirota–Maccari system, many researchers have examined a lot of techniques in order to find the exact solutions for this system, such as the extended trial equation and the generalized Kudryashov [28], tanh-coth, sec-tan, rational sinh-cosh and sech-csch methods [29], (G'/G)-expansion [30], Hirota bilinear method [31], Weierstrass elliptic function expansion [32], Painleve approach [33], Painleve test [34], general projective Riccati equation and improved $tan(\frac{\phi(\theta)}{2})$-expansion method [35] and complex hyperbolic-function [36]. While the exact solutions of stochastic Hirota–Maccari system have been studied in [37] in the Itô sense by using three different methods: Riccati–Bernoulli sub-ODE, sine-cosine and He's semi-inverse.

The originality of this paper is to acquire the analytical solutions of the SFSHMs (1-2). This work is the first to attain the exact solutions of the SFSHMs (1-2). We employ the Jacobi elliptic functions approach to obtain a broad range of solutions, including hyperbolic, trigonometric and rational functions. Moreover, to study the effects of Brownian motion on the solutions of the SFSHMs (1-2), we build 3D graphs for some of the developed solutions by using MATLAB tools.

This is how the paper is organized: We use a suitable wave transformation in Section 2 to provide the wave equation of SFSHMs. We employ the Jacobi elliptic functions approach in Section 3 to obtain the analytical solutions of the SFSHMs (1-2). In Section 4, we look at how the Brownian motion affects the generated solutions. Finally, we state the conclusions of this paper.

2. Wave Equation for SFSHMs

To get the wave equation of the SFSHMs (1-2), let us utilize the following transformation:

$$\Phi(x,y,t) = Q(\zeta)e^{i\theta-\sigma W(t)-\sigma^2 t}, \ \Psi(x,y,t) = P(\zeta)e^{-2\sigma W(t)-2\sigma^2 t}, \tag{5}$$

with

$$\zeta = (\frac{\zeta_1}{\alpha}x^\alpha + \frac{\zeta_2}{\alpha}y^\alpha + \zeta_3 t), \ \theta = \frac{\theta_1}{\alpha}x^\alpha + \frac{\theta_2}{\alpha}y^\alpha + \theta_3 t,$$

where θ_k, ζ_k for $k = 1, 2, 3$ are nonzero constants. We substitute Equation (5) into Equations (1-2), and use

$$\begin{aligned}\frac{d\Phi}{dt} &= (\zeta_3 Q' + i\theta_3 Q - \sigma Q W_t + \frac{1}{2}\sigma^2 Q - \sigma^2 Q)e^{i\theta-\sigma W(t)-\sigma^2 t}, \\ &= (\zeta_3 Q' + i\theta_3 Q - \sigma Q W_t - \frac{1}{2}\sigma^2 Q)e^{i\theta-\sigma W(t)-\sigma^2 t}, \\ &= (\zeta_3 Q' + i\theta_3 Q - \sigma Q \circ W_t)e^{i\theta-\sigma W(t)-\sigma^2 t},\end{aligned}$$

and

$$\begin{aligned}\mathcal{D}_x^\alpha \Phi &= (\zeta_1 Q' + i\theta_1 Q)e^{i\theta-\sigma W(t)-\sigma^2 t}, \ \mathcal{D}_y^\alpha \Phi(|\Phi|^2) = \zeta_2 (Q^2)' e^{-2\sigma W(t)-2\sigma^2 t}, \\ \mathcal{D}_{xxx}^\alpha \Phi &= (\zeta_1^3 Q''' + 3i\theta_1\zeta_1^2 Q'' - 2\theta_1^2\zeta_1 Q' - \theta_1^2\zeta_1 Q' - i\theta_1^3 Q)e^{i\theta-\sigma W(t)-\sigma^2 t}, \\ \mathcal{D}_{xy}^\alpha \Phi &= (\zeta_1\zeta_2 Q'' + i\zeta_1\theta_2 Q' + i\zeta_2\theta_1 Q' - \theta_1\theta_2 Q)e^{i\theta-\sigma W(t)-\sigma^2 t},\end{aligned}$$

to obtain for the real part

$$(\zeta_1\zeta_2 - \theta_1\zeta_1^2)Q'' - (\theta_3 + \theta_1\theta_2 - \theta_1^3)Q + QPe^{-2\sigma W(t)-2\sigma^2 t} = 0, \tag{6}$$

$$3\zeta_1 P' + \zeta_2 (Q^2)' = 0. \tag{7}$$

Integrating Equation (7), we have

$$P = \frac{-\zeta_2}{3\zeta_1}Q^2. \tag{8}$$

Setting Equation (8) into Equation (6) we obtain

$$Q'' - A_1 Q^3 e^{-2\sigma W(t)-2\sigma^2 t} - A_2 Q = 0, \tag{9}$$

where

$$A_1 = \frac{\zeta_2}{3\zeta_1(\zeta_1\zeta_2 - \theta_1\zeta_1^2)} \quad \text{and} \quad A_2 = \frac{\theta_3 + \theta_1\theta_2 - \theta_1^3}{\zeta_1\zeta_2 - \theta_1\zeta_1^2}. \tag{10}$$

Taking expectation $\mathbb{E}(\cdot)$ on both sides for Equation (9), we attain

$$Q'' - A_1 Q^3 e^{-2\sigma^2 t}\mathbb{E}(e^{-2\sigma W(t)}) - A_2 Q = 0. \tag{11}$$

Since $W(t)$ is a normal process, then $\mathbb{E}(e^{-2\sigma W(t)}) = e^{2\sigma^2 t}$. Therefore Equation (11) becomes

$$Q'' - A_1 Q^3 - A_2 Q = 0. \tag{12}$$

3. The Analytical Solutions of the SFSHMs

In this section, we use the Jacobi elliptic functions method [38] to acquire the solutions to Equation (12). Consequently, we obtain the analytical solutions of the SFSHMs (1-2).

3.1. Method Description

Let the solutions of Equation (12) have the form

$$Q(\zeta) = \sum_{i=1}^{N} a_i \mathcal{Z}^i(\zeta), \tag{13}$$

where $\mathcal{Z}$ solves

$$\mathcal{Z}' = \sqrt{\frac{1}{2}\ell_1 \mathcal{Z}^4 + \ell_2 \mathcal{Z}^2 + \ell_3}, \tag{14}$$

where ℓ_1, ℓ_2 and ℓ_3 are real parameters and N is a positive integer number.

We notice that Equation (14) has a variety of solutions depending on ℓ_1, ℓ_2 and ℓ_3 as in the following Table 1 :

Table 1. All possible solutions for Equation (14) for different values of ℓ_1, ℓ_2 and ℓ_3.

Case	ℓ_1	ℓ_2	ℓ_3	$\mathcal{Z}(\zeta)$
1	$2\mathbf{m}^2$	$-(1+\mathbf{m}^2)$	1	$sn(\zeta)$
2	2	$2\mathbf{m}^2 - 1$	$-\mathbf{m}^2(1-\mathbf{m}^2)$	$ds(\zeta)$
3	2	$2-\mathbf{m}^2$	$(1-\mathbf{m}^2)$	$cs(\zeta)$
4	$-2\mathbf{m}^2$	$2\mathbf{m}^2 - 1$	$(1-\mathbf{m}^2)$	$cn(\zeta)$
5	-2	$2-\mathbf{m}^2$	$(\mathbf{m}^2-1)$	$dn(\zeta)$
6	$\frac{\mathbf{m}^2}{2}$	$\frac{(\mathbf{m}^2-2)}{2}$	$\frac{1}{4}$	$\frac{sn(\zeta)}{1\pm dn(\zeta)}$
7	$\frac{\mathbf{m}^2}{2}$	$\frac{(\mathbf{m}^2-2)}{2}$	$\frac{\mathbf{m}^2}{4}$	$\frac{sn(\zeta)}{1\pm dn(\zeta)}$
8	$\frac{-1}{2}$	$\frac{(\mathbf{m}^2+1)}{2}$	$\frac{-(1-\mathbf{m}^2)^2}{4}$	$\mathbf{m}cn(\zeta) \pm dn(\zeta)$
9	$\frac{\mathbf{m}^2-1}{2}$	$\frac{(\mathbf{m}^2+1)}{2}$	$\frac{(\mathbf{m}^2-1)}{4}$	$\frac{dn(\zeta)}{1\pm sn(\zeta)}$
10	$\frac{1-\mathbf{m}^2}{2}$	$\frac{(1-\mathbf{m}^2)}{2}$	$\frac{(1-\mathbf{m}^2)}{4}$	$\frac{cn(\zeta)}{1\pm sn(\zeta)}$
11	$\frac{(1-\mathbf{m}^2)^2}{2}$	$\frac{(1-\mathbf{m}^2)^2}{2}$	$\frac{1}{4}$	$\frac{sn(\zeta)}{dn\pm cn(\zeta)}$
12	2	0	0	$\frac{c}{\zeta}$
13	0	1	0	ce^{ζ}

Where $dn(\zeta) = dn(\zeta, \mathbf{m})$, $cn(\zeta) = cn(\zeta, \mathbf{m})$, $sn(\zeta) = sn(\zeta, \mathbf{m})$ are the Jacobi elliptic functions (JEFs) for $0 < \mathbf{m} < 1$. If $\mathbf{m} \to 1$, then the JEFs are transformed into the following hyperbolic functions:

$$\begin{aligned} cs(\zeta) &\to \operatorname{csch}(\zeta), \quad sn(\zeta) \to \tanh(\zeta), \quad cn(\zeta) \to \operatorname{sech}(\zeta), \\ dn(\zeta) &\to \operatorname{sech}(\zeta), \quad ds \to \operatorname{csch}(\zeta). \end{aligned}$$

3.2. Solutions of SFSHMs

Let us balance Q'' with Q^3 in Equation (12) to define N as follows:

$$N + 2 = 3N \Longrightarrow N = 1. \tag{15}$$

Equation (14) is rewritten with $N = 1$ as

$$Q(\zeta) = a_0 + a_1 \mathcal{Z}(\zeta). \tag{16}$$

Differentiating Equation (16) twice, we have, by using (14),

$$Q'' = a_1 \ell_2 \mathcal{Z} + a_1 \ell_1 \mathcal{Z}^3. \tag{17}$$

Plugging Equation (16) and Equation (17) into Equation (12) we have

$$(a_1\ell_1 - A_1a_1^3)\mathcal{Z}^3 - 3a_0a_1^2A_1\mathcal{Z}^2 + (a_1\ell_2 - 3A_1a_0^2a_1 + A_2a_1)\mathcal{Z} - (A_1a_0^3 - A_2a_0) = 0.$$

Setting each coefficient of $\mathcal{Z}^k$ for $k = 0, 1, 2, 3$ equal to zero, we attain

$$a_1\ell_1 - A_1a_1^3 = 0,$$

$$3a_0a_1^2A_1 = 0,$$

$$a_1\ell_2 - 3A_1a_0^2a_1 + A_2a_1 = 0,$$

and

$$A_1a_0^3 - A_2a_0 = 0.$$

We obtain by solving these equations

$$a_0 = 0, \;\; a_1 = \pm\sqrt{\frac{\ell_1}{A_1}}, \;\; \ell_2 = -A_2.$$

Thus, Equation (12) has the following solution

$$Q(\zeta) = \pm\sqrt{\frac{\ell_1}{A_1}}\mathcal{Z}(\zeta), \;\; \text{for} \;\; \frac{\ell_1}{A_1} > 0. \tag{18}$$

The following are two sets that depend on ℓ_1 and A_1 :

First set: If $\ell_1 > 0$ (from Table 1)and $A_1 > 0$, then the wave Equation (12) has the solution $Q(\zeta)$ as in the following Table 2:

Table 2. All possible solutions for wave Equation (12) when $\ell_1 > 0$.

Case	ℓ_1	ℓ_2	ℓ_3	$\mathcal{Z}(\zeta)$	$Q(\zeta)$
1	$2m^2$	$-(1+\mathbf{m}^2)$	1	$sn(\zeta)$	$\pm\sqrt{\frac{\ell_1}{A_1}}sn(\zeta)$
2	2	$2\mathbf{m}^2-1$	$-\mathbf{m}^2(1-\mathbf{m}^2)$	$ds(\zeta)$	$\pm\sqrt{\frac{\ell_1}{A_1}}ds(\zeta)$
3	2	$2-\mathbf{m}^2$	$(1-\mathbf{m}^2)$	$cs(\zeta)$	$\pm\sqrt{\frac{\ell_1}{A_1}}cs(\zeta)$
4	$\frac{\mathbf{m}^2}{2}$	$\frac{(\mathbf{m}^2-2)}{2}$	$\frac{1}{4}$ or $\frac{\mathbf{m}^2}{4}$	$\frac{sn(\zeta)}{1\pm dn(\zeta)}$	$\pm\sqrt{\frac{\ell_1}{A_1}}\frac{sn(\zeta)}{1\pm dn(\zeta)}$
5	$\frac{1-\mathbf{m}^2}{2}$	$\frac{(1-\mathbf{m}^2)}{2}$	$\frac{(1-\mathbf{m}^2)}{4}$	$\frac{cn(\zeta)}{1\pm sn(\zeta)}$	$\pm\sqrt{\frac{\ell_1}{A_1}}\frac{cn(\zeta)}{1\pm sn(\zeta)}$
6	$\frac{(1-\mathbf{m}^2)^2}{2}$	$\frac{(1-\mathbf{m}^2)^2}{2}$	$\frac{1}{4}$	$\frac{sn(\zeta)}{dn\pm cn(\zeta)}$	$\pm\sqrt{\frac{\ell_1}{A_1}}\frac{sn(\zeta)}{dn\pm cn(\zeta)}$
7	2	0	0	$\frac{c}{\zeta}$	$\pm\sqrt{\frac{\ell_1}{A_1}}\frac{c}{\zeta}$

If $\mathbf{m} \to 1$, then the previous Table 2 becomes

Table 3. All possible solutions for wave Equation (12) when $\ell_1 > 0$ and $\mathbf{m} \to 1$.

Case	ℓ_1	ℓ_2	ℓ_3	$\mathcal{Z}(\zeta)$	$Q(\zeta)$
1	2	-2	1	$\tanh(\zeta)$	$\pm\sqrt{\frac{\ell_1}{A_1}}\tanh(\zeta)$
2	2	1	0	$\mathrm{sech}(\zeta)$	$\pm\sqrt{\frac{\ell_1}{A_1}}\mathrm{sech}(\zeta)$
3	2	1	0	$\mathrm{csch}(\zeta)$	$\pm\sqrt{\frac{\ell_1}{A_1}}\mathrm{csch}(\zeta)$
4	$\frac{1}{2}$	$\frac{-1}{2}$	$\frac{1}{4}$	$\frac{\tanh(\zeta)}{1\pm\mathrm{sech}(\zeta)}$	$\pm\sqrt{\frac{\ell_1}{A_1}}\frac{\tanh(\zeta)}{1\pm\mathrm{sech}(\zeta)}$
5	2	0	0	$\frac{c}{\zeta}$	$\pm\sqrt{\frac{\ell_1}{A_1}}\frac{c}{\zeta}$

Now, using the previous Table 2 (or Table 3 when $\mathbf{m} \to 1$) and Equations (5) and (18), we obtain the exact solutions of the SFSHMs (1-2), for $\frac{\ell_1}{A_1} > 0$, as follows:

$$\Phi(x,y,t) = Q(\zeta)e^{(i\theta-\sigma W(t)-\sigma^2 t)}, \tag{19}$$

$$\Psi(x,y,t) = \frac{-\zeta_2}{3\zeta_1}Q^2(\zeta)e^{(-2\sigma W(t)-2\sigma^2 t)}, \tag{20}$$

where $\zeta = (\frac{\zeta_1}{\alpha}x^\alpha + \frac{\zeta_2}{\alpha}y^\alpha + \zeta_3 t)$, $\theta = \frac{\theta_1}{\alpha}x^\alpha + \frac{\theta_2}{\alpha}y^\alpha + \theta_3 t$.

Second set: If $\ell_1 < 0$ and $A_1 < 0$, then the solutions $Q(\zeta)$ of the wave Equation (12) are

Table 4. All possible solutions for wave Equation (12) when $\ell_1 < 0$.

Case	ℓ_1	ℓ_2	ℓ_3	$\mathcal{Z}(\zeta)$	$Q(\zeta)$
1	$-2\mathbf{m}^2$	$2\mathbf{m}^2 - 1$	$(1-\mathbf{m}^2)$	$cn(\zeta)$	$\pm\sqrt{\frac{\ell_1}{A_1}}cn(\zeta)$
2	-2	$2-\mathbf{m}^2$	$(\mathbf{m}^2-1)$	$dn(\zeta)$	$\pm\sqrt{\frac{\ell_1}{A_1}}dn(\zeta)$
3	$\frac{-1}{2}$	$\frac{(\mathbf{m}^2+1)}{2}$	$\frac{-(1-\mathbf{m}^2)^2}{4}$	$\mathbf{m}cn(\zeta)\pm dn(\zeta)$	$\pm\sqrt{\frac{\ell_1}{A_1}}[\mathbf{m}cn(\zeta)\pm dn(\zeta)]$
4	$\frac{\mathbf{m}^2-1}{2}$	$\frac{(\mathbf{m}^2+1)}{2}$	$\frac{(\mathbf{m}^2-1)}{4}$	$\frac{dn(\zeta)}{1\pm sn(\zeta)}$	$\pm\sqrt{\frac{\ell_1}{A_1}}\frac{dn(\zeta)}{1\pm sn(\zeta)}$

If $\mathbf{m} \to 1$, then the previous Table 4 becomes

Table 5. All possible solutions for wave Equation (12) when $\ell_1 < 0$ and $\mathbf{m} \to 1$.

Case	ℓ_1	ℓ_2	ℓ_3	$\mathcal{Z}(\zeta)$	$Q(\zeta)$
1	-2	1	0	$\mathrm{sech}(\zeta)$	$\pm\sqrt{\frac{\ell_1}{A_1}}\mathrm{sech}(\zeta)$
2	$\frac{-1}{2}$	2	0	$2\mathrm{sech}(\zeta)$	$\pm2\sqrt{\frac{\ell_1}{A_1}}\mathrm{sech}(\zeta)$

In this situation, we may obtain the analytical solutions of the SFSHMs (1-2) as reported in Equations (19) and (20) by utilizing the previous Table 4 (or Table 5 when $\mathbf{m} \to 1$).

4. The Effect of Noise and Fractional Derivative on Solutions

In this article, the impact of noise and fractional derivative on the acquired solutions of the SFSHMs (1-2) is discussed. We utilize the MATLAB tools to create some graphs, for various noise strength σ, for the following solutions:

$$\Phi(x,y,t) = \sqrt{\frac{\ell_1}{A_1}}sn(\frac{\zeta_1}{\alpha}x^\alpha + \frac{\zeta_2}{\alpha}y^\alpha + \zeta_3 t)e^{(i\theta-\sigma W(t)-\sigma^2 t)}, \tag{21}$$

$$\Psi(x,y,t) = \frac{-\zeta_2 \ell_1}{3\zeta_1 A_1} sn^2 (\frac{\zeta_1}{\alpha} x^\alpha + \frac{\zeta_2}{\alpha} y^\alpha + \zeta_3 t) e^{-2\sigma W(t) - 2\sigma^2 t}. \tag{22}$$

Fixing the following parameters: $\zeta_1 = \zeta_2 = \theta_2 = 1$, $\theta_1 = 0.5$, $\theta_3 = 0.4$, and $y = 0.5$, then $\zeta_3 = -2$, and $A_1 = \frac{2}{3}$. In this case $\mathbf{m} = 0.5$, $\ell_1 = 0.5$ and $\zeta = \frac{1}{\alpha} x^\alpha + \frac{1}{\alpha} (0.5)^\alpha - 2t$.

Firstly the effect of noise: In the next Figure 1, when $\sigma = 0$, we observe that the surface fluctuates

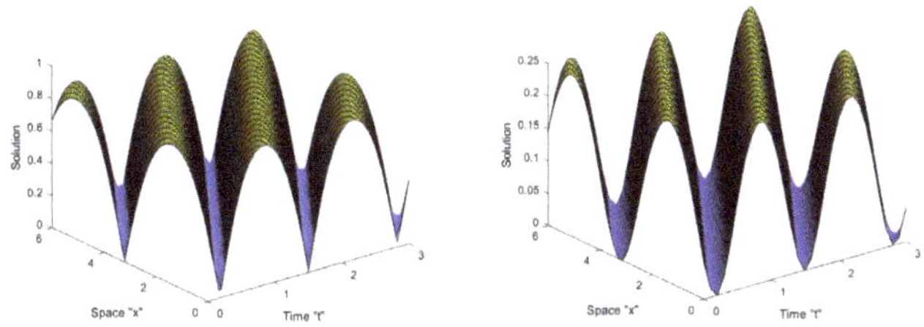

Equation (21) with $\sigma = 0$ Equation (22) with $\sigma = 0$

Figure 1. 3D profile of Equations (21) and (22) with $\sigma = 0$.

Furthermore, in Figure 2, if the noise intensity is raised, the surface becomes more planar after small transit behaviors as follows:

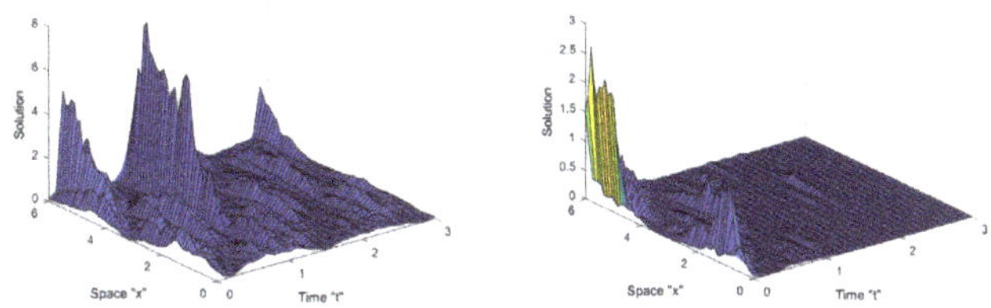

Equation (21) with $\sigma = 1$ Equation (22) with $\sigma = 1$

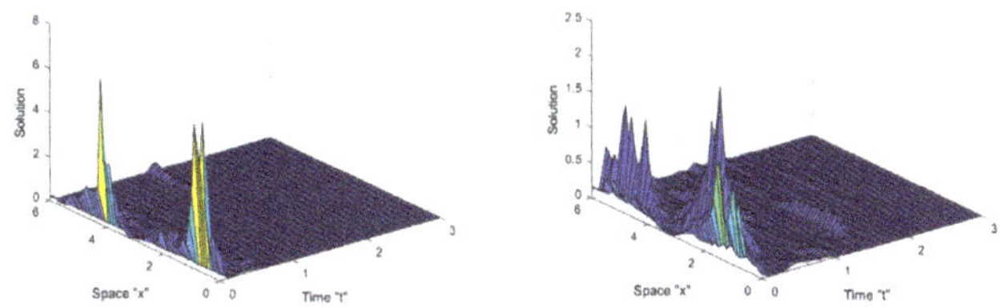

Equation (21) with $\sigma = 2$ Equation (22) with $\sigma = 2$

Figure 2. 3D profile of Equations (21) and (22) with $\sigma = 1, 2$.

Secondly the effect of fractional order: In Figures 3 and 4, if $\sigma = 0$, we can observe that as α increases, the surface extends:

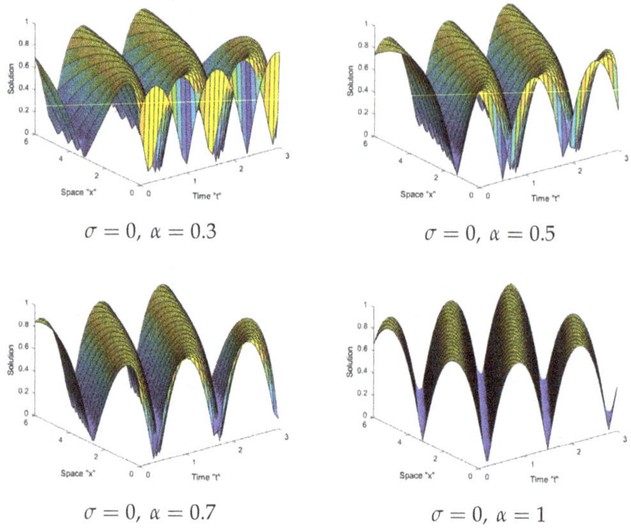

Figure 3. 3D profile of Equation (21) with $\sigma = 0$ and various α.

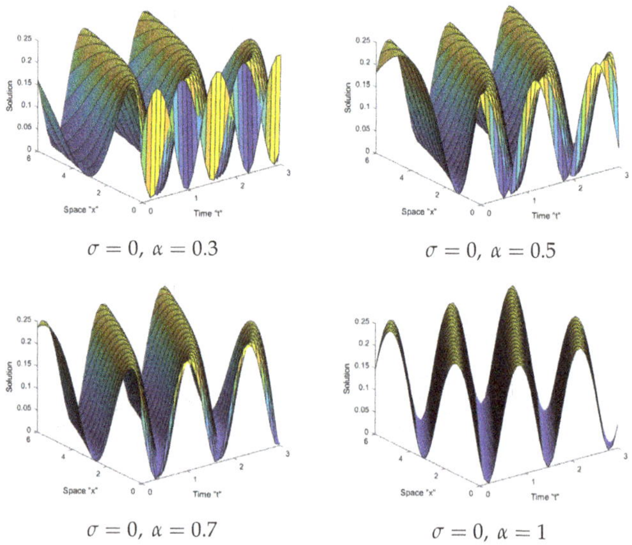

Figure 4. 3D profile of Equation (22) with $\sigma = 0$ and various α.

5. Conclusions

The stochastic fractional-space Hirota–Maccari system (1-2) were taken into consideration in this work. To obtain stochastic trigonometric, elliptic, rational solutions, we used the Jacobi elliptic functions approach. The obtained solutions will be very helpful for further research in disciplines such as optical fibers and others. Finally, an illustration is provided of how multiplicative Brownian motion affects the exact solutions of the SFSHMs (1-2). In future studies, we can consider SDSEs with additive noise.

Author Contributions: Data curation, F.M.A.-A. and M.E.-M.; Formal analysis, W.W.M., F.M.A.-A. and C.C.; Funding acquisition, F.M.A.-A.; Methodology, C.C. and M.E.-M.; Project administration, W.W.M.; Software, W.W.M. and M.E.-M.; Supervision, C.C.; Visualization, F.M.A.-A.; Writing—original draft, M.E.-M.; Writing—review & editing, W.W.M. and C.C. All authors have read and agreed to the published version of the manuscript.

Funding: This research received no external funding.

Institutional Review Board Statement: Not applicable.

Informed Consent Statement: Not applicable.

Data Availability Statement: Not applicable.

Acknowledgments: Princess Nourah bint Abdulrahman University Researchers Supporting Project number (PNURSP2022R273), Princess Nourah bint Abdulrahman University, Riyadh, Saudi Arabia.

Conflicts of Interest: The authors declare no conflict of interest.

References

1. Yuste, S.B.; Acedo, L.; Lindenberg, K. Reaction front in an $A + B \rightarrow C$ reaction–subdiffusion process. *Phys. Rev. E* **2004**, *69*, 036126. [CrossRef] [PubMed]
2. Mohammed, W.W.; Iqbal, N.; Botmart, T. Additive noise effects on the stabilization of fractional-space diffusion equation solutions. *Mathematics* **2022**, *10*, 130. [CrossRef]
3. Benson, D.A.; Wheatcraft, S.W.; Meerschaert, M.M. The fractional-order governing equation of Lévy motion. *Water Resour.* **2000**, *36*, 1413–1423. [CrossRef]
4. Mohammed, W.W.; Aly, E.S.; Matouk, A.E.; Albosaily, S.; EM Elabbasy, E.M. An analytical study of the dynamic behavior of Lotka-Volterra based models of COVID-19. *Phys. Rev. Lett.* **2001**, *87*, 118301. [CrossRef] [PubMed]
5. Mohammed, W.W.; Bazighifan, O.; Al-Sawalha M.M.; Almatroud, A.O.; Aly, E.S. The influence of noise on the exact solutions of the stochastic fractional-space chiral nonlinear schrdinger equation. *Fractal Fract.* **2021**, *5*, 262. [CrossRef]
6. Barkai, E.; Metzler, R.; Klafter, J. From continuous time random walks to the fractional Fokker–Planck equation. *Phys. Rev.* **2000**, *61*, 132–138. [CrossRef]
7. Mohammed, W.W.; Blömker, D. Fast-diffusion limit for reaction-diffusion equations with multiplicative noise. *J. Math. Anal. Appl.* **2021**, *496*, 124808. [CrossRef]
8. Weinan, E.; Li, X.; Vanden-Eijnden, E. Some recent progress in multiscale modeling. *Multiscale Model. Simul.* **2004**, *39*, 3–21.
9. Imkeller, P.; Monahan, A.H. Conceptual stochastic climate models. *Stoch. Dynam.* **2002**, *2*, 311–326. [CrossRef]
10. Mohammed, W.W. Modulation equation for the stochastic Swift–Hohenberg equation with cubic and quintic nonlinearities on the Real Line. *Mathematics* **2020**, *6*, 1217. [CrossRef]
11. Rezazadeh, H.; Mirzazadeh, M.; Mirhosseini-Alizamini, S.M.; Neirameh, A.; Eslami, M.; Zhou, Q. Optical solitons of Lakshmanan–Porsezian–Daniel model with a couple of nonlinearities. *Optik* **2018**, *164*, 414–423. [CrossRef]
12. Arshed, S.; Raza, N.; Alansari, M. Soliton solutions of the generalized Davey-Stewartson equation with full nonlinearities via three integrating schemes. *Ain Shams Eng. J.* **2021**, *12*, 3091–3098. [CrossRef]
13. Wang, M.L.; Li, X.Z.; Zhang, J.L. The $(\frac{G'}{G})$-expansion method and travelling wave solutions of nonlinear evolution equations in mathematical physics. *Phys. Lett. A* **2008**, *372*, 417–423. [CrossRef]
14. Mirzazadeh, M.; Eslami, M.; Milovic, D.; Biswas, A. Topological solitons of resonant nonlinear Schödinger's equation with dual-power law nonlinearity by $(\frac{G'}{G})$-expansion technique. *Optik* **2014**, *125*, 5480–5489. [CrossRef]
15. Biswas, A.; Zhou, Q.; Moshokoa, S.P.; Triki, H.; Belic, M.; Alqahtani, R. Resonant 1-soliton solution in anti-cubic nonlinear medium with perturbations. *Optik* **2017**, *145*, 14–17. [CrossRef]
16. Savescu, M.; Bhrawy, A.H.; Hilal, E.M.; Alshaery, A.A.; Biswas, A. Optical Solitons in Birefringent Fibers with Four-Wave Mixing for Kerr Law Nonlinearity. *Rom. J. Phys.* **2014**, *59*, 582–589.
17. Blömker, D.; Mohammed, W.W. Amplitude equations for SPDEs with cubic nonlinearities. *Stochastics Int. J. Probability Stoch. Process.* **2013**, *85*, 181–215. [CrossRef]
18. Mohammed, W.W. Amplitude equation with quintic nonlinearities for the generalized Swift-Hohenberg equation with additive degenerate noise. *Adv. Differ. Equ.* **2016**, *1*, 1–18. [CrossRef]
19. Wen-Xiu, M.; Sumayah, B. A binary darboux transformation for multicomponent NLS equations and their reductions. *Anal. Math. Phys.* **2021**, *11* 44.
20. Al-Askar, F.M.; Mohammed, W.W.; Albalahi, A.M.; El-Morshedy, M. The Impact of the Wiener process on the analytical solutions of the stochastic (2+ 1)-dimensional breaking soliton equation by using tanh–coth method. *Mathematics* **2022**, *10*, 817. [CrossRef]
21. Malfliet, W.; Hereman, W. The tanh method. I. Exact solutions of nonlinear evolution and wave equations. *Phys. Scr.* **1996**, *54*, 563–568. [CrossRef]
22. Khan, K.; Akbar, M.A. The $exp(-\Phi(\varsigma))$ -expansion method for finding travelling wave solutions of Vakhnenko-Parkes equation. *Int. J. Dyn. Syst. Differ. Equ.* **2014**, *5*, 72–83.

23. Yan, Z.L. Abunbant families of Jacobi elliptic function solutions of the-dimensional integrable Davey-Stewartson-type equation via a new method. *Chaos Solitons Fractals* **2003**, *18*, 299–309. [CrossRef]
24. Mohammed, W.W.; FM Al-Askar, F.M.; Cesarano, C.; El-Morshedy, M. The Optical Solutions of the Stochastic Fractional Kundu-Mukherjee-Naskar Model by Two Different Methods. *Mathematics* **2020**, *10*, 1465. [CrossRef]
25. Khalil, R.; Horani, M.A.; Yousef, A.; Sababheh, M. A new definition of fractional derivative. *J. Comput. Appl. Math.* **2014**, *264*, 65–70. [CrossRef]
26. Kloeden, P.E.; Platen, E. *Numerical Solution of Stochastic Differential Equations*; Springer: New York, NY, USA, 1995.
27. Maccari, A. A generalized Hirota equation in (2+1) dimensions. *J. Math. Phys.* **1998**, *39*, 6547–6551. [CrossRef]
28. Demiray, S.T.; Pandir, Y.; Bulut, H. All exact travelling wave solutions of Hirota equation and Hirota-Maccari system. *Opt. Int. J. Light Electron Opt.* **2016**, *127*, 1848–1859. [CrossRef]
29. Wazwaz, A.M. Abundant soliton and periodic wave solutions for the coupled Higgs eld equation, the Maccari system and the Hirota-Maccari system. *Phys. Scr.* **2012**, *85*, 1–10. [CrossRef]
30. Malik, A.; Chand, F.; Khatri, H. Exact solutions of some physical models using the (G'/G)-expansion method. *Pramana* **2012**, *78*, 513. [CrossRef]
31. Yu, X.; Gao, Y.T.; Sun, Z.Y.; Meng, X.H.; Liu, Y.; Feng, Q.; Wang, M.Z. N-soliton solutions for the (2+1)-dimensional Hirota-Maccari equation in fluids, plasmas and optical bers. *J. Math. Anal. Appl.* **2011**, *378*, 519–527. [CrossRef]
32. Chen, Y.; Yan, Z. The Weierstrass elliptic function expansion method and its applications in nonlinear wave equations. *Chaos Solitons Fractals* **2006**, *29*, 948–964. [CrossRef]
33. Liang, Z.F.; Tang, X.Y. Modulational instability and variable separation solution for a generalized (2+1)-dimensional Hirota equation. *Chin. Phys. Lett.* **2010**, *27*, 1–4.
34. Xu, G.Q.; Li, Z.B. The Painleve test of nonlinear partial differential equations and its implementation using Maple. *Comput. Algebr. Geom. Algebra Appl.* **2005**, *3519*, 179–190.
35. Raza, N.; Jhangeery, A.; Rezazadehz, H.; Bekir, A. Explicit solutions of the (2 + 1)-dimensional Hirota-Maccarisystem arising in nonlinear optics. *Int. J. Mod. Phys. B* **2019**, *33*, 1950360. [CrossRef]
36. Bai, C.L.; Zhao, H. Complex hyperbolic-function method and its applications to nonlinear equations. *Phys. Lett. A* **2006**, *355*, 32–38. [CrossRef]
37. Mohammed, W.W.; Ahmad, H.; Boulares, H.; Khelifi, F.; El-Morshedy, M. Exact solutions of Hirota–Maccari system forced by multiplicative noise in the Itô sense. Journal of Low Frequency Noise. *Vib. Act. Control* **2022**, *41*, 74–84.
38. Peng, Y.Z. Exact solutions for some nonlinear partial differential equations. *Phys. Lett. A* **2013**, *314*, 401–408. [CrossRef]

axioms

MDPI

Article

Iterative Approximate Solutions for Variational Problems in Hadamard Manifold

Mohammad Dilshad [1,*], Doaa Filali [2,*], Sumit Chandok [3] and Mohammad Akram [4]

1 Department of Mathematics, Faculty of Science, University of Tabuk, P.O. Box 741, Tabuk 71491, Saudi Arabia
2 Department of Mathematical Science, College of Sciences, Princess Nourah Bint Abdulrahman University, Riyadh 84428, Saudi Arabia
3 School of Mathematics, Thapar Institute of Engineering & Technology, Patiala 147004, Punjab, India; sumit.chandok@thapar.edu
4 Department of Mathematics, Faculty of Science, Islamic University of Madinah, P.O. Box 170, Madinah 42351, Saudi Arabia; akramkhan_20@rediffmail.com
* Correspondence: mdilshaad@gmail.com (M.D.); dkfilali@pnu.edu.sa (D.F.)

Abstract: The goal of this paper is to propose and investigate new iterative methods for examining an approximate solution of a fixed-point problem, an equilibrium problem, and a finite collection of variational inclusions in the Hadamard manifold's structure. Operating under some assumptions, we extend the proximal point algorithm to estimate the common solution of stated problems and obtain a strong convergence theorem for the common solution. We also present several consequences of the proposed iterative methods and their convergence results.

Keywords: proximal point method; equilibrium problem; fixed-point problem; variational inclusion problem; Hadamard manifold

MSC: 47J20; 47H10; 49J40

Citation: Dilshad, M.; Filali, D.; Chandok, S.; Akram, M. Iterative Approximate Solutions for Variational Problems in Hadamard Manifold. *Axioms* **2022**, *11*, 352. https://doi.org/10.3390/axioms11070352

Academic Editor: Clemente Cesarano

Received: 18 June 2022
Accepted: 18 July 2022
Published: 21 July 2022

1. Introduction

Many nonlinear problems, such as equilibrium, optimization, variational inequality, and fixed-point problems, have recently been transformed from linear spaces to Hadamard manifolds; see [1–15]. Fan [16] initiated the equilibrium problem (EP), which was later developed by Blum and Oettli [17] in real Hilbert space. It was Colao [5] who studied the equilibrium problem for the first time on the Hadamard manifold. For a bi-function $F : K \times K \to \mathbb{R}$, such that $F(u, u) = 0$, $\forall u \in K$, K is a nonempty subset of the Hadamard manifold $\mathbb{X}$. The equilibrium problem is to locate a point $u^\star \in K$, such that

$$F(u^\star, u) \geq 0, \forall u \in K. \tag{1}$$

They studied the existence of equilibrium point of equilibrium problem (1), and utilized their results to find the solution of mixed variational inequality problems, fixed-point problems and Nash equilibrium problems in Hadamard manifolds. They also introduced the Picard iterative method to approximate a solution of the equilibrium problem (1). Recently, Khammahawong et al. [10,18] studied the splitting type algorithms for equilibrium and inclusion problems on Hadamard manifolds. We denote by $\mathrm{EP}(F)$ the set of equilibrium points of the equilibrium problem (1).

The variational inclusion problem in Hilbert space $\mathbb{H}$ is to locate a point $u \in D$, such that

$$0 \in V(u) + G(u), \tag{2}$$

where $V : D \to \mathbb{H}$ and $G : D \to 2^{\mathbb{H}}$ are single valued and set-valued mappings, respectively, defined on a nonempty subset D of Hilbert space $\mathbb{H}$. The solution set of the problem (2) is denoted by $(V+G)^{-1}(0)$.

Due to its application-oriented nature, the problem (2) has been investigated extensively by a number of researchers in diverse directions.The proximal point method due to Martinet [19] is a fundamental approach for solving the inclusion problem $u \in G^{-1}(0)$, and Rockafellar [15] generalized this strategy to solve the variational inclusion problem (2). Li et al. [11] introduced the proximal point method for the inclusion problem in Hadamard manifold. Ansari et al. [2] examined Korpelevich's method to find the solution of the variational inclusion problem (2) in the structure of the Hadamard manifold $\mathbb{X}$.

Recently, Ansari and Babu [3] investigated the variational inclusion problem (2) using the proximal point method in the Hadamard manifold, as follows:

Let $u_0 \in \mathbb{X}$ and $\lambda_k > 0$, define u_{k+1}, such that

$$\mathbf{0} \in \mathrm{P}_{u_{k+1},u_k} V(u_k) + G(u_{k+1}) - \tfrac{1}{\lambda_k}\exp^{-1}_{u_{k+1}} u_k, \tag{3}$$

where P_{u_{k+1},u_k} is the parallel transport of $T_{u_k}\mathbb{X}$ to $T_{u_{k+1}}\mathbb{X}$ on the tangent bundle of $T\mathbb{X}$, exp is the exponential mapping, V and G are single valued and set-valued monotone vector fields, respectively defined on $K \subseteq \mathbb{X}$.

Several practical problems can be formulated as a fixed-point problem:

$$S(u) = u, \tag{4}$$

where S is a nonlinear mapping. The solutions of this equation are called fixed points of S, which is denoted by $\mathrm{Fix}(S)$. Li et al. [13] extended the Mann and Halpern iteration scheme to find the fixed point of nonexpansive mappings from Hilbert spaces to Hadamard manifolds. Recently, Al-Homidan et al. [1] proposed and analyzed the Halpern and Mann-type iterative methods to find the solution of a variational inclusion problem (2) and fixed-point problem (4) of self nonexpansive mapping S in the Hadamard manifold, which is to locate $u \in K$, such that

$$u \in \mathrm{Fix}(S) \cap (V+G)^{-1}(0). \tag{5}$$

Most of the problems originating in nonlinear science, such as signal processing, image recovery, signal processing, optimization, machine learning, etc., are switchable to either variational inclusion, an equilibrium problem or a fixed-point problem. Therefore, many mathematicians have recently transformed and studied the inclusion problems, equilibrium problems and fixed-point problems in different directions from linear to nonlinear spaces; for examples, see [1–3,6,7,9,11–13,20–22] and references cited therein.

As zero of the sum of monotone mapping $V + G$ is the fixed point of resolvent $J^G_\lambda(\exp_x(-\lambda V(x))), \lambda > 0$, following the work of Ansari et al. [2], and Al-Homidan et al. [1], Chang et al. [4] investigated the problem:

$$\text{Find } u \in K \text{ such that } u \in \mathrm{Fix}(S) \bigcap_{i=1}^{N} (V_i + G)^{-1}(0) \bigcap \mathrm{EP}(F), \tag{6}$$

where $\mathrm{Fix}(S)$ and $\mathrm{EP}(F)$ represent the set of fixed points of the mapping S and equilibrium points of equilibrium function F, respectively, and $\bigcap_{i=1}^{N} (V_i + G)^{-1}(0)$ is the set of common singularities of N variational inclusion problems, defined as:

$$\text{Find } u \in K \text{ such that } 0 \in V_i(u) + G(u),\ \forall\, i \in \{1, 2 \cdots N\}.$$

If $V_i = V$, for all $i = 1, 2, \cdots N$, we have

$$\text{Find } u \in K \text{ such that } u \in \mathrm{Fix}(S) \bigcap (V+G)^{-1}(0) \bigcap \mathrm{EP}(F). \tag{7}$$

Inspired by the works of Ansari and Babu [3], Al-Homidan et al. [1] and following contemporary research work, our motive in this article is to propose new iterative algorithms to solve problems (5)–(7) in the setting of Hadamard manifold. We also bring out some consequences of proposed iterative algorithms. The following section contains some definitions, symbols, and useful results on Riemannian manifolds. Section 3 contains the main results describing the iterative algorithms for the problems (5)–(7). In the last section, we discuss some of the consequences of the suggested algorithms and their convergence results for solving variational inequality problems with equilibrium and fixed-point problems.

2. Preliminaries

We consider $\mathbb{X}$ to be a differentiable manifold of finite dimension. Let $T_u\mathbb{X}$ indicate the tangent space of $\mathbb{X}$ at u, and the tangent bundle of $\mathbb{X}$ is indicated by $T\mathbb{X} = \cup_{u\in\mathbb{X}} T_u\mathbb{X}$, which is obviously a manifold. An inner product $\langle\cdot,\cdot\rangle_u$ on $T_u\mathbb{X}$ is termed as Riemannian metric on $T_u\mathbb{X}$. A tensor $\langle\cdot,\cdot\rangle : u \to \langle\cdot,\cdot\rangle_u$ is said to be the Riemannian metric on $T_u\mathbb{X}$, if $\langle\cdot,\cdot\rangle_u$ is a Riemannian metric on $T_u\mathbb{X}$ for each $u \in \mathbb{X}$. We denote the Riemannian metric on $\mathbb{X}$ by $\langle\cdot,\cdot\rangle_u$ and corresponding norm by $\|\cdot\|_u$, which is given by $\|w\|_u = \sqrt{\langle w,w\rangle_u}$, for all $w \in T_u\mathbb{X}$. We assume that $\mathbb{X}$ is equipped with the Riemannian metric $\langle\cdot,\cdot\rangle_u$ and its corresponding norm is $\|\cdot\|_u$. For simplicity, we omit the subscript.

The length of a piecewise smooth curve joining u to v (i.e., $\gamma(u) = a$ and $\gamma(v) = b$) is defined as $L(\gamma) = \int_a^b \|\gamma^{'}(x)\|dx$. The Riemannian distance $d(u,v)$ yields the original topology on $\mathbb{X}$, which minimizes the length over the set of all such curves which connect u and v.

We denote the Levi-Civita connection associated to $\mathbb{X}$ by ∇. We know that if $\nabla_{\gamma'(\kappa)} F = 0$, the vector field F is parallel along a smooth curve γ. If $\gamma^{'}$ is parallel along γ, then γ is said to be geodesic and in this case $\|\gamma^{'}\|$ is constant. γ is called a normalized geodesic, if $\|\gamma^{'}\| = 1$. A minimal geodesic is a geodesic connecting u to v in $\mathbb{X}$ with the length equal to $d(u,v)$. A complete Riemannian manifold is one in which for any $u \in \mathbb{X}$. All geodesics that originate from u are defined for all real numbers $\kappa \in (-\infty,\infty)$. Due to Hopf–Rinow Theorem [23], it is known to us that in a complete Riemannian manifold $\mathbb{X}$, any $u,v \in \mathbb{X}$ can be attached through a minimal geodesic.

Moreover, the exponential map $\exp_u : T_u\mathbb{X} \to \mathbb{X}$ at u is defined by $\exp_u(w) = \gamma_w(1,u)$ for each $w \in T_u\mathbb{X}$, where $\gamma_w(\cdot,u)$ is the geodesic starting from u with velocity w (that is, $\gamma_w(0,u) = u$ and $\gamma_w^{'}(0,u) = w$). We know that $\exp_u(tw) = \gamma_w(t,u)$ for each real number t and $\exp_u 0 = \gamma_w(0;u) = u$. It is known to us that for any $u \in \mathbb{X}$, the exponential map $\exp_u$ is differentiable on $T_u\mathbb{X}$ and the derivative of $\exp_u(\mathbf{0})$ is the identity vector of $T_u\mathbb{X}$. Hence, using inverse mapping theorem, there is an inverse exponential map $\exp_u^{-1} : \mathbb{X} \to T_u\mathbb{X}$. Moreover, for any $u,v \in \mathbb{X}$, we have $d(u,v) = \|\exp_u^{-1} v\| = \|\exp_v^{-1} u\|$, where $\|\exp_u^{-1} v\| = \sqrt{\langle \exp_u^{-1} v, \exp_u^{-1} v\rangle}$. In particular, if $\mathbb{X} = \mathbb{R}^n$ the Euclidian space, then $\exp_u^{-1} v = v - u$ for all $u,v \in \mathbb{R}^n$.

A Hadamard manifold is a Riemannian manifold with nonpositive sectional curvature which is complete and simply connected.

Lemma 1 ([23]). *Let $\mathbb{X}$ be a finite dimensional manifold and $\gamma : [0,1] \to \mathbb{X}$ be a geodesic joining u to v. Then,*

$$d(\gamma(\kappa_1),\gamma(\kappa_2)) = |\kappa_1 - \kappa_2| d(u,v), \quad \textit{for all } \kappa_1,\kappa_2 \in [0,1]. \tag{8}$$

Proposition 1 ([23]). *Let $\mathbb{X}$ be a Hadamard manifold. Then*

(i) The exponential map $\exp_u : T_u\mathbb{X} \to \mathbb{X}$ is a diffeomorphism for all $u \in \mathbb{X}$.

(ii) For any pair of point $u,v \in \mathbb{X}$, there exists a unique normalized geodesic $\gamma : [0,1] \to \mathbb{X}$ joining $u = \gamma(0)$ to $v = \gamma(1)$, which is in fact a minimal geodesic defined by

$$\gamma(\kappa) = \exp_u \kappa \exp_u^{-1} v, \text{ for all } \kappa \in [0,1].$$

A subset K of Hadamard manifold $\mathbb{X}$ is called a convex set if, for any $u, v \in K$, any geodesic joining u and v must be in K. In other words, if $\gamma : [a, b] \to \mathbb{X}$ is a geodesic, such that $u = \gamma(a)$ and $v = \gamma(b)$, then $\gamma((1-\kappa)a + \kappa b) \in K$, for all $\kappa \in [0, 1]$.

A function $h : K \to (-\infty, \infty]$ is called a geodesic convex function, if for any geodesic $\gamma : [a, b] \to \mathbb{X}$, the composition function $h \circ \gamma : [a, b] \to \mathbb{R}$ is convex; that is,

$$(h \circ \gamma)(t_1\kappa + (1-\kappa)t_2) \le \kappa(h \circ \gamma)(t_1) + (1-\kappa)(h \circ \gamma)(t_2),\ \forall\, \kappa \in [0,1] \text{ and } \forall\, t_1, t_2 \in \mathbb{R}.$$

Proposition 2 ([23]). *The Riemannian distance $d : \mathbb{X} \times \mathbb{X} \to \mathbb{R}$ is a convex function with respect to the product Riemannian metric, i.e., given any pair of geodesics $\gamma_1 : [0,1] \to \mathbb{X}$ and $\gamma_2 : [0,1] \to \mathbb{X}$, the following inequality holds for all $\kappa \in [0,1]$:*

$$d(\gamma_1(\kappa), \gamma_2(\kappa)) \le (1-\kappa)d(\gamma_1(0), \gamma_2(0)) + \kappa d(\gamma_1(1), \gamma_2(1)). \tag{9}$$

In particular, for each $u \in \mathbb{X}$, the function $d(\cdot, u) : \mathbb{X} \to \mathbb{R}$ is a convex function.

For n-dimensional manifold $\mathbb{X}$, we conclude by Proposition 1 that $\mathbb{X}$ is diffeomorphic to the Euclidean space $\mathbb{R}^n$; hence, $\mathbb{X}$ and $\mathbb{R}^n$ have the same differential structure and topology. Moreover, Euclidean spaces and Hadamard manifold have certain identical geometric prospects. Some of these are stated in the following results.

In a Riemannian manifold $\mathbb{X}$, geodesic triangle $\Delta(r_1, r_2, r_3)$ is a collection of three points r_1, r_2 and r_3 and the three minimal geodesics γ_k joining ϕ_k to ϕ_{k+1}, where $k = 1, 2, 3 \bmod (3)$.

Lemma 2 ([13]). *Let $\Delta(r_1, r_2, r_3)$ be a geodesic triangle in Hadamard manifold $\mathbb{X}$. Then, $r_1', r_2', r_3' \in \mathbb{R}^2$, such that*

$$d(r_1, r_2) = \|r_1' - r_2'\|, \quad d(r_2, r_3) = \|r_2' - r_3'\|, \quad \textit{and} \quad d(r_3, r_1) = \|r_3' - r_1'\|.$$

The points r_1', r_2', r_3' are called the comparison points to r_1, r_2, r_3, respectively. The triangle $\Delta(r_1', r_2', r_3')$ is called the comparison triangle of the geodesic triangle $\Delta(r_1, r_2, r_3)$, which is unique to the isometry of $\mathbb{X}$.

Lemma 3 ([13]). *Let $\Delta(r_1, r_2, r_3)$ be a geodesic triangle in Hadamard manifold $\mathbb{X}$ and $\Delta(r_1', r_2', r_3') \in \mathbb{R}^2$ be its comparison triangle.*

(i) Let $\theta_1, \theta_2, \theta_3$ (respectively, $\theta_1', \theta_2', \theta_3'$) be the angles of $\Delta(r_1, r_2, a_3)$ (respectively, $\Delta(r_1', r_2', r_3')$) at the vertices (r_1, r_2, r_3) (respectively, r_1', r_2', r_3'). Then, the following inequalities hold:

$$\theta_1' \ge \theta_1, \quad \theta_2' \ge \theta_2, \quad \theta_3' \ge \theta_3.$$

(ii) Let v be a point on the geodesic joining r_1 to r_2 and v' be its comparison point in the interval $[r_1', r_2']$. Suppose that $d(v, r_1) = \|v' - r_1'\|$ and $d(v, r_2) = \|v' - r_2'\|$. Then,

$$d(v, r_3) \le \|v' - r_3'\|.$$

Proposition 3 ([23]). (Comparison Theorem for Triangle) *Let $\Delta(r_1, r_2, r_3)$ be a geodesic triangle. Denote, for each $k = 1, 2, 3 \bmod (3)$, by $\gamma_k : [0, l_k] \to \mathbb{X}$ geodesic joining r_k to r_{k+1} and set $l_k = L(\gamma_k), \theta_k = \angle(\gamma_k'(0) - \gamma_{k-1}'(l_{k-1}))$. Then,*

$$\theta_1 + \theta_2 + \theta_3 \le \pi, \tag{10}$$

$$l_k^2 + l_{k+1}^2 - 2l_k l_{k+1} \cos\theta_{k+1} \le l_{k-1}^2. \tag{11}$$

In terms of d and $\exp$, (11) can be expressed as

$$d^2(r_k, r_{k+1}) + d^2(r_{k+1}, r_{k+2}) - 2\langle \exp_{r_{k+1}}^{-1} r_k,\ \exp_{r_{k+1}}^{-1} r_{k+2}\rangle \le d^2(r_{k-1}, r_k), \tag{12}$$

since

$$\langle \exp^{-1}_{r_{k+1}} r_k, \exp^{-1}_{r_{k+1}} r_{k+2} \rangle = d(r_k, r_{k+1}) d(r_{k+1}, r_{k+2}) \cos \theta_{k+1}. \tag{13}$$

The parallel transport $P_{\gamma,\gamma(d),\gamma(c)} : T_{\gamma(x)}\mathbb{X} \to T_{\gamma(y)}\mathbb{X}$ on the tangent bundle $T\mathbb{X}$ along $\gamma : [c,d] \to \mathbb{R}$, with respect to ∇, is defined by

$$P_{\gamma,\gamma(d)\gamma(c)}(u) = V(\gamma(d)), \ \forall\, c,d \in \mathbb{R},\ u \in T_{\gamma(c)}\mathbb{X},$$

such that $\nabla_{\gamma'(t)} V = 0$, for all $t \in [c,d]$ and $V\gamma(c)) = u$, where V is the unique vector field. If γ is the minimal geodesic from u to v, then we write $P_{v,u}$ in place of $P_{\gamma,v,u}$. Moreover, $P_{v,u}$ is an isometry from $T_u\mathbb{X}$ to $T_v\mathbb{X}$, which means that parallel transport preserves the inner product, $\langle P_{v,u}w, P_{y,x}z \rangle = \langle w, z \rangle_u, \forall\, w,z \in T_u\mathbb{X}$.

Lemma 4 ([11]). *Let $u_0 \in \mathbb{X}$ and $\{u_k\} \subset \mathbb{X}$ with $u_k \to u_0$. Then, the following assertions hold:*

(i) For any $v \in \mathbb{X}$, we have $\exp^{-1}_{u_k} v \to \exp^{-1}_{u_0} v$ and $\exp^{-1}_{v} u_k \to \exp^{-1}_{v} u_0$.

(ii) If $z_k \in T_{u_k}\mathbb{X}$ and $z_k \to z_0$, then $z_0 \in T_{u_0}\mathbb{X}$

(iii) Let $z_k, y_k \in T_{u_k}\mathbb{X}$ and $z_0, y_0 \in T_{u_0}\mathbb{X}$, if $z_k \to z_0$ and $y_k \to y_0$ then $\langle z_k, y_k \rangle \to \langle z_0, y_0 \rangle$.

(iv) For any $z \in T_{u_0}\mathbb{X}$, the function $\psi : \mathbb{X} \to T\mathbb{X}$, defined by $\psi(u) = P_{u,u_0} z$ for all $u \in \mathbb{X}$, is continuous on $\mathbb{X}$.

We denote by $\Omega(\mathbb{X})$, the set of all single-valued vector fields $V : \mathbb{X} \to T\mathbb{X}$, such that $V(u) \in T_u(\mathbb{X})$ for all $u \in \mathbb{X}$ and by $\chi(\mathbb{X})$ the set of all set-valued vector fields, $G : \mathbb{X} \rightrightarrows T\mathbb{X}$, such that $G(u) \subseteq T_u(\mathbb{X})$ for all $u \in dom(G)$, where $dom(G)$ is the domain of G defined as $dom(G) = \{u \in \mathbb{X} : G(u) \neq \emptyset\}$.

Definition 1 ([24]). *A single-valued vector field $V \in \Omega(\mathbb{X})$ is said to be*

(i) Monotone if

$$\langle V(u), \exp^{-1}_u v \rangle \leq \langle V(v), -\exp^{-1}_v u \rangle, \ \forall\, u,v \in \mathbb{X}.$$

(ii) Strongly monotone if there exists a constant $\eta > 0$ such that

$$\langle V(u), \exp^{-1}_u v \rangle + \langle V(v), -\exp^{-1}_v u \rangle \leq -\eta d^2(u,v), \ \forall\, u,v \in \mathbb{X}.$$

(iii) φ-Lipschitz continuous if there exists a constant $\varphi > 0$, such that

$$\|P_{u,v} V(u) - V(v)\| \leq \varphi d(u,v), \ \forall\, u,v \in \mathbb{X}.$$

Definition 2 ([25]). *A set-valued vector field $G \in \chi(\mathbb{X})$ is said to be*

(i) Monotone if for all $u, v \in D(\mathbb{X})$,

$$\langle w, \exp^{-1}_u v \rangle \leq \langle z, -\exp^{-1}_v u \rangle, \ \forall w \in G(u), \forall z \in G(v).$$

(ii) Maximal monotone if G is monotone and for $u \in D(G)$ and $w \in T_u(\mathbb{X})$, the condition

$$\langle w, \exp^{-1}_u v \rangle \leq \langle z, -\exp^{-1}_v u \rangle,$$

implies $w \in G(u)$.

Definition 3 ([25]). *A set-valued vector field $G \in \chi(\mathbb{X})$ is called upper Kuratowski semicontinuous at $u \in D(G)$ if, for any sequence $\{u_k\} \subseteq D(G)$ and $\{v_k\} \subseteq T\mathbb{X}$ with $v_k \in G(u_k)$, the relation $\lim_{k\to\infty} v_k = v$ and $\lim_{k\to\infty} u_k = u$ imply $v \in G(u)$. Moreover, G is called upper Kuratowski semicontinuous on $\mathbb{X}$ if it is Kuratowski semicontinuous at each $u \in D(G)$.*

Definition 4. *Let (X,d) be a complete metric space and $K \subseteq X$ be a nonempty set. A sequence $\{u_n\}$ in X is called Fejér convergent to K if, for all $u \in K$ and $k \geq 0$,*

$$d(u_{k+1}, u) \leq d(u_k, u).$$

Lemma 5 ([8])**.** *Let (X,d) be a complete metric space. If $u_k \subset X$ is a Fejér convergent to a nonempty set $K \subseteq X$, then $\{u_k\}$ is bounded. Moreover, if cluster point u of $\{u_k\}$ belongs to K, then $\{u_k\}$ converges to u.*

Let $K \subseteq \mathbb{X}$ and $F : K \times K \to \mathbb{R}$ be a bifunction satisfying the following conditions:

(A) $F(u,u) \geq 0, \forall u \in K$;
(B) F is monotone; that is, for all $u, v \in K, F(u,v) + F(v,u) \leq 0$;
(C) For every $v \in K$, $u \to F(u,v)$ is upper semicontinuous;
(D) For all $u \in K$, $v \to F(u,v)$ is geodesic convex and lower semicontinuous;
(E) There exists a compact set $C \subset \mathbb{X}$ and a point $u \in C \cap K$, such that

$$F(u,v) < 0, \ \ \forall\, v \in K \backslash C,$$

The resolvent $T_t^F : \mathbb{X} \rightrightarrows K$ of a bifunction F, a set-valued operator introduced by Colao [5] in the setting of the Hadamard manifold, is defined by

$$T_t^F(u) = \{w \in K : F(w,v) - \frac{1}{t}\langle \exp_w^{-1} u, \, \exp_w^{-1} v \rangle \geq 0, \forall\, v \in K\}, \forall\, u \in \mathbb{X}.$$

Lemma 6 ([5])**.** *Let $K \subseteq \mathbb{X}$ and $F : K \times K \to \mathbb{R}$ be a bifunction satisfying (A)–(E). Then, for $t > 0$,*

(a) The resolvent T_t^F of F is nonempty and single valued;
(b) The resolvent T_t^F of F is firmly nonexpansive;
(c) The fixed point of T_t^F is the equilibrium point set of F;
(d) The equilibrium point set EP(F) *is closed and geodesic convex.*

3. Main Results

The solution to problem (6) is assumed to be consistent, and it is denoted by Γ. We propose the following iterative procedure to solve the problem (6) in $\mathbb{X}$, based on the proximal point method (3).

Algorithm 1. *Suppose that $V_i \in \Omega(\mathbb{X})$, $(i = 1, \cdots, N)$, $G \in \chi((\mathbb{X}), F, S$ and T_t^F are the same as described above. Choose arbitrary $z_0 \in K$, to define the sequences $\{u_k^i\}, i \in \{1, 2, \cdots, N\}$, $\{v_k\}$ and $\{z_k\}$ as follows:*

$$\begin{aligned} \mathbf{0} &\in \mathrm{P}_{u_k^i, z_k} V_i(z_k) + G(u_k^i) - \frac{1}{\lambda_k} \exp_{u_k^i}^{-1} z_k, \\ v_k &= \exp_{z_k}(1 - \alpha_k) \exp_{z_k}^{-1} T_t^F(u_k^{k_i}), \\ z_{k+1} &= \exp_{z_k}(1 - \varrho\beta_k) \exp_{z_k}^{-1} S(v_k), \end{aligned}$$

where $k_i \in \{1, 2, \cdots N\}$ such that $d(u_k^{k_i}, z_k) = \max_{i=1,\cdots,N} \{d(u_k^i, z_k)\}$, $\alpha_n, \beta_n \in (0,1)$, $0 < \varrho < 1$ and $\lambda_k > 0$.

If $V_i = V$ for all $i \in \{1, 2, \cdots N\}$, we have the following iterative algorithm to solve the problem (7).

Algorithm 2. *For arbitrary $z_0 \in K$, obtain the sequences $\{u_k\}$, $\{v_k\}$ and $\{z_k\}$ as follows:*

$$\begin{aligned} \mathbf{0} &\in \mathrm{P}_{u_k,z_k}V(z_k) + G(u_k) - \frac{1}{\lambda_k}\exp_{u_k}^{-1}z_k, \\ v_k &= \exp_{z_k}(1-\alpha_k)\exp_{z_k}^{-1}T_t^F(u_k), \\ z_{k+1} &= \exp_{z_k}(1-\varrho\beta_k)\exp_{z_k}^{-1}S(v_k), \end{aligned}$$

where $\alpha_k, \beta_k \in (0,1)$, $0 < \varrho < 1$ and $\lambda_k > 0$.

If $V_i = V$ for all $i \in \{1,2,\cdots N\}$ and $F = 0$, then we have the following iterative algorithm to solve the problem (5).

Algorithm 3. *For arbitrary $z_0 \in K$, obtain the sequences $\{u_k\}$ and $\{z_k\}$ as follows:*

$$\begin{aligned} \mathbf{0} &\in \mathrm{P}_{u_k,z_k}V(z_k) + G(u_k) - \frac{1}{\lambda_k}\exp_{u_k}^{-1}z_k, \\ z_{k+1} &= \exp_{z_k}(1-\varrho\beta_k)\exp_{z_k}^{-1}S(u_k), \end{aligned}$$

where $\beta_k \in (0,1)$, $0 < \varrho < 1$ and $\lambda_k > 0$.

Theorem 1. *Let K be the nonempty, closed and geodesic convex subset of $\mathbb{X}$. Suppose that for every $i \in \{1,2\cdots,N\}$, vector field $V_i \in \Omega(\mathbb{X})$ is η_i-strongly monotone and φ_i-Lipschitz continuous and $G \in \chi(\mathbb{X})$ is maximally monotone. Let $F : K \times K \to \mathbb{R}$ be a bifunction enjoying the conditions $(A)-(E)$ and T_t^F be the resolvent of F, $S : K \to K$ as a nonexpansive mapping. If $\Gamma \neq \emptyset$ and $\eta = \min_{\{i=1,2\cdots N\}}\{\eta_i\}$, $\varphi = \max_{\{i=1,2\cdots N\}}\{\varphi_i\}$, $\alpha_n, \beta_n \in (0,1)$, $0 < \varrho < 1$ and $\lambda_k > 0$ satisfy the following conditions:*

(H1) $0 < \bar{\lambda} < \lambda_k < \lambda < \frac{1}{2\eta}$, *and* $\varphi < 2\eta$.

(H2) $\sum_{k=0}^{\infty} \beta_k = \infty$.

(H3) $0 < b < \alpha_k,\ \beta_k < c < 1$.

Then, the sequence $\{z_k\}$ obtained from Algorithm 1 converges to an element in Γ.

Proof. The proof is divided into the following three steps:
Step I. First, we justify that the sequence $\{z_k\}$ is Fejér monotone with respect to Γ.

Let $z^\star \in \Gamma$, then $-V_i(z^\star) \in G(z^\star)$ for each $i \in \{1,2,\cdots N\}$. For any arbitrary $z_0 \in K$, from Algorithm 1, we have

$$-\mathrm{P}_{u_k^i,z_k}V_i(z_k) + \frac{1}{\lambda_k}\exp_{u_k^i}^{-1}z_k \in G(u_k^i),$$

with monotonicity of G, which implies that

$$\Big\langle -\mathrm{P}_{u_k^i,z_k}V_i(z_k) + \frac{1}{\lambda_k}\exp_{u_k^i}^{-1}z_k,\ \exp_{u_k^i}^{-1}z^\star\Big\rangle \leq \Big\langle -V_i(z^\star),\ -\exp_{u_k^i}^{-1}z^\star\Big\rangle. \tag{14}$$

Since V_i is η_i-strongly monotone vector field for each $i \in \{1,2\cdots N\}$, then

$$\big\langle V_i(z^\star),\ \exp_{z^\star}^{-1}u_k^i\big\rangle \leq \big\langle -V_i(u_k^i),\ \exp_{u_k^i}^{-1}z^\star\big\rangle - \eta_i d^2(u_k^i, z^\star). \tag{15}$$

Combining (14) and (15), we get

$$\Big\langle -\mathrm{P}_{u_k^i,z_k}V_i(z_k) + \frac{1}{\lambda_k}\exp_{u_k^i}^{-1}z_k,\ \exp_{u_k^i}^{-1}z^\star\Big\rangle \leq \big\langle -V_i(z^\star),\ \exp_{u_k^i}^{-1}z^\star\big\rangle - \eta_i d^2(u_k^i, z^\star),$$

or,

$$\langle \exp^{-1}_{u^i_k} z_k,\ \exp^{-1}_{u^i_k} z^\star \rangle \leq \lambda_k \langle \mathrm{P}_{u^i_k, z_k} V_i(z_k) - V_i(u^i_k),\ \exp^{-1}_{u^i_k} z^\star \rangle - \eta_i d^2(u^i_k, z^\star). \tag{16}$$

Since V_i is φ_i-Lipschitz continuous monotone vector field for each $i \in \{1, 2 \cdots N\}$ and $\varphi = \max_{\{i=1,2\cdots N\}} \{\varphi_i\}$, using Cauchy–Schwartz inequality, we get

$$\begin{aligned} \langle \mathrm{P}_{u^i_k, z_k} V_i(z_k) - V_i(u^i_k),\ \exp^{-1}_{u^i_k} z^\star \rangle &\leq \|\mathrm{P}_{u^i_k, z_k} V_i(z_k) - V_i(u^i_k)\| \|\exp^{-1}_{u^i_k} z^\star\| \\ &\leq \varphi_i d(u^i_k, z_k) \|\exp^{-1}_{u^i_k} z^\star\| \\ &= \varphi_i \|\exp^{-1}_{u^i_k} z_k\| \|\exp^{-1}_{u^i_k} z^\star\| \\ &\leq \frac{\varphi}{2} \left\{ \|\exp^{-1}_{u^i_k} z_k\|^2 + \|\exp^{-1}_{u^i_k} z^\star\|^2 \right\} \\ &\leq \frac{\varphi}{2} \left\{ d^2(z_k, u^i_k) + d^2(u^i_k, z^\star) \right\}. \end{aligned}$$

Thus, inequality (16) becomes

$$2\langle \exp^{-1}_{u^i_k} z_k),\ \exp^{-1}_{u^i_k} z^\star \rangle \leq \varphi \lambda_k \left\{ d^2(z_k, u^i_k) + d^2(u^i_k, z^\star) \right\} - 2\eta_i d^2(u^i_k, z^\star). \tag{17}$$

For fixed $k \in \mathbb{N}$ and $i \in \{1, 2 \cdots N\}$, let $\triangle(z_k, u^i_k, z^\star) \subseteq \mathbb{X}$. Then, using (12), we get

$$d^2(z_k, u^i_k) + d^2(u^i_k, z^\star) - 2\langle \exp^{-1}_{u^i_k} z_k,\ \exp^{-1}_{u^i_k} z^\star \rangle \leq d^2(z_k, z^\star). \tag{18}$$

From inequalities (17) and (18), and using $\eta = \min_{\{i=1,2\cdots N\}} \{\eta_i\}$, we have

$$d^2(z_k, u^i_k) + d^2(u^i_k, z^\star) \leq \varphi \lambda_k d^2(z_k, u^i_k) + \varphi \lambda_k d^2(u^i_k, z^\star) + d^2(z_k, z^\star) - 2\eta \lambda_k d^2(u_k, z^\star).$$

Since, $0 < \bar{\lambda} < \lambda_k < \lambda < \frac{1}{2\eta}$ and $\varphi < 2\eta$, we have

$$d^2(z_k, u^i_k) + d^2(u^i_k, z^\star) \leq \varphi \lambda d^2(z_k, u^i_k) + d^2(z_k, z^\star),$$

or

$$d^2(u^i_k, z^\star) \leq d^2(z_k, z^\star) - (1 - \varphi \lambda) d^2(z_k, u^i_k). \tag{19}$$

Since $\lambda < \frac{1}{2\eta}$ and $\varphi < 2\eta$, implies that $\varphi \lambda < 1$, we get

$$d^2(u^i_k, z^\star) \leq d^2(z_k, z^\star), \ \ i \in \{1, 2, \cdots N\},\ k \in \mathbb{N}. \tag{20}$$

Let $k_i \in \{1, 2, \cdots N\}$ such that $d(u^{k_i}_k, z^\star) = \max_{k \in \{1,2\cdots,N\}} \{d(u^i_k, z^\star)\} \leq d(z_k, z^\star)$. From (20), Algorithm 1, we have

$$\begin{aligned} d(v_k, z^\star) &= d(\gamma_k(1 - \alpha_k), z^\star) \\ &\leq (1 - \alpha_n) d(\gamma_k(0), z^\star) + \alpha_n d(\gamma_k(1), z^\star) \\ &= (1 - \alpha_k) d(z_k, z^\star) + \alpha_n d(T^F_t(u^{k_i}_k), z^\star) \\ &\leq (1 - \alpha_k) d(z_k, z^\star) + \alpha_n d(u^{k_i}_k, z^\star) \\ &\leq (1 - \alpha_k) d(z_k, z^\star) + \alpha_n d(z_k, z^\star) \\ &= d(z_k, z^\star). \end{aligned} \tag{21}$$

From Algorithm 1, (21) and using the nonexpansiveness of S, we get

$$\begin{aligned} d(z_{k+1}, z^\star) &= d(\gamma_k(1-\varrho\beta_n), z^\star) \\ &\leq (1-\varrho\beta_n)d(\gamma_k(0), z^\star) + \varrho\beta_n d(\gamma_k(1), z^\star) \\ &= (1-\varrho\beta_n)d(z_k, z^\star) + \varrho\beta_n d(S(v_k), z^\star) \\ &\leq (1-\varrho\beta_n)d(z_k, z^\star) + \varrho\beta_n d(v_k, z^\star) \\ &\leq (1-\varrho\beta_n)d(z_k, z^\star) + \varrho\beta_n d(z_k, z^\star) \\ &= d(z_k, z^\star). \end{aligned} \tag{22}$$

that is, $\{z_k\}$ is Fejér monotone and hence bounded by Lemma 5, and therefore the sequence $\{u_k\}, \{v_k\}$ all are bounded and $\lim_{k\to\infty} d(z_k, z^\star)$ exists.

Step II. Next, we show that $d(z_k, u_k) = 0$, $d(z_k, v_k) = 0$ and $d(z_{k+1}, z_k) = 0$, as $n \to \infty$. Since $z_{k+1} = \gamma_k(1-\varrho\beta_k)$, then applying geodesic convexity of d, we get

$$\begin{aligned} d(z_{k+1}, z_k) &= d(\gamma_k(1-\varrho\beta_k), z_k) \\ &\leq (1-\varrho\beta_k)d(\gamma_k(0), z_k) + \varrho\beta_k d(\gamma_k(1), z_k) \\ &\leq (1-\varrho\beta_k)d(z_k, z_k) + \varrho\beta_k d(S(v_k), z_k) \\ &\leq \varrho\beta_k d(S(v_k), z_k). \end{aligned} \tag{23}$$

For fixed $k \in \mathbb{N}$, let $p_k = S(v_k)$ and $\triangle(z_k, p_k, z^\star)$ be the geodesic triangle and $\triangle(\tilde{x}_k, \tilde{p}_k, \tilde{x}) \subseteq \mathbb{X}$ be the comparison triangle. Then, we have

$$\begin{aligned} d^2(z_{k+1}, z^\star) &\leq \|\tilde{x}_{k+1} - \tilde{x}\|^2 \\ &= \|(1-\varrho\beta_k)\tilde{x} + \varrho\beta_k\tilde{p}_k - \tilde{x}\|^2 \\ &= \|(1-\varrho\beta_k)(\tilde{x}_k - \tilde{x}) + \varrho\beta_k\|\tilde{x} - \tilde{p}_k\|^2 \\ &= (1-\varrho\beta_k)\|\tilde{x}_k - \tilde{x}\|^2 + \varrho\beta_k\|\tilde{p}_k - \tilde{x}\|^2 - \varrho\beta_k(1-\varrho\beta_k)\|\tilde{p}_k - \tilde{x}_k\|^2 \\ &\leq (1-\varrho\beta_k)d^2(z_k, z^\star) + \varrho\beta_k d^2(p_k, z^\star) - \varrho\beta_k(1-\varrho\beta_k)d^2(p_k, z_k) \\ &\leq (1-\varrho\beta_k)d^2(z_k, z^\star) + \varrho\beta_k d^2(S(v_k), z^\star) - \varrho\beta_k(1-\varrho\beta_k)d^2(S(v_k), z_k) \\ &\leq (1-\varrho\beta_k)d^2(z_k, z^\star) + \varrho\beta_k d^2(z_k, z^\star) - \varrho\beta_k(1-\varrho\beta_k)d^2(S(v_k, z_k)) \\ &\leq d^2(z_k, z^\star) - \varrho\beta_k(1-\varrho\beta_k)d^2(S(v_k), z_k) \end{aligned}$$

or,

$$d^2(S(v_k), z_k) \leq \frac{1}{\varrho\beta_k(1-\varrho\beta_k)}\Big\{d^2(z_k, z^\star) - d^2(z_{k+1}, z^\star)\Big\}. \tag{24}$$

Further, using condition (H3), we have

$$d^2(z_k, S(v_k)) \leq \frac{1}{\varrho b(1-\varrho c)}\Big\{d^2(z_k, z^\star) - d^2(z_{k+1}, z^\star)\Big\}. \tag{25}$$

Since $\{z_k\}$ is Fejér monotone with respect to Γ, $\lim_{k\to\infty} d(z_k, z^\star)$ exists; hence, we get

$$d(z_k, S(v_k)) = 0,\ k \to \infty. \tag{26}$$

Using (23) and (26), we obtain

$$d(z_{k+1}, z_k) = 0,\ k \to \infty. \tag{27}$$

Since $\{z_k\}$, $\{v_k\}$, are bounded, there exists $N_1 > 0$ with $d(z_k, z^\star) \leq N_1$, and for each $k \in \mathbb{N}$, we have

$$\begin{aligned} d(z_k, z^\star) &\leq d(\gamma_{k-1}(1-\varrho\beta_k), z^\star) \\ &\leq (1-\varrho\beta_{k-1})d(\gamma_{k-1}(0), z^\star) + \varrho\beta_{k-1}d(\gamma_{k-1}(1), z^\star) \\ &= (1-\varrho\beta_{k-1})d(z_k, z^\star) + \varrho\beta_{k-1}d(S(v_{k-1}), z^\star) \\ &\leq (1-\varrho\beta_{k-1})d(z_k, z^\star) + \varrho\beta_{k-1}d(v_{k-1}, z^\star). \end{aligned} \tag{28}$$

For any integer $m \leq k-1$, we can write

$$d(z_k, z^\star) \leq N_1 \sum_{j=m}^{k-1} \{(1-\varrho\beta_j) \prod_{n=j+1}^{k-1} \varrho\beta_n\} + N_1 \prod_{j=m}^{k-1} \varrho\beta_j. \tag{29}$$

From (20), (22) and (29), we achieve

$$\begin{aligned} d(z_k, u_k^i) &= d(z_k, z_{k+1}) + d(z_{k+1}, z^\star) + d(u_k^i, z^\star) \\ &= d(z_k, z_{k+1}) + d(z_{k+1}, z^\star) + d(z_k, z^\star) \\ &\leq d(z_k, z_{k+1}) + d(z_k, z^\star) + d(z_k, z^\star) \\ &= d(z_k, z_{k+1}) + 2d(z_k, z^\star) \\ &\leq d(z_k, z_{k+1}) + 2N_1 \sum_{j=m}^{k-1} \{(1-\varrho\beta_j) \prod_{n=j+1}^{k-1} \varrho\beta_n\} + 2N_1 \prod_{j=m}^{k-1} \varrho\beta_j. \end{aligned}$$

Using condition (H2), we have

$$\lim_{m\to\infty} \sum_{j=m}^{\infty} \{(1-\varrho\beta_j) \prod_{n=j+1}^{\infty} \varrho\beta_n\} = 0, \quad \lim_{m\to\infty} \prod_{j=m}^{\infty} \varrho\beta_j = 0.$$

Thus, using (27), we get

$$\lim_{k\to\infty} d(z_k, u_k^i) = 0, \ k \to \infty \ \text{ for each } i \in \{1, \cdots, N\}. \tag{30}$$

Furthermore, for each $i \in \{1, 2, \cdots N\}$

$$\begin{aligned} d(z_k, T_t^F(u_k^i)) &= d(z_k, z_{k+1}) + d(z_{k+1}, z^\star) + d(T_t^F(u_k^i), z^\star) \\ &\leq d(z_k, z_{k+1}) + d(z_{k+1}, z^\star) + d(u_k^i, z^\star) \\ &\leq d(z_k, z_{k+1}) + d(z_{k+1}, z^\star) + d(z_k, z^\star) \to 0, k \to \infty, \end{aligned} \tag{31}$$

and

$$\begin{aligned} d(z_k, v_k) &= d(z_k, z_{k+1}) + d(z_{k+1}, z^\star) + d(v_k, z^\star) \\ &\leq d(z_k, z_{k+1}) + d(z_{k+1}, z^\star) + d(z_k, z^\star) \to 0, k \to \infty. \end{aligned} \tag{32}$$

Step III. Finally, we show that the limit of a sequence $\{z_k\}$ belongs in Γ.

From step I, we know that the sequence $\{z_k\}$ is bounded, so there is a subsequence $\{z_{k_n}\}$ of $\{z_k\}$ converging to a cluster point $w^\star$ of $\{z_k\}$. From (26), we have $v_{k_n} \to w^\star$, and (32) implies $d(z_{k_n}, S(v_{k_n})) \to 0$ as $n \to \infty$; thus, due to the nonexpansiveness of S, we get

$$\begin{aligned} d(S(w^\star), w^\star) &= d(S(w^\star), S(v_{k_n})) + d(S(v_{k_n}), z_{k_n}) + d(z_{k_n}, w^\star) \\ &\leq d(w^\star, v_{k_n}) + d(S(v_{k_n}), z_{k_n}) + d(z_{k_n}, w^\star) \to 0, \ n \to \infty, \end{aligned}$$

Thus, we obtain $w^\star \in \text{Fix(S)}$.

Since T_t^F is also nonexpansive, using (31), we get

$$\begin{aligned} d(T_t^F(w^\star), w^\star) &= d(T_t^F(w^\star), T_t^F(u^i_{k_n})) + d(T_t^F(u^i_{k_n}), z_{k_n}) + d(z_{k_n}, w^\star) \\ &\leq d(w^\star, u^i_{k_n}) + d(T_t^F(u^i_{k_n}), z_{k_n}) + d(z_{k_n}, w^\star) \to 0,\ n \to \infty, \end{aligned} \tag{33}$$

which amounts to $w^\star \in \mathrm{Fix}(T_t^F)$.

From Algorithm 1, we have

$$\psi_{k_n+1} = -\mathrm{P}_{u^i_{k_n}, z_{k_n}} V_i(z_{k_n}) + \frac{1}{\lambda_{k_n}} \exp^{-1}_{u^i_{k_n}} z_{k_n} \in G(u^i_{k_n}). \tag{34}$$

From (30), we have $\lim_{k\to\infty} d(z_k, u^i_k) = 0$ and sine $0 < \bar{\lambda} < \lambda_k < \lambda < 1$, and we deduce that $\lim_{k\to\infty} \frac{1}{\lambda_k} d(z_k, u^i_k) = 0$, for every $i \in \{1, 2, \cdots N\}$. Thus, we have

$$\lim_{n\to\infty} \frac{1}{\lambda_{k_n}} \|\exp^{-1}_{u^i_{k_n}} z_{k_n}\| = \lim_{n\to\infty} \frac{1}{\lambda_{k_n}} d(u^i_{k_n}, z_{k_n}) = 0, \tag{35}$$

and so,

$$\lim_{n\to\infty} \frac{1}{\lambda_{k_n}} \exp^{-1}_{u^i_{k_n}} z_{k_n} = 0. \tag{36}$$

Since V_i is the Lipschitz continuous vector field and $z_{k_n} \to w^\star$ as $n \to \infty$, taking into account (34) and (36), we get

$$\lim_{n\to\infty} \psi_{k_n+1} = -V_i(w^\star),\ i \in \{1, 2, \cdots N\}. \tag{37}$$

G is upper Kuratowski semicontinuous, as it is maximally monotone; then, we have $-V_i(w^\star) \in G(w^\star)$, for every $i \in \{1, 2, \cdots N\}$, that is $w^\star \in \bigcap_{i=1}^{N} (V_i + G)^{-1}(\mathbf{0})$. Hence, $w^\star \in \Gamma$. This completes the proof by appealing to Lemma 5. □

If $V_i = V$, then we have the following convergence result for Algorithm 2.

Corollary 1. *Let K be nonempty, closed and geodesic convex subset of $\mathbb{X}$. Let vector field $V \in \Omega(\mathbb{X})$ be a η-strongly monotone and φ-Lipschitz continuous; $G \in \chi(\mathbb{X})$ is maximally monotone. Let $F : K \times K \to \mathbb{R}$ be a bifunction enjoying the conditions $(A) - (E)$, and T_t^F be the resolvent of F, $S : K \to K$ be a nonexpansive mapping. If $\mathrm{Fix}(S) \cap (V + G)^{-1}(\mathbf{0}) \cap \mathrm{EP}(F) \neq \emptyset$ and $\alpha_n, \beta_n \in (0, 1)$, $0 < \varrho < 1$ and $\lambda_k > 0$ satisfy the following conditions (H1)–(H3), then the sequence $\{z_k\}$ obtained by Algorithm 2 converges to the solution of problem* (7).

For Algorithm 3, we have the following result to solve $\mathrm{Fix}(S) \cap (V + G)^{-1}(\mathbf{0})$.

Corollary 2. *Let K be a nonempty, closed and geodesic convex subset of $\mathbb{X}$ and vector field $V \in \Omega(\mathbb{X})$ be η-strongly monotone and φ-Lipschitz continuous. $G \in \chi(\mathbb{X})$ is maximally monotone and $S : K \to K$ is a nonexpansive mapping. If $\mathrm{Fix} \cap (S)(V + G)^{-1}(\mathbf{0}) \neq \emptyset$ and $\beta_n \in (0, 1)$, $0 < \varrho < 1$ and $\lambda_k > 0$ satisfy the following conditions (H1)–(H3), then the sequence $\{z_k\}$ obtained by Algorithm 3 converges to the solution of problem* (5).

4. Consequences

Németh [14], introduced and studied the following variational inequality problem $VI(V, K)$: Find $u \in K$, such that

$$\langle V(u), \exp^{-1}_u v\rangle \geq 0, \quad \text{for all } v \in K, \tag{38}$$

where $V : K \to T\mathbb{X}$ is a single-valued vector field defined on $K \subseteq \mathbb{X}$.

We know that $u \in K$ is a solution of $VI(V,K)$ if and only if u satisfies

$$0 \in V(u) + N_K(u), \tag{39}$$

where $N_K(u)$ is the normal cone to K at $u \in K$, defined by

$$N_K(u) = \{p \in T_u\mathbb{X} : \langle p, \exp_u^{-1} v\rangle \leq 0, \text{ for all } v \in K\}.$$

The indicator function γ_K of K is defined by

$$\gamma_K(u) = \begin{cases} 0, & if\ u \in K, \\ +\infty, & if\ u \notin K. \end{cases}$$

Since γ_K is proper, lower semicontinuous, then the differential $\partial\gamma_K(u)$ of γ_K is maximally monotone, which is defined by

$$\partial\gamma_K(u) = \{p \in T_u\mathbb{X} : \langle p, \exp_u^{-1} v\rangle \quad \leq \quad \gamma_K(v) - \gamma_K(u) = 0\}.$$

Thus, we have

$$\begin{aligned} \partial I_K(u) &= \{p \in T_u\mathbb{X} : \langle p, \exp_u^{-1} v\rangle \leq 0\} \\ &= N_K(u). \end{aligned} \tag{40}$$

For $\lambda > 0$, the resolvent of $\partial\gamma_K$, defined by

$$J_\lambda^{\partial\gamma_K}(u) = \{q \in \mathbb{X} : u \in \exp_q \lambda\partial\gamma_K(q)\} = P_K(u), \text{ for all } u \in \mathbb{X}.$$

Thus, for $V : K \to \mathbb{X}$ and for all $u \in K$, we have

$$\begin{aligned} u \in (V + \partial\gamma_K)^{-1}(0) &= 0 \in V(u) + \partial\gamma_K(u) = -V(u) \in \partial\gamma_K(u) \\ &\iff \langle -V(u), \exp_u^{-1} v\rangle \leq 0, \text{ for all } v \in K \\ &\iff u \in VI(V,K). \end{aligned} \tag{41}$$

Let $V_i : K \to T\mathbb{X}, i \in \{1,2,\cdots N\}$ be a finite collection of monotone mappings, then the variational inequality problem for V_i is defined as

$$\langle V_i(u^\star), \exp_{u^\star}^{-1} v\rangle \geq 0, \ \forall v \in K \text{ and } i \in \{1,2,\cdots,N\}, \tag{42}$$

and the solution set is denoted by $\bigcap_{i=1}^{N} VI(V_i,K)$.

Algorithm 4. *For an arbitrary $z_0 \in K$, compute the sequences $\{u_k^i\}, i \in \{1,2,\cdots\}$, $\{v_k\}$ and $\{z_k\}$ as follows:*

$$\begin{aligned} \mathbf{0} &\in \mathrm{P}_{u_k,z_k} V_i(z_k) + \partial^i\gamma_K(u_k^i) - \frac{1}{\lambda_k}\exp_{u_k^i}^{-1} z_k, \\ v_k &= \exp_{z_k}(1-\alpha_k)\exp_{z_k}^{-1} T_t^F(u_k^{k_i}), \\ z_{k+1} &= \exp_{z_k}(1-\varrho\beta_k)\exp_{z_k}^{-1} S(v_k), \end{aligned}$$

where $k_i \in \{1,2,\cdots N\}$ such that $d(u_k^{k_i}, z_k) = \max_{i=1,\cdots,N}\{d(u_k^i, z_k)\}$, $\alpha_k, \beta_k \in (0,1)$, $0 < \varrho < 1$ and $\lambda_k > 0$.

If $V_i = V$ for all $i \in \{1,2,\cdots N\}$, then we give the following algorithm to solve $\mathrm{Fix}(S) \bigcap VI(V,K) \bigcap \mathrm{EP}(F)$.

Algorithm 5. *For arbitrary $z_0 \in K$, compute the sequences $\{u_k\}$, $\{v_k\}$ and $\{z_k\}$ as follows:*

$$\begin{aligned} \mathbf{0} &\in \mathrm{P}_{u_k,z_k} V(z_k) + \partial\gamma_K(u_k) - \frac{1}{\lambda_k}\exp_{u_k}^{-1} z_k, \\ v_k &= \exp_{z_k}(1-\alpha_k)\exp_{z_k}^{-1} T_t^F(u_k), \\ z_{k+1} &= \exp_{z_k}(1-\varrho\beta_k)\exp_{z_k}^{-1} S(v_k), \end{aligned}$$

where $\alpha_k, \beta_k \in (0,1)$, $0 < \varrho < 1$ and $\lambda_k > 0$.

If $V_i = V$ for all $i \in \{1, 2, \cdots N\}$ and $F = 0$, then we propose the following algorithm to solve $\mathrm{Fix}(S) \bigcap VI(V, K)$.

Algorithm 6. *For arbitrary $z_0 \in K$, compute the sequences $\{u_k\}$ and $\{z_k\}$ as follows:*

$$\begin{aligned} \mathbf{0} &\in \mathrm{P}_{u_k,z_k} V(z_k) + \partial\gamma_K(u_k) - \frac{1}{\lambda_k}\exp_{u_k}^{-1} z_k, \\ z_{k+1} &= \exp_{z_k}(1-\varrho\beta_k)\exp_{z_k}^{-1} S(u_k), \end{aligned}$$

where $\beta_k \in (0,1)$, $0 < \varrho < 1$ and $\lambda_k > 0$.

Corollary 3. *Let $V_i \in \Omega(\mathbb{X})$ be η_i-strongly monotone and φ_i-Lipschitz continuous monotone vector fields for each $i \in \{1, 2\cdots, N\}$. Let $F : K \times K \to \mathbb{R}$ be a bifunction satisfying the conditions (A)–(E) and T_t^F be the resolvent of F, $S : K \to K$, which is a nonexpansive mapping. If $\mathrm{Fix}(S) \bigcap_{i=1}^{N} VI(V_i, K) \bigcap \mathrm{EP}(F) \neq \emptyset$ and $\eta = \min_{\{i=1,2\cdots N\}} \{\eta_i\}$, $\varphi = \max_{\{i=1,2\cdots N\}} \{\varphi_i\}$, $\alpha_k, \beta_k \in (0,1)$, $0 < \varrho < 1$ and $\lambda_k > 0$ satisfy the conditions given in Theorem 1. Then, the sequence $\{z_k\}$ obtained by Algorithm 4 converges to an element in $\mathrm{Fix}(S) \bigcap_{i=1}^{N} VI(V_i, K) \bigcap \mathrm{EP}(F)$.*

Corollary 4. *Let $V \in \Omega(\mathbb{X})$ be η-strongly monotone and φ-Lipschitz continuous monotone vector field. Let $F : K \times K \to \mathbb{R}$ be a bifunction satisfying the conditions (A)–(E) and T_t^F be the resolvent of F, $S : K \to K$ be a nonexpansive mapping. If $\mathrm{Fix}(S) \bigcap VI(V, K) \bigcap \mathrm{EP}(F) \neq \emptyset$, $\alpha_k, \beta_k \in (0,1)$, $0 < \varrho < 1$ and $\lambda_k > 0$ satisfy the conditions given in Theorem 1, then the sequence $\{z_k\}$ obtained by Algorithm 5 converges to an element in $\mathrm{Fix}(S) \bigcap VI(V, K) \bigcap \mathrm{EP}(F)$.*

Corollary 5. *Let $V \in \Omega(\mathbb{X})$ be η-strongly monotone and φ-Lipschitz continuous monotone vector field. Let $S : K \to K$ be a nonexpansive mapping. If $\mathrm{Fix}(S) \bigcap VI(V, K) \neq \emptyset$, $\beta_k \in (0,1)$, $0 < \varrho < 1$ and $\lambda_k > 0$ satisfy the conditions given in Theorem 1. Then the sequence $\{z_k\}$ obtained by Algorithm 6 converges to an element in $\mathrm{Fix}(S) \bigcap VI(V, K)$.*

5. Conclusions

This work is concerned with the investigation of the common solution of a fixed-point problem, an equilibrium problem and a finite collection of variational inclusion problems. Our proposed algorithms are advanced and can be considered improvements to the methods discussed in the paper [3]. Several consequences of the suggested algorithms are discussed for variational inequalities, equilibrium and fixed-point problems. We anticipate that the methods presented in this paper can be extended to more general settings; for example, hyperbolic spaces, geodesic spaces and a CAT(0) space.

Author Contributions: Conceptualization, M.D.; methodology, D.F.; validation, M.A.; formal analysis, D.F.; investigation, S.C.; writing, original draft preparation, M.D.; funding acquisition, D.F.; writing, review and editing, M.A. All authors have read and agreed to the published version of the manuscript.

Funding: This research was funded by the Deanship of Scientific Research at Princess Nourah bint Abdulrahman University through the Fast-track Research Funding Program.

Institutional Review Board Statement: Not applicable.

Informed Consent Statement: Not applicable.

Data Availability Statement: Not applicable.

Acknowledgments: This research was funded by the Deanship of Scientific Research at Princess Nourah bint Abdulrahman University through the Fast-track Research Funding Program. The authors sincerely thank the unknown reviewers for their worthy suggestions and helpful comments that have led to the present form of the original manuscript.

Conflicts of Interest: The authors declare no conflict of interest.

References

1. Al-Homidan, S.; Ansari, Q.H.; Babu, F. Halpern and Mann type algorithms for fixed points and inclusion problems on Hadamard manifolds. *Numer. Funct. Anal. Optim.* **2019**, *40*, 621–653. [CrossRef]
2. Ansari, Q.H.; Babu, F.; Li, X.-B. Variational inclusion problems on Hadamard manifolds. *J. Nonlinear Convex Anal.* **2018**, *19*, 219–237.
3. Ansari, Q.H.; Babu, F. Proximal point algorithm for inclusion problems in Hadamard manifolds with applications. *Optim. Lett.* **2021**, *15*, 901–921. [CrossRef]
4. Chang, S.S.; Yao, J.C.; Yang, L.; Wen, C.F.; Wu, D.P. Convergence analysis for variational inclusion problems equilibrium problems and fixed point in Hadamard manifolds. *Numer. Funct. Anal. Appl.* **2021**, *42*, 567–582. [CrossRef]
5. Colao, V.; López, G.; Marino, G.; Martín-Márquez, V. Equilibrium problems in Hadamard manifolds. *J. Math. Anal. Appl.* **2012**, *388*, 61–71. [CrossRef]
6. Dilshad, M. Solving Yosida inclusion problem in Hadamard manifold. *Arab. J. Math.* **2020**, *9*, 357–366. [CrossRef]
7. Dilshad, M.; Khan, A.; Akram, M. Splitting type viscosity methods for inclusion and fixed point problems on Hadamard manifolds. *AIMS Math.* **2021**, *6*, 5205–5221. [CrossRef]
8. Ferreira, O.P.; Oliveira, P.R. Proximal point algorithm on Riemannian manifold. *Optimization* **2002**, *51*, 257–270. [CrossRef]
9. Filali, D.; Dilshad, M.; Akram, M.; Babu, F.; Ahmad, I. Viscosity method for hierarchical variational inequalities and variational inclusions on Hadamard manifolds. *J. Inequalities Appl.* **2021**, *2021*, 66. [CrossRef]
10. Khammahawong, K.; Kumam, P.; Chaipunya, P. Splitting algorithms of common solutions between equilibrium and inclusion problems on Hadamard manifold. *Linear Nonlinear Anal.* **2020**, *6*, 227–243.
11. Li, C.; Lopez, G.; Márquez, V.M. Monotone vector fields and the proximal point algorithm on Hadamard manifolds. *J. Lond. Math. Soc.* **2009**, *79*, 663–683. [CrossRef]
12. Li, C.; López, G.; Márquez, V.M.; Wang, J.H. Resolvent of set-valued monotone vector fields in Hadamard manifolds. *J. Set-Valued Anal.* **2011**, *19*, 361–383. [CrossRef]
13. Li, C.; López, G.; Martín-Márquez, V. Iterative algorithms for nonexpansive mappings on Hadamard manifolds. *Taiwan. J. Math.* **2010**, *14*, 541–559.
14. Németh, S.Z. Variational inequalities on Hadamard manifolds. *Nonlinear Anal.* **2003**, *52*, 1491–1498. [CrossRef]
15. Rockafellar, R.T. Monotone operators and the proximal point algorithm. *SIAM J. Control Optim.* **1976**, *14*, 877–898. [CrossRef]
16. Fan, K. *A Minimax Inequality and Applications*; Academic Press: New York, NY, USA, 1972; pp. 103–113.
17. Blum, E.; Oetteli, W. From optomization and variational inequalities to equilibrium problems. *Math. Stud.* **1994**, *63*, 123–145.
18. Khammahawong, K.; Kumam, P.; Chaipunya, P. Splitting Algorithms for Equilibrium Problems and Inclusion Problems on Hadamard Manifolds. *Numer. Funct. Anal. Optim.* **2021**, *42*, 1645–1682. [CrossRef]
19. Martinet, B. Régularisation d'inequations variationnelles par approximations successives. *Rev. Fr. Inform. Oper.* **1970**, *4*, 154–158.
20. Walter, R. On the metric projections onto convex sets in Riemannian spaces. *Arch. Math.* **1974**, *25*, 91–98. [CrossRef]
21. Khammahawong, K.; Kumam, P.; Chaipunya, P.; Martinez-Marino, J. Tseng's method for inclusion problem on Hadamard manifolds. *Optimization* **2021**. [CrossRef]
22. Rapcsák, T. *Smooth Nonlinear Optimization in* $\mathbb{R}^n$; Kluwer Academic Publishers: Dordrecht, The Netherlands, 1997.
23. Sakai, T. *Riemannian Geomety, Translations of Mathematical Monograph*; American Mathematical Society: Providence, RI, USA, 1996.
24. Németh, S.Z. Monotone vector fields. *Publ. Math. Debrecen* **1999**, *54*, 437–449.
25. Da Cruz Neto, J.X.; Ferreira, O.P.; Lucambio Pérez, L.R. Monotone point-to-set vector fields. *Balk. J. Geom. Appl.* **2000**, *5*, 69–79.

axioms MDPI

Article

Numerical Processes for Approximating Solutions of Nonlinear Equations

Samundra Regmi [1,*], Ioannis K. Argyros [2], Santhosh George [3] and Christopher I. Argyros [4]

1 Department of Mathematics, University of Houston, Houston, TX 77204, USA
2 Department of Mathematical Sciences, Cameron University, Lawton, OK 73505, USA; iargyros@cameron.edu
3 Department of Mathematical and Computational Sciences, National Institute of Technology Karnataka, Mangaluru 575 025, India; sgeorge@nitk.edu.in
4 Department of Computing and Technology, Cameron University, Lawton, OK 73505, USA; christopher.argyros@cameron.edu
* Correspondence: sregmi5@uh.edu

Abstract: In this article, we present generalized conditions of three-step iterative schemes for solving nonlinear equations. The convergence order is shown using Taylor series, but the existence of high-order derivatives is assumed. However, only the first derivative appears on these schemes. Therefore, the hypotheses limit the utilization of the schemes to operators that are at least nine times differentiable, although the schemes may converge. To the best of our knowledge, no semi-local convergence has been given in the setting of a Banach space. Our goal is to extend the applicability of these schemes in both the local and semi-local convergence cases. Moreover, we use our idea of recurrent functions and conditions only on the derivative or divided differences of order one that appear in these schemes. This idea can be applied to extend other high convergence multipoint and multistep schemes. Numerical applications where the convergence criteria are tested complement this article.

Keywords: iterative schemes; Banach space; convergence criterion

MSC: 49M15; 47H17; 65J15; 65G99; 41A25

Citation: Regmi, S.; Argyros, I.K.; George, S.; Argyros, C.I. Numerical Processes for Approximating Solutions of Nonlinear Equations. *Axioms* **2022**, *11*, 307. https://doi.org/10.3390/axioms11070307

Academic Editor: Clemente Cesarano

Received: 24 May 2022
Accepted: 23 June 2022
Published: 24 June 2022

1. Introduction

Let M and M_1 denote Banach spaces, D stand for an open set and $F : D \subset M \to M_1$ be a continuous operator.

We denote by x^* a solution of the nonlinear equation

$$F(x) = 0. \tag{1}$$

Iterative schemes are utilized for solving the nonlinear Equation (1). A plethora of iterative schemes have been employed for approximating x^* [1,2].

In this article, we study the generalized three-step iterative schemes defined for $n = 0, 1, 2, \ldots$, by

$$\begin{aligned} y_n &= x_n - M_{1,n}^{-1}F(x_n) \\ z_n &= y_n - M_{2,n}^{-1}F(y_n) \\ x_{n+1} &= z_n - M_{3,n}^{-1}F(z_n), \end{aligned} \tag{2}$$

where $M_{1,n} = M_1(x_n), M_1 : D \longrightarrow L(M, M_1)$, $M_{2,n} = M_2(x_n, y_n), M_2 : D \times D \longrightarrow L(M, M_1)$, $M_{3,n} = M_3(x_n, y_n, z_n)$, and $M_3 : D \times D \times D \longrightarrow L(M, M_1)$.

This scheme generalizes numerous others already in the literature [3–5]. If, e.g.,

$$M_{1,n} = M_{2,n} = F'(x_n),\ M_{3,n} = O, \tag{3}$$

or

$$M_{1,n} = M_{2,n} = M_{3,n} = F'(x_n) \tag{4}$$

or

$$M_{1,n} = F'(x_n), M_{2,n} = F'(y_n) \text{ and } M_{3,n} = F'(z_n), \tag{5}$$

then Newton–Traub-type methods are obtained.

The convergence order of the specialized schemes was shown to be three, five, and eight, respectively, using Taylor expansions. In the case of order three, the fourth derivative is used. Hence, the assumptions on the ninth derivative reduce the applicability of these schemes [2,4–6]. In particular, even a simple scalar equation cannot be handled with the existing results.

For example: Let $M = M_1 = \mathbb{R}$, $D = [-0.5, 1.5]$. Define scalar function λ on D by

$$\lambda(t) = \begin{cases} t^3 \log t^2 + t^5 - t^4 & if\ t \neq 0 \\ 0 & if\ t = 0. \end{cases}$$

Notice that $t^* = 1$ solves equation $\lambda(t) = 0$ and the third derivative is given by

$$\lambda'''(t) = 6 \log t^2 + 60t^2 - 24t + 22.$$

Obviously, $\lambda'''(t)$ is not bounded on D. Therefore, the convergence of the scheme (2) is not guaranteed by the previous analyses in [2,4–8]. A plethora of other choices can be found in [4–8]. Therefore, it is important to study the local as well as the semi-local convergence under unifying convergence and weaker than before criteria.

There are two important types of convergence: The semi-local and the local. The semi-local is based on the information about an initial guess to provide criteria guaranteeing the convergence of the scheme; while the local one is based on the information around a solution to find estimates of the radii of the convergence balls.

The local convergence results are important, although the solution is generally unknown since the convergence order of the scheme can be determined. This type of result also demonstrates the degree of difficulty in choosing initial guesses. There are cases when the radius of convergence of the scheme can be found without knowing the solution.

As an example, let $M = M_1 = \mathbb{R}$. Suppose that function F satisfies an autonomous differential [4,6] equation of the form

$$S(F(t)) = F'(t),$$

where S is a continuous function. Notice that $S(F(t_*)) = F'(t_*)$ or $F'(t_*) = S(0)$. In the case of $F(t) = e^t - 1$, we can choose $S(t) = t + 1$ (see also the numerical section).

Moreover, the local results can apply to projection schemes such as Arnoldi's, the generalized minimum residual scheme (GMRES), the generalized conjugate scheme (GCS) for combined Newton/finite projection schemes, and in relation to the mesh independence principle to develop the cheapest and most efficient mesh refinement techniques [5,7,9].

In this article, we introduce a majorant sequence and also use our idea of recurrent functions to extend the applicability of the scheme (2). Our analysis includes error bounds and results on the uniqueness of x^* based on computable Lipschitz constants not given before in [2,4–8] and in other similar studies using the Taylor series. Our idea is very general. Therefore, it applies to other schemes too [9–14].

The rest of the article is set up as follows: In Section 2, we present the results of the local analysis. Section 3 contains the semi-local analysis, whereas in Section 4, special cases are discussed. The numerical experiments are presented in Section 5. Concluding remarks are given in the last Section 6.

2. Local Analysis

Let ℓ_1, ℓ_2 and ℓ_3 be given positive constants. Define function φ_1 on the interval $[0, \frac{1}{\ell_1})$ by

$$\varphi_1(t) = \frac{(\ell_0 + 2\ell_1)t}{2(1 - \ell_1 t)}.$$

Notice that $r_1 = \frac{2}{\ell_0 + 4\ell_1}$ solves equation $\varphi_1(t) - 1 = 0$. Set $\rho_1 = \min\{\frac{1}{\ell_1}, \frac{1}{\ell_2}\}$. Moreover, define function φ_2 on the interval $[0, \rho_1)$ by

$$\varphi_2(t) = \frac{\ell_2 + \frac{\ell_0}{2}\varphi_1(t))t}{1 - \ell_2 t}.$$

Then, $\varphi_2(0) = -1$ and $\varphi_2(t) \longrightarrow \infty$ as $t \longrightarrow \rho_1^-$. Denote by r_2 the minimal root of function $\varphi_2(t) - 1$ guaranteed to exist by the intermediate value theorem on the interval $(0, \rho_1)$. Furthermore, define function φ_3 on the interval $[0, \rho_2)$ by

$$\varphi_3(t) = \frac{(\ell_3 + \frac{\ell_0}{2}\varphi_2(t))t}{1 - \ell_3 t},$$

for $\rho_2 = \min\{\frac{1}{\ell_3}, \rho_1\}$. It follows that $\varphi_3(0) = -1$ and $\varphi_3(t) \longrightarrow \infty$ as $t \longrightarrow \rho_2^-$. Denote by r_3 the minimal root of function $\varphi_3(t) - 1$ in the interval $(0, \rho_2)$.

We then show that r defined by

$$r = \min\{r_1, r_2, r_3\} \tag{6}$$

is a radius of convergence for scheme (2). Set $T = [0, r)$. It then follows that for all $t \in T$

$$\ell_1 t < 1, \ \ell_2 t < 1, \ \ell_3 t < 1, \tag{7}$$

$$0 \le \varphi_1(t) < 1, \tag{8}$$

$$0 \le \varphi_2(t) < 1, \tag{9}$$

and

$$0 \le \varphi_3(t) < 1 \tag{10}$$

hold.

Denote by $U(x, \rho)$ the open ball with center $x \in M$ and of radius $\rho > 0$. Moreover, the ball $U[x, \rho]$ denotes the closure of the ball $U(x, \rho)$. Furthermore, by F', we denote the Fréchet derivative of operator F.

The following conditions are needed to show the local convergence of scheme (2). Suppose:

(A1) There exists a simple solution $x^* \in D$ of equation $F(x) = 0$.

(A2) $\|F'(x^*)^{-1}(M_1(x) - F'(x^*))\| \le \ell_1\|x - x^*\|$ for all $x \in D$ and some $\ell_1 > 0$. Set $D_1 = U(x^*, \frac{1}{\ell_1}) \cap D$.

(A3) $\|F'(x^*)^{-1}(F'(x) - F'(x^*))\| \le \ell_0\|x - x^*\|$ for all $x \in D_1$ and some $\ell_0 > 0$.

(A4) $\|F'(x^*)^{-1}(M_2(x, y) - F'(x^*))\| \le \ell_2\|x - x^*\|$ for all $x \in D_1$, $y = x - F'(x)^{-1}F(x)$, and some constant $\ell_2 > 0$.

(A5) $\|F'(x^*)^{-1}(M_3(x, y, z) - F'(x^*))\| \le \ell_3\|x - x^*\|$ for all $x \in D_1$, $z = y - M_2(x, y)^{-1}F(y)$, and some constant $\ell_3 > 0$.

(A6) $U[x^*, r] \subset D$.

The main local convergence result follows for scheme (2).

Proof. Consider $\tilde{x} \in D_2$ with $F(\tilde{x}) = 0$. Define the linear operator $Q = \int_0^1 F'(x^* + \theta(\tilde{x} - x^*))d\theta$. Then, by applying condition (A3)

$$\|F'(x^*)^{-1}(Q - F'(x^*))\| \leq \ell_0 \int_0^1 \|x^* + \theta(\tilde{x} - x^*)) - x^*\|d\theta$$
$$\ell_0 \int_0^1 \theta\|\tilde{x} - x^*\|d\theta < \frac{\ell_0}{2}\frac{2}{\ell_0} = 1. \tag{24}$$

It follows that the linear operator Q is invertible. Then, the approximation $Q(\tilde{x} - x^*) = F(\tilde{x}) - F(x^*) = 0 - 0 = 0$, gives $\tilde{x} - x = Q^{-1}(0) = 0$. Hence, we conclude that $\tilde{x} = x^*$. □

Remark 1. *A similar result was given in ([15], Theorem 1) in the special case when* $M = M_1 = \mathbb{R}$ *and* $M_{1,n} = F'(x_n)$. *However, this non-affine invariant form result is not correct, since it corresponds to the (11) estimate which is*

$$\|y_n - x^*\| \leq \frac{\ell_1\|x_n - x^*\|^2}{2(1 - \ell_1\|x_n - x^*\|)}$$

but which is not implied by (A2). Hence, the proof of Theorem 1 in [15] breaks down at this point. Notice also that in [15] they used $\bar{M}_{1,n} = F'(x_n)^{-1}$, $\bar{M}_{2,n} = M_{2,n}^{-1}$ *and* $\bar{M}_{3,n} = M_{3,n}^{-1}$.

3. Semi-Local Analysis

The semi-local analysis of iterative scheme (2) is based on some Lipschitz-type conditions relating operators F, F', and linear operators $M_{j,n}$ to some parameters. Moreover, sequence $\{x_n\}$ is majorized by some scalar sequences depending on some parameters. Suppose:

(H1) There exist $x_0 \in D$, $\eta \geq 0$ such that $F'(x_0)^{-1}, M_{1,0}^{-1} \in L(M_1, M)$ and $\|M_{1,0}^{-1}F(x_0)\| \leq \eta$.

(H2) $\|F'(x_0)^{-1}(M_1(x) - F'(x_0))\| \leq a_1\|x - x_0\|$ for all $x \in D$ and some $a_1 > 0$. Set $D_3 = U(x_0, \frac{1}{a_1}) \cap D$.

(H3) $\| \int_0^1 F'(x_0)^{-1}(F'(z + \theta(x - z)) - M_3(x, y, z))d\theta\| \leq b_1$

$$\| \int_0^1 F'(x_0)^{-1}(F'(x + \theta(y - x)) - M_1(x))d\theta\| \leq b_2,$$

$$\| \int_0^1 F'(x_0)^{-1}(F'(y + \theta(z - y)) - M_2(x, y))d\theta\| \leq b_3,$$

$$\|F'(x_0)^{-1}(M_2(x, y) - F'(x_0))\| \leq a_2\|y - x_0\|,$$

$$\|F'(x_0)^{-1}(M_3(x, y, z) - F'(x_0))\| \leq a_3\|z - x_0\|,$$

where for all $\theta \in [0, 1], x \in D_3$ and y, z are taken from method (26) (or for all $y, z \in D_3$), and b_1, b_2, b_3, a_2 and a_3 are positive constants depending on operators F, F' and $M_{j,n}$.

(H4) $U[x_0, \rho] \subset D$ for some $\rho > 0$ to be given later.

As can be seen by the proof of Theorem 2 that follows the iterates, $\{x_n\}$ lies in the set D_3 which is a more accurate domain than D, since $D_3 \subset D$. This way, at least as tight constants are obtained than if conditions (H3) and (H4) hold only in D (see also the numerical section).

We chose the last two conditions in (H3) this way. However, other choices are also possible [1–4]. Notice that if $a_1\eta < 1$ and $\tilde{D} = U(y_0, \frac{1}{a_1} - \eta) \cap D$, then $\tilde{D} \subset D_3$,, respectively, and even smaller constants "a" are obtained, if $\tilde{D}$ replaces D_3.

Moreover, we define the scalar sequence $\{t_n\}$ by

$$\begin{aligned} t_0 &= 0,\, s_0 = \eta \\ u_n &= s_n + \frac{b_2(s_n - t_n)}{1 - a_2 s_n} \qquad (25) \\ t_{n+1} &= u_n + \frac{b_3(u_n - s_n)}{1 - a_3 u_n}, \qquad (26) \\ s_{n+1} &= t_{n+1} + \frac{b_1(t_{n+1} - u_n)}{1 - a_1 t_{n+1}}. \end{aligned}$$

This sequence shall be shown to be majorizing for scheme $\{x_n\}$ in Theorem 2. However, first, a convergence result for it is needed.

We then develop results on the convergence of sequence $\{t_n\}$.

Lemma 1. *Suppose*

$$a_2 s_n < 1,\ a_3 u_n < 1 \text{ and } a_1 t_{n+1} < 1 \qquad (27)$$

hold for all $n = 0, 1, 2, \ldots$. *Then, sequence* $\{t_n\}$ *is such that* $s_n \le u_n \le t_{n+1} < \frac{1}{a_1}$ *and* $\lim_{n \longrightarrow \infty} t_n = t^* \le \frac{1}{a_1}$.

Proof. It follows from (26) and (27) that sequence $\{t_n\}$ is nondecreasing, bounded from above by $\frac{1}{a_1}$ and as such it converges to its unique least upper bound $t^* \in [0, \frac{1}{a_1}]$. □

The semi-local convergence of method (2) follows next.

Theorem 2. *Under conditions (H1)–(H4), further suppose: conditions of Lemma 1 hold and* $\rho = t^*$ *in (H4). Then, the sequence* $\{x_n\}$ *generated by method (2) exists in* $U(x_0, t^*)$, *stays in* $U(x_0, t^*)$ *and converges to a solution* $x^* \in U[x_0, t^*]$ *of equation* $F(x) = 0$. *Moreover, the following estimates hold*

$$\|y_n - x_n\| \le s_n - t_n \qquad (28)$$

$$\|z_n - y_n\| \le u_n - s_n, \qquad (29)$$

and

$$\|x_{n+1} - z_n\| \le t_{n+1} - u_n. \qquad (30)$$

Proof. Mathematical induction is used to show (29)–(31). Using (H1) and (27)

$$\|y_0 - x_0\| = \|M_{1,0}^{-1} F(x_0)\| \le \eta = s_0 - t_0,$$

so iterate $y_0 \in U(x_0, t^*)$ and (56) holds for $n = 0$. Let $v \in U(x_0, t^*)$. It then follows from (H3) that

$$\|F'(x_0)^{-1}(M_2(x_0, y_0) - F'(x_0))\| \le a_2 \|y_0 - x_0\| < a_2 t^* < 1.$$

That is, $M_2(x_0, y_0)^{-1} \in L(M_1, M)$,

$$\|M_2(x_0, y_0)^{-1} F(x_0)\| \le \frac{1}{1 - a_2\|y_0 - x_0\|}, \qquad (31)$$

and iterate z_0 is well defined by the second substep of method (26) for $n = 0$. By the first substep of method (2)

$$F(y_0) = F(y_0) - F(x_0) - M_{1,0}(y_0 - x_0),$$

$$F'(x_0)^{-1} F(y_0) = \int_0^1 F'(x_0)^{-1}(F'(x_0 + \theta(y_0 - x_0)) - M_1(x_0)) d\theta (y_0 - x_0),$$

Proof. Induction is utilized for items

$$0 \leq \frac{L(s_k - t_k)}{2(1 - L_0 s_k)} \leq \gamma, \tag{47}$$

$$0 \leq \frac{L(u_k - s_k)}{2(1 - L_0 u_k)} \leq \gamma, \tag{48}$$

$$0 \leq \frac{L(t_{k+1} - u_k)}{2(1 - L_0 t_{k+1})} \leq \gamma, \tag{49}$$

and

$$t_k \leq s_k \leq u_k \leq t_{k+1}. \tag{50}$$

These estimates hold for $k = 0$ by (34) and (43). Suppose they hold for all integers smaller or equal to k. Then, we obtain

$$\begin{aligned}
t_{k+1} &\leq u_k + \gamma^{2k+2}\eta \leq s_k + \gamma^{2k+1}\eta + \gamma^{2k+2}\eta \\
&\leq t_k + \gamma^{2k}\eta + \gamma^{2k+1}\eta + \gamma^{2k+2}\eta \\
&\vdots \\
&\leq t_0 + \gamma\eta + \cdots + \gamma^{2k+2}\eta \\
&= \frac{1 - \gamma^{2k+3}}{1 - \gamma}\eta < \frac{\eta}{1 - \gamma} = t^{**},
\end{aligned}$$

similarly,

$$s_k \leq \frac{1 - \gamma^{2k+1}}{1 - \gamma}\eta \text{ and } u_k = \frac{1 - \gamma^{2k+2}}{1 - \gamma}\eta.$$

Then, evidently, (47) holds if

$$\frac{L}{2}\gamma^{2k}\eta + L_0\gamma\frac{1 - \gamma^{2k+1}}{1 - \gamma}\eta - \gamma \leq 0$$

or

$$f_k^{(1)}(t) \leq 0 \text{ at } t = \gamma. \tag{51}$$

By the definition of $f_k^{(1)}$, we can find a relationship between two consecutive functions:

$$\begin{aligned}
f_{k+1}^{(1)}(t) &= f_{k+1}^{(1)}(t) - f_k^{(1)}(t) + f_k^{(1)}(t) \\
&= f_k^{(1)}(t) + \frac{L}{2}t^{2k+1}\eta + L_0(1 + t + \ldots + t^{2k+2})\eta - 1 \\
&\quad -\frac{L}{2}t^{2k+1}\eta - L_0(1 + t + \ldots + t^{2k})\eta + 1 \\
&= f_k^{(1)}(t) + p(t)t^{2k+1}\eta.
\end{aligned} \tag{52}$$

In particular, by the definition of p, we obtain

$$f_{k+1}^{(1)} = f_k^{(1)}(t) \text{ at } t = \gamma. \tag{53}$$

Let function

$$f_\infty^{(1)}(t) = \lim_{k \longrightarrow \infty} f_k^{(1)}(t). \tag{54}$$

It follows by the definition of $f_k^{(1)}$ and (54) that

$$f_\infty^{(1)}(t) = \frac{L_0\eta}{1 - t} - 1.$$

Consequently, assertion (51) holds if

$$f_\infty^{(1)}(t) \leq 0 \text{ at } t = \gamma,$$

which is true by the right hand side of inequality (43). Similarly, to show (48)

$$\frac{L}{2}\gamma^{2k+1}\eta + L_0\gamma\frac{1-\gamma^{2k+2}}{1-\gamma}\eta - \gamma \leq 0$$

or

$$f_k^{(2)}(t) \leq 0 \text{ at } t = \gamma.$$

This time, we also have

$$f_{k+1}^{(2)}(t) = f_k^{(2)}(t) + p(t)t^{2k}\eta,$$

and for

$$f_\infty^{(2)}(t) = \lim_{k\longrightarrow\infty} f_k^{(2)}(t) = \frac{L_0\eta}{1-t} - 1 \leq 0$$

at $t = \gamma$. Moreover, (49) holds if

$$\frac{L}{2}\gamma^{2k+2}\eta + \gamma L_0\frac{1-\gamma^{2k+3}}{1-\gamma}\eta - \gamma \leq 0$$

or

$$f_k^{(3)}(t) \leq 0 \text{ at } t = \gamma. \tag{55}$$

However, we have

$$f_{k+1}^{(3)}(t) = f_k^{(3)}(t) + p(t)t^{2k+1}\gamma,$$

so

$$f_{k+1}^{(3)}(t) = f_k^{(3)}(t), \text{ at } t = \gamma.$$

That is, (55) holds if $f_\infty^{(3)}(t) = \lim_{k\longrightarrow\infty} f_k^{(3)}(t) \leq 0$, at $t = \gamma$. However, again, we obtain

$$f_\infty^{(3)}(t) = \frac{L_0\eta}{1-t} - 1.$$

Therefore, assertion (55) holds again by (45). Furthermore, (50) holds by (34) and (47)–(49). The induction for items (47)–(50) is completed. Hence, we deduce $t_k \leq s_k \leq t_{k+1}$ and $\lim_{k\longrightarrow\infty} t_k = t^*$. □

5. Numerical Example

We verify convergence criteria using method (32). Moreover, we compare Lipschitz constants L_0, L, L_1 and K. In particular, the first example is used to show that the ratio $\frac{L_0}{L_1}$ can be arbitrarily small.

Example 1. *Let $M = M_1 = \mathbb{R}$. Define function*

$$\psi(t) = \delta_0 t + \delta_1 + \delta_2 \sin \delta_3 t,\ t_0 = 0,$$

where δ_j, $j = 0, 1, 2, 3$ are fixed parameters. Then, clearly for δ_3 large and δ_2 small, $\frac{L_0}{L_1}$ can be (arbitrarily) small, so that $\frac{L_0}{L_1} \longrightarrow 0$.

The parameters L_0, L, K and L_1 are computed in the next example. Moreover, the convergence criteria (46)–(48) and those of Lemma 3 are compared.

Example 2. *Let $M = M_1 = \mathbb{R}$. Let us consider a scalar function F defined on the set $D = U[x_0, 1-q]$ for $q \in (0, \frac{1}{2})$ by*

$$F(x) = x^3 - q.$$

Choose $x_0 = 1$. Then, we obtain the estimates $\eta = \frac{1-q}{3}$,

$$\begin{aligned} |F'(x_0)^{-1}(F'(x) - F'(x_0))| &= |x^2 - x_0^2| \\ &\leq |x + x_0||x - x_0| \leq (|x - x_0| + 2|x_0|)|x - x_0| \\ &= (1 - q + 2)|x - x_0| = (3 - q)|x - x_0|, \end{aligned}$$

for all $x \in D$, so $L_0 = 3 - q$, $D_0 = U(x_0, \frac{1}{L_0}) \cap D = U(x_0, \frac{1}{L_0})$,

$$\begin{aligned} |F'(x_0)^{-1}(F'(y) - F'(x)| &= |y^2 - x^2| \\ &\leq |y + x||y - x| \leq (|y - x_0 + x - x_0 + 2x_0)||y - x| \\ &= (|y - x_0| + |x - x_0| + 2|x_0|)|y - x| \\ &\leq (\frac{1}{L_0} + \frac{1}{L_0} + 2)|y - x| = 2(1 + \frac{1}{L_0})|y - x|, \end{aligned}$$

for all $x, y \in D$ and so $K = 2(1 + \frac{1}{L_0})$.

$$\begin{aligned} |F'(x_0)^{-1}(F'(y) - F'(x)| &= (|y - x_0| + |x - x_0| + 2|x_0|)|y - x| \\ &\leq (1 - q + 1 - q + 2)|y - x| = 2(2 - q)|y - x|, \end{aligned}$$

for all $x, y \in D$ and $L_1 = 2(2 - q)$.

Notice that for all $q \in (0, \frac{1}{2})$

$$L_0 < K < L_1.$$

Next, set $y = x - F'(x)^{-1}F(x), x \in D$. Then, we have

$$y + x = x - F'(x)^{-1}F(x) + x = \frac{5x^3 + q}{3x^2}.$$

Define function $\bar{F}$ on the interval $D = [q, 2 - q]$ by

$$\bar{F}(x) = \frac{5x^3 + q}{3x^2}.$$

Then, we obtain by this definition that

$$\begin{aligned} \bar{F}'(x) &= \frac{15x^4 - 6xq}{9x^4} \\ &= \frac{5(x - q)(x^2 + xq + q^2)}{3x^3}, \end{aligned}$$

where $p = \sqrt[3]{\frac{2q}{5}}$ is the critical point of function $\bar{F}$. Notice that $q < p < 2 - q$. It follows that this function is decreasing on the interval (q, p) and increasing on the interval $(q, 2 - q)$, since $x^2 + xq + q^2 > 0$ and $x^3 > 0$. So, we can set

$$K_2 = \frac{5(2 - q)^2 + q}{9(2 - q)^2}$$

and

$$K_2 < L_0.$$

However, if $x \in D_0 = [1 - \frac{1}{L_0}, 1 + \frac{1}{L_0}]$, *then*

$$L = \frac{5\varrho^3 + q}{9\varrho^2},$$

where $\varrho = \frac{4-q}{3-q}$ *and* $K < K_1$ *for all* $q \in (0, \frac{1}{2})$. *Then, criterion (39) is not satisfied for all* $q \in (0, \frac{1}{2})$. *Hence, there is no guarantee that scheme (34) converges to* $x^* = \sqrt[3]{q}$. *Moreover, our earlier criterion (38) holds for* $q \in (0.4620, 1]$. *Furthermore, the new criterion by solving becomes*

$$2\bar{L}\eta \leq 1,$$

where $\bar{L} = \frac{1}{8}(4L_0 + L + \sqrt{L^2 + 8L_0 L})$. *This condition holds for* $q \in (0.4047, 1)$. *Clearly, the new results extend the range of values q for which scheme (34) converges.*

This range can be extended even further if we apply Lemma 2. Indeed, choose $q = 0.4$, *and we have the following Table 1, showing that the conditions of Lemma 2 are satisfied.*

Table 1. Sequence (32).

n	1	2	3	4	5	6
u_i	0.2330	0.2945	0.3008	0.3009	0.3009	0.3009
s_i	0.2000	0.2896	0.3008	0.3009	0.3009	0.3009
t_{n+1}	0.2341	0.2946	0.3008	0.3009	0.3009	0.3009
$L_0 s_i$	0.5200	0.7530	0.7820	0.7824	0.7824	0.7824
$L_0 u_i$	0.6058	0.7658	0.7822	0.7824	0.7824	0.7824
$L_0 t_{i+1}$	0.6087	0.7659	0.7822	0.7824	0.7824	0.7824

Example 3. *Consider* $M = M_1 = C[0,1]$ *and* $D = U[0,1]$. *Then, the boundary value problem (BVP) [4]*

$$\varsigma(0) = 0, \varsigma(1) = 1,$$
$$\varsigma'' = -\varsigma - \sigma\varsigma^2$$

can be also given as

$$\varsigma(s) = s + \int_0^1 G(s,t)(\varsigma^3(t) + \sigma\varsigma^2(t))dt$$

where σ *is a constant and* $G(s,t)$ *is the Green's function*

$$G(s,t) = \begin{cases} t(1-s), & t \leq s \\ s(1-t), & s < t. \end{cases}$$

Consider $F : D \longrightarrow M_1$ *as*

$$[F(x)](s) = x(s) - s - \int_0^1 G(s,t)(x^3(t) + \sigma x^2(t))dt.$$

Let us set $\varsigma_0(s) = s$ *and* $D = U(\varsigma_0, \rho_0)$. *Then, clearly* $U(\varsigma_0, \rho_0) \subset U(0, \rho_0 + 1)$, *since* $\|\varsigma_0\| = 1$. *If* $2\sigma < 5$. *Then, conditions (H1)–(H4) are satisfied for*

$$L_0 = \frac{2\sigma + 3\rho_0 + 6}{8}, L = \frac{\sigma + 6\rho_0 + 3}{4}.$$

Hence, $L_0 < L_1$.

The next two examples concern the local convergence of method (34) and the radii r_j, r were computed using Formula (6) and the functions φ_j.

Example 4. *If* $M = M_1 = C[0,1]$ *is equipped with the max-norm,* $D = U[0,1]$*, consider* $Q : D \longrightarrow M_1$ *given as*

$$Q(\lambda)(x) = \varphi(x) - 5\int_0^1 x\tau\lambda(\tau)^3 d\tau. \tag{56}$$

We obtain

$$Q'(\lambda(\xi))(x) = \xi(x) - 15\int_0^1 x\tau\lambda(\tau)^2\xi(\tau)d\tau, \text{ for each } \xi \in D.$$

Then, since $x^* = 0$*, conditions (A1)–(A5) hold provided that* $\ell_0 = \ell_1 = \ell_2 = \ell_3 = 7.5$*. Then, the radii are:*

$$r_1 = 0.0533 = r,\ r_2 = 0.1499, \text{ and } r_3 = 0.1660.$$

Example 5. *Consider the motion system*

$$\mathcal{H}_1'(w_1) = e^{w_1},\ \mathcal{H}_2'(w_2) = (e-1)w_2 + 1,\ \mathcal{H}_3'(w_3) = 1$$

with $\mathcal{H}_1(0) = \mathcal{H}_2(0) = \mathcal{H}_3(0) = 0$*. Let* $\mathcal{H} = (\mathcal{H}_1, \mathcal{H}_2, \mathcal{H}_3)$*. Let* $M = M_1 = \mathbb{R}^3$*,* $D = U[0,1]$*,* $x^* = (0,0,0)^{tr}$*. Let function* $\mathcal{H}$ *on* D *for* $w = (w_1, w_2, w_3)^{tr}$ *given as*

$$\mathcal{H}(w) = (e^{w_1} - 1, \frac{e-1}{2}w_2^2 + w_2, w_3)^{tr}.$$

The Fréchet derivative is given by

$$\mathcal{H}'(w) = \begin{bmatrix} e^x & 0 & 0 \\ 0 & (e-1)w_2 + 1 & 0 \\ 0 & 0 & 1 \end{bmatrix}.$$

Notice that $\mathcal{H}'(x^*) = I$*. Let* $w \in \mathbb{R}^3$ *with* $w = (w_1, w_2, w_3)^{tr}$*. Moreover, the nor for* $M \in \mathbb{R}^3 \times \mathbb{R}^3$ *is*

$$\|M\| = \max_{1 \le k \le 3} \sum_{i=1}^{3} \|m_{k,i}\|.$$

We need to verify conditions (A1)–(A5). To achieve this, we study $\mathcal{G}(t) = e^t - 1$ *on* $D = [-1,1]$*. We have* $t^* = 1$*, hence* $\mathcal{G}'(t^*) = 1$*, and*

$$\begin{aligned} |\mathcal{G}'(t) - \mathcal{G}'(t^*)| &= |t + \frac{t^2}{2} + \ldots + \frac{t^n}{n!} + \ldots| \\ &= |1 + \frac{t-0}{2!} + \ldots + \frac{(t-0)^{n-1}}{n!} + \ldots||t - o| \end{aligned}$$

so $\ell_1 = e - 1$*. Then,* $D_1 = U(x^*, \frac{1}{e-1}) \cap D = U(x^*, \frac{1}{e-1})$*. This time we obtain*

$$|\mathcal{G}'(t) - \mathcal{G}'(t^*)| \le \ell_0|t - 0|,$$

where

$$\ell_0 = 1 + \frac{1}{(e-1)2!} + \ldots + \frac{1}{(e-1)^{n-1}n!} + \ldots \approx 1.43 < \ell_1.$$

Then, we have for $t \in D_1$

$$\begin{aligned} |s| &= |t - \mathcal{G}'(t)^{-1}\mathcal{G}(t)| = |t - 1 + e^{-t}| \\ &= |\frac{(-t)^2}{2!} + \ldots + \frac{(-t)^n}{n!} + \ldots| \\ &= |t|(\frac{|t|}{2!} + \ldots + \frac{|t|^{n-1}}{n!} + \ldots) \le \frac{\ell_0 - 1}{e - 1}. \end{aligned}$$

Moreover,

$$\begin{aligned} |F'(s) - F'(t^*)| &= |e^s - 1| \\ &\leq |s|(1 + \frac{|s|}{2!} + \ldots + \frac{|s|^{n-1}}{n!} + \ldots) \\ &\leq |t|\frac{\ell_0 - 1}{e-1}(1 + \frac{\ell_0 - 1}{(e-1)2!} + \ldots + \left(\frac{\ell_0 - 1}{e-1}\right)^{n-1}\frac{1}{n!} + \ldots) \\ &= \ell_2(t - 0), \end{aligned}$$

where $\ell_2 \approx 0.49 < \ell_1$. *We can set* $\ell_3 = \ell_2$.

Then, the radii are:

$$r_1 = 0.2409 = r,\ r_2 = 0.3101, \text{ and } r_3 = 0.3588.$$

In the last example, we revisit the motivational example given in the introduction, where we apply scheme (32).

Example 6. *The iterates for the motivational example with* $x_0 = 0.85$ *are given in Table 2.*

Table 2. Sequence (32).

n	1	2	3	4	5	6
y_i	1.1609	0.2067	0.0846	0.0377	0.0174	0.0081
z_i	0.3121	0.1640	0.0695	0.0313	0.0145	0.0068
x_i	0.8500	0.3985	0.1399	0.0605	0.0274	0.0127

6. Conclusions

Conditions for the convergence of generalized three-step schemes are presented for both the local as well as semi-local case. The sequences generated by these schemes approximate solutions of equation $F(x) = 0$ that are locally unique. The convergence conditions depend on the divided difference of the order of one or the derivative, which appears on the schemes. However, this is not the case with earlier articles utilizing high-order derivatives, which do not appear in the schemes. Moreover, the error analysis is tighter because we show that the iterates remain in a stricter domain than in earlier articles. Hence, the utilization of these schemes is extended with the same or even weaker conditions. Our process does not depend on these schemes. Therefore, it can be employed similarly to extend the usage of the other schemes [9,10,15–18].

Author Contributions: Conceptualization, S.R., I.K.A., S.G. and C.I.A.; methodology, S.R., I.K.A., S.G. and C.I.A.; software, S.R., I.K.A., S.G. and C.I.A.; validation, S.R., I.K.A., S.G. and C.I.A.; formal analysis, S.R., I.K.A., S.G. and C.I.A.; investigation, S.R., I.K.A., S.G. and C.I.A.; resources, S.R., I.K.A., S.G. and C.I.A.; data curation, S.R., I.K.A., S.G. and C.I.A.; writing—original draft preparation, S.R., I.K.A., S.G. and C.I.A.; writing—review and editing, S.R., I.K.A., S.G. and C.I.A.; visualization, S.R., I.K.A., S.G. and C.I.A.; supervision, S.R., I.K.A., S.G. and C.I.A.; project administration, S.R., I.K.A., S.G. and C.I.A.; funding acquisition, S.R., I.K.A., S.G. and C.I.A. All authors have read and agreed to the published version of the manuscript.

Funding: This research received no external funding.

Institutional Review Board Statement: Not applicable.

Informed Consent Statement: Not applicable.

Data Availability Statement: Not applicable.

Acknowledgments: We would like to express our gratitude to the reviewers for the constructive criticism of this article.

Conflicts of Interest: The authors declare no conflict of interest.

References

1. Argyros, I.K.; Hilout, S. Weaker conditions for the convergence of Newton's method. *J. Complex.* **2012**, *28*, 364–387. [CrossRef]
2. Cordero, A.; Torregrosa, J.R. Variants of Newton's method using fifth-order quadrature formulas. *Appl. Math. Comput.* **2007**, *190*, 686–698. [CrossRef]
3. Argyros, I.K. Unified Convergence Criteria for Iterative Banach Space Valued Methods with Applications. *Mathematics* **2021**, *9*, 1942. [CrossRef]
4. Argyros, I.K. *The Theory and Applications of Iteration Methods*, 2nd ed.; Engineering Series; CRC Press, Taylor and Francis Group: Boca Raton, FL, USA, 2022.
5. Kou, J.; Wang, X.; Li, Y. Some eight order root finding three-step methods, Commun. *Nonlinear Sci. Numer. Simulat.* **2010**, *15*, 536–544. [CrossRef]
6. Argyros, I.K.; Magrenan, A.A. *A Contemporary Study of Iterative Methods*; Elsevier (Academic Press): New York, NY, USA, 2018.
7. Grau-Sanchez, M.; Grau, A.; Noguera, M. Ostrowski type methods for solving system of nonlinear equations. *Appl. Math. Comput.* **2011**, *218*, 2377–2385. [CrossRef]
8. Homeier, H.H.H. A modified Newton method with cubic convergence: The multivariate case. *J. Comput. Appl. Math.* **2004**, *169*, 161–169. [CrossRef]
9. Kantorovich, L.V.; Akilov, G.P. *Functional Analysis*; Pergamon Press: Oxford, UK, 1982.
10. Proinov, P.D. New general convergence theory for iterative processes and its applications to Newton–Kantorovich type theorems. *J. Complex.* **2010**, *26*, 3–42. [CrossRef]
11. Sharma, J.R.; Arora, H. Efficient derivative - free numerical methods for solving systems of nonlinear equations. *Comp. Appl. Math.* **2016**, *35*, 269–284. [CrossRef]
12. Xiao, X.; Yin, H. Achieving higher order of convergence for solving systems of nonlinear equations. *Appl. Math. Comput.* **2017**, *311*, 251–261. [CrossRef]
13. Noor, M.A.; Waseem, M. Some iterative methods for solving a system of nonlinear equations. *Comput. Math. Appl.* **2009**, *57*, 101–106. [CrossRef]
14. Traub, J.F. *Iterative Methods for the Solution of Equations*; Prentice Hall: Englewood Cliffs, NJ, USA, 1964.
15. Ezquerro, J.A.; Hernandez, M.A. *Newton's Method: An Updated Approach of Kantorovich's Theory*; Birkhäuser: Cham, Switzerland, 2018.
16. Nashed, M.Z.; Chen, X. Convergence of Newton-like methods for singular operator equations using outer inverses. *Numer. Math.* **1993**, *66*, 235–257. [CrossRef]
17. Shakhno, S.M.; Gnatyshyn, O.P. On an iterative Method of order 1.839... for solving nonlinear least squares problems. *Appl. Math. Appl.* **2005**, *161*, 253–264.
18. Verma, R. *New Trends in Fractional Programming*; Nova Science Publisher: New York, NY, USA, 2019.

axioms

MDPI

Article

Development of Patent Technology Prediction Model Based on Machine Learning

Chih-Wei Lee [1], Feng Tao [1], Yu-Yu Ma [2] and Hung-Lung Lin [3,*]

1 Institute of Industrial Economics, Jinan University, Guangzhou 510632, China; alanlee99983@gmail.com (C.-W.L.); fengtao@jnu.edu.cn (F.T.)
2 School of Education Science, Minnan Normal University, No. 36 Shi Qian Zhi St., Zhangzhou 363000, China; misssuperyoyo@gmail.com
3 School of Economics and Management, Sanming University, No. 25 Ching-Tung Rd., Sanming 365004, China
* Correspondence: hsa8936.hsa8936@msa.hinet.net

Abstract: Intellectual property rights have a great impact on the development of the automobile industry. Issues related to the timeliness of patent applications often arise, such as the inability of firms to predict new technologies and patents developed by peers. To find the proper direction of product development, the R&D departments of enterprises need to accurately predict the technology trends. Machine learning adopts calculation through a large amount of data through mathematical models and methods and finds the best solution at the fastest speed through repeated simulation and experiments, to provide decision makers with a reference basis. Therefore, this paper provides accurate forecasts through established models. In terms of the significance of management, the planning of future enterprise strategy can be divided into three stages as a short-term plan of 1–3 years, a medium-term plan of 3–5 years, and a long-term plan of 5–10 years. This study will give appropriate suggestions for the development of automobile industry technology.

Keywords: patent technology; intellectual property; automobile industry; artificial neural network; machine learning; ensemble learning

MSC: 68Uxx; 68Wxx

Citation: Lee, C.-W.; Tao, F.; Ma, Y.-Y.; Lin, H.-L. Development of Patent Technology Prediction Model Based on Machine Learning. *Axioms* **2022**, *11*, 253. https://doi.org/10.3390/axioms11060253

Academic Editor: Clemente Cesarano

Received: 27 March 2022
Accepted: 24 May 2022
Published: 26 May 2022

1. Introduction

With the development of China's economy, China's automobile industry has transformed from original equipment manufacturer (OEM) services between 2000 and 2010, to a new stage of independent research, development, and production of domestic brand cars through drawing lessons from the world's famed factories. According to the survey report of the China Association of Automobile Manufacturers, the sales volume of China's brands has increased year by year from USD 2.943 million in 2011 to USD 7.749 million in 2020, with an increase rate of about 263% [1]. In addition, the market share of China's domestic automobile brands has grown year by year from 29% in 2011 to 38.4% in 2020. This shows that the innovation and R&D achievements of Chinese domestic automobile brands through OEM and technical cooperation have won the recognition of market consumers.

Because of the progress and development of information technology, many products have been designed to provide customers with a combination of Internet Plus and the intellectualized experience of new-generation products. Just like the theory of the product lifecycle (PLC), every product must go through stages of development, growth, maturity, and decline [2]. To survive in the competitive environment, every enterprise must launch new products through innovation and R&D before reaching the final stage of its lifecycle. As stated by Pryshlakivsky and Searcy, enterprises should adopt different measures to launch new products or services and give new value to products or services at different stages of the product lifecycle to hold advantage in the highly competitive market and achieve the goal of sustainable operation [3].

Similarly, in the rapidly changing market environment of science and technology, the automobile industry needs to keep innovating. Based on the analysis of 13 years' patent data of 39 innovative enterprises in China's telecommunications, electrical machinery, automobile, and pharmaceutical industries, the cooperation breadth of employees has a positive impact on the innovation performance of enterprises [4]. The development of new automobile products refers to a series of decision-making processes from the research for selecting products that meet the needs of the market through to product design, and on to manufacturing process design, until normal production. Product development involves a wide range of aspects including design, engineering analysis, trial production, and experimentation with the components or technologies of new vehicles, such as improvement of automobile engine power, vehicle crash tests, computer-aided AEB automatic brakes, and so on [5]. Hence, the investment in automobile products must allocate limited resources to the projects which need to be developed effectively to achieve the best results.

The key process of the development of new automobile products is to accurately determine the direction of a new product's development. Automobile products differ from other products in the characteristics of its products, in addition to both innovation and science and technology, and the safety requirements are critical. As a consequence, it is very important to select the right direction to reduce the risks in development. Many studies have pointed out the risks of new product development, which can be manifested in the following aspects [6–8]:

(1) Technology development risk:

This refers to the requirement that the developed technology conform to scientific principles, but the reasons for development failure are complicated. For example, it is difficult to complete the research or meet technical difficulties because of the immature technology at the present stage. Chin et al. [9] proposed several new product development risks, which are described as follows. (a) The production risk refers to the failure to meet production requirements within a predetermined time. (b) The R&D risks caused by a person who cannot complete the product specification design within the expected time. (c) Supplier risk means that the supplier may not provide good materials or may not provide them within the expected period. (d) Product reliability risk refers to the risk that the expected performance will not be achieved under normal manufacturing procedures. It may be that inadequate conditions lead to the failure of the research, or it may be that the preconceived ideas of the participants turn out to be wrong and unworkable.

(2) Market competition risk:

This refers to the risk caused by market competition in the market. According to Allayannis et al. [10] and Guay and Kothari [11], the risk of market competition is composed of the following factors. (a) The scale of market competition: the greater the competitive power and cost of competitors, the greater the market risk will be (Allayannis et al., 2001). (b) The intensity of market competition: this is mainly reflected in the competition for market share to improve sales and profitability (Guay and Kothari, 2003). (c) R&D competition: this happens when the technology is still in progress and has been successfully developed by other researchers.

(3) Risk of an objective environment:

Due to changes in the objective social, economic, and technological environment, the original technological development is out of date or no longer necessary. The automobile industry is a typical intellectual-property-intensive industry, and its development depends heavily on intellectual property rights. In particular, the global automobile industry is at a critical moment of industrial restructuring and technological transformation. As an important force in the global automobile industry, intellectual property rights are indispensable.

Generally speaking, before developing a new technology or innovative products, the enterprise will first check the patent application data to determine whether there is similar technologies or products extant in the industry. In the process of patent inquiry, the timeliness of an application for patent certification is crucial; otherwise, the technology or product in the certification or research and development process cannot be queried correctly. For example, it is nearly impossible to know whether other companies are developing the same innovative technology or product, or whether the competition is still applying for certification. Finally, after the completion of technology or product development, the patent application often leads to disputes, thus causing significant damage to enterprises. According to the State Intellectual Property Office [12], the number of intellectual property rights and competition dispute cases in the automobile industry showed an increasing trend year by year from 2009 to 2018, with an average annual increase rate of 28.22%. Among the intellectual property and improper competition disputes in the automobile industry (manufacturing) in 2019, intellectual property infringement disputes accounted for 76.83%, unfair competition disputes accounted for 13.26%, and intellectual property contract disputes accounted for 9.45%. Presently, the global automobile industry is in a critical moment of industrial restructuring and technological transformation. As an important force in the global automobile industry, China's intellectual property rights of new patented technologies must be a top priority, whether this involves setting up joint ventures with famous overseas automobile enterprises, carrying out technology research and development cooperation projects with all parties, or designing and implementing OEM models. In the process of new product technology research and development, new patent disputes are an important issue worthy of attention. For example, in 2020, the proportion of patent infringement in China is as high as 10.8% [12].

In the automobile industry, many scholars have proposed effective methods to predict the technology, production, inventory, sales, and market conditions of the automobile industry, such as Yuan and Cai [13]. The growth curve method and entropy method were proposed to predict the future situation of vehicle power energy. The research results show that hybrid electric vehicles have the most promising future development prospects, followed by battery electric vehicles and traditional internal combustion engine vehicles. The development of fuel cell electric vehicles is slow. Hanggara [14] used the method of moving average combined with market supply and demand to forecast the automobile production in Indonesia, to reasonably estimate the production volume and solve the problem of overproduction. Babai et al. [15] put forward Bayesian parametric frequency and non-parametric methods for empirical evaluation of the demand of about 3000 inventory units in the automobile industry, and compared the proposed method with other methods. The results also proved that the proposed method could provide a more accurate decision-making reference for the inventory management plan of the automobile industry. Wan et al. [16] proposed the integration of principal component regression with neural network, support vector machine, and other methods, aiming to formulate a sales prediction model for electric vehicles. Wan et al., (2021) proposed the integration of principal component regression with a neural network, a support vector machine, and other methods for a sales prediction model of electric vehicles (EV). After an example analysis, it was verified that the integrated model had a good practical forecasting effect. The principal component regression–back propagation (PCR-BP) model and the principal component regression–support vector machine (PCR-SVM) model are better than a single model, such as the support vector machine model alone. Tsang et al. [17] proposed the fuzzy-based battery lifecycle prediction framework (FBLPF) to effectively manage the automobile market. This framework integrated the multi-responses Taguchi method (MRTM) and the adaptive neuro-fuzzy inference system (ANFIS), and the market forecast of the product lifecycle of electric vehicles can be carried out through the integrated method. The research results prove the accuracy of the proposed method and put forward corresponding plans and countermeasures for the sustainable development of energy and environmental protection in the automobile industry. Although these methods can effectively forecast the market profile and development prospects of the automobile industry, they must also reduce the risk involved in the automobile industry for enterprises in the process of product production, sales, and R&D. However, for professional managers or decision makers, the mathematical calculation process is complicated and tedious. Based on this point of view, many researchers have adopted machine learning methods to predict the technology development in the automobile industry. For instance, Lee M. [18] adopted the text mining model method of machine learning. Research on AI algorithm classification using patent data submitted from 1980 to 2017 can demonstrate the dynamic change pattern of the fusion of AI and EV technology. Wang et al. [19] stated that new product development in China's automobile industry can be predicted by machine learning methods. From 2001 to 2014, they obtained 1088 valid sample datasets from the Chinese automobile industry to construct an evaluation indicator system. Choi et al. [20] raised a hybrid method, which takes into account expert opinions, patents, and machine learning methods, analyzes the results, and combines semi-supervised learning with active learning to effectively find emerging and promising technologies. Lee et al. [21] helped pharmaceutical technology identify emerging patented technologies through machine learning and multilayer neural network model calculation and simulation. Teng et al. [22] used a VSM (vector space model) and K-MEAN to solve the technical problem of batteries developed by new technologies through machine learning. Suhail et al. [23] used machine learning to integrate random forest and decision tree to carry out calculations and simulations to help dentists make decisions during tooth extraction, avoiding errors caused by human judgment. Barrera-Animas et al. [24] used machine learning to conduct simulation and prediction, employing linear regression and a support vector model, etc., to solve the expensive and complex problems faced by the existing five major cities in the UK in meteorological forecasting. Ensafi et al. [25] adopted machine learning to predict the sales of seasonal goods with ARIMA and convolutional neural networks (CNN). Its advantage is that it can find out the most accurate trend of commodity sales through repeated calculation, help enterprises accurately forecast sales volume, and avoid the problem of overproduction and inventory in order to provide decision makers with a quick method for judgment. Machine learning adopts calculation through a large amount of data using mathematical models and methods and finds the best solution at the fastest speed through repeated simulation and experiment, providing decision makers a reference basis. Many studies also show the practicability and value of machine learning methods. Therefore, this paper proposes a new prediction method—"The concept of technology maturity combined with machine learning model". This method can model and forecast the status quo of patent technology in the automobile industry, aiming to provide decision makers and managers in the automobile industry with an accurate prediction of the trends of new technologies or products in the future market, before investing in research and development. Finally, the method reduces the significant losses caused by the patent disputes mentioned above. In addition, this study takes a case study of patented body technology in China's automobile industry for modeling and analysis, and compares the model accuracy of traditional time series and non-traditional machine learning methods, respectively, to prove that the proposed method is more accurate and stable than others, thus proving the stability and applicability of the model. Importantly, the proposed method can provide a systematic and scientific reference for decision makers and managers in the automobile industry to initiate technology or product R&D plans, and put forward valuable suggestions for researchers and enterprises.

To sum up, the background and purpose of this study are introduced in the introduction, and the main research structure and core are specifically divided into the following four parts. The literature review in Section 2 includes the technology forecasting method and the research on innovation for R&D and patent market forecasting. Section 3 mainly concerns the construction of the trend model of the R&D patent market, including a machine-learning-building, integrated-learning prediction model. Section 4 presents a case study analysis, including research analysis, model verification and discussion, and prediction of future development trends. The conclusion, presented in Section 5, summarizes the management and academic aspects of the proposed method.

2. Literature Review

2.1. Technology Prediction Methods for Innovation and R&D

A prediction is an estimate or calculation made about a future outcome that people are concerned about, or about an uncertain event that people want to comprehend in advance [26]. Making predictions is very important for business operations. Through different forecasting methods, decision makers of enterprises can understand the economic development or the future changes of the market to form the goals or decisions of their enterprises. Through scientific management methods, the risks and costs of enterprise operation can be reduced, and the enterprise objectives can be achieved smoothly [21]. Commonly used innovation and R&D technology forecasting methods can be divided into the following categories.

(1) Quantitative prediction method [21–27].

Quantitative prediction methods include trend extrapolation, analogies, causal models, and so on. Trend extrapolation is similar to the autoregressive integrated moving average model (ARIMA). Analogies are similar to support vector machines (SVM). Causal models are similar to linear regression (LR). Quantitative analysis has been successfully applied to different fields and to solve related problems. For example, it has been used to analyze the new patented technology of mobile communication in South Korea, based on the ARIMA model, and the information system of the Korean Intellectual Property Office (KIPO) was adopted for data collection [27]. According to the International Patent Classification (IPC), 20,294 patents were classified into 152 categories. Finally, Korea's major mobile communication technologies were classified into four categories. This provides an important reference standard for decision makers in government departments and related industries when investing in R&D. Researchers have used metrology and patent analysis to analyze the S curve in the logistic growth curve model of hydrogen energy and fuel cell technology, and they determined the best patent strategy for the fuel cell industry [28]. The results show that the S curve is an efficient means of quantifying a method of predicting the technology of cumulative published patent numbers. Researchers have used regression analysis to evaluate weapons technology in the defense industry, and proposed a method of constructing a technology map, which divides technologies into four categories according to their technical effects [29].

These studies confirmed the advantages of quantitative analysis, as follows: (a) different standards or variables can be considered at the same time, that is, an approach can include different standard variables in experiments and analyses in different environments to obtain the best results; (b) technology forecasts can be adapted to different industries; (c) quantitative forecasts can be applied to different products.

(2) Qualitative prediction methods and the combination of qualitative and quantitative methods [30–32].

Expert group judgment has different applications, such as the Delphi technique, interview, brainstorming, and nominal group techniques. The Delphi technique is an expert judgment method often used in technical forecasting, which is especially applicable when historical data are insufficient and require objectivity and independence of expert judgment compared with the other three methods.

(3) The combination of qualitative and quantitative methods [30–32].

By and large, the Delphi technique, focus group interviews, and brainstorming are commonly used to cope with multicriteria decision-making methods of quantitative analysis, such as analytic hierarchy process (AHP), analytic network process (ANP), entropy, and the technique for order preference by similarity to an ideal solution (TOPSIS). This combination has been successfully applied in different fields and solved related problems. For example, researchers used the expert interview method and ANP to predict the warehousing operation of out-stock and in-stock of the logistics center of a chain supermarket and optimized its warehousing classification management [30]. Researchers have used the Delphi technique and AHP to evaluate the factors that affect the success of start-up companies when rice bran polysaccharide is used in the Taiwan venture capital industry [31]. Researchers have used expert groups combined with entropy and TOPSIS to classify and forecast the warehouse management of green plant e-commerce vendors, and they developed methods for warehouse optimization [32]. These studies confirm the advantages of combining qualitative and quantitative methods, for example, (a) obtaining a variety of different but valuable perspectives; (b) being able to apply these perspectives to long-term and new products' forecasting.

To sum up, technological innovation prediction is the premise and basis of enterprise technological innovation decision making. Through the evaluation of innovation or research and development, enterprises can obtain an accurate sense of future technological development and the changing trends. This provides a scientific basis for enterprises to reduce subjectivity and blindness in processes of technological innovation decision making. In the competitive market and complicated environments, an enterprise's technological innovation determines its survival and development. Therefore, to ensure the correctness of technological innovation, enterprises should choose appropriate forecasting methods according to different environmental factors, such as time and place, to reduce the risks involved in enterprise operation.

2.2. *Research on Innovation, R&D, and Patent Market Prediction*

There have been many studies using various forecasting methods in patent R&D demand or market demand as follows.

(1) Research on traditional forecasting methods in patent technology and market demand.

Researchers have proposed that the future market trend and new patents of the home appliance industry can be predicted by combining the pearl curve with related indicators of home appliance isolation technology, and the results showed that the proposed method is effective in application [33]. Researchers classified and predicted the patent of "coherent light generator" based on bass and the ARIMA time series model, they and proposed a new classification standard for this technology (mainly divided into the first class and subclasses) [34]. Finally, viewpoints and countermeasures have been put forward for the future trend of first-class patents and subclasses of technologies through the analysis results. The authors of [35] proposed the use of LR and clustering technology to predict the future trend of new product development, supply, and demand in many global industries. The research revealed that the innovation of technology will accelerate the development of PLC for the uncertainty of products and sales demand, and proved that the proposed method can be used as an effective tool for decision making. The authors of [36] proposed the application of patent analysis with the concept of growth curve and technology maturity to predict the development of spare wind turbine technology.

The results show that the technology of jet engine wind turbines is in the early-maturity stage, the gearless wind turbine is at the end of its growth curve, and the airborne wind turbine is at the end of the maturity stage on the growth curve, which proves the effectiveness of the proposed method. The authors of [37] used support vector machines (SVMs) to conduct progressive analysis of difficult classification problems of patents. The results indicated that the proposed method can effectively classify patents and provide an important reference standard for inventors or lawyers when facing related problems. The authors of [38] used the S-curve and LR method to analyze the data of the United States Patent and Trademark Office (USPTO). New patents for unmanned vessel technologies (UVTs) were studied and the current technology stage of UVT was determined. The result reflected that UVTs are in the growth stage of their technology lifecycle and represents an emerging technology with future investment value.

(2) Research on machine learning in patent technology prediction.

The authors of [39] stated an improved method of machine learning to predict emerging technologies and verified it with the patent data provided by the United States Patent and Trademark Office. The research presented that the proposed method can effectively predict the future development of new technologies with an accuracy of up to 70%, which helps enterprises reduce costs and risks in the process of innovation and R&D, and enables enterprises to effectively carry out strategic investment. The authors of [40] applied patent and machine learning methods to design a new method combining coding and tag coding based on existing research on patent grant term prediction. The results show that the proposed method can effectively confirm the patent application grant period in the data of the Indian Patent Office. The authors of [41] used patent-related data provided by the United States Patent and Trademark Office to predict patents in the healthcare industry and classified different technologies by using the standard of cooperative patent classification. This study assessed the potential of different technology clusters in foreign countries to provide a reference for decision makers or managers of enterprises or national regulatory authorities regarding future investment in innovative R&D.

Cho et al., (2021) first constructed a communication network with association rules. Machine learning methods were then used to predict the future using various link prediction indices, and finally latent Dirichlet assignment (LDA) topic modeling was used to identify keywords related to the technology that is expected to converge [42]. The analysis of patent data of 2012–2014 from the US Patent and Trademark Office in the chemical engineering and environmental technology fields showed that the random forest model in machine learning has the best prediction effect on a 4-year interval. By predicting the new technology fields that may emerge in the future, the study could provide direction suggestions for companies focused on technological advances. The authors of [43] analyzed complex patent problems by combining self-organizing map (SOM), principal component analysis (PCA), and support vector machine calculus with machine learning methods, then compared it with a single machine learning method. The results showed that the proposed integrated machine learning method was more accurate and saved more resources than the single machine learning method. Using a machine learning and multilayer neural network method, researchers selected 18 input and 3 output indicators from the database of the United States Patent and Trademark Office for pharmaceutical technology and explored the nonlinear relationship between input and output indicators [21]. The result indicated that the multiple patent indicators can be used to identify whether a drug is worth developing at an early stage, before it was developed into a new pharmaceutical technology. The authors of [44] put forward the method of machine learning and semantic analysis of patented text information to judge the patented technology of vehicle signal and electronic message transmission, and to predict the trend of future development.

In summary, traditional patent and market demand forecasting has proved that the proposed methods can measure the utility value of new products or technologies in the input process and reduce the risk of enterprises, such as the dispute cases of new patents. However, these traditional methods also have many disadvantages or deficiencies, such as cumbersome and slow calculation processes, difficult data collection, uncertain information, and other problems [45–47]. Therefore, many studies put forward machine learning to replace traditional prediction methods, and the above research has proved the effectiveness of machine learning as a prediction method. Based on the existing research, this paper proposes various prediction and integration algorithms of machine learning, compared the time series methods, and proposed the feasibility of an innovative patent prediction method after a comprehensive comparison. Table 1 presents a comparison of the advantages and disadvantages of the proposed method and other model methods.

Table 1. Comparison of the advantages and disadvantages of the proposed method and other model methods.

Aspects	Prosed Method	Other Methods (Qualitative/Quantitative)
Advantages	(1) It can be combined with other classification and regression algorithms to improve its accuracy and stability and avoid overfitting by reducing the variation of results. (2) It is composed of processing nodes similar to human brain neurons. The greatest advantage of a neural network is that it can accurately predict complex problems. (3) The support vector machine method can effectively solve the classification and regression problems of high-dimensional features.	(1) A variety of different and valuable points of view can be gained. (2) It is suitable for long-term prediction and prediction of new products, and can be used when historical data is insufficient. (3) This method can make up for the lack of basic information.
Disadvantages	(1) This method is prone to overfitting. (2) This method is sensitive to missing data. (3) There are many neural network parameters in this method.	(1) It is less reliable for product prediction by region. (2) Qualitative advice is sometimes incomplete or impractical. (3) Generally, it is only applicable to the prediction of the total amount, but it has poor reliability when applied to regions, customers, and product categories.
Summary	After comparison, there are three reasons for choosing this scheme: (1) the calculation will be faster; (2) the obtained model will be more accurate; (3) it is suitable for a large amount of data and for the method of applying mathematics to assist in making decisions.	

3. Model Construction of R&D Patent Market Trend

This paper will build the model in separate three stages. The first stage is "machine learning-the construction of the ensemble learning prediction model". The theory of the model and the constructing procedure will be explained in this stage. The second stage is "the model validation". In this stage, the data of car body patent applications in China's automobile industry will be taken as a case study. In this paper, the relevant data collected by the Chinese Intellectual Property Office are used for modeling and analysis, and the errors between the proposed model and the traditional prediction model are compared to prove the accuracy and applicability of the proposed method. The third stage is "the forecast for future trends". Some suggestions and countermeasures are put forward for the analysis of market demand information of the automobile industry, providing a reference for use by the relevant personnel of the automobile industry and scholars. The construction process of this research model is described as follows, and the specific research framework is illustrated in Figure 1.

3.1. Stage 1: Machine Learning—The Construction of the Ensemble Learning Prediction Model

According to the research framework in Figure 1, the first stage, Stage 3.1, is machine learning—the construction of the ensemble learning prediction model. It includes data mining and the construction of the ensemble learning model and the ensemble learning prediction model.

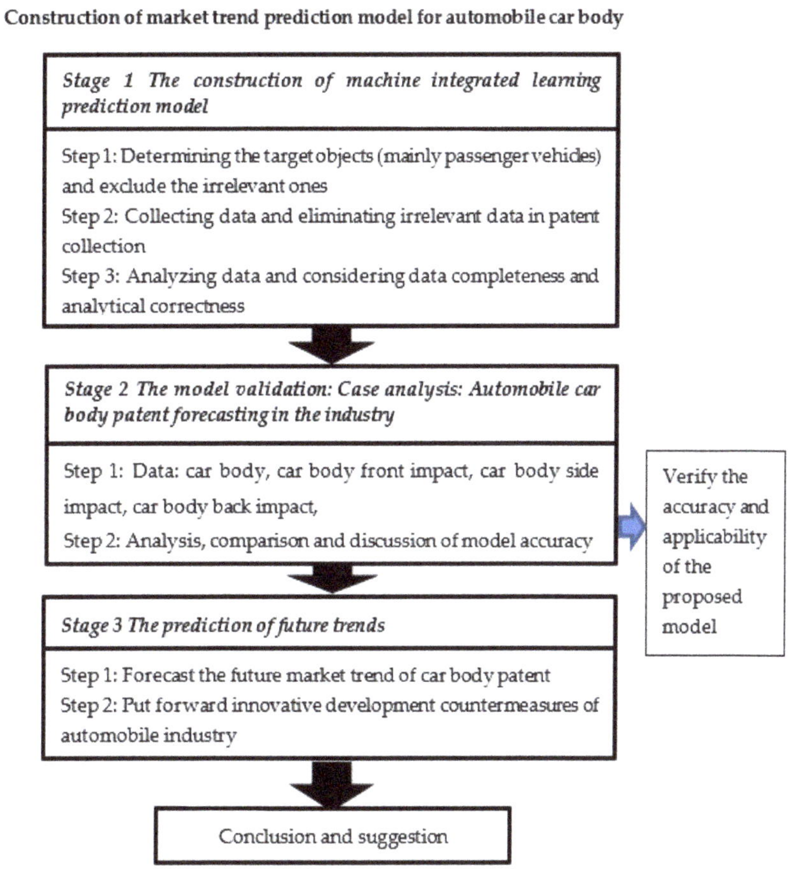

Figure 1. Research framework diagram.

3.1.1. Data Mining and Machine Learning—Ensemble Learning Model

First proposed by Breiman [46], bagging (bootstrap aggregating) is an ensemble learning algorithm for machine learning. Bagging combines the prediction results of each learning model through voting rules to make the final classification prediction. First, train all the other algorithms with the data, and then take all the predictions of the other algorithms as additional input. In general, bagging is an isomorphic model, and the same model is used for training in other learning model algorithms. After that, hard voting or soft voting rules are used to combine the prediction input of the other algorithms mentioned above to obtain the final prediction classification result.

Breiman [46] proposed the bagging (bootstrap aggregating) method, which combines multiple different prediction models by voting or averaging. Although each prediction model uses the same learning algorithm, they all adopt different training datasets. A schematic diagram of the bagging algorithm is shown in Figure 2.

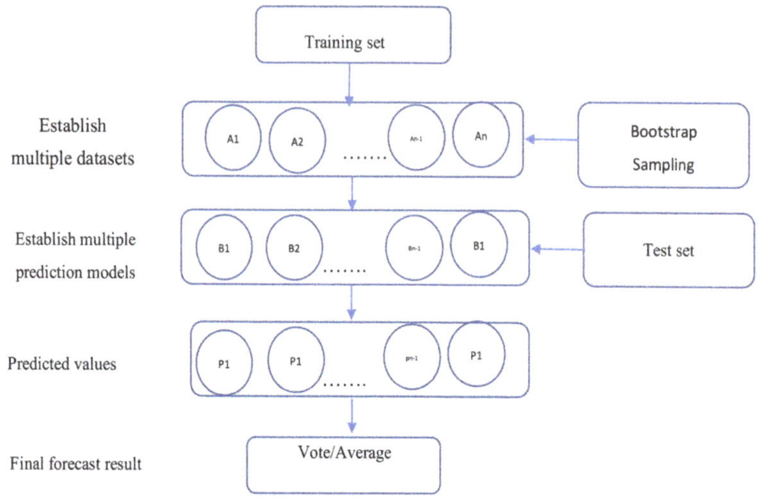

Figure 2. Schematic diagram of the bagging algorithm.

The principle of the bagging algorithm is as follows: Given a training set, D, with size N, the bagging method selects m subsets D_i with size N uniformly, and with the return (using the self-help sample method) as a new training set. M models can be obtained by using classification and regression algorithms on m training sets, and then the results of the bagging method can be obtained by taking average values and majority votes. In the end, the accuracy and stability are improved, while the variance of results is reduced to avoid the occurrence of overfitting.

The principle of the Bagging algorithm is described as follows. When a given dataset is $L = \{(x_1, y_1), \ldots, (x_m, y_m)\}$, the basic learner is $h(x, L)$. If the input is x, then Y is predicted by $h(x, L)$. Suppose that there is a dataset $\{L_k\}$ sequence, each consisting of M independent observations from the same distribution as L. The task was to obtain better learning results by using $\{L_k\}$, which was stronger than learning $h(x, L)$ in a single dataset. This requires the use of learning $\{h(x, L_K)\}$ sequences. If y is a number, then the process is to replace $\{h(x, L_K)\}$ with the average of $\{h(x, L_K)\}$ over K, that is, $h_A(x) = E_L h(x, L)$. Where E_L represents the mathematical expectation of L, and the subscript A of h_A represents a composition. If $h(x, L)$ predicts class $j \in \{1, \ldots J\}$, then one way to synthesize $h(x, L_K)$ is by voting. Let $M_j = \#\{K, h(x, L_K) = j\}$ so that will be $h_A(x) = \arg_j \max M_j$.

Step 1: Determining the target objects.

Firstly, the number of global body patents is taken as the target to predict the number of future patents.

Step 2: Collecting data.

Next, the patent data provided by the Chinese Intellectual Property Office are used to screen the patent data, patent classification, and the patent pool through retrieval. A total of 46 years of statistical data from 1974 to 2020 were used to collect and preprocess the data.

Step 3: Analyzing data.

Finally, WEKA software is applied to perform data mining tasks. After the process of data preprocessing, clustering, classification, and testing the model and the parameters, the machine learning technology is applied to automatically perform a calculation to obtain the model and the parameter values.

3.1.2. On the Basis of Machine Learning—The Construction of the Ensemble Learning Prediction Model

Ensemble learning, also known as multiple classifier systems, is composed of multiple base learners whose spirit is to gather the "wisdom of crowds". The generalization ability of ensemble learning is usually stronger than that of a base learner. The base learner can be generated by substituting the base learning algorithm into the training sample, and such a base algorithm includes a decision tree, a neural network, etc., though most ensemble learning methods use a single base.

A learning algorithm is used to produce homogeneous base learners; there are still other methods that use different learning algorithms to produce heterogeneous learners. Additionally, because there is no single base learning algorithm, basic learners can also be used as component learners or individual learners.

In principle, ensemble learning is divided into two steps. First, several basic learners are generated in parallel or sequential patterns. Later, all the basic learners are used together, and common merging methods include the concept of majority voting (classification problems) and the concept of weighted averaging (regression problems). Generally speaking, to attain a good ensemble learning model, the base learner should be as accurate as possible, but also as diverse as possible. The accuracy of a learner can be measured using cross-validation or hold-out tests, but there is no rigorous measure of diversity.

There are many approaches to ensemble learning, three of which are described in detail here.

1. Leo Breiman proposed bagging, also known as bootstrap aggregation or bootstrap, as a simple and powerful ensemble learning method. Meanwhile, many homogeneous weak learners are considered, and these weak learners are independent and parallel-constructed; their respective results are determined by averaging or voting [46].
2. Boosting, first put forward by Freund [47], is also a weak learner with a good deal of homogeneity. Unlike bagging, these basic models adapt and learn sequentially and combine the results in a deterministic strategy.
3. Stacking is a weak learner using heterogeneity. It can construct the respective models in parallel and combine the prediction results of different weak learners to train a metamodel and draw conclusions.

Ensemble learning is a kind of supervised learning. This method establishes multiple hypotheses by multiple learning algorithms, and combines them into a whole hypothesis by way of weight, so as to make a reasonable prediction of the test data. Many studies have shown that prediction using ensemble learning is more accurate than a single hypothesis.

In the learning algorithm, the training data need to be set up first. Each training material is made up of a special vector and a category tag, Y. Secondly, the real function is computed. Suppose the real function, f, exists, such that the identity $y = f(x)$ is true. Finally, the learning algorithm and hypothesis are verified. The goal of the learning algorithm is to find a hypothesis, h, such that $h \approx f$ formula.

The ensemble learning model consists of a set of hypotheses $\{h_1, h_2, \ldots, h_n\}$ and a set of hypothesis weights $\{W_1, W_2, \ldots, W_n\}$, as shown in Formula (1):

$$h(x) = W_1 h_1(x) + W_2 h_2(x) + \ldots \ldots \ldots + W_n h_n(x) \tag{1}$$

where $h(x)$ is the ensemble learning model, $\{h_1, h_2, \ldots, h_n\}$ is a set of hypotheses constructed by multiple learning algorithms, $\{W_1, W_2, \ldots, W_n\}$ is the corresponding weight of each hypothesis, and the final prediction is obtained by combining the weight of each hypothesis and individual hypotheses. For example, first, apply the WEKA software, then select the decision stump classifier, and select tenfold cross-validation for test option training and evaluation. Next, select the AdaboostM1 classifier, which is an ensemble learner using the lifting algorithm. To compare with the decision stump classifier, the base classifier of AdaboostM1 is set as the decision stump classifier. After confirmation, select the training button for training, and there are multiple classifiers to choose from. The number of iterations in the parameter setting is set to 10 by default, that is, the training will carry out the decision stump classifier 10 times. The schematic diagram of the ensemble learning model of this paper is shown in Figure 3.

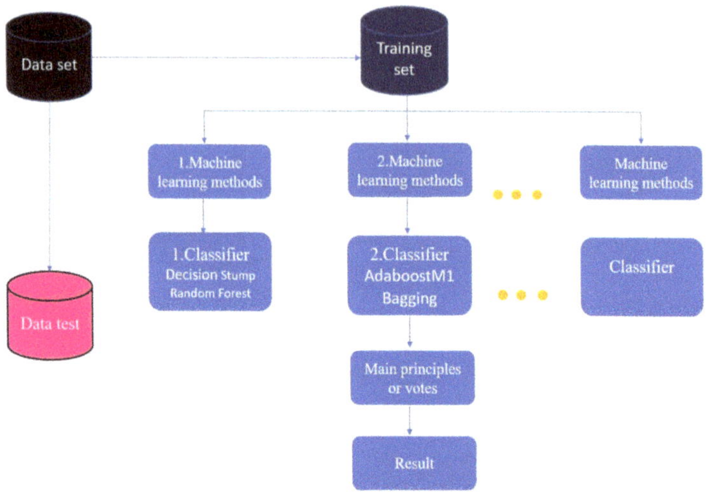

Figure 3. The schematic diagram of the ensemble learning model.

4. Research Analysis—Car Body Patent Forecasting for the Automobile Industry

The main content of Section 4 includes the following three parts. Section 4.1 is the research analysis. This part mainly explains the source and basis of the collected data. Section 4.2 is the model verification and discussion. This part focuses on analyzing each model based on the data in Section 4.1 to verify the accuracy of the proposed model and each model. Section 4.3 is the forecast of the future trend.

4.1. The Research Analysis

This paper takes vehicle safety collisions as samples. The main reason is that in addition to the safety of the car body, it also includes seat belts, airbags, safety seats, and automatic emergency braking, etc. The development and manufacture of these safety protection measures will be based on the main consideration of car body safety collision. For example, when the car body design is not secure, safety belts, airbags, and seats cannot be functional in protecting life safety [48]. In addition, the body structure has also been affected by environmental protection policies in recent years. For example, strengthening the rigid structure of the body will increase the weight of the body, which may cause more fuel or electricity consumption. Therefore, this paper will take the body collision as the research sample, and is expected to put forward specific development countermeasures and suggestions for future patent research and development of the automobile industry through the examination results.

Step 1: The collection of sample data.

The patent database provided by the Intellectual Property Office of the People's Republic of China was used as the basis for data analysis. It is difficult to search for the correct patent data of safety car bodies. This is mainly because of the large amount of literature, and the number of preliminarily searched studies reached 30,000. In addition, the International Patent Classification (IPC) standard used does not classify according to different models (such as trucks, small buses, buses, etc.), and there is no unified standard for some key components (such as beams, plates, columns, etc.). Therefore, the classification systems of Japan and the United States were adopted in this study as the main retrieval basis, and then the keywords of IPC classification were used for retrieval (as shown in Table 2). Finally, the recall rates of the three famous Japanese automobile companies, including Toyota Auto Corporation, Mazda Motor Corporation, and Mitsubishi Auto Industry Corporation, were taken as data samples. For American studies, 90 studies were randomly selected for manual reading, and 83 studies related to the retrieval subject were obtained, with an accuracy of about 92%. Finally, the accuracy was 100% by manual work. The scope of patent data is a total of 46 years from 1974 to 2020.

Table 2. Table of automobile crash safety technology.

Level 1 Classification	Level 2 Classification	Level 3 Classification
Safe car body (B62D21, B62D23, B62D25)	Car body that reduces front impact damage (B62D 21/00; B62D 23/00; B62D 25/00)	Front cross member Front rail Impact energy absorbing device A pillar Upper rail Door panel Front floor Front panel Subframe Splash shield stiffener Combinatorial optimization and others
	Car body that reduces side impact damage (B62D 21/00; B62D 23/00; B62D 25/00)	B pillar Lower rail Door panel and guard assay Floor assembly Roof member Combinatorial optimization and others
	Car body that reduces rear impact damage (B62D 21/00; B62D 23/00; B62D 25/00)	C pillar Back floor Back rail Back cross member Combinatorial optimization and others

Step 2: Pretest the predicted data.

The classification of automobile industry technologies in this study is shown in Table 2. The first level of classification is the safe car body, and the second level of classification is subdivided into the front-collision-damage-reduction car body, side-collision-damage-reduction car body, and rear-collision-damage-reduction car body, and finally corresponds to the parts of the third level of classification.

The development of the retrieval strategy, using the International Patent Classification (IPC) as a large category, is coordinated with Table 2. For example, when the keyword B62D corresponds to the safe car body, it can combine the standard classification with the actual terms used in the automobile industry.

The data were taken as samples from 1974 to 2011, and the linear regression method in machine learning was used to establish the mathematical model and judge whether the fitting was feasible. For example, Rsq > 80%: if the model is established, then patent data can be further predicted. First, the accumulative number of automobile body patents is predicted to be 4772 in 2012 and 5484 in 2016. It can be judged that the model is regular and predictive. Second, the cumulative number of predicted patents for the front collision of the car body is 2856 in 2012 to 3144 in 2016, showing that the model is regular and predictive. Third, the accumulative number of side collision patents was 1511 in 2012, but it could not predict the number in 2016, so it showed that the model did not have regularity and predictability. For the fourth, the accumulative number of rear collision patents for the car body was 454 in 2012, but the number in 2016 could not be predicted, so the model can be considered to not have regularity and predictability.

Therefore, the car body patent data using International Patent Classification (IPC) and level 1 classification are regular and predictive. The data of the International Patent Classification (IPC) and the level 2 classification, such as front, side, or back collision, are not regular and predictable, so it is easy to misjudge the prediction of the technology lifecycle. Consequently, the subsequent use of data will mainly be International Patent Classification (IPC) and level 1 classification of the car body patent.

Step 3: The consistency test.

The model adaptability was tested with the level 1 data of the safe car body according to the results of the pretest in Step 2 in this paper. The general methods of ensemble learning include voting, boosting, and bagging. In terms of effect, the AdaBoostM1 algorithm of boosting is the most effective. The idea of the bagging method is to train multiple classifiers with random sampling which are put back so that the "lower-level" classifiers pay more attention to the misclassified data of the "upper level". Finally, the result of each classifier is weighed and combined to make the decision. Voting applies multiple classifiers for optional combinations, but the disadvantage is that the majority rules can only avoid the worst-case scenarios. Therefore, in this study, boosting and bagging were used to test adaptability, and voting was excluded.

A decision stump was used as a classifier to verify the adaptability of boosting. The accuracy rate of the test results of the first training was 76.59%. The higher the accuracy rate is, the better result it is, and it is considered practical when the accuracy rate is over 80%. If it cannot meet the standard, then data training needs to be redone to improve the accuracy rate. In the method of improving the accuracy of data, AdaboostM1 was used to train the data, and the parameters were set to 10 iterations. The final classification accuracy was 100%, which represented the adaptability of the boosting method in this paper.

In this paper, folding cross-validation was used as the test option for training and evaluation of bagging adaptability, and the classification accuracy rate was 96.69%. The accuracy of the bagging method meets the requirements as long as it reaches 80%, but in this paper, the classifier training was carried out for the second time in pursuit of higher accuracy and the Automobile WEKA was used to improve the performance of the ensemble learner. The random forest classifier was used as the comparison standard, and the final classification accuracy rate was 98.88%, which showed that the results could make a correct judgment.

In brief, the results of the above two stages showed that the adaptability test of this paper corresponds to the hypothesis of the theory, so the results can provide a relatively reliable guarantee for the subsequent prediction results.

Step 4: The error result prediction.

Based on the test results of Step 3, this study used the ensemble bagging method to make a prediction and compared the errors of each period through the historical data from 2001 to 2020. The prediction results of each period are shown in Table 2. The average absolute error was 55.25, which was more accurate than other single prediction models. In order to verify the accuracy of the proposed model, this paper analyzes and compares the traditional prediction methods in Section 4.2 to prove the feasibility and applicability of the proposed model in patent prediction.

4.2. Validation and Discussion of the Model

In order to verify the accuracy of the model, this study is explained in three parts, as follows. The first part is to compare the accuracy with different prediction methods. In this study, absolute error was used to verify the accuracy of the proposed model and other methods, such as pearl curve, the ARIMA method, the regression method, the support vector machine (SVR) method, and the ensemble bagging method of neural networks (BPR), to prove the validity of the proposed method. The second part is to compare the accuracy with the posterior error test. In this study, the method proposed by Julong, D [49] was used to calculate the error of the prediction results, to judge the reliability of the prediction model.

The third part is the co-integration test (CI) and the error correction model (ECM). The CI method was proposed by Engle and Granger [50], and it mainly conducts unit root test on the residual of the regression equation. If the residual sequence is stationary, then it indicates that there is a co-integration relationship between the variables of the equation, otherwise there is no co-integration relationship. The ECM, proposed by Davidson et al. [51], is mainly the influence of short-term fluctuations of variables. Secondly, variables deviate from the long-term equilibrium relationship in short-term fluctuations. These three parts are described below.

(1) The comparison of the accuracy with different prediction methods.

To verify the accuracy of the proposed model, pearl curve, ARIMA, the regression method, the support vector machine (SVM) method, the neural network (BPR), ensemble learning (bag method), and other methods are compared, respectively. The actual value, the theoretical value, the absolute error, and the mean absolute error of each period from 2001 to 2020 are presented in Table 3. According to the mean absolute error analysis, the ensemble learning (bagging method) is 55 and the pearl curve is 73.8, which shows that the bagging method model proposed in this paper is more accurate than the other models.

Table 3. Predictive performance and absolute error of global body patents.

Year	Patent	Pearl Curve		ARIMA		Regression		Support Vector Machine		Neural Network		Ensemble (Bagging)	
	Actual Value	Predictive Value	Error	Predictive Value	Error	Predictive Value	Error	Predictive Value	Error	Predictive Value	Error	Predictive Value	Error
2001	209	206	3	217.5	9	185	24	333	124	217	8	189	20
2002	178	222	44	230.8	53	182	4	251	73	251	73	176	2
2003	241	234	7	244.9	4	180	61	233	8	212	29	181	60
2004	243	243	0	258.1	15	178	65	343	100	215	28	188	55
2005	358	247	111	271.5	87	175	183	246	112	224	134	191	167
2006	304	246	58	284.4	20	173	131	372	68	227	77	232	72
2007	364	240	124	297.2	67	171	193	198	166	250	114	254	110
2008	405	231	174	309.7	95	169	236	256	149	224	181	286	119
2009	368	217	151	321.9	46	167	201	483	115	225	143	320	48
2010	376	201	175	334	42	165	211	322	54	228	148	349	27
2011	219	184	35	345.8	127	163	56	418	199	227	8	165	54
2012	69	221	152	357.3	288	161	92	408	339	240	171	155	86
2013	124	205	81	368.6	245	159	35	421	297	224	100	145	21
2014	89	187	98	379.7	291	157	68	450	361	224	135	168	79
2015	95	170	75	390.6	296	155	60	457	362	224	129	168	73
2016	91	152	61	401.2	310	153	62	444	353	224	133	98	7
2017	110	136	26	411.5	302	151	41	434	324	229	119	102	8
2018	92	120	28	421.7	330	149	57	440	348	225	133	113	21
2019	105	106	1	431.5	327	148	43	438	333	225	120	93	12
2020	164	92	72	441.2	277	146	18	415	251	226	62	100	64
Mean absolute error	NA	NA	73.8	NA	161.39	NA	92.05	NA	206.8	NA	102.25	NA	55.25

It can be further observed from Figure 4 that the red curve is the number of existing patents (the actual value). After comparing with the theories predicted by other models, it can be concluded that ARIMA is more accurate in the early stage (2001–2009), and the proposed model (ensemble bagging) is more accurate in the middle stage (2010–2012) and the latter stage (2013–2020). However, they will lose accuracy in different intervals, and the method proposed in this paper has stronger stability. In addition, from the analysis results of the trend criterion, it can be observed that the bagging method stage result is better, and the stability of the three stages will be observed in the following part.

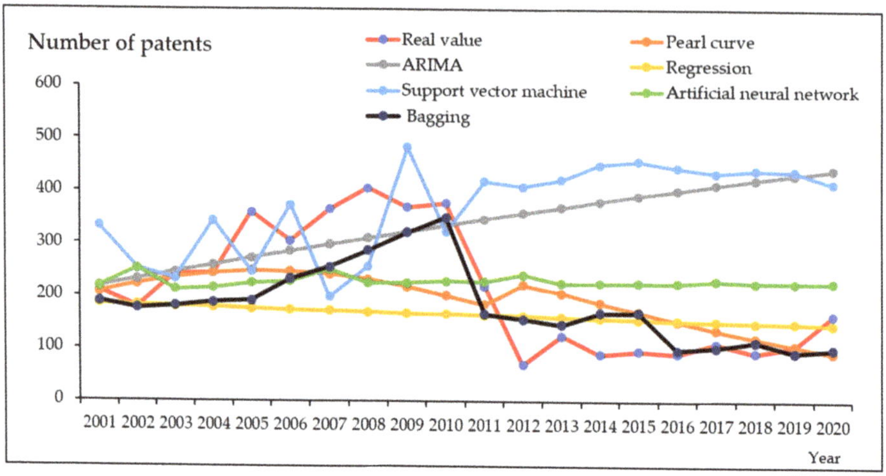

Figure 4. The trend of the actual patent number and various prediction methods.

As shown in Figure 4, the results of comparing the three intervals from the average absolute errors of different intervals are as follows. The first interval is from 2001 to 2009, in which ARIMA is the most accurate, with an error of 44. The second interval is from 2010 to 2012, during which the proposed model (the true ensemble bagging method) is the most accurate, with an error of 196. The third segment is from 2013 to 2020, which is also the most accurate model (the true ensemble bagging method), with an error value of 36. By comprehensive observation of Figures 4 and 5, although each method has its accuracy interval or period in different intervals or periods, the accuracy of the model proposed in this study (the true ensemble bagging method) is more accurate than other models in the overall trend (different intervals or periods).

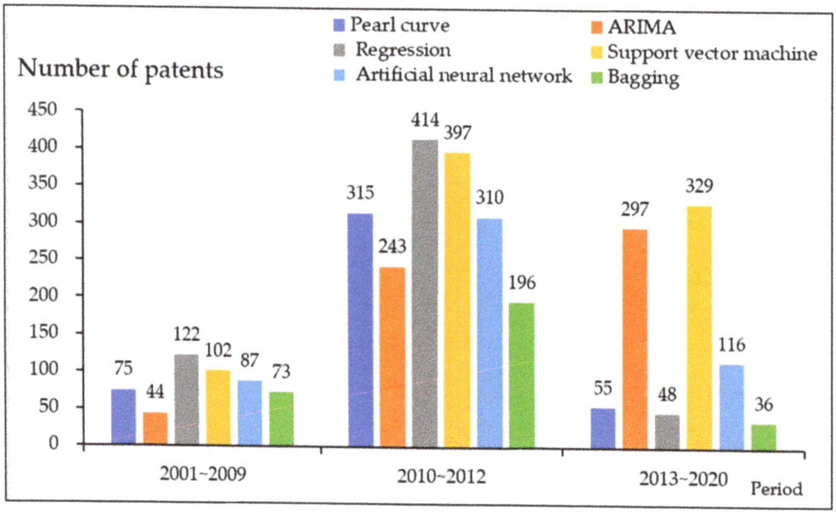

Figure 5. Mean absolute error (lower means more accurate).

(2) The posterior error test method.

After establishing the integrated bagging model, the usability and reliability of the model were tested. In this paper, the posterior error test method was adopted. Let

$\delta_i = f_i - \overline{f}_i (i = 1, 2, 3, \ldots, n)$, where f_i is the number of patent applications in a certain year, $\overline{f}_i$ is the estimated amount calculated by the integrated bagging model, and δ_i is the residual.

$\overline{f} = \frac{1}{n}\sum_{i=1}^{n} f_i$; $\overline{\delta} = \frac{1}{n}\sum_{i=1}^{n} \delta_i$; Standard deviation of raw data $S_1 = \sqrt{\frac{1}{n}\sum_{i=1}^{n}\left(f_i - \overline{f}\right)^2}$;

Standard deviation of residual $S_2 = \sqrt{\frac{1}{n}\sum_{i=1}^{n}\left(\delta_i - \overline{\delta}\right)^2}$.

Calculate variance ratio $c = \frac{S_2}{S_1}$ and small error probability $p = p\{|\delta_i - \overline{\delta}| \langle 0.6745 S_1 \}$.

According to the values of C index and p index, the model level is determined as shown in Table 4. According to Table 5 data, $\overline{f}$ = 210.2, $\overline{\delta}$ = 26.55, S1 = 115.74, S2 = 65.86. The posterior error ratio C = 0.56 and the small error probability p = 1 were calculated. By comparing the posterior test table (see Table 4), it can be concluded that the prediction of patent application volume by the integrated bagging model is level 3 (generally satisfied). The verification of the actual application data above shows that the bagging model has high reliability for patent prediction.

Table 4. Posterior error test table.

p Index	*C* Index	Model Class
>0.95	<0.35	Level 1 (very satisfied)
>0.8	<0.5	Level 2 (satisfied)
>0.7	<0.65	Level 3 (generally satisfied)
<0.7	≤0.7	Level 4 (unqualified)

Table 5. Actual and forecast number of patents.

Year	Quantity (Actual Value)	Forecast Quantity	Residual Error
2001	209	189	20
2002	178	176	2
2003	241	181	60
2004	243	188	55
2005	358	191	167
2006	304	232	72
2007	364	254	110
2008	405	286	119
2009	368	320	48
2010	376	349	27
2011	219	165	54
2012	69	155	−86
2013	124	145	−21
2014	89	168	−79
2015	95	168	−73
2016	91	98	−7
2017	110	102	8
2018	92	113	−21
2019	105	93	12
2020	164	100	64

(3) Co-Integration and Error Correction Model (ECM).

The main theoretical basis of CI and ECM is that in many time series studies, the data fluctuation is not a stationary phenomenon, but a random process. In this method, difference methods (DM) are used to change the original unstable sequence into a stable one. For example, the equilibrium degree of short-term and long-term fluctuations is used to provide the model with higher prediction accuracy [52]. Therefore, this paper will verify the accuracy of the model again through this method, and the main analysis process is described below.

Step 1: The first step is to perform a unit root test on the actual value (variable A).

First of all, the trend chart is made for the actual value (variable A) data, as shown in Figure 6, from which the phenomenon of data containing the trend can be judged. Subsequently, augmented Dickey–Fuller (ADF) was used for testing. It can be seen from Table 6 that the insignificant *p*-Value in the original sequence test column (0.6869) means that the actual value (variable A) was non-stationary and there a unit root, so difference processing was required. Finally, the first-order difference sequence unit root test was performed on the actual sequence value (variable A). It can be seen from Table 6 that the *p*-Value in the column of the first-order difference sequence was significant (0.0430), which means that the sequence data of the actual value (variable A) was stationary. If the *p*-Value of the original sequence test was not significant, then the difference method would continue to process until the *p*-Value became significant.

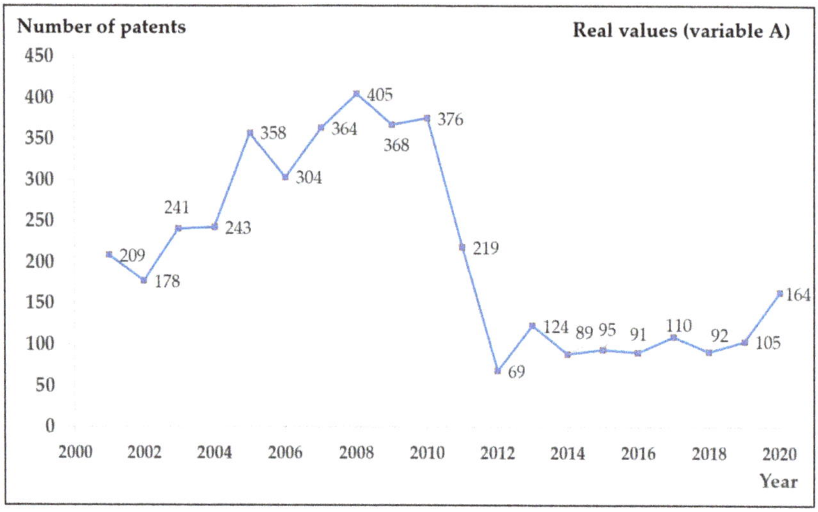

Figure 6. Trend diagram of real values (variable A).

Table 6. Unit root test results of actual values (variable A).

Process		Level	t-Statistic	Prob. *
Original sequence test	ADFTS Test critical values	1%	−1.752625 −4.532598	0.6869
First order difference sequence	ADFTS Test critical values	1%	−3.775465 −4.571559	0.0430 *

Note 1: Augmented Dickey–Fuller Test Statistic (ADFTS). Note 2: * = $p < 0.05$.

Step 2: The second step is to perform unit root test on the theoretical predicted value (variable B).

This step was tested in the same way as the previous step, with a unit and test for the theoretically predicted value (variable B). Figure 7 shows that the data of the theoretically predicted value has a tendency, so the ADF test was carried out. The results of the ADF test are shown in Table 7. The insignificant *p*-Value (0.6280) in the sequence test column indicates that the theoretically predicted value (variable B) was a non-stationary phenomenon with a unit root, so differential processing was required. Finally, the first-order difference sequence unit root test was performed on the predicted value of sequence theory (variable B). It can be seen from Table 7 that the *p*-Value in the column of the first-order difference sequence was significant (0.0245), which means that the sequence data of the theoretically predicted value (variable B) was a stationary phenomenon.

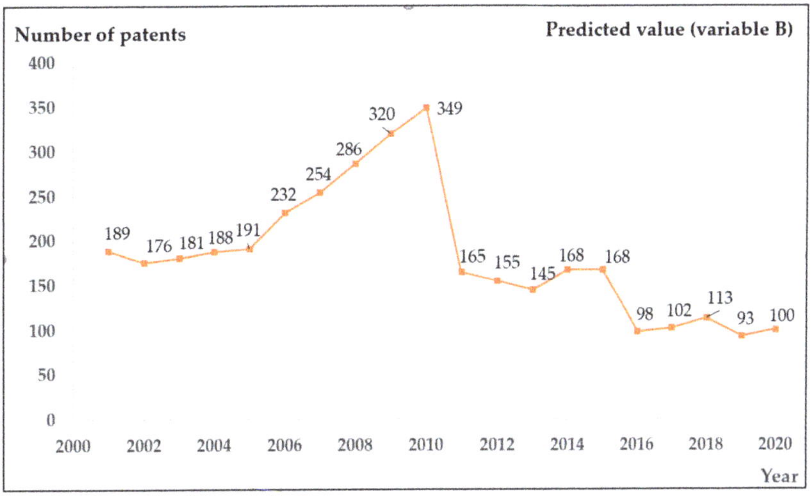

Figure 7. Trend diagram of predicted value (variable B).

Table 7. Unit root test results of actual values (variable B).

Process		Level	t-Statistic	Prob. *
Original sequence test	ADFTS Test critical values	1%	−1.874321 −4.532598	0.6280
First order difference sequence	ADFTS Test critical values	1%	−4.087372 −4.571559	0.0245 *

Note 1: Augmented Dickey–Fuller Test Statistic (ADFTS). Note 2: * = $p < 0.05$.

Step 3: Third step is to test the stationarity of the residual sequence.

First, both the actual value and the theoretical prediction (variable A and variable B) are first-order differences, so A regression model can be established for co-integration analysis. Then, the least square method is used to estimate the regression model, and the residual sequence value can be obtained. Figure 8 shows the trend diagram of residual sequence values in each period. Finally, the unit root of residual error between the actual value and the theoretical value (variables A and B) was tested, and the results are shown in Table 8. It can be seen from Table 8 that the p-Value of ADF test result was significant (0.0000), which means that the residual sequence data were stable and the co-integration relationship between variables existed.

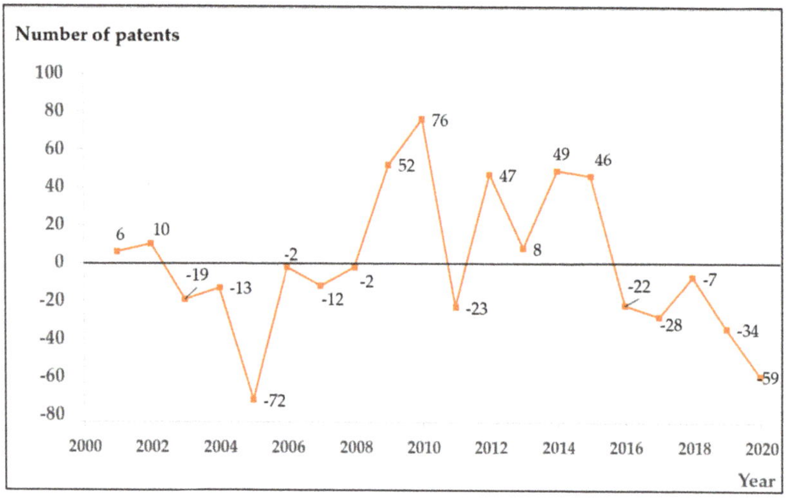

Figure 8. Residual sequence trend diagram of actual value and theoretical value (A and B variables).

Table 8. Residual unit root test results of actual and theoretical values (A and B variables).

Values / Tests	t-Statistic	Prob.*
ADFTS	−6.740233	0.0000 **
Test critical values: 1% level	−2.699769	

Note 1: Augmented Dickey–Fuller Test Statistic (ADFTS). Note 2: * = $p < 0.05$, ** = $p < 0.01$

Step 4: Error correction model (ECM).

It is generated according to the first-order autoregressive distributed lag model (ECM), which describes the short-term fluctuation Δyt of the explained variable. $\left(\frac{\beta_0}{\beta_1-1} + y + \frac{\beta_2+\beta_3}{\beta_1-1}x_t - 1\right)$ is the error correction term, and $(\beta_1 - 1)$ is the coefficient of the error term, also known as the adjustment coefficient, which reflects the degree to which the short-term fluctuation of the variable deviates from the long-term equilibrium. Since there was a co-integration relationship between variables A and B, the ECM model could be established, and the residual sequence of the regression model obtained was the value of the error correction term ECM. We inputted the variables of the error correction term model, selected OLS for estimation, and obtained the error correction model results, as shown in Table 9. The coefficient of the error correction term ECM(−1) was estimated to be significant at the 20% test level, reflecting the extent to which the short-term error fluctuation of −0.107 deviates from the long-term equilibrium.

Table 9. Error correction model and equation estimation.

Process	Variable	Coefficient	Std. Error	t-Statistic	Prob.
EECM (short-term error level)	C	−2.503389	12.14467	−0.206131	0.8397
	D(INC02)	0.359942	0.177777	2.024687	0.0624
	ECM(−1)	−0.107066	0.331128	−0.323337	0.7512
EECM (long-term error level)	C	−3.844246	10.35557	−0.371225	0.7151
	D(INC02)	0.354652	0.156139	2.271378	0.0364

Note: estimation of error correction model (EECM).

As shown in Table 9, the coefficient of short-term error correction term [ECM(−1)] verified in this study was −0.107, taking the absolute value, so the estimated value of test error tended to 11%. Similarly, the coefficient with a long-term error level of [D(INC02)] was 0.354652, so the estimated test error was close to 35%. In summary, according to Lin et al. [53], as long as the estimated short-term test error value is less than 30% and the estimated long-term test error value is less than 37%, the model is feasible. However, the long-term estimated value of this study was 35% and the short-term estimated value was 10%. Therefore, the model error of this study is feasible.

In summary, there are three error verification methods in this study, the first is the accuracy comparison of different prediction methods, the second is the method using the posterior error test, and the third is the co-integration and error correction model. The results of the above three kinds of test errors show that the prediction method proposed in this study is reliable in error precision determination.

We adopted three error verification methods. The first is the accuracy comparison of different prediction methods, the second is the method of posterior error test, and the third is the co-integration and error correction model. According to the analysis results, the first ensemble (bagging) method was more accurate, the second model was generally satisfied, and the third model had a short-term fluctuation of $-0.10 < -0.30$. According to Lin et al. (2011), as long as <0.3, the model is an adaptation. Therefore, the model error of this paper is acceptable.

4.3. Forecast the Future Development Trend

In this study, the validity of the proposed method was verified by the accuracy of the validation results, so the global car body patent was forecast for the next 10 years. It can be observed from the predicted results that the number of patents decreased year by year from 161 in 2020 to 144 in 2030, with a projected decline rate of 15.28% over the next 10 years (Figure 9).

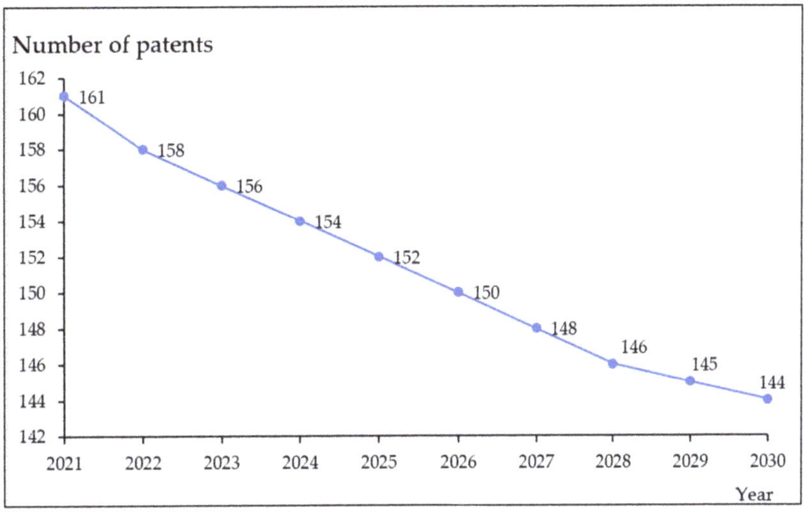

Figure 9. Prediction of number of patents by ensemble learning bagging method.

From 161 cases in 2021 to 154 cases in 2024, and to 148 cases in 2027, a decline is predicted in the rate of every three years. The total number of cases will drop 15.28 percent to 144 cases by 2030. This shows that the product technology lifecycle moves from maturity period to decline period. The results indicate that the research and development of rigid strength of car body are in a mature stage. At present, the development patents of body patent technology mostly take body rigidity as the main research and development technology. Although the body rigidity is strengthened to meet the requirements of safety materials (such as steel plates as structural parts and cover parts), it also increases the load of the car itself. It may cause problems in environmental protection and energy-saving that do not conform to economic effects and carbon emissions. Therefore, new and other technologies (such as energy-saving engines) should be developed at the same time to overcome such problems. In the research conclusion, this study will put forward future suggestions on the analysis results.

5. Conclusions

In this study, a new forecasting method, the "concept of technology maturity combined with machine learning model" was proposed to model and forecast the status quo of patented technology in the automobile industry. It is expected that the proposed method can provide decision makers and managers in the automotive industry with an accurate prediction of the future trend of new technologies or products in the industry market before investing in new technologies or product research and development, so as to reduce the significant losses of enterprises caused by patent disputes. In addition, this study was modeled and analyzed by a case study of body patent technology in China's automobile industry, and the results prove that the proposed model has stability and applicability in patent prediction results. What is important is that this method can provide a systematic and scientific decision-making reference for decision makers or managers in the automotive industry to use when making new technology or product research and development plans, and bring value to academic and practical circles. Finally, according to the results of this study, suggestions for the industry and academia are put forward as follows.

First, our advice to the industry is as follows: According to the S-curve of the theory of inventive problem-solving theory (TIPS) [54], the technological evolution of products can be divided into infancy (initial stage), the growth stage, the maturity stage, and the decline stage. The lifecycle of the technical system can be judged according to the curve characteristics of the product.

According to the comparison of patent quantity and the S-shaped curve in Figure 10, patents in the whole region started between 1980 and 2030. From 1980 to 1990 is the beginning period. From 2001 to 2010, the number of cases increased from 209 to 376, belonging to the growth stage. From 2011 to 2020, the number of cases decreased from 219 to 164, belonging to the mature stage. The number of cases is expected to decrease from 164 to 144 between 2020 and 2030. The maturity period is characterized by a slight decrease in the number of patents every year, and a slight increase in performance parameters and the invention level, which belong to the first level. Therefore, it is judged that the maturity period of automobile body technology will gradually decline until 2030. The predicted value is the same as the PLC theory (S-shaped curve), so specific countermeasures are proposed for the future. It is suggested to follow the TIPS theory to improve the ideal degree law, improve the system parameters at the present stage, and reduce the production cost. Where possible, patents can cross-license patents to other companies and predict the patented technology and efficiency of other parts of the car. For example, for the front-body collision technology, the application of the technology route can plan the product technology blueprint and the layout of key patents in the next 5–10 years, so as to increase the company's research and development competitiveness, and can also authorize patents to increase corporate profits.

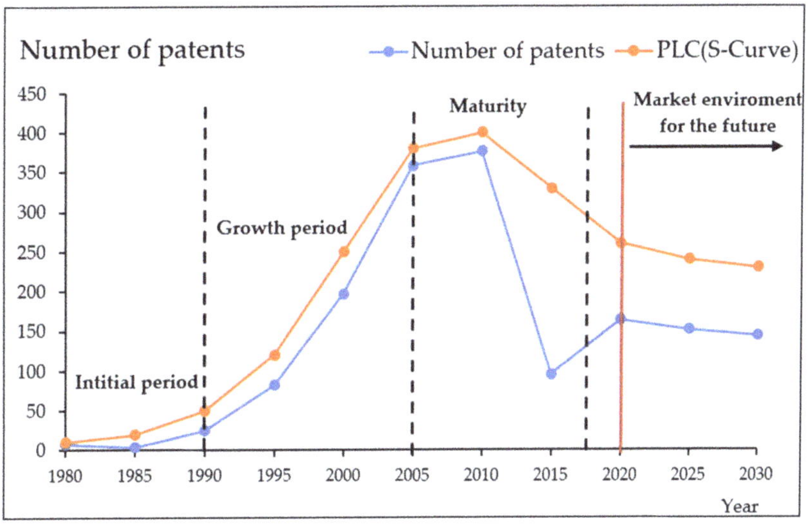

Figure 10. Comparison of patent quantity and S-shaped curve.

Based on the results of the analysis, the load problems related to the current body rigidity design and research and the development objectives of the automotive industry in the next 10 years are described as follows.

(1) Strategic objectives for short-term development (1–3 years):

Starting from 2021, the short-term trend is 161–156 patents. It is suggested that aluminum, magnesium alloy, and fiber-reinforced composite materials should be selected appropriately for short-term strategic development. In terms of design, optimization design should be carried out according to material characteristics and performance requirements. Cold forming should be the main process, and hot forming, roll forming, and laser welding should be the minor methods. The short-term goal is to reduce body weight by 18%.

(2) Strategic objectives of medium-term development (1–5 years):

In the medium term, the number of patents went from 161 to 152. In the mid-term strategic development, the application of aluminum, magnesium alloy, and carbon fiber-reinforced composite materials in the car body should be expanded. Structured materials with performance-integrated lightweight multi objective collaborative optimization designs should be adopted. In terms of technology, hot forming, warm forming, and internal high-pressure forming should be the main processes, and extrusion forming, bending, and thermosetting fiber material should be supplementary processes. The mid-term goal is to reduce body weight by 30%

(3) Strategic objectives of long-term development (1–10 years):

In the long term, the number of patents went from 161 to 144. In the long-term strategic development, the selection of materials should be mainly fiber composite materials, supplemented by light alloy and high strength steel. The design can be integrated with the requirements of the manufacturing process and cost control. In terms of technology, thermoplastic fiber material forming, extrusion forming, bending forming, warm forming, and hot forming should be considered supplementary. The long-term goal is to reduce body weight by 40%. Automobile body patent technology may have produced core technologies, so the number of patent applications will decrease. Hence, patent types will be mainly related to application methods in the future.

Second, our advice to academics is as follows: In this study, traditional statistical methods and machine learning were used to predict the number of patents, while continuous quantification was also used to predict the number of patents. It is suggested that the application of text-based machine learning to patent analysis could be further studied. Secondly, in recent years, the growth of new energy vehicles has been substantial, and the technical problems encountered by the development of traditional fuel vehicles in the automobile body are worth studying.

Author Contributions: Conceptualization, H.-L.L.; methodology, H.-L.L. and C.-W.L.; formal analysis, C.-W.L.; writing—original draft preparation, C.-W.L.; writing—review and editing, H.-L.L.; and Y.-Y.M.; supervision, H.-L.L. and F.T. All authors have read and agreed to the published version of the manuscript.

Funding: This research received no external funding.

Institutional Review Board Statement: Not applicable.

Informed Consent Statement: Not applicable.

Data Availability Statement: Not applicable.

Conflicts of Interest: The authors declare no conflict of interest.

References

1. Author Group of China Automobile Industry Association. *Economic Operation of Automobile Industry in 2021, China*; China Automobile Industry Association: Beijing, China, 2022. Available online: http://www.caam.org.cn (accessed on 1 January 2020).
2. Vernon, R. The product cycle hypothesis in a new international environment. *Oxf. Bull. Econ. Stat.* **1979**, *41*, 255–267.
3. Pryshlakivsky, J.; Searcy, C. Life Cycle Assessment as a decision-making tool: Practitioner and managerial considerations. *J. Clean. Prod.* **2021**, *309*, 127344. [CrossRef]
4. Zhang, G.; Tang, C. How could firm's internal R&D collaboration bring more innovation? *Technol. Forecast. Soc. Change* **2017**, *125*, 299–308.
5. Canuto da Silva, G.; Kaminski, P.C. Proposal of framework to managing the automobilemotive product development process. *Cogent Eng.* **2017**, *4*, 1317318.
6. Mousavi, S.A.; Seiti, H.; Hafezalkotob, A.; Asian, S.; Mobarra, R. Application of risk-based fuzzy decision support systems in new product development: An R-VIKOR approach. *Appl. Soft Comput.* **2021**, *109*, 107456. [CrossRef]
7. Fontem, B.; Smith, J. Analysis of a chance-constrained new product risk model with multiple customer classes. *Eur. J. Oper. Res.* **2019**, *272*, 999–1016. [CrossRef]
8. Adler, T.R.; Pittz, T.G.; Meredith, J. An analysis of risk sharing in strategic R&D and new product development projects. *Int. J. Proj. Manag.* **2016**, *34*, 914–922.
9. Chin, K.S.; Tang, D.W.; Yang, J.B.; Wong, S.Y.; Wang, H. Assessing new product development project risk by Bayesian network with a systematic probability generation methodology. *Expert Syst. Appl.* **2009**, *36*, 9879–9890.
10. Allayannis, G.; Ofek, E. Exchange rate exposure, hedging, and the use of foreign currency derivatives. *J. Int. Money Financ.* **2001**, *20*, 273–296. [CrossRef]
11. Guay, W.; Kothari, S.P. How much do firms hedge with derivatives? *J. Financ. Econ.* **2003**, *70*, 423–461. [CrossRef]
12. Gan, S.; Ge, S.; Han, X.; Yan, S.; Liu, J. *2020 China Patent Investigation Report*; Intellectual Property Development Research Center of State Intellectual Property Office: Beijing, China, 2021.
13. Yuan, X.; Cai, Y. Forecasting the development trend of low emission vehicle technologies: Based on patent data. *Technol. Forecast. Soc. Change* **2021**, *166*, 120651. [CrossRef]
14. Hanggara, F.D. Forecasting Car Demand in Indonesia with Moving Average Method. *J. Eng. Sci. Technol. Manag. JES-TM* **2021**, *1*, 1–6.
15. Babai, M.Z.; Chen, H.; Syntetos, A.A.; Lengu, D. A compound-Poisson Bayesian approach for spare parts inventory forecasting. *Int. J. Prod. Econ.* **2021**, *232*, 107954. [CrossRef]
16. Wan, J.P.; Xie, L.Q.; Hu, X.F. Study on the electric vehicle sales forecast with TEI@ I methodology. *Int. J. Knowl. Eng. Data Min.* **2021**, *7*, 1–38. [CrossRef]
17. Tsang, Y.P.; Wong, W.C.; Huang, G.Q.; Wu, C.H.; Kuo, Y.H.; Choy, K.L. A fuzzy-based product life cycle prediction for sustainable development in the electric vehicle industry. *Energies* **2020**, *13*, 3918. [CrossRef]
18. Lee, M. An analysis of the effects of artificial intelligence on electric vehicle technology innovation using patent data. *World Pat. Inf.* **2020**, *63*, 102002. [CrossRef]
19. Wang, X.; Zeng, D.; Dai, H.; Zhu, Y. Making the right business decision: Forecasting the binary NPD strategy in Chinese automotive industry with machine learning methods. *Technol. Forecast. Soc. Change* **2020**, *155*, 120032. [CrossRef]
20. Choi, Y.; Park, S.; Lee, S. Identifying emerging technologies to envision a future innovation ecosystem: A machine learning approach to patent data. *Scientometrics* **2021**, *126*, 5431–5476. [CrossRef]

21. Lee, C.; Kwon, O.; Kim, M.; Kwon, D. Early identification of emerging technologies: A machine learning approach using multiple patent indicators. *Technol. Forecast. Soc. Change* **2018**, *127*, 291–303. [CrossRef]
22. Teng, F.; Sun, Y.; Chen, F.; Qin, A.; Zhang, Q. Technology opportunity discovery of proton exchange membrane fuel cells based on generative topographic mapping. *Technol. Forecast. Soc. Change* **2021**, *169*, 120859. [CrossRef]
23. Suhail, Y.; Upadhyay, M.; Chhibber, A. Machine learning for the diagnosis of orthodontic extractions: A computational analysis using ensemble learning. *Bioengineering* **2020**, *7*, 55. [CrossRef]
24. Barrera-Animas, A.Y.; Oyedele, L.O.; Bilal, M.; Akinosho, T.D.; Delgado, J.M.D.; Akanbi, L.A. Rainfall prediction: A comparative analysis of modern machine learning algorithms for time-series forecasting. *Mach. Learn. Appl.* **2022**, *7*, 100204. [CrossRef]
25. Ensafi, Y.; Amin, S.H.; Zhang, G.; Shah, B. Time-series forecasting of seasonal items sales using machine learning—A comparative analysis. *Int. J. Inf. Manag. Data Insights* **2022**, *2*, 100058. [CrossRef]
26. Lin, S.; Lin, R.; Sun, J.; Wang, F.; Wu, W. Dynamically evaluating technological innovation efficiency of high-tech industry in China: Provincial, regional and industrial perspective. *Socio-Econ. Plan. Sci.* **2021**, *74*, 100939. [CrossRef]
27. Kim, J.E.; Cho, Y.S.; Kim, Y.R. The Major Common Technology Field Analysis of Domestic Mobile Carriers based on Patent Information Data. *J. Korea Acad.-Ind. Coop. Soc.* **2017**, *18*, 723–737.
28. Chen, Y.H.; Chen, C.Y.; Lee, S.C. Technology forecasting and patent strategy of hydrogen energy and fuel cell technologies. *Int. J. Hydrogen Energy* **2011**, *36*, 6957–6969. [CrossRef]
29. Altuntas, S.; Dereli, T. A Regression-Based "Patent Data Analysis" Approach: A Case Study for "Weapon Technology" Evaluation Process. *IEEE Trans. Eng. Manag.* **2021**, 1–13. [CrossRef]
30. Lin, H.L.; Ma, Y.Y. A New Method of Storage Management Based on ABC Classification: A Case Study in Chinese Supermarkets' Distribution Center. *SAGE Open* **2021**, *11*, 21582440211023193. [CrossRef]
31. Lin, C.W.; Kao, C.S.; Chien, C.S. The Evaluation of Venture Capital in the Biotech Investment of Taiwan Rice-Bran Polysaccharide. *Adv. Manag. Appl. Econ.* **2020**, *10*, 151–172.
32. Lin, H.L.; Cho, C.C.; Ma, Y.Y.; Hu, Y.Q.; Yang, Z.H. Optimization plan for excess warehouse storage in e-commerce–based plant shops: A case study for Chinese plant industrial. *J. Bus. Econ. Manag.* **2019**, *20*, 897–919. [CrossRef]
33. Karakan, G.; Koc, T. Technology forecasting methods and an application to white goods sector. *J. Ind. Eng. Turk. Chamb. Mech. Eng.* **2008**, *20*, 29–38.
34. You, H.; Li, M.; Hipel, K.W.; Jiang, J.; Ge, B.; Duan, H. Development trend forecasting for coherent light generator technology based on patent citation network analysis. *Scientometrics* **2017**, *111*, 297–315. [CrossRef]
35. Jose Basallo-Triana, M.; Rodriguez-Sarasty, J.A.; Dario Benitez-Restrepo, H. Analogue-based demand forecasting of short life-cycle products: A regression approach and a comprehensive assessment. *Int. J. Prod. Res.* **2016**, *55*, 2336–2350. [CrossRef]
36. Phan, K.; Daim, T. Forecasting the maturity of alternate wind turbine technologies through patent analysis. In *Research and Technology Management in the Electricity Industry*; Springer: London, UK, 2013; pp. 189–211.
37. Yun, J.; Geum, Y. Automobilemated classification of patents: A topic modeling approach. *Comput. Ind. Eng.* **2020**, *147*, 106636. [CrossRef]
38. Altuntaş, F.; Yilmaz, M. Patent analizi ile teknoloji ağlarının oluşturulması. *J. Entrep. Innov. Manag.* **2017**, *6*, 97–129.
39. Kyebambe, M.N.; Cheng, G.; Huang, Y.; He, C.; Zhang, Z. Forecasting emerging technologies: A supervised learning approach through patent analysis. *Technol. Forecast. Soc. Change* **2017**, *125*, 236–244. [CrossRef]
40. Dutt, R.; Rathi, P.; Krishna, V. Novel mixed-encoding for forecasting patent grant duration. *World Pat. Inf.* **2021**, *64*, 102007. [CrossRef]
41. Kim, G.; Bae, J. A novel approach to forecast promising technology through patent analysis. *Technol. Forecast. Soc. Change* **2017**, *117*, 228–237. [CrossRef]
42. Cho, J.H.; Lee, J.; Sohn, S.Y. Predicting future technological convergence patterns based on machine learning using link prediction. *Scientometrics* **2021**, *126*, 5413–5429. [CrossRef]
43. Chang, P.C.; Wu, J.L.; Tsao, C.C.; Lin, M.H. A patent quality classification system using a kernel-pca with svm. In Proceedings of the ADVCOMP 2015: The Ninth International Conference on Advanced Engineering Computing and Applications in Sciences, Nice, France, 19–24 July 2015.
44. San Kim, T.; Sohn, S.Y. Machine-learning-based deep semantic analysis approach for forecasting new technology convergence. *Technol. Forecast. Soc. Change* **2020**, *157*, 120095.
45. Lin, C.C.; Lin, C.L.; Shyu, J.Z. Hybrid multi-model forecasting system: A case study on display market. *Knowl.-Based Syst.* **2014**, *71*, 279–289. [CrossRef]
46. Breiman, L. Bagging predictors. *Mach. Learn.* **1996**, *24*, 123–140. [CrossRef]
47. Freund, Y.; Schapire, R.E. Experiments with a new boosting algorithm. In *Proceedings of the ICML'96: Proceedings of the Thirteenth International Conference on Machine Learning, Bari, Italy, 3–6 July 1996*; Morgan Kaufmann Publishers Inc.: San Francisco, CA, USA, 1996.
48. Xiao, F.; Gao, X. The ring-shaped route body structure design and evaluation method. In Proceedings of the FISITA 2012 World Automotive Congress; Springer: Berlin/Heidelberg, Germany, 2013; pp. 447–461.
49. Julong, D. Introduction to grey system theory. *J. Grey Syst.* **1989**, *1*, 1–24.
50. Engle, R.F.; Granger, C.W.J. Cointegration and Error Correction: Representation, Estimation and Testing. *Econometrica* **1987**, *55*, 251–276. [CrossRef]

51. Davidson, J.E.; Hendry, D.F.; Srba, F.; Yeo, S. Econometric modelling of the aggregate time-series relationship between consumers' expenditure and income in the United Kingdom. *Econ. J.* **1978**, *88*, 661–692. [CrossRef]
52. Duan, L.; Liu, Z.; Yu, W.; Chen, W.; Jin, D.; Li, D.; Sun, S.; Dai, R. Modeling Analysis and Comparision of Neural Network Simulation Based on ECM and LSTM. *J. Phys. Conf. Ser.* **2021**, *2068*, 012041. [CrossRef]
53. Lin, Y.; Chen, J.; Chen, Y. Dynamic relationships of knowledge creation activities in supply chains: Evidence from patent data in the US auto industry. *Afr. J. Bus. Manag.* **2011**, *5*, 12563–12576.
54. Altshuller, G.S.; Shapiro, R.B. On the psychology of inventive creativity. *Quest. Psychol.* **1956**, *6*, 37–49. (In Russian)

axioms

MDPI

Article

Modeling Preferences through Personality and Satisfaction to Guide the Decision Making of a Virtual Agent

Jorge Castro-Rivera [1], María Lucila Morales-Rodríguez [1], Nelson Rangel-Valdez [2,*], Claudia Gómez-Santillán [1] and Luciano Aguilera-Vázquez [1]

[1] División de Estudios de Posgrado e Investigación, Tecnológico Nacional de México, Instituto Tecnológico de Ciudad Madero, Los Mangos 89440, Mexico; D10070283@cdmadero.tecnm.mx (J.C.-R.); lucila.mr@cdmadero.tecnm.mx (M.L.M.-R.); claudia.gs@cdmadero.tecnm.mx (C.G.-S.); luciano.av@cdmadero.tecnm.mx (L.A.-V.)

[2] División de Estudios de Posgrado e Investigación, CONACyT—Tecnológico Nacional de Mexico, Instituto Tecnológico de Ciudad Madero, Los Mangos 89440, Mexico

* Correspondence: nelson.rv@cdmadero.tecnm.mx

Abstract: Satisfaction is relevant for decision makers (DM, Decision Makers). Satisfaction is the feeling produced in individuals by executing actions to satisfy their needs, for example, the payment of debts, jobs, or academic achievements, and the acquisition of goods or services. In the satisfaction literature, some theories model the satisfaction of individuals from job and customer approaches. However, considering personality elements to influence satisfaction and define preferences in strategies that optimize decision making provides the unique characteristics of a DM. These characteristics favor the scope of solutions closer to the satisfaction expectation. Satisfaction theories do not include specific elements of personality and preferences, so integrating these elements will offer more efficient decisions in computable models. In this work, a model of satisfaction with personality characteristics that influence the preferences of a DM is proposed. The proposed model is integrated into a preference-based optimizer that improves the decision-making process of a Virtual Decision Maker (VDM) in an optimization context. The optimization context addressed in this work is the product selection process within a food product shopping problem. An experimental design is proposed that compares two configurations that represent the cognitive part of an agent's decision process to validate the operation of the proposed model in the context of optimization: (1) satisfaction, personality, and preferences, and (2) personality and preferences. The results show that considering satisfaction and personality in combination with preferences provides solutions closer to the interests of an individual, reflecting a more realistic behavior. Furthermore, this work demonstrates that it is possible to create a configurable model that allows adapting to different aptitudes and reflecting them in a computable model.

Keywords: Decision Maker; satisfaction; personality; preferences; Virtual Decision Maker

MSC: 93A30; 68T05

Citation: Casto-Rivera, J.; Moralez-Rodriguez, M.L.; Rangel-Valdez, N.; Gomez-Santillan, C.; Aguilera-Vazquez, L. Modeling Preferences through Personality and Satisfaction to Guide the Decision Making of a Virtual Agent. *Axioms* **2022**, *11*, 232. https://doi.org/10.3390/axioms11050232

Academic Editor: Clemente Cesarano

Received: 31 March 2022
Accepted: 13 May 2022
Published: 17 May 2022

1. Introduction

Satisfaction is a factor that represents the perception of individuals about the final result of a decision process, where elements such as cognitive effort and level of satisfaction intervene. Currently, organizations and institutions resort to strategies aimed at recognizing the expectation of satisfaction that meets the needs of decision makers (DM, Decision Maker). In this way, it is possible to offer goods and services closer to what the individual expects to obtain beyond their preferences.

For example, the preference for dark clothing does not imply that any dark garment meets the individual's expectations. Said garment may cover all the preferred search criteria (price, fabric quality, size, among others). However, it may be that the garment is not to the individual's liking when trying it on. The above is related to causes associated with the individual's personality, which reflect traits that help define their level of satisfaction. Knowing this type of characteristics related to satisfaction (personality and preferences) guarantees suggestions of goods and services with a high expectation of satisfaction.

According to the previous idea, if organizations or institutions adopt this type of optimization mechanism, the existing link with their established market could be strengthened by offering their goods or services personalized. They are even making it possible to venture into a new potential market due to the new and efficient attention, which can be interpreted as profits. These gains are the result of addressing the perception of the preferences of each individual, in particular, considerably reducing results perceived as unfavorable by the individual.

For example, the authors Cruz-Reyes et al. [1] provide a study focused on the integration of the perception of individuals through their preferences to optimize decision processes, reflecting in some way their satisfaction. Another study that can be highlighted is that of the authors Castro-Rivera et al. [2], where they were not limited to integrating only the preferences of the individual but also their personality to give a better approximation to what satisfies them according to a decision context.

In general, profits play an essential role in different works that provide studies in favor of integrating the perception of individuals through their preferences. Such a link between profits, perception, and preferences is built to gain an advantage in computable optimization processes so that better solutions can be achieved [1,2]. Hence, the profits can be seen as a means of characterizing the impact of a particular individual's perception over distinct alternatives, which can vary. For example, from the perspective of some individuals, it may be healthy to consume coffee with a lot of sugar, but for others, it is a precursor to disease. The example above is a clear manifestation of preferences and the influence of satisfaction on them.

Satisfaction modeling is related to decision making, representing DM satisfaction through conceptual models. These models seek to provide various components that visualize the decisions of individuals and their agreement on the results. These components have been grouped into satisfaction models under the job and customer approaches. Both approaches share a relationship between their main components to represent the satisfaction of individuals. For example, they share emotional factors, motivation, commitment, equity factors, and strengthening the quality of goods and services. In addition, these models can model satisfaction from questionnaires provided by the DM, generating representative values of their satisfaction expectations.

The job and customer satisfaction approaches aim to reflect the satisfaction of the DM by providing the degree of satisfaction concerning a decisional context [3,4]. However, representing the satisfaction of the DM is a problem that requires involving more characteristics, such as preferences and personality.

The reason for considering personality as a characteristic to achieve the satisfaction of the DM is that preferences are particularities derived from personality; that is, personality influences preferences. Additionally, personality distinguishes the DM's behavior relative to others in the decision-making process. For example, when buying products, an individual with a relaxed personality tends to see product attributes with similar relevance, regardless of whether the quality is lower than the price. On the other hand, an authoritarian personality emphasizes a preference for one of the product's attributes over another. To emulate this type of behavior in decision making, indirect strategies are applied [1,5], and optimizers are based on preferences and influences of personality [2].

Personality influences not only the DM's preferences but also their satisfaction. The satisfaction characteristic allows one to observe the influence of personality through satisfaction, showing that each individual expresses what uniquely satisfies them. The DM's level or degree of satisfaction indicates if the expectation of satisfaction concerning the results from a decision-making process has been achieved. Results can be obtained through a strategy based on preferences, such as HHGA-SPP (Hyper-Heuristic Genetic Algorithm for Social Portfolio Problem) [6], RPM (Robust Portfolio Modeling) [7], or NOSGA-II (Non-Outranking Sorting Genetic Algorithm) [8].

Integrating characteristics such as personality and satisfaction in an optimization strategy based on preferences from the literature could offer more representative solutions for the interest of the DM. These alternatives are evaluated to see if they meet the DM's expectations or degree of satisfaction. This type of satisfaction indicator, together with the influence of personality on preferences, is an innovative feature of the proposed satisfaction model. Furthermore, the integration of satisfaction in metaheuristic algorithms has not been applied previously.

In this work, a satisfaction model with personality characteristics is proposed to influence the preferences of the DM seeking to improve the decision-making process of a VDM under an optimization context. Optimization context addresses the product selection process within a food product shopping problem. This context will serve to evaluate the functioning of the proposed satisfaction model. In this case study, the intelligent agent is virtual and takes on the role of a sales assistant who offers the user food product suggestions according to interests through an optimization strategy based on preferences.

The configuration of the suggestions was classified according to the elements with which they were generated. This classification consists of two elements: (1) suggestions generated with satisfaction, personality, and preferences, and (2) suggestions generated with personality and preferences. These suggestions will be compared with each other and evaluated with user satisfaction. It is expected that the suggestions of group 1 meet the satisfaction expectation of the individual concerning the suggestions of the other group.

The main contributions of this work revolve around a satisfaction model and an architecture of intelligent agents to facilitate an interaction mechanism with the user. The proposed satisfaction model uses personality properties to influence an individual's preferences through preference-based solution strategies. Influencing an individual's preferences through these characteristics is the most remarkable contribution of this work. The developed architecture of intelligent agents integrates into its cognitive process the assisted satisfaction model with personality attributes and a strategy based on preferences in its deliberative process. Both the personality attributes and the preference-based optimization strategy come from the literature. The optimization strategy within the deliberative process is influenced by the features provided by the satisfaction model. This architecture is the means to represent the cognitive part of the decision process of an intelligent agent with the role of a VDM.

This research's main objective is to model a DM's preferences influenced by personality characteristics and satisfaction level to improve the decision-making processes of a virtual agent in an optimization context. Furthermore, this objective intends to demonstrate that the integration of a satisfaction model that reflects the degree of satisfaction of an individual in optimization problems that consider the characteristics of their personality and preferences will provide better solutions than processes that do not integrate a model of satisfaction. This hypothesis is discussed extensively in Section 5.6.

The following describes how the sections of this document are organized. Section 2 presents the theoretical foundation that supports the realization of this work. Section 3 shows the general architecture of the VDM project. Section 4 presents the satisfaction model proposed in this work and the description of its components. Section 5 presents the formulas involved in the satisfaction model and the evaluation of the model's performance through a case study, as well as the experimental design. Section 6 corresponds to the discussion about the results achieved in the experimentation. Finally, Section 7 corresponds to the conclusions of this work.

2. Background

2.1. Approaches to Satisfaction in the Literature

The main concepts for developing theories and models of satisfaction are addressed in the literature from two approaches: the job and customer approach. In most jobs, job satisfaction is the most recurrent concerning the satisfaction of individuals. Job satisfaction is made up of emotional and cognitive processes, and through these, the individual evaluates their experience at work [9,10]. Cognitive job satisfaction arises from evaluating job characteristics more consciously and comparing them with a cognitive standard [10,11]. On the other hand, affective or emotional job satisfaction represents a positive emotional response from the employee towards work as a whole [10,12].

In addition to job satisfaction, another recurring concept in the literature is the concept of customer satisfaction. The wealth of companies comes mainly from having their customers satisfied. According to the above, it is necessary to have robust processes and qualified personnel who provide the consumer's service or product quality. Measuring customer satisfaction allows one to know if the conditions in which said processes and personnel are carried out are adequate and, in this way, to predict the consumption of sales. Therefore, it is relevant to know the opinion of consumers about the service provided [13]. The concepts of customer satisfaction are illustrated through customer satisfaction models, which are based on market research and are classified as macro- and micro-models [4].

Some of the most recurrent theories or models under the approach to job satisfaction are: the theory of affect [14], the theory of the two factors, the model of expectations of Porter and Lawler [15], Fit-Job theory [16], among others. On the other hand, customer satisfaction models are divided into macro-models and micro-models. Macro-models highlight consumer satisfaction by comparing performance standards of services or products. Some of these macro-models are the traditional model, the models based on the value chain, and the perceived quality of the service. On the other hand, micro-models look more directly at customer satisfaction. The micro-models are listed in seven types [4,17], such as the model of disconfirmation of expectations, model of perceived performance, model of norms, model of multiple processes, models of attribution, affective models, and models of equity.

The job and customer satisfaction theories can be associated with personality theories and agent architectures to develop support models in decision making that make satisfaction explicit through traits, types, emotions, cognitive elements, and real-world symbology. According to the above, the models of job satisfaction that, at first glance, show more similarities at the conceptual level with the theories of personality and the architectures of agents are the Theory of Labor Adjustment or Fit-Job (it belongs to the emotional approaches) and Comparison Theory (belongs to a Motivational approach). In the case of customer models, the Traditional Model has more similarities with personality theories and agent architectures, followed by the Value Chain Model.

The Fit-Job satisfaction models, Comparison Theory, Traditional Model, and the Value Chain Model are functional for developing a decision-making model in an intelligent virtual agent that integrates the satisfaction and personality of the individuals in various decision contexts.

2.2. *Personality*

Personality is commonly seen as the set of behaviors that make up a person's individuality and is regularly used to describe and classify a person's behavior. The personality includes the external behavior of the person (gestures, behaviors, and observable events) and the internal experience of the person (desires, thoughts, feelings, and beliefs), which will produce observable events in the environment [18].

Studies on personality are supported by Personality Theories based on psychology, which explain the behavior of humans through two study approaches personality traits and types [19]. Both approaches seek to describe the personality of individuals through their strengths, weaknesses, preferences to act, and emotional states.

2.2.1. Personality Traits

In the development of systems that interact with people (simulators of human behavior), personality traits cannot be ignored due to their influence. They constitute a decisive part of human reasoning and behavior, mainly if one agent's emotional state can influence the decisions. Furthermore, some personality traits can influence the definition of emotions and their intensity, as is the case with neuroticism, which reflects the mood of the person [20].

In contemporary psychology, a personality model seeks to describe the characteristics of human behavior that constitute its individuality. In general, some of the most spread trait-based personality models are: big three [21,22], the big five [23,24], and the Five-Factor Model (FFM) (also known as OCEAN (Openness, Conscientiousness, Extraversion, Agreeableness, Neuroticism) [25]. According to McCrae and John [25] and Penn-State [26], six facets are derived from each of the five dimensions or factors of the OCEAN model, which are: (1) Extraversion: friendliness, gregariousness, assertiveness, activity level, excitement-seeking, and cheerfulness. (2) Agreeableness: trust, morality, altruism, cooperation, modesty, and sympathy. (3) Conscientiousness: self-efficacy, orderliness, dutifulness, achievement-striving, self-discipline, and cautiousness. (4) Neuroticism: anxiety, anger, depression, self-consciousness, immoderation, and vulnerability. (5) Openness: imagination, artistic interests, emotionality, adventurousness, intellect, and liberalism.

2.2.2. Personality Types

Personality types represent another of the approaches that conceptualize personality. In this approach, each of the humans presents a different vision of the world, making it clear that each individual is unique and independent in their behavior [27].

There are models of personality that employ Jung's theory. This theory consists of three dichotomies that explain how humans differ in the way they perceive their environment, interact with others, and how they make their decisions based on these personality types [27]. Some of these models are MBTI (Myers-Briggs Type Indicator) [28], and the Keirsey Temperament Sorted (KTS) model of temperaments [29], which is based on MBTI. Of these two grand theories of personality on human behavior, the FFM and MBTI models stand out as the most recurrent in the scientific literature. These types of models are commonly used to model socio-emotional agents. In addition, they could influence decision making through metaheuristics, mainly those that take into account other behavioral factors, such as preferences.

2.3. Solution Strategy That Integrates the Preferences of a DM, NOSGA-II

Most current multi-objective evolutionary optimization literature approaches focus on adopting an evolutionary algorithm to generate an approximation of the Pareto Frontier. For example, the NOSGA-II (Non-Outranking Sorting Genetic Algorithm) algorithm [8] characterizes the best compromise solution of a multi-objective optimization problem by increasing the selective pressure toward the most satisfactory solutions. In this way, it integrates the preferences of a DM established a priori in a genetic algorithm [8,30].

In this work, NOSGA-II is used to integrate the preferences of a DM and generate alternatives influenced by a personality profile and satisfaction factors to further facilitate decision making. The configuration applied in this work for the operation of NOSGA-II is described in the work of the authors Fernández et al. [8].

In Section 2.4, it is possible to find some works related to strategies that integrate the preferences of a DM, as well as research that offers a proposal to influence personality factors in this type of metaheuristics.

2.4. State the Art Analysis

Various investigations reveal the importance of personality and preferences on human behavior in different situations, particularly decision making. They hypothetically visualize that these characteristics allow them to reach the expectations of satisfaction of the individuals through the results of the application of their methodologies. However, the satisfaction of individuals is an issue whose characteristics must be considered in decision-making processes.

The absence of some of the distinctive factors of human behavior mentioned above is usually observed in the literature. For example, the work of Delgado-Hernández et al. [31] characterizes a dialogue with personality elements and selects the sentences of the conversation with a preference-based optimizer. However, it does not consider characteristics of satisfaction.

On the other hand, in the work of Seltzer et al. [32], the characteristics of satisfaction are considered. They relate personality, life, and job satisfaction to highlight the influence of personality on satisfaction. However, they do not consider the DM's preferences and are relevant to satisfaction. For example, a person whose job is not to their liking is more likely to harm their satisfaction than someone who performs a job to their liking.

Bradea et al. [33] propose a management tool for the selection of assets that provide optimal returns in the market. They use the preferences of the DM through an optimizer for decision making. In this work, characteristics of satisfaction and personality are not considered, so the results could improve in its experimental simulation when considering these factors.

According to the reviewed literature, no proposals were found that consider the three topics of human behavior (personality, preferences, and satisfaction) interacting in a computable model. For this reason, the proposal of a satisfaction model influenced by a personality that helps model the preferences of a DM is one of the novel characteristics of this research work.

3. General Architecture of VDM

This section deals with a proposed architecture of a virtual agent with human-like behavioral traits [34] through satisfaction, personality, and preference models. This architecture represents a VDM with the role of a decision maker.

The architecture of this work has a degree of topological and mathematical abstraction [35]. The VDM and the flow of its components are modeled through a diagram. The data flow between its components comes from applying models that resort to mathematical formulations, as is the case of the proposed satisfaction model in this work.

In addition, the proposed architecture is based on the structure of a utility-based agent [36] and on the fundamentals of a BDI (Beliefs, Desires, and Intentions) architecture [37,38]. This work aims to provide a framework [39,40] that facilitates the development of various decision contexts in which the VDM and a real DM can interact.

Figure 1 shows the general scheme of the VDM, whose structure has been developed to work in any case study. The operation of the architecture consists of selecting from the knowledge base the contextual elements, information on personality (through the MBTI [28] and IPIP-NEO [26] questionnaires), the Corpus Processed representative of the preferences (with the questionnaire proposed by Castro et al. [2]), and the DM satisfaction profile. With this information, it will be possible to obtain preferential parameters influenced by the VDM's personality and approximate the degree of personal satisfaction.

In this project, the PMUDC-I model (Personality Model Under a Decision Context I) [2] is responsible for generating personality parameters, as well as preferential parameters. Therefore, the PMUDC-I is the basis for concluding with the development of the PMUDC-II model. However, this investigation will not address its calculation procedure until future investigations.

Satisfaction-based personality traits (detailed in Section 5) are generated by the PMUDC-II model. Therefore, the satisfaction metric to evaluate the results of the deliberative process conformed by NOSGA-II comes from the satisfaction model.

In general terms, the VDM architecture aims to emulate a DM's characteristics through a decision context. For example, the emulation of the skills of a laboratory technician, developing experimentation in a virtual laboratory as if they were the DM. This document focuses on the blocks within the dotted area of the agent architecture (Figure 1). Section 4 presents the characteristics of the satisfaction model proposed in this work.

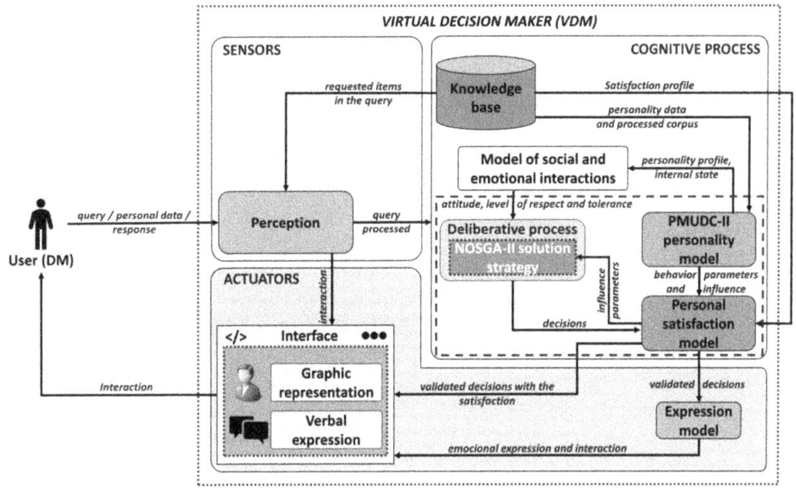

Figure 1. VDM architecture is composed of the satisfaction model, NOSGA-II, and PMUDC-II.

4. Personal Satisfaction Model

The module of the personal satisfaction model is part of the cognitive process of the agent or VDM. This model provides the parameters that reveal the satisfaction of the DM. This model comprises the customer satisfaction models, which are the Traditional Model and the Theory of Value, as well as the theories of job satisfaction, which are the Comparison Theory and the Fit-Job Theory.

The personal satisfaction model has three process blocks: definition of satisfaction parameters, parameter update, and satisfaction level validation module. Figure 2 shows the personal satisfaction model with its process blocks. The interaction with the PMUDC-II model, the knowledge base, and the agent's deliberative process (NOSGA-II) is mainly observed. Sections 4.1–4.3 describe the three process blocks of the personal satisfaction model proposed in this work.

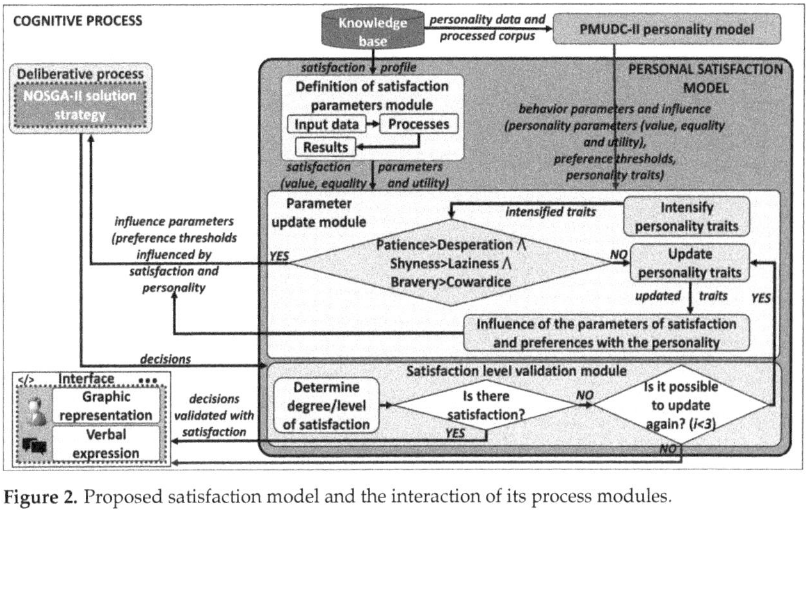

Figure 2. Proposed satisfaction model and the interaction of its process modules.

4.1. Definition of Satisfaction Parameters Module

The definition of satisfaction parameters module consists of three internal blocks, which are: input data, processes, and results, which are composed of a combination of the approaches of job satisfaction and customer satisfaction for their relationship in similar processes.

In short, the block input data is responsible for retrieving the information from the satisfaction profile, which contains the attributes of the service-product (s-p). These attributes are: expected performance, quality, quality-performance standards, emotional value, RIASEC test [41], and the ideal-real expectations of the s-p. The block process compares quality and performance with quality standards to interpret satisfaction, comparing ideal and actual expectations, reporting whether or not there is satisfaction with the s-p. Finally, it retrieves the RIASEC test score. The block process defines satisfaction parameters named value, equality, and utility.

Specifically, the parameter value is made up of information on the perceived performance of the p-s, combining characteristics of the Traditional Model and the Theory of Value. Furthermore, the parameter equality compares the ideal-real expectations based on the Comparison Theory. Finally, the utility parameter obtains the evaluation provided by the RIASEC test, which comes from the Fit-Job theory.

Once the satisfaction parameters are generated, they are sent to the block parameter update module.

4.2. Parameter Update Module

The block parameter update module is made up of the following blocks: intensify personality traits, update personality traits, and influence parameters of satisfaction and preferences with personality. In general terms, the parameter update module readjusts the parameters of satisfaction, personality traits, and preferences to reflect the DV's behavior in more satisfying and personality-influenced decision making.

Personality traits are given by the PMUDC-II model and are based on satisfaction attributes. These traits come from a set of personality parameters called value, equality, and utility and are intended to characterize satisfaction attributes, which are supported by satisfaction models in the literature [3,4].

By way of clarification, from the perspective of satisfaction, the parameter value is developed from the traditional models, and value theory [4] and represents the sentimental value of the goods or services that produce well-being. On the other hand, from the perspective of personality, the parameter value comes from the facets of the OCEAN dimension agreeableness and represents the moral values of the individual, which can produce satisfaction and well-being by correctly orienting their actions towards society.

In the case of the satisfaction parameter equality, it is based on the comparison theory [3,42], and represents the satisfaction or dissatisfaction in the expectation of a service or product. The personality parameter equality is based on the OCEAN facets of the factor neuroticism and represents dissatisfaction if conditions of equality with others do not exist.

Finally, the satisfaction parameter utility is based on the Job Fit theory [16] and aims to highlight the skills of the person in the work areas where they perform best and feel satisfied. The personality parameter utility is based on the facets of the extraversion, conscientiousness, neuroticism, and openness factors, reflecting aspects that intervene in decision making, favoring or limiting the results. For example, a shy person may lose opportunities in their environment due to self-consciousness; on the contrary, a naive person could make unreasonable decisions.

Through the personality parameters (value, equality, and utility), a set of personality traits associated with satisfaction are derived. These traits are quantified through the intensifies personality traits block described below.

The block intensify personality traits assigns the value of the OCEAN facets (discussed in Section 5.3) to the set of personality traits proposed in this work (discussed in

Table 1). This assignment of values gives intensity to personality traits, thus influencing the representative parameters of satisfaction and preferences.

Table 1. Classification of personality traits.

Updating Cycle	Influence of Parameters		
Utility	Value	Equality	Utility
Patience Desperation Shyness Laziness Bravery Cowardice	Ethic Humility	Cruelty Generosity	Conceit Egoism Naivety

The intensity of personality traits determines how much influence they can provide on the parameters mentioned above. Intensity is obtained through the IPIP-NEO (International Personality Item Pool-Neuroticism, Extraversion, and Openness) [26] questionnaire.

The relationship between the OCEAN facets and personality traits is possible through the similarities in its description's attributes. In the case of facets, their descriptions have been taken from the OCEAN model [25,26]. The descriptions or definitions of the personality traits proposed in this work have been taken from the RAE [43].

For example, according to OCEAN, the gregariousness facet of the extraversion dimension mentions that gregarious people find the company of others rewarding and enjoy the excitement of crowds. However, people with low scores tend to feel overwhelmed by large crowds. This description has similarities to the shyness trait, so the gregariousness facet score can be assigned to the shyness trait. This assignment of values can be consulted in Section 5.3, where the assignment of the values obtained from each facet to the personality traits through the IPIP-NEO questionnaire is observed.

Yet another example of similarity in their descriptions is the facet activity level and the trait laziness. The facet activity level refers to participation in multiple activities. Low scores on this facet indicate a very relaxed pace. The personality trait laziness describes a person as being too lax in carrying out their tasks. The relationship of the rest of the facets with the personality traits can be consulted in [44].

The block update personality traits receives the intensified personality traits to update other personality traits, according to the classification presented in Table 1. Personality traits are classified in two ways: traits that control the update cycle of parameters and traits that influence preferences, satisfaction, and even other elements of personality. The traits belonging to the utility parameter, such as patience, desperation, laziness, timidity, bravery, and cowardice, control the update cycle of the parameters. Other personality traits that also belong to the utility parameter, as well as to the value and equality parameters, influence the elements of satisfaction, preferences, and personality.

Once the personality traits are updated, they will be sent to the influence parameters of satisfaction and preferences with a personality block to influence the satisfaction parameters (value, equality, and utility) and in the preference thresholds given by PMUDC-I. After the previous process, the influenced parameters will be sent to the deliberative process (to NOSGA-II) to integrate the preference thresholds. Solutions given by NOSGA-II will be evaluated by the Satisfaction level validation module.

4.3. Satisfaction Level Validation Module

The satisfaction level validation module receives the solution alternatives from the deliberative process and validates them through the satisfaction characteristics, which make up the DM degree of satisfaction, in addition to the query or request formulated from the beginning by the DM.

The solution alternatives of the deliberative process and the DM request are composed of criteria or attributes. Depending on the context, these criteria may be colors, sizes, and costs, which may be about selling or offering services. The criteria DM's request consists of a value, which must be accumulated to be compared with the accumulated total of the solution alternatives obtained together with the representative tolerance of the DM. For example, if a request is made under an element selection context, whose criteria or attributes are its color and size, assuming that each attribute has a weight, the procedure to perform to obtain the accumulated total is to add the weights of each criterion. Afterward, the accumulated total is evaluated with the tolerance, representing the deviation or distance between the expectation (request) and the reality (alternatives).

If the accumulated value of an alternative received criterion does not exceed the tolerated percentage, it will be counted as a hit. The more hits an alternative has, the more satisfaction it will reflect. For example, a received or suggested alternative or list containing three items governed by two criteria would generate a maximum of six hits and a minimum of zero. Satisfaction is subjective, so an alternative with three correct answers out of six may be considered satisfactory if the individual's tolerance allows it. On the contrary, an alternative with five correct answers out of six may not be acceptable. The above depends a lot on the personality profile of the individual.

If the solution alternatives are close to those expected by the DM, they are sent to the graphical interface. Otherwise, the parameters will be updated again to reach a level of satisfaction more appropriate for the DM, as the update cycle allows (e.g., $iteration < 3$). The iteration limit avoids spending too much time searching for an improvement that may no longer exist because it has already been achieved. The equations and the procedure explained above can be consulted in the topic Section 5.7.

Section 5 presents how satisfaction is modeled through the characteristics of four individuals under a case study. In addition, the experimental design and the analysis of the results are described.

5. Analysis and Results

This section shows how the satisfaction model works using a food purchase case study. The calculation of parameters and values of each of the modules or process blocks presented in Section 4, corresponding to the personal satisfaction model, will be shown.

In Section 5.7, the case study will be addressed through two analysis cases. The first case analyzes an individual's satisfaction with a collaborative personality profile. The second case analyzes the satisfaction of an individual corresponding to the rest of the personality profiles (optimistic, inquirer, and strict). The food products consider the price and content criteria in both analysis cases.

The representation of the shopping list is based on the Project Portfolio (PP) problem [45]. The personality profiles, the preferential parameters, and the tolerance parameter are based on the work of Castro-Rivera et al. [2].

Table 2 shows the input data for the first case of analysis, belonging to a DM with a collaborative profile. These data are preference thresholds representative of the food product shopping context, the tolerance parameter, and the personality parameters from the perspective of satisfaction (Table 1). In the second case of analysis, the input data will be detailed in Section 5.7.

Table 2. Collaborative profile individual and its parameters.

Parmeter | Threshold	Price	Contents	Value	Personality Parameters
Indifference (q)	23.78	185.37	—	Value = 0.4
Preveto (u)	31.81	271.58	—	Equality = 0.37
Veto (v)	39.85	357.79	—	Utility = 0.65
Credibility (λ)	—	—	0.71	
Asymmetry (β)	—	—	0.08	
Symmetry (ϵ)	—	—	0.04	
Tolerance (φ)	—	—	0.58125	

The satisfaction parameters, developed from the information provided from the satisfaction profile, have been used in the experiments of the four individuals under analysis. The above is to observe the positive impact of the influence of satisfaction on the decision making regardless of the personality/decision profile of the DM. On the other hand, observe the contrast of the analysis of the results when there is no influence of satisfaction in decision making.

The process blocks of the satisfaction model are described through Sections 5.1–5.5. In Sections 5.1 and 5.2, the modeled satisfaction parameters are described. Sections 5.3 and 5.4 show how personality traits influence satisfaction characteristics. Finally, Section 5.5 presents the influence of satisfaction parameters and personality traits on preference modeling.

5.1. *Interpretation of the Satisfaction Profile*

The personal satisfaction model requires a series of input parameters for its operation, including the satisfaction profile. This profile is obtained from a questionnaire with five questions structured according to the Linkert scale (Appendix E). Each question represents the concepts of satisfaction models from the literature.

The description of each question and the satisfaction model supporting it are as follows: Question 1. The expected performance of the s-p is based on the Traditional Model and Theory of Value; Question 2. Quality is expected to perceive and is built from the Theory of Value; Question 3. Emotional value for the s-p is based on the Theory of Value; Question 4. Finally, the ideal expectation of s-p takes its elements from the Comparison Theory; Question 5. The fulfillment of realistic expectations of the s-p is based on the Comparison Theory.

In addition, the satisfaction profile provides quality standards, which are elements required by the Traditional Model to compare the quality and performance of the s-p. These standards represent elements of the context previously-stored and evaluated according to different opinions collected from users. This profile also provides the result of the RIASEC test (based on Fit-Job Theory) [16] to take into account the capabilities of the individual in the areas that satisfy him at work.

Through the satisfaction profile, you can obtain a minimum of 1 and a maximum of 5 points. The result of the satisfaction profile is shown in Table 3 as an example, together with the literals that identify each concept.

Table 3. A hypothetical score of the satisfaction profile questionnaire.

Satisfaction Profile Concept	Points
Performance (D)	5
Quality (C)	5
Value (V)	5
Ideal expectation (A)	5
Real expectation (B)	4
RIASEC test (R)	7
RIASEC test (I)	4
RIASEC test (A)	5

Table 4 aims to illustrate the quality and performance standards according to the decision context or case study (purchase of products). However, the values corresponding to performance Y and quality Z in the calculations have been proposed and not taken from a collection of authentic standards. From these data, the perceived disagreement (d) can be calculated, which is a concept of the traditional model that measures the negative-positive impact of s-p.

Once the satisfaction profile data is known, it is possible to define the satisfaction parameters, named as value, equality, and utility.

Table 4. A hypothetical example of the context element standards.

Item	Type	Color	Contents	Availability	...	Performance (*Y*)	Quality (*Z*)
1	Product	Coffee	3 pieces	—	...	3	5
2	Service	—	—	—	...	—	—
4	Product	...	...	...	...	3	4
3	Product	...	...	...	...	...	...

5.2. Procedure for Defining Satisfaction Parameters

After obtaining the input data of the satisfaction profile, inside block processes define the parameter value the performance (*Y*) and the quality (*Z*) of the standards for obtain the perceived disconfirmation (*d*). This calculation consists of taking only those values closest to the quality (*C*) and performance (*D*) given in the satisfaction profile. The selected Y and Z values will be averaged. The Equation (1) shows the sum of the average between Y and Z, as well as the sum between C and D, resulting in d.

$$d = (\overline{Y} + \overline{Z}) + (D + C) \tag{1}$$

Within the block processes, D, C, V, and d are used to interpret the DM's satisfaction (s) with the s-p through Equation (2).

$$s = \frac{D \times C \times V}{d} \tag{2}$$

To calculate the equality parameter, the ideal expectation must be compared with the real expectation of the s-p, according to the Theory of Comparison. The Equation (3) shows the comparison procedure between A and B.

$$\begin{aligned} A = B &\rightarrow satisfaction \\ A > B &\rightarrow dissatisfaction \\ A < B &\rightarrow guilty, \quad inequity, \quad discomfort \end{aligned} \tag{3}$$

Within the results block, the level of dissatisfaction or guilt obtained by the Equation (3) is defined using the absolute difference (k) between the ideal expected A and the real expectation B of the s-p. Equation (4) shows this operation. The value resulting from applying Equation (4) is the result of calculating the parameter equality.

$$k = |A - B| \tag{4}$$

Finally, within the block results, the utility parameter is defined, taking the values of the RIASEC test. According to what is specified in the RIASEC test, the highest score that can be obtained with the three literals (M) is 21; that is, 7 points for each literal. In Equation (5), a conversion of the total score to a scale of 10 is performed for easier handling, where it is assumed that each literal has a maximum score of 7. The definition of the parameter utility can be seen in Equation (6), where the value of L in each literal corresponds to that of the answered RIASEC test.

$$m = \frac{M_1 + M_2 + M_3}{10} \tag{5}$$

$$u = \frac{L_1 + L_2 + L_3}{m} \tag{6}$$

Table 5 shows, in a summarized way, the calculation of the satisfaction parameters using the equations and tables previously exposed. The data substituted in each equation (EQ) correspond to those obtained by the satisfaction profile.

Table 5. Definition of satisfaction parameters named as value, equality, and utility.

Parameter	EQ Used	Substitution of Values in EQ	Result
Value	(2)	$s = (5 \times 5 \times 5) \div 17$	7.36
Equality	(4)	$k = \|5 - 4\|$	1
Utility	(6)	$u = (7 + 4 + 5) \div 2.1$	7.62

5.3. *Procedure for the Intensification or Quantification of Personality Traits*

Personality traits are quantified in the intensify personality traits block. This process is possible through the facets of the OCEAN model and the scores provided by the IPIP-NEO questionnaire (addressed in Section 4.2). Table 6 shows the quantification of personality traits through the most similar facet. For example, the values shown in this table represent an individual with a collaborative decision profile. The value assigned to each trait will be the representative intensity, how shy, ethical, or desperate the person is, and influence the parameters in general. There are similarities of a personality trait with more than one facet in some cases, so it must be averaged to obtain its intensity value.

Table 6. Intensification of personality traits through the OCEAN facets [25] and IPIP-NEO questionnaire [26].

OCEAN Factors	Facets	Value with IPIP-NEO	Personality Trait	Value with Facet	Personality Parameter
Extraversion	Activity Level	0.80	Laziness	0.80	Utility
	Gregariousness	0.55	Shyness		
	Excitement-Seeking	0.17	Bravery	0.17	
Agreeableness	Morality	0.89	Ethic	0.89	Value
	Modesty	0.65	Humility	0.65	
	Altruism	0.95	Generosity	0.95	
Conscient.	Self-Efficacy	0.80	Patience	0.80	
	Cautiousness	0.72	Shyness	Average: 0.63	Utility
			Cowardice	0.72	
Neuroticism	Anxiety	0.64	Desperation	0.64	Utility
	Angry	0.27	Egoism	0.27	Utility
			Cruelty		Equality
	Immoderation	0.48	Conceit	0.48	Utility
			Cruelty	Average: 0.37	Equality
Openness	Imagination	0.50	Naivety	0.50	Utility

5.4. *Personality Traits Update Procedure*

The module personality traits update procedure is responsible for updating the personality traits displayed in the Table 1. Updating is possible through the association of the description between the characteristics of these features (according to [44]). In this case, the related traits are ethics with patience, which have peaceful and correct behavior in common; humility and shyness, which recognize their ability; conceit and bravery, which both emit arrogance. Table 7 shows the value of the intensity of said traits, according to the quantification presented in Table 6. This intensity value will be used to calculate the update of the decision and influence characteristics.

Table 7. The intensity of personality traits is classified as decisive.

i	Influence Traits (n_i)	Intensity (n_i)	Decision Traits (w_i)	Intensity (w_i)
1	Ethic	0.89	Patience	0.80
2	Humility	0.65	Shyness	0.63
3	Conceit	0.48	Bravery	0.17

Equation (7) shows the rules that must be followed to apply influence to decision traits; that is, if the intensity of the traits desperation, laziness, and cowardice does not exceed the intensity of the traits patience, shyness, and bravery, the latter will not be influenced, keeping their value, otherwise they will be influenced by applying Equation (8). This last equation increases a small percentage, representing the influence trait update over the decision trait. For example, the trait of patience increases due to the feedback it has with the ethics part, so that it can overcome desperation.

$$w_i^* = \begin{cases} w_i & \text{if} \quad \begin{array}{l} patience > desperation \quad \wedge \\ shyness > laziness \quad \wedge \\ bravery > cowardice \end{array} \\ (n_i \times w_i) + w_i & \text{if} \quad \begin{array}{l} patience < desperation \quad \wedge \\ shyness < laziness \quad \wedge \\ bravery < cowardice \end{array} \end{cases} \tag{7}$$

$$w_2^* = (n_2 \times w_2) + w_2 = 1.03 \rightarrow shyness^* \tag{8}$$

Updating the egoism, generosity, cruelty, and naivete traits is conducted in a similar way as explained for the previous traits. The common characteristics of these traits are intended to update the preference thresholds given by the PMUDC-I model. The relationship between the characteristics of both approaches (decision and influence) is observed as follows: egoism and laziness, both are interested only in themselves; generosity and cowardice, both have neither humor nor courage to do harm; cruelty and desperation, present a state of mind altered by anger; naivety and patience handle simplicity without alterations.

Table 8 shows the intensity corresponding to each trait based on Table 6. The influence traits are updated by applying Equation (9), except for the trait humility, which is calculated using the Equation (10). The relationship between the traits egoism, generosity, cruelty, and naivety and preference thresholds will be discussed in the topic Section 5.5.

$$n_1^* = (n_1 \times w_1) + n_1 = 0.48 \rightarrow Egoism^* \tag{9}$$

$$Humility = \frac{(Egoism^* + Generosity^*)}{2} = 1.05 \tag{10}$$

Table 8. The intensity of personality traits is classified as influential.

i	Influence Traits (n_i)	Intensity (n_i)	Decision Traits (w_i)	Intensity (w_i)
1	Egoism	0.27	Laziness	0.80
2	Generosity	0.95	Cowardice	0.72
3	Cruelty	0.37	Desperation	0.64
2	Naivety	0.50	Patience	0.80

In Table 9, the decision traits will be used to control a cycle that will determine if the influence traits should be updated or not. In addition, influence traits will serve to update preference thresholds and satisfaction parameters. Table 9 is a summary of the results of the influence on each of the personality traits. This influence is the result of applying Equations (7)–(10). Finally, it only remains to send them to the following process to influence the satisfaction and preference parameters (thresholds).

Table 9. Results of the influence calculation of the decision and influence traits.

Influenced Decision Traits	Intensity	Influenced Traits of Influence	Intensity
Patience	1.512	Egoism	0.48
Shyness	1.03	Generosity	1.63
Bravery	0.25	Humility	1.05
—	—	Cruelty	0.60
—	—	Naivety	0.90

5.5. Procedure of Influence of the Parameters of Satisfaction and Preferences with the Personality

Within the procedure Procedure of influence of the parameters of satisfaction and preferences with the personality the following elements are required: personality traits (Table 9), satisfaction parameters (Table 5), personality parameters, and preference thresholds (Table 2).

Equation (11) shows the process of influencing the satisfaction parameters with the personality parameters (relationship addressed in Section 4.2), where the parameters belonging to the same group will perform the influence or update.

Equation (12) shows as an example the calculation of the influence of the satisfaction parameter value (V_iS_j) by substituting the values from Table 10 in Equation (11) according to their corresponding group. The satisfaction parameters were taken from Table 5 and the personality parameters are found in Table 2.

$$\begin{aligned} V_iS_j^* &= (V_iS_j \times V_iP_j) + V_iS_j \\ E_iS_j^* &= (E_iS_j \times E_iP_j) + E_iS_j \\ U_iS_j^* &= (U_iS_j \times U_iP_j) + U_iS_j \end{aligned} \tag{11}$$

$$\begin{aligned} &V_iS_j^* = (V_iS_j \times V_iP_j) + V_iS_j \\ &\text{Parameter Value}^* = (7.36 \times 0.4) + 7.36 = 10.304 \end{aligned} \tag{12}$$

Table 10. Influence of personality on satisfaction through the parameters value, equality, and utility.

Params. (i)	Satisf. Params. (S_j)	Pers. Params. (P_j)	Influence of Pers. on Satisf.
Value (V_i)	7.36	0.4	10.304
Equality (E_i)	1	0.37	1.37
Utility (U_i)	7.62	0.65	12.573

The influence traits presented in Table 9 influence the preference thresholds. The preference thresholds indicate the differences between comparisons of alternatives through a strategy that integrates preferences of a DM, such as NOSGA-II [8]. The preference thresholds will be provided by the PMUDC-I model preferential impact model [2].

In general terms, the description of the threshold q indicates the minor differences between one alternative and another to consider them negligible. On the other hand, the description of the threshold v points out the significant differences between alternatives, considering one of them preferred over the other. Finally, the description of the threshold u shows the magnitude of the differences between alternatives when the veto conditions begin to be observed. These descriptions have been taken from Rivera-Zárate's work [46]

The description of the trait generosity indicates sensitivity and compassion for the misfortunes of others. The egoism trait describes excessive attention to oneself without caring about others. In the case of the humility trait, it indicates the virtue of recognizing one's limitations and weaknesses. These definitions or descriptions have been taken from RAE [43]

Through the provided descriptions of the preference thresholds and the traits generosity, egoism, and humility, it is possible to visualize a relationship in common and, in this way, influence thresholds of preference with the personality traits mentioned above. In the case of the threshold q and the trait generosity, they have in common that they are indifferent to minimal situations. The threshold v and the trait egoism reflect a restrictive character. Finally, the threshold u and the trait humility share that they both recognize their limitations, but it does not represent any problem.

Table 11 shows the satisfaction parameters and the result of the influence of personality traits. The threshold-related trait q (generosity) represents the least stringent trait; therefore, the satisfaction parameter with the least weight will be influenced by generosity, and the strictest trait egoism, will influence the parameter with the highest weight.

In Table 11, the satisfaction parameters have been ordered in ascending order and placed with the corresponding personality trait, influencing said parameter through its intensity, generating a small percentage of equivalent increases of the trait over the parameter. Through Equation (13), it is possible to influence the satisfaction parameters with personality traits to affect the DM preference thresholds later. The Table 11 shows the result of applying Equation (13).

$$\begin{aligned} &Equality^* = (Equality \times \text{Generosity Intensity}) + Equality \\ &Value^* = (Value \times \text{Humility Intensity}) + Value \\ &Utility^* = (Utility \times \text{Egoism Intensity}) + Utility \\ &\text{Parameter } Equality^* = (1.37 \times 1.63) + 1.37 = 3.60 \end{aligned} \tag{13}$$

Table 11. Results of the influence of the satisfaction parameters with personality traits.

Parameter	Parameter Value	Influence Traits	Intensity	Result of Influence
Equality	1.37	Generosity	1.63	3.60
Value	10.304	Humility	1.05	21.12
Utility	12.573	Egoism	0.48	18.60

After influencing the parameters of satisfaction with personality, they are converted to a percentage to affect the preference thresholds consistently and moderately, increasing the equivalent percentage of each parameter over each of the thresholds. Table 12 shows the conversion of each parameter to a percentage. Equation (14) shows how the calculation of the influence of the preference parameters is carried out with the satisfaction parameters influenced by personality, and Table 13 shows the results of the influence of each threshold.

$$\begin{aligned} &q^* = (q \times Equality) + q \\ &u^* = (u \times Value) + u \\ &v^* = (v \times Utility) + v \\ &\text{Parameter } q^* = (23.78 \times 0.036) + 23.78 = 24.63 \end{aligned} \tag{14}$$

Table 12. Conversion of the satisfaction parameters to a percentage fraction.

Parameter	Influenced Parameter Value	Conversion to %	%
Equality	3.60	3.60 ÷ 100	0.036
Value	21.12	21.12 ÷ 100	0.2112
Utility	18.60	18.60 ÷ 100	0.186

Table 13. Preference thresholds influenced by satisfaction parameters from Table 12.

Threshold	Threshold Value	Satisf. Param.	Param. Value	Result of Influence
q	23.78	Equality	0.036	24.63
u	31.81	Value	0.2112	38.52
v	39.85	Utility	0.186	47.26

The influence of the preference thresholds λ (credibility), β (asymmetry), and ε (symmetry) is completed in the same way as with the thresholds q, u, and v. In this case, the traits used to influence are cruelty, naivety, and humility.

According to the description of the threshold λ, it is associated with credibility. The more value you have, the more credibile and strict the character. The threshold β indicates a preferential distinction between comparisons of alternatives. Finally, the threshold ε establishes indifference in comparing alternatives. These descriptions or definitions were interpreted from the work of Fernández et al. [47].

In the case of personality traits, the trait description or definition of cruelty reflects a fierce or impious state of mind. The trait naivety indicates sincerity, straightforwardness, and lack of malice. The humility trait mentions recognizing limitations and weaknesses. These definitions or descriptions are based on RAE [43].

Through the provided descriptions of the thresholds λ, β, and ε, and of the traits cruelty, naivety, and humility, it is possible to visualize a common relationship and influence the aforementioned thresholds with personality traits. The common description between the threshold λ and the trait cruelty is that they both share a strong and strict character. The relationship between the threshold β and the trait humility is that they recognize their limitations. Finally, the threshold ε and the trait naivety share an opening character.

Equation (15) shows how to calculate the influence of the parameters of satisfaction with personality traits. Finally, Table 14 shows the result of calculating the influence of personality on satisfaction parameters. According to their standard description, the parameters have been ordered in descending order and with the corresponding personality trait.

$$\begin{array}{l} Utility^* = (Utility \times \text{Cruelty Intensity}) + Utility \\ Value^* = (Value \times \text{Humility Intensity}) + Value \\ Equality^* = (Equality \times \text{Naivety Intensity}) + Equality \\ \text{Parameter utility}^* = (12.573 \times 0.60) + 12.573 = 20.11 \end{array} \tag{15}$$

Table 14. Calculation of the influence of the parameters of satisfaction with the traits in order with the thresholds λ, β, and ε.

Parameter	Parameter Value	Influence Traits	Intensity	Result of Influence
Utility	12.573	Cruelty	0.60	20.11
Value	10.304	Humility	1.05	21.12
Equality	1.37	Naivety	0.90	2.60

Table 15 shows the conversion of the satisfaction parameters to generate a moderate increase in the influence of personality and satisfaction on the thresholds λ, β, and ε.

Table 15. Conversion of satisfaction parameters.

Parameter	Influenced Parameter Value	Conversion to %	%
Utility	20.11	20.11 ÷ 100	0.2011
Value	21.12	21.12 ÷ 100	0.2112
Equality	2.60	2.60 ÷ 100	0.026

Equation (16) shows how to calculate the influence of the thresholds λ, β, and ε with the satisfaction parameters. Finally, Table 16 shows the thresholds influenced by the satisfaction parameters ordered from strictest to most relaxed (in the same way as in Table 14).

$$\begin{array}{l} \lambda^* = (\lambda \times Utility) + \lambda \\ \beta^* = (\beta \times Value) + \beta \\ \varepsilon^* = (\varepsilon \times Equality) + \varepsilon \\ \text{Parameter } \lambda^* = (0.71 \times 0.2011) + 0.71 = 0.85 \end{array} \tag{16}$$

Table 16. Result of preference thresholds influenced by satisfaction.

Threshold	Threshold Value	Satisf. Param.	Param. Value	Result of Influence
λ	0.71	Utility	0.2011	0.85
β	0.08	Value	0.2112	0.096
ε	0.04	Equality	0.026	0.041

Table 17 shows the preference thresholds finally calculated and ready to be sent to the deliberative process. The increase in each parameter can be seen with the naked eye, where said increase represents the influence of satisfaction and personality on preferences during the decision-making process.

Table 17. Summary of preference thresholds influenced by satisfaction and personality.

Threshold	Threshold Value
Indifference (q)	24.63
Preveto (u)	38.52
Veto (v)	47.26
Credibility (λ)	0.85
Asymmetry (β)	0.096
Symmetry (ε)	0.041

5.6. Experimental Design

The experimental design validates the functioning of the proposed satisfaction model integrated into the cognitive process of an intelligent agent. Furthermore, the hypothesis to be validated shows that integrating the degree of satisfaction of an individual in optimization problems that take into account personality and preferences generates better solutions than process solutions that do not incorporate satisfaction. The validation is carried out through a case study that addresses the purchase of food products.

The solutions that integrate characteristics of satisfaction, personality, and preferences of the DM, come from the process of applying the satisfaction model proposed in this work, the NOSGA-II metaheuristic based on preferences [8], and a personality model (PMUDC -II). On the other hand, the solutions that only integrate personality characteristics and DM preferences come from the application of the PMUDC-I [2] personality model and the NOSGA-II strategy. These solutions represent a set of shopping lists with the products desired by the DM, which the VDM suggests. Both sets of shopping lists (generated with/without satisfaction characteristics) will be compared to validate the proposed hypothesis.

The hypothesis validation experiment will be applied to four individuals that reflect different characteristics to contrast the solutions generated. These individuals will be identified under the optimistic, collaborative, inquirer, and strict personality profiles. A parameter will indicate their tolerance for solutions differently from their decision, and a set of parameters will quantify their satisfaction from a personality perspective. To collect information on the personality of individuals, the questionnaire based on personality types of the MBTI model is used [28] and the IPIP-NEO [26] questionnaire will be applied, which is based on personality traits from the FFM-OCEAN model [25]. The personality profiles and the tolerance parameter will be taken from the PMUDC-I model [2]. The personality parameters that characterize satisfaction will be taken from the PMUDC-II model, which uses the PMUDC-I model for its development. The PMUDC-II model will be addressed in future research. The result of applying the personality questionnaire can be seen in Appendices B and C.

Information on the preferences of the individuals under experimentation will be collected through a questionnaire based on a specific decision context. In this case, the context is the purchase of food products. In this way, it will be possible to generate representative parameters of the preferences of a DM, which are: indifference, preveto, veto, credibility, asymmetry, and symmetry. The questionnaire and the preference parameters will be provided through the preferential impact model of the PMUDC-I model [2]. The result of applying the preferences questionnaire can be seen in Appendix D, and the product database can be found in Appendix A.

The information on the satisfaction profile will be obtained through a questionnaire proposed in this work, whose structure is presented in Section 5.1. The information from the satisfaction profile (results of the satisfaction questionnaire and the RIASEC test [16,41]) will be used in the experimentation with the four study subjects to influence the cognitive and deliberative process. The reason for experimenting with the same set in the decision process of the four individuals is to observe the positive impact of satisfaction on preferences regardless of the personality characteristics of the DM. The result of applying the satisfaction questionnaire can be seen in Appendix E. The result of applying the RIASEC test can be seen in Appendix F.

Using the information of the individuals mentioned above, the VDM will provide a set of instances generated with the influence of the satisfaction model and without the intervention of said influence. Each instance will be evaluated using the degree of satisfaction metric proposed in this work to determine if it meets its expectations. These instances are composed of a series of food products requested by the individual. In this set, it is simulated that the four study subjects want or request to acquire the same type of products (for example, water, milk, and bread).

The results obtained from evaluating the set of instances of the individuals' understudy will be compared through the Wilcoxon non-parametric statistical test. This statistical test will indicate whether or not there are significant differences between the solutions or instances generated with the satisfaction model and without the said model. This statistical test will reinforce the hypothesis that guides this research work.

5.7. The Evaluation Process of the Degree or Level of Satisfaction (Satisfaction Metric)

The satisfaction metric is responsible for evaluating the solution alternatives provided by the deliberative process. These solutions come from the NOSGA-II solution strategy, which integrates the preference thresholds influenced by satisfaction and personality. Therefore, the alternative solutions (decisions) provided by NOSGA-II somehow reflect the DM's satisfaction, preferences, and personality. In addition, the satisfaction metric ensures that the solutions are closest to the DM's satisfaction expectations imposed, that is, to their initial request, which, according to the case study of product shopping, is a shopping list with certain products selected by the user (DM).

The evaluation consists of taking the DM's initial request or product list as a reference and comparing it with the solution alternatives given by the NOSGA-II strategy, preventing them from exceeding the tolerance ($\varphi*$) allowed for deviation from their ideal satisfaction.

In the work of Castro-Rivera et al. [2], a method to calculate tolerance (φ) allowed for distance concerning alternative solutions other than your preference has been proposed. However, this tolerance (φ) does not reflect the DM's satisfaction. Equation (17) shows how to integrate satisfaction into tolerance ($\varphi*$), where μ represents the union of the set of satisfaction parameters and φ represents the tolerance of the DM without reflecting satisfaction.

The calculation of μ is proposed through the union of the satisfaction parameters calculated in Table 12, whose result is 0.4332. The reason for using the satisfaction parameters to influence q, u, and v, is because these preference parameters represent a less strict character with respect to the thresholds (λ, β, and ϵ), according to the description provided in Section 5.5. The above reason make them more suitable for calculating $\varphi*$ since tolerance indicates relaxation and not restriction. After calculating $\varphi*$, it is necessary to know the accumulated value of each criterion, both the DM's request and the solution alternatives given by the deliberative process (NOSGA-II), to compare them with $varfi*$.

$$\varphi* = (\varphi \times \mu) + \varphi \tag{17}$$

Table 18 shows the structure of both the query or list of products requested, as well as the alternative solutions, where R represents the set of suggested alternatives/lists/shopping baskets, be it the request or the alternatives delivered by the deliberative processes (NOSGA-II strategy). This set goes from R_1 to R_m and is made up of n elements or products x characterized by benefits, criteria, or attributes b that go from b_1 to b_p. Table 18 also shows the total sum of each of the criteria ($S_{b_{R_{mp}}}$), which is formally expressed in Equation (18). The total sum of each criterion, determined by $S_{b_{R_{mp}}}$, will be compared with $\varphi*$ using Equation (19) as the first measure of evaluation of the satisfaction.

$$S_{b_{R_{k|k \in \{1,2,\dots,m\}}} j|j \in \{1,2,\dots,p\}} = \sum_{i=1}^{n} b_{R_k j} x_{R_k} i \tag{18}$$

Table 18. Structure of the requested shopping list and solution alternatives/suggested shopping lists.

Lists	Products	Criteria			
R_1	$x_{R_{11}}, x_{R_{12}}, \dots, x_{R_{1n}}$	$b_{R_{11}}$	$b_{R_{12}}$	$\dots$	$b_{R_{1p}}$
	$x_{R_1 1}$	$b_{R_1 1 x_{R_1} 1}$	$b_{R_1 2 x_{R_1} 1}$	$\dots$	$b_{R_{1p} x R_1 1}$
	$x_{R_1 2}$	$b_{R_1 1 x_{R_1} 2}$	$b_{R_1 2 x_{R_1} 2}$	$\dots$	$b_{R_1 p x_{R_1} 2}$
	$\vdots$	$\vdots$	$\vdots$	$\vdots$	$\vdots$
	$x_{R_1} n$	$b_{R_1 1 x_{R_1} n}$	$b_{R_1 2 x_{R_1} n}$	$\dots$	$b_{R_1 p x_{R_1} n}$
		$S_{b_{R_1} 1}$	$S_{b_{R_1} 2}$	$\dots$	$S_{b_{R_1} p}$
$\vdots$	$\vdots$	$\vdots$	$\vdots$	$\vdots$	$\vdots$
R_m	$x_{R_{m1}}, x_{R_{m2}}, \dots, x_{R_{mn}}$	$b_{R_{m1}}$	$b_{R_{m2}}$	$\dots$	$b_{R_{mp}}$
	$x_{R_{m1}}$	$b_{R_m 1 x_{R_m} 1}$	$b_{R_m 2 x_{R_m} 1}$	$\dots$	$b_{R_m p x_{R_m} 1}$
	$x_{R_{m2}}$	$b_{R_m 1 x_{R_m} 2}$	$b_{R_m 2 x_{R_m} 2}$	$\dots$	$b_{R_m p x_{R_m} 2}$
	$\vdots$	$\vdots$	$\vdots$	$\vdots$	$\vdots$
	$x_{R_{mn}}$	$b_{R_m 1 x_{R_m} n}$	$b_{R_m 2 x_{R_m} n}$	$\dots$	$b_{R_m p x_{R_m} n}$
		$S_{b_{R_{m1}}}$	$S_{b_{R_{m2}}}$	$\dots$	$S_{b_{R_{mp}}}$

Table 19 shows the structure of a list/request/alternative solution (Table 18) with the accumulated total of each of its criteria (Equation (18)). In this case, said list represents the query or shopping list of food products requested by the DM. This shopping list comprises three products and two criteria, the price and the content.

Table 19. DM's initial shopping list for the VDM.

Product	Price	Contents
Natural water	5.80	600
Soluble coffee	38	180
Sweetbread	9.90	62
—	$S_{b_{R_{01}}}$: 53.70	$S_{b_{R_{02}}}$: 842

In Table 20, there are alternative solutions or shopping lists suggested by the VDM, generated with the NOSGA-II strategy. These lists are based on the shopping list requested by the DM. Suggested lists by VDM try to cover the objectives from the list requested by DM, improving either in some criterion or in both (price or content). In addition, the suggested lists reflect the preferences, personality, and satisfaction of the DM due to the preference thresholds (Table 17) that were provided to NOSGA-II.

Table 20. Solution alternatives generated with NOSGA-II based on the list in Table 19.

List	Product	Price	Contents
List 1	Natural water	8.50	600
	Soluble coffee	41	180
	Sweetbread	14	200
		$S_{bR_{11}}$: 63.50	$S_{bR_{12}}$: 980
List 2	Natural water	8.50	600
	Soluble coffee	41	180
	Sweetbread	9.90	62
		$S_{bR_{21}}$: 59.40	$S_{bR_{22}}$: 842
List 3	Natural water	8.50	600
	Natural water	12.60	1500
	Soluble coffee	38	180
	Sweetbread	14	200
		$S_{bR_{21}}$: 73.10	$S_{bR_{22}}$: 2480

The first strategy is to evaluate what was obtained against what was expected. That is to say, the requested list with the lists suggested by the VDM. Then, it is necessary to calculate the proportion that exceeds each criterion of the suggested lists to the criteria of the requested list. In this work, it is proposed to compare the proportion of differences between criteria with the tolerance ($\varphi*$), ensuring that the total sum of each criterion ($S_{bR_{mp}}$) of the suggested lists does not exceed what is allowed by $\varphi*$. It will be counted as a hit (A_b). The higher the number of hits the set of suggested lists has ($R = \{1, 2, \ldots, m\}$), the closer the DM's satisfaction will be. In Equation (19), the procedure described above is presented.

$$\begin{array}{lll} A_b = A_b + 1 & \text{si} & \varphi* \geq \frac{|S_{bR_{01}} - S_{bR_{11}}|}{S_{bR_{01}}}, \frac{|S_{bR_{02}} - S_{bR_{12}}|}{S_{bR_{02}}}, \ldots, \frac{|S_{bR_{0p}} - S_{bR_{1p}}|}{S_{bR_{0p}}} \\ A_b = A_{b+1} & \text{si} & \varphi* \geq \frac{|S_{bR_{01}} - S_{bR_{21}}|}{S_{bR_{01}}}, \frac{|S_{bR_{02}} - S_{bR_{22}}|}{S_{bR_{02}}}, \ldots, \frac{|S_{bR_{0p}} - S_{bR_{2p}}|}{S_{bR_{0p}}} \\ \vdots & \vdots & \qquad\qquad\qquad \vdots \\ A_b = A_b + 1 & \text{si} & \varphi* \geq \frac{|S_{bR_{01}} - S_{bR_{m1}}|}{S_{bR_{01}}}, \frac{|S_{bR_{02}} - S_{bR_{m2}}|}{S_{bR_{02}}}, \ldots, \frac{|S_{bR_{0p}} - S_{bR_{mp}}|}{S_{bR_{0p}}} \end{array} \quad (19)$$

In Table 21, Equation (19) is replaced with the values of the suggested shopping lists (Table 20) and the list requested by the DM (Table 19). In this evaluation, the total hits of the set of suggested lists have been five hits out of six. Each list can obtain two maximum hits due to its two criteria and a minimum of zero hits.

Table 21. Substitution of values in Equation (19).

List	Criteria	Operation	Comparison with $\varphi*$	Hit (A_b)
List 1	Price	$\|53.70 - 63.50\| \div 53.70 = 0.182$	$0.8330475 \geq 0.182$	$A_b = 1$
	Contents	$\|842 - 980\| \div 842 = 0.163$	$0.8330475 \geq 0.163$	$A_b = 2$
List 2	Price	$\|53.70 - 59.40\| \div 53.70 = 0.106$	$0.8330475 \geq 0.106$	$A_b = 3$
	Contents	$\|842 - 842\| \div 842 = 0$	$0.8330475 \geq 0$	$A_b = 4$
List 3	Price	$\|53.70 - 73.10\| \div 53.70 = 0.361$	$0.8330475 \geq 0.361$	$A_b = 5$
	Contents	$\|842 - 2480\| \div 842 = 1.945$	$0.8330475 \geq 1.945$	$A_b = 5$

After counting the total hits of the solution alternatives (set R), verifying if the said number of hits comes close to the DM's ideal satisfaction expectation is necessary. For evaluation satisfaction of the lists suggested by the VDM, the proportion represented by the hits in the m lists of the set R must first be obtained. Then, with this proportion, it will be possible to know the percentage of satisfaction that the correct answers cover in the p criteria. Finally, this percentage should be compared to the satisfaction expectation of the DM.

If the percentage of correct answers exceeds or equals the satisfaction expectation, then the set R is accepted; otherwise, it will be necessary to readjust the satisfaction, preferences, and personality parameters. Equation (20) shows the procedure described above, in addition to the substitution of the values presented above, where $A_b = 5$, $m = 3$, $p = 2$ and $\varphi* = 0.8330475$. The result indicates that the set of lists R reaches the satisfaction expectation so that the solution alternatives are satisfactory and efficient for the interests of the DM.

$$\begin{array}{ll} \text{There is satisfaction if}\ldots & \frac{A_b}{m \times p} \geq |1 - \varphi *| \\ \text{Substituting}\ldots & \frac{5}{(3 \times 2)} = 0.84 \\ & |1 - 0.8330475| = 0.1669525 \\ \text{Yes, there is satisfaction} & 0.84 \geq 0.1669525 \end{array} \tag{20}$$

Tables 22 and 23 show the data used in each individual to generate the lists and the evaluation of the results. In Table 23, personality parameters corresponding to each decision profile are used to influence satisfaction and preferences. The same satisfaction parameters (Table 10) were applied in the experiments of the three individuals with different profiles. The above is the purpose of observing the impact of the personality on the results, despite having the same satisfaction or expectation, and observing how it complements the satisfaction, producing highly satisfactory results when both factors are present.

In Table 24, the previous experiment has been replicated, only that this time three different personality-decision profiles are involved than that of the previously analyzed individual (cooperative decision profile). In this experiment, the results of six lists with/without satisfaction for each decision profile (strict, optimistic, and inquirer) have been evaluated. That is, solutions generated with the presence of satisfaction and without its presence are evaluated. These lists also consider only two criteria.

Table 22. Information from three individuals under studies with different decision profiles.

Profile	Status	Criteria	Thresholds						Tol.
		b	q	u	v	λ	β	ϵ	$\varphi*$
Strict	WS	Price	15.23	18.85	22.14	1.07	0.20	0.08	0.23
		Contents	150.72	223.56	298.05				
	WoS	Price	14.88	16.49	18.11	0.92	0.17	0.08	0.166
		Contents	147.27	195.53	243.8				
Optimistic	WS	Price	36.71	47.20	56.28	0.63	0.02	0.01	1.23
		Contents	800.54	1039.43	1248.25				
	WoS	Price	35.93	41.63	47.33	0.54	0.02	0.01	0.91
		Contents	783.41	916.62	1049.83				
Inquirer	WS	Price	35.01	44.38	49.28	0.93	0.13	0.06	0.39
		Contents	179.95	343.55	483.67				
	WoS	Price	34.39	38.8	43.21	0.8	0.12	0.06	0.30
		Contents	176.76	300.4	424.05				

Table 23. Personality parameters corresponding to each decision profile.

Factor	Profile	Parameters		
	—	**Value**	**Equality**	**Utility**
Personality	Strict	0.253846154	0.26	0.353846154
	Optimistic	0.053076923	0.175384615	0.247692308
	Inquirer	0.27	0.2715385	0.4715385
Satisfaction	—	7.34	1	7.62

Table 24. Experimentation of the impact of satisfaction in three individuals with different decision profiles.

Profile	Status	Lists			Hits (A_b)	Satisf. (Equation (20))
			Prices	**Contents**		
Strict	With satisfaction	List 1	57.8	980	5 de 6	YES
		List 2	65.70	2342		
		List 3	53.69	842		
	Without satisfaction	List 1	69.90	1942	0 de 6	NO
		List 2	70.70	1042		
		List 3	72.00	2342		
			Price	**Contents**		
Optimistic	With satisfaction	List 1	60.00	1880	4 de 6	YES
		List 2	65.80	2480		
		List 3	75.69	1110		
	Without satisfaction	List 1	62.69	2342	3 de 6	YES
		List 2	67.70	2842		
		List 3	67	2380		
			Price	**Contents**		
Inquirer	With satisfaction	List 1	70.40	1042	5 de 6	YES
		List 2	70.90	2442		
		List 3	60.50	980		
	Without satisfaction	List 1	56.40	842	3 de 6	NO
		List 2	67.00	2880		
		List 3	75.50	3480		

The resulting shopping lists are shown in Table 24; each decision profile presents three lists for each strategy (with/without satisfaction) with the accumulated values of the price and content criteria. The lists of each strategy have been selected from the deliberative process (NOSGA-II) and represent the most optimal set of solutions suggested by the VDM concerning the satisfaction, preferences, and personality of a DM.

The results of the experiment with three individuals with different profiles in Table 24 indicate that the optimistic profile has a similar performance in both cases (with/without satisfaction). The above is due to its high tolerance since optimistic or relaxed individuals are very open to decisions other than their preferred ones. Hence, their satisfaction is high, possibly in most decision contexts, so lists with the influence of satisfaction meet the expectations of the optimistic DM. In contrast, in the case of the inquirer and strict profile, the satisfaction-influenced lists have a more substantial advantage in meeting the satisfaction expectation.

In Table 25, the same instances of the experiment above (Table 24) have been used, but evaluating each of the three decision profiles (with/without satisfaction) has. In the said table, similar behavior is observed concerning the results of Table 24, where an optimistic individual in both cases (with/without satisfaction) shows a very high tolerance. In the case of the individual with the strict profile, only the instance I1 was accepted as satisfactory, and the difference in results can be seen when satisfaction is present and when it is not present. In the inquirer profile, instances I2 and I5 show that the presence of satisfaction represents a difference concerning its absence. In Table 25, the terminology used is as follows: H (Hits), WS (With satisfaction), WoS (Without satisfaction), S (Satisfaction), Y (Yes), N (No), and I (Instance).

Table 25. Experimentation with three decision profiles using six data instances.

Instance	Values		Profile											
			Strict				Optimistic				Inquirer			
	Price	Content	WS		WoS		WS		WoS		WS		WoS	
			H	S	H	S	H	S	H	S	H	S	H	S
I1	57.8 65.7 53.69	980 2342 842	5	Y	4	N	5	Y	5	Y	5	Y	5	Y
I2	69.9 70.70 72.00	1942 1042 2342	0	N	0	N	4	Y	4	Y	4	Y	1	N
I3	60.00 65.80 75.69	1880 2480 1110	2	N	1	N	4	Y	4	Y	3	N	3	N
I4	62.69 67.70 67.00	2342 2842 2380	1	N	0	N	3	Y	3	Y	3	N	3	N
I5	70.40 70.9 60.50	1042 2442 980	2	N	2	N	5	Y	5	Y	5	Y	3	N
I6	56.40 67.00 75.50	842 2880 3480	2	N	2	N	4	Y	4	Y	3	N	3	N

The results of Table 25 were subjected to a statistical analysis taking the Hits (H) column of the WS and WoS groups of the six instances evaluated with the three profiles of the DMs'. The statistical test applied was Wilcoxon to compare both groups and determine significant differences between them. The significance level used for the test was 0.05, obtaining a p-value of 0.0393, which means that the difference in means of both groups is the same, so the null hypothesis is rejected. The preceding affirms a significant difference when a satisfaction model is integrated into an optimization problem than when its integration is not considered.

6. Discussion of Results

In this research work, the satisfaction model proposed was subjected to experimentation, validating whether the definition of the satisfaction parameters of this model generates a significant and positive influence on the preferences of a DM, improving the deliberative process of a virtual agent.

Four types of individuals were required in food product shopping to test the satisfaction model. The strategy applied to ensure that these individuals provided distinctive characteristics to the experimentation was through the PMUDC-I model [2]. PMUDC-I provides a way to identify individuals through personality and decision profiling. These profiles are optimistic, collaborative, inquirer, and strict. In addition, NOSGA-II [8] was used like an optimization strategy that acts as the deliberative process of the VDM, producing the shopping lists requested by individuals according to their preferences, satisfaction, and personality.

In the results of the experimentation shown in Table 21, carried out with the collaborative profile DM, the comparison between the criteria of the products expected by the DM and the lists suggested by the VDM could be observed. In said comparison, the level of correct answers was very significant, achieving a total of five correct answers out of six.

The more correct answers, the greater the possibility of covering the satisfaction expectation of the DM. The above could be corroborated by applying Equation (20), showing that the DM with collaborative characteristics is 84% satisfied with the suggestions given by the VDM.

The data provided in Tables 22 and 23 were used to replicate the previous experiment, generating instances or shopping lists suggested by the VDM for three different individuals. These individuals are identified under the strict, optimistic/relaxed, and inquirer profiles. The total number of instances generated was six, of which two of them were generated through the corresponding data of each individual, integrating and restricting the influence of the satisfaction model.

Table 24 shows the results of the experimentation with the six instances generated with the three individuals. These results clearly show that integrating a satisfaction model to influence an agent's deliberation positively impacts the scope of the satisfaction expectation concerning when it is not integrated. It is worth mentioning that the optimistic DM was the only one that managed to reach the satisfaction expectation in both cases due to their flexible characteristics being satisfied more easily and thus, reflected in a high tolerance. The correct answers more clearly describe the scope of the satisfaction expectation according to the profile of each DM. For example, in the case of the strict DM, the hits highlight that integrating a satisfaction model improves the scope of the satisfaction expectation. When integrating the characteristics of satisfaction, five out of six correct answers were obtained. On the contrary, zero of six correct answers were obtained by not integrating satisfaction.

In the experiment presented in Table 25, the six instances of the experiment in Table 24 were used. In this new experiment, the six instances with the three individuals (strict, optimistic, and inquirer) were evaluated using the satisfaction metric proposed in Equation (20). From this new experimental case, we observed that the optimistic DM reached their satisfaction expectation regardless of whether or not there was any influence on satisfaction. In the strict DM, it can be seen that only one instance (I1) covers the level of satisfaction required by said individual, showing five of six correct answers when satisfaction was integrated compared to four of six correct answers when satisfaction does not influence. In the rest of the instances of the strict profile, the number of correct answers did not exceed two. In the case of the inquirer DM, it was possible to meet the expectation of satisfaction in three instances, of which instance I2 stands out, due to it showing a clear significant difference when integrating satisfaction with four of six correct answers concerning one of six correct answers when satisfaction is not integrated.

To strengthen the results obtained from the experiment presented in Table 25, they were subjected to the Wilcoxon statistical test. The results reveal the feasibility of considering the characteristics of satisfaction in a computable model to improve the cognitive process of a virtual agent.

The experimentation presented in this work confirms that the proposed satisfaction model is a novel contribution to behavioral simulation. However, despite the results and the consistent behavior of each individual, it is necessary to strengthen these advantages. The above could be through the integration of personality traits more representative of satisfaction or other elements that assist in modeling the satisfaction of individuals more precisely. The preceding could give rise to future research that generates more significant advantages in the experimentation results than that reported in this work.

7. Conclusions

In this document, a satisfaction model capable of influencing and improving the decision-making process of a virtual agent in an optimization context was developed. The above was possible by integrating models from the literature aimed at assisting in the simulation of behaviors, such as the NOSGA-II preference-based strategy, the PMUDC-I model, and its predecessor in the development phase PMUDC-II, as well as models of satisfaction with work and customer, approaches.

According to the above, the main objective of this research was achieved by using the attributes provided by the PMUDC-I, PMUDC-II models, and the satisfaction model to assist in modeling and influencing the preferences of a DM, managing to improve the cognitive process of a virtual agent, as observed in the experimentation carried out in this work.

The integration of parameters and attributes of personality and satisfaction generate an impact on preferences confirming the hypothesis that arises from the main objective of this work, demonstrating that better solutions are provided by integrating a satisfaction model compared to processes that do not consider integrating it.

In addition to contributing to developing a satisfaction model, an intelligent agent architecture was also developed to facilitate an interaction mechanism with the DM. The satisfaction model was integrated with the personality model and the NOSGA-II metaheuristic in the deliberative process.

However, despite contributing to a satisfaction model that provides excellent scope for improving optimization process solutions focused on behavior simulation, there are still certain unknowns that limit the efficiency of the results in some way. These deficiencies or unknowns could be resolved by modeling other significant impacts, such as those addressed. Nevertheless, the above is a reason to continue research and analyze the emulation of human behavior through computable models that provide credibility in the development of virtual entities.

Author Contributions: Conceptualization, J.C.-R. and M.L.M.-R.; methodology, J.C.-R. and N.R.-V.; software, J.C.-R.; validation, C.G.-S. and L.A.-V.; formal analysis, N.R.-V. and M.L.M.-R.; investigation, J.C.-R.; resources, L.A.-V. and C.G.-S.; data curation, J.C.-R. and M.L.M.-R.; writing—original draft preparation, J.C.-R. and M.L.M.-R.; writing—review and editing, N.R.-V., L.A.-V. and C.G.-S.; visualization, J.C.-R.; supervision, M.L.M.-R. and N.R.-V.; project administration, M.L.M.-R. All authors have read and agreed to the published version of the manuscript.

Funding: This research received no external funding.

Institutional Review Board Statement: Not applicable.

Informed Consent Statement: Not applicable.

Data Availability Statement: Not applicable.

Acknowledgments: The authors thanks CONACyT for the support granted through the Scholarship for Postgraduate Studies with CVU 784035, and the projects no. 3058, A1-S-11012. Moreover, we thank the Laboratorio Nacional de Tecnologías de la Informaci6n (LANTI), and acknowledge the support of ITCM, and the TECNM project 14612.22-P.

Conflicts of Interest: The authors declare no conflict of interest.

Sample Availability: Not applicable.

Abbreviations

The following abbreviations are used in this manuscript:

NOSGA-II	Non-Outranking Sorting Genetic Algorithm
DM	Decision-Maker
VDM	Virtual Decision-Maker
IVA	Intelligent Virtual Agent
PMUDC	Personality Model Under Decision Context
FFM-OCEAN	Five-Factor Model-Openness, Conscientiousness, Extraversion, Agreeableness, Neuroticism
MBTI	Myers-Brigg Type Indicator
KTS	Keirsey Temperament Sorted

Appendix A. Case of the Study Details

The Table A1 present the products used in the food shopping case study, which consists of 55 product variants.

Table A1. Table of products used in the experimentation with the case study of foods products.

No.	Product	Price	Content	No.	Product	Price	Content
1	Water	5.8	600	29	Milk	21	1000
2	Water	6	1000	30	Milk	28.3	1500
3	Water	8	1500	31	Milkshake	7.2	250
4	Water	12	2000	32	Milkshake	8.5	200
5	Water	8.5	600	33	Milkshake	7.2	250
6	Water	12.6	1500	34	Milkshake	21.5	1000
7	Water	6	500	35	Wholemeal bread	29.5	480
8	Water	9	1500	36	Wholemeal bread	34.5	680
9	Water	9	2000	37	Wholemeal bread	30.7	567
10	Instant coffee	38	180	38	Wholemeal bread	82	540
11	Instant coffee	41	180	39	Wholemeal bread	64	450
12	Instant coffee	63	205	40	Sweetbread	32	240
13	Instant coffee	90	225	41	Sweetbread	9.9	62
14	Instant coffee	155.5	350	42	Sweetbread	32.9	240
15	Instant coffee	399	1200	43	Sweetbread	31.9	330
16	Instant coffee	62	120	44	Sweetbread	14	200
17	Soda	13.1	600	45	Dessert	115	700
18	Soda	12	355	46	Dessert	11	114
19	Soda	29	2000	47	Dessert	24.5	324
20	Soda	30.6	2500	48	Dessert	15.4	14
21	Soda	34.5	3000	49	Instant coffee	47.5	180
22	Soda	10	600	50	Milk	50	1000
23	Soda	8	355	51	Milkshake	50	1000
24	Soda	21.9	2000	52	Instant coffee	41.9	250
25	Soda	24	2500	53	Sweetbread	13.9	125
26	Soda	25	3000	54	Milkshake	8.5	200
27	Milk	19.9	1000	55	Sweetbread	6	100
28	Milk	18.9	1000				

Appendix B. Results from the Types-Based Personality Questionnaire

This section presents the results of the MBTI personality model questionnaire based on personality types [28]. This questionnaire consists of 4 questions that try to recognize the preference of individuals to act in their environment. These characteristics are represented by a label consisting of 4 dichotomies or letters that form the individual's personality profile. These dichotomies come from a set of 8 letters with which a total of 16 personality profiles can be formed. The results of the application of this questionnaire are presented in Table A2, where the MBTI profile of the four individuals or DM with whom the experimentation was carried out in this work and their decision profile is given by the PMUDC-I model [2] to identify the DM in decision-making more accurately.

Table A2. According to [2,28], the MBTI questionnaire results were applied to four DM.

No. of DM	MBTI Profile	PMUDC-I Profile
1	ESFP	Optimistic
2	ISFJ	Collaborative
3	INTP	Inquirer
4	ISTJ	Strict

Appendix C. Results from Traits-Based Personality Questionnaire

This section presents the results of the IPIP-NEO questionnaire [26] based on personality traits from the FFM-OCEAN model [25]. The questionnaire consists of 120 questions (reduced version) that aim to collect information about the strengths and weaknesses of an individual. Table A3 presents the results of the questionnaire applied to the four individuals mentioned in Table A2, where the values of the facets of interest in this work are observed according to each DM. In general, this table shows the dimensions or factors of OCEAN, the value of the dimension (factor value), the facets of each dimension, and the DM identified through the profile provided by PMUDC-I [2].

Table A3. Results of the IPIP-NEO questionnaire [26] belonging to the four DM under study.

		PMUDC-I Profile			
OCEAN Factors	**OCEAN Facets**	**Optimistic (DM 1)**	**Collaborative (DM 2)**	**Inquirer (DM 3)**	**Strict (DM 4)**
Extraversion	Activity Level	0.3	0.80	0.27	0.78
	Gregariousness	0.75	0.55	0.08	0.17
	Excitement-Seeking	0.41	0.17	0.04	0.38
	Factor value	0.60	0.70	0.21	0.38
Agreeableness	Morality	0.83	0.89	0.61	0.17
	Modesty	0.69	0.65	0.89	0.35
	Altruism	0.38	0.95	0.33	0.34
	Factor value	0.18	0.88	0.60	0.05
Conscientiousness	Self-Efficacy	0.34	0.8	0.01	0.58
	Cautiousness	0.93	0.72	0.64	0.64
	Factor value	0.17	0.65	0.18	0.59
Neuroticism	Anxiety	0.3	0.64	0.55	0.3
	Anger	0.27	0.27	0.2	0.65
	Immoderation	0.42	0.48	0.38	0.31
	Factor value	0.30	0.43	0.52	0.42
Openness	Imagination	0.74	0.5	0.19	0.17
	Factor value	0.34	0.59	0.51	0.20

Appendix D. Results form Preferences Questionnaire

This section presents the questionnaire proposed by Castro et al. [2], necessary to generate representative parameters of the preferences of a DM through the PMUDC-I model. The questionnaire aims to collect information on the preferences of the DM according to a decision context, which in this work was applied under a context of shopping of food products. The way in which this shopping context is expressed is through presenting the DM with a set of food products from which he must select the ones of his preference, as well as forming shopping lists with said products, according to what is requested. in the questionnaire. In this way, it is possible to collect the DM's preferences in this shopping environment and form parameters representative of the DM's preferences. The food products presented in Table A1 are the ones that the questionnaire uses to acquire the preferential information of the DM. Table A4 shows the results of the questionnaire applied to the four DM mentioned in Table A2, where the parameters or preference thresholds given by the PMUDC-I model are presented with the influence of satisfaction (WS) and without the influence of satisfaction (WoS). The values presented were rounded to two figures after the point.

Table A4. Preference thresholds resulting from the application of the preference questionnaire in the four DM under study

Profile	Status	Thresholds						
		Criteria	q	u	v	λ	β	ϵ
Optimistic (DM 1)	WS	Price	36.71	47.20	56.28	0.63	0.02	0.01
		Contents	800.54	1039.43	1248.25			
	WoS	Price	35.93	41.63	47.33	0.54	0.02	0.01
		Contents	783.41	916.62	1049.83			
Collaborative (DM 2)	WS	Price	24.63	38.52	47.26	0.85	0.096	0.041
		Contents	192.04	328.93	424.33			
	WoS	Price	23.78	31.81	39.85	0.71	0.08	0.04
		Contents	185.37	271.58	357.79			
Inquirer (DM 3)	WS	Price	35.01	44.38	49.28	0.93	0.13	0.06
		Contents	179.95	343.55	483.67			
	WoS	Price	34.39	38.8	43.21	0.8	0.12	0.06
		Contents	176.76	300.4	424.05			
Strict (DM 4)	WS	Price	15.23	18.85	22.14	1.07	0.20	0.08
		Contents	150.72	223.56	298.05			
	WoS	Price	14.88	16.49	18.11	0.92	0.17	0.08
		Contents	147.27	195.53	243.8			

Appendix E. Satisfaction Questionnaire (Satisfaction Profile of the DM) and Results

This section presents the questionnaire proposed in this work, which collects information on the satisfaction of the DM. This questionnaire consists of five questions that meet the satisfaction expectation of the DM according to a service or product. Table A5 shows the satisfaction questionnaire, which gathers the satisfaction characteristics of the DM to form a satisfaction profile.

Table A5. Satisfaction questionnaire (satisfaction profile of the DM).

No.	Question
1	What is the expected performance of your product? __Very low __low __Medium __Good __Very good
2	What is the quality you expect to perceive from your product? __Very low __low __Medium __Good __Very good
3	Does the product represent any emotional value to you? __Very little __Little __Regular __A lot of __Too much
4	In general terms, what is the expectation you expect from the product? __Very little __Little __Regular __A lot of __Too much
5	Do you think the product will meet your expectations? __Very little __Little __Regular __A lot of __Too much

Derived from the results of the proposed satisfaction questionnaire, representative parameters of DM satisfaction are generated. These parameters are calculated using the strategies shown in Sections 5.1 and 5.2. The values of these parameters are representative for the four DM under study. The parameters and their values are as follows: value −7.34; equality −1; and utility −7.62.

Appendix F. Results from RIASEC Test

This Section presents the result of the application of the RIASEC [16,41] test. This questionnaire consists of 6 dimensions and 42 questions that collect information on the work areas you perform best. The six dimensions comprise the RIASEC literals, where each literal comprises seven questions. The result is a label formed by the three literals with the highest score.

As in the previous Appendix E, the RIASEC result was used for the four studied individuals. The RIASEC result and its values are as follows: R (REALISTIC) −7; I (INVESTIGATIVE) −5 and A (ARTISTIC) −5.

This questionnaire is related to job satisfaction because it exposes the areas where the individual has a better performance and, therefore, greater satisfaction.

References

1. Cruz-Reyes, L.; Fernández, E.; Rangel-Valdez, N. A Metaheuristic Optimization-Based Indirect Elicitation of Preference Parameters for Solving Many-Objective Problems. *Int. J. Comput. Intell. Syst.* **2017**, *10*, 56–77. [CrossRef]
2. Castro-Rivera, J.; Morales-Rodríguez, M.L.; Rangel-Valdez, N.; Cruz-Reyes, L.; Pazos R., R.A. Prioritization of Elements Selection in Order-Picking Problems through a Preference Model Influenced by Personality. In *Handbook of Research on Metaheuristics for Order Picking Optimization in Warehouses to Smart Cities*; Ortiz-Zezzatti, A.O., Rivera, G., Gómez-Santillán, C., Sánchez-Lara, B., Eds.; IGI Global: Hershey, PA, USA, 2019; pp. 117–142. [CrossRef]
3. Mallareddy, T. Employee job satisfaction a Case Study of South Central Railway. Ph.D. Thesis, Gulbarga University, Kalaburagi, Karnataka, India, 2015.
4. Hom, W. *An Overview of Customer Satisfaction Models*; Reports—Descriptive 141; ERIC: Pacific Grove, CA, USA, 2000.
5. Frikha, H.M.; Charfi, S. Inferring an ELECTRE I model from binary outranking relations. *Int. J. Multicriteria Decis. Mak.* **2018**, *7*, 263–275. [CrossRef]
6. García-Rodríguez, R. Hiper-heurístico para Resolver el Problema de Cartera de Proyectos Sociales. Master's Thesis, Instituto Tecnológico de Ciudad Madero, Cd. Madero, Tamaulipas, Mexico, 2010.
7. Liesiö, J.; Mild, P.; Salo, A. Preference programming for robust portfolio modeling and project selection. *Eur. J. Oper. Res.* **2007**, *181*, 1488–1505. [CrossRef]
8. Fernández, E.; López, E.; López, F.; Coello-Coello, C.A. Increasing Selective Pressure Toward the Best Compromise in Evolutionary Multiobjective Optimization: The Extended NOSGA Method. *J. Inf. Sci. Int. J.* **2011**, *181*, 44–56. [CrossRef]
9. Brief, A.P. *Attitudes in and around Organizations*; SAGE Publications: Thousand Oaks, CA, USA, 1998; Volume 9.
10. Pujol-Cols, L.J.; Dabos, G.E. Satisfacción laboral: Una revisión de la literatura acerca de sus principales determinantes. *Estud. Gerenciales* **2018**, *34*, 3–18. [CrossRef]
11. Moorman, R.H. The Influence of Cognitive and Affective Based Job Satisfaction Measures on the Relationship Between Satisfaction and Organizational Citizenship Behavior. *SAGE Publ.* **1993**, *46*, 759–776. [CrossRef]
12. Spector, P.E. *Job Satisfaction: Application, Assessment, Causes, and Consequences*; SAGE Publications: Thousand Oaks, CA, USA, 1997; Volume 1.
13. Flores-Juárez, J.B. ¿Por qué Medir la SatisfaccióN del Cliente? 2019. Available online: https://circulotne.com/por-que-medir-la-satisfaccion-del-cliente.html (accessed on 30 April 2022).
14. Locke, E.A. The nature and causes of job satisfaction. In *Handbook of Industrial and Organizational Psychology*; Dunnette, M.D., Ed.; Rand McNally College Pub. Co.: Chicago, IL, USA, 1976; pp. 1297–1349.
15. Porter, L.W.; Lawler, E.E. *Managerial Attitudes and Performance*; Irwin-Dorsey Series in Behavioral Science in Business; R.D. Irwin, Inc.: Homewood, IL, USA, 1968; Volume 1.
16. Deng, C.P.; Armstrong, P.I.; Rounds, J. The fit of Holland's RIASEC model to US occupations. *J. Vocat. Behav.* **2007**, *71*, 1–22. [CrossRef]
17. Erevelles, S.; Leavitt, C. A Comparison of Current Models of Consumer Satisfaction/Dissatisfaction. *J. Consum. Satisf. Dissatisf. Complain. Behav.* **1992**, *5*, 114–194.
18. Polaino-Lorente, A.; Cabanyes-Truffino, J.; Pozo-Armentia, A.d. *Fundamentos de Psicología de la Personalidad*, 2nd ed.; Rialp Editions: Madrid, Spain, 2003; Volume 1.
19. Ahrndt, S.; Fähndrich, J.; Albayrak, S. Modelling of Personality in Agents: From Psycology to Implementation. In *Proceeding of the Fourth International Workshop on Human-Agent Interaction Design and Models (HAIDM 2015), Co-Located with AAMAS 2015*; Bordini, R.H., Elkind, E., Weiss, G., Yolum, P., Eds.; IFAAMAS: Istanbul, Turkey, 2015; pp. 1–16.
20. Pérez-Pinillos, D.; Fernández, S.; Borrajo, D. Modeling Motivations, Personality Traits and Emotional States in Deliberative Agents Based on Automated Planning. In *International Conference on Agents and Artificial Intelligence: Agents and Artificial Intelligence*; Filipe, J., Fred, A., Eds.; Springer: Berlin/Heidelberg, Germany, 2013; Volume 271, pp. 146–160. [CrossRef]
21. Eysenck, H.J.; Eysenck, S.B.G. *Psychoticism as a Dimension of Personality*; Crane, Russak: New York, NY, USA, 1977; Volume 1.
22. Eysenck, H.J. *Dimensions of Personality*; Transaction Publishers: London, UK, 1998; Volume 1.
23. Cattell, R.B. *Personality: A Systematic Theoretical and Factual Study*, 1st ed.; McGraw-Hill Publications in Psychology; McGraw-Hill: New York, NY, USA, 1950; Volume 1.
24. Cattell, H.E.; Mead, A.D. The Sixteen Personality Factor Questionnaire. In *The Sage Handbook of Personality Theory and Assessment*; Boyle, G.J., Matthews, G., Saklofske, D.H., Eds.; SAGE Publications: Thousand Oaks, CA, USA, 2008; Volume 2, pp. 135–159.

25. McCrae, R.; John, O. An introduction to the Five-Factor Model and Its Applications. *J. Personal.* **1992**, *60*, 175–215. [CrossRef] [PubMed]
26. Penn-State. The IPIP-NEO (International Personality Item Pool Representation of the NEO PI-R). 2018. Available online: http://www.personal.psu.edu/~j5j/IPIP/ (accessed on 30 April 2022).
27. Salvit, J.; Sklar, E. Modulating Agent Behavior using Human Personality Type. In *Workshop on Human-Agent Interaction Design and Models (HAIDM) at Autonomous Agents and MultiAgent Systems (AAMAS)*; IFAAMAS: Valencia, Spain, 2012; pp. 145–160.
28. The-Myers-Briggs-Foundation. The Myers & Briggs Foundation. 2022. Available online: http://www.myersbriggs.org/my-mbti-personality-type/ (accessed on 30 April 2022).
29. Keirsey, D. *Please Understand Me II: Temperament Character Intelligence*, 1st ed.; Prometheus Nemesis Book Company: Del Mar, CA, USA, 2006.
30. Fernández, E.; López, E.; Navarro, J.; Vega, I. Aplicación de metaheurísticas multiobjetivo a la solución de problemas de cartera de proyectos públicos con una valoración multidimensional de su impacto. *Gestión Y Política Pública* **2011**, *20*, 381–432.
31. Delgado-Hernández, X.; Morales-Rodríguez, M.; Rangel-Valdez, N.; Cruz Reyes, L.; Castro-Rivera, J. Development of Conversational Deliberative Agents Driven by Personality via Fuzzy Outranking Relations. *Int. J. Fuzzy Syst.* **2020**, *22*, 2720–2734. [CrossRef]
32. Seltzer, B.K.; Ones, D.S.; Tatar, A. Using Personality Facets to Understand the Nature of Personality-Satisfaction Relationships: Findings from Meta-Analytic Bifactor Latent Modeling. *Career Dev. Int.* **2017**, *22*, 477–506. [CrossRef]
33. Boloș, M.I.; Bradea, I.A.; Delcea, C. A Fuzzy Logic Algorithm for Optimizing the Investment Decisions within Companies. *Symmetry* **2019**, *11*, 186. [CrossRef]
34. Morales-Rodríguez, M.L.; Medellín-Martínez, F.; González B., J.J. Modeling Facial Expression of Intelligent Virtual Agents. In *Soft Computing for Intelligent Control and Mobile Robotics*; Castillo, O., Kacprzyk, J., Pedrycz, W., Eds.; Springer: Berlin/Heidelberg, Germany, 2010; Volume 318, pp. 303–313. [CrossRef]
35. Carvajal-Villaplana, Z. Teorías y modelos: Formas de representación de la realidad. *Comunicación* **2002**, *12*, 1–14.
36. Russell, S.J.; Norvig, P.; Davis, E. *Artificial Intelligence: A Modern Approach*, 3rd ed.; Prentice Hall Series in Artificial Intelligence; Pearson Education, Inc.: Upper Saddle River, NJ, USA, 2010; Volume 1.
37. Iglesias-Fernández, C. Definición de una Metodología para el Desarrollo de Sistemas Multiagente. Ph.D. Thesis, Universidad Politécnica de Madrid, Madrid, Spain, 1998.
38. Wooldridge, M.J. *An Introduction to MultiAgent Systems*, 2nd ed.; John Wiley & Sons Ltd.: London, UK, 2002; Volume 1.
39. Gutiérrez, J.J. ¿Qué es un Framework Web? 2005. Available online: http://www.lsi.us.es/~javierj/investigacion_ficheros/Framework.pdf (accessed on 30 April 2022).
40. Sarasty-España, H.F. Documentación y AnáLisis de los Principales Frameworks de Arquitectura de Software en Aplicaciones Empresariales. Specialty Thesis, Facultad de InformáTica—Universidad Nacional de La Plata, Buenos Aires, Argentina, 2015.
41. Career and Technical Education. Hawai'I Career Pathway System Handbook. 2022. Available online: http://www.hawaiipublicschools.org/DOE%20Forms/CTE/CTEhandbook.pdf (accessed on 30 April 2022).
42. Furnham, A. *The Psychology of Behaviour at Work: The Individual in the Organization*, 2nd ed.; Taylor & Francis: Abingdon, UK, 2012; Volume 2.
43. RAE. Diccionario de la Lengua EspañOla, 23rd ed. 2022. Available online: https://dle.rae.es/ (accessed on 9 May 2022).
44. Castro-Rivera, J. Cuantificación de Rasgos de la Personalidad a TravéS del Modelo OCEAN para Influir en la Toma de Decisiones. 2021. Available online: https://www.academia.edu/61508873/Cuantificaci%C3%B3n_de_rasgos_de_la_personalidad_a_trav%C3%A9s_del_modelo_OCEAN_para_influir_en_la_toma_de_decisiones (accessed on 11 November 2021).
45. Carazo, A.F.; Gómez, T.; Molina, J.; Hernández-Díaz, A.G.; Guerrero, F.M.; Caballero, R. Solving a comprehensive model for multiobjective project portfolio selection. *Comput. Oper. Res.* **2010**, *37*, 630–639. [CrossRef]
46. Rivera-Zárate, G. Enfoque MetaheuríStico HíBrido para el Manejo de Muchos Objetivos en OptimizacióN de Cartera de Proyectos Interdependientes con Decisiones de Apoyo Parcial. Doctoral Thesis, Instituto Tecnológico de Tijuana, Tijuana, Baja California, Mexico, 2015.
47. Fernández, E.; López, E.; Mazcorro, G.; Olmedo, R.; Coello-Coello, C.A. Application of the Non-Outranked Sorting Genetic Algorithm to Public Project Portfolio Selection. *J. Inf. Sci.* **2013**, *228*, 131–149. [CrossRef]

axioms

MDPI

Article

The Classification of All Singular Nonsymmetric Macdonald Polynomials

Charles F. Dunkl

Department of Mathematics, University of Virginia, Charlottesville, VA 22904-4137, USA; cfd5z@virginia.edu

Abstract: The affine Hecke algebra of type A has two parameters (q,t) and acts on polynomials in N variables. There are two important pairwise commuting sets of elements in the algebra: the Cherednik operators and the Jucys–Murphy elements whose simultaneous eigenfunctions are the nonsymmetric Macdonald polynomials, and basis vectors of irreducible modules of the Hecke algebra, respectively. For certain parameter values, it is possible for special polynomials to be simultaneous eigenfunctions with equal corresponding eigenvalues of both sets of operators. These are called singular polynomials. The possible parameter values are of the form $q^m = t^{-n}$ with $2 \leq n \leq N$. For a fixed parameter, the singular polynomials span an irreducible module of the Hecke algebra. Colmenarejo and the author (SIGMA 16 (2020), 010) showed that there exist singular polynomials for each of these parameter values, they coincide with specializations of nonsymmetric Macdonald polynomials, and the isotype (a partition of N) of the Hecke algebra module is $(dn-1, n-1, \ldots, n-1, r)$ for some $d \geq 1$. In the present paper, it is shown that there are no other singular polynomials.

Keywords: nonsymmetric Macdonald polynomials; the affine Hecke algebra of type A; Young tableaux; Jucys–Murphy operators

MSC: 33D52; 20C08; 05E10

Citation: Dunkl, C.F. The Classification of All Singular Nonsymmetric Macdonald Polynomials. *Axioms* **2022**, *11*, 208. https://doi.org/10.3390/axioms11050208

Academic Editor: Clemente Cesarano

Received: 30 March 2022
Accepted: 24 April 2022
Published: 29 April 2022

1. Introduction

Many structures arise from the action of the symmetric group on polynomials in N variables. Among them are the Hecke algebra and the affine Hecke algebra of type A. This paper concerns polynomials with noteworthy properties with respect to these algebras. The symmetric group $\mathcal{S}_N$ is generated by the simple reflections $s_i, 1 \leq i < N$, where

$$xs_i := \left(x_1, \ldots, \overset{i}{x_{i+1}}, \overset{i+1}{x_i}, \ldots, x_N\right);$$

they satisfy the braid relations $s_i s_{i+1} s_i = s_{i+1} s_i s_{i+1}$ and $s_i s_j = s_j s_i$ for $|i-j| \geq 2$. Let q,t be parameters satisfying $t^n \neq 1$ for $2 \leq n \leq N$ and $q,t \neq 0$. Define $\mathcal{P} = \mathbb{K}[x_1, \ldots, x_N]$ where $\mathbb{K}$ is a field containing $\mathbb{Q}(q,t)$. The Hecke algebra $\mathcal{H}_N(t)$ is generated by Demazure operators (with $p \in \mathcal{P}$ and $1 \leq i < N$)

$$T_i p(x) := (1-t) x_{i+1} \frac{p(x) - p(xs_i)}{x_i - x_{i+1}} + tp(xs_i);$$

they satisfy the same braid relations $T_i T_{i+1} T_i = T_{i+1} T_i T_{i+1}$ and $T_i T_j = T_j T_i$ for $|i-j| \geq 2$, as well as the quadratic relations $(T_i - t)(T_i + 1) = 0$. The affine Hecke algebra $\mathcal{H}_N(t;q)$ is obtained by adjoining the q-shift

$$wp(x) := p(qx_N, x_1, x_2, \ldots, x_{N-1})$$

and defining

$$T_0 p(x) := wT_1 w^{-1} p(x) = (1-t)x_1 \frac{p(x) - p(xs_0)}{qx_N - x_1} + tp(xs_0),$$
$$xs_0 := (qx_N, x_2, \ldots, x_{N-1}, x_1/q).$$

Then $wT_{i+1} = T_i w$ where the indices are taken mod N. (That is, $w^2 T_1 = T_{N-1} w^2$.) The quadratic relations imply $T_i^{-1} = t^{-1}(T_i + (1-t))$. There are two commutative families of operators in $\mathcal{H}_N(t;q)$ (each indexed $1 \le i \le N$): the Cherednik operators (see [1])

$$\xi_i := t^{i-1} T_i T_{i+1} \cdots T_{N-1} w T_1^{-1} T_2^{-1} \cdots T_{i-1}^{-1}$$

and the Jucys–Murphy operators

$$\omega_i = t^{i-N} T_i T_{i+1} \cdots T_{N-1} T_{N-1} T_{N-2} \cdots T_i.$$

Note that $\xi_i = t^{-1} T_i \xi_{i+1} T_i$ and $\omega_i = t^{-1} T_i \omega_{i+1} T_i$ for $i < N$. The simultaneous eigenfunctions of the Cherednik operators are the nonsymmetric Macdonald polynomials and the simultaneous eigenvectors of the Jucys–Murphy operators span irreducible representations of $\mathcal{H}_N(t)$. Our concern is to determine all polynomials which are simultaneous eigenfunctions of both sets of operators, more specifically, when q, t satisfy a relation of the form $q^m t^n = 1$ to determine the homogeneous polynomials p such that $\xi_i p = \omega_i p$ for all i. These are called *singular polynomials* with singular parameter $q^m = t^{-n}$. In a previous paper [2] Colmenarejo and the author found a large class of such polynomials associated with tableaux of quasi-staircase shape. In this paper, we will show that there are no other occurrences.

Affine Hecke algebras were used by Kirillov and Noumi [3] to derive important results about the coefficients of Macdonald polynomials. Mimachi and Noumi [4] found double sums for reproducing kernels for series in nonsymmetric Macdonald polynomials. The paper [5] by Baker and Forrester is a source of some background for the present paper.

In Section 2, we collect the needed definitions and results about the Hecke algebra action on polynomials, Cherednik operators, nonsymmetric Macdonald polynomials, and the representation theory of Hecke algebra of type A. The definition of singular polynomials and its consequences, that is, necessary conditions, are presented in Section 3. This section also explains the known existence theorem. Section 4 concerns the method of restriction to produce singular polynomials with a smaller number of variables and this leads into Section 5 where our main nonexistence theorem is proved.

2. Preliminary Results

In this section, we present background information and computational results dealing with $\mathcal{H}_N(t)$ and the action on polynomials.

Lemma 1. *If $j > i+1$ or $j < i$ then $T_i \omega_j = \omega_j T_i$, and $T_i \omega_i = (t-1)\omega_i + \omega_{i+1} T_i$, $T_i \omega_{i+1} = \omega_i T_i - (t-1)\omega_i$.*

Proof. If $j > i+1$ then T_i commutes with each factor of ω_j. Suppose $j = i-1$ then by the braid relations

$$\begin{aligned} T_i \omega_{i-1} &= t^{i-1-N} T_i T_{i-1} T_i T_{i+1} \cdots T_i T_{i-1} = t^{i-1-N} T_{i-1} T_i T_{i-1} T_{i+1} \cdots T_i T_{i-1} \\ &= t^{i-1-N} T_{i-1} T_{i+1} T_{i+2} \cdots T_{i-1} T_i T_{i-1} \\ &= t^{i-1-N} T_{i-1} T_i T_{i+1} \cdots T_i T_{i-1} T_i = \omega_{i-1} T_i. \end{aligned}$$

Suppose $j < i-1$ then $\omega_j = t^{j-i+1} T_j T_{j+1} \cdots T_{i-2} \omega_{i-1} T_{i-2} \cdots T_j$ and T_i commutes with each factor in this product. If $j = i$ then

$$\begin{aligned} T_i \omega_i &= t^{-1} T_i^2 \omega_{i+1} T_i = t^{-1}\{(t-1)T_i + t\}\omega_{i+1} T_i \\ &= (t-1)\omega_i + \omega_{i+1} T_i, \end{aligned}$$

and similarly $\omega_i T_i = t^{-1} T_i \omega_{i+1} T_i^2 = (t-1)\omega_i + T_i \omega_{i+1}$. □

Lemma 2. *If $j > i+1$ or $j < i$ then $T_i \xi_j = \xi_j T_i$, and $T_i \xi_i = (t-1)\xi_i + \xi_{i+1} T_i$, $T_i \xi_{i+1} = \xi_i T_i - (t-1)\xi_i$.*

Proof. Recall $wT_{i+1} = T_i w$, $w^2 T_1 = T_{N-1} w^2$. Suppose $j = i-1$ then

$$\begin{aligned} T_i \xi_{i-1} &= t^{i-1-N} T_i T_{i-1} T_i T_{i+1} \cdots T_{N-1} w T_1^{-1} \cdots T_{i-2}^{-1} \\ &= t^{i-1-N} T_{i-1} T_i T_{i-1} T_{i+1} \cdots T_{N-1} w T_1^{-1} \cdots T_{i-2}^{-1} \\ &= t^{i-1-N} T_{i-1} T_i T_{i+1} \cdots T_{N-1} T_{i-1} w T_1^{-1} \cdots T_{i-2}^{-1} \\ &= t^{i-1-N} T_{i-1} T_i T_{i+1} \cdots T_{N-1} w T_i T_1^{-1} \cdots T_{i-2}^{-1} = \xi_{i-1} T_i. \end{aligned}$$

The analogous argument as in the previous lemma shows $T_i \xi_j = \xi_j T_i$ for $j < i-1$. Suppose $j > i+1$ then

$$\begin{aligned} T_i \xi_j &= t^{j-N} T_i T_j T_{j+1} \cdots T_{N-1} w T_1^{-1} \cdots T_{j-1}^{-1} = t^{j-N} T_j T_{j+1} \cdots T_{N-1} T_i w T_1^{-1} \cdots T_{j-1}^{-1} \\ &= t^{j-N} T_j T_{j+1} \cdots T_{N-1} w T_{i+1} T_1^{-1} \cdots T_{j-1}^{-1} \\ &= t^{j-N} T_j \cdots T_{N-1} w T_1^{-1} \cdots T_{i-1} T_{i-2}^{-1} T_{i-1}^{-1} \cdots T_{j-1}^{-1}. \end{aligned}$$

The modified braid relations $aba = bab \Leftrightarrow ab^{-1}a^{-1} = b^{-1}a^{-1}b$ imply $T_{i+1} T_i^{-1} T_{i+1}^{-1} = T_i^{-1} T_{i+1}^{-1} T_i$ and thus $T_i \xi_j = \xi_j T_i$. As before

$$\begin{aligned} &T_i \xi_i = t^{-1} T_i^2 \xi_{i+1} T_i = t^{-1}\{(t-1)T_i + t\}\xi_{i+1} T_i = (t-1)\xi_i + \xi_{i+1} T_i. \\ &\xi_i T_i = (t-1)\xi_i + T_i \xi_{i+1}. \end{aligned}$$

□

Polynomials are spanned by monomials $x^\alpha = \prod_{i=1}^{N} x_i^{\alpha_i}, \alpha \in \mathbb{N}_0^N$. For $\alpha \in \mathbb{N}_0^N$ set $s_i\alpha = \left(\alpha_1, \ldots, \overset{i}{\alpha_{i+1}}, \overset{i+1}{\alpha_i}, \ldots\right)$ for $1 \le i < N$, and $|\alpha| = \sum_{j=1}^N \alpha_j$ (the degree of x^α). Let $\mathbb{N}_0^{N,+} = \{\alpha \in \mathbb{N}_0^N : \alpha_1 \ge \alpha_2 \ge \ldots \ge \alpha_N\}$, the set of partitions of length $\le N$. Let α^+ denote the nonincreasing rearrangement of α (thus $\alpha^+ \in \mathbb{N}_0^{N,+}$). There is a partial order on $\mathbb{N}_0^N$

$$\begin{aligned} \alpha \prec \beta &\Longleftrightarrow \sum_{j=1}^{i} \alpha_j \le \sum_{j=1}^{i} \beta_j,\ 1 \le i \le N,\ \alpha \ne \beta, \\ \alpha \lhd \beta &\Longleftrightarrow (|\alpha| = |\beta|) \wedge \left[(\alpha^+ \prec \beta^+) \vee (\alpha^+ = \beta^+ \wedge \alpha \prec \beta)\right], \end{aligned}$$

and a rank function ($1 \le i \le N$)

$$r_\alpha(i) := \#\{j : \alpha_j > \alpha_i\} + \#\{j : 1 \le j \le i, \alpha_j = \alpha_i\}.$$

Note $\alpha_i = \alpha^+_{r_\alpha(i)}$.

2.1. Nonsymmetric Macdonald Polynomials

The key fact about the Cherednik operators is the triangular property (see [5])

$$\xi_i x^\alpha = q^{\alpha_i} t^{N-r_\alpha(i)} x^\alpha + \sum_{\beta \lhd \alpha} c_{\alpha,\beta}(q,t) x^\beta, \tag{1}$$

where the coefficients $c_{\alpha,\beta}(q,t)$ are polynomials in q,t. For generic (q,t) (this means $q^m t^n \neq 1, 0$ for $m \geq 0$ and $1 \leq n \leq N$) there is a basis of $\mathcal{P}$, for $\alpha \in \mathbb{N}_0^N$

$$M_\alpha(x) = q^{b(\alpha)} t^{e(\alpha)} x^\alpha + \sum_{\beta \lhd \alpha} A_{\alpha,\beta}(q,t) x^\beta$$

(where $A_{\alpha,\beta}(q,t)$ is a rational function of (q,t) with no poles when (q,t) is generic) and for $1 \leq i \leq N$

$$\xi_i M_\alpha = q^{\alpha_i} t^{N-r_\alpha(i)} M_\alpha.$$

The exponents are $b(\alpha) = \frac{1}{2} \sum_{i=1}^N \alpha_i(\alpha_i - 1)$ and $e(\alpha) = \sum_{i=1}^N \alpha_i^+(N - 2i + 1) - \operatorname{inv}(\alpha)$, with $\operatorname{inv}(\alpha) := \#\{(i,j) : 1 \leq i < j \leq N, \alpha_i < \alpha_j\}$; there is an equivalent formula:

$$e(\alpha) = \frac{1}{2} \sum_{1 \leq i < j \leq N} \left(|\alpha_i - \alpha_j| + |\alpha_i - \alpha_j + 1| - 1\right).$$

These powers arise from the Yang-Baxter graph method of constructing the M_α, and are not actually needed here. The *spectral vector* of M_α is $[\zeta_\alpha(i)]_{i=1}^N$ with $\zeta_\alpha(i) = q^{\alpha_i} t^{N-r_\alpha(i)}$. We will need the formulas for the action of T_i on M_α. Suppose $\alpha_i < \alpha_{i+1}$ and $z = \zeta_\alpha(i+1)/\zeta_\alpha(i) = q^{\alpha_{i+1}-\alpha_i} t^{r_\alpha(i) - r_\alpha(i+1)}$ then

$$T_i M_\alpha = M_{s_i\alpha} - \frac{1-t}{1-z} M_\alpha, \tag{2}$$

$$T_i M_{s_i\alpha} = \frac{(1-zt)(t-z)}{(1-z)^2} M_\alpha + \frac{z(1-t)}{(1-z)} M_{s_i\alpha}. \tag{3}$$

If $\alpha_i = \alpha_{i+1}$ then $T_i M_\alpha = t M_\alpha$. The quadratic relation appears as

$$\left(T_i + \frac{1-t}{1-z}\right)\left(T_i - \frac{z(1-t)}{1-z}\right) = \frac{(1-zt)(t-z)}{(1-z)^2}.$$

2.2. Action of T_i on Polynomials and $\rhd$-Maximal Terms

The following are routine computations:

Lemma 3. *Suppose $\gamma \in \mathbb{N}_0^N$ and $1 \leq i < N$. Set $x' = \prod_{j \neq i,i+1} x^{\gamma_j}$. Then*

(1) $\gamma_i > \gamma_{i+1} + 1$ implies $T_i x^\gamma = (1-t)x' \sum_{j=0}^{\gamma_i - \gamma_{i+1} - 1} x_i^{\gamma_i - j - 1} x_{i+1}^{\gamma_{i+1}+j+1} + t x^{s_i\gamma}$;

(2) $\gamma_i = \gamma_{i+1} + 1$ implies $T_i x^\gamma = x^{s_i\gamma}$;

(3) $\gamma_i = \gamma_{i+1}$ implies $T_i x^\gamma = t x^\gamma$;

(4) $\gamma_i = \gamma_{i+1} - 1$ implies $T_i x^\gamma = t x^{s_i\gamma} + (t-1)x^\gamma$;

(5) $\gamma_i < \gamma_{i+1} - 1$ implies $T_i x^\gamma = (t-1)x' \sum_{j=0}^{\gamma_{i+1} - \gamma_i - 1} x_i^{\gamma_i + j} x_{i+1}^{\gamma_{i+1} - j} + t x^{s_i\gamma}$.

Lemma 4. *Suppose $\lambda \in \mathbb{N}_0^{N,+}, \lambda_i > \lambda_j + 1$ $(i > j)$ and $1 \leq s < \lambda_i - \lambda_j$, $\mu \in \mathbb{N}_0^N$ such that $\mu_k = \lambda_k$ for $k \neq i, j$, $\mu_i = \lambda_i - s$, $\mu_j = \lambda_j + s$ then $\lambda \succ \mu^+$.*

(The proof is left as an exercise.)

In (1) above let $\alpha_k = \gamma_k$ for $k \neq i, i+1$ and $\alpha_i = \gamma_i - j - 1, \alpha_{i+1} = \gamma_{i+1} + j + 1$ with $1 \leq j + 1 < \gamma_i - \gamma_{i+1}$ then the Lemma with $\lambda = \gamma^+$ and $\mu^+ = \alpha^+$ shows $\gamma^+ \succ a^+$ (the other term in (1) is $x^{s_i\gamma}$ and $\gamma \succ s_i\gamma$). Similarly in (5) let $\alpha_i = \gamma_i + j, \alpha_{i+1} = \gamma_{i+1} - j$ with $1 \le j \le \gamma_{i+1} - \gamma_i - 1$, thus $\gamma^+ \succ a^+$ (the other term in (5) for $j = 0$ is x^γ and $s_i\gamma \succ \gamma$.

Proposition 1. *Suppose α is $\rhd$-maximal in $p = \sum_\delta c_\delta x^\delta$ (a homogeneous polynomial, $|\delta| = |\alpha|$), that is, $c_\alpha \neq 0$ and if some $\delta \trianglerighteq \alpha$ with $c_\delta \neq 0$ then $\delta = \alpha$. Furthermore suppose $\alpha_{i+1} > \alpha_i$ for some i and x^β with $\beta \rhd s_i\alpha$ appears in $(T_i + c)p$ then $\beta^+ = \alpha^+$ and $\beta \succ s_i\alpha$.*

Proof. Suppose x^β appears in $T_i x^\gamma$ (with $c_\gamma \neq 0$) in one of the five cases of Lemma 3 and $\beta^+ \succ (s_i\alpha)^+ = \alpha^+$. Every term satisfies $\gamma^+ \succ \beta^+$ or $\gamma^+ = \beta^+$ but then $\gamma^+ \succeq \beta^+ \succ \alpha^+$ and $\gamma \rhd \alpha$, a contradiction. Suppose $\beta^+ = \alpha^+$ then $\beta \rhd s_i\alpha$ implies $\beta \succ s_i\alpha$. □

Corollary 1. *If α is $\rhd$-maximal in $p = \sum_\delta c_\delta x^\delta$ and x^β appears in $(T_i + c)p$ with $\beta \trianglerighteq s_i\alpha$ then either $\beta = s_i\alpha$ or $\beta^+ = \alpha^+$ and $\beta \succ s_i\alpha$ with $\beta = s_i\gamma$ where x^γ appears in p.*

Proof. If β occurs in case (1) or case (5) of Lemma 3 and $\beta \neq \gamma, s_i\gamma$ (for x^γ appearing in p) then $\gamma^+ \succ \beta^+ \succ s_i\alpha \succ \alpha$ which violates the $\rhd$-maximality of α, this leaves only $\beta = s_i\gamma$. □

Note $\beta = s_i\gamma$ does not imply $s_i\beta \succ \alpha$, for example let $\beta = (4,1,3,2)$ and $s_1\alpha = (3,2,1,4)$ then $\beta \succ s_1\alpha$ but $s_1\beta = (1,4,3,2)$ and $\alpha = (2,3,1,4)$ are not $\rhd$-comparable.

2.3. Irreducible Representations of the Hecke Algebra

Irreducible representations of $\mathcal{H}_N(t)$ are indexed by partitions of N (for background see Dipper and James [6]). Given a partition $\tau \in \mathbb{N}_0^{N,+}$ with $|\tau| = N$ there is a *Ferrers diagram*: boxes at (i,j) with $1 \le i \le \ell(\tau) = \max\{j : \tau_j > 0\}$ and $1 \le j \le \tau_i$. The module is spanned by reverse standard Young tableaux (abbr. RSYT) of shape τ (denoted $\mathcal{Y}_\tau$): the numbers $1, \ldots, N$ are inserted into the Ferrers diagram so that the entries in each row and in each column are decreasing. The module $\mathrm{span}_{\mathbb{K}}\{Y : Y \in \mathcal{Y}_\tau\}$ is said to be of isotype τ. If k is in cell (i,j) of RSYT Y (denoted $Y[i,j] = k$) then the *content* $c(k,Y) := j - i$; the *content vector* $[c(k,Y)]_{k=1}^N$ determines Y uniquely. The action of $\mathcal{H}_N(t)$ is specified by the formulas for T_iY:

- If $c(i,Y) - c(i+1,Y) = 1$ then $T_iY = tY$;
- If $c(i,Y) - c(i+1,Y) = -1$ then $T_iY = -Y$;
- If $|c(i,Y) - c(i+1,Y)| \ge 2$ then let $Y^{(i)}$ denote the RSYT obtained by interchanging i and $i+1$ in Y and set $z = t^{c(i+1,Y) - c(i,Y)}$: if $c(i,Y) - c(i+1,Y) \ge 2$, then
$$T_iY = Y^{(i)} - \frac{1-t}{1-z}Y;$$
if $c(i,Y) - c(i+1,Y) \le -2$, then
$$T_iY = \frac{(1-zt)(t-z)}{(1-z)^2}Y^{(i)} - \frac{1-t}{1-z}Y.$$

From these relations it follows that $\omega_iY = t^{c(i,Y)}Y$ for $1 \le i \le N$. Call the vector $\left[t^{c(i,Y)}\right]_{i=1}^N$ the t-exponential content vector of Y, or the t^C-vector for short. Note $c(N,Y) = 0$ always and $\omega_N := 1$.

So if one finds a simultaneous eigenfunction of $\{\omega_i\}$ then the eigenvalues determine an RSYT and the isotype (partition) of an irreducible representation.

2.4. Singular Parameters

For integers m and n such that $m \ge 1$ and $2 \le n \le N$ we consider *singular* parameters (q,t) satisfying $q^mt^n = 1$ with the property that if $q^at^b = 1$ then $a = rm, b = rn$ for some $r \in \mathbb{Z}$.

Definition 1. *Let $g = \gcd(m,n)$ and let $z = \exp\left(\frac{2\pi ik}{m}\right)$ with $\gcd(k,g) = 1$, that is, $z^{m/g}$ is a primitive g^{th} root of unity. If $g = 1$ then set $z = 1$. Define $\varpi := (q,t) = \left(zu^{-n/g}, u^{m/g}\right)$ where u is not a root of unity and $u \neq 0$.*

Lemma 5. *If $q^a t^b|_{\varpi} = 1$ for some integers a, b then $a = rm, b = rn$ for some $r \in \mathbb{Z}$.*

Proof. By hypothesis $z^a u^{-an/g+bm/g} = 1$ and, since u is not a root of unity, $-a\frac{n}{g} + b\frac{m}{g} = 0$. From $\gcd\left(\frac{n}{g}, \frac{m}{g}\right) = 1$, it follows that $a = p'\frac{m}{g}$ and $b = p'\frac{n}{g}$, for some $p' \in \mathbb{Z}$. Thus, $1 = z^a = \exp\left(\frac{2\pi ik}{m}\frac{mp'}{g}\right) = \exp\left(\frac{2\pi ik}{g}p'\right)$. Moreover, since $\gcd(k,g) = 1$, $p' = pg$ with $p \in \mathbb{Z}$. Hence $a = pm$ and $b = pn$. □

In fact, to describe all the possibilities for ϖ, it suffices to let $1 \leq k < g$. To be precise, ϖ is not a single point but a variety in $(\mathbb{C}\backslash\{0\})^2$.

3. Necessary Conditions for Singular Polynomials

By using the degree-lowering (q-Dunkl) operators defined by Baker and Forrester [5] we find another characterization of singular polynomials.

Definition 2. *Suppose $p \in \mathcal{P}$ then*

$$\begin{aligned} D_N p(x) &:= \frac{1}{x_N}(1 - \xi_N)p(x), \\ D_i p(x) &:= \frac{1}{t} T_i D_{i+1} T_i p(x),\ i < N. \end{aligned}$$

Proposition 2. *A polynomial p is singular if and only if $D_i p = 0$ for $1 \leq i \leq N$.*

Proof. The proof is by downward induction on i. Since $\omega_N = 1$, it follows that $D_N p = 0$ iff $\xi_N p = p = \omega_N p$. Suppose that $D_i p = 0$ iff $\xi_i p = \omega_i p$ for all p and $k \leq i \leq N$. Then $D_{k-1}p = 0$ iff $t^{-1}T_{k-1}D_k T_{k-1}p = 0$ iff $D_k T_{k-1}p = 0$ iff $\xi_k T_{k-1}p = \omega_k T_{k-1}p$ iff $t^{-1}T_{k-1}\xi_k T_{k-1}p = t^{-1}T_{k-1}\omega_k T_{k-1}p$. □

First we show that any singular polynomial generates an $\mathcal{H}_N(t)$-module consisting of singular polynomials. This allows the use of the representation theory of $\mathcal{H}_N(t)$.

Proposition 3. *Suppose p is singular and $1 \leq i < N$, then $T_i p$ is singular.*

Proof. The commutation relations from Lemmas 1 and 2 are used. Suppose $j < i$ or $j > i+1$ then $\xi_j T_i p = T_i \xi_j p = T_i \omega_j p = \omega_j T_i p$. Case $j = i$:

$$\begin{aligned} \xi_i T_i p &= \{(t-1)\xi_i + T_i \xi_{i+1}\}p = (t-1)\omega_i p + T_i \omega_{i+1} p \\ &= \{(t-1)\omega_i + T_i \omega_{i+1}\}p = \omega_i T_i p. \end{aligned}$$

Case $j = i+1$

$$\begin{aligned} \xi_{i+1} T_i p &= \{T_i \xi_i - (t-1)\xi_i\}p = T_i \omega_i p - (t-1)\omega_i p \\ &= \{T_i \omega_i - (t-1)\omega_i\}p = \omega_{i+1} T_i p. \end{aligned}$$

□

Proposition 4. *Suppose p is singular then $\mathcal{M} = \mathcal{H}_N(t)p$ is a linear space of singular polynomials, and it is closed under the actions of ξ_i, ω_i. for $1 \leq i \leq N$, and w.*

Proof. By definition of ω_i we see that $f \in \mathcal{M}$ implies $\omega_i f \in \mathcal{M}$, and by definition $\xi_i f = \omega_i f \in \mathcal{M}$. Also

$$\begin{aligned}\xi_1 p &= T_1 T_2 \cdots T_{N-1} w p \\ &= \omega_1 p = t^{1-N} T_1 T_2 \ldots \cdots T_{N-1} T_{N-1} T_{N-2} \cdots T_1 p\end{aligned}$$

thus $wp = t^{1-N} T_{N-1} T_{N-2} \cdots T_1 p$. □

Note that $\mathcal{M}$ is also a module of the affine Hecke algebra. By the representation theory of $\mathcal{H}_N(t)$ the module has a basis of $\{\omega_i\}$-simultaneous eigenfunctions and by definition these are $\{\xi_i\}$-simultaneous eigenfunctions - note we are not claiming they are specializations of nonsymmetric Macdonald polynomials at ϖ. Suppose f is such an eigenfunction and let α be $\rhd$-maximal in the expression $f(x) = \sum_\beta c_\beta x^\beta$. Then $\xi_i f = q^{\alpha_i} t^{N-r_\alpha(i)} f$ because by the triangularity property of ξ_i (see (1)) x^α can only appear in $\xi_i f$ in the term $\xi_i x^\alpha$. Furthermore $\xi_i f = \omega_i f$ implies $q^{\alpha_i} t^{N-r_\alpha(i)} = t^{c(i,Y)}$ for some RSYT Y, at ϖ. As well we can conclude $\alpha_i = mr, N - r_\alpha(i) - c(i,Y) = nr$ for some $r \in \mathbb{N}$ (Lemma 5). The next step is to produce a simultaneous eigenfunction which has a $\rhd$-maximal term x^λ with $\lambda \in \mathbb{N}_0^{N,+}$.

Proposition 5. *There exists $f \in \mathcal{M}$ which is a simultaneous $\{\omega_i\}$-eigenfunction and $f = c_\lambda x^\lambda + \sum_{\beta \lhd \lambda} c_\beta x^\beta + \sum_\gamma c_\gamma x^\gamma$ where γ is not $\rhd$-comparable to λ, and $\lambda \in \mathbb{N}_0^{N,+}$.*

Proof. Suppose $f = \sum c_\alpha x^\alpha$ is an eigenfunction and there is a $\rhd$-maximal α with x^α (i.e., $c_\alpha \neq 0$) appearing in f, and $\alpha_i < \alpha_{i+1}$ then $T_i f \neq f$ and the coefficient of $x^{s_i\alpha}$ is tc_α; let $\omega_j f = \mu_j f$ for $1 \le j \le N$ and $\mu_{i+1} \neq \mu_i$ (because $c(i,Y) \neq c(i+1,Y)$ for any RSYT) so that

$$g := T_i f + \frac{t-1}{\mu_{i+1}/\mu_i - 1} f$$

is a simultaneous eigenfunction with $\rhd$-maximal β such that $\beta^+ = \alpha^+$ and $\beta \succeq s_i\alpha$, (by Proposition 1) and eigenvalues $\ldots \mu_{i+1}, \mu_i \ldots$ In general this formula could produce a zero function g but this does not happen here because the coefficient of $x^{s_i\alpha}$ in g is not zero. Repeating these steps eventually produces a $\rhd$-maximal term x^λ with $\lambda \in \mathbb{N}_0^{N,+}$ (at most $\operatorname{inv}(\alpha)$ steps). □

At this point we have shown if there is a singular polynomial then there is a partition $\lambda \in \mathbb{N}_0^{N,+}$ and an RSYT Y such that $q^{\lambda_i} t^{N-i} = t^{c(i,Y)}$ at ϖ, for $1 \le i \le N$. Next we determine necessary conditions on λ for the existence of Y, in other words, when $\left[q^{\lambda_i} t^{N-i}\right]_{i=1}^N$ at ϖ is a valid t^C-vector. The equations $\lambda_i = mr_i, N - i - c(i,Y) = nr_i$ for $1 \le i \le N$ show that λ can be replaced by $\frac{1}{m}\lambda$ and ϖ by $qt^n = 1$ (simply $q = t^{-n}$), also $n\lambda_i = N - i - c(i,Y)$.

The following is a restatement of the development in [2] with significant differences in notation. First there is an informal discussion of the beginning of the process of building Y by placing $N, N-1, N-2, \ldots$ in possible locations and determining $\lambda_N, \lambda_{N-1}, \lambda_{N-2}, \ldots$ accordingly. Abbreviate $c_i = c(i,Y)$.

Suppose λ_{N-k} is the last nonzero entry of λ ($\lambda_i = 0$ for $i > N-k$) then $k - c_{N-k} = n\lambda_{N-k}$ ($c_{N-j} = j$ for $0 \le j < k$ implies $Y[1,j] = N - j - 1$); the entry $N-k$ in Y is at $[1, k+1]$ or $[2,1]$ thus $c_{N-k} = k, \lambda_{N-k} = 0$ (contra) or $c_{N-k} = -1, n\lambda_{N-k} = k+1$. Set $\lambda_{N-k} = d_1$ and $k = nd_1 - 1$.The entry $N-k-1$ in Y is in one of $[3,1], [2,2], [1,k+1]$ with contents $-2, 0, k$, respectively, yielding the equations $n\lambda_{N-k-1} = k + 1 - c_{N-k-1} = k-1, k+1, 1 = nd_1 - 2, nd_1, 1$, respectively. If $n > 2$ then only $[2,2]$ is possible and $\lambda_{N-k-1} = d_1$. If $n = 2$ then $[3,1], \lambda_{N-k-1} = d_1 + 1$ and $[2,2], \lambda_{N-k-1} = d_1$ are possible.

Theorem 1. *There are numbers $d_1 \ge d_2 \ge \ldots \ge d_L \ge 1$ such that with $\gamma_s := \sum_{i=1}^{s-1} d_i$ and $0 \le r_{L+1} < N - n\gamma_{L+1} + L \le nd_L - 1$ the entries in row s of Y are $R_s := \{i : n\gamma_s - s + 1 \le$*

$N-i \leq n\gamma_{s+1}-s-1\}$ *for* $1 \leq s \leq L$, $R_{L+1} = \{i : n\gamma_{L+1}-L \leq N-i \leq N-1\}$ *and* $\lambda_i = \gamma_s$ *for* $i \in R_s$. *The isotype of* Y *is* $\tau := (nd_1-1, nd_2-1, \ldots, nd_L-1, r_{L+1})$.

Proof. By way of induction suppose there are numbers $d_1 \geq d_2 \geq \ldots \geq d_{k-1} > 0$ such that the entries in row s of Y are $R_s = \{i : n\gamma_s - s+1 \leq N-i \leq n\gamma_{s+1}-s-1\}$ and $\lambda_i = \gamma_s$ for $i \in R_s$. Assume this has been proven for $1 \leq s < k$ and for row k up to $n\gamma_k - k+1 \leq N-i \leq n\gamma_k - k+\ell$ with $\ell \leq nd_{k-1}-1$ (the length $\#R_{k-1}$ of row $k-1$). Consider the possible locations for the next entry $p = N-(n\gamma_k - k+\ell+1)$. The possible boxes are (1) $[s, nd_s]$ ($s<k$ and $d_s < d_{s-1}$ or $s=1$), (2) $[k, \ell+1]$, (3) $[k+1, 1]$ with contents $nd_s - s, \ell+1-k, -k$, respectively. The equations

$$\begin{aligned} n\lambda_p &= N-p-c_p = n\gamma_k - k+\ell+1-c_p \\ n(\lambda_p-\gamma_k) &= -k+\ell+1-c_p \end{aligned}$$

must hold;
case (1): (note $\ell+1 \leq nd_{k-1}$)

$$\begin{aligned} n(\lambda_p-\gamma_k) &= -k+\ell+1-nd_s+s \\ n(\lambda_p-\gamma_k+d_s) &= -k+s+1+\ell \leq -k+s+nd_{k-1} \\ n(\lambda_p-\gamma_k+d_s-d_{k-1}) &\leq s-k<0 \end{aligned}$$

$\lambda_p \geq \gamma_k = \lambda_{p+1}$ and $d_s \geq d_{k-1}$ by inductive hypothesis, so the left side ≥ 0 and there is a contradiction.
case (2):

$$\begin{aligned} n(\lambda_p-\gamma_k) &= -k+\ell+1-(\ell+1-k) = 0 \\ \lambda_p &= \gamma_k \end{aligned}$$

and the inductive hypothesis is proved for $n\gamma_k - k+1 \leq N-i \leq n\gamma_k - k+\ell+1$, entries in row k.
case (3)

$$n(\lambda_p-\gamma_k) = -k+\ell+1+k = \ell+1$$

set $\ell = nd_k - 1$ and $\gamma_{k+1} = \gamma_k + d_k, \lambda_p = \gamma_{k+1}$. The inductive step has been proven for k and for $k+1$ with $Y[k+1,1] = N - n\gamma_{k+1}+k$. By induction this uses up all the entries. Let row $L+1$ be the last row of Y and of length r_{L+1}, then $N = \sum_{i=1}^{L}(nd_i-1)+r_{L+1}$ and $r_{L+1} \leq nd_L - 1$. □

Corollary 2. *Suppose* $\varpi = (q,t)$ *as in Definition 1 and* p *is singular. Then* $\mathcal{H}_N(t)p$ *contains a* $\{\omega_i, \xi_i\}$ *simultaneous eigenfunction* $f = c_\lambda x^\lambda + \sum_{\beta \lhd \lambda} c_\beta x^\beta + \sum_\gamma c_\gamma x^\gamma$ *with* γ *not* $\rhd$*-comparable to* λ *so that* $\lambda_i = m\gamma_s$ *if* $i \in R_s$, *in the notation of the Theorem.*

We have shown if α is $\rhd$-maximal in a simultaneous $\{\omega_i, \xi_i\}$ eigenfunction then there is an eigenfunction in which α^+ is $\rhd$-maximal. Now the eigenvalues are determined by Y and it follows that $\alpha^+ = \lambda$ as constructed above. Hence each term x^γ in an eigenfunction satisfies $\gamma \unlhd \lambda$. (Suppose at some stage γ is $\rhd$-maximal then there is a simultaneous eigenfunction with γ^+ being $\rhd$-maximal and the construction produces an RSYT of the same isotype τ and the numbers $N, N-1, \ldots$ are entered row-by-row forcing $\gamma^+ = \lambda$.)

Theorem 2 ([2]). *In the notation of Theorem 1 if* $d_i = 1$ *for* $i \geq 2$ *then* $M_\lambda(x)$ *specialized to* ϖ *has no poles and is singular. The module* $\mathcal{H}_N(t)M_\lambda$ *is spanned by* $M_{\alpha(Y)}$ *where* $Y \in \mathcal{Y}_\tau$, $\tau = \left(nd_1-1, (n-1)^{L-1}, r_{L+1}\right)$ *and* $\alpha(Y)_i = m(d_1+s-2)$ *if* $Y[s,k] = i$ *for* $s \geq 2$ *and some* k, *otherwise* ($Y[1,k] = i$) $\alpha(Y)_i = 0$.

The Ferrers diagram of λ (from Theorem 1) is called a quasi-staircase, the shape suggested when French notation with row 1 on the bottom is used.

We have reached the main purpose of this paper: to show there are no other singular polynomials.

4. Restrictions

In this section, we show that the desired nonexistence result can be reduced to the simpler two-row situation.

Suppose $\alpha \in \mathbb{N}_0^N$ and $r_\alpha(1) = 1$ (that is, $\alpha_i \leq \alpha_1$ for all i). Let $\alpha' = (\alpha_2, \ldots, \alpha_N)$ and $Y' = Y\backslash\{1\}$ (the RSYT where the entry 1 is deleted) and f satisfies $\xi_i f = q^{\alpha_i} t^{N-r_\alpha(i)} f$, at ϖ. First we will show that $f_{\alpha'} := \operatorname{coeff}(x_1^{\alpha_1}, f)$ is an eigenfunction of ξ_i' with eigenvalue $q^{\alpha_i} t^{N-r_\alpha(i)}$ for $2 \leq i \leq N$ where

$$w'p(x) := p(qx_N, x_2, x_3, \ldots, x_{N-1}),$$
$$\xi_i' p(x) := t^{i-2} T_i T_{i+1} \cdots T_{N-1} w' T_2^{-1} \cdots T_{i-1}^{-1} p(x)$$

Lemma 6. *Let $f = x_1^{\alpha_1} x_2^{\alpha_2} p(x_3, \ldots, x_N)$ with $\alpha_1 \geq \alpha_2$ then*

$$\operatorname{coeff}\left(x_1^{\alpha_1}, wT_1^{-1} f\right) = t^{-1} w' \operatorname{coeff}(x_1^{\alpha_1}, f).$$

Proof. By definition

$$\begin{aligned} T_1^{-1} f &= \frac{1-t}{t} x_1 \frac{f(x) - f(xs_1)}{x_1 - x_2} + t^{-1} f(xs_1) \\ &= \frac{1-t}{t} x_1^{1+\alpha_2} x_2^{\alpha_2} \frac{x_1^{\alpha_1-\alpha_2} - x_2^{\alpha_1-\alpha_2}}{x_1 - x_2} p + t^{-1} x_1^{\alpha_2} x_2^{\alpha_1} p(x_3, \ldots, x_N) \\ &= \frac{1-t}{t} \sum_{i=0}^{\alpha_1-\alpha_2-1} x_1^{\alpha_1-i} x_2^{\alpha_2+i} p + t^{-1} x_1^{\alpha_2} x_2^{\alpha_1} p(x_3, \ldots, x_N) \end{aligned}$$

then

$$\begin{aligned} wT_1^{-1} f = &\frac{1-t}{t} \sum_{i=0}^{\alpha_1-\alpha_2-1} (qx_N)^{\alpha_1-i} x_1^{\alpha_2+i} p(x_2, x_3, \ldots, x_{N-1}) \\ &+ x_1^{\alpha_1} (qx_N)^{\alpha_2} t^{-1} p(x_2, x_3, \ldots, x_{N-1}). \end{aligned}$$

The highest power of x_1 in the first term is $\alpha_1 - 1$ thus

$$\operatorname{coeff}\left(x_1^n, wT_1^{-1} f\right) = (qx_N)^{\alpha_2} t^{-1} p(x_2, x_3, \ldots, x_{N-1})$$

and the right hand side is $t^{-1} w' x_2^{\alpha_2} p(x_3, \ldots, x_N)$. $\square$

Let $\pi_n f := \operatorname{coeff}(x_1^n, f)$.

Theorem 3. *Suppose $f = \sum_\alpha c_\alpha x^\alpha$ with $\max_i \alpha_i = n$ then $\pi_n \xi_i f = \xi_i' \pi_n f$ for $2 \leq i \leq N$.*

Proof. Let $i > 1$ then

$$\begin{aligned}\pi_n \xi_i f &= t^{i-1}\pi_n T_i T_{i+1}\cdots T_{N-1} w T_1^{-1} T_2^{-1}\cdots T_{i-1}^{-1} f(x)\\ &= t^{i-1} T_i T_{i+1}\cdots T_{N-1}\pi_n w T_1^{-1} T_2^{-1}\cdots T_{i-1}^{-1} f(x)\\ &= t^{i-2} T_i T_{i+1}\cdots T_{N-1} w' \pi_n T_2^{-1}\cdots T_{i-1}^{-1} f(x)\\ &= t^{i-2} T_i T_{i+1}\cdots T_{N-1} w' T_2^{-1}\cdots T_{i-1}^{-1}\pi_n f(x)\\ &= \xi_i' \pi_n f;\end{aligned}$$

this uses the Lemma and the fact that $\xi_i f$ and $T_2^{-1}\cdots T_{i-1}^{-1} f$ are sums of monomials x^β with $\beta_j \leq n$ for $j \geq 1$ (properties of the order $\rhd$ and of T_j^{-1}). If $i = 2$ then the empty product $T_2^{-1}\cdots T_{i-1}^{-1}$ reduces to 1. □

Suppose $\alpha, \beta \in \mathbb{N}_0^{N-1}$ (indexed $2 \leq i \leq N$) and $|\alpha| = |\beta|$, set $\alpha' = (n, \alpha), \beta' := (n, \beta)$ (so that $|\alpha'| = |\beta'|$).

Lemma 7. *Suppose* $\max_i \alpha_i \leq n$ *and* $\max_i \beta_i \leq n$ *then* $\alpha'^+ = (n, \alpha^+), \beta'^+ = (n, \beta^+)$ *and* $\alpha' \succ \beta'$ *iff* $\alpha \succ \beta$, $\alpha' \rhd \beta'$ *iff* $\alpha \rhd \beta$.

Proof. By hypothesis $(\alpha'^+)_1 = n$ and $\alpha'^+ = (n, \alpha^+)$, similarly $\beta'^+ = (n, \beta^+)$. Furthermore

$$\begin{aligned}\alpha' \succ \beta' &\Longleftrightarrow n + \sum_{j=2}^{i} \alpha_j \geq n + \sum_{j=2}^{i} \beta_j \ \forall i \geq 2\\ &\Longleftrightarrow \alpha \succ \beta\end{aligned}$$

Then

$$\begin{aligned}\alpha \rhd \beta &\Longleftrightarrow (\alpha^+ \succ \beta^+) \vee (\alpha^+ = \beta^+ \wedge \alpha \succ \beta)\\ \alpha' \rhd \beta' &\Longleftrightarrow (\alpha'^+ \succ \beta'^+) \vee (\alpha'^+ = \beta'^+ \wedge \alpha' \succ \beta')\end{aligned}$$

and $\alpha \rhd \beta \Longleftrightarrow \alpha' \rhd \beta'$. □

Proposition 6. *Let f be the $\{\omega_i, \xi_i\}$ simultaneous eigenfunction from Corollary 2 with eigenvalues $q^{\lambda_i} t^{N-i} = t^{c(i,Y)}$ at $q^m t^n = 1$ for $1 \leq i \leq N$ and $\lambda_2 > 0$. Then $\pi_{\lambda_1} f$ is a nonzero $\{\omega_i, \xi_i' : i \geq 2\}$ simultaneous eigenfunction with the same eigenvalues as f for $i \geq 2$ with $c(i, Y) = c(i, Y\backslash\{1\})$. Here $Y\backslash\{1\}$ is the RSYT obtained by removing the box containing 1 from Y.*

Proof. We showed that each term x^α appearing in f satisfies $\lambda \trianglerighteq \alpha$ and $\alpha_1 \leq \lambda_1$ for all i. Apply π_{λ_1} to f then by Lemma 7 $\beta \trianglelefteq (\lambda_2, \lambda_3, \ldots, \lambda_N)$ for each x^β appearing in $\pi_{\lambda_1} f$. For $i \geq 2$ ω_i commutes with π_{λ_1} and by Theorem 3 $\pi_{\lambda_1}\xi_i f = \xi_i' \pi_{\lambda_1} f$. Thus $\omega_i \pi_{\lambda_1} f = \xi_i' \pi_{\lambda_1} f$ for $i \geq 2$. Furthermore, $(\lambda_2, \lambda_3, \ldots, \lambda_N) \in \mathbb{N}_0^{N-1,+}$ is $\rhd$-maximal in $\pi_{\lambda_1} f$. □

The definition of RSYT has been slightly modified to allow filling with $2, 3, \ldots, N$. The isotype of $\pi_{\lambda_1} f$ is $\tau' := (nd_1 - 1, nd_2 - 1, \ldots, nd_L - 1, r_{L+1} - 1)$.

Theorem 4. *In the notation of Theorem 1 if $d_2 \geq 2$ then there is a singular polynomial for the parameter ϖ in $n(d_1 + 1) - 1$ variables with $\lambda = \left((md_1)^n, 0^{nd_1 - 1}\right)$, of isotype $(nd_1 - 1, n)$.*

Proof. Apply Proposition 6 repeatedly, and by hypothesis $nd_2 - 1 \geq 2n - 1 > n$. The remaining RSYT is

$$Y' = \begin{bmatrix} N & N-1 & \ldots & \ldots & \ldots & N - nd_1 + 2 \\ N - nd_1 + 1 & \ldots & N - nd_1 - n + 2 & & & \end{bmatrix},$$

and has the t^C-vector $\left[t^{n-2}, t^{n-3}, \ldots, 1, t^{-1}, t^{nd_1-2}, t^{nd_1-3}, \ldots, t, 1\right]$. □

5. Concluding Argument

Re-index the variables by replacing $d_1 \geq 2$ (implied by $d_2 \geq 2$) by d, N by $N = nd - 1 + n$ and

$$Y'' = \begin{bmatrix} nd-1+n & nd-2+n & \ldots & \ldots & \ldots & n+1 \\ n & \ldots & 1 & & & \end{bmatrix}.$$

Proposition 7. *Suppose* $\lambda = \left(d^n, 0^{nd-1}\right)$ *and* $\gamma \in \mathbb{N}_0^K$ *for some* $K \geq N$ *satisfies* $|\gamma| = nd$ *and* $C_i : n(\lambda_i - \gamma_i) = r_\gamma(i) - i$ *for* $1 \leq i \leq K$ *(setting* $\lambda_i = 0$ *for* $i > N$*) then* $\gamma = \lambda$ *or* $\gamma = \beta := \left(0^n, 1^{nd}\right)$.

Proof. By condition C_{n+1} we have $(r_\gamma(n+1) - n - 1) = -n\gamma_{n+1}$ so that $\gamma_{n+1} = 1 - \frac{1}{n}(r_\gamma(n+1) - 1) \leq 1$ and thus $\gamma_{n+1} = 1$ or $\gamma_{n+1} = 0$. If $\gamma_{n+1} = 1$ then $r_\gamma(n+1) = 1$, which implies $\gamma_i = 0$ for $1 \leq i \leq n$ and $\gamma_i \leq 1$ for $i > n+1$. If $j > n$ and $\gamma_j = 0$ then by C_j $r_\gamma(j) = j = \#\{k <= j : \gamma_k \geq 0\} + \#\{k > j : \gamma_k > 0\}$ so that $k > j$ implies $\gamma_k = 0$. Since $|\gamma| = |\lambda| = nd$ we see that $\gamma_{n+1} = 1$ implies $\gamma^+ = \left(1^{nd}\right)$ and in fact $\gamma_i = 1$ for $n+1 \leq i \leq n(d+1)$, since $\gamma_j = 0$ and $\gamma_{j+1} = 1$ is impossible for any $j > n$. If $1 \leq j \leq n$ then $r_\gamma(j) = nd + j$ and $n(\lambda_i - \gamma_i) = nd = r_\gamma(j) - j$, thus satisfying C_j. The other conditions C_i are verified similarly. Thus, $\gamma = \beta$.

If $\gamma_{n+1} = 0$ then $r_\gamma(n+1) = n+1$ and $\ell(\gamma) = n$. Suppose $1 \leq j \leq n$ then C_j states $n(\lambda_j - \gamma_j) = r_\gamma(j) - j$ and the bounds $1 \leq j, r_\gamma(j) \leq n$ imply $|r_\gamma(j) - j| \leq n - 1$ and thus $\gamma_j = \lambda_j$. □

Corollary 3. *Suppose* $\lambda = \left((md)^n, 0^{nd-1}\right) \in \mathbb{N}_0^{N,+}$. *The coefficients of* $M_\lambda(x)$ *have no poles at* ϖ.

Proof. $M_\lambda(x)$ is a nonzero multiple of $x^\lambda + \sum_{\beta \lhd \lambda} A_{\lambda,\beta} x^\beta$. For each $\beta \lhd \lambda$ there is at least one index j_β such that $\zeta_\lambda(i_\beta) \neq \zeta_\beta(i_\beta)$ at ϖ or else $q^{\lambda_i - \beta_i} t^{r_\beta(i) - i} = 1$ for all $i \leq N$. In this case by Lemma 5 $(\lambda_i - \beta_i) = ms_i, r_\beta(i) - i = ns_i$ for some $s_i \in \mathbb{Z}$. Set $\lambda' = \frac{1}{m}\lambda, \beta' = \frac{1}{m}\beta$ then $n(\lambda'_i - \beta'_i) = r_\beta(i) - i$ for all i and by the Proposition $\beta' = \lambda'$ or $\beta' = \left(0^n, 1^{nd}\right)$ but the latter is impossible because $\left(0^n, 1^{nd}\right) \notin \mathbb{N}_0^N$. Finally (this works because there is a triangular expansion $x^\lambda = cM_\lambda + \sum_{\beta \lhd \lambda} A'_{\beta,\lambda} M_\beta$ which holds for generic (q,t))

$$M_\lambda(x) = c \prod_{\beta \lhd \lambda} \frac{\xi_{i_\beta} - \zeta_\beta(i_\beta)}{\zeta_\lambda(i_\beta) - \zeta_\beta(i_\beta)} x^\lambda.$$

This shows that the poles of M_λ are of the form $q^a t^b - 1 = 0$ and ϖ is not a pole. □

Proposition 8. *Suppose* f *is as in Theorem 4 then* $f(x) = cM_\lambda(x)$ *at* ϖ *for some constant* $c \neq 0$.

Proof. By matching coefficients of x^λ find c so that $\operatorname{coeff}(x^\lambda, f - cM_\lambda) = 0$. If $g := f - cM_\lambda \neq 0$ then there exists β such that x^β is $\rhd$-maximal in g. By $\rhd$-triangularity $\xi_i g = q^{\beta_i} t^{N - r_\beta(i)} g$ (at ϖ) for all i. However, g has the same eigenvalues as M_λ, that is, $q^{\beta_i} t^{N - r_\beta(i)} = q^{\lambda_i} t^{N-i}$ at ϖ and the proof of the Corollary showed that $\beta = \lambda$, contradicting $g \neq 0$. □

Recall the transformation Formula (3) for M_α for $\alpha_i > \alpha_{i+1}$ with $z = \frac{\zeta_\alpha(i+1)}{\zeta_\alpha(z)}$

$$M_{s_i\alpha} = \frac{(1-z)^2}{(1-zt)(t-z)}\left(T_i + \frac{1-t}{1-z}\right)M_\alpha.$$

If M_α has no pole at ϖ and $z \neq 1, t, t^{-1}$ then $M_{s_i\alpha}$ has no pole at ϖ. When $\alpha^+ = \lambda$ then $\alpha_i > \alpha_{i+1}$ implies $\alpha_i = md$ and $\alpha_{i+1} = 0, z = q^{-md}t^{r_\alpha(i)-r_\alpha(i+1)} = t^{nd+r_\alpha(i)-r_\alpha(i+1)}$ at ϖ. In the substring $(\alpha_1, \ldots, \alpha_i, \alpha_{i+1})$ there are $r_\alpha(i)$ values md and $i+1-r_\alpha(i)$ zeros, thus $r_\alpha(i+1) = n+i+1-r_\alpha(i)$. Thus, $z = t^b$ with $b = nd+2r_\alpha(i)-n-i-1$. Suppose $r_\alpha(i) = n$, thus $i \geq n$ and s_i can act on α without introducing a pole at ϖ if $nd+n-i-1 > 1$, that is $i < nd+n-2 = N-1$. The last permitted occurrence of md in α is $i = N-2$. Next move the second last occurrence of md in α as far as possible without a pole: set $r_\alpha(i) = n-1$ and require $nd+2(n-1)-n-i-1 > 1$, that is, $i < nd+n-4 = N-3$, thus $i = N-4$ is the last permitted value. More generally let $r_\alpha(i) = n-j$ (with $0 \leq j \leq n-1$) then require $nd+2(n-j)-n-i-1 > 1$, that is, $nd+n-2j-2 > i$ or $i < N-1-2j$; the last permitted value is $i = N-2(j+1)$.

Let

$$\alpha = \left(0^{nd-n-1}, md, 0, md, 0 \ldots, md, 0\right)$$
$$\zeta_\alpha = \left[t^{N-n-1}, \ldots, t^n, q^{md}t^{N-1}, t^{n-1}, \ldots, q^{md}t^{N-n}, 1\right].$$

We showed that M_α has no poles at ϖ, and if M_λ at ϖ is singular then so is M_α. The spectral vector ζ_α at ϖ coincides with the t^C-vector of the RSYT

$$Y_0 = \begin{bmatrix} N & N-2 & \cdots & N-2n+2 & N-2n & \cdots & 1 \\ N-1 & N-3 & \cdots & N-2n+1 & & & \end{bmatrix},$$

and thus $\omega_{N-1}Y_0 = t^{-1}Y_0$; by construction $\zeta_\alpha(N-1) = q^{md}t^{N-n} = t^{-nd+N-n} = t^{-1}$. If M_α at ϖ is singular then $\omega_{N-1}M_\alpha = \xi_{N-1}M_\alpha = t^{-1}M_\alpha$; this means

$$\begin{aligned} t^{-1}T_{N-1}T_{N-1}M_\alpha &= t^{-1}M_\alpha \\ ((t-1)T_{N-1}+t)M_\alpha &= M_\alpha \\ (t-1)T_{N-1}M_\alpha &= (1-t)M_\alpha \\ (T_{N-1}+1)M_\alpha &= 0. \end{aligned}$$

For the next step we recall some standard definitions: the q-Pochhammer symbol is $(a;q)_k = \prod_{i=1}^{k}(1-aq^{i-1})$ and the generalized (q,t)-Pochhammer symbol for $\lambda \in \mathbb{N}_0^{N,+}$ is

$$(v;q,t) = \prod_{i=1}^{N}\left(vt^{1-i};q\right)_{\lambda_i}.$$

In the context of the Ferrers diagram representation of a composition $\alpha \in \mathbb{N}_0^N$, $\{(i,j) : 1 \leq i \leq N, 1 \leq j \leq \alpha_i\}$ (the rows with $\alpha_i = 0$ are empty) define the arm-length and leg-length of a box in the diagram ($\lambda \in \mathbb{N}_0^{N,+}$)

$$\begin{aligned} \mathrm{arm}(i,j;\lambda) &:= \lambda_i - j, \\ \mathrm{arm}(i,j;\alpha) &:= \alpha_i - j, \\ \mathrm{leg}(i,j;\lambda) &:= \#\{l : i < l \leq N, j \leq \lambda_l\}, \end{aligned}$$

$$\mathrm{leg}(i,j;\alpha) := \#\{r : r > i, j \leq \alpha_r \leq \alpha_i\} + \#\{r : r < i, j \leq \alpha_r + 1 \leq \alpha_i\}.$$

The (q,t)-hook product is

$$h_{q,t}(v;\alpha) = \prod_{(i,j)\in\alpha} \left(1 - vq^{\mathrm{arm}(i,j;\alpha)} t^{\mathrm{leg}(i,j;\alpha)}\right).$$

There is an evaluation at a special point (see [Cor. 7] [7]): let $x^{(0)} := \left(1, t, t^2, \ldots, t^{N-1}\right)$, then for any $\beta \in \mathbb{N}_0^N$

$$M_\beta\left(x^{(0)}\right) = q^{b(\beta)} t^{e'(\beta^+)} \frac{\left(qt^N; q,t\right)_{\beta^+}}{h_{q,t}(qt;\beta)},$$

where $b(\beta) = \sum_{i=1}^N \binom{\beta_i}{2}, e'(\beta^+) = \sum_{i=1}^N \beta_i^+(N-i)$.

Theorem 5. *$(T_{N-1}+1)M_\alpha \neq 0$ at ϖ and M_α is not singular.*

Proof. For any polynomial p let $x = x^{(0)}$ in $T_i p(x) = (1-t)x_{i+1}\frac{p(x)-p(xs_i)}{x_i - x_{i+1}} + tp(xs_i)$ then $T_i p\left(x^{(0)}\right) = t\left(p\left(x^{(0)}\right) - p\left(x^{(0)}s_i\right)\right) + tp\left(x^{(0)}s_i\right) = tp\left(x^{(0)}\right)$ (since $x_{i+1}^{(0)} = tx_i^{(0)}$). Set $b_0 = b(\alpha) = n\binom{md}{2}$, $e_0 = e'(\alpha^+) = \frac{1}{2}mdn(2N-n-1)$ then

$$\begin{aligned} T_{N-1}M_\alpha\left(x^{(0)}\right) + M_\alpha\left(x^{(0)}\right) &= (t+1)M_\alpha\left(x^{(0)}\right) \\ &= q^{b_0}t^{e_0}(t+1)\frac{\left(q^N t; q,t\right)_{\alpha^+}}{h_{q,t}(qt;\alpha)}. \end{aligned}$$

The numerator is

$$\left(q^N t; q,t\right)_{\alpha^+} = \prod_{i=1}^n \left(qt^{N-i+1}; q\right)_{md} = \prod_{i=1}^n \prod_{j=1}^{dm} \left(1 - q^j t^{nd+n-i}\right),$$

where the only term vanishing at ϖ is for $i = n, j = dm$ (for suppose $j = rm$ with $r \leq d, nd+n-i = rn$ for some $r \in \mathbb{N}$ then $n \geq i = n(d-r+1)$ and $d-r+1 \leq 1$, that is, $r \geq d$, hence $r = d, i = n$). For the hook product observe that if $1 \leq j \leq n$ then $\mathrm{leg}(\alpha; N-2j+1, 1) = nd-2$ because there are $nd-1-j$ zero values in $\left(\alpha_1, \ldots, \alpha_{N-2j+1}\right)$ and $j-1$ values of md in $\left(\alpha_{N-2j+2}, \ldots, \alpha_N\right)$. Since $\mathrm{arm}(\alpha; N-2j+1, 1) = dm-1$ we find that the boxes $\{[N-2j+1, 1] : 1 \leq j \leq n\}$ contribute $\left(1 - q^{dm}t^{nd-1}\right)^n$ to $h_{q,t}(qt;\alpha)$. This term becomes $\left(1-t^{-1}\right)^n$ at ϖ. The other boxes in the diagram of α are $\{[N-2j+1, k] : 1 \leq j \leq n, 2 \leq k \leq md\}$ and $\mathrm{leg}(\alpha; N-2j+1, k) = j-1$, $\mathrm{arm}(\alpha; N-2j+1, k) = dm-k$. Thus

$$\begin{aligned} h_{q,t}(qt;\alpha) &= \left(1 - q^{dm}t^{nd-1}\right)^n \prod_{j=1}^n \prod_{k=1}^{dm} \left(1 - q^{dm-k+1}t^j\right) \\ &= \left(1 - q^{dm}t^{nd-1}\right)^n \prod_{j=1}^n \prod_{i=1}^{dm} \left(1 - q^i t^j\right). \end{aligned}$$

The only term in the product vanishing at ϖ is for $i = m, j = n$. Thus, the term $(1 - q^m t^n)$ cancels out in $\frac{\left(q^N t; q,t\right)_{\alpha^+}}{h_{q,t}(qt;\alpha)}$ and $(T_{N-1}+1)M_\alpha\left(x^{(0)}\right) \neq 0$. □

Example 1. *Let $N = 5$, $n = 2$, $m = 1$, $d = 2$ then $\alpha = (0,2,0,2,0)$ and $\varpi = \left(t^{-2}, t\right)$ (that is, $qt^2 = 1$) The spectral vector of α is $\left[t^2, q^2t^4, t, q^2t^3, 1\right]$ which equals $\left[t^2, 1, t, t^{-1}, 1\right]$ at $q = t^{-2}$.*

The expression for M_α is too large to display here (32 monomials); the denominators of the coefficients are factors of $qt-1$, $(q^2t^3-1)^2$ and

$$M_\alpha\left(1,t,t^2,t^3,t^4\right) = q^2t^{14}\frac{(qt^2+1)(qt^4-1)(qt^5-1)(q^2t^5-1)}{(q^2t^3-1)^2(qt-1)}$$

which does not vanish at $q=t^{-2}$. However, the same polynomial is singular with $n=4$, $d=1$, $m=2$ and $q=-t^{-2}$ (that is, $q^2t^4=1$ but $qt^2\neq 1$). The singularity can be proven by direct computation and the vanishing of $M_\alpha(1,\ldots,t^4)$ is only a necessary condition.

We have shown if there is a singular polynomial as described in Theorem 1 and $d_2 \geq 2$ then by using the restriction Proposition 6 repeatedly there is a singular polynomial of isotype (nd_1-1,n), which in turn implies that M_α is singular. This is impossible and we conclude that $d_2=1$ is necessary, and all singular polynomials have been determined.

Funding: This research received no external funding.

Data Availability Statement: Not applicable.

Conflicts of Interest: The author declares no conflict of interest.

References

1. Cherednik, I. Nonsymmetric Macdonald polynomials. *Int. Math. Res. Not.* **1995**, *1995*, 483–515. [CrossRef]
2. Colmenarejo, L.; Dunkl, C.F. Singular nonsymmetric Macdonald polynomials and quasistaircases. *SIGMA Symmetry Integr. Geom. Methods Appl.* **2020**, *16*, 010. [CrossRef]
3. Kirillov, A.N.; Noumi, M. Affine Hecke algebras and raising operators for Macdonald polynomials. *Duke Math. J.* **1998**, *93*, 1–39. [CrossRef]
4. Mimachi, K.; Noumi, M. A reproducing kernel for nonsymmetric Macdonald polynomials. *Duke Math. J.* **1998**, *91*, 621–634. [CrossRef]
5. Baker, T.H.; Forrester, P.J. A q-analogue of the type A Dunkl operator and integral kernel. *Int. Math. Res. Not.* **1997**, *14*, 667–686. [CrossRef]
6. Dipper, R.; James, G. Representations of Hecke algebras of general linear groups. *Proc. Lond. Math. Soc.* **1986**, *52*, 2–52. [CrossRef]
7. Dunkl, C.F.; Luque, J.-G. Clustering properties of rectangular Macdonald polynomials. *Annales de l'Institut Henri Poincaré D* **2015**, *2*, 263–307. [CrossRef]

MDPI AG
St. Alban-Anlage 66
4052 Basel
Switzerland
www.mdpi.com

Axioms Editorial Office
E-mail: axioms@mdpi.com
www.mdpi.com/journal/axioms

www.ingramcontent.com/pod-product-compliance
Lightning Source LLC
Chambersburg PA
CBHW061504220926
51850CB00004B/169
9783725812547